Oil Paintings in Public Ownership in Essex

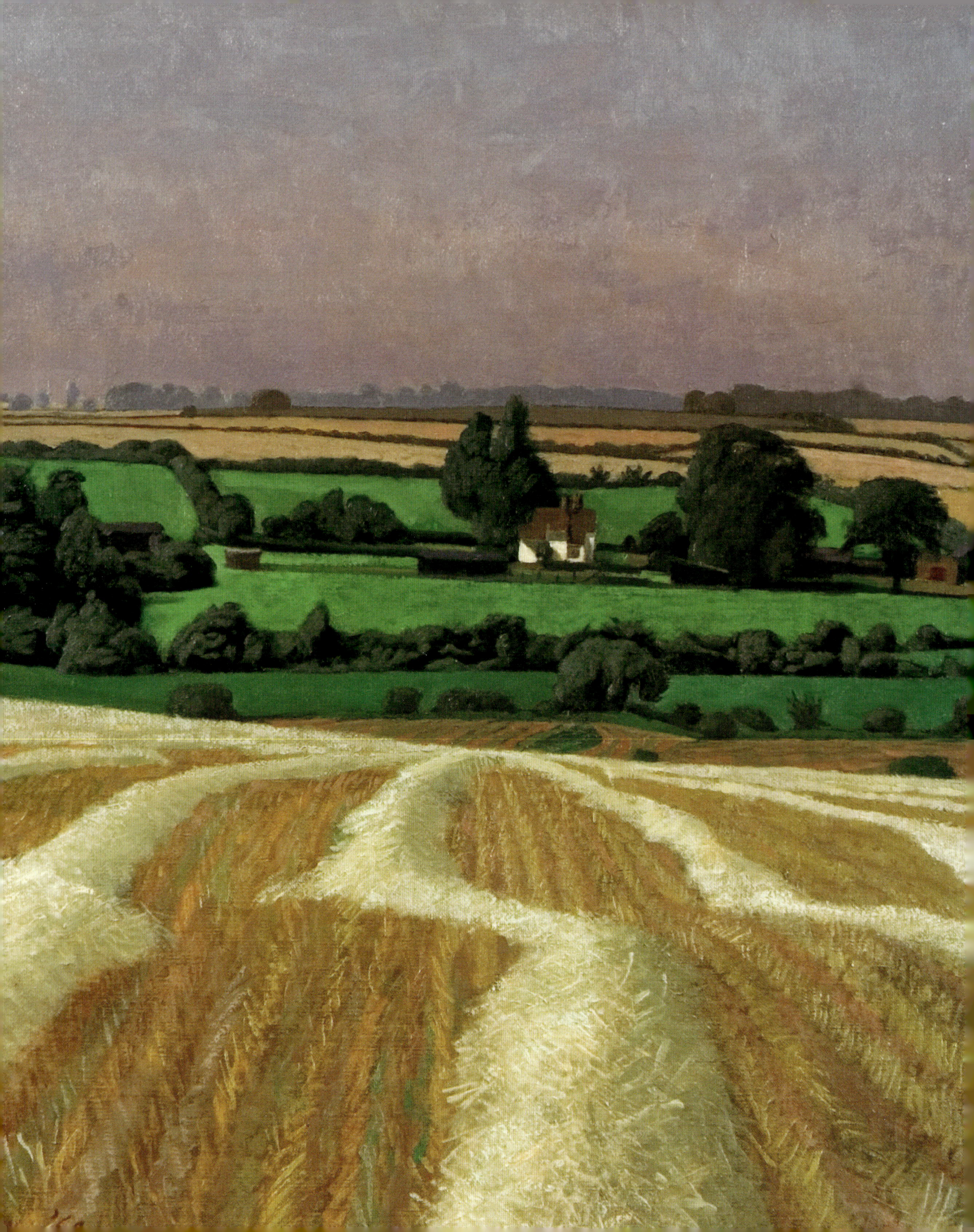

Oil Paintings in Public Ownership in

Essex

The Public Catalogue Foundation

Andrew Ellis, Director
Sonia Roe, Editor
Julia Abel Smith, Essex Coordinator
Nick Moss, Todd-White Art Photography

First published in 2006 by the Public Catalogue Foundation, St Vincent House, 30 Orange Street, London, WC2H 7HH

The responsibility for the accuracy of the information presented in this catalogue lies solely with the holding collections. Suggestions that might improve the accuracy of the information contained in this catalogue should be sent to the relevant collection and emailed to info@thepcf.org.uk.

ISBN 1-904931-14-6 (hardback)
ISBN 1-904931-15-4 (paperback)

Essex photography: Nick Moss, Todd-White Art Photography

Designed by Jeffery Design, London

Distributed by the Public Catalogue Foundation, St Vincent House, 30 Orange Street, London, WC2H 7HH
Telephone 020 7747 5936

Printed and bound in the UK by Butler & Tanner Ltd, Frome, Somerset

Cover image:

Castle, Lucy b.1977
The Kursaal II (detail), 2001
Southend Museums Service (see p. 256)

Image opposite title page:

Aldridge, John Arthur Malcolm 1905–1983
Stubble Field, Thaxted (detail), 1968
Southend Museums Service (see p.248)

Back cover images (from top to bottom):

Larusdottir, Karolina b.1944
Sunday Visit to the Summerhouse (detail), 1994
Southend Museums Service (see p. 271)

unknown artist early 17th C
Portrait of a Lady in an Embroidered Dress
Essex Record Office (see p. 64)

Lamb, Lynton Harold 1907–1977
The Crown
Essex County Council (see p. 53)

Contents

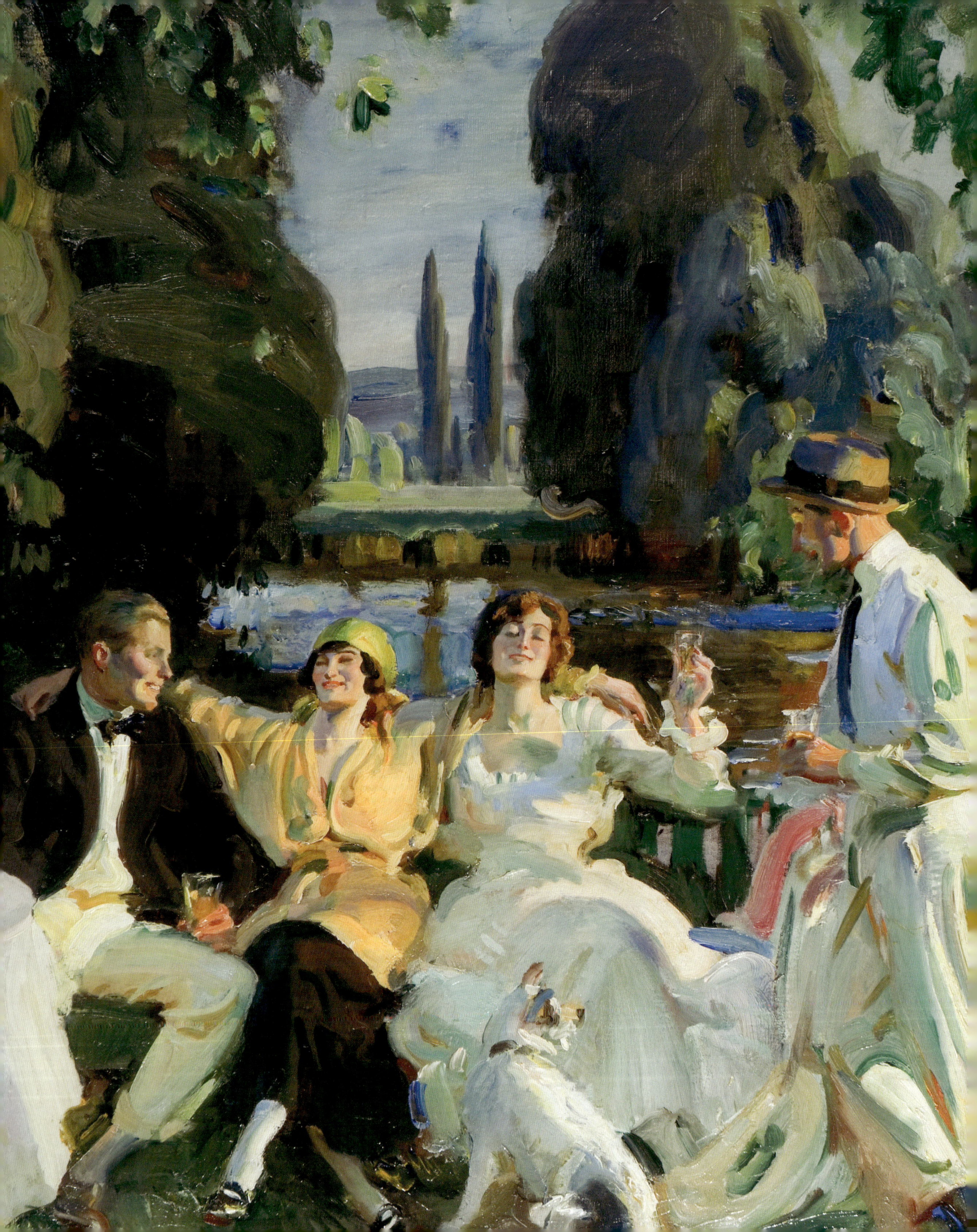

Foreword

Each and every one of the Foundation's catalogues is, by definition, a revelation and the Essex catalogue ranks with the best of them. Yet, while the worth of the Foundation's work is becoming more apparent to more and more people, we can still find a County Council (the first ever to adopt this position) able to state that not only will it not provide a whisper of funding, but neither will it permit its paintings to be included in our catalogue of that county. Weirder yet is the letter from a museum that attracts 10,000 visitors a year (and charges them all an entrance fee of £1.50 each), stating that the management did not wish the paintings in the collection to be publicised on the Internet or anywhere else.

We shall win, so it is with enormous happiness therefore that I read Lord Hanningfield's words in his introduction to the Essex County Council collection. For Lord Hanningfield, who is leader of that Council, says that our catalogue prompts him 'to reacquaint myself with the wonderful collection of oil paintings the county of Essex enjoys'. That reaction, when matched with the comment by David Beevers, Keeper of Art at Brighton – 'I do not know how we managed without (the catalogue). An open copy is always beside me' – and similar remarks by countless other curators, brings into stark focus a key problem.

It is not simply that, if you tuck 80% of our paintings away in back rooms we the public cannot see them. It is equally the case that their custodians cannot see them either. Both ends of this equation need to be awakened to what we own – or we are on a sure course to disaster. Which compels me to reiterate a truth of equal importance: whereas we may have thought at the outset that the lack of catalogues was merely a gallery-related problem, it soon became evident that it was at least a county one; then, we began to see that it was a national one. Now, as North American and European interest begins to appear, it is beginning to look as if it is a wider issue of Western art recording generally. There is a long way still to go but with this, our twelfth volume, I began to sense the swell of a greater wave behind us. Thanks and praise to Lord Hanningfield, and would that every Council Leader were as enlightened.

I owe a great debt of gratitude to Simon Heffer, an Essex resident who has not only consistently supported our work but who introduced us to Julia Abel Smith, our highly-skilled County Coordinator on this catalogue.

There are over 2,100 paintings in public ownership in 60 collections in Essex. It is one of the largest counties in England and recording these riches has sometimes been a logistic challenge. The fine and varied collections in Colchester for example, are located in no fewer than nine sites. We have, however, met everywhere with enormous enthusiasm and helpfulness and our sincere thanks go to all the curators and officers who have smoothed our, at times tortuous, path. Finally, great gratitude is due to George Courtauld, who with humour and hard work has enabled us to raise the money to produce this catalogue.

Fred Hohler, Chairman

Facing page: Munnings, Alfred James, 1878–1959, *Tagg's Island* (detail), 1920, Sir Alfred Munnings Art Museum, (p. 102)

The Public Catalogue Foundation

The United Kingdom holds in its galleries and civic buildings arguably the greatest publicly owned collection of oil paintings in the world. However, an alarming four in five of these paintings are not on view. Whilst many galleries make strenuous efforts to display their collections, too many paintings across the country are held in storage, usually because there are insufficient funds and space to show them. Furthermore, very few galleries have created a complete photographic record of their paintings, let alone a comprehensive illustrated catalogue of their collections. In short, what is publicly owned is not publicly accessible.

The Public Catalogue Foundation, a registered charity, has three aims. First, it intends to create a complete record of the nation's collection of oil, tempera and acrylic paintings in public ownership. Second, it intends to make this accessible to the public through a series of affordable catalogues and, after a suitable delay, through a free Internet website. Finally, it aims to raise funds through the sale of catalogues in gallery shops for the conservation and restoration of oil paintings in these collections and for gallery education.

The initial focus of the project is on collections outside London. Highlighting the richness and diversity of collections outside the capital should bring major benefits to regional collections around the country. The benefits also include a revenue stream for conservation, restoration, gallery education and the digitisation of collections' paintings, thereby allowing them to put the images on the Internet if they so desire. These substantial benefits to galleries around the country come at no financial cost to the collections themselves.

The project should be of enormous benefit and inspiration to students of art and to members of the general public with an interest in art. It will also provide a major source of material for scholarly research into art history.

Financial Supporters

The Public Catalogue Foundation would like to express its profound appreciation to the following organisations and individuals who have made the publication of this catalogue possible.

Donations of £10,000 or more

The Foyle Foundation

Donations of £5,000 or more

The Leche Trust
The Manifold Trust
The Monument Trust

Donations of £1,000 or more

The AIM Foundation
Braxted Park Estate
Essex County Council
Marc Fitch Fund
Christopher & Catherine Foyle
Friends of Historic Essex
Paul & Kathrine Haworth
Michael A. Lambert
National Gallery Trust
P. F. Charitable Trust
The Pilgrim Trust
University of Essex
Wilkin & Sons Ltd
Peter Wolton Charitable Trust

Other Donations

Mr & Mrs Charles Arthur
Mr & Mrs Edward Astle
Dr & Mrs James Bettley
Mr & Mrs P. Boulding
Braintree District Museum Trust
Dr Sibel Bulinger-Peck
Meg & Tom Clarke
Polly Clarke
Sonia Coode-Adams
Mrs Claire Cottrell
The Reverend Christopher Courtauld
George Courtauld, DL
Julien & Paddy Courtauld
Mr & Mrs Simon Eccles Williams
Robert & Brenda Ellis
H. F. A. Engleheart
Mr & Mrs R. Erith
The Essex Club
Friends of Braintree District Museum
Patrick & Sally Hearne
Mrs Patricia Herrmann
Mr & Mrs Adrian Holmes
Sir Alex & Lady Jarratt
Mr Hugh Johnson
Mr Lance Lepper
Lady Lewis
M. C. Malone-Lee
Norman Marshall
Mr Sam Metson
Milsom Hotels Ltd
Julius A. S. Neave
The Baroness Platt of Writtle
Hugh & Marion Scantlebury
Sir Alastair & Lady Stewart
Roger & Barbara Stratton-Smith
Mrs Diana Thompson
Jonathan Trower
G. C. Waterer
Andrew Widdowson
I. & P. A. Williams
Mr & Mrs John Wolton

National Supporters

The Bulldog Trust
The John S. Cohen Foundation
Hiscox plc
National Gallery Trust
Stavros S. Niarchos Foundation
The Manifold Trust
The Monument Trust
P. F. Charitable Trust
Garfield Weston Foundation

National Sponsor

Christie's

Acknowledgements

The Public Catalogue Foundation would like to thank the individual artists and copyright holders for their permission to reproduce for free the paintings in this catalogue. Exhaustive efforts have been made to locate the copyright owners of all the images included within this catalogue and to meet their requirements. Copyright credit lines for copyright owners who have been traced are listed in the Further Information section.

The Public Catalogue Foundation would like to express its great appreciation to the following organisations for their great assistance in the preparation of this catalogue:

Bridgeman Art Library
Flowers East
Marlborough Fine Art
National Association of Decorative and Fine Art Societies (NADFAS)
National Gallery, London
National Portrait Gallery, London
Royal Academy of Arts, London
Tate

The participating collections included in the catalogue would like to express their appreciation to the many individuals who have contributed so generously to the county's collections and those who continue to do so. They would also like to express their thanks to the following organisations which have so generously enabled them to acquire paintings featured in this catalogue:

Basildon Arts Trust
Constable Trust
Contemporary Art Society
Essex Heritage Fund
Friends of the Beecroft Art Gallery
Friends of Chelmsford Museums
Friends of Colchester Museum
Friends of Historic Essex
Friends of Wat Tyler County Park
Maldon Art Society
National Art Collections Fund
Olive Cook Bequest
Resource/Victoria & Albert Purchase Grant Fund
Thorpe-Smith Bequest
Victor Batte-Lay Trust
Waltham Abbey Historical Society

Catalogue Scope and Organisation

Medium and Support
The principal focus of this series is oil paintings. However, tempera and acrylic are also included as well as mixed media, where oil is the predominant constituent. Paintings on all forms of support (e.g. canvas, panel, etc.) are included as long as the support is portable. The principal exclusions are miniatures, hatchments or other purely heraldic paintings and wall paintings *in situ*.

Public Ownership
Public ownership has been taken to mean any paintings that are directly owned by the public purse, made accessible to the public by means of public subsidy or generally perceived to be in public ownership. The term 'public' refers to both central government and local government. Paintings held by national museums, local authority museums, English Heritage and independent museums, where there is at least some form of public subsidy, are included. Paintings held in civic buildings such as local government offices, town halls, guildhalls, public libraries, universities, hospitals, crematoria, fire stations and police stations are also included. Paintings held in central government buildings as part of the Government Art Collection and MoD collections are not included in the county-by-county series but should be included later in the series on a national basis.

Geographical Boundaries of Catalogues
The geographical boundary of each county is the 'ceremonial county' boundary. This county definition includes all unitary authorities. Counties that have a particularly large number of paintings are divided between two or more catalogues on a geographical basis.

Criteria for Inclusion
As long as paintings meet the requirements above, all paintings are included irrespective of their condition and perceived quality. However, painting reproductions can only be included with the agreement of the participating collections and, where appropriate, the relevant copyright owner. It is rare that a collection forbids the inclusion of its paintings. Where this is the case and it is possible to obtain a list of paintings, this list is given in the Paintings Without Reproductions section. Where copyright consent is refused, the paintings are also listed in the Paintings Without Reproductions section. All paintings in collections' stacks and stores are included, as well as those on display. Paintings which have been lent to other institutions, whether for short-term exhibition or long-term loan, are listed under the owner collection. In addition, paintings on long-term loan are also included under the borrowing institution when they are likely to remain there for at least another five years from the date of publication of this catalogue. Information relating to owners and borrowers is listed in the Further Information section.

Layout
Collections are grouped together under their home town. These locations are listed in alphabetical order. In some cases collections that are spread over a number of locations are included under a single owner collection. A number of collections, principally the larger ones, are preceded by curatorial forewords. Within each collection paintings are listed in order of artist surname. Where there is more than one painting by the same artist, the paintings are listed chronologically, according to their execution date.

The few paintings that are not accompanied by photographs are listed in the Paintings Without Reproductions section.

There is additional reference material in the Further Information section at the back of the catalogue. This gives the full names of artists, titles and media if it has not been possible to include these in full in the main section. It also provides acquisition credit lines and information about loans in and out, as well as copyright and photographic credits for each painting. Finally, there is an index of artists' surnames.

Key to Painting Information

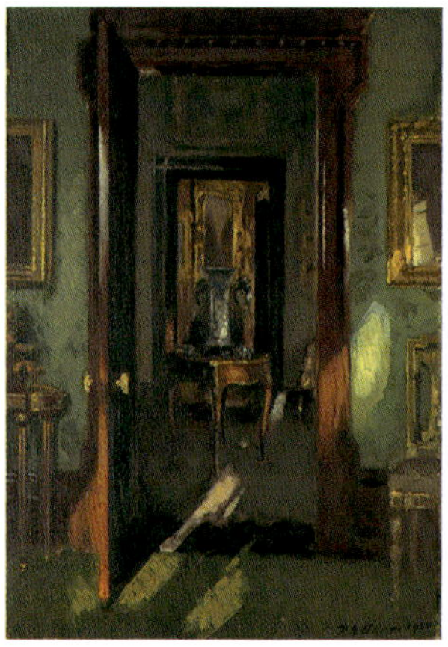

Almost all paintings are reproduced in the catalogue. Where this is not the case they are listed in the Paintings Without Reproductions section. Where paintings are missing or have been stolen, the best possible photograph on record has been reproduced. In some cases this may be black and white. Paintings that have been stolen are highlighted with a red border. Some paintings are shown with conservation tissue attached to parts of the painting surface.

Adam, Patrick William 1854–1929
Interior, Rutland Lodge: Vista through Open Doors 1920
oil on canvas 67.3 × 45.7
LEEAG.PA.1925.0671.LACF ✱

Artist name This is shown as surname first. Where the artist is listed on the Getty Union List of Artist Names (ULAN), ULAN's preferred presentation of the name is always given. In a number of cases the name may not be a firm attribution and this is made clear. Where the artist name is not known, a school may be given instead. Where the school is not known, the painter name is listed as *unknown artist*. If the artist name is too long for the space, as much of the name is given as possible followed by (...). This indicates the full name is given at the rear of the catalogue in the Further Information section.

Painting title A painting followed by *(?)* indicates that the title is in doubt. Where the alternative title to the painting is considered to be better known than the original, the alternative title is given in parentheses. Where the collection has not given a painting a title, the publisher does so instead and marks this with an asterisk. If the title is too long for the space, as much of the title is given as possible followed by *(...)* and the full title is given in the Further Information section.

Medium and support Where the precise material used in the support is known, this is given.

Artist dates Where known, the years of birth and death of the artist are given. In some cases one or both dates may not be known with certainty, and this is marked. No date indicates that even an approximate date is not known. Where only the period in which the artist was active is known, these dates are given and preceded with the word *active*.

Execution date In some cases the precise year of execution may not be known for certain. Instead an approximate date will be given or no date at all.

Dimensions All measurements refer to the unframed painting and are given in cm with up to one decimal point. In all cases the height is shown before the width. Where the painting has been measured in its frame, the dimensions are estimates and are marked with (E). If the painting is circular, the single dimension is the diameter. If the painting is oval, the dimensions are height and width.

Collection inventory number In the case of paintings owned by museums, this number will always be the accession number. In all other cases it will be a unique inventory number of the owner institution. (P) indicates that a painting is a private loan. Details can be found in the Further Information section. The ✱ symbol indicates that the reproduction is based on a Bridgeman Art Library transparency (go to www.bridgeman.co.uk) or that the Bridgeman administers the copyright for that artist.

Facing page: Blamey, Norman, 1914–1999, *Proximity* (detail), 1960s, Southend Museums Service, (p. 253)

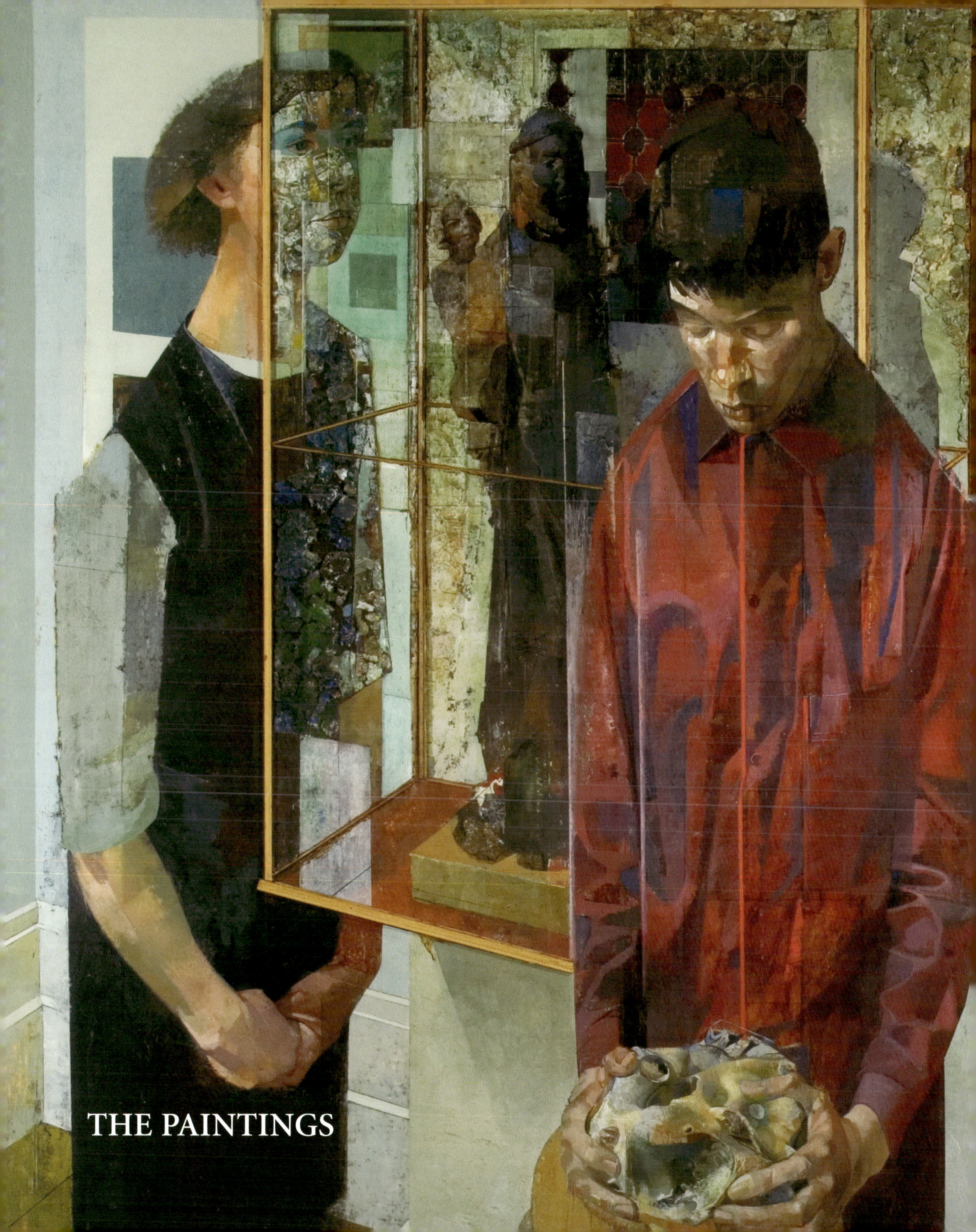

THE PAINTINGS

Basildon Arts Trust

Kenneth Cotton (whose wife was the architect of St Martin's Church, Basildon), Stewart Mason and Derrick Fisher set up Basildon Arts Trust in 1978. Some of the works came from the Stuyvesant Collection, through connections with the cigarette manufacturers, Carreras, whose head office was based in Basildon and employed many people from the district. Carreras' policy was to give back to the community. Additional works were acquired over time with grants from the Regional Arts board and are now held in trust for the people of Basildon.

Basildon Arts Trust is a good representative collection of what was happening in British art during the second half of the twentieth century. It represents a cross-section of local, international, contemporary and traditional artists' work since the 1950s.

By the time the collection was started in the late 1960s, British artists had the chance to absorb the continental influences prior to the Second World War, ranging from Picasso and Cubism to Mondrian and geometrical abstraction. After the war came the impact of American Abstract Expressionism.

In a typically British way, some artists chose to ignore these powerful influences, others absorbed them in modified form and some embraced them wholeheartedly. The British are a literary people. They like pictures that tell a story and are generally suspicious of abstract art, with no obvious narrative or recognisable object. Yet many of our painters and sculptors have made important contributions to abstraction, including several in this collection. Such artists very often begin producing representational paintings, but, in striving for a purer form, move towards abstraction.

Two examples are Ivon Hitchens and William Scott. Both were capable of depicting anything with near-photographic accuracy. However, Hitchens' canvases of the landscape around his home in West Sussex became progressively more non-representative throughout his life, as he strove to abstract what he saw as the essence of landscape. Scott's early still lifes were compositions of recognisable tables, pots and pans which later became just squares and rectangles.

Terry Frost is another artist who moved towards abstraction. His picture here can be viewed as simple shapes, yet the boat profiles which he saw around him in the Cornish port of St Ives were an important influence. Another Cornish artist, Patrick Heron, embraced abstraction whole-heartedly, producing canvases filled with lozenges and bands of life-enhancing rich colour, complete in themselves.

Over the years, British artists have produced a string of pictures with a strong personal imagery. Alan Davie and Peter Unsworth are in this tradition. Their unique images challenge the viewer to use his or her imagination to make a personal interpretation, adding to the picture's memorability.

The sponsors of the Basildon Arts Trust collection, Cleanaway Pitsea Marsh Fund, the Essex Arts Development Fund and Basildon District Council, must be congratulated for making this interesting group of pictures available for wider public enjoyment. In 2006 the collection was displayed in the Eastgate

Shopping Centre in Basildon where it was hugely popular and a new location is currently being sought. The paintings are now back in the Basildon Art Trust Gallery, in the Basildon Centre, as well as in the foyer of the Towngate Theatre.

David Buckman, a friend of Basildon Arts Trust

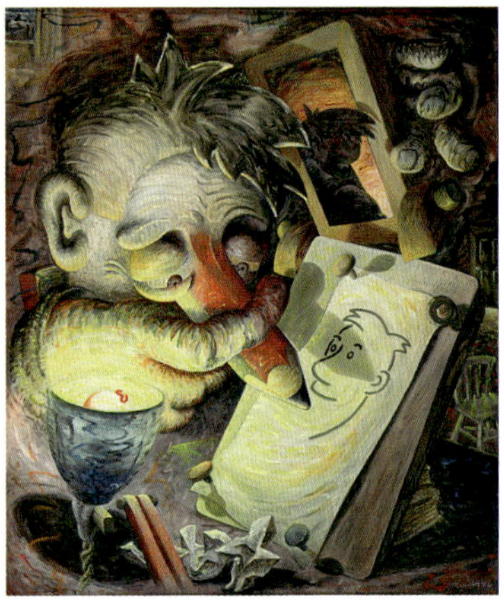

Crowley, Graham b.1950
3B 1982
oil on canvas 137 x 114
64

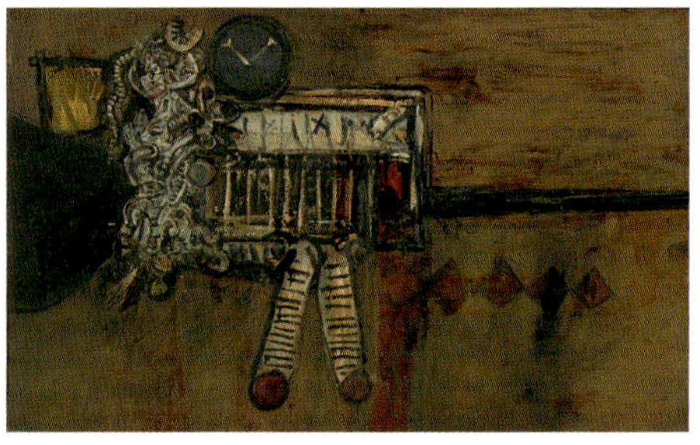

Davie, Alan b.1920
White Magician 1979
oil on board 152 x 244
20

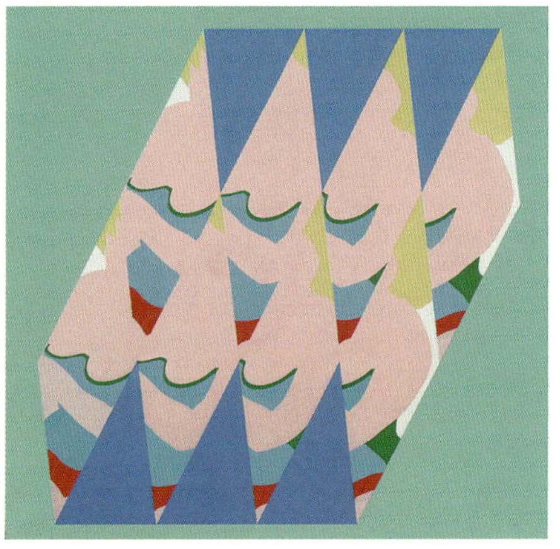

Donaldson, Antony b.1939
Zigzag Past an Aurelia 1964
oil on canvas 168 x 168
21

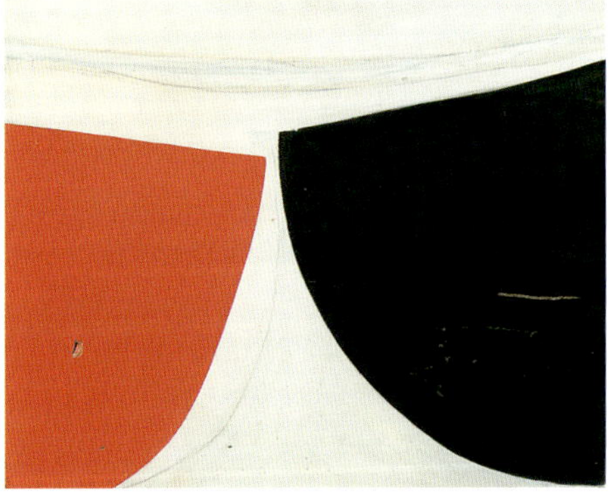

Frost, Terry 1915–2003
Red and Black
oil on canvas 128 x 153
22

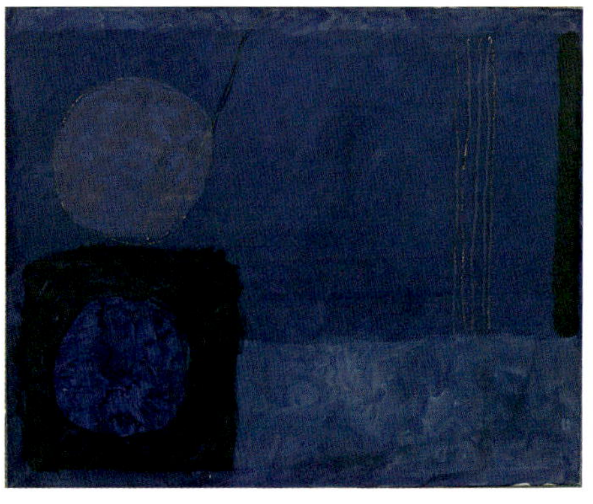

Heron, Patrick 1920–1999
*Study in Blue**
oil on canvas 153 x 183
23

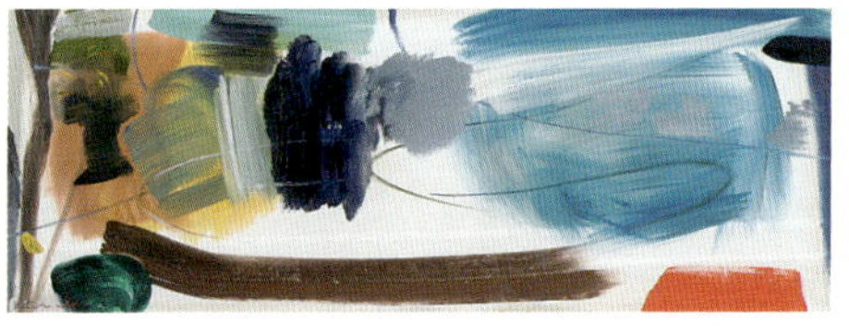

Hitchens, Ivon 1893–1979
Blue November
oil on canvas 57 x 154
25

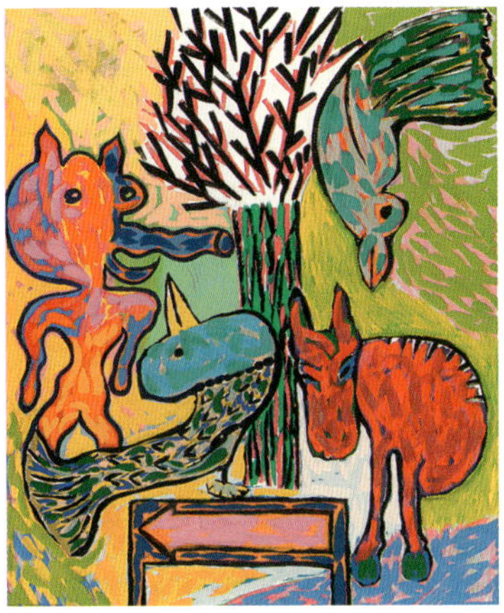

Mullaniff, Kathleen b.1957
*Birds and Animals by a Tree**
acrylic on board 149 x 120
65

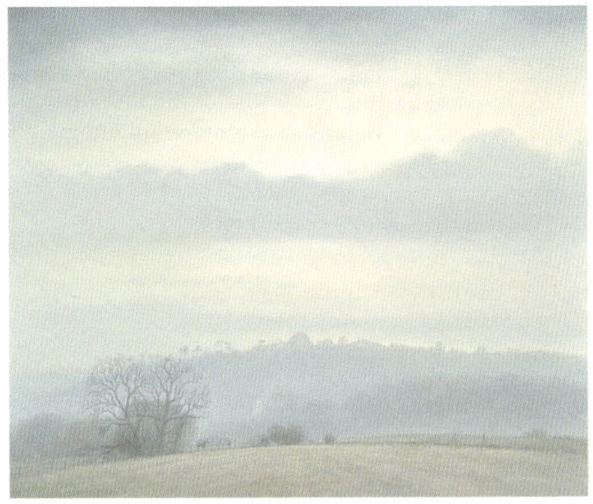

Outram, Steven b.1953
Landscape: A Late February Afternoon
oil on board 49.5 x 60
28

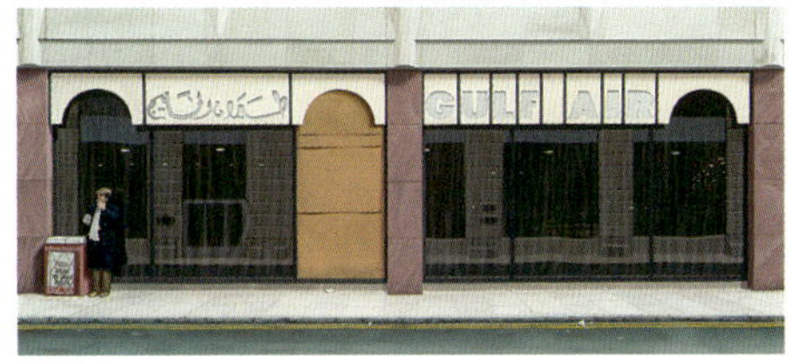

Redfern, David b.1947
The Shah's Riot 1980
oil on canvas 59 x 129
39

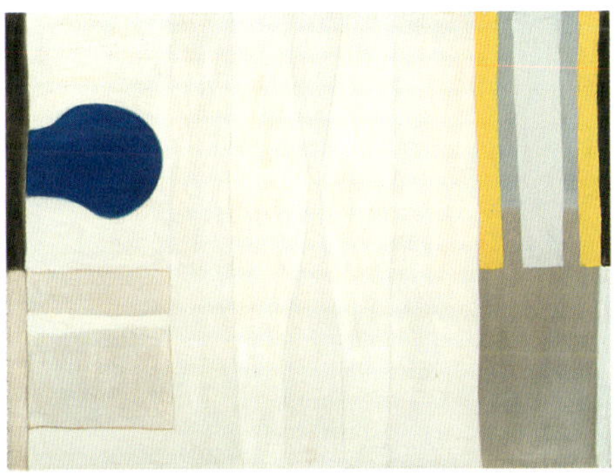

Scott, William George 1913–1989
Blue Form on White 1964
oil on canvas 155 x 200
26

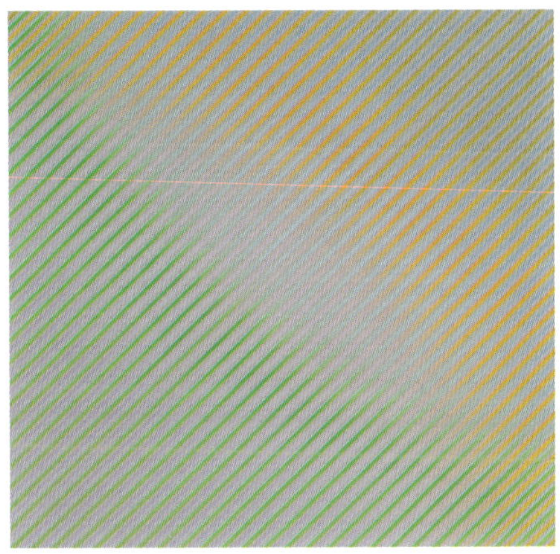

Sedgley, Peter b.1930
Oranges and Lemons 1980
acrylic on card 69 x 69
37

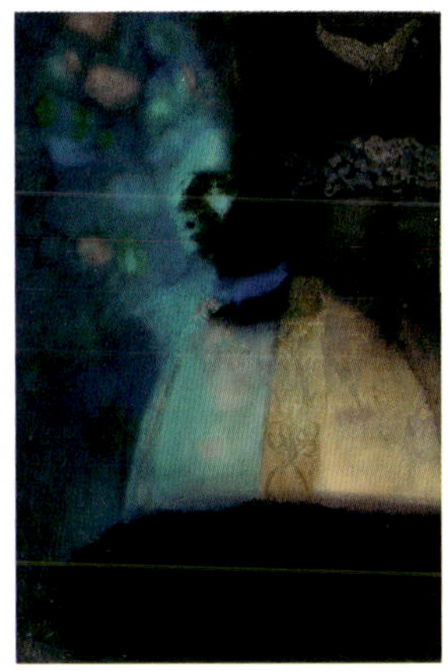

Unsworth, Peter b.1937
Owl and Clergyman
oil on canvas 92 x 61
29

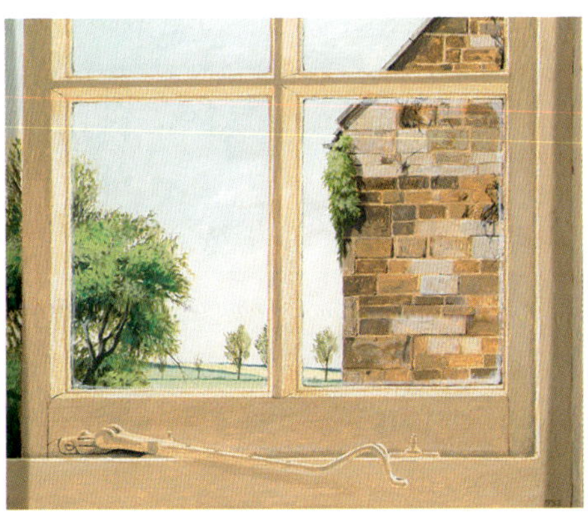

Waldron, Dylan b.1953
Farmhouse Corner 1982
tempera on board 17 x 20
59

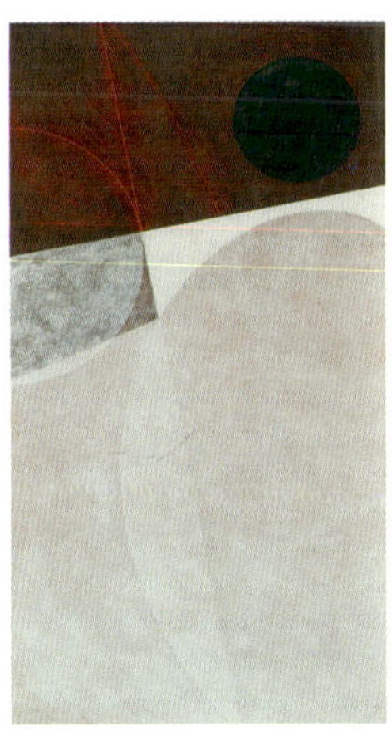

Wells, John 1907–2000
*Study in Grey and Brown**
oil on board 121 x 60
27

Basildon District Council

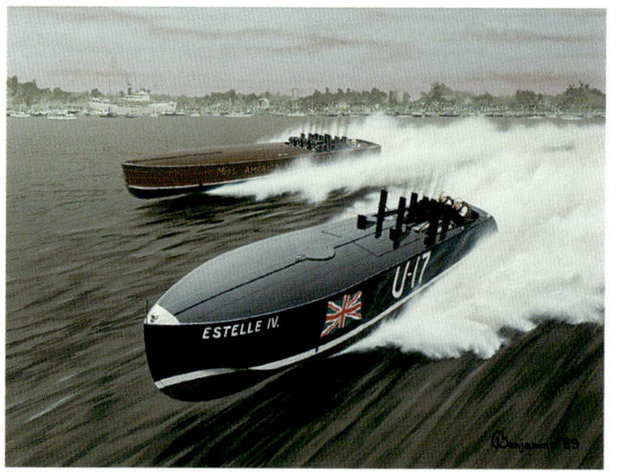

Benjamins, Arthur b.1953
'Estelle IV' at Detroit, 1930 (Miss Carstairs leading the race for the Harmsworth Trophy) 1989
oil on board 59 x 90
1

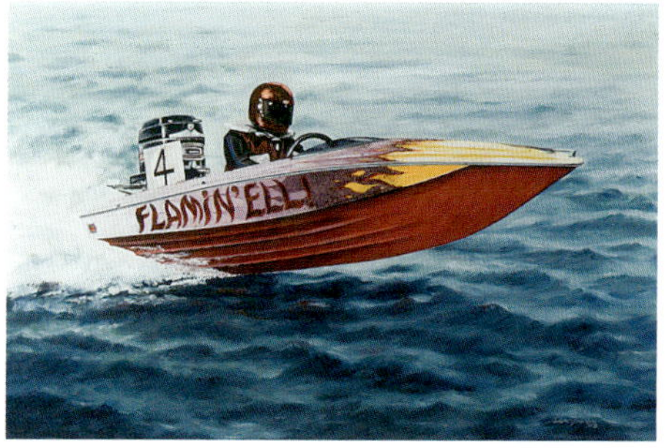

Franks, Dave
Eric Blunden in 'Flamin' 'Ell!' 1973
oil on board 40 x 59.5
3

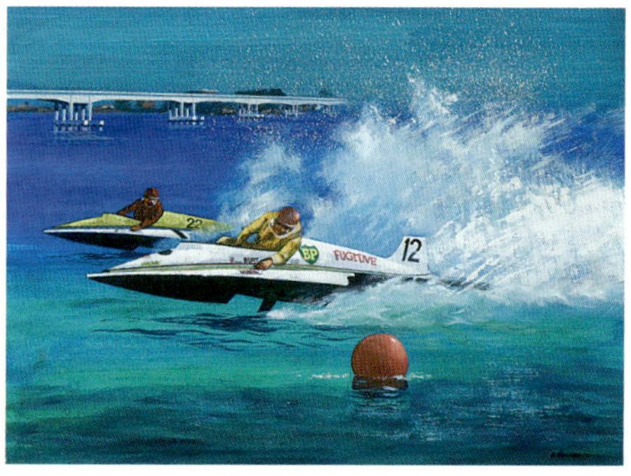

Hawkins, G.
Burt Noone in His Racing Boat 'Fugitive' 1971
acrylic on board 44 x 60
2

Belchamp St Paul Community House

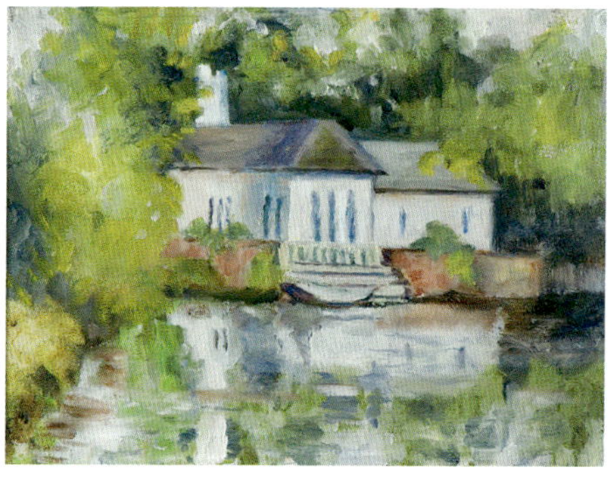

May, Margaret d. after 1993
The House by the Lake (Kyrenia)
oil on canvas 30 x 40
2

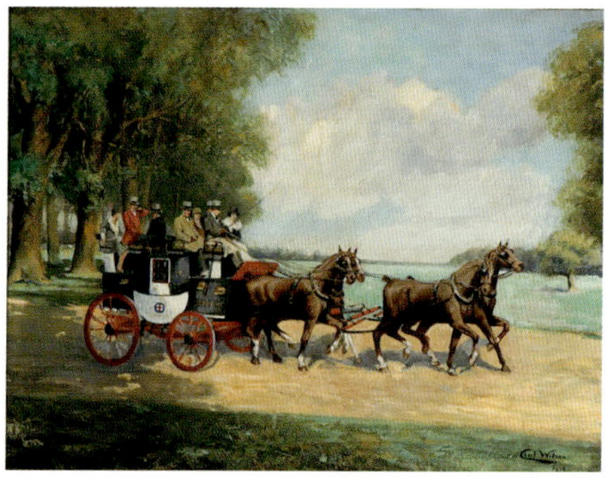

Wilson, Cecil active c.1900–1934
The Stagecoach, 'Venture' 1928
oil on canvas 83 x 106
1

Castle Point Borough Council

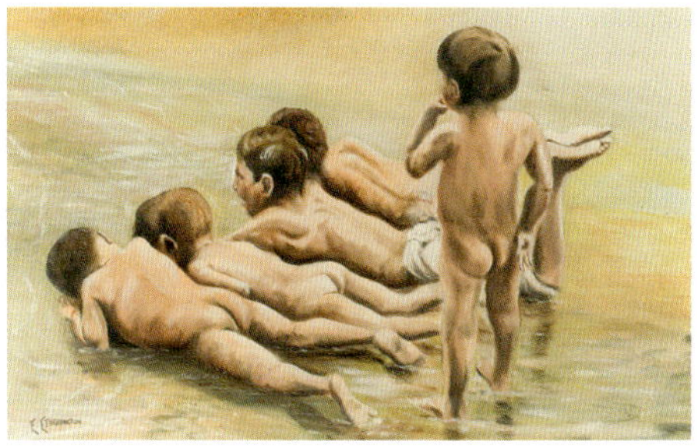

Etherington, E.
Children Lying in the Surf
oil on board 44 x 70
69

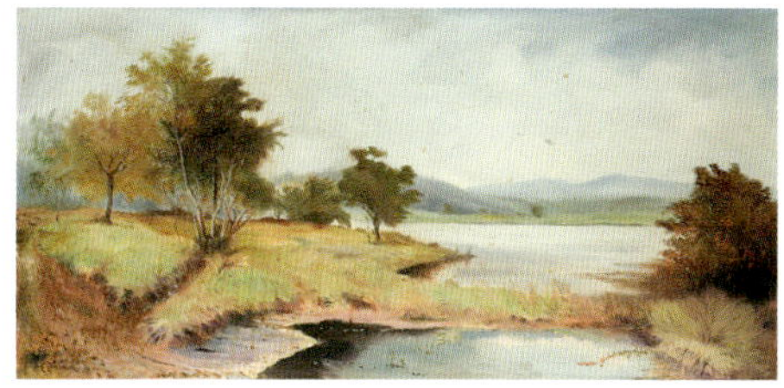

Etherington, E.
Countryside River Scene
oil on board 60 x 121
70

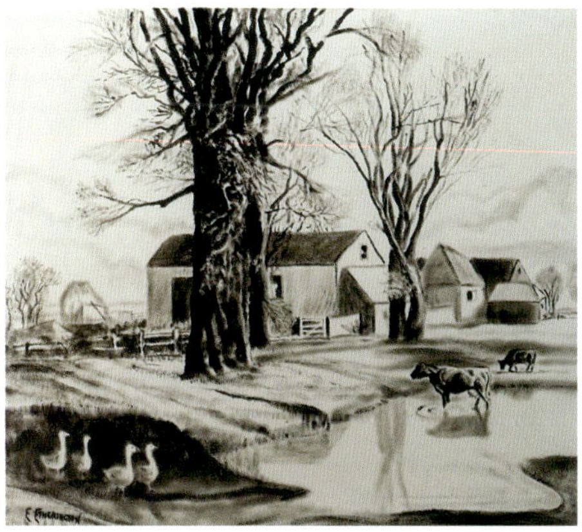

Etherington, E.
Farmyard Scene
oil on board 68 x 75
50

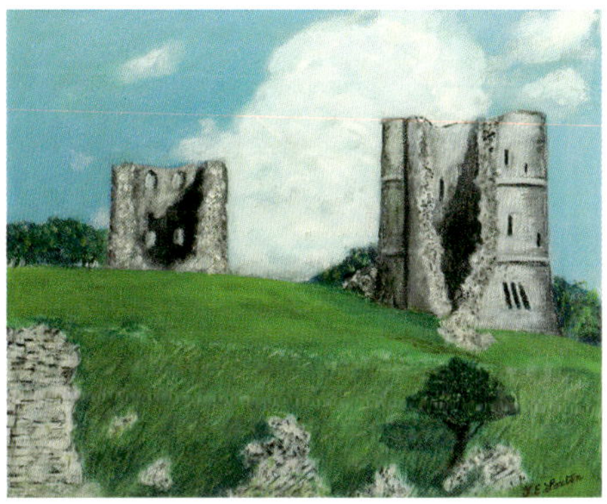

Loxton, J. E.
Hadleigh Castle
oil on board 41.5 x 49
49

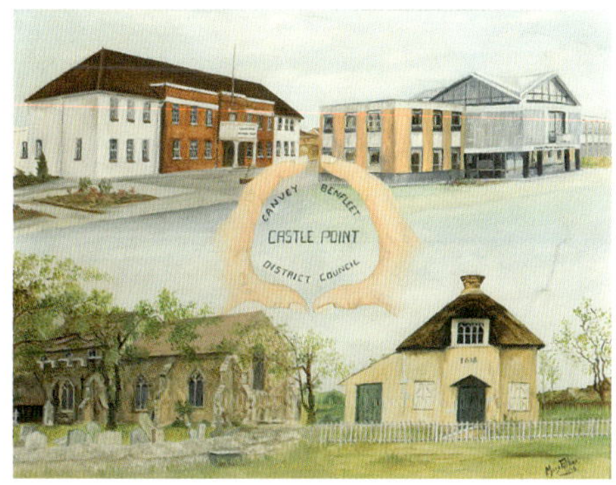

Parker, Mary
Old Canvey Council Offices; Benfleet Council Offices, South Benfleet; St Mary the Virgin; Dutch Cottage Museum, Canvey Island 1976
oil on board 44.5 x 54
25

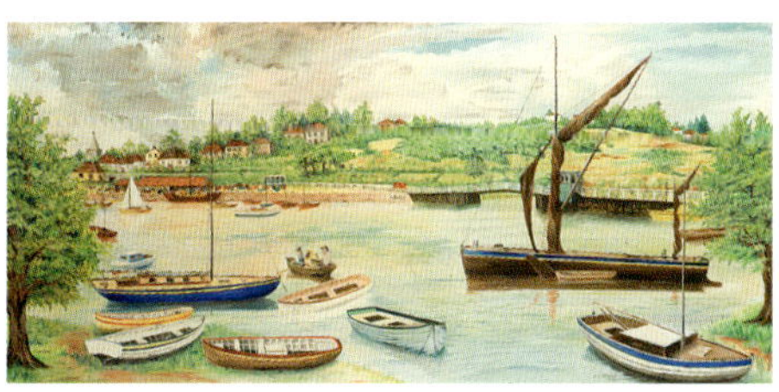

Pound, F. C.
Folding Bridge and Creek between the Mainland and Canvey Island 1970
oil on board 59.5 x 122
18

Dutch Cottage Museum

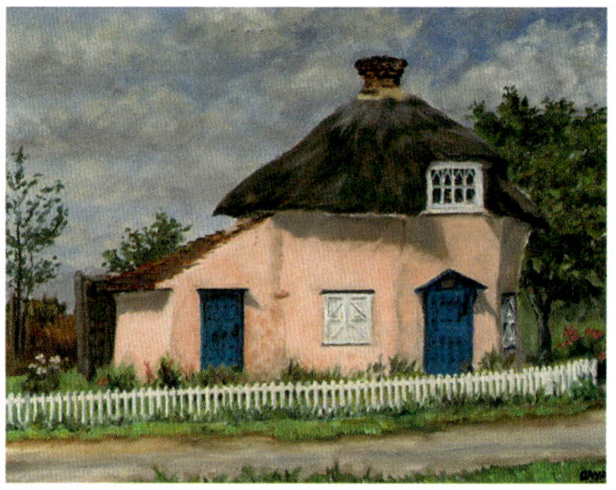

Amos, Gay
The Dutch Cottage Museum c.1975
oil on hardboard 31 x 39.5
2

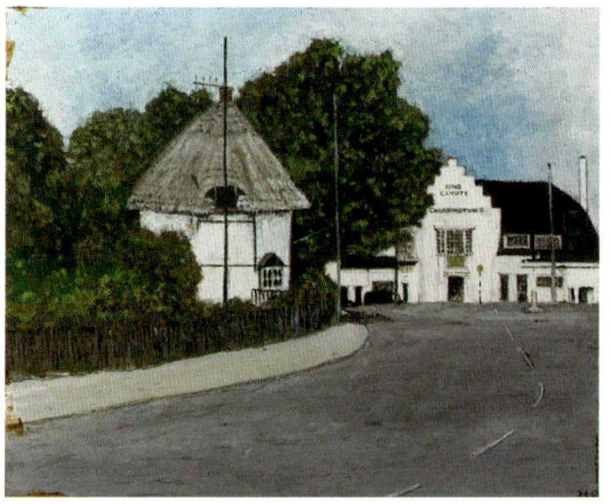

Kerwood, G.
Dutch Cottage, Haven Road 1965
oil on hardboard 47 x 57
4

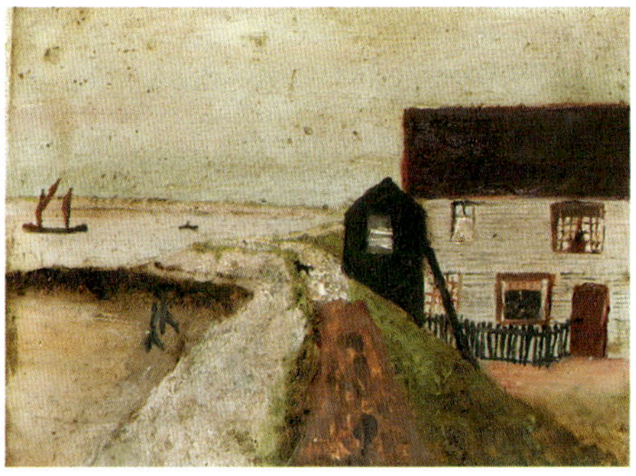

unknown artist
The Lobster Smack, Canvey Island c.1900
oil on panel 11 x 14
1

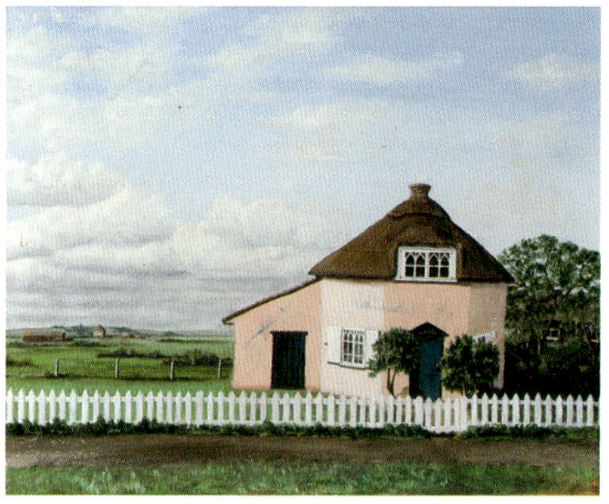

unknown artist
The Dutch Cottage Museum c.1970
oil on hardboard 40 x 50
3

Braintree District Museum

Nestling in the middle of North Essex, the local authority district of Braintree is widespread, and its rural charm is punctuated by a surprising industrial heritage. The artistic paternalism of industrial benefactors is well represented within the small art collection of Braintree District Museum. This began with the collection of a local clerk, Alfred Hills, being displayed within Braintree Town Hall. After a succession of different homes, the collection was eventually housed in the Braintree District Museum, which opened in the former Manor Street School in 1993.

Braintree Town Hall opened in 1928 to the designs of Emanuel Vincent Harris (1879–1971) and was the gift of Sir William Julien Courtauld (1870–1940), who commissioned the series of eight murals painted on copper from Maurice Greiffenhagen, RA (1862–1931). The donor's intention was to decorate the Council Chamber and to portray some of the history of Braintree.

Either side of the staircase are portraits by Greiffenhagen of Sir William Julien Courtauld, presented by his wife, and George Thomas Thorpe Bartram, in recognition of 50 years of service as a local councillor and of his role as Chairman of the Urban District Council at the opening of the Town Hall.

The long history of the silk industry that shaped the industrial development of many local communities is illustrated in the mural, commissioned in 1957 by Sir Reginald Mathys, Deputy Chairman of Courtaulds Ltd, from Anna Zinkeisen (1901–1976). Scenes include Egyptian textiles; Chinese silk; Medieval tapestry weaving; French silk industry; the cities of Coventry and London; spinning; the discovery of artificial fibres, and a couple which probably represents George Courtauld and his wife.

Engineering was another important local industry and Crittall Manufacturing Company Ltd commissioned the *Old Iron* collection of 47 known portraits of its employees between 1926 and 1930. Sir George Clausen, and Professors Rothenstein, Russell and Tonks nominated the 25 rising artists who undertook the commission, probably for the 'Guv'nor', Francis Henry Crittall (1860–1935). They were first exhibited together for the opening of Silver End Village Hall in 1928. The garden village was created by Francis Henry in 1926 as a site for a new Crittall metal window factory, modernist housing and all the facilities for the employees to be completely self-sufficient. So far, 22 portraits have been brought into the Museum and we are grateful for the loan of the collection from Crittall Windows Ltd. Research continues into this fascinating glimpse of the lives of company employees from the Crittall family, who owned the metal window company, to the workers on the shop floor.

The tradition of accepting the work of local artists such as Olive de Horne Vaizey of Bocking, and John Aldridge (1905–1983) of Great Bardfield, has broadened and continues with the selection of one work every year from the Braintree District Arts *Open Art and Craft Exhibition*. Braintree District Museum will also continue to liaise with other local museums and heritage centres within the district, which own art collections. Future collecting is dependent upon the generosity of donors and funding bodies.

We applaud the benefits of the work of the Public Catalogue Foundation, not only in improving the profile of the Museum's oil paintings but also in raising funds for the conservation of this important local collection for the future enjoyment of inhabitants and visitors to Braintree District.

Robert Rose, Collections and Heritage Manager

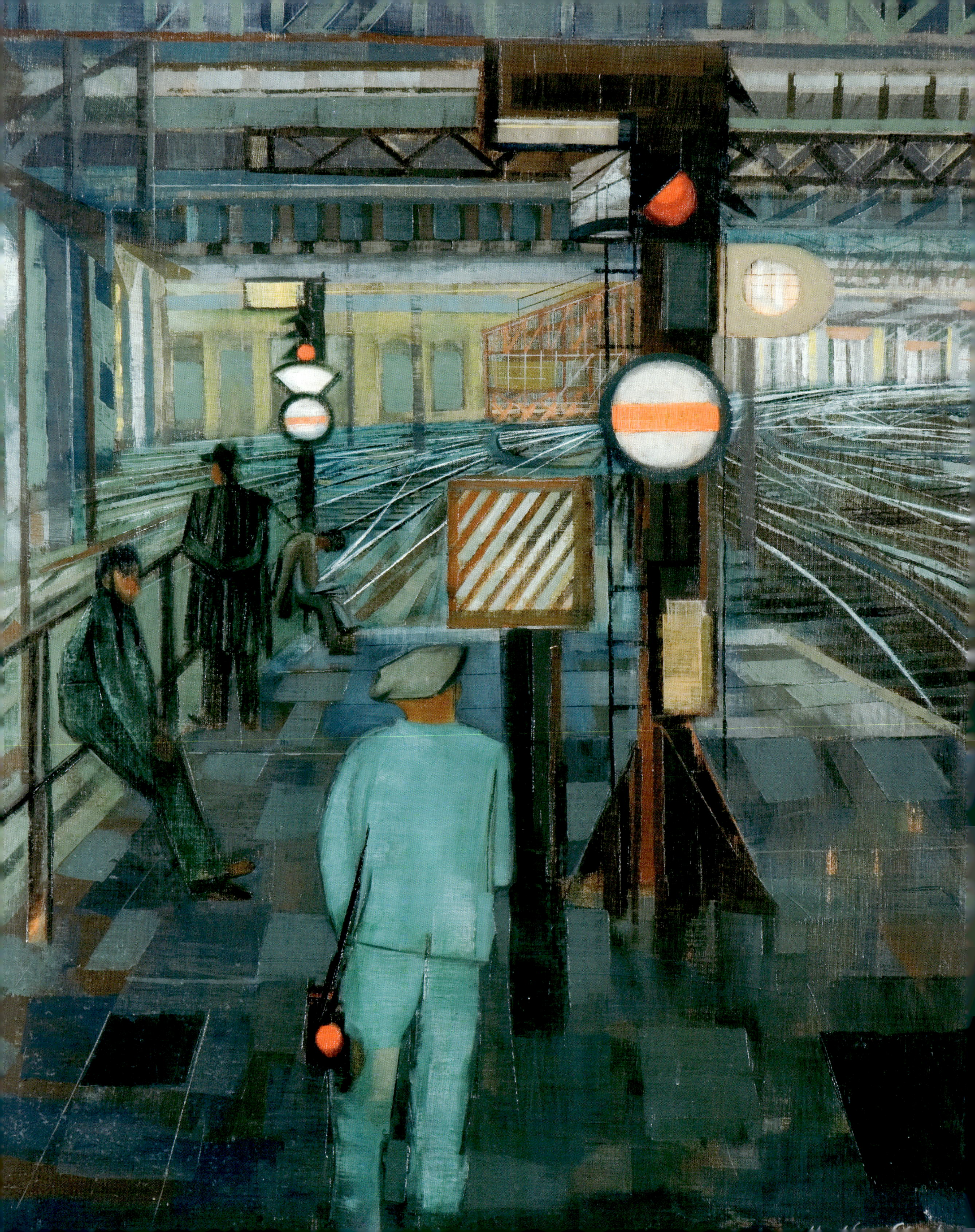

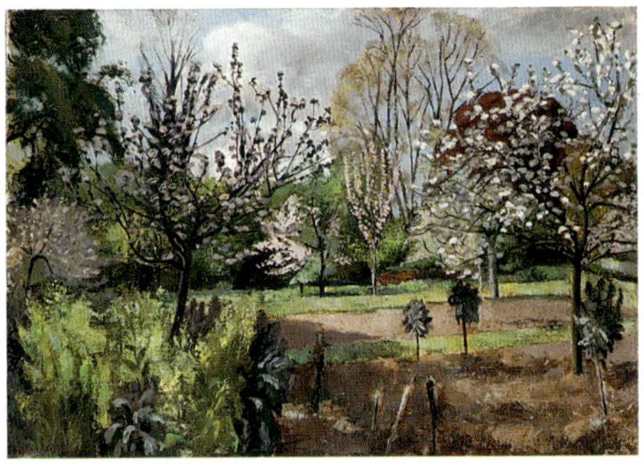

Aldridge, John Arthur Malcolm 1905–1983
The Orchard, the Place House, Great Bardfield c.1948
oil on board 47.8 x 66.1
BRNTM 2005.28

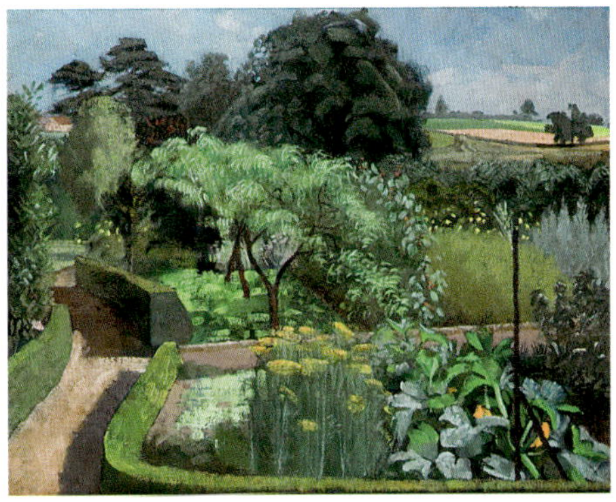

Aldridge, John Arthur Malcolm 1905–1983
The Vegetable Garden, the Place House, Great Bardfield 1966
oil on canvas 50.5 x 60.8
BRNTM 2005.29

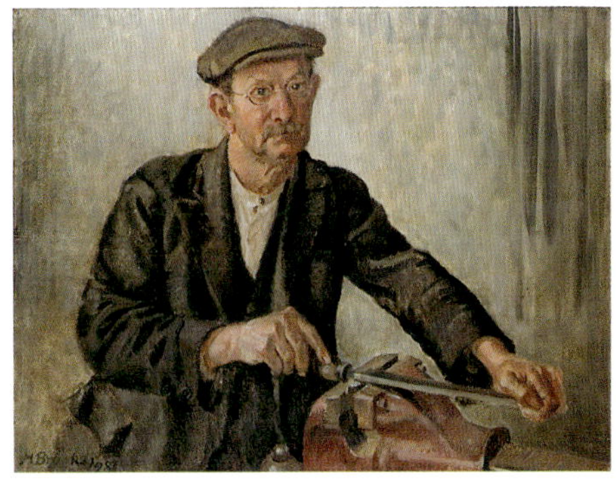

Brooks, Marjorie 1904–1980
W. Griggs (Old Iron Portrait Collection) 1928
oil on canvas 61 x 76.5
BRNTM 1989.82.7

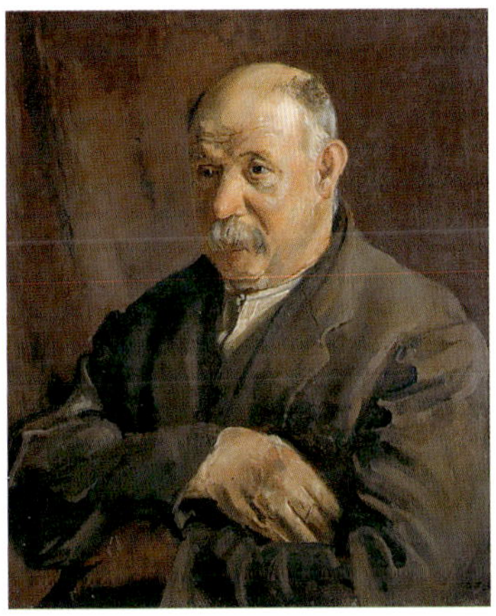

Burn, Rodney Joseph 1899–1984
A. North (Old Iron Portrait Collection) 1927
oil on canvas 61.8 x 51
BRNTM 1989.82.13

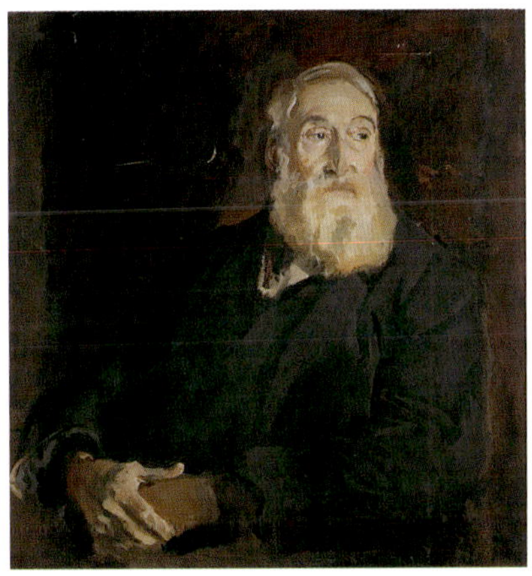

Burn, Rodney Joseph 1899–1984
A. T Strutt (Old Iron Portrait Collection) 1927
oil on canvas 68.8 x 63.6
BRNTM 1989.82.10 (P)

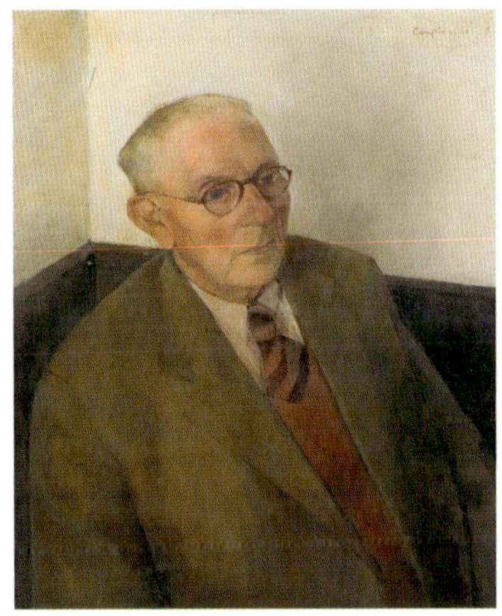

Campion, Oliver 1928–2000
J. W. Caton 1958
oil on canvas 61 x 50.8
BRNTM 1996.81

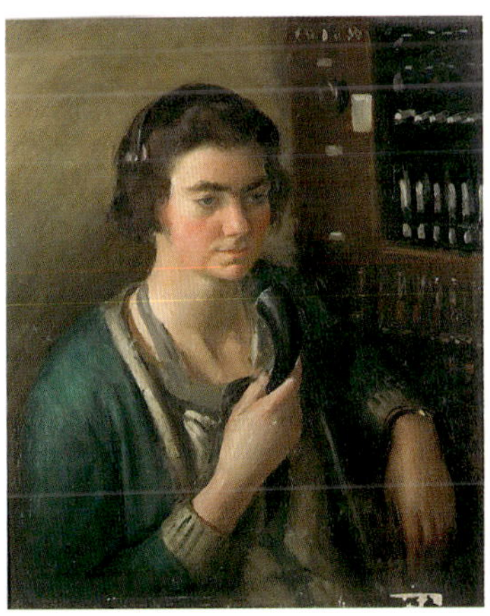

Carr, Henry Marvell 1894–1970
Miss H. Dearlove (Old Iron Portrait Collection) c.1927
oil on canvas 61.2 x 50.8
BRNTM 1989.82.9 (P)

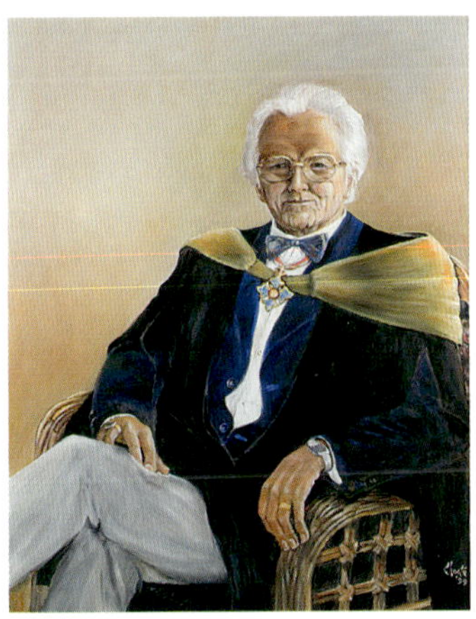

Choate, Francis Desmond 1916–2001
Iorwerth Williams, CBE (b.1926) 1999
oil on canvas 91.1 x 71
BRNTM 2005.26

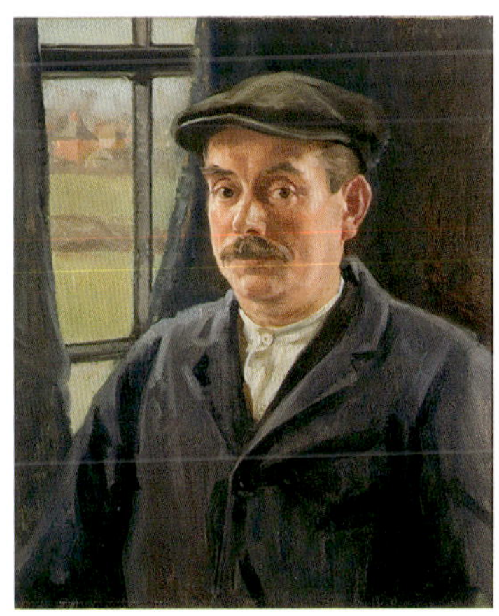

Christie, Alexander b.1901
G. Monk (Old Iron Portrait Collection) 1928
oil on canvas 61.1 x 51
BRNTM 1989.82.5 (P)

Facing page: Spender, John Humphrey, 1910–2005, *Station Scene* (detail), 1953, University of Essex, (p. 179)

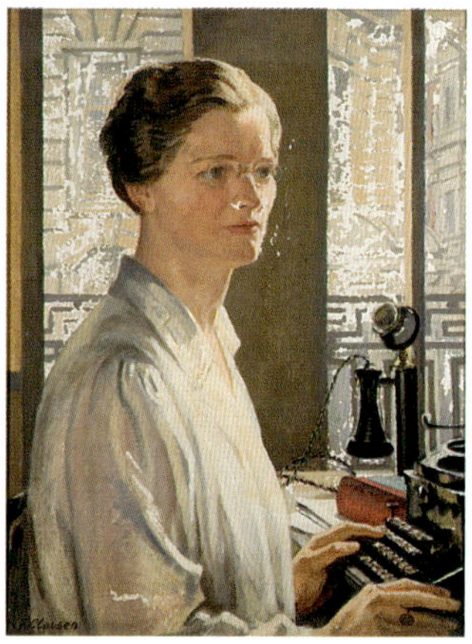

Clausen, Katharine Frances 1886–1936
I. M. Coope (Old Iron Portrait Collection) c.1927
oil on canvas 68.9 x 51
BRNTM 2005.36 (P)

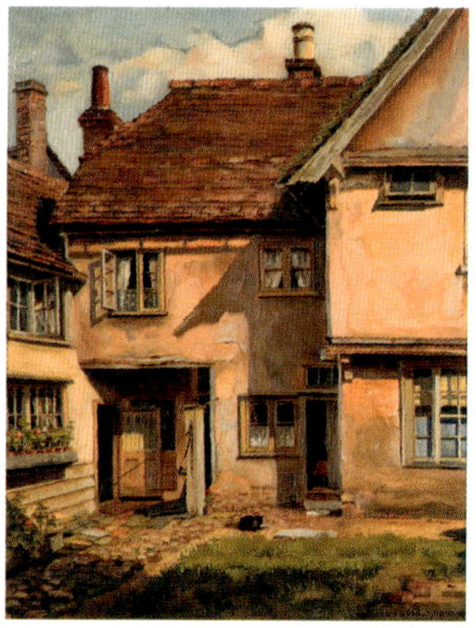

Cole, Elsie Vera 1885–1968
Rear of 23 Bradford Street, Bocking 1910
oil on canvas 45.8 x 35.7
BRNTM 2005.23

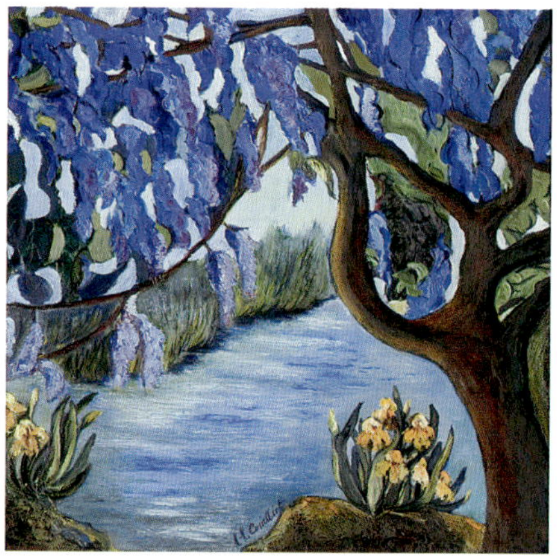

Couilliot, Marguerite
Purple Landscape c.1998
oil on board 44 x 44 (E)
BRNTM 2005.20

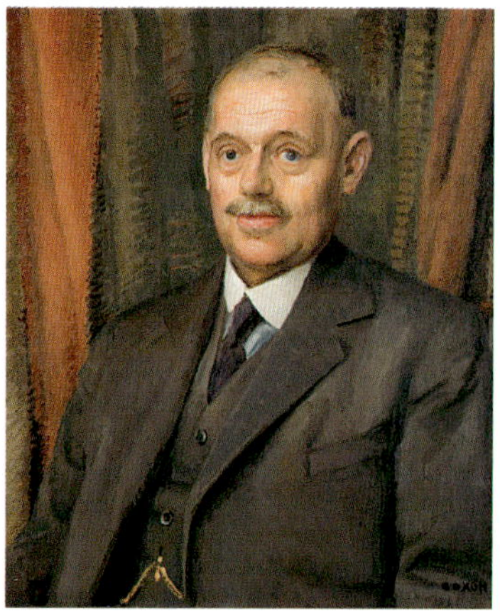

Coxon, Raymond James 1896–1997
H. S. Usher (Old Iron Portrait Collection) 1926
oil on canvas 61.2 x 51.1
BRNTM 1989.82.14

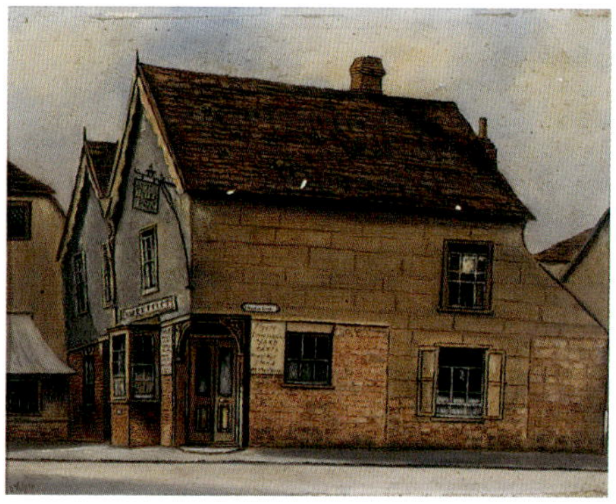

de Horne Vaizey, Olive active c.1932–1959
Old Six Bells Inn, Church Lane, Bocking c.1932
oil on canvas 20.2 x 25.5
BRNTM 2005.27

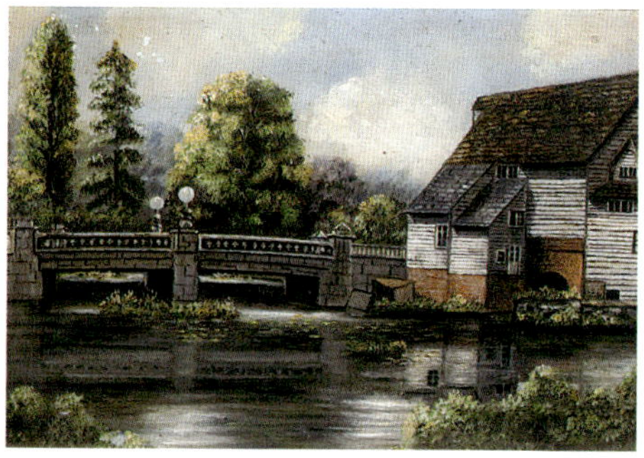

de Horne Vaizey, Olive active c.1932–1959
Cane's Mill, Bocking c.1940–1959
oil on canvas 17.8 x 25.4
BRNTM 1975.2286

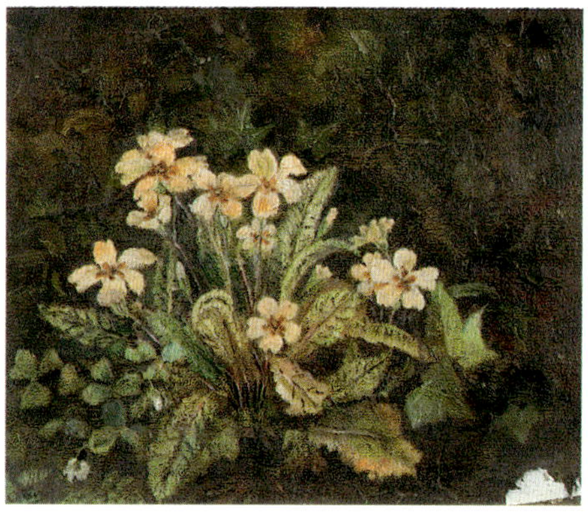

de Horne Vaizey, Olive active c.1932–1959
My Peaceful Home c.1940–1959
oil on board 17.8 x 21
BRNTM 1975.2288

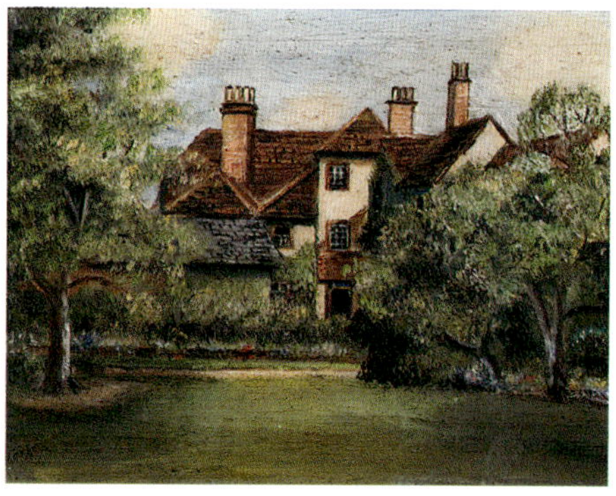

de Horne Vaizey, Olive active c.1932–1959
Back of Maysent House, Bradford Street, Bocking 1945
oil on board 11.4 x 15.3 (E)
BRNTM 1975.2287

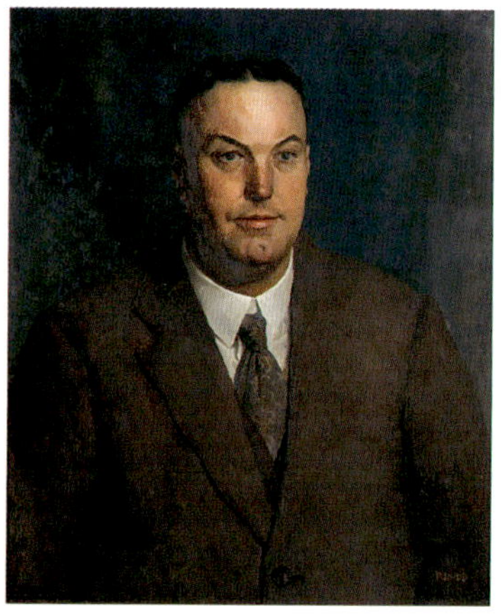

Dodd, Phyllis 1899–1995
F. Rogers (Old Iron Portrait Collection) c.1927
oil on canvas 61.1 x 50.8
BRNTM 1989.82.20

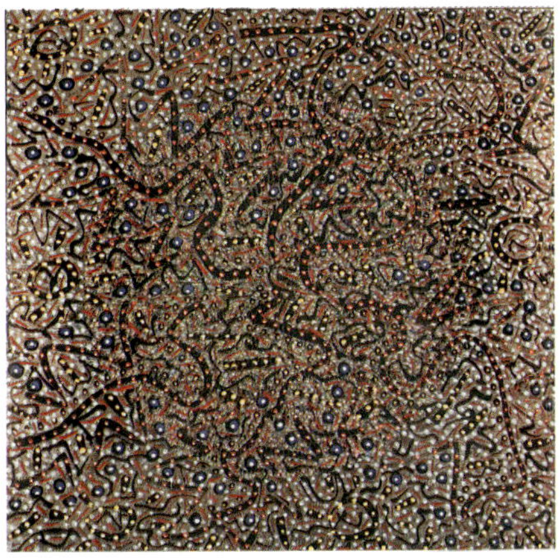

Downey, Steve b.1945
Yantra 2: Circle of Indifference 1993
oil on board 107 x 107
BRNTM 2005.21

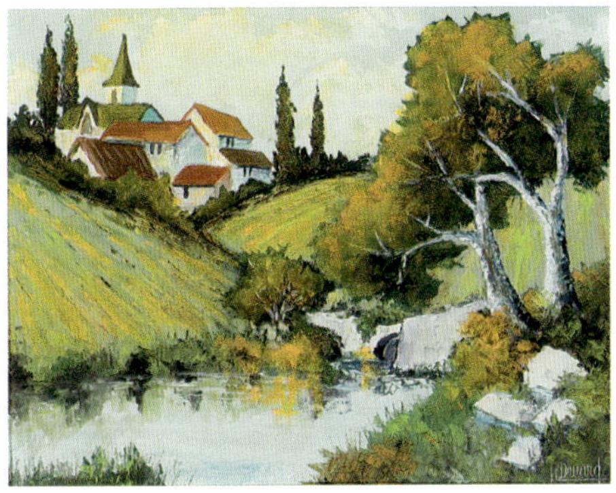

Druard, R.
L'étang, St Pierre 1998
oil on board 33 x 41
BRNTM 2005.22

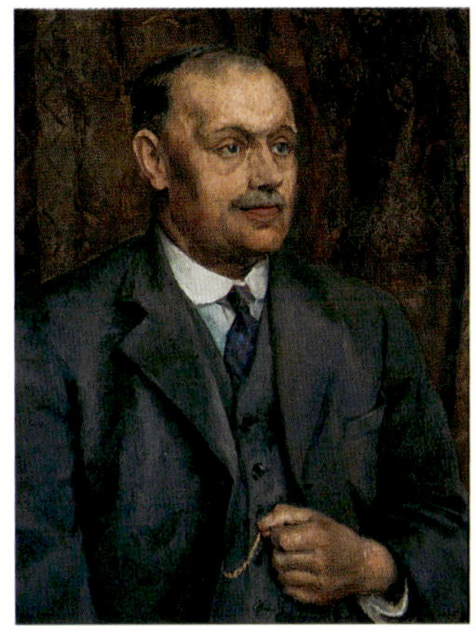

Gines, A.
H. S. Usher 1928
oil on canvas 60.5 x 45.4
BRNTM 1989.82.21

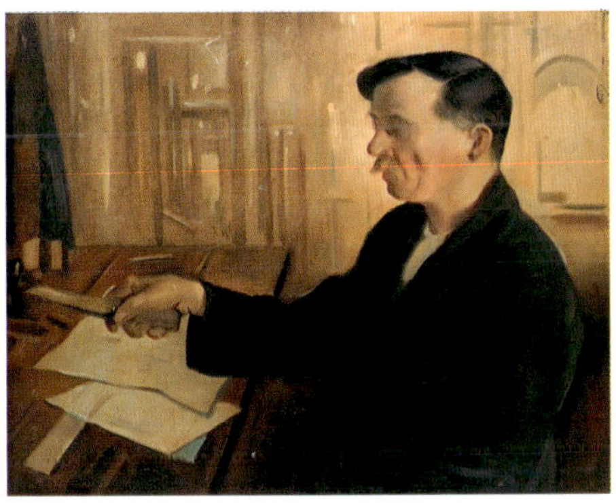

Greenham, Robert Duckworth 1906–1976
E. Byford (Old Iron Portrait Collection) 1928
oil on canvas 63.8 x 76.6
BRNTM 2005.37 (P)

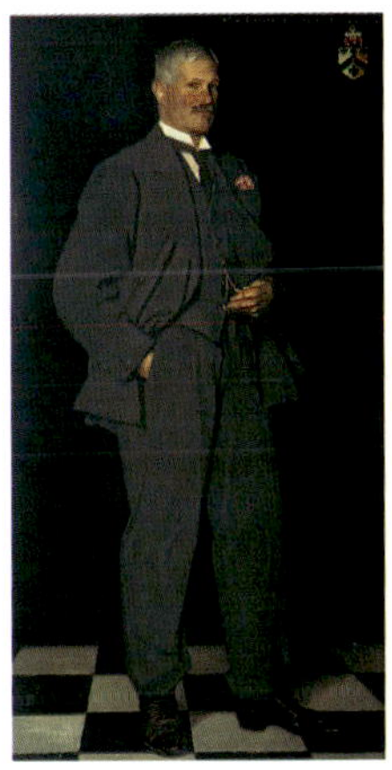

Greiffenhagen, Maurice 1862–1931
Sir William Julien Courtauld, BT, JP, CC (1870–1940), the Donor of the Town Hall to Braintree 1928
oil on canvas 194 x 90 (E)
BRNTM 2005.17

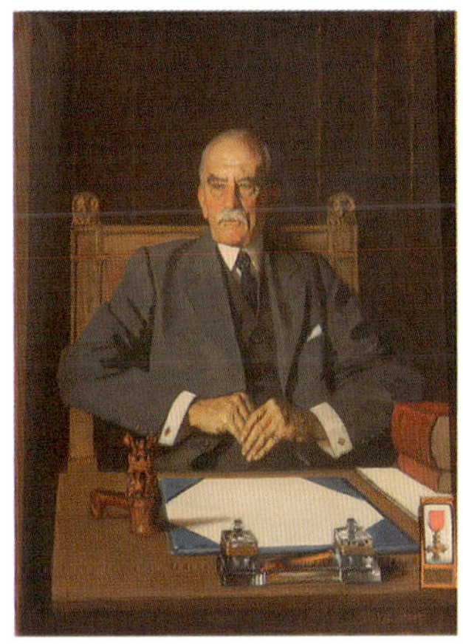

Greiffenhagen, Maurice 1862–1931
George Thomas Thorpe Bartram, JP, CA 1929
oil on panel 137 x 101 (E)
BRNTM 2005.30

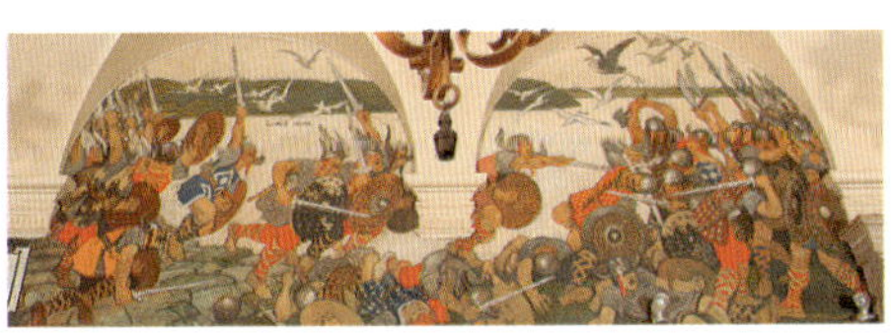

Greiffenhagen, Maurice 1862–1931
Battle of Maldon, 991 1930
oil on copper 150 x 488 (E)
BRNTM 2005.34.4

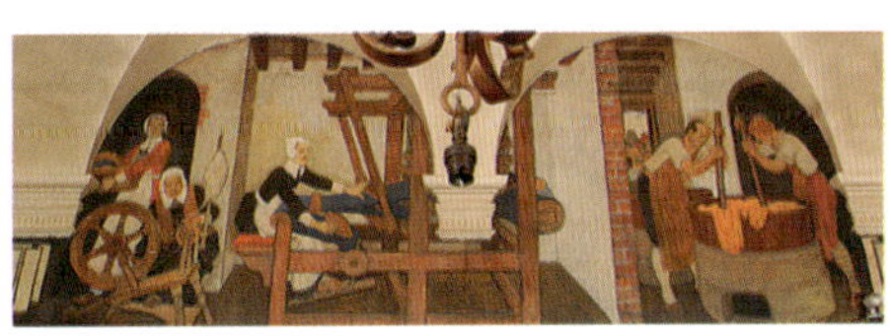

Greiffenhagen, Maurice 1862–1931
Huguenots Spinning, Weaving and Dyeing, 1690 1930
oil on copper 150 x 480 (E)
BRNTM 2005.34.8

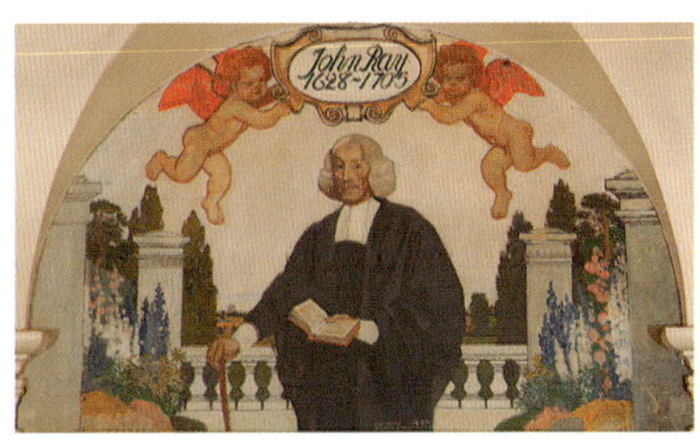

Greiffenhagen, Maurice 1862–1931
John Ray (1628–1705) 1930
oil on copper 120 x 177 (E)
BRNTM 2005.34.5

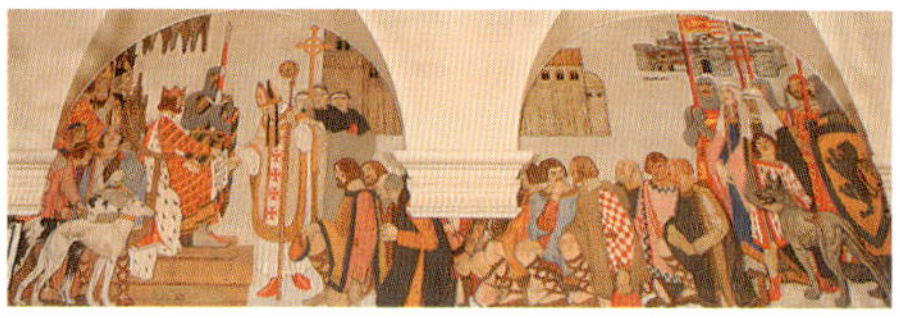

Greiffenhagen, Maurice 1862–1931
King John Presents the Bishop of London with the Charter for Braintree, 1199 1930
oil on copper 150 x 600 (E)
BRNTM 2005.34.3

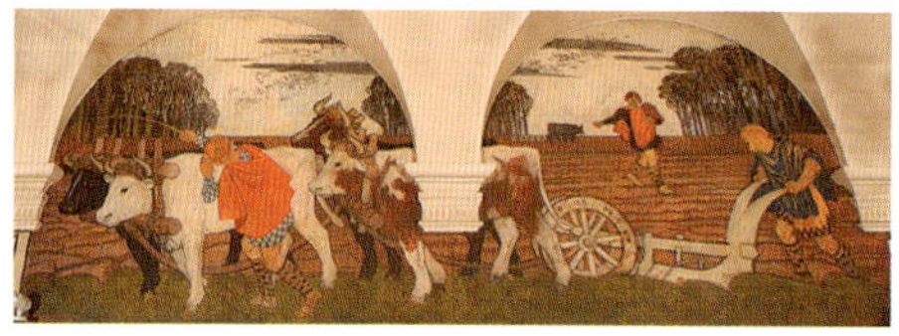

Greiffenhagen, Maurice 1862–1931
Ploughing, Sowing and Harrowing, c.1060 1930
oil on copper 150 x 500 (E)
BRNTM 2005.34.2

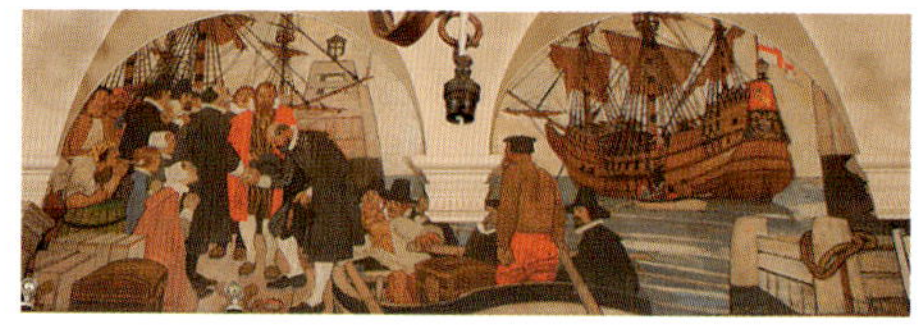

Greiffenhagen, Maurice 1862–1931
Sailing of the Braintree Company in the 'Lyon', 1632 1930
oil on copper 150 x 480 (E)
BRNTM 2005.34.6

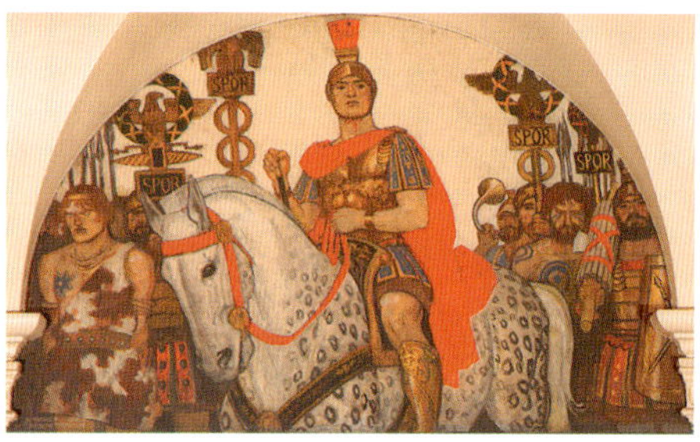

Greiffenhagen, Maurice 1862–1931
Soldier on a Horse, Depicting the History of the Township of Braintree 1930
oil on copper 150 x 223 (E)
BRNTM 2005.34.1

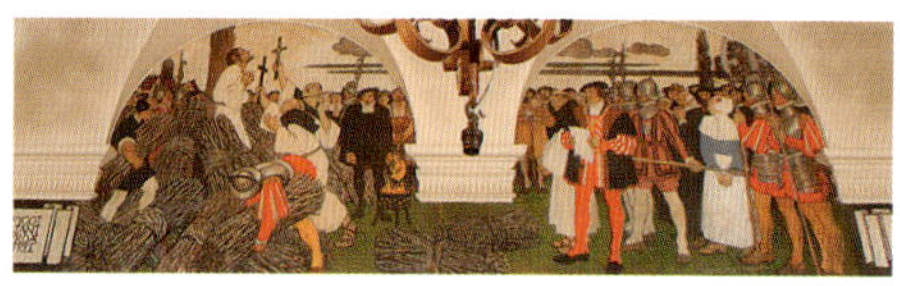

Greiffenhagen, Maurice 1862–1931
William Pygot, Protestant Martyred at Braintree, 28 March 1555 1930
oil on copper 140 x 600 (E)
BRNTM 2005.34.7

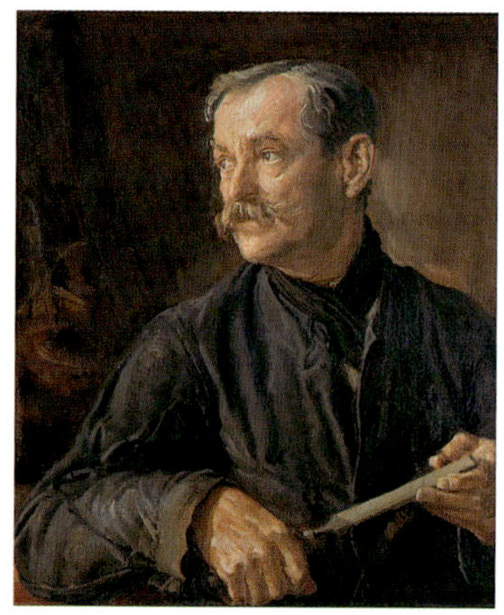

Guthrie, Robin 1902–1971
H. Walford (Old Iron Portrait Collection) c.1927
oil on canvas 61.2 x 50.8
BRNTM 1989.82.4

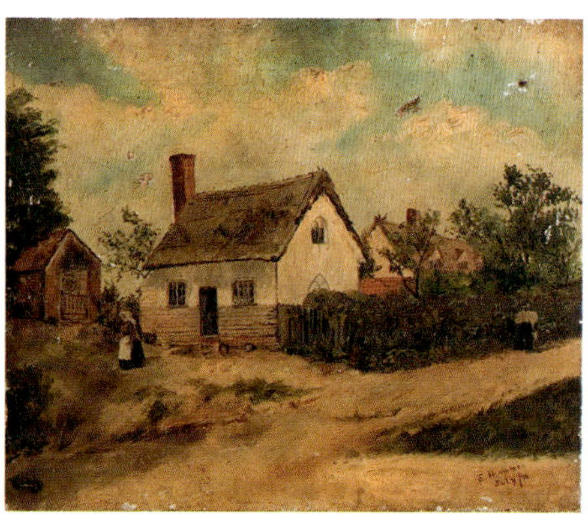

Hawkes, S.
Mary's Cottage, Rayne 1896
oil on canvas 30.5 x 35.5
BRNTM 1989.20

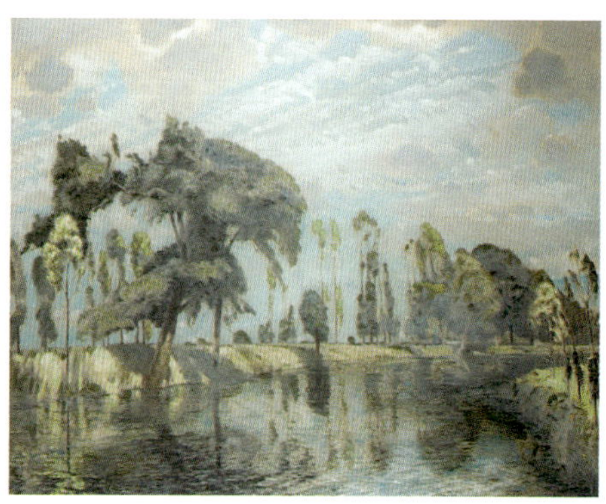

Hood, William T.
Essex Landscape: The Heybridge Canal near Maldon 1948
oil on canvas 69 x 85 (E)
BRNTM 2005.19

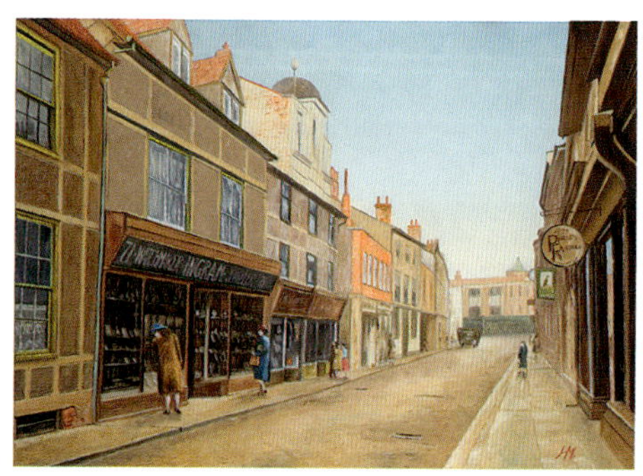

H. M.
High Street, Braintree 1939–1945
oil on board 45.3 x 60
BRNTM 1995.276

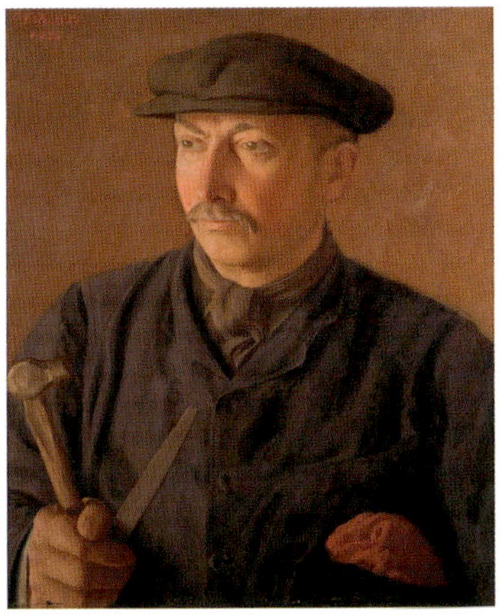

Ososki, Gerald Judah 1903–1981
A. Franklin (Old Iron Portrait Collection) 1928
oil on canvas 61 x 51.1
BRNTM 1989.82.1 (P)

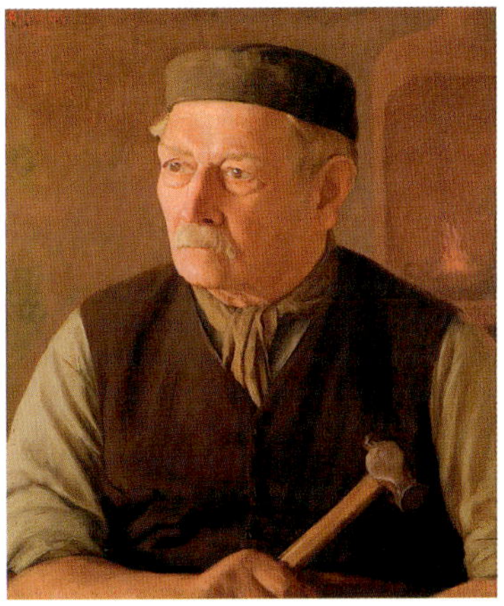

Ososki, Gerald Judah 1903–1981
George 'Doc' Harvey (Old Iron Portrait Collection) 1928
oil on canvas 61.1 x 51.1
BRNTM 2005.25

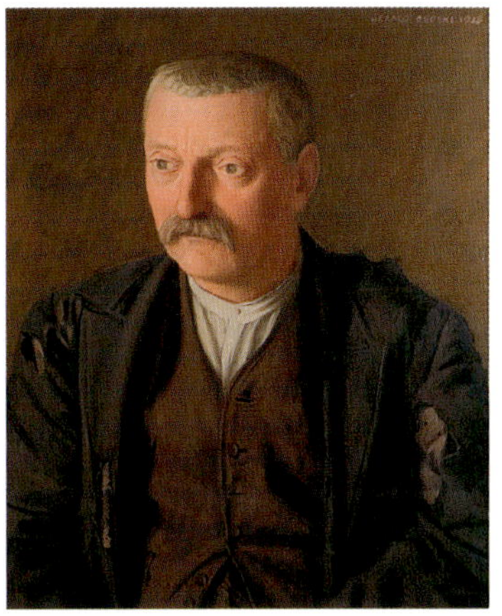

Ososki, Gerald Judah 1903–1981
H. White (Old Iron Portrait Collection) 1928
oil on canvas 61 x 51
BRNTM 1989.82.18

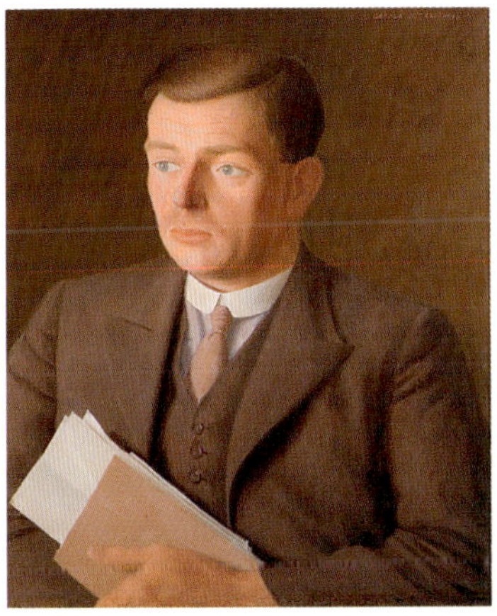

Ososki, Gerald Judah 1903–1981
S. H. Wordley (Old Iron Portrait Collection) 1928
oil on canvas 61 x 51
BRNTM 1989.82.17 (P)

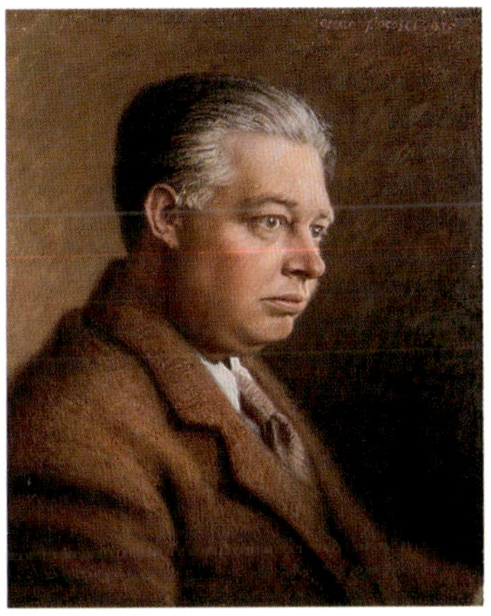

Ososki, Gerald Judah 1903–1981
Sir Valentine Crittall, JP (1884–1961), Lord Braintree (Old Iron Portrait Collection) 1930
oil on canvas 69.3 x 56.3
BRNTM 1989.82.11 (P)

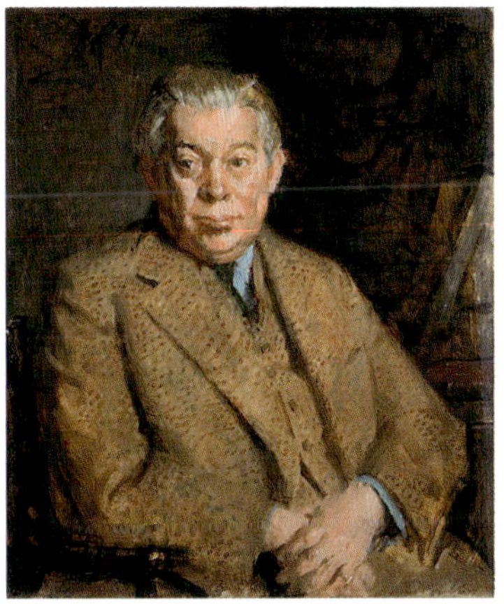

Phillips, A. active 1927–1939
Sir Valentine Crittall, JP (1884–1961), Lord Braintree
oil on canvas 80.8 x 68
BRNTM 1989.82.19

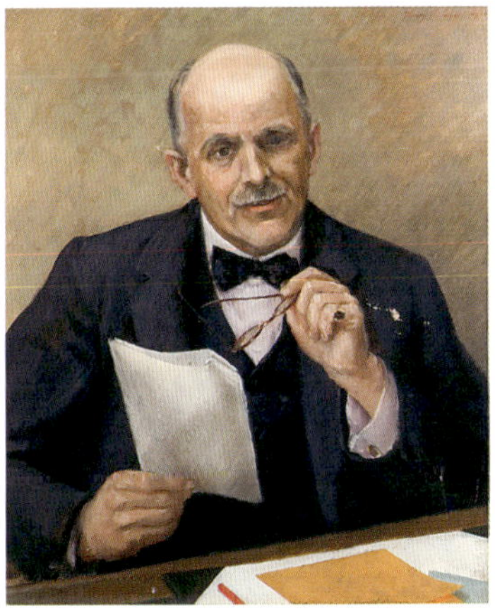

Sands, Henry Southgate b.1900
H. S. Munns (Old Iron Portrait Collection) 1928
oil on canvas 61 x 51
BRNTM 1989.82.2 (P)

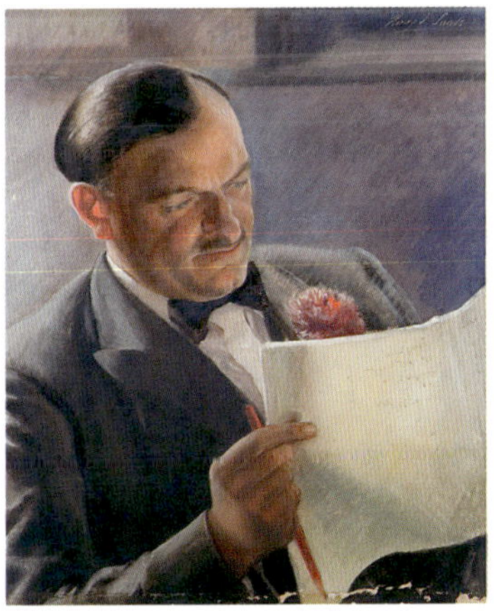

Sands, Henry Southgate b.1900
W. C. C. Bywater (Old Iron Portrait Collection) 1928
oil on canvas 61.5 x 51
BRNTM 1989.82.3 (P)

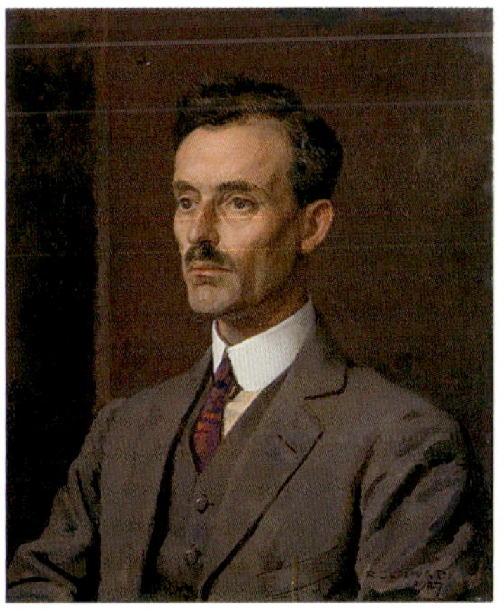

Schwabe, Randolph 1885–1948
Frederick Gold Rogers (Old Iron Portrait Collection) 1927
oil on canvas 61.3 x 51.4
BRNTM 2005.24

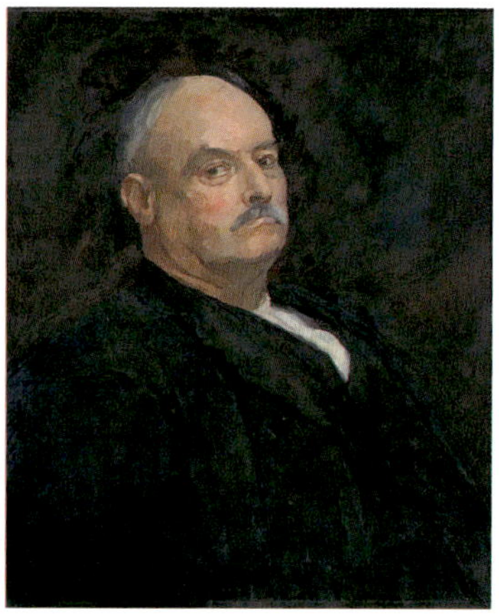

Towner, Donald Chisholm 1903–1985
C. Conroy (Old Iron Portrait Collection) 1927
oil on canvas 60.8 x 50.9
BRNTM 1989.82.15

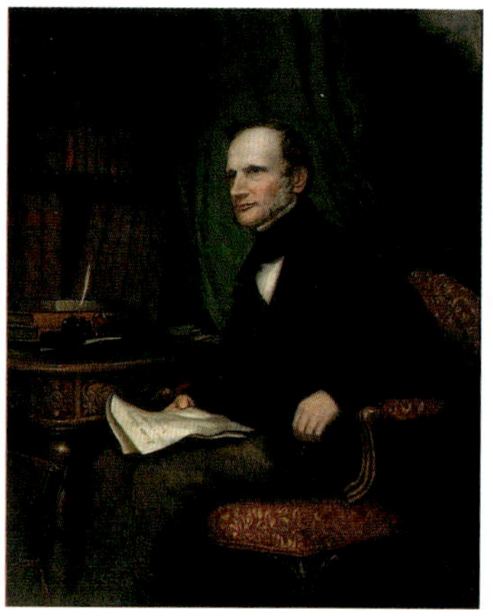

unknown artist early 19th C
George Courtauld, Donor of Braintree Literary and Mechanics Institution (1802–1861)
oil on canvas 125.5 x 100.4 (E)
BRNTM 1967.258

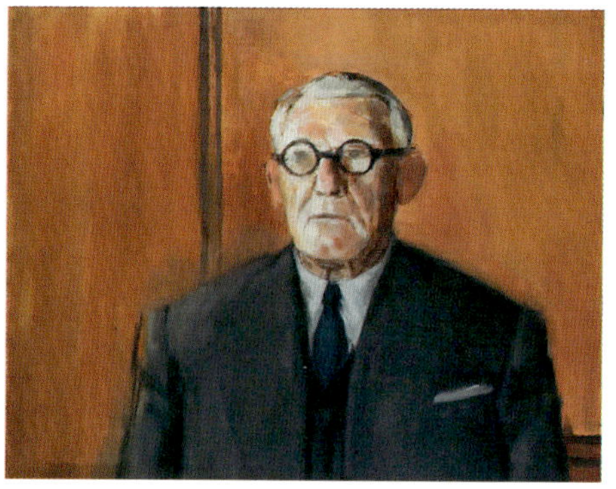

unknown artist
Victor Attwood c.1967–1973
oil on canvas 50.5 x 60.7
BRNTM 2005.18

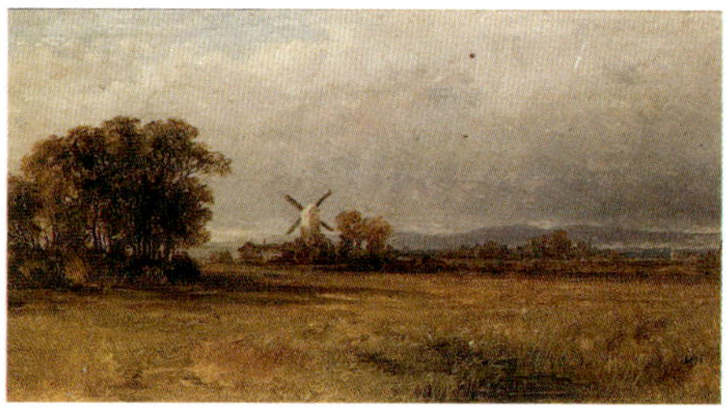

Vaizey, A. early 19th C
Bocking Post Mill
oil on board 17.4 x 31 (E)
BRNTM 1975.2275

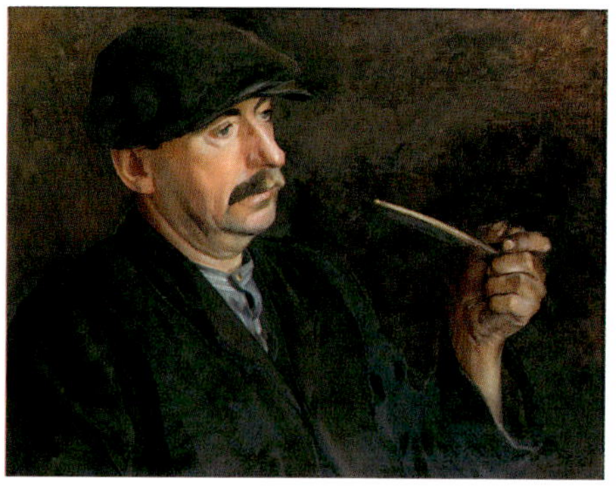

Wells, Leonard Harry b.1903
J. 'Ramsey' Willison (Old Iron Portrait Collection) c.1927
oil on canvas 50.8 x 61.6
BRNTM 1989.82.16

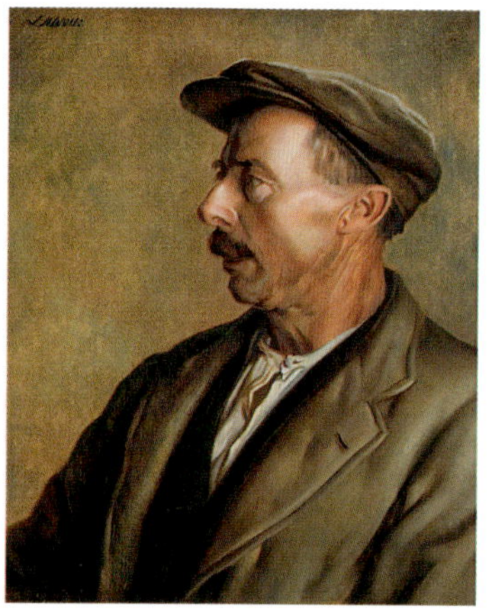

Wells, Leonard Harry b.1903
G. Usher (Old Iron Portrait Collection) 1928
oil on canvas 56 x 45.8
BRNTM 1989.82.6 (P)

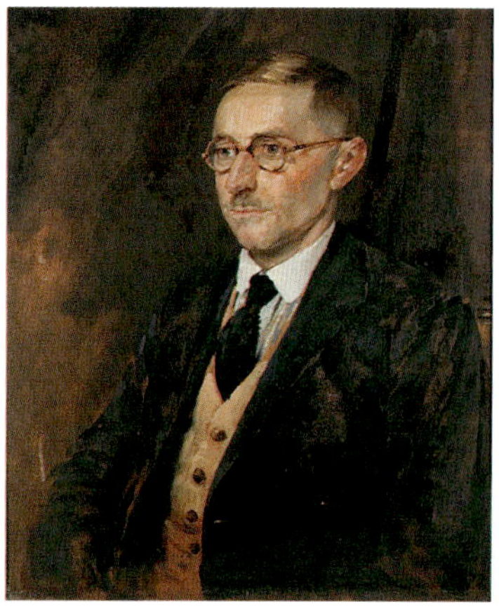

Wilkie, James 1890–1957
H. H. Wrate (Old Iron Portrait Collection) c.1927
oil on canvas 61.5 x 50.8
BRNTM 1989.82.8 (P)

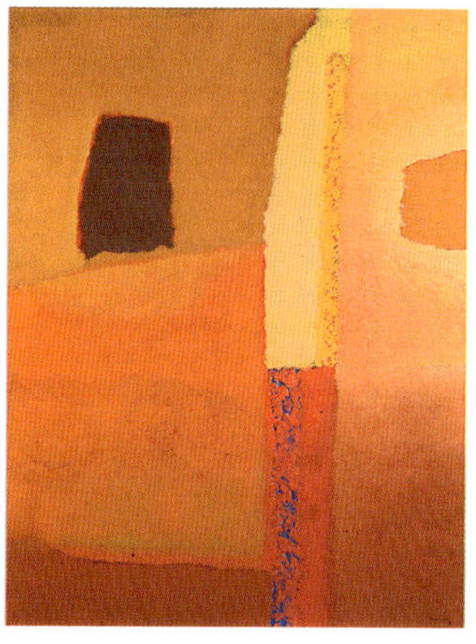

Winn, Hugh b.1940
Resurrection 1994
oil on board 73.5 x 58.2 (E)
BRNTM 2005.33

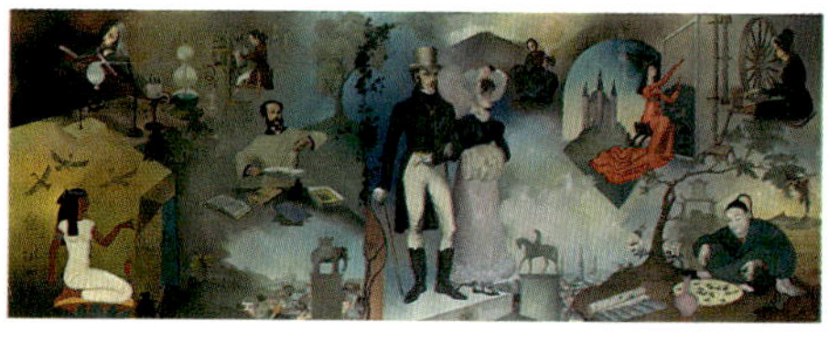

Zinkeisen, Anna Katrina 1901–1976
The Evolution of the Textile Industry 1957–1958
oil on board 206 x 539
BRNTM 2005.31

Braintree Library

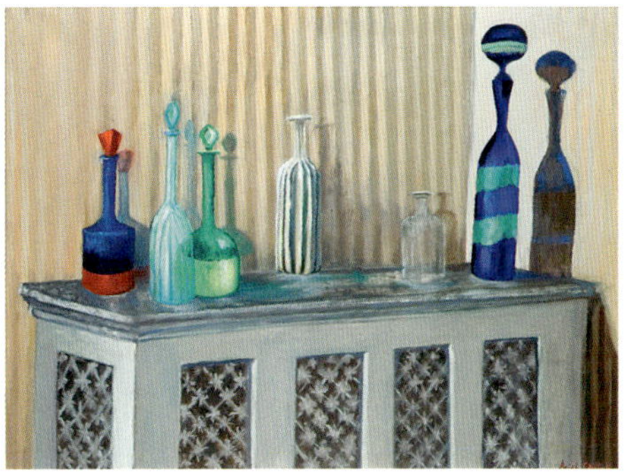

Crittall, Ariel b.1914
Venetian Bottles c.1994
oil on canvas 71.1 x 91.3
34

Great Bardfield Historical Society

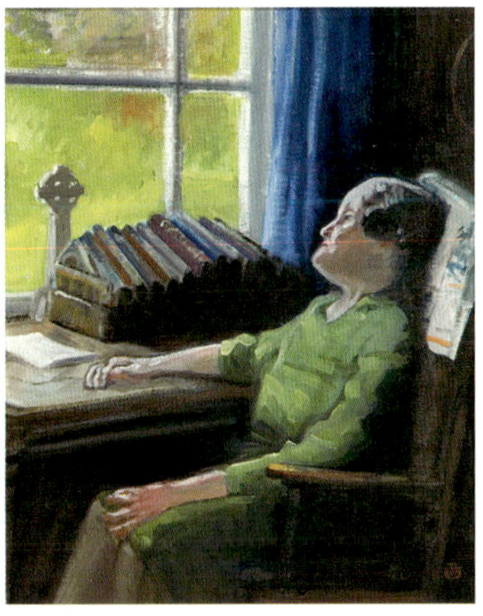

Thomas, Philippa Mary b.1919
Mrs Alington c.1973
oil on canvas 50.6 x 40.9
1

Brentwood Museum

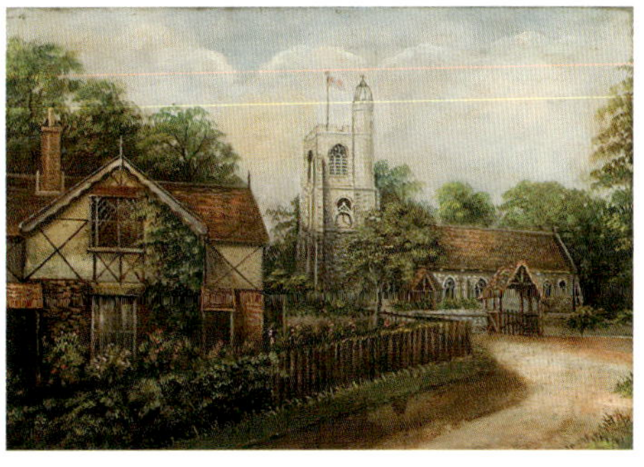

Gutheridge, W. G. active 1902–1910
St Peter, South Weald 1909
oil on board 43 x 61
1

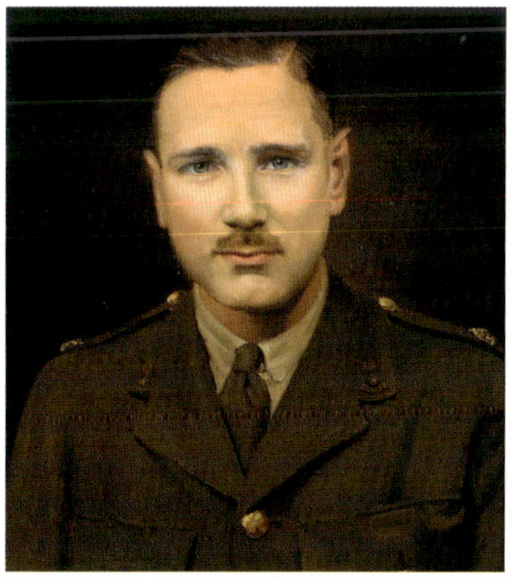

unknown artist
Roger Chester Nightingale (1909–1944)
oil on board 49 x 44.5
2

Burnham-on-Crouch and District Local Society

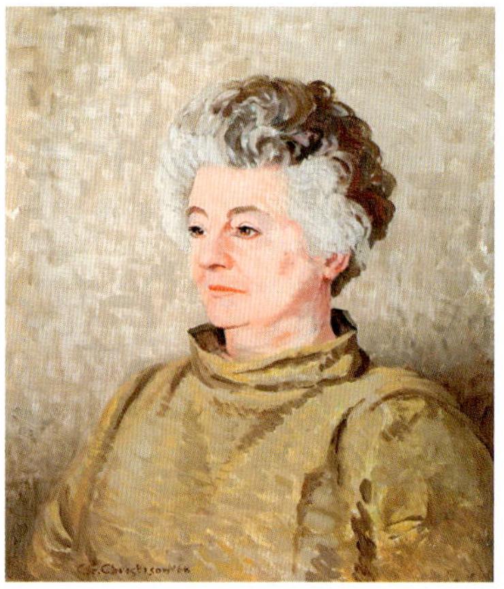

Christison, C. G.
Betty Perren, Founder of the Museum 1968
oil on board 53 x 45
2

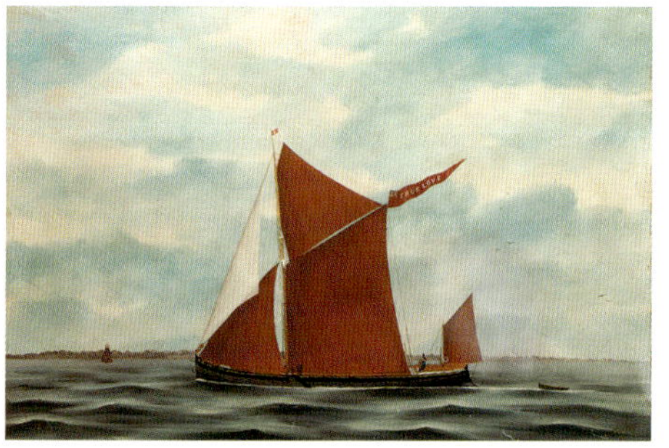

Cossey, George
The Thames Barge 'Truelove' 1904
oil on board 54 x 79.5
402

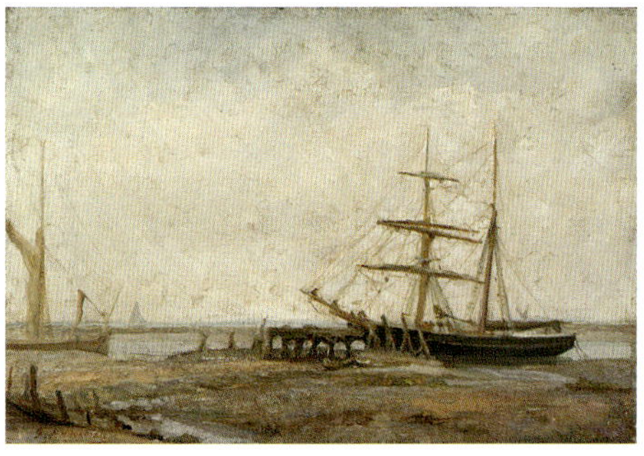

Hackman, Frederick James
active 1908–1922
Schooner and Barge Loading at Bradwell Quay
c.1910
oil on canvas 35 x 50
1

Anglia Ruskin University

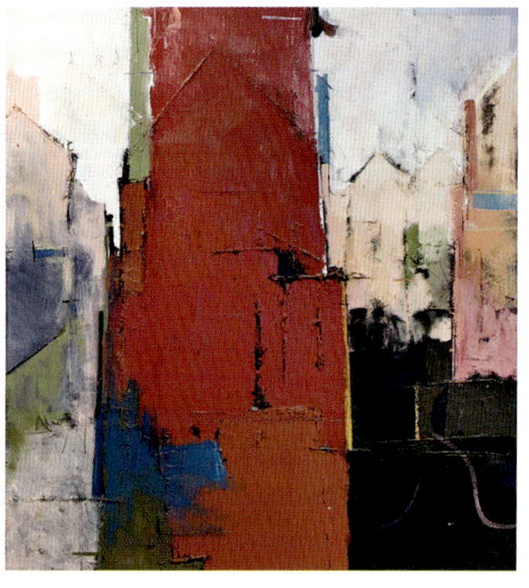

Gibbs, Andrew Robert
Harmonics of Duality c.1994
oil on canvas 157 x 142
1

Broomfield Hospital

Scientific evidence shows that art within hospitals helps with the healing process, so Broomfield Hospital has an Arts Project for the benefit of patients, visitors, staff and the community. The Broomfield Arts Project team commissions, buys, rents and exhibits a wide range of works of art to display at the Hospital.

Established in 1997, the initial goal of the Arts Project was to commission a wide range of public artworks for the new East Wing of Broomfield Hospital. This goal was completed in January 2002, by which time over 50 original paintings, sculptures, stained glass works, prints, mosaics, ceramics and textiles were commissioned from artists across the UK. The artists were selected by staff of the hospital from over 2,000 responses to a national advertisement.

The Broomfield Art Gallery was established in the main entrance corridor to the East Wing, featuring a series of art exhibitions by artists across the UK. The clear link between the arts and health has been recognised since the time of the ancient Greeks. This is confirmed by recent research, which shows that patients react favourably to suitably selected and placed artworks, which produce reductions in levels of stress and the need for anti-pain drugs, encouraging a faster recuperation.

The Broomfield Arts Project has been prominently promoted through press and media coverage, and was featured in the Arts Council of England publication and CD-Rom *Arts in Hospitals.* It is a registered charity and is funded entirely through grants, donations and sponsorships.

Christopher Walker, Chairman of Broomfield Arts Project

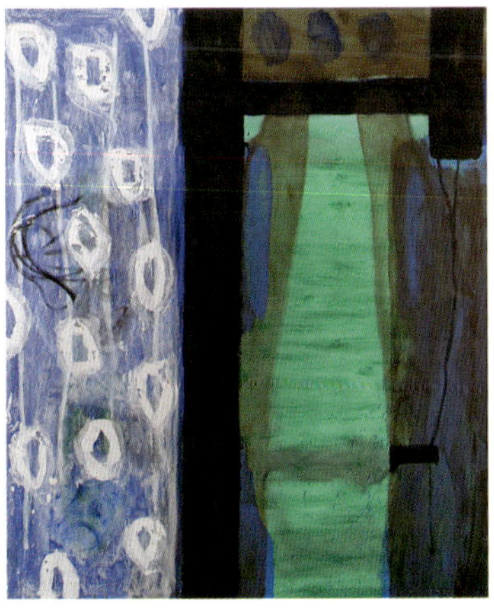

Bicknell, John b.1958
Untitled
oil on canvas 203 x 165
28

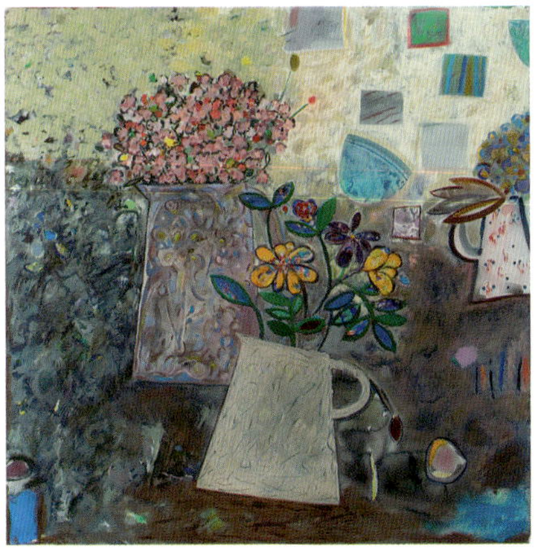

Cain, Jean
Still Life 1986
acrylic on paper 111 x 98
54

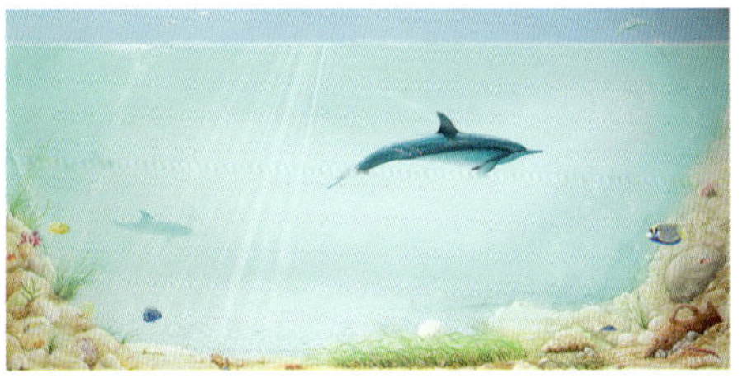

Hocombe, Sarah b.1963
Dolphin Mural
acrylic on wood 112 x 244
33.1

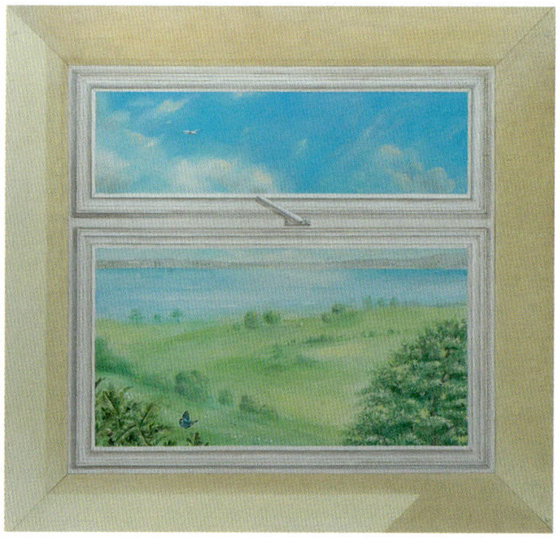

Hocombe, Sarah b.1963
Hadleigh Castle
acrylic on board 100 x 100
52a

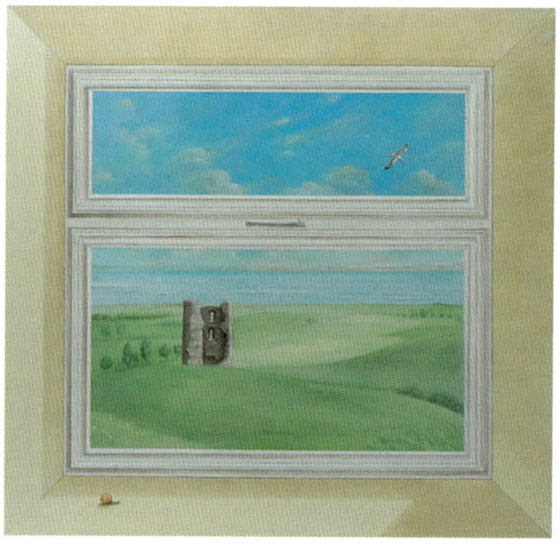

Hocombe, Sarah b.1963
Hadleigh Castle
acrylic on board 100 x 100
52b

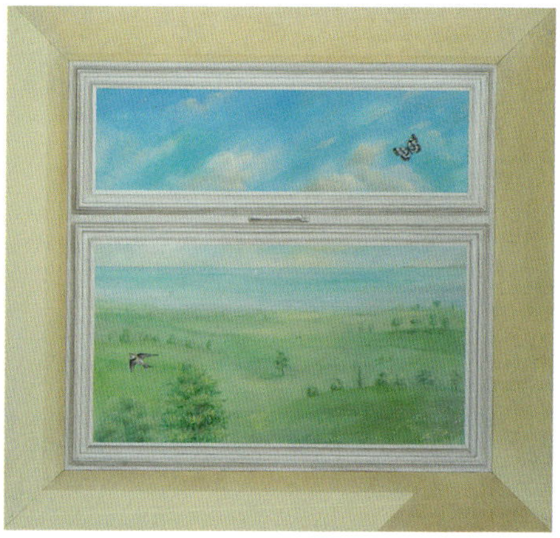

Hocombe, Sarah b.1963
Hadleigh Castle
acrylic on board 100 x 100
52c

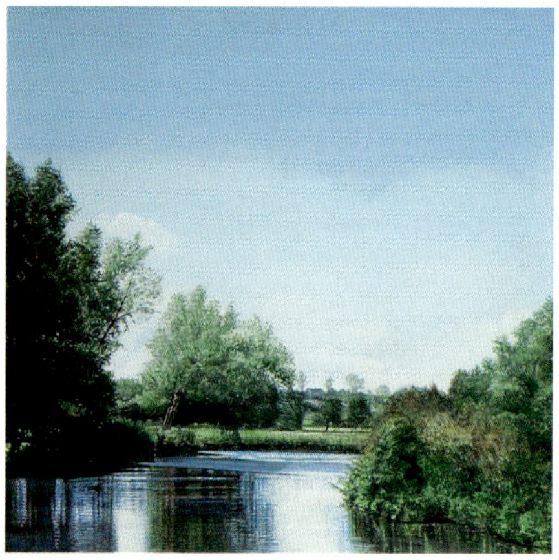

Hocombe, Sarah b.1963
Landscape 1
acrylic on board 60 x 50 (E)
61

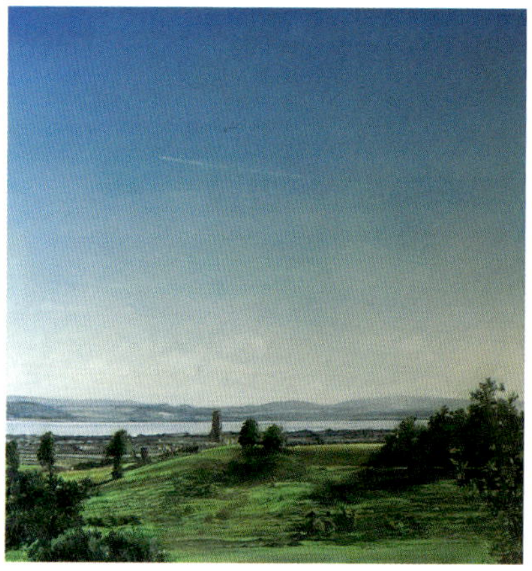

Hocombe, Sarah b.1963
Landscape 2
acrylic on board 60 x 50 (E)
62

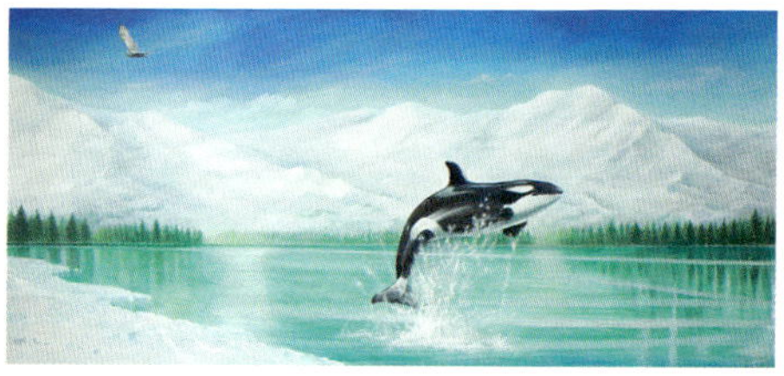

Hocombe, Sarah b.1963
Orca
acrylic on board 116 x 228
112

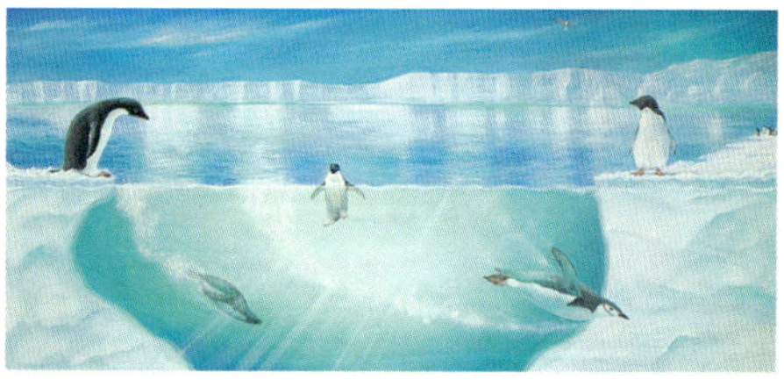

Hocombe, Sarah b.1963
Penguins in an Icy Landscape
acrylic on board 109 x 232
111

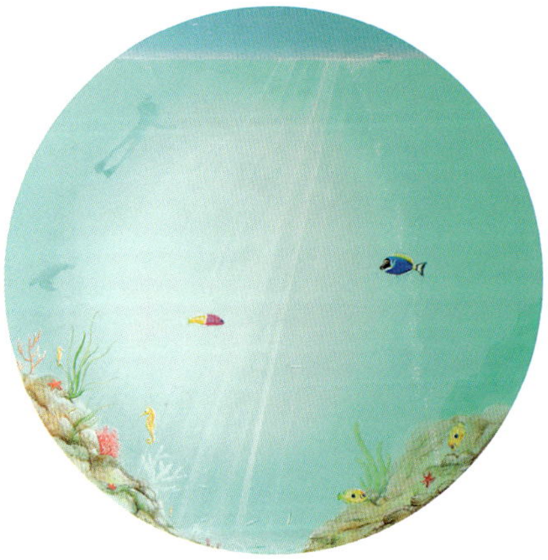

Hocombe, Sarah b.1963
Porthole
acrylic on wood 122
34.2

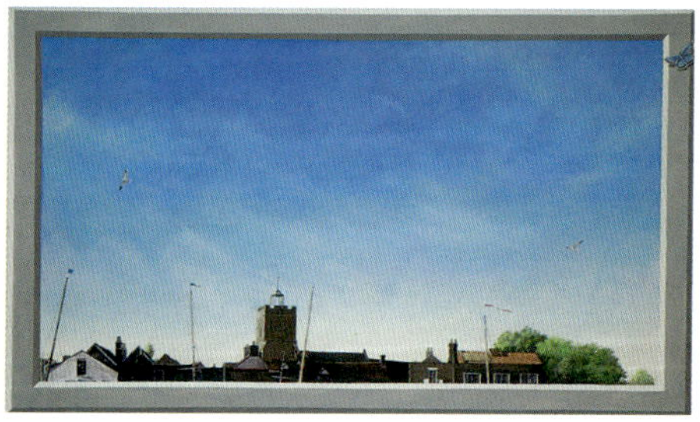

Hocombe, Sarah b.1963
Skyscape 1, View of Wivenhoe
acrylic on board 70 x 116
63

Facing page: Jackson, Gilbert (attributed to), active 1621–1640, *Portrait of a Lady with a Lace Collar Holding a Tulip* (detail), 1633, Saffron Walden Museum, (p. 238)

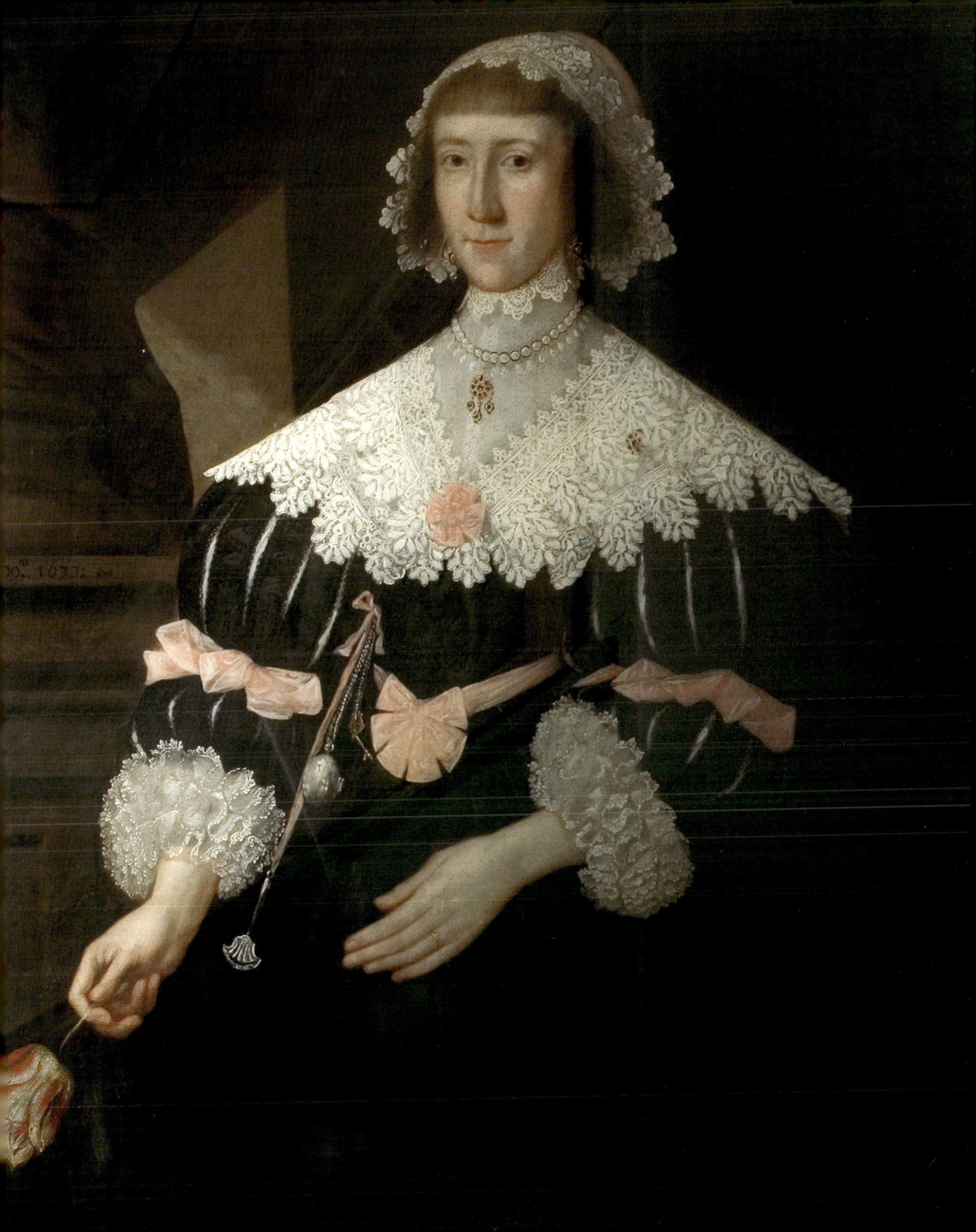

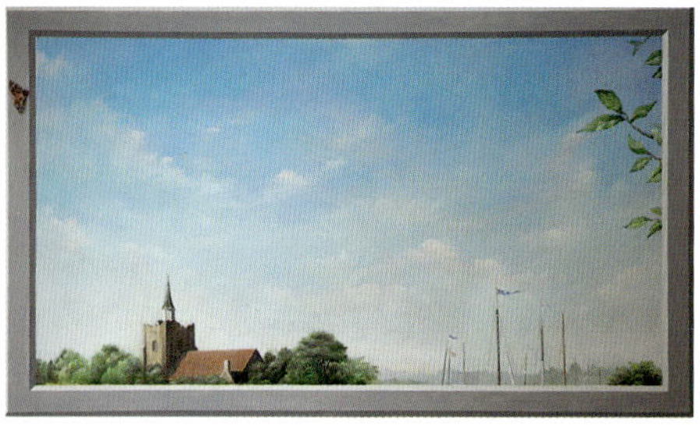

Hocombe, Sarah b.1963
Skyscape 2, View of Maldon
acrylic on board 70 x 116
64

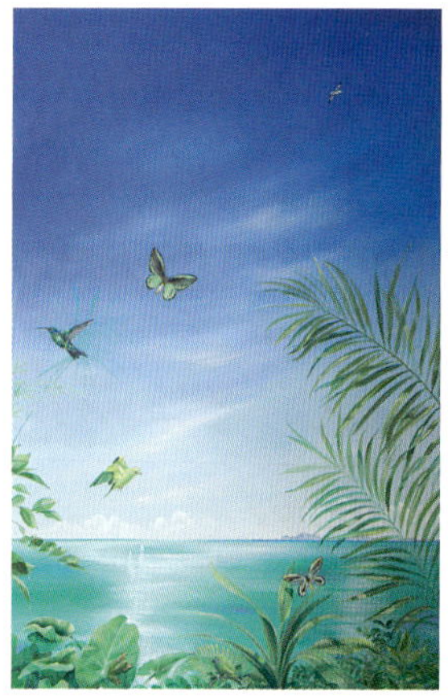

Hocombe, Sarah b.1963
Tropical Forest, Day
acrylic on board 137 x 88
110

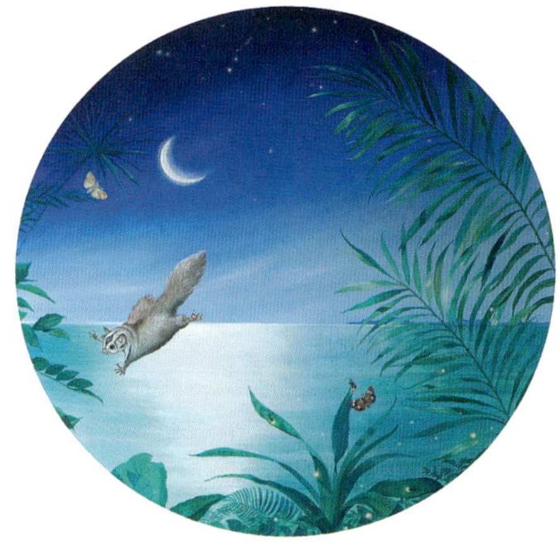

Hocombe, Sarah b.1963
Tropical Forest, Night
acrylic on board 92
113

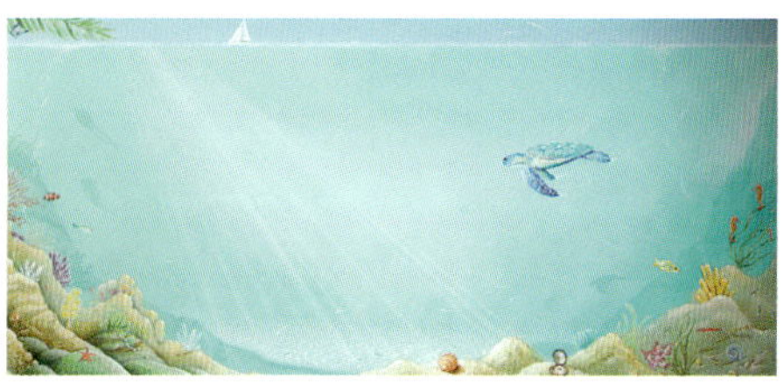

Hocombe, Sarah b.1963
Turtle Mural
acrylic on wood 116 x 228
34.1

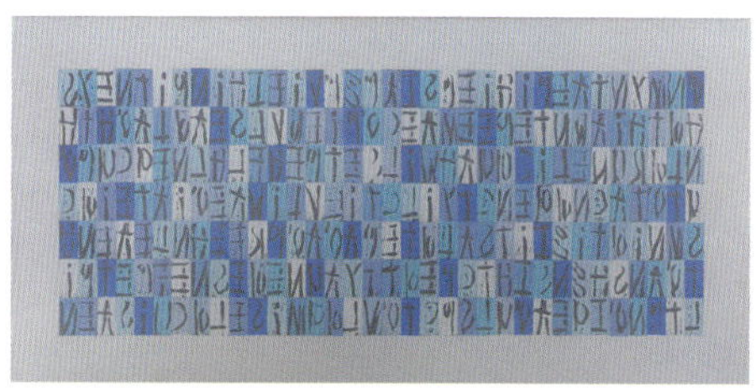

Marine, Tom b.1963 & **Relton, Christine** b.1959
White Text
acrylic on canvas 105 x 266
30

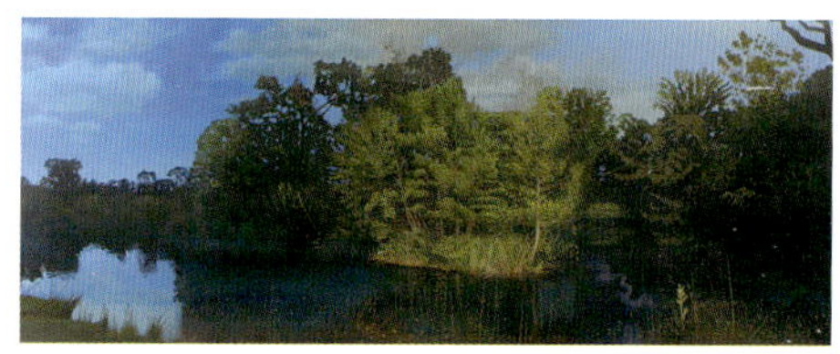

Priseman, Robert b.1965
Hatfield Forest, Night and Day
oil on canvas 90 x 197
46

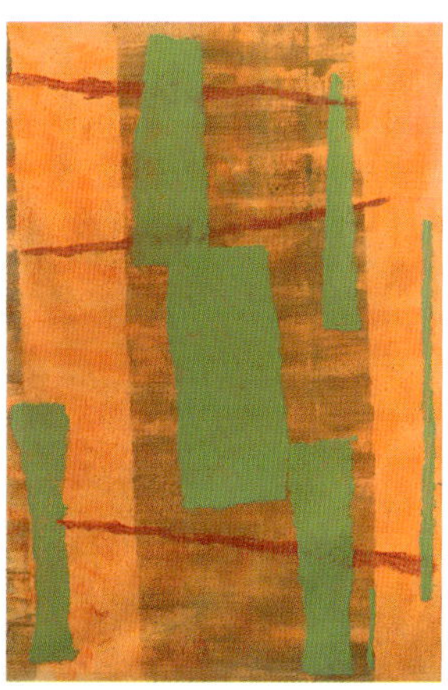

Smith, Dillwyn b.1958
Untitled
oil on canvas 204 x 136
27

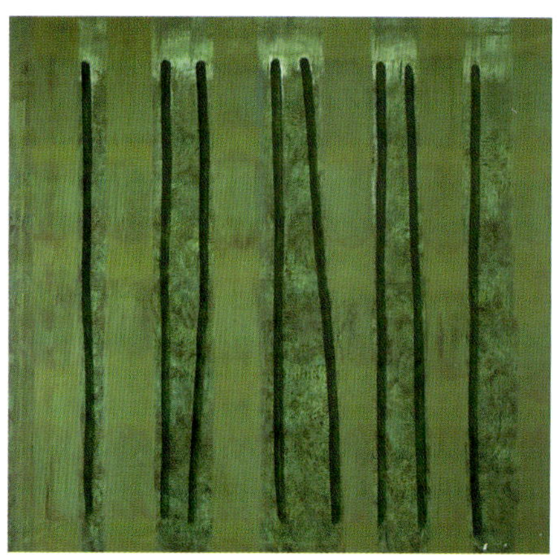

Thompson, Estelle b.1960
Garden Picture
oil on linen 152 x 152
29

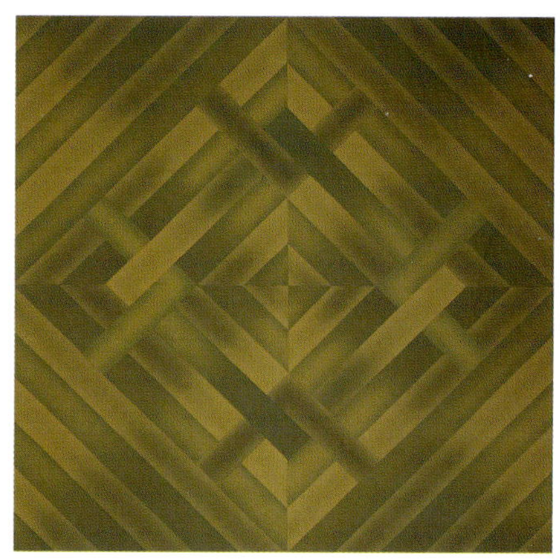

unknown artist
Brown Abstract
acrylic on canvas 152 x 152
65

Chelmsford Museums

Chelmsford Museum was founded by Chelmsford Philosophical Society in 1835, and has been run by Chelmsford District (later Borough) Council, from early in the twentieth century. In 1930, the Museum moved to its present home in Oaklands House, an 1860s villa in its own park on the south of the town. An extension housing the Essex Regiment Museum was opened by HRH Princess Margaret in 1973.

Few pictures remain from the Museum's nineteenth century collections. The rood screen panels from Latchingdon Church are a primary example. Otherwise, the first certain acquisition records for pictures now in the collection are from 1907. These are for a group of topographical watercolours of old buildings in the Chelmsford area by Alfred Bennett Bamford, a teacher at the School of Art. This sets the course for most of the Museum's pictures: many views of the town and area, nearly all by Essex artists, and mostly on paper. Among the oils are the fine view of *The Shire Hall,* painted by Philip Reinagle in 1794 for its architect John Johnson; the finest of the portraits are probably two of Juliana Waltersdorff, mistress of Hylands House, painted by her Danish compatriot Jens Juel: *Juliana Margaretta Waltersdorff (later Mrs Cornelius Kortright)*, c.1780s–c.1790 and *Juliana, Wife of Cornelius Kortright*, c.1800–1801 (after seven childbirths). Later in the nineteenth century, *Ear Inspection in a Russian Hospital* by Emily Shanks, painted in Moscow c.1890s, is possibly the only painting by this artist in an English public collection.

During the second half of the twentieth century, the Museum acquired work by Essex-based artists: John Aldridge, Maggi Hambling, Cedric Morris, John O'Connor and others. Lynton Harold Lamb, best known as an illustrator, lived close to Chelmsford. Collecting has been constrained by lack of space as well as of money, but at the time of writing the Council has agreed to extend Oaklands House to cope with modern requirements, probably in 2007–2008.

Anne Lutyens-Humfrey, Keeper of Art

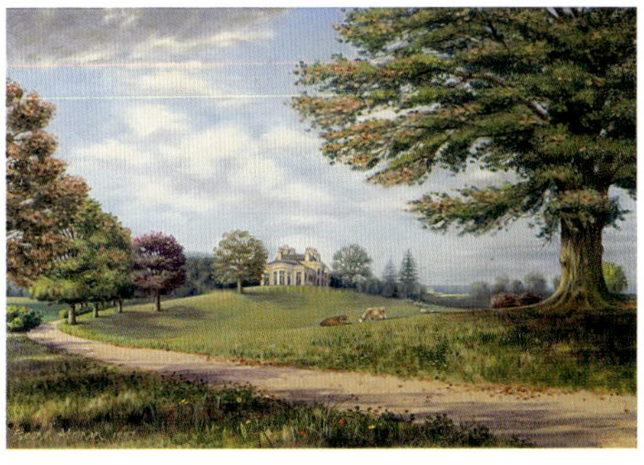

Abraham, Esmond b.1935
Hylands in 1803 (after George Whitmore) 1997
oil on canvas 76.8 x 107
1999.183

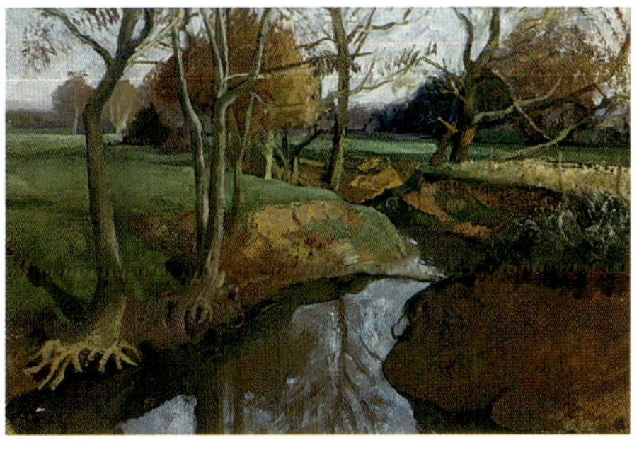

Aldridge, John Arthur Malcolm 1905–1983
The River Pant near Sculpin's Bridge 1961
oil on board 23 x 32
M28322

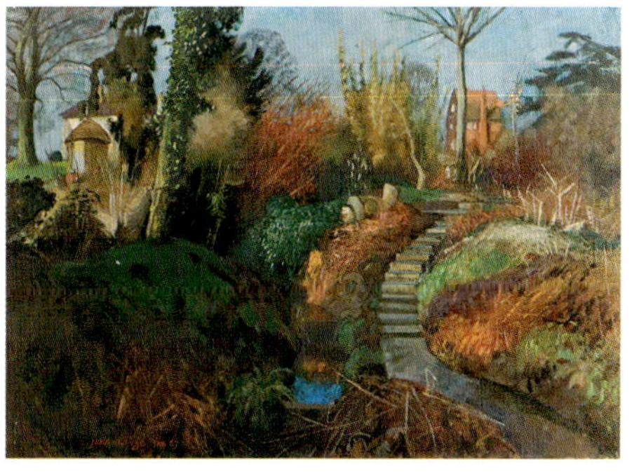

Aldridge, John Arthur Malcolm 1905–1983
Garden in January 1967
oil on canvas 52 x 76
1988.268

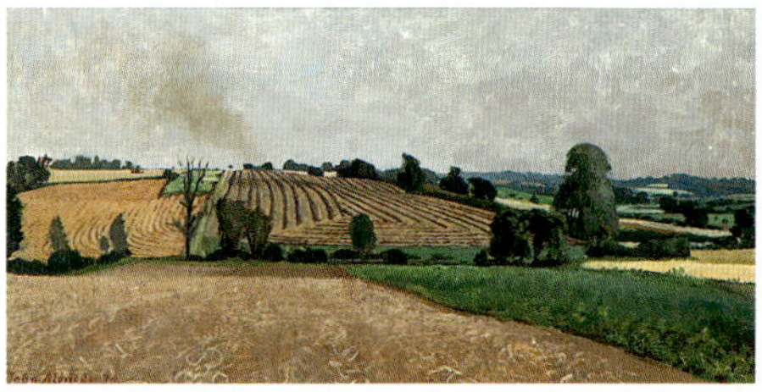

Aldridge, John Arthur Malcolm 1905–1983
Harvest Fields, Duton Hill, near Dunmow 1974
oil on canvas 30.5 x 56
1988.269

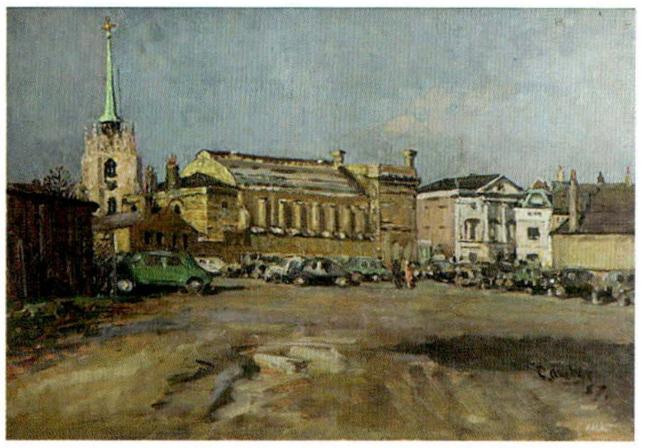

Archer, Charles 1904–1993
The Old Corn Exchange and Market 1957
oil on board 44.3 x 64.7
M28340

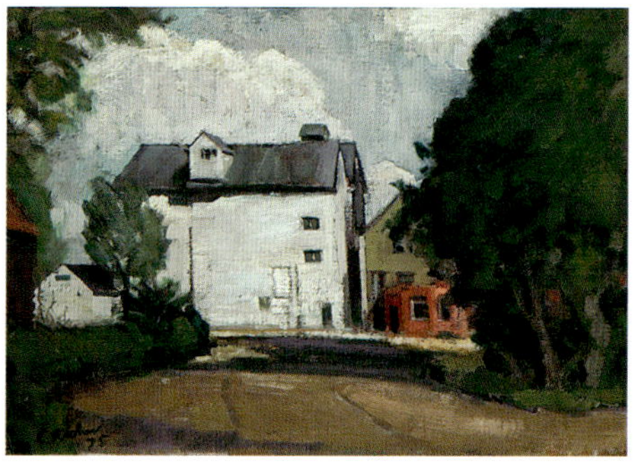

Archer, Charles 1904–1993
Moulsham Mill, Chelmsford 1975
oil on board 39.4 x 49.5
1980.124

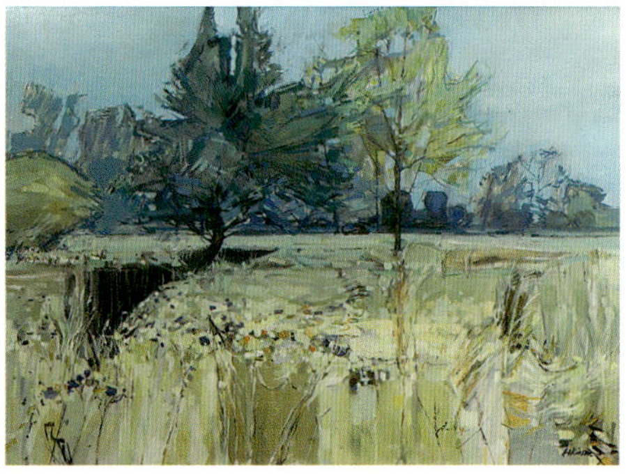

Atkinson, Anthony b.1929
Water Meadows, Boxted c.1960s
oil on canvas 76 x 101.6
M28342

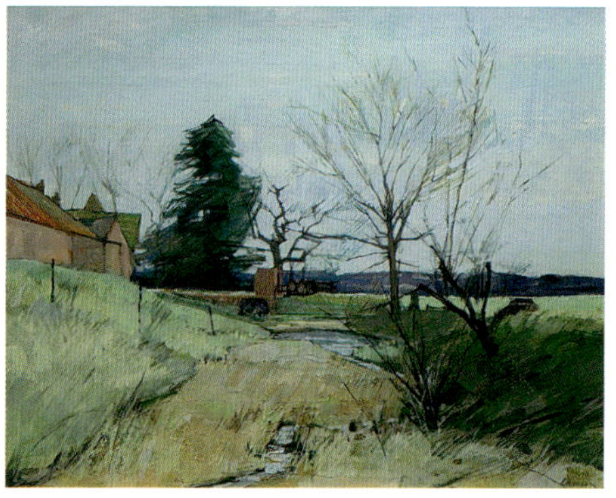

Atkinson, Anthony b.1929
Farm at West Bergholt
oil on canvas 63.5 x 76.2
1974.321

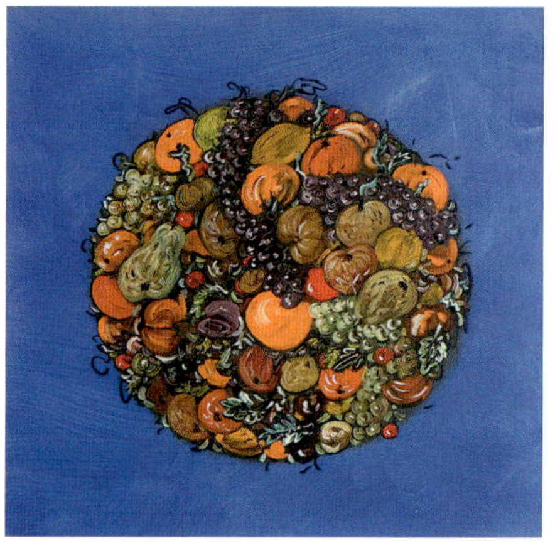

Austen, David b.1960
Giotto's Basket 1980s
oil on canvas 61 x 61
1988.236

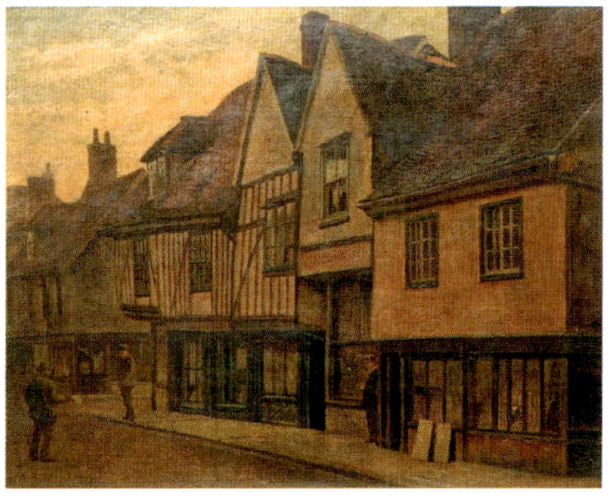

Bamford, Alfred Bennett 1857–1939
Old Houses, the Friars, Moulsham Street, Chelmsford 1881
oil on canvas 25.4 x 29.2
M28342A

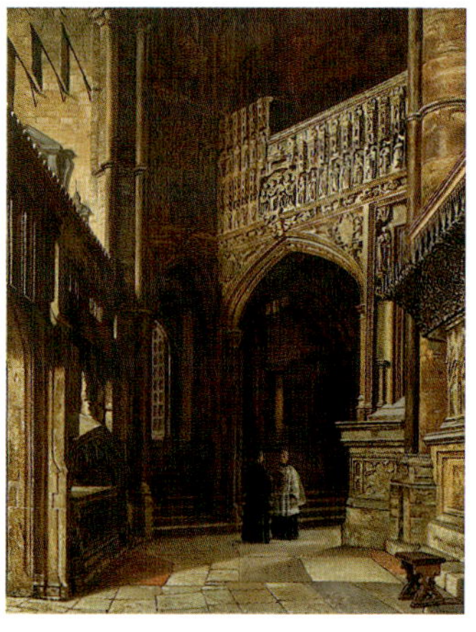

Bamford, Alfred Bennett 1857–1939
North Ambulatory, Westminster Abbey 1884
oil on canvas 46.2 x 36
1997.220

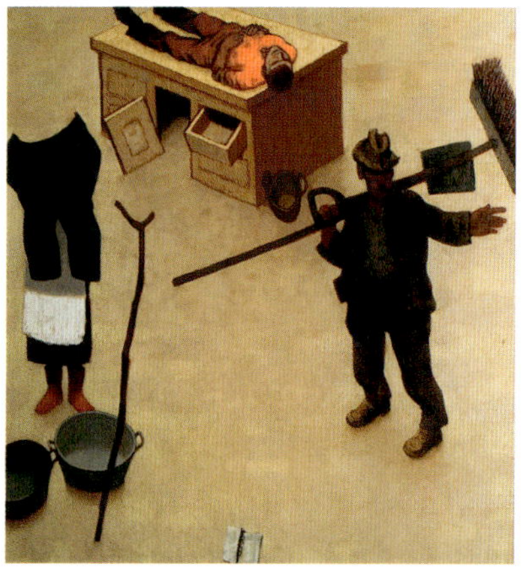

Barrett, Roderic 1920–2000
Separate Relations 1970s
oil on canvas 120.7 x 120.7 (E)
1979.402

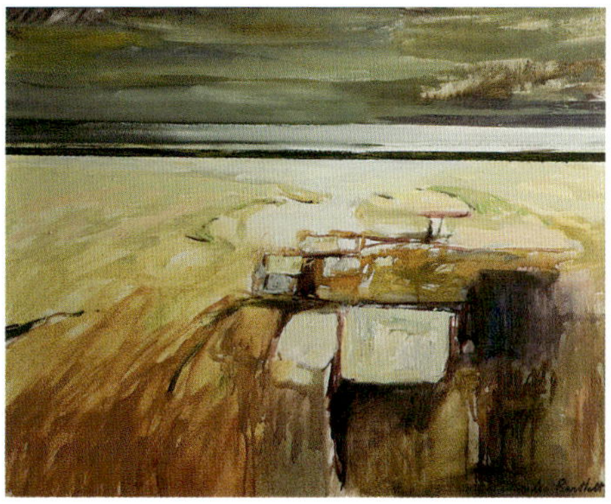

Bartlett, Charles b.1921
Essex Estuary 1976?
oil on canvas 50.5 x 60
1976.601

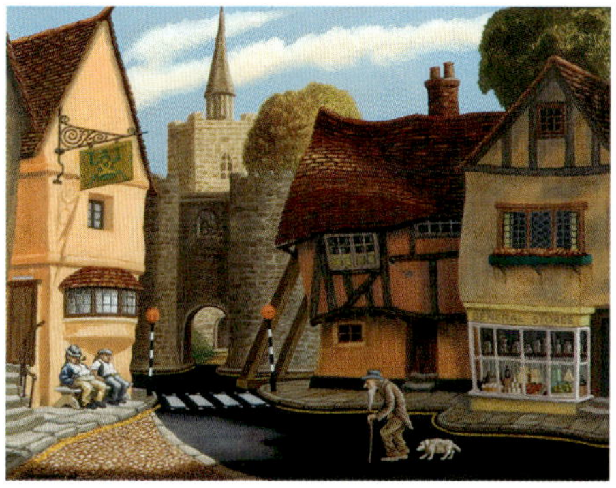

Barton, Charles H. 1908–1979
Imaginary Townscape 1967
oil on canvas 40 x 50.5
1979.599

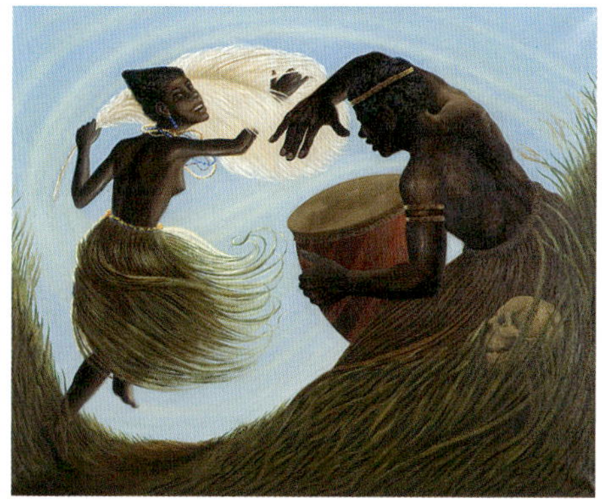

Barton, Charles H. 1908–1979
Zambezi Ritual Dance 1967
oil on canvas 50 x 59.5
1979.601

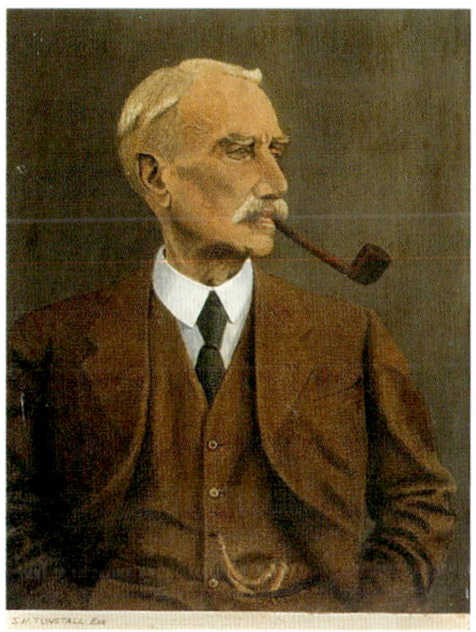

Barton, Charles H. 1908–1979
S. H. Tunstall
oil on canvas board 30.5 x 24
1979.598

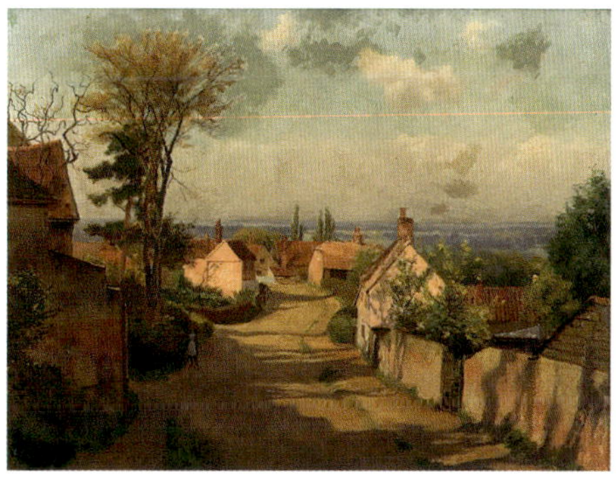

Beckingham, Arthur 1855–1920
Village Street, Danbury c.1885–c.1910?
oil on canvas 43 x 59
1997.614

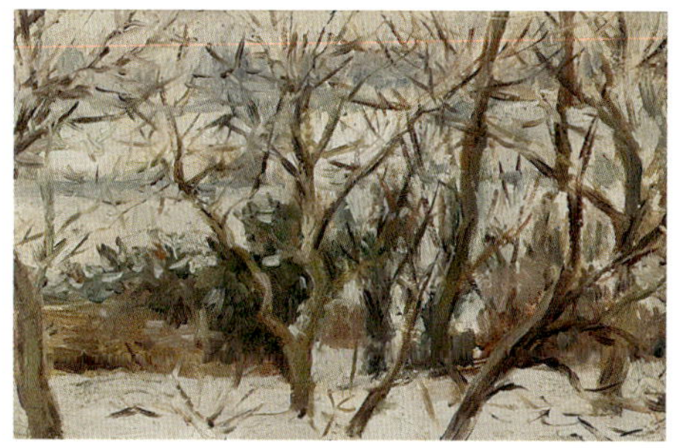

Bellingham-Smith, Elinor 1906–1988
Orchard Snowscape, Felsted 1944
oil on canvas 14 x 22
2003.294

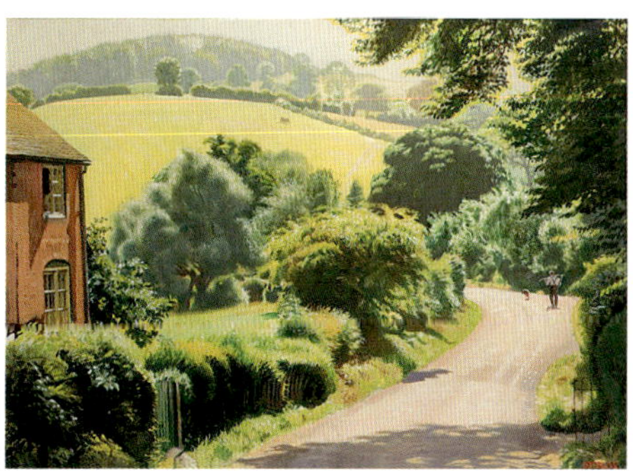

Bliss, Douglas Percy 1900–1984
High Noon, Windley 1951
oil on canvas 74.3 x 99.7
1985.080

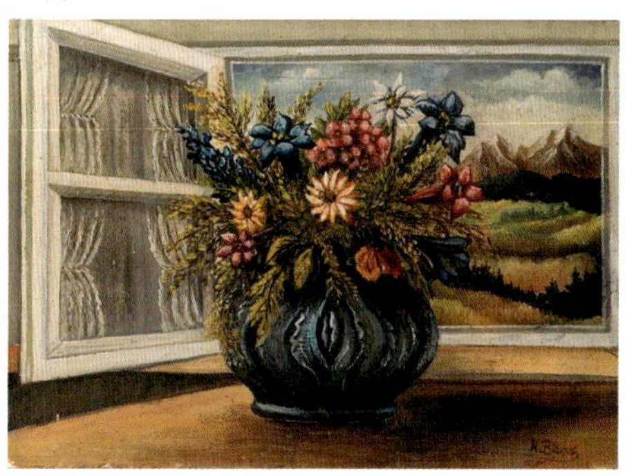

Bottefer, M. (attributed to)
Vase of Flowers with Mountain View
oil on canvas 32 x 44
ER043

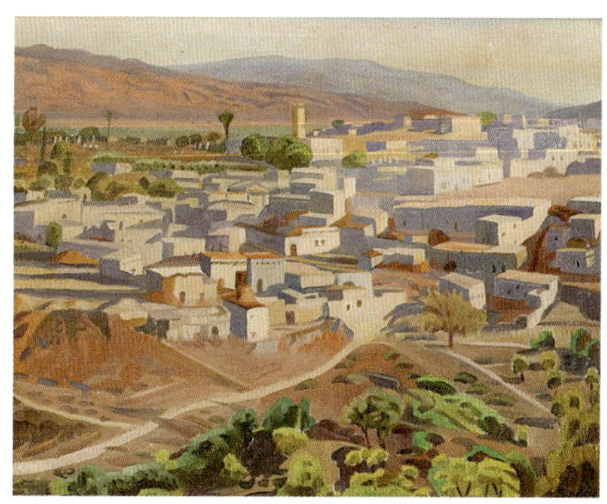

Boulton-Maude, Doris 1893–1961
View of a Village and River (possibly the Nile)
1920s
oil on canvas 38.5 x 46
1971.011

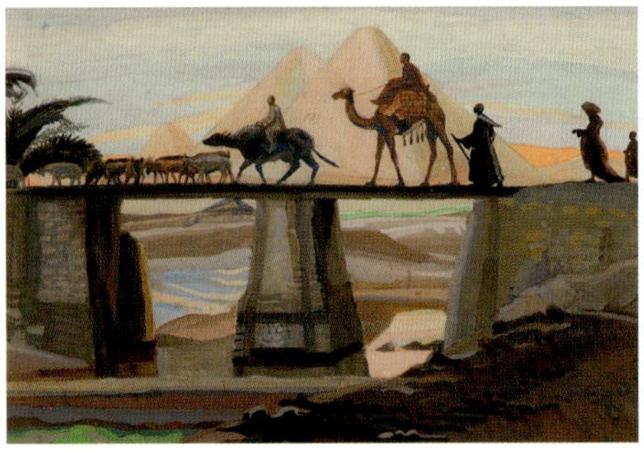

Boulton-Maude, Doris 1893–1961
The Return c.1920s
tempera on board 31.7 x 45
1971.010

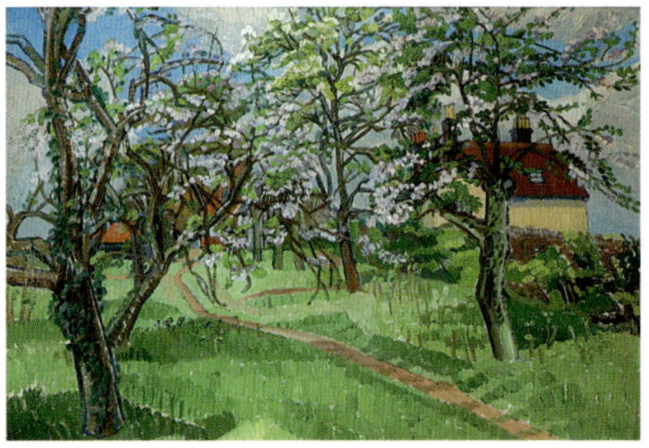

Boulton-Maude, Doris 1893–1961
Orchard in Blossom c.1930s–c.1950?
oil on canvas 50 x 70
1993.894

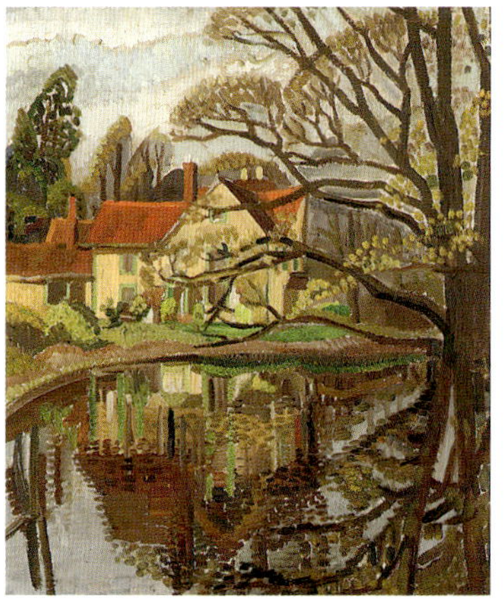

Boulton-Maude, Doris 1893–1961
Mayes Farm, Sandon c.1940
oil on canvas 61 x 51
2003.016

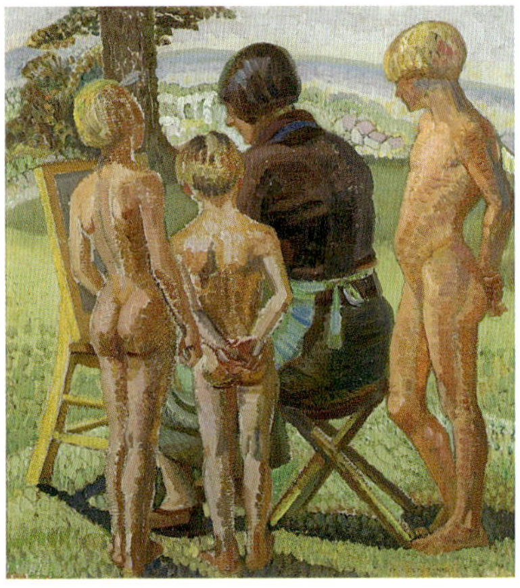

Boulton-Maude, Doris 1893–1961
Point of View 1949
oil on canvas 53.8 x 49.3
1971.005

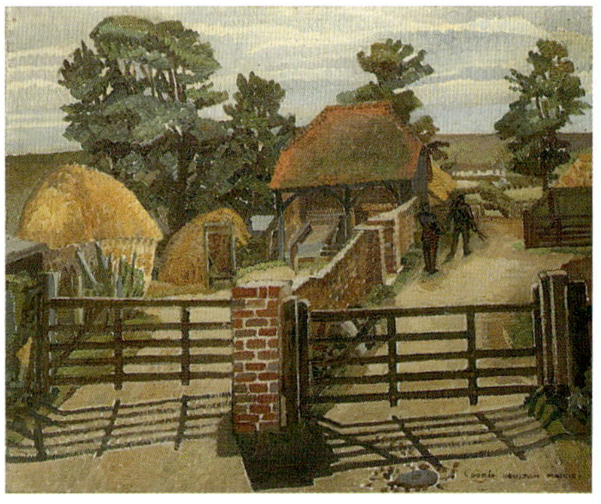

Boulton-Maude, Doris 1893–1961
Farmyard, Fordingbridge c.1940s
oil on canvas 50.8 x 61.3
1971.008

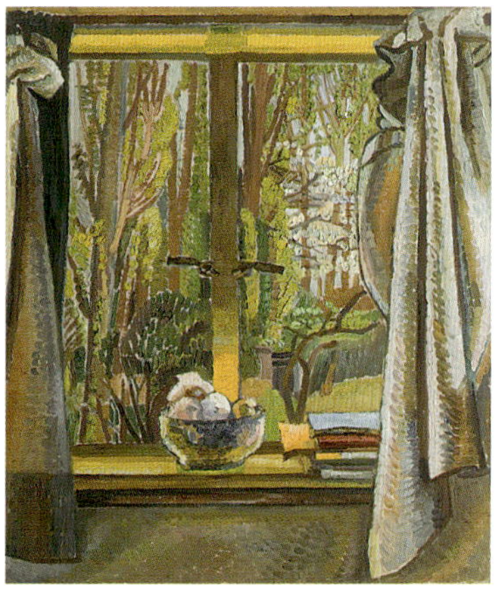

Boulton-Maude, Doris 1893–1961
The Garden Window c.1940s
oil on canvas 61 x 51
1971.007

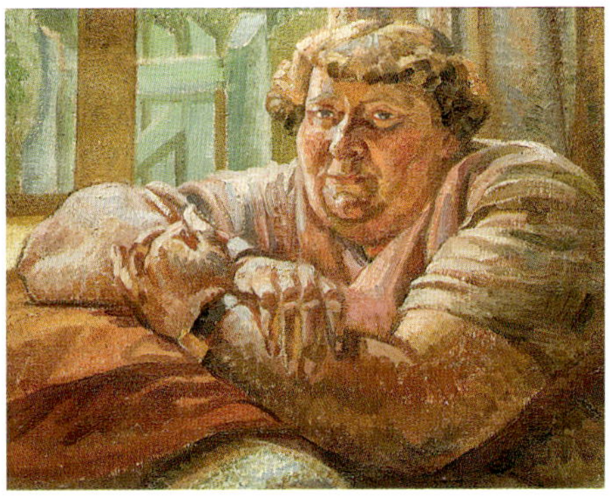

Boulton-Maude, Doris 1893–1961
Isobel Barnes
oil on canvas 36.5 x 44.5
1971.009

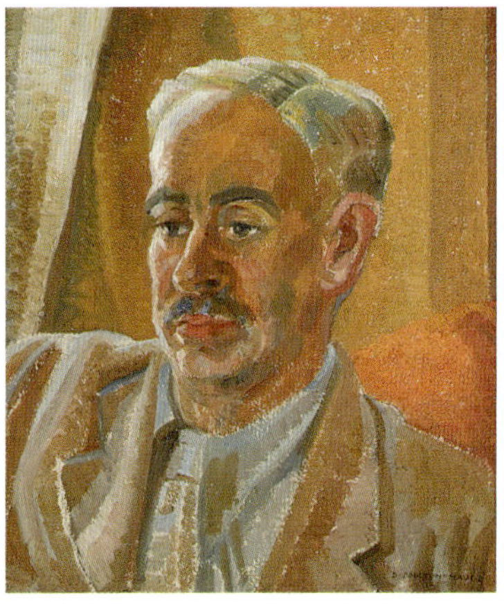

Boulton-Maude, Doris 1893–1961
Lionel Maude
oil on canvas 40.7 x 35.5
LOAN032 (P)

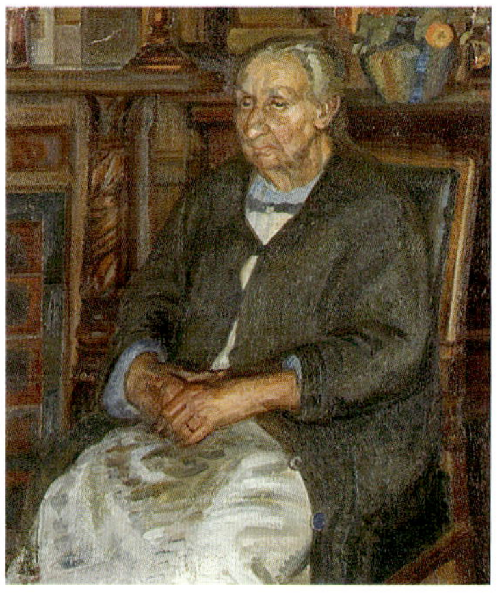

Boulton-Maude, Doris 1893–1961
Louise Maude, née Shanks (1855–1939)
oil on canvas 60.2 x 50.2
LOAN031 (P)

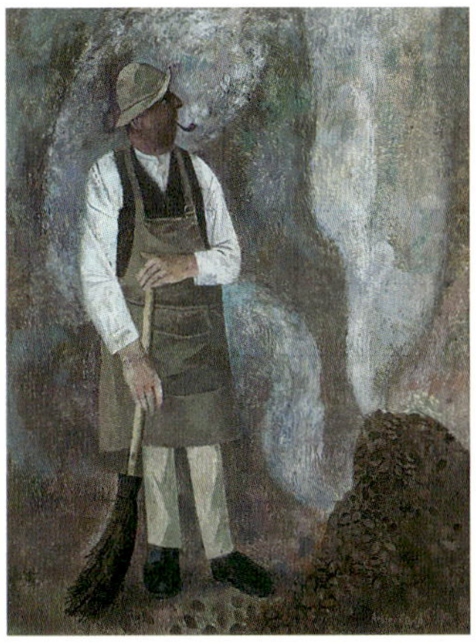

Brill, Reginald 1902–1974
Smoke c.1974?
oil on board 67 x 49.1
1974.220

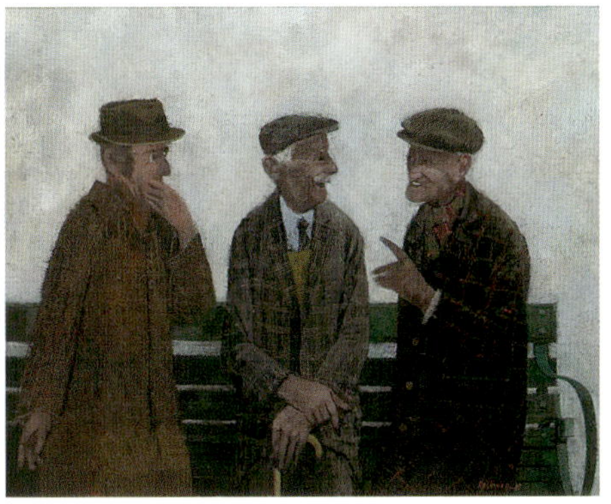

Brill, Reginald 1902–1974
Three Men ('Have You Heard This One?')
oil on board 43.5 x 51.8
1974.221

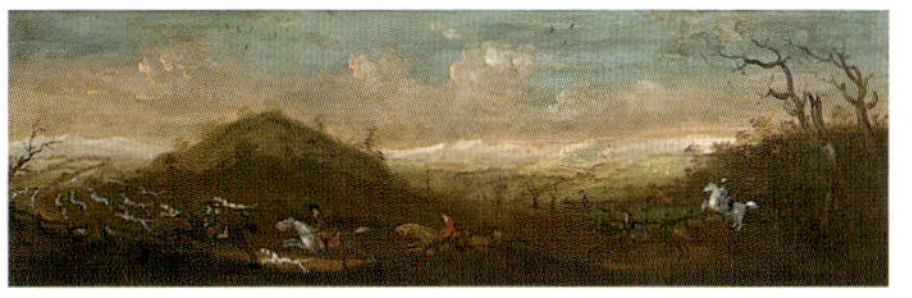

British (English) School
The Hunt at Galleywood? c.1700
oil on board 51.5 x 157
1999.431

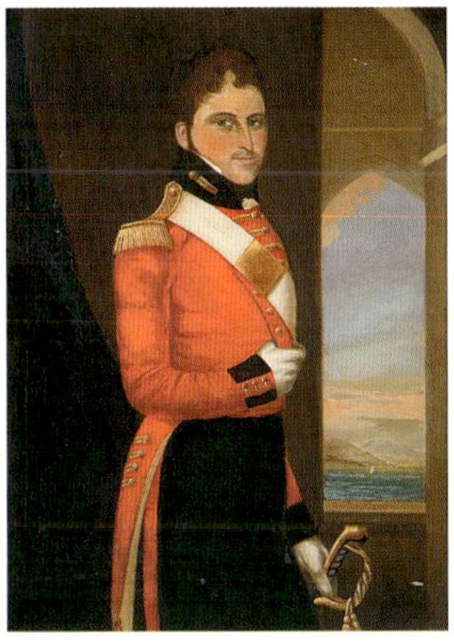

British (English) School
Captain William Thorne, 56th Regiment (d.1844) 1799
oil on canvas 51 x 37.5
ER0032

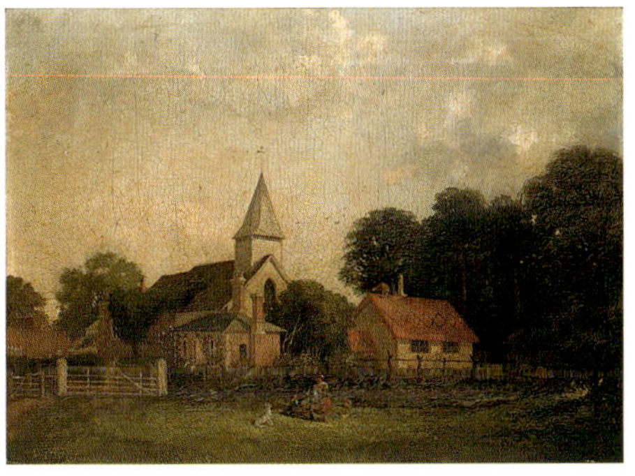

Brown, William 1822/1823–1899
Widford Old Church 1858
oil on canvas 28 x 37
1973.221

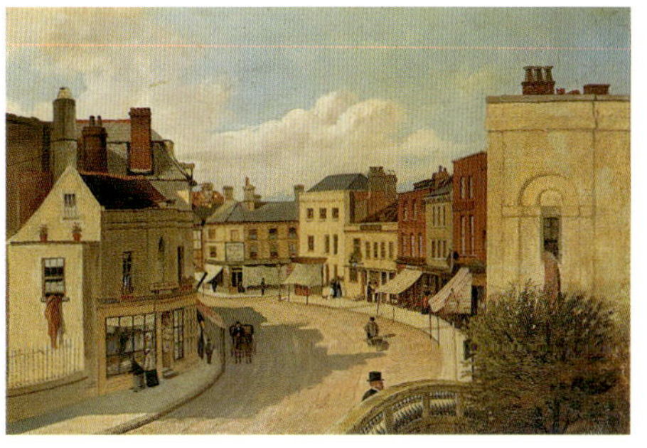

Brown, William 1822/1823–1899
Chelmsford High Street, from above the Stone Bridge 1890
oil on canvas 22.8 x 41.7
1973.218

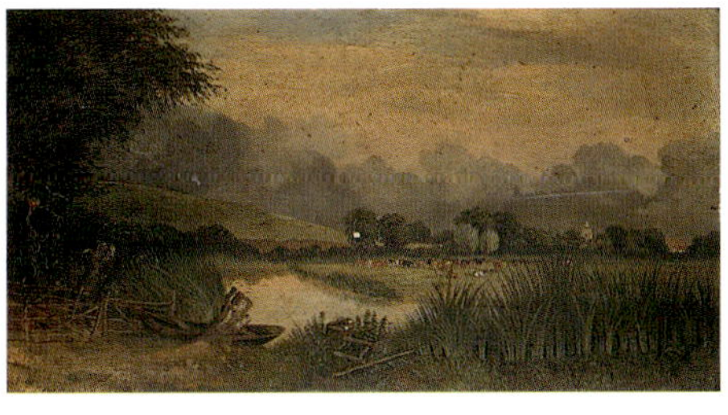

Brown, William 1822/1823–1899
River Chelmer at Broomfield
oil on board 19 x 34.5
1973.220

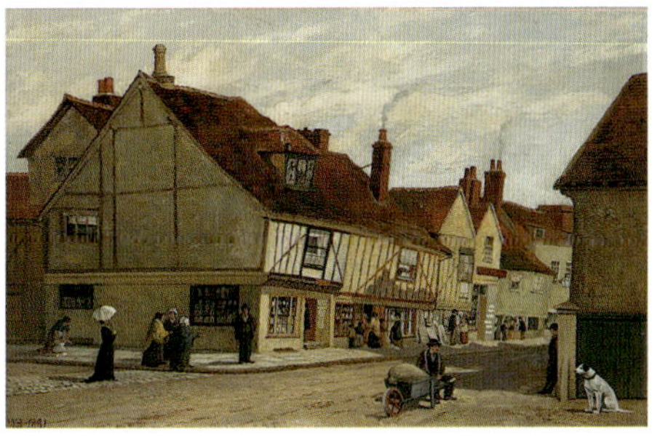

Brown, William (attributed to)
1822/1823–1899
Friars' Place and Moulsham Street 1881
oil on canvas 31.8 x 44.7
M28332

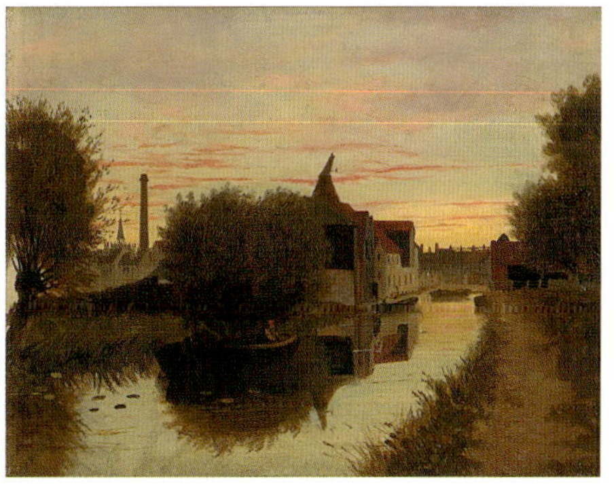

Brown, William (attributed to)
1822/1823–1899
Springfield Wharf
oil on canvas 19 x 24.1
M28293

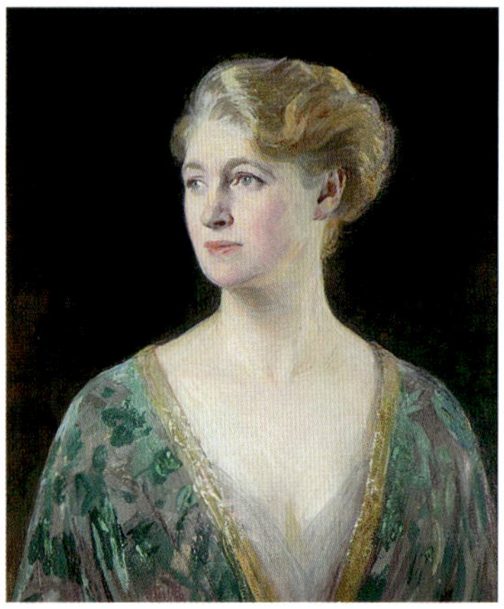

Buchel, Charles A. 1872–1950
Christine, Mrs John Hanbury
oil on canvas 68.6 x 61
1997.016

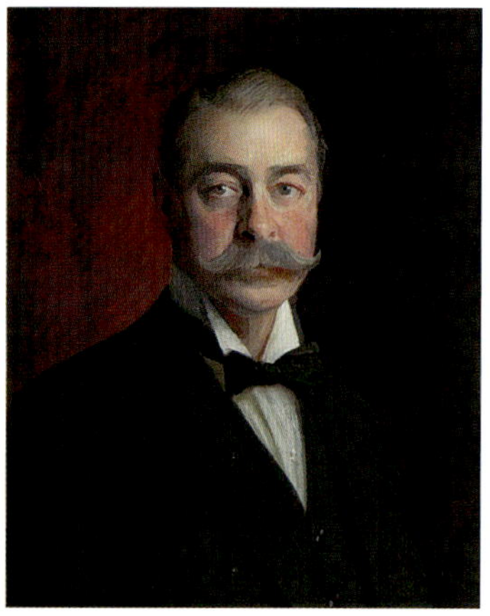

Buchel, Charles A. 1872–1950
John Hanbury
oil on canvas 68 x 61
1997.017

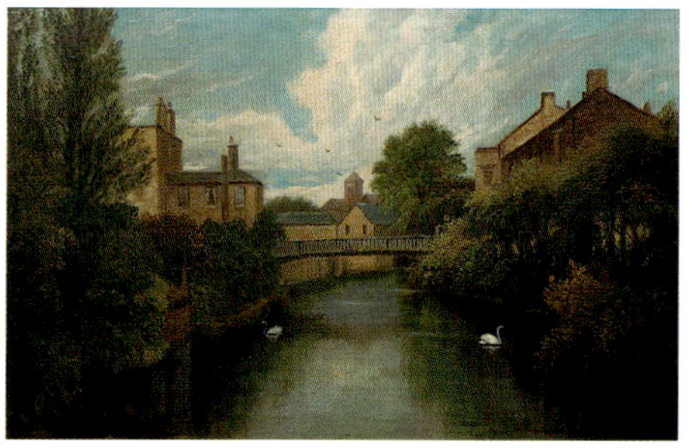

Buckler, E.
The Iron Bridge, Chelmsford
oil on canvas 49.5 x 75
M28337

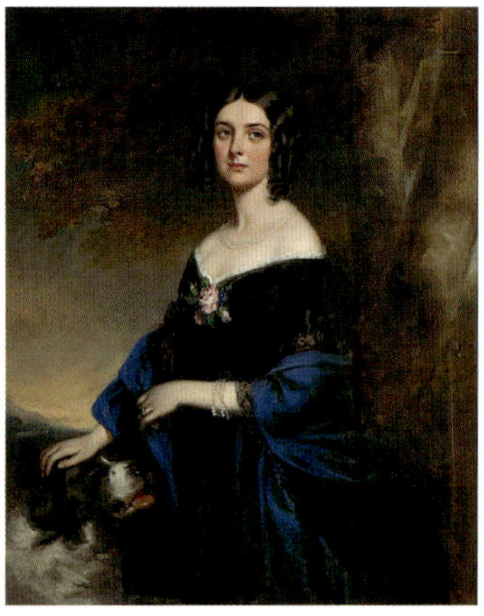

Buckner, Richard 1812–1883
Margaret Laetitia, Lady Western, née Bushby (1798–1872) 1849
oil on canvas 124 x 99
M28243

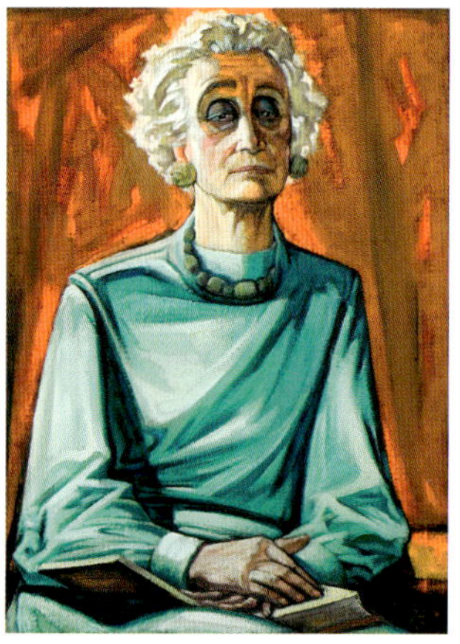

Burnand, Geoffrey Norman 1912–1996
Mrs Kathleen May Andrews 1975
oil on canvas 81.3 x 58.4
1980.430

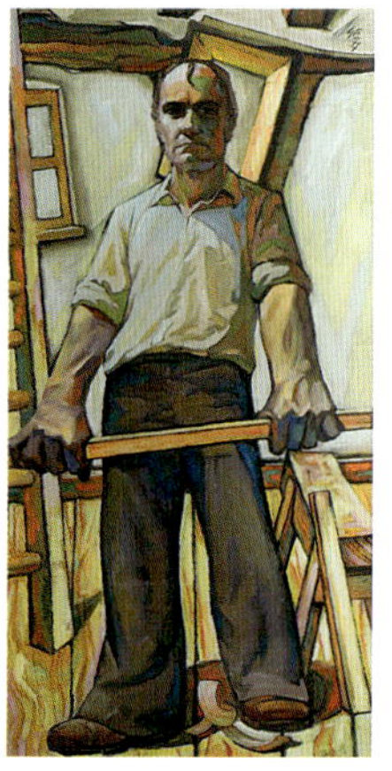

Burnand, Geoffrey Norman 1912–1996
The Carpenter 1977
oil on canvas 167 x 83
1986.842

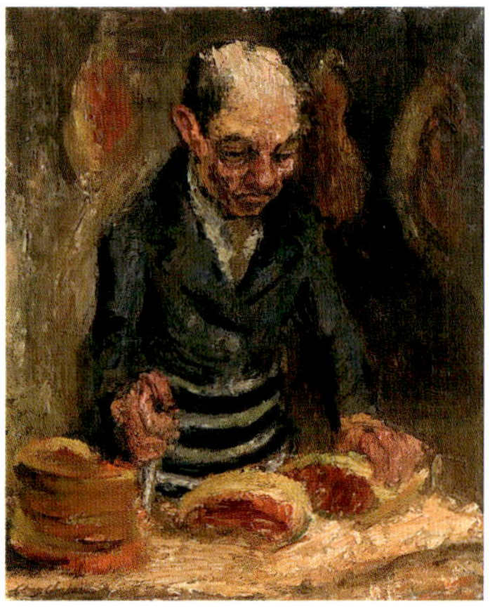

Chapman, George 1908–1993
Mr Bone, the Butcher of Great Bardfield
c.1948–c.1950
oil on canvas 61 x 48
1990.183

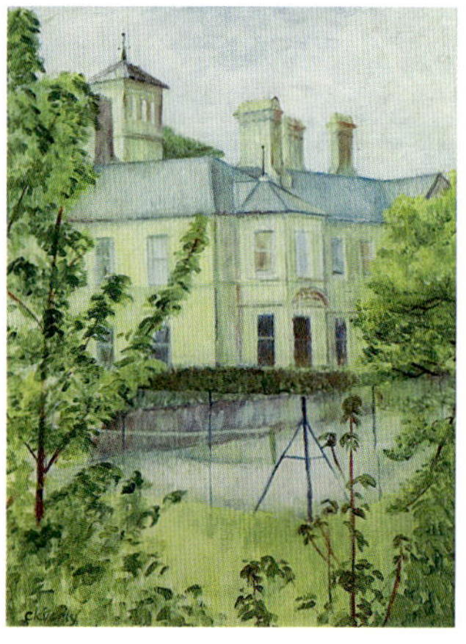

Cleverly, Peter b.1943
Oaklands House, Moulsham Street, Chelmsford
1994
oil on canvas 65 x 45.7
1994.316

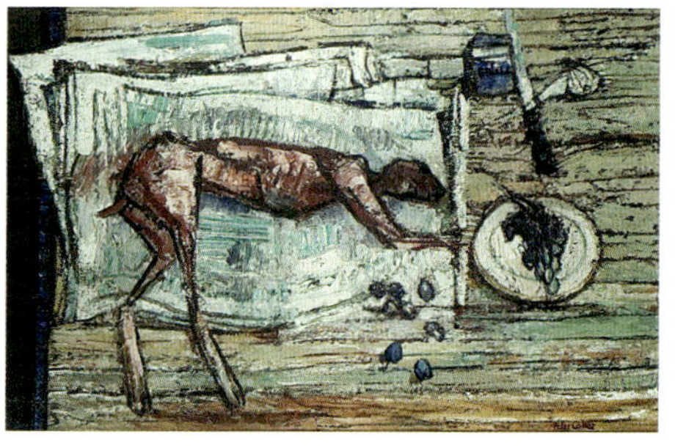

Coker, Peter 1926–2004
Still Life with Hare and Grapes 1955
oil on board 79 x 122
1987.383

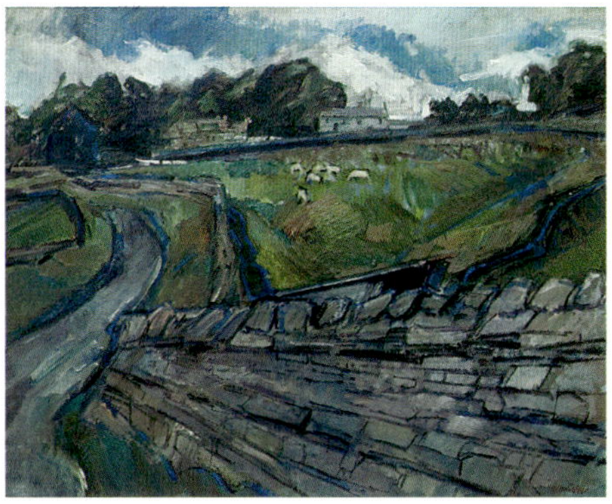

Coker, Peter 1926–2004
Leadgate, Cumbria 1970
oil on canvas 62.2 x 75.5
1973.266

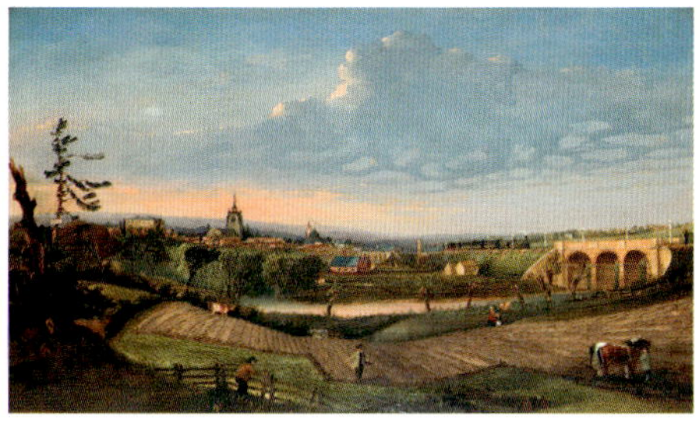

Colkett, Samuel David (attributed to)
1806–1863
Chelmsford from Springfield Hill 1847
oil on canvas 62 x 100.3
M28321

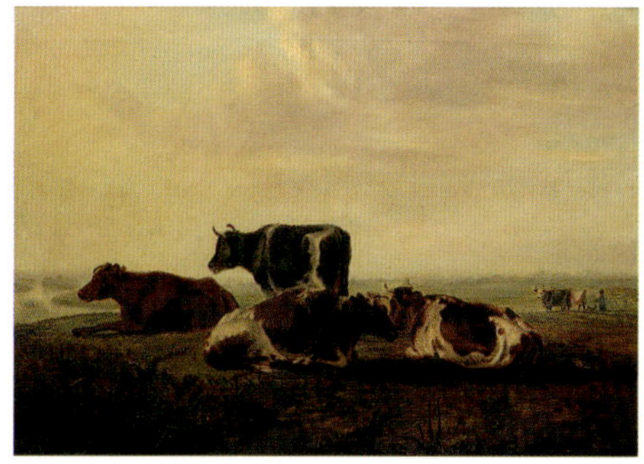

Cooper, Thomas Sidney (circle of)
1803–1902
Pastoral Scene with Cows
oil on canvas 51 x 68.6
M28252

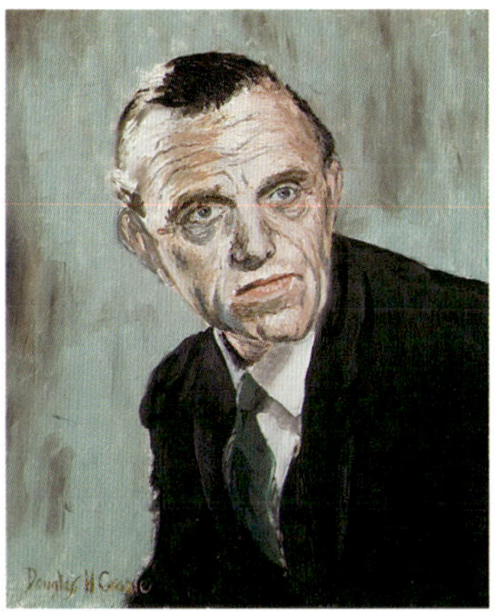

Crome, Douglas H.
Councillor Fred Richardson c.1975
oil on board 51 x 41
1986.001

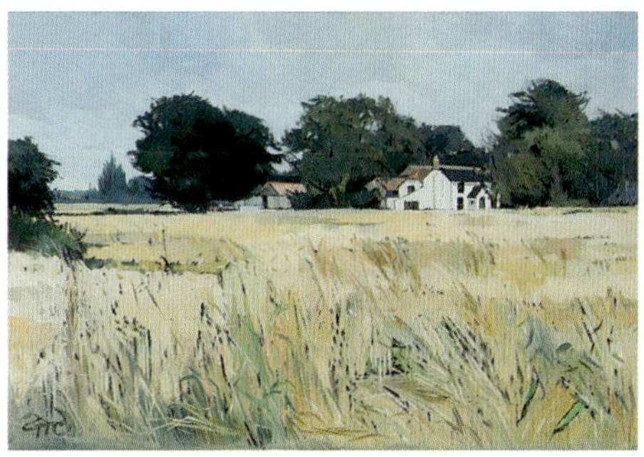

Crossley, Gordon b.1929
Gladwyns Farmhouse, Sheering 1975
oil on canvas 25.5 x 34.8
1975.373

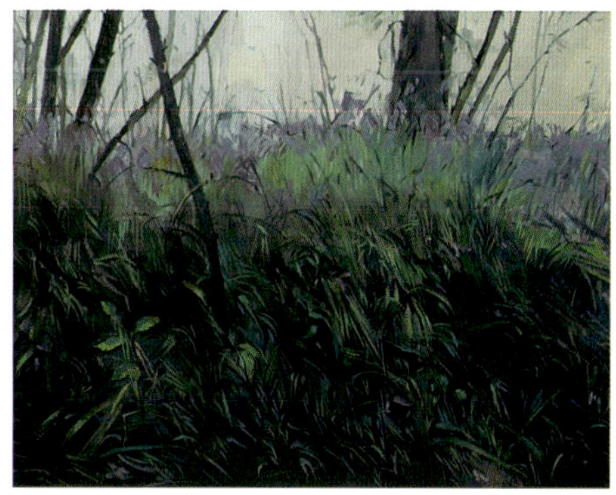

Crossley, Gordon b.1929
Edge of a Wood
oil on canvas 38.7 x 49.2
1975.374

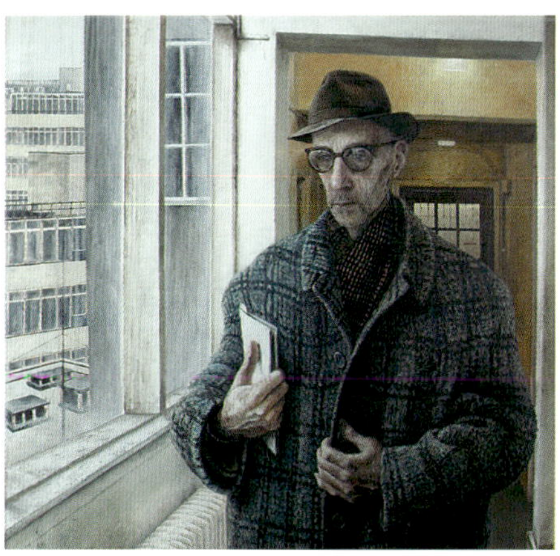

Cuthbert, Rosalind b.1951
Cecil Collins at the Central School of Art, London (detail of full-length) 1982
oil on canvas 202 x 67
1986.487

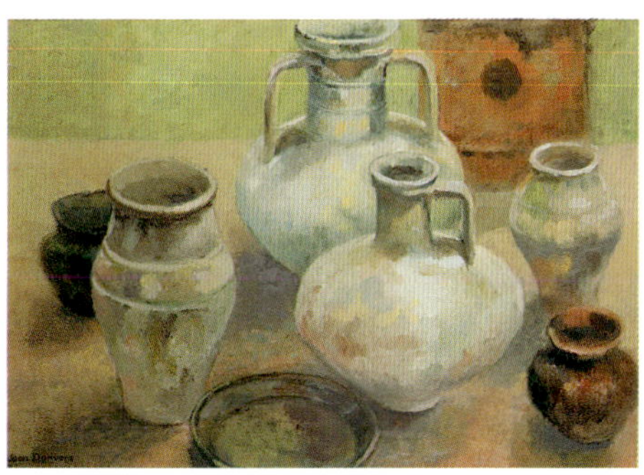

Danvers, Joan b.1919
Pots from the Little Waltham Dig 1972–1973
oil on hardboard 44.5 x 59.7
1973.216

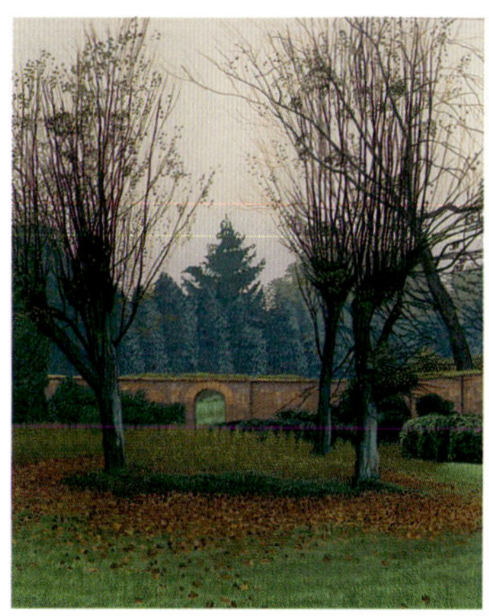

Deakins, Thomas William b.1957
December Dusk 1995?
oil on board 29.1 x 24.1
1997.008

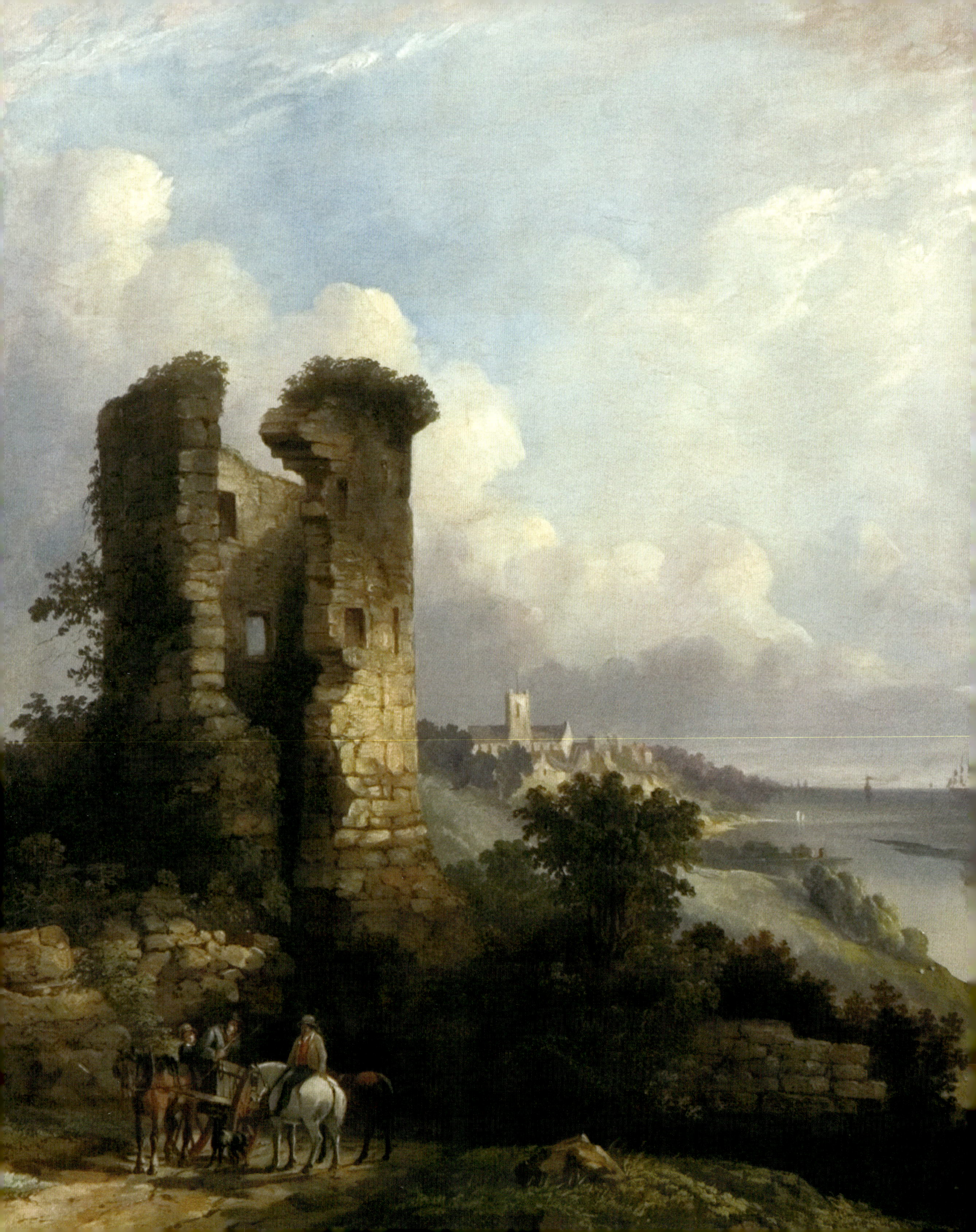

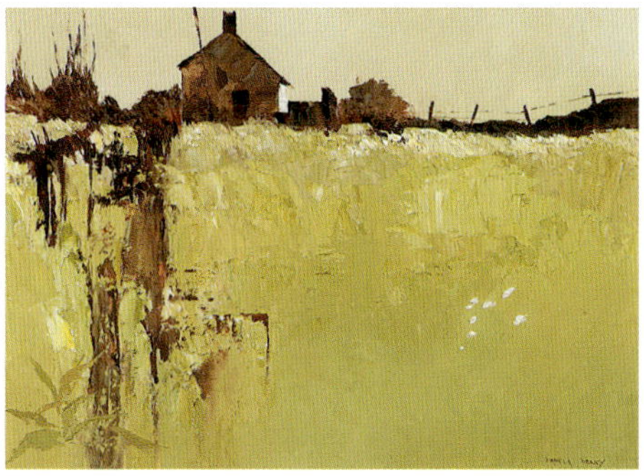

Derry, Pamela 1932–2002
Now Summer Has Come
oil on board 43.1 x 58.4
1977.113

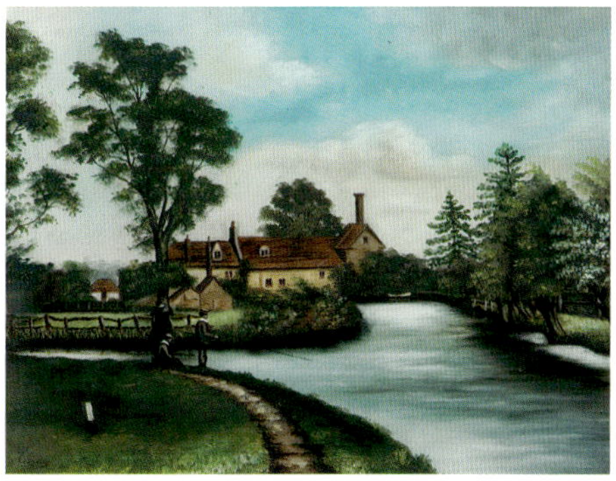

Dudley, Robert d.c.1893
River Scene with View of a Mill
oil on canvas 38 x 48
M28255

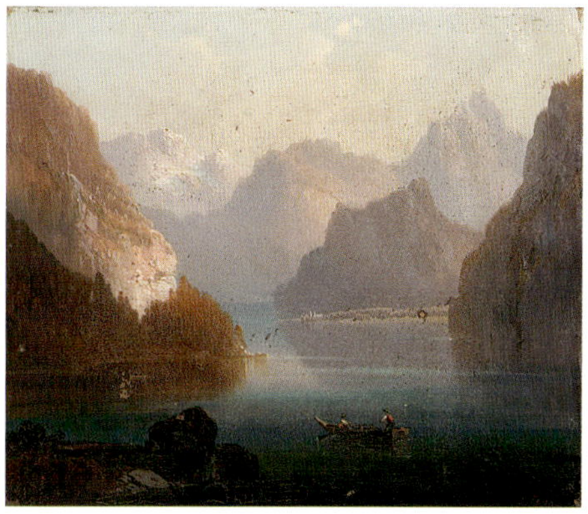

Feldh, F. C. active 19th C
Mountain Lake
oil on canvas 34.5 x 39
chmer3080

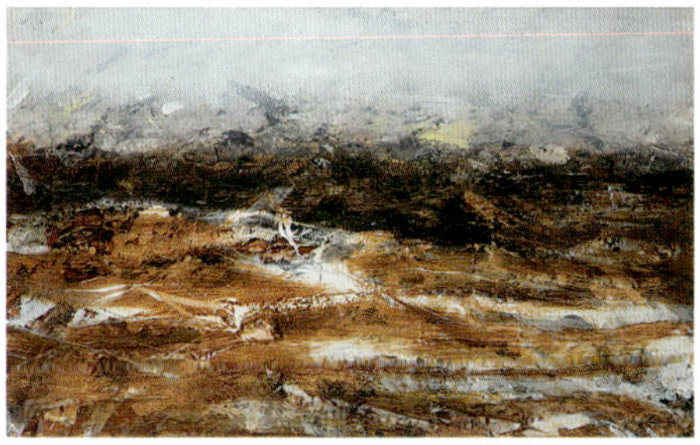

Francis, Mark b.1962
Trassey
oil on paper 46.1 x 72.2
1990.052

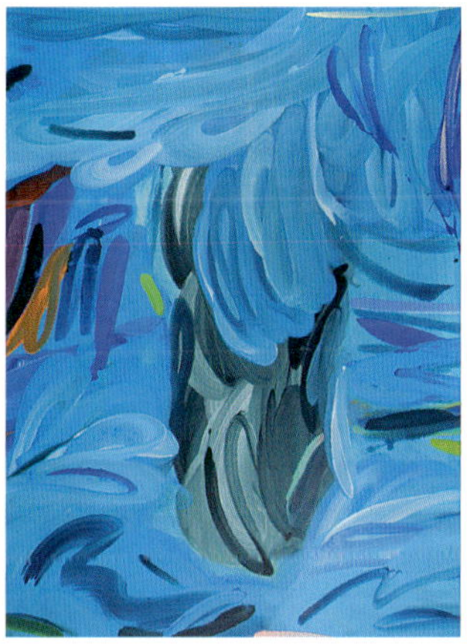

Fraser, Alexander b.1940
Guild Street No.3 1983
acrylic on canvas 213.4 x 125
1992.126

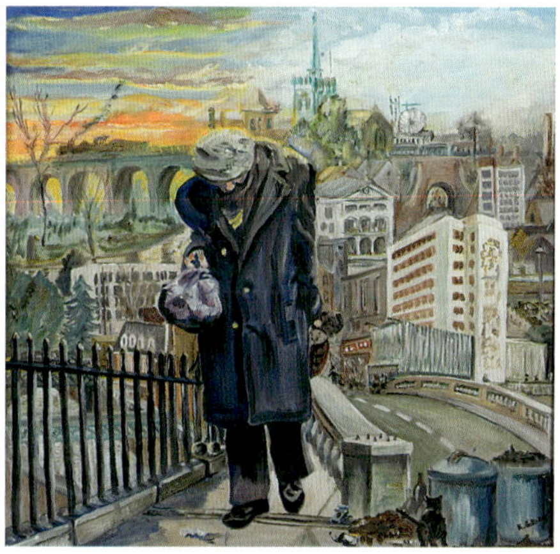

Gilbey, Kathrine b.1932
Bundles 1975–1976
oil & acrylic on board 48.4 x 50.4
1977.039

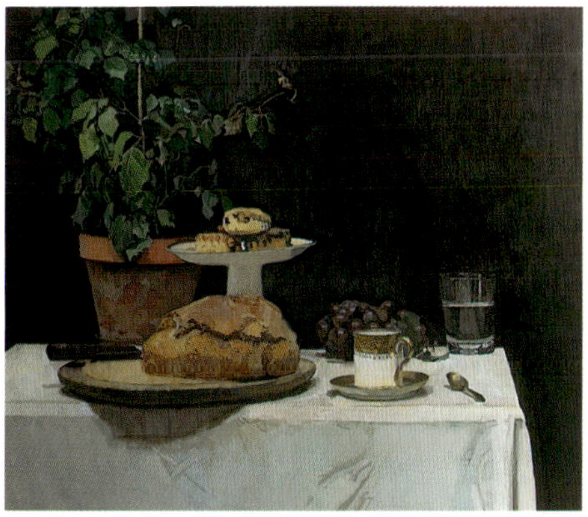

Gopal-Chowdhury, Paul b.1949
Still Life with Bread 1981
oil on canvas 59 x 74.2
1983.045

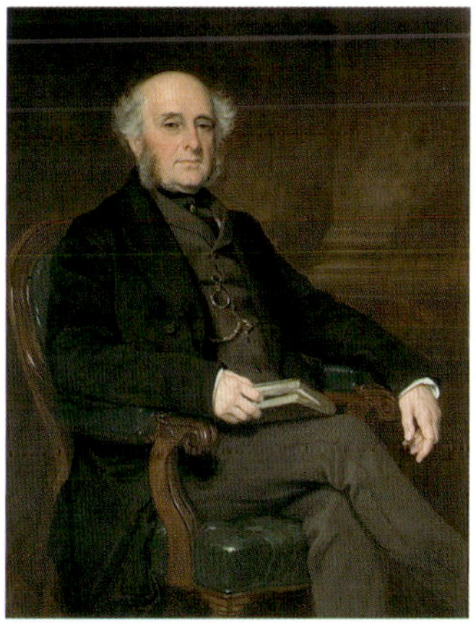

Grant, Francis 1803–1878
Sir Thomas Burch Western, Lord Lieutenant and Custos Rotulorum of the County of Essex 1864
oil on canvas 127.2 x 103
M28244

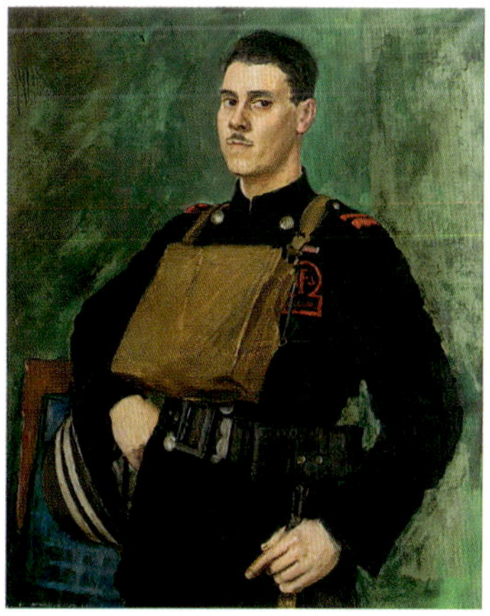

Hailstone, Bernard 1910–1987
District Officer F. G. Keen of Chelmsford, OBE, Auxiliary Fire Service 1942
oil on canvas 104 x 78.8
M28248

Facing page: Bright, Henry, 1814–1873, *Hadleigh Castle* (detail), c.1840, Southend Museums Service, (p. 254)

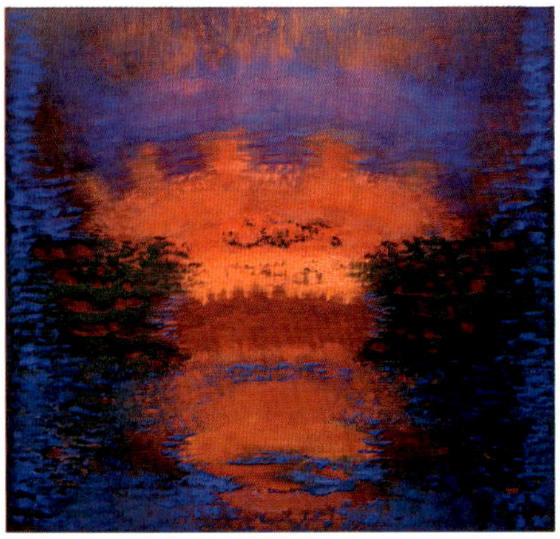

Hambling, Maggi b.1945
Mourning Sunset 1988
oil on canvas 144.8 x 149.8
1992.555

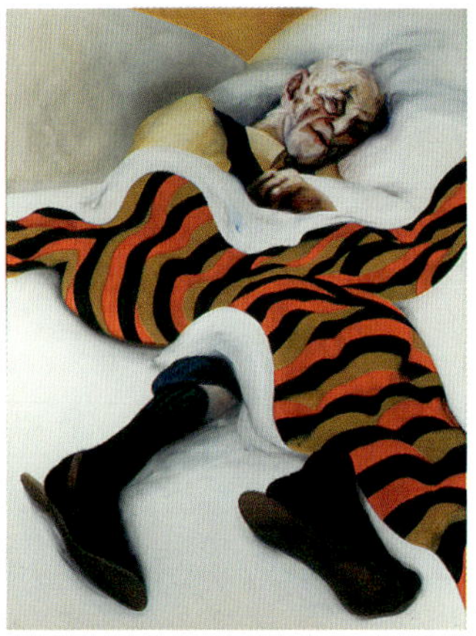

Hambling, Maggi b.1945
Lett Dreaming
oil on canvas 163 x 122
1986.843

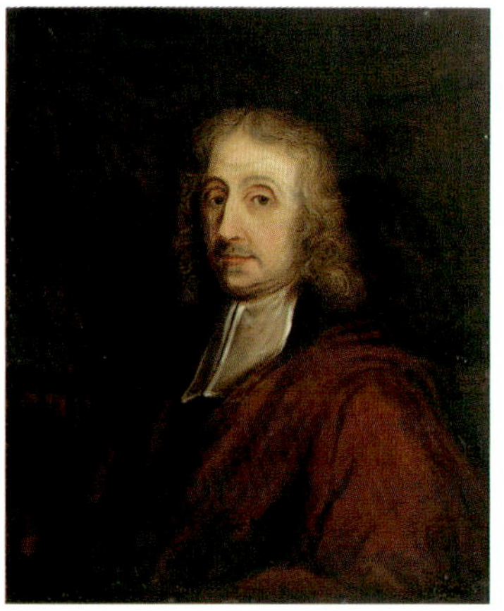

Harraden, Richard Banks 1778–1862
John Ray (1628–1705) (copy after Thomas Hudson) 1847
oil on canvas 76.7 x 63.3
M28242

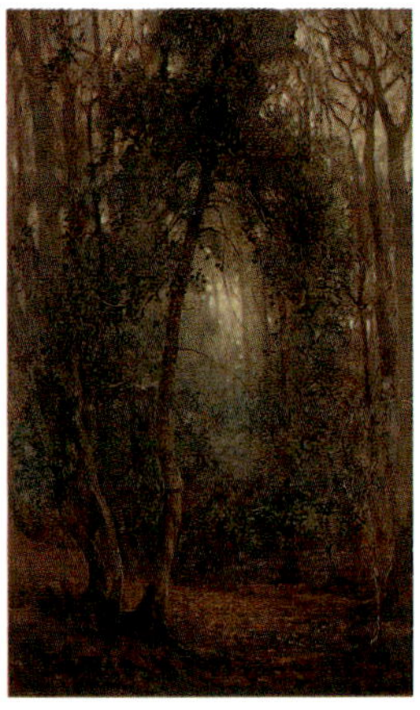

Haughton, Benjamin 1865–1924
A Woodland Vista
oil on board 43 x 26
M28265

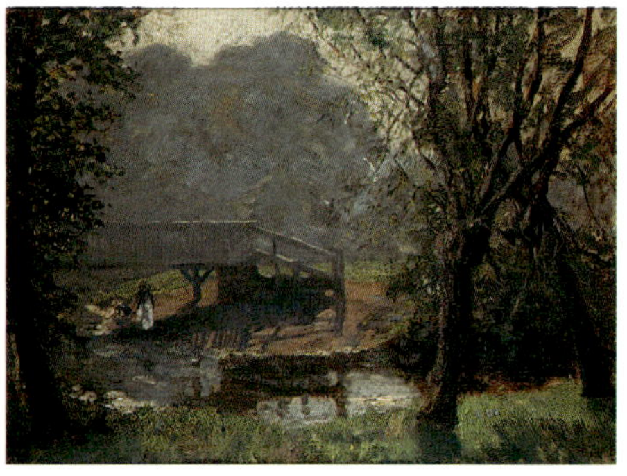

Haughton, Benjamin 1865–1924
On the Yeo
oil on canvas 35 x 45
M28267A

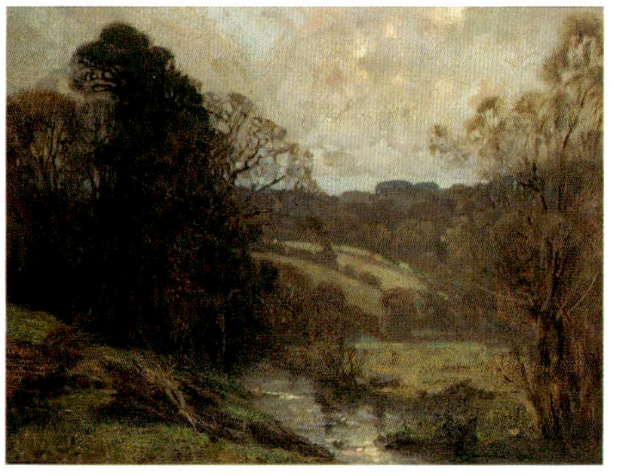

Haughton, Benjamin 1865–1924
Spring Evening
oil on canvas 34 x 43
M28267B

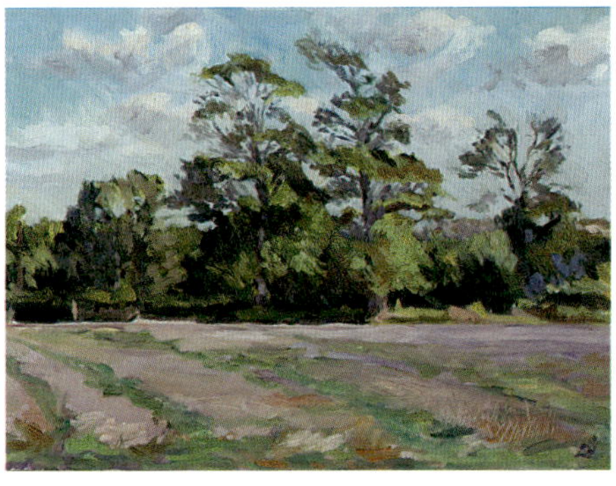

Hughes, Diane b.1943
Across the Fields after Harvest 1990
oil on canvas 30.5 x 49.5
1998.085

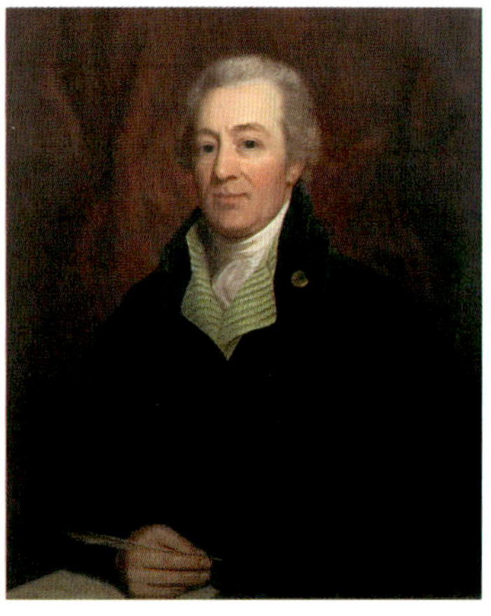

Jackson, John 1778–1831
Robert Tindal of Coval Hall (1749–1833), Father of Sir Nicholas Tindal c.1800
oil on canvas 73 x 59.5
1986.845

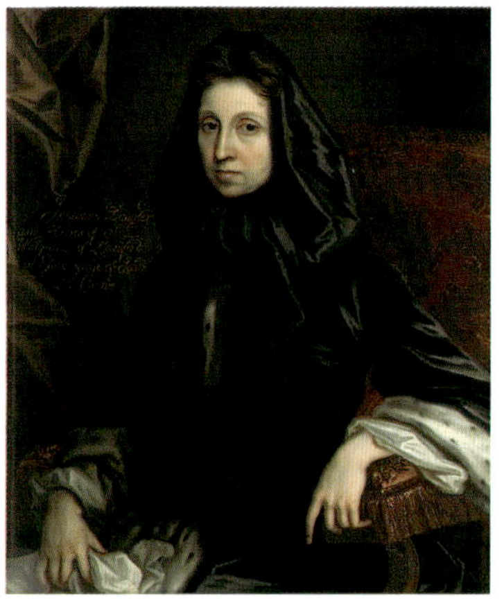

Janssens van Ceulen, Cornelis (circle of) 1593–1661
Jemima Waldegrave, Lady Crewe c.1620
oil on canvas 93 x 72.3
M28324

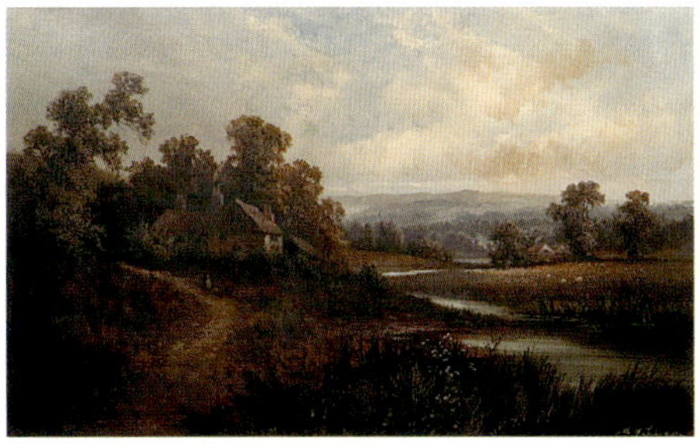

Johnson, Sidney Yates active 1892–1929
Landscape 1902
oil on canvas 51 x 76
M28250

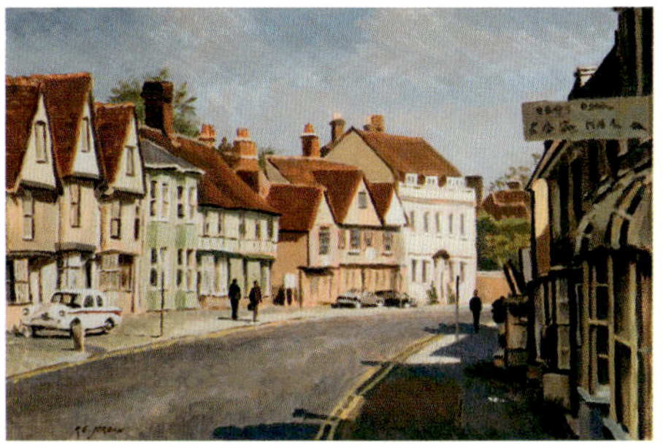

Jordan, R. E.
Bradford Street, Bocking 1979
oil on board 37 x 52
1979.226

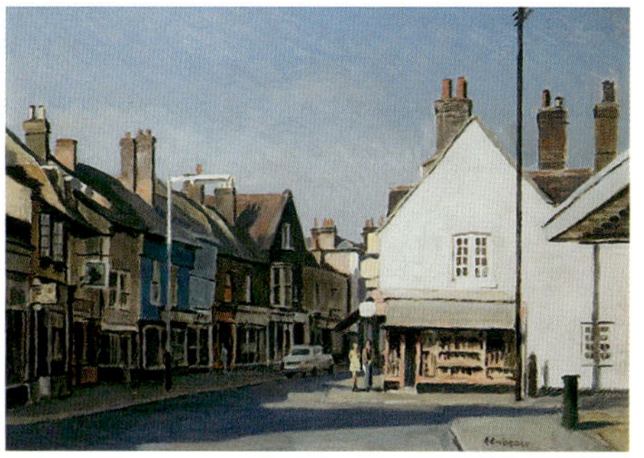

Jordan, R. E.
Baddow Road, Chelmsford
oil on board 26.6 x 36
1973.073

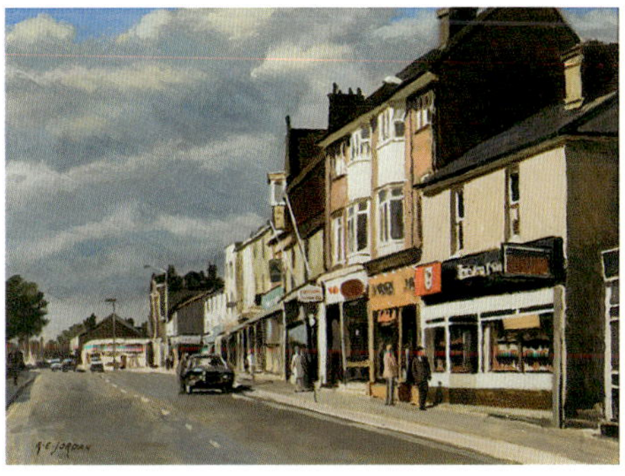

Jordan, R. E.
Duke Street, Chelmsford
oil on board 36 x 48.6
1975.370

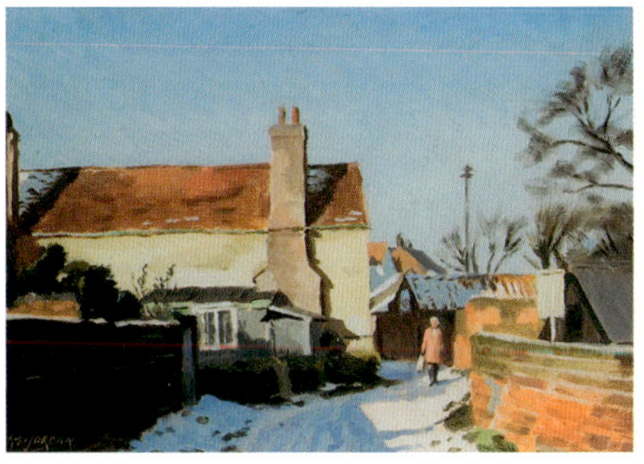

Jordan, R. E.
Snow at Writtle
oil on board 26.6 x 36
1975.365

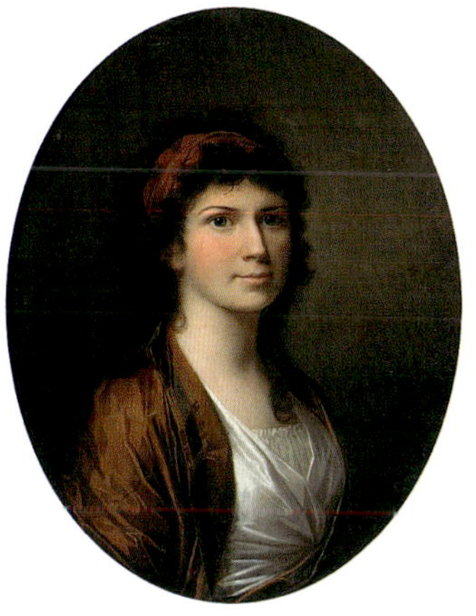

Juel, Jens 1745–1802
Juliana Margaretta Waltersdorff (later Mrs Cornelius Kortright) c.1780s–c.1790
oil on canvas 70 x 54
2001.302

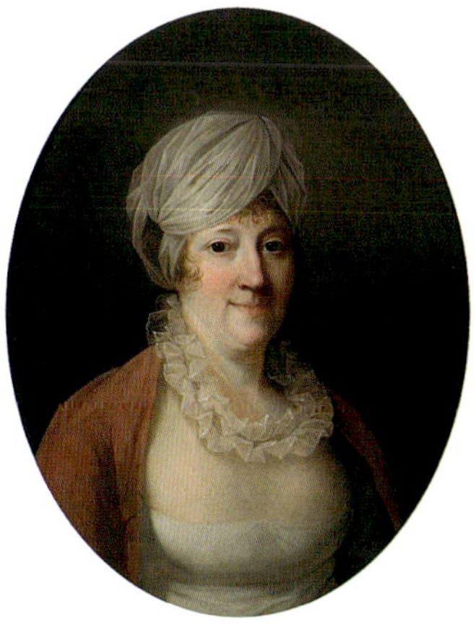

Juel, Jens 1745–1802
Juliana, Wife of Cornelius Kortright c.1800–1801
oil on canvas 68 x 52.5
2002.123

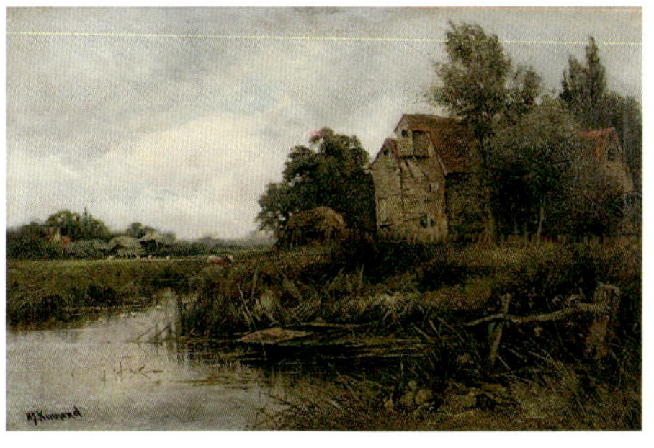

Kinnaird, Henry John active 1880–1920
Old Mill near Little Baddow c.1880s–c.1893
oil on canvas 50.7 x 76.3
1999.428

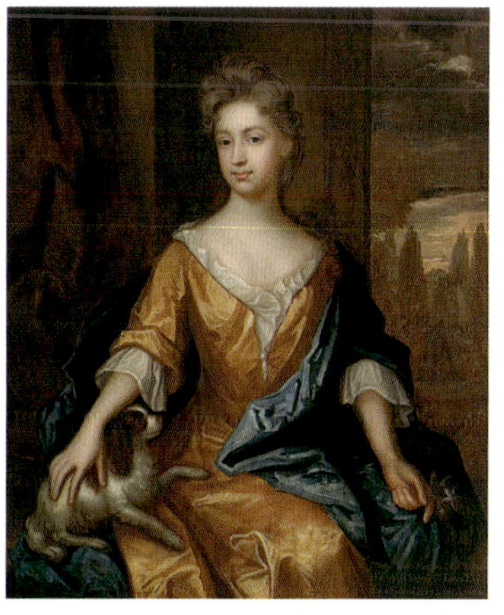

Kneller, Godfrey (circle of) 1646–1723
Dorothy, Lady Monoux 1705?
oil on canvas 125.7 x 102
M28325

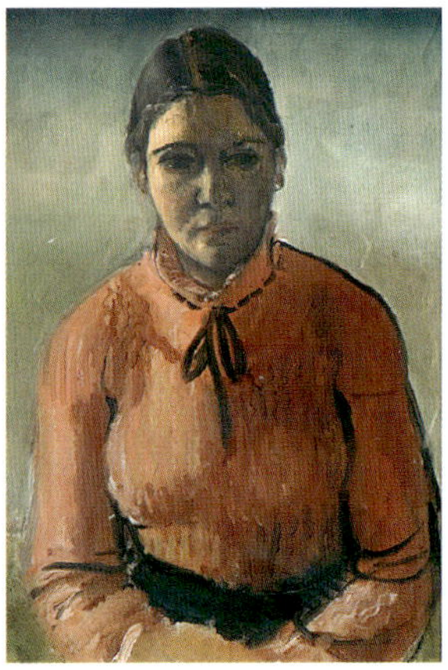

Lamb, Lynton Harold 1907–1977
Lila late 1920s–1930s?
oil on canvas 50.5 x 35
1991.132

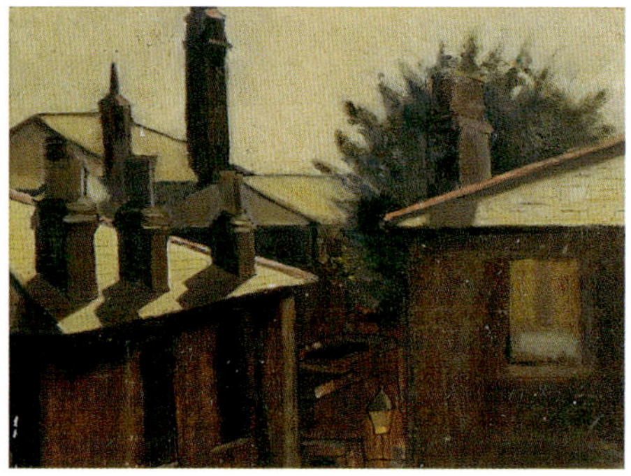

Lamb, Lynton Harold 1907–1977
Rooftops 1928
oil on board 27 x 35
1997.516

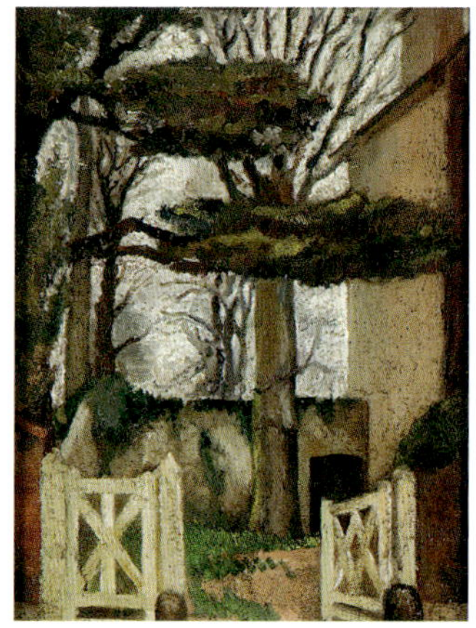

Lamb, Lynton Harold 1907–1977
Elms, Sydenham 1930
oil on canvas 38.2 x 28
1999.002

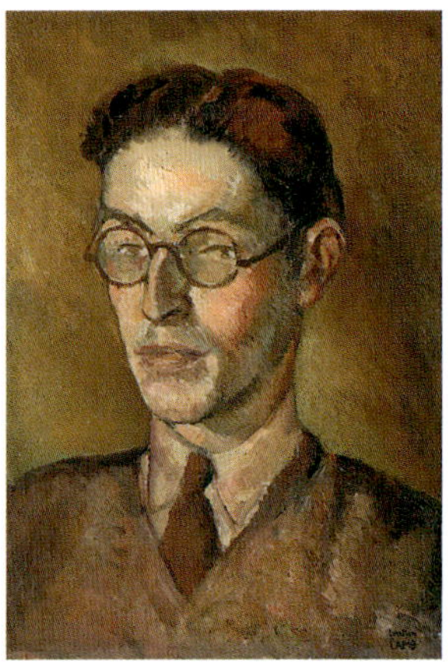

Lamb, Lynton Harold 1907–1977
Geoffrey Luling c.1930s
oil on canvas 49.5 x 34
1991.130

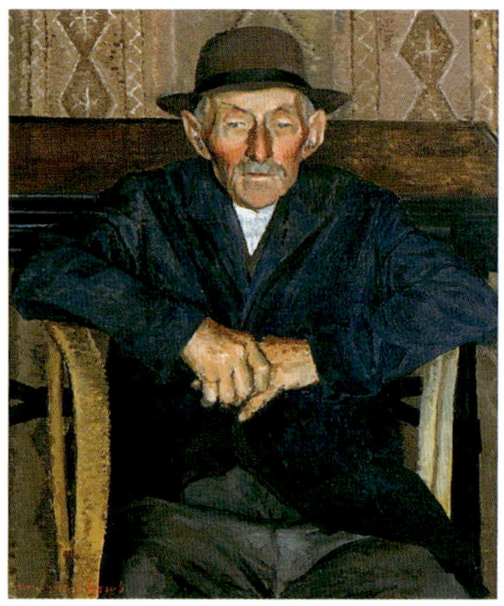

Lamb, Lynton Harold 1907–1977
Mr Mayhew of Sandon 1957
oil on canvas 61.5 x 51
M28326

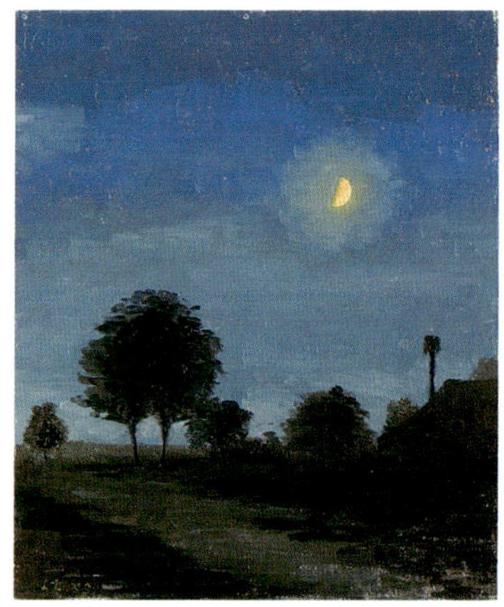

Lamb, Lynton Harold 1907–1977
A Lane near Ludlow by Moonlight 1959
oil on canvas 49.5 x 39.5
1991.134

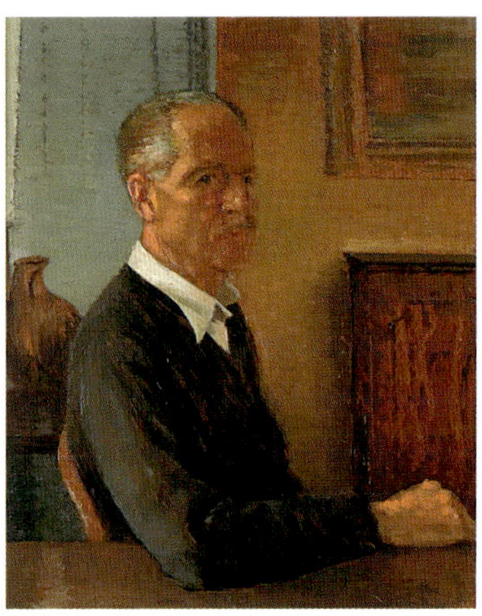

Lamb, Lynton Harold 1907–1977
Self Portrait 1959
oil on board 55 x 45
1991.129

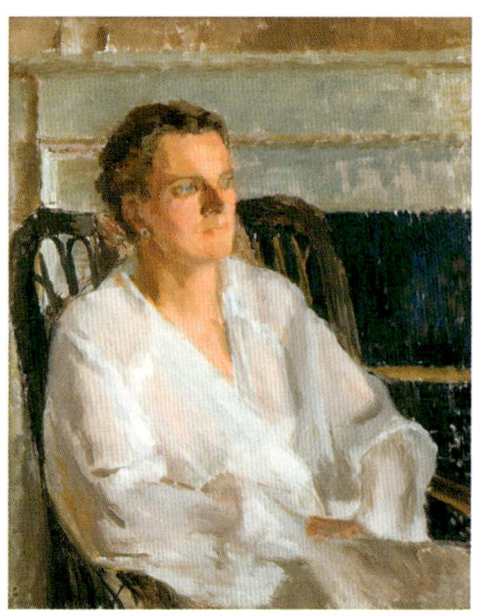

Lamb, Lynton Harold 1907–1977
Biddy, Mrs Lynton Lamb 1950s
oil on canvas 61 x 50.9
2003.032

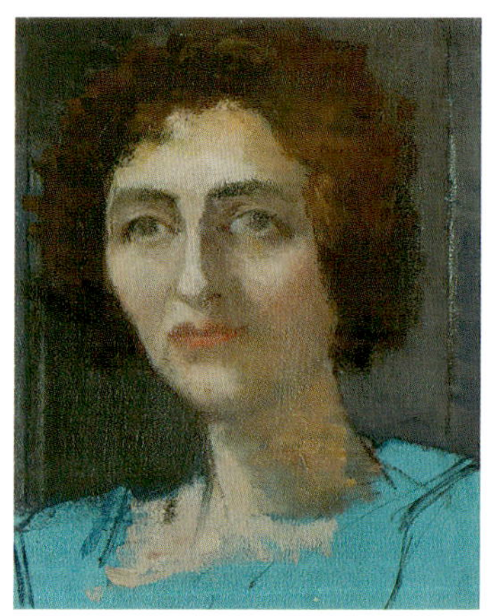

Lamb, Lynton Harold 1907–1977
Jocelyn Newbery late 1950s–1960s
oil on canvas 35 x 23
1991.131

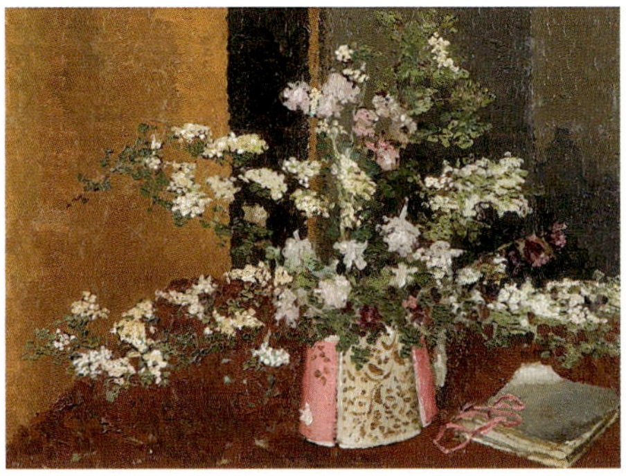

Lamb, Lynton Harold 1907–1977
Still Life with Flowers c.1950s
oil on canvas 44.5 x 59.5
1991.133

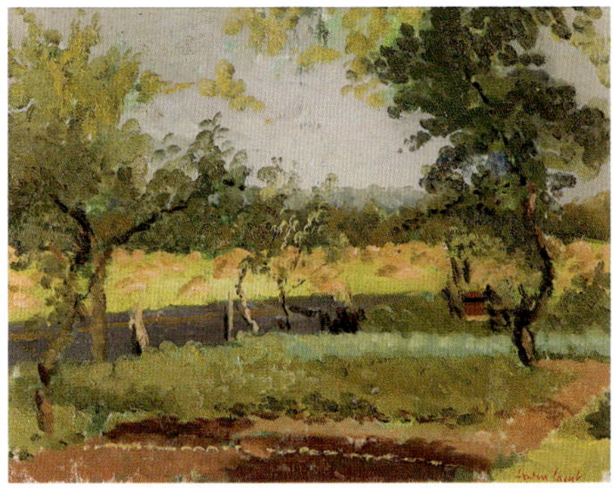

Lamb, Lynton Harold 1907–1977
The Garden at Rose Cottage, Sandon c.1960
oil on canvas 38.3 x 48.4
1999.005

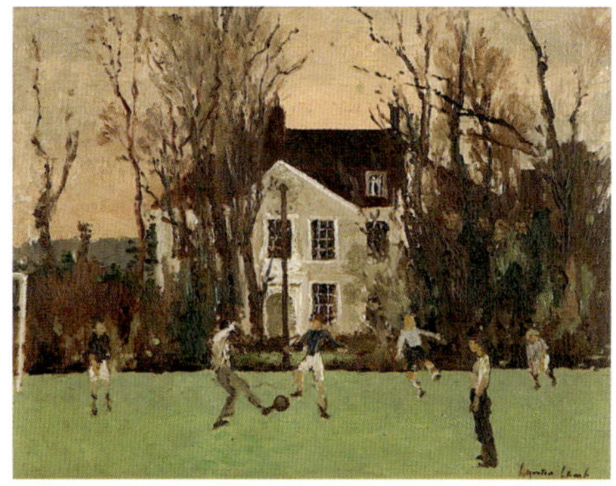

Lamb, Lynton Harold 1907–1977
Old Rectory, Sandon (Football Match) c.1960s
oil on canvas 38.2 x 48.8
1999.001

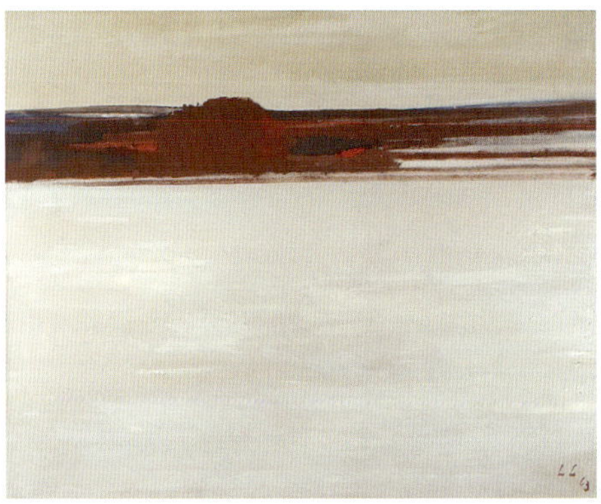

Lamb, Lynton Harold 1907–1977
Winter Landscape: Essex 1963
oil on canvas 61.5 x 73.5
1994.398

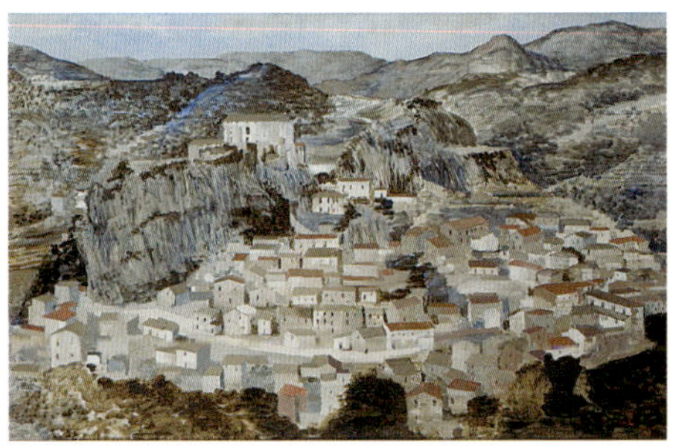

Lamb, Lynton Harold 1907–1977
Calabria 1965
oil on canvas 60.5 x 91
M28347/A

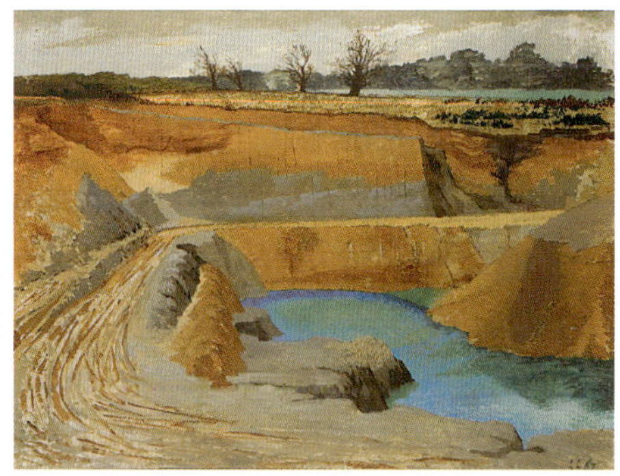

Lamb, Lynton Harold 1907–1977
No.1 Ballast Workings, Sandon 1967
oil on board 80.8 x 103.3
M28346

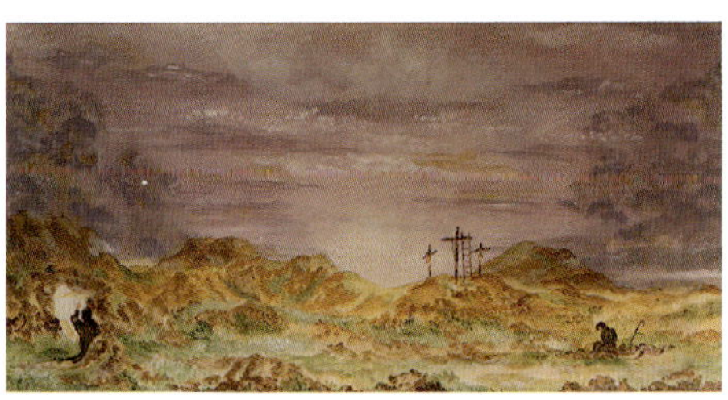

Longley, F. C. active 1970s
The Dawn of Christianity 1975
acrylic on hardboard 59.5 x 111.3
1975.277

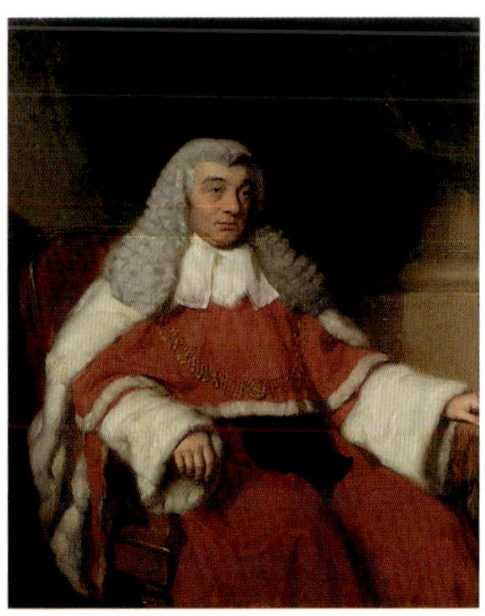

Lucas, John 1807–1874
Sir Nicholas Tindal (1776–1846), Chief Justice of the Common Pleas c.1835–c.1855
oil on canvas 127.2 x 101.7
1977.245

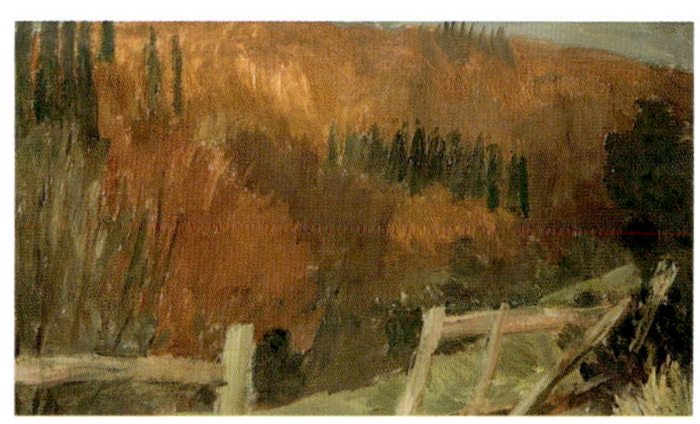

Lysaght, Edward 1902–1997
Late Autumn, Whitebrook Valley 1970s?
oil on paper 45.5 x 73
chmer3082

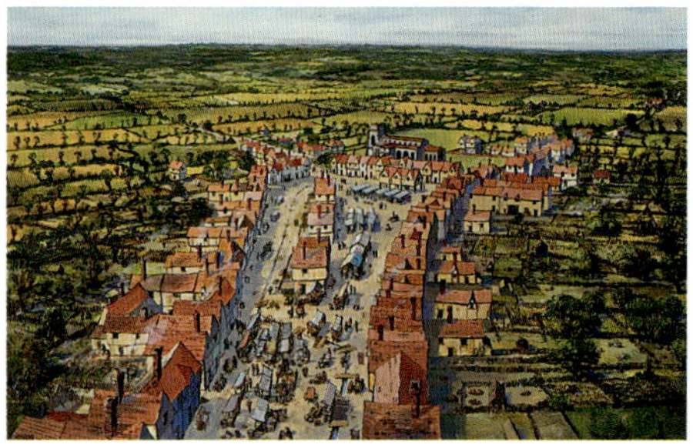

Massey-Ryan, Roger b.1959
Chelmsford Town and Market in 1591 1999
oil on board 45 x 69
1999.514

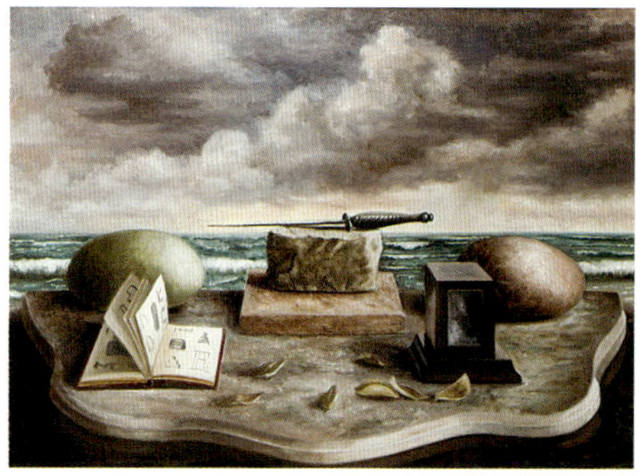

McKenna, Stephen b.1939
Heroic Still Life 1981
oil on canvas 68.6 x 89.2
1983.125

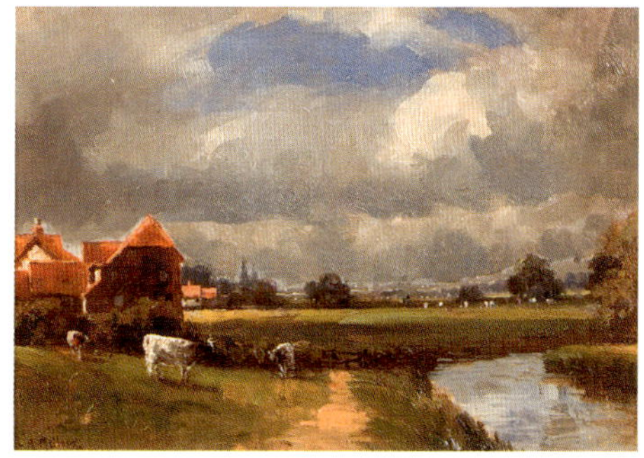

Mellon, Campbell A. 1876–1955
Baddow Meads, Chelmsford
oil on board 25.5 x 35.5
1995.370

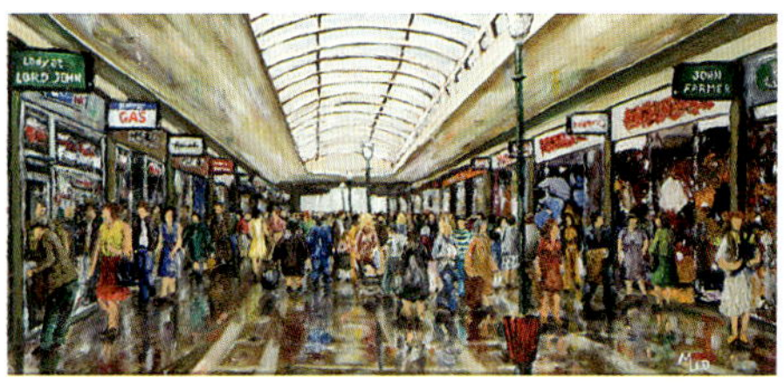

Middleton, Charles
Chelmsford Shoppers c.1980
oil on canvas 43.3 x 89.2
1981.380

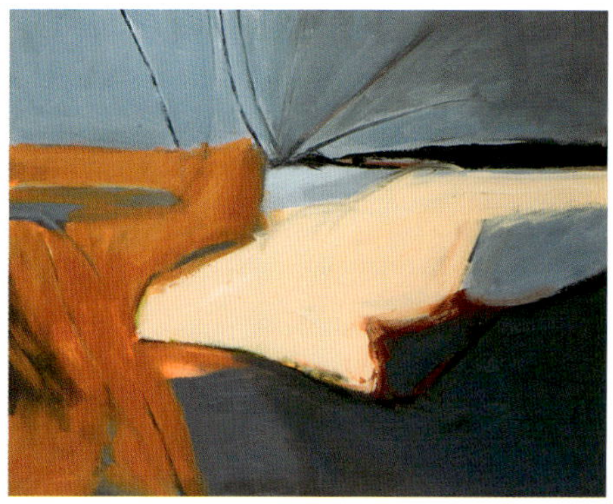

Mileham, Anthony active 1950–1975
Landscape: Galleywood Common 1974
acrylic on canvas 62.2 x 74.9
1977.244

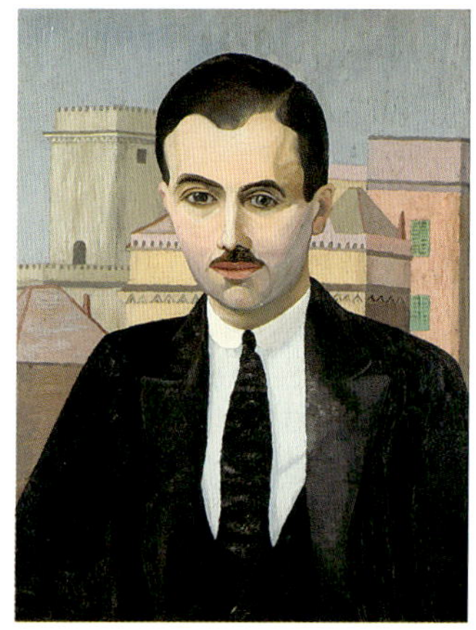

Morris, Cedric Lockwood 1889–1982
The Swiss Visitor 1925
oil on canvas 79.8 x 63.5
1982.159

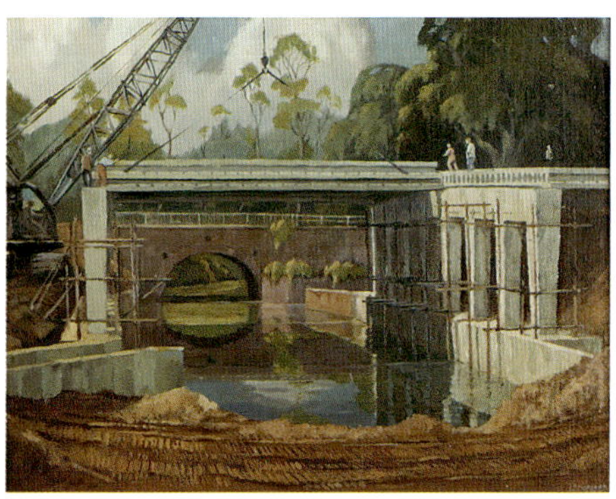

Norman, R. F. d.1978?
Progress 1964
oil on board 45.7 x 59.8
M28335

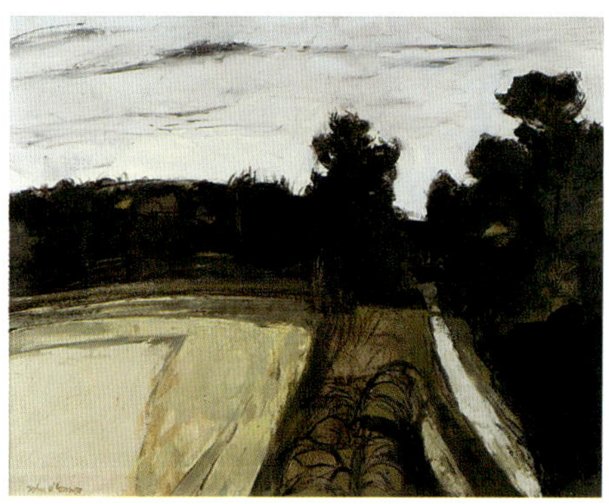

O'Connor, John Scorror 1913–2004
Track to Corbel's Farm 1950s–1960s
oil on canvas 59 x 74
M28338

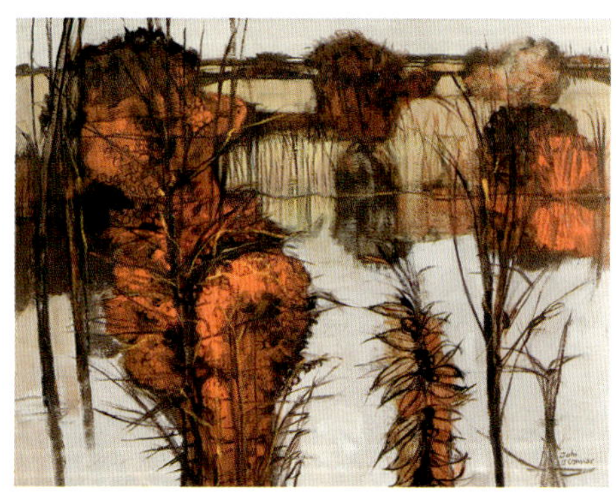

O'Connor, John Scorror 1913–2004
Pond on Tollesbury Marshes 1961
oil on canvas 61 x 75
M28318

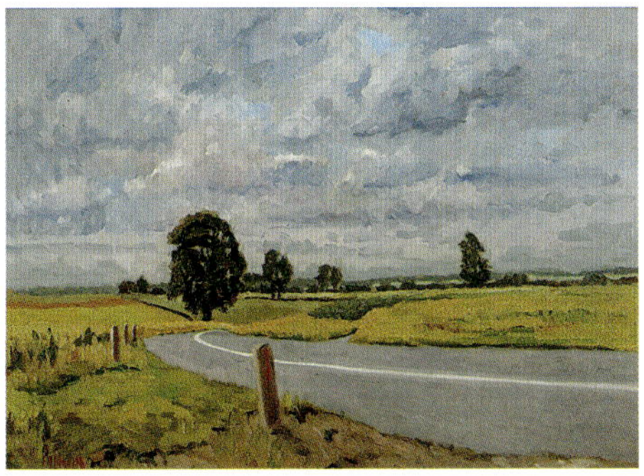

Popham, James Kidwell 1884–c.1960
The Road to Little Waltham
oil on canvas 43 x 57
M28343

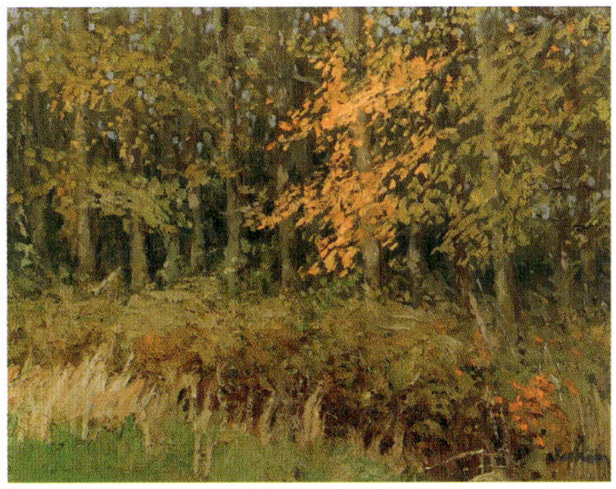

Popham, James Kidwell 1884–c.1960
The Wood in Autumn
oil on canvas 38.4 x 49
M28251

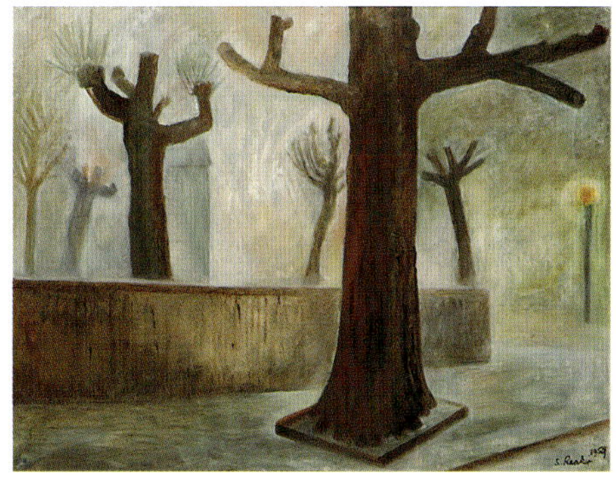

Rankin, Stella b.1915
London Fog 1953
oil on paper 43.4 x 55.3
1996.300

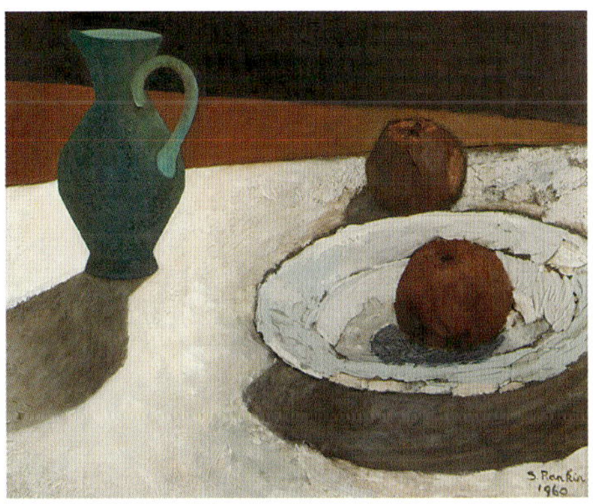

Rankin, Stella b.1915
Jug and Apples 1960
oil on hardboard 40.4 x 48
1992.449

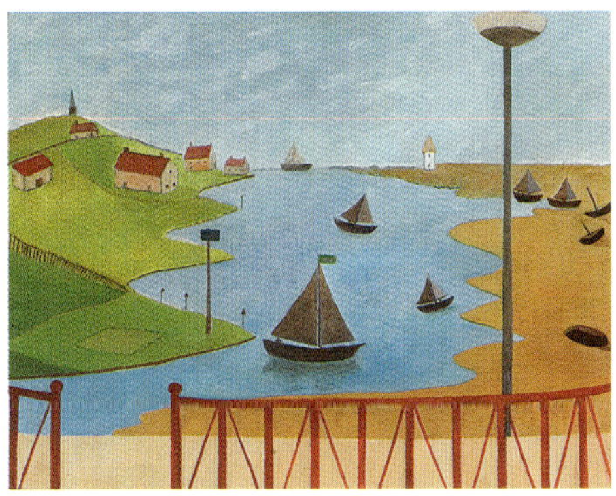

Rankin, Stella b.1915
Estuary Threatened by a Marina 1991
oil on board 39.3 x 49.5
1992.447

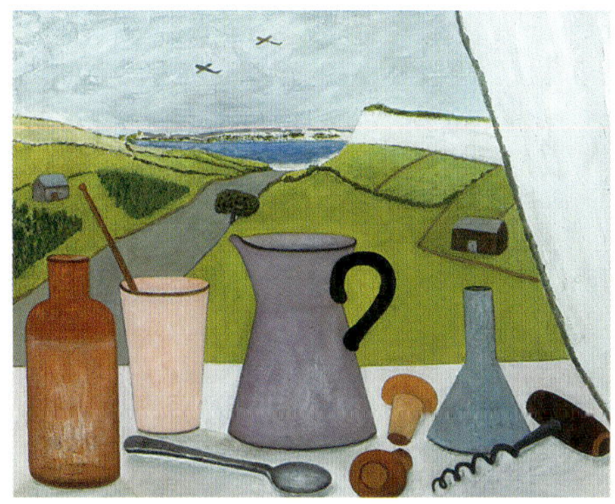

Rankin, Stella b.1915
Still Life and Landscape 1991
oil on canvas 30.5 x 38
1992.448

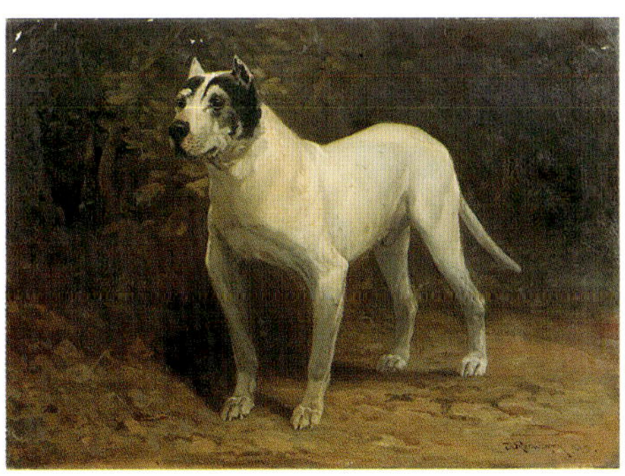

Redworth, William Josiah 1873–1947
Captain Arthur Hill's 'Mike' 1903
oil on canvas 35.5 x 61
M28350

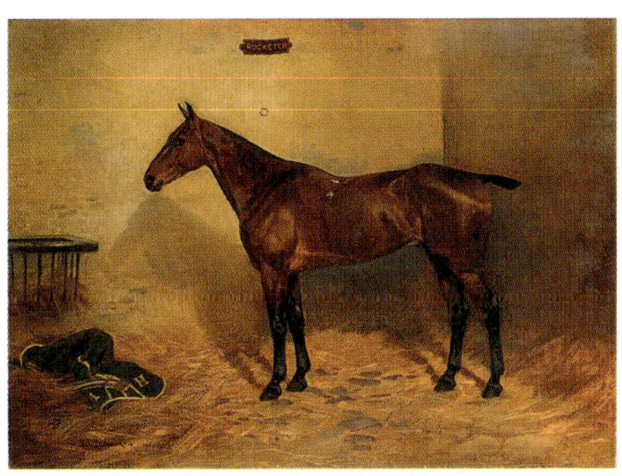

Redworth, William Josiah 1873–1947
'Rocketer' 1903
oil on canvas 49.5 x 59.7
M28349

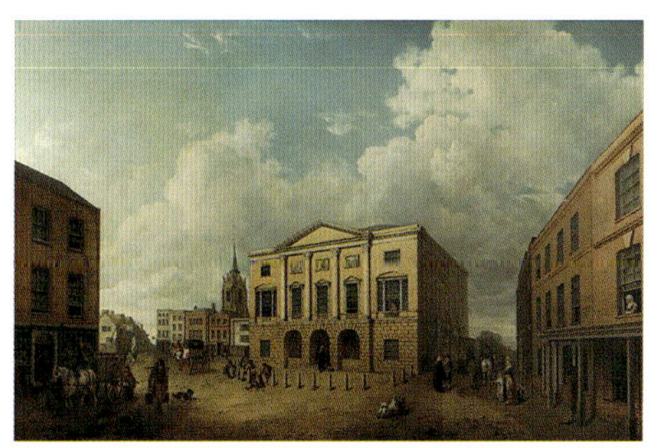

Reinagle, Philip 1749–1833
The Shire Hall, Chelmsford 1794
oil on canvas 65.1 x 99.8
M28333

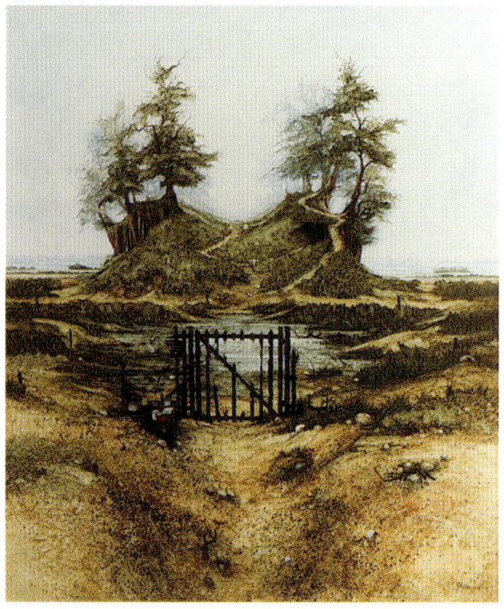

Ridgewell, John b.1937
Gate 1972
oil on canvas 111.7 x 94
1981.283

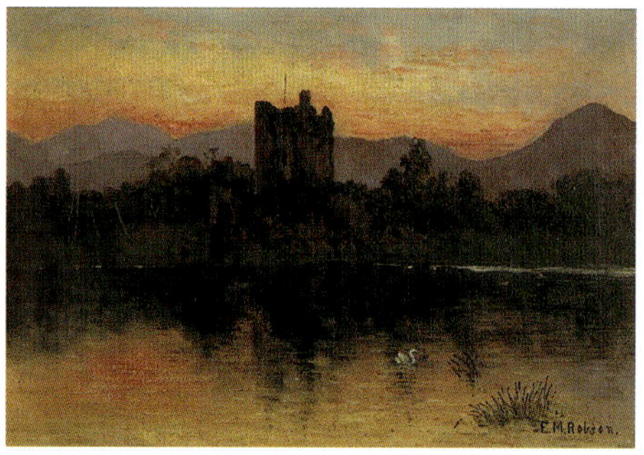

Robson, Elsie May active c.1910–1938
Landscape with Ruined Castle c.1910–c.1915
oil on canvas 24 x 33
1974.005.B

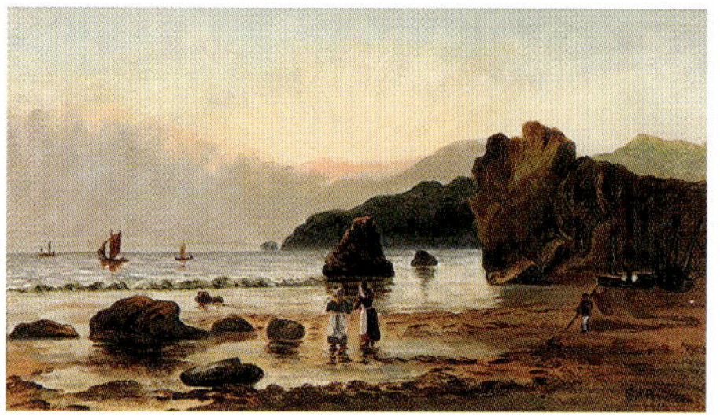

Robson, Elsie May active c.1910–1938
Landscape (Rocky Bay) 1912
oil on canvas 29.2 x 49.6
1974.008

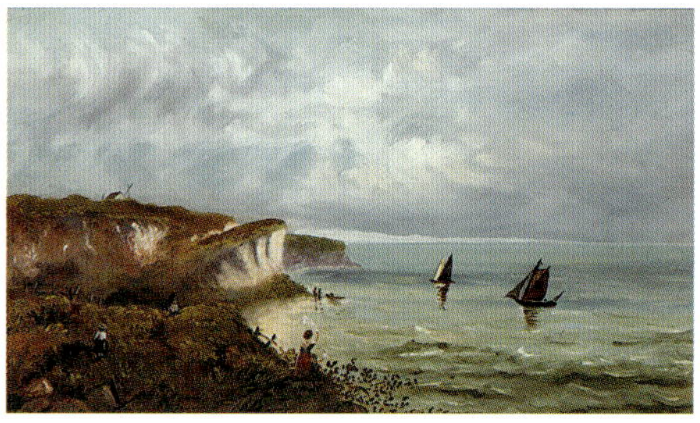

Robson, Elsie May active c.1910–1938
Seascape (from cliffs) 1912
oil on canvas 29.2 x 49.5
1974.007

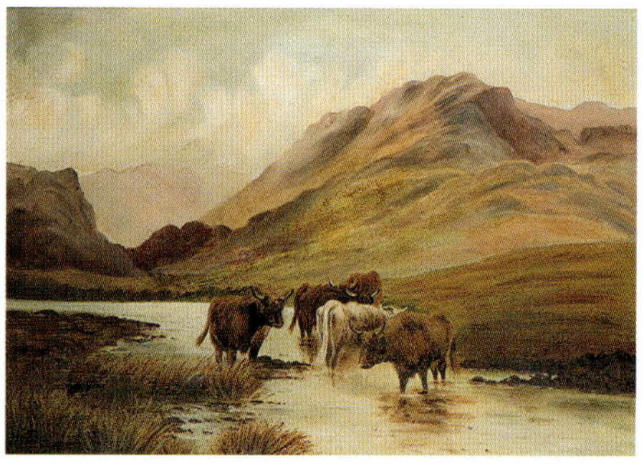

Robson, Elsie May active c.1910–1938
Landscape with Highland Cattle 1913
oil on canvas 50 x 67
1974.009

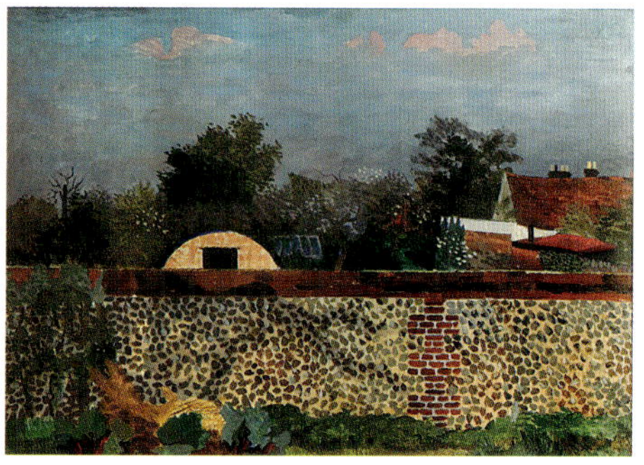

Rowntree, Kenneth 1915–1997
Summer Gardens, Bardfield c.1940s
oil on canvas 57.4 x 77.8
1986.840

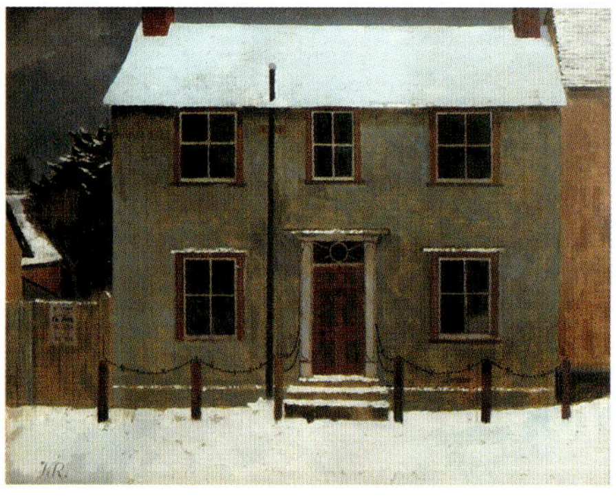

Rowntree, Kenneth 1915–1997
Ethel House, Great Bardfield 1942
oil on canvas on board 61.6 x 77.4
1986.841

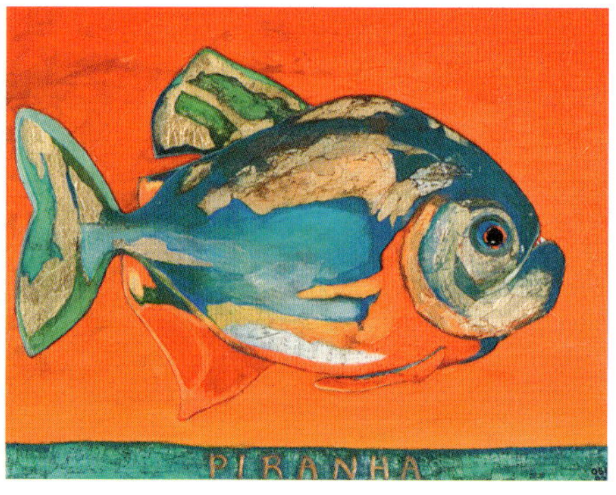

Schwegmann-Fielding, Anne b.1967
Piranha 1997
mixed media on board 61 x 77.8
1997.463

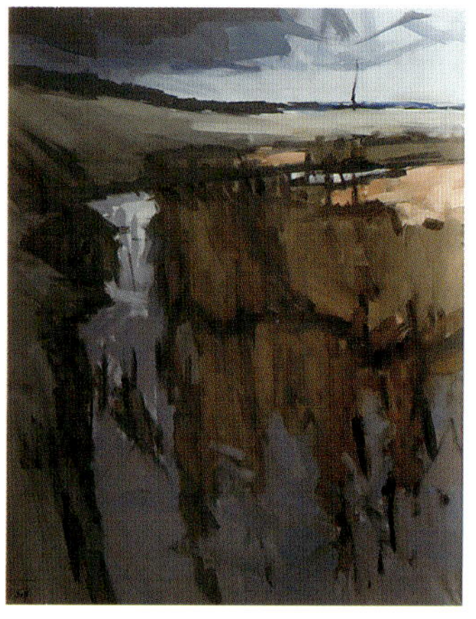

Self, Lawrence 1924–2002
Saltings, Shingle Street c.1960s
oil on canvas 101.5 x 75.2
M28349A

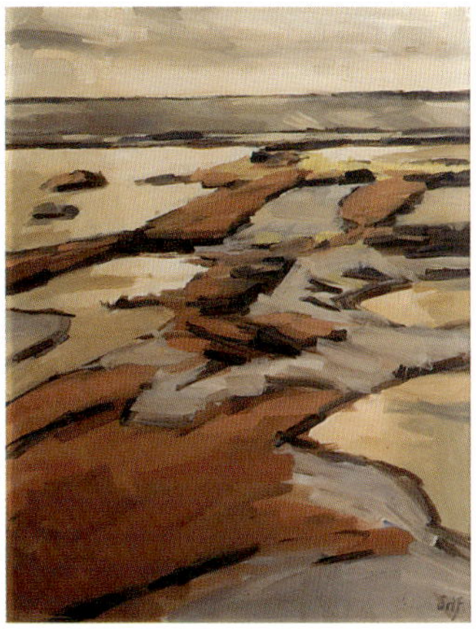

Self, Lawrence 1924–2002
Sunlight and Sea Wall, Walberswick 1968
oil on canvas 101.5 x 76.2
M28350A

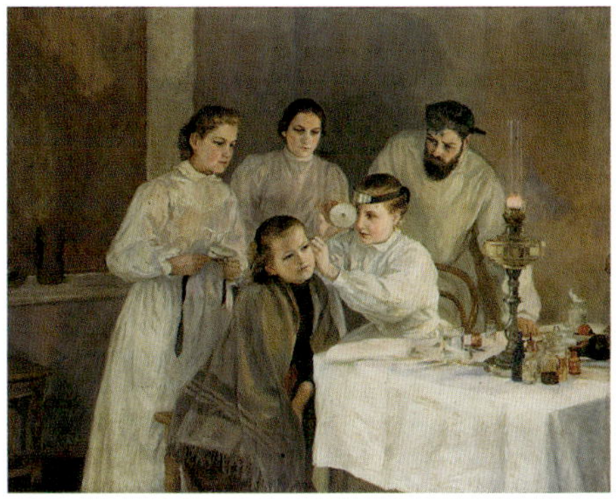

Shanks, Emily 1857–1936
Ear Inspection in a Russian Hospital c.1890s
oil on canvas 88.8 x 106.6
M28336

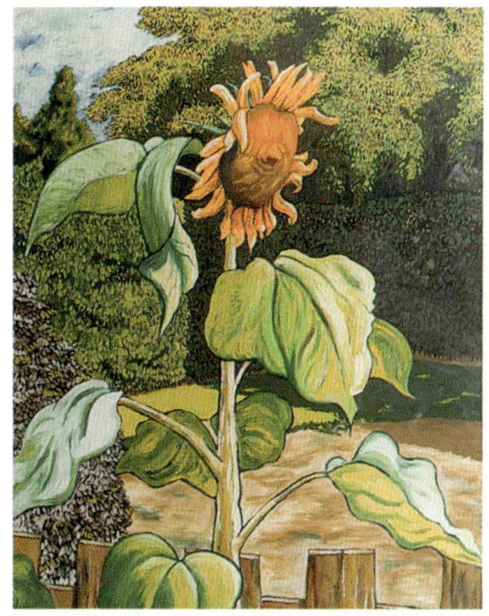

Shirlaw, George 1934–2005
Sunflower
oil on canvas 118 x 92.5
1979.108

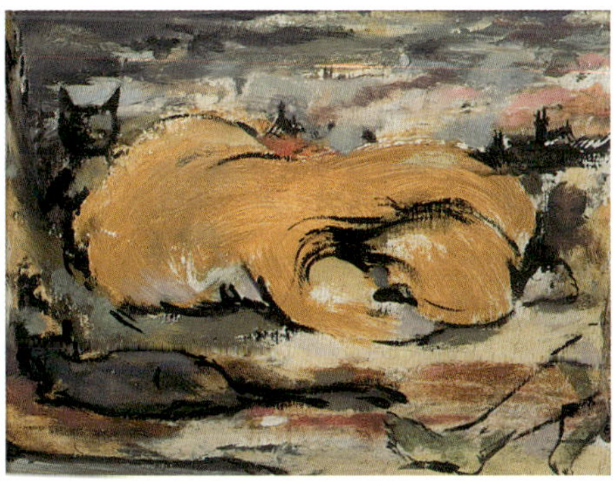

Smith, Edwin 1912–1971
War Unmasked 1942
oil on board 23 x 30.5
2003.092

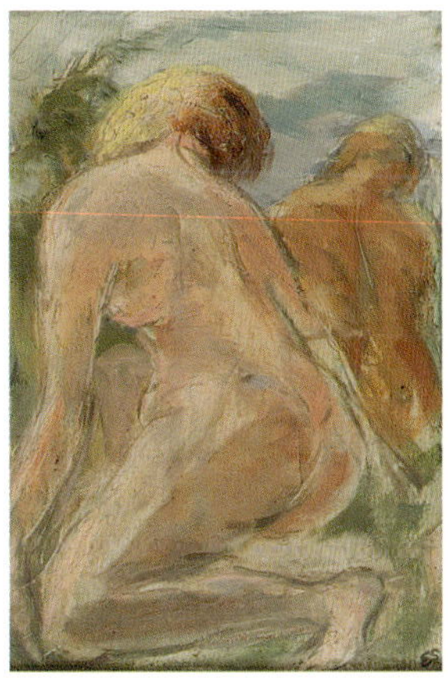

Smith, Edwin 1912–1971
The Eloquent Backs 1942–1943
oil on board 24.4 x 16.4
2003.091

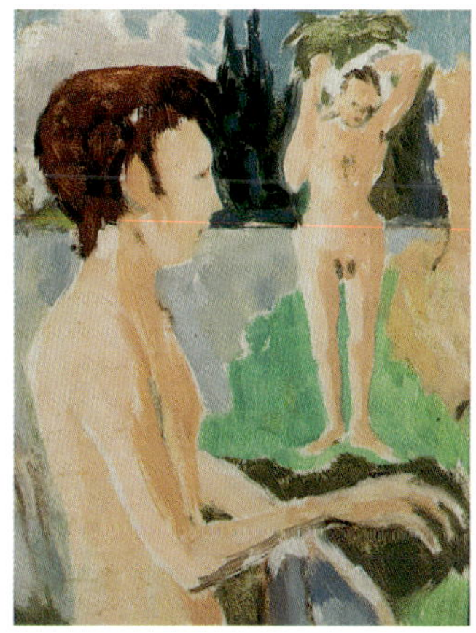

Smith, Edwin 1912–1971
Boy Shapes 1944
oil on board 31.5 x 24
2003.093

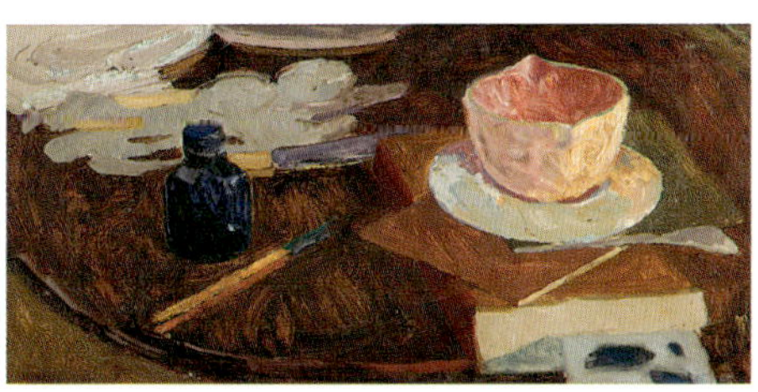

Smith, Edwin 1912–1971
Still Life with Pens, Ink and Jug 1948
oil on canvas 30.5 x 61
2003.094

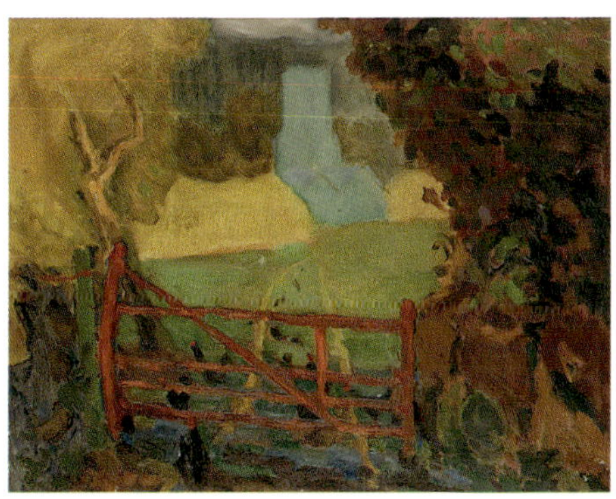

Smith, Edwin 1912–1971
The Red Gate 1948
oil on canvas 55 x 68
2003.096

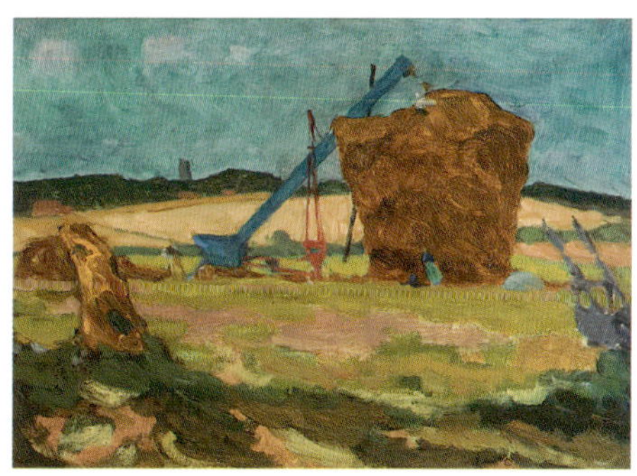

Smith, Edwin 1912–1971
Stacking Peas (with a view of Waveney Church, Norfolk) 1948–1949
oil on board 44 x 60
2003.095

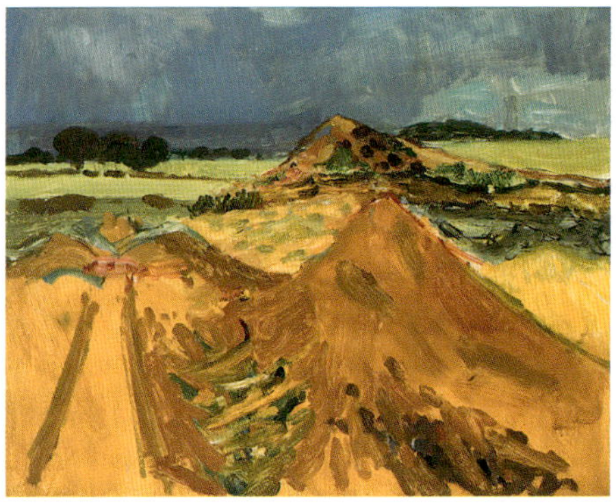

Smith, Edwin 1912–1971
Norfolk Sandpit 1958
oil on board 26.5 x 76.4
2003.097

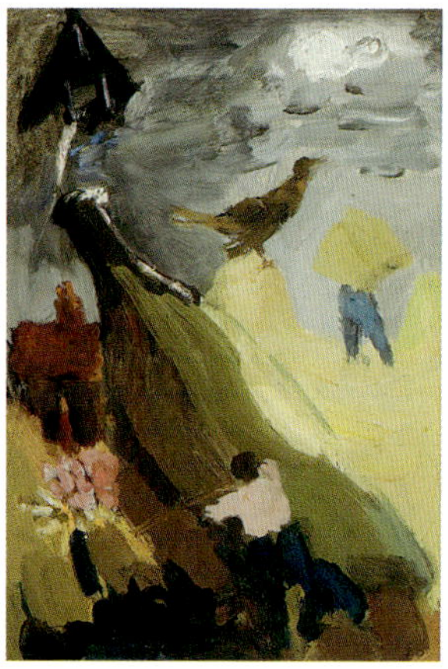

Smith, Edwin 1912–1971
Southwold (Landscape with Jet) 1960–1961
oil on board 35.3 x 25
2003.098

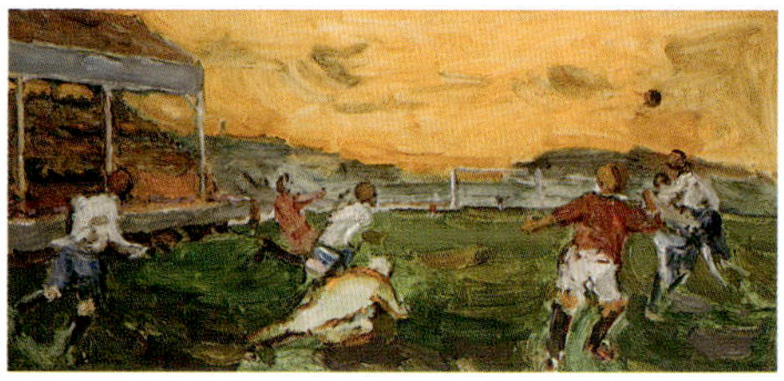

Smith, Edwin 1912–1971
Playing for the Painter 1979?
oil on board 60 x 122
2003.099

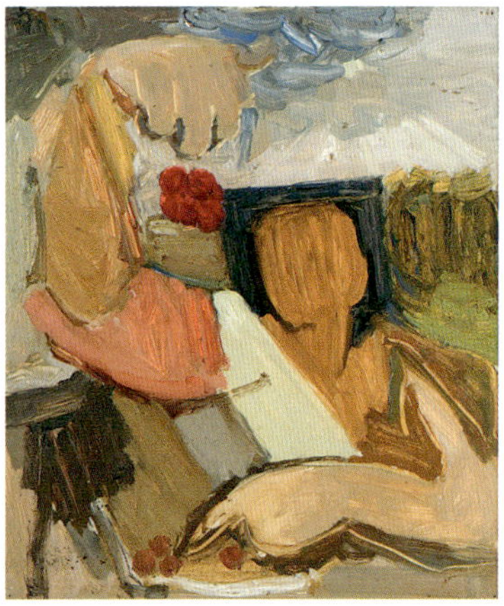

Smith, Edwin 1912–1971
Cherry Picker
oil on board 61 x 50.7
2003.103

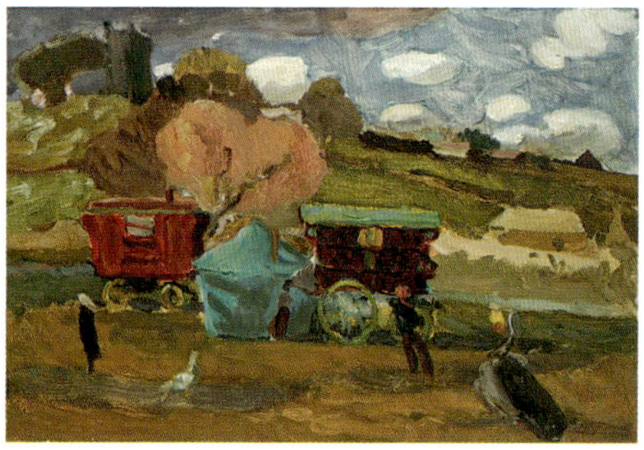

Smith, Edwin 1912–1971
Gypsy Encampment
oil on canvas 54 x 76.5
2003.102

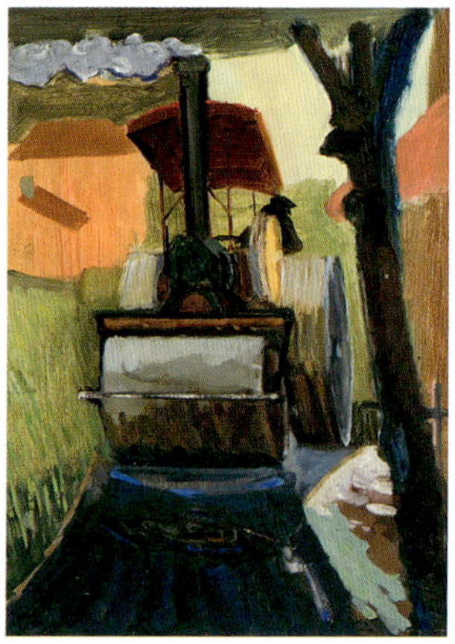

Smith, Edwin 1912–1971
Steam Roller
oil on board 94 x 61
2003.101

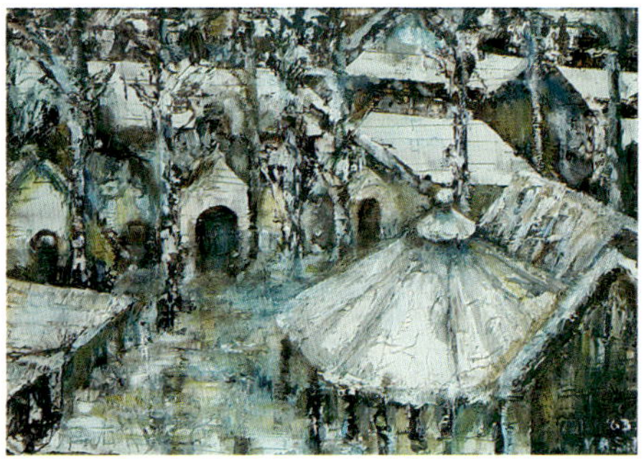

Spencer-Phillips, Valerie b.1923
Chelmsford in Winter (The Old Cattle Market)
1963
oil on board 29 x 40
1992.136

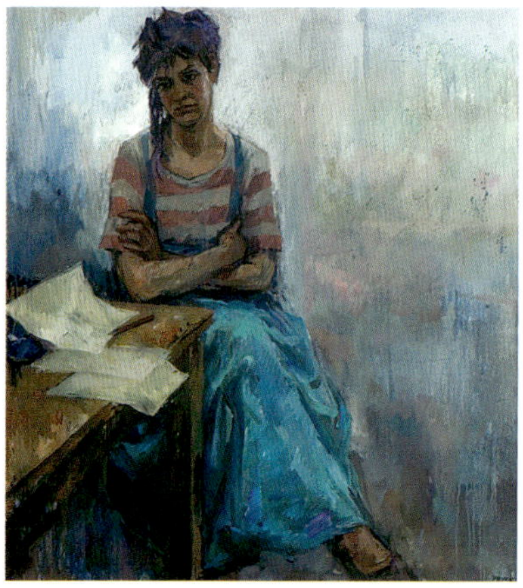

Spencer-Pryse, Tessa b.1940
Poverty 1985
oil on canvas 106.7 x 101.6
1986.406

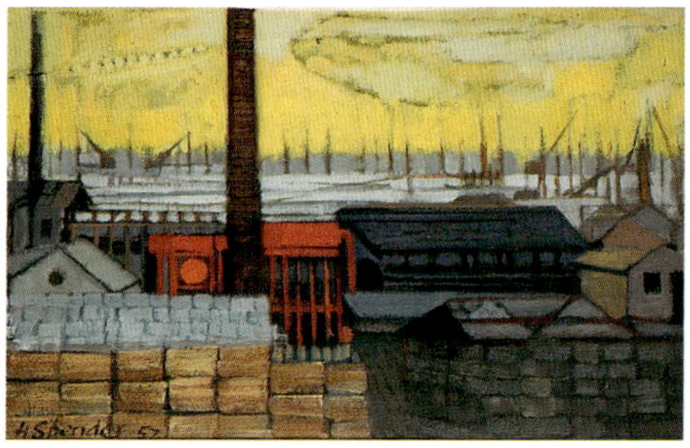

Spender, John Humphrey 1910–2005
Paper Mills 1957
oil on board 40.1 x 56.1
1986.889

Facing page: Martínez, Raúl, 1927–1995, *Repetitions with a Flag* (detail), 1966, University of Essex, Collection of Latin American Art, (p. 188)

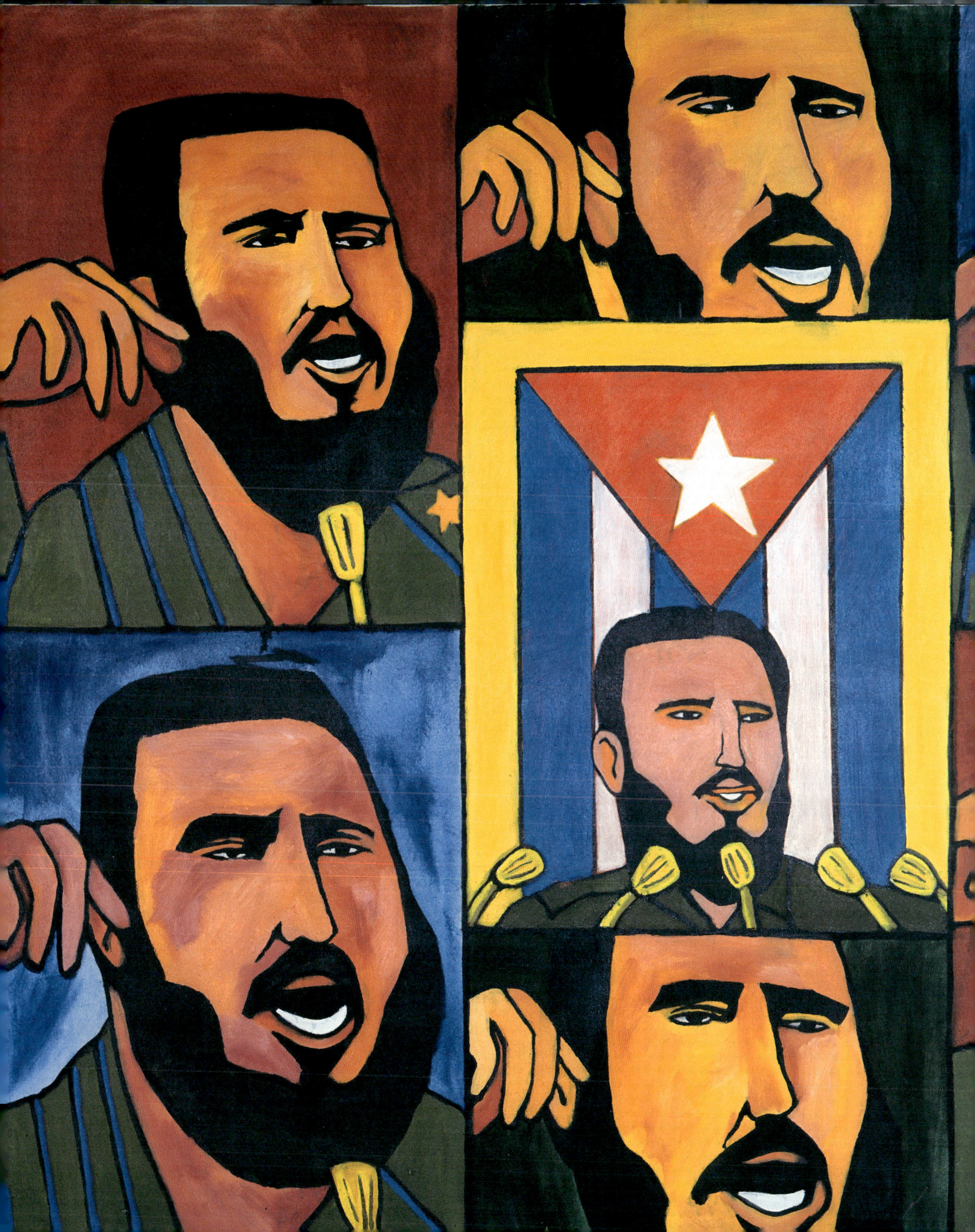

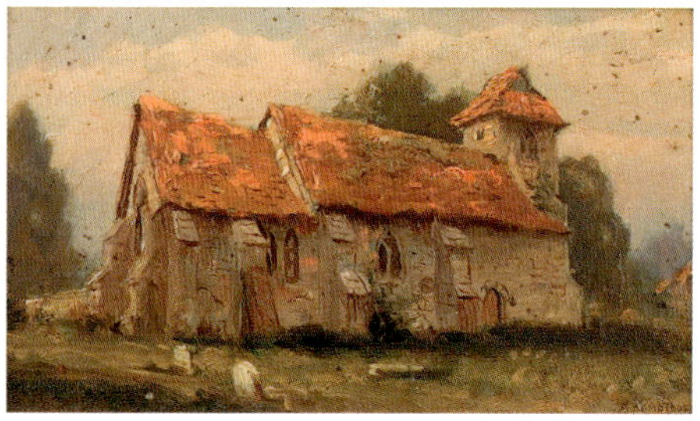

Tebby, Arthur Kemp c.1865–c.1935
Ashingdon, St Andrew (before the north vestry was added by Sir Charles Nicholson, 1921)
oil on board 12 x 20.6
1975.569

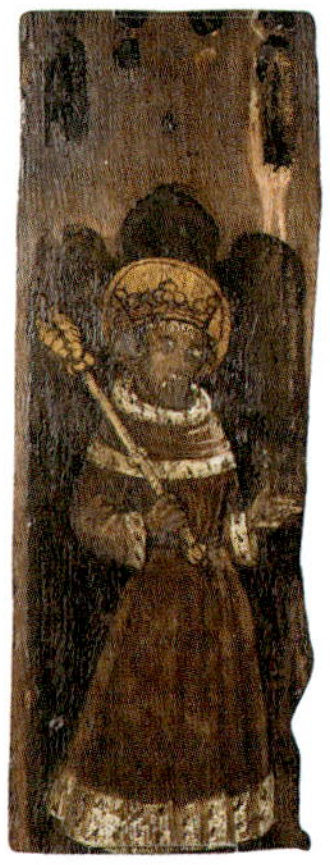

unknown artist early 15th C
King with Gold Crown, possibly Edward the Confessor
oil & tempera on panel 63.5 x 21.2
N22098.006

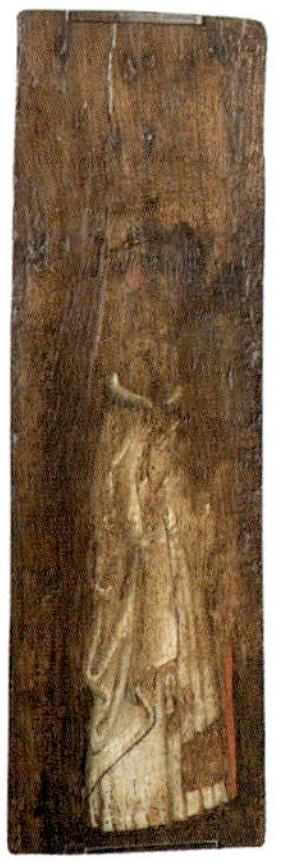

unknown artist early 15th C
Pope with Tiara with Gold Ball and Cross
oil & tempera on panel 63.2 x 19.5
N22098.007

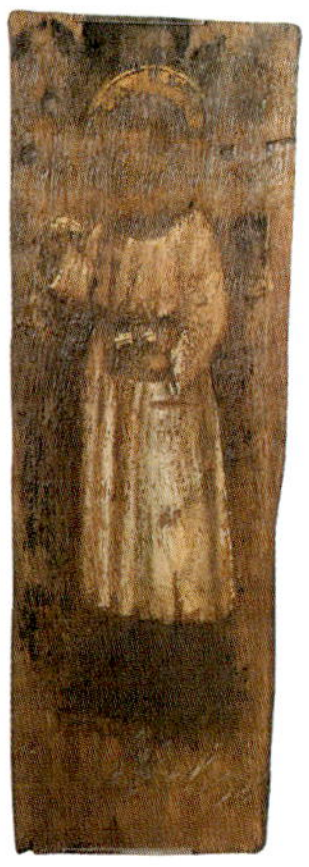

unknown artist early 15th C
Saint with Book
oil & tempera on panel 65 x 22.5
N22098.009

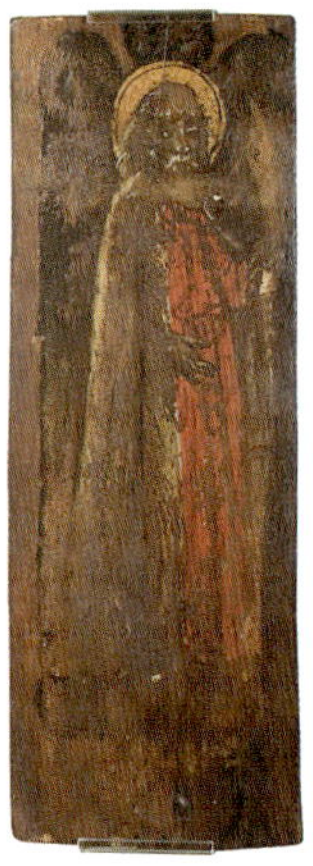

unknown artist early 15th C
St Bartholomew
oil & tempera on panel 64.5 x 22.8
N22098.001

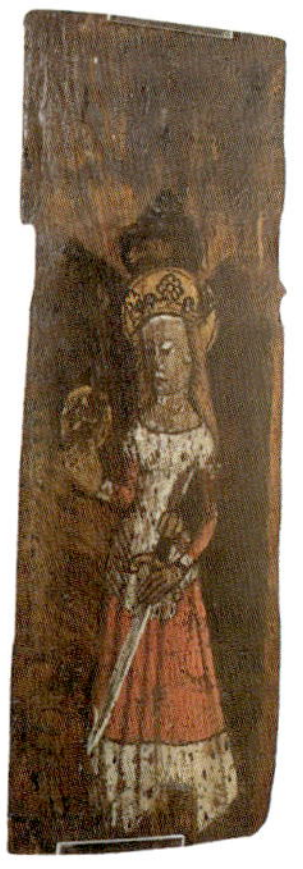

unknown artist early 15th C
St Catherine of Alexandria
oil & tempera on panel 63.5 x 22
N22098.010

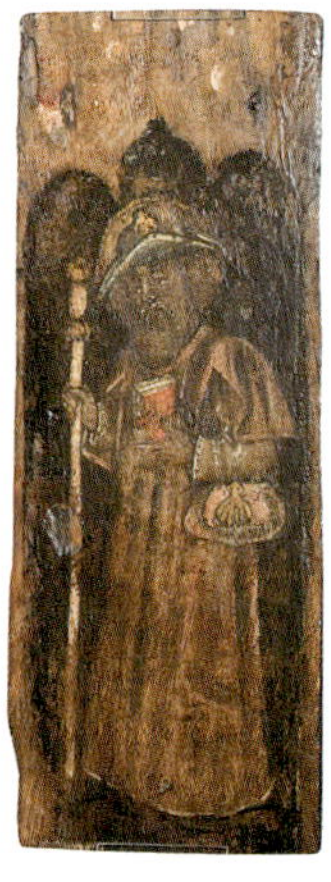

unknown artist early 15th C
St James the Great
oil & tempera on panel 62.7 x 24.6
N22098.004

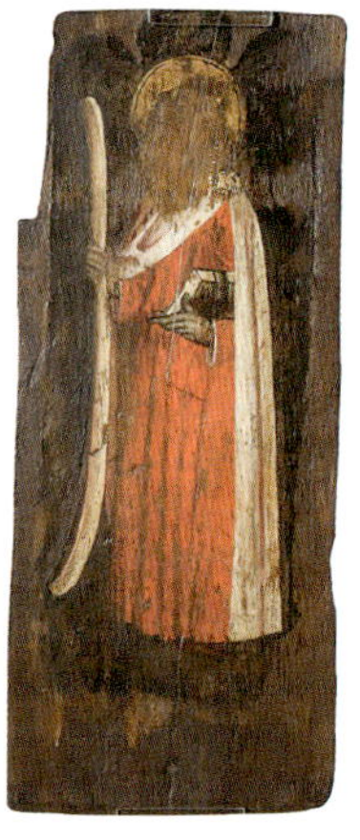

unknown artist early 15th C
St James the Less
oil & tempera on panel 64.5 x 25.9
N22098.005

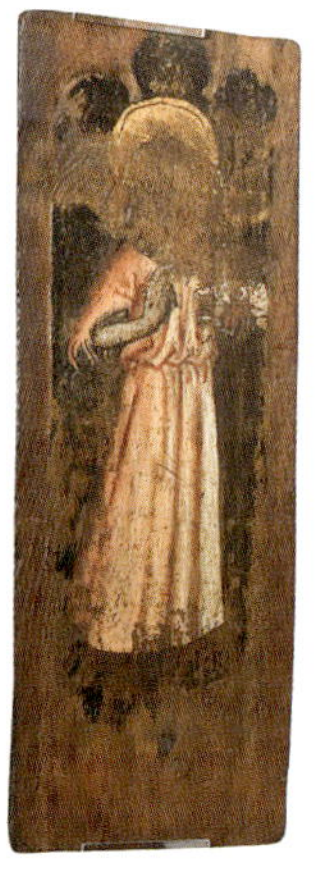

unknown artist early 15th C
St John Baptist
oil & tempera on panel 64.6 x 22.4
N22098.008

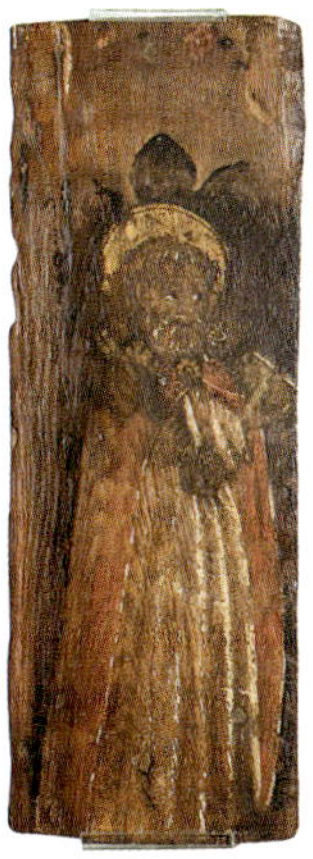

unknown artist early 15th C
St Peter
oil & tempera on panel 62 x 22
N22098.003

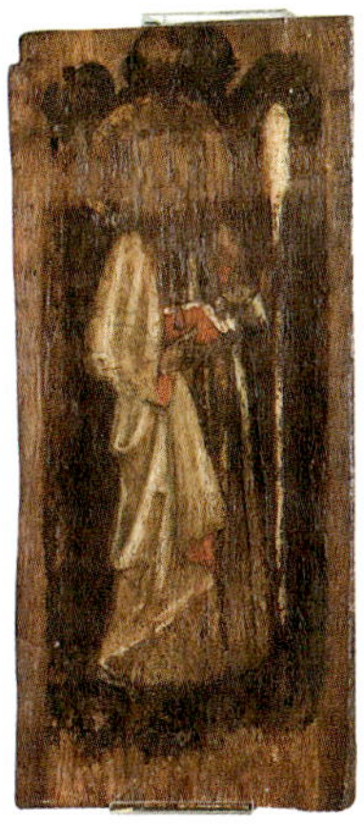

unknown artist early 15th C
St Simon
oil & tempera on panel 64 x 24
N22098.002

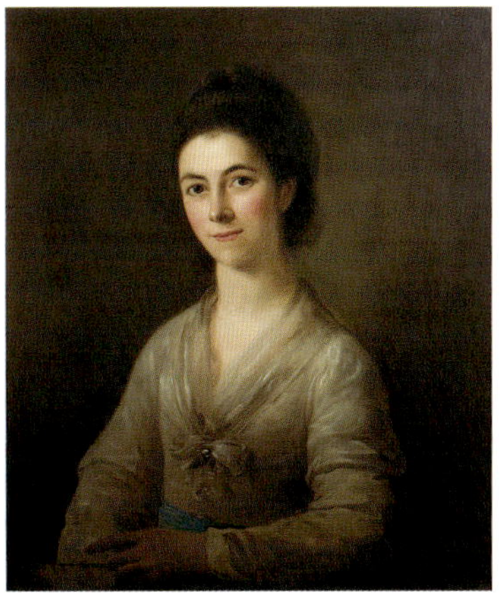

unknown artist
Sally, née Pocock (1755–1818), Wife of Robert Tindal, Mother of Sir Nicholas Tindal c.1780s
oil on canvas 74 x 61.5
1986.846

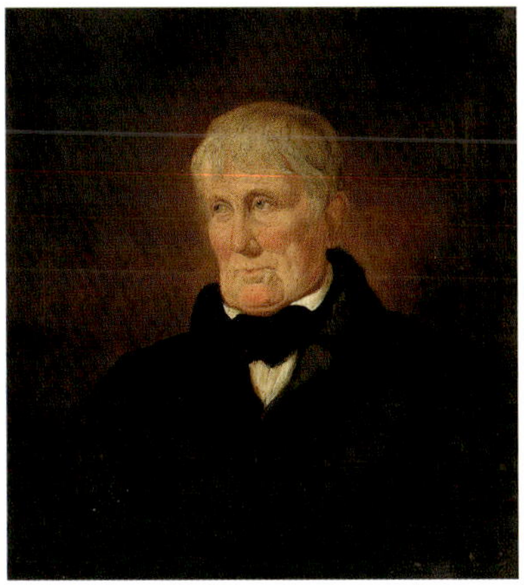

unknown artist
Mr Brady Wood of Sparrows Farm, Terling
c.1800–1830
oil on canvas 76.2 x 63.4
1979.335

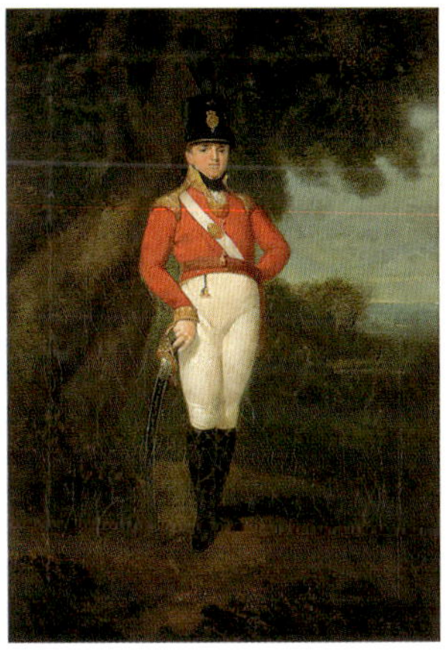

unknown artist
Captain George Cheveley of the Roxwell Volunteers 1803
oil on canvas 74 x 52
M28246

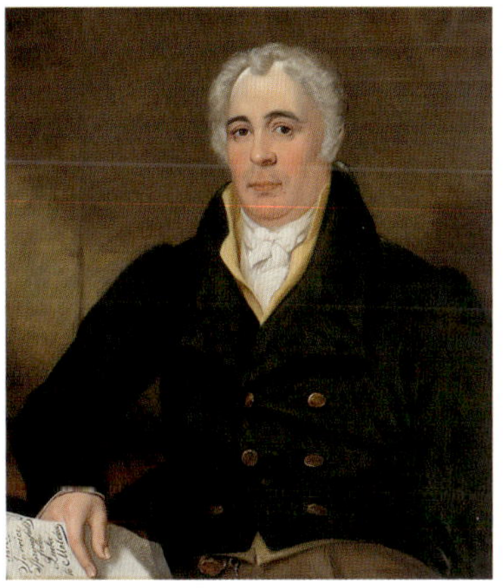

unknown artist
Richard Coates of Maldon (1763–1822) 1812?
oil on canvas 77.3 x 67.3
M28245

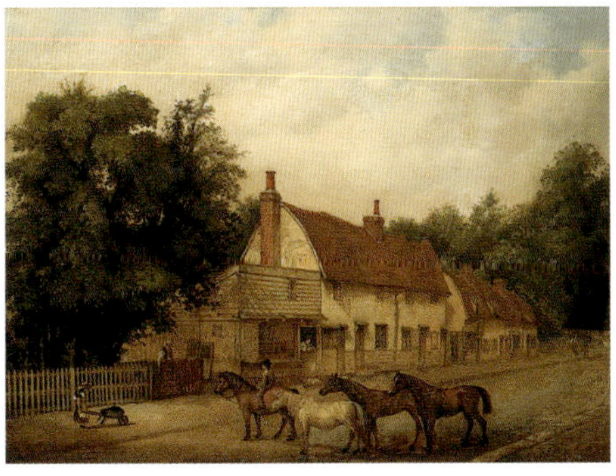

unknown artist
Old Cottages, Duke Street, Chelmsford
before 1871
oil on canvas 39 x 49.5
1974.334

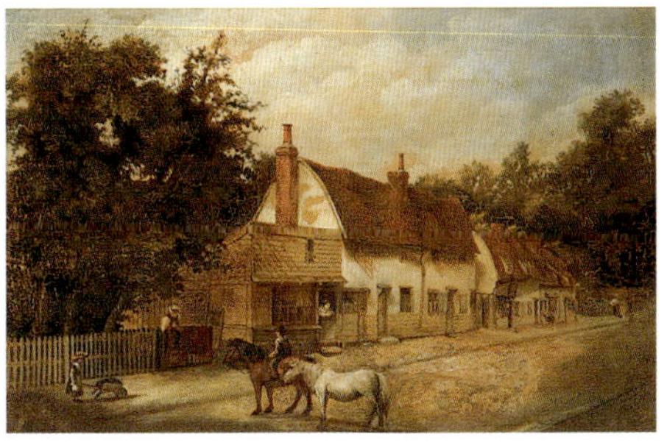

unknown artist
Old Cottages, Duke Street, Chelmsford
before 1875
oil on canvas 34 x 49.5
M28358

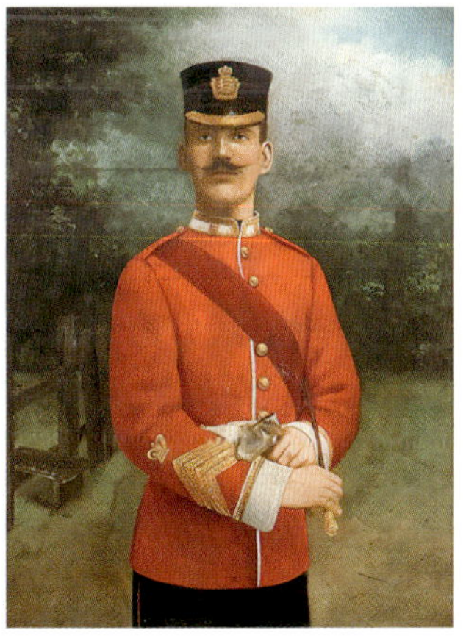

unknown artist
Sergeant-Major James Mitchell 1891
oil on canvas 59 x 43
ER16571

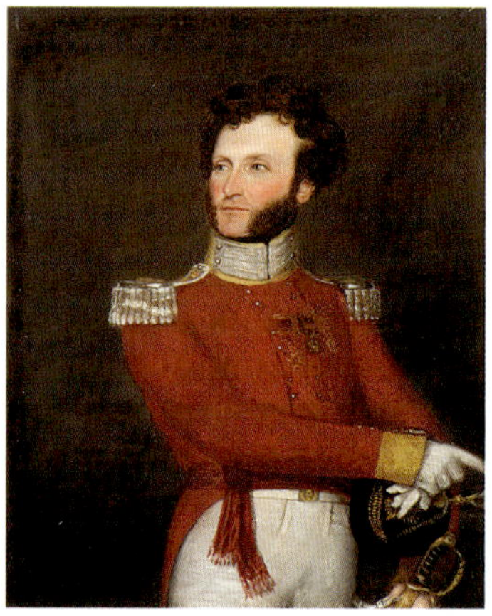

unknown artist early 19th C
Major-General George O'Malley GCB, 88th Regiment (1780–1843)
oil on canvas? 50.7 x 40.9
ER3281

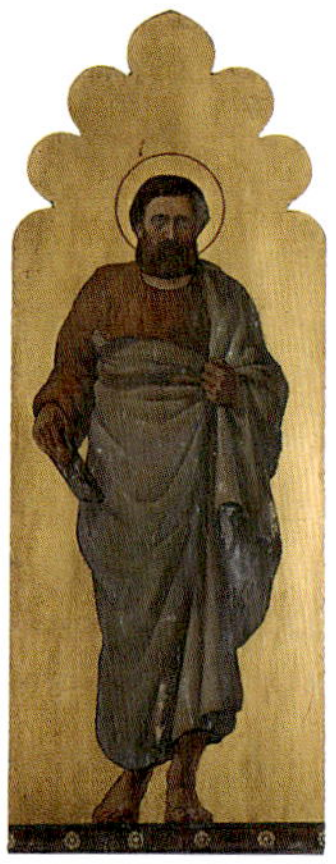

unknown artist late 19th C
Saint with Book
oil on panel 89 x 33
chmer3691.3

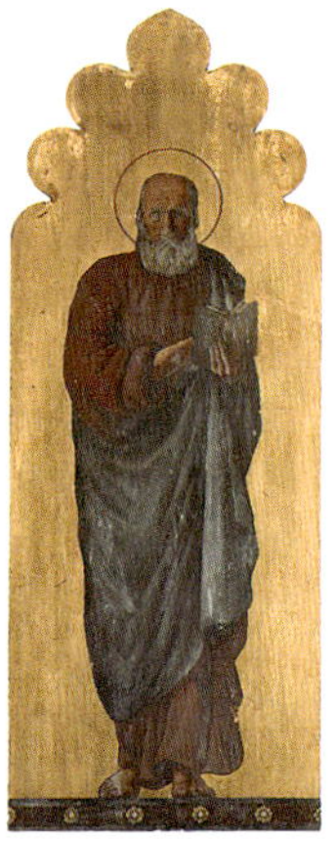

unknown artist late 19th C
Saint with Book
oil on panel 89 x 33
chmer3691.6

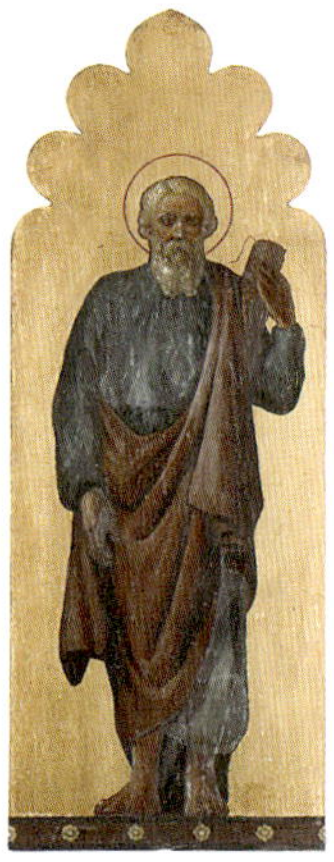

unknown artist late 19th C
Saint with Canister
oil on panel 89 x 33
chmer3691.5

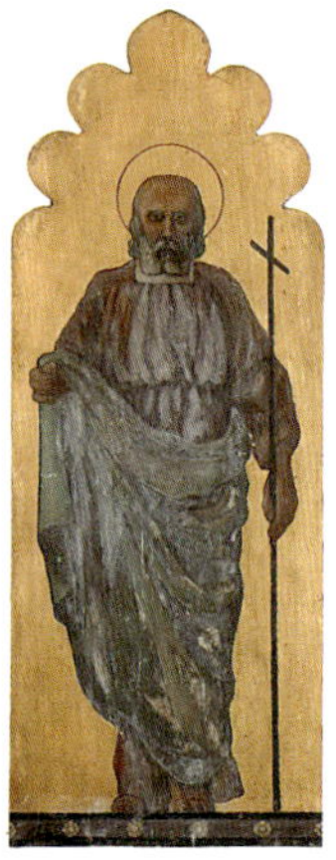

unknown artist late 19th C
Saint with Cross (possibly St Paul)
oil on panel 89 x 33
chmer3691.1

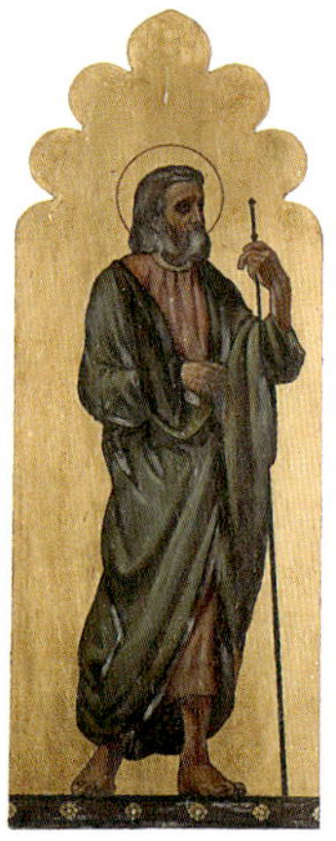

unknown artist late 19th C
Saint with Staff
oil on panel 89 x 33
chmer3691.8

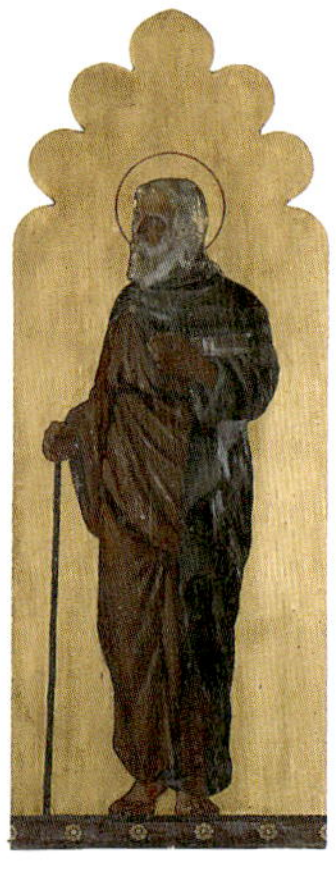

unknown artist late 19th C
Saint with Stick and Book
oil on panel 89 x 33
chmer3691.7

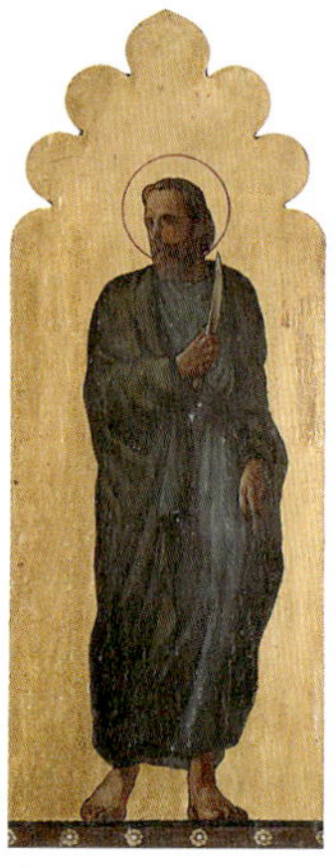

unknown artist late 19th C
St Bartholomew with Knife
oil on panel 89 x 33
chmer3691.2

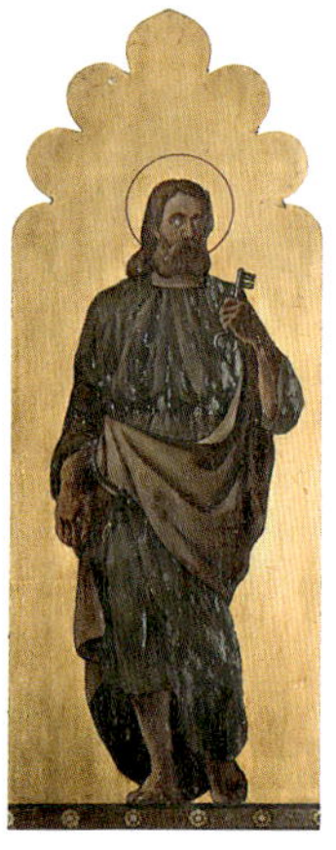

unknown artist late 19th C
St Peter
oil on panel 89 x 33
chmer3691.4

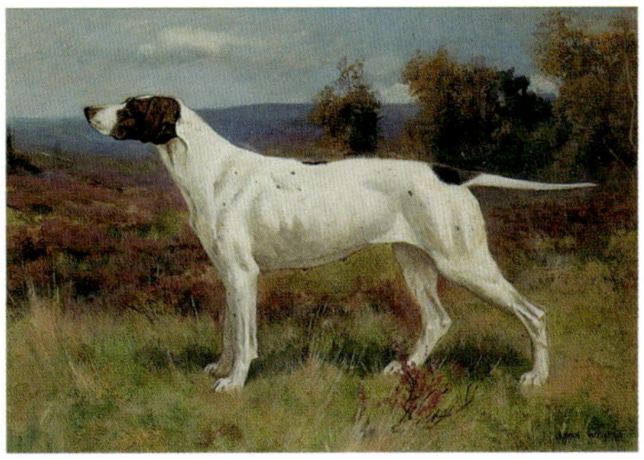

Wardle, Arthur 1864–1949
Study of a Pointer
oil on canvas 21 x 30
M28351

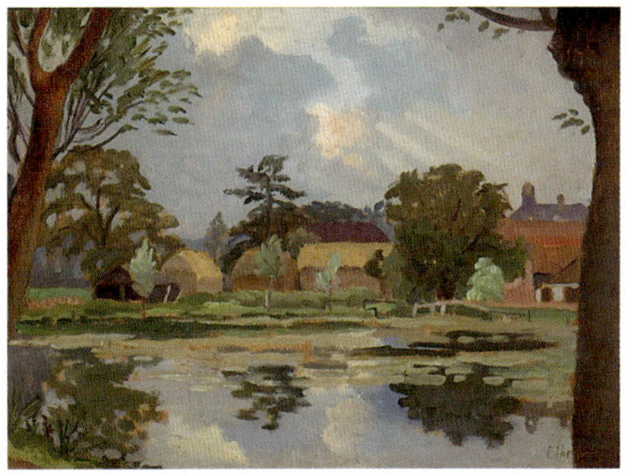

White, Ethelbert 1891–1972
New Hall Farm, Boreham
oil on board 27 x 35.5
1988.154

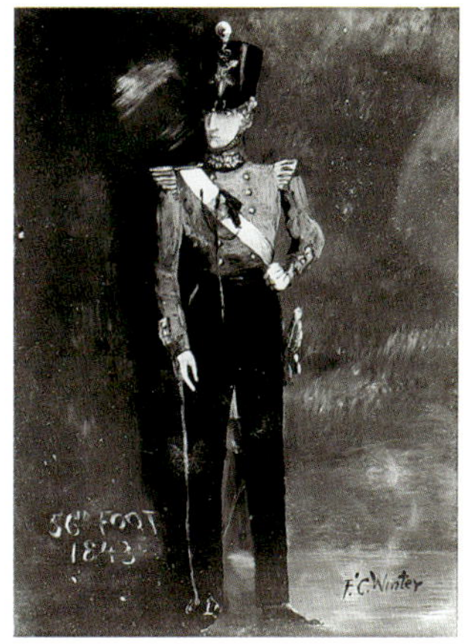

Winter, Frederick Charles
active 1891–1930s
An Officer of the 56th Foot, 1843
oil on board 20.2 x 15
ER0056

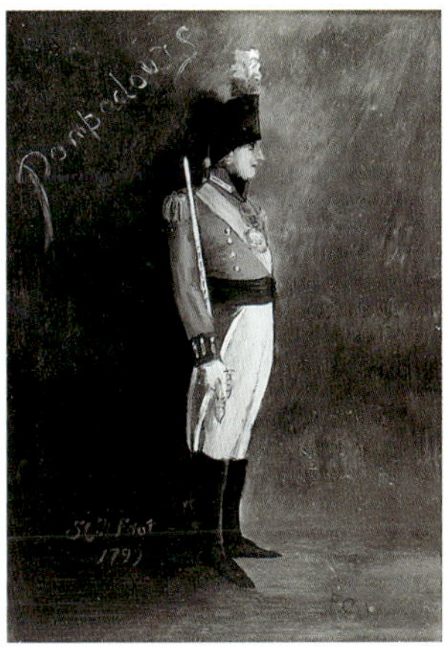

Winter, Frederick Charles
active 1891–1930s
An Officer of the Pompadours (56th Light Foot, 1799)
oil on board 21.5 x 14
ER0025

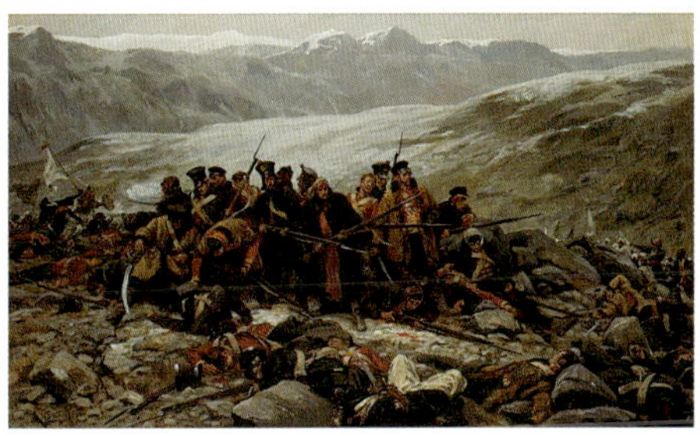

Wollen, William Barnes 1857–1936
The Last Stand of the 44th Foot at Gundermuck, 1842 1898
oil on canvas 75.9 x 122
ER11094

Essex County Council

Let me start by saying thank you to the Public Catalogue Foundation: their commendable efforts have prompted me to reacquaint myself with the wonderful collection of oil paintings the County of Essex enjoys.

The Essex County Council Collection began shortly after the County Council was established in 1898 and it is thanks largely to this inaugural County Council that we possess the majority of the collection that we enjoy today.

The collection is comprised of an eclectic mix of Old Dutch and English oils dating back to the seventeenth century, complemented by a collection of more modern portraits. Today the main body of the collection is displayed in a number of locations in central Chelmsford, with two important works on loan to Hylands House.

We owe the core collection of Dutch and English oils to the prescience of a young Deputy Clerk of the Peace and the generosity of a wealthy Essex gentleman. According to early records, in 1898, D. P. Sellar Esq. presented a collection of 30 oils to the County of Essex. These represented part of a larger collection he had previously offered to the Corporation of London, who had declined his generous offer due to uncertain provenance of parts of the collection. Indignant at the Corporation's rejection, Sellar held an exhibition of the collection at Grafton Galleries. The exhibition was visited by Mr H. W. Gibson, Deputy Clerk of the Peace, who suggested that Sellar might like to present his paintings to the County of Essex, for the purposes of decorating the Shire Hall.

During this period both the County Council and the Quarter Sessions Court were seen as jointly embodying the 'County of Essex', and shared responsibility for the Shire Hall. Stellar agreed and a delegation led by Lord Rookwood, an artist himself, and Admiral Sir W. G. Luard, visited the exhibition and selected the oil paintings on behalf of the County.

The collection was originally hung in what later became known as the Picture Room in Shire Hall. The oils from the Sellar collection were complemented by a number of portraits of notable local figures, mainly members of the Bramston family. The first County Council Chairman Andrew Johnston is credited with securing these for the County, although there is no record of how he achieved this. Of particular note is one the oldest portraits, a large oil on canvas of Lord Chief Justice Sir John Bramston, painted some time after 1635.

Several important additions were made to the collection in 1938. As part of the decoration for the newly built County Hall, Councillor Sir William Julien Courtauld personally commissioned four large oils. These paintings depict scenes from the history of Essex and were hung in the Octagon Room at the Royal Academy Exhibition of the same year. Today they still hang on the north wall of the Council Chamber.

The abolition of the Quarter Sessions Court in 1970 heralded a moment of crisis for the collection. The Quarter Sessions, whose functions were subsumed by the Crown Court, had jointly accepted the Sellar collection in 1898 on behalf of the 'County of Essex'. At the prospect of their demise there followed a period of dispute over the ownership of this part of the collection. The County

Council argued persuasively that the paintings had come to be regarded as County Council property and succeeded in retaining possession of the collection.

In subsequent years, the collection has grown through gifts and the continuing practice of commissioned portraiture of County Council Chairmen. Lord Kenyon of Gredington presented the nineteenth century portrait of Sir John Tyssen Tyrrel, which is currently on loan to Hylands House, to the County of Essex in 1959. More recently the Essex Yeomanry Association presented two portraits of Sir Francis Whitmore, former Lord Lieutenant of Essex. Of particular interest is the portrait painted by the artist Frank Dicksee, who was once President of the Royal Academy.

Unfortunately the statutory services we provide are under constant financial pressure, so collecting oil paintings has become a luxury that the County Council can no longer afford. However, we do continue the time-honoured practice, which began with the first County Council Chairman Andrew Johnston, of commissioning a portrait of departing Chairmen. Many of these continue to be painted in oils, as well as my own portrait, which was painted in 1992 by June Mendoza. We also remain committed to preserving all the paintings in our care and have conducted some important restoration work in recent years.

I applaud the work of the Public Catalogue Foundation and hope that the publication of the Essex Catalogue inspires people to take pleasure in the beautiful collection oil paintings we enjoy in Essex.

Lord Hanningfield, Leader of Essex County Council

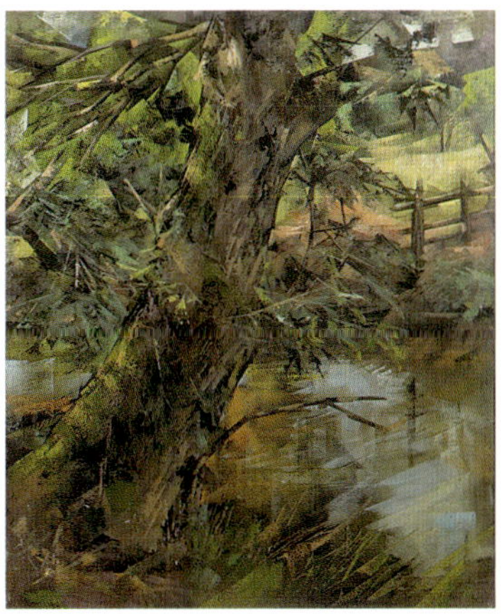

Appelbee, Leonard 1914–2000
Tree and Stream with Stile
oil on board 59.5 x 49.5
208

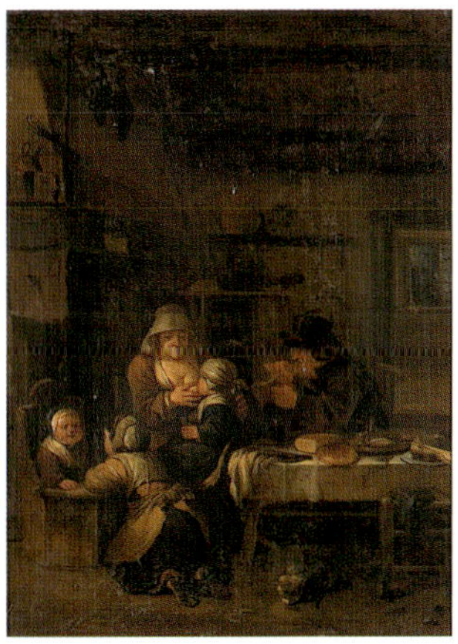

Bega, Cornelis Pietersz. (follower of)
1631/1632–1664
Interior with Mother Suckling Her Child
oil on panel 36 x 26
8

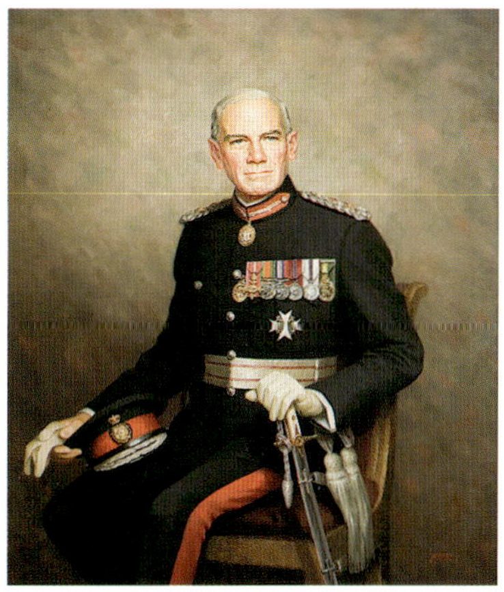

Boden, Leonard 1911–1999
Colonel Sir John Ruggles-Brise, Bt, CB, OBE, TD, JP of Spains Hall, Finchingfield, Lord Lieutenant of Essex (1958–1978) 1978
oil on canvas 130 x 100
99

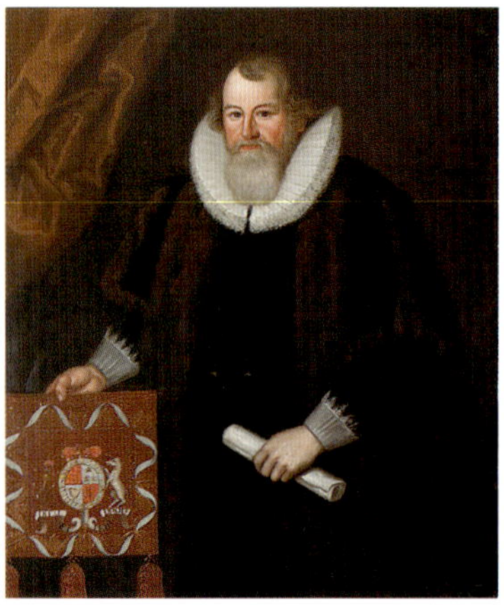

British (English) School
Portrait of a Bearded Gentleman (possibly Francis Bacon, 1st Baron Verulam and Viscount St Albans) c.1610
oil on canvas 124 x 100
60

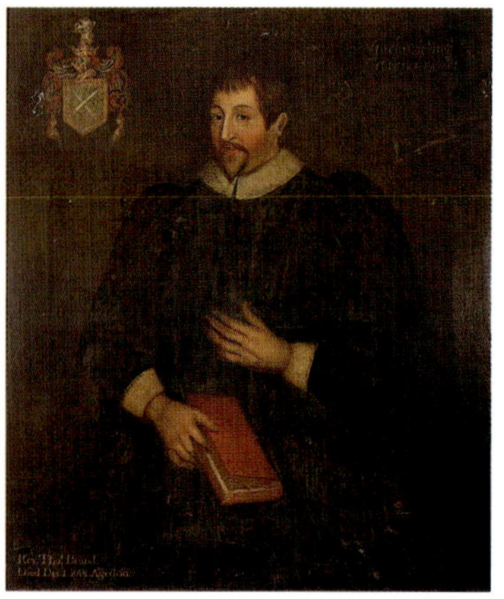

British (English) School 17th C
Reverend Thomas Brand
oil on canvas 105 x 87
68

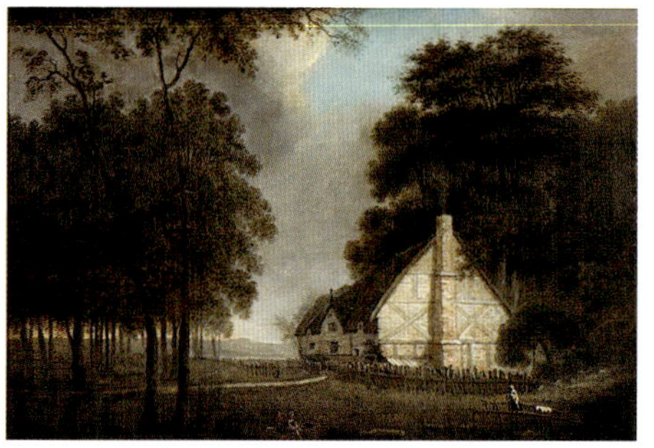

British (English) School
Wooded Landscape with Thatched Cottage c.1760
oil on canvas 67 x 97
17

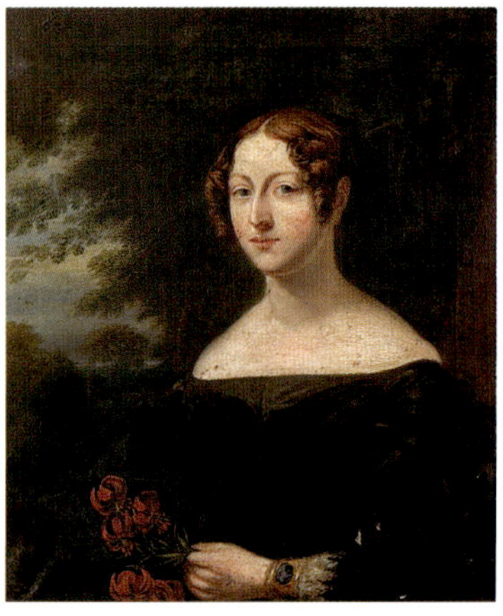

British (English) School 19th C
Portrait of a Lady
oil on canvas 74 x 62
96

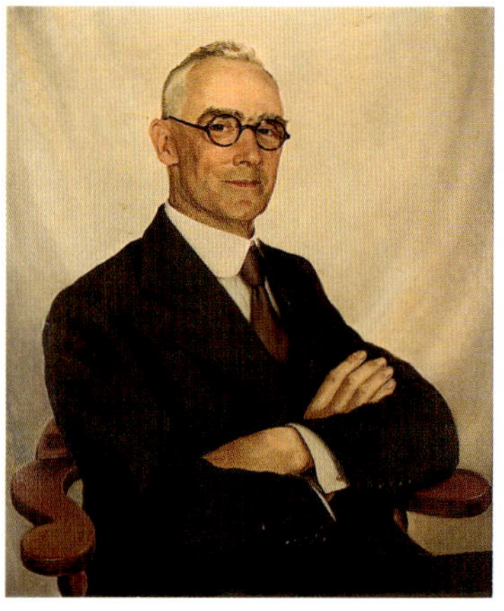

British (English) School 20th C
Joseph Hewett, JP
oil on canvas 74 x 62
37

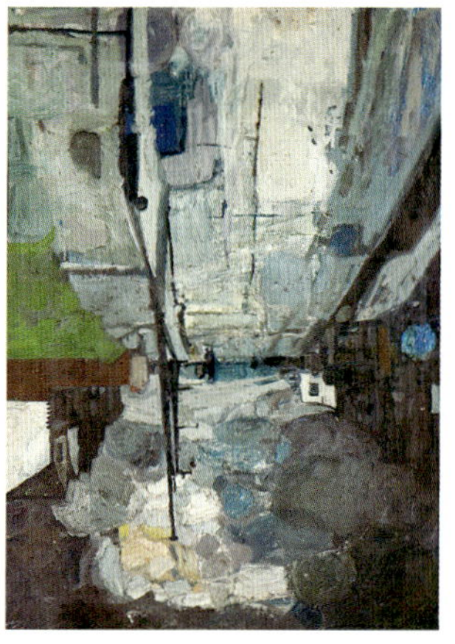

Carlson, Ronald b.1936
Welsh Street
oil on board 120 x 84.5
18a

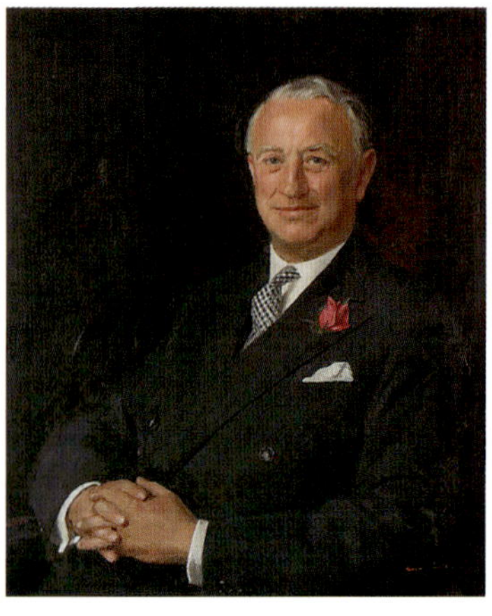

Carr, Henry Marvell 1894–1970
George Frederick Chaplin, CBE, JP, DL 1961
oil on canvas 75 x 62
42

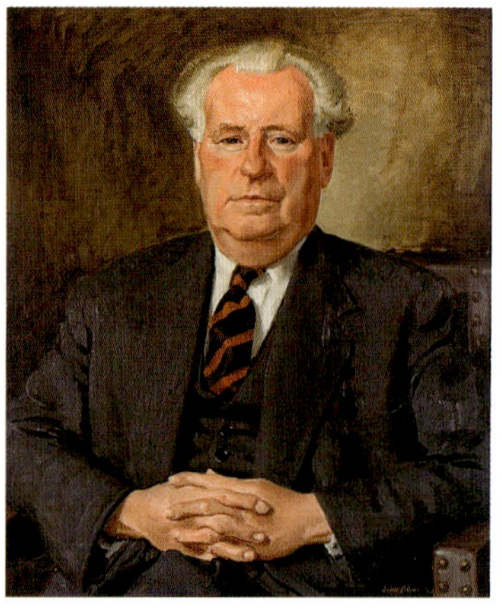

Codner, John b.1913
Charles Edward Leatherland, OBE, JP, DL 1960
oil on canvas 75 x 62
44

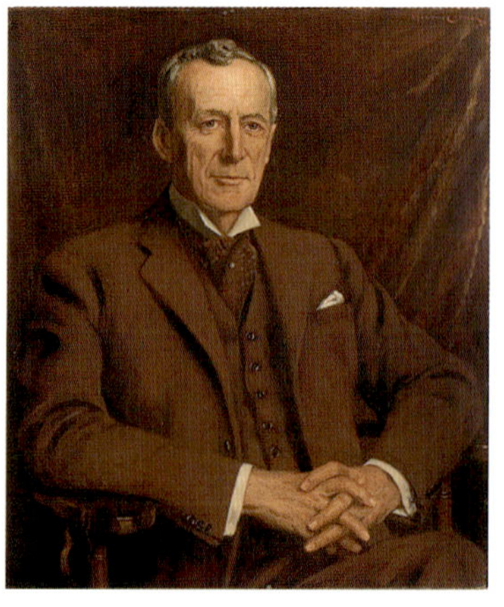

Codner, Maurice Frederick 1888–1958
Colonel Sir Gilbertson Smith, TD, DL 1944
oil on canvas 74.5 x 62.5
55

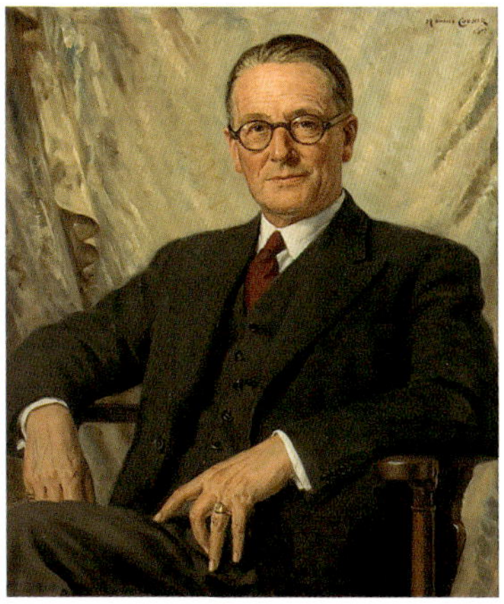

Codner, Maurice Frederick 1888–1958
Percy Astins, CBE, JP 1949
oil on canvas 74.5 x 72 (E)
40

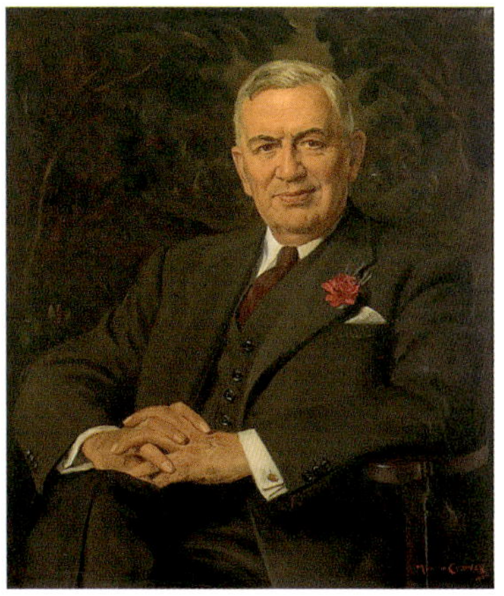

Codner, Maurice Frederick 1888–1958
Frank Savin Foster, CBE, JP 1950
oil on canvas 75 x 62
38

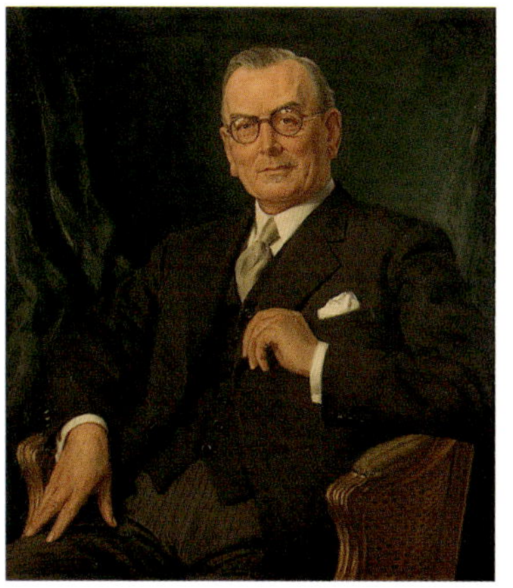

Codner, Maurice Frederick 1888–1958
William James Bennett, CBE, JP, DL 1952
oil on canvas 70 x 62
39

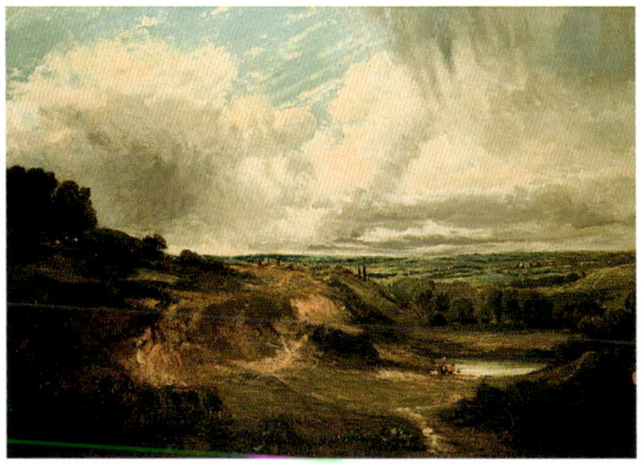

Constable, John (follower of) 1776–1837
View of Hampstead Heath 19th C
oil on canvas 69 x 95
22

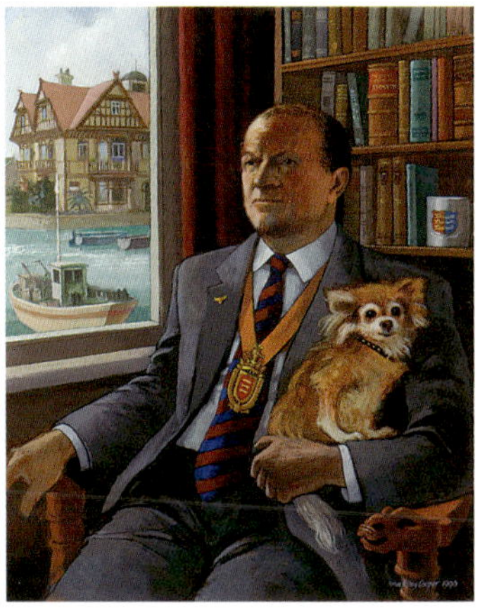

Cooper, John Riley
Councillor Thomas Edward Dale, DL, Chairman (1994–1995) 1996
oil on canvas 74.5 x 59.5
183

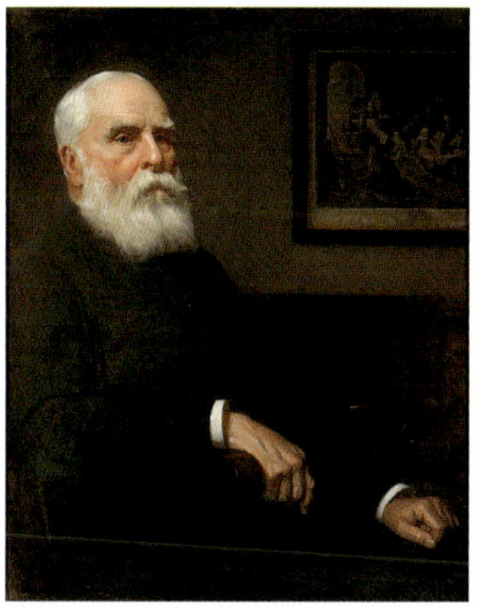

Daniell, Frank 1866–1932
Andrew Johnston, First Chairman of the Essex County Council (1835–1922) 1929
oil on canvas 91 x 70.5
50

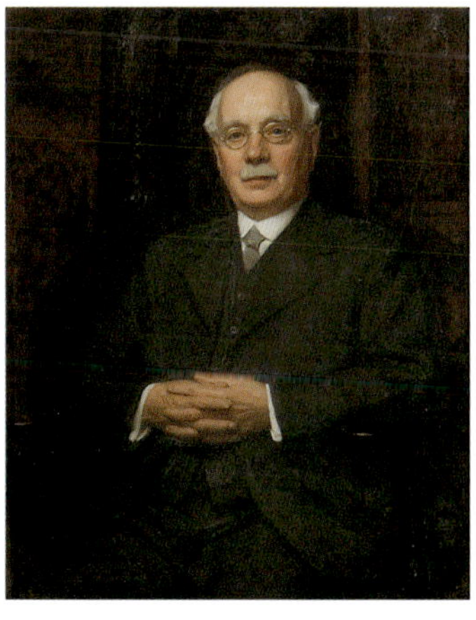

Daniell, Frank 1866–1932
J. H. Burrows, JP (1854–1935), Chairman (1931) 1938?
oil on canvas 90 x 69.5
53

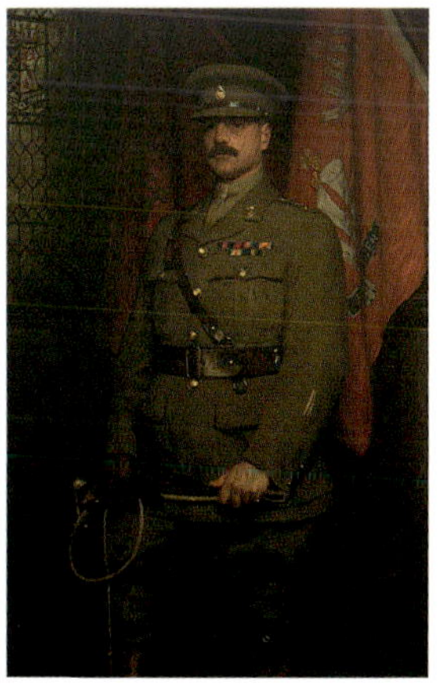

Dicksee, Frank 1853–1928
Colonel Sir Francis H. D. C. Whitmore, Bt, KCB, CMG, DSO, TD, JP of Orsett Hall, Lord Lieutenant of Essex (1936–1958) 1919
oil on canvas 145 x 94.5
101

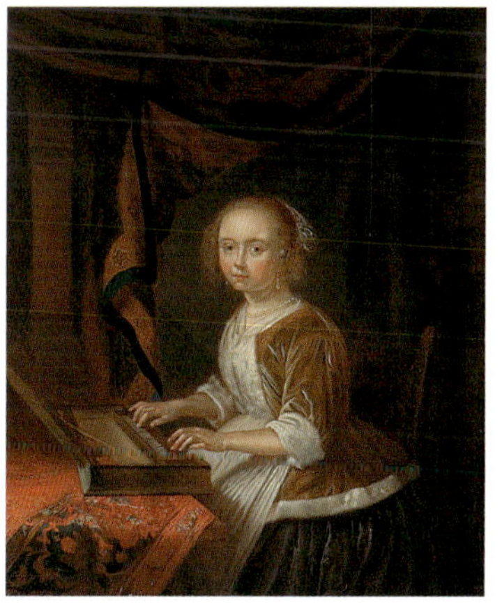

Dou, Gerrit (after) 1613–1675
Girl Playing a Virginal
oil on panel 33 x 27.5
10

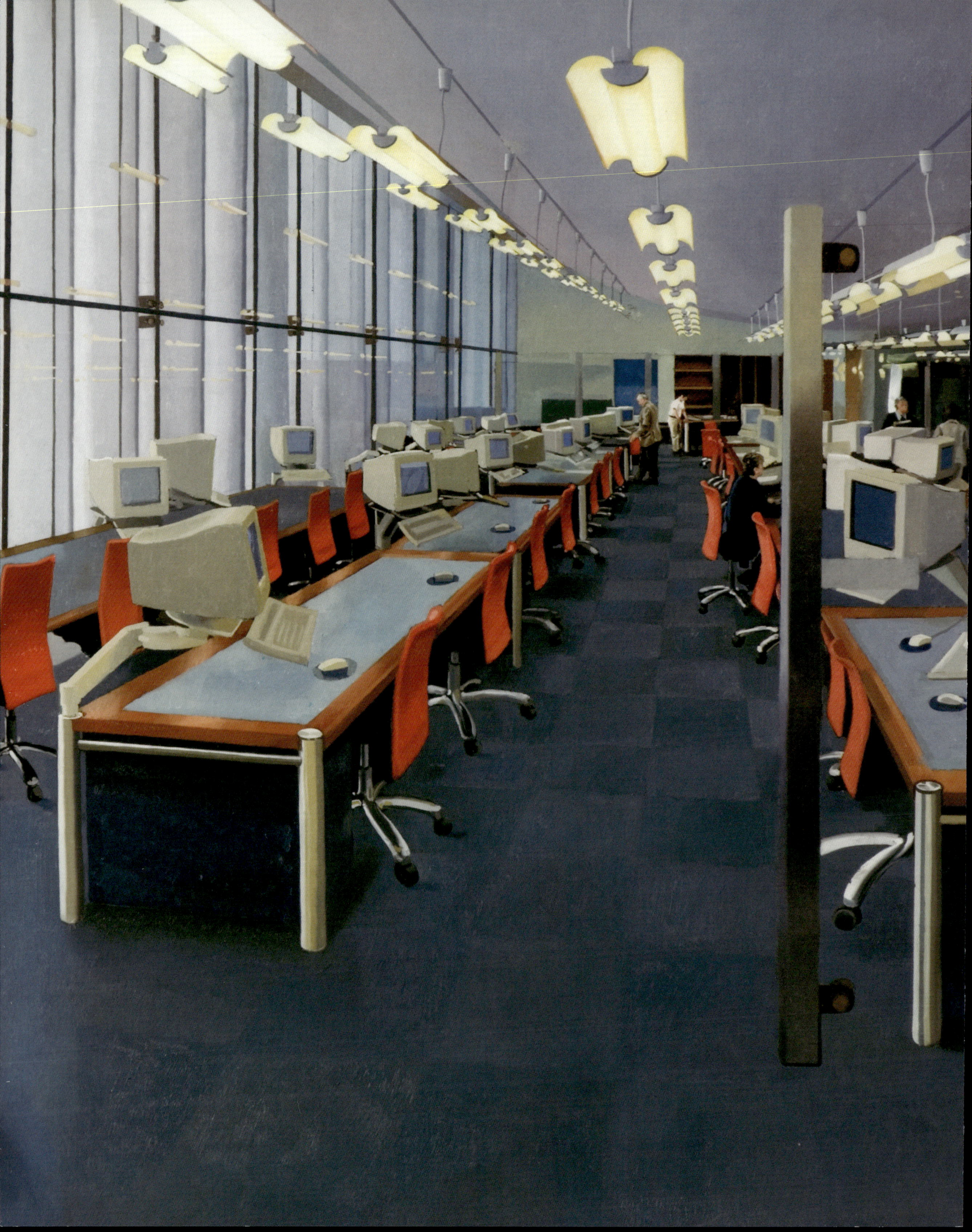

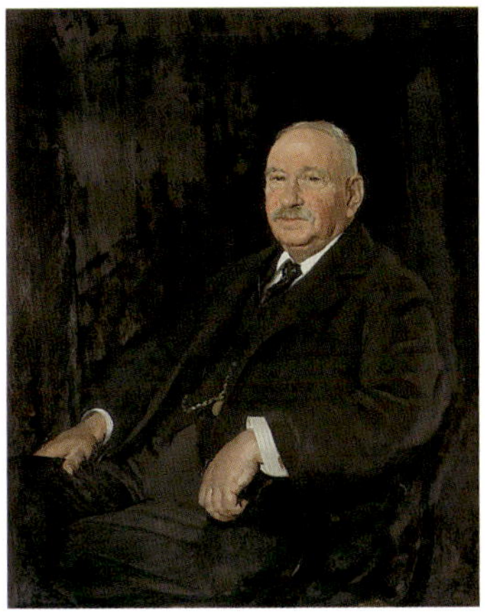

Dugdale, Thomas Cantrell 1880–1952
Sir Christopher Musgrave, JP, CA (1856–1929) 1926
oil on canvas 111 x 85
54

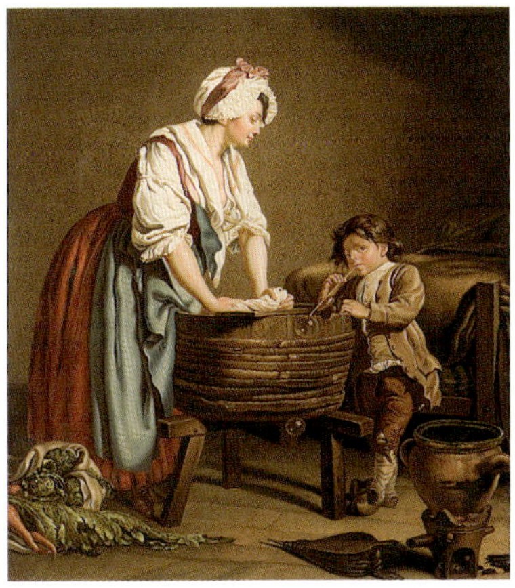

Dyckmans, Josephus Laurentius 1811–1888
Lady Standing at a Wash Tub
oil on canvas 74.9 x 63.5
14

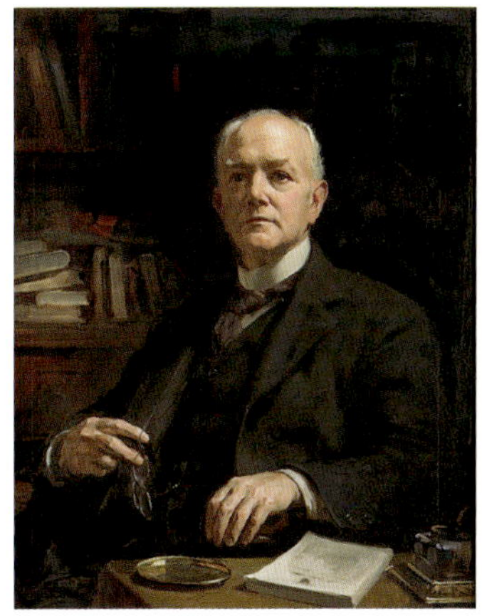

Eastman, Frank S. 1878–1964
W. Swaine Chisenhale-Marsh (1857–1929), Chairman (1916–1929), High Sheriff of Essex (1892) 1929
oil on canvas 90.5 x 70
51

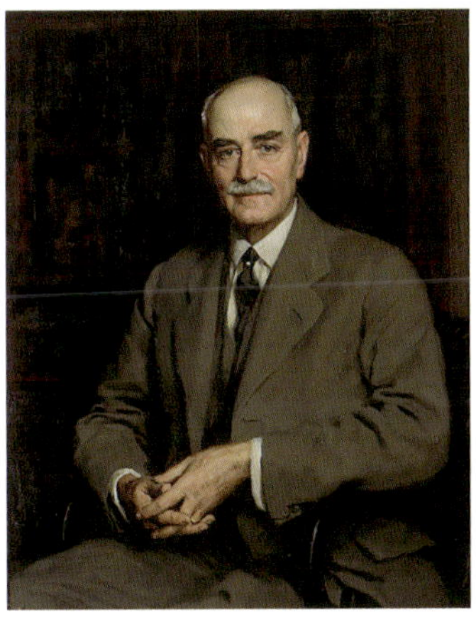

Eastman, Frank S. 1878–1964
Herbert Edmund Brooks, DL, JP (1860–1931), Chairman (1929) 1930
oil on canvas 90 x 70
52

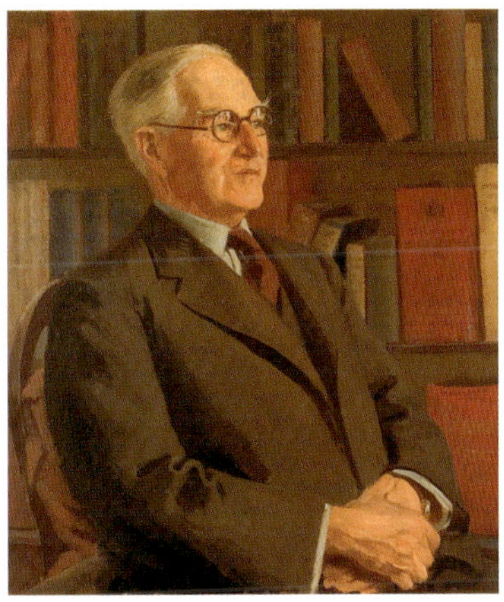

Eastman, Mary active c.1932–1970
H. de Havilland, MA 1941
oil on canvas 74 x 62
56

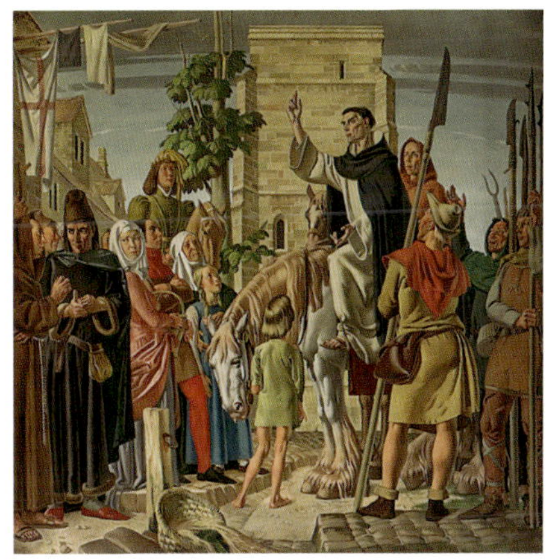

Fleetwood-Walker, Bernard 1893–1965
John Ball Preaching at Brentwood, 1381 1938
oil on canvas 370 x 380 (E)
213

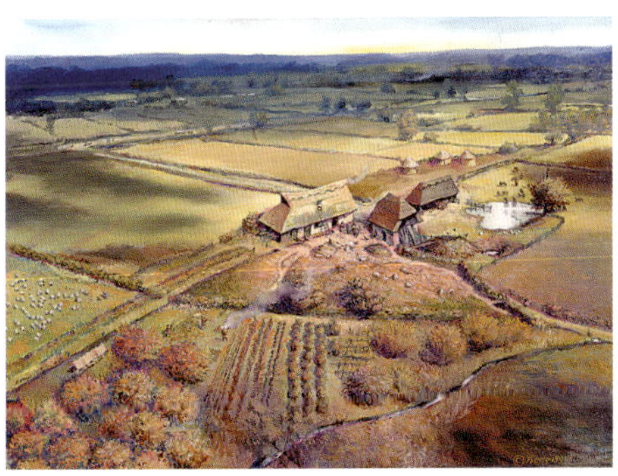

Froste, Peter b.1935
Medieval Farmstead at Stebbingford 1995
oil on board 48 x 60 (E)

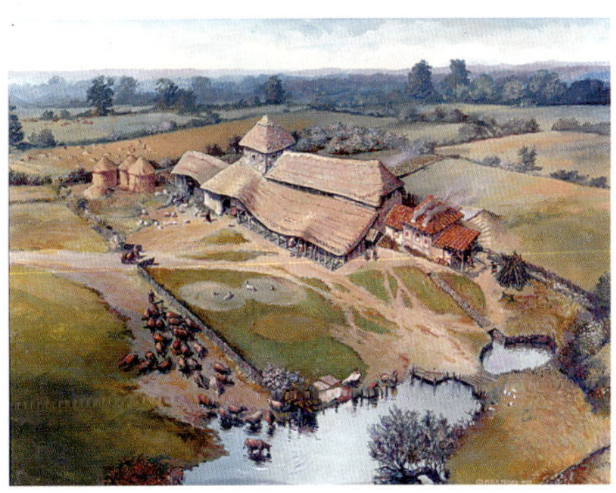

Froste, Peter b.1935
Roman Villa at Great Holts, Boreham 1995
oil on board 48 x 60 (E)

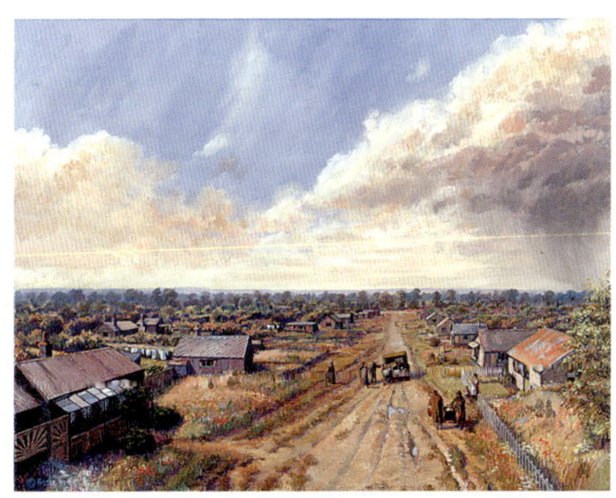

Froste, Peter b.1935
Plotlands at Basildon in the 1940s 1999
oil on board 48 x 60 (E)

Facing page: Priseman, Robert, b.1965, *The Search Room at the Essex Record Office* (detail), 2003, Essex Record Office, (p. 63)

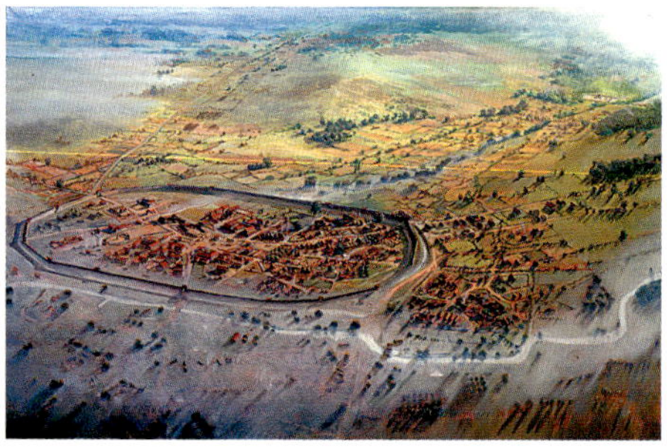

Froste, Peter b.1935
Roman Settlement at Great Chesterford
oil on board 48 x 60 (E)

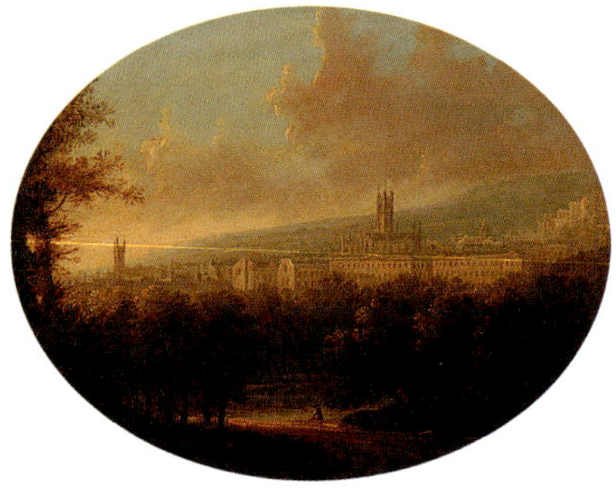

Garvey, Edmund (after) c.1740–1813
View of Bath 1840
oil on canvas 40 x 51
11

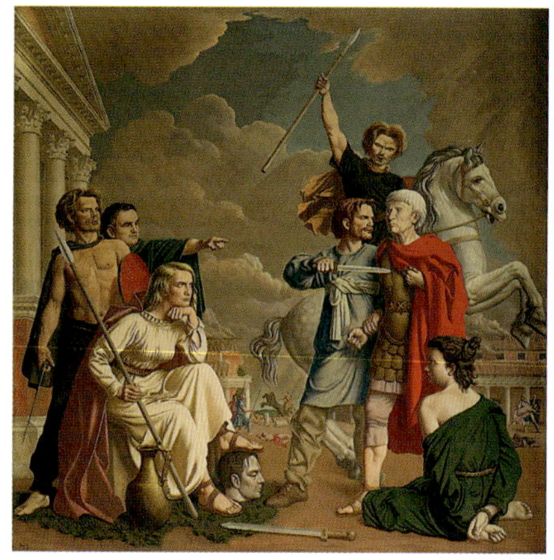

Gill, Colin Unwin 1892–1940
Boadicea at Colchester, 61 AD 1938
oil on canvas 370 x 380 (E)
214

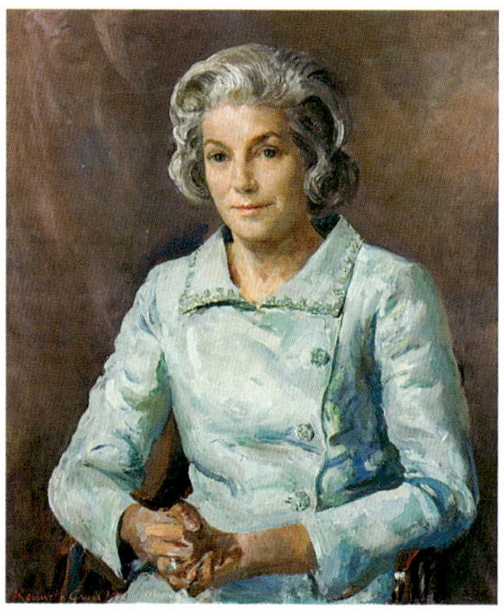

Green, Kenneth 1905–1986
Elizabeth Coker 1971
oil on canvas 75 x 62
46

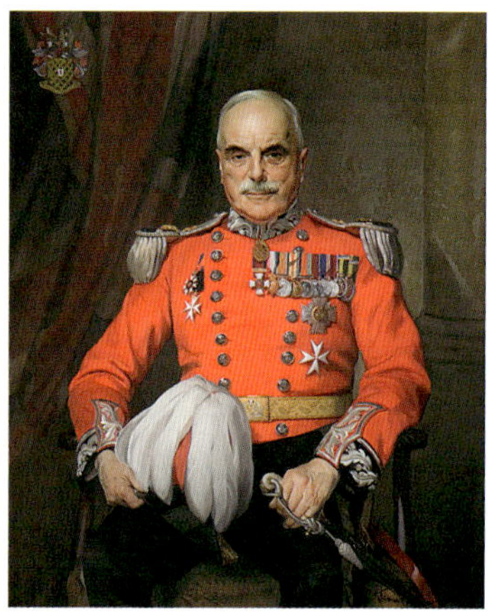

Gunn, Herbert James 1893–1964
Colonel Sir Francis H. D. C. Whitmore, Bt, KCB, CMG, DSO, TD, JP of Orsett Hall, Lord Lieutenant of Essex (1936–1958)
oil on canvas 130 x 100
36

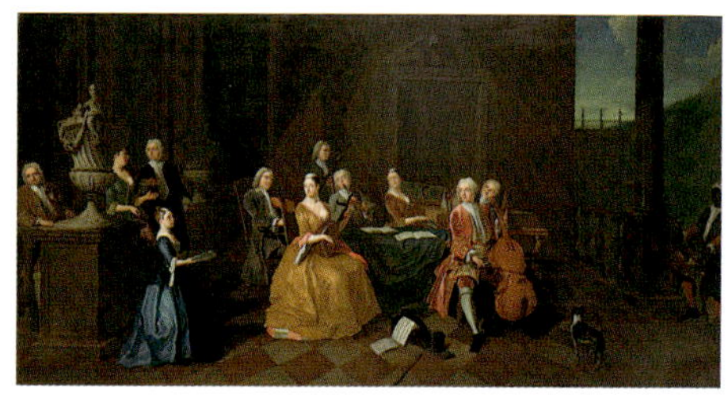

Haecken, Alexander van 1701–1758
A Fashionable Music Party
oil on canvas 28 x 51.5
30

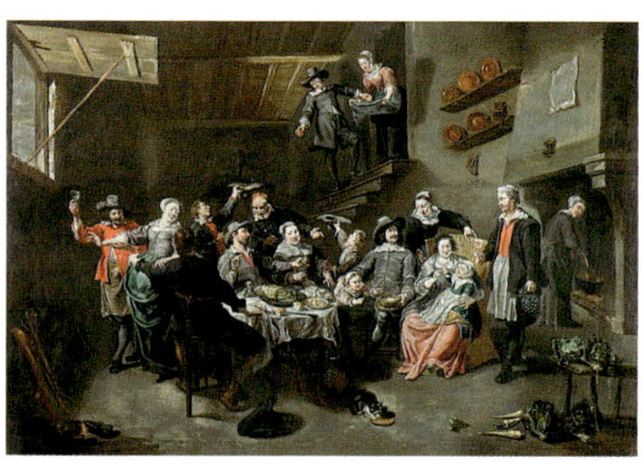

Herp, Willem van I c.1614–1677
Interior with Figures Eating and Drinking
oil on canvas 78 x 114
15

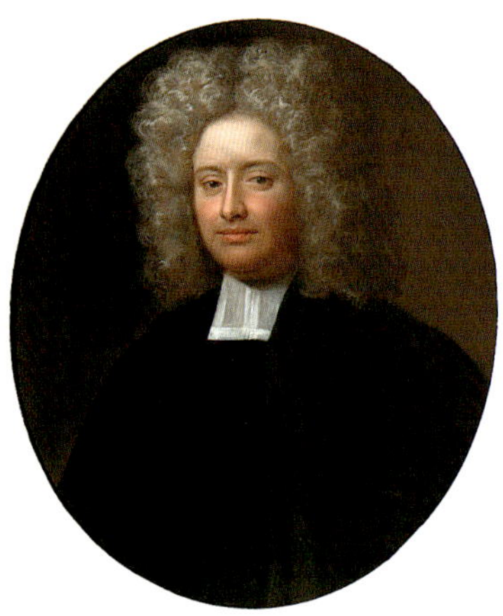

Highmore, Joseph (follower of) 1692–1780
Reverend Joseph Avery of Kirby-le-Soken
oil on canvas 73 x 61
61

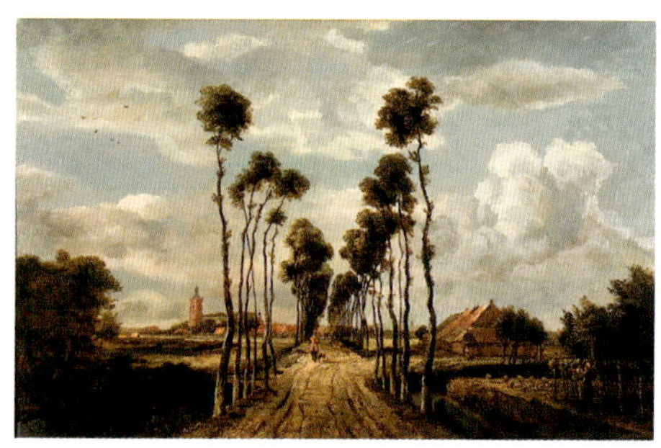

Hobbema, Meindert (after) 1638–1709
The Avenue at Middleharnis
oil on canvas 59 x 90
23

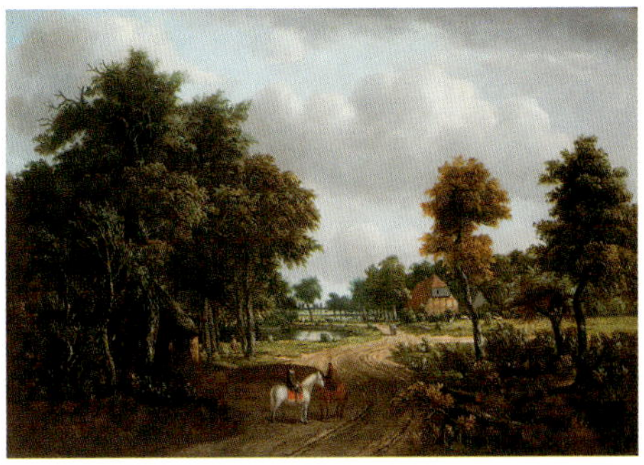

Hobbema, Meindert (style of) 1638–1709
Wooded Landscape with Horsemen Resting by a House early 19th C
oil on canvas 56 x 77
24

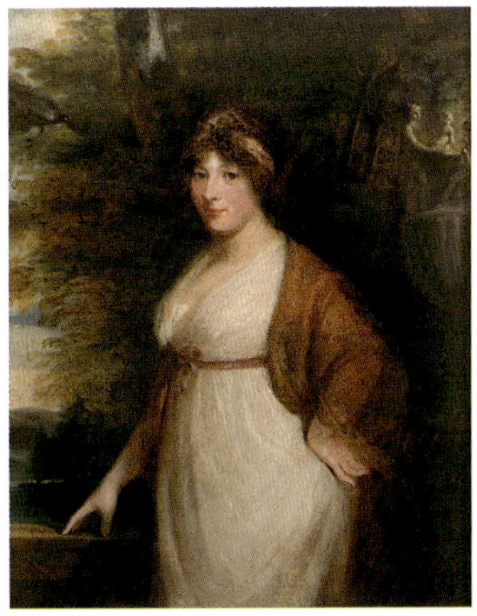

Hoppner, John (follower of) 1758–1810
Portrait of a Lady
oil on canvas 119 x 92
21

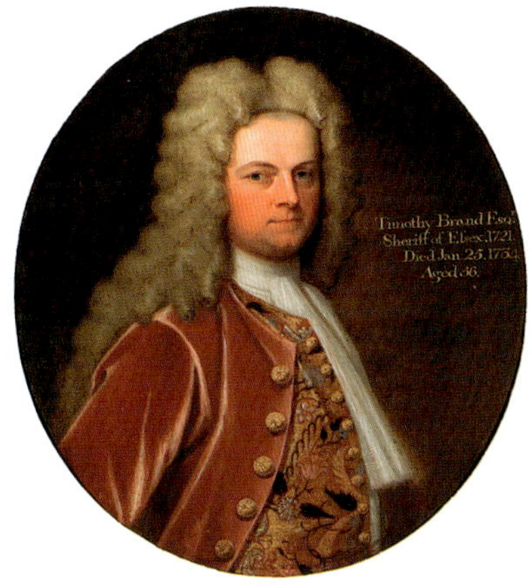

Hysing, Hans (attributed to) 1678–1753
Timothy Brand, Sheriff of Essex (1721)
oil on canvas 75 x 63.5
29

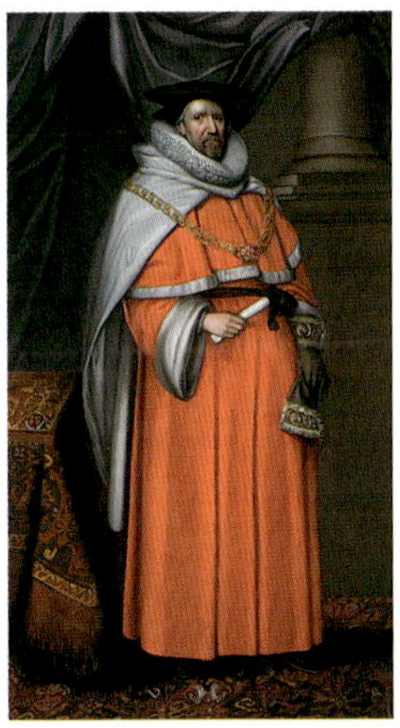

Janssens van Ceulen, Cornelis (style of) 1593–1661
Sir John Bramston, Lord Chief Justice (1635) c.1635–1700
oil on canvas 213.3 x 119.4
16

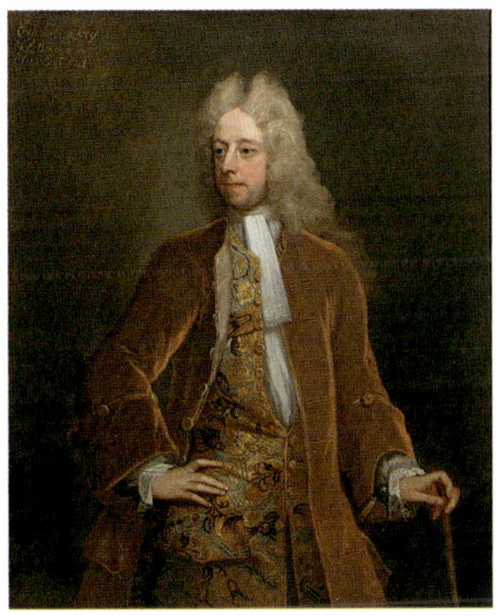

Kneller, Godfrey (attributed to) 1646–1723
Edmund Humfrey of Rettendon 1712
oil on canvas 125.5 x 101
59

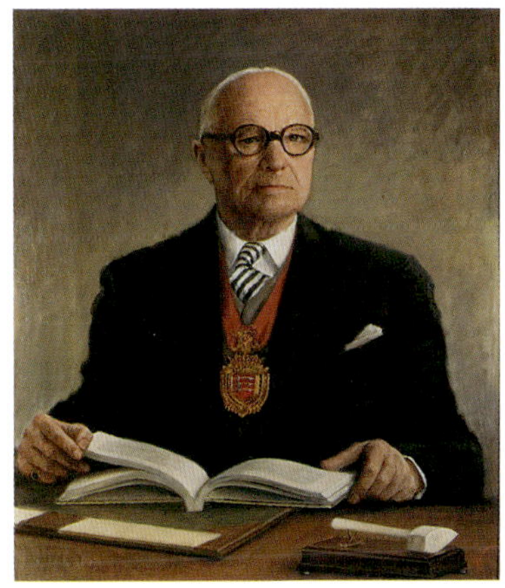

Kwarte, Felix
Sidney Woodfull Millard
oil on canvas 75 x 62.4
41

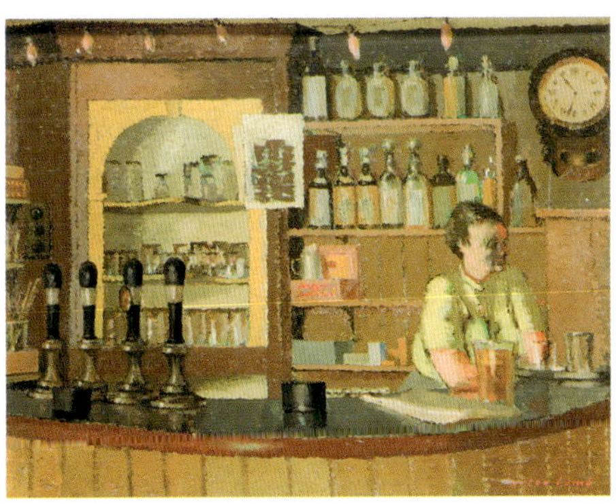

Lamb, Lynton Harold 1907–1977
The Crown
oil on canvas 63 x 76
19a

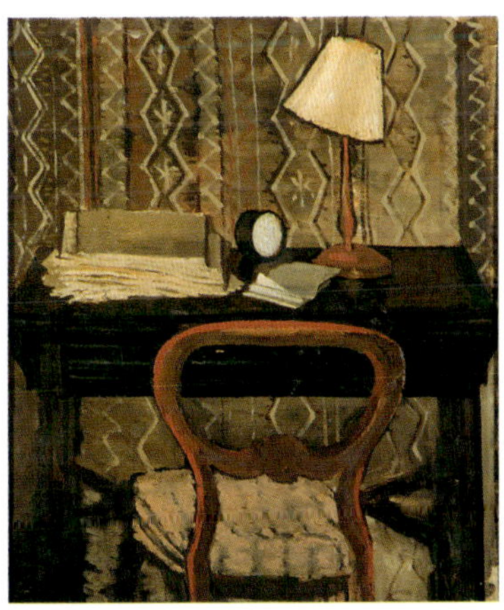

Lamb, Lynton Harold 1907–1977
Work Table
oil on canvas 60 x 50
20a

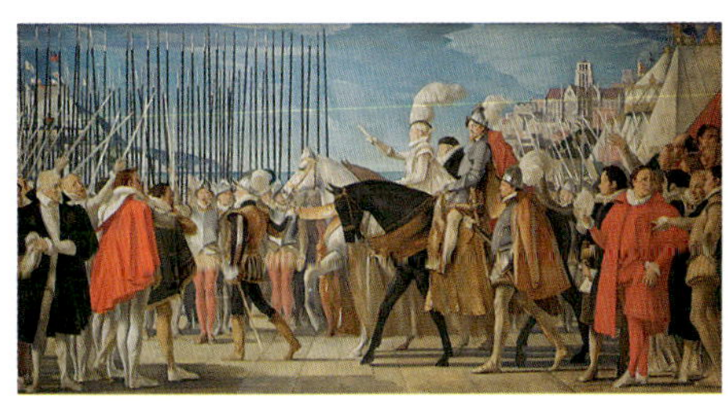

Lawrence, Alfred Kingsley 1893–1975
Queen Elizabeth I at Tilbury, 1588 c.1938
oil on canvas 255 x 510
157

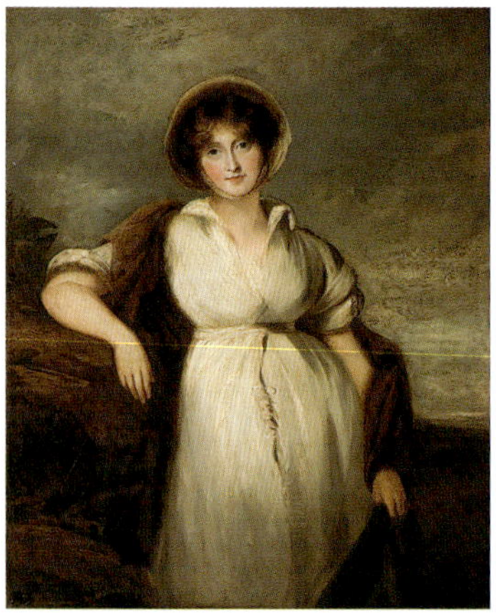

Lawrence, Thomas (follower of) 1769–1830
Queen Caroline (1768–1821)
oil on canvas 123 x 97.5
25

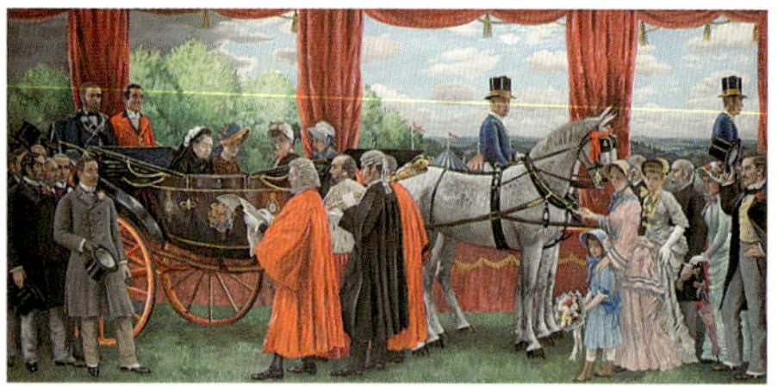

Lewis, Neville 1895–1972
Queen Victoria at Epping Forest, 1882 c.1938
oil on canvas 255 x 510
158

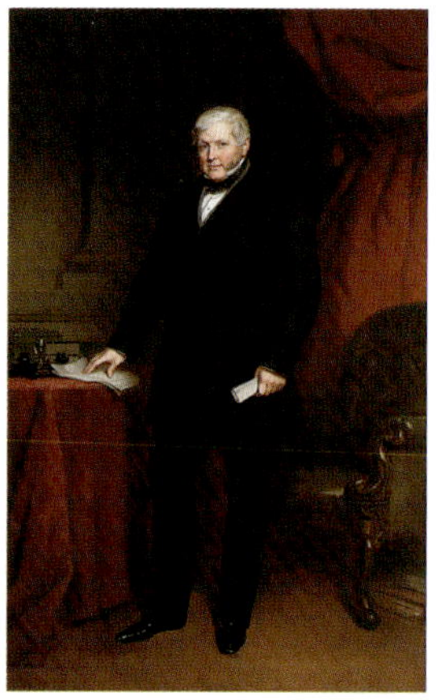

Lonsdale, James (attributed to) 1777–1839
Sir John Tyssen Tyrell, Bt, MP of Boreham (1795–1877) c.1830–1839
oil on canvas 239.4 x 147
35

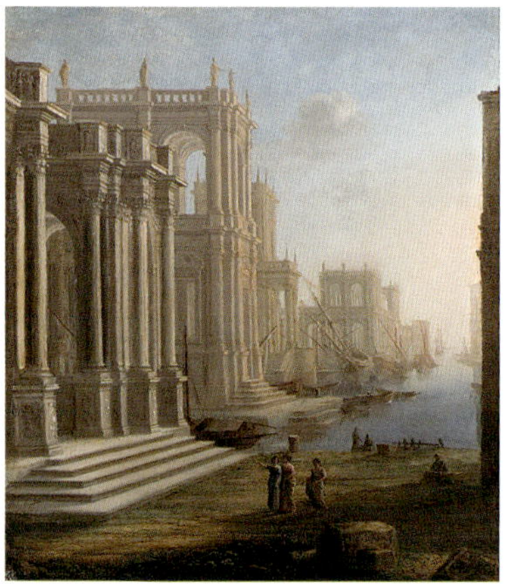

Lorrain, Claude (follower of) 1604–1682
Capriccio with Harbour
oil on canvas 90 x 77
18

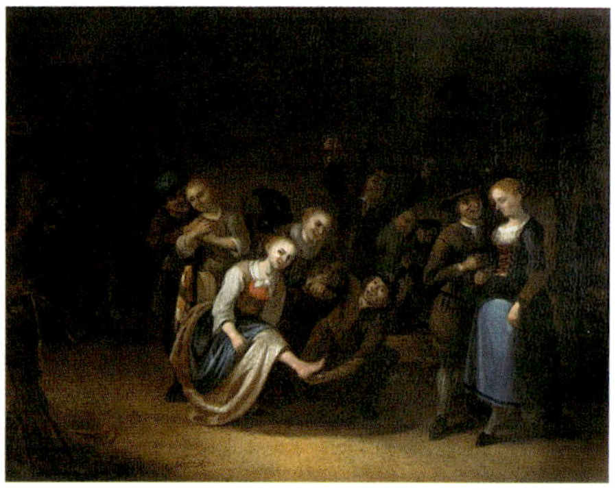

Lundens, Gerrit 1622–after 1683
Dutch Company Merrymaking
oil on canvas 33 x 42.5
27

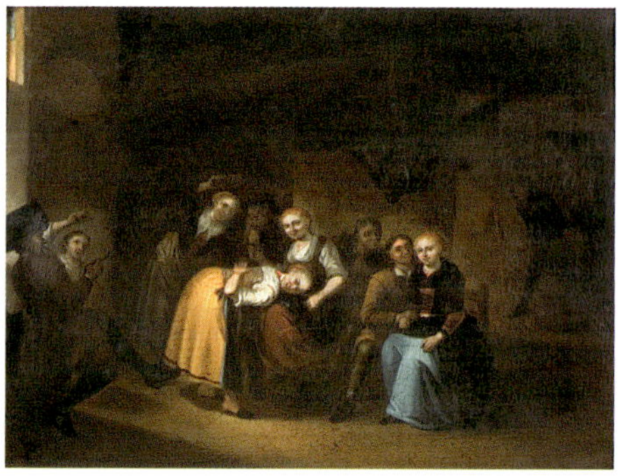

Lundens, Gerrit 1622–after 1683
'La main chaude', Dutch Party Playing Games in an Interior
oil on panel 34 x 44.5
26

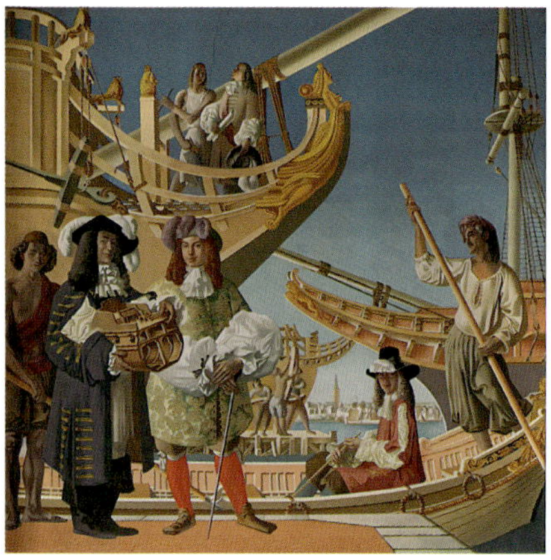

Lyon, Robert 1894–1978
Harwich in the Late XVII Century (Samuel Pepys, MP for Harwich inspecting the King's Navy) 1938
oil on canvas 370 x 380 (E)
211

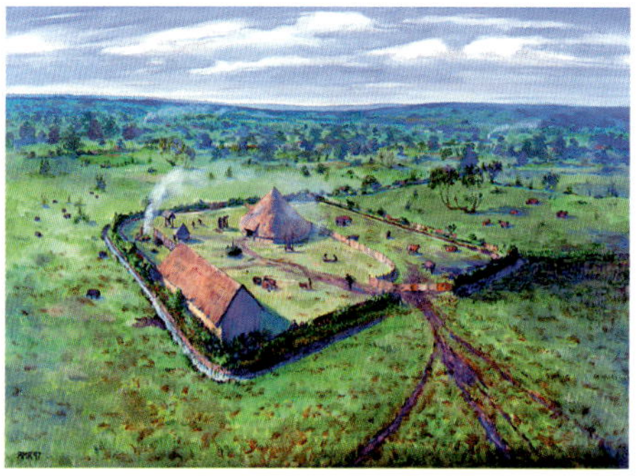

Massey-Ryan, Roger b.1959
Iron Age Settlement at Lofts Farm, near Maldon, c.850 BC 1997
oil on board 48 x 60 (E)

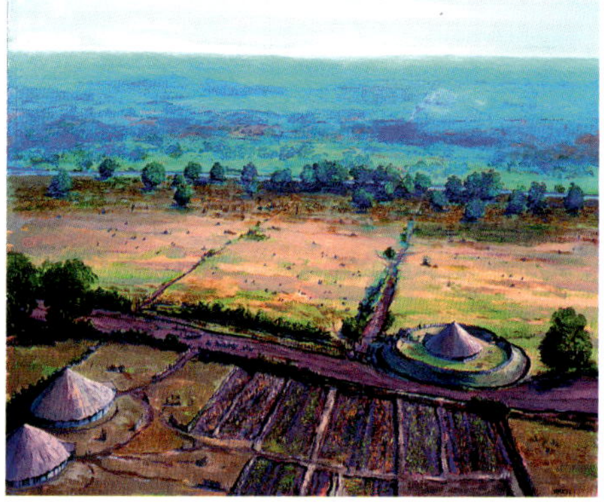

Massey-Ryan, Roger b.1959
Late Bronze Age Landscape at South Hornchurch 2003
oil on board 55 x 60 (E)

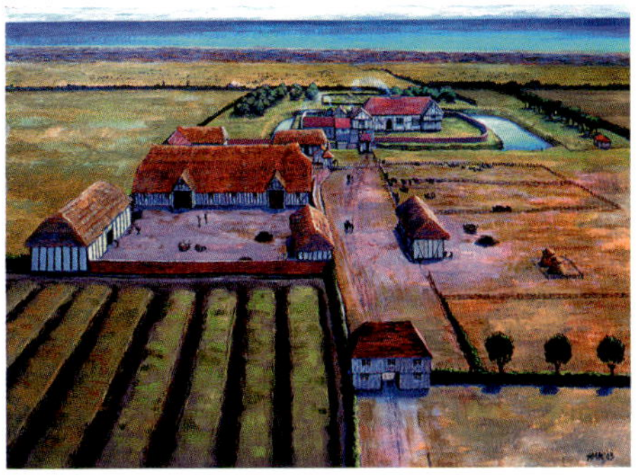

Massey-Ryan, Roger b.1959
Medieval Manorial Complex at Southchurch Hall, c.1400 2003
oil on board 48 x 60 (E)

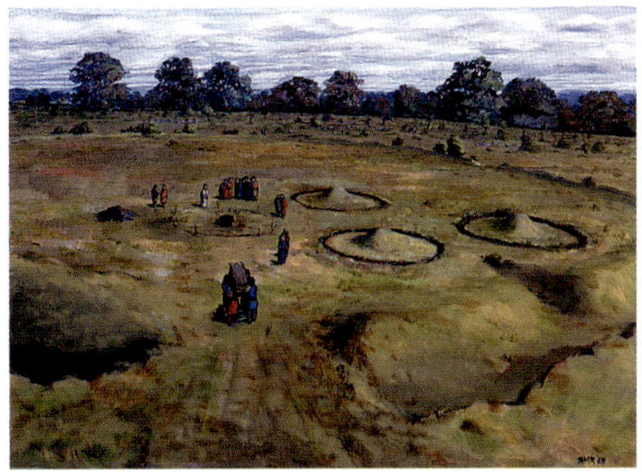

Massey-Ryan, Roger b.1959
Saxon Cemetery within Prehistoric Remains at Orsett 2003
oil on board 48 x 60 (E)

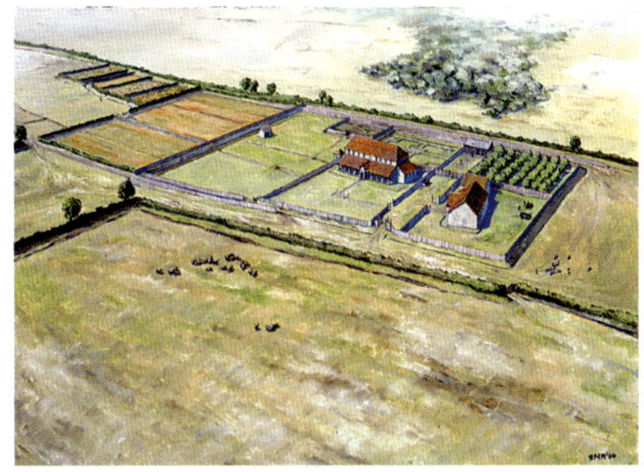

Massey-Ryan, Roger b.1959
Roman Villa at Mucking 2004
oil on board 48 x 60 (E)

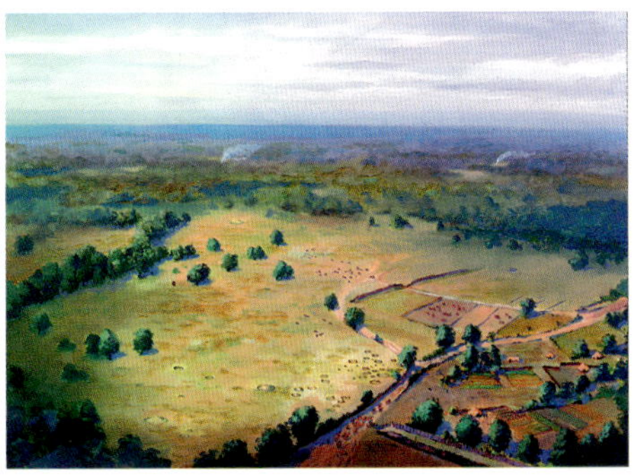

Massey-Ryan, Roger b.1959
Bronze Age Landscape at Ardleigh, c.1200 BC
oil on board 48 x 60 (E)

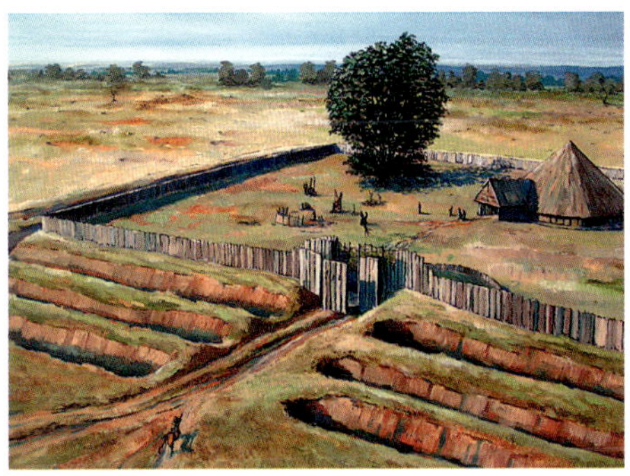

Massey-Ryan, Roger b.1959
Triple-Ditch, Pre-Conquest, Iron Age Enclosure at Orsett Cock
oil on board 48 x 60 (E)

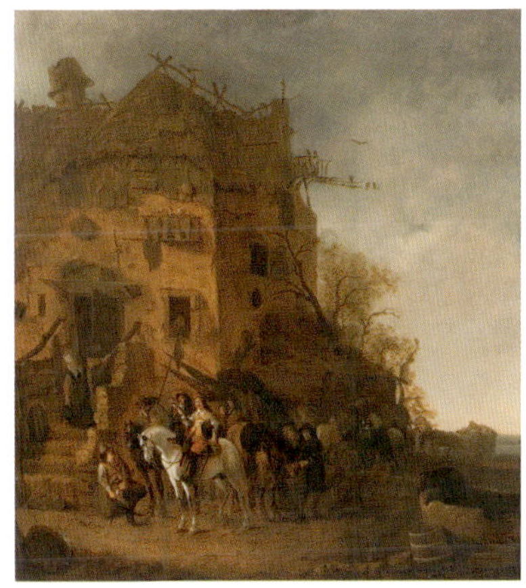

Meijer, Hendrick de c.1600–c.1690
Horsemen Resting by a House 1648
oil on panel 98 x 86
1

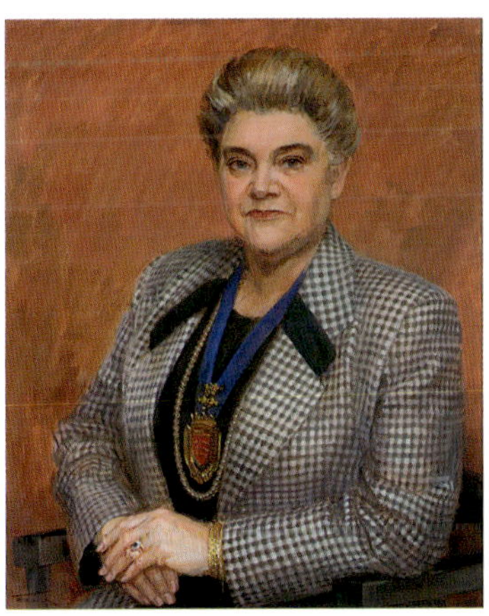

Mendoza, June active 1960–2006
Councillor Mrs Kathleen Nolan, DL, Chairman (1992–1993)
oil on canvas 74.5 x 59
97

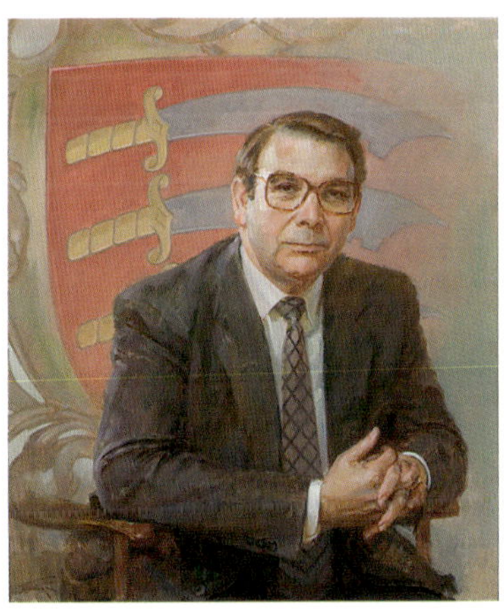

Mendoza, June active 1960–2006
Councillor Paul Edward Winston White, DL (Lord Hanningfield), Chairman (1989–1992)
oil on canvas 74.5 x 61.5
64

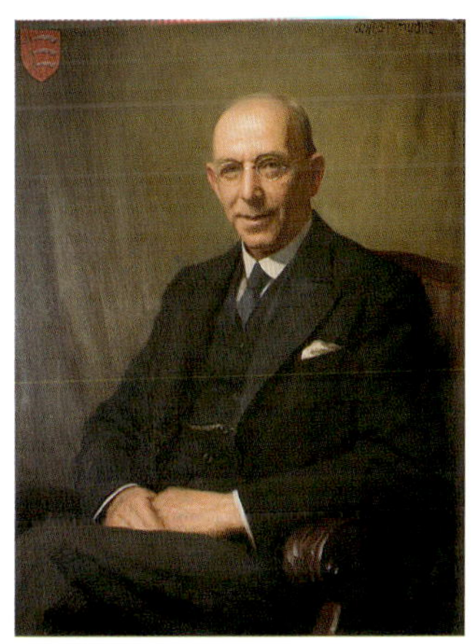

Moore, Ernest 1865–1940
Arthur Porter, JP
oil on canvas 90 x 69.5
57

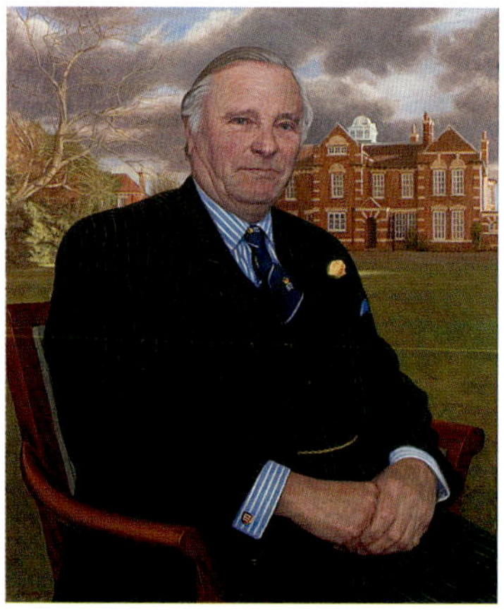

Oakshea, Anthony
Anthony Peel in front of the Police Headquarters at Springfield 2004
oil on canvas 75 x 62
209

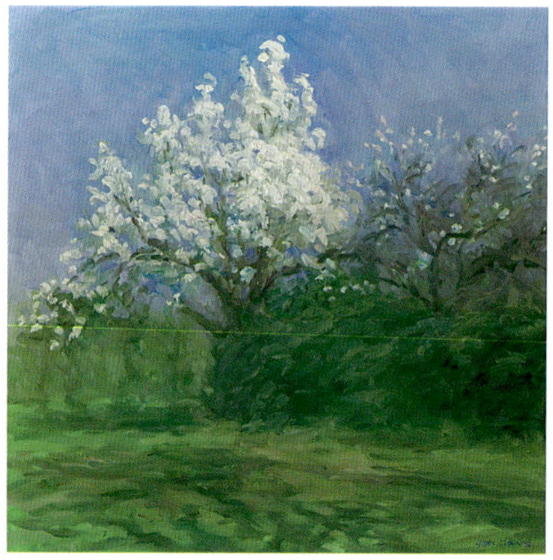

Osborne, John b.1939
A White Blossom Tree
oil on board 44.3 x 44.3
72

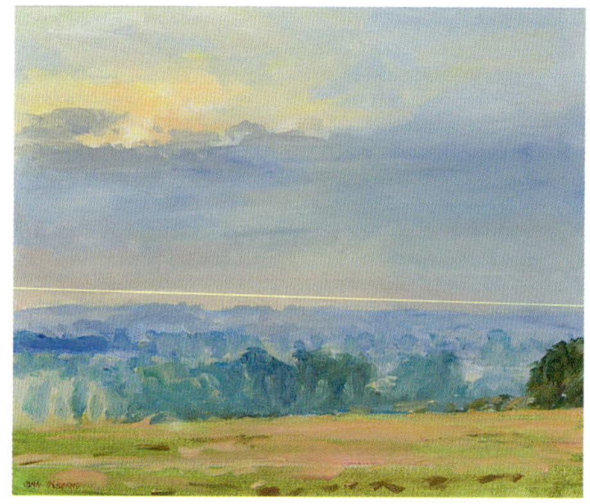

Osborne, John b.1939
Field at Sunset
oil on board 29.5 x 34.5
77

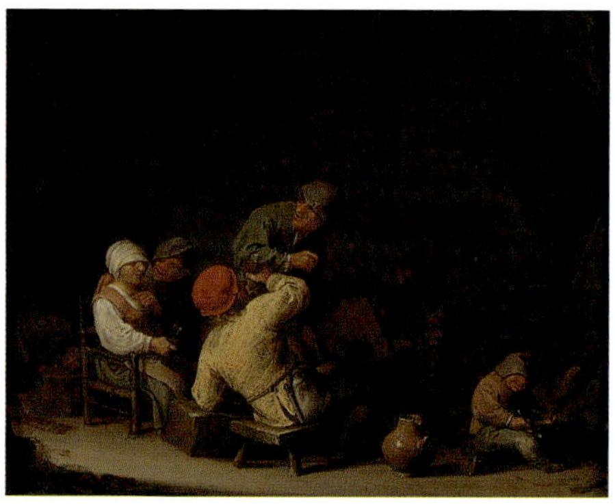

Ostade, Adriaen van (follower of)
1610–1685
Interior with Dutch Peasants Drinking
oil on panel 27 x 33
9

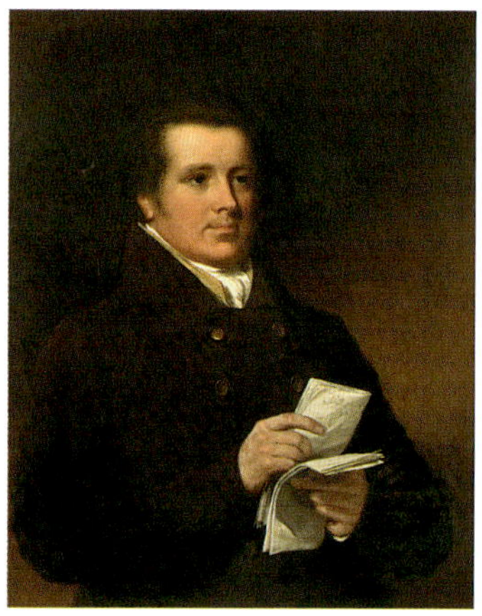

Phillips, Thomas (circle of) 1770–1845
Thomas Gardiner Bramston
oil on canvas 35.5 x 27.5
19

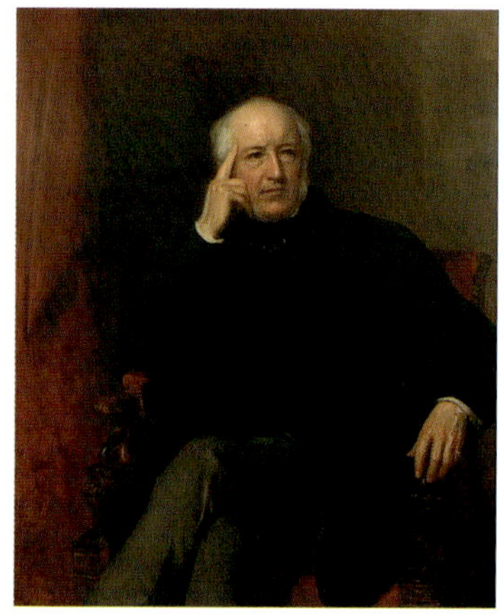

Pickersgill, Henry William (circle of)
1782–1875
William Bramston 1865
oil on canvas 90 x 69
20

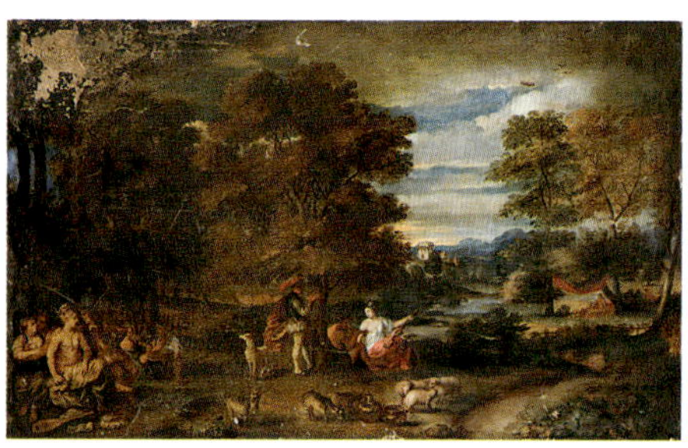

Poussin, Nicolas (school of) 1594–1665
Bacchanalia
oil on canvas 76 x 121
163

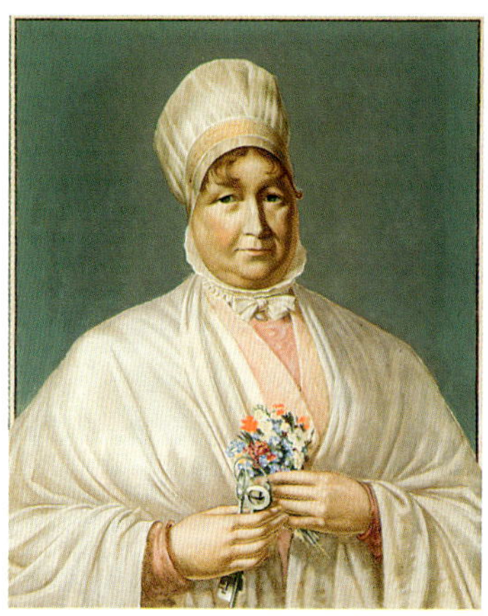

Rushbury, Henry 1889–1968
Elizabeth Fry of Plashet (East Ham), the Friend of Prisoners (1780–1845) c.1938
oil on canvas 190 x 120 (E)
218

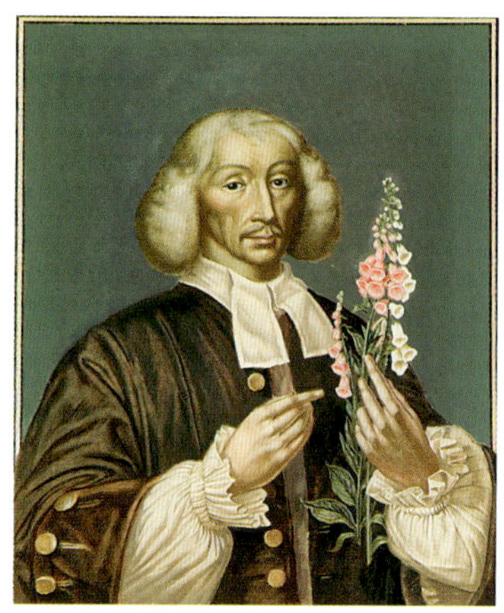

Rushbury, Henry 1889–1968
John Ray of Black Notley, Father of Natural History (1627–1703) c.1938
oil on canvas 190 x 120 (E)
217

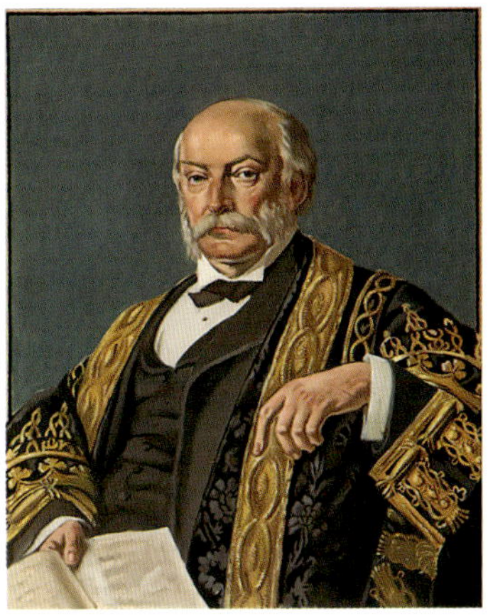

Rushbury, Henry 1889–1968
Lord Rayleigh of Terling, President of the Royal Society (1842–1919) c.1938
oil on canvas 190 x 120 (E)
221

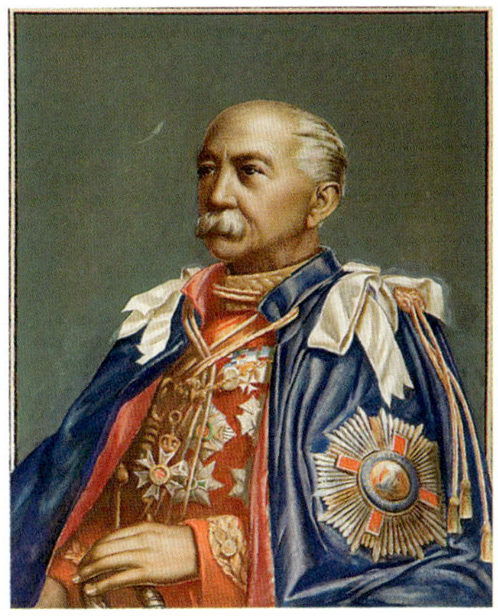

Rushbury, Henry 1889–1968
Sir Evelyn Wood of Harlow, Soldier (1858–1919) c.1938
oil on canvas 190 x 120 (E)
220

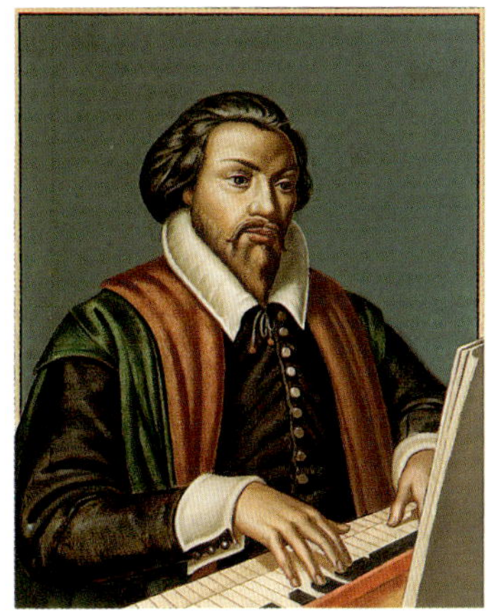

Rushbury, Henry 1889–1968
William Byrd of Stondon Place, Composer and Musician (1558–1625) c.1938
oil on canvas 190 x 120 (E)
216

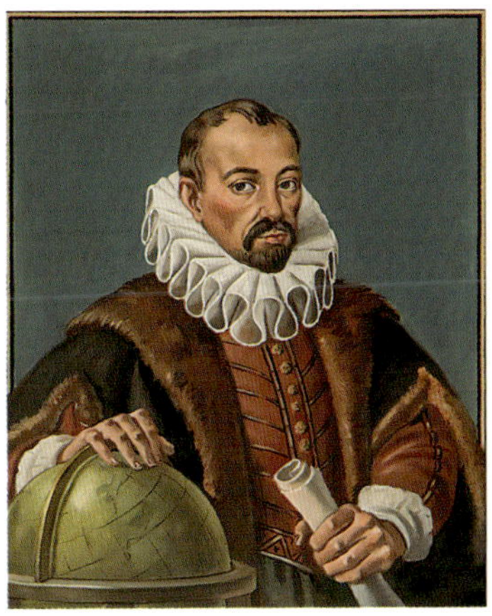

Rushbury, Henry 1889–1968
William Gilberd of Colchester, Pioneer of Electrical Science (1540–1603) c.1938
oil on canvas 190 x 120 (E)
215

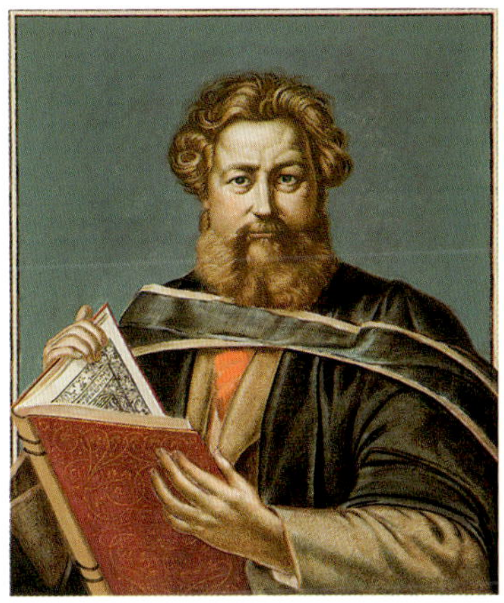

Rushbury, Henry 1889–1968
William Morris of Walthamstow, Poet and Craftsman (1834–1896) c.1938
oil on canvas 190 x 120 (E)
219

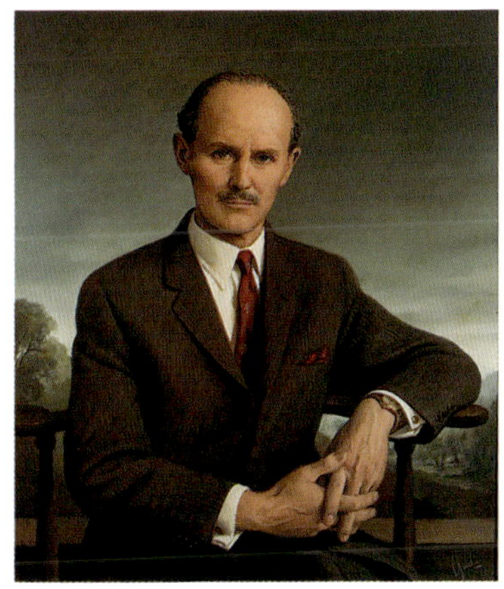

Sancha, Carlos Luis 1920–2001
Thomas Frederick James Collins, CBE, DL 1970
oil on canvas 77 x 65
43

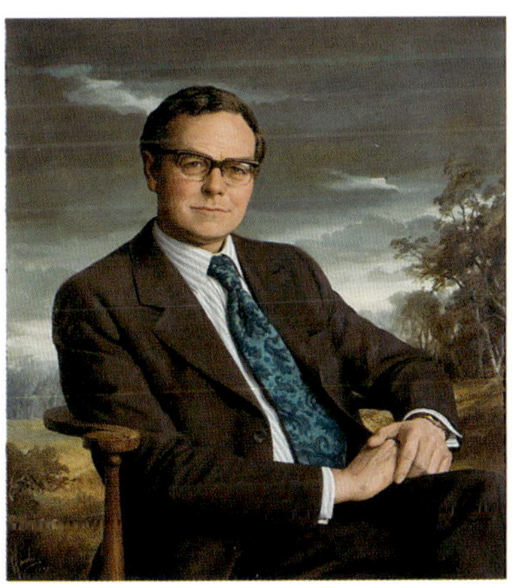

Sancha, Carlos Luis 1920–2001
Geoffrey Claud Waterer, DL 1977
oil on canvas 77.5 x 68.5
45

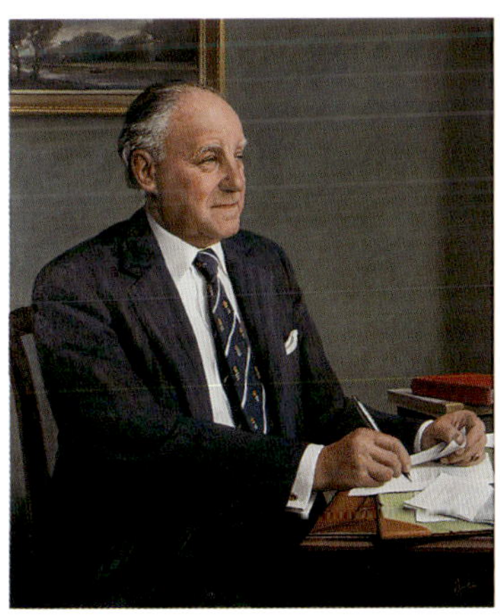

Sancha, Carlos Luis 1920–2001
Robert George Reginald Daniels, JP, DL 1983
oil on canvas 75 x 62
48

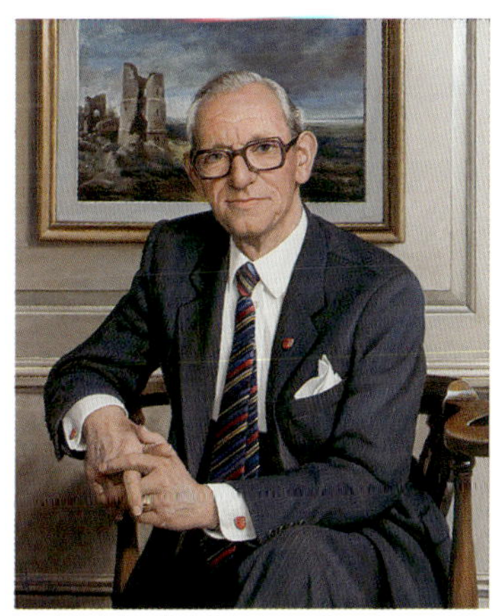

Sancha, Carlos Luis 1920–2001
Ronald Millward Williams, DL 1986
oil on canvas 75 x 62
49

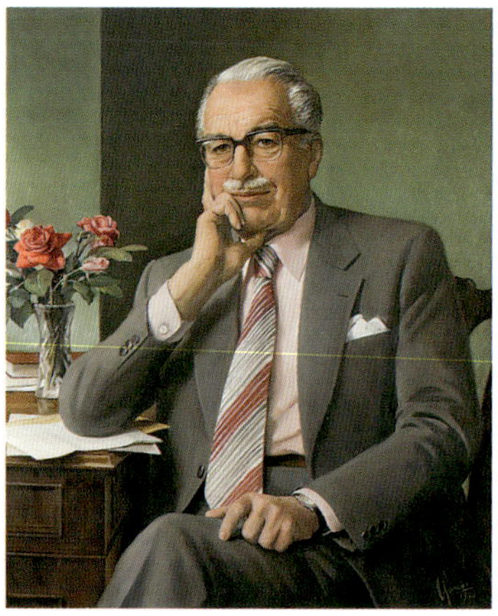

Sancha, Carlos Luis 1920–2001
Stanley George Barnett 1988
oil on canvas 75 x 62
47

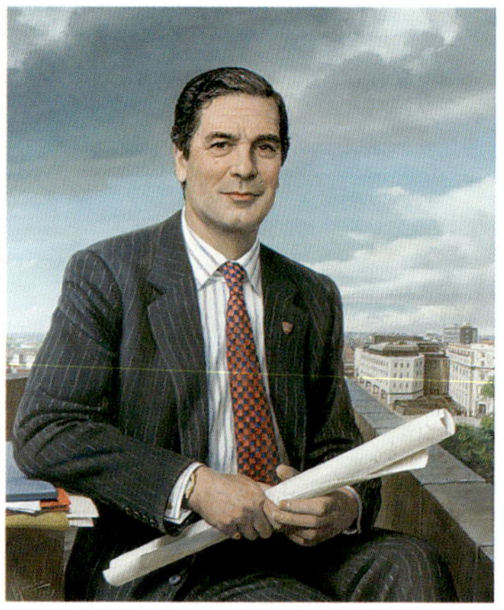

Sancha, Carlos Luis 1920–2001
Robert William Dixon Smith 1989
oil on canvas 75 x 62.5
63

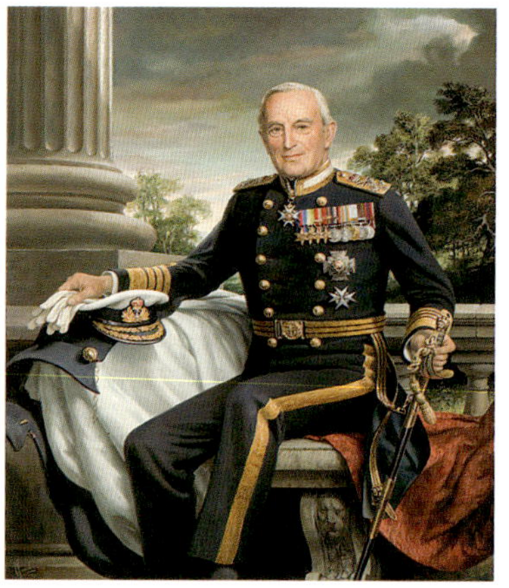

Sancha, Carlos Luis 1920–2001
Admiral Sir Andrew Lewis, KCB, JP, Lord Lieutenant of Essex (1978–1992) 1991
oil on canvas 130 x 100
100

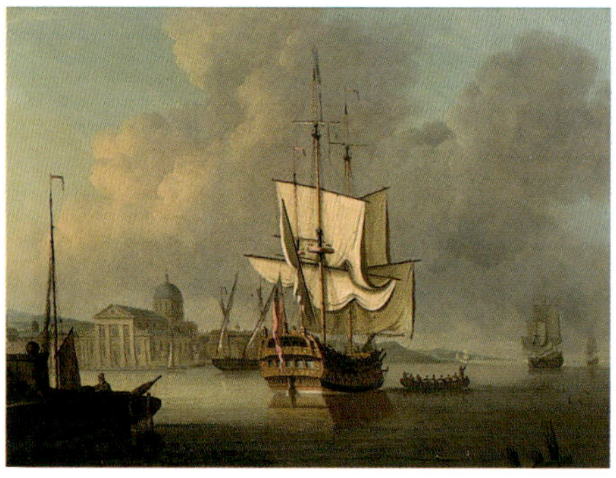

Serres, John Thomas (follower of) 1759–1825
Capriccio with a British Man o' War
oil on canvas 68 x 89
28

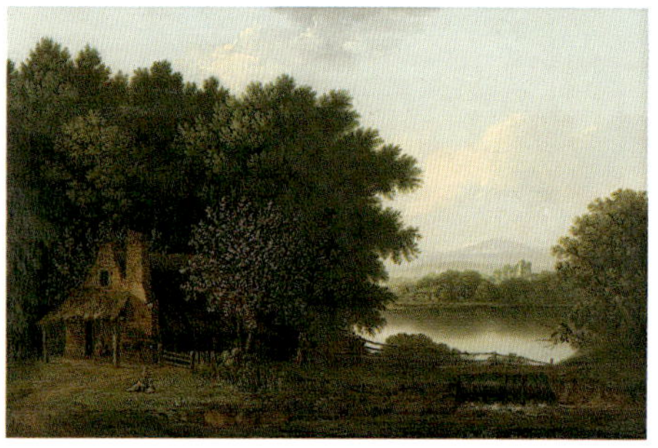

Smith, John (attributed to) c.1717–1764
Wooded Lake with Thatched Cottage
oil on canvas 42 x 62.5
12

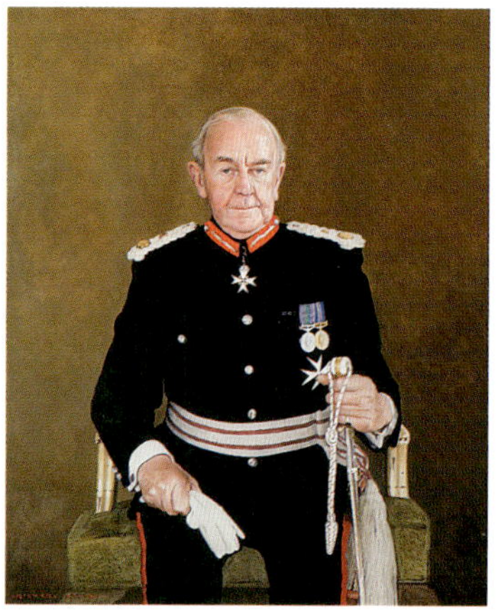

Stone, Richard b.1951
The Right Honourable the Lord Braybrooke, Knight of St John, MA, JP, Lord Lieutenant of Essex (1992–2002)
oil on canvas 130 x 100
210

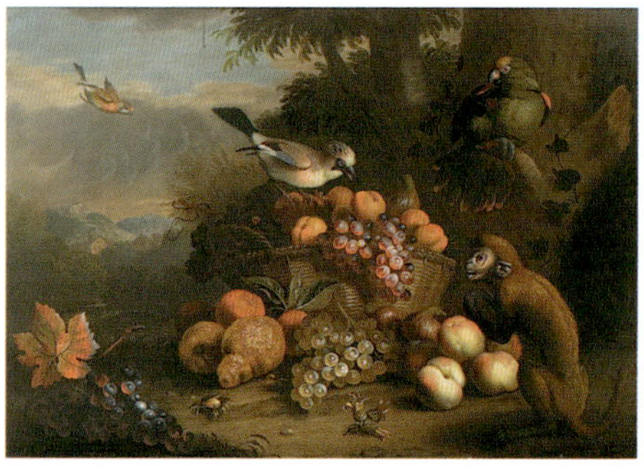

Stranovius, Tobias (studio of) 1684–1731
Still Life with a Monkey, Jay and Parrot
oil on canvas 88 x 121
4

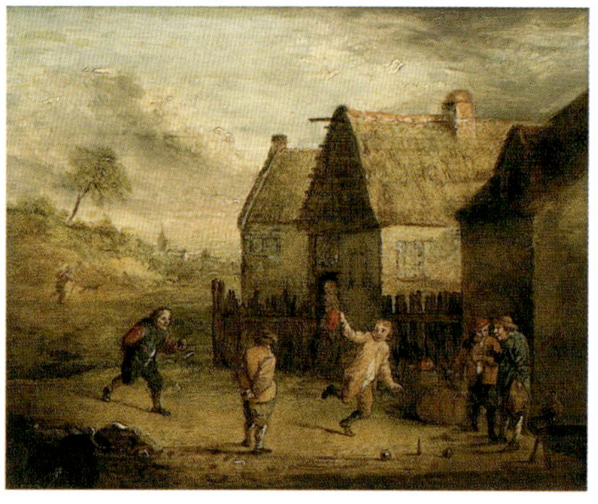

Teniers, David II (after) 1610–1690
Rural Scene with Figures Playing Skittles
oil on panel 22 x 26
129

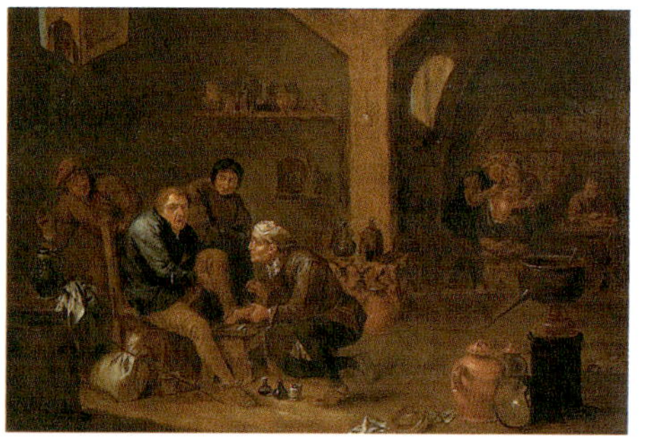

Teniers, David II (follower of) 1610–1690
Surgery with Chiropodist
oil on canvas 38 x 55
6

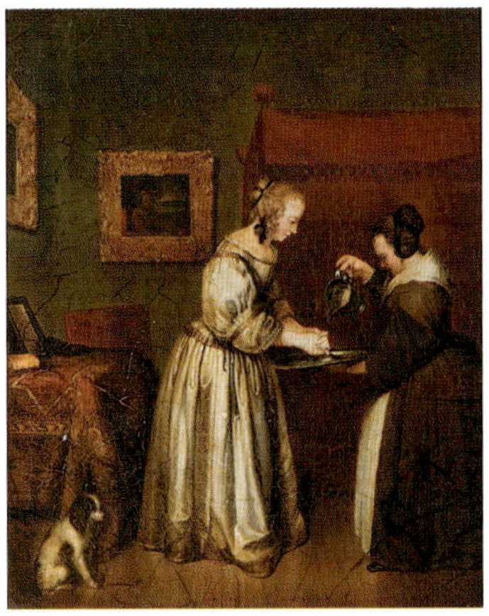

Terborch, Gerard II (after) 1617–1681
Interior with Lady Washing Her Hands
oil on canvas 43 x 33
13

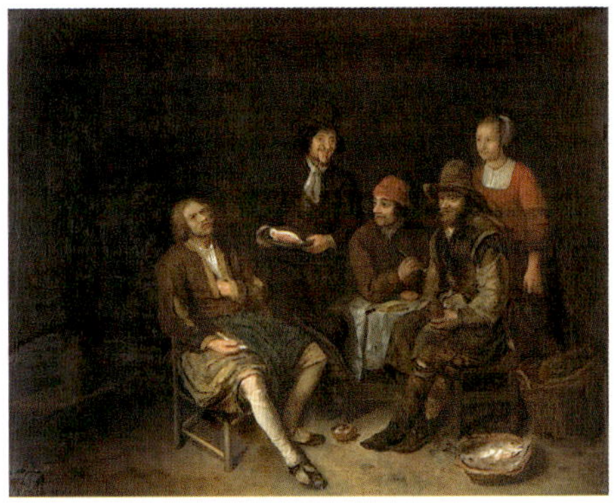

Terborch, Gerard II (follower of)
1617–1681
Interior with Peasants
oil on canvas 52 x 63
2

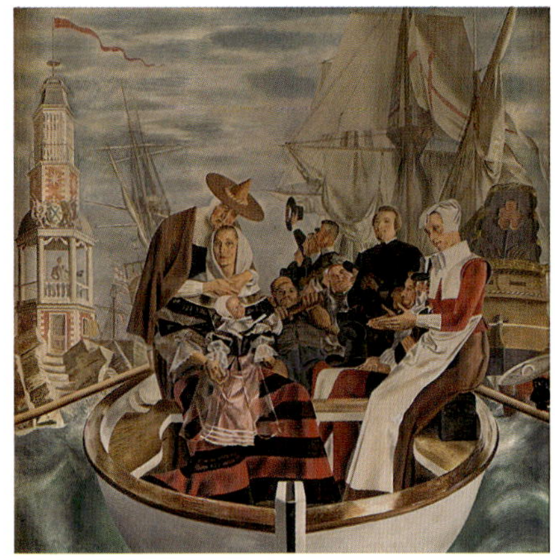

Thompson, Anthony
The 'Mayflower' Leaving Plymouth, 1620
1938
oil on canvas 370 x 380 (E)
212

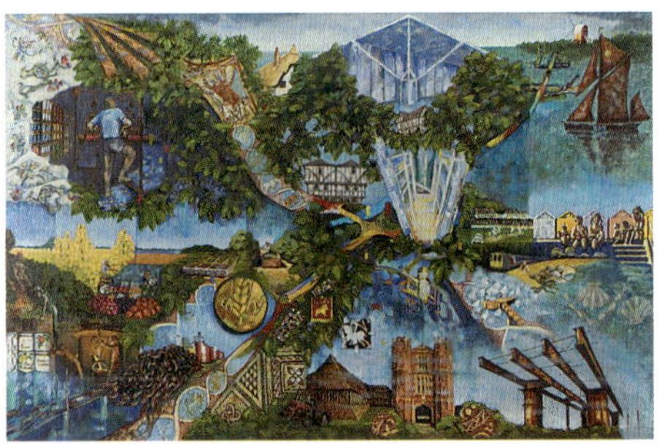

Wigley, Eileen b.1946
My Personal View of Essex 1992
oil on canvas 178 x 267
87

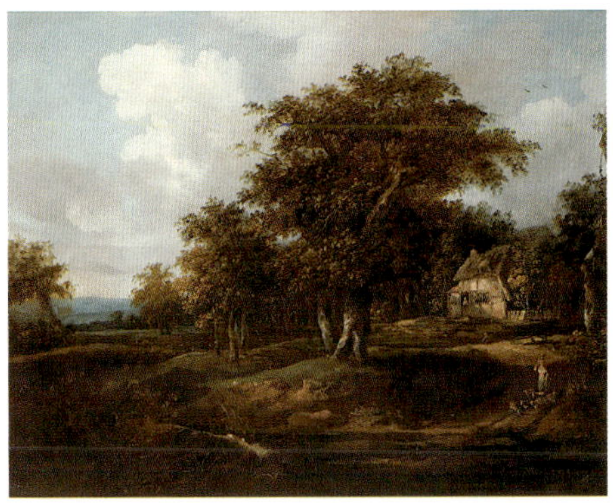

Williams, Edward (circle of) 1782–1855
Wooded Landscape with Thatched Cottage
oil on canvas 59.5 x 72
3

Essex Police Museum

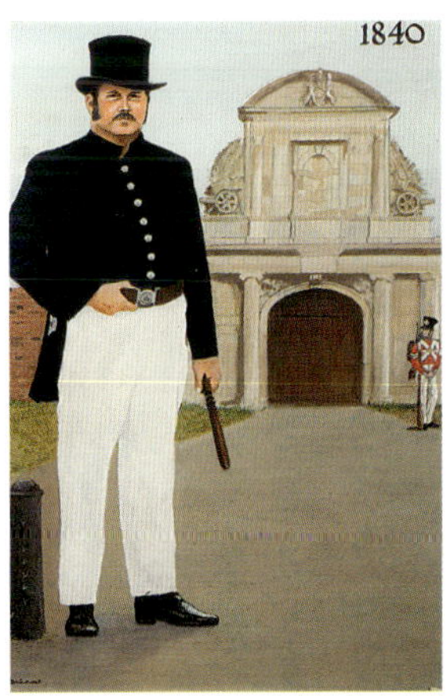

Bridge, Jack
Essex Police, 1840 (Tilbury) 1990
oil on board 37 x 27
IR0417

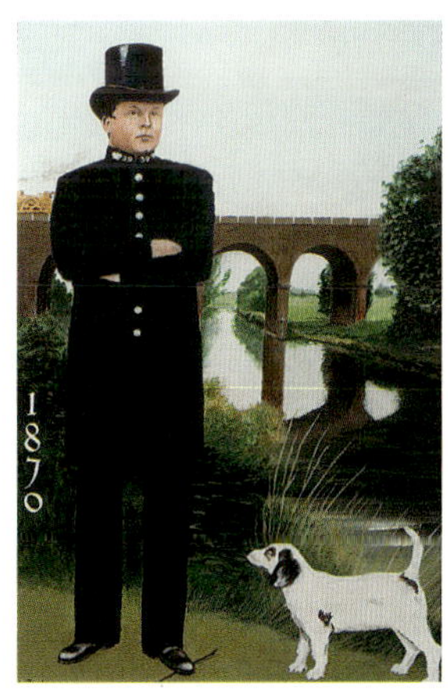

Bridge, Jack
Essex Police, 1870 (Chappel) 1990
oil on board 37 x 27
IR0418

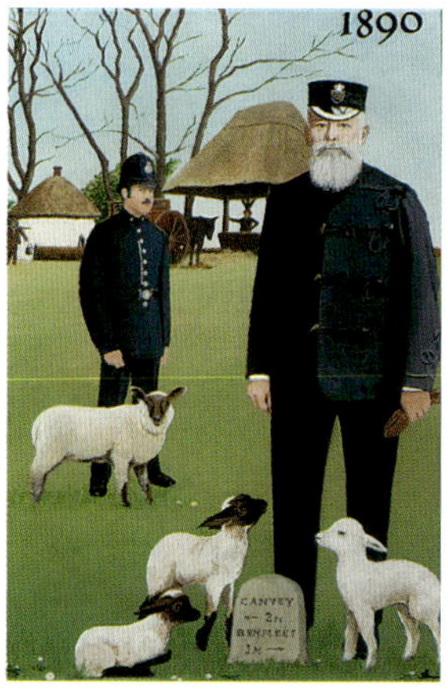

Bridge, Jack
Essex Police, 1890 1990
oil on board 37 x 27
IR0419

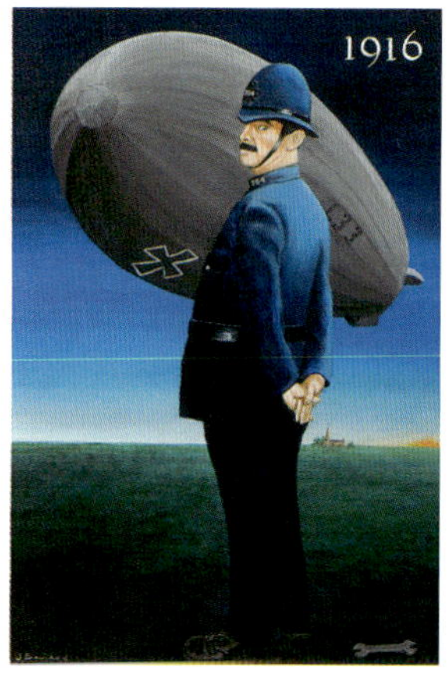

Bridge, Jack
Essex Police, 1916 (L.33 over Little Wigborough) 1990
oil on board 37 x 27
IR0420

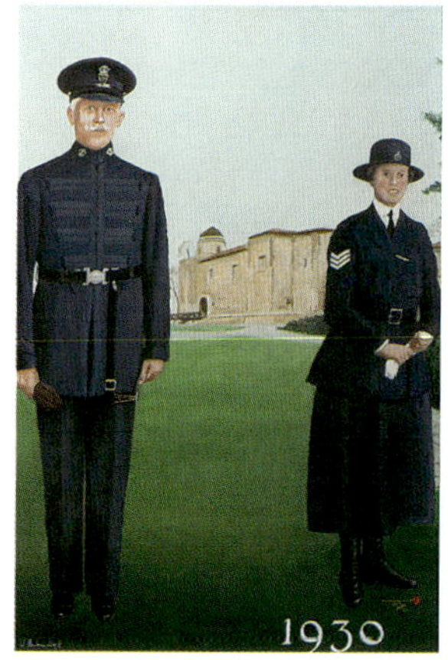

Bridge, Jack
Essex Police, 1930 (Colchester) 1990
oil on board 37 x 27
IR0421

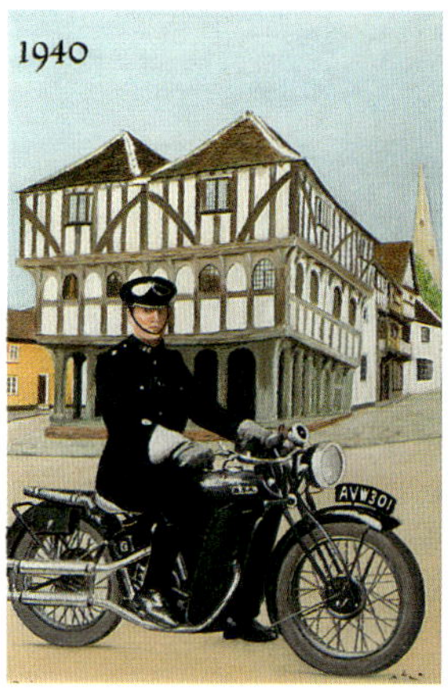

Bridge, Jack
Essex Police, 1940 (Thaxted) 1990
oil on board 37 x 27
IR0422

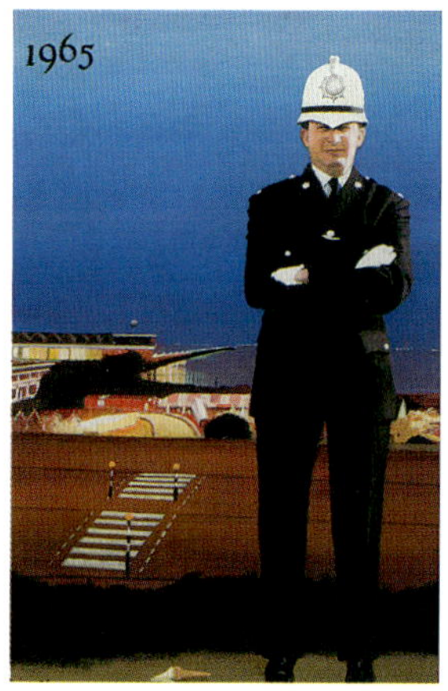

Bridge, Jack
Essex Police, 1965 (Southend-on-Sea) 1990
oil on board 37 x 27
IR0423

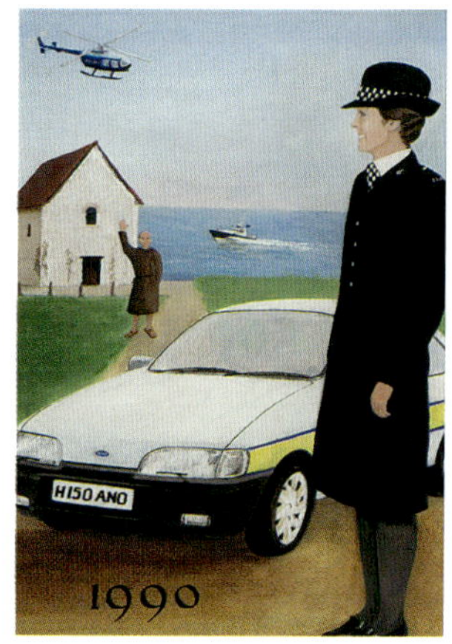

Bridge, Jack
Essex Police, 1990 (Bradwell-on-Sea) 1990
oil on board 37 x 27
IR0424

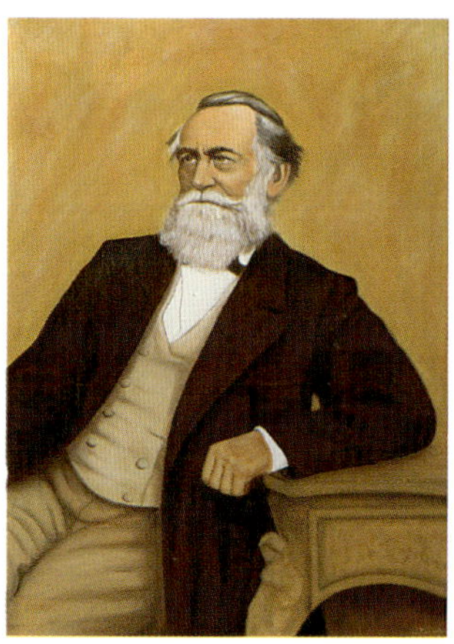

Bridge, Jack
Admiral John McHardy, Chief Constable of Essex (1840–1881)
oil on canvas 48 x 38
IR0436

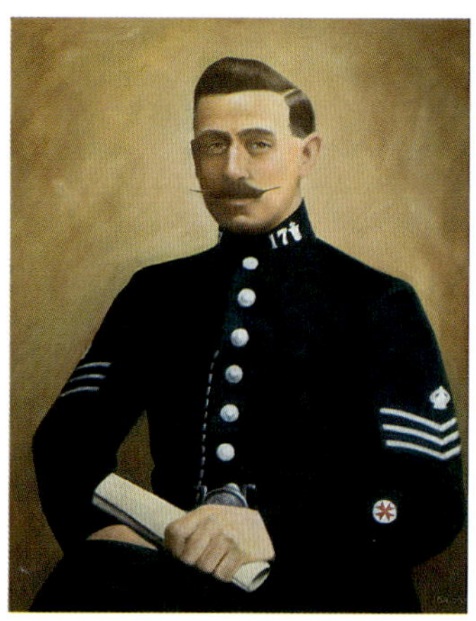

Bridge, Jack
Constable Charles 'Zepp' Smith (arrested the crew of a zeppelin which crashed at Little Wigborough, 1916)
oil on canvas 60 x 46
IR0787

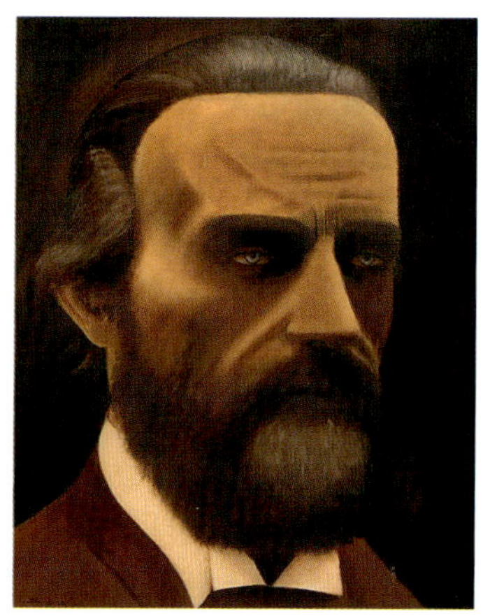

Bridge, Jack
James Lee (hanged for the murder of Inspector Simmons)
oil on canvas 50 x 40
IR0457

Facing page: Weight, Carel Victor Morlais, 1908–1997, *Death of Lucretia No.1* (detail), Southend Museums Service: Beecroft Art Gallery, (p. 289)

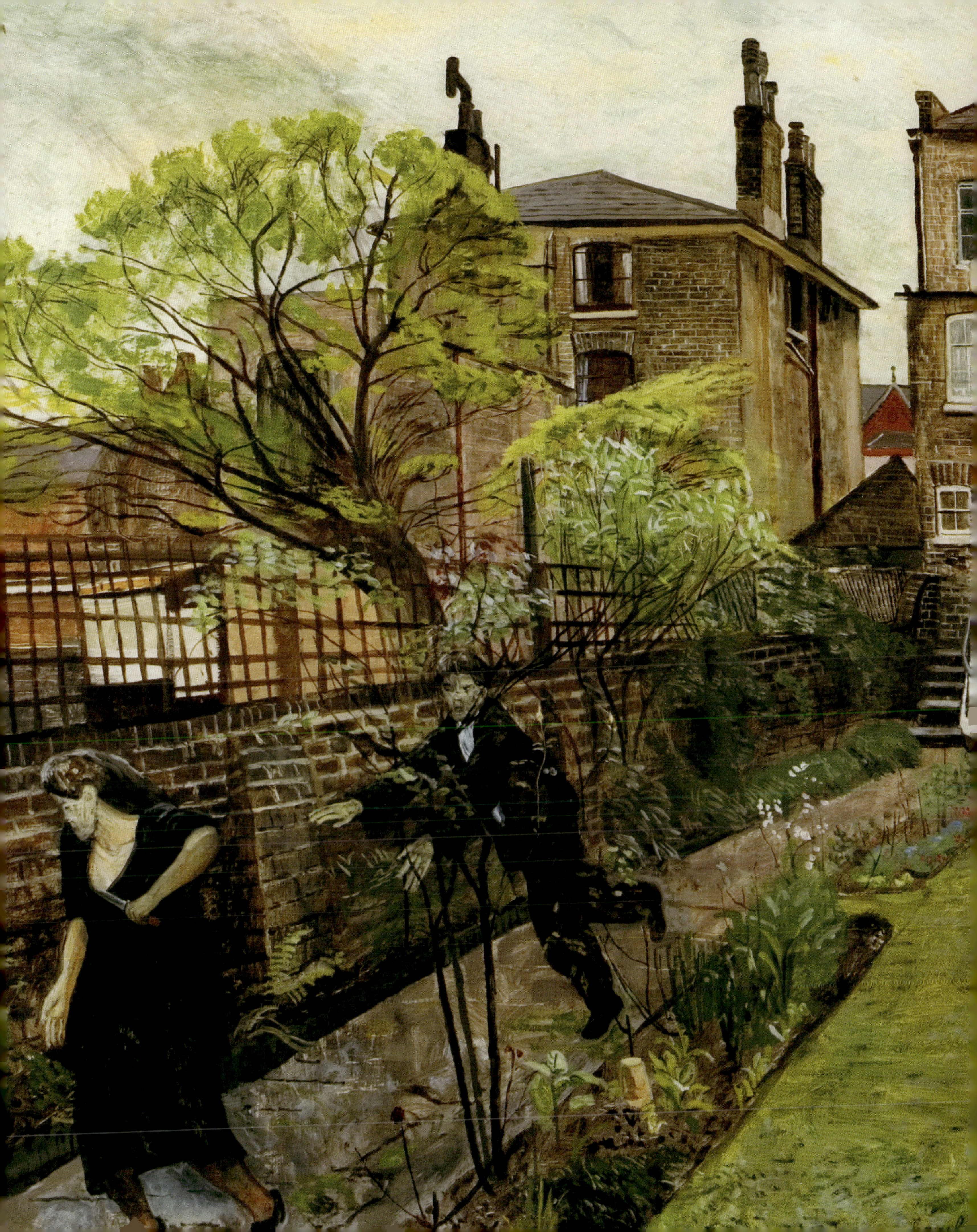

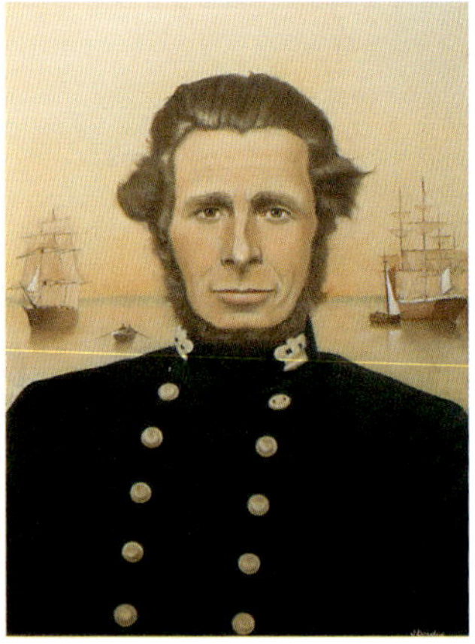

Bridge, Jack
John Bausor, an Early Inspector of the Essex Constabulary
oil on canvas 50 x 40
IR0365

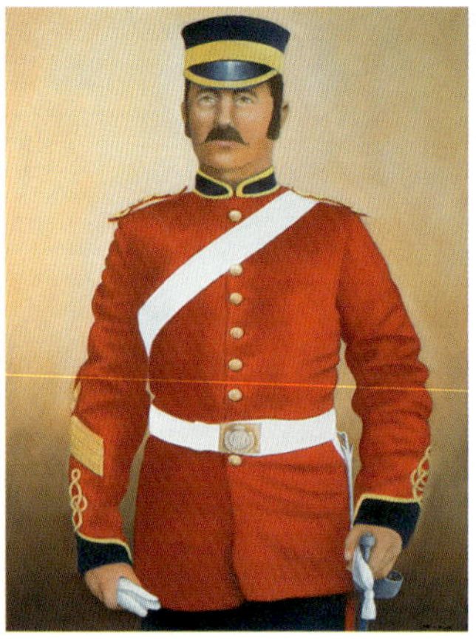

Bridge, Jack
Samuel Dougal in Staff Sergeant's Military Dress (Murderer of Camille Holland, Moat Farm, Clavering)
oil on canvas 72 x 57
IR0546

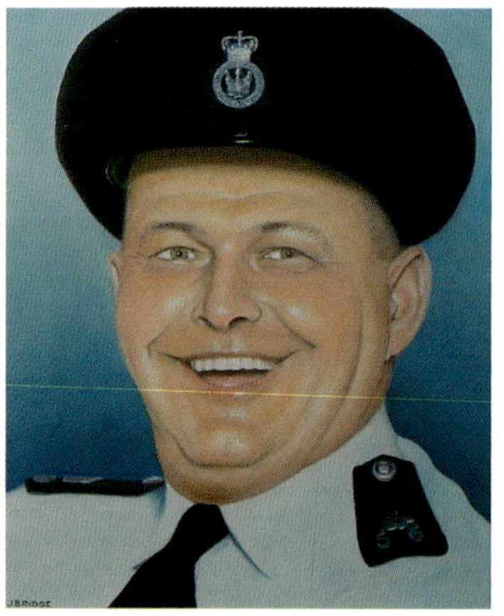

Bridge, Jack
Sergeant Bill Gosling (Southend-on-Sea Constabulary)
oil on canvas 42 x 37
IR0458

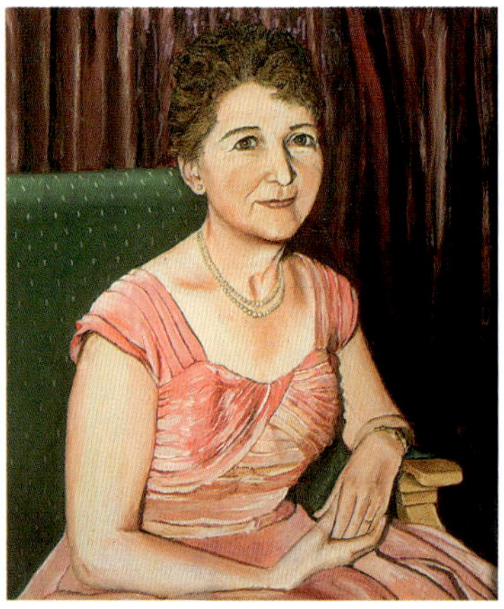

Hodges, George d.1980s
Dorothy Jordan, First Woman Police Inspector of Essex Constabulary (1944)
oil on canvas 80 x 60 (E)
IR0237

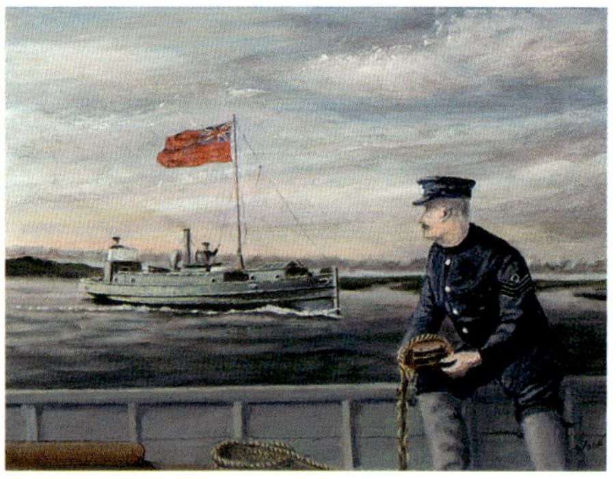

Woon, Des
Police Launch
oil on canvas 39 x 49
IR0054

Essex Record Office

The Essex Record Office's function is to preserve the archival heritage of the county, written, printed and electronic. It has a large collection of pictorial material that consists in the main of prints, drawings, watercolours and photographs. These have been collected for their value as historical evidence, rather than for their artistic merit, or have come to the Office as part of larger collections of documentary material. There are comparatively few oil paintings; most of these were acquired in the mid-twentieth century, when family portraits and anonymous landscapes were regarded as of little or no commercial value.

The largest single group comprises the portraits of the Baynes family of Bower House, Havering atte Bower along with two anonymous views of the house, all of which formerly hung in the house itself.

The Record Office is part of Essex County Council, and over the years pictures have been transferred between it and other County Council collections. The two Lynton Lamb paintings, for instance, were originally from a collection that the County Council used to maintain for loan to schools and other establishments. For this reason they can be seen under the Essex County Council collection entry in this catalogue.

The only one of the paintings that is on permanent display is a view of the Record Office Searchroom by the contemporary artist, Robert Priseman, that was presented to the Office by its Friends Organisation. Unfortunately, there is not space to display any of the others, and they can be viewed only by written request.

Richard Harris, Archive Service Manager

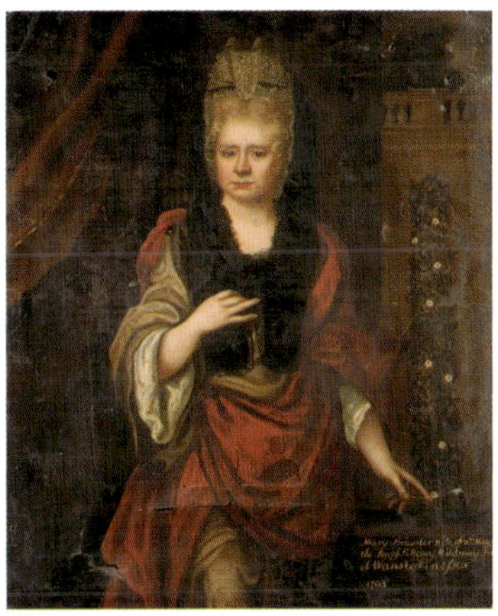

Burgoyne, P.
Mary Brewster, Wife of William Mildmay 1703
oil on canvas 127 x 102
17

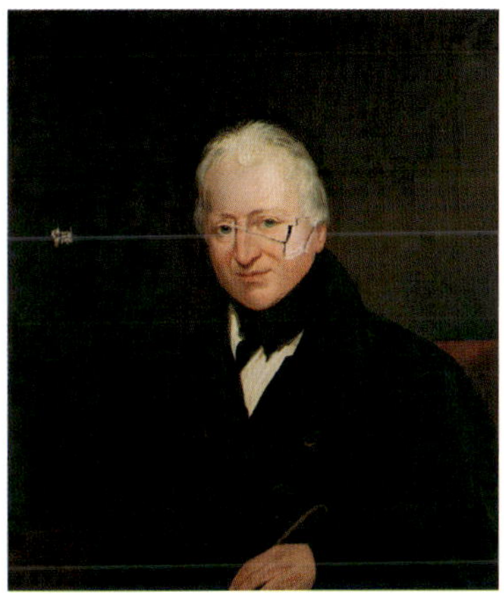

Carse, James (attributed to)
active c.1836–1848
Ellys Anderson Stephens of Bower Hall (demolished in 1926) (...) c.1836
oil on canvas 76.5 x 62
13 (P)

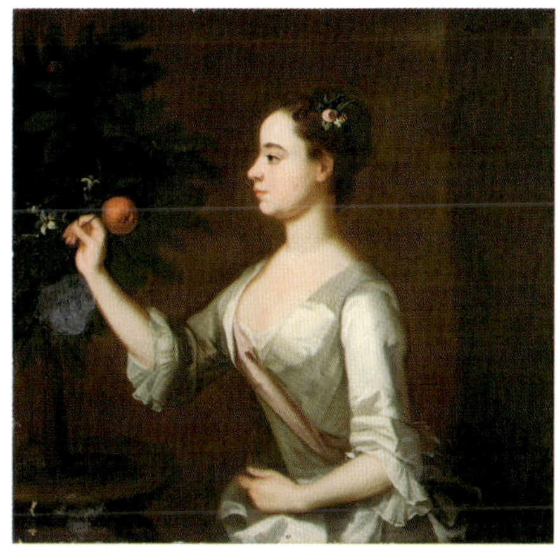

Hogarth, William (school of) 1697–1764
Lucy Baynes Plucking an Orange
oil on canvas 92 x 92
12

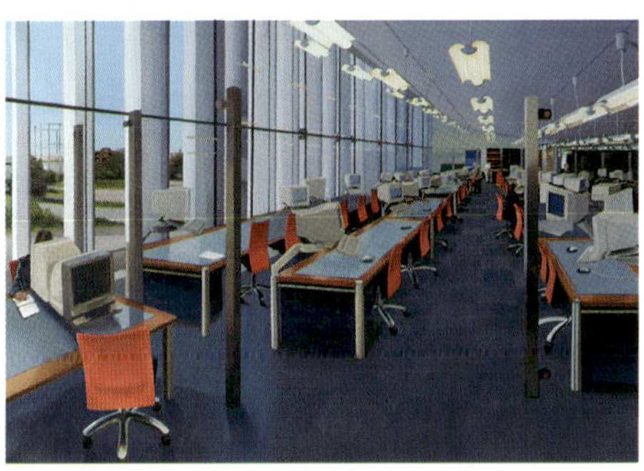

Priseman, Robert b.1965
The Search Room at Essex Record Office 2003
oil on canvas 75 x 106
1

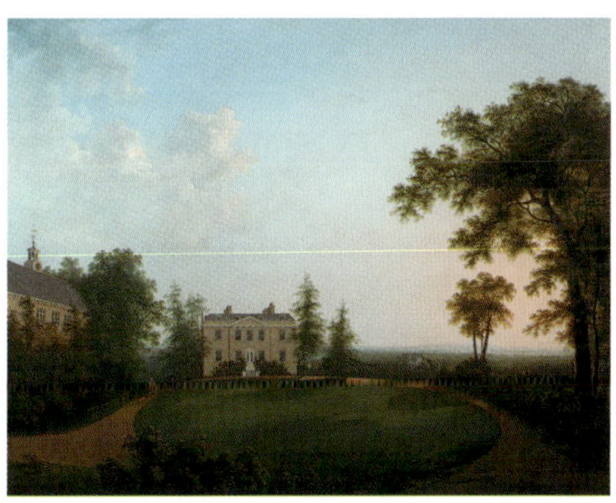

J. S.
A View of the North Front of Bower House, Havering atte Bower 1791
oil on canvas 112 x 140.5
2

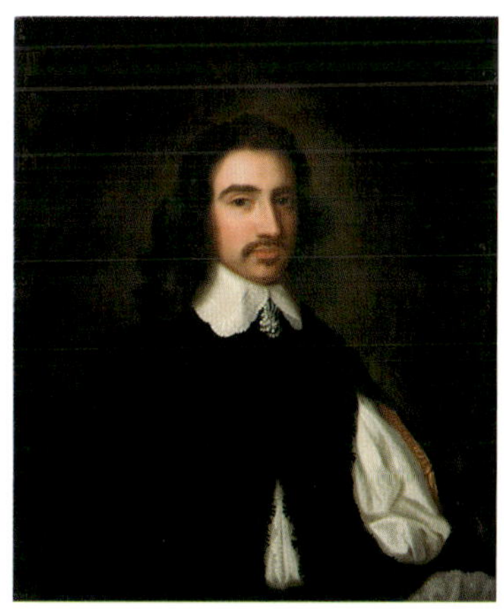

unknown artist early 17th C
Portrait of a Gentleman in a Black Doublet and Lace Collar
oil on canvas 76 x 63
10

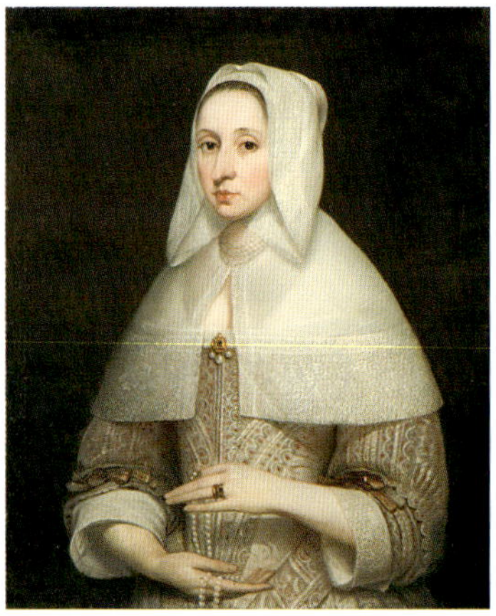

unknown artist early 17th C
Portrait of a Lady in an Embroidered Dress
oil on canvas 76 x 61
11

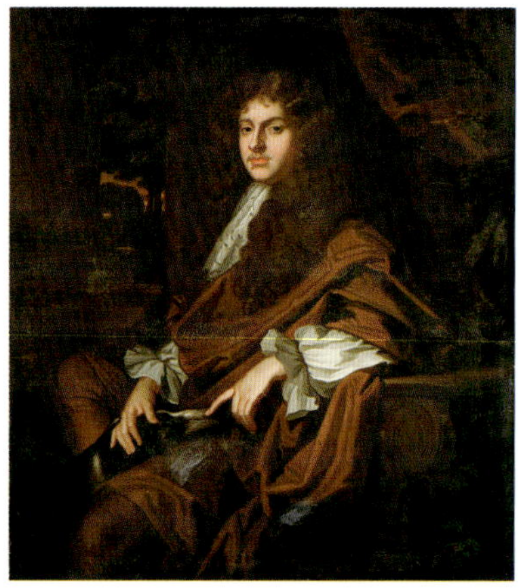

unknown artist late 17th C
Portrait of a Gentleman in a Long Wig and a Brown Cloak, with a Dog
oil on canvas 131 x 114
9

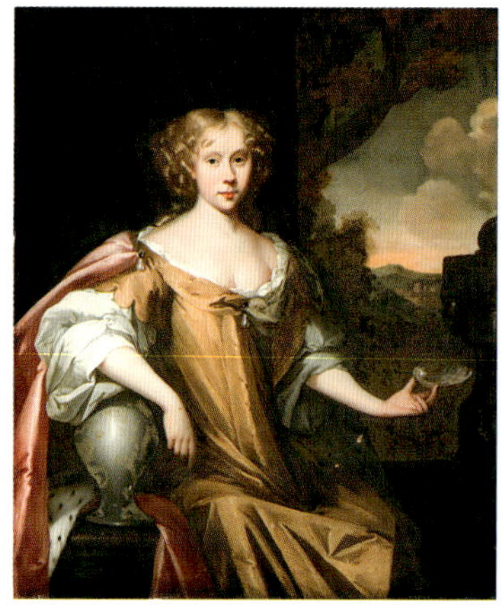

unknown artist late 17th C
Portrait of a Young Lady in a Brown Dress and Pink Cloak
oil on canvas 130 x 103
4

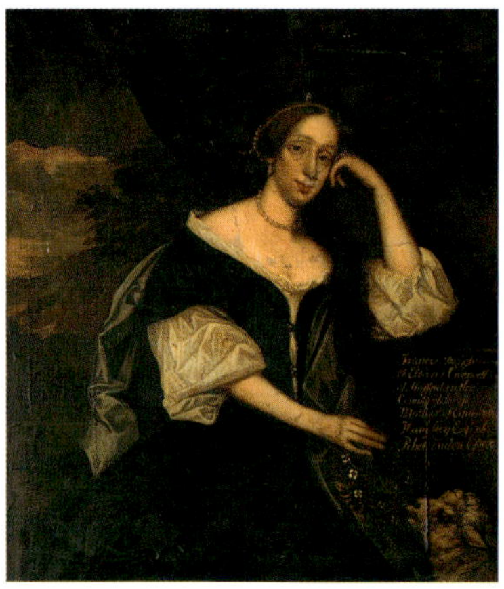

unknown artist
Frances Carswell, Mother of Edmund Humfrey of Rettendon c.1700
oil on canvas 115 x 99
15

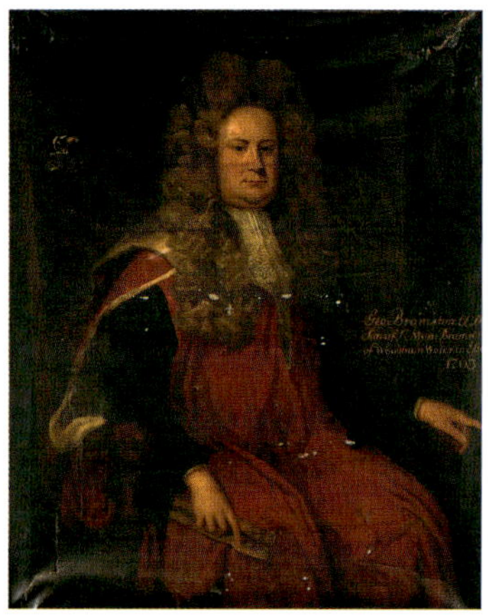

unknown artist
George Bramston, LLD, of Woodham Walter 1703
oil on canvas 126 x 101
14

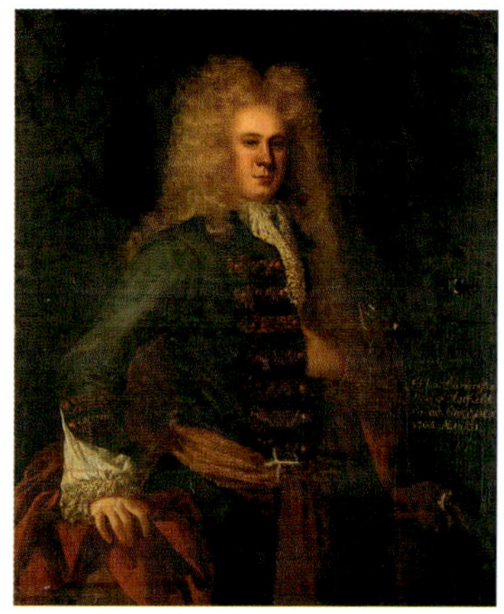

unknown artist
Sir Charles Barrington of Hatfield Broad Oak, Aged 31 1703
oil on canvas 126 x 102
16

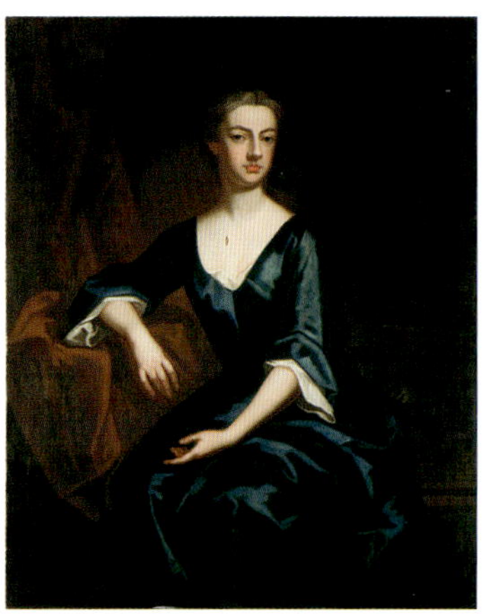

unknown artist
Mary Beke (d.1771), Wife of John Baynes c.1722
oil on canvas 129 x 101
6

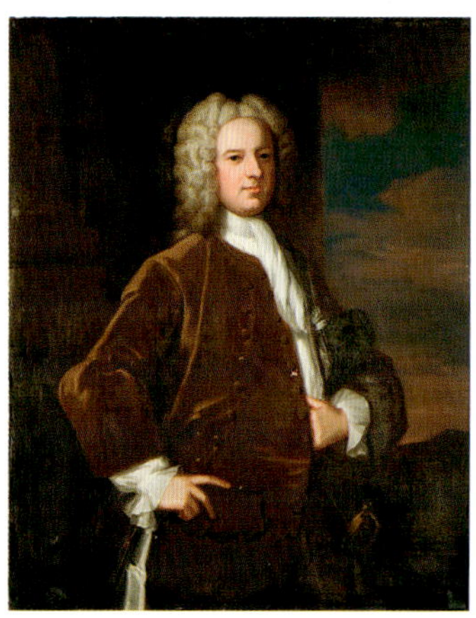

unknown artist early 18th C
Portrait of a Gentleman in a Brown Coat (believed to be Francis Lee, possibly the husband of Lucy Baynes)
oil on canvas 131 x 101
5

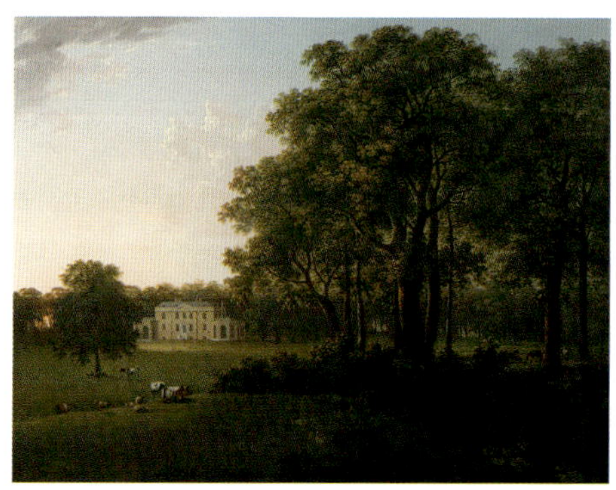

unknown artist
A View of the South Front of Bower House, Havering atte Bower c.1840?
oil on canvas 113 x 141
3

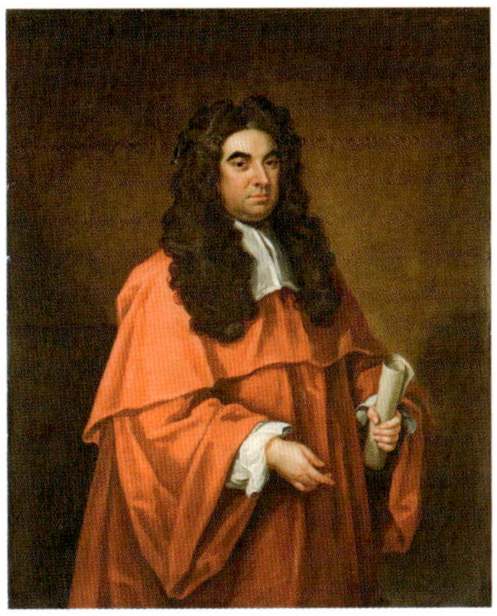

Vanderbank, John c.1694–1739
John Baynes, Sergeant-at-Law, d.1737 (builder of Bower House, Havering atte Bower) 1727
oil on canvas 131 x 101
7

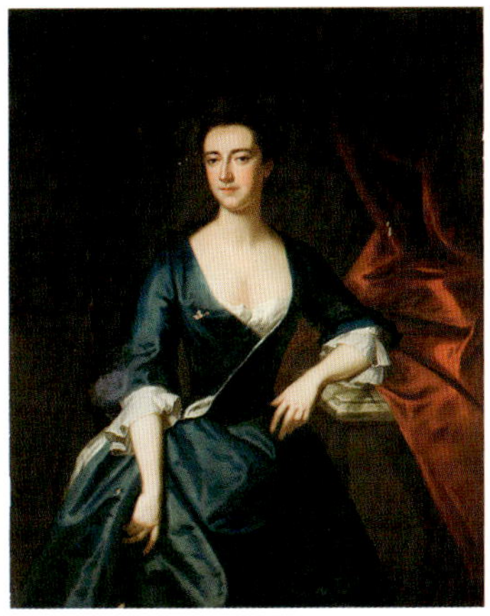

Vanderbank, John c.1694–1739
Mary (d.1771), Wife of John Baynes 1727
oil on canvas 129 x 102
8

Colchester Archaeological Trust

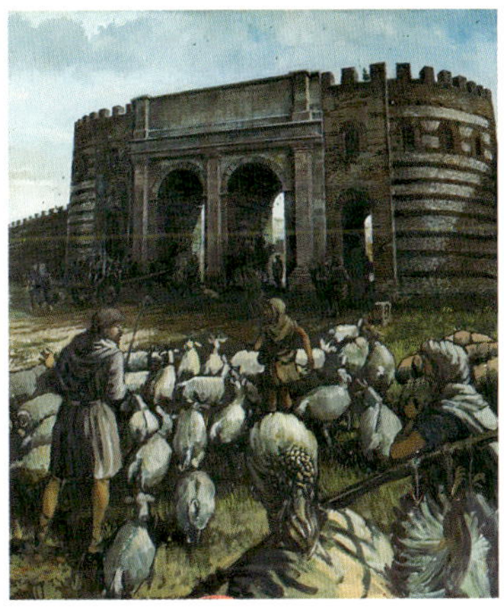

Froste, Peter b.1935
Balkerne Gate, Colchester c.1974
oil on board 61 x 50
2

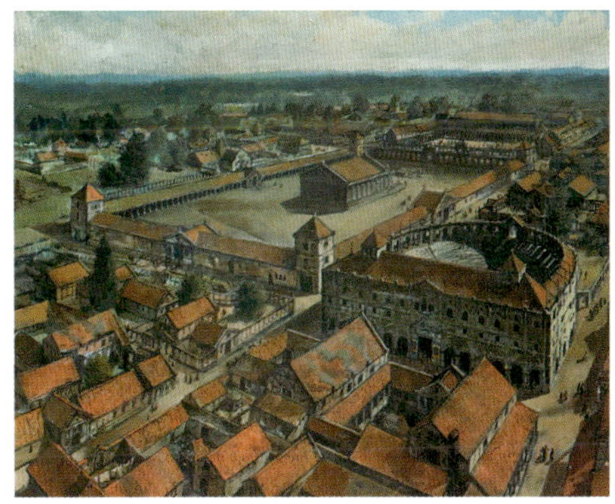

Froste, Peter b.1935
Roman Theatre and Temple of Claudius, Colchester c.1983
oil on board 50 x 60
1

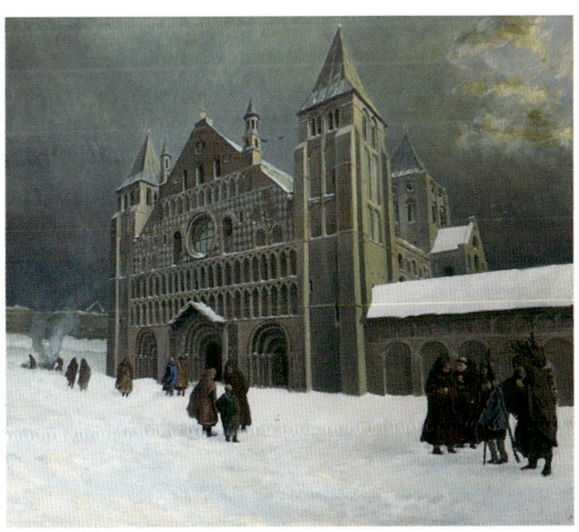

Froste, Peter b.1935
West Front, St Botolph's Priory, Colchester c.1991
oil on board 77 x 84
3

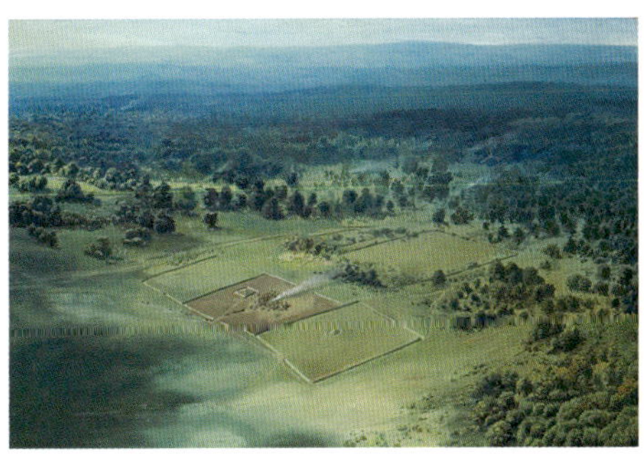

Froste, Peter b.1935
The Stanway Burials c.65 AD c.1995
oil on board 49 x 72
4

Colchester County High School

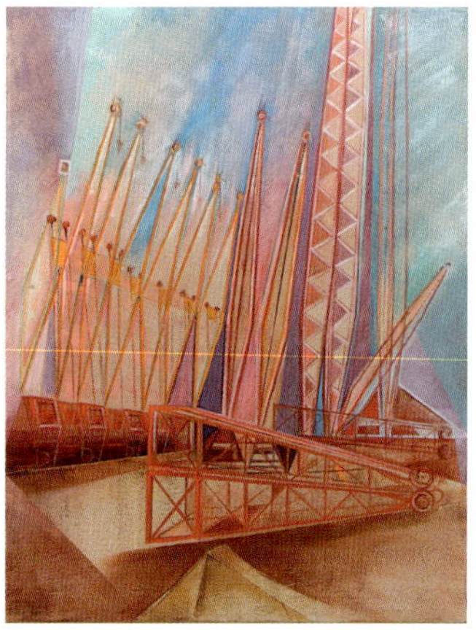

Pallot, Joyce 1912–2004
Cranes
oil on canvas 103 x 77
23

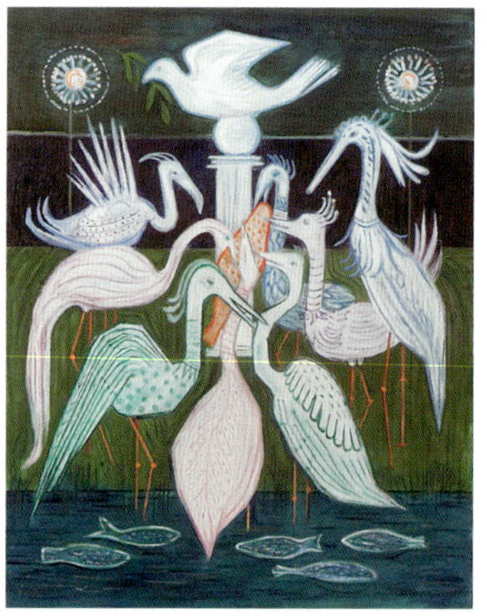

Pallot, Joyce 1912–2004
Flamingoes and Fish
oil on canvas 101.5 x 77
22

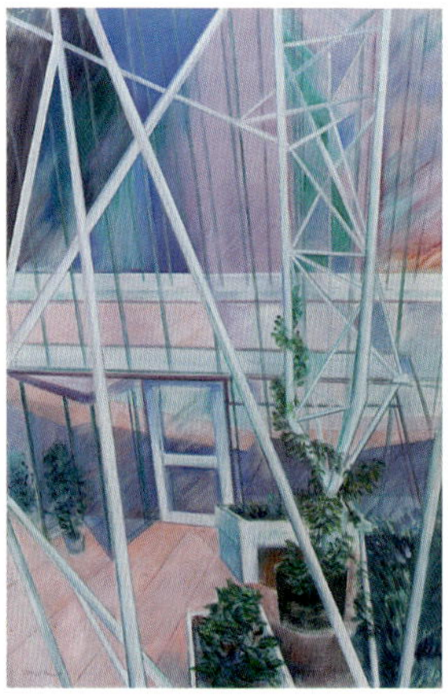

Pallot, Joyce 1912–2004
Glazed Vestibule
oil on canvas 97 x 61
143

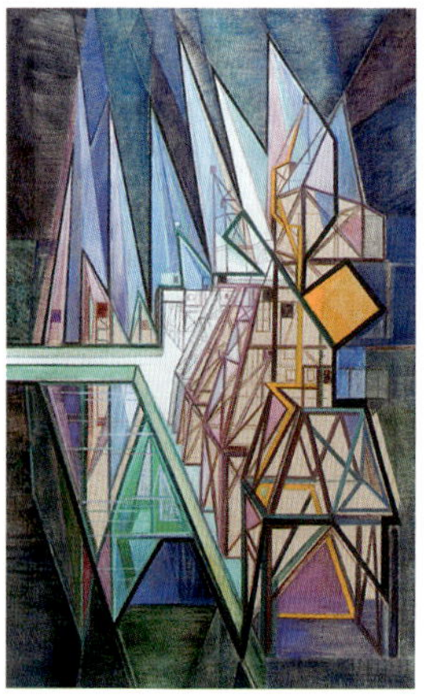

Pallot, Joyce 1912–2004
Quayside Reflections
oil on canvas 117 x 71
21

Colchester Museums

The origins of Colchester Museums lie in 1846 when a museum collection was established in response to the Museum Act of the previous year. Works of art were collected from the start. This has resulted in a large art collection, in Essex terms, with particularly strong holdings of local topographic scenes as well as depictions of members of the local community, with relatively few examples being of wider artistic significance.

A major element within the collection is the paintings that were commissioned to furnish Colchester Town Hall, which opened in 1902 to the design of Sir John Belcher. The building is a fine example of civic grandeur and the paintings support this endeavour by commemorating the great and the good of the town. Artists including Harry Becker, Frank Daniell, Charles Head and John L. Reilly painted numerous portraits among which can be found copies of earlier works where the sitters were no longer alive. In subsequent years Colchester Borough Council has commissioned further portraits by such artists as Maurice Codner in the 1950s, and most notably, the local artist, Richard Stone. His portrait of the Queen from 1991 is one of the best-known images of the monarch.

Two further noteworthy paintings acquired for display in the Town Hall are portraits of Viscount and Viscountess Cowdray by John Macdonald Aiken that were given by Viscountess Cowdray in 1931.

There are only a few paintings earlier than 1800 in the collection. *Flemish Village Merrymaking* by David Vinckboons is perhaps the most important painting in the collection. There are two Flemish School paintings on copper, *The Transfiguration* and *The Visitation* from the New Testament. The early seventeenth century portrait of local magnate, Sir Thomas Lucas, attributed to Robert Peake, was purchased in 1993 with help from the National Art Collections Fund. There is also an interesting pair of mid-seventeenth century portraits of Sir Thomas Honywood and his wife, Hester. Included within the collection, although on loan from the Victor Batte-Lay Trust, is an intriguing painting of the Golden Horn at Constantinople. This exotic view has a Dalmatian in the foreground, which gives the painting its current name, *The Spotted Dog*. It has been attributed to Otto Hoynk and most probably found its way to Colchester through the trading links of a local family.

There are a number of well-known artists with strong local connections who are represented in the collection. First and foremost is John Constable through his portrait of the Reverend Thomas Lechmere Grimwood, Headmaster of Dedham Grammar School. The collection also holds *Flatford Lock*, the only securely attributed painting by the East Bergholt artist, John Dunthorne (1770–1844), who encouraged Constable in his early career. There is a fine portrait by John James Halls of his daughter, Julia. *Willy Lott's Cottage* at Flatford by Roger Fry and *The Garden in Winter* by John Nash, a founder member of the Colchester Art Society, were both purchased in 1993. In 1998 *The Acacia Tree*, painted by Lucien Pissarro in the garden of the Minories in Colchester during one of his visits to his relations, was acquired. It joined *St Lawrence Church near Southminster* and *Colchester from Sheepen Hill* by the same artist, already in the collection. Also worthy of attention is the nineteenth century artist, John Vine, who, despite being born with only rudimentary arms and hands, became an accomplished painter whose speciality was animal portraits. The museum has two of his paintings of horses as well as portraits of Mr and Mrs James Cobb.

The museum is actively engaged in an initiative to build up a collection of prints by current and recent artists with local connections. However, there are no plans for active collecting of oil paintings as the cost, even when offset by grant-aid, would be prohibitive. The acquisition of paintings by gift, bequest and perhaps the occasional one-off purchase will continue.

Tom Hodgson, Curator of Social History

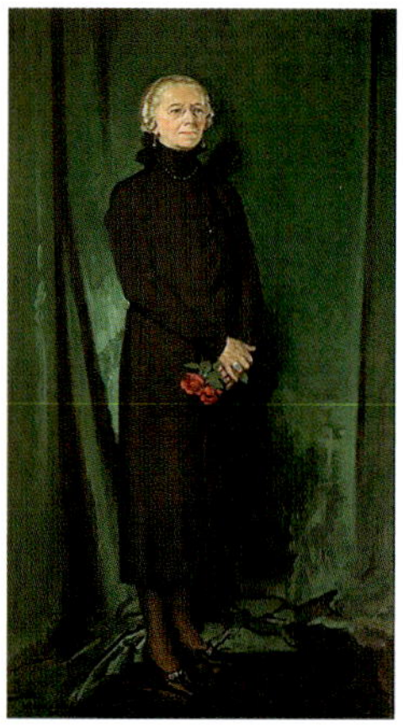

Aiken, John MacDonald 1880–1961
Annie, Viscountess Cowdray, High Steward of Colchester (copy after William Orpen) c.1920
oil on canvas 203.2 x 104.1
COLEM : 207A

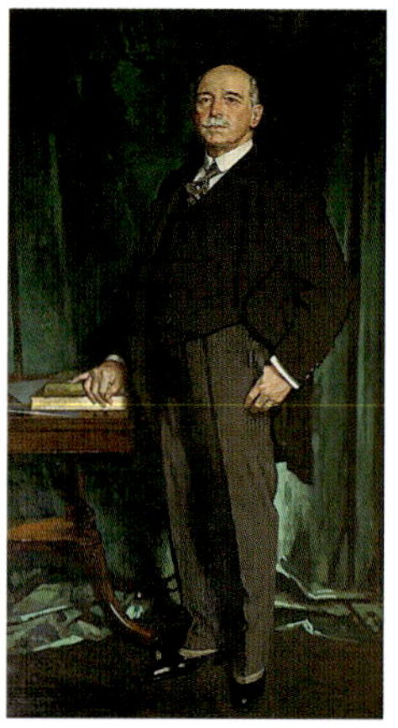

Aiken, John MacDonald 1880–1961
The Right Honourable Weetman Dickinson Pearson, 1st Viscount Cowdray PC, GCVO (1856–1927) (...) c.1920
oil on canvas 203.2 x 104.1
COLEM : 208A

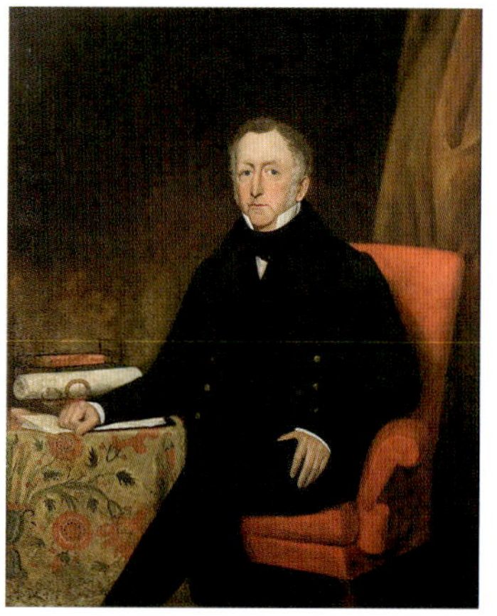

Archer, Archibald active 1810–1845
Sir George Henry Smythe 1840?
oil on canvas 137.2 x 109.2
COLEM : 186A

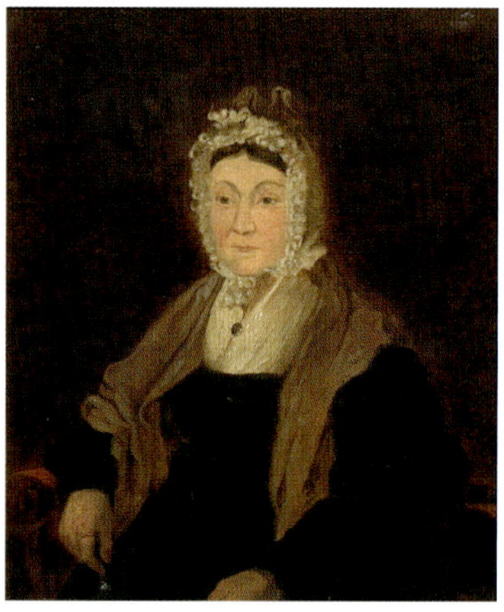

Bamfield, W. B.
Susannah Wiseman (after William Allsworth)
oil on canvas 30.5 x 25.4
COLEM : 1942.193

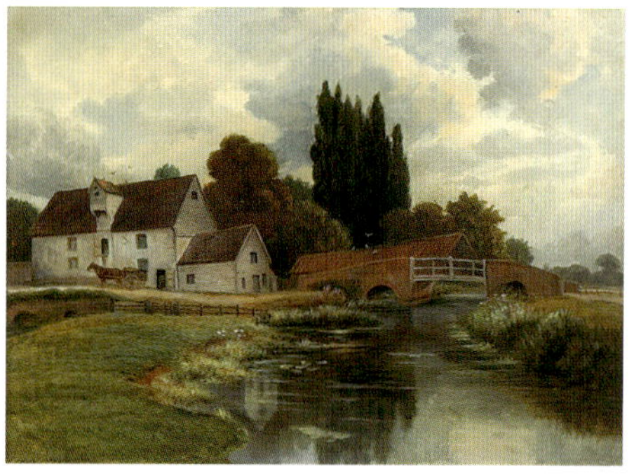

Barber, Alfred R. 1841–1925
Langham Mill c.1920
oil on canvas 46 x 61
COLEM : 77A

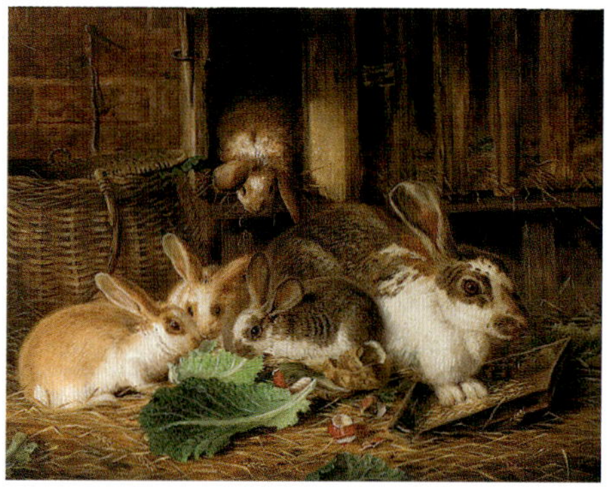

Barber, Alfred R. 1841–1925
Five Rabbits
oil on canvas 51 x 65
COLEM : 1990.110

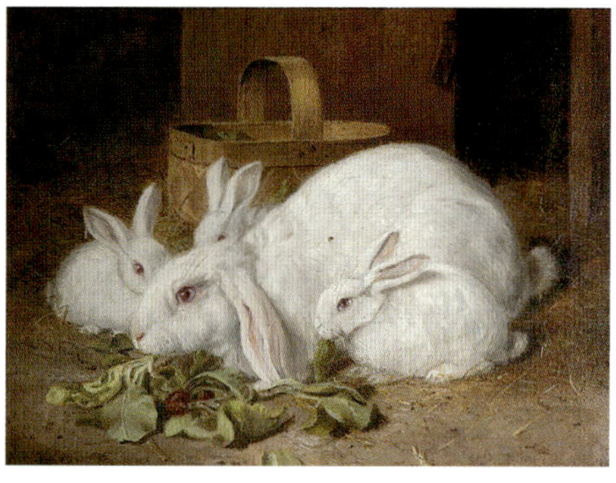

Barber, Alfred R. 1841–1925
Four White Rabbits
oil on canvas 35.6 x 45.7
COLEM : 1970.36

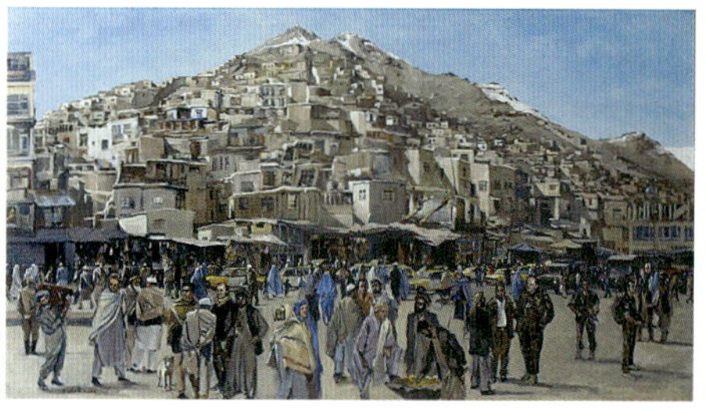

Bashall, Nick b.1956
Bed Street, Kabul 2002
oil on canvas 79 x 126
COLEM : 2005.125

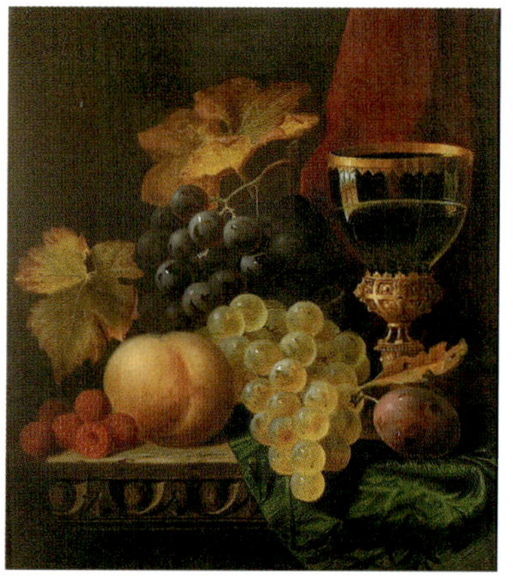

Baskett, Charles E. 1845–1929
Still Life with Wine Glass
oil on canvas 35 x 30
COLEM : 82A

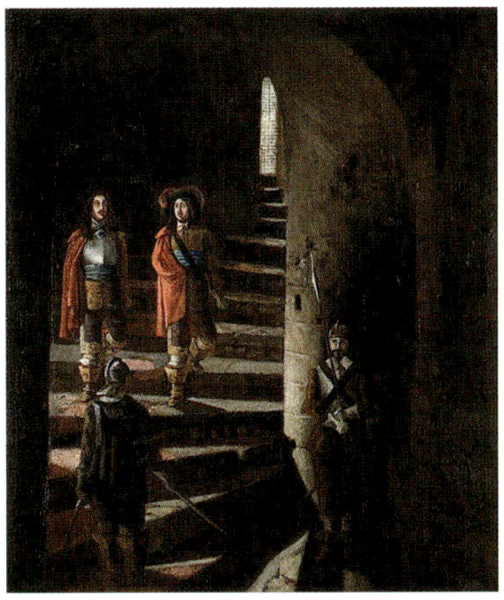

Becker, Harry 1865–1928
Lucas and Lisle Descending the Great Stair, Colchester Castle 1900–1920
oil on canvas 61 x 50.8
COLEM : 260A

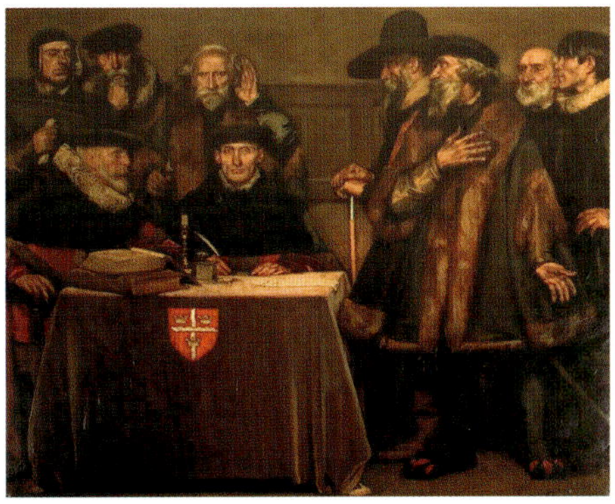

Becker, Harry 1865–1928
Dutch Refugees Fleeing from the Persecution of the Duke of Alva, Praying Permission of the Bailiffs of Colchester to Settle (...) 1913
oil on canvas 202 x 241
COLEM : 269A

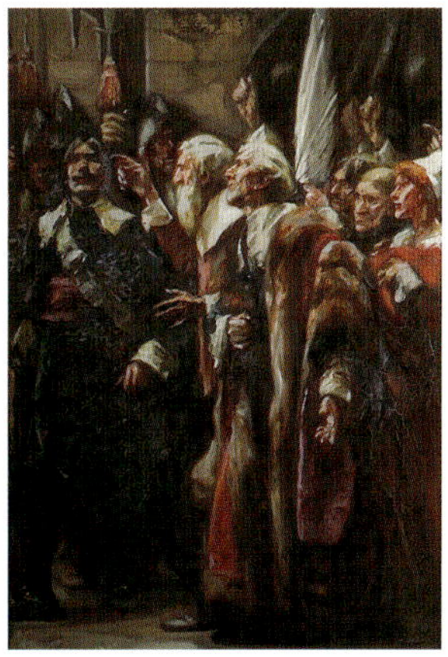

Becker, Harry 1865–1928
An Incident at the Siege of Colchester, 1648
oil on canvas 82.6 x 58.4
COLEM : 267A

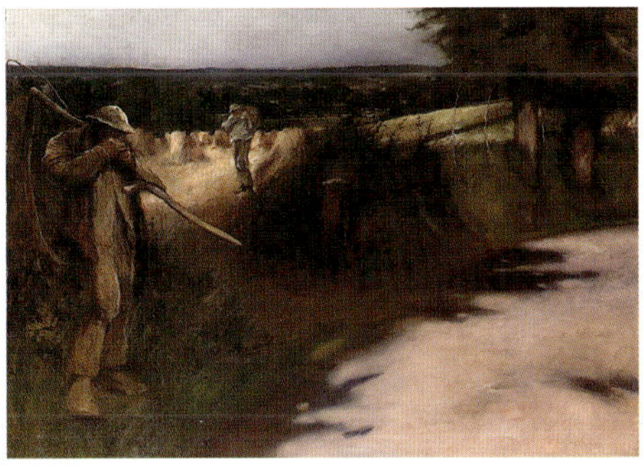

Becker, Harry 1865–1928
Harvesters, Suffolk
oil on canvas 60.5 x 81
COLEM : 1993.17

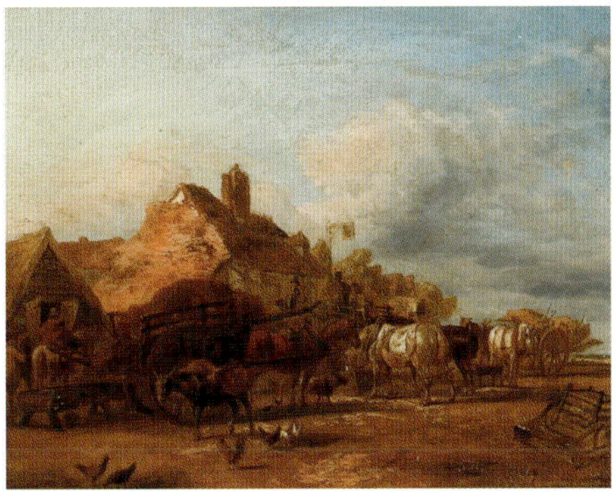

Bell, Thomas Currie 1873–1946
A Country Inn 1896?
oil on canvas 21.6 x 26.7
COLEM : 1972.124

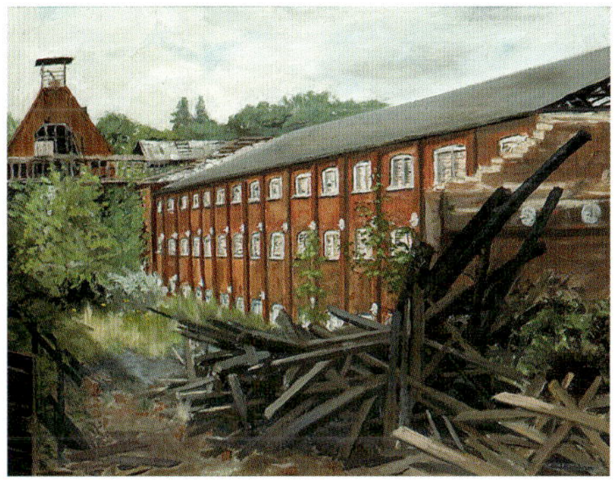

Benham, Barbara J. 1912–1999
The Maltings at the Hythe, Colchester c.1970
oil on board 39 x 49
COLEM : 1978.51

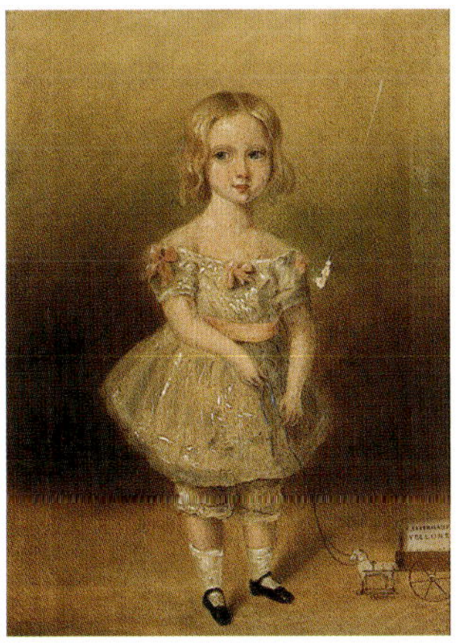

Beyerhaus, E. active 1857–1862
Charlotte Eleanor Cooper
oil on canvas 27.9 x 20.3
COLEM : 1966.OS.252

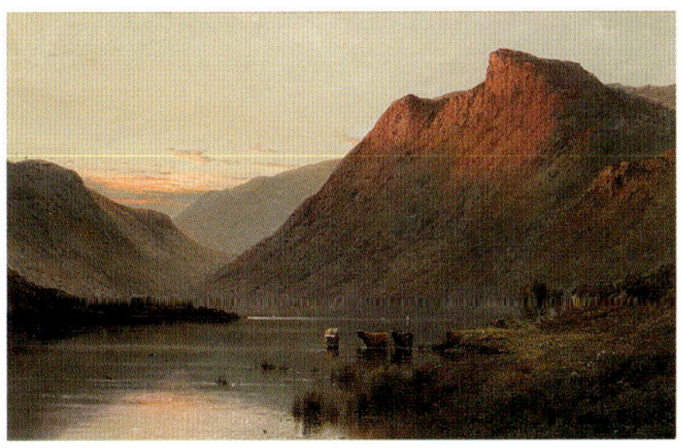

Breanski, Alfred de 1852–1928
Evening, Wonders of the Loch
oil on canvas 51 x 76.5
COLEM : 275A

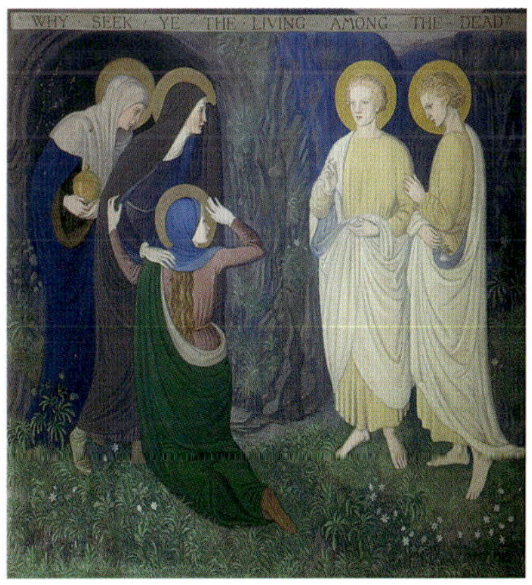

Bryans, H. W. active 1891–c.1922
The Three Marys at the Sepulchre c.1922
oil on canvas 104.5 x 98
COLEM : 1979.74

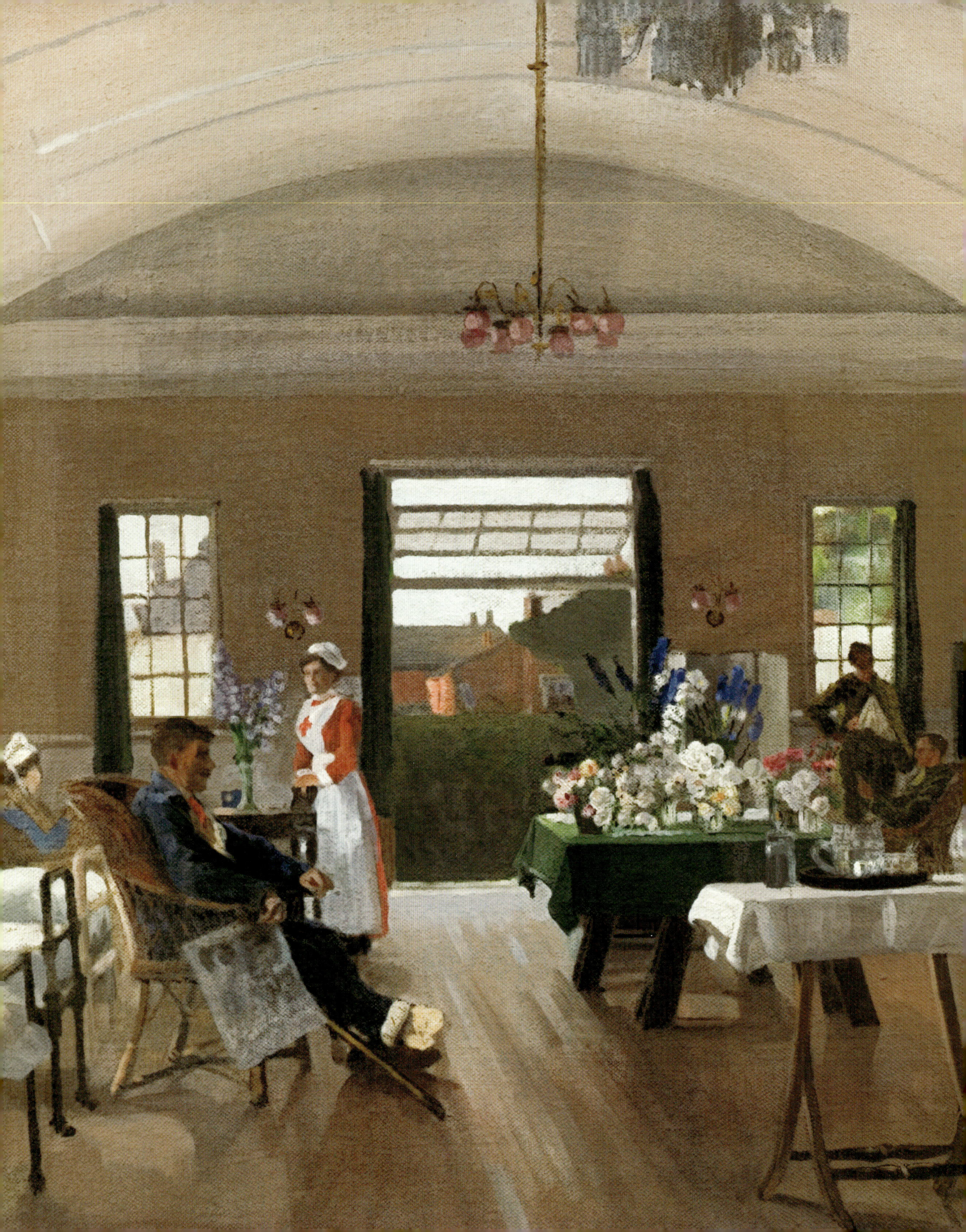

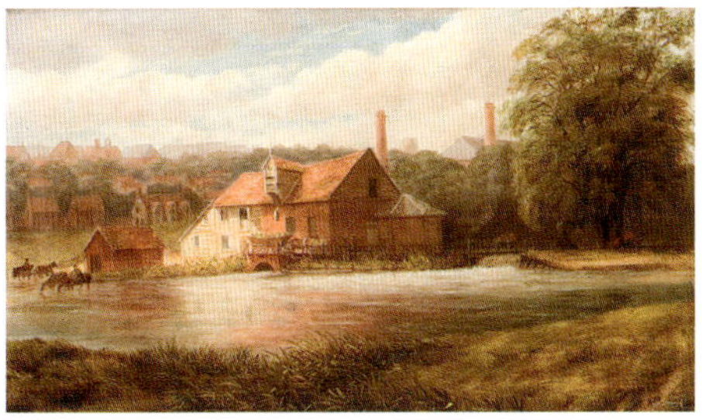

Buck, William active 1864–1900
Choppings Mill, Colchester 1900
oil on canvas 24.1 x 38.7
COLEM : 1955.2169A

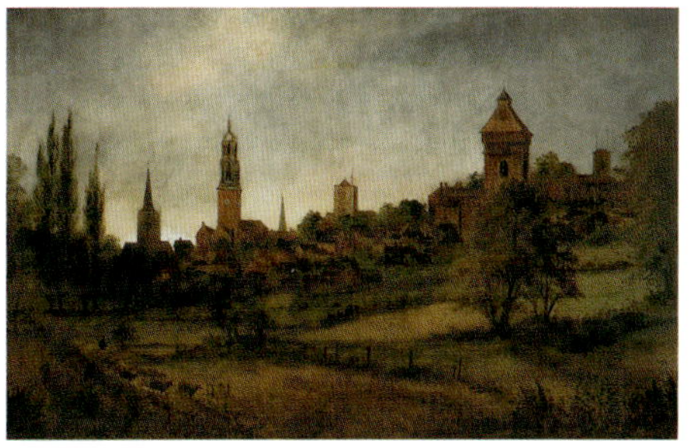

Bull, J.
Colchester, Dawn c.1900
oil on canvas 74 x 123
COLEM : 1986.16

Burton, Hal
Tram Crossing the North Bridge, Colchester
oil on board 23.5 x 38.1
COLEM : 1963.551

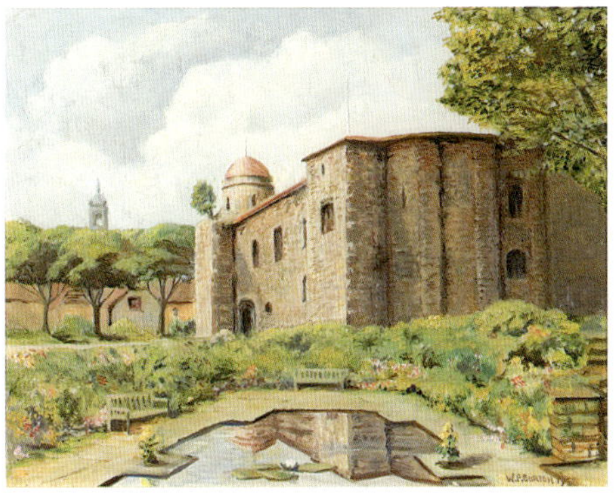

Burton, William Francis 1907–1995
Colchester Castle 1956
oil on board 37.5 x 50
COLEM : 1990.41

Campion, C. S.
Sir William Campion (killed at the Siege of Colchester, 1648)
oil on canvas 76.2 x 63.5
COLEM : 190A

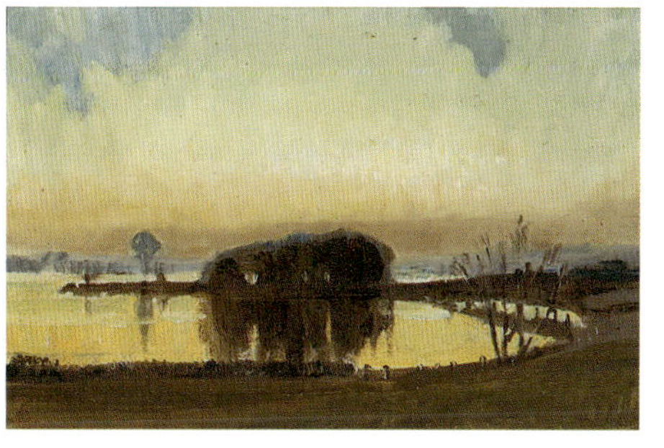

Carter, H. Malcolm
Abberton Reservoir at Sunset c.1970
oil on board 28 x 42
COLEM : 1984.61

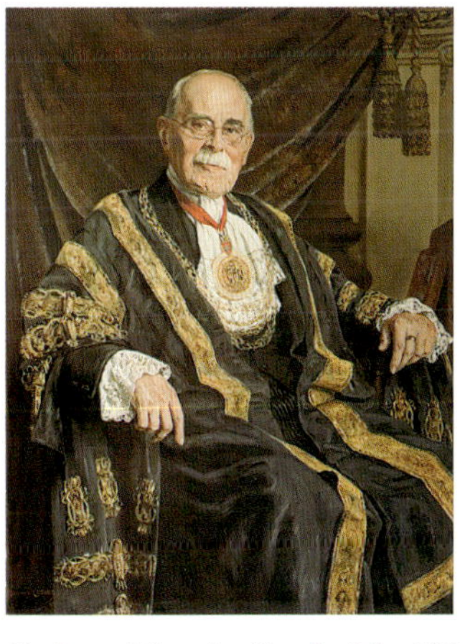

Codner, Maurice Frederick 1888–1958
Sir Gurney Benham (1859–1944), Mayor of Colchester 1942
oil on canvas 109.2 x 91.4
COLEM : 146A

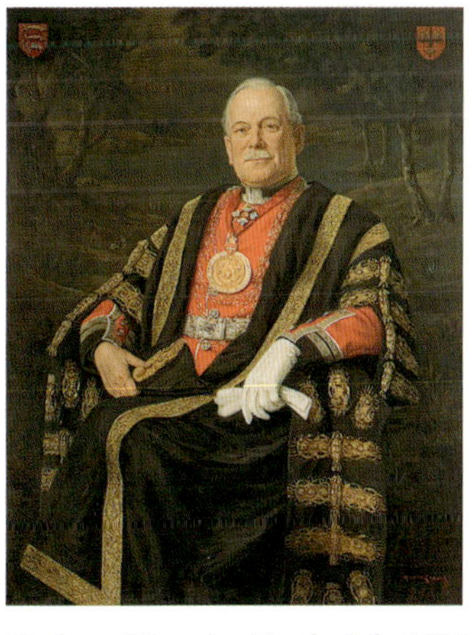

Codner, Maurice Frederick 1888–1958
Alderman Percy A. Sanders, CBE, DG, JP (Mayor of Colchester 1922 & 1939–1942) 1953
oil on canvas 134.6 x 109.2
COLEM : 148A

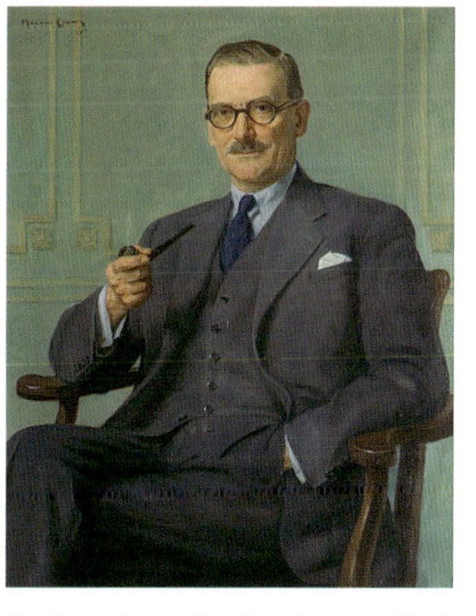

Codner, Maurice Frederick 1888–1958
Bernard Mason 1954
oil on canvas 91.5 x 71
COLEM : 1984.192

Facing page: Rose, George, 1882–1955, *The Ballroom at Budworth Hall, Ongar* (detail), 1915, Ongar War Memorial Hospital, (p. 218)

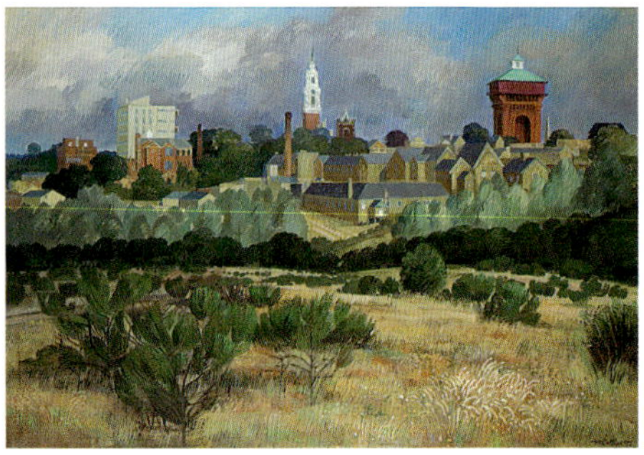

Collins, Henry 1910–1994
Sheepen, Colchester 1977
oil on canvas 75 x 105
COLEM : 1995.1

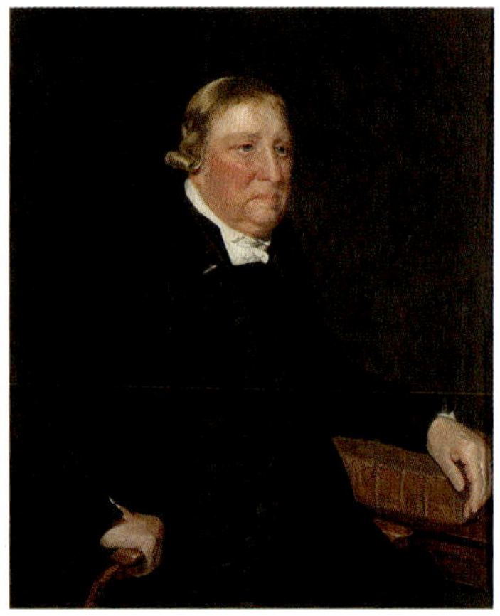

Constable, John 1776–1837
Reverend Thomas Lechmere Grimwood, DD (1740–1809), Headmaster of Dedham Grammar School
oil on canvas 90 x 72
COLEM : 191A

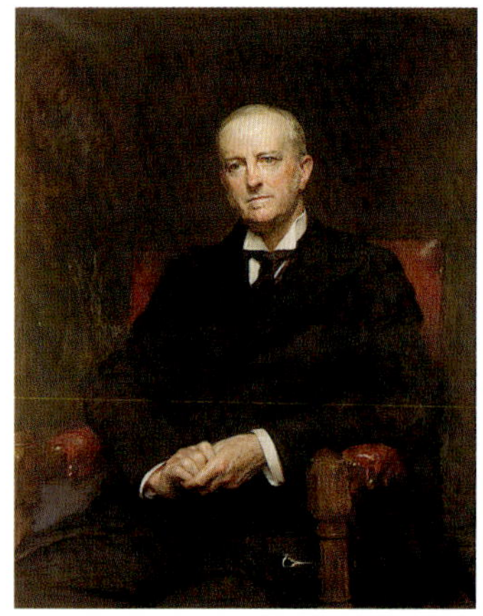

Cope, Arthur Stockdale 1857–1940
The Right Honourable James Round of Birch Hall, PC (1842–1916) c.1900
oil on canvas 109.2 x 86.4
COLEM : 161A

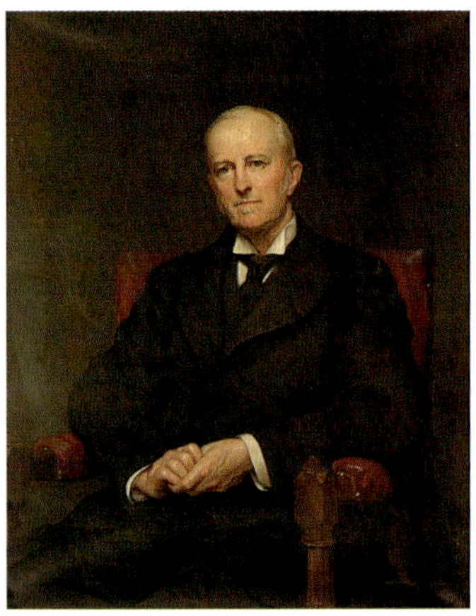

Cope, Arthur Stockdale (copy of) 1857–1940
The Right Honourable James Round of Birch Hall, PC (1842–1916)
oil on canvas 104.1 x 83.8
COLEM : 263A

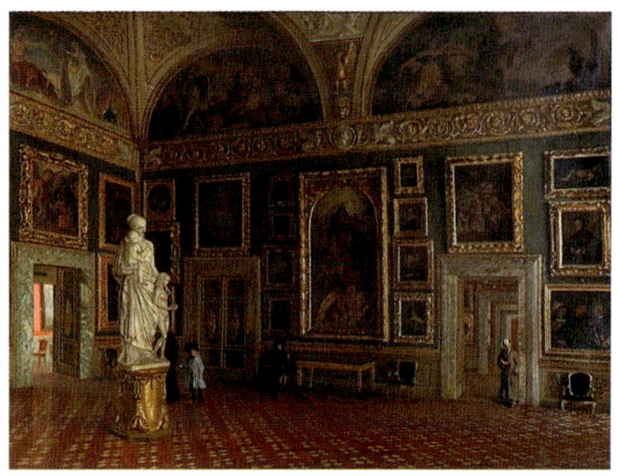

Corsi, Santi b.1871 & **Lavery, John** 1856–1941
Pitti Palace, Florence
oil on canvas 96.5 x 123
COLEM : 272A

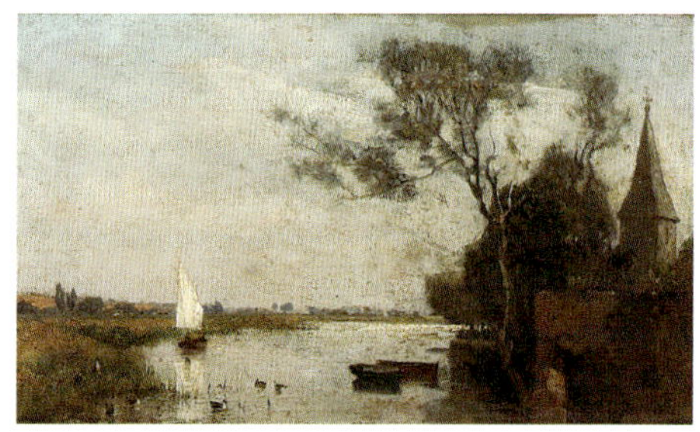

Cotman, Frederick George 1850–1920
At Fordwich, Kent
oil on board 25.4 x 40.6
COLEM : 283A

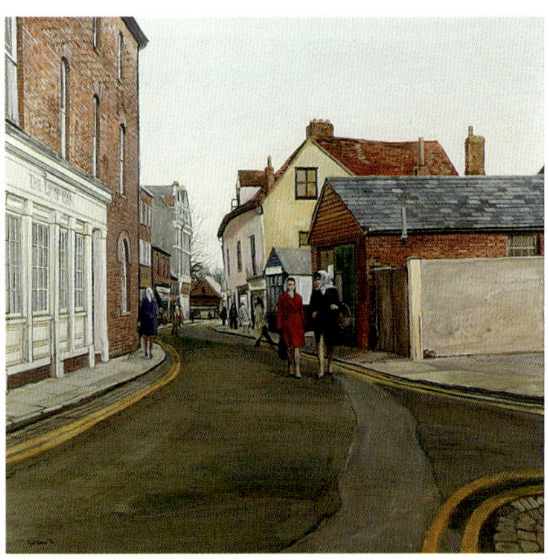

Cross, Gail
Culver Street, Colchester 1971
oil on board 91.4 x 91.4
COLEM : 1971.125

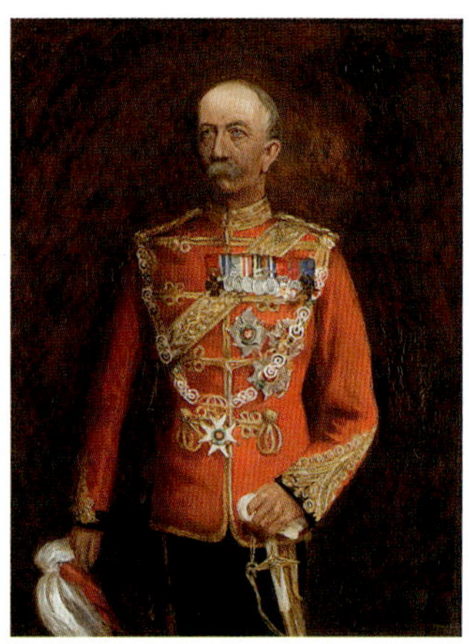

Cunningham, C. H.
Field Marshal Sir Evelyn Wood, VC, GCB, GCMG (commanded Colchester Garrison, 1886–1889) 1899
oil on panel 43.2 x 33
COLEM : 187A

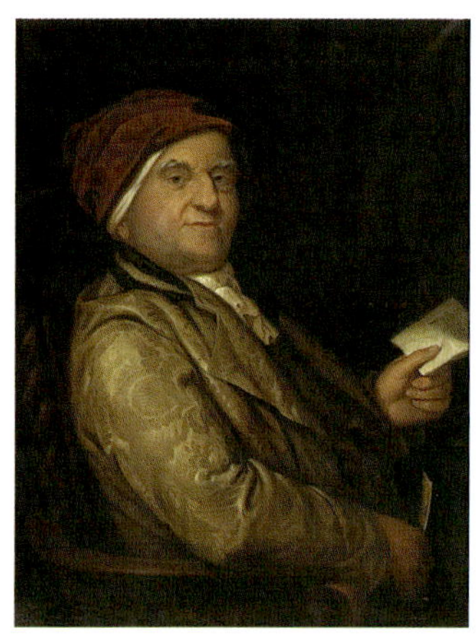

Dance, George the younger (copy of) 1741–1825
Reverend Samuel Parr, LLD (1742–1825), Headmaster of Colchester Grammar School
oil on canvas 88.9 x 71.1
COLEM : 277A

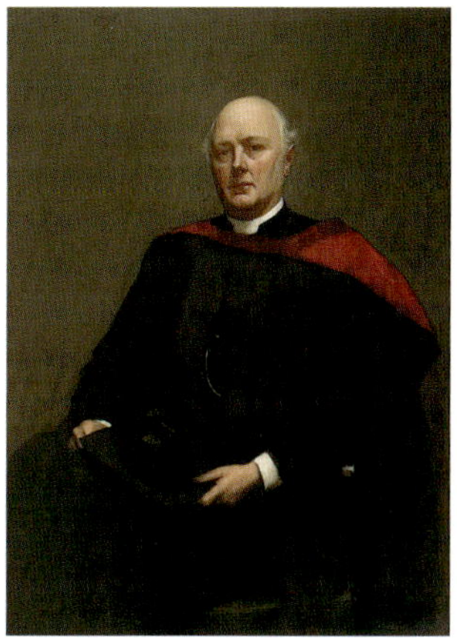

Daniell, Frank 1866–1932
Canon Irvine, MA 1895
oil on canvas 132.1 x 116.8
COLEM : 194A

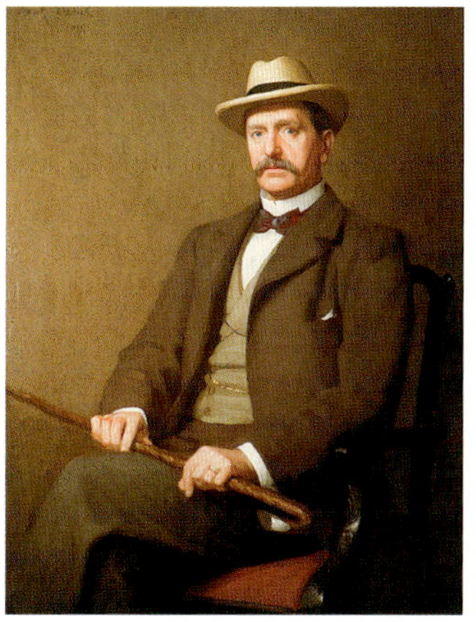

Daniell, Frank 1866–1932
John Kavanagh 1897
oil on canvas 116.8 x 88.9
COLEM : 1970.8

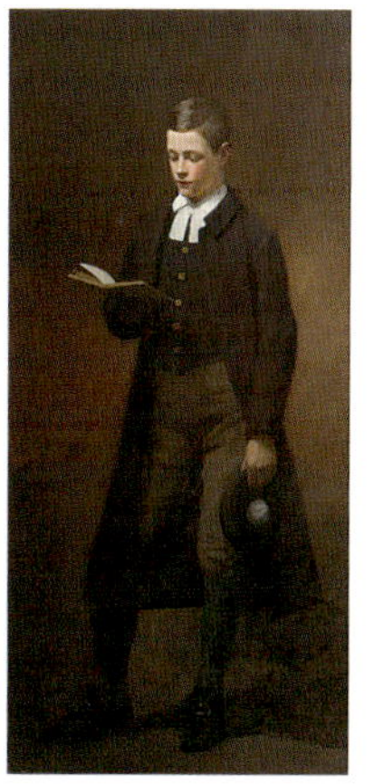

Daniell, Frank 1866–1932
Colchester Blue Coat School Boy c.1914
oil on canvas 175.9 x 80
COLEM : 270A

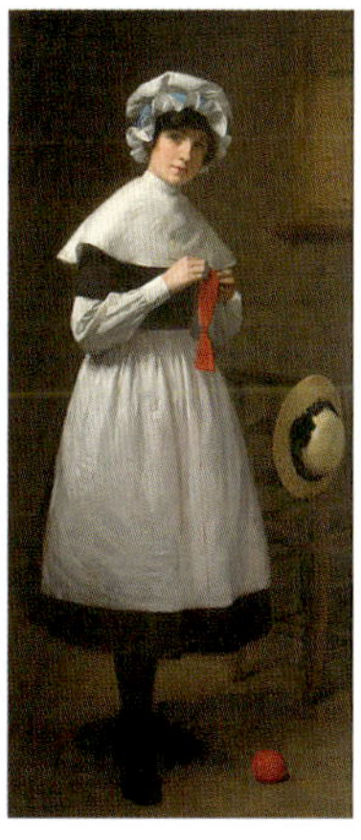

Daniell, Frank 1866–1932
Colchester Blue Coat School Girl c.1914
oil on canvas 175.9 x 80
COLEM : 268A

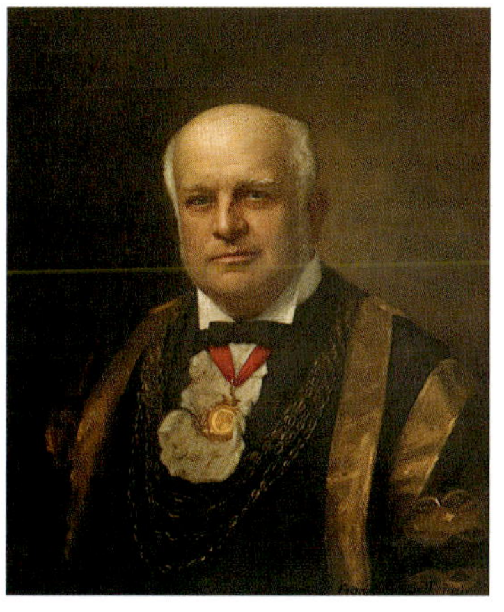

Daniell, Frank 1866–1932
Alderman Henry Goody, JP, Mayor of Colchester (1893, 1894 & 1905–1906) 1921
oil on canvas 76.2 x 63.5
COLEM : 180A

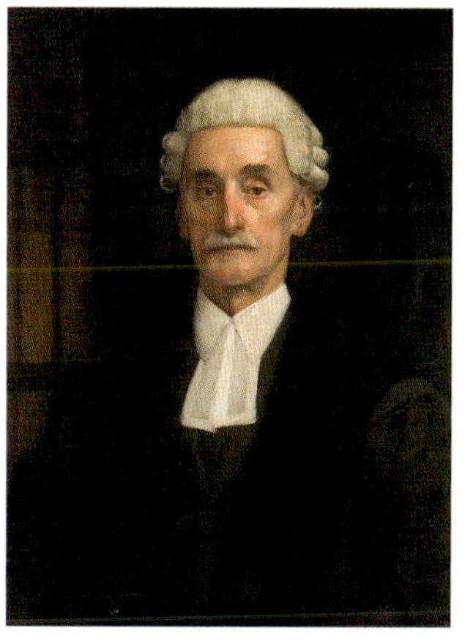

Daniell, Frank 1866–1932
Henry Charles Wanklyn, Town Clerk c.1925
oil on canvas 82.6 x 59.7
COLEM : 200A

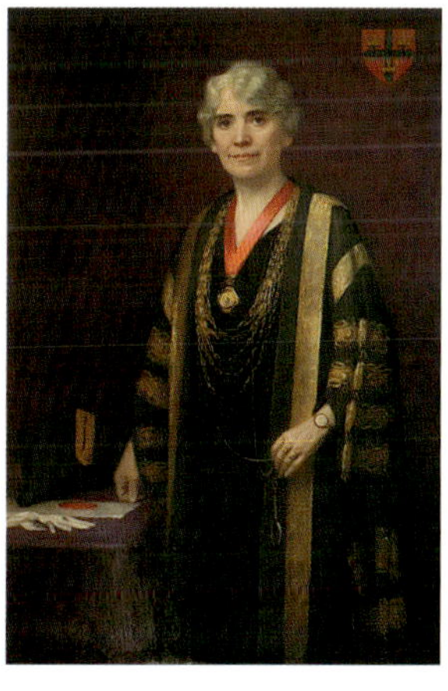

Daniell, Frank 1866–1932
Councillor Catherine Buchanan Alderton, JP (The first woman Mayor of Colchester, 1923–1924) 1926
oil on canvas 121.9 x 91.4
COLEM : 147A

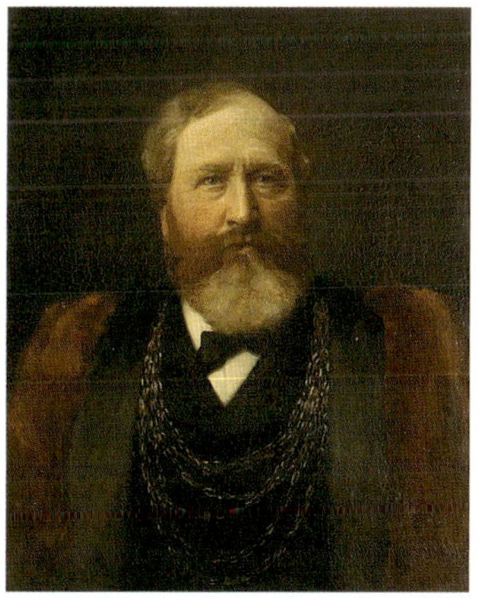

Daniell, Frank 1866–1932
Alderman Alfred Francis, Mayor of Colchester (1883)
oil on canvas 66 x 61
COLEM : 184A

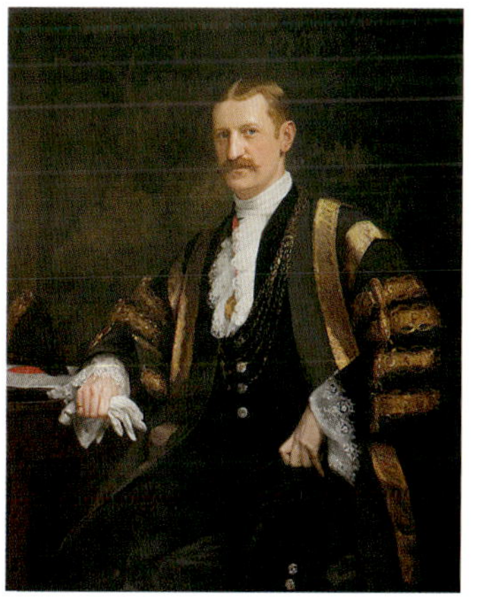

Daniell, Frank 1866–1932
Alderman Claude Egerton-Green, JP, Mayor of Colchester (1894–1895 & 1900–1901)
oil on canvas 124.5 x 99.1
COLEM : 144A

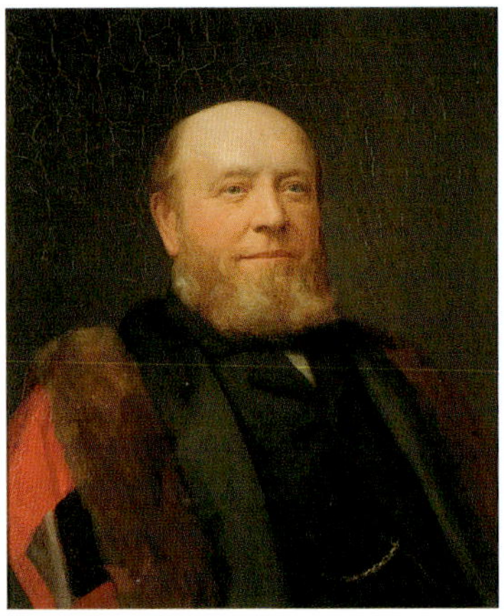

Daniell, Frank 1866–1932
Alderman Edwin Beard, JP
oil on canvas 61 x 50.8
COLEM : 176A

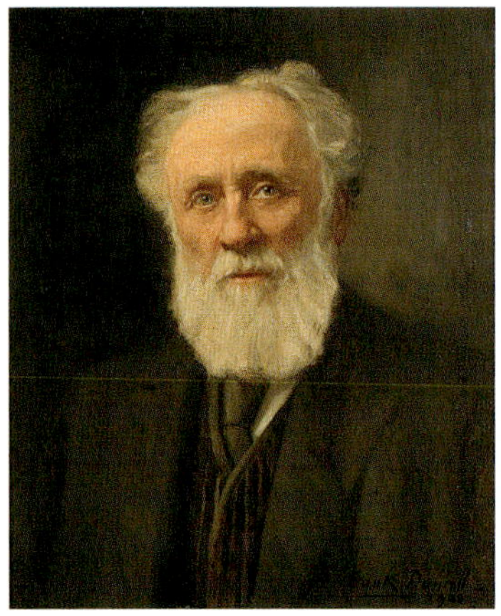

Daniell, Frank 1866–1932
Alderman Henry Laver, JP, FSA
oil on canvas 58.4 x 48.3
COLEM : 178A

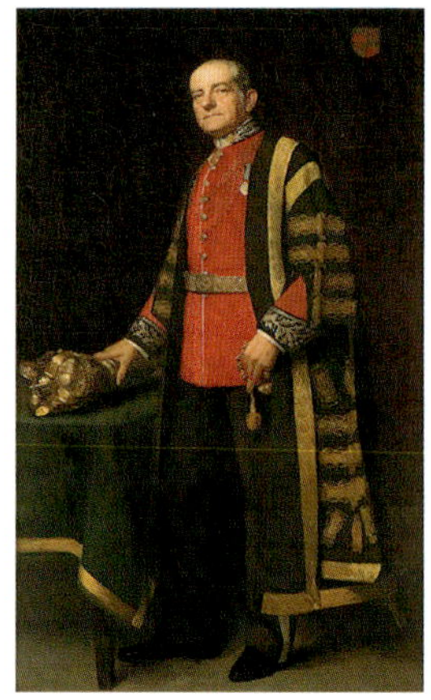

Daniell, Frank 1866–1932
Alderman Horace Egerton-Green, JP, DL, Mayor of Colchester (1886–1887 & 1898–1899)
oil on canvas 213.4 x 121.9
COLEM : 142A

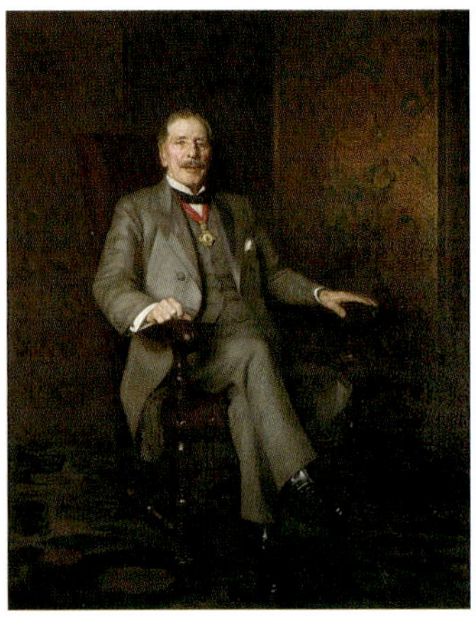

Daniell, Frank 1866–1932
Alderman James N. Paxman, CE (1832–1922), Mayor of Colchester (1887–1888 & 1897–1898)
oil on canvas 177.8 x 134.6
COLEM : 175A

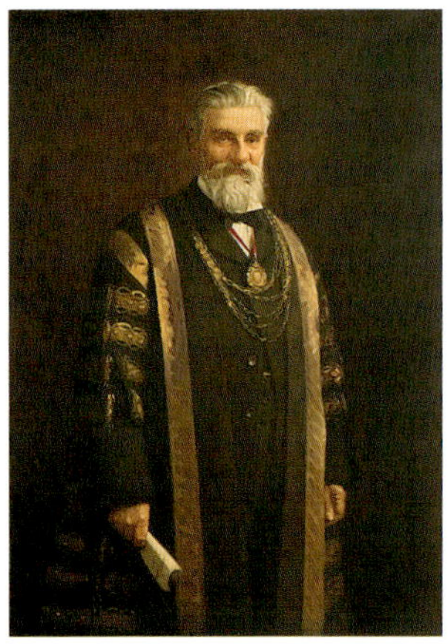

Daniell, Frank 1866–1932
Alderman James Wicks, JP, Mayor of Colchester (1895–1896)
oil on canvas 139.7 x 94
COLEM : 160A

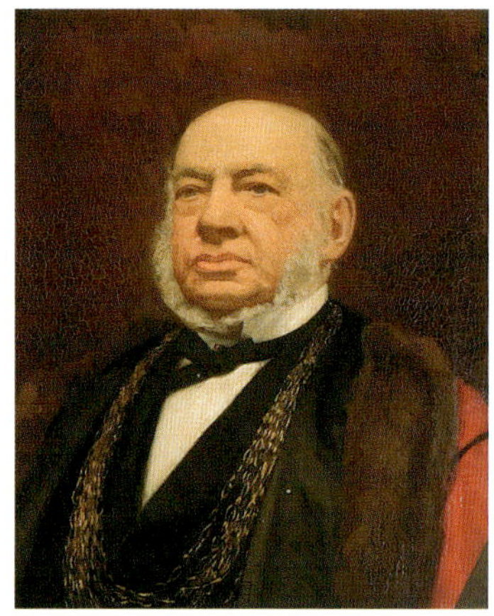

Daniell, Frank 1866–1932
Alderman John Kent (1805–1896), Mayor (1879)
oil on canvas 58.4 x 50.8
COLEM : 179A

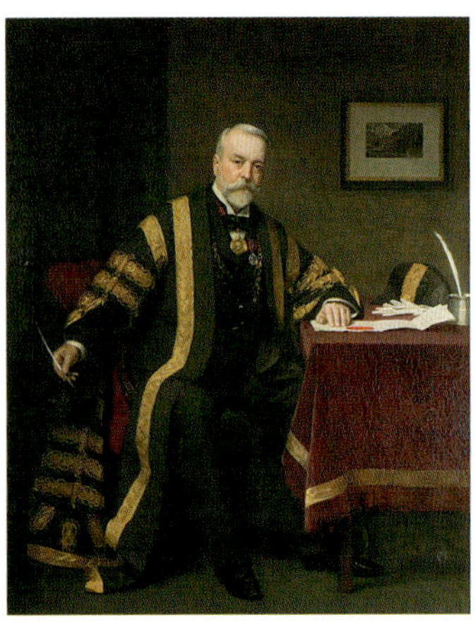

Daniell, Frank 1866–1932
Alderman Wilson Marriage, JP, Portreeve of Colchester
oil on canvas 182.9 x 144.8
COLEM : 210A

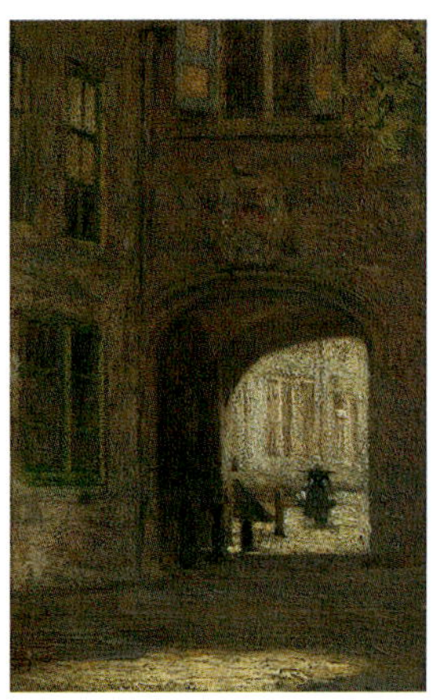

Daniell, Frank 1866–1932
Entrance at Middleburg, Holland
oil on board 22.9 x 15.2
COLEM : 1967.72

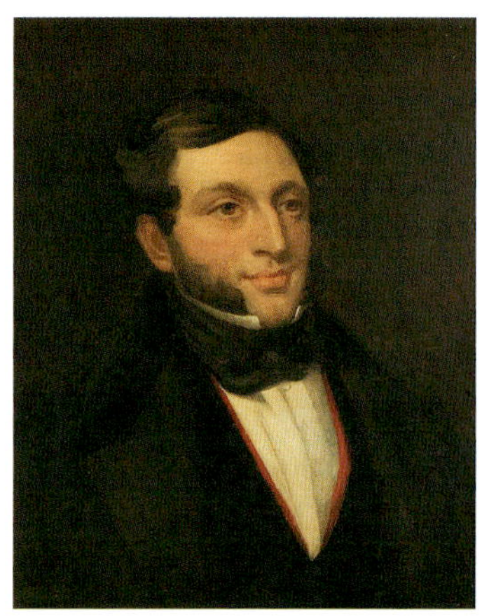

Daniell, Frank 1866–1932
George Bawtree
oil on canvas 68.6 x 50.8
COLEM : 181A

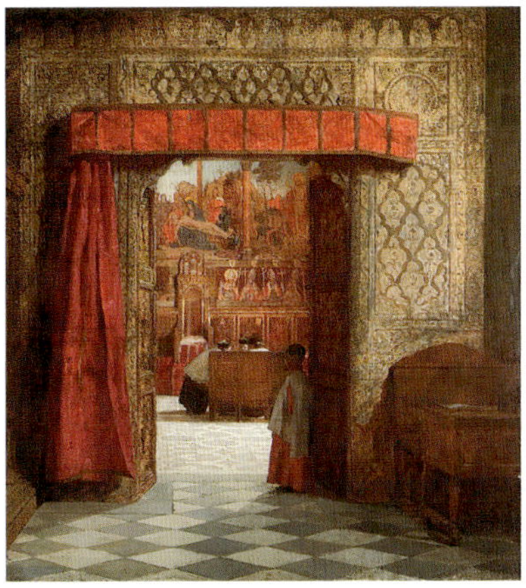

Daniell, Frank 1866–1932
Toledo Cathedral
oil on canvas 68.5 x 60.5
COLEM : 1984.276A

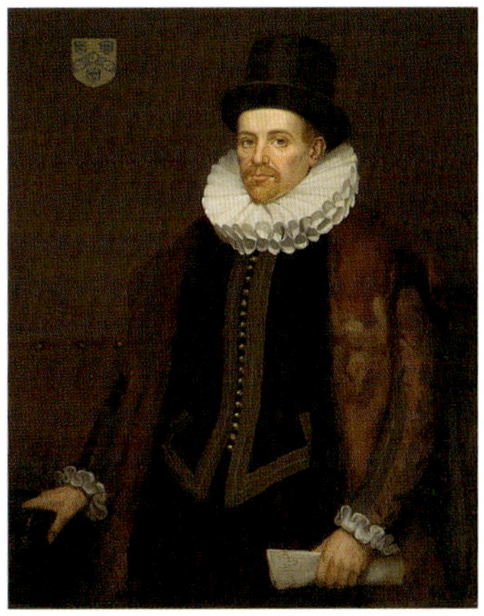

Daniell, Frank 1866–1932
William Gilberd of Colchester (1540–1603), Physician to Queen Elizabeth and King James, Founder of the Science of Magnetism
oil on canvas 119.4 x 88.9
COLEM : 150A

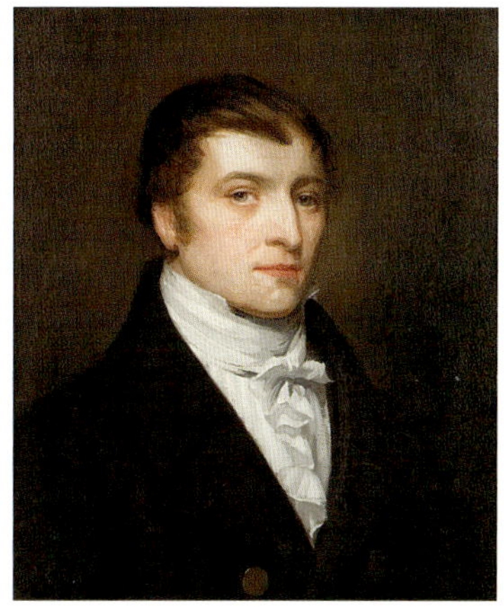

Daniell, Frank 1866–1932
William Sparling
oil on canvas 58.4 x 48.3
COLEM : 177A

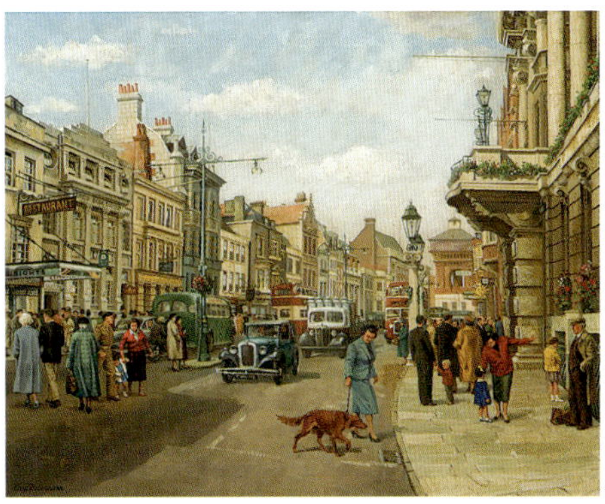

Debenham, Charles b.1933
High Street, Colchester, 1950 1955–1958
oil on canvas 50 x 59.5
COLEM : 2003.24

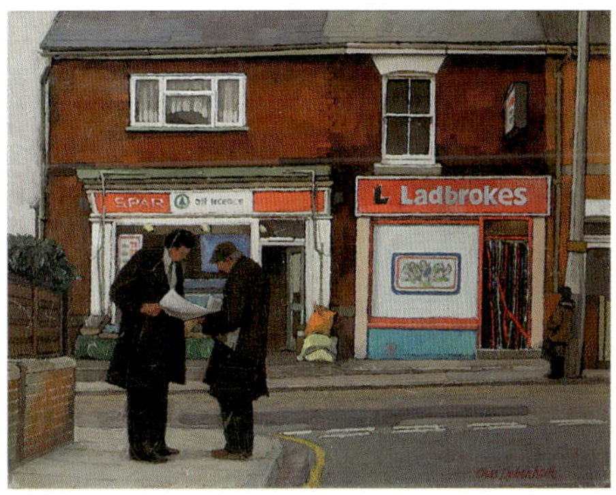

Debenham, Charles b.1933
Bourne Road Bookies, Colchester c.1990
oil on panel 20.5 x 25.5
COLEM : 1997.3.2

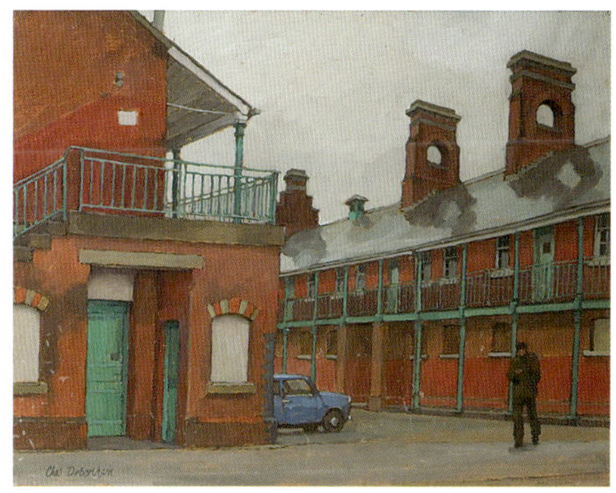

Debenham, Charles b.1933
Cavalry Barracks, Colchester c.1990
oil on panel 20.5 x 25.5
COLEM : 1997.3.3

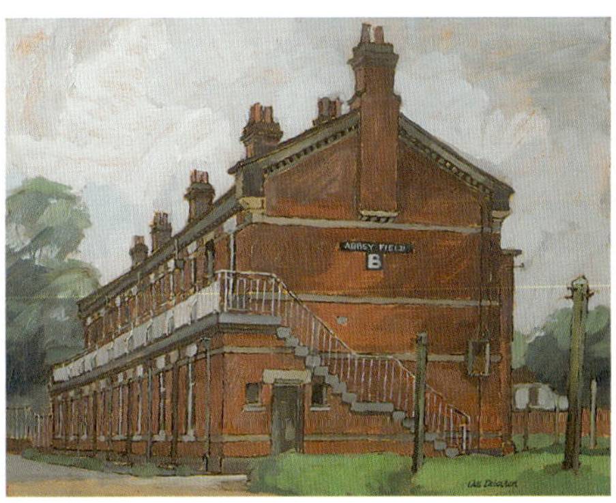

Debenham, Charles b.1933
Married Quarters, Abbey Fields c.1990
oil on panel 20.5 x 25.5
COLEM : 1997.3.4

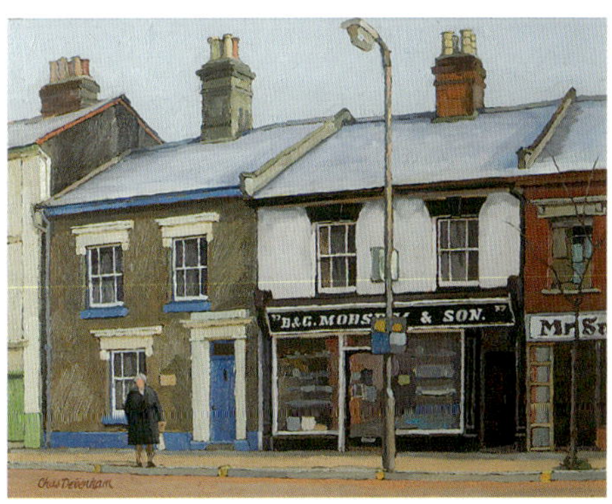

Debenham, Charles b.1933
North Station Road, Colchester c.1990
oil on panel 20.5 x 25
COLEM : 1997.3.1

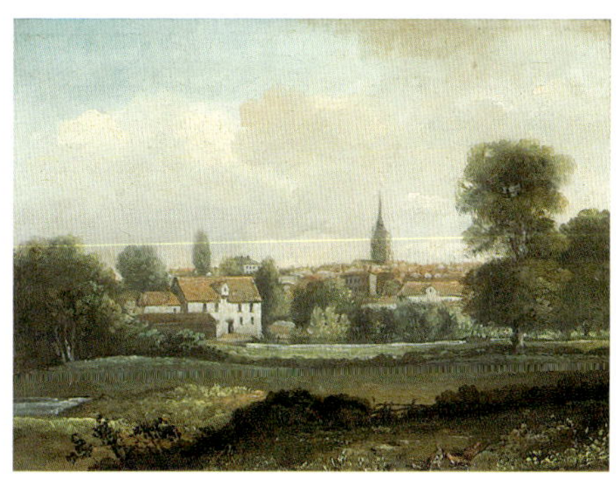

Dunthorne, James I (attributed to) 1730–1815
Colchester from Middle Mill
oil on board 19.1 x 25.4
COLEM : 1954.344

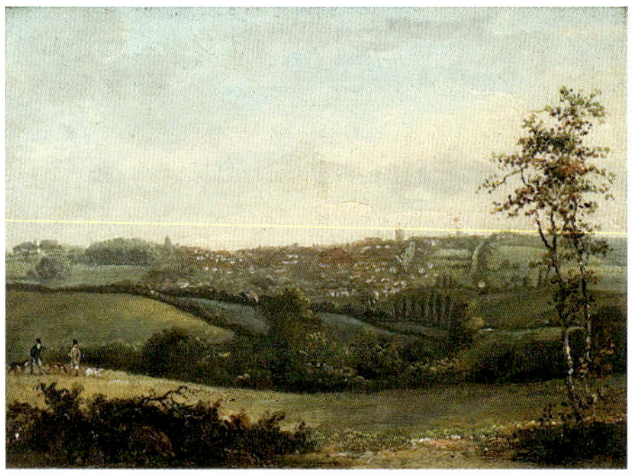

Dunthorne, James I (attributed to) 1730–1815
Colchester from the North-West
oil on board 19.1 x 25.4
COLEM : 1954.345

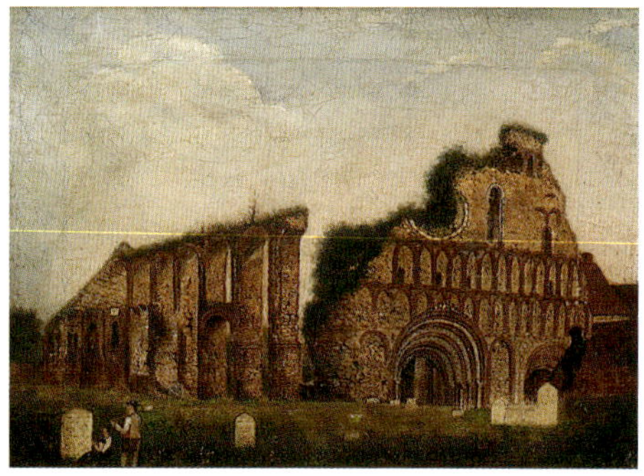

Dunthorne, James I (attributed to) 1730–1815
St Botolph's Priory, Colchester
oil on canvas 28.6 x 38.7
COLEM : 1966.OS.177

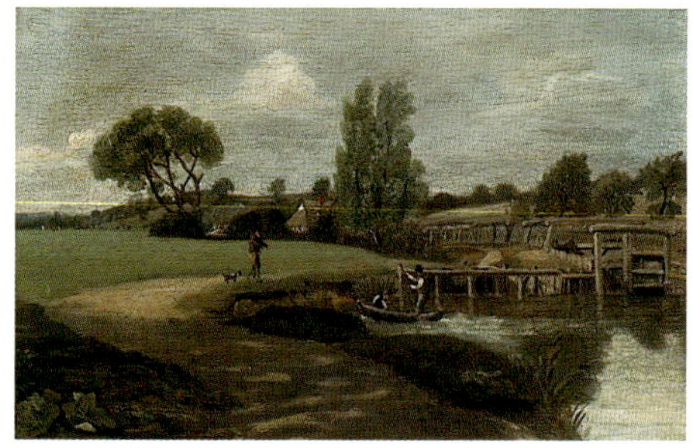

Dunthorne, John III 1770–1844
Flatford Lock, Suffolk 1814
oil on panel 23.5 x 35.9
COLEM : 1966.OS.176

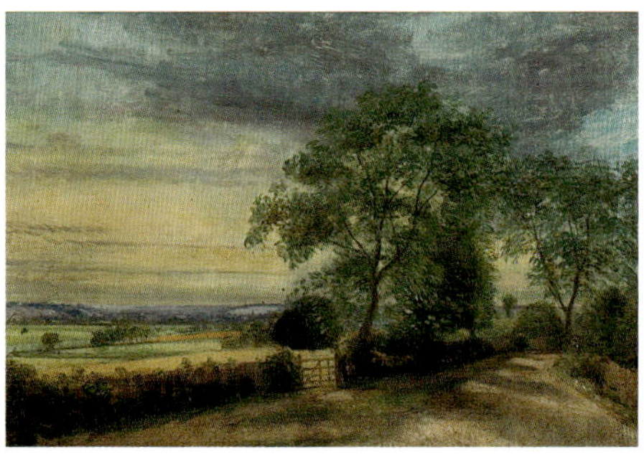

Dunthorne, John IV 1798–1832
A Country Lane
oil on canvas 22.9 x 33.7
COLEM : 1966.OS.86

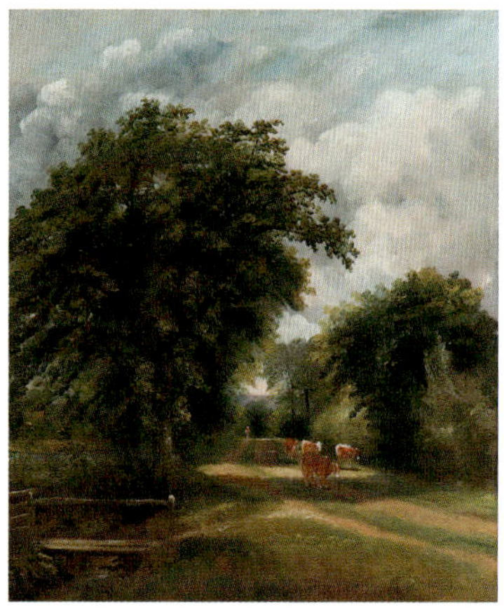

Dunthorne, John IV 1798–1832
Cows on a Country Lane
oil on canvas 36 x 30
COLEM : 1966.OS.273

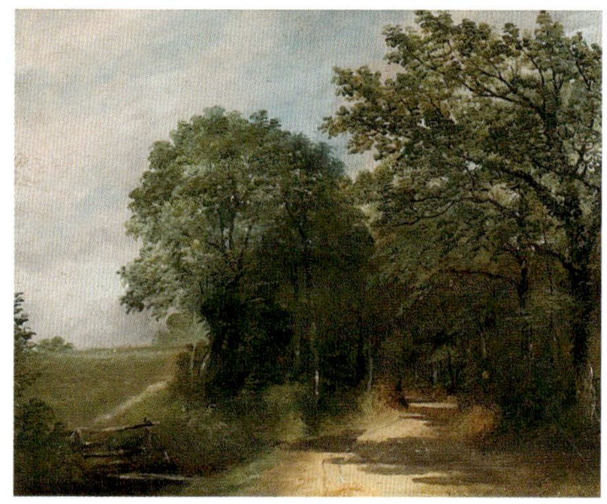

Dunthorne, John IV 1798–1832
Lane with Stile and Field, Dedham Vale
oil on board 24.1 x 28.6
COLEM : 1966.OS.91

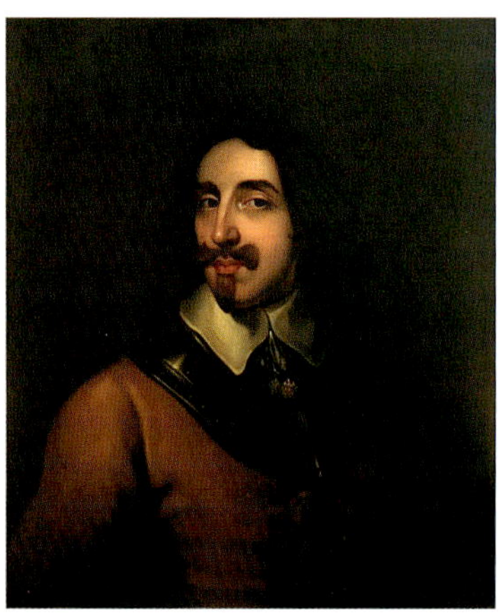

Dyck, Anthony van (after) 1599–1641
Arthur Capel 1900
oil on canvas 78.7 x 68.6
COLEM : 171A

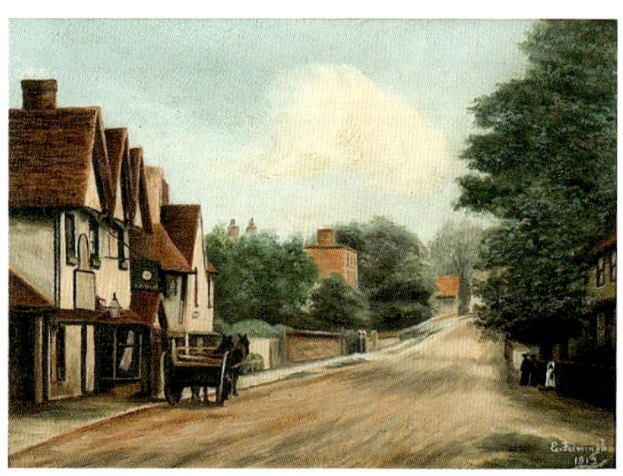

Felmingham, E.
Kelvedon High Street 1912
oil on canvas 43.5 x 59
COLEM : 1985.104

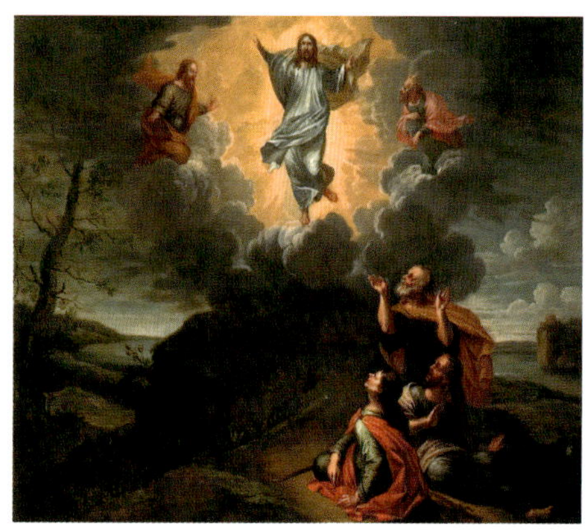

Flemish School
The Transfiguration
oil on copper 84 x 104
COLEM : 75A

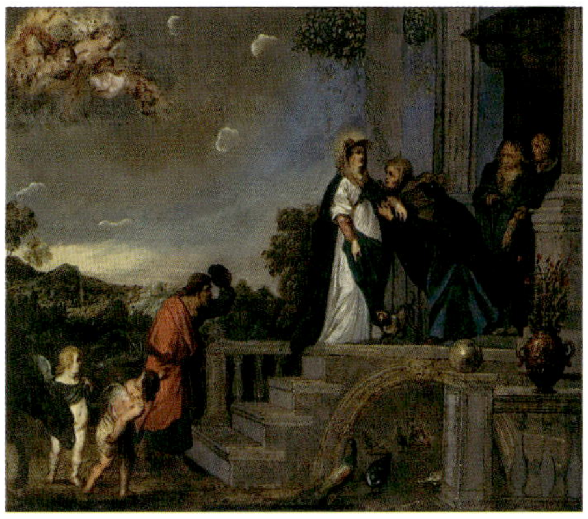

Flemish School
The Visitation
oil on copper 69.5 x 87
COLEM : 76A

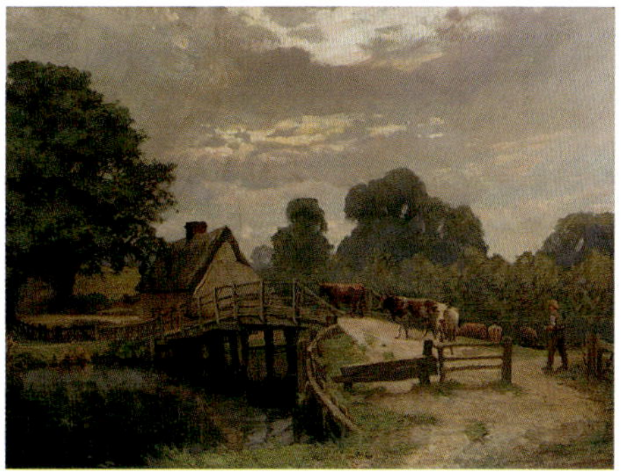

Friswell, Harry P. Hain 1857–after 1906
Flatford Bridge, Suffolk
oil on canvas 70 x 90
COLEM : 265A

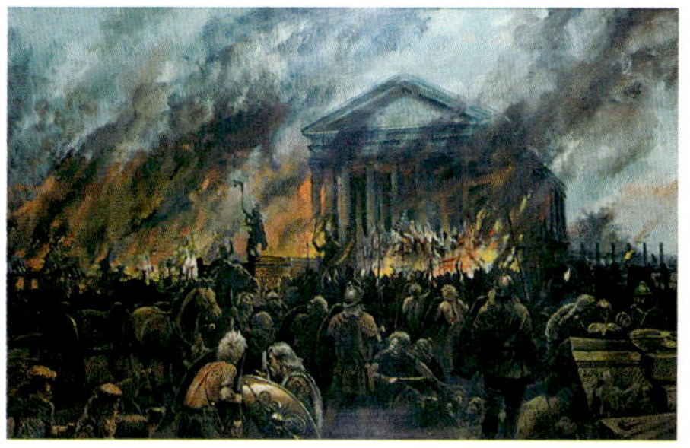

Froste, Peter b.1935
Sack of the Temple of Claudius, Colchester
1991
oil on canvas 62 x 90
COLEM : 1991.67

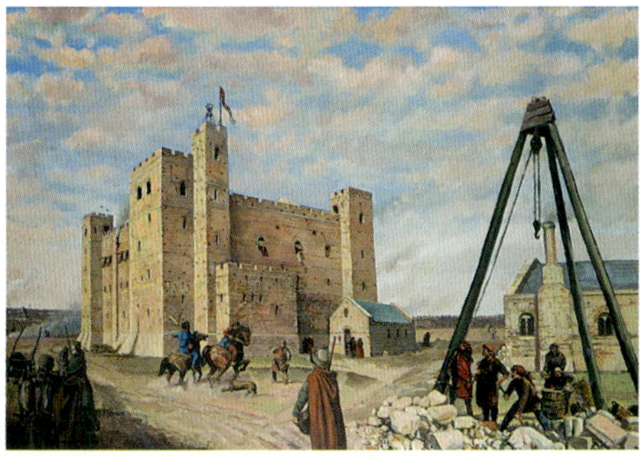

Froste, Peter b.1935
Colchester Castle under Construction
oil on wood 61 x 85
COLEM : 1998.89.1

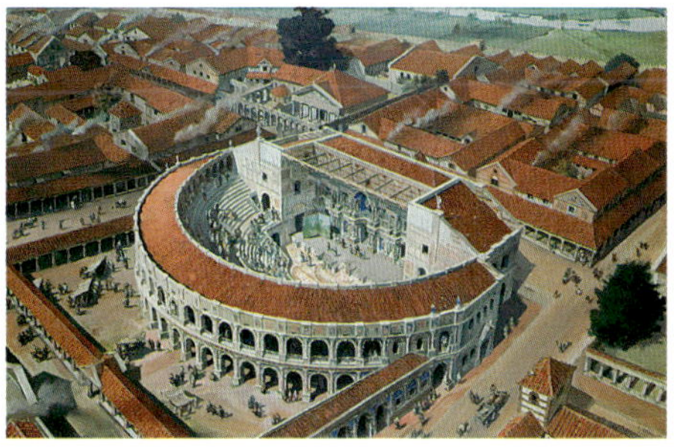

Froste, Peter b.1935
Roman Theatre, Colchester
oil on board 58 x 88
COLEM : 1998.89.2

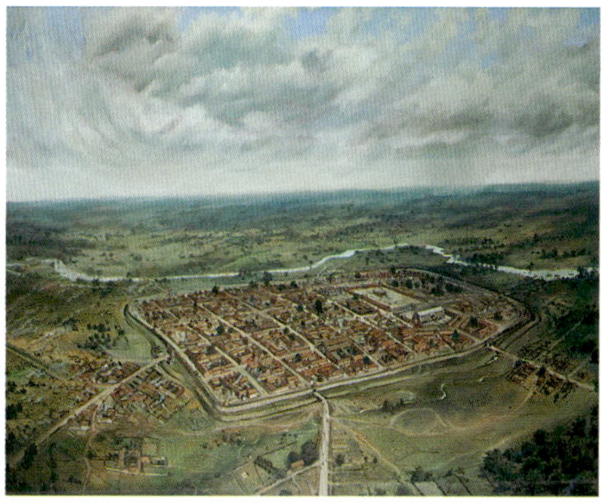

Froste, Peter b.1935
View of Roman Colchester from the South-West
acrylic on canvas 77 x 84
COLEM : 1992.49

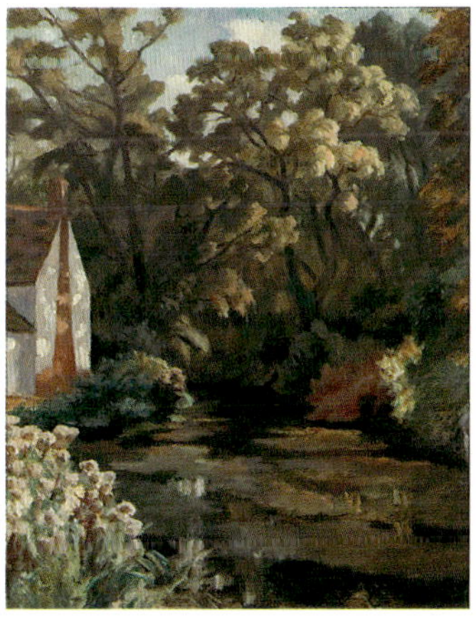

Fry, Roger Eliot 1866–1934
Willy Lott's Cottage, Flatford
oil on canvas 54.5 x 43
COLEM : 1993.16

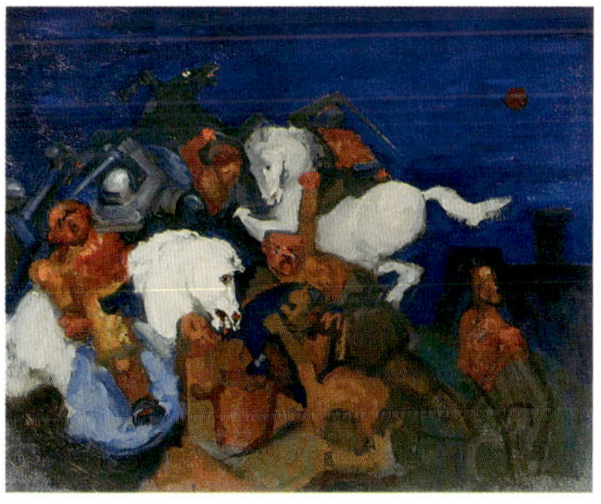

Fussell, Michael 1927–1974
A Scene from the Siege of Colchester
oil on canvas 91 x 108.5
COLEM : 1993.63

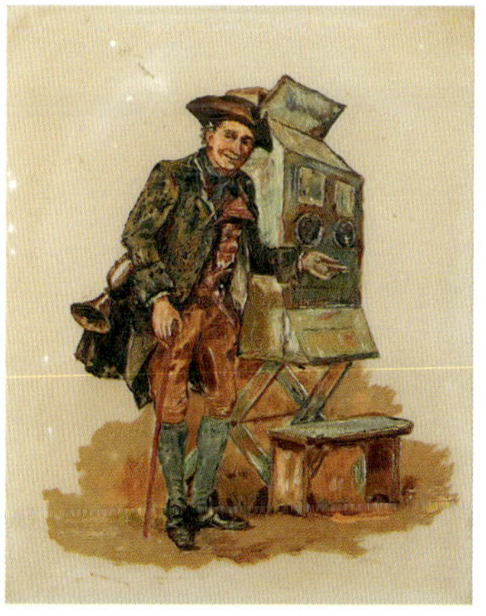

Gale, Charles T.
The Peep Show Man 1890–1893
oil on clay 23 x 18.5
COLEM : 1969.16

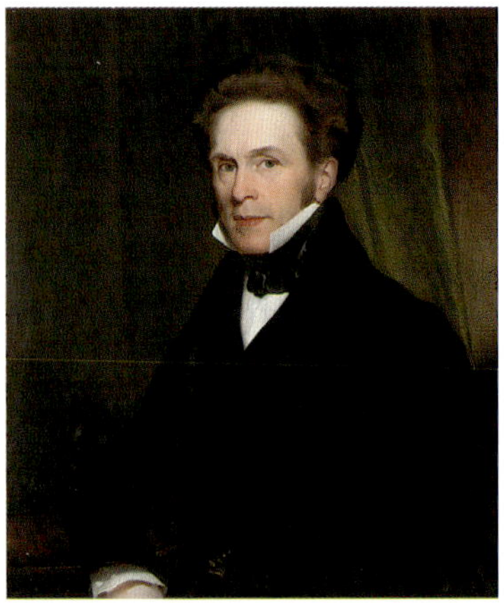

Gilbert, Josiah 1814–1892
Isaac Taylor II
oil on canvas 76 x 63
COLEM : 1953.407

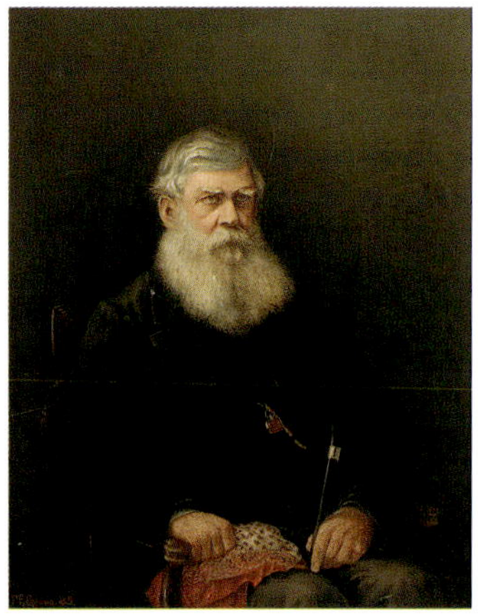

Grone, Ferdinand E. c.1845–1920
Edward Marriage, President of the Colchester Friends' Adult Schools 1895
oil on canvas 109.2 x 83.8
COLEM : 162A

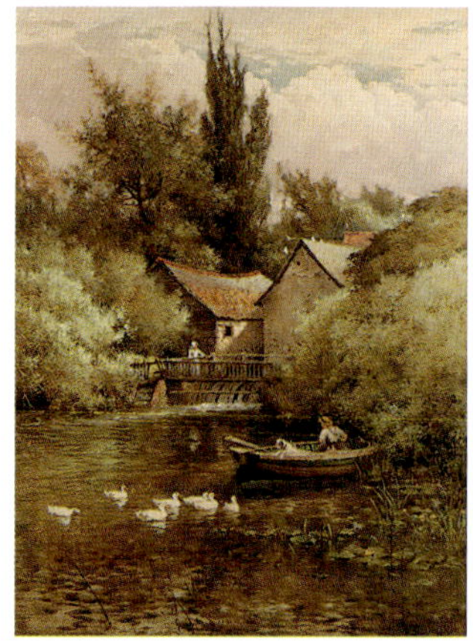

Grone, Ferdinand E. c.1845–1920
Flatford Mill, Suffolk
oil on canvas 126.4 x 90.8
COLEM : 271A

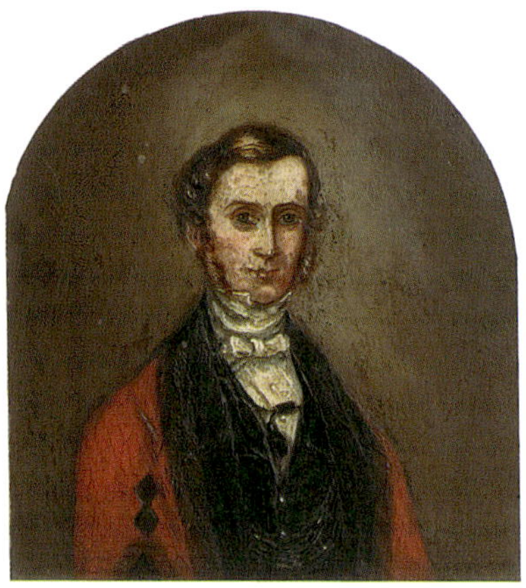

Haddock, Jesse E.
Charles H. Hawkins, JP (Mayor of Colchester 1848–1849, 1865, 1870 & 1871) 1849
oil on panel 15.2 x 14
COLEM : 149A

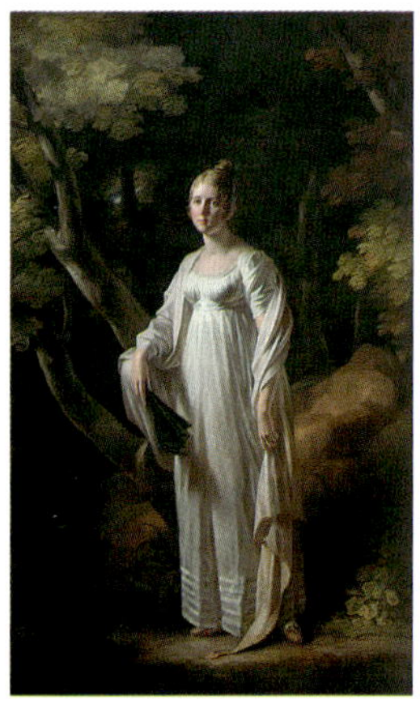

Halls, John James 1776–1834
Julia Halls Holding an Umbrella 1800–1825?
oil on canvas 237.2 x 146.5
COLEM : 1984.117

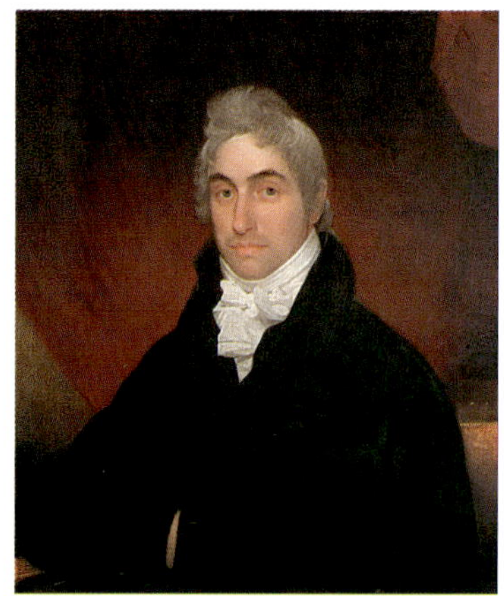

Halls, John James 1776–1834
Reverend John Savill (1780–1826) 1811
oil on canvas 77 x 63
COLEM : 202A

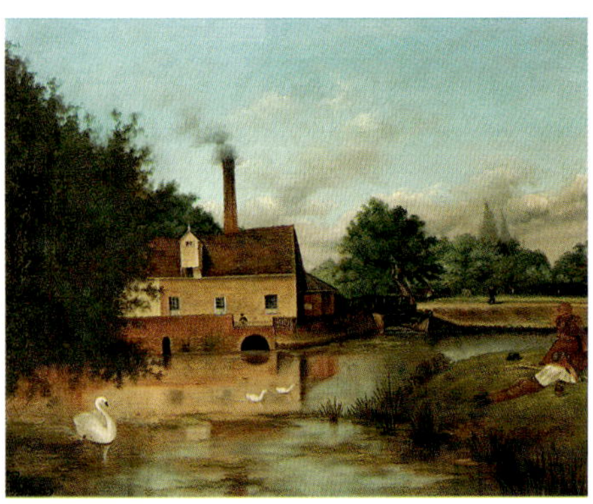

Hansard, W. D.
Middle Mill, Colchester 1896
oil on canvas 48.9 x 59.1
COLEM : 1944.56

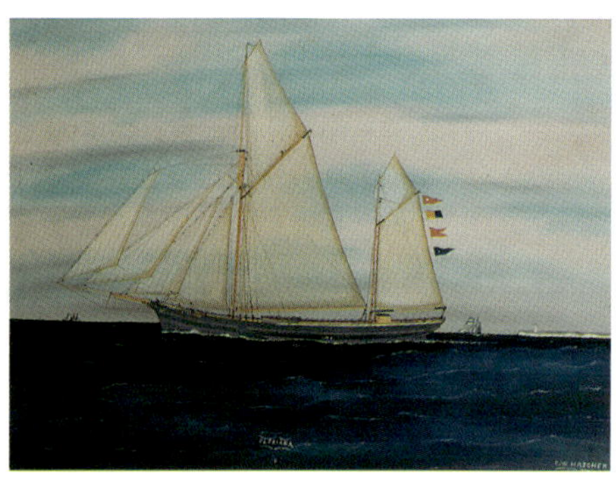

Hatcher, E. W.
'Cloriana' 1890
oil on canvas 40.6 x 61
COLEM : 31A

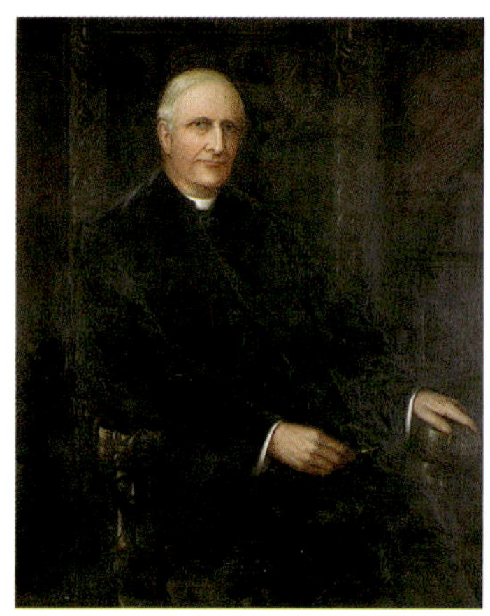

Head, Charles 1850–1926
Reverend Sabine Baring-Gould (1834–1924), Rector of East Mersea (1871–1881) 1911
oil on canvas 127 x 101.6
COLEM : 196A

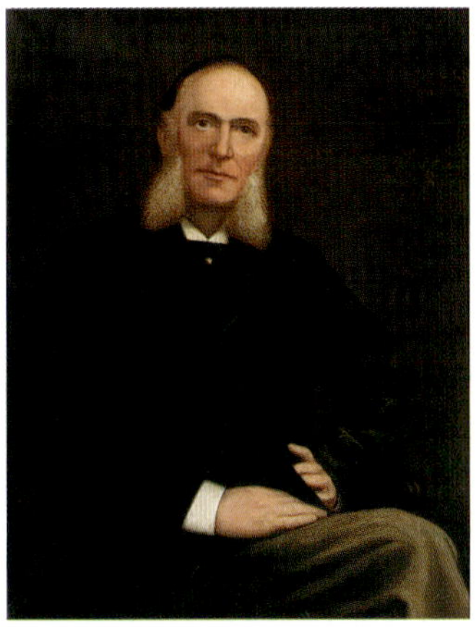

Head, Charles 1850–1926
Benjamin Revett Cant, the Eminent Rosarian
oil on canvas 99.1 x 73.7
COLEM : 199A

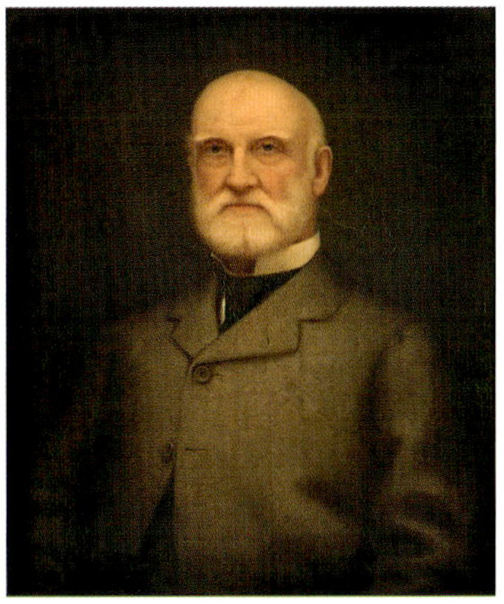

Head, Charles 1850–1926
Charles Henry Hawkins, JP
oil on canvas 76.2 x 63.5
COLEM : 183A

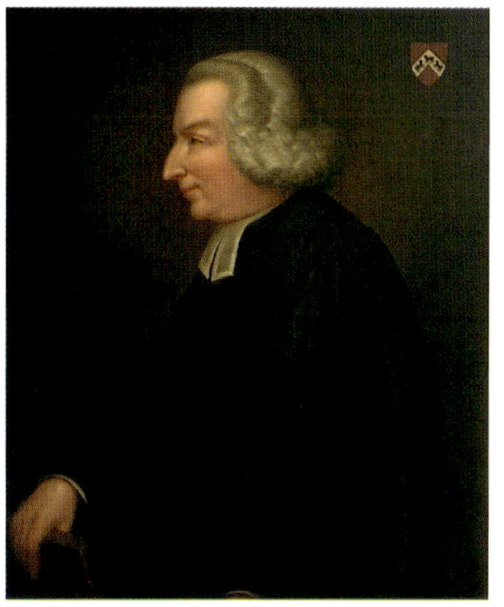

Head, Charles 1850–1926
Reverend Philip Morant (1700–1770), Historian of Essex and Colchester
oil on canvas 94 x 78.7
COLEM : 163A

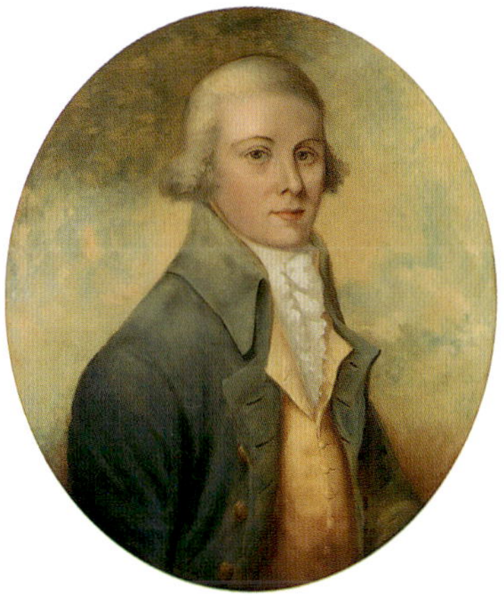

Head, Charles 1850–1926
William Mason (d.1802) Alderman of the Borough of Colchester, Mayor (1796–1797)
oil on canvas 76.2 x 63.5
COLEM : 157A

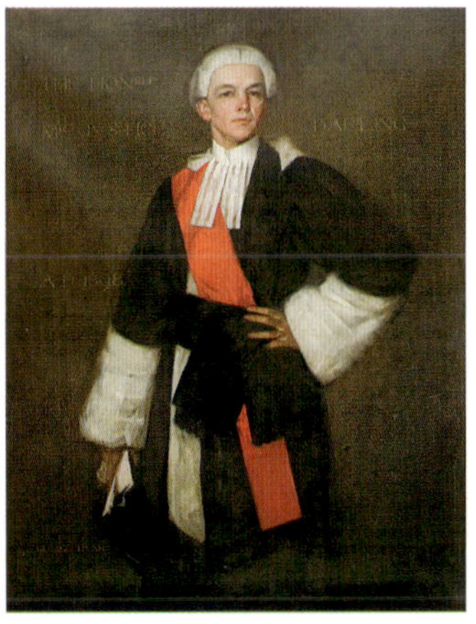

Henry, George F. 1858–1943
The Honourable Mr Justice Darling (1849–1936), Judge of the King's Bench (1897–1936) 1898
oil on canvas 142.2 x 114.3
COLEM . 140A

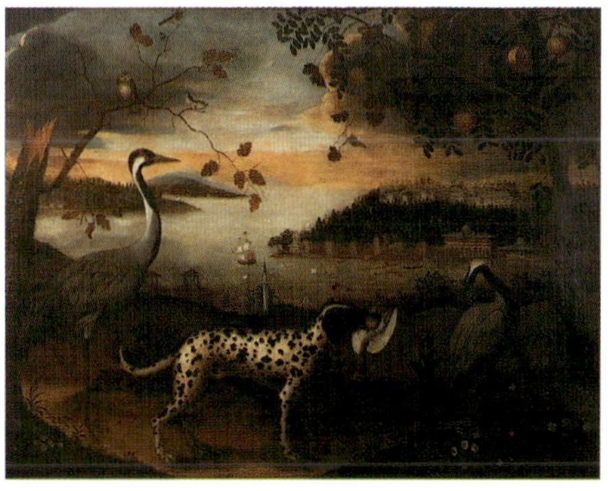

Hoynk, Otto (attributed to) c.1630–c.1686
The Spotted Dog (The Golden Horn at Constantinople)
oil on canvas on wooden panel 170 x 214
COLEM : 2005.66

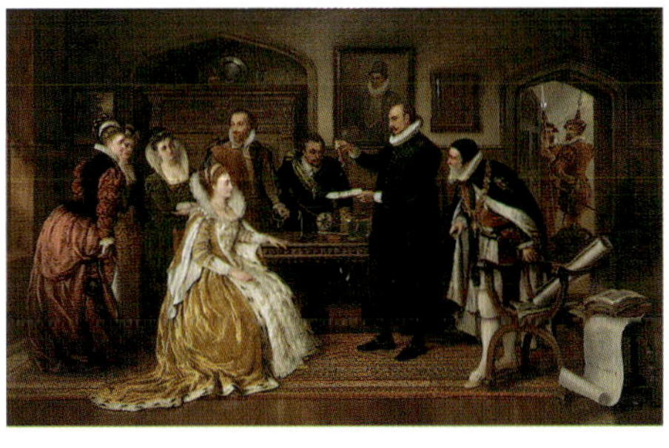

Hunt, Arthur Ackland active 1865–1902
Dr William Gilberd Showing His Experiments on Electricity to Queen Elizabeth and Her Court
oil on canvas 142.2 x 218.4
COLEM : 151A

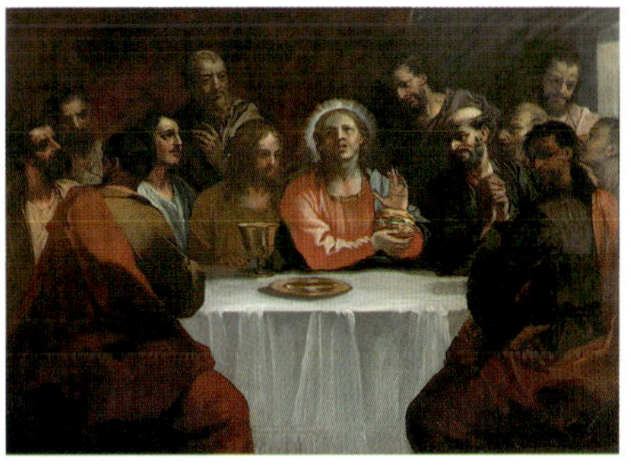

Italian (Venetian) School
The Last Supper c.1700
oil on canvas 135 x 184
COLEM : 1984.111

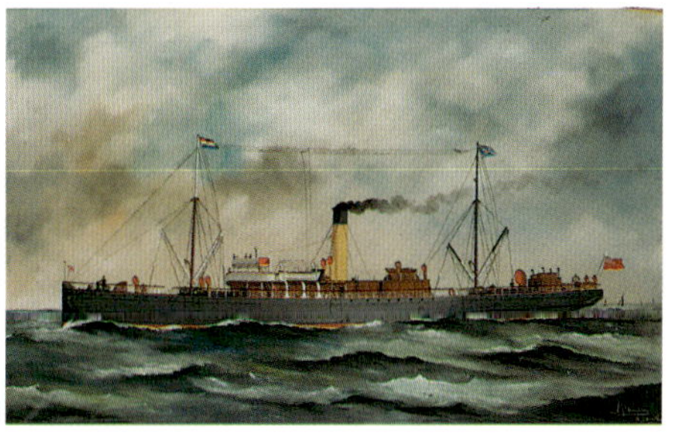

Jensen, Alfred 1859–1935
'SS Colchester' 1915
oil on canvas 50 x 77.5
COLEM : 1984.197

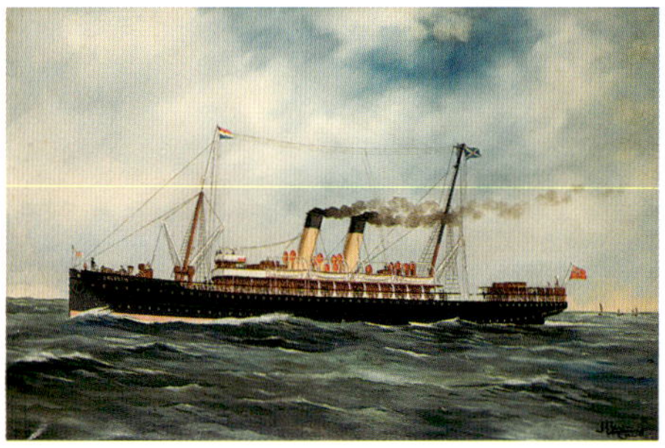

Jensen, Alfred 1859–1935
'SS Dresden' 1915
oil on canvas 49.5 x 73.7
COLEM : 1963.614.4

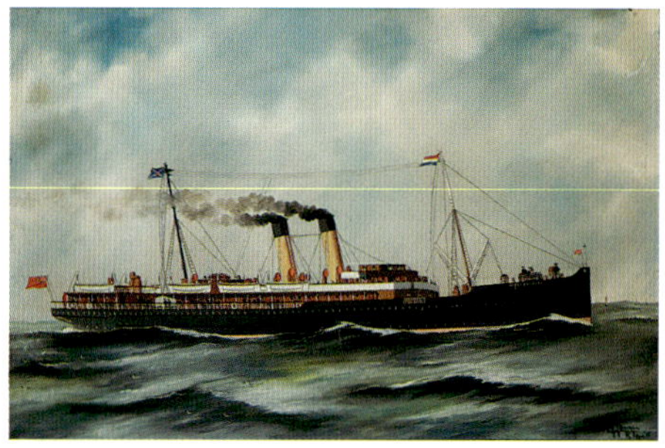

Jensen, Alfred 1859–1935
'SS St Petersburg' 1915
oil on canvas 49.5 x 73.7
COLEM : 1963.614.5

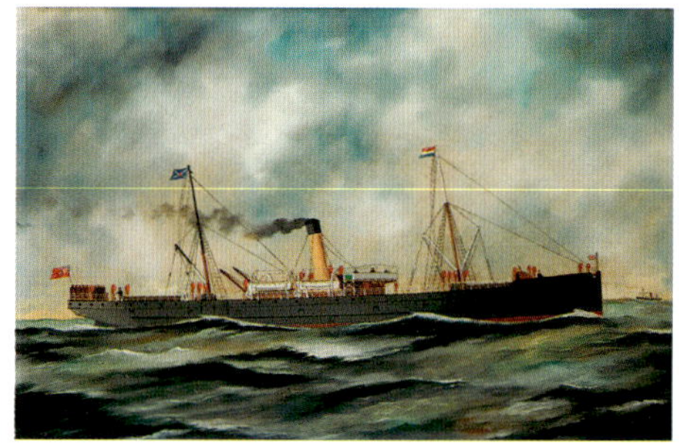

Jensen, Alfred 1859–1935
'SS Cromer' c.1915
oil on canvas 49.5 x 73.7 (E)
COLEM : 1963.614.1

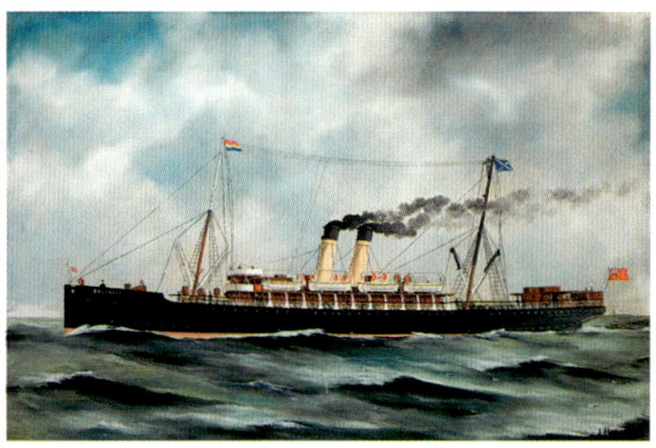

Jensen, Alfred 1859–1935
'SS Brussels' 1917
oil on canvas 49.5 x 73.7 (E)
COLEM : 1963.614.3

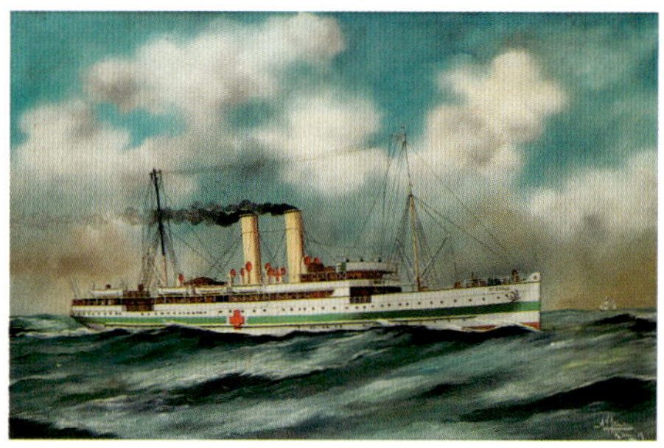

Jensen, Alfred 1859–1935
'SS St Denis' 1917
oil on canvas 49.5 x 73.7 (E)
COLEM : 1963.614.2

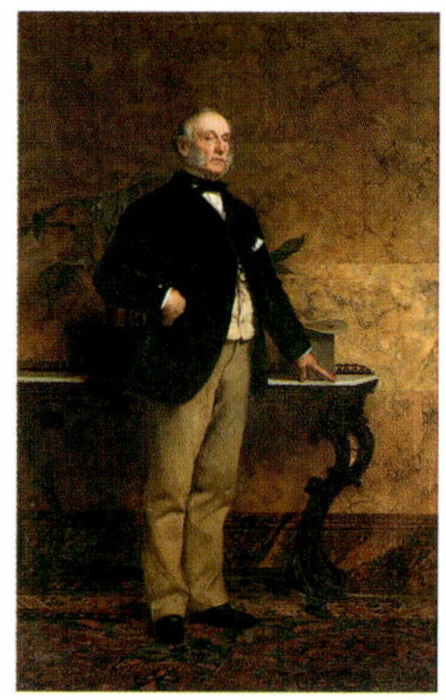

Johnson, Cyrus 1848–1925
George Henry Errington, High Steward of Colchester 1879
oil on canvas 243.8 x 152.4
COLEM : 209A

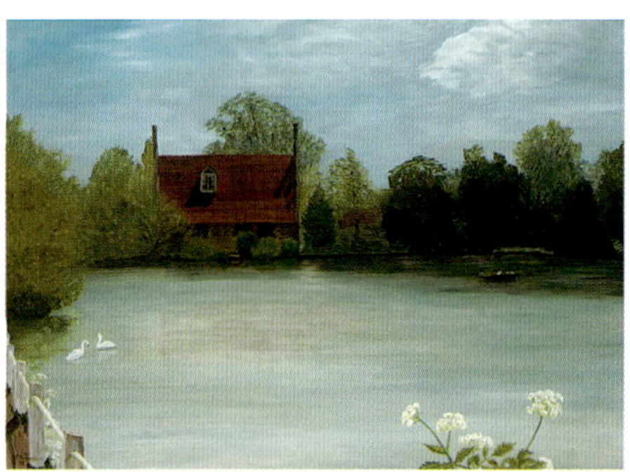

Johnson, F. R. active 1978–1979
Bourne Mill, Colchester 1978
oil on hardboard 66 x 75
COLEM : 1992.114

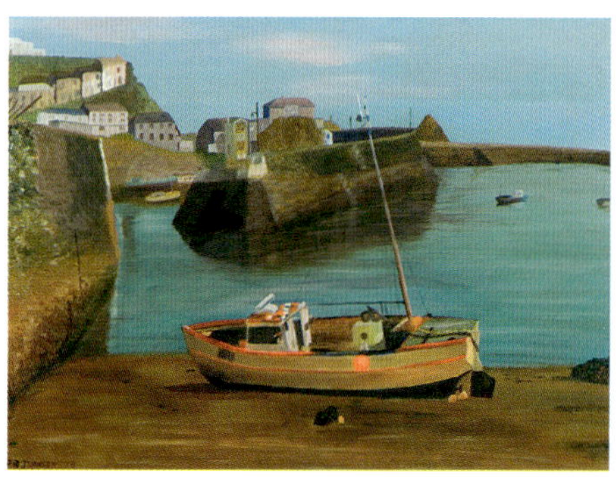

Johnson, F. R. active 1978–1979
Mevagissey, Cornwall 1979
oil on board 44 x 60
COLEM : 2005.129

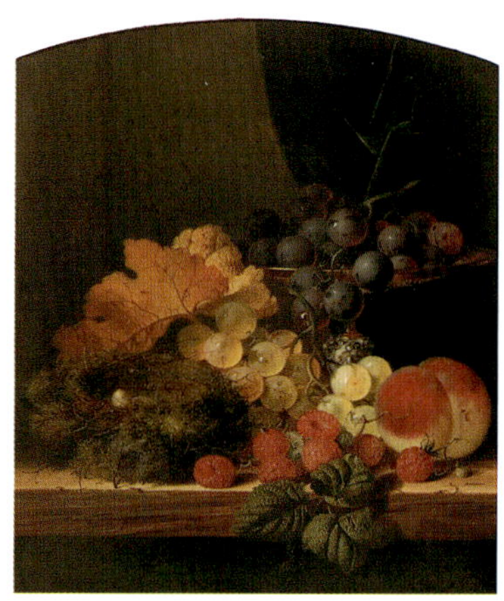

Ladell, Edward 1821–1886
Still Life with Fruit and a Bird's Nest
oil on canvas 36.5 x 30
COLEM : 81A

Facing page: Bellany, John, b.1942, *Woman of the North Sea* (detail), Fry Art Gallery, (p. 229)

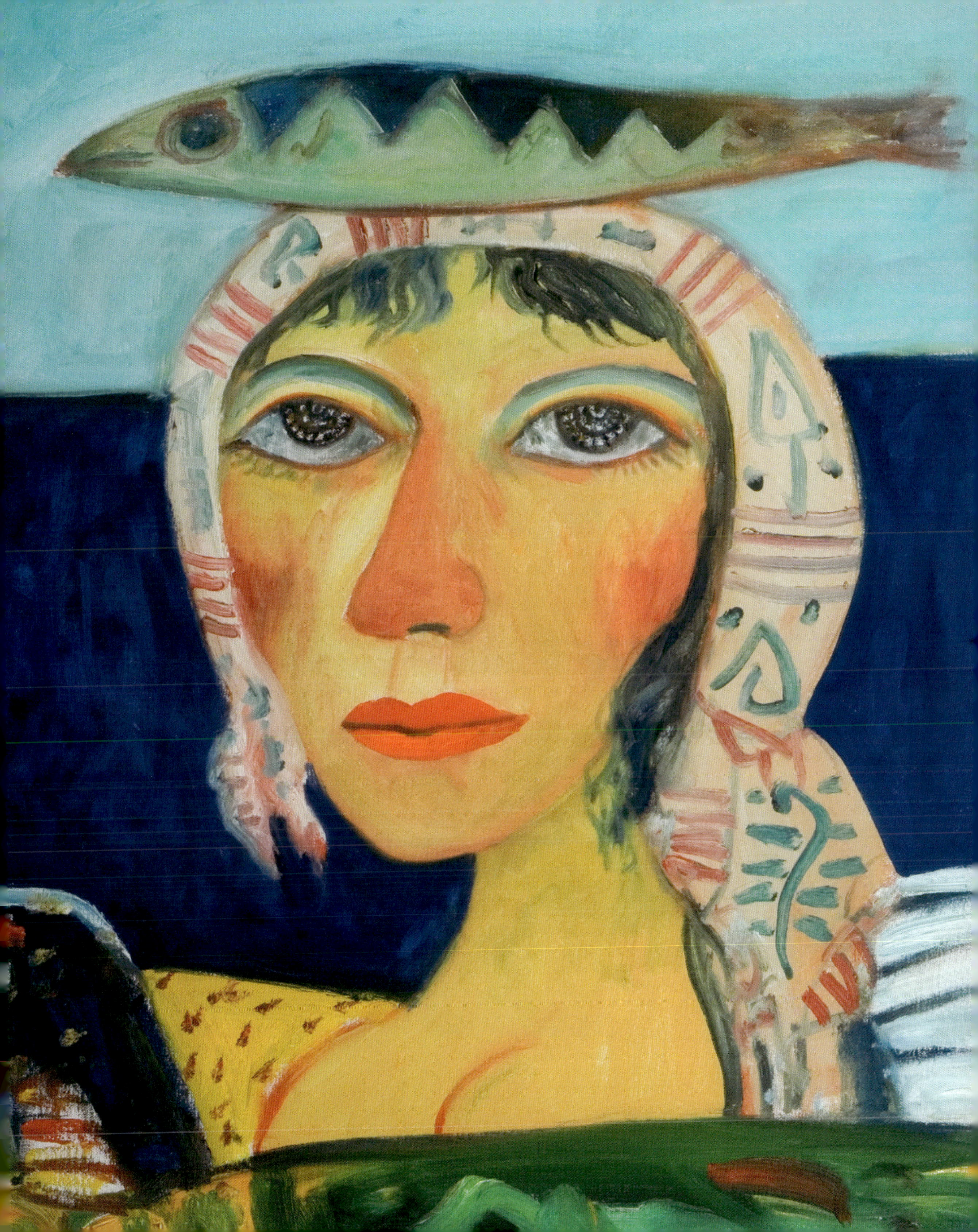

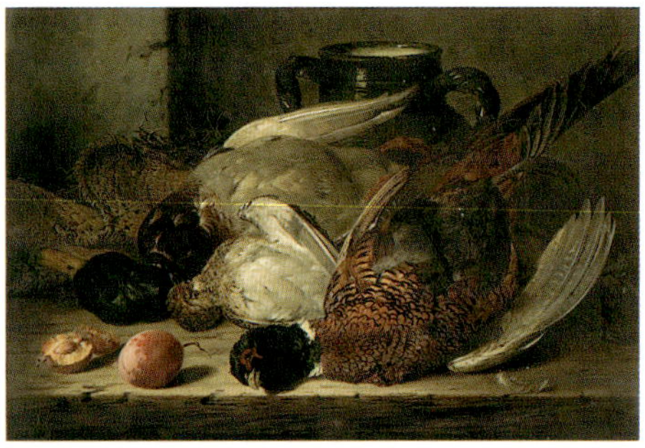

Ladell, Edward 1821–1886
Still Life with Pheasant, Partridge and Duck
oil on canvas 44 x 66
COLEM : 266A

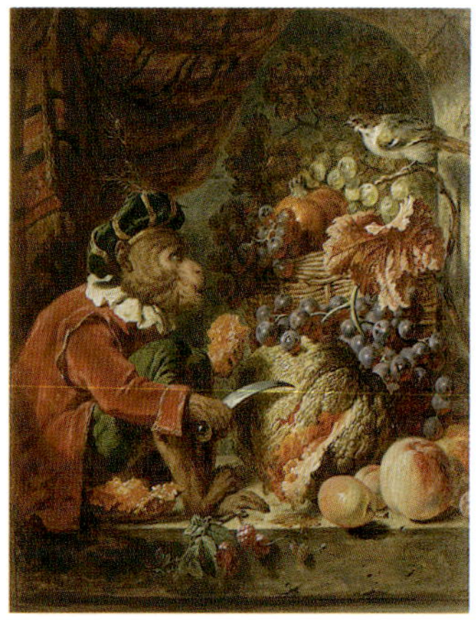

Lance, George 1802–1864
Still Life with Monkey, Sparrow and Fruit c.1850
oil on canvas 54.6 x 47.6
COLEM : 264A

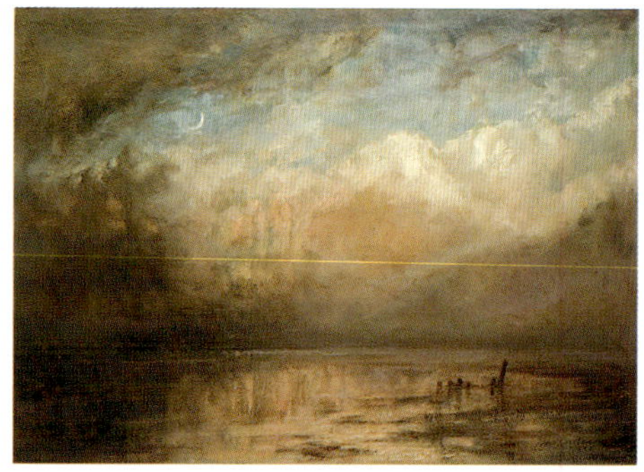

Landon, Charles Paul 1760–1826
Landscape: Water, Clouds and Moon
oil on canvas 40 x 53.3
COLEM : 1966.OS.88

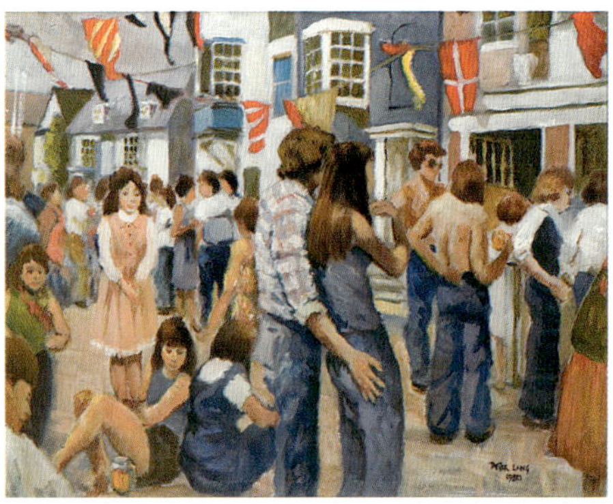

Lang, Peter
Wivenhoe Quay 1980
acrylic on canvas 49 x 58
COLEM : 1980.272

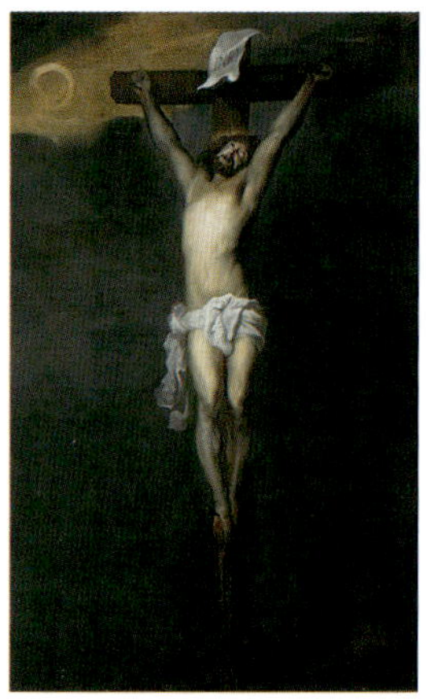

Largillière, Nicolas de (after) 1656–1746
The Crucifixion
oil on canvas 133 x 100
COLEM : 74A

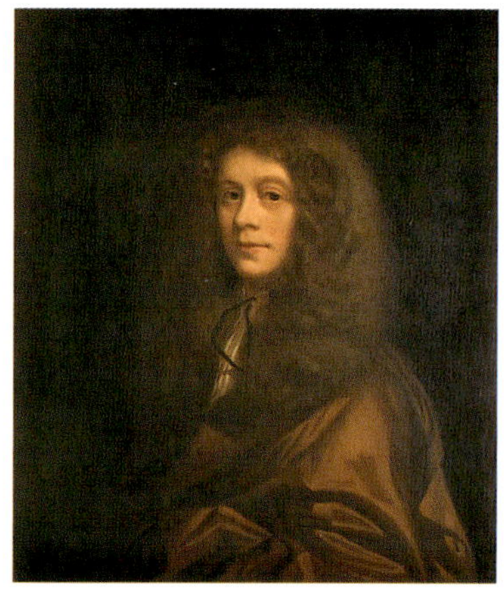

Lely, Peter (after) 1618–1680
Arthur Barnadiston, Recorder of Colchester (1649)
oil on canvas 73.6 x 63.5
COLEM : 156A

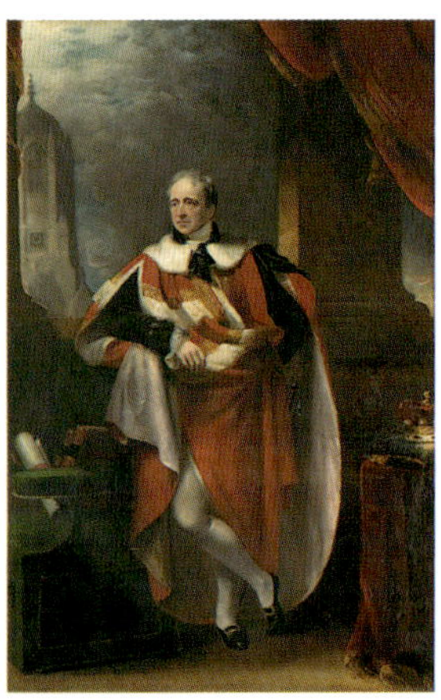

Lonsdale, James 1777–1839
Charles Abbot, 1st Baron Colchester (1757–1829) 1817
oil on canvas 236.2 x 152.4
COLEM : 172A

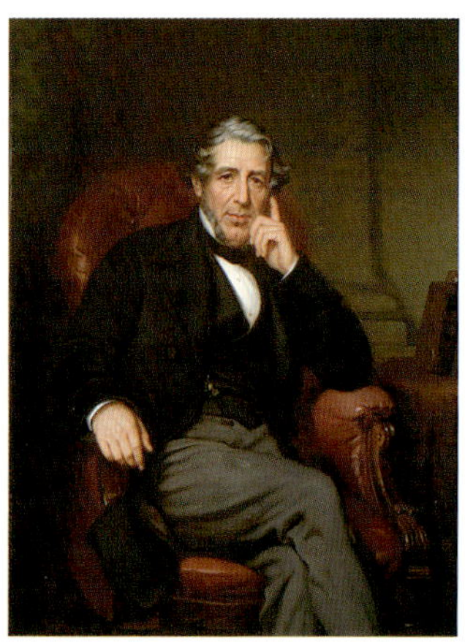

Lucas, John 1807–1874
George Round (1803–1857), High Sheriff of Essex (1845) c.1850
oil on canvas 120.5 x 90.5
COLEM : 165A

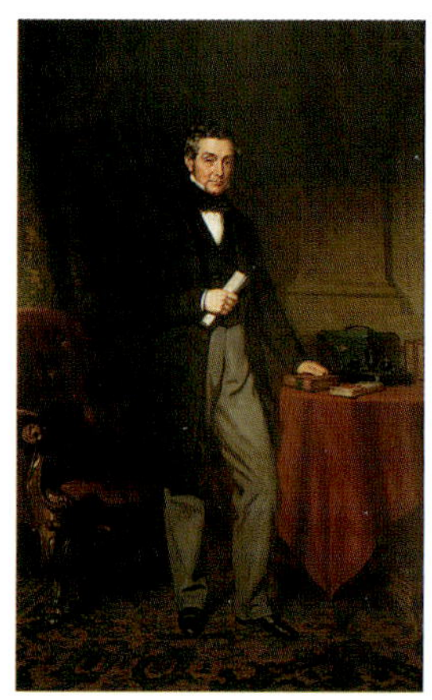

Lucas, John 1807–1874
Charles Gray Round, MA 1863
oil on canvas 243.8 x 152.4
COLEM : 143A

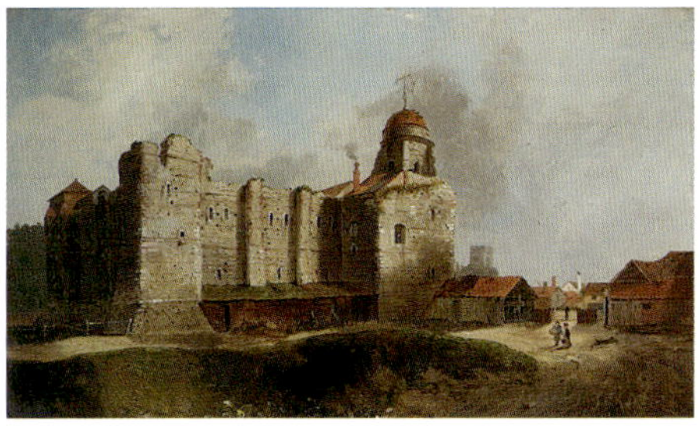

Miles, G.
Colchester Castle 1841
oil on board 29.2 x 48.3
COLEM : 1972.126

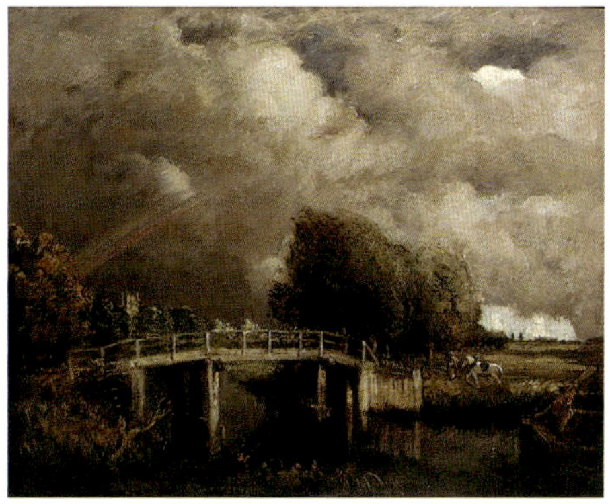

Muirhead, David 1867–1930
The Fen Bridge, near Dedham (Constable's Country)
oil on canvas 89.5 x 104.8
COLEM : 273A

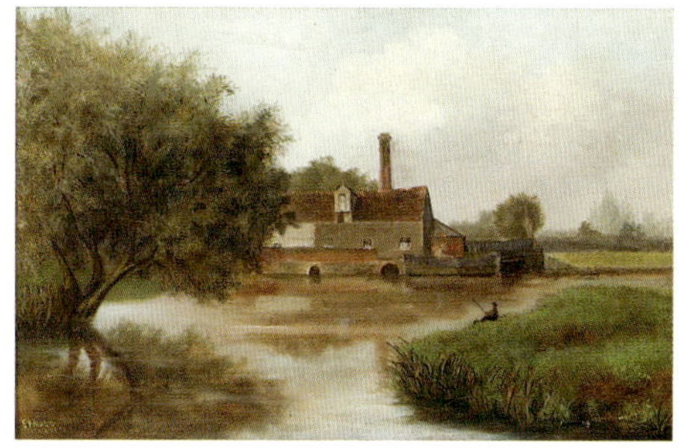

Nagle, I.
Middle Mill, Colchester 1892
oil on canvas 35 x 53
COLEM : 1970.12

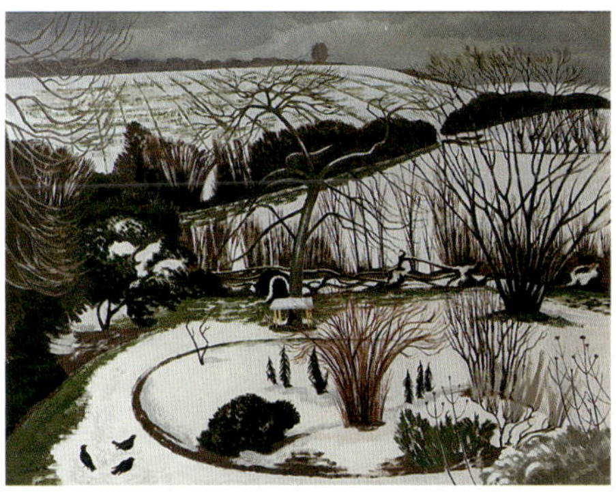

Nash, John Northcote 1893–1977
The Garden in Winter 1943–1967
oil on canvas 64 x 77
COLEM : 1993.15

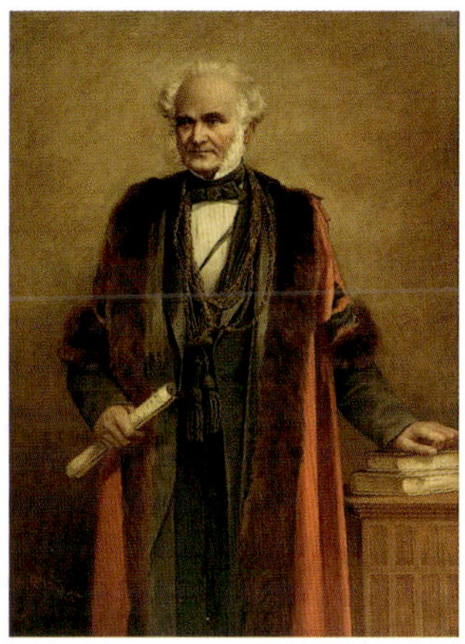

Nicholson, E. W. active 1901–1902
John Bawtree Harvey, JP (1809–1890), Mayor of Colchester (1881–1883) 1901
oil on canvas 152.4 x 106.7
COLEM : 139A

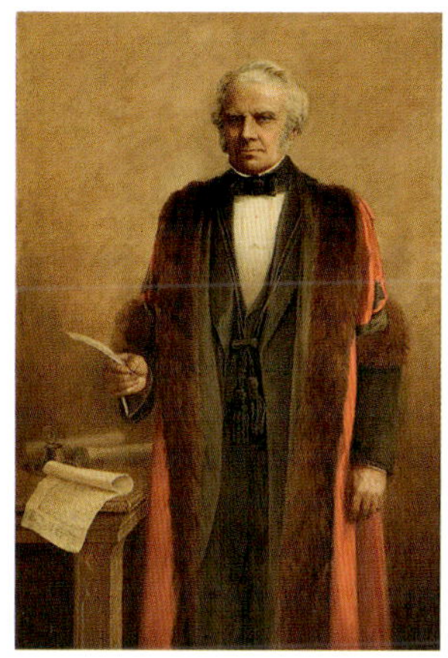

Nicholson, E. W. active 1901–1902
Henry Sidney Goody 1902
oil on canvas 154.9 x 104.1
COLEM : 141A

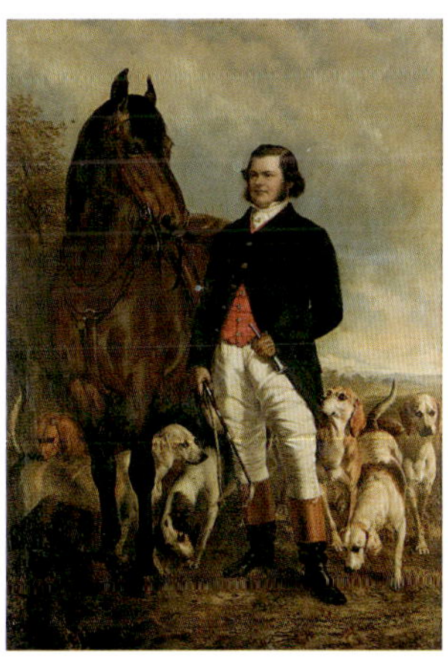

Nightingale, Robert 1815–1895
William Philip Honywood of Markshall, near Coggeshall (1823–1859), High Sheriff (1851) c.1859
oil on canvas 261.5 x 180.3 (E)
COLEM : 1994.12

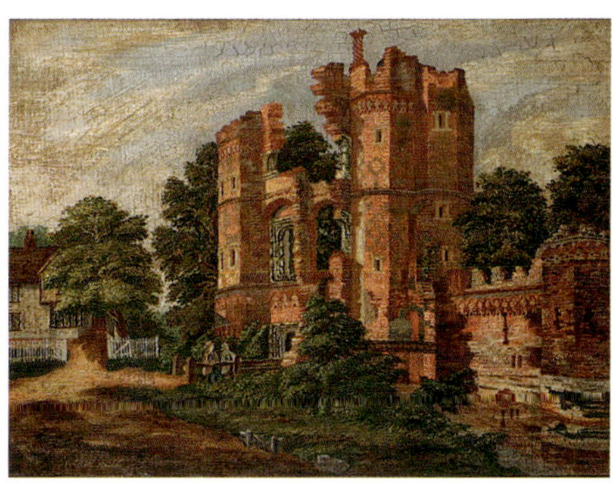

Parish, Josiah 1834–1882
Nether Hall, Roydon 1870–1880
oil on canvas 42 x 54
COLEM : 1957.323

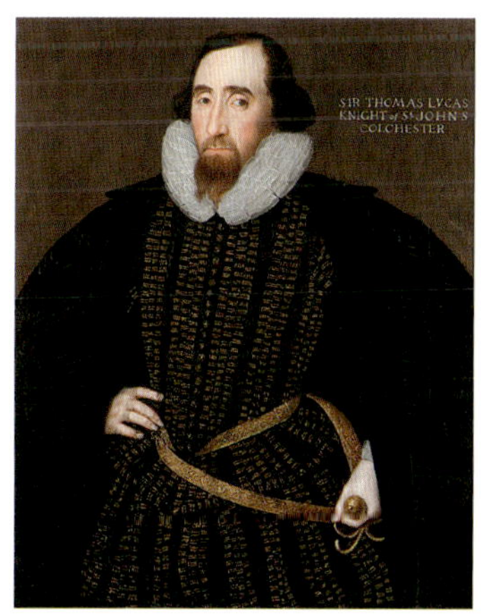

Peake, Robert (attributed to) c.1551–1619
Sir Thomas Lucas, Knight of St John, Colchester c.1580
oil on panel 90.5 x 73.5
COLEM : 1993.62

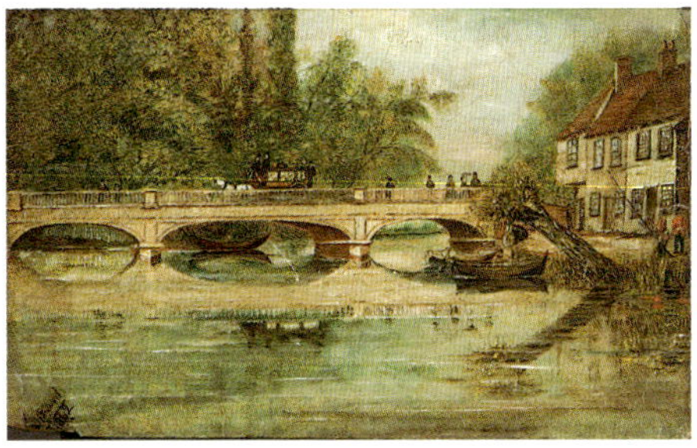

Percival, W. H. active 1862–1906
North Bridge, Colchester 1862
oil on board 21 x 33
COLEM : 1966.OS.84

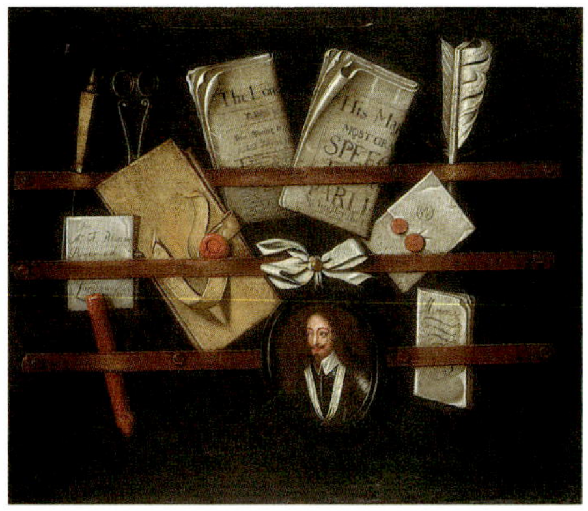

Peterson, Otto Fredrik 1672–1729
King Charles I before 1720
oil on canvas 63.5 x 76.2
COLEM : 1972.128

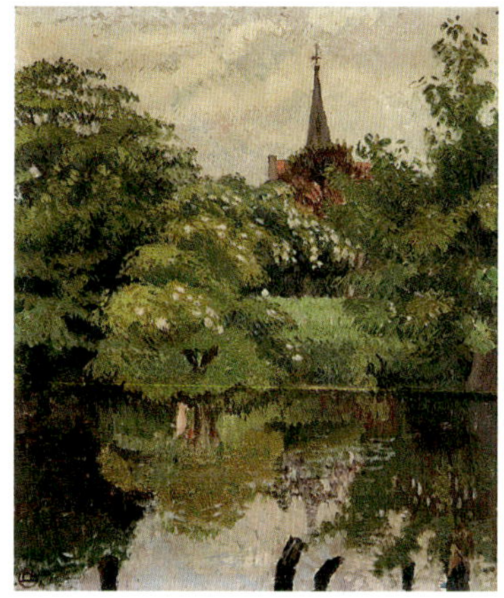

Pissarro, Lucien 1863–1944
St Lawrence's Church, near Southminster 1903
oil on canvas 56 x 46
COLEM : 80A

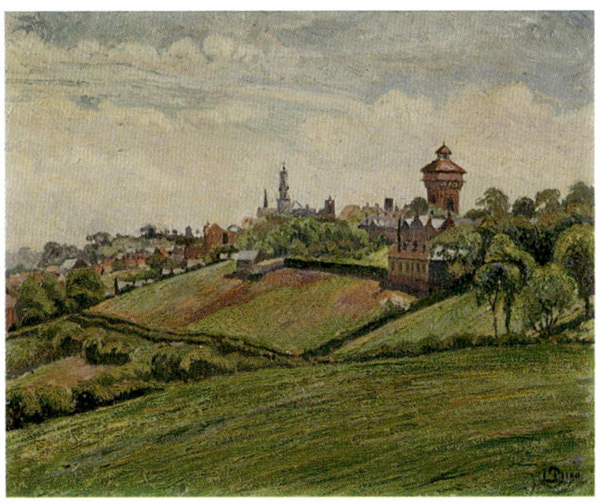

Pissarro, Lucien 1863–1944
Colchester from Sheepen Hill 1911
oil on canvas 54 x 64.5
COLEM : 78A

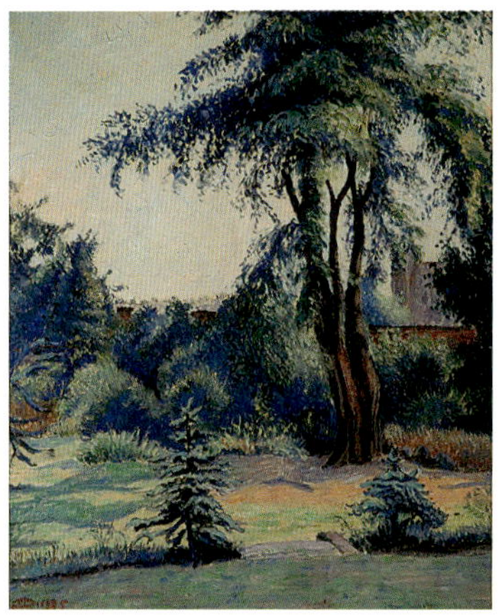

Pissarro, Lucien 1863–1944
The Acacia Tree at the Minories, Colchester
1935
oil on canvas 53 x 44
COLEM : 1998.73

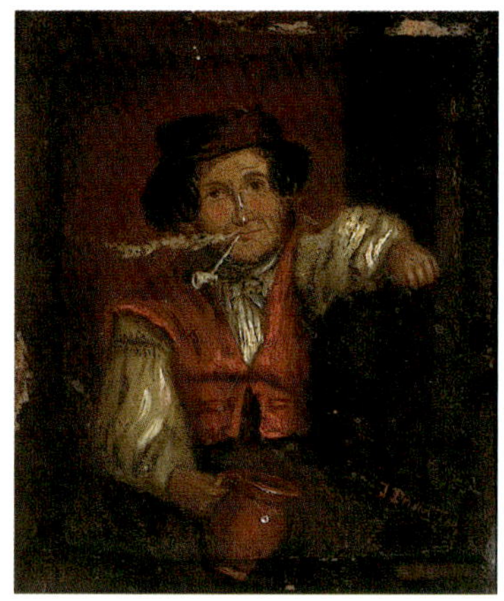

Prentice, James active 1846
A Yokel 1846
oil on board 14 x 11.4
COLEM : 1968.23

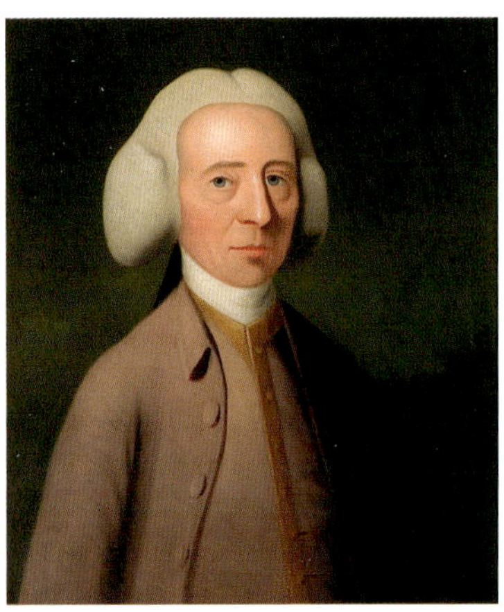

Reilly, John Lewis active 1857–1899
Charles Gray (1696–1782), MP for Colchester in Five Parliaments (copy after Thomas Gainsborough) 1899
oil on canvas 61 x 51
COLEM : 278A

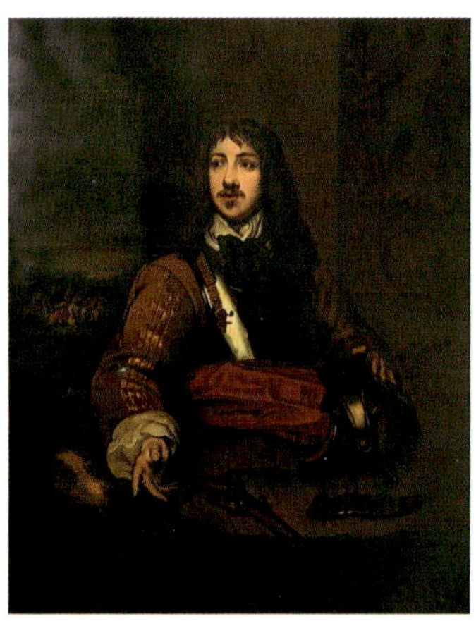

Reilly, John Lewis active 1857–1899
Colonel Neville (copy after William Charles Thomas Dobson) 1899
oil on canvas 145 x 116.8
COLEM : 206A

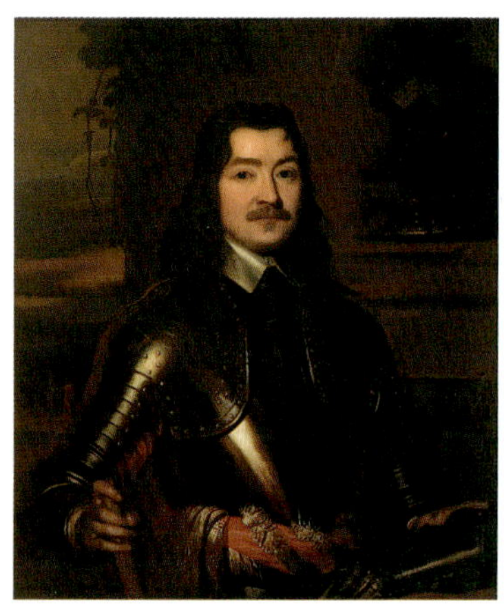

Reilly, John Lewis active 1857–1899
Sir Charles Lucas, Leader of the Royalist Forces at the Siege of Colchester (after William Charles Thomas Dobson) 1899
oil on canvas 99.1 x 83.8
COLEM : 170A

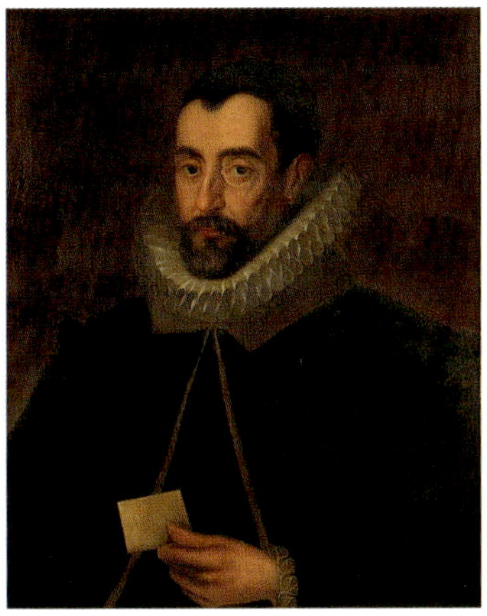

Reilly, John Lewis active 1857–1899
Sir Francis Walsingham, Secretary of State, Recorder of Colchester (d.1590) c.1899
oil on canvas 70 x 56
COLEM : 262A

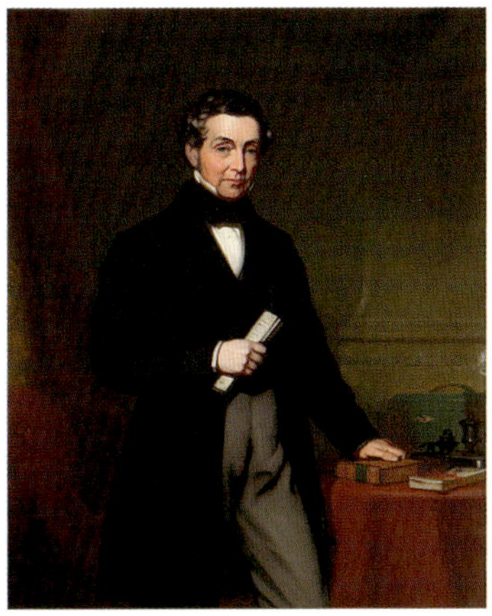

Reilly, John Lewis active 1857–1899
Charles Gray Round (copy after John Lucas)
oil on canvas 141 x 110.5
COLEM : 1966.93

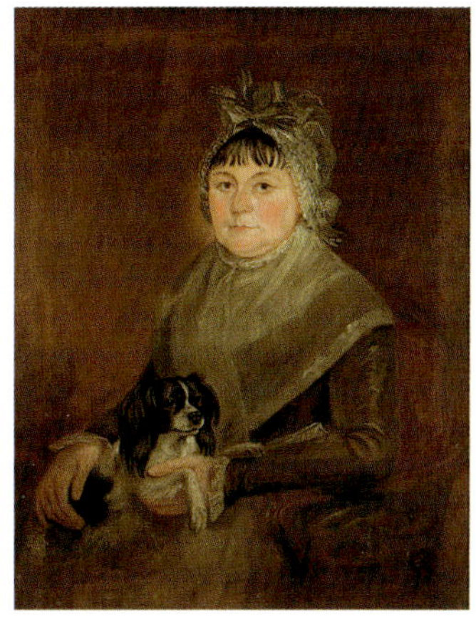

Reinagle, Ramsay Richard (copy of) 1775–1862
Ann Constable (1748–1815) c.1830
oil on canvas 90 x 69
COLEM : 192A

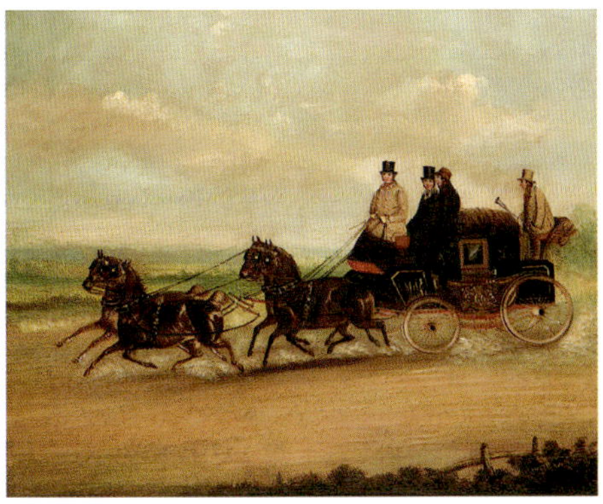

Roberts, Henry Benjamin 1832–1915
London Stage Coach c.1870
oil on canvas 48.3 x 59.4
COLEM : 1966.OS.179

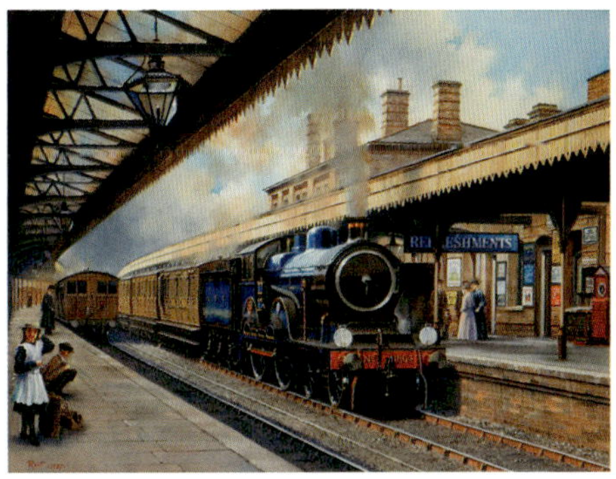

Root, Malcolm b.1950
Train at Colchester Station 1987
oil on canvas 59 x 76
COLEM : 1989.1

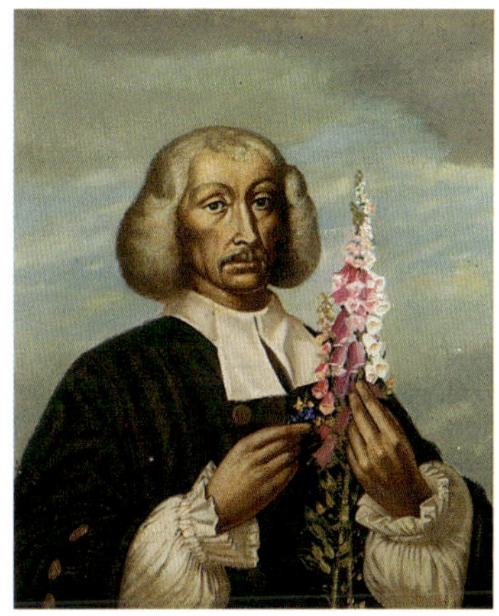

Rushbury, Henry 1889–1968
John Ray of Black Notley, Father of Natural History (1627–1703) 1938
oil on canvas 49 x 39
COLEM : 2005.63

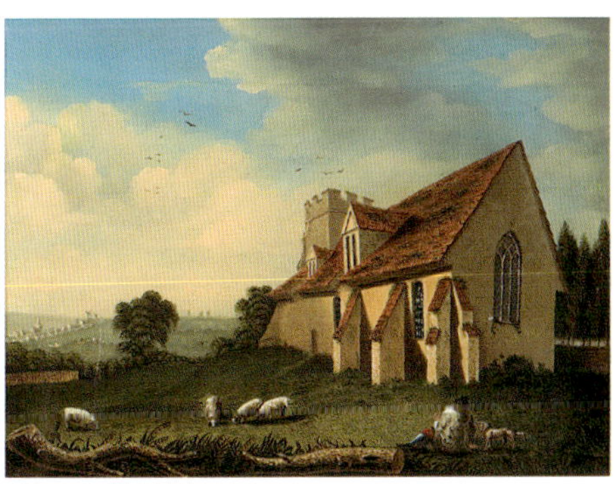

Savage, James Henry active c.1820–1853
Greenstead Church, Colchester (copy after John Greig) c.1820
oil on canvas 27.3 x 35.9
COLEM : 1953.295

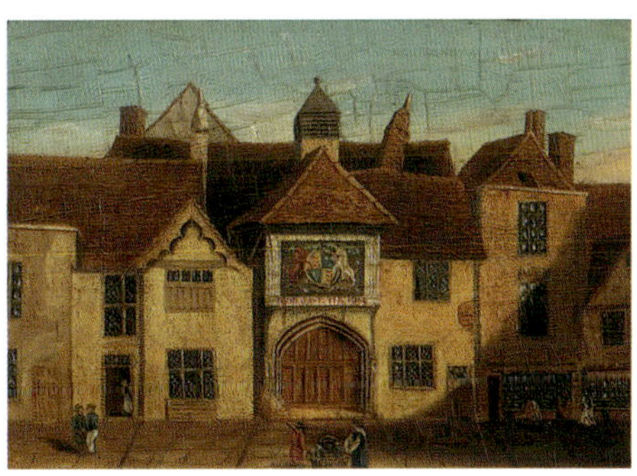

Savage, James Henry active c.1820–1853
The Old Moot Hall, Colchester c.1821
oil on panel 17.8 x 24.1
COLEM : 1968.106

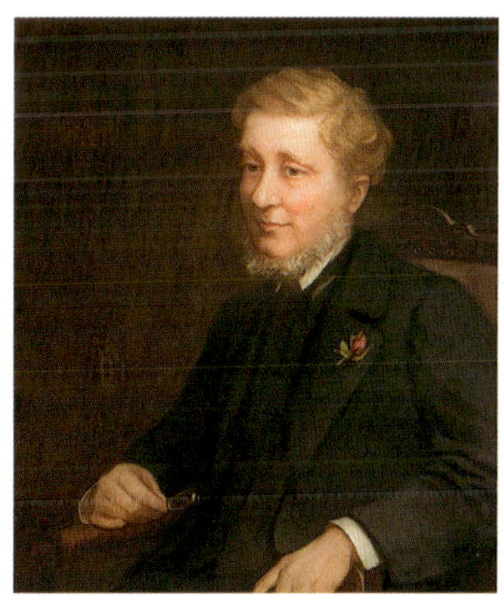

Saville, Josephine active 1863–1906
John Stock Barnes, Clerk of the Peace (1836–1887) 1875–c.1900
oil on canvas 75 x 62
COLEM : 198A

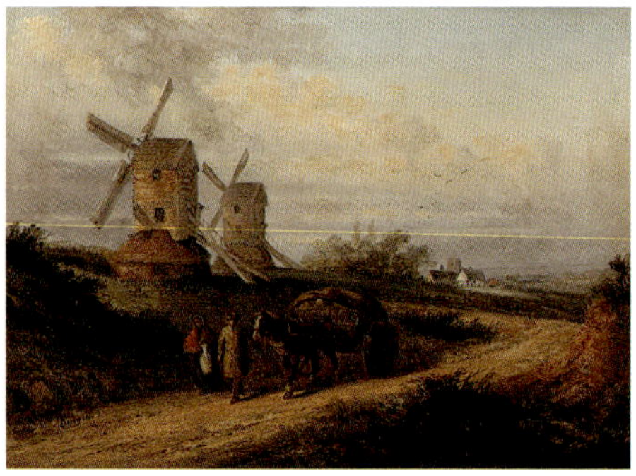

Smythe, Thomas 1825–1907
Country Scene with Two Windmills
oil on canvas 30.5 x 40.6
COLEM : 284A

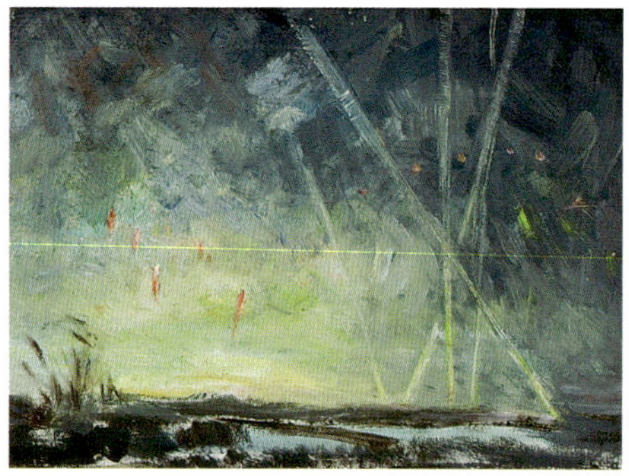

St George, Sylvia 1881–1950
Air Raid over Colchester at Night 1940–1944
oil on canvas 24.1 x 33
COLEM : 1968.56.1

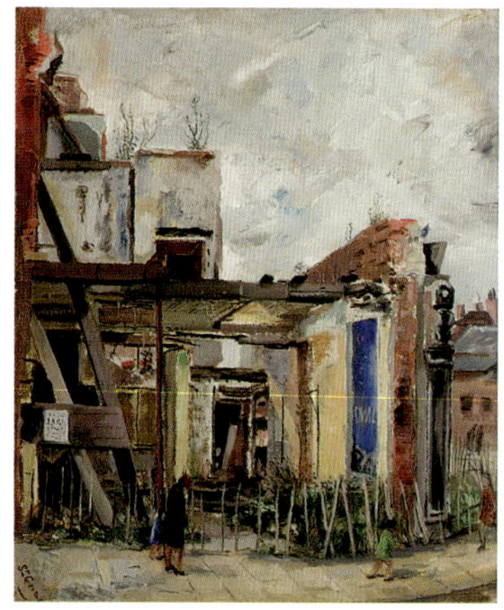

St George, Sylvia 1881–1950
St Botolph's, Colchester, a Bombed House
c.1944
oil on canvas 61 x 50.2
COLEM : 1968.56.2

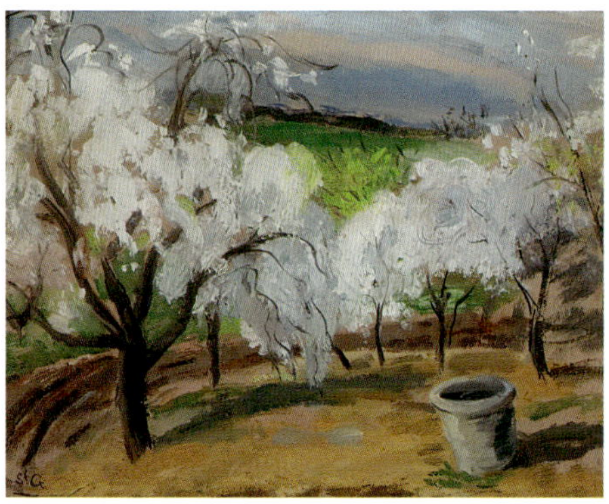

St George, Sylvia 1881–1950
Cherry Blossom, Boxted
oil on board 52 x 60
COLEM : 2004.366.3

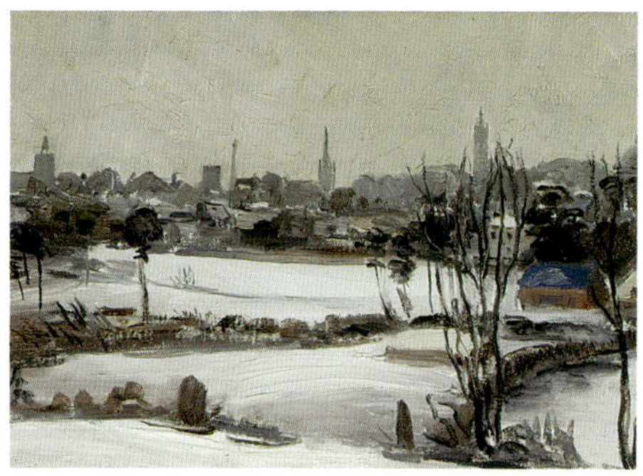

St George, Sylvia 1881–1950
Colchester in Winter
oil & resin on canvas 25 x 34
COLEM : 1997.9.1

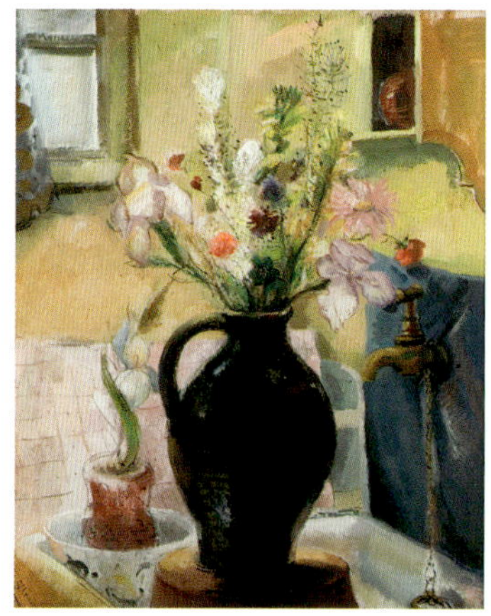

St George, Sylvia 1881–1950
Flowers in the Sink
oil on board 61 x 50
COLEM : 2004.366.6

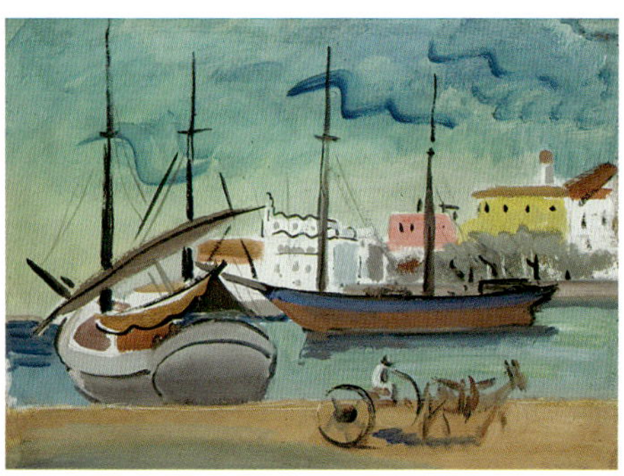

St George, Sylvia 1881–1950
Malaga, Spain
oil on board 34 x 45
COLEM : 2004.366.5

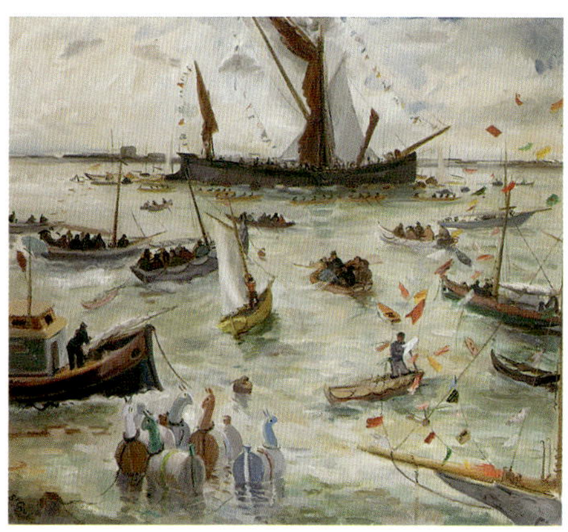

St George, Sylvia 1881–1950
Regatta at Burnham-on-Crouch
oil on canvas 83 x 90
COLEM : 2004.366.1

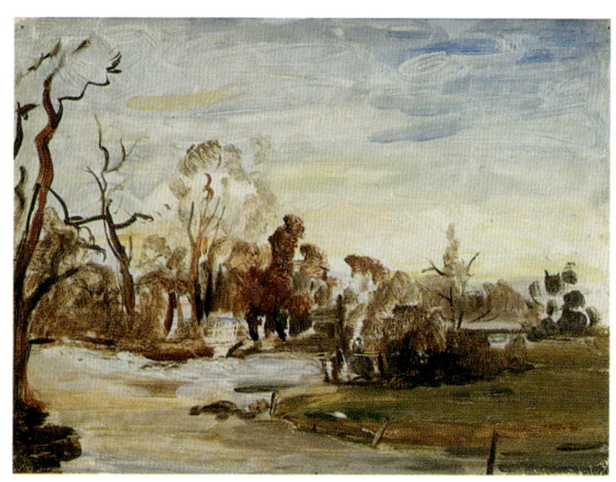

St George, Sylvia 1881–1950
River Stour in Flood, Essex
oil on board 27 x 34
COLEM : 2004.366.2

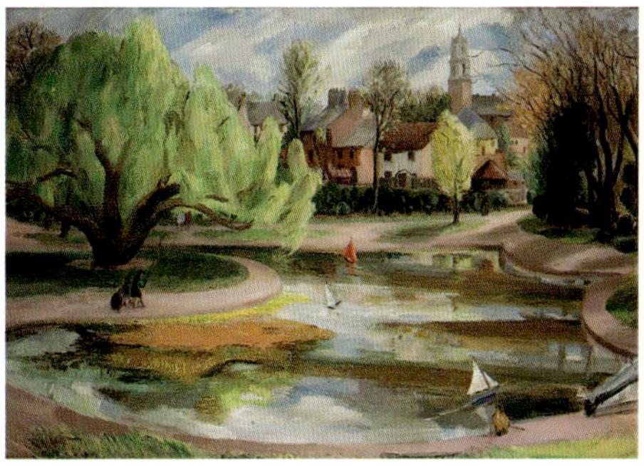

St George, Sylvia 1881–1950
The Parks, Colchester
oil & resin on canvas 68 x 93
COLEM : 1997.9.2

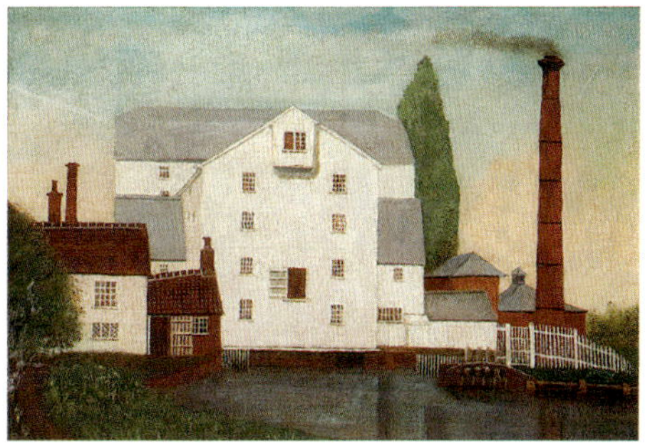

Stannard, F.
Nayland Mill, Suffolk c.1890
oil on board 24.5 x 34.5
COLEM : 1931A

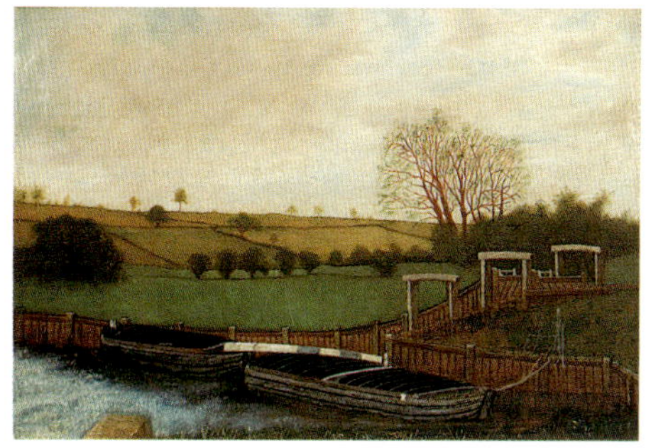

Stannard, F.
Wissington Locks, Barges and Floodgate c.1890
oil on board 24.5 x 34.5
COLEM : 1931B

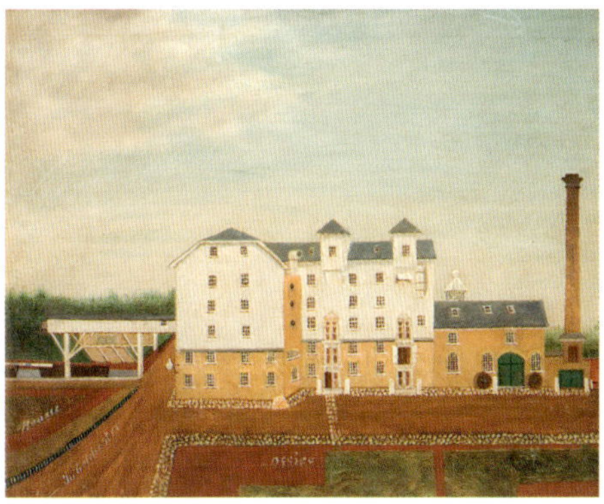

Stannard, F.
Wissington Mill, Suffolk c.1890
oil on board 29 x 34.5
COLEM : 1931

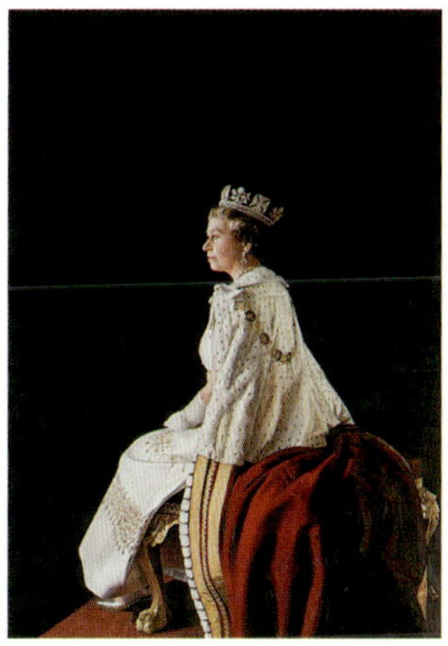

Stone, Richard b.1951
Queen Elizabeth II (b.1926) 1991
oil on canvas 210 x 147 (E)
COLEM : 2001.114

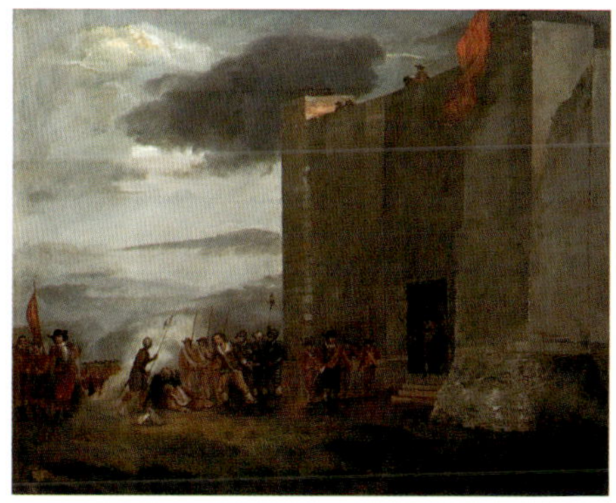

Strutt, Benjamin 1754–1857
Execution of Sir Charles Lucas and Sir George Lisle at Colchester, 28 August 1648 c.1800
oil on canvas 55.9 x 66
COLEM : 122A

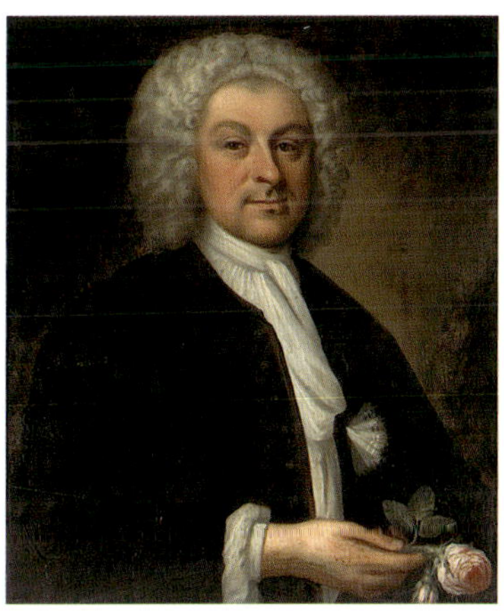

Summers, S. N. active 1764–1806
Dr Robert Potter
oil on canvas 71.1 x 61
COLEM : 159A

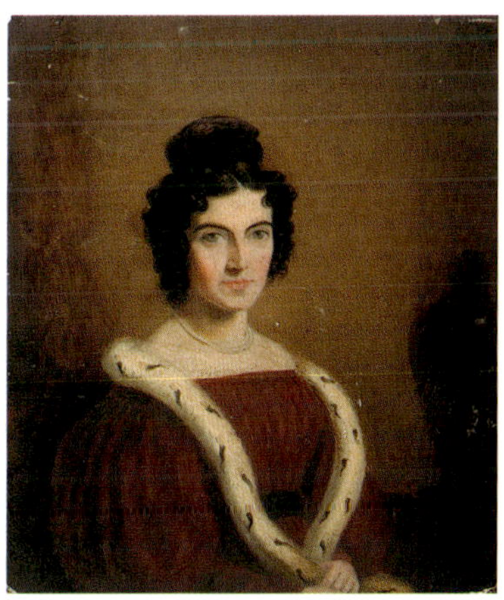

Taylor, R.
Lady in an Ermine Robe
oil on board 35.5 x 30
COLEM : 1930.527

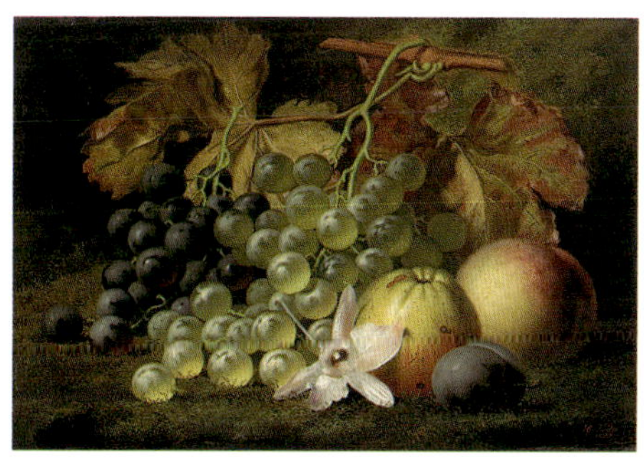

Todd, F. G.
Still Life with Fruit 1886
oil on canvas 22 x 32
COLEM : 1980.273

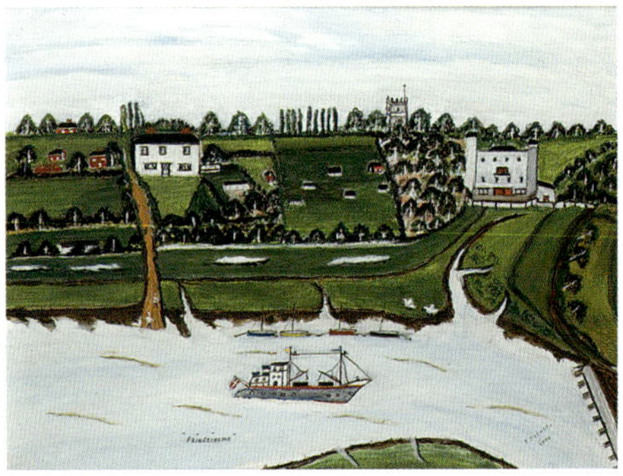

Turner, Ernie d.1977
Fingringhoe 1976
oil on board 50 x 59 (E)
COLEM : 1978.5

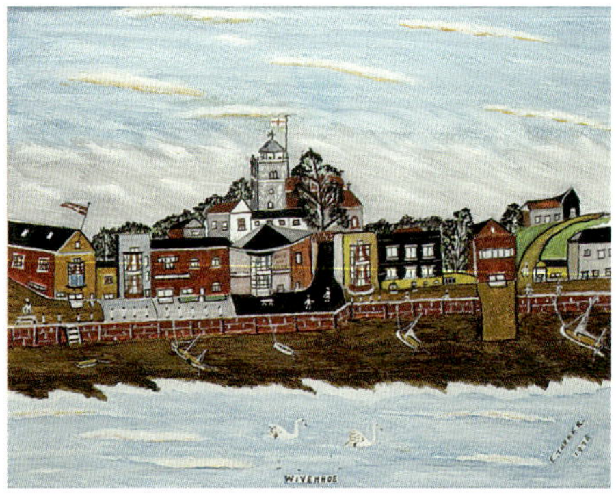

Turner, Ernie d.1977
Wivenhoe 1976
oil on board 50 x 59 (E)
COLEM : 1978.4

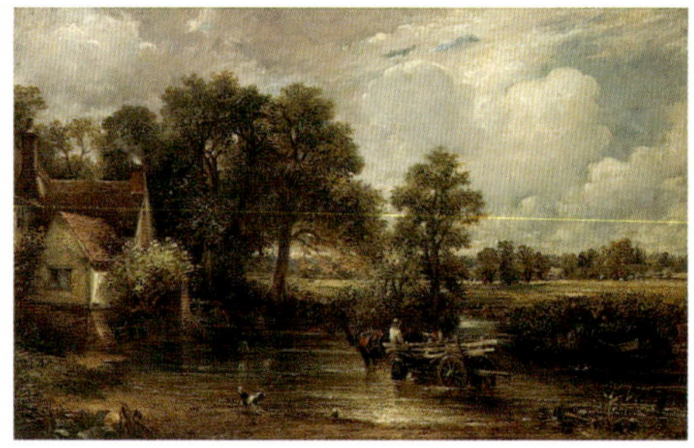

Turner, F. Claridge active 1872–1893
The Haywain (after John Constable)
oil on canvas 49 x 75
COLEM : 73A

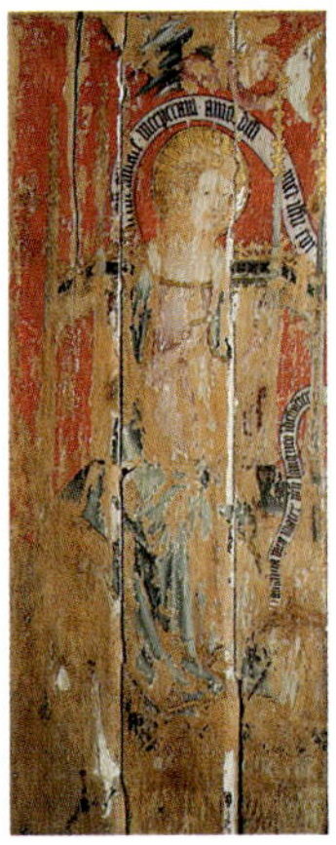

unknown artist
The Virgin 1395
oil on panel 84 x 47.5
COLEM : 2000.11

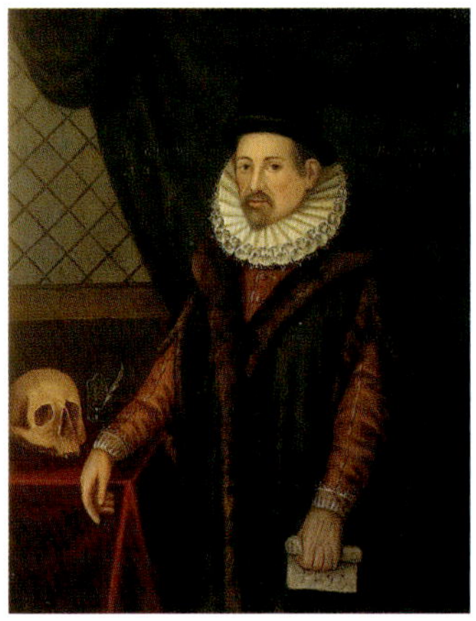

unknown artist
Dr William Gilberd, MD 1591
oil on oak panel 31.8 x 25.4
COLEM : 1968.108

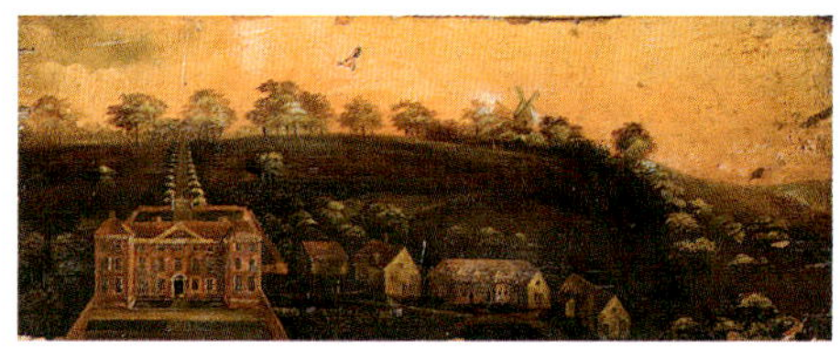

unknown artist 17th C
Bower Hall, Steeple Bumpstead (demolished in 1926)
oil on panel 36.8 x 86.4
COLEM : 1966.OS.210

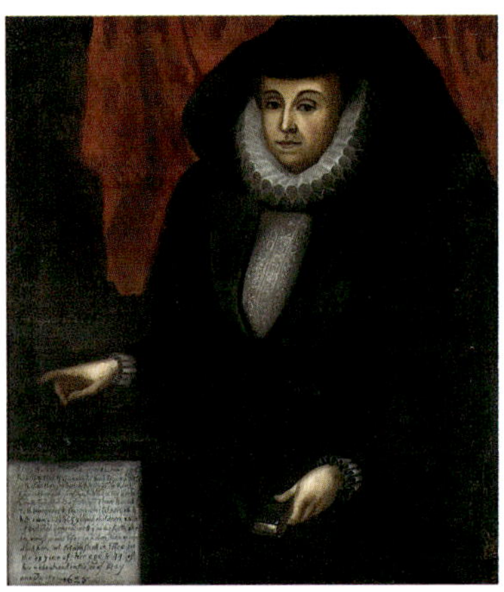

unknown artist 17th C
Mary Honywood (née Waters) of Markshall, Essex (d.1625)
oil on canvas 83 x 70.5
COLEM : 1966.OS.141

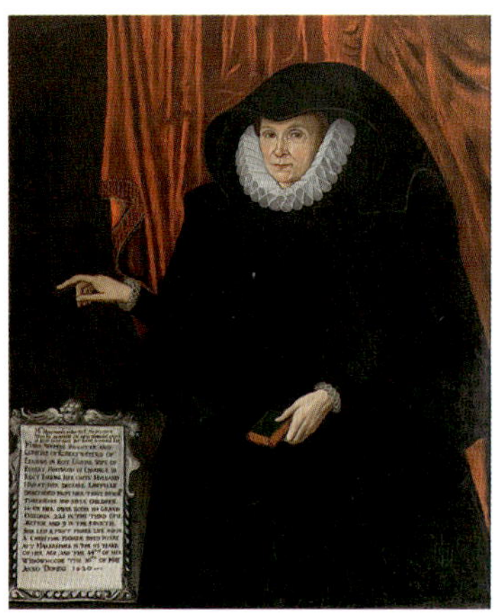

unknown artist 17th C
Mary Honywood (née Waters) of Markshall, Essex (d.1625)
oil on canvas 104.1 x 88.9
COLEM : 1972.129

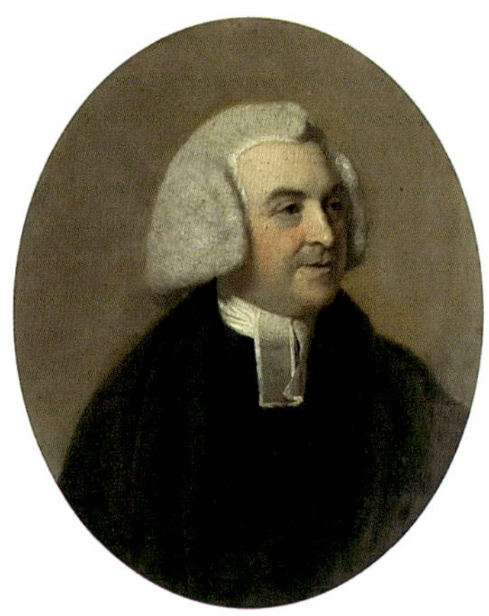

unknown artist 18th C
Bishop Warburton (1698–1769)
oil on panel 23.5 x 19.1
COLEM : 1966.OS.249

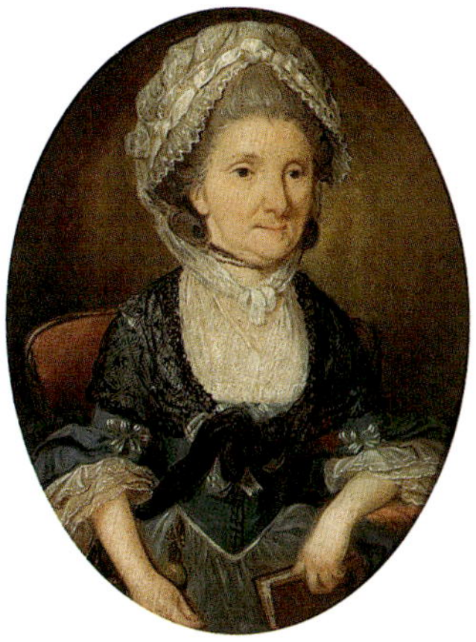

unknown artist 18th C
Miss Anne Lisle
oil on canvas 34 x 26
COLEM : 201A

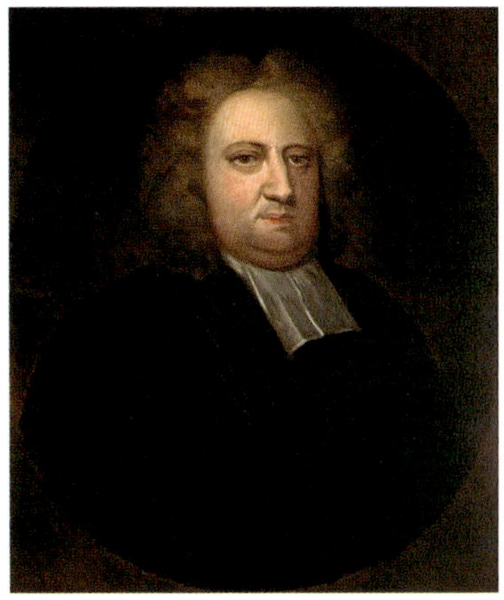

unknown artist 18th C
Mr Boys
oil on canvas 76 x 63.5
COLEM : 1985.106

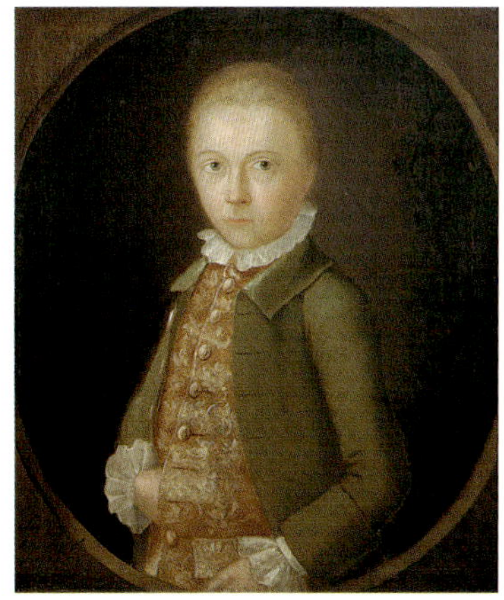

unknown artist 18th C
Samuel Claye (b.1752)
oil on canvas 61 x 50.8
COLEM : 1966.57

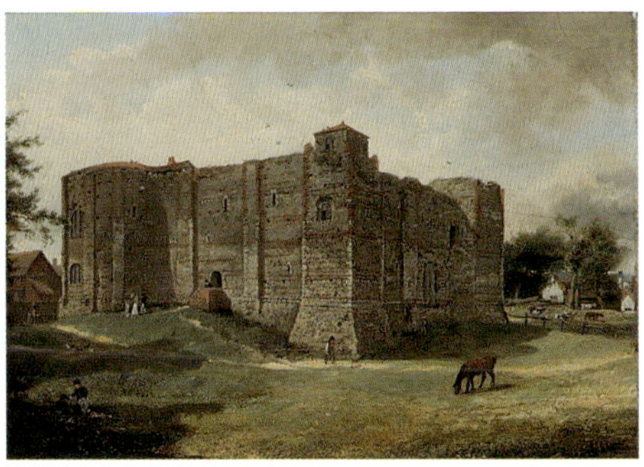

unknown artist
Colchester Castle 1800–1825?
oil on canvas 38.1 x 50.8
COLEM : 1972.125

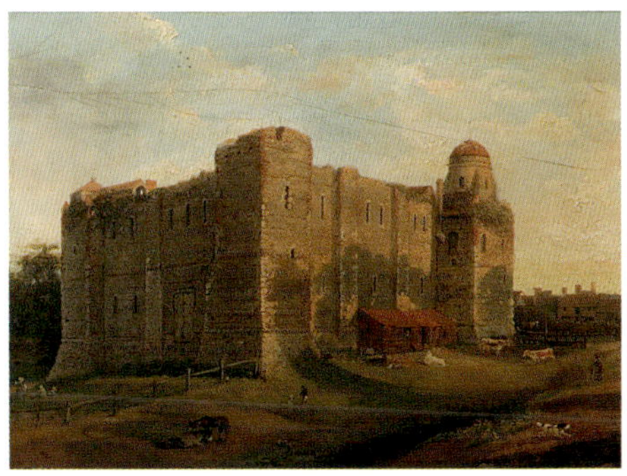

unknown artist
North-West View of Colchester Castle 1820
oil on wood 38.1 x 53.3
COLEM : 1969.21

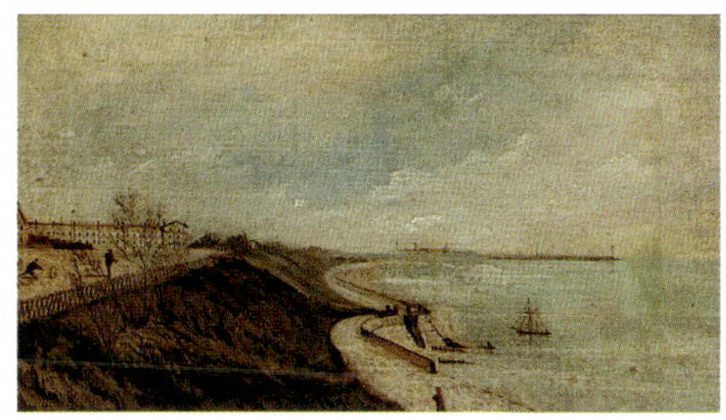

unknown artist
Cliffs and Seashore, Harwich and Dovercourt
c.1840
oil on canvas 20 x 35.9
COLEM : 1958.29

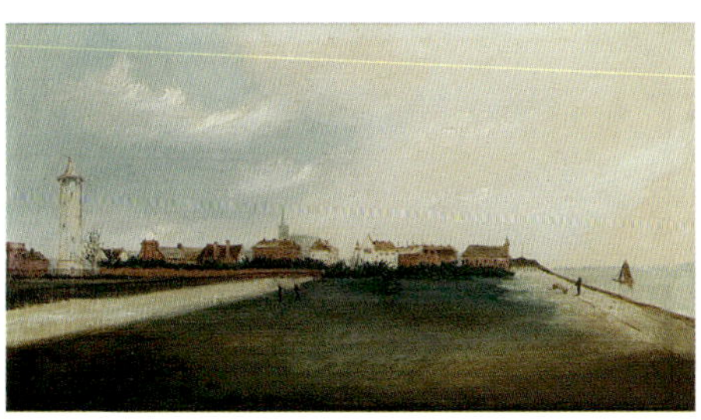

unknown artist
Harwich and Dovercourt c.1840
oil on canvas 19.7 x 34.8
COLEM : 1958.30

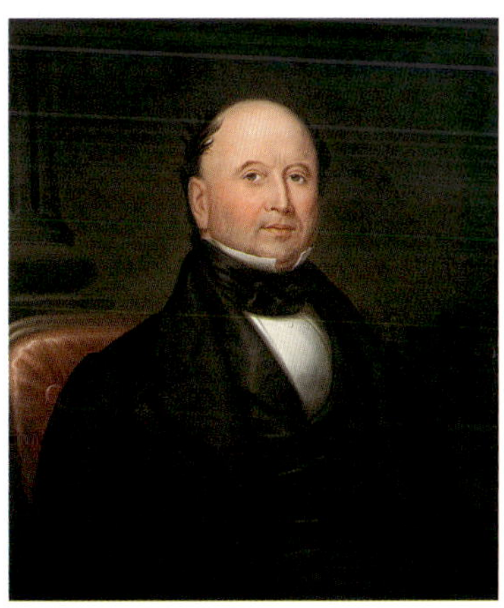

unknown artist
Mr Thomas Moore 1848
oil on canvas 75 x 63
COLEM : 2004.364.1

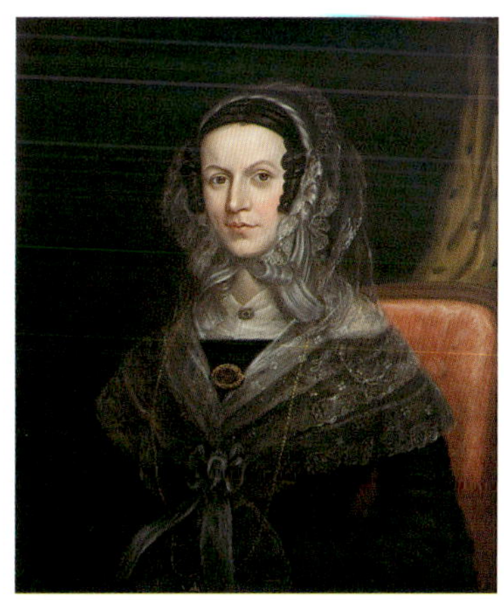

unknown artist
Mrs Thomas Moore 1848
oil on canvas 75 x 63
COLEM : 2004.364.2

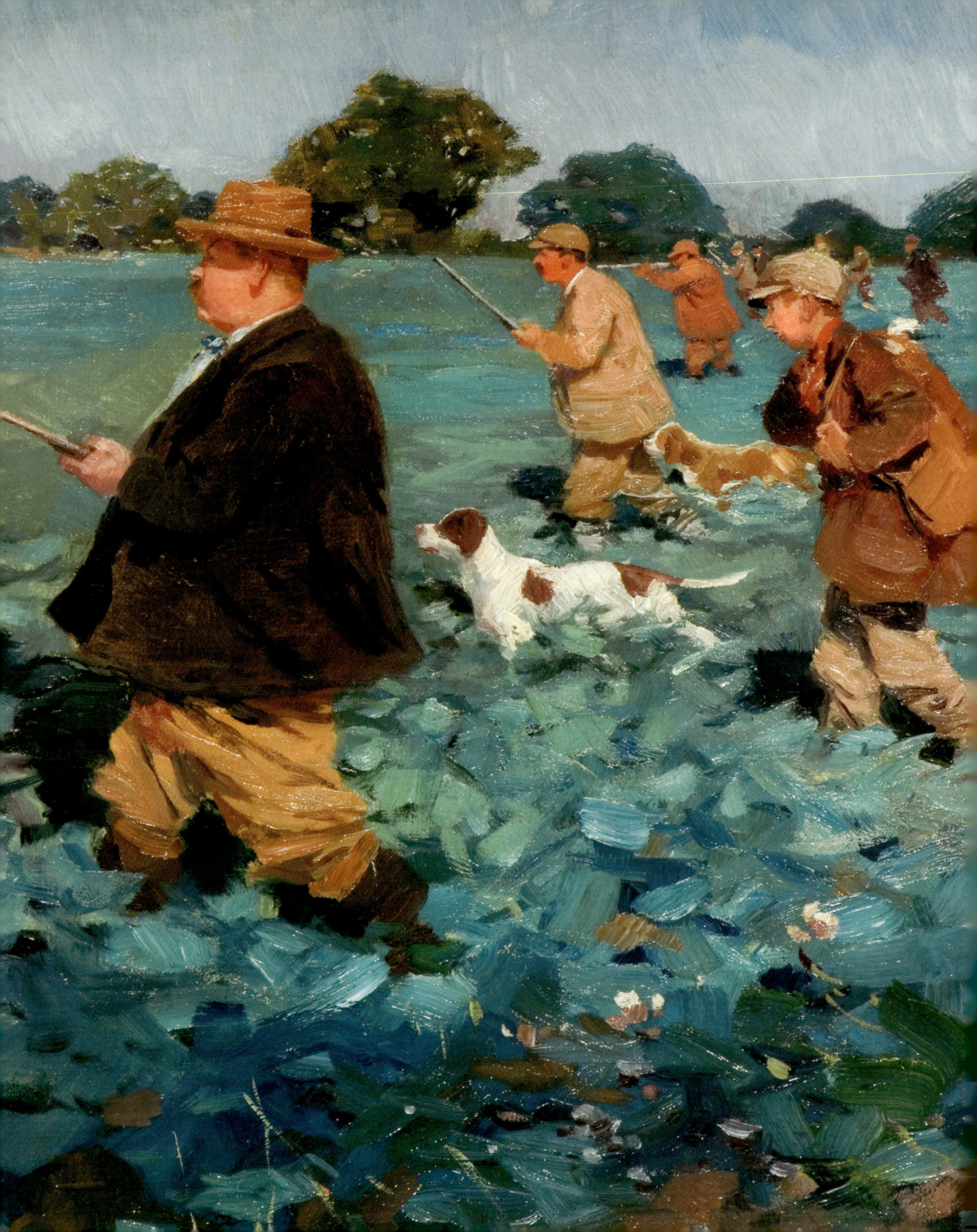

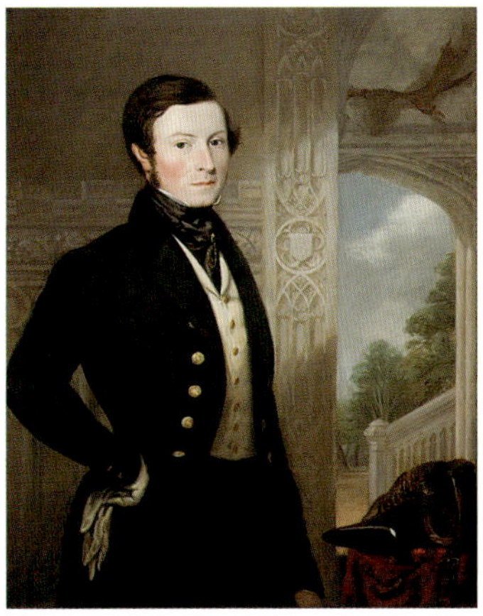

unknown artist
Portrait of a Gentleman in a Gothic Hall
c.1850
oil on canvas 140 x 116
COLEM : 2004.364.3

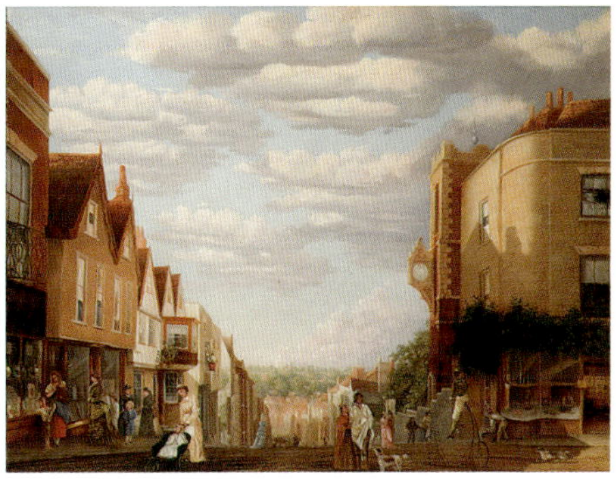

unknown artist
North Hill, Colchester 1875
oil on canvas 61 x 76.5
COLEM : 1955.2252

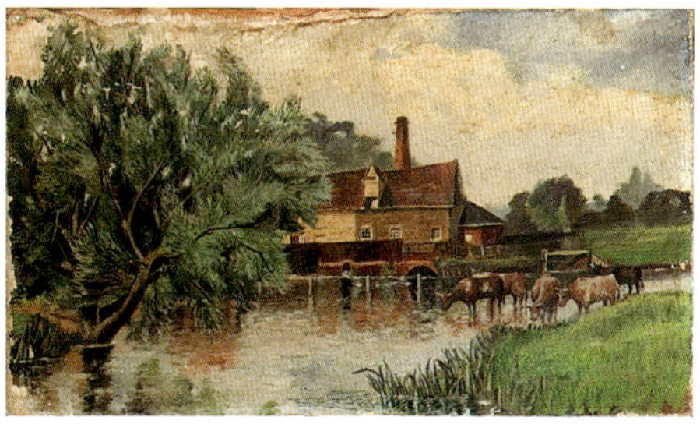

unknown artist
Middle Mill, Colchester from East Stream
c.1885
oil on canvas 30.2 x 50.5
COLEM : 1934.145

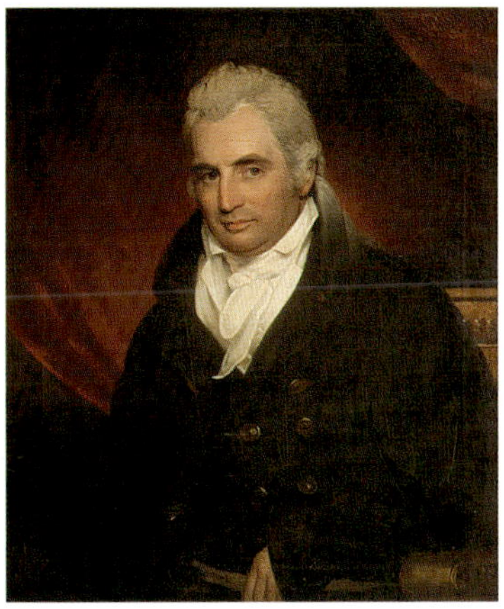

unknown artist early 19th C
John Bawtree (1760–1824), Deputy Lieutenant for the County of Essex, JP
oil on canvas 76.2 x 63.5
COLEM : 155A

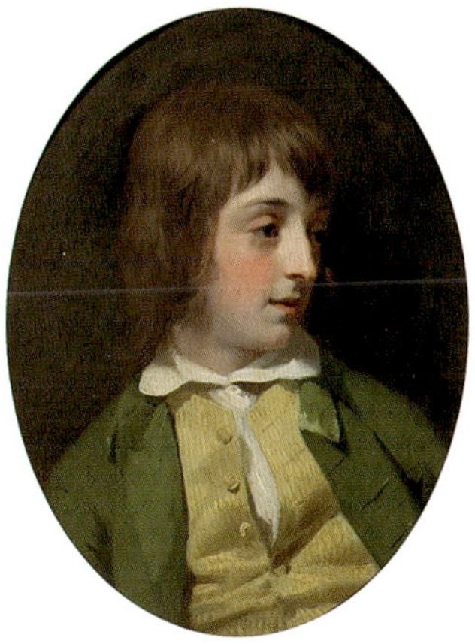

unknown artist early 19th C
Portrait of a Boy
oil on panel 22.9 x 17.8
COLEM : 20A

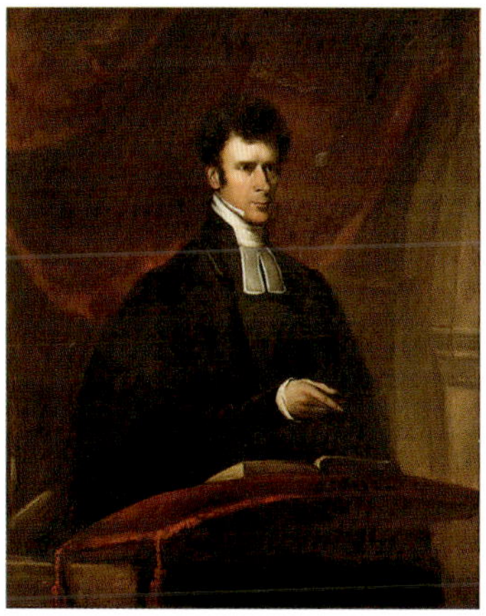

unknown artist early 19th C
Reverend Samuel Carr, MA (1791–1854), Vicar of St Peter's, Colchester (1829–1854)
oil on canvas 127 x 99
COLEM : 197A

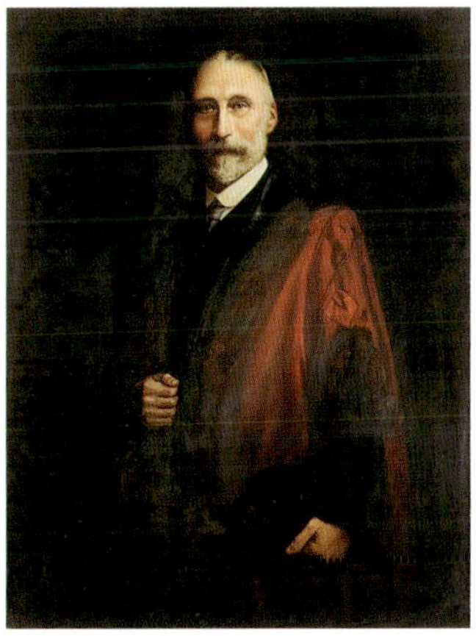

unknown artist 19th C
Alderman William Cheshire
oil on canvas 63.5 x 45.7
COLEM : 204A

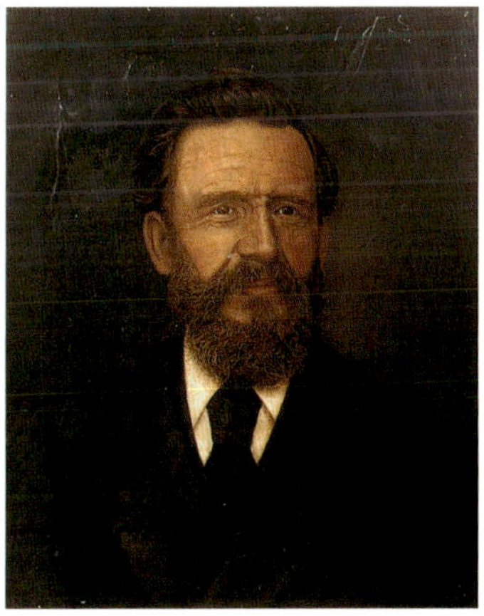

unknown artist 19th C
Benjamin Monson, the First Colchester Photographer
oil on canvas 53.3 x 43.2
COLEM : 1949.97

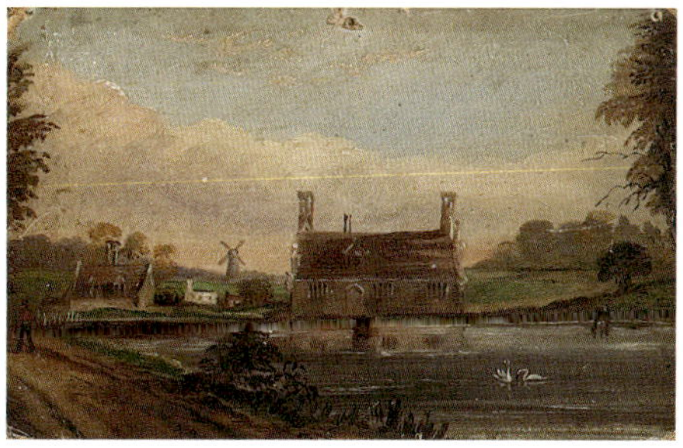

unknown artist 19th C
Bourne Mill, Colchester
oil on card 16 x 25.2
COLEM : 1996.57

Facing page: Munnings, Alfred James, 1878–1959, *A Shoot in a Sweed Field* (detail), 1901, Sir Alfred Munnings Art Museum, (p. 97)

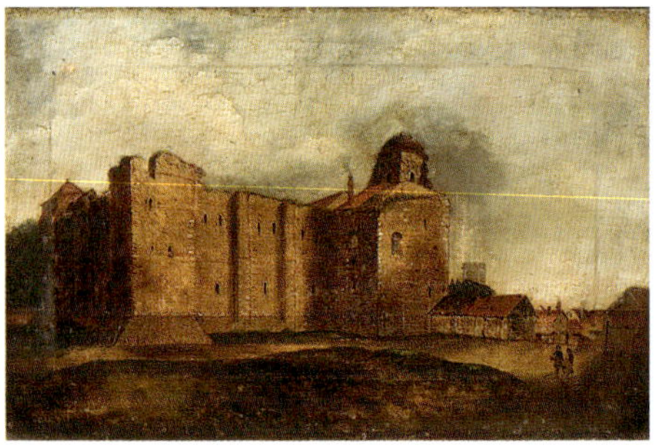

unknown artist 19th C
Colchester Castle
oil on canvas 29.8 x 45.1
COLEM : 1966.OS.90

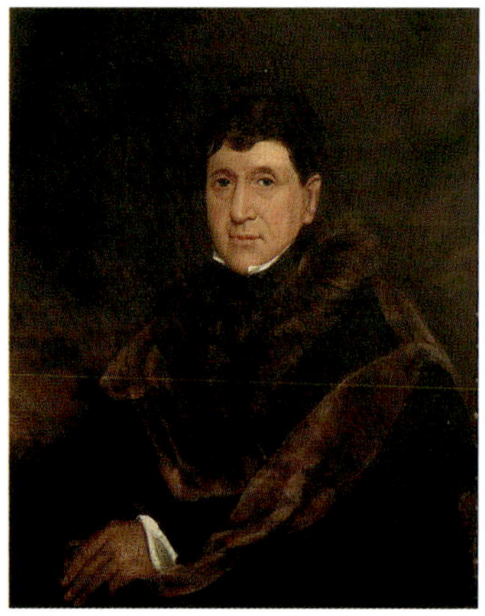

unknown artist 19th C
General Francis Slater Rebow (1770–1845), Owner of Wivenhoe Park and Patron of John Constable
oil on canvas 76 x 63
COLEM : 1985.109

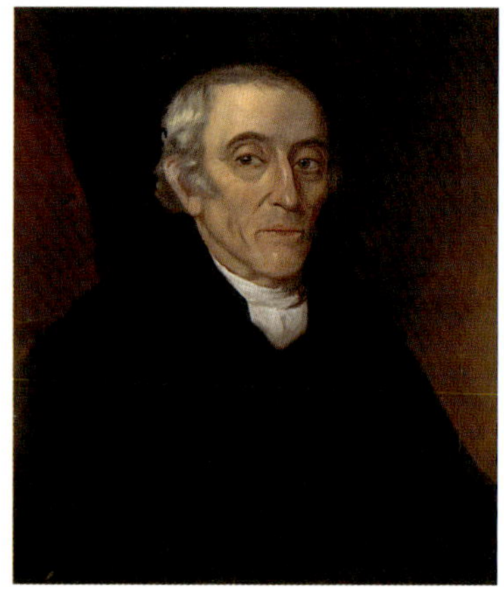

unknown artist 19th C
John Eley of Kelvedon
oil on canvas 61 x 50.4
COLEM : 1984.206

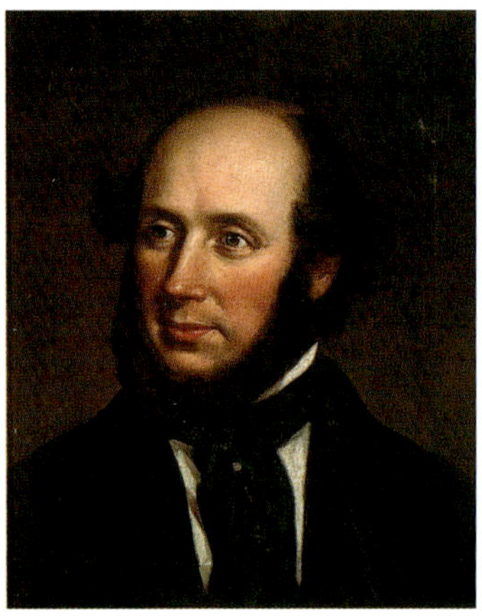

unknown artist 19th C
John Grimwade
oil on canvas 50 x 40.4
COLEM : 1972.106

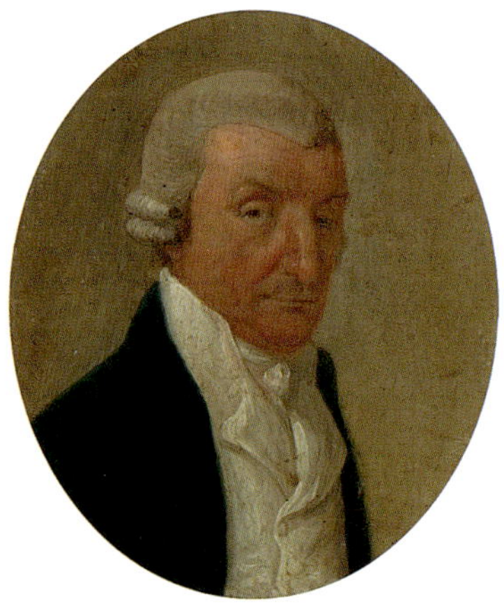

unknown artist 19th C
Lieutenant John Andrews (d.1817)
oil on board 13 x 10
COLEM : 2005.64

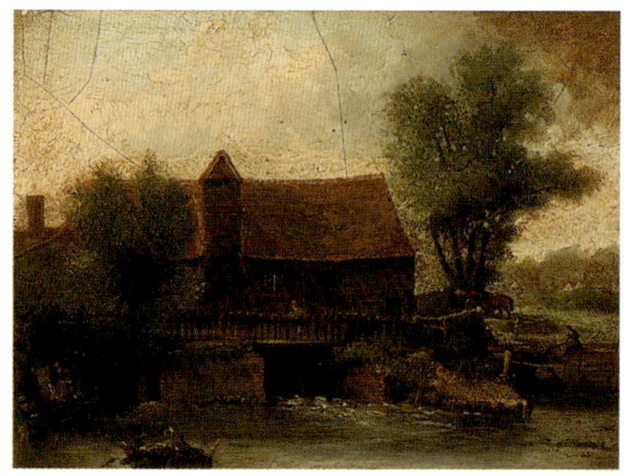

unknown artist 19th C
Middle Mill, Colchester
oil on board 20 x 26.5
COLEM : 72A

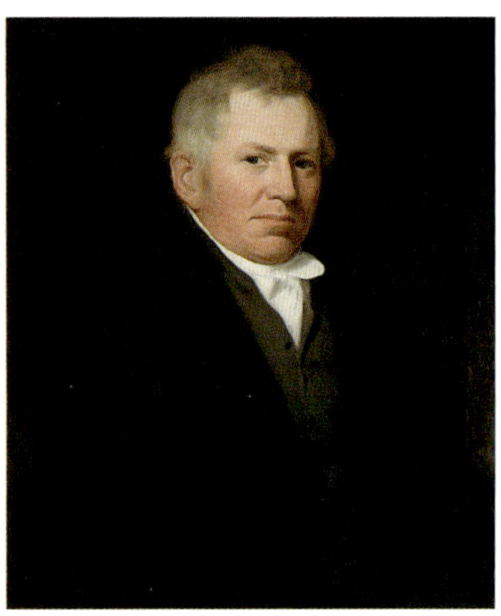

unknown artist 19th C
Sergeant Lay
oil on canvas 76 x 63
COLEM : 1985.107

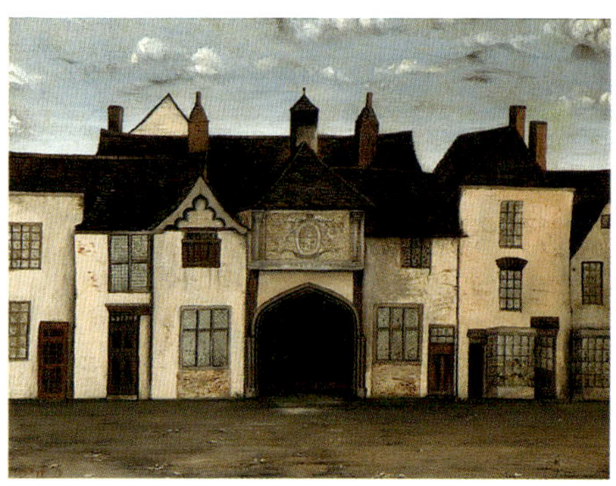

unknown artist 19th C
The Old Moot Hall, Colchester
oil on canvas 40.6 x 50.8
COLEM : 1954.576

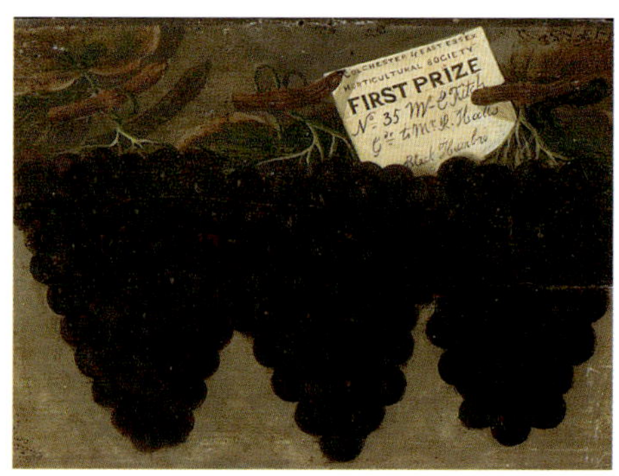

unknown artist 19th C
Three Bunches of First Prize Black Grapes
oil on board 25.4 x 34.3
COLEM : 1969.81.2

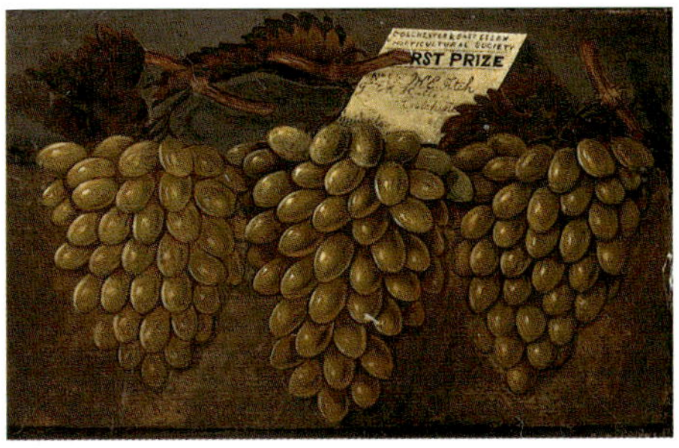

unknown artist 19th C
Three Bunches of First Prize Green Grapes
oil on board 24.8 x 36.8
COLEM : 1969.81.1

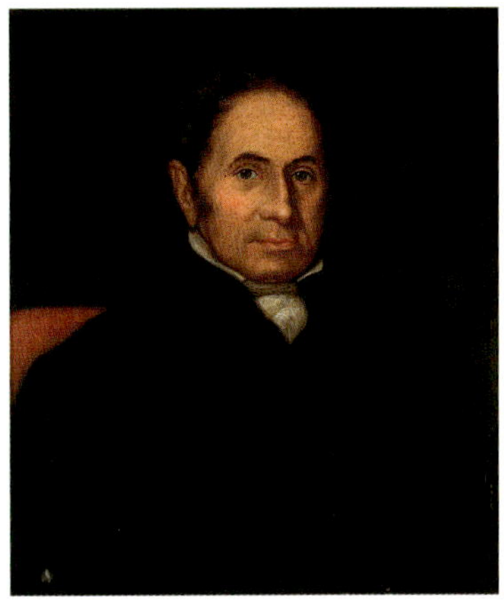

unknown artist 19th C
Walter Swinborne
oil on canvas 61 x 50.8
COLEM : 185A

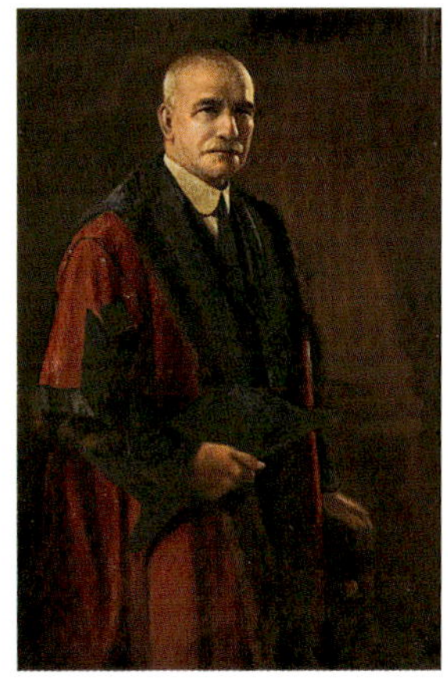

unknown artist
Alderman Walter Littlebury, JP 1911–1926?
oil on canvas 61 x 40.6
COLEM : 195A

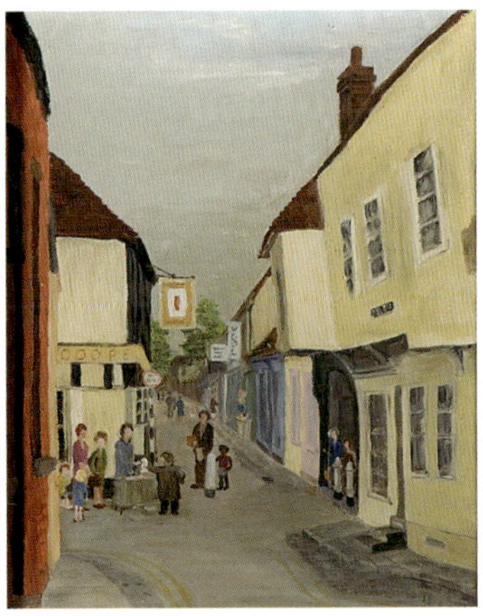

unknown artist
Eld Lane, Colchester c.1967
oil on canvas 62 x 42.5
COLEM : 2004.363

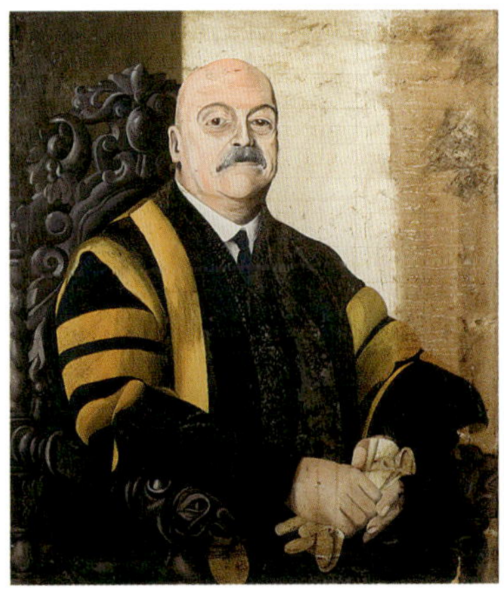

unknown artist 20th C
Councillor Chopping
oil on canvas 61 x 51
COLEM : 2002.41.2

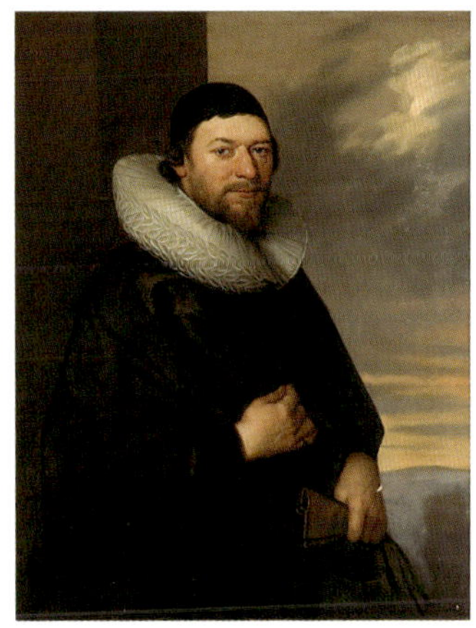

unknown artist
Charles Tayspill (1600–1662)
oil on canvas 113 x 85
COLEM : 166A

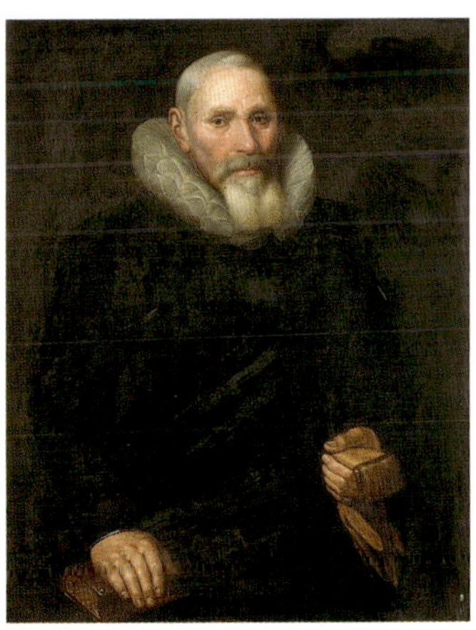

unknown artist
Giles Tayspill
oil on canvas 96.5 x 73.7
COLEM : 167A

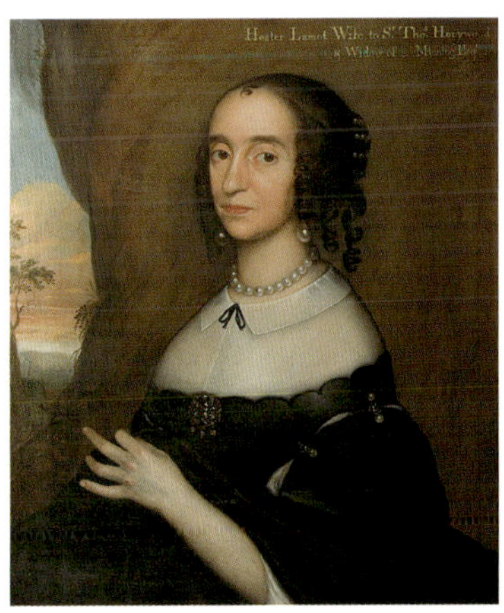

unknown artist
Hester, Lady Honywood, née Lamont (1607–1681)
oil on canvas 71.1 x 61
COLEM : 173A

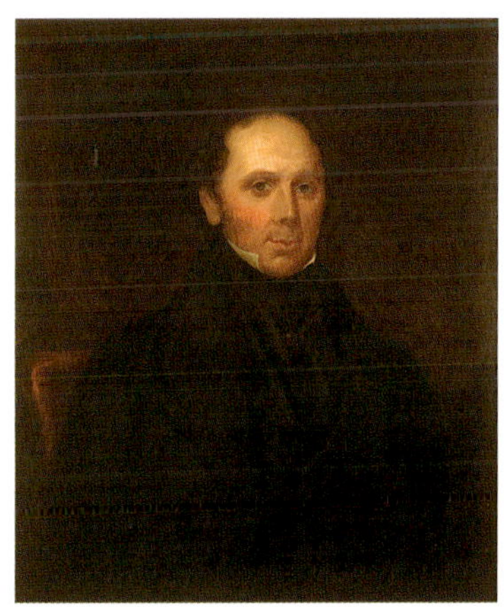

unknown artist
John Chaplin (1795–1858), Mayor of Colchester (1836)
oil on canvas 76.2 x 63.5
COLEM : 158A

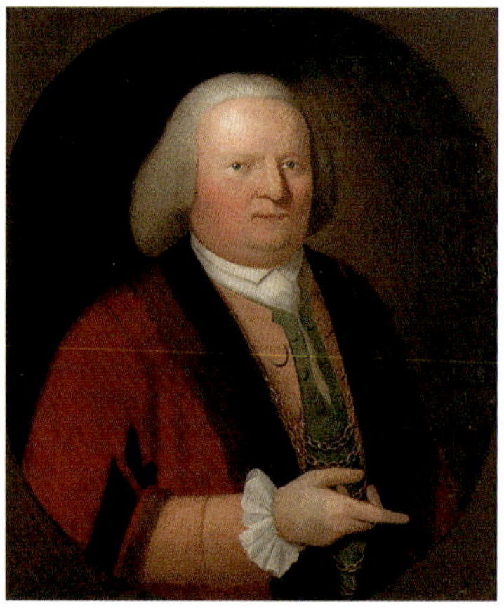

unknown artist
John King, Mayor of Colchester (1775–1778 & 1781)
oil on canvas 73.7 x 61
COLEM : 145A

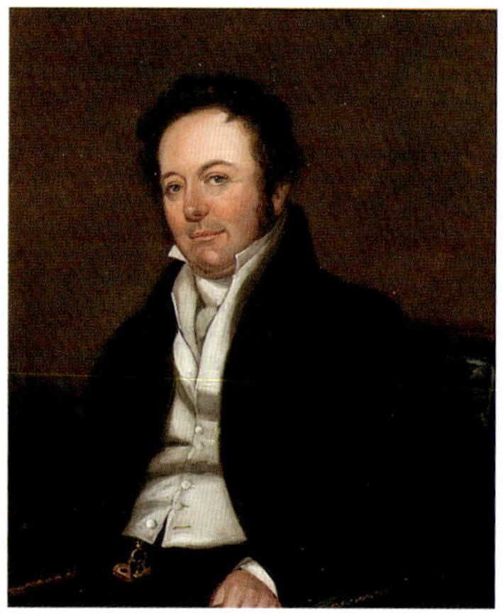

unknown artist
Roger Nunn, MD, Mayor of Colchester (1834 & 1842)
oil on canvas 76.2 x 63.5
COLEM : 182A

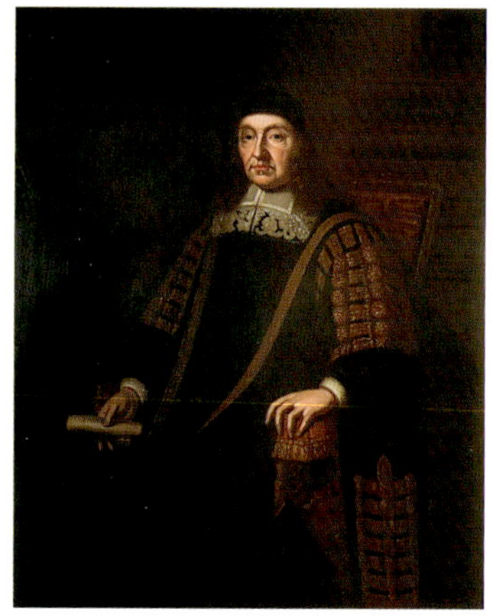

unknown artist
Sir Harbottle Grimston, PC (1603–1685), Speaker of the House of Commons, Master of the Rolls
oil on canvas 127 x 101.6
COLEM : 164A

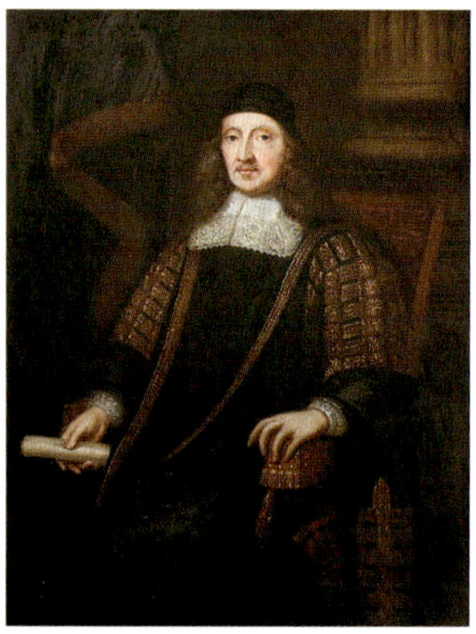

unknown artist
Sir Harbottle Grimston, PC (1603–1685) Speaker of the House of Commons, Master of the Rolls
oil on canvas 121.9 x 88.9
COLEM : 203A

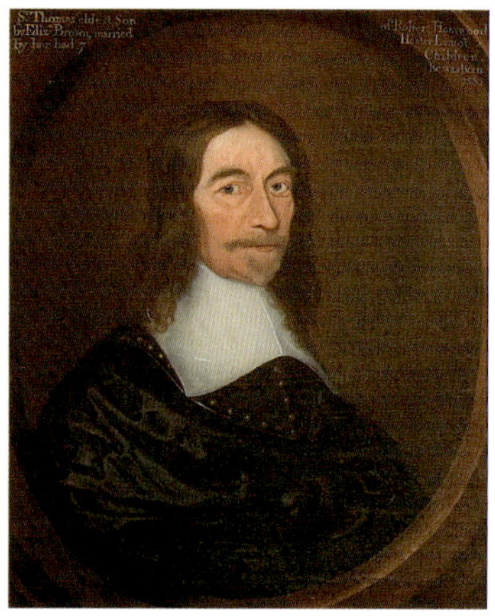

unknown artist
Sir Thomas Honywood (1586–1666)
oil on canvas 72.4 x 61
COLEM : 174A

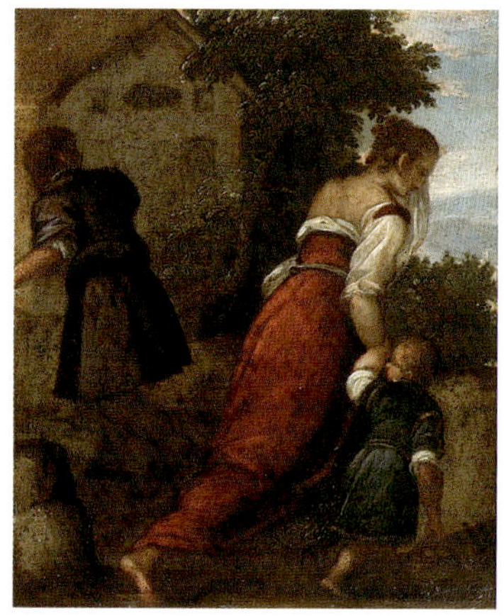

unknown artist
The Casting Out of Hagar
oil on metal 29.8 x 23.5
COLEM : 1966.OS.213

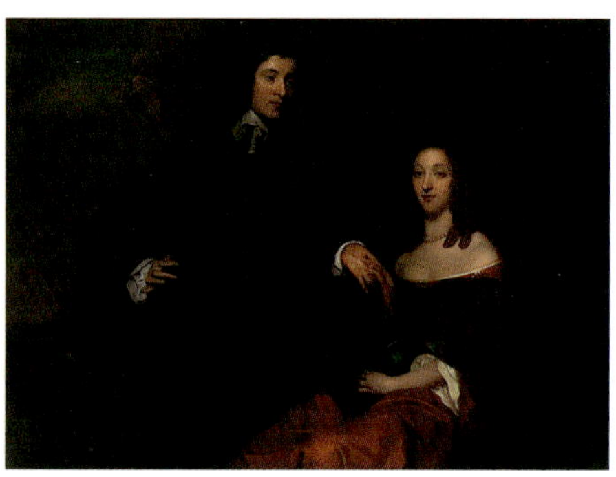

unknown artist
Thomas, 3rd Lord Fairfax (1612–1671), and His Wife, Anne (1614–1665) (after William Charles Thomas Dobson)
oil on canvas 139.7 x 182.9
COLEM : 169A

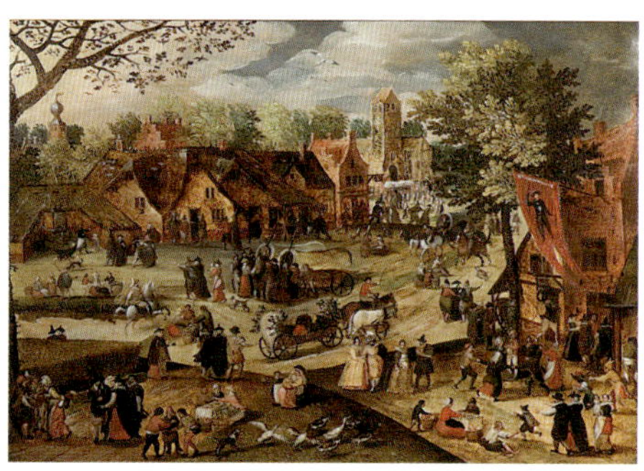

Vinckboons, David 1576–c.1632
Flemish Village Merrymaking
oil on oak panel 76.8 x 109.2
COLEM : 118A

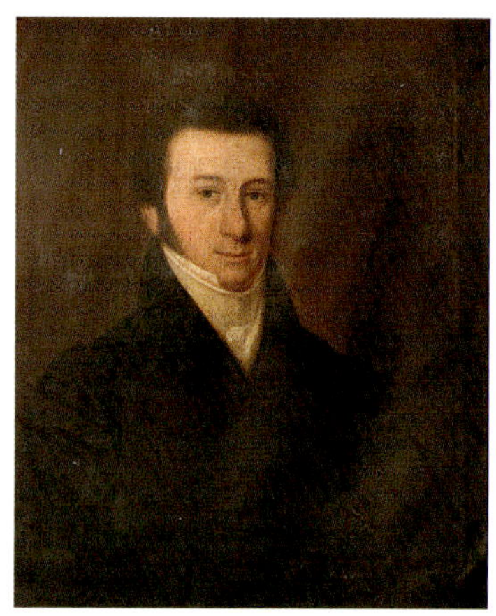

Vine, John c.1809–1867
James Cobb of 16 High Street, Colchester c.1840
oil on canvas 63.5 x 50.8
COLEM : 153A

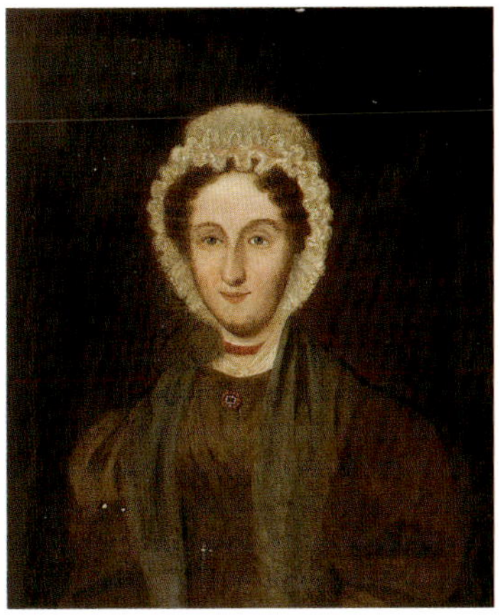

Vine, John c.1809–1867
Mrs James Cobb of Colchester c.1840
oil on canvas 63.5 x 50.8
COLEM : 154A

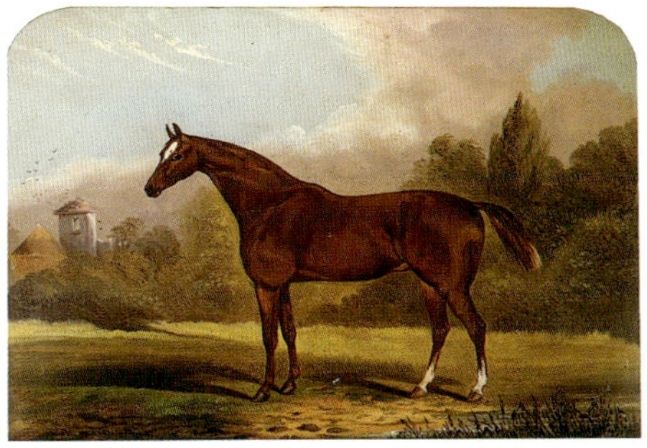

Vine, John c.1809–1867
Chestnut Horse 1858
oil on card 45.5 x 61
COLEM : 1985.146

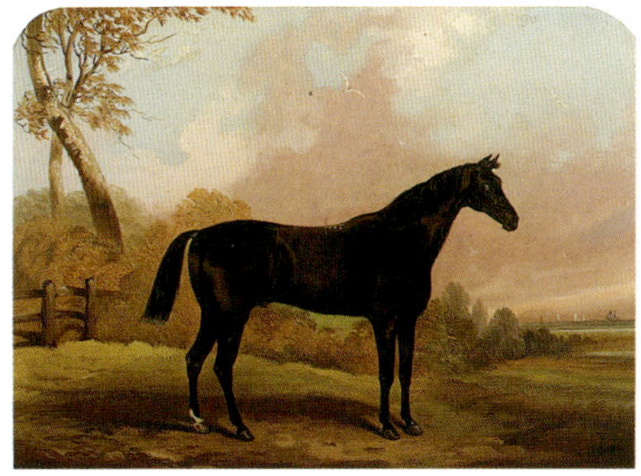

Vine, John c.1809–1867
Black Horse
oil on card 45.5 x 60.5
COLEM : 1985.145

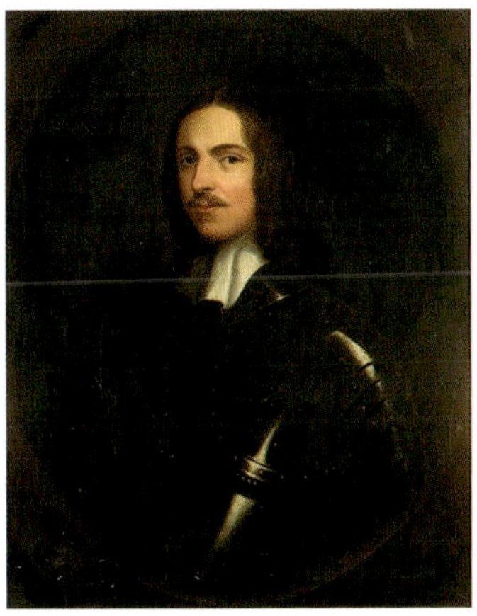

Walker, Robert (after) c.1600–c.1659
General Henry Ireton
oil on canvas 90 x 69
COLEM : 168A

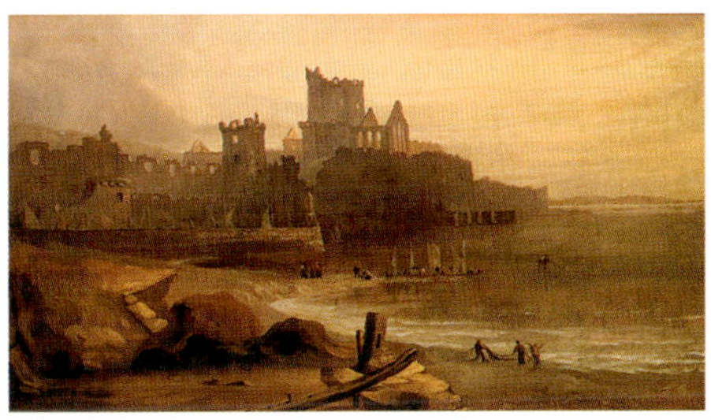

Williams, R. active 1842
Peel Castle, Isle of Man
oil on canvas 54 x 91
COLEM : 279A

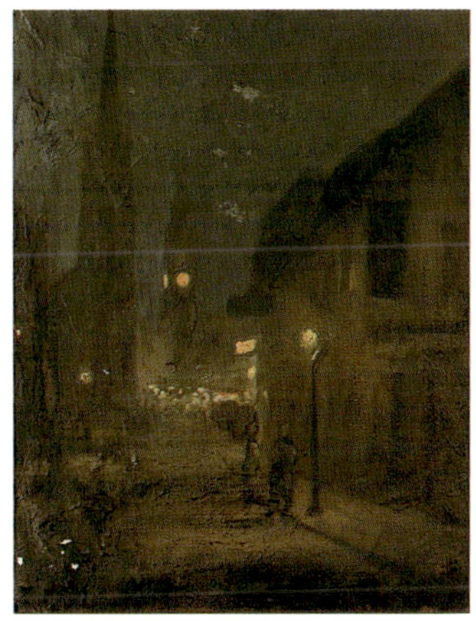

Winch, Miller J. active 1891–c.1920
High Street, Colchester at Night c.1920
oil on canvas 46 x 36
COLEM : 1975.93

Feering & Kelvedon Local History Museum

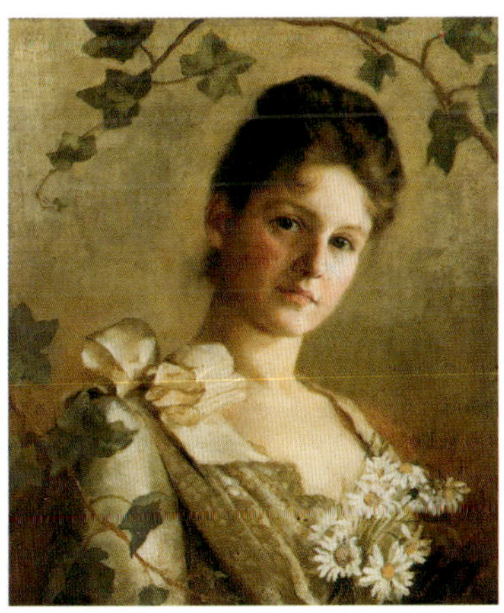

Durell, Amy Clara b.1865
Miss Ada Cecilia Lance (b.1866) of the Red House, Kelvedon 1888
oil on canvas 62 x 54
9076

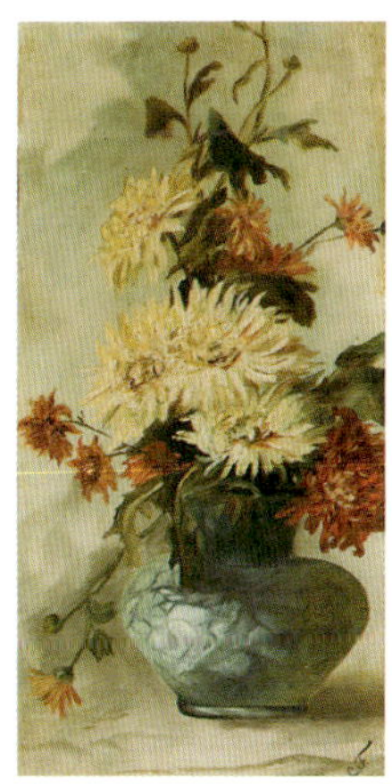

Foster, C.
Chrysanthemums in a Jug c.1880
oil on canvas 60 x 30
9075

Sir Alfred Munnings Art Museum

The Museum is situated at Castle House, Dedham, which Sir Alfred Munnings bought in 1919. He put up a studio building in the garden and lived and worked here for the rest of his life. He married Violet McBride, a noted horsewoman, in 1920 and after his death in 1959, she decided to devote the house to his memory by establishing a museum to display those pictures which were still in her possession. Castle House was first opened to the public in 1961 and a year later she set up the Violet Munnings Trust Fund, formed for the purpose of financing an art museum. Four years later the Castle House Trust came into existence as a charitable organisation. The ownership of the house, its furnishings and Sir Alfred's paintings, together with some 40 acres of surrounding land and an endowment fund, were vested in the Trustees.

The greater part of the picture collection consisted of juvenilia, early advertising work, drawings and sketches, works dating from the artist's youth in Norfolk and landscapes which Sir Alfred had painted for his own satisfaction in and around Dedham. However, most periods of his life are represented. There are figure subjects done when he studied as a young man at the Atelier Julian in Paris; scenes of gipsy life; pictures painted at Lamorna in Cornwall, where he had a studio for a while attracted by the Newlyn School; military subjects which he painted in France in 1918 in his capacity as an official War Artist attached to the Canadian Cavalry Brigade; and scenes of Exmoor, where he and Violet lived during the Second World War while Castle House was requisitioned by the army. In 1919 Munnings was elected an Associate of the Royal Academy and he received his knighthood on becoming its President in 1944. From the First World War onwards, he concentrated increasingly on equestrian portraits, paintings of horses and hunting and racing scenes. Since most of these were commissioned, they are hardly represented in the collection but there are a number of studies of horses and jockeys at the starting gate and in the unsaddling enclosure.

Lady Munnings died in 1971 and shortly afterwards the Trustees decided to add to the collection whenever possible. The first purchases, made in 1973, were *A Suffolk Horse Fair, Lavenham* (1901), *Flower Girl, Violets* (c.1904), *A Gipsy Camp Fire* (1910), *Tagg's Island* (1920) and *A Shoot in a Swede Field* (1901). Other early pictures were acquired in subsequent years but by the mid-1980s, the rising price of paintings by Munnings, even early or unusual ones, had become prohibitive and the Trust lacked the means to compete in the open market for any major work. Fortunately, since then some welcome gifts have been received and a magnificent picture of *'Shrimp' on a White Welsh Pony* was bequeathed to the Museum in 2002.

Michael Archer, Trustee

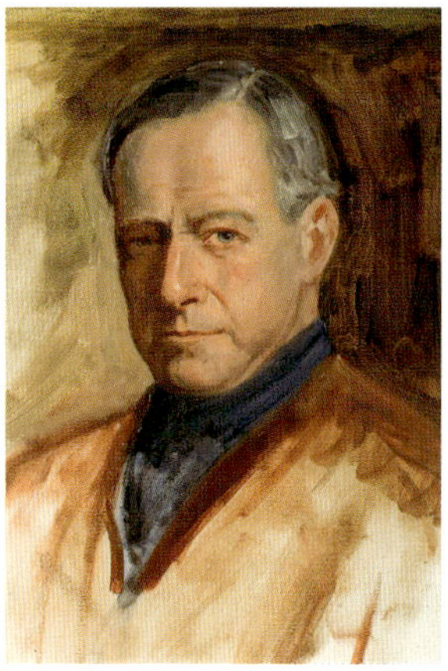

Codner, Maurice Frederick 1888–1958
Sir Alfred Munnings
oil on canvas 31.2 x 29.2
Misc3

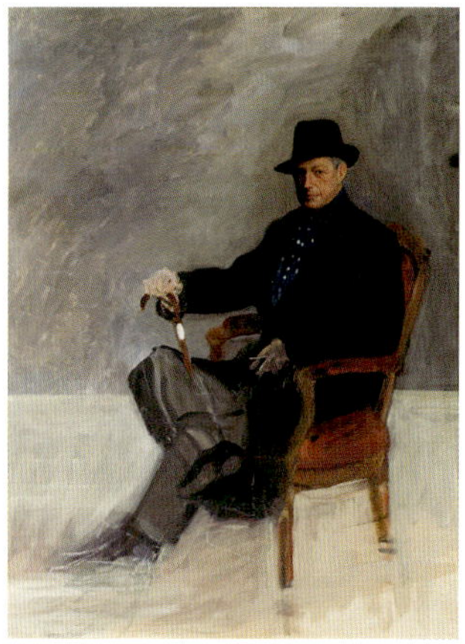

Codner, Maurice Frederick 1888–1958
Sir Alfred Munnings Seated
oil on canvas 111.8 x 81.3
Misc4

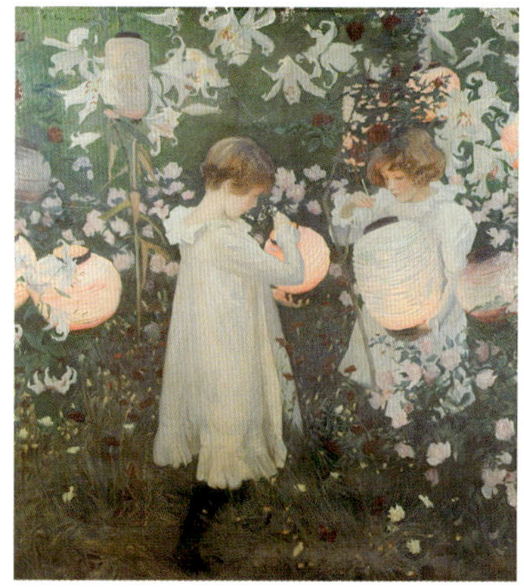

Eves, Reginald Grenville 1876–1941
'Lily, Carnation, Lily, Rose' (copy of John Singer Sargent)
oil on canvas 42.9 x 37.4
Misc5

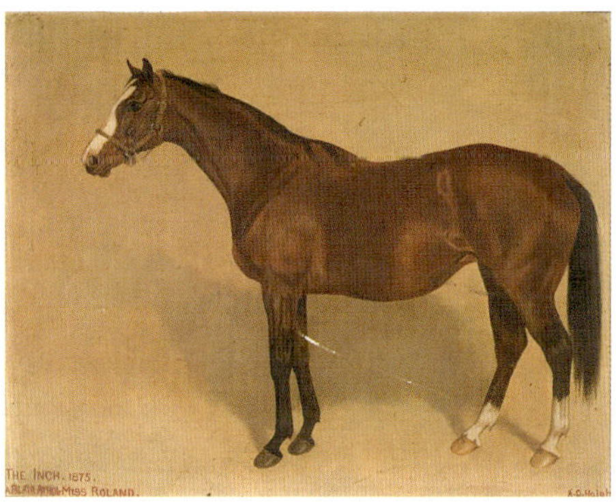

Haigh, Alfred G. 1870–1963
The Inch 1875
oil on canvas 67.7 x 83.9
Misc1

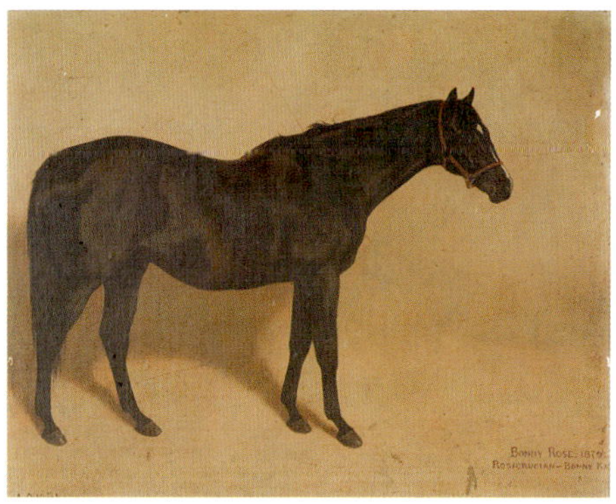

Haigh, Alfred G. 1870–1963
Bonny Rose 1879
oil on canvas 69.4 x 82.3
Misc2

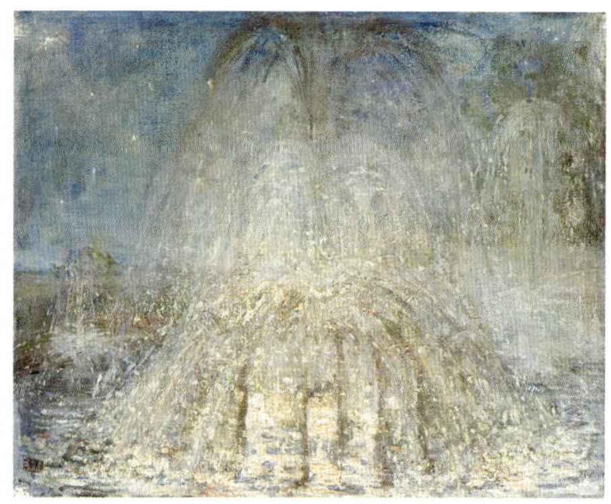

E. F. M.
Fountain of Lights
oil on canvas 50.5 x 61
Misc7

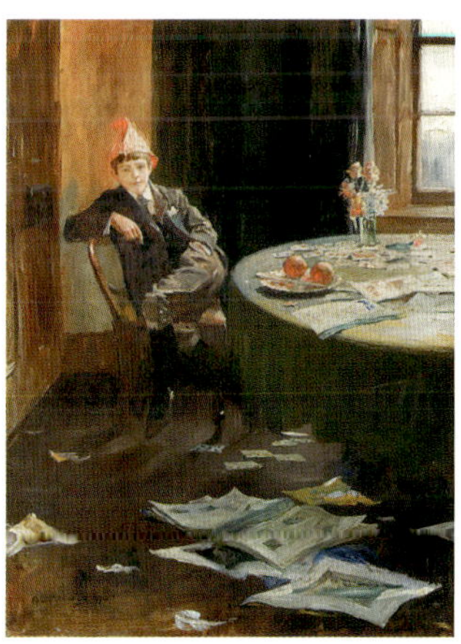

Munnings, Alfred James 1878–1959
After the Party 1897
oil on canvas 76.2 x 55.9
209

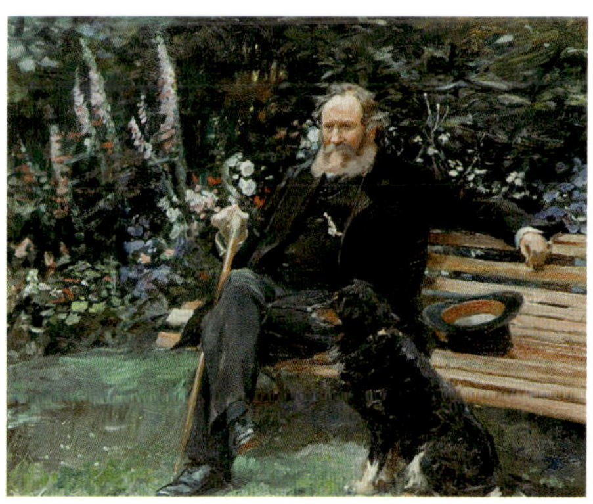

Munnings, Alfred James 1878–1959
Daniel Tomkins and His Dog 1898
oil on canvas 55.9 x 66
637

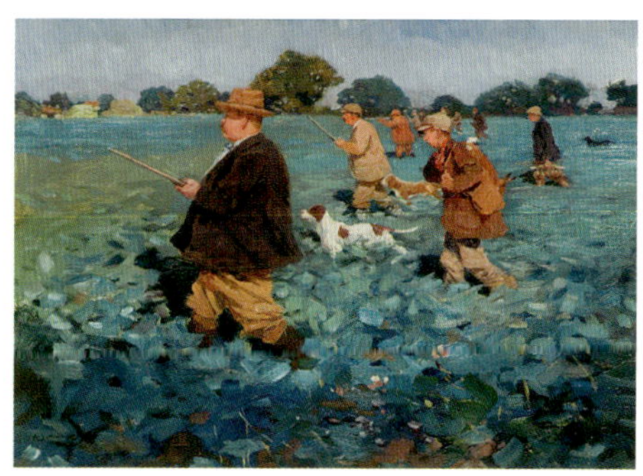

Munnings, Alfred James 1878–1959
A Shoot in a Swede Field 1901
oil on canvas 41.3 x 55.9
633

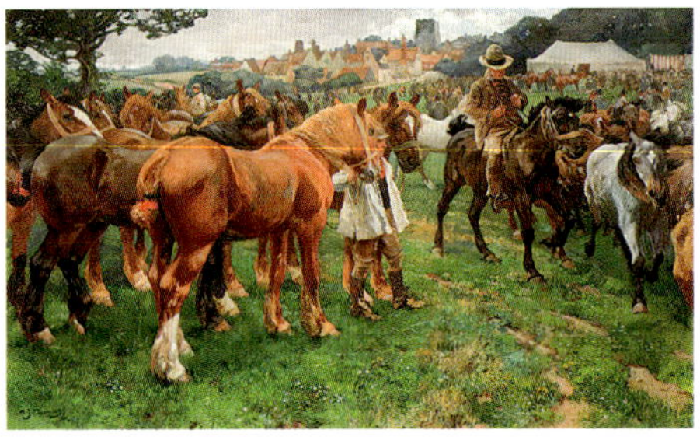

Munnings, Alfred James 1878–1959
A Suffolk Horse Fair, Lavenham 1901
oil on canvas 127 x 203.2
634

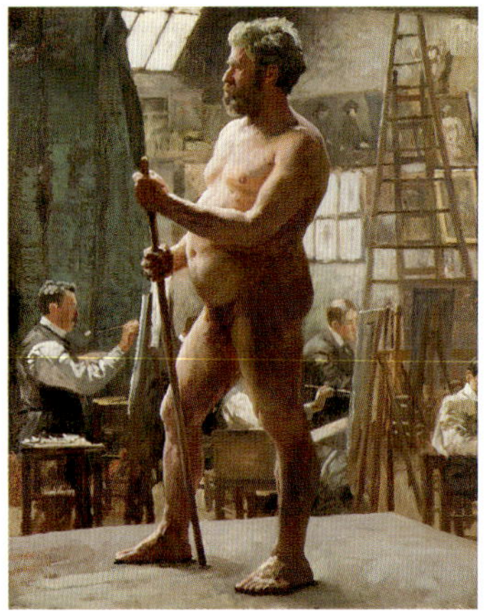

Munnings, Alfred James 1878–1959
Study of a Male Nude in Julian's Atelier 1901
oil on canvas 81.3 x 64.8
432

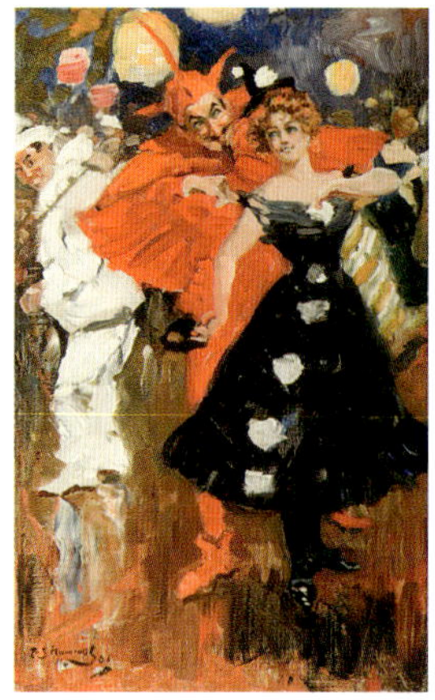

Munnings, Alfred James 1878–1959
The Fancy Dress Ball 1901
oil on canvas 50.8 x 30.8
L3:2005 (P)

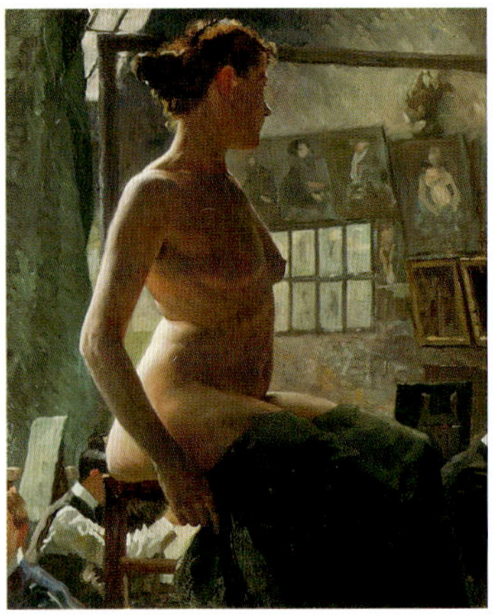

Munnings, Alfred James 1878–1959
A Female Nude Seated at Julian's Atelier, Rue du Dragon 1902
oil on canvas 82.6 x 66
204

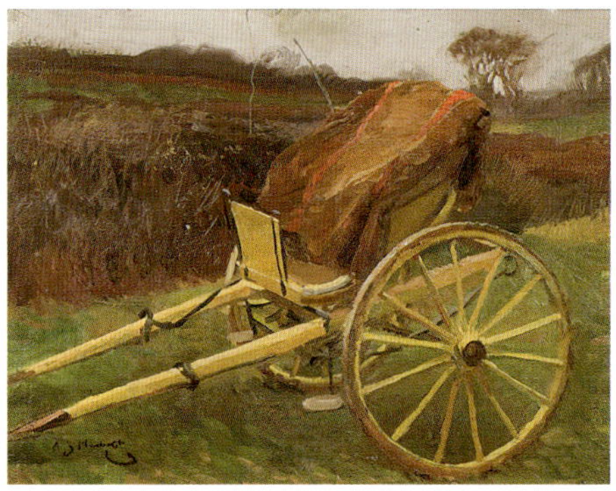

Munnings, Alfred James 1878–1959
Colt Breaker's Gig 1902
oil on canvas 35.6 x 45.7
3

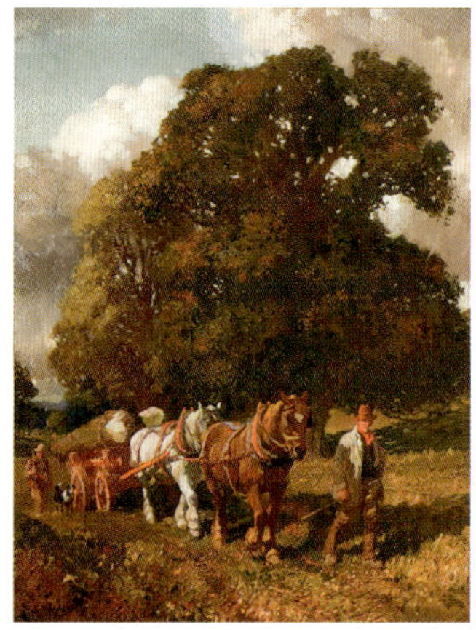

Munnings, Alfred James 1878–1959
The Timber Gill 1902
oil on canvas 142.2 x 111.8
144

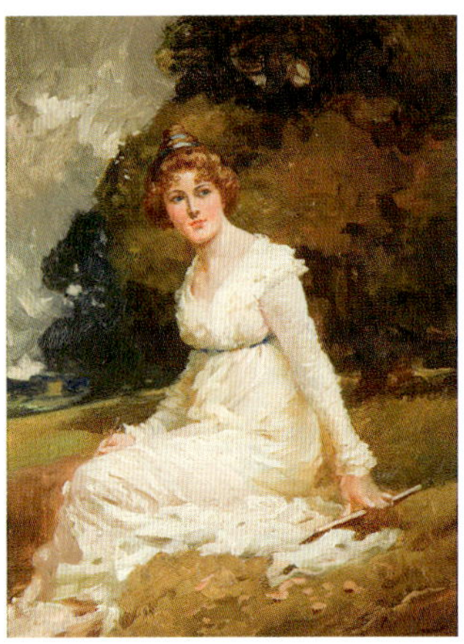

Munnings, Alfred James 1878–1959
A Lady Seated in a Park 1903
oil on canvas 40.6 x 30.5
658

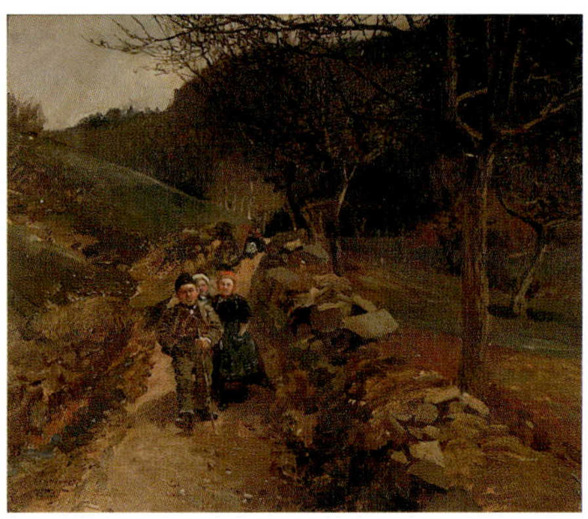

Munnings, Alfred James 1878–1959
Hornberg, Black Forest 1903
oil on canvas 35.6 x 40.6
646

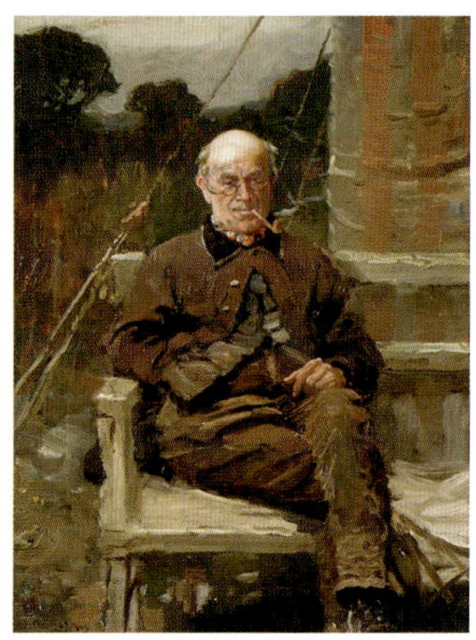

Munnings, Alfred James 1878–1959
Old Gray 1903
oil on canvas 40.6 x 30.5
662

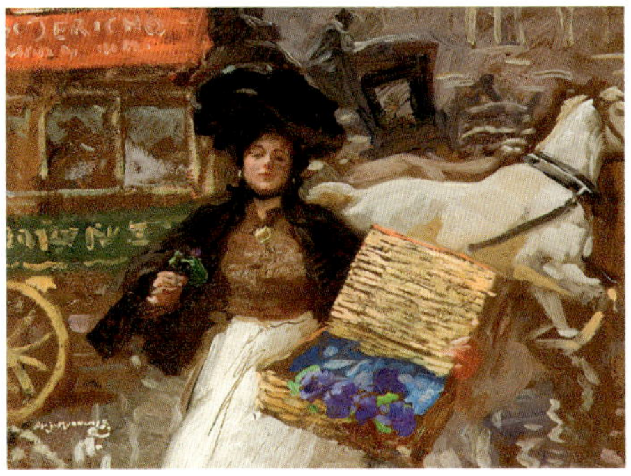

Munnings, Alfred James 1878–1959
Flower Girl, Violets c.1904
oil on canvas 35.6 x 45.7
631

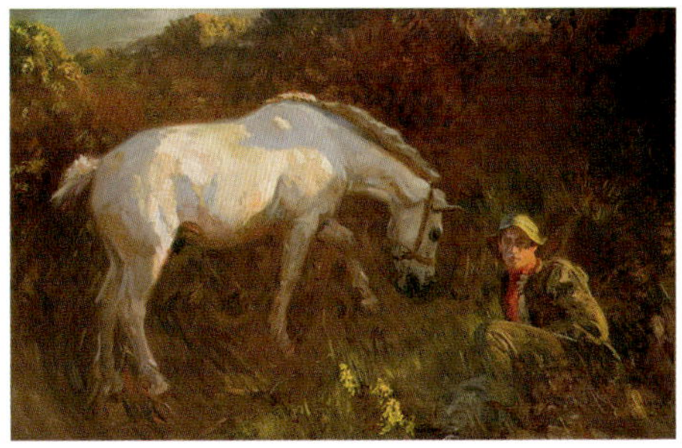

Munnings, Alfred James 1878–1959
The Grey Pony, Augereau, in a Sandpit with Groom, George Curzon 1905
oil on canvas 125.7 x 202.6
79

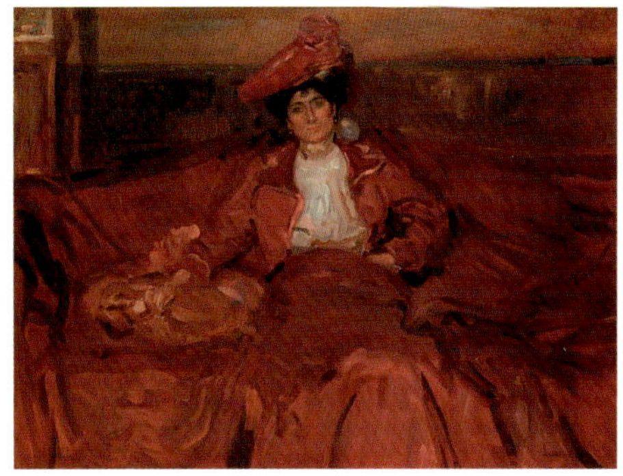

Munnings, Alfred James 1878–1959
Nelly Gray 1907
oil on canvas 72.4 x 92.7
654

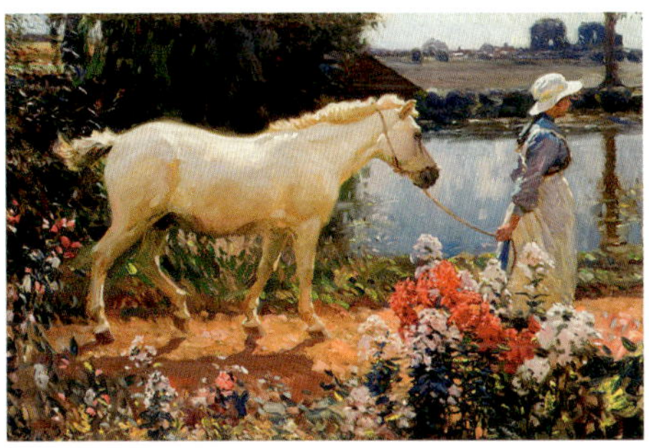

Munnings, Alfred James 1878–1959
Path to the Orchard 1908
oil on canvas 76.2 x 106.7
635

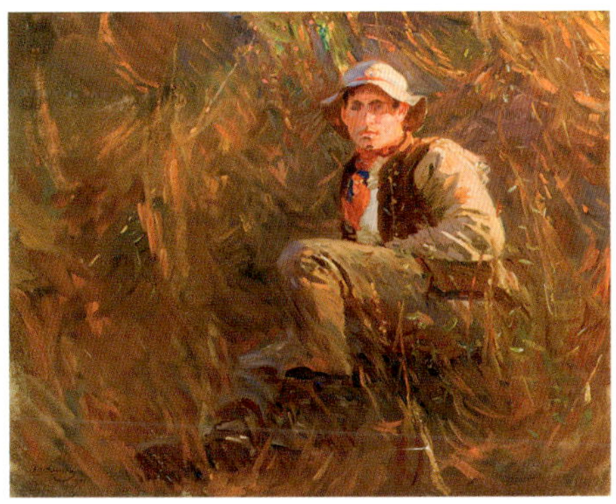

Munnings, Alfred James 1878–1959
Study of George Curzon, Groom 1908
oil on canvas 60.4 x 76.4
205

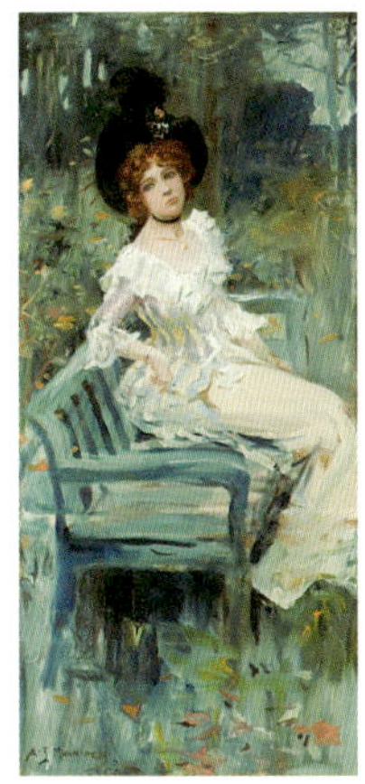

Munnings, Alfred James 1878–1959
Cassie Jeweller 1909
oil on canvas 163 x 87
650

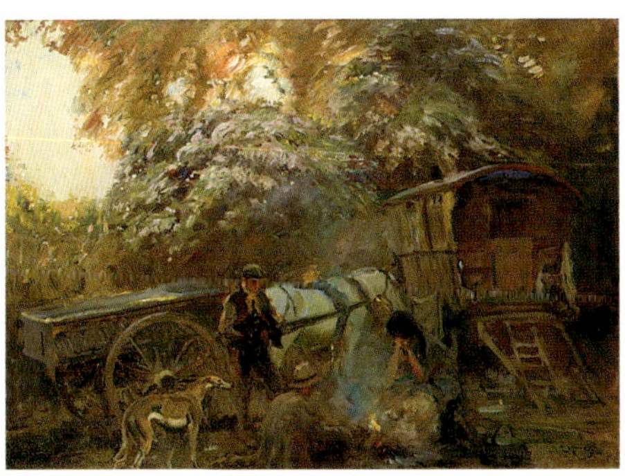

Munnings, Alfred James 1878–1959
A Gipsy Campfire 1910
oil on canvas 76.2 x 101.6
632

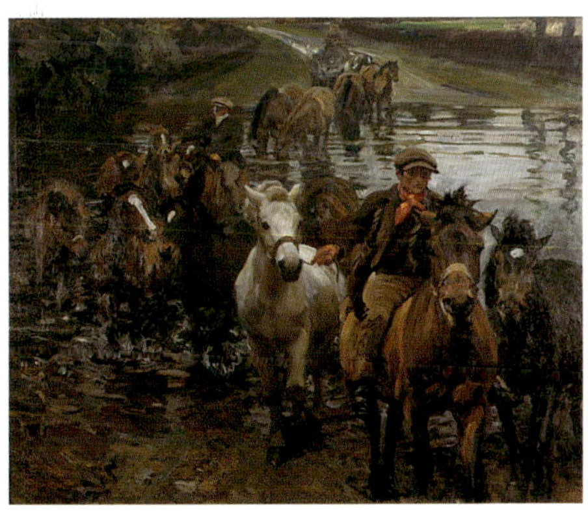

Munnings, Alfred James 1878–1959
The Ford 1910
oil on canvas 134.6 x 162.6
132

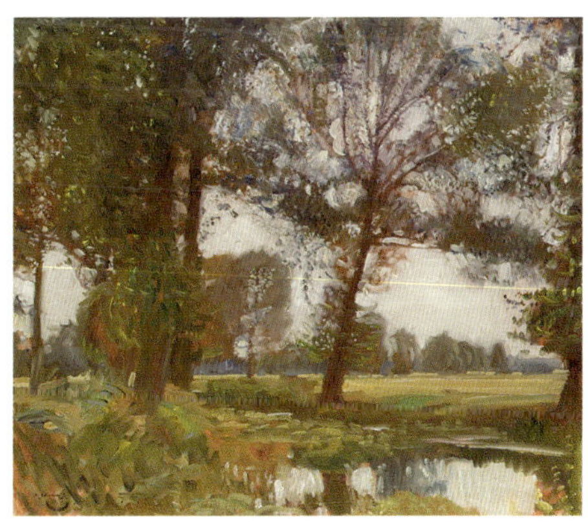

Munnings, Alfred James 1878–1959
Poplars, River Waveney 1911
oil on canvas 64.8 x 71.8
54

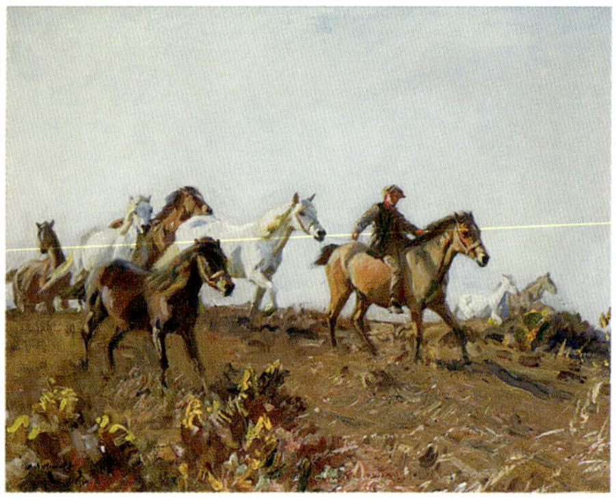

Munnings, Alfred James 1878–1959
'Shrimp' Leading Ponies across a Norfolk Common 1911
oil on canvas 62.2 x 74.9
653

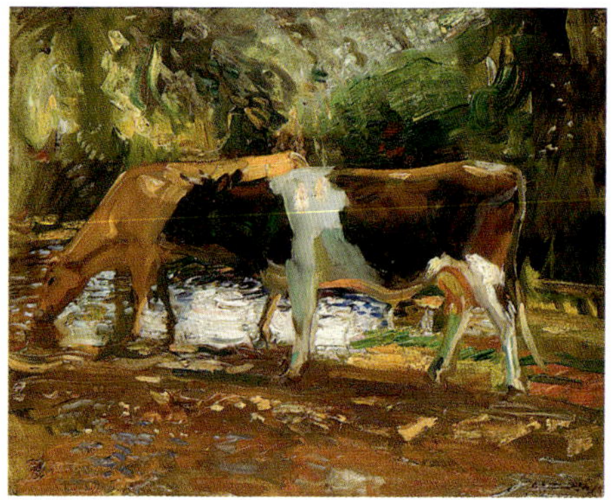

Munnings, Alfred James 1878–1959
Cattle Watering in a Stream, Zennor, Cornwall 1912
oil on canvas 63.5 x 76.2
142

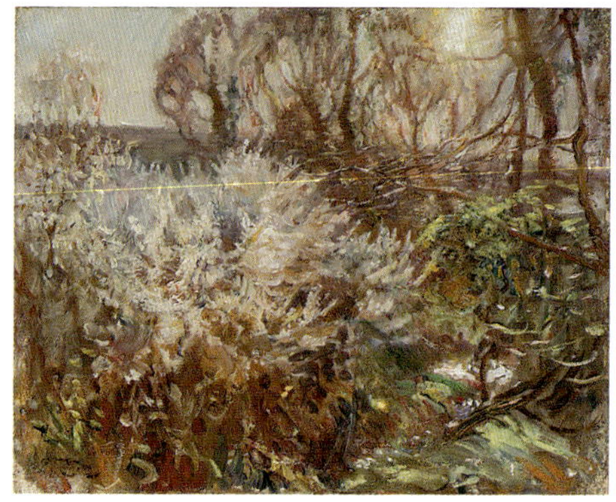

Munnings, Alfred James 1878–1959
Cornwall, Blossom 1912
oil on canvas 50.8 x 61
17

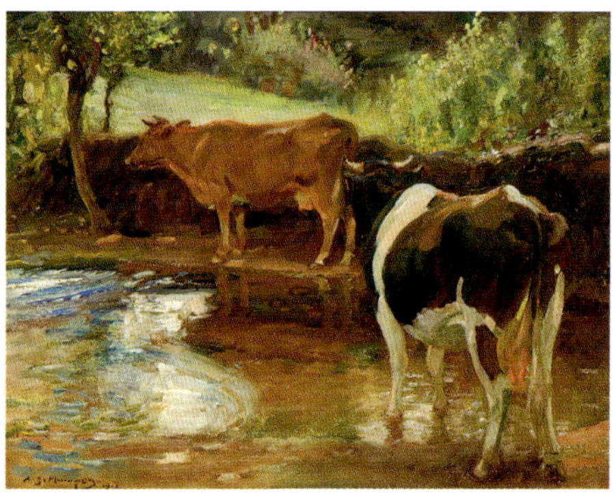

Munnings, Alfred James 1878–1959
Cows at Water, Lamorna 1912
oil on canvas 35.6 x 43.2
74

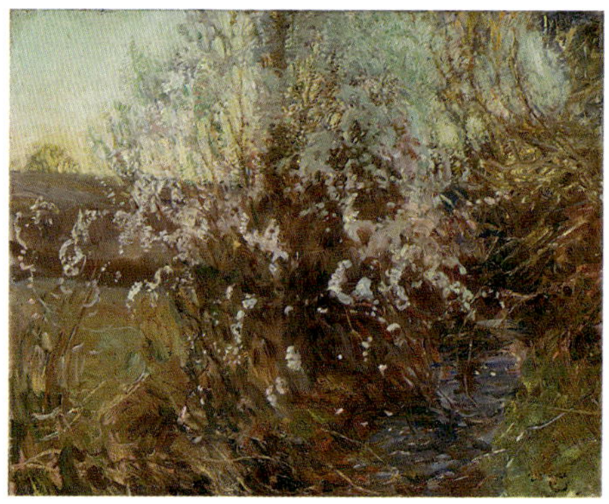

Munnings, Alfred James 1878–1959
Spring in a Cornish Valley 1912
oil on canvas 63.5 x 76.2
148

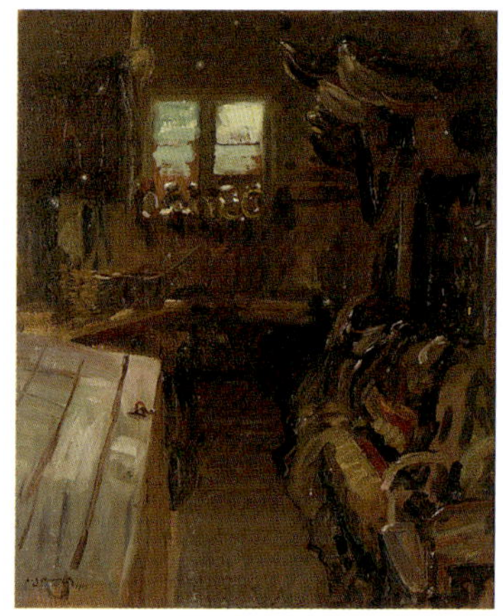

Munnings, Alfred James 1878–1959
The Harness Room 1912
oil on panel 40.6 x 33
321

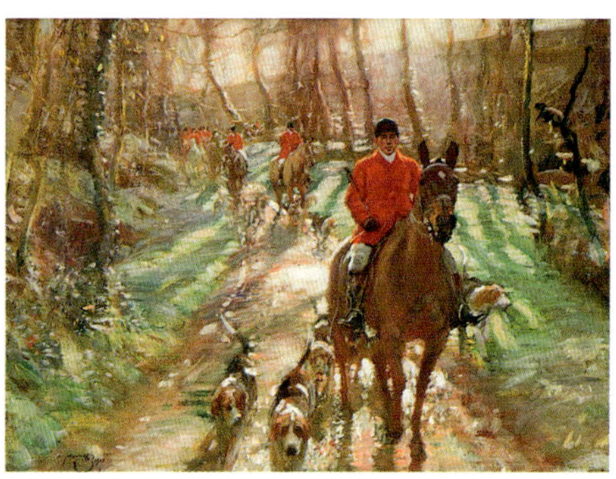

Munnings, Alfred James 1878–1959
Hunting Morning 1913
oil on board 52.1 x 66.7
636

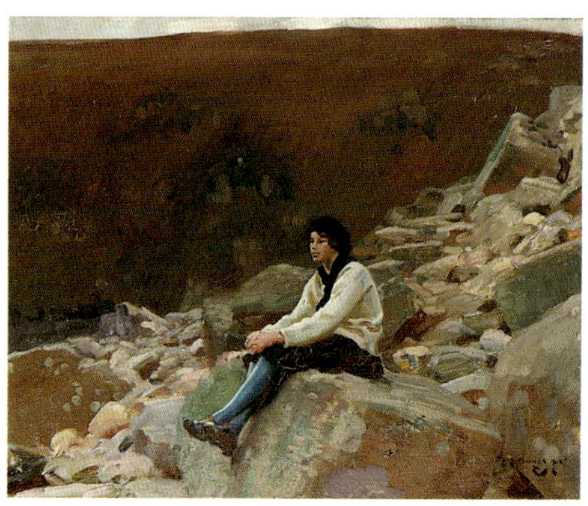

Munnings, Alfred James 1878–1959
Phyllis Crocker 1913
oil on canvas 48.3 x 55.9
147

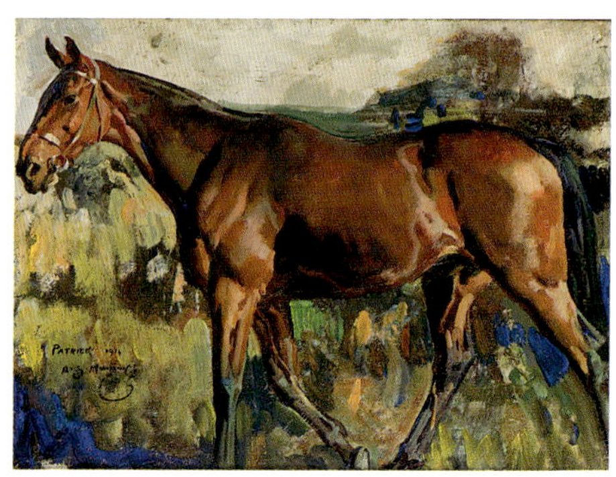

Munnings, Alfred James 1878–1959
The Bay Horse, 'Patrick', Bought in Dublin with Grey Mare 1914
oil on canvas 35.6 x 45.7
36

Facing page: Wade, Maurice, 1917–1991, *Canal at Longport* (detail), Southend Museums Service, (p. 288)

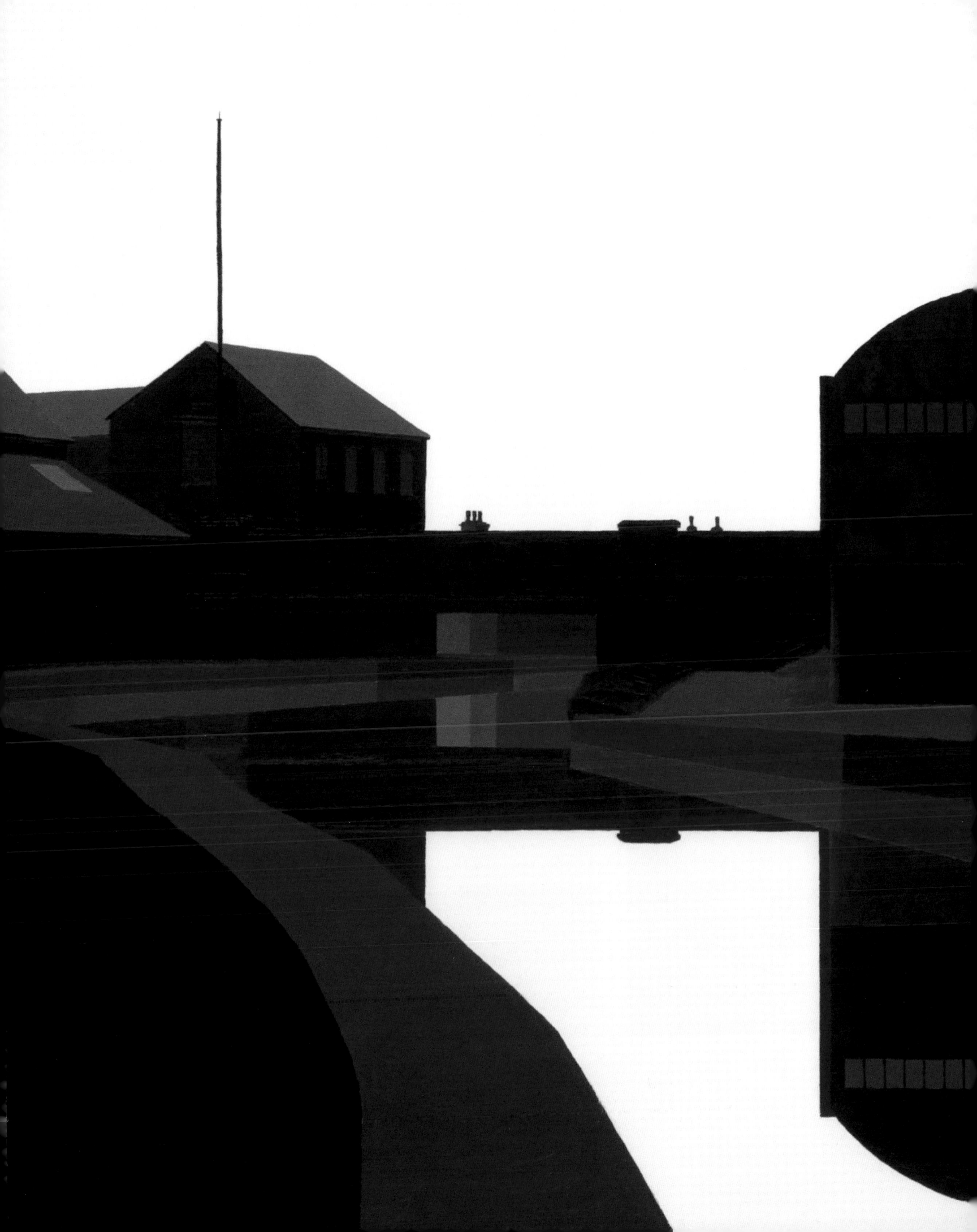

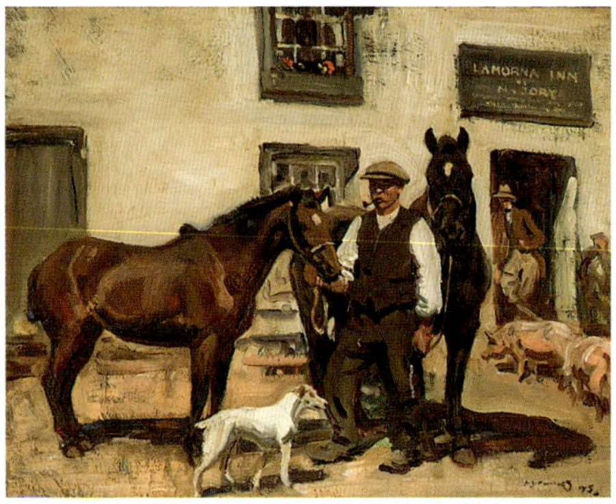

Munnings, Alfred James 1878–1959
Lamorna Inn 1915
oil on canvas 50.8 x 61
638

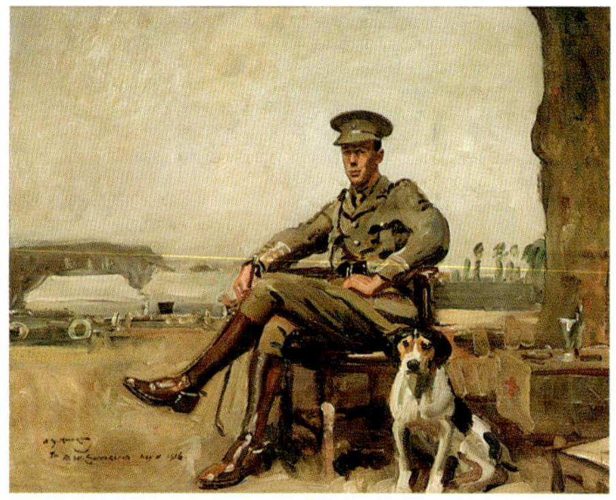

Munnings, Alfred James 1878–1959
R. W. Sutherland, Cavalry Officer 1916
oil on board 50.8 x 61
220

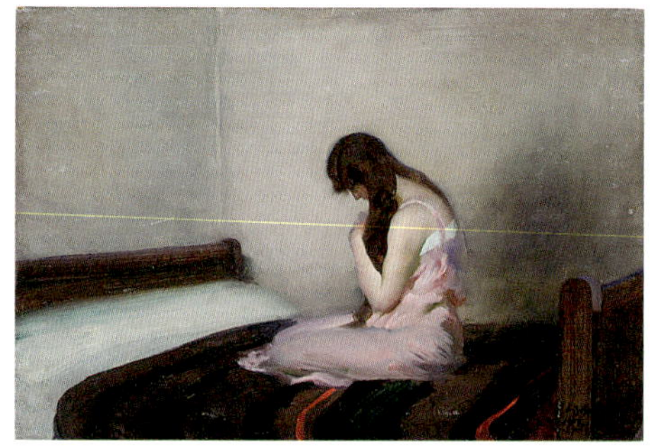

Munnings, Alfred James 1878–1959
A Girl on a Bed 1917
oil on panel 25.4 x 35.6
573

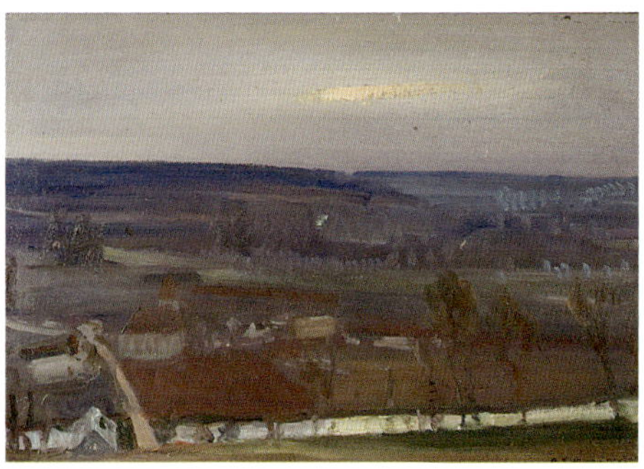

Munnings, Alfred James 1878–1959
Study in the Eure Valley, France, with the Canadian Army 1917
oil on panel 25.4 x 34.9
548

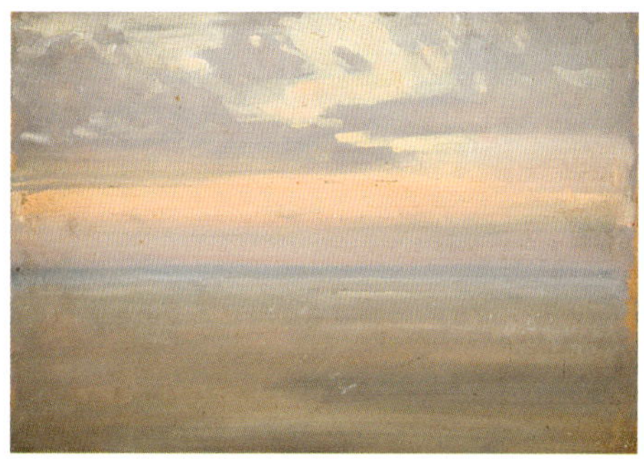

Munnings, Alfred James 1878–1959
Study of Dawn Effect, France, 2 April 1918
1918
oil on board 25.4 x 35.6
666

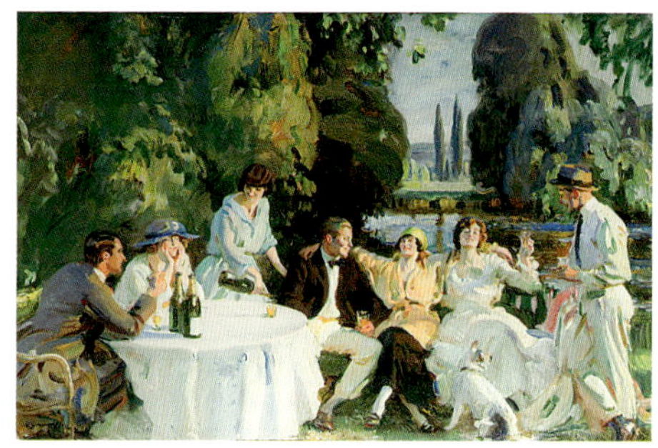

Munnings, Alfred James 1878–1959
Tagg's Island 1920
oil on canvas 88.9 x 127
630

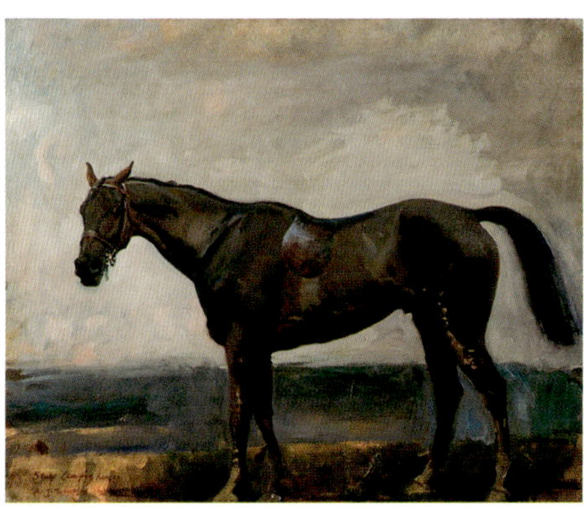

Munnings, Alfred James 1878–1959
A Dark Bay Hunter 1922
oil on canvas 50.8 x 63
22

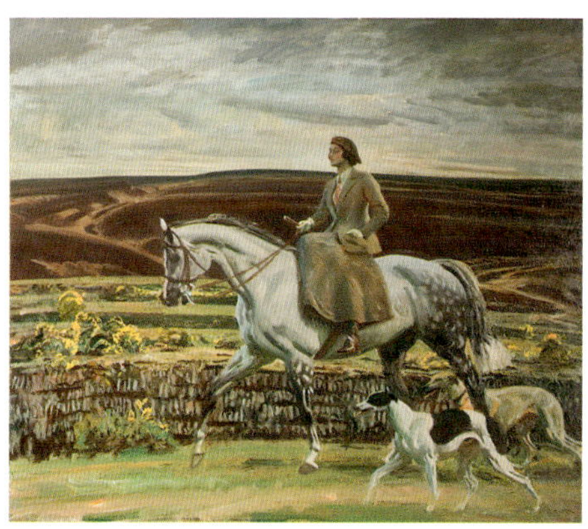

Munnings, Alfred James 1878–1959
Lady Munnings Riding a Grey Hunter ('Magnolia') Side-Saddle, with Her Dogs on Exmoor 1924
oil on canvas 176.7 x 187
76

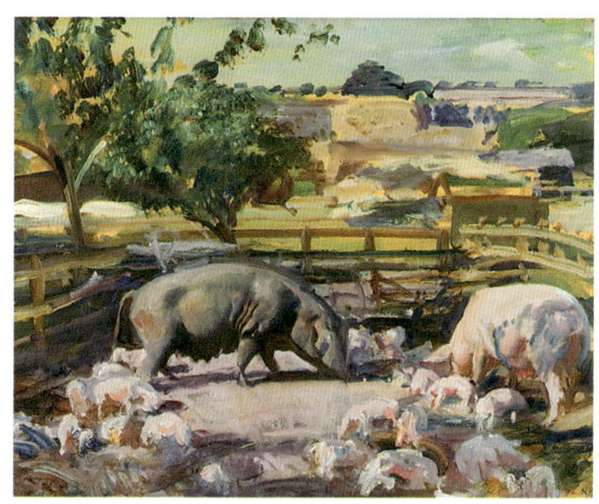

Munnings, Alfred James 1878–1959
Sow and Pigs, Great Thurlow, Suffolk 1926
oil on canvas 51.4 x 61
362

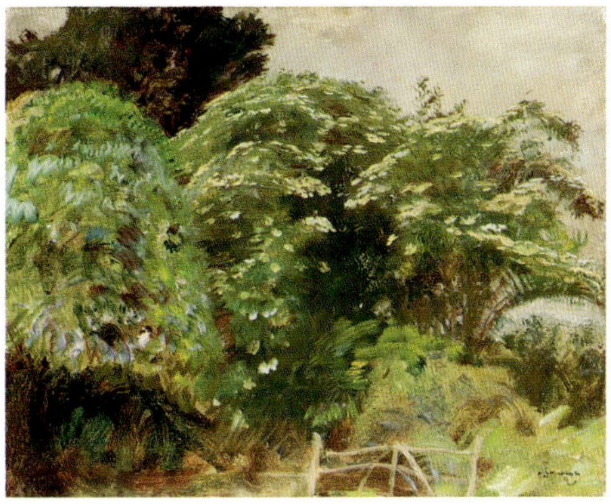

Munnings, Alfred James 1878–1959
Elder Blossom 1935
oil on canvas 50.8 x 61 (E)
527

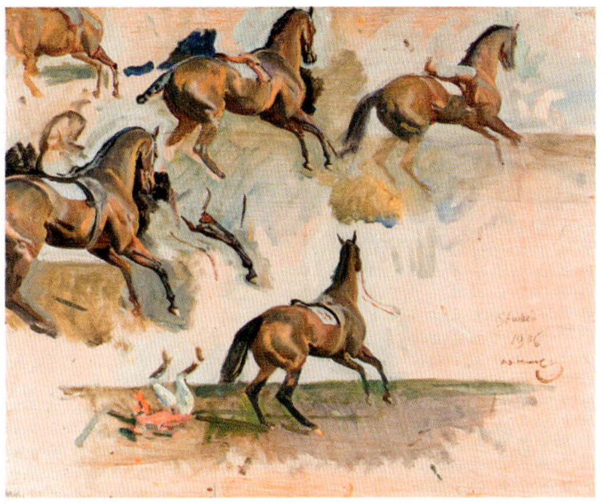

Munnings, Alfred James 1878–1959
Horse Studies (recto) 1936
oil on board 50.8 x 61 (E)
152

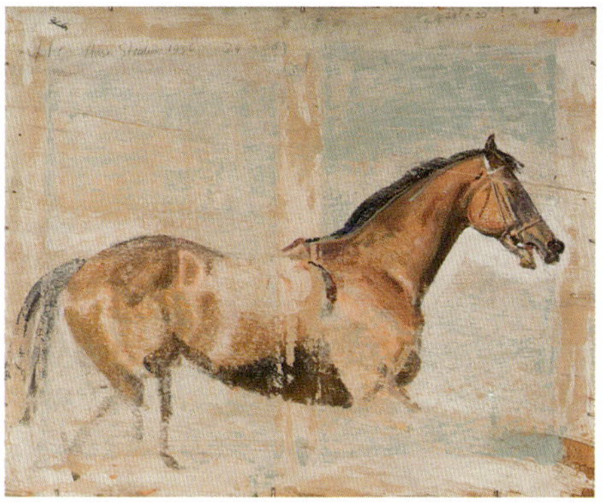

Munnings, Alfred James 1878–1959
Horse Study (verso) 1936
oil on board 50.8 x 61 (E)
152A

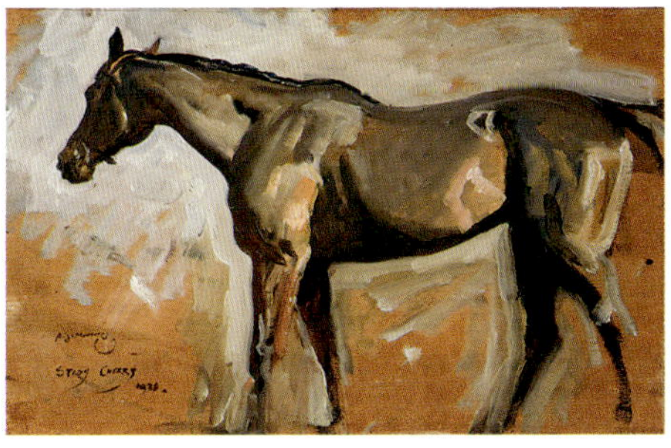

Munnings, Alfred James 1878–1959
Study of a Clipped Hunter Mare 1936
oil on panel 38.1 x 50.8
643

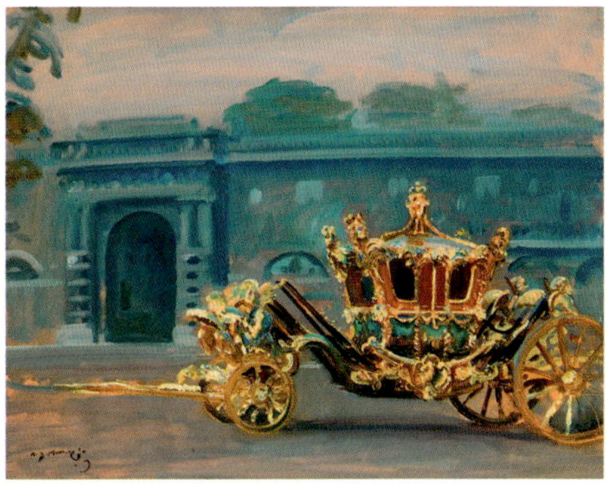

Munnings, Alfred James 1878–1959
The Gilded Coach, Painted in the Palace Yard in Grey Weather 1936
oil on canvas 50.8 x 62.2
140

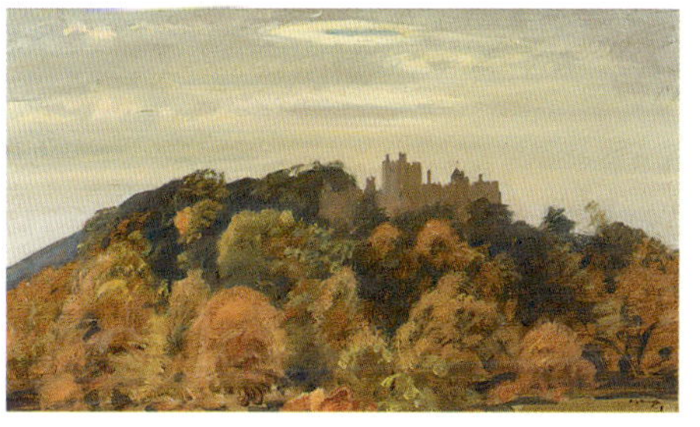

Munnings, Alfred James 1878–1959
Dunster Castle, Somerset 1938
oil on board 42 x 69
354

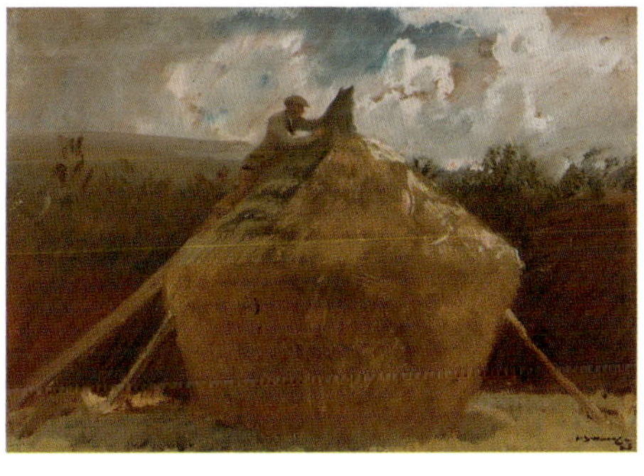

Munnings, Alfred James 1878–1959
Thatching an Oat Stack with Rushes, Exmoor 1938
oil on board 24.8 x 35.6
603

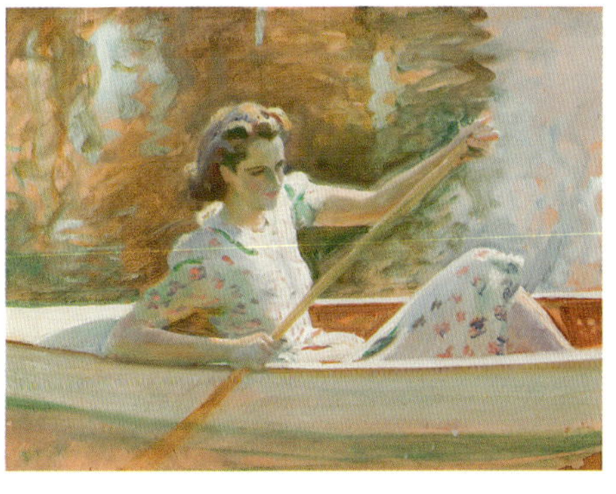

Munnings, Alfred James 1878–1959
Study for 'The White Canoe' 1939
oil on board 35 x 44
199

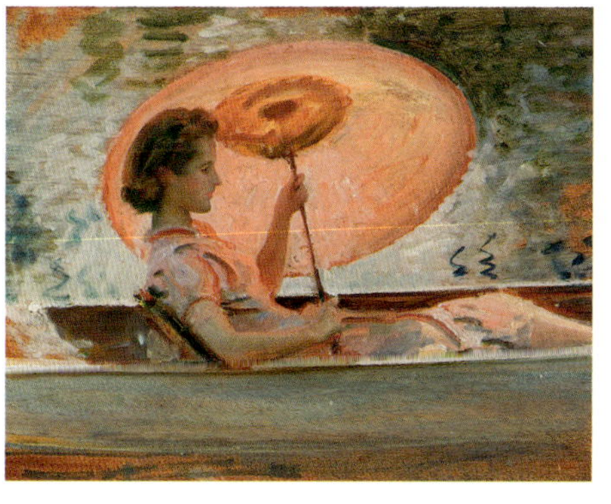

Munnings, Alfred James 1878–1959
Study for 'The White Canoe' 1939
oil on board 36 x 43
200

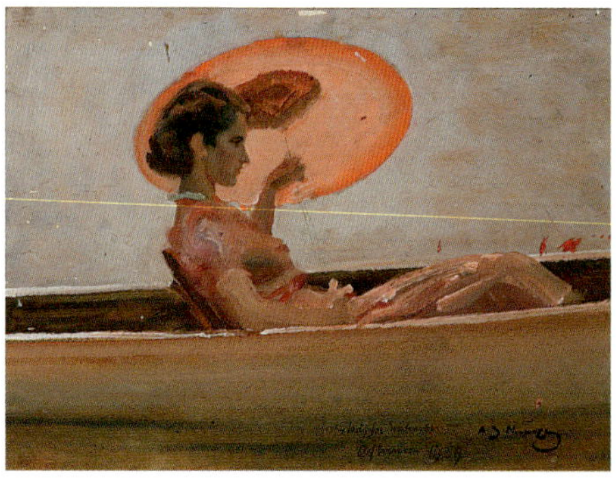

Munnings, Alfred James 1878–1959
Study for 'The White Canoe' (recto) 1939
oil on board 28 x 38 (E)
606

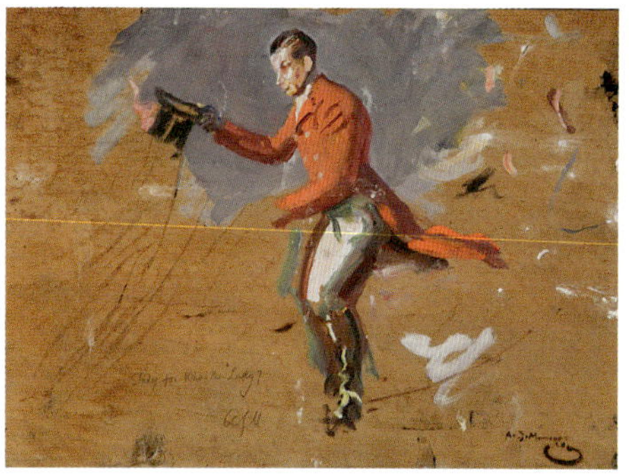

Munnings, Alfred James 1878–1959
Study of a Huntsman for 'Who's the Lady?' (verso)
oil on board 28 x 38 (E)
606A

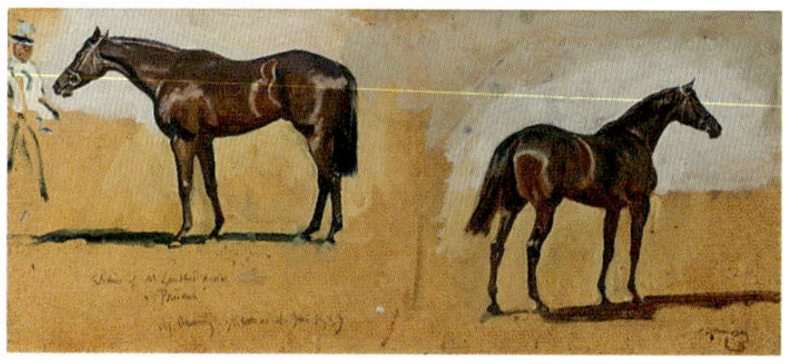

Munnings, Alfred James 1878–1959
Two Studies of Mr George Lambton's Horse, 'Pricket' 1939
oil on board 30.5 x 66
114

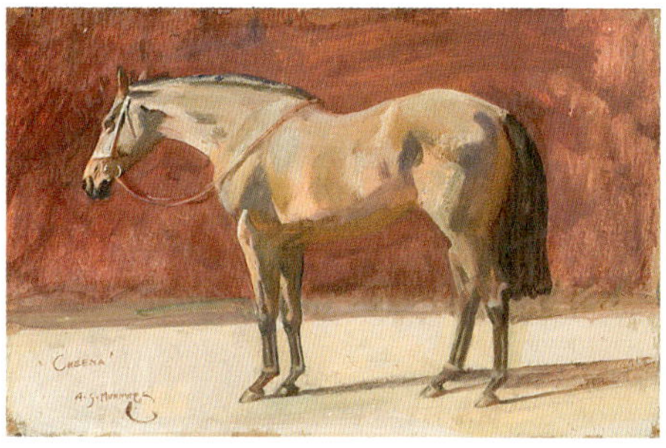

Munnings, Alfred James 1878–1959
'Cheena', a Study of Lady Munnings' Mare 1940
oil on board 25.4 x 38.1
309

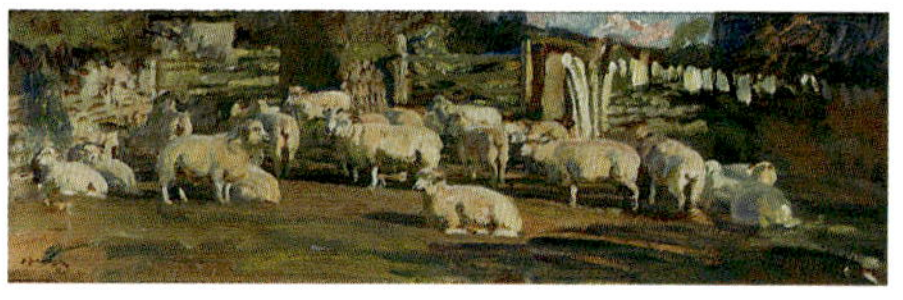

Munnings, Alfred James 1878–1959
Exmoor Sheep (recto) 1940
oil on board 21.5 x 67 (E)
274

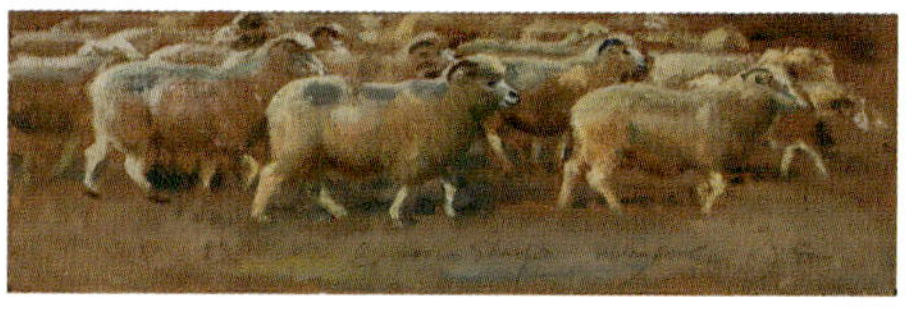

Munnings, Alfred James 1878–1959
Sheep Studies (verso) 1940
oil on board 21.5 x 67 (E)
274A

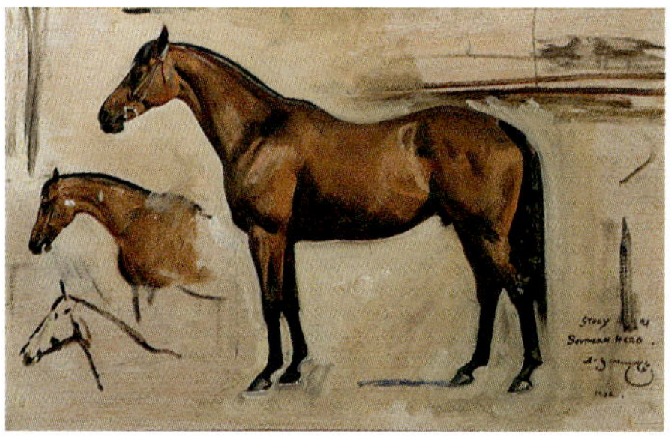

Munnings, Alfred James 1878–1959
Study for 'Southern Hero' 1942
oil on board 40.6 x 61
136

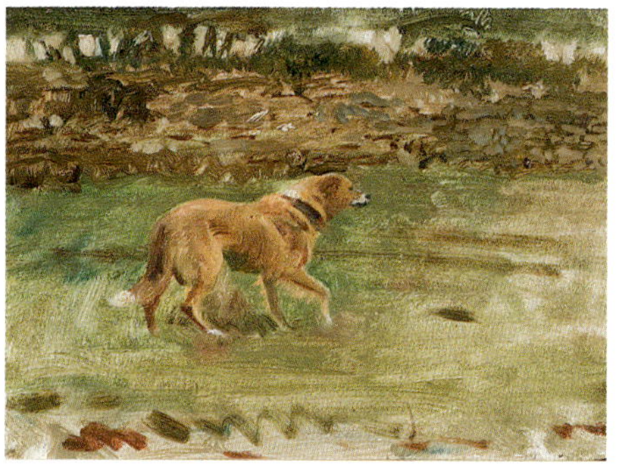

Munnings, Alfred James 1878–1959
A Sheepdog at Withypool, Exmoor 1943
oil on board 24 x 32
194

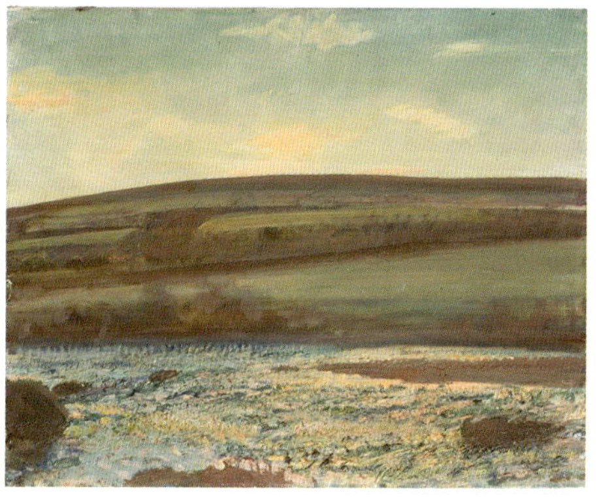

Munnings, Alfred James 1878–1959
Brightworthy Ford, Withypool, Exmoor, Evening 1943
oil on canvas 50.8 x 61
519

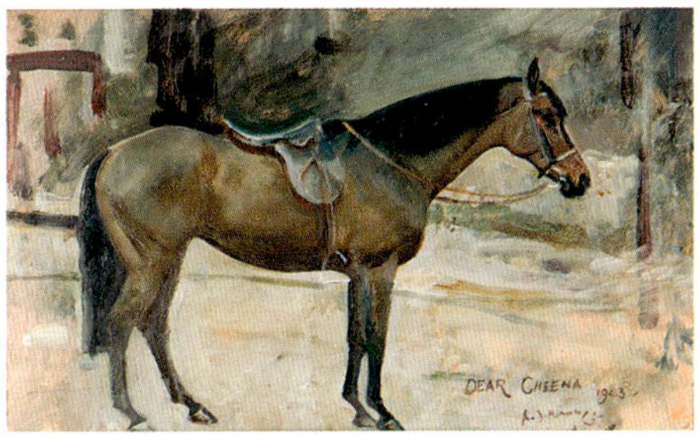

Munnings, Alfred James 1878–1959
'Dear Cheena', a Bay Hunter 1943
oil on board 22.2 x 34.9
5

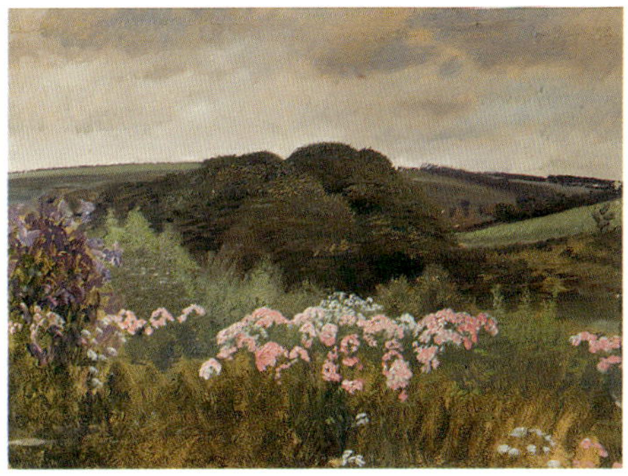

Munnings, Alfred James 1878–1959
Garden at Withypool, Exmoor 1943
oil on board 38.1 x 50.8
43

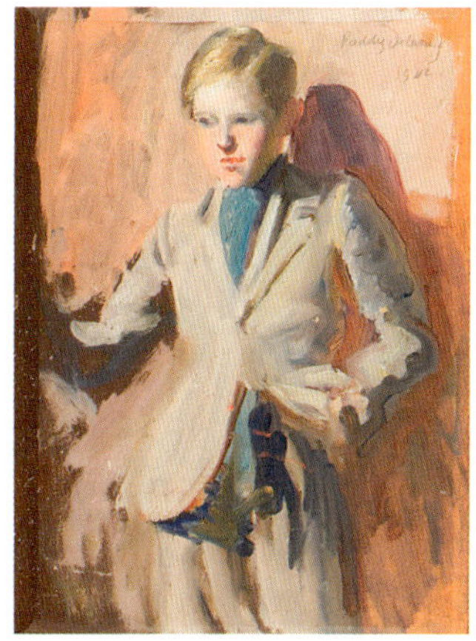

Munnings, Alfred James 1878–1959
Study of Paul Delaney, Withypool, Exmoor 1943
oil on board 34.9 x 25.4
238

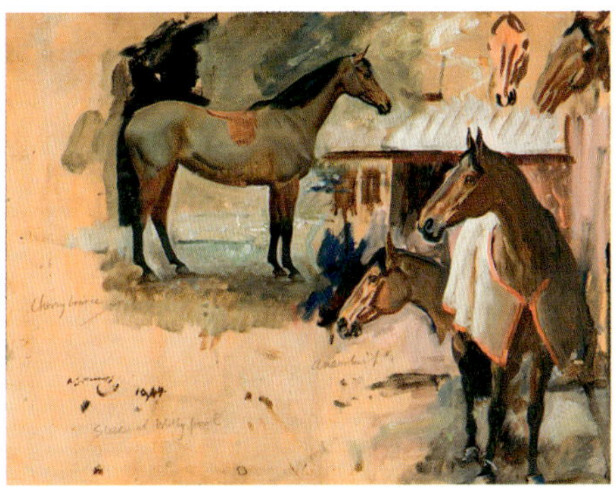

Munnings, Alfred James 1878–1959
Stables at Withypool, Exmoor, Studies of 'Cherrybounce' and 'Anarchist' 1944
oil on board 40.6 x 50.8
189

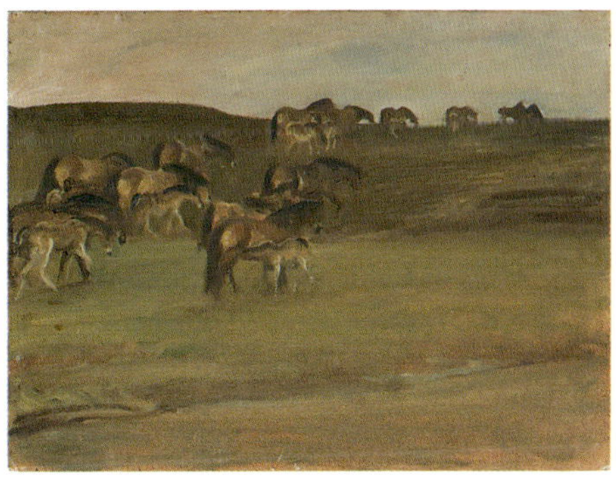

Munnings, Alfred James 1878–1959
Exmoor Ponies c.1944/1945
oil on canvas laid on board 35.6 x 45.7
476

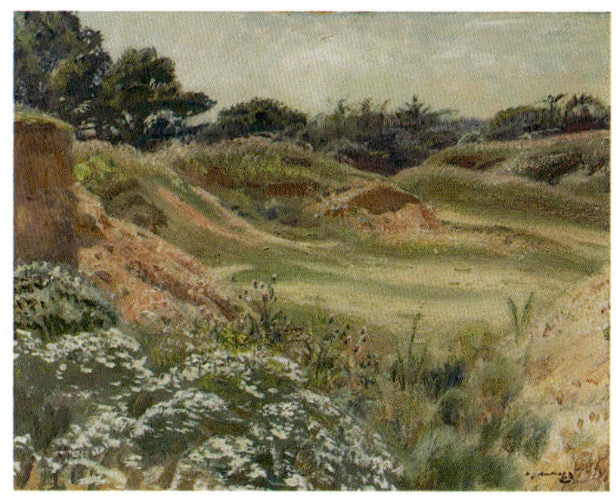

Munnings, Alfred James 1878–1959
An Old Gravel Pit 1946
oil on board 33 x 41.3
245

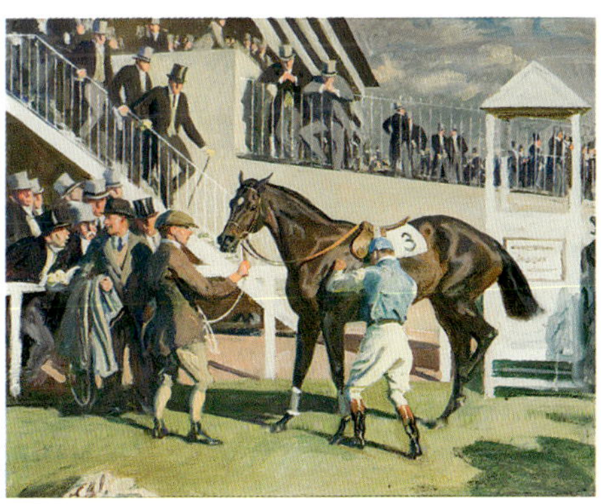

Munnings, Alfred James 1878–1959
The Unsaddling Enclosure, Epsom 1948
oil on canvas 63.5 x 76.2
15

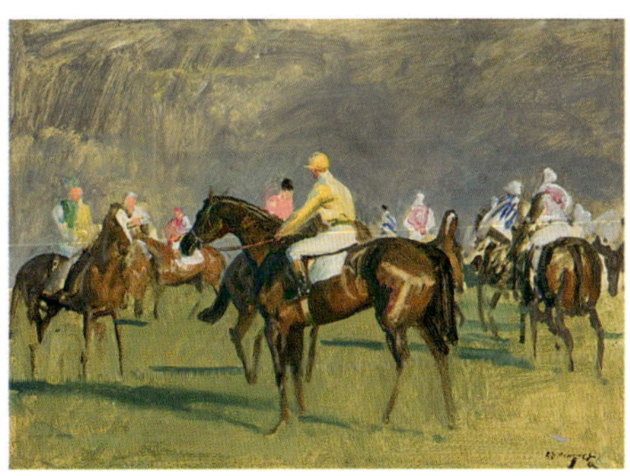

Munnings, Alfred James 1878–1959
Before the Start, Newmarket 1949
oil on panel 45.7 x 61
445

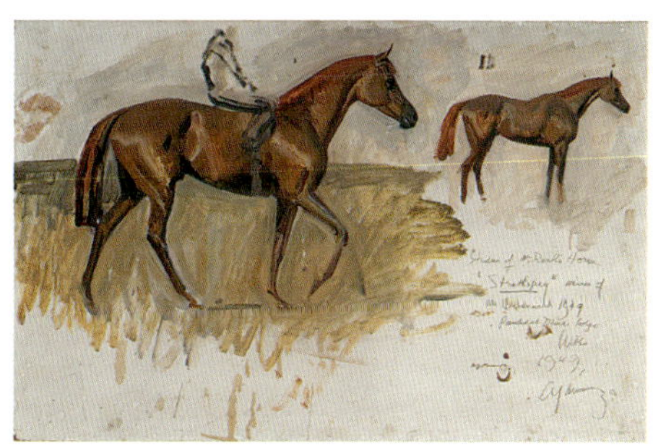

Munnings, Alfred James 1878–1959
Studies of Mr Rank's Horse, 'Strathspey', Winner of 1949 Cesarewitch (painted at Druids' Lodge) 1949
oil on board 50.5 x 76.2
117

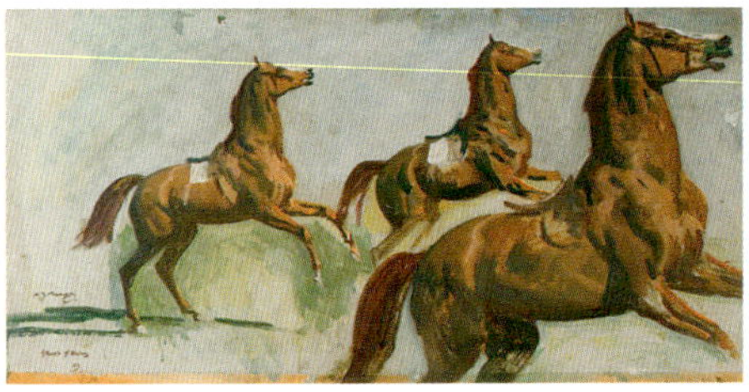

Munnings, Alfred James 1878–1959
Studies of 'Rufus' 1949
oil on board 37.5 x 71.8
499

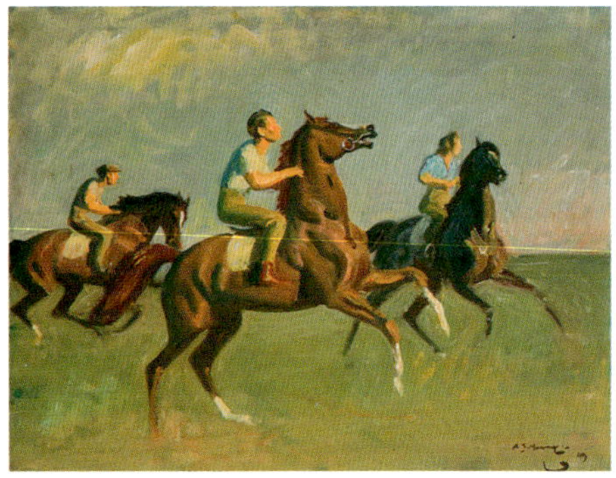

Munnings, Alfred James 1878–1959
Study for 'Early Morning, Newmarket' 1949
oil on panel 36.8 x 47
375

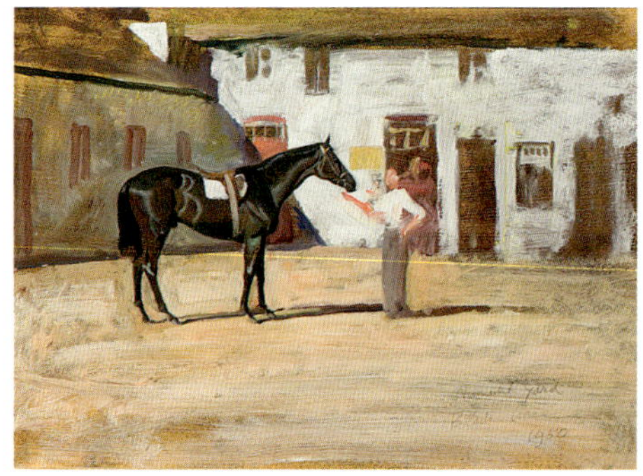

Munnings, Alfred James 1878–1959
A Black Horse at Newmarket 1950
oil on board 45.7 x 61
443

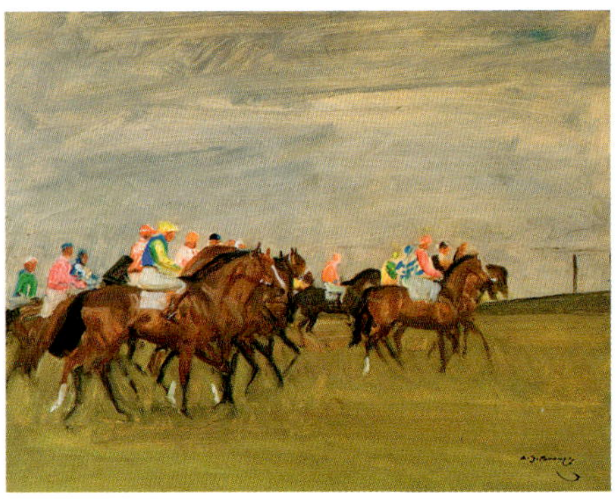

Munnings, Alfred James 1878–1959
Moving up for the Start (painted after the last race in the artist's studio, Newmarket) 1950
oil on board 40.6 x 50.8
120

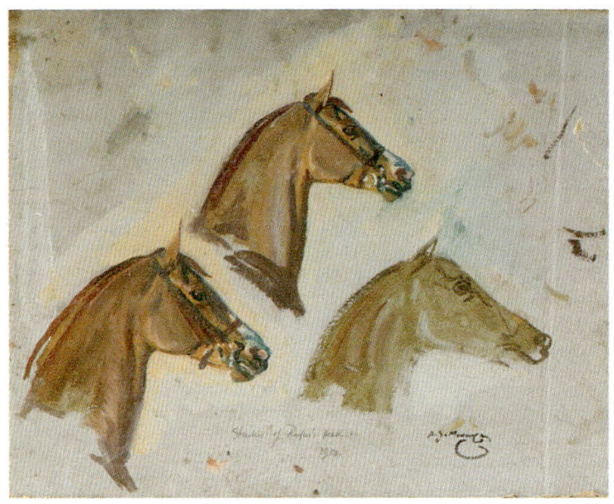

Munnings, Alfred James 1878–1959
Studies of 'Rufus's' Head 1950
oil on board 34.3 x 42.5
393

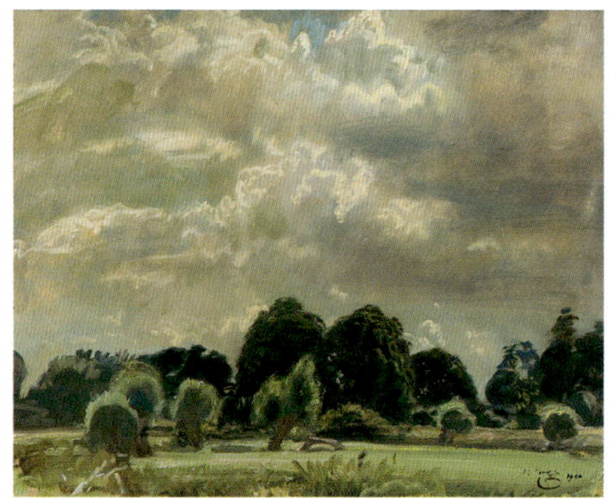

Munnings, Alfred James 1878–1959
Trees by the Edge of a Field 1950
oil on board 50.8 x 61
530

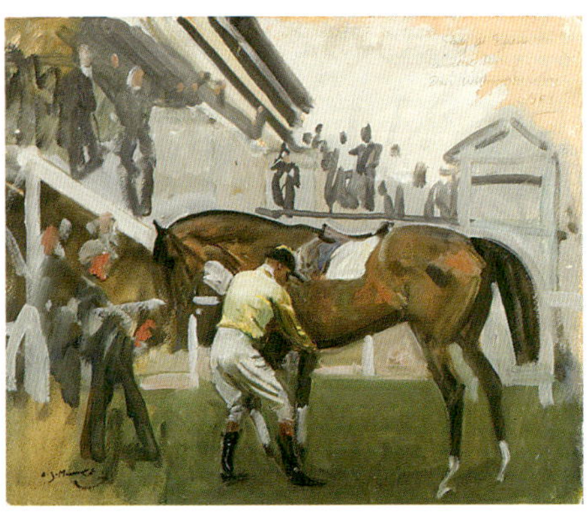

Munnings, Alfred James 1878–1959
Study for 'The Unsaddling Enclosure, Epsom' 1951
oil on board 40.6 x 48.3
384

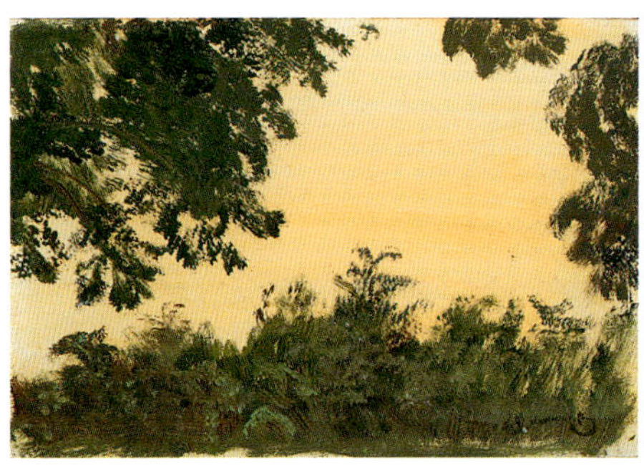

Munnings, Alfred James 1878–1959
Study of Foliage and Sky 1951
oil on board 17.8 x 25.4
1

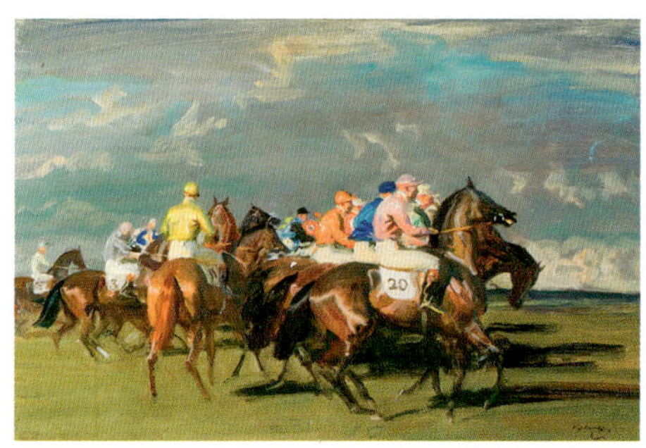

Munnings, Alfred James 1878–1959
Study of 'The Start' (done in studio on heath after racing) 1951
oil on board 45.1 x 66
129

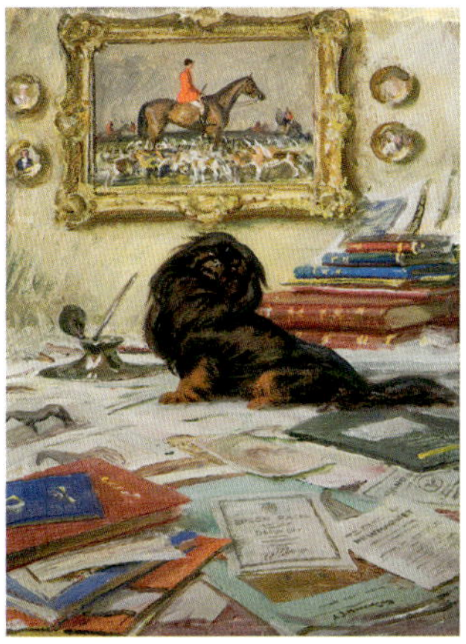

Munnings, Alfred James 1878–1959
'Black Knight' Finishes His Diary 1954
oil on board 45.7 x 31.8
66

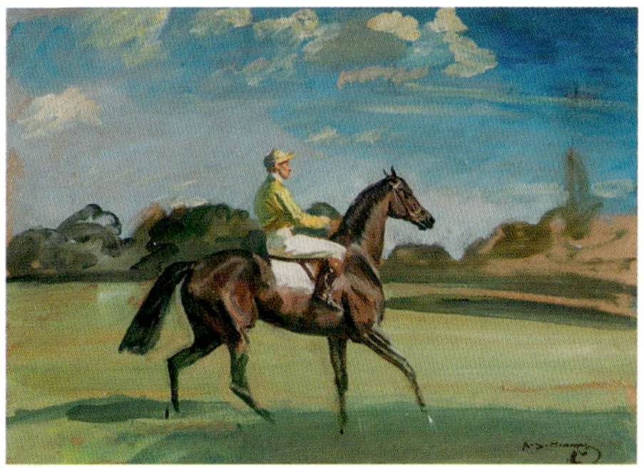

Munnings, Alfred James 1878–1959
Study of a Yellow Jockey on My Mare, 'Irish Smock' 1954
oil on board 47 x 60.3 (E)
20

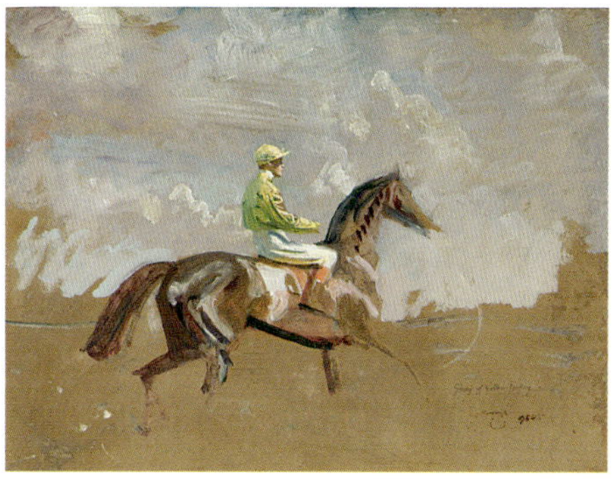

Munnings, Alfred James 1878–1959
Study of the Yellow Jockey 1954
oil on canvas 47 x 60 (E)
376

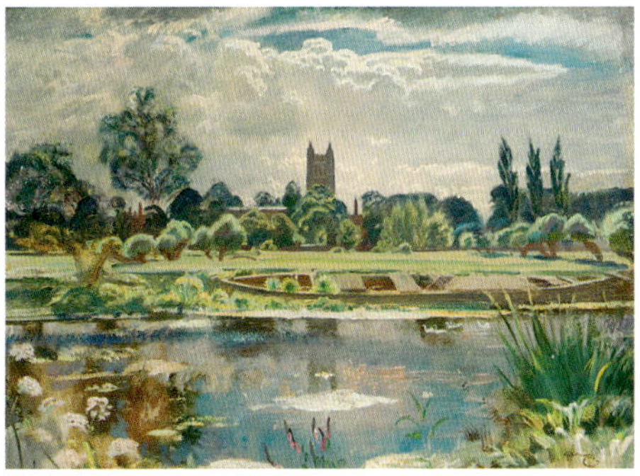

Munnings, Alfred James 1878–1959
A Barge on the Stour at Dedham
oil on canvas 61 x 81.3
435

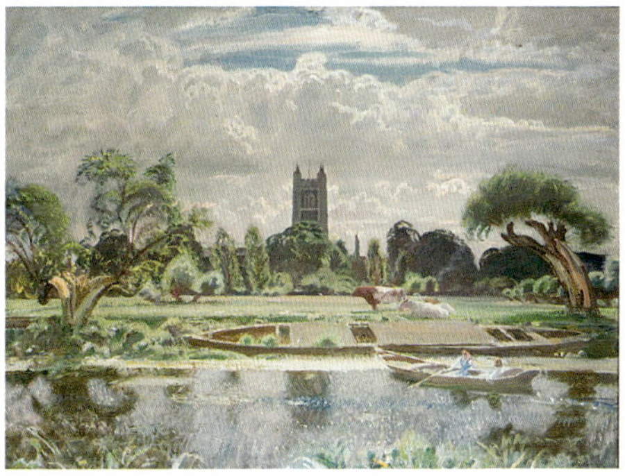

Munnings, Alfred James 1878–1959
A Barge on the Stour at Dedham
oil on canvas 81.3 x 104.1
647

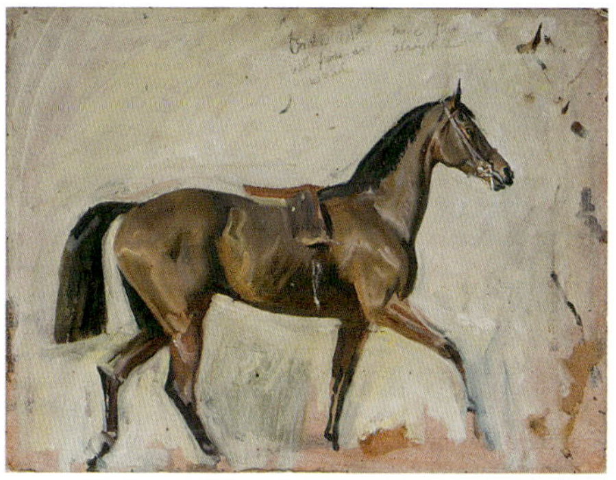

Munnings, Alfred James 1878–1959
A Bay Horse
oil on board 33 x 46
262

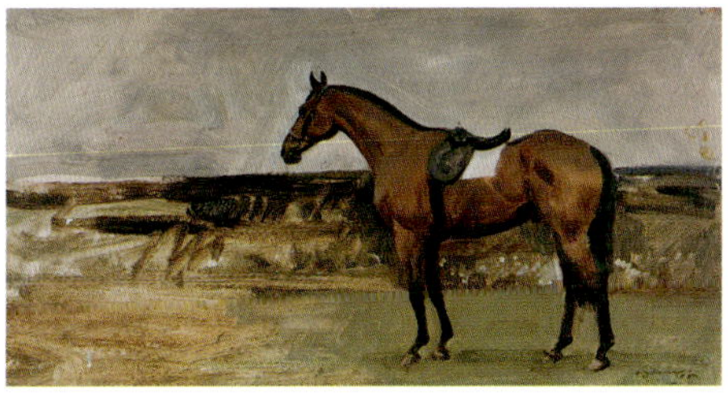

Munnings, Alfred James 1878–1959
A Bay Horse in a Landscape
oil on board 26 x 47
258

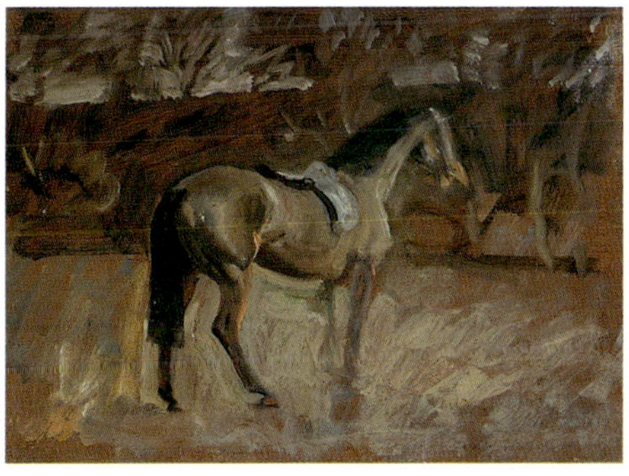

Munnings, Alfred James 1878–1959
A Bay Horse in a Landscape
oil on panel 30.5 x 40.6
590

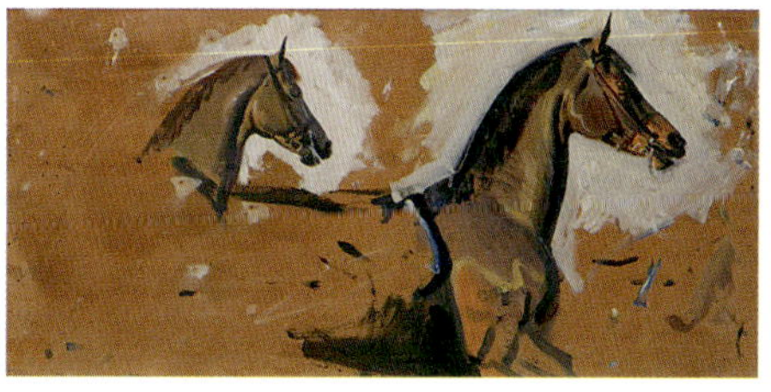

Munnings, Alfred James 1878–1959
A Bay Horse in a Stable (recto)
oil on board 34.9 x 70.5
184

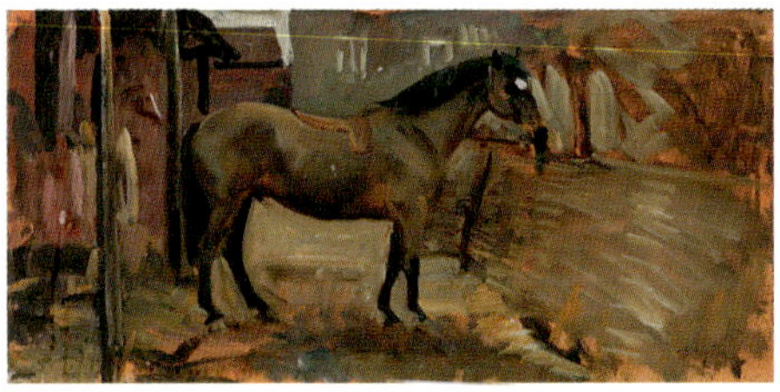

Munnings, Alfred James 1878–1959
Studies of a Horse's Head (verso)
oil on board 34.9 x 70.5
184A

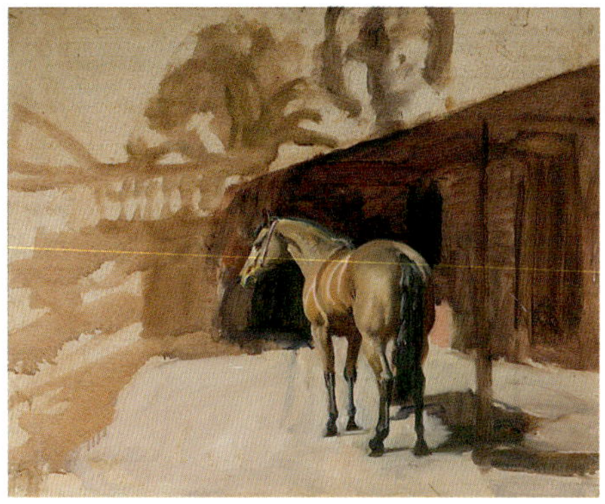

Munnings, Alfred James 1878–1959
A Bay Horse near a Building
oil on board 50.8 x 61
455

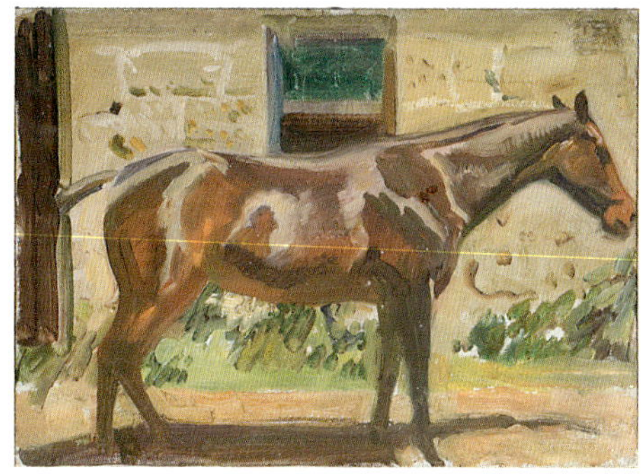

Munnings, Alfred James 1878–1959
A Bay Hunter
oil on canvas laid on board 30.5 x 40.6
583

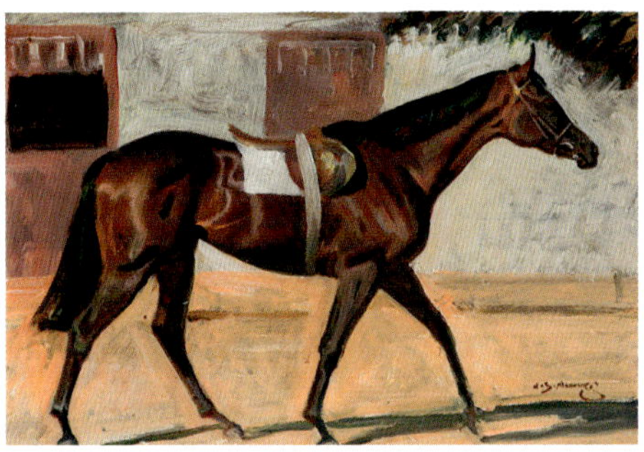

Munnings, Alfred James 1878–1959
A Bay Racehorse by a Stable
oil on board 27.9 x 39.4
195

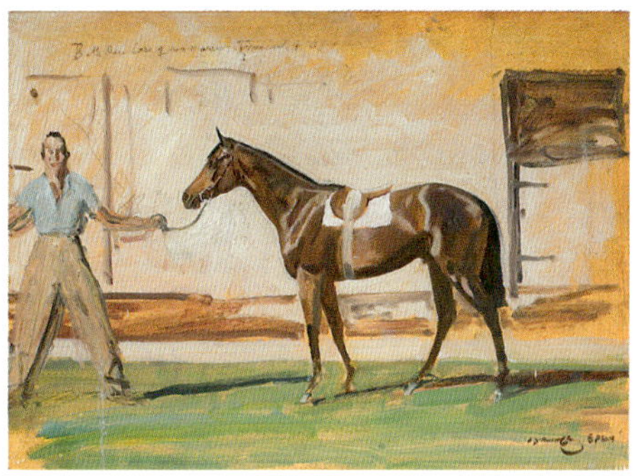

Munnings, Alfred James 1878–1959
A Bay Racehorse with a Groom
oil on board 45.7 x 61
109

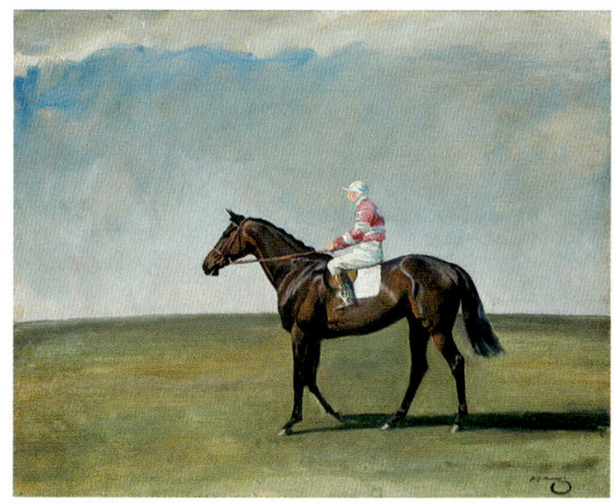

Munnings, Alfred James 1878–1959
A Bay Racehorse with Jockey up, in Pink and White Striped Colours, in a Landscape
oil on canvas 64.1 x 76.2
107

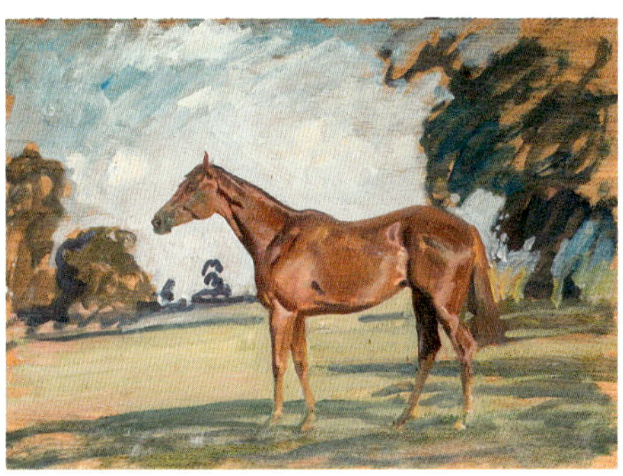

Munnings, Alfred James 1878–1959
A Chestnut Horse in a Landscape
oil on board 39.4 x 53.3
416

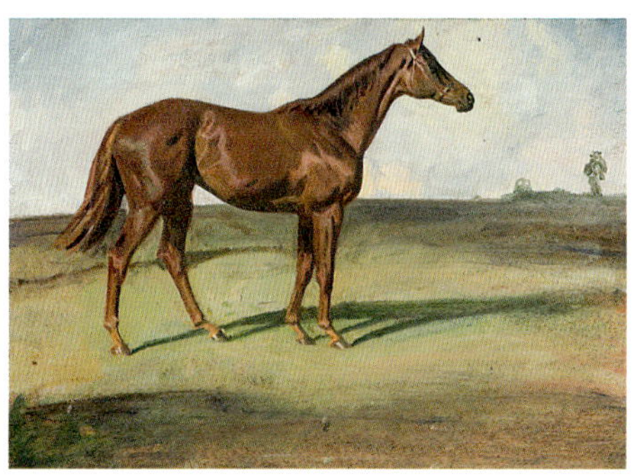

Munnings, Alfred James 1878–1959
A Chestnut Horse in a Landscape ('Happy Laughter')
oil on board 45.7 x 61
113

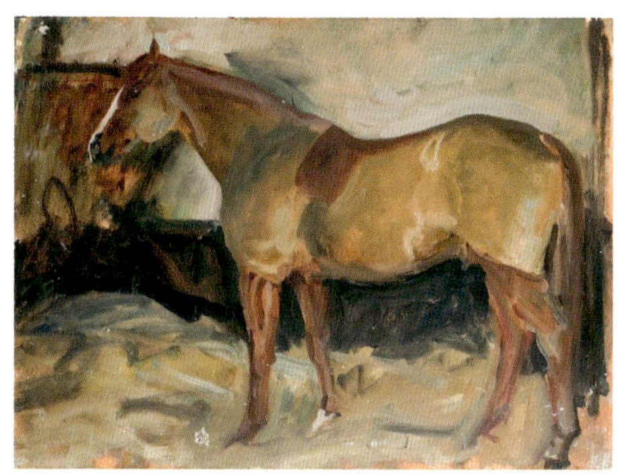

Munnings, Alfred James 1878–1959
A Chestnut Horse in a Stable
oil on board 50.8 x 61
451

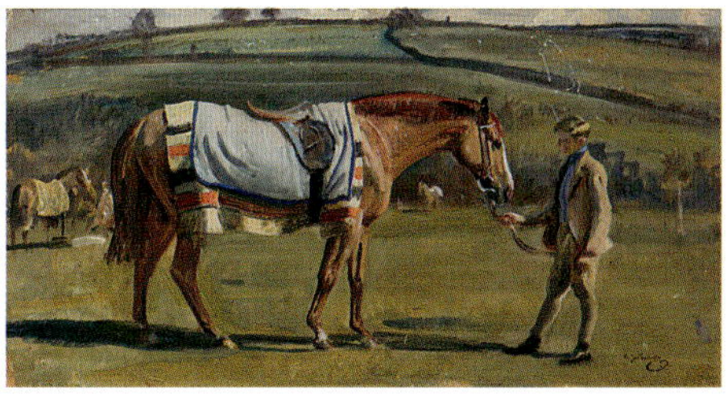

Munnings, Alfred James 1878–1959
A Chestnut Racehorse Held by a Boy in a Landscape
oil on panel 30.5 x 55.2
57

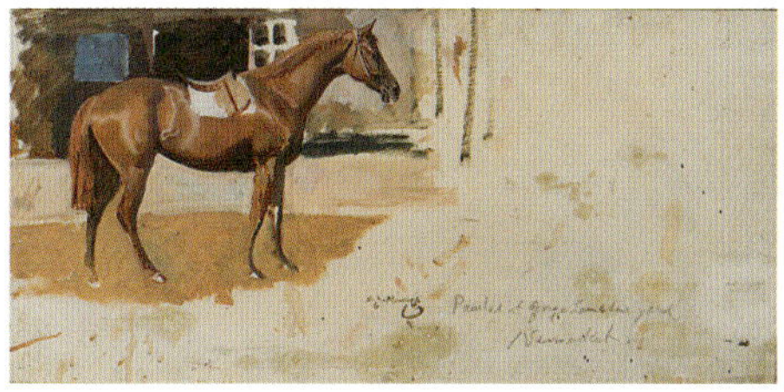

Munnings, Alfred James 1878–1959
A Chestnut Racehorse Painted at George Lambton's Yard, Newmarket
oil on board 30.5 x 61
359

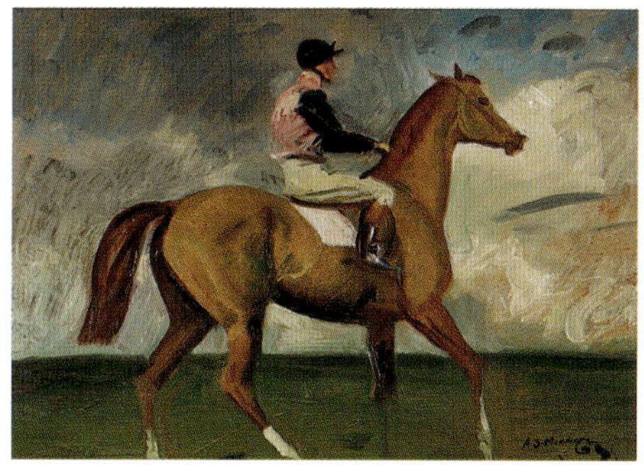

Munnings, Alfred James 1878–1959
A Chestnut Racehorse with Jockey up in a Landscape
oil on board 24.8 x 33
127

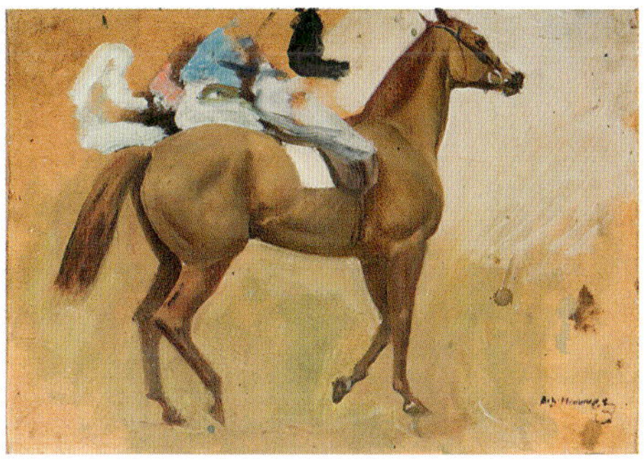

Munnings, Alfred James 1878–1959
A Chestnut with Jockey up
oil on board 25.4 x 35.6
4

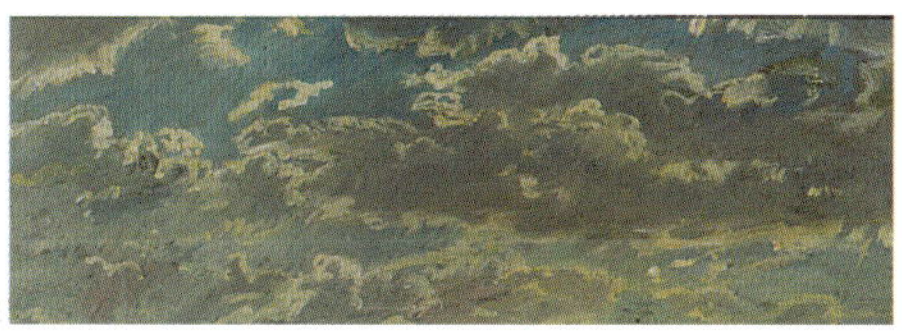

Munnings, Alfred James 1878–1959
A Cloud Study
oil on board 24.1 x 66.7
271

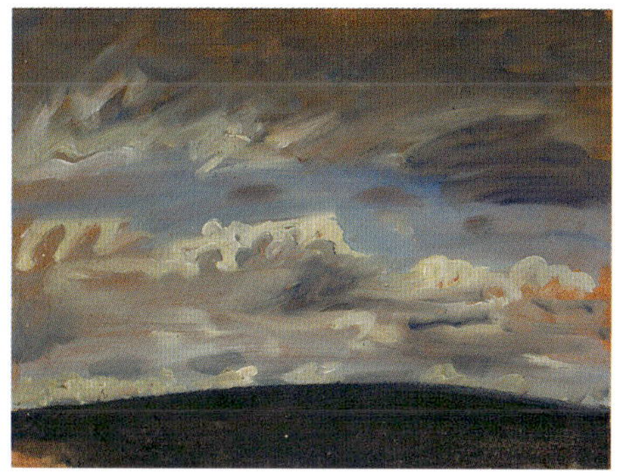

Munnings, Alfred James 1878–1959
A Cloud Study
oil on canvas laid on board 35.6 x 45.7
479

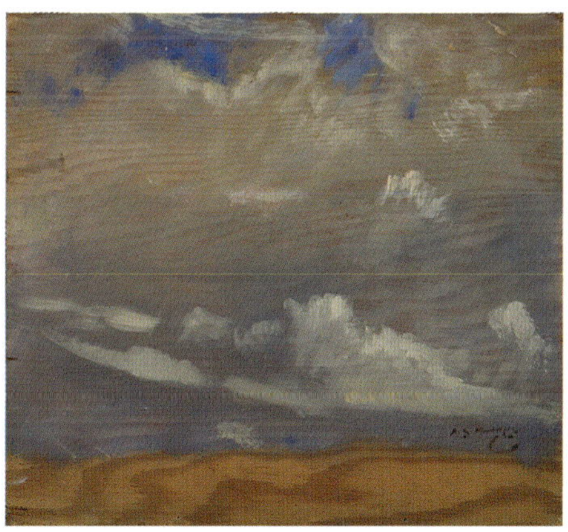

Munnings, Alfred James 1878–1959
A Cloud Study
oil on board 27.9 x 29.8
534

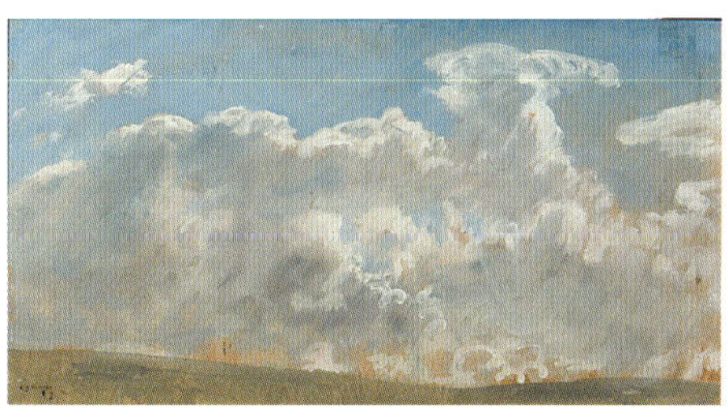

Munnings, Alfred James 1878–1959
A Cloud Study, Exmoor
oil on board 33.7 x 61
475

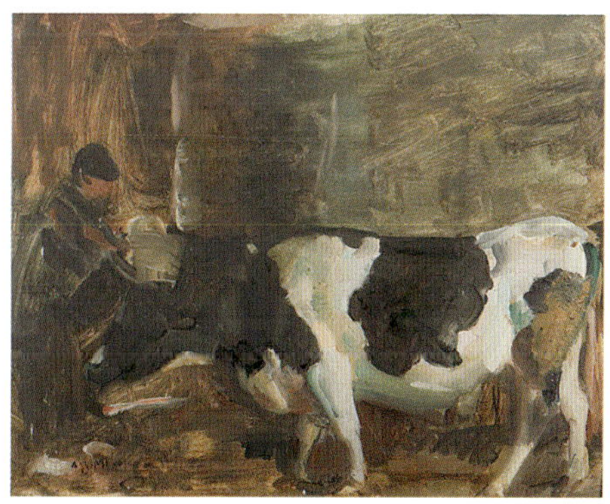

Munnings, Alfred James 1878–1959
A Cow and a Figure in a Stable
oil on board 33 x 40.6
42

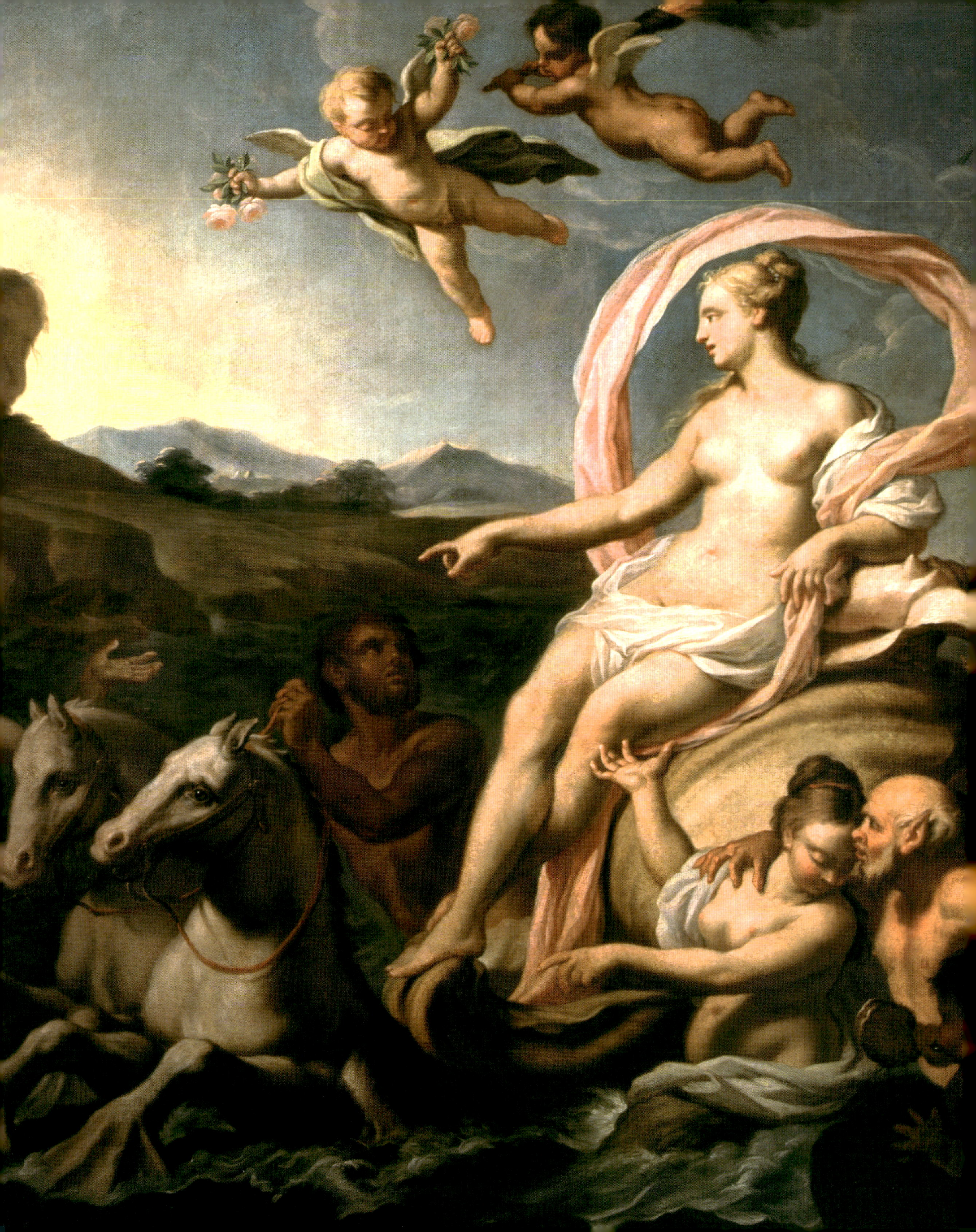

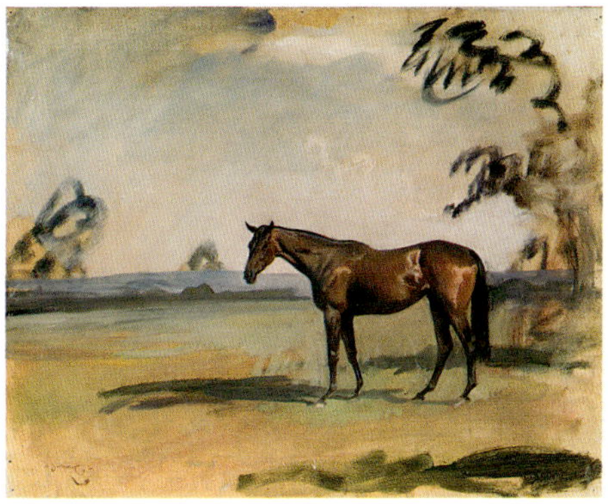

Munnings, Alfred James 1878–1959
A Dark Bay Horse in a Landscape
oil on canvas 52.1 x 62.2
448

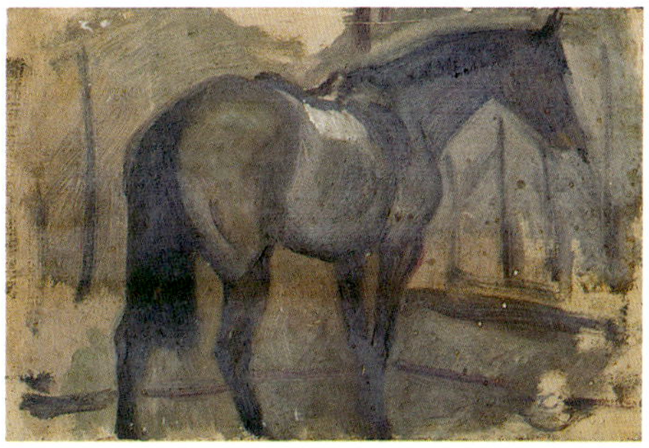

Munnings, Alfred James 1878–1959
A Dark Bay Racehorse in a Stable
oil on board 20.3 x 29.8
312

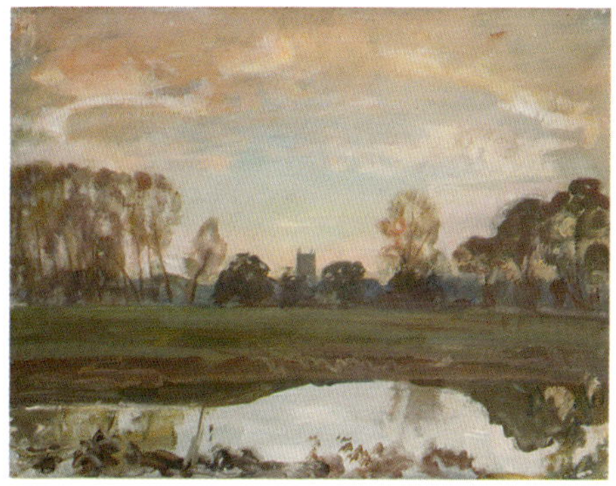

Munnings, Alfred James 1878–1959
A Distant View of Dedham from the Stour at Sunset
oil on canvas 57.2 x 72.4
85

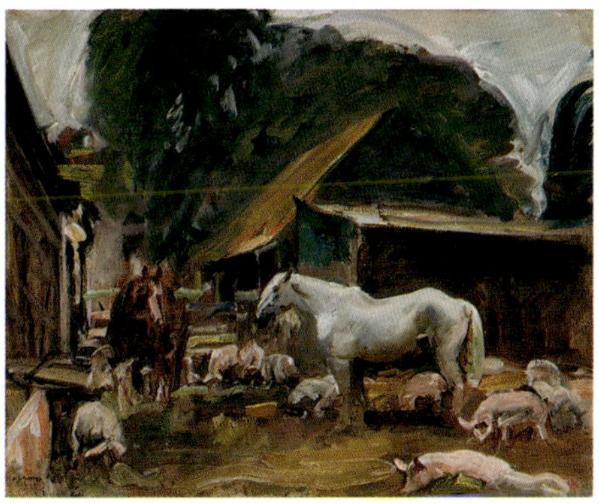

Munnings, Alfred James 1878–1959
A Farmyard Scene
oil on canvas 50.8 x 61
143

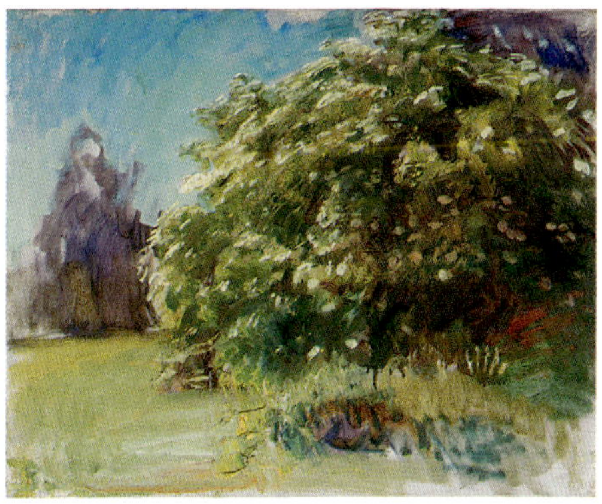

Munnings, Alfred James 1878–1959
A Garden Scene
oil on canvas 51.4 x 61
270

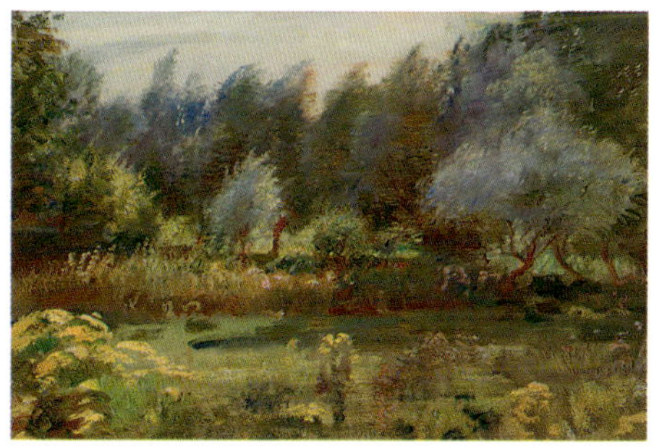

Munnings, Alfred James 1878–1959
A Garden Scene
oil on canvas 45.7 x 64.8
280

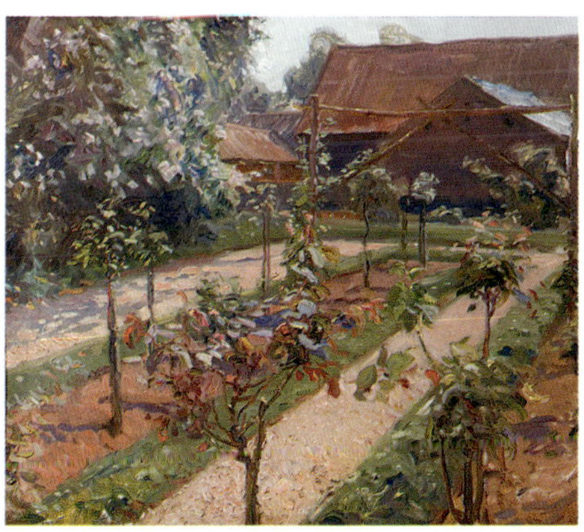

Munnings, Alfred James 1878–1959
A Garden Scene
oil on canvas 63.5 x 71.1
433

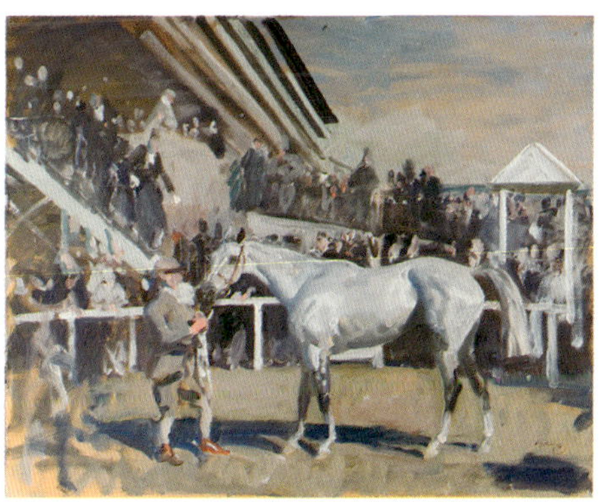

Munnings, Alfred James 1878–1959
A Grey Horse in the Unsaddling Paddock, Epsom
oil on canvas 63.5 x 76.2
332

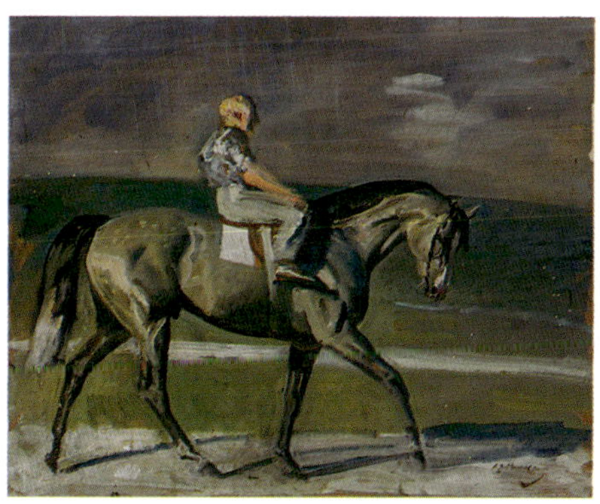

Munnings, Alfred James 1878–1959
A Grey Racehorse with a Lad up
oil on board 50.2 x 61
465

Facing page: Grassi, Nicola, 1682–1748, *The Triumph of Amphitrite* (detail), Southend Museums Service, (p. 264)

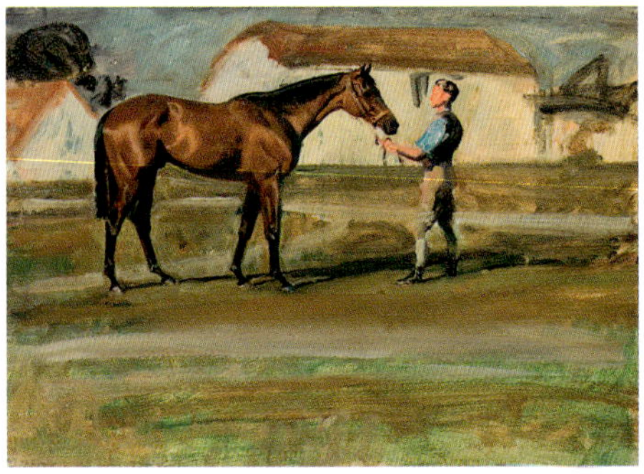

Munnings, Alfred James 1878–1959
A Groom Holding a Bay Horse, near Stables
oil on board 45.7 x 61
417

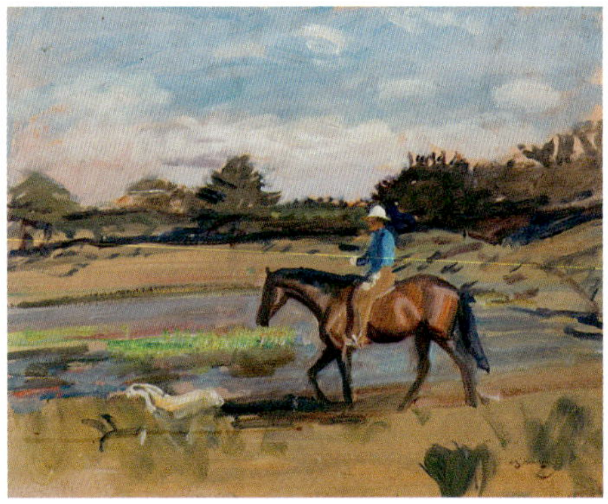

Munnings, Alfred James 1878–1959
A Horse and Rider in a Landscape
oil on board 50.8 x 61
457

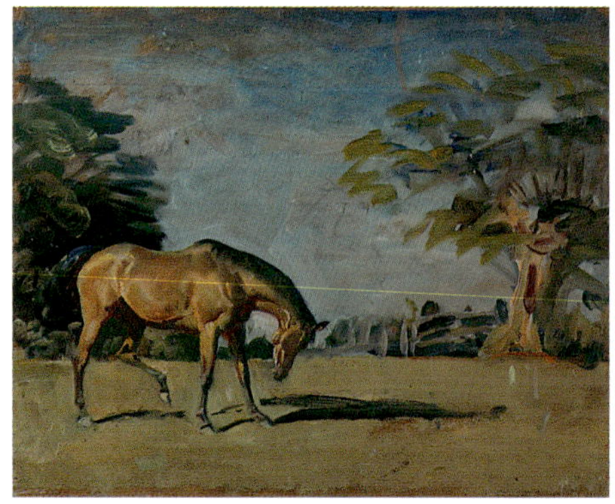

Munnings, Alfred James 1878–1959
A Horse in a Landscape
oil on board 50.8 x 61
449

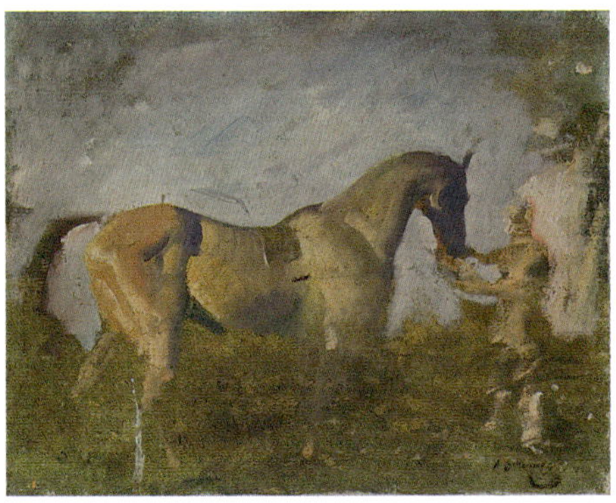

Munnings, Alfred James 1878–1959
A Horse with a Groom
oil on canvas 35.6 x 45.7
477

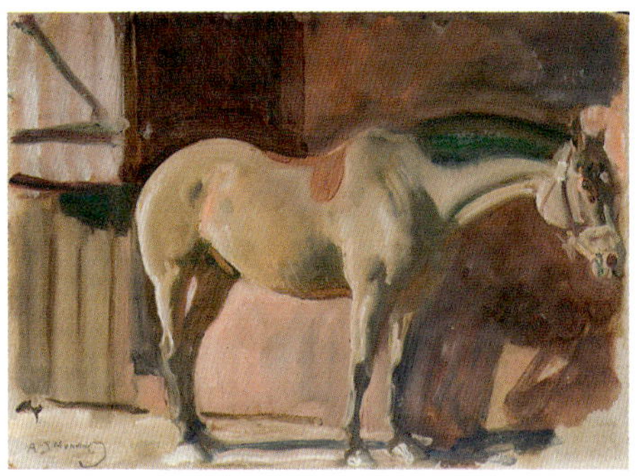

Munnings, Alfred James 1878–1959
A Hunter in a Stable
oil on panel 24.1 x 33
68

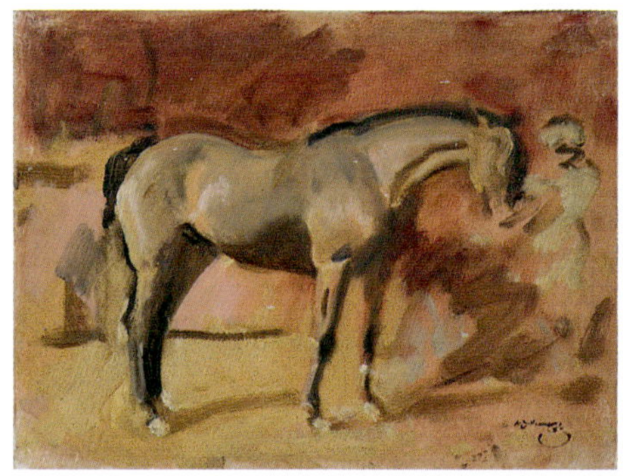

Munnings, Alfred James 1878–1959
A Hunter in a Stable
oil on canvas 35.6 x 45.7
470

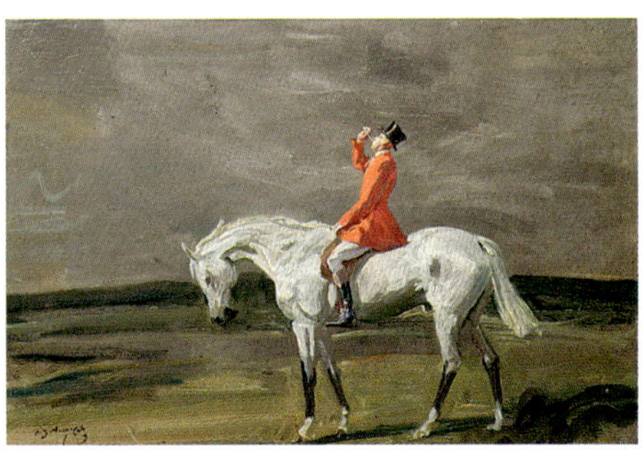

Munnings, Alfred James 1878–1959
A Huntsman on a Grey in a Landscape
oil on canvas 35.6 x 50.8
105

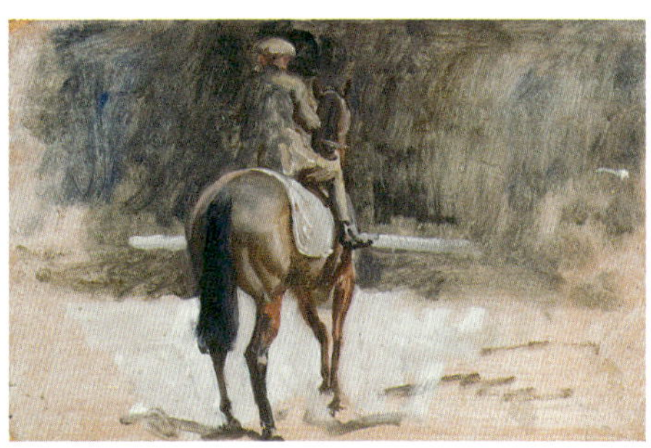

Munnings, Alfred James 1878–1959
A Lad Exercising a Racehorse
oil on board 22.9 x 33.7
542

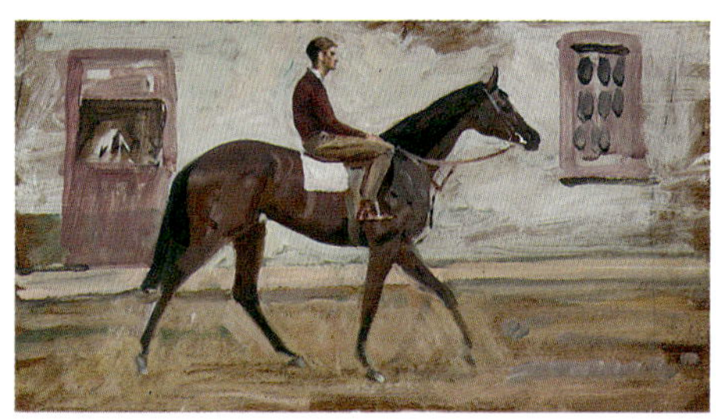

Munnings, Alfred James 1878–1959
A Lad on a Racehorse
oil on board 24.8 x 43.2
571

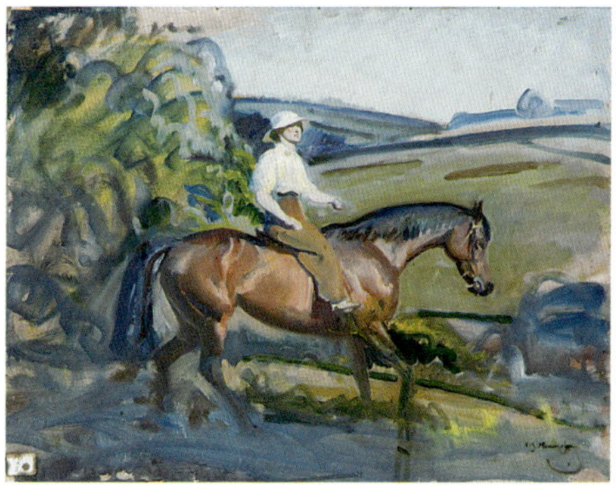

Munnings, Alfred James 1878–1959
A Lady Riding a Bay Hunter
oil on board 40.6 x 50.2
169

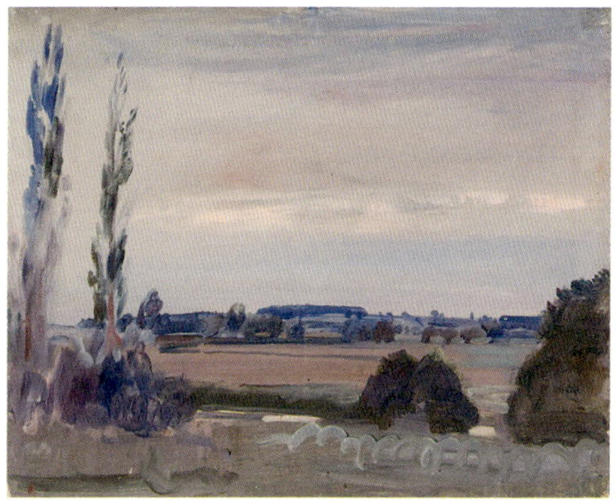

Munnings, Alfred James 1878–1959
A Landscape
oil on canvas 50.8 x 61
506

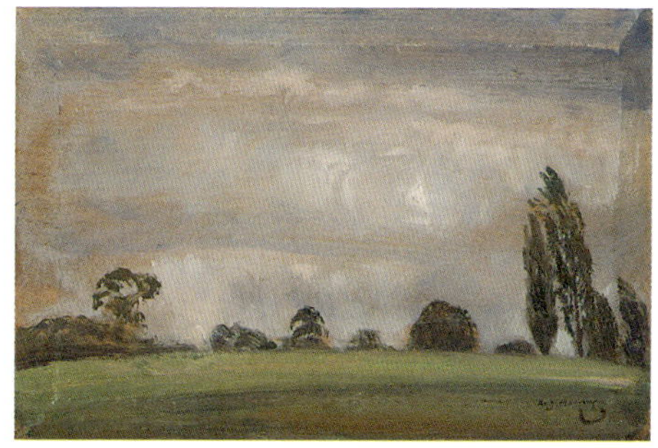

Munnings, Alfred James 1878–1959
A Landscape (recto)
oil on panel 17.8 x 25.4
558

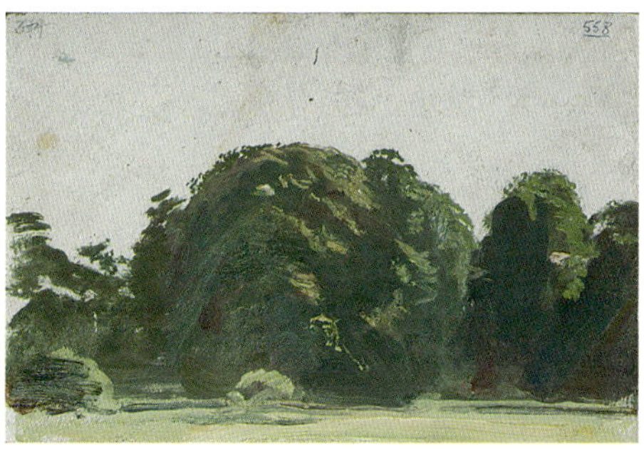

Munnings, Alfred James 1878–1959
Study of Trees (verso)
oil on panel 17.8 x 25.4
558A

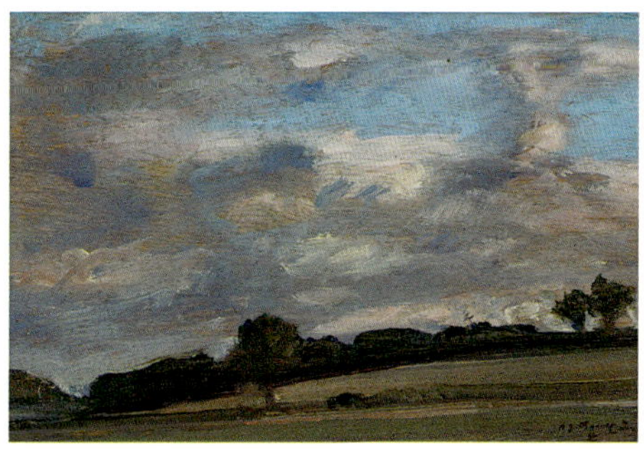

Munnings, Alfred James 1878–1959
A Landscape of Fields and Hedgerows in Deep Shadow
oil on panel 21 x 29.8
559

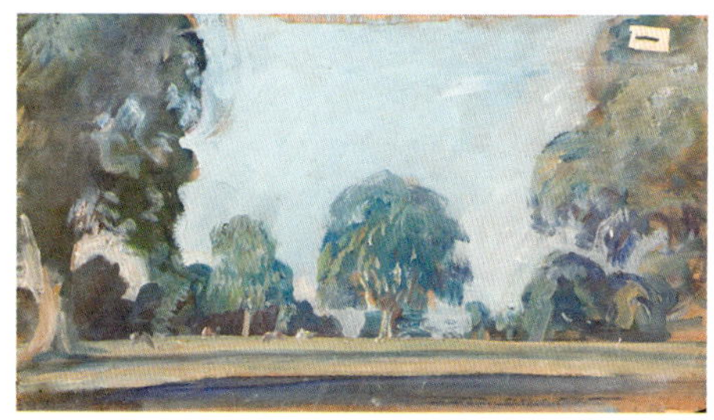

Munnings, Alfred James 1878–1959
A Landscape of Trees and Grazing Sheep
oil on board 38.1 x 64.8
396

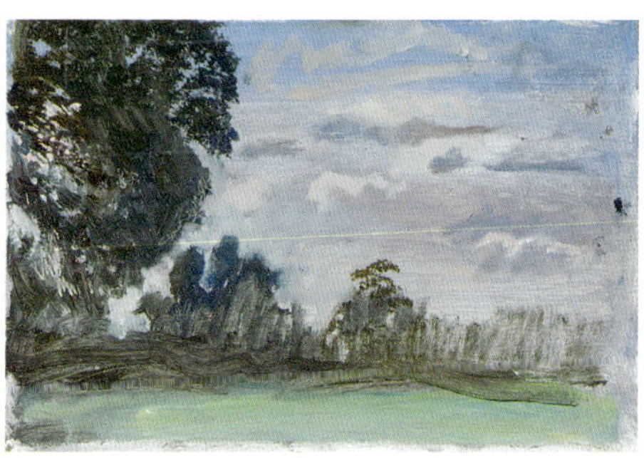

Munnings, Alfred James 1878–1959
A Landscape, Study with Trees
oil on board 17.8 x 25.4
536

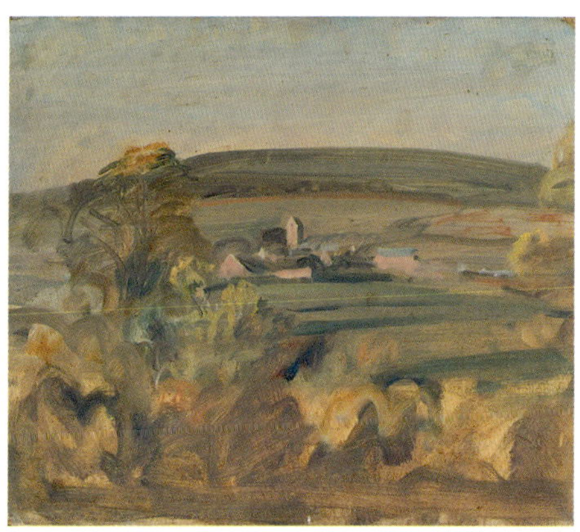

Munnings, Alfred James 1878–1959
A Landscape with a Distant Village (possibly French)
oil on board 40.6 x 44.5
289

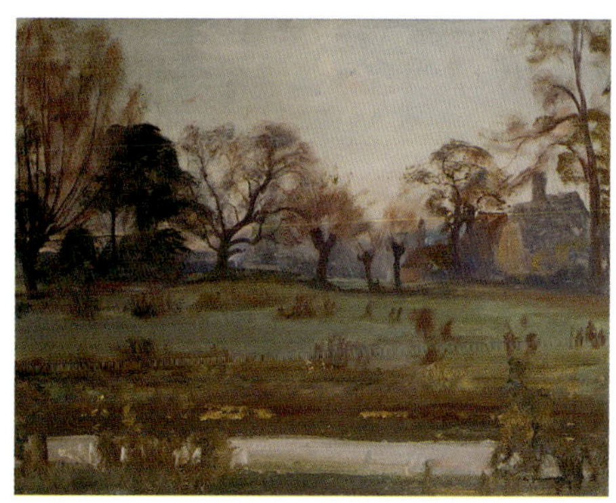

Munnings, Alfred James 1878–1959
A Landscape with Cottage
oil on canvas 46.4 x 55.9
522

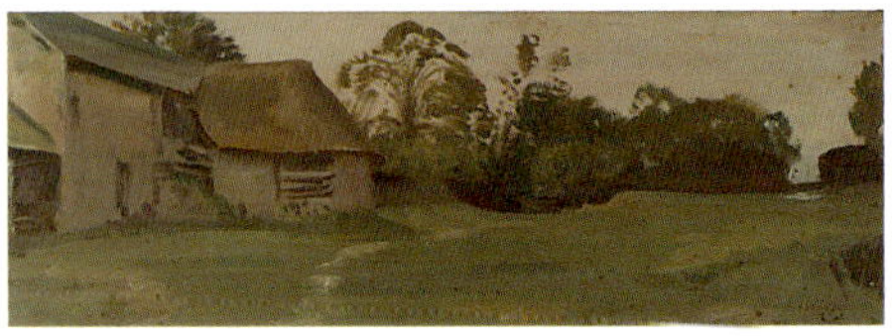

Munnings, Alfred James 1878–1959
A Landscape with Farm Buildings
oil on board 26 x 71.1
104

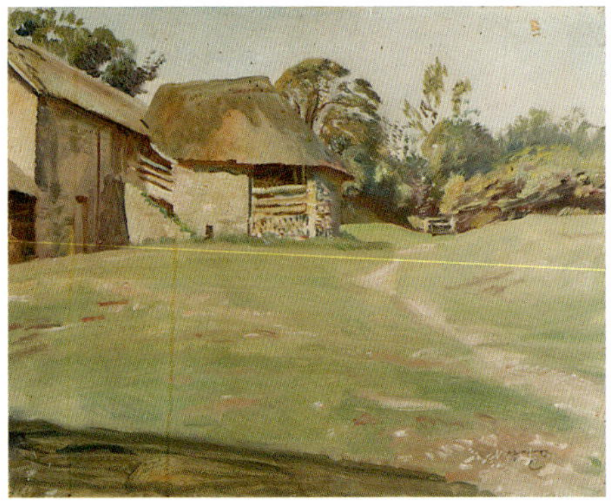

Munnings, Alfred James 1878–1959
A Landscape with Farm Buildings
oil on board 50.8 x 61
485

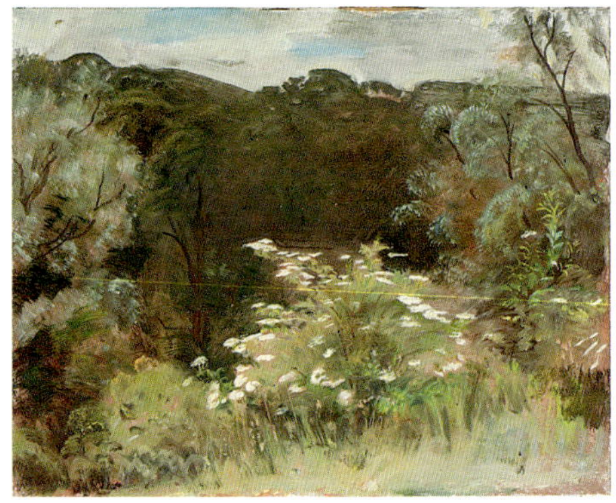

Munnings, Alfred James 1878–1959
A Landscape with Foliage
oil on canvas 50.8 x 61
513

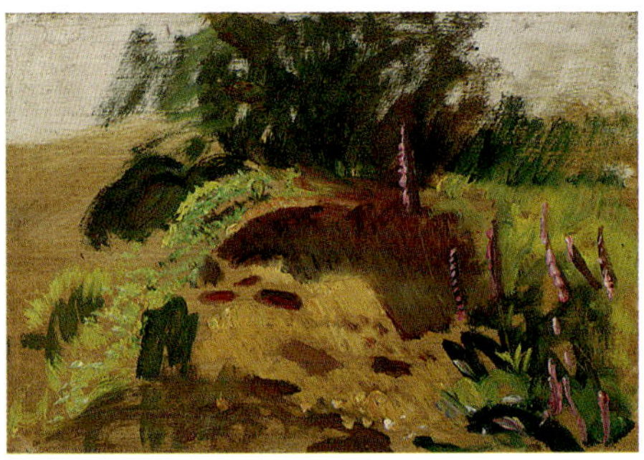

Munnings, Alfred James 1878–1959
A Landscape with Foxgloves
oil on board 17.8 x 25.4
597

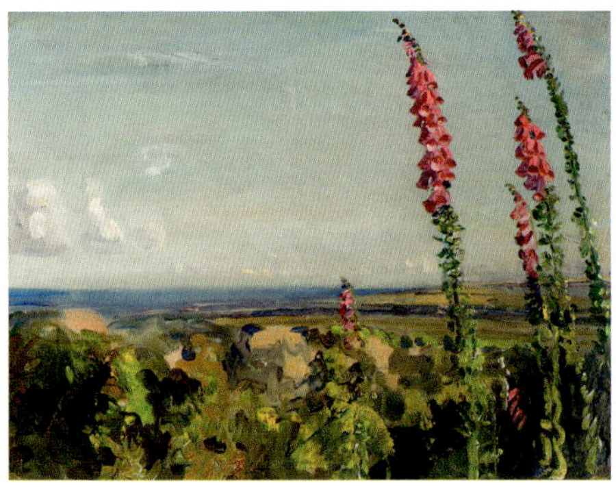

Munnings, Alfred James 1878–1959
A Landscape with Foxgloves in the Foreground
oil on canvas 35.6 x 45.7
401

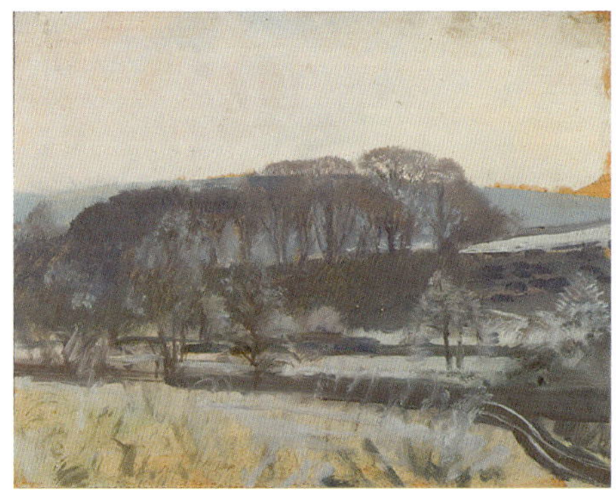

Munnings, Alfred James 1878–1959
A Landscape with Trees
oil on panel 33 x 42.5
315

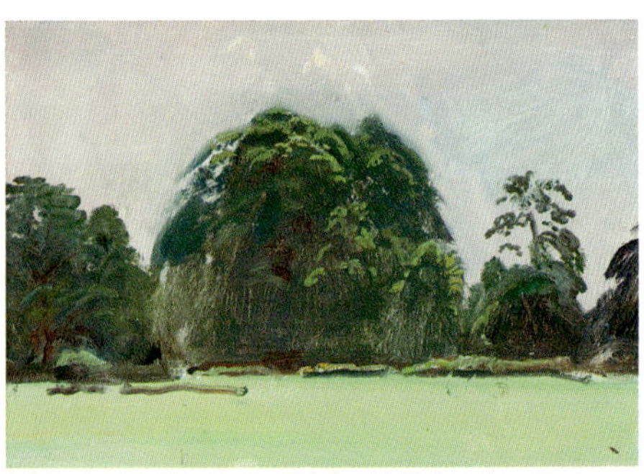

Munnings, Alfred James 1878–1959
A Landscape with Trees by a Field
oil on panel 17.8 x 25.4
593

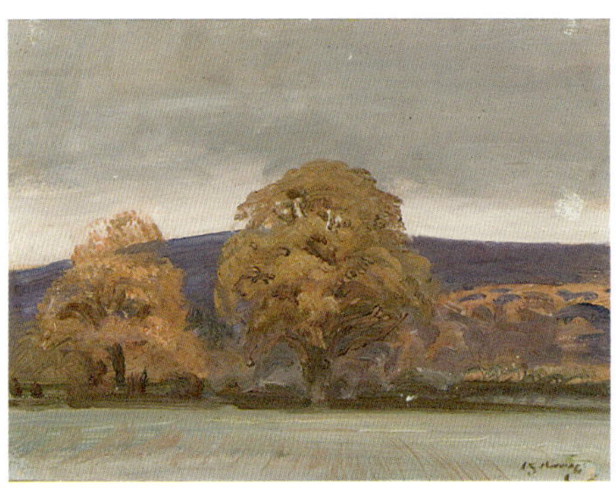

Munnings, Alfred James 1878–1959
A Landscape with Trees on the Edge of a Field (recto)
oil on board 31.8 x 35.6
316

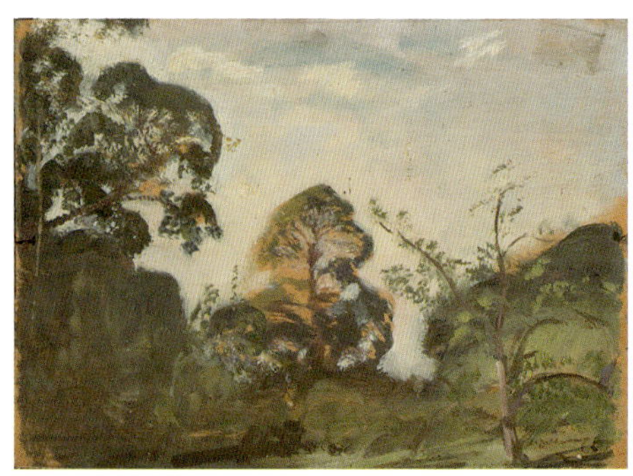

Munnings, Alfred James 1878–1959
Study of Trees (verso)
oil on board 31.8 x 35.6
316A

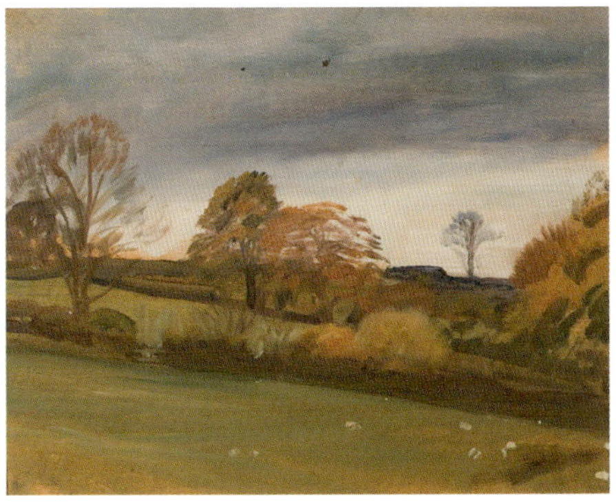

Munnings, Alfred James 1878–1959
A Landscape with Trees on the Edge of a Field
oil on panel 32.4 x 41.3
317

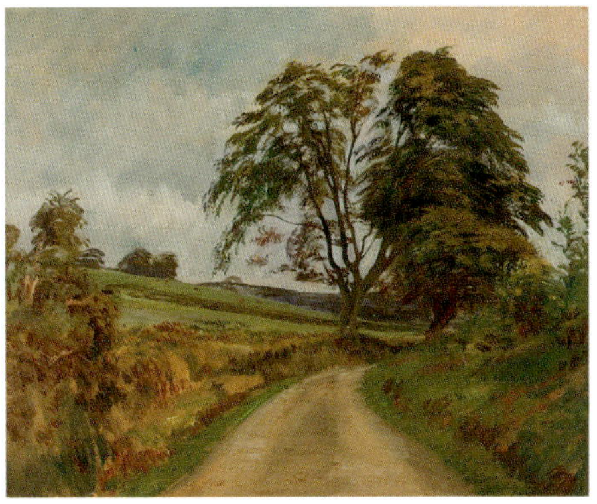

Munnings, Alfred James 1878–1959
A Lane at Exford, Exmoor (study of a tree)
oil on board 50.8 x 60.3
145

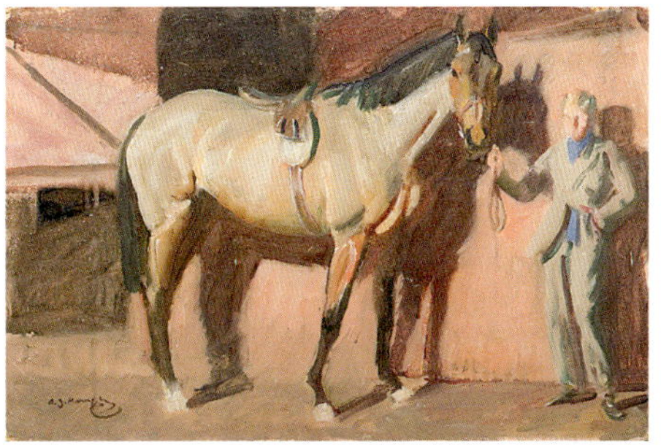

Munnings, Alfred James 1878–1959
A Light Bay Horse with a Stable Boy
oil on board 27.9 x 40.6
187

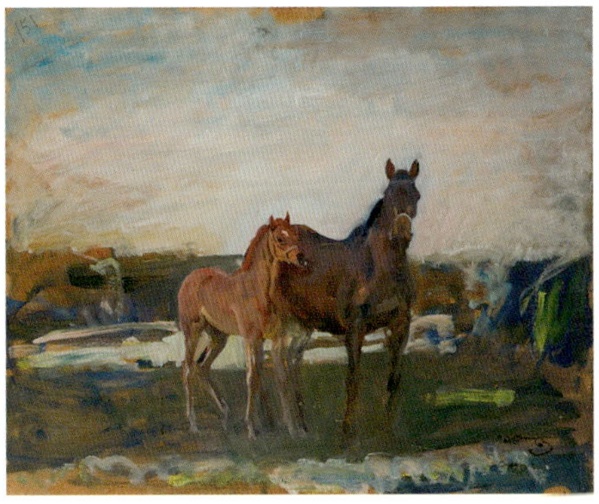

Munnings, Alfred James 1878–1959
A Mare and Foal
oil on board 50.8 x 61
371

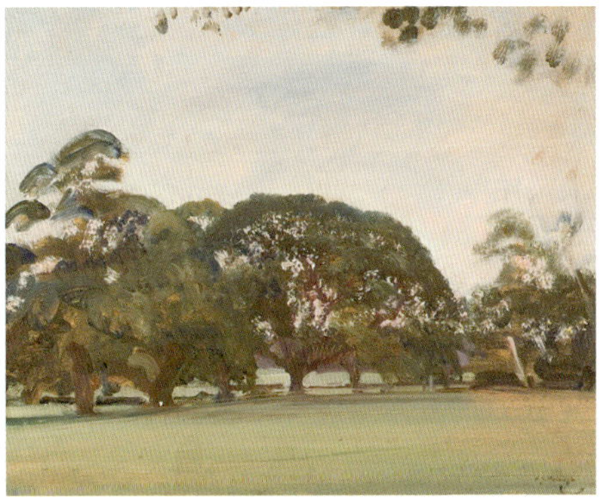

Munnings, Alfred James 1878–1959
A Parkland Scene with Trees
oil on board 33 x 40.6
6

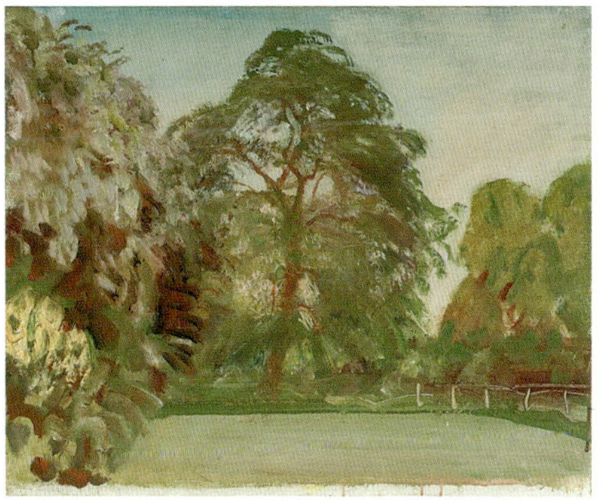

Munnings, Alfred James 1878–1959
A Parkland Scene with Trees
oil on canvas 50.8 x 61
27

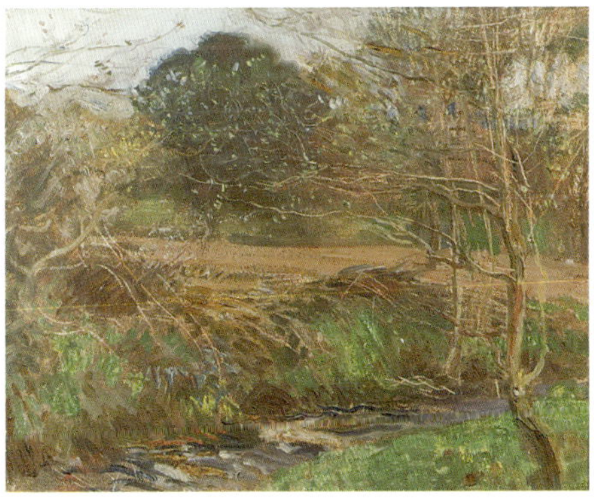

Munnings, Alfred James 1878–1959
A Pastoral Scene with Trees and a Stream in the Foreground
oil on canvas 50.8 x 61
30

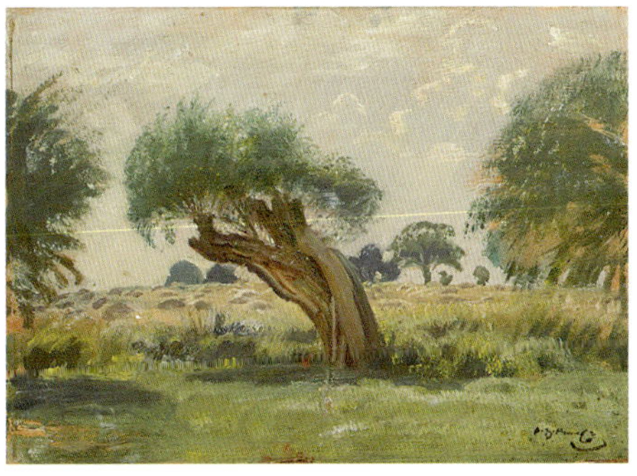

Munnings, Alfred James 1878–1959
A Pollarded Willow (recto)
oil on board 25.4 x 33.7
554

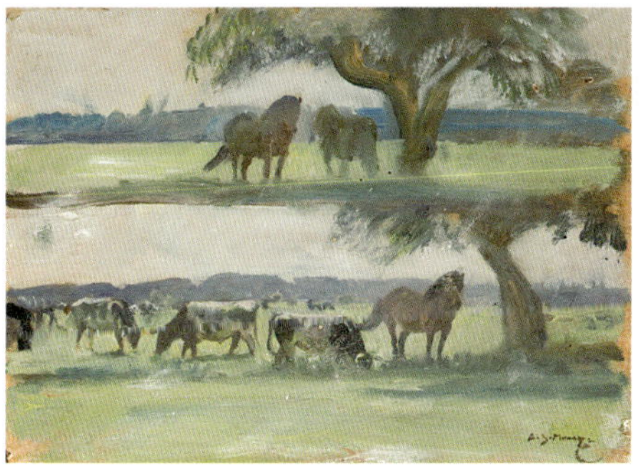

Munnings, Alfred James 1878–1959
Studies of Ponies and Cattle (verso)
oil on board 25.4 x 33.7
554A

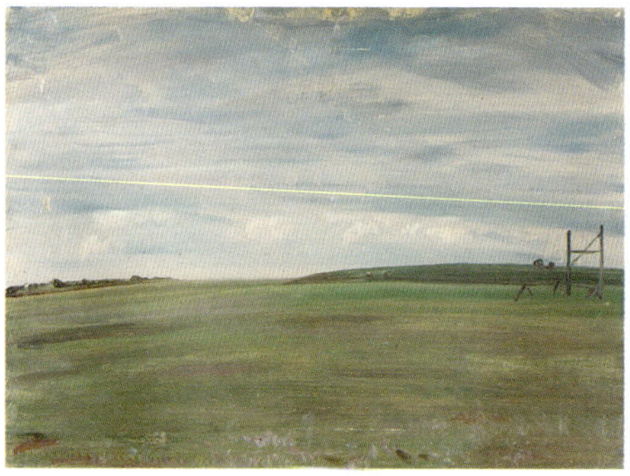

Munnings, Alfred James 1878–1959
A Racecourse
oil on board 45.7 x 61
523

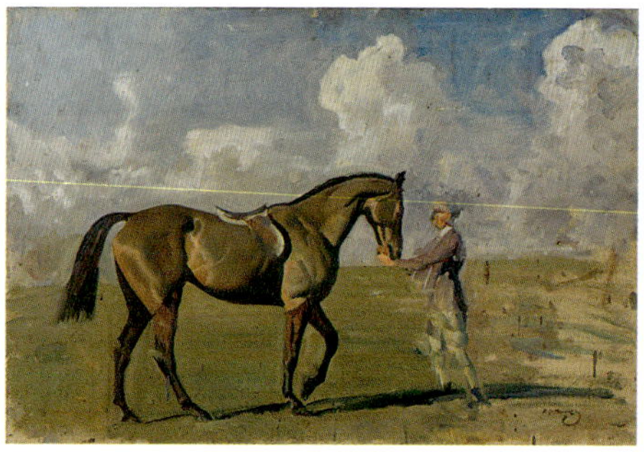

Munnings, Alfred James 1878–1959
A Racehorse Held by a Groom
oil on board 45.7 x 66
442

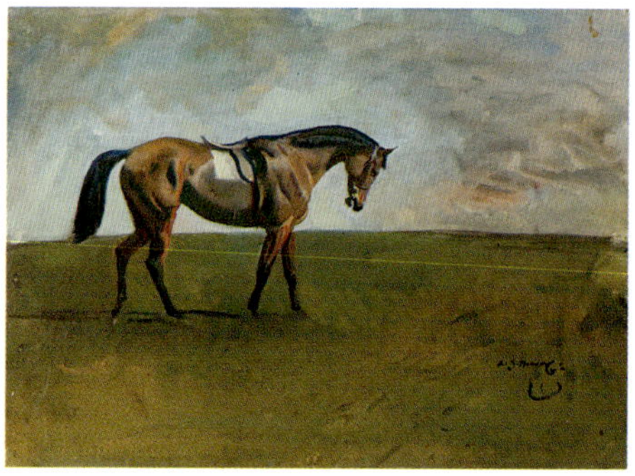

Munnings, Alfred James 1878–1959
A Racehorse in a Landscape
oil on board 35.6 x 47.6
176

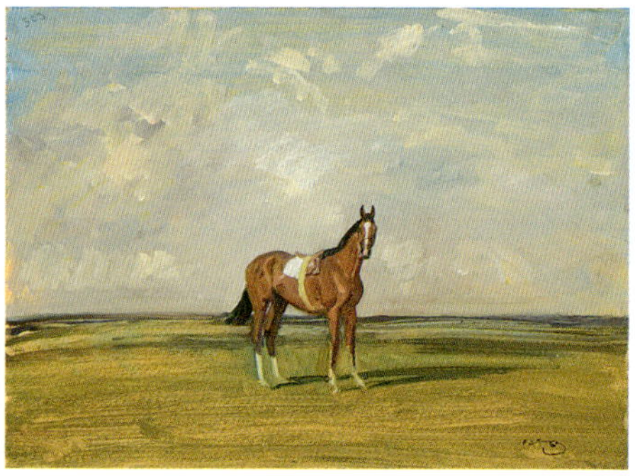

Munnings, Alfred James 1878–1959
A Racehorse in a Landscape
oil on board 45.7 x 61
450

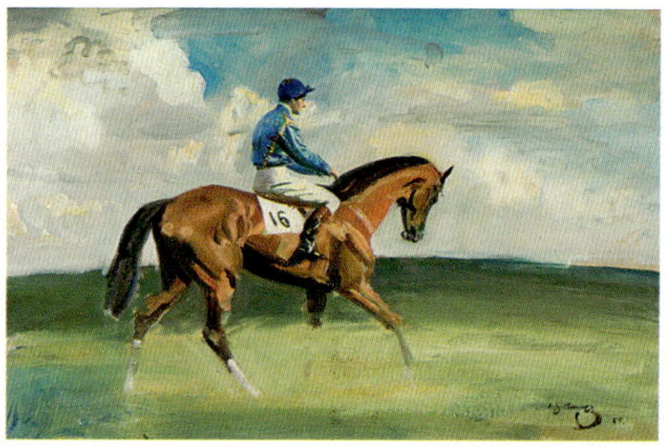

Munnings, Alfred James 1878–1959
A Racehorse with Jockey up, Wearing Blue with Yellow Ribbon
oil on canvas 35.6 x 53.3
414

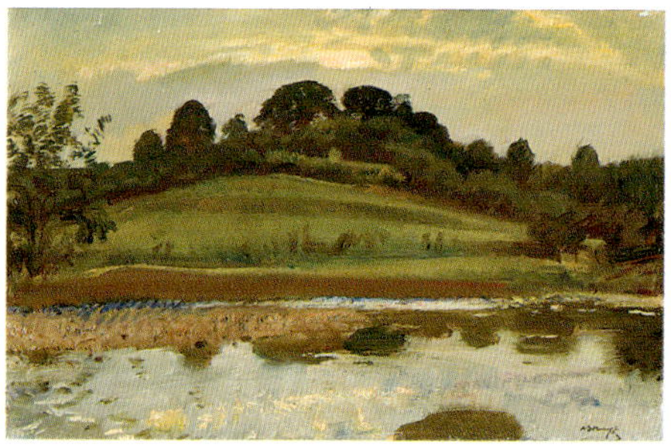

Munnings, Alfred James 1878–1959
A River Landscape on Exmoor
oil on canvas 51.4 x 76.8
329

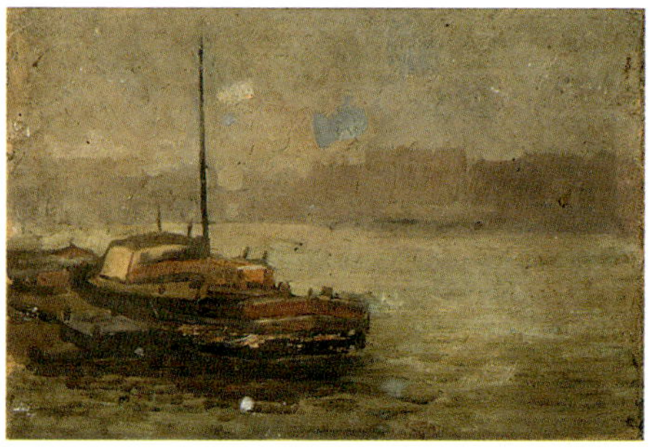

Munnings, Alfred James 1878–1959
A River Scene with a Tug
oil on board 20.3 x 29.2
257

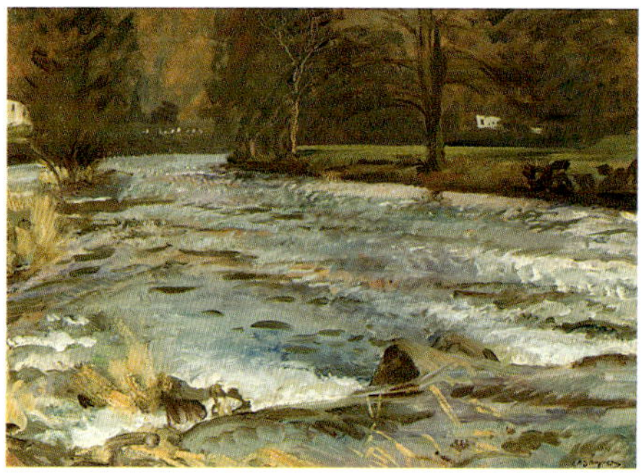

Munnings, Alfred James 1878–1959
A River Scene with Trees
oil on canvas 52.7 x 71.8
324

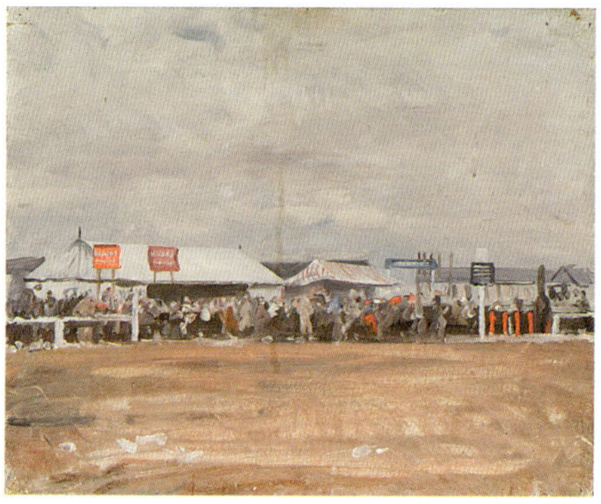

Munnings, Alfred James 1878–1959
A Scene at Newmarket
oil on board 50.8 x 61
405

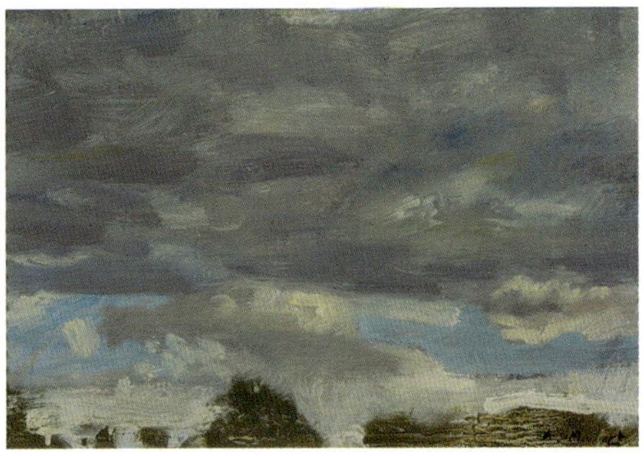

Munnings, Alfred James 1878–1959
A Sky Study
oil on board 25.4 x 34.9
545

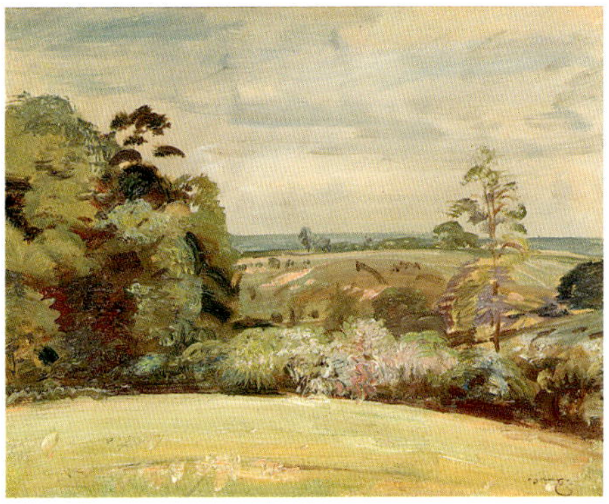

Munnings, Alfred James 1878–1959
A Spring Landscape, Raydon, Suffolk
oil on canvas 50 x 60
364

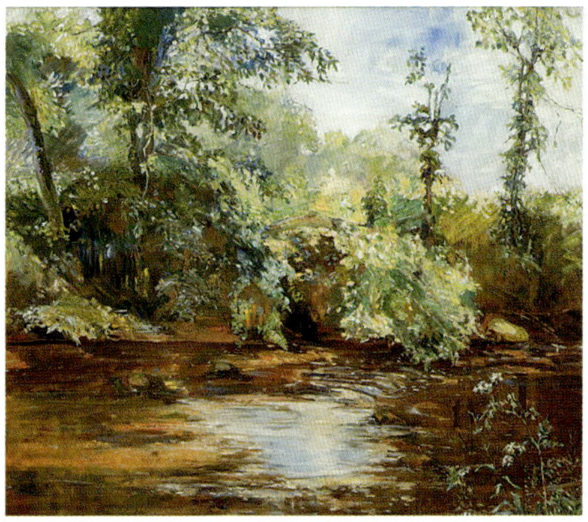

Munnings, Alfred James 1878–1959
A Stream Overhung by Trees
oil on canvas 101.6 x 127
625

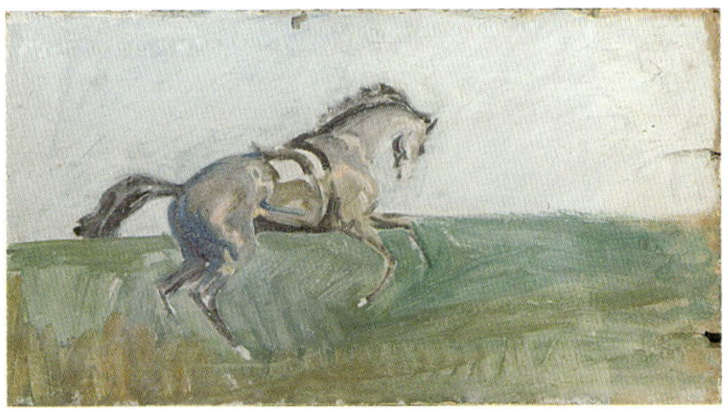

Munnings, Alfred James 1878–1959
A Study from Memory of an Eager Horse
oil on board 30.5 x 55.2
394

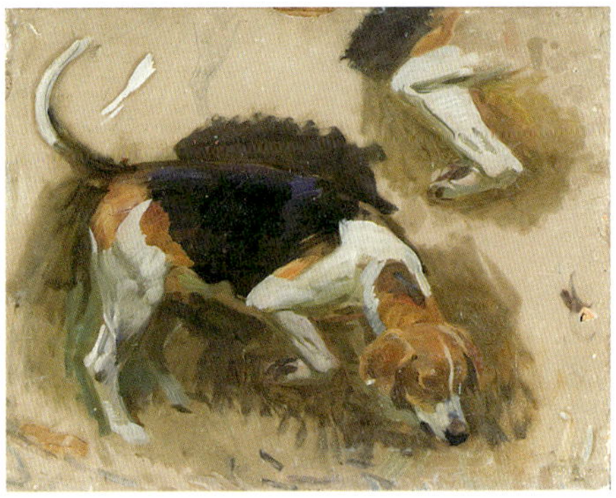

Munnings, Alfred James 1878–1959
A Study of a Hound (recto)
oil on paper mounted on board 47 x 58.4 (E)
242

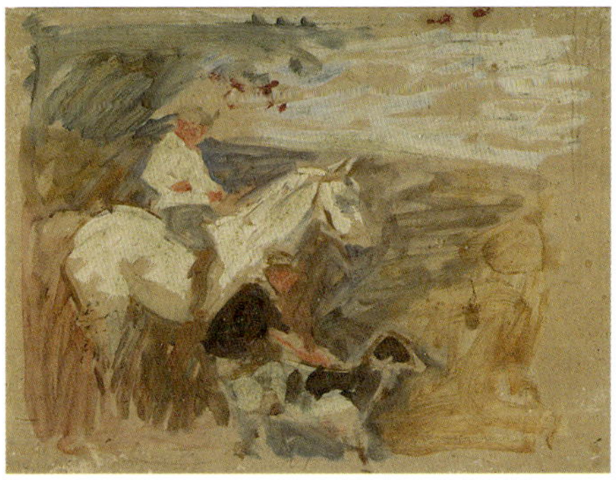

Munnings, Alfred James 1878–1959
Study of a Rider with Man and Calf (verso)
oil on paper mounted on board 47 x 58.4 (E)
242A

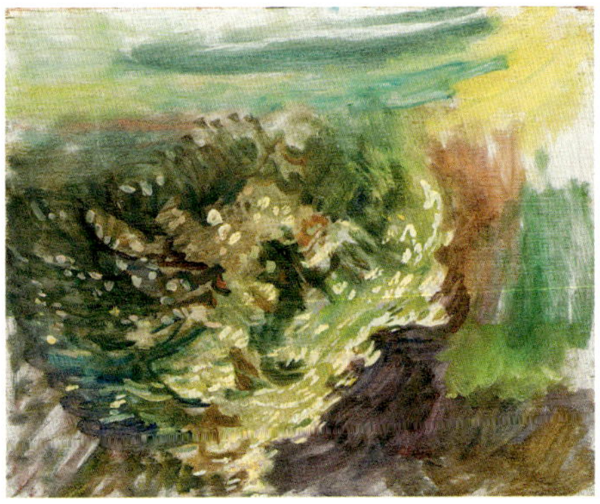

Munnings, Alfred James 1878–1959
A Study of Blossom
oil on board 50.8 x 61
409

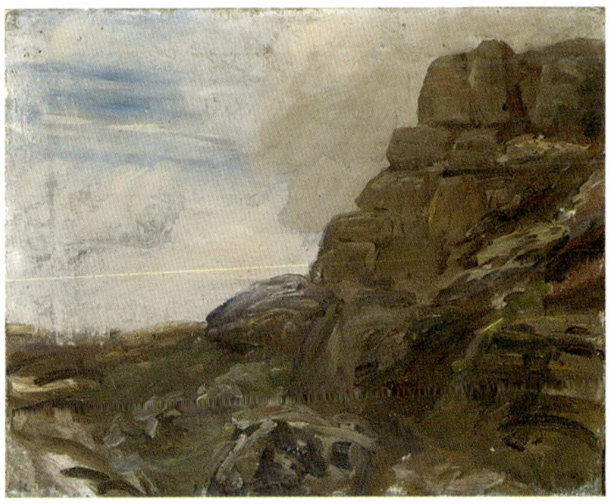

Munnings, Alfred James 1878–1959
A Study of Rocks, Lamorna Cove
oil on canvas 45.7 x 55.9
408

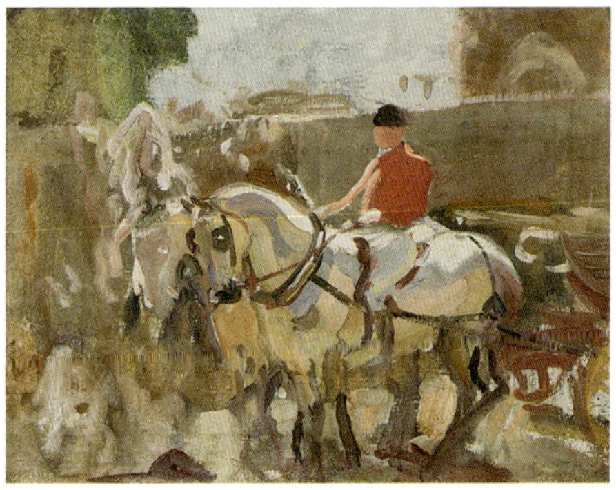

Munnings, Alfred James 1878–1959
A Study of the Windsor Greys
oil on canvas 35.6 x 45.7
35

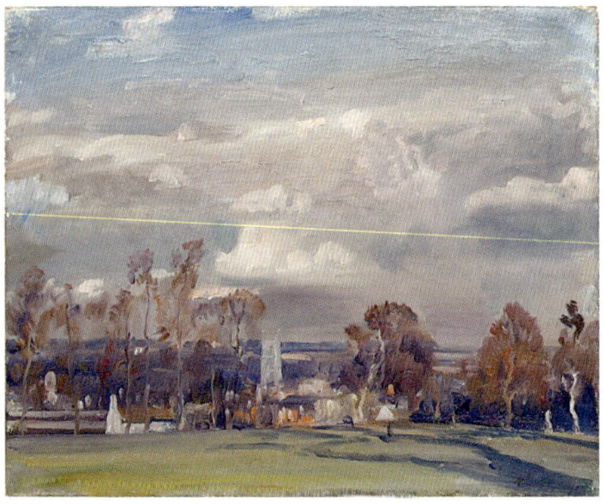

Munnings, Alfred James 1878–1959
A Suffolk Landscape
oil on canvas 51.4 x 61.6
508

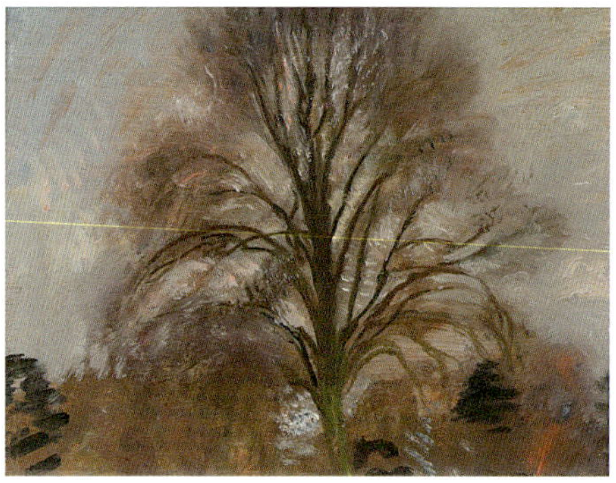

Munnings, Alfred James 1878–1959
A Tree Study (recto)
oil on panel 24.8 x 31.8 (E)
549

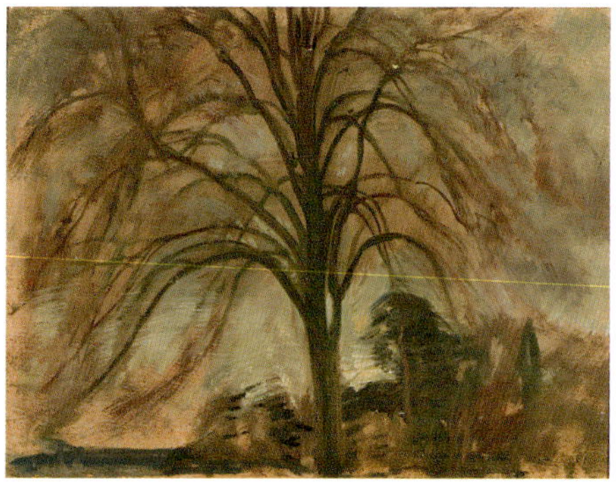

Munnings, Alfred James 1878–1959
A Tree Study (verso)
oil on panel 24.8 x 31.8 (E)
549A

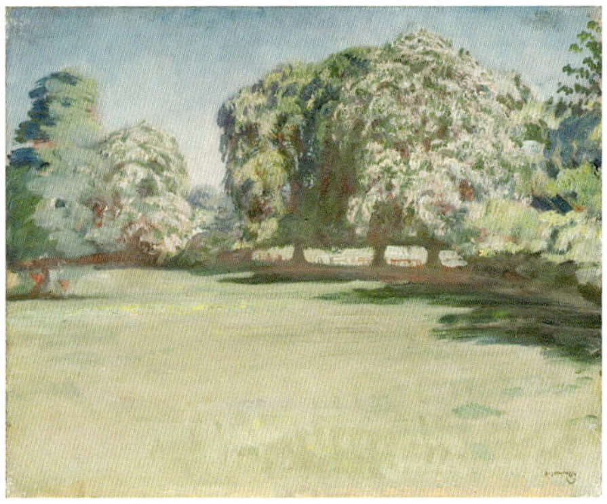

Munnings, Alfred James 1878–1959
A View at Castle House
oil on canvas 50.8 x 61
525

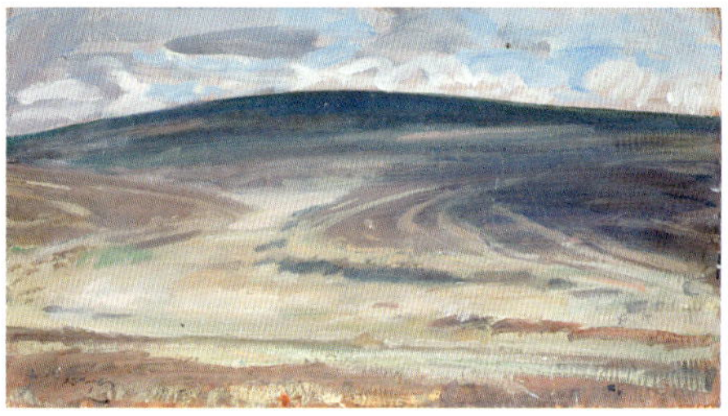

Munnings, Alfred James 1878–1959
A View in Exmoor, Distant Hill in Shadow
oil on board 33 x 58.4
395

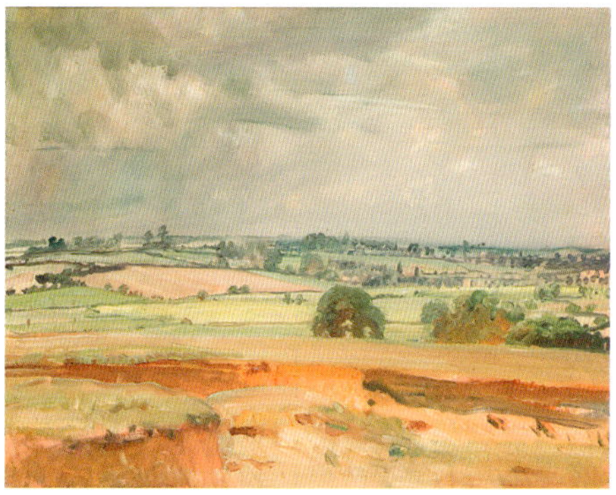

Munnings, Alfred James 1878–1959
A View in Suffolk
oil on canvas 59.7 x 72.4
251

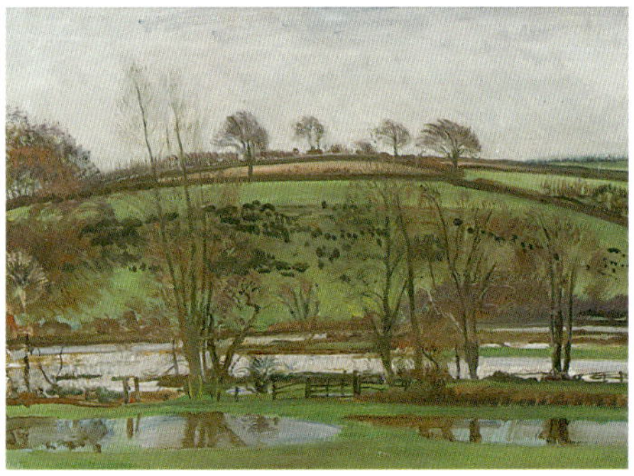

Munnings, Alfred James 1878–1959
A View near Withypool, Exmoor, with Flood Water
oil on panel 45.7 x 60.3
272

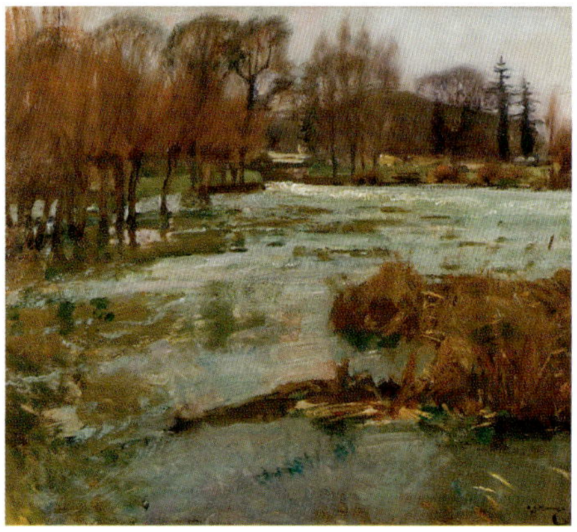

Munnings, Alfred James 1878–1959
A View of Boxted Mill
oil on canvas 68 x 76.5
108

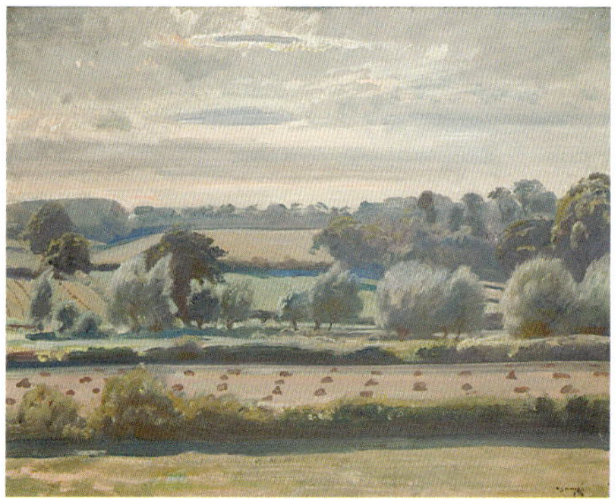

Munnings, Alfred James 1878–1959
A View of Dedham Vale with Stacks in a Field
oil on board 63.5 x 76.2
434

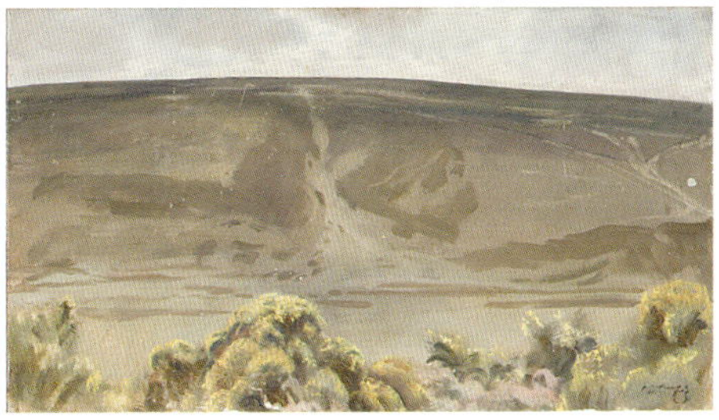

Munnings, Alfred James 1878–1959
A View of Exmoor, Gorse Bushes in Foreground
oil on panel 35.6 x 61
24

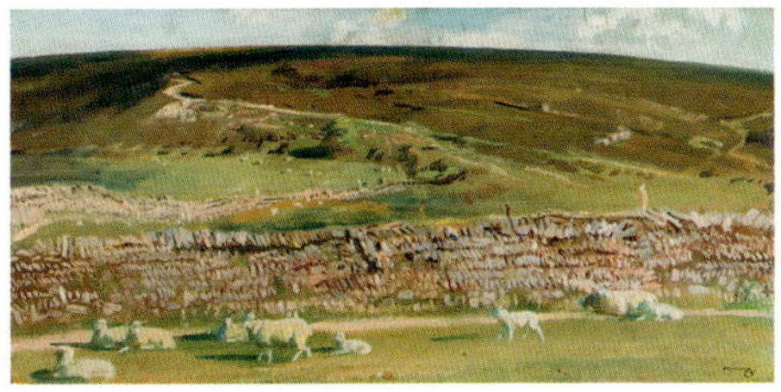

Munnings, Alfred James 1878–1959
A View of Exmoor, Sheep by the Wall in the Foreground
oil on board 45 x 91
52

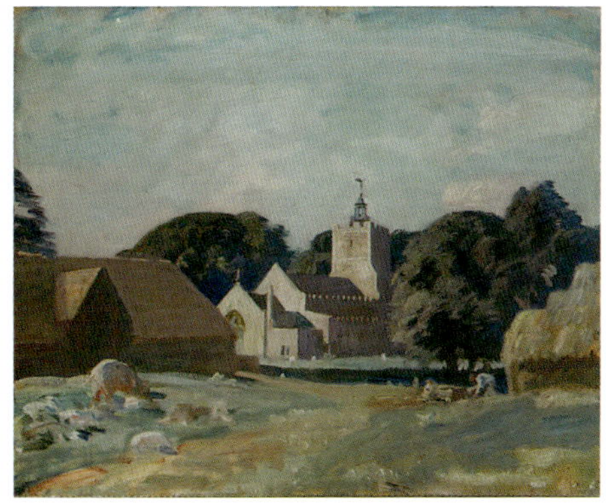

Munnings, Alfred James 1878–1959
A View of Great Thurlow, Suffolk
oil on canvas 63.5 x 76.2
84

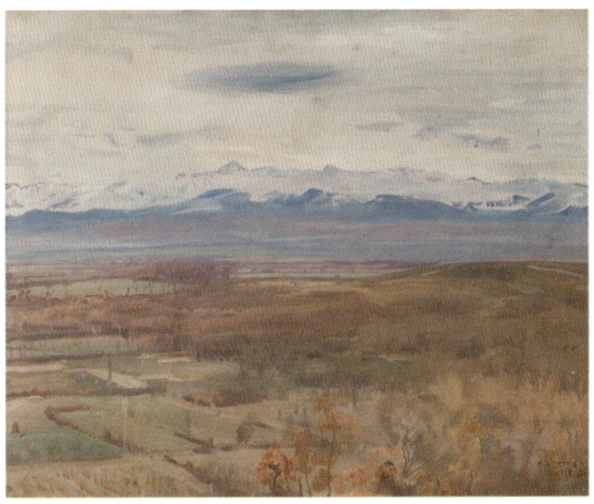

Munnings, Alfred James 1878–1959
A View of the Pyrenees from Pau
oil on canvas 50.8 x 61.6
346

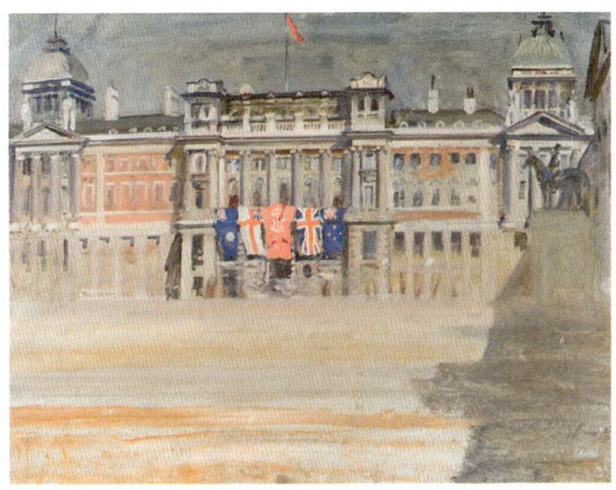

Munnings, Alfred James 1878–1959
A View of Whitehall
oil on canvas 55.9 x 71.1
335

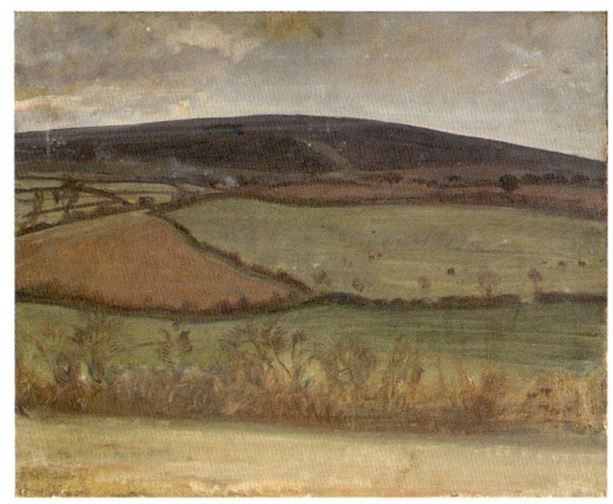

Munnings, Alfred James 1878–1959
A View on Exmoor
oil on board 50.8 x 61
503

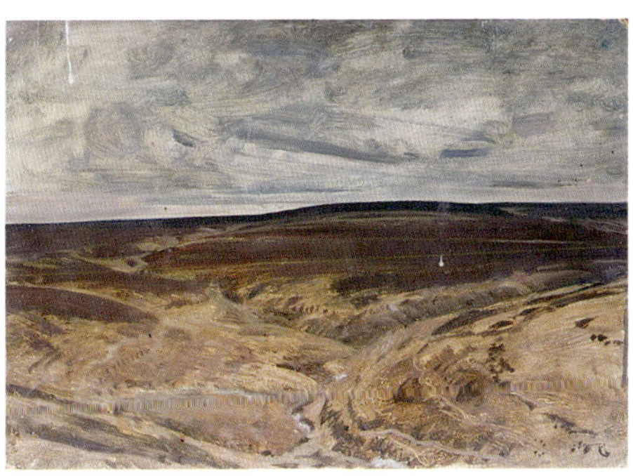

Munnings, Alfred James 1878–1959
A View on Exmoor
oil on board 44.5 x 60.3
505

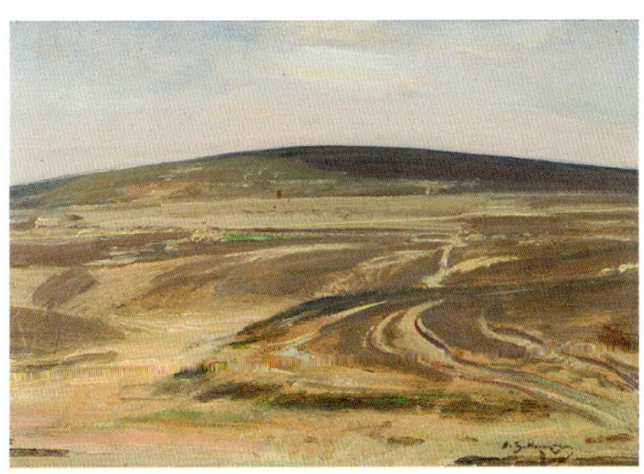

Munnings, Alfred James 1878–1959
A View on Exmoor
oil on panel 25.4 x 34.9
547

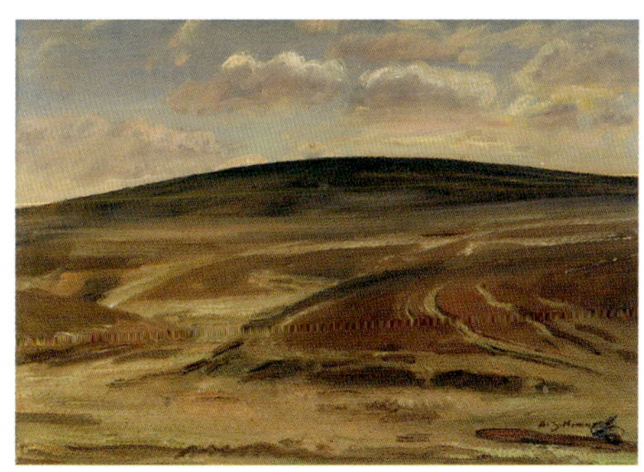

Munnings, Alfred James 1878–1959
A View on Exmoor
oil on panel 25.4 x 35.6
550

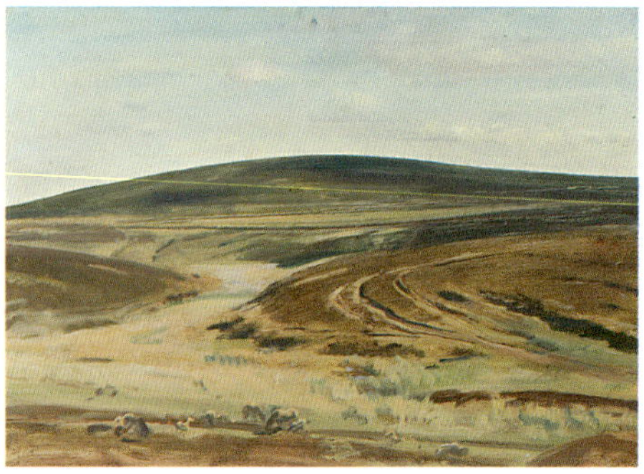

Munnings, Alfred James 1878–1959
A View on Exmoor, Ponies in the Foreground (recto)
oil on panel 44.5 x 60.3 (E)
353

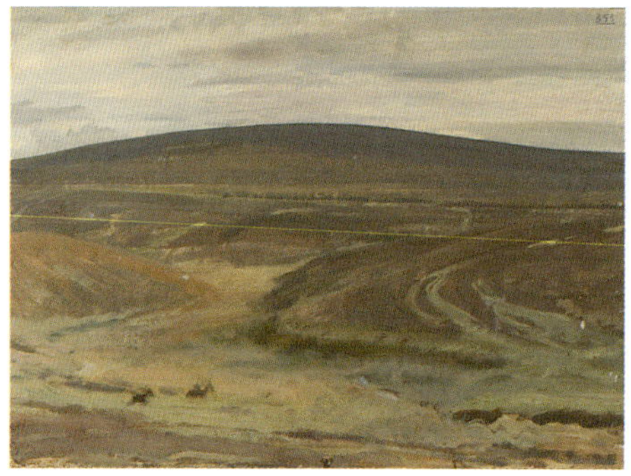

Munnings, Alfred James 1878–1959
Study of a Landscape (verso)
oil on panel 44.5 x 60.3 (E)
353A

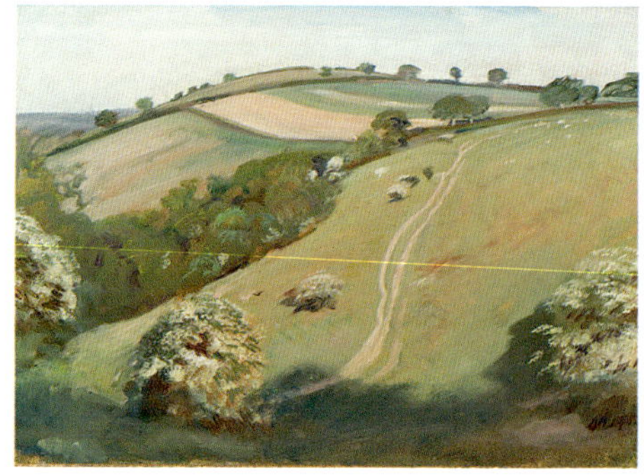

Munnings, Alfred James 1878–1959
A View on Exmoor with Bushes in Blossom
oil on canvas 52.7 x 71.1
110

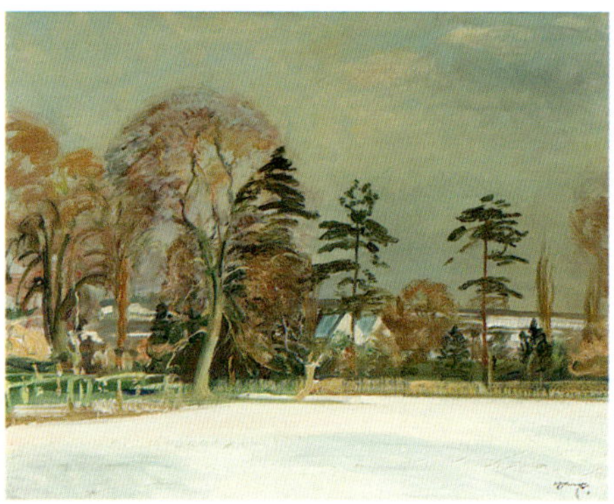

Munnings, Alfred James 1878–1959
A Winter Landscape
oil on board 63.5 x 76.2
339

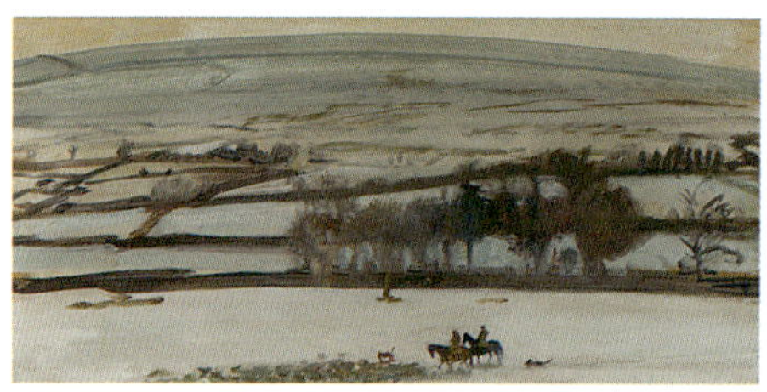

Munnings, Alfred James 1878–1959
A Winter Landscape, Exmoor, Figures on Horseback in the Foreground
oil on board 35.6 x 71.1
267

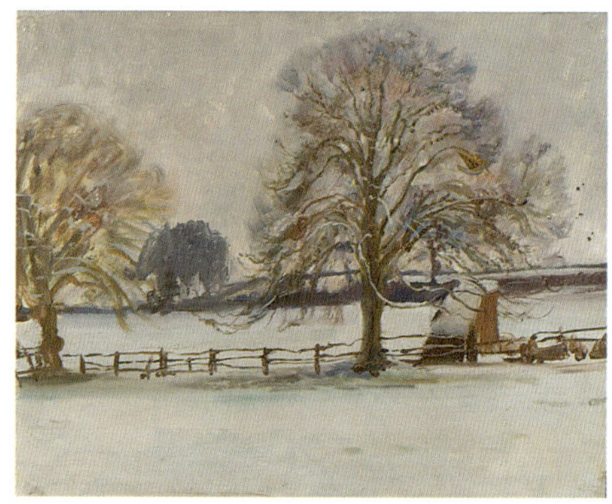

Munnings, Alfred James 1878–1959
A Winter Landscape with Trees
oil on canvas 50.8 x 61
18

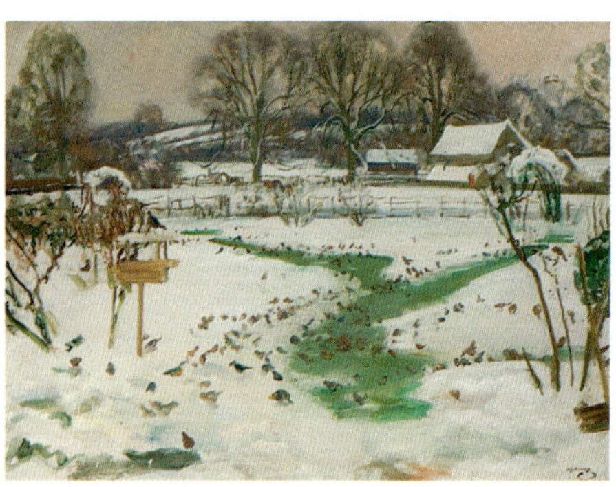

Munnings, Alfred James 1878–1959
A Winter Scene at Castle House with Birds Feeding
oil on canvas 81.3 x 105.4
424

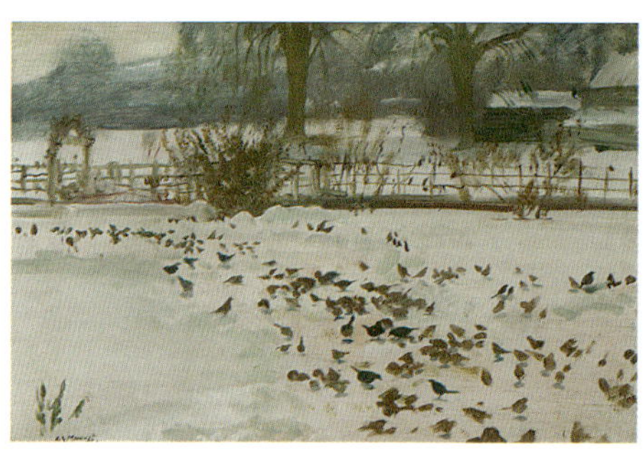

Munnings, Alfred James 1878–1959
A Winter Scene at Castle House with Birds in the Foreground
oil on board 41.3 x 61
295

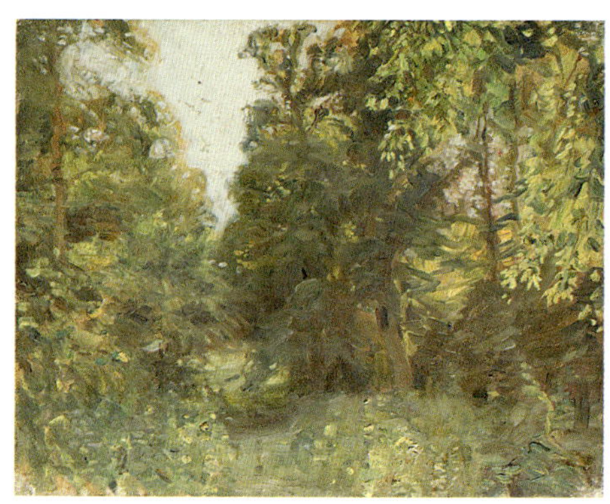

Munnings, Alfred James 1878–1959
A Wooded Landscape
oil on canvas 50.8 x 61
29

Facing page: Wood, Christopher, 1901–1930, *Mlle Bourgoint* (detail), 1929, University of Essex, (p. 180)

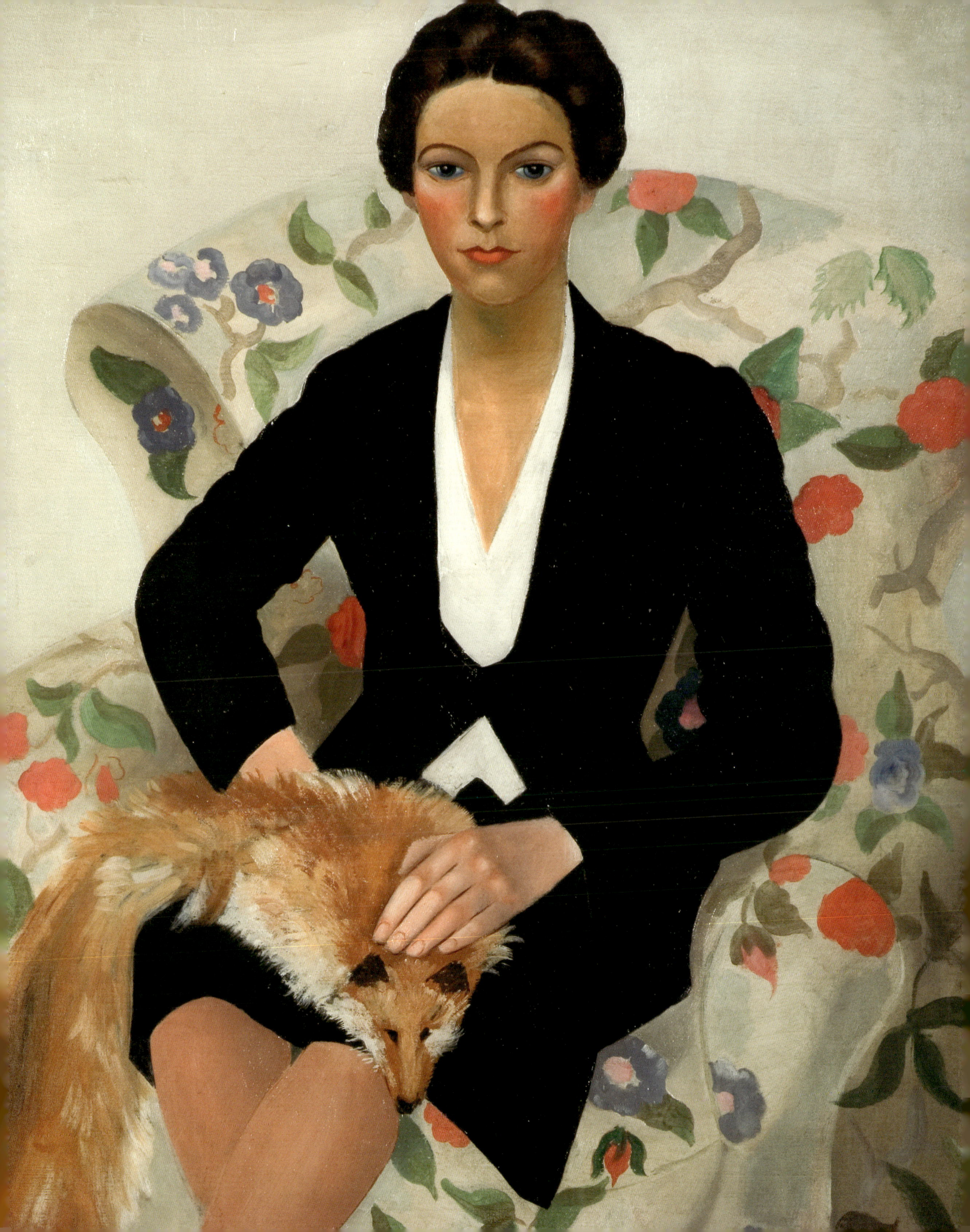

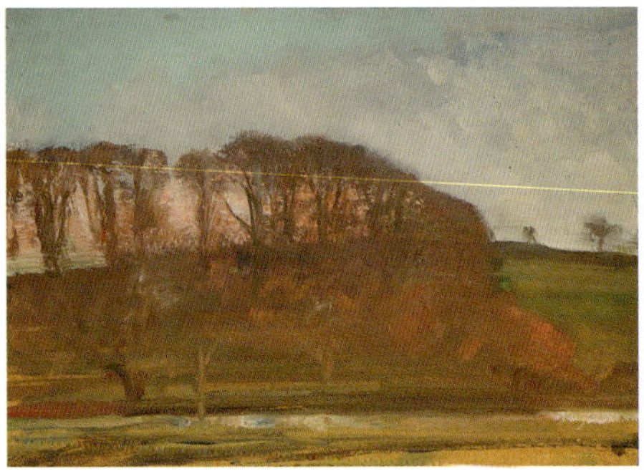

Munnings, Alfred James 1878–1959
A Wooded Landscape
oil on panel 38.1 x 50.8
356

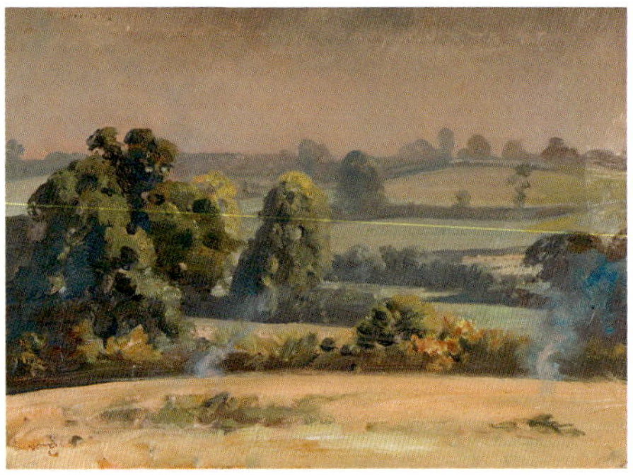

Munnings, Alfred James 1878–1959
A Wooded Landscape
oil on canvas 45.7 x 61
509

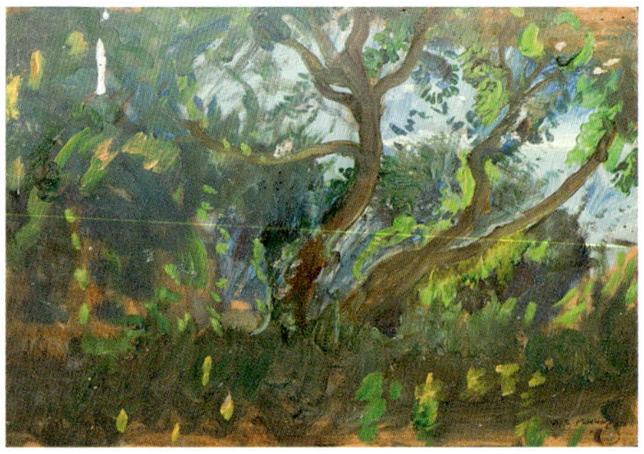

Munnings, Alfred James 1878–1959
A Woodland Scene
oil on panel 25.4 x 35.6
565

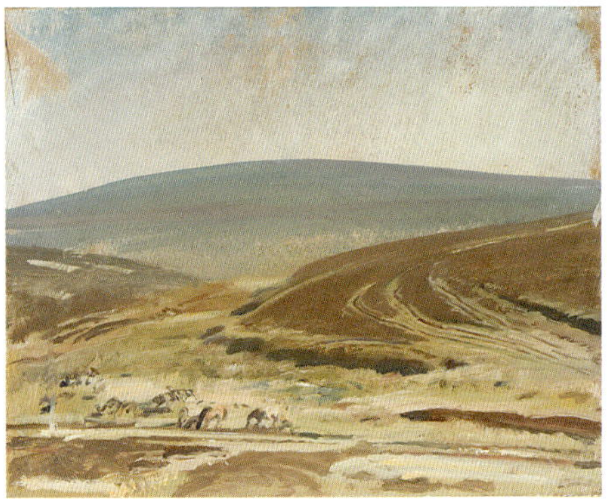

Munnings, Alfred James 1878–1959
An Autumn Exmoor Landscape
oil on board 50.8 x 61
492

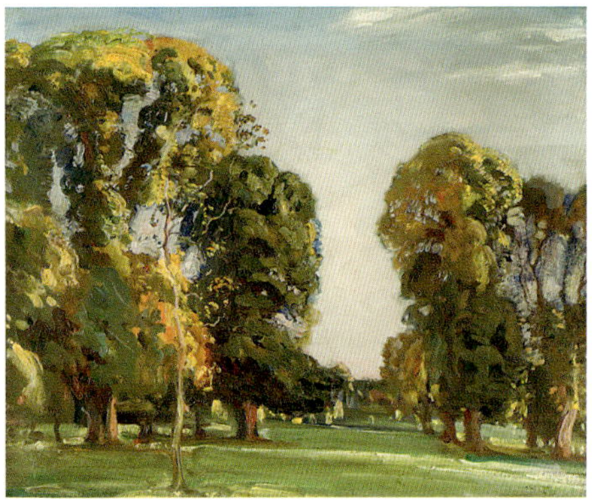

Munnings, Alfred James 1878–1959
An Avenue of Trees
oil on canvas 76.2 x 88.9
366

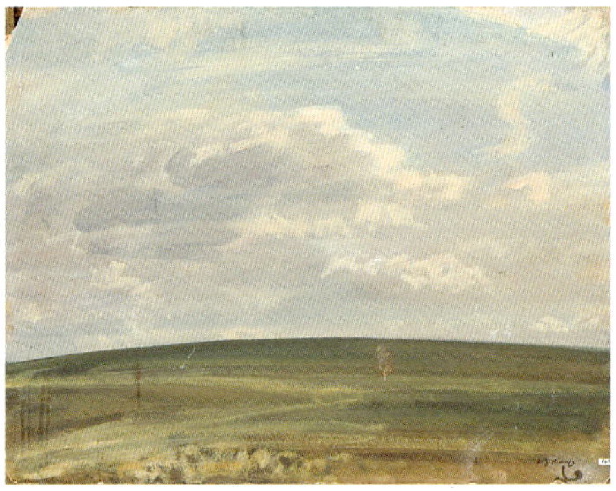

Munnings, Alfred James 1878–1959
An Exmoor Landscape (recto)
oil on board 47 x 59.7
491

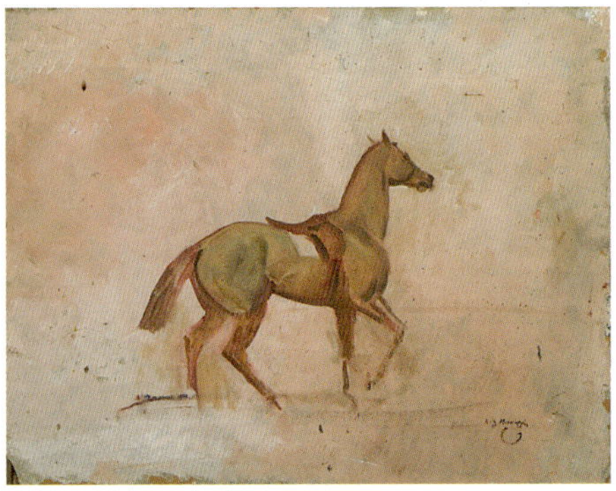

Munnings, Alfred James 1878–1959
Study of a Horse (verso)
oil on board 47 x 59.7
491A

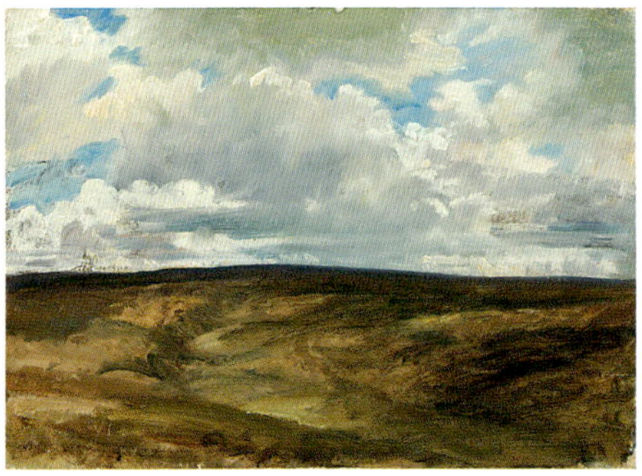

Munnings, Alfred James 1878–1959
An Exmoor Landscape
oil on board 45.7 x 60.3
495

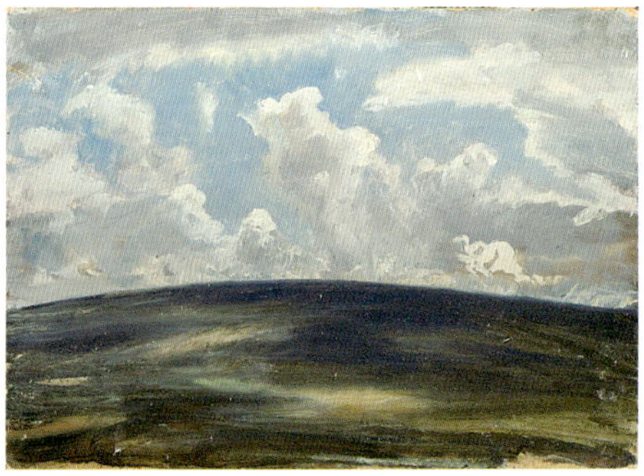

Munnings, Alfred James 1878–1959
An Exmoor Landscape
oil on board 44.5 x 61
497

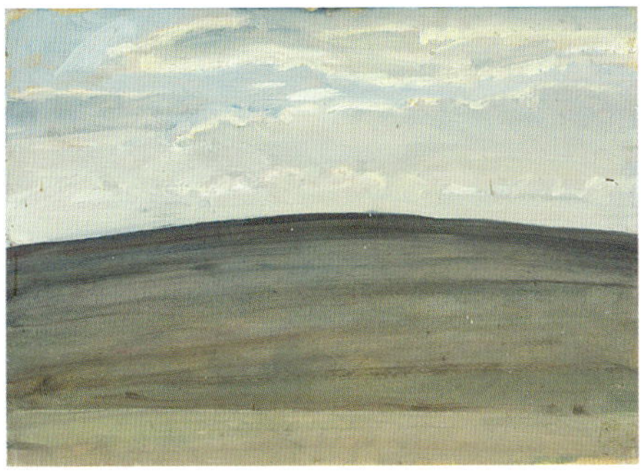

Munnings, Alfred James 1878–1959
An Exmoor Landscape
oil on board 43.8 x 61
500

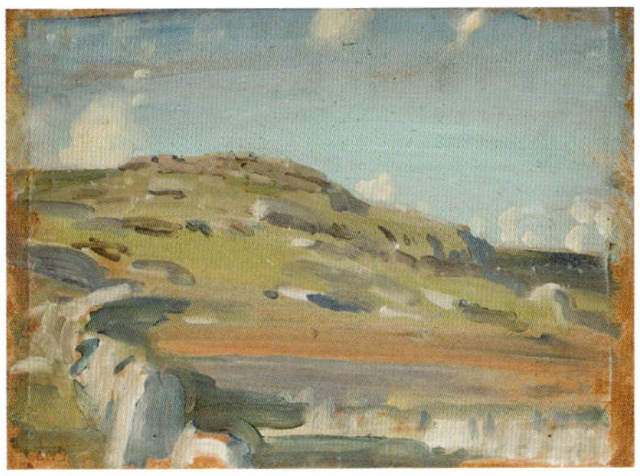

Munnings, Alfred James 1878–1959
An Exmoor Landscape (recto)
oil on panel 30.5 x 40.6
577

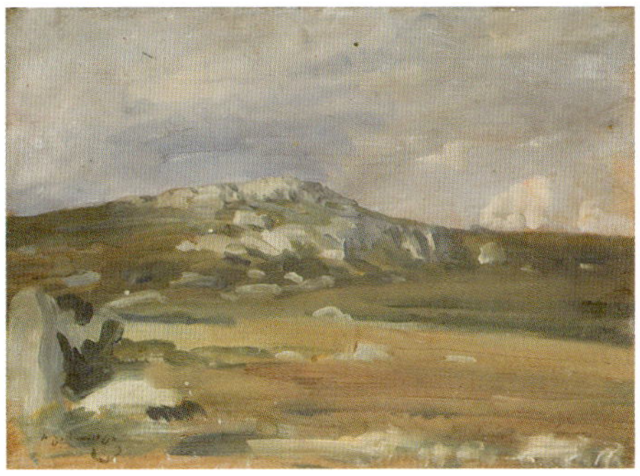

Munnings, Alfred James 1878–1959
An Exmoor Landscape (verso)
oil on panel 30.5 x 40.6
577A

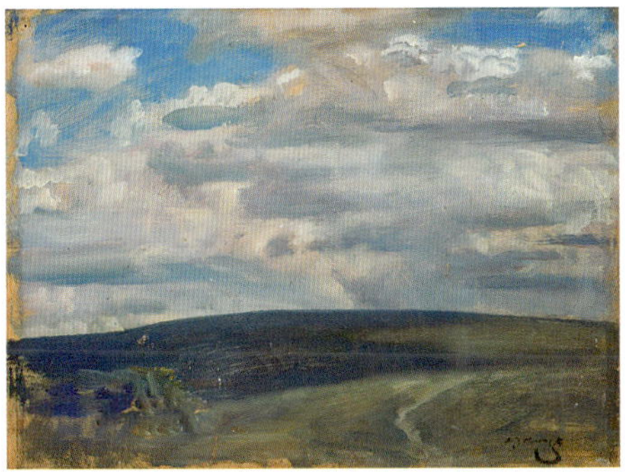

Munnings, Alfred James 1878–1959
An Exmoor Landscape (recto)
oil on panel 30.5 x 40.6
580

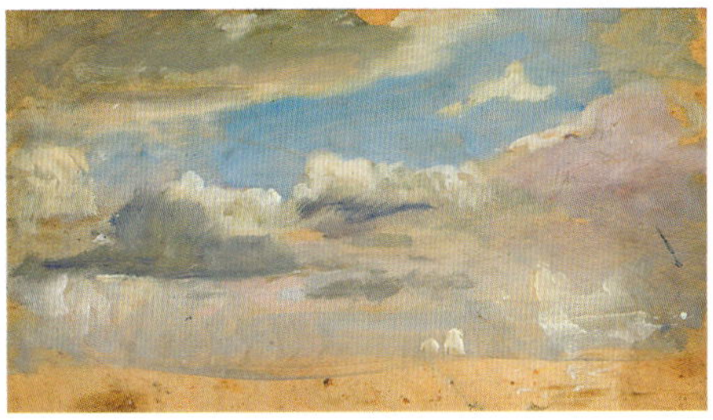

Munnings, Alfred James 1878–1959
Study of Clouds (verso)
oil on panel 30.5 x 40.6
580A

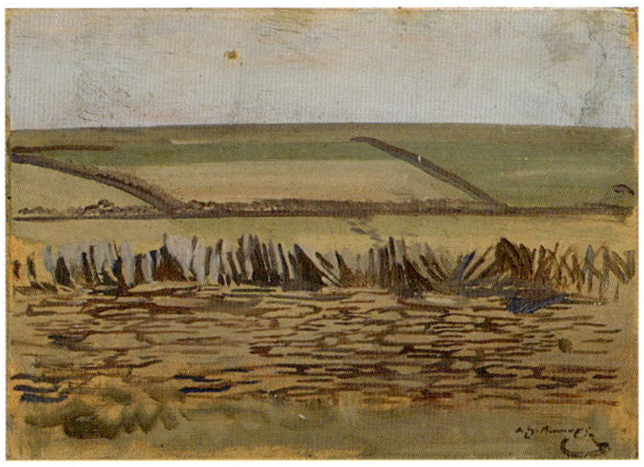

Munnings, Alfred James 1878–1959
An Exmoor Landscape with a Wall (recto)
oil on board 25.4 x 35.6
555

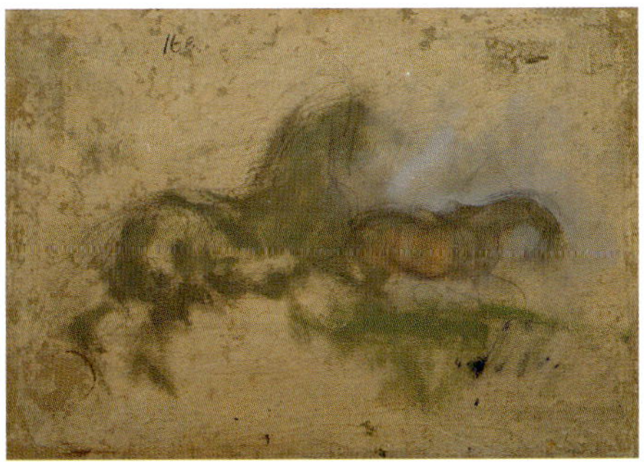

Munnings, Alfred James 1878–1959
Horse Studies (verso)
oil on board 25.4 x 35.6
555A

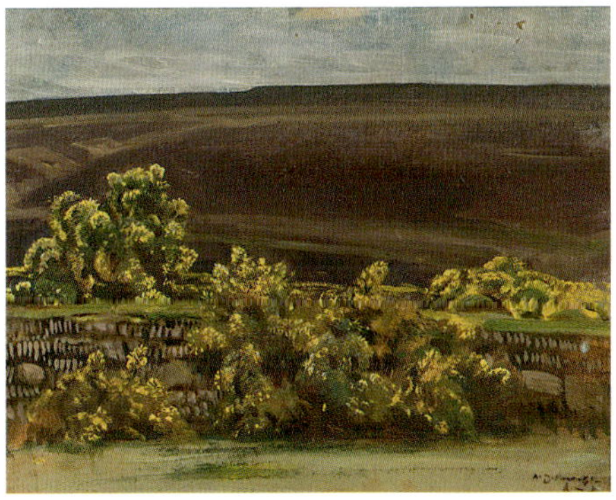

Munnings, Alfred James 1878–1959
An Exmoor Landscape with Gorse (recto)
oil on panel 36 x 46 (E)
341

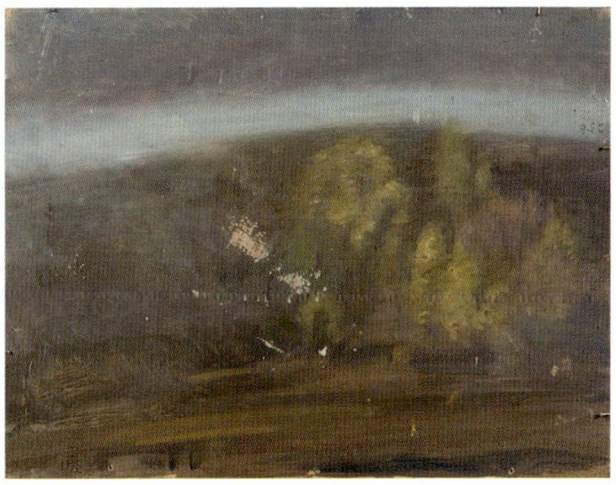

Munnings, Alfred James 1878–1959
Trees in a Landscape (verso)
oil on panel 36 x 46 (E)
341A

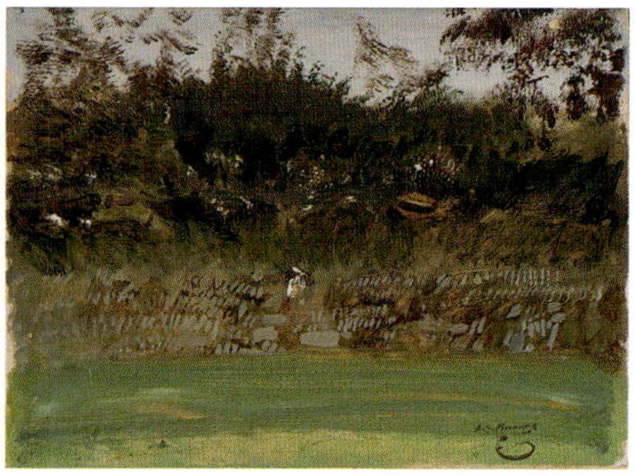

Munnings, Alfred James 1878–1959
An Exmoor Scene
oil on board 25.9 x 35.6
574

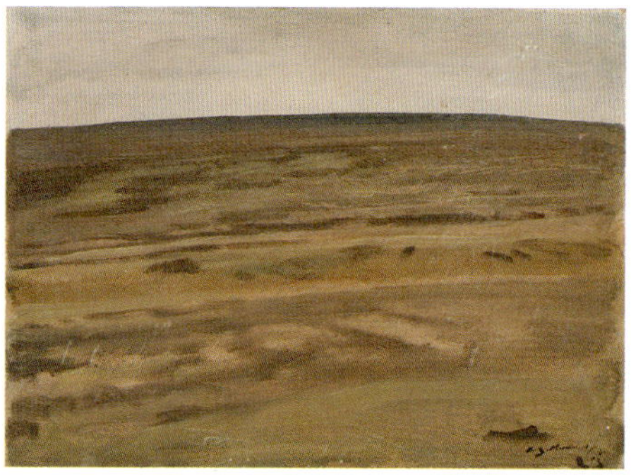

Munnings, Alfred James 1878–1959
An Exmoor View (recto)
oil on panel 24.8 x 33
543

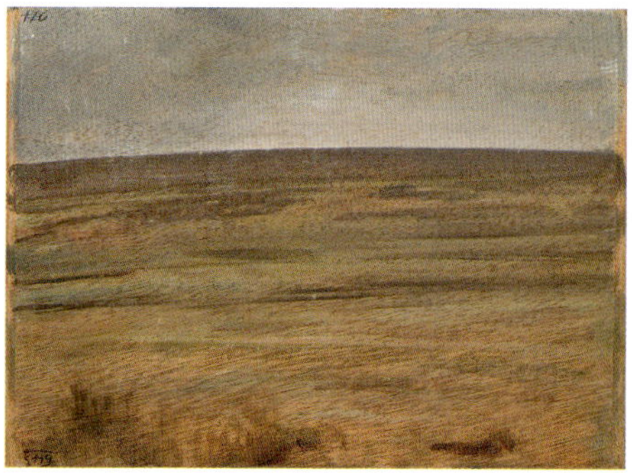

Munnings, Alfred James 1878–1959
An Exmoor View (verso)
oil on panel 24.8 x 33
543A

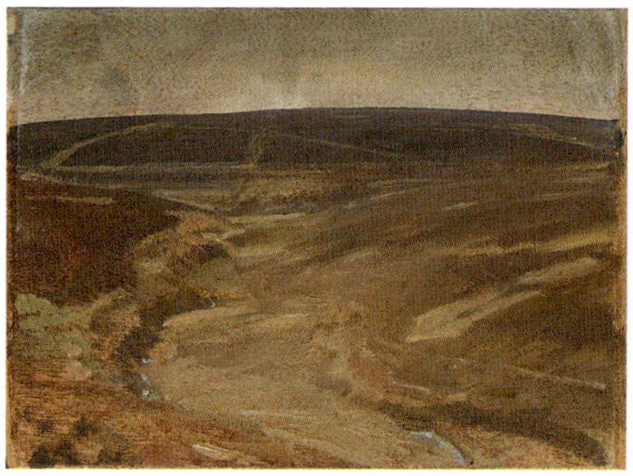

Munnings, Alfred James 1878–1959
An Exmoor View (recto)
oil on panel 24.8 x 33
567

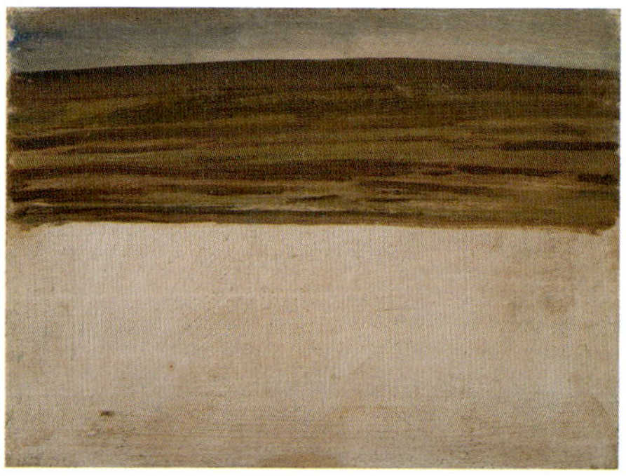

Munnings, Alfred James 1878–1959
An Exmoor View (verso)
oil on panel 24.8 x 33
567A

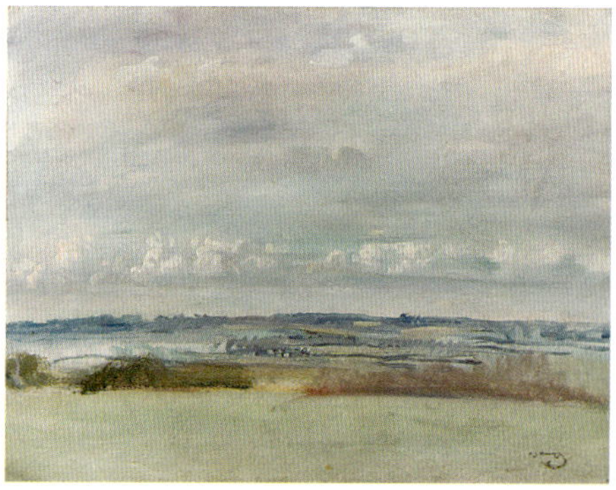

Munnings, Alfred James 1878–1959
An Extensive Landscape
oil on board 55.9 x 71.1
345

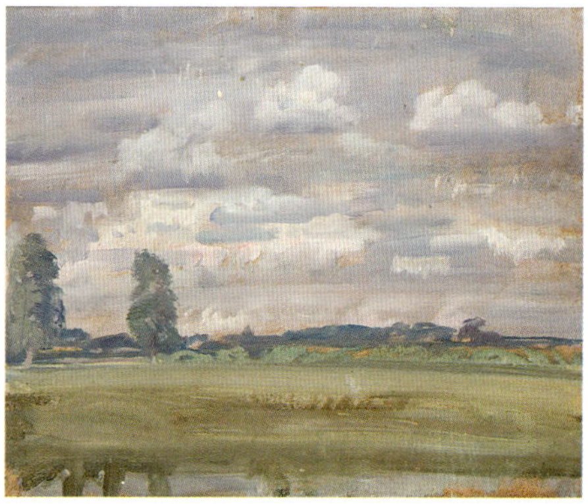

Munnings, Alfred James 1878–1959
An Extensive Landscape
oil on board 50.8 x 61
406

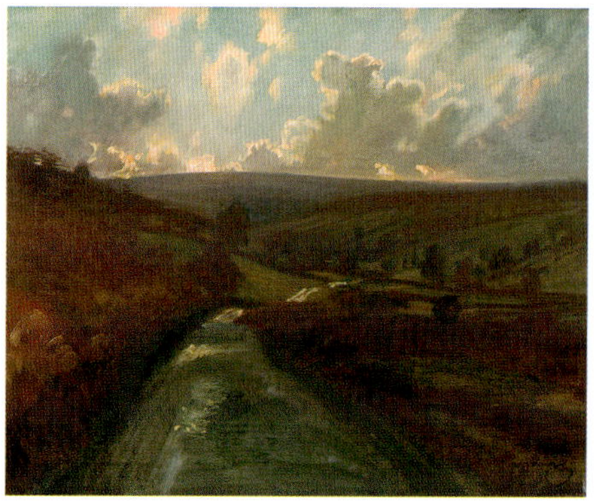

Munnings, Alfred James 1878–1959
An Extensive Landscape with a Road
oil on canvas 50.8 x 61.6
361

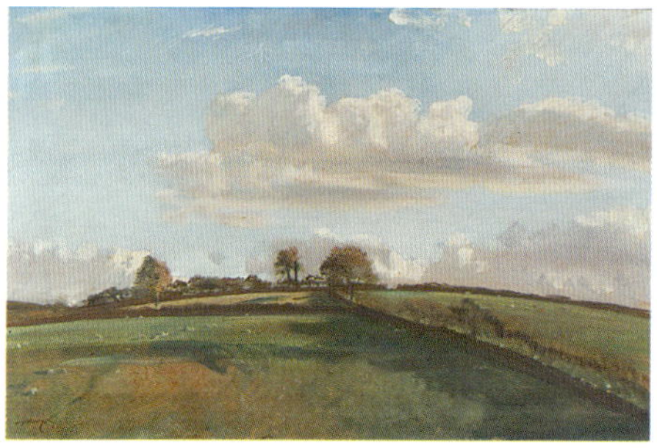

Munnings, Alfred James 1878–1959
An Extensive Landscape with Sheep Grazing in the Fields
oil on board 50.2 x 76.2
253

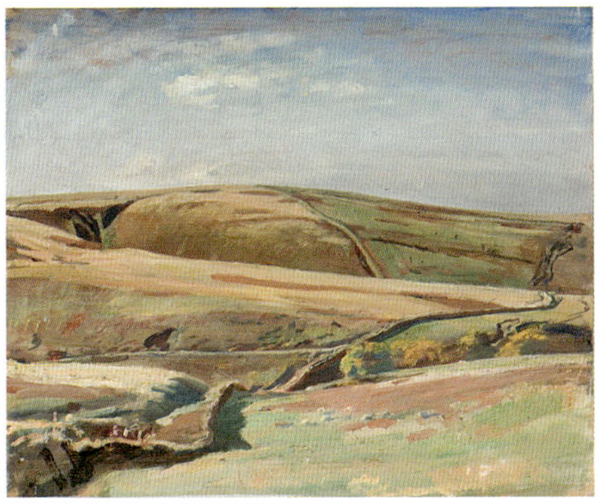

Munnings, Alfred James 1878–1959
An Extensive View of Exmoor
oil on panel 50.8 x 61
10

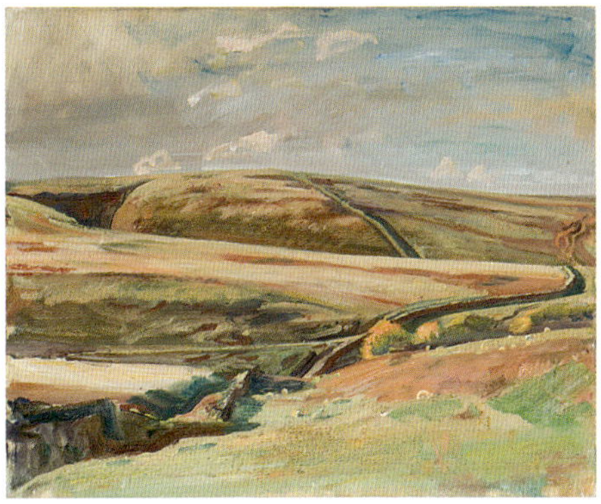

Munnings, Alfred James 1878–1959
An Extensive View of Exmoor
oil on canvas 50.8 x 61
23

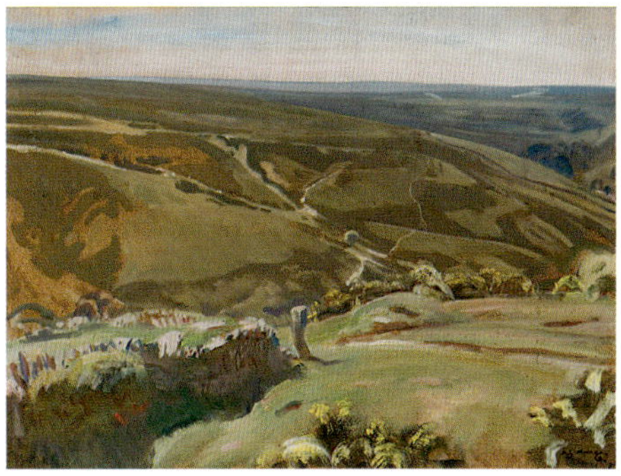

Munnings, Alfred James 1878–1959
An Extensive View of Exmoor
oil on board 45.7 x 61
501

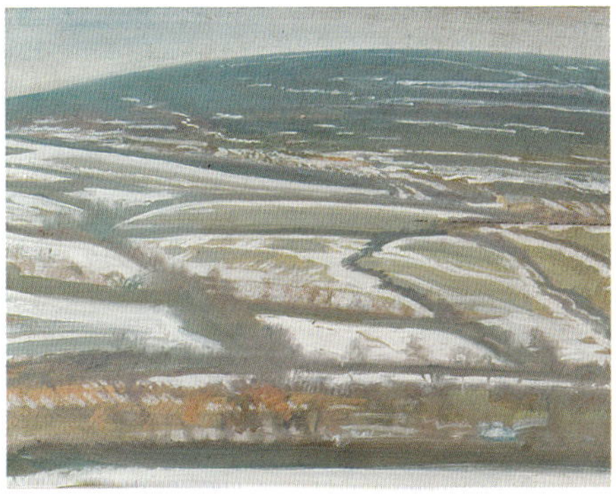

Munnings, Alfred James 1878–1959
An Extensive Winter Landscape, Exmoor (recto)
oil on board 35.6 x 45.7
350

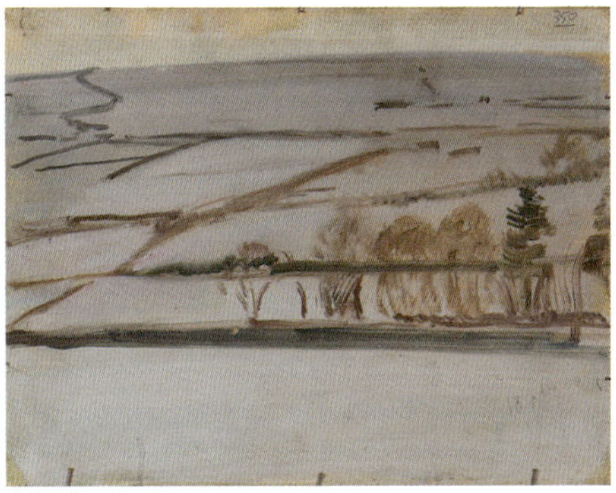

Munnings, Alfred James 1878–1959
Study of a Winter Landscape (verso)
oil on board 35.6 x 45.7
350A

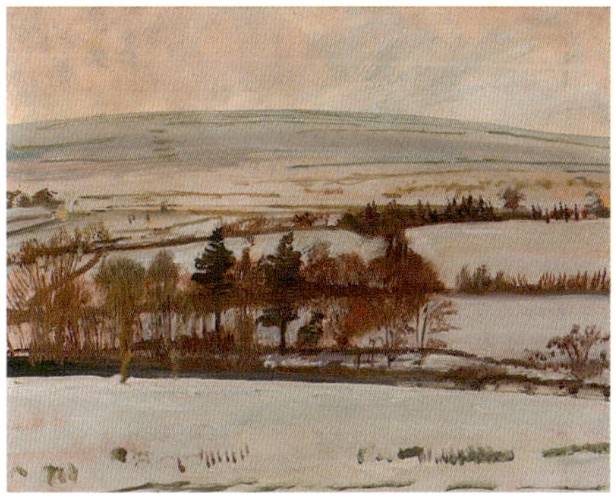

Munnings, Alfred James 1878–1959
An Extensive Winter Landscape, Withypool, Exmoor
oil on board 40.6 x 50.8
413

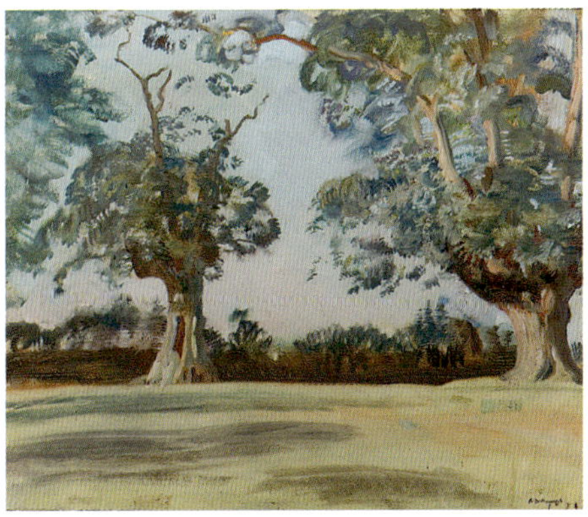

Munnings, Alfred James 1878–1959
An Oak Grove, Nayland, Suffolk
oil on canvas 50.8 x 63.5
149

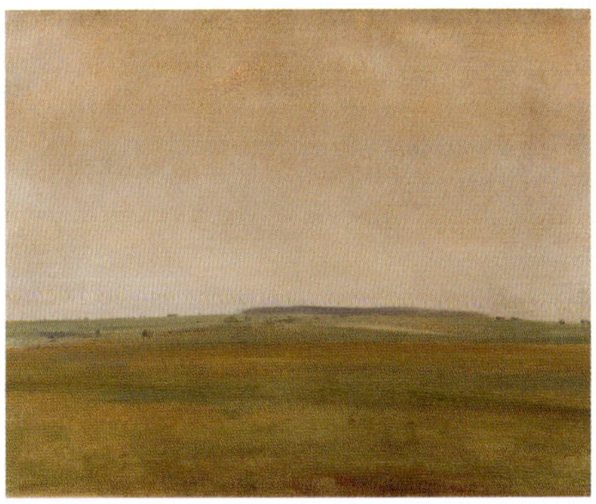

Munnings, Alfred James 1878–1959
An Open Landscape
oil on canvas 45.7 x 55.9
380

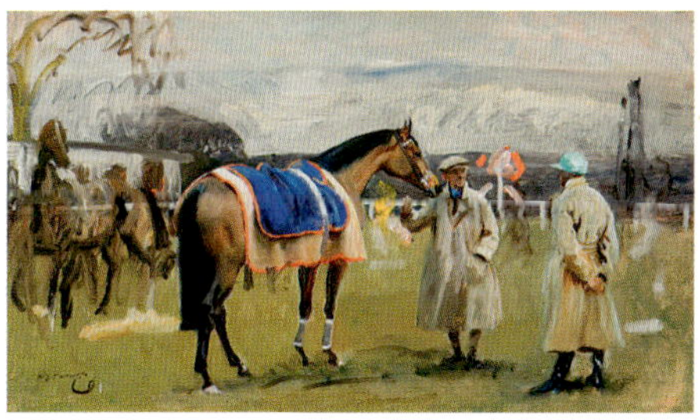

Munnings, Alfred James 1878–1959
'Anarchist'
oil on board 35.6 x 63.5
188

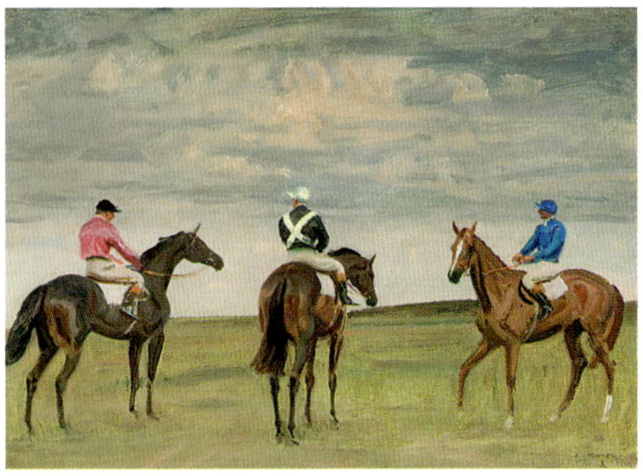

Munnings, Alfred James 1878–1959
At the Half Mile, Newmarket, Three Runners
oil on board 45.7 x 61
273

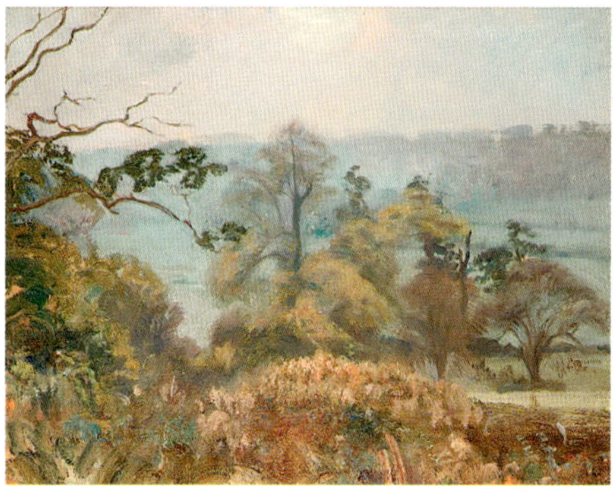

Munnings, Alfred James 1878–1959
Autumn, near Stoke by Nayland
oil on canvas 46.4 x 55.9
355

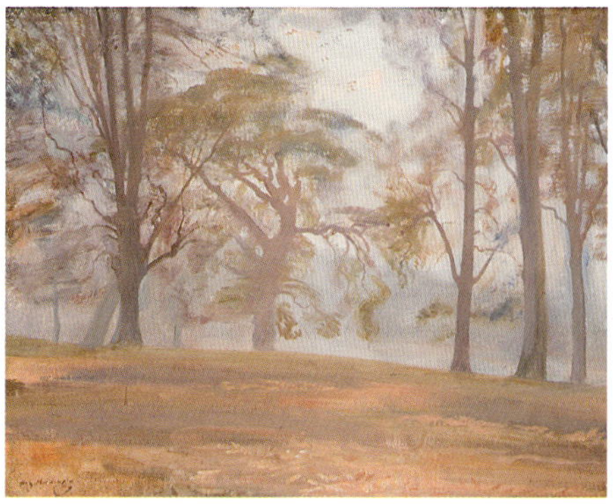

Munnings, Alfred James 1878–1959
Autumn, Richmond Park
oil on canvas 71.1 x 85.1
119

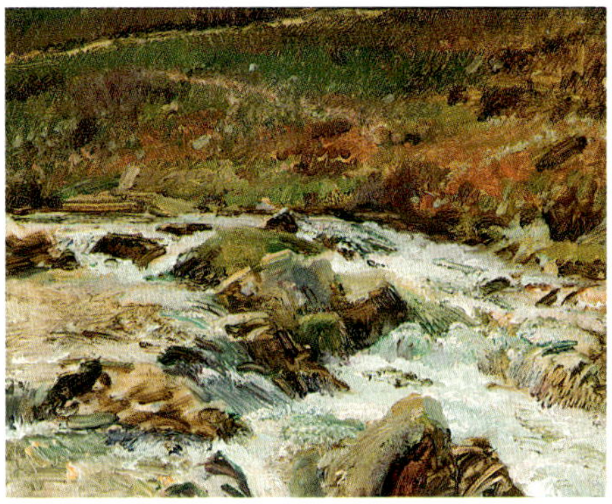

Munnings, Alfred James 1878–1959
Bagsworthy Water, Exmoor
oil on board 50.2 x 61
121

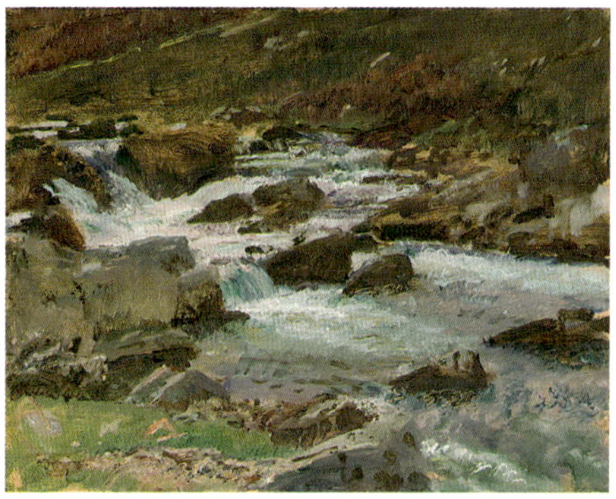

Munnings, Alfred James 1878–1959
Bagsworthy Water, Exmoor, at Cloud
oil on panel 33 x 40.6
56

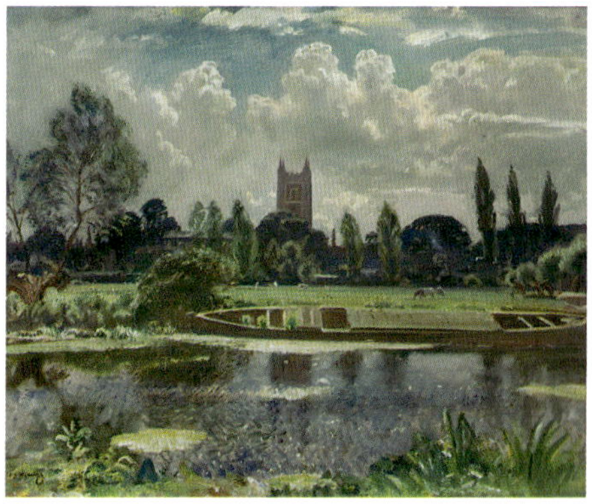

Munnings, Alfred James 1878–1959
Barge on the Stour at Dedham
oil on canvas 48.3 x 58.4
L2:1987 (P)

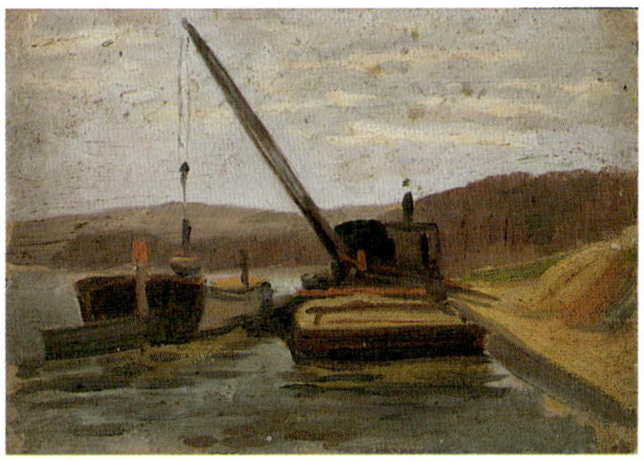

Munnings, Alfred James 1878–1959
Barges on a River
oil on pressed paper board 20.3 x 28.6
256

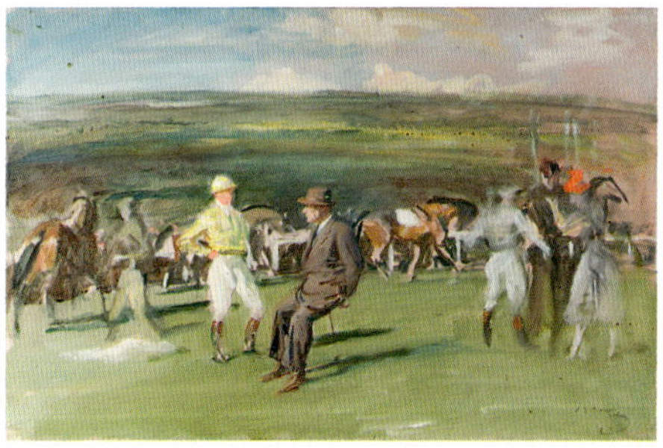

Munnings, Alfred James 1878–1959
Before the Race
oil on canvas 50.8 x 76.2
82

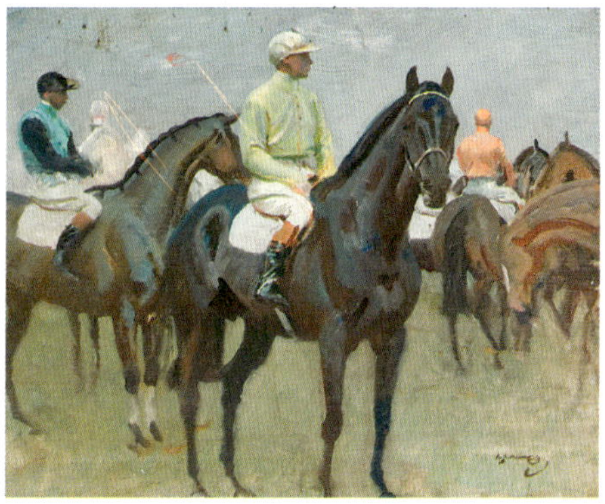

Munnings, Alfred James 1878–1959
Before the Race
oil on panel 50.8 x 60.3
269

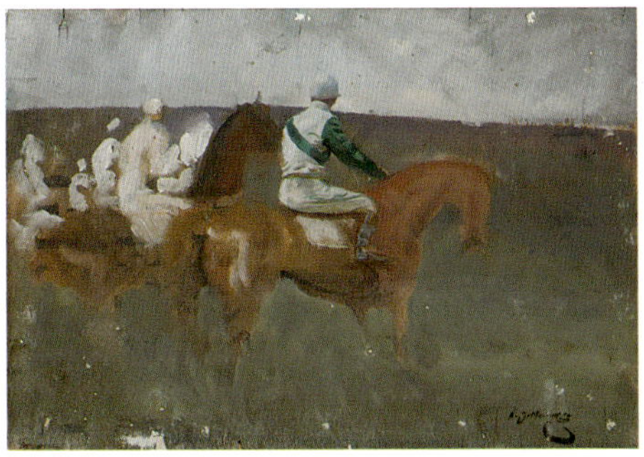

Munnings, Alfred James 1878–1959
Before the Race
oil on board 30.5 x 41.9
304

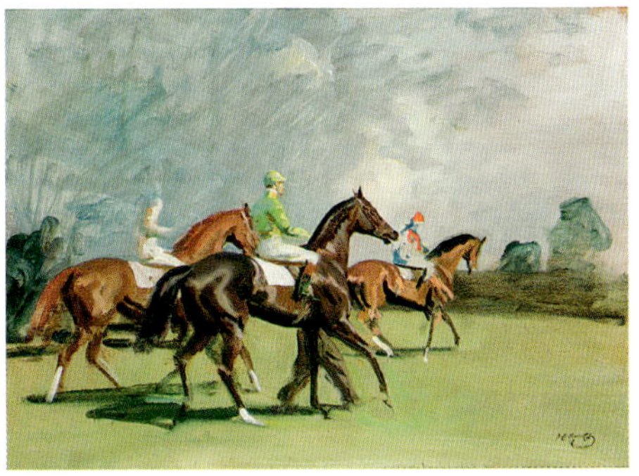

Munnings, Alfred James 1878–1959
Before the Race
oil on panel 55.9 x 75.6
342

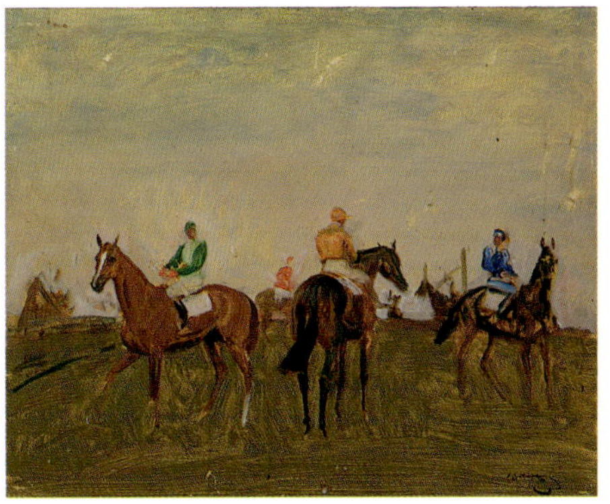

Munnings, Alfred James 1878–1959
Before the Start
oil on board 50.8 x 61
452

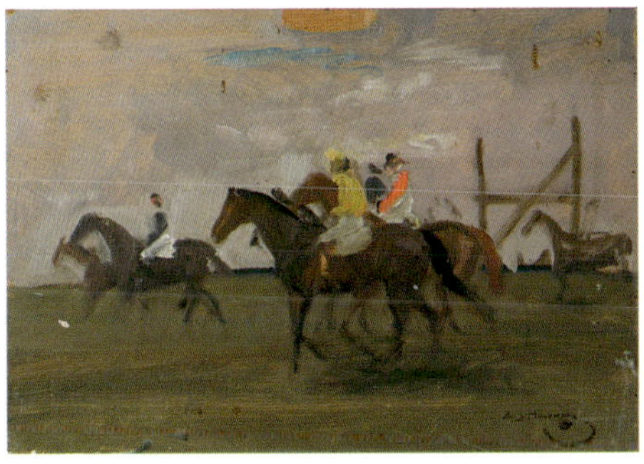

Munnings, Alfred James 1878–1959
Before the Start
oil on panel 25.4 x 35.6
531

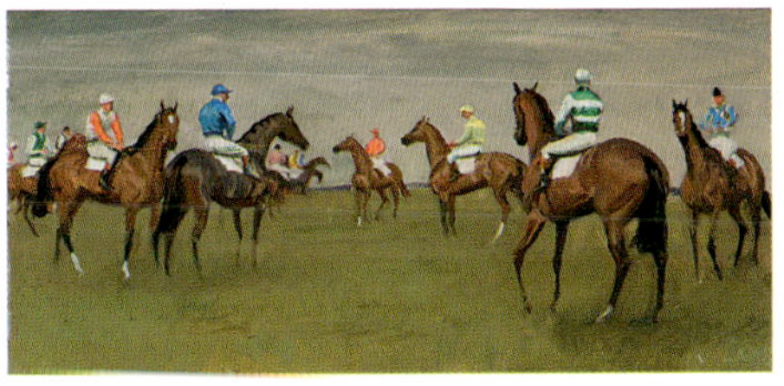

Munnings, Alfred James 1878–1959
Before the Start, Newmarket
oil on board 30.5 x 61
134

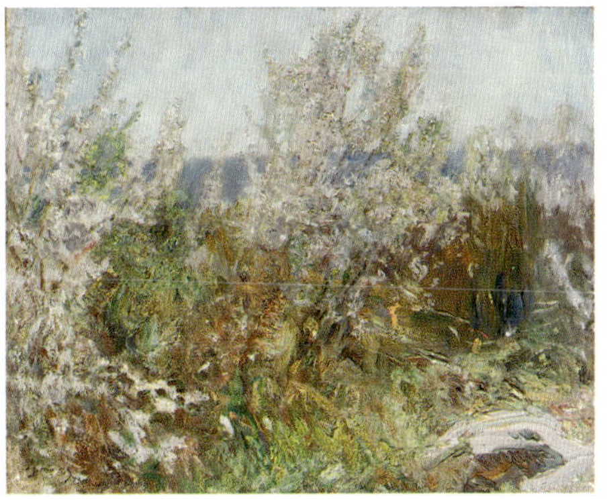

Munnings, Alfred James 1878–1959
Blossom
oil on canvas 50.8 x 61
521

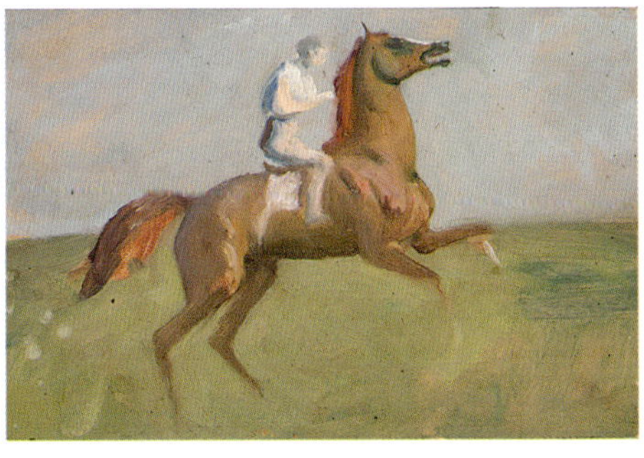

Munnings, Alfred James 1878–1959
Boy and Racehorse Study
oil on panel 17.8 x 24.8
595

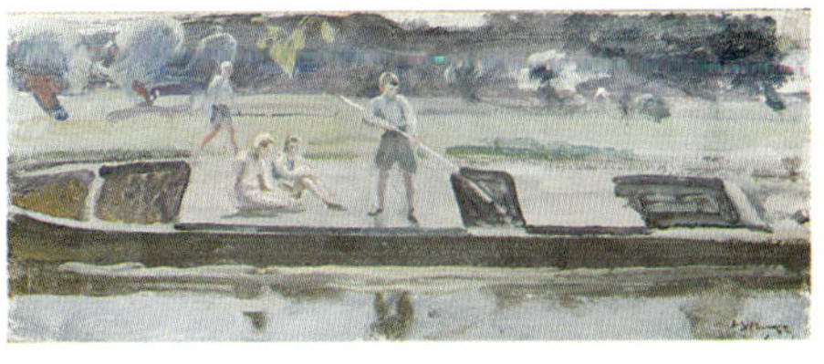

Munnings, Alfred James 1878–1959
Boys on a Barge
oil on panel 22.2 x 52.7
259

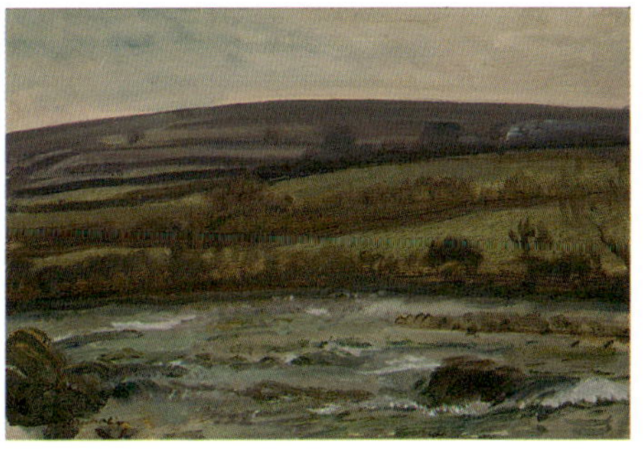

Munnings, Alfred James 1878–1959
Brightworthy Ford, Exmoor (recto)
oil on board 17.1 x 24.8
600

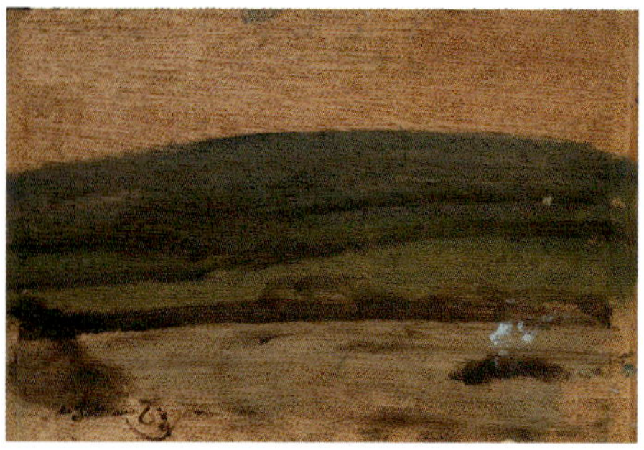

Munnings, Alfred James 1878–1959
Brightworthy Ford, Withypool, Exmoor (verso)
oil on board 17.1 x 24.8
600A

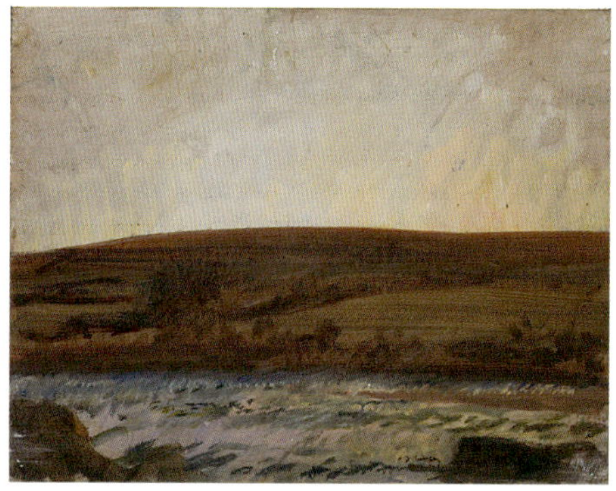

Munnings, Alfred James 1878–1959
Brightworthy Ford, Withypool, Exmoor (recto)
oil on panel 40.6 x 50.8
415

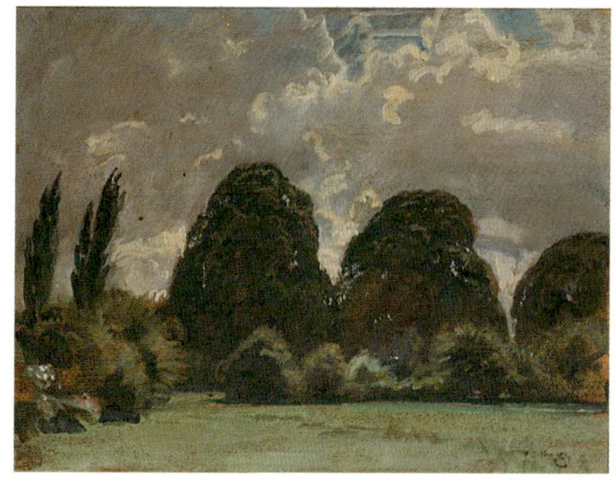

Munnings, Alfred James 1878–1959
Elm Trees (verso)
oil on panel 40.6 x 50.8
415A

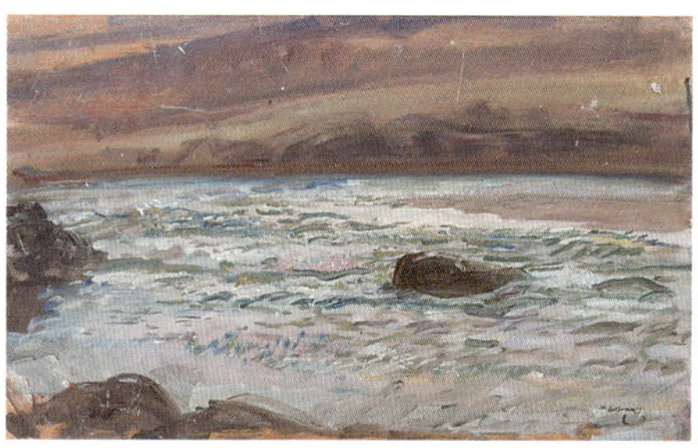

Munnings, Alfred James 1878–1959
Brightworthy Ford, Withypool, Exmoor (recto)
oil on board 38.1 x 61
388

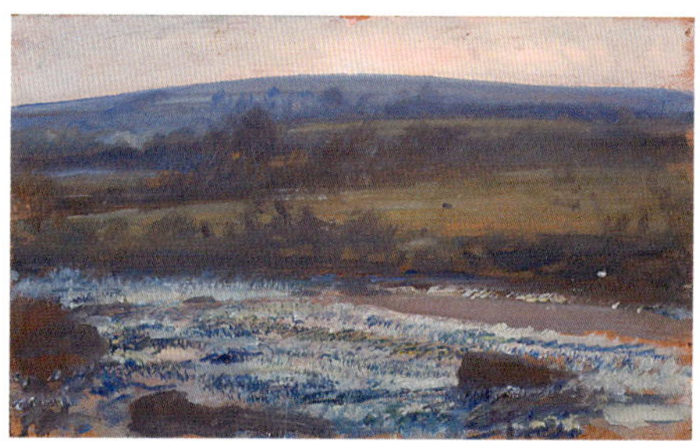

Munnings, Alfred James 1878–1959
Brightworthy Ford, Withypool, Exmoor (verso)
oil on board 38.1 x 61
388A

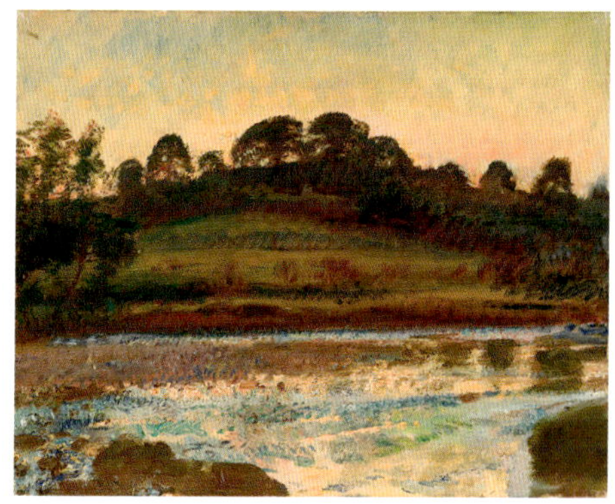

Munnings, Alfred James 1878–1959
Brightworthy Ford, Withypool, Exmoor
oil on canvas 50.8 x 61
33

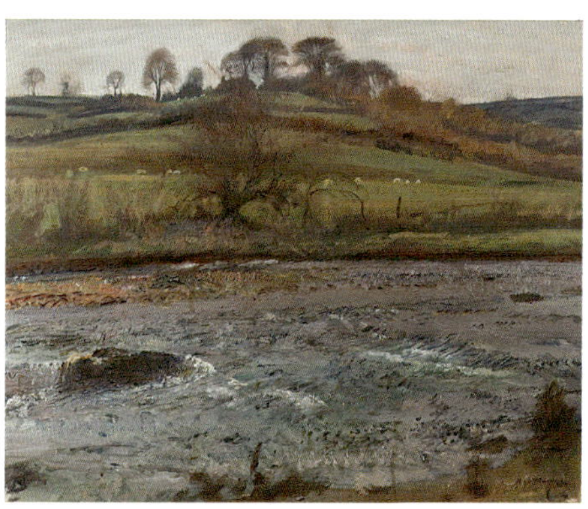

Munnings, Alfred James 1878–1959
Brightworthy Ford, Withypool, Exmoor
oil on canvas 50.8 x 61
146

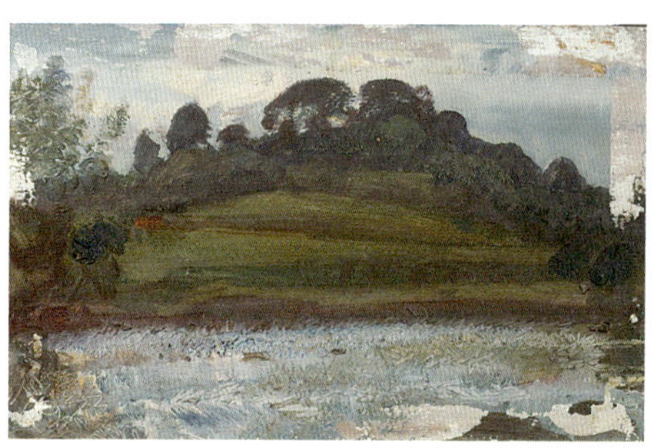

Munnings, Alfred James 1878–1959
Brightworthy Ford, Withypool, Exmoor
oil on board 27.9 x 41.9
244

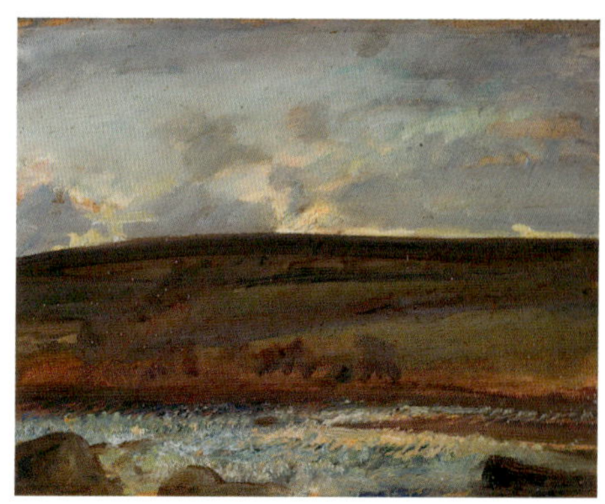

Munnings, Alfred James 1878–1959
Brightworthy Ford, Withypool, Exmoor (recto)
oil on board 33 x 40.6
299

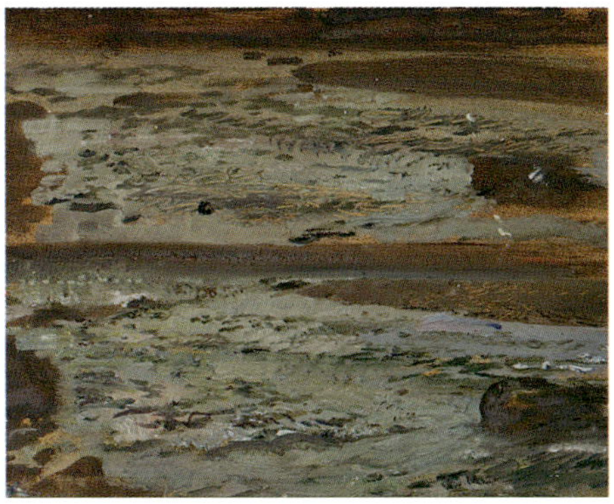

Munnings, Alfred James 1878–1959
Study (verso)
oil on board 33 x 40.6
299A

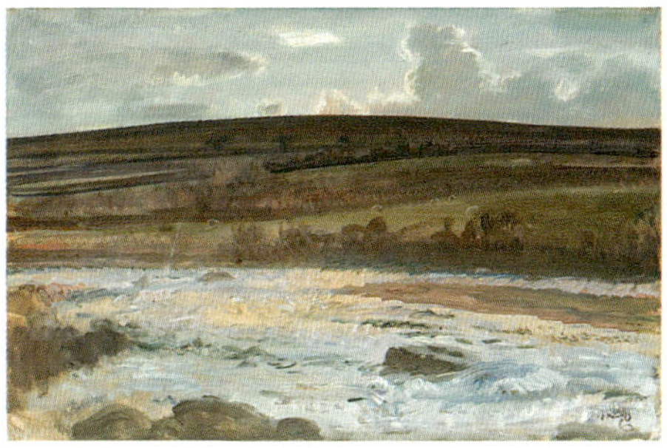

Munnings, Alfred James 1878–1959
Brightworthy Ford, Withypool, Exmoor
oil on canvas 50.8 x 76.2
322

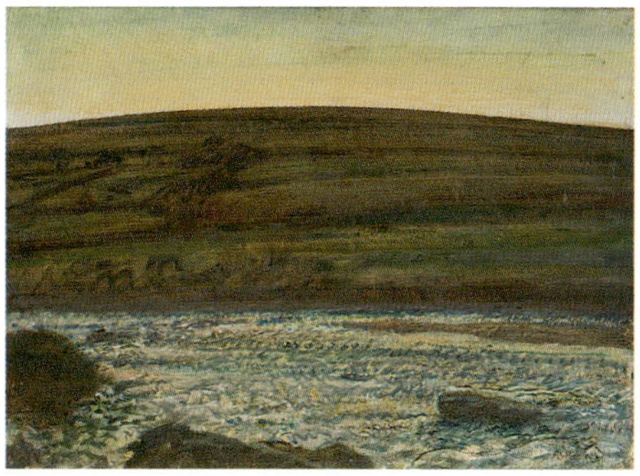

Munnings, Alfred James 1878–1959
Brightworthy Ford, Withypool, Exmoor
oil on canvas 52.1 x 70.5
323

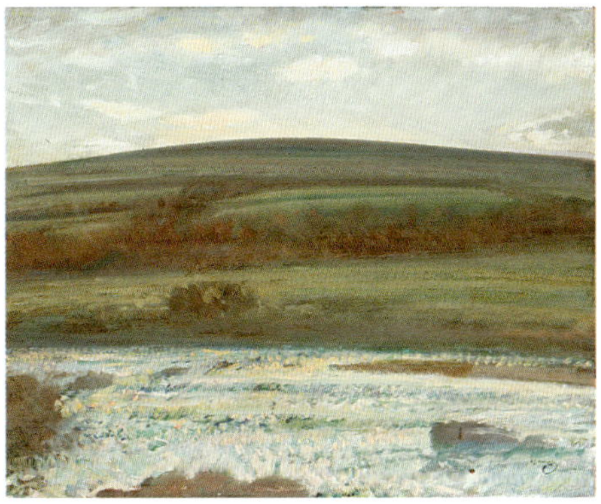

Munnings, Alfred James 1878–1959
Brightworthy Ford, Withypool, Exmoor
oil on canvas 63.5 x 76.2
333

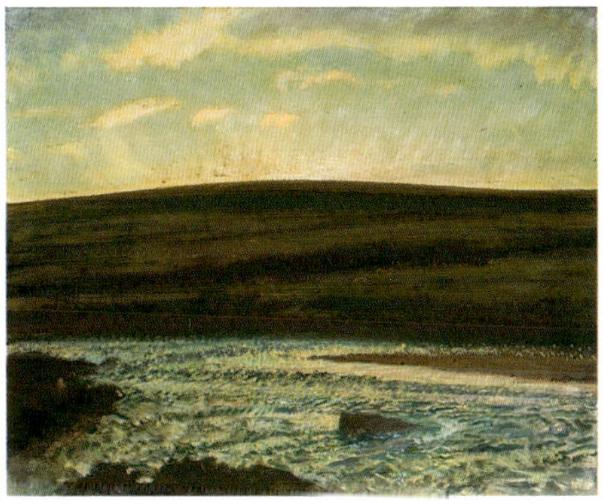

Munnings, Alfred James 1878–1959
Brightworthy Ford, Withypool, Exmoor
oil on canvas 63.5 x 76.2
334

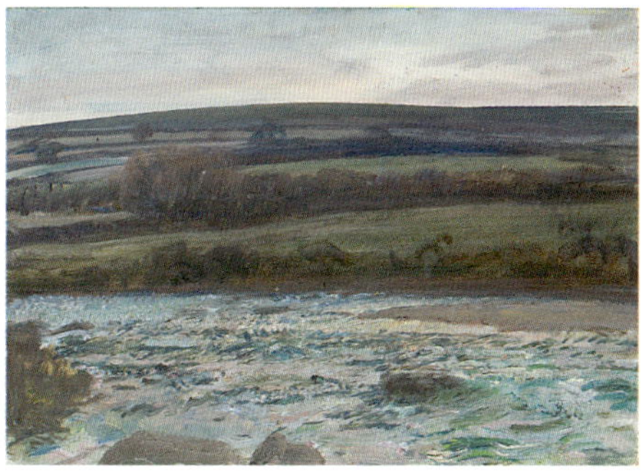

Munnings, Alfred James 1878–1959
Brightworthy Ford, Withypool, Exmoor
oil on board 43.8 x 61
347

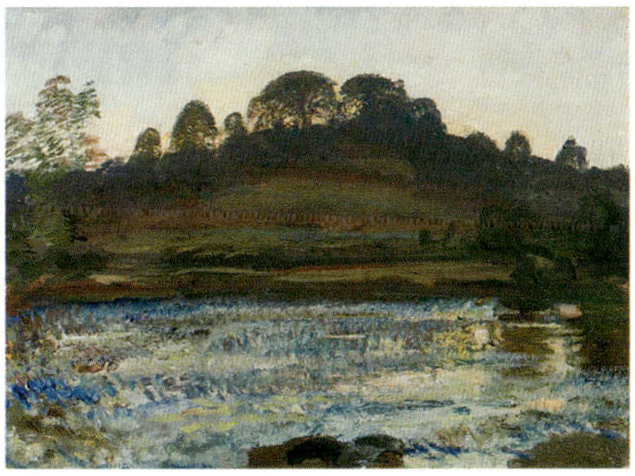

Munnings, Alfred James 1878–1959
Brightworthy Ford, Withypool, Exmoor
oil on canvas 45.7 x 61
373

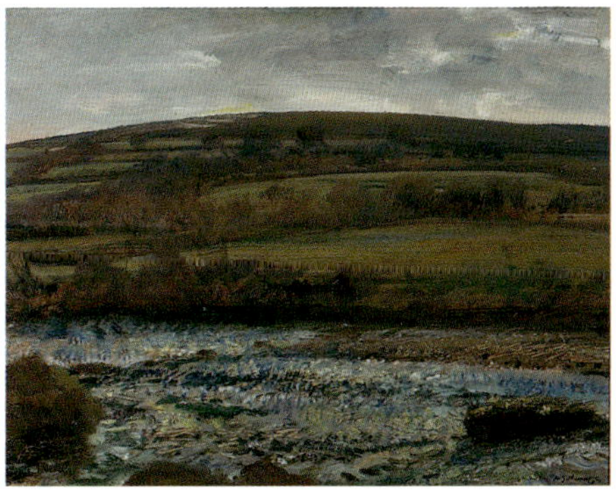

Munnings, Alfred James 1878–1959
Brightworthy Ford, Withypool, Exmoor
oil on panel 40.6 x 50.8
378

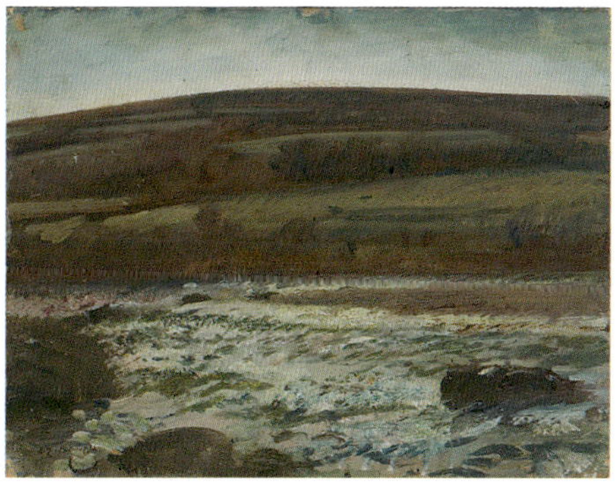

Munnings, Alfred James 1878–1959
Brightworthy Ford, Withypool, Exmoor
oil on canvas laid on board 35.6 x 45.7
478

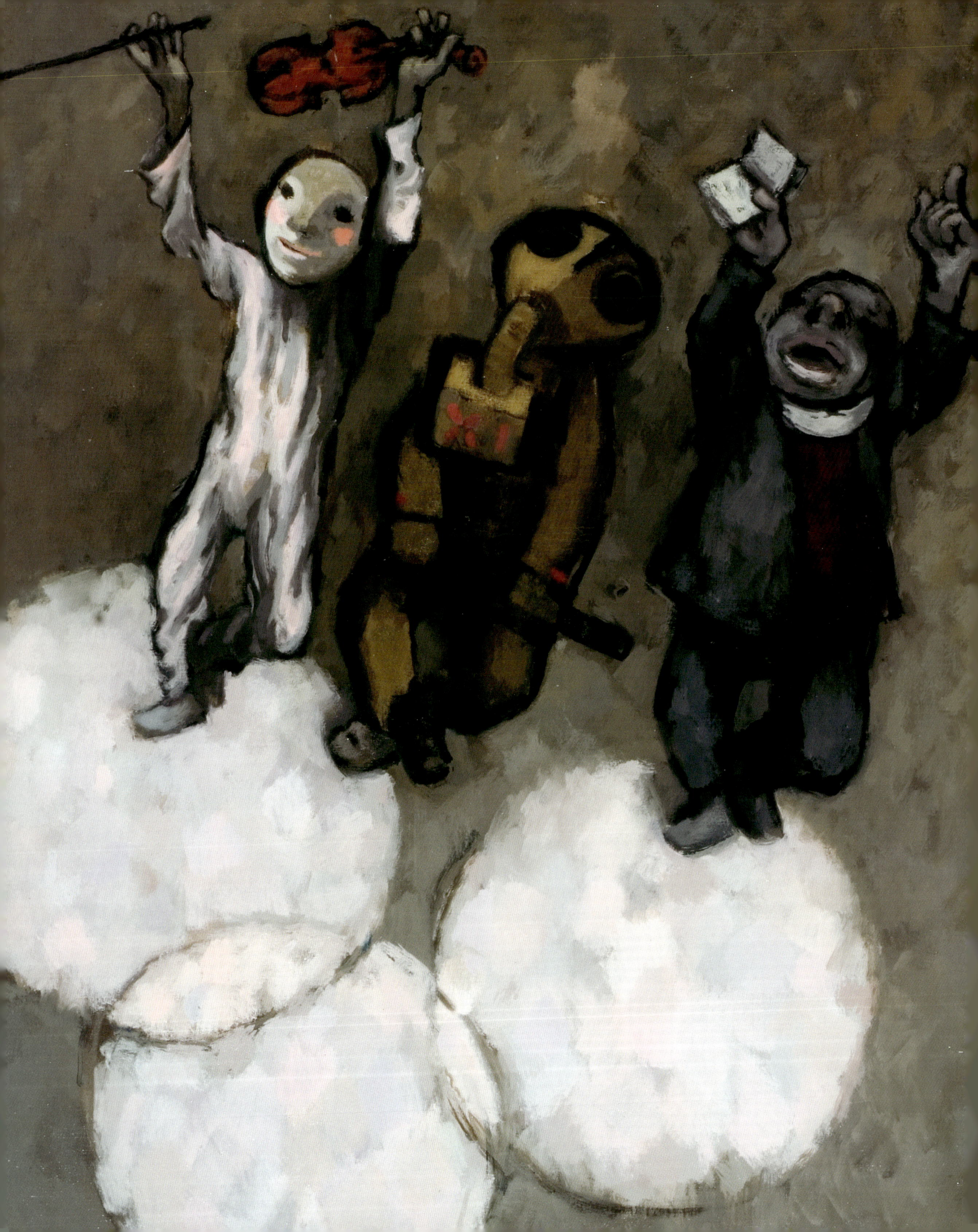

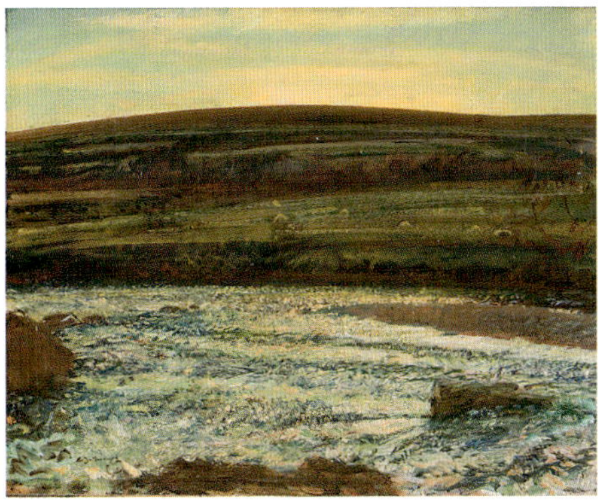

Munnings, Alfred James 1878–1959
Brightworthy Ford, Withypool, Exmoor
oil on board 50.8 x 61
488

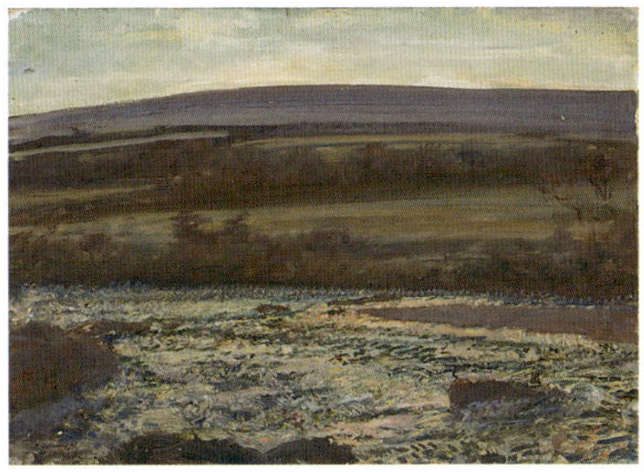

Munnings, Alfred James 1878–1959
Brightworthy Ford, Withypool, Exmoor
oil on board 44.5 x 60.3
496

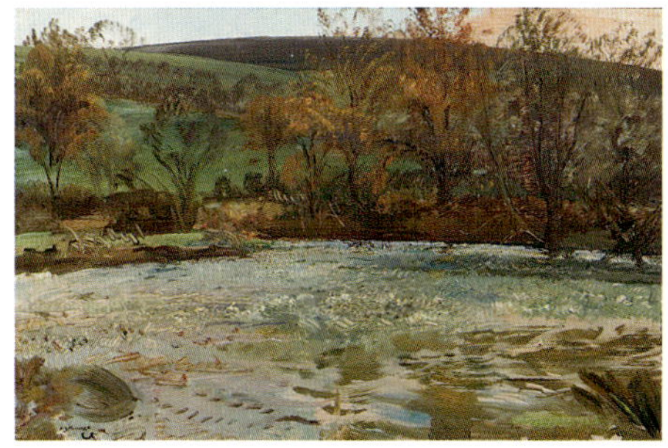

Munnings, Alfred James 1878–1959
Brightworthy Ford, Withypool, Exmoor
oil on panel 50.2 x 75.6
504

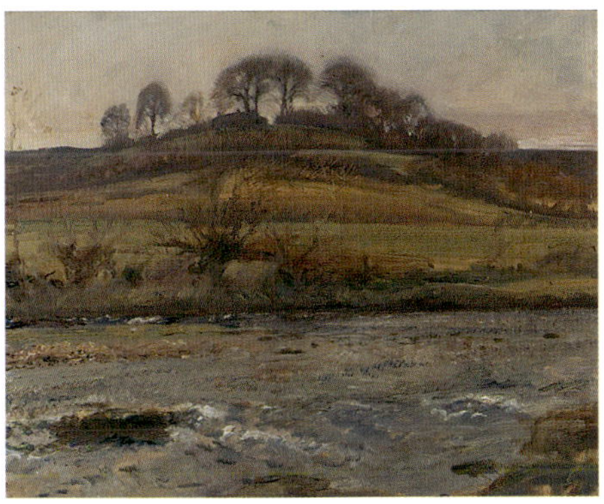

Munnings, Alfred James 1878–1959
Brightworthy Ford, Withypool, Exmoor
oil on board 50.8 x 61
358

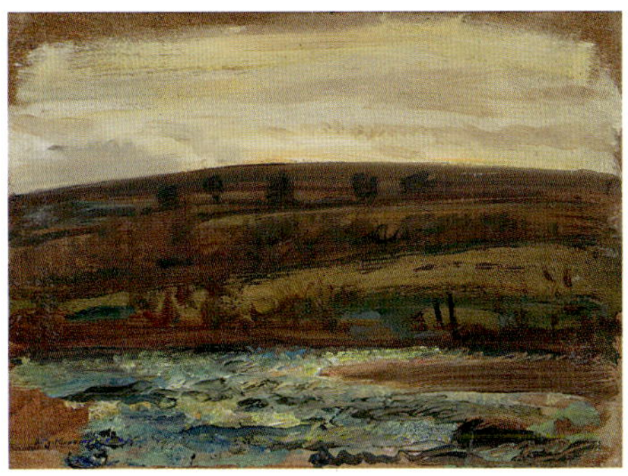

Munnings, Alfred James 1878–1959
Brightworthy Ford, Withypool, Exmoor
oil on panel 24.8 x 33
560

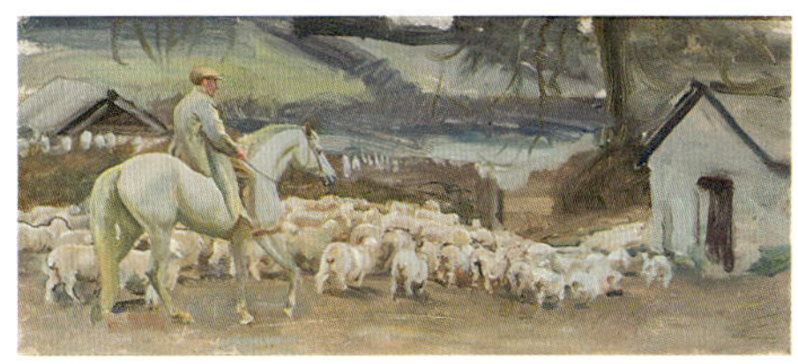

Munnings, Alfred James 1878–1959
Bringing Home the Sheep, Withypool, Exmoor
oil on board 27 x 60.5
268

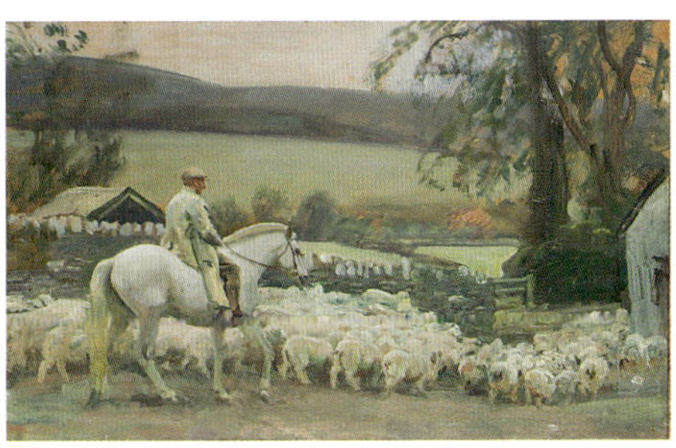

Munnings, Alfred James 1878–1959
Bringing Home the Sheep, Withypool, Exmoor
oil on board 50 x 76
340

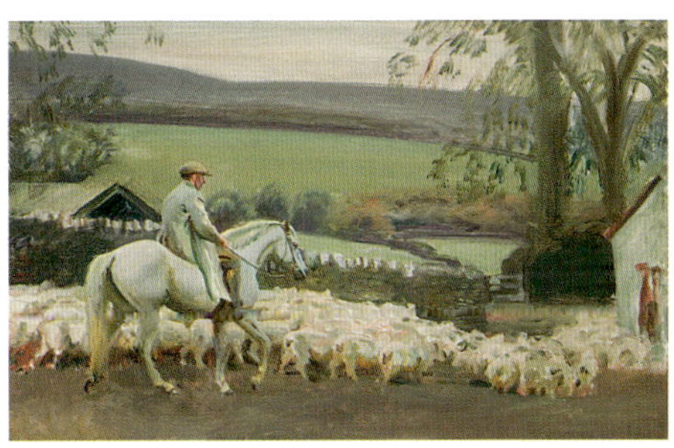

Munnings, Alfred James 1878–1959
Bringing Home the Sheep, Withypool, Exmoor
oil on canvas 50.8 x 76.2
241

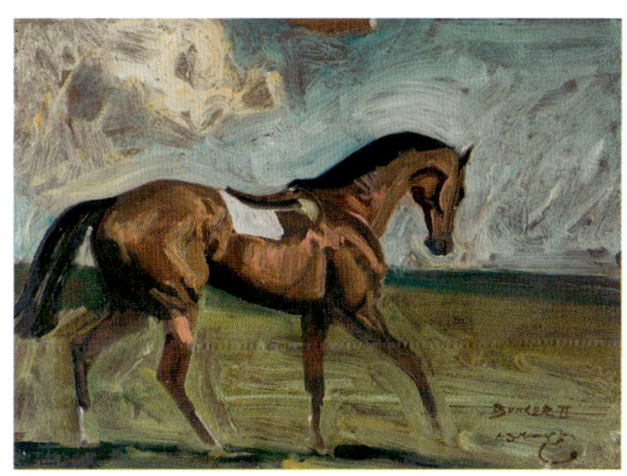

Munnings, Alfred James 1878–1959
'Bunker II', a Bay Racehorse
oil on panel 30.5 x 40.6
570

Facing page: Barrett, Roderic, 1920–2000, *The Arts, Army and Church, Dance* (detail), 1989, Epping Forest District Museum, (p. 293)

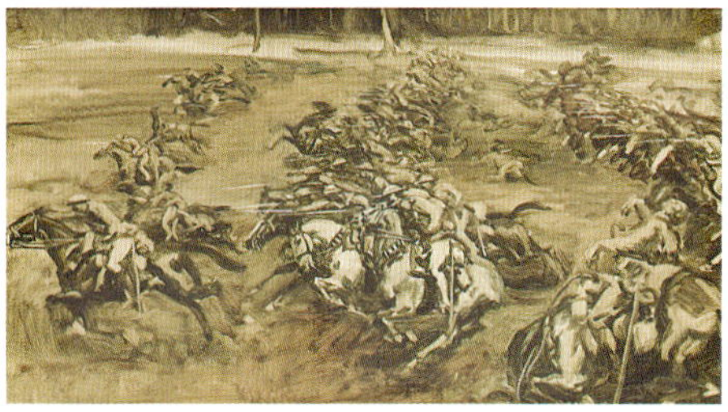

Munnings, Alfred James 1878–1959
Cavalry Charge Led by Lieutenant G. M. Flowerdew, VC
oil on canvas 54.6 x 91.4
426

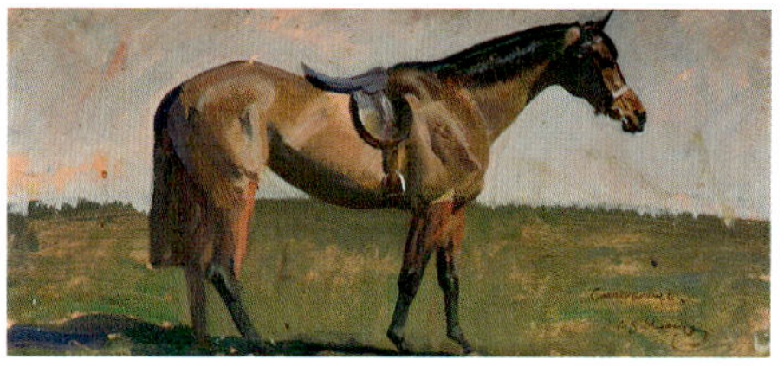

Munnings, Alfred James 1878–1959
'Cherrybounce'
oil on board 19.7 x 40.6
311

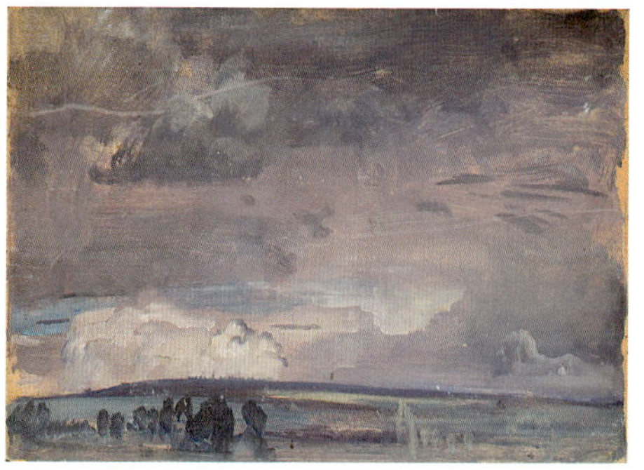

Munnings, Alfred James 1878–1959
Cloud Studies (recto)
oil on panel 30.5 x 40.6
586

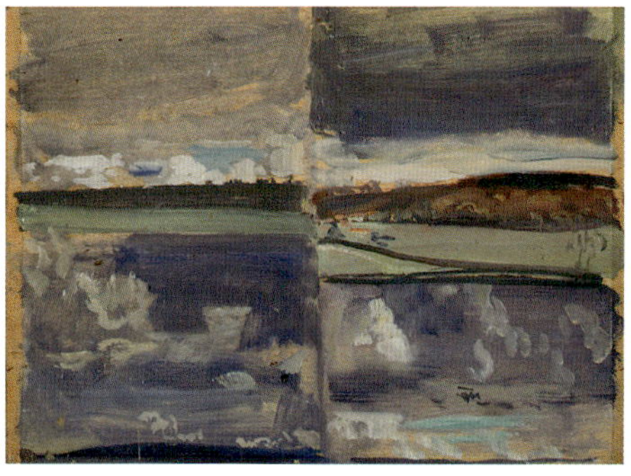

Munnings, Alfred James 1878–1959
Cloud Studies (verso)
oil on panel 30.5 x 40.6
586A

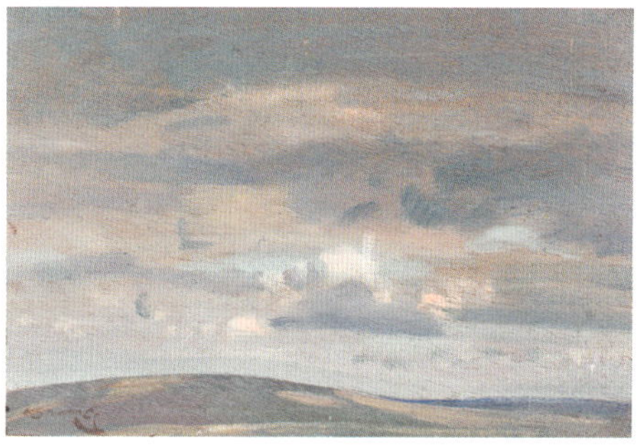

Munnings, Alfred James 1878–1959
Cloud Study (recto)
oil on board 17.1 x 24.8 (E)
613

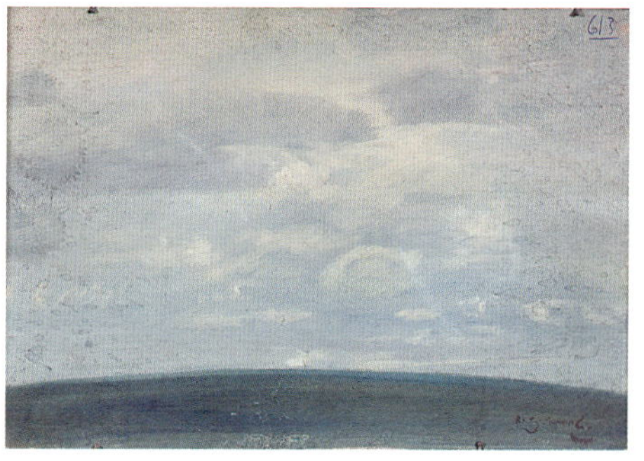

Munnings, Alfred James 1878–1959
Cloud Study (verso)
oil on board 17.1 x 24.8 (E)
613A

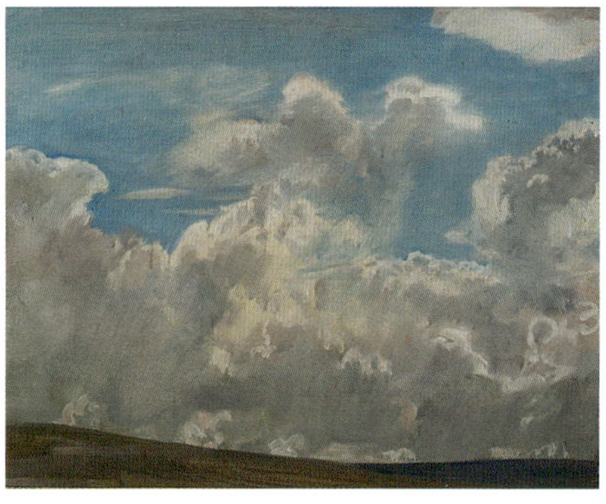

Munnings, Alfred James 1878–1959
Cloud Study, Exmoor
oil on board 40.6 x 50.8
419

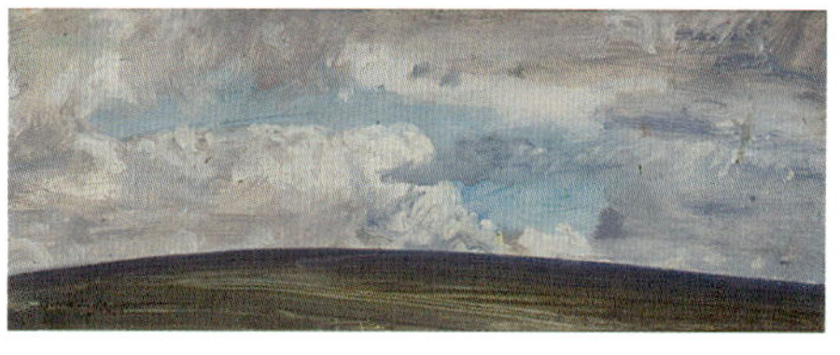

Munnings, Alfred James 1878–1959
Cloud Study on Exmoor
oil on board 19.7 x 50.2
255

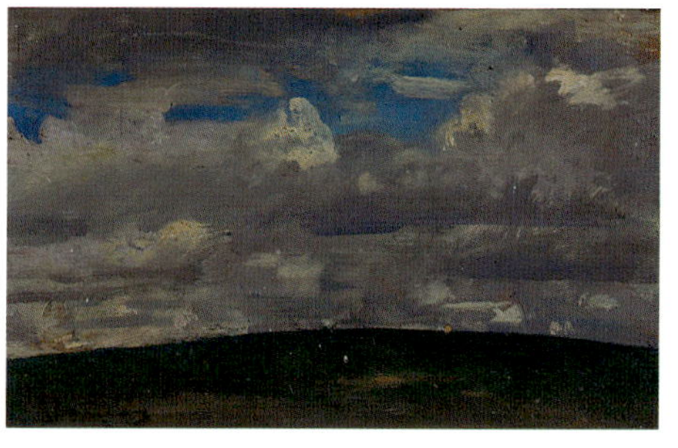

Munnings, Alfred James 1878–1959
Clouds on Exmoor
oil on board 27 x 41.5
303

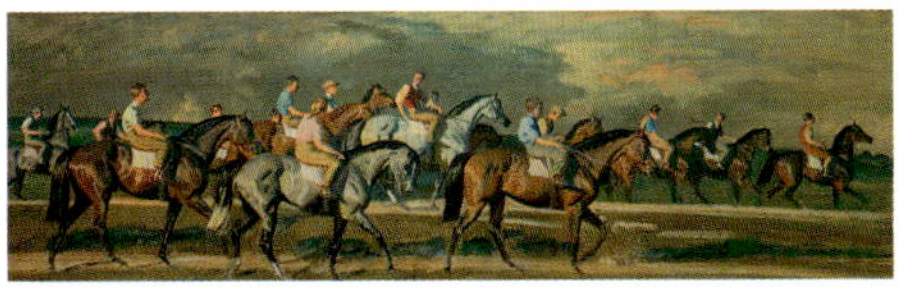

Munnings, Alfred James 1878–1959
Coming off the Heath, Exercising the Horses, Newmarket
oil on board 58.4 x 182.9
168

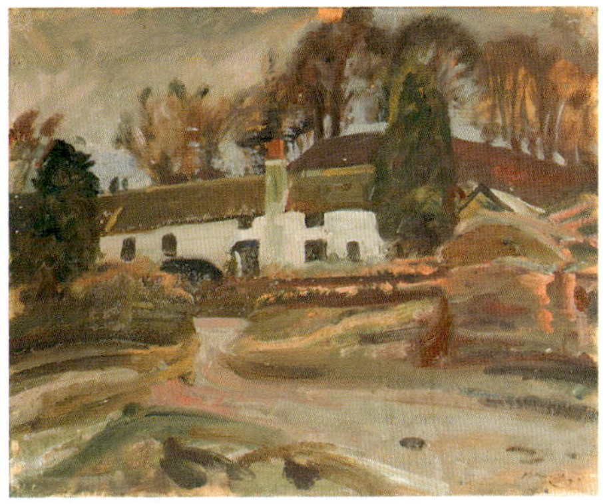

Munnings, Alfred James 1878–1959
Cottages by a River
oil on canvas 50.8 x 61
412

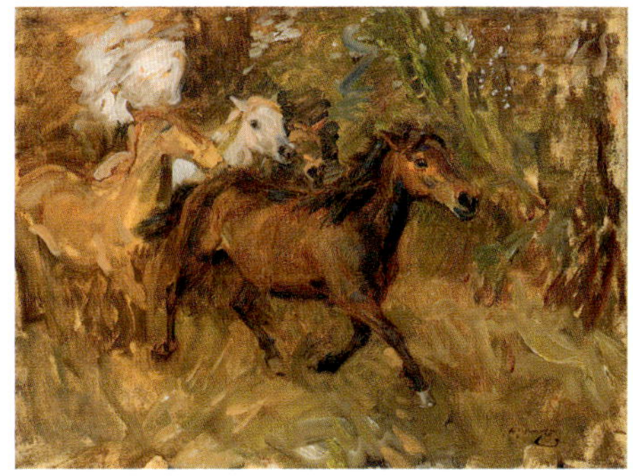

Munnings, Alfred James 1878–1959
Crossing the Ford
oil on canvas 43.2 x 56.5
75

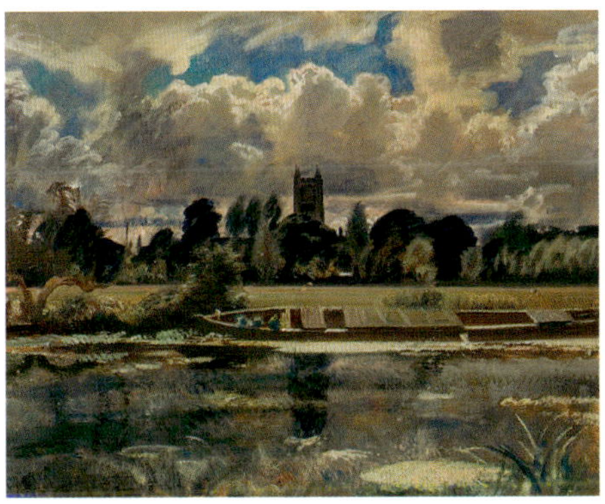

Munnings, Alfred James 1878–1959
Dedham Painted from Lock Cottage
oil on canvas 51 x 61
139

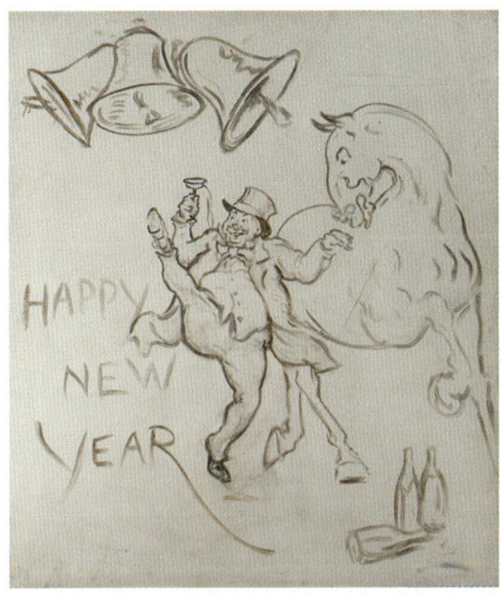

Munnings, Alfred James 1878–1959
Design for Happy New Year Greeting
oil on canvas 152.4 x 127
427

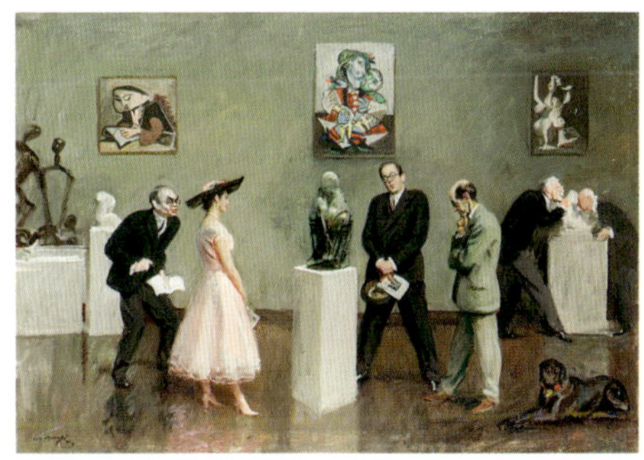

Munnings, Alfred James 1878–1959
Does the Subject Matter?
oil on canvas 76.2 x 108.6
53

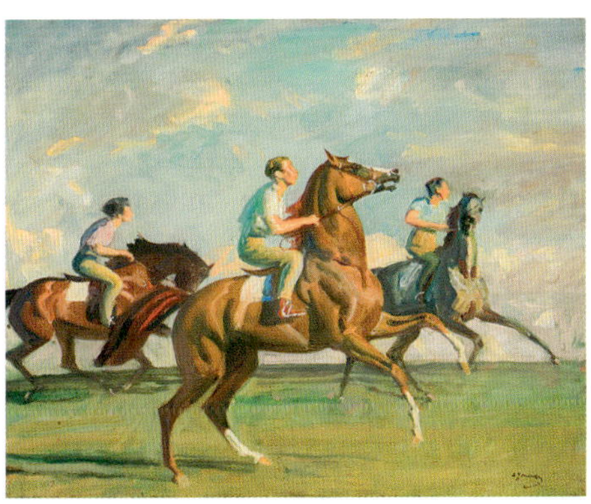

Munnings, Alfred James 1878–1959
Early Morning, Newmarket
oil on board 59.4 x 69.9
170

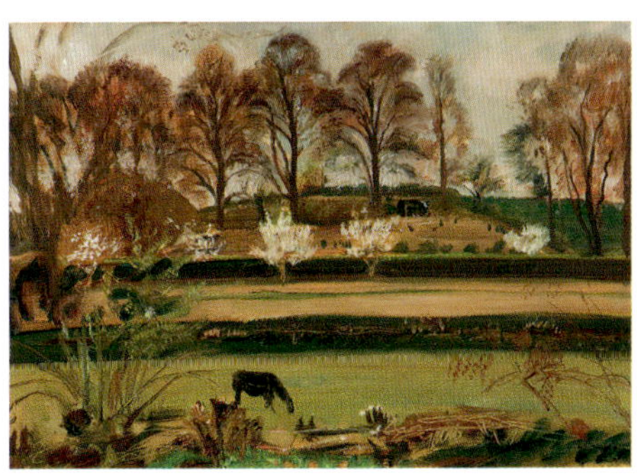

Munnings, Alfred James 1878–1959
Early Spring Landscape, Dedham
oil on panel 50.8 x 71.1
275

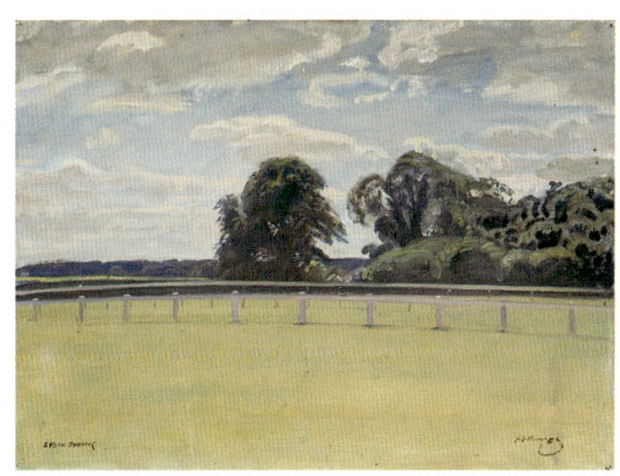

Munnings, Alfred James 1878–1959
Epsom Paddock
oil on board 45.7 x 61
518

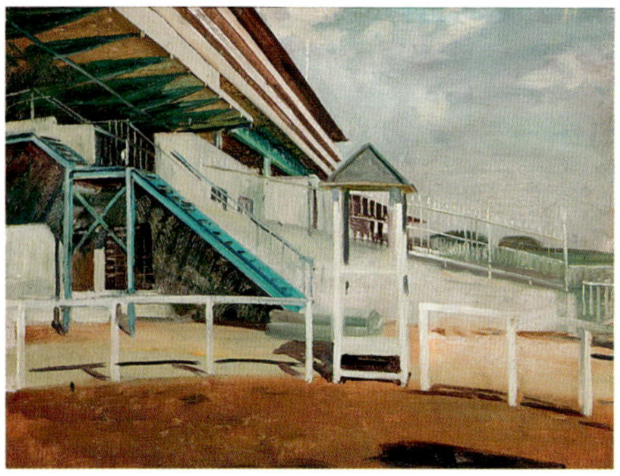

Munnings, Alfred James 1878–1959
Epsom Paddock and Stands
oil on canvas 55.9 x 71.1
328

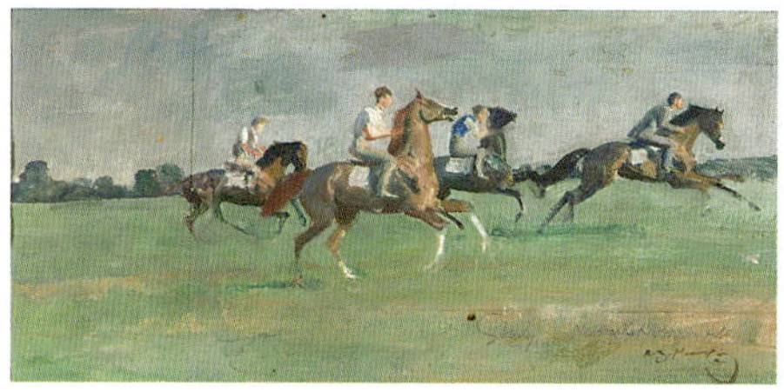

Munnings, Alfred James 1878–1959
Exercising Horses on Warren Hill, Newmarket
oil on board 26.7 x 48.3
400

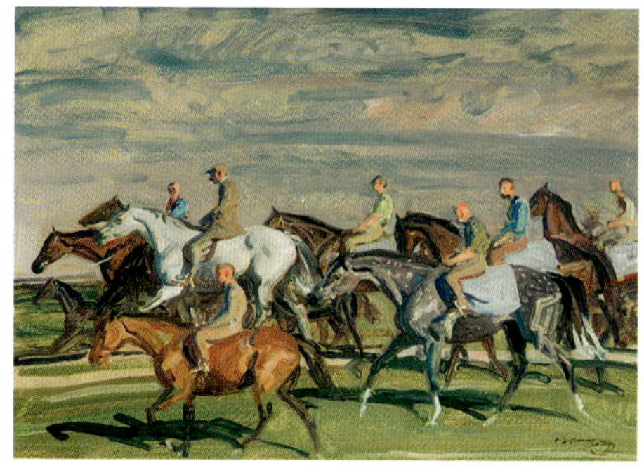

Munnings, Alfred James 1878–1959
Exercising the Horses
oil on panel 45.7 x 61
266

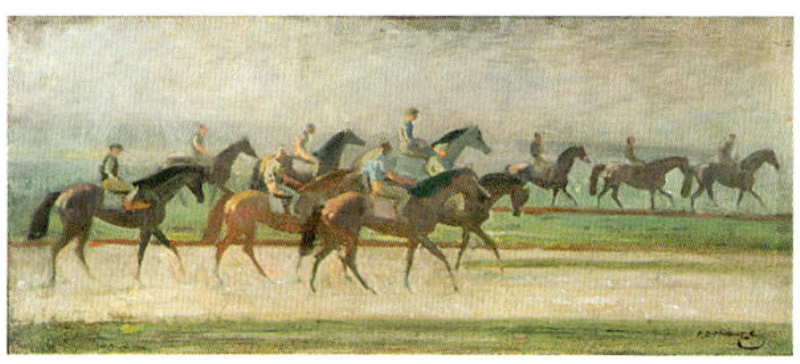

Munnings, Alfred James 1878–1959
Exercising the Horses
oil on panel 29.2 x 66
397

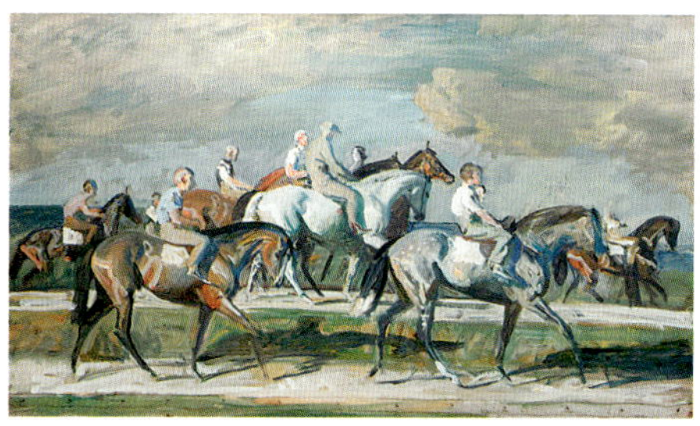

Munnings, Alfred James 1878–1959
Exercising the Horses
oil on canvas 76.2 x 127
425

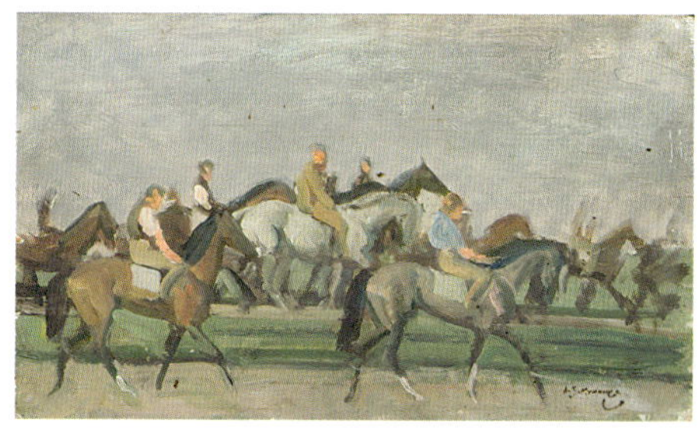

Munnings, Alfred James 1878–1959
Exercising the Horses
oil on board 22.2 x 35.6
618

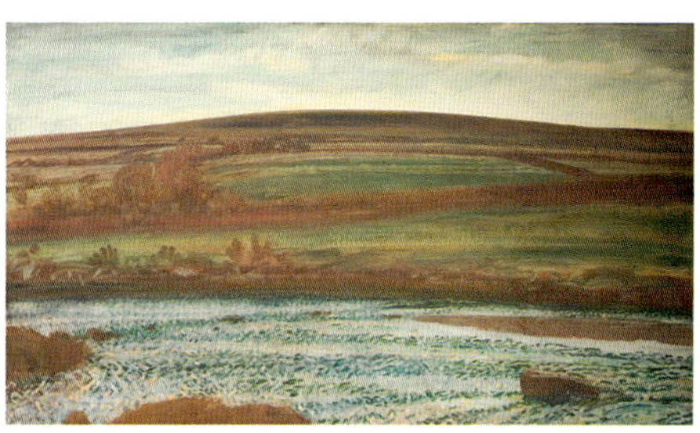

Munnings, Alfred James 1878–1959
Exmoor
oil on board 98.4 x 163.8
430

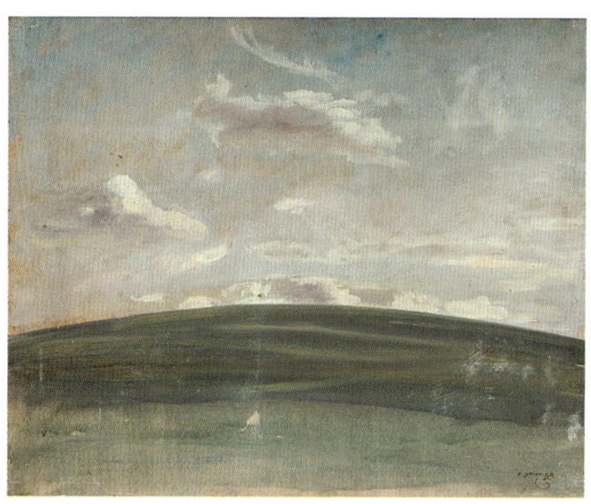

Munnings, Alfred James 1878–1959
Exmoor
oil on board 50.8 x 61
493

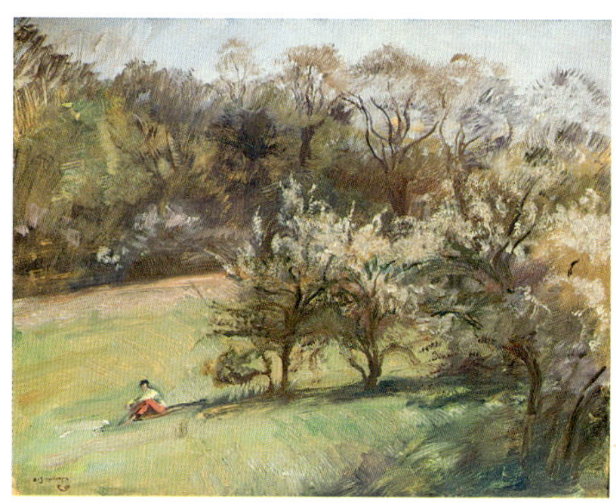

Munnings, Alfred James 1878–1959
Exmoor, Blackthorne
oil on board 50.8 x 61
50

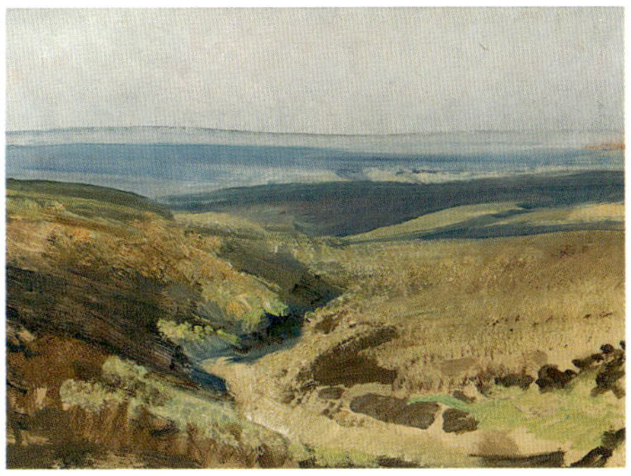

Munnings, Alfred James 1878–1959
Exmoor Landscape
oil on board 45.7 x 61
348

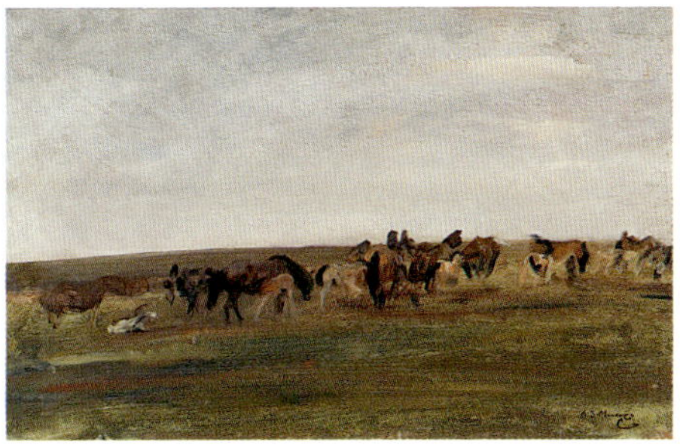

Munnings, Alfred James 1878–1959
Exmoor Ponies
oil on panel 40.6 x 60.3
305

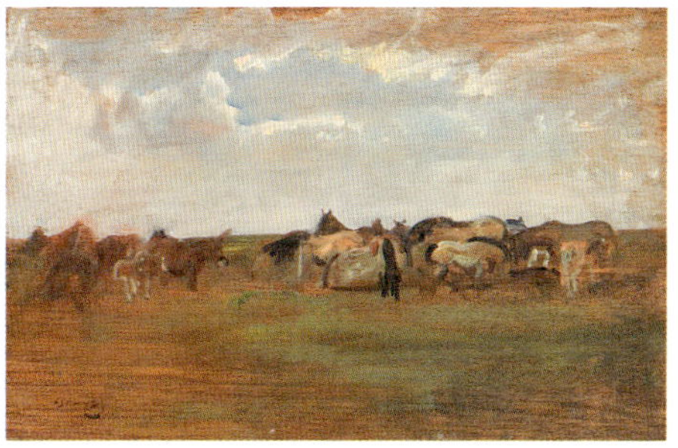

Munnings, Alfred James 1878–1959
Exmoor Ponies
oil on panel 40.6 x 61
387

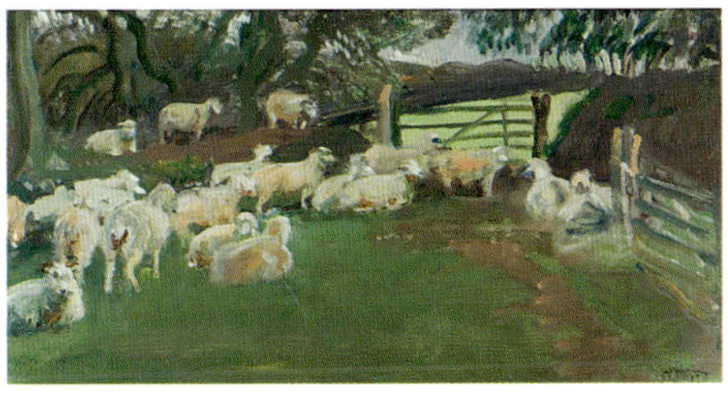

Munnings, Alfred James 1878–1959
Exmoor Sheep
oil on board 33 x 60.5
265

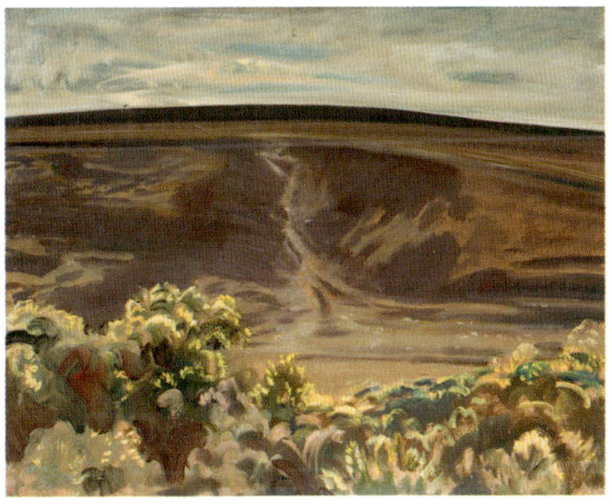

Munnings, Alfred James 1878–1959
Exmoor with Gorse
oil on panel 50.8 x 61
526

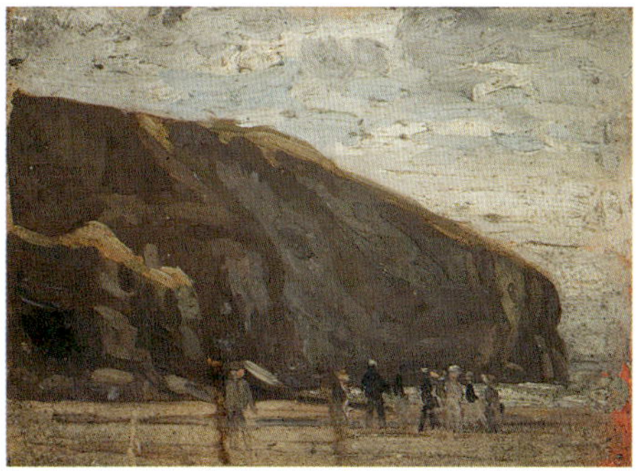

Munnings, Alfred James 1878–1959
Figures on a Beach below Cliffs (possibly Cornwall)
oil on board 17.1 x 22.9
669

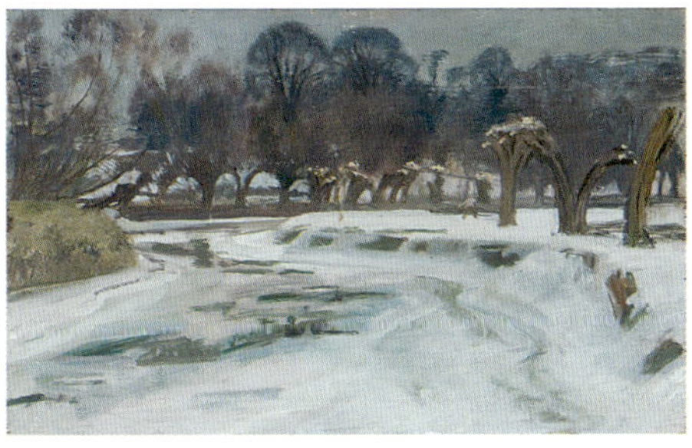

Munnings, Alfred James 1878–1959
First Study for 'Frozen River'
oil on board 45.7 x 61
418

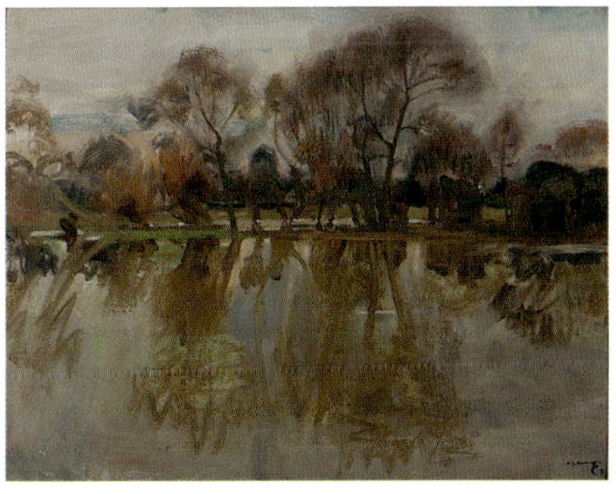

Munnings, Alfred James 1878–1959
Floods near Nayland
oil on canvas 57.2 x 72.4
125

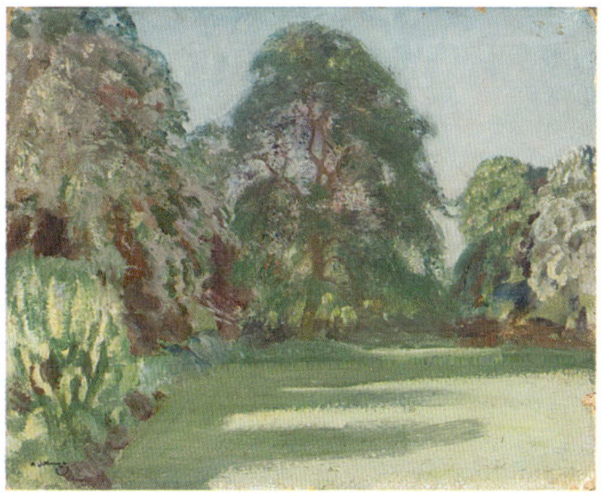

Munnings, Alfred James 1878–1959
Gardens, Dedham
oil on board 50.2 x 61
490

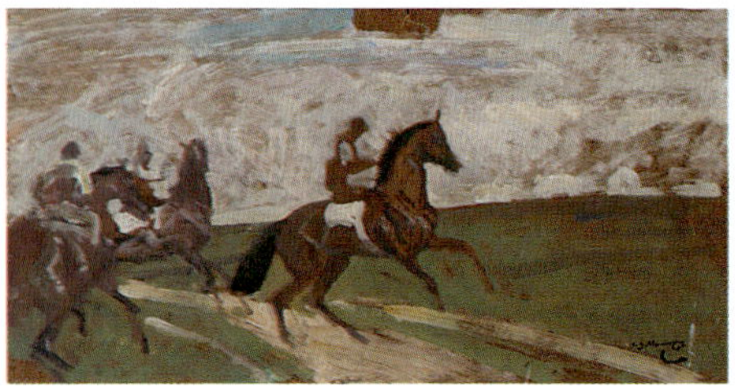

Munnings, Alfred James 1878–1959
Going to the Start
oil on board 24.8 x 45.7
310

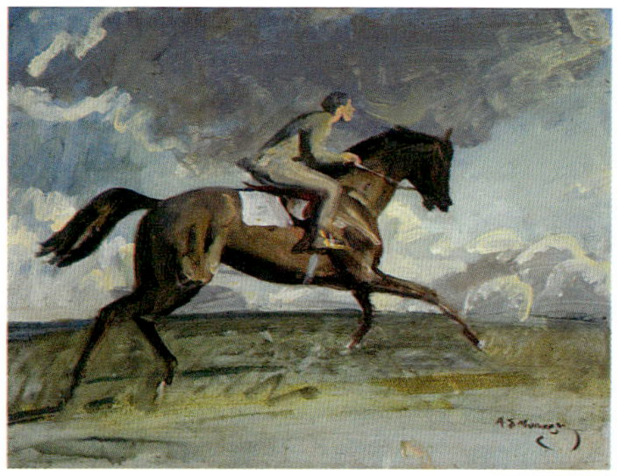

Munnings, Alfred James 1878–1959
Going up the Canter, a Boy Exercising a Racehorse
oil on panel 35.6 x 45.7
59

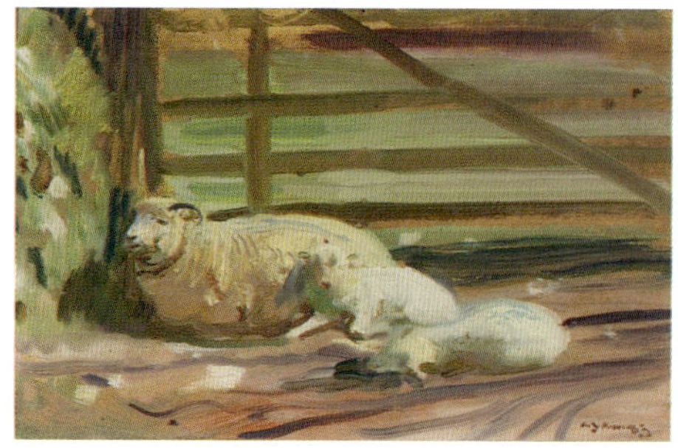

Munnings, Alfred James 1878–1959
Good Pasture beyond the Gate
oil on board 19 x 29.5
679

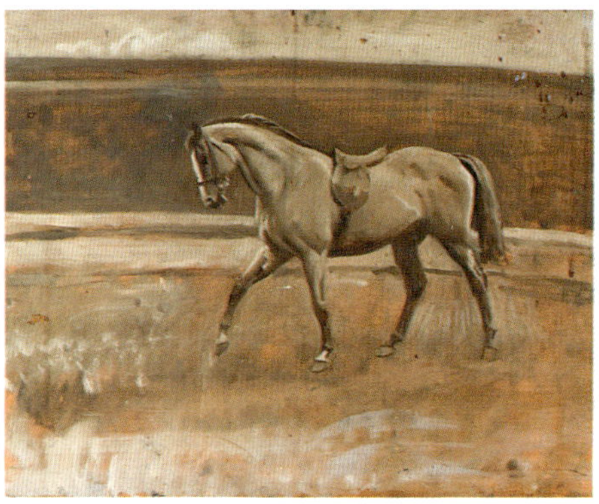

Munnings, Alfred James 1878–1959
Grisaille Study of a Hunter
oil on board 50.8 x 58.4
439

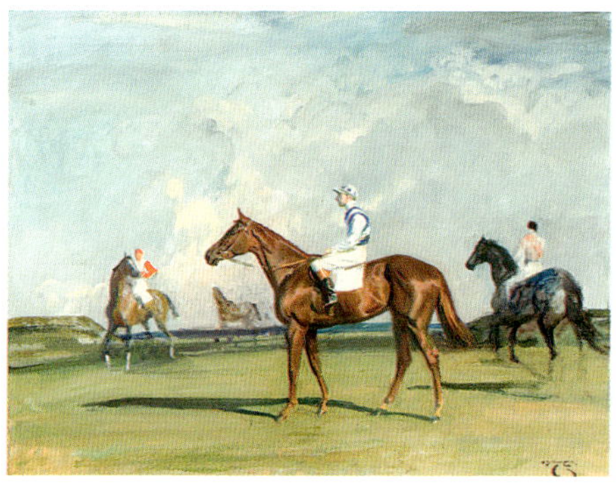

Munnings, Alfred James 1878–1959
'Happy Laughter', a Chestnut Racehorse, with Jockey up in a Landscape
oil on canvas 72.3 x 91.4
111

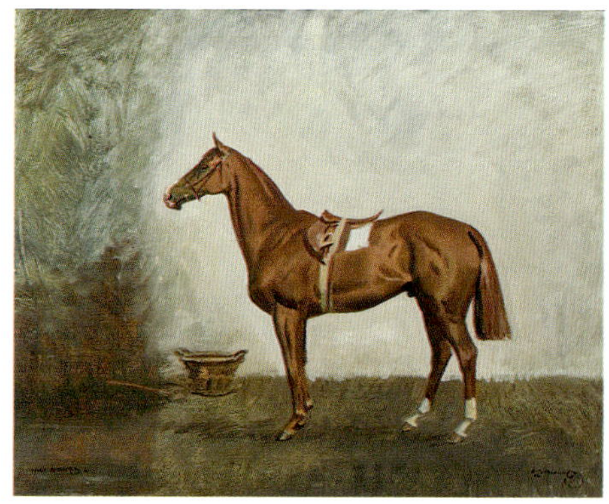

Munnings, Alfred James 1878–1959
'High Stakes', Lord Astor's Horse
oil on panel 50.8 x 61
141

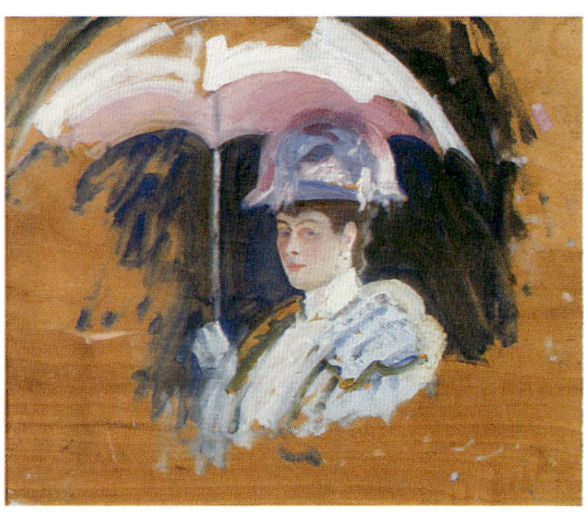

Munnings, Alfred James 1878–1959
HM Queen Mary, a Study for 'Driving to Ascot'
oil on panel 30.5 x 37.5
219

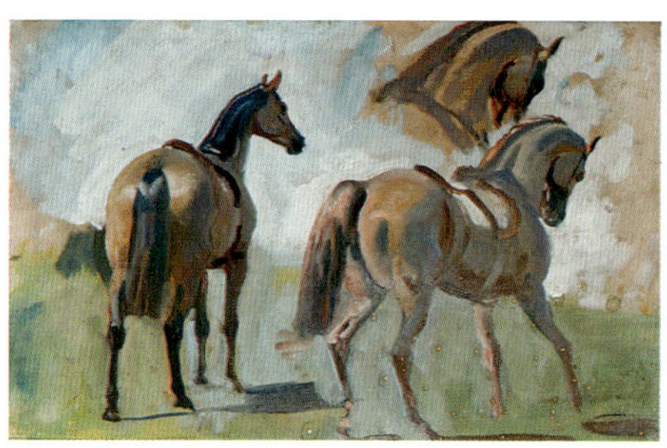

Munnings, Alfred James 1878–1959
Horse Studies
oil on board 24.8 x 38.1
617

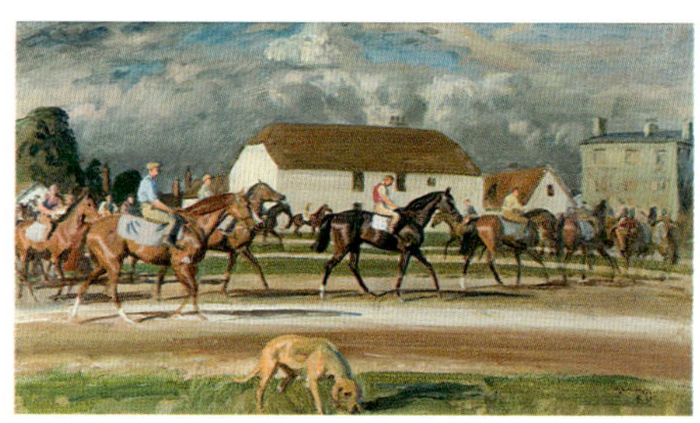

Munnings, Alfred James 1878–1959
Horses with Stable Lads up at Newmarket
oil on board 45.1 x 74.3
16

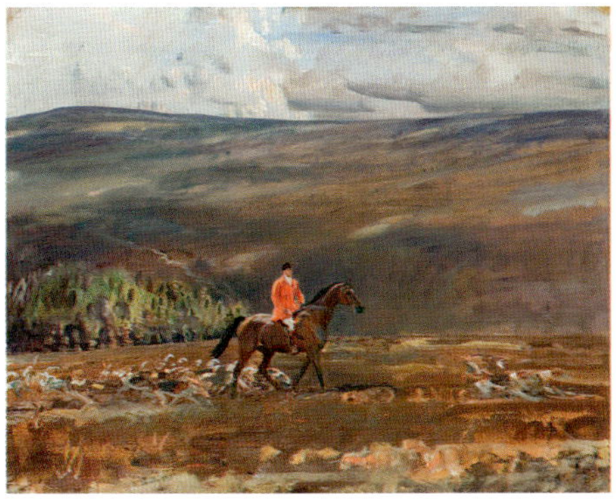

Munnings, Alfred James 1878–1959
Huntsman Crossing the Dunkery Beacon, Exmoor
oil on canvas 63.5 x 76.2
150

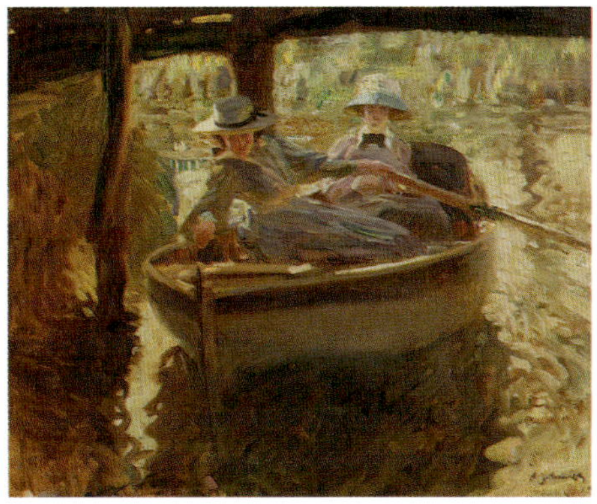

Munnings, Alfred James 1878–1959
Idle Moments
oil on canvas 316.1 x 387
L7:1997 (P)

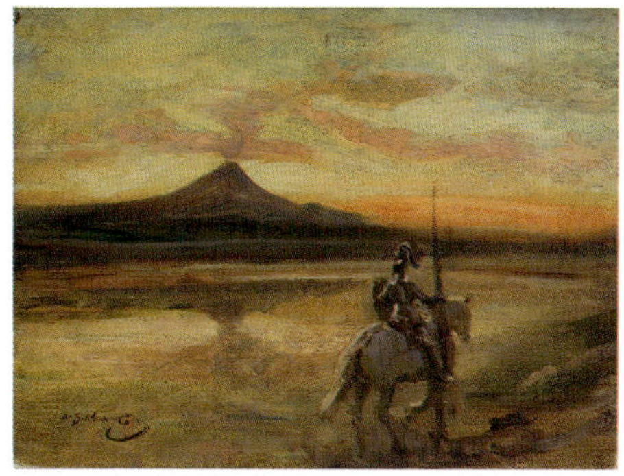

Munnings, Alfred James 1878–1959
Knight Riding by a Lake (recto)
oil on panel 26.7 x 34.9
532

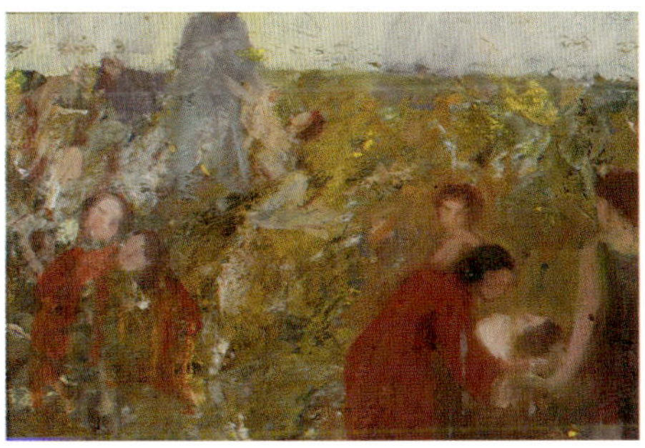

Munnings, Alfred James 1878–1959
A Scene from the New Testament (verso)
oil on panel 26.7 x 34.9
532A

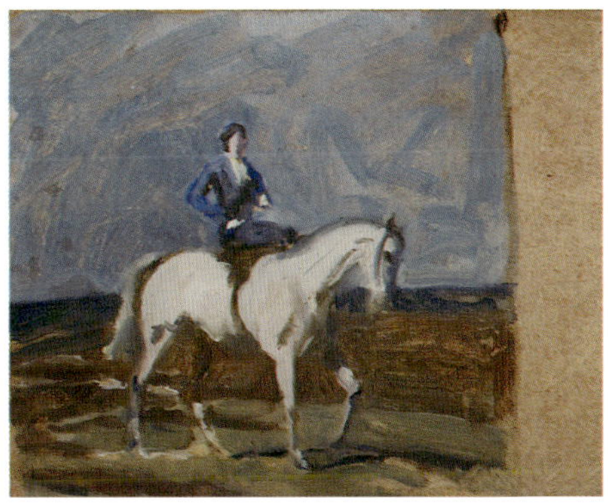

Munnings, Alfred James 1878–1959
Lady Munnings on a Grey Hunter
oil on board 15.2 x 22.9
537

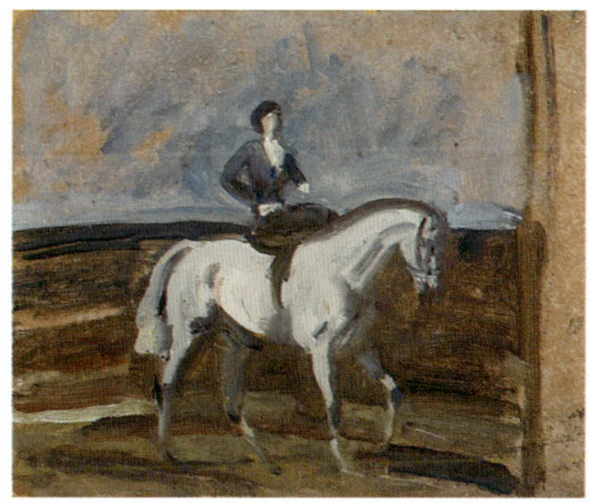

Munnings, Alfred James 1878–1959
Lady Munnings on a Grey Hunter
oil on board 15.9 x 22.9
596

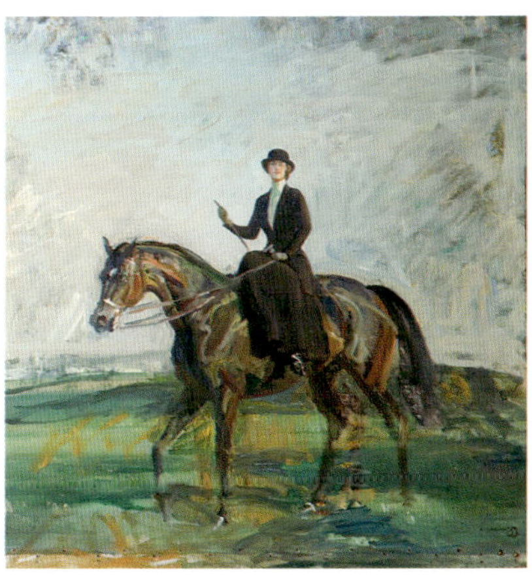

Munnings, Alfred James 1878–1959
Lady Munnings Riding a Bay Hunter
oil on canvas 88.9 x 83.8
279

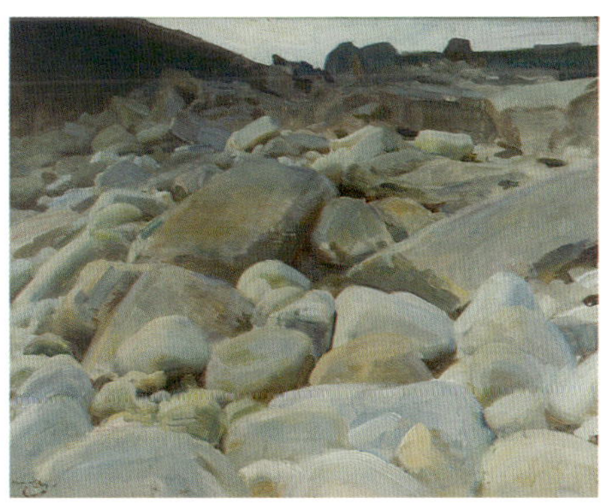

Munnings, Alfred James 1878–1959
Lamorna Cove, Cornwall
oil on canvas 59 x 73
124

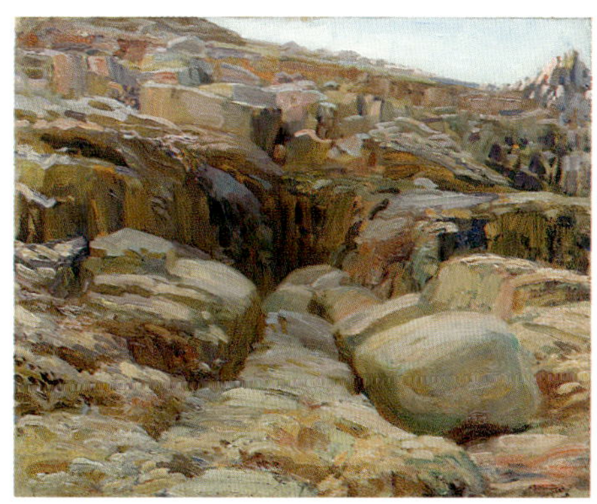

Munnings, Alfred James 1878–1959
Lamorna Cove, Cornwall
oil on canvas 50.8 x 61
411

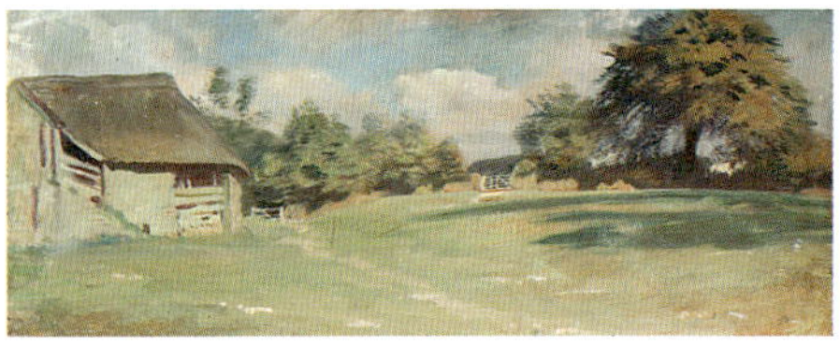

Munnings, Alfred James 1878–1959
Landscape with a Barn
oil on board 28.6 x 71.1
398

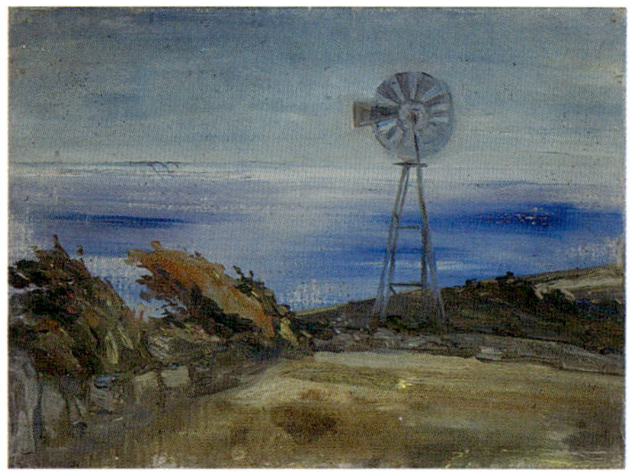

Munnings, Alfred James 1878–1959
Landscape with a Windmill
oil on canvas board 30.5 x 40.6
602

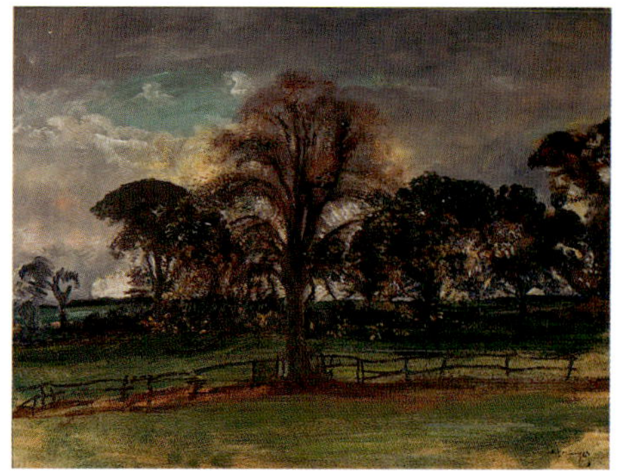

Munnings, Alfred James 1878–1959
Landscape with Trees
oil on canvas 57.8 x 72.4
252

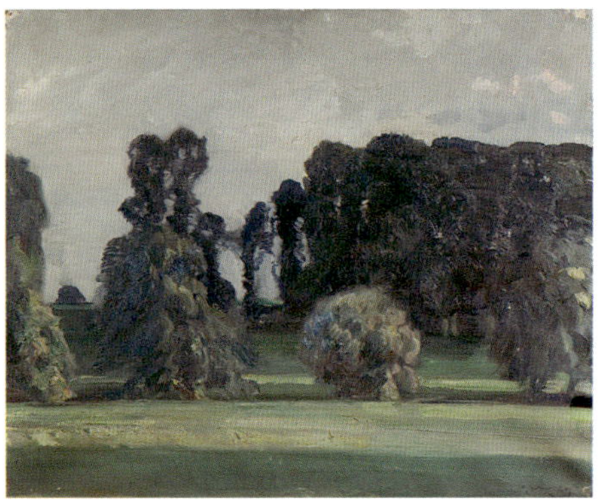

Munnings, Alfred James 1878–1959
Landscape with Trees
oil on canvas 129 x 154.8
L4:2005 (P)

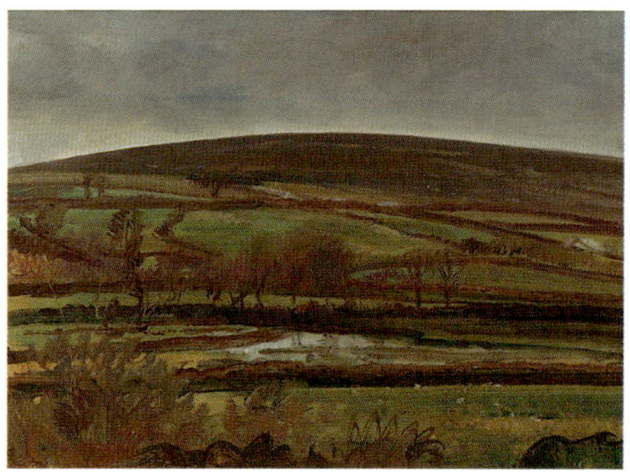

Munnings, Alfred James 1878–1959
Landscape, Withypool, Exmoor, Winter
oil on board 45.7 x 61
494

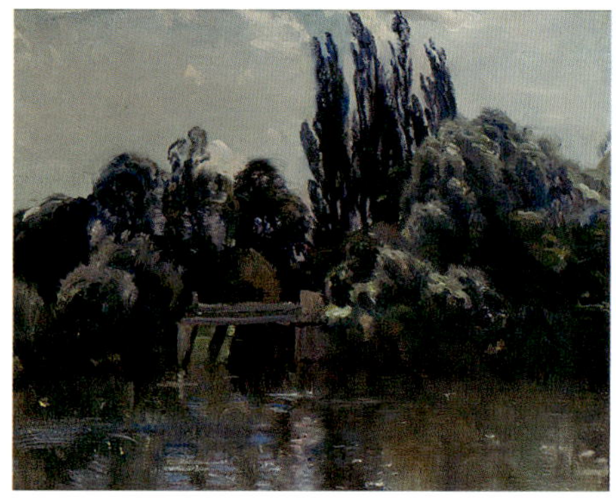

Munnings, Alfred James 1878–1959
Langham Mill Pool on the Stour
oil on canvas 50.8 x 61
32

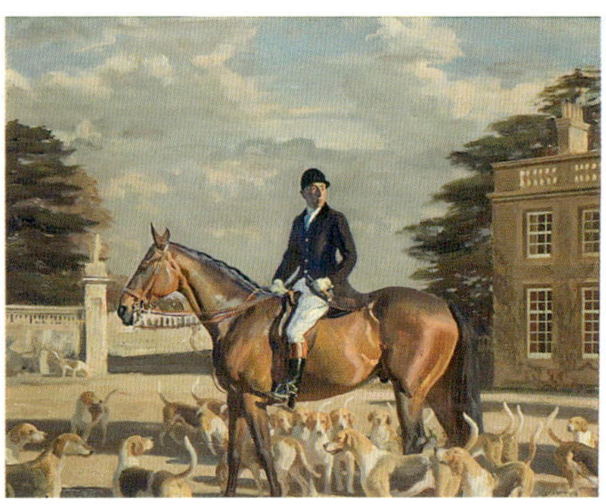

Munnings, Alfred James 1878–1959
Major E. Shackle, Buckinghamshire Farmers' Hunt
oil on canvas 63.5 x 76.2
651

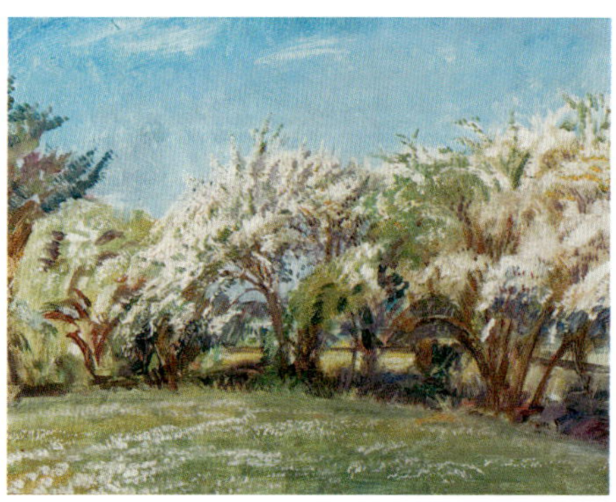

Munnings, Alfred James 1878–1959
May Blossom
oil on board 40 x 50.5
357

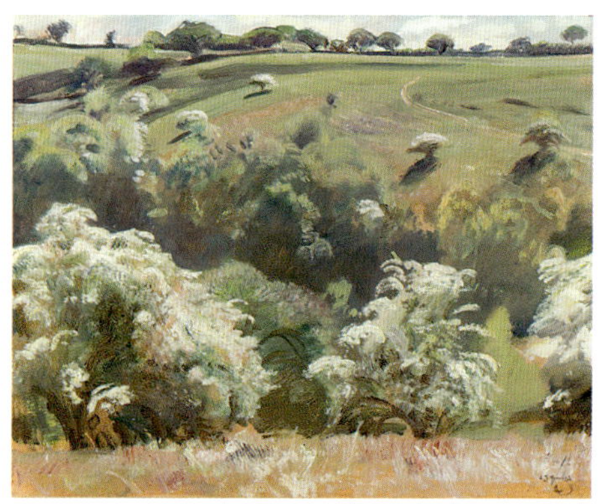

Munnings, Alfred James 1878–1959
May on Exmoor
oil on board 50 x 61
122

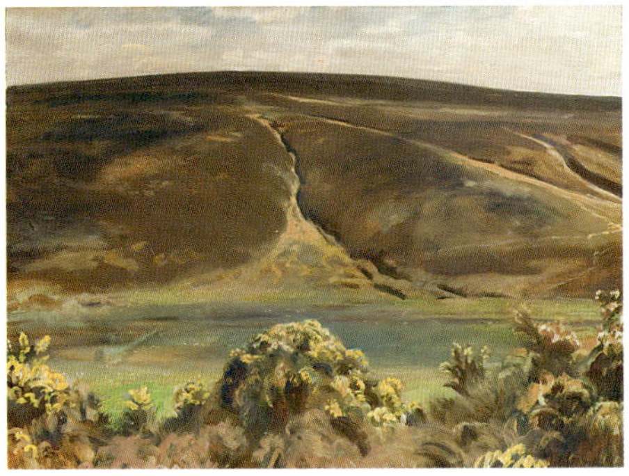

Munnings, Alfred James 1878–1959
Mill Hill, Oar, Exmoor
oil on canvas 71.8 x 91.4
45

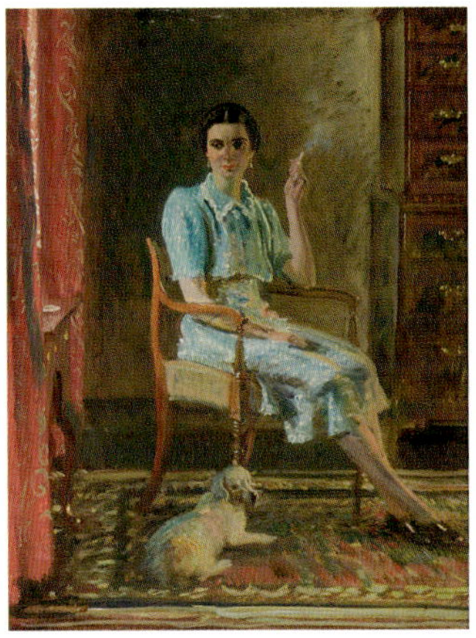

Munnings, Alfred James 1878–1959
Miss Hancock, Seated Smoking with a Dog in an Interior
oil on canvas 68.6 x 50.8
153

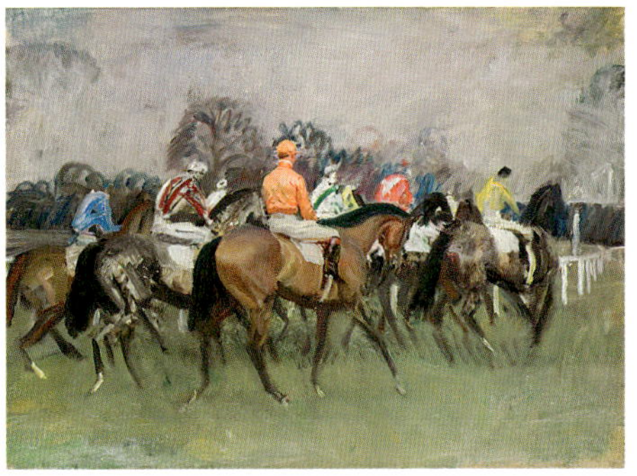

Munnings, Alfred James 1878–1959
Moving up to the Start
oil on canvas 88.9 x 119.4
423

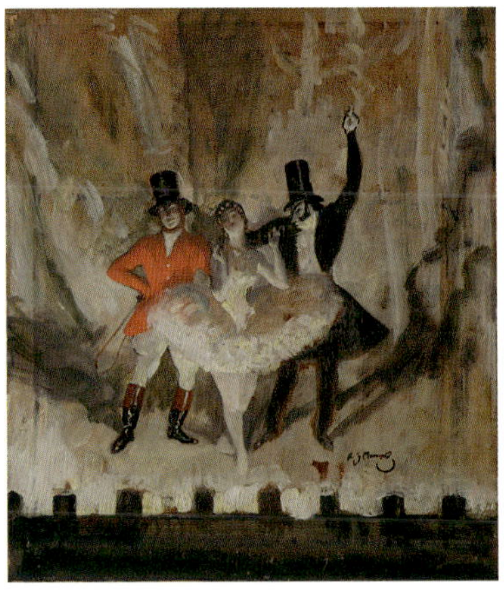

Munnings, Alfred James 1878–1959
Mr Sponge on the Go
oil on board 61 x 51
502

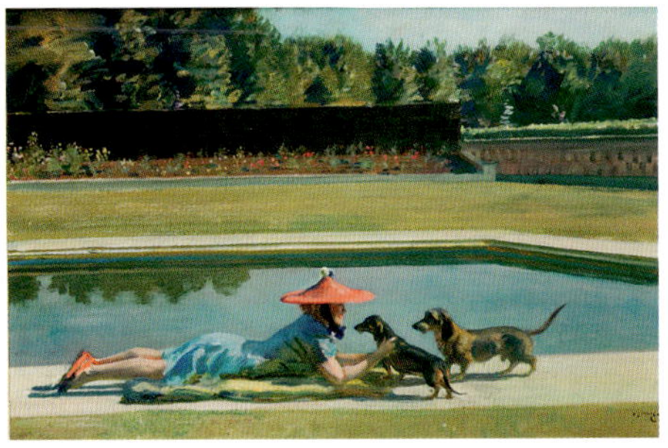

Munnings, Alfred James 1878–1959
Mrs J. V. Rank at Druids' Lodge by the Swimming Pool
oil on canvas 49.5 x 74.9
655

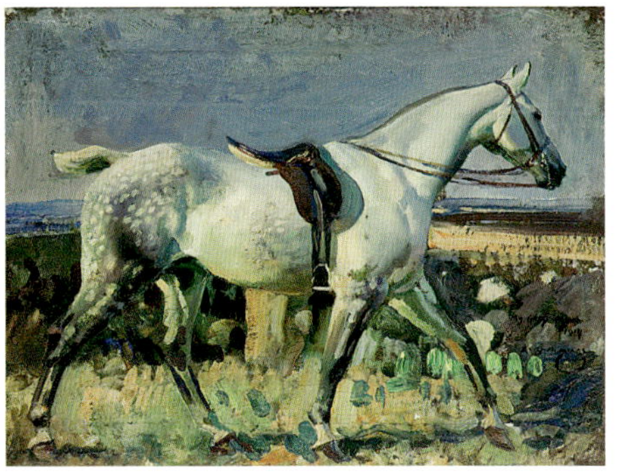

Munnings, Alfred James 1878–1959
My Grey Mare
oil on canvas 35.6 x 45.7
34

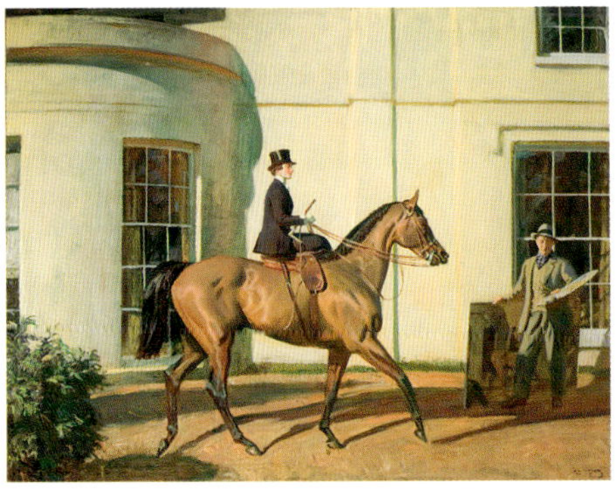

Munnings, Alfred James 1878–1959
My Wife, My Horse and Myself
oil on canvas 101 x 126.4
51

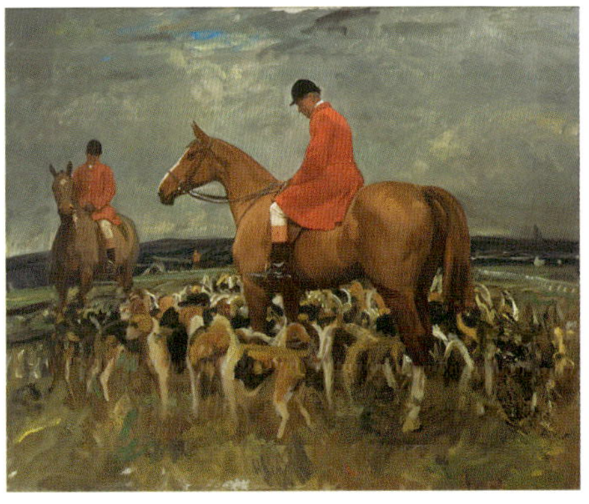

Munnings, Alfred James 1878–1959
Nobby Gray with the Hunt
oil on canvas 158.8 x 199.4
81

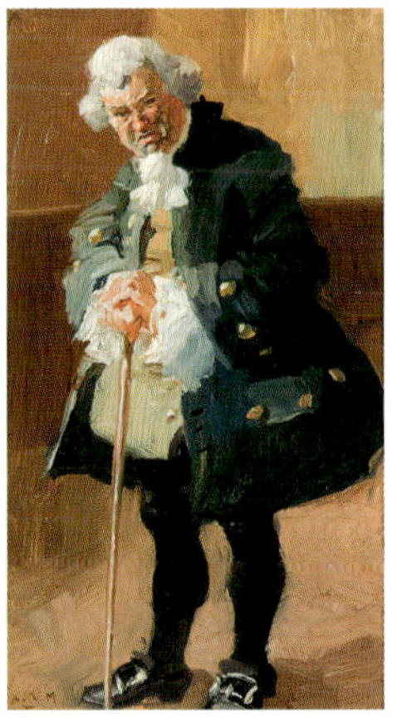

Munnings, Alfred James 1878–1959
Old Gentleman in Period Costume with Walking Stick
oil on canvas 35.7 x 20.2
661

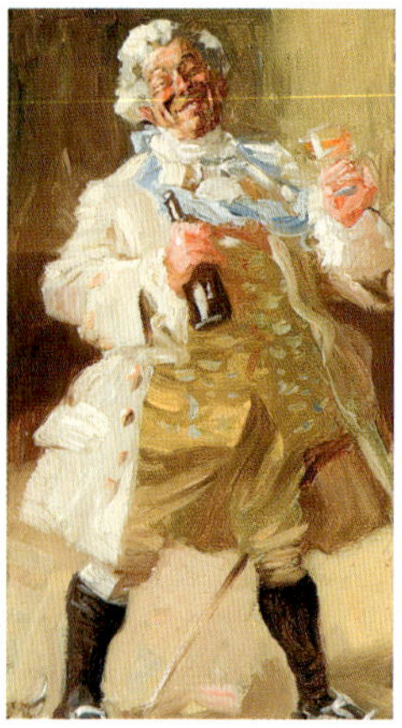

Munnings, Alfred James 1878–1959
Old Man in Period Costume Holding a Bottle and Glass
oil on canvas 35.7 x 20.2
660

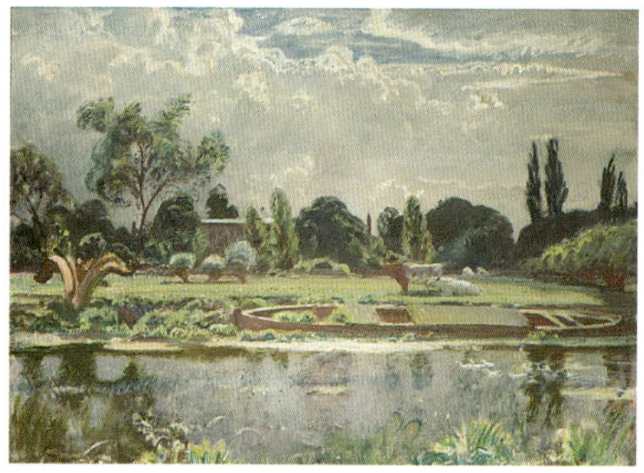

Munnings, Alfred James 1878–1959
On the Stour, Dedham
oil on canvas 76.2 x 101.6
236

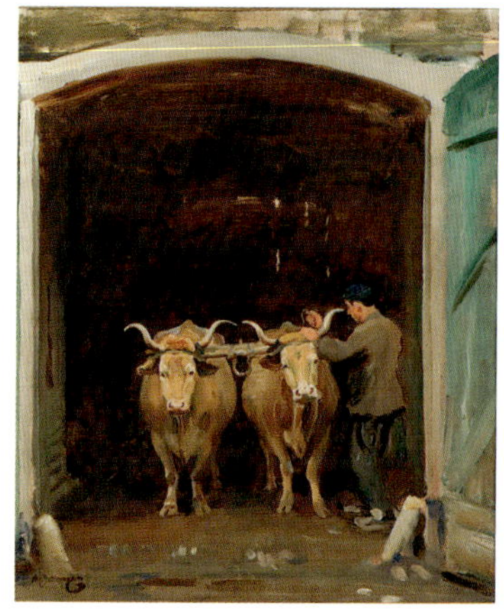

Munnings, Alfred James 1878–1959
Oxen at an Archway Being Yoked, at Baron Robert's Estate, Chantilly
oil on canvas 65 x 55
55

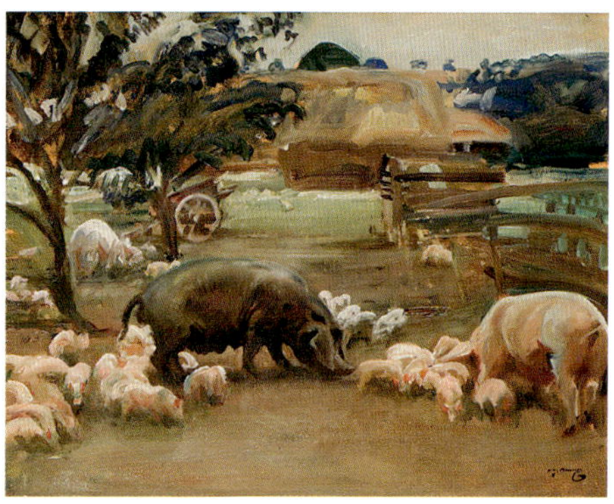

Munnings, Alfred James 1878–1959
Pigs at Great Thurlow, Suffolk
oil on canvas 51.4 x 61
118

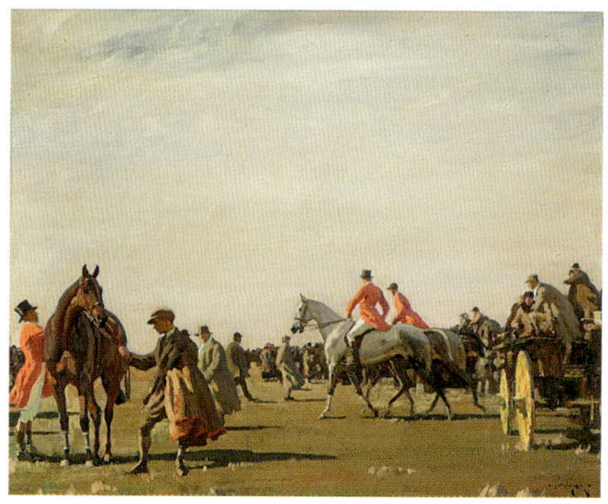

Munnings, Alfred James 1878–1959
Point-to-Point
oil on canvas 72.4 x 90.2
1927.8

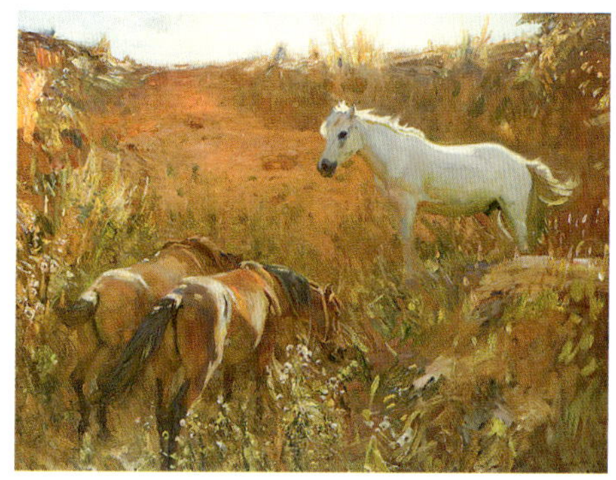

Munnings, Alfred James 1878–1959
Ponies in a Sandpit, Ringland Hills, Norfolk
oil on canvas 102.9 x 127
116

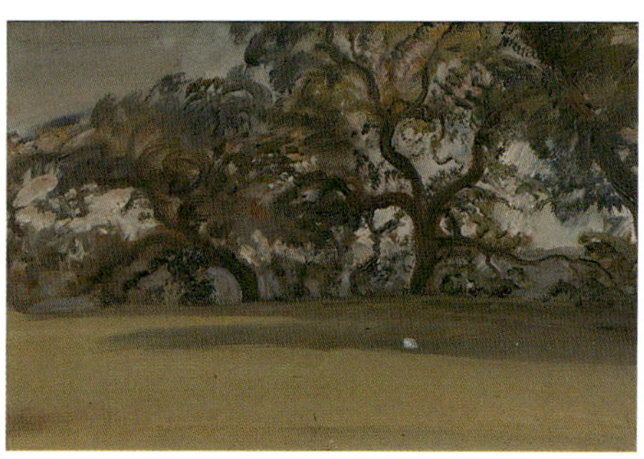

Munnings, Alfred James 1878–1959
Porlock Studies, Trees by the Edge of a Field (recto)
oil on board 23.5 x 34.9 (E)
619

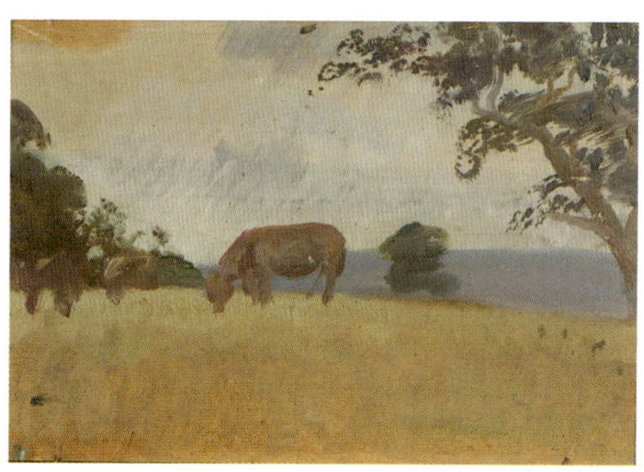

Munnings, Alfred James 1878–1959
Study of Cattle Grazing (verso)
oil on board 23.5 x 34.9 (E)
619A

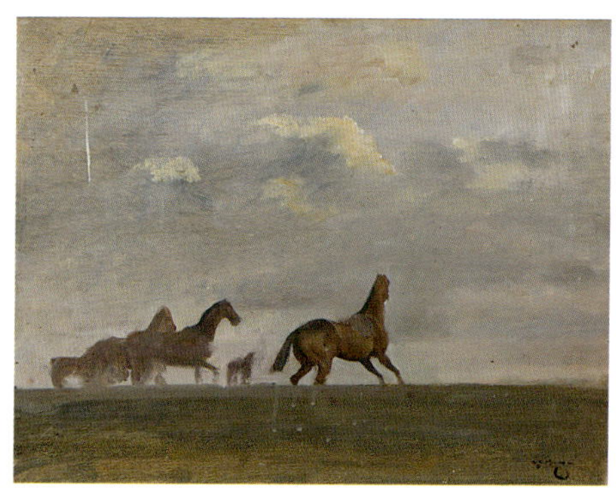

Munnings, Alfred James 1878–1959
Racehorses in a Landscape
oil on board 40.6 x 50.8
386

Facing page: Ogborne, David, c.1700–1768, *The Flitch Procession Moving away from Little Dunmow Priory Church* (detail), c.1751, Great Dunmow Town Council, (p. 196)

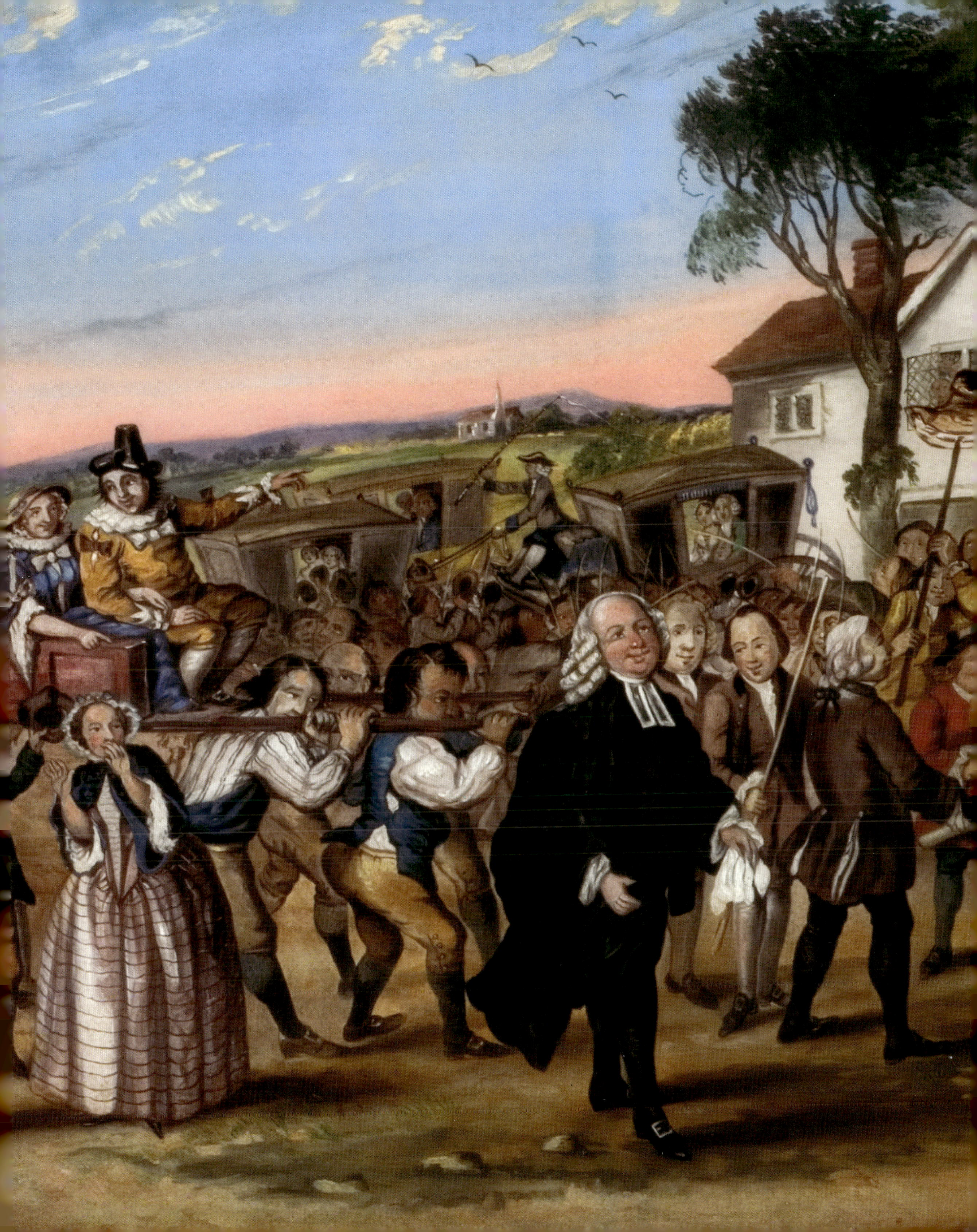

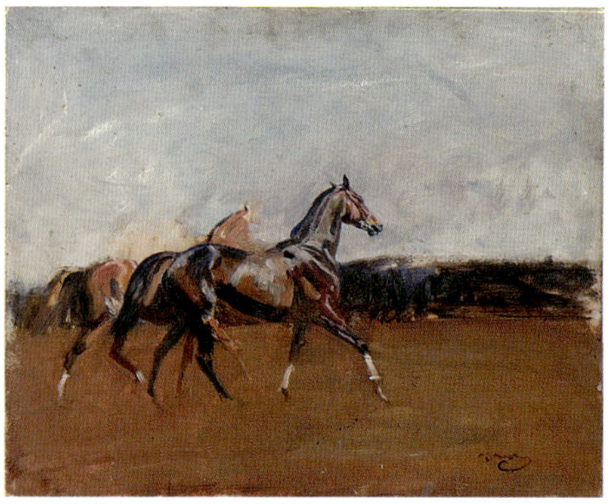

Munnings, Alfred James 1878–1959
Racehorses in a Landscape
oil on panel 50.8 x 60.3
458

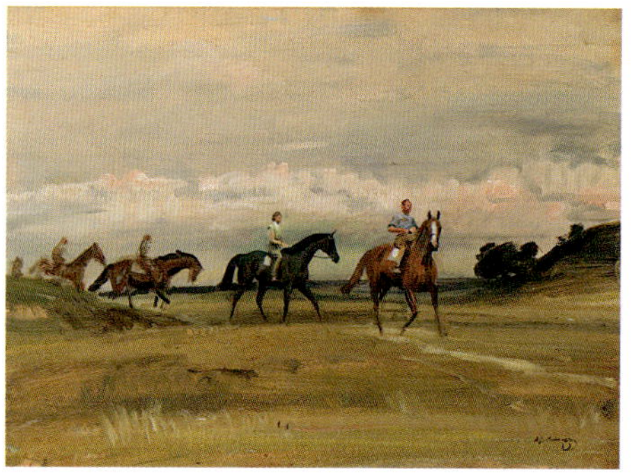

Munnings, Alfred James 1878–1959
Racehorses Training in a Landscape
oil on board 45.7 x 60.3
372

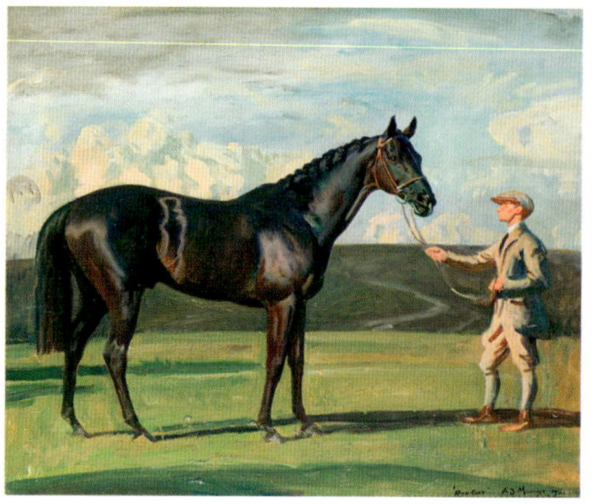

Munnings, Alfred James 1878–1959
'Rich Gift'
oil on canvas 66 x 76.2
14

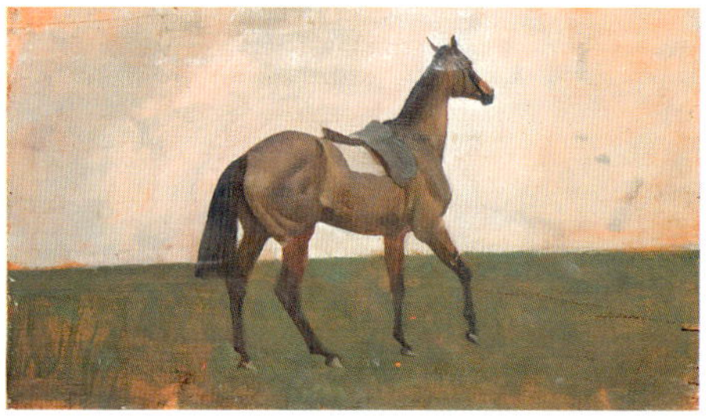

Munnings, Alfred James 1878–1959
Riderless Horse
oil on board 22.9 x 38.1
604

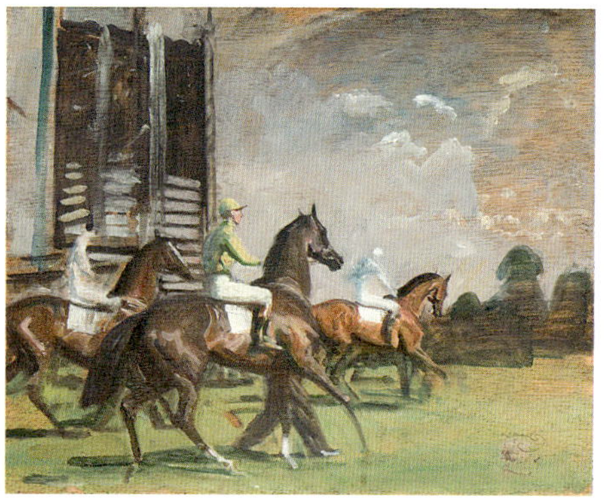

Munnings, Alfred James 1878–1959
Riding to the Start
oil on board 50.2 x 61
291

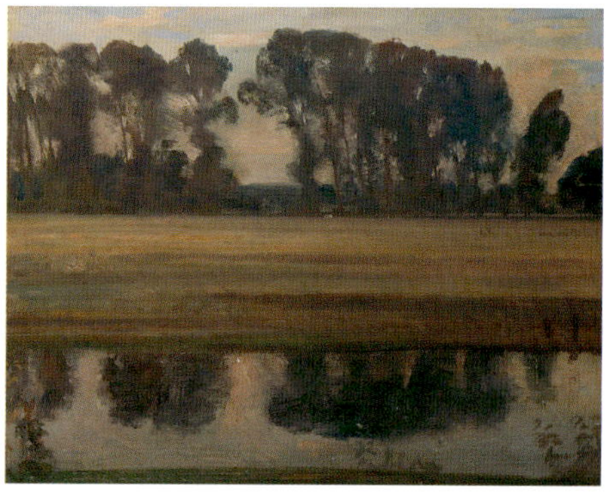

Munnings, Alfred James 1878–1959
River Landscape with Trees
oil on board 50.8 x 61
507

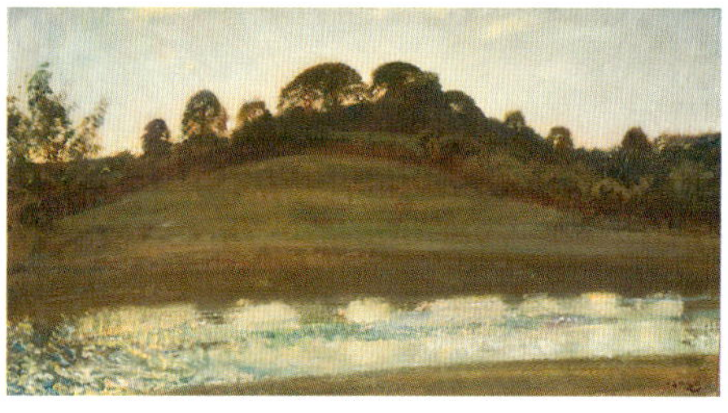

Munnings, Alfred James 1878–1959
River Scene at Brightworthy, Withypool, Exmoor, Evening Light
oil on canvas 54.6 x 94
436

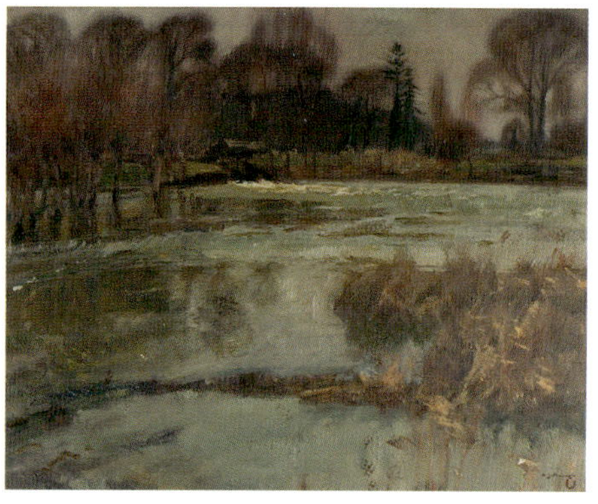

Munnings, Alfred James 1878–1959
River Scene, Boxted Mill
oil on canvas 63.5 x 76.2
682

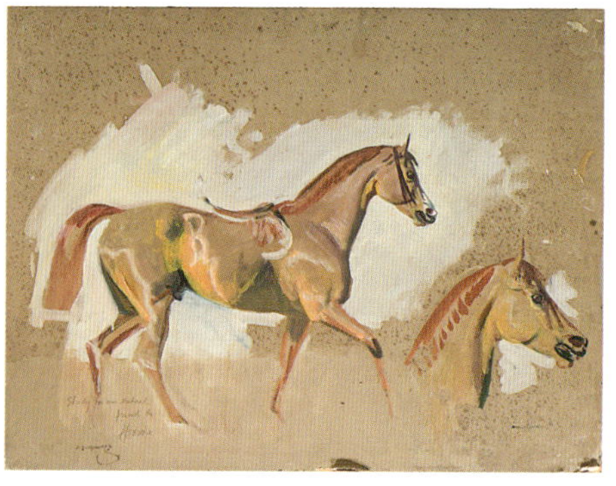

Munnings, Alfred James 1878–1959
'Rufus', a Study for 'Our Mutual Friend the Horse'
oil on board 46 x 58.5
466

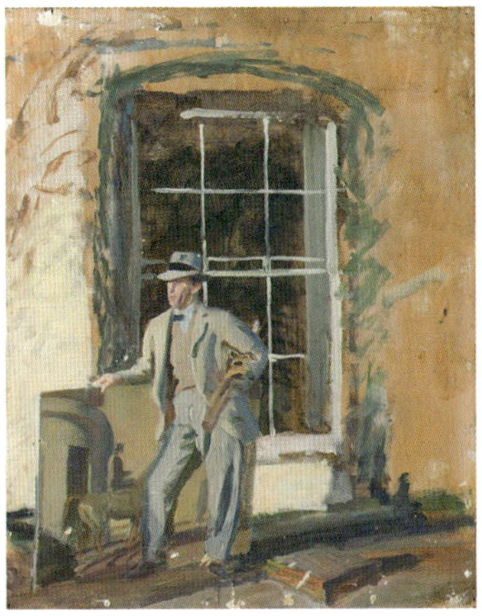

Munnings, Alfred James 1878–1959
Self Portrait (recto)
oil on board 58.5 x 46
498

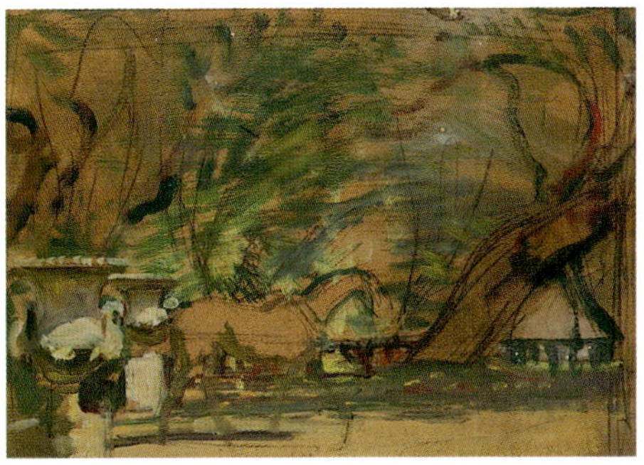

Munnings, Alfred James 1878–1959
Study (verso)
oil on board 46 x 58.5
498A

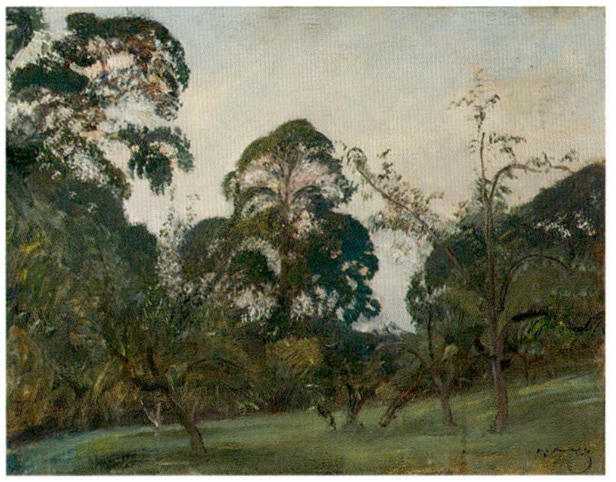

Munnings, Alfred James 1878–1959
Selworthy, West Somerset
oil on board 35.6 x 45.7
286

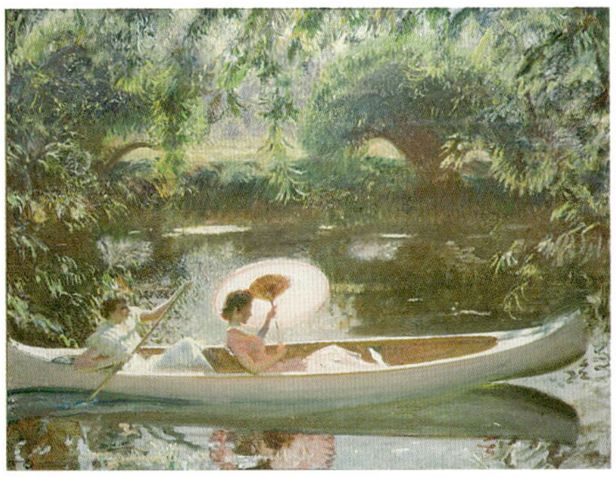

Munnings, Alfred James 1878–1959
September Afternoon on the Stour, Dedham
oil on canvas 100.3 x 125.7
210

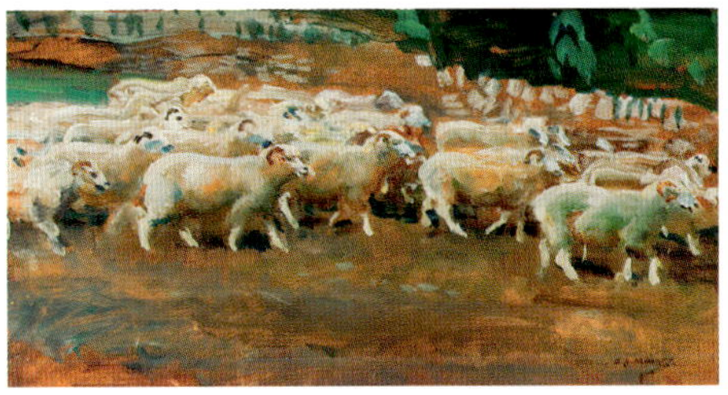

Munnings, Alfred James 1878–1959
Sheep on Exmoor
oil on panel 30.5 x 61
260

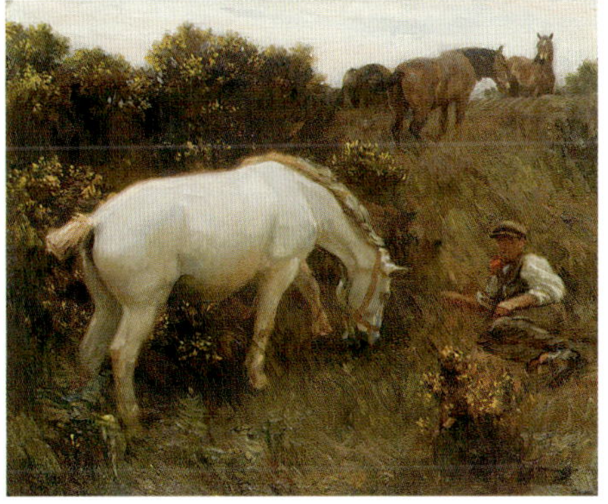

Munnings, Alfred James 1878–1959
'Shrimp' and 'Augereau' in Ringland Hills
oil on canvas 61 x 66
644

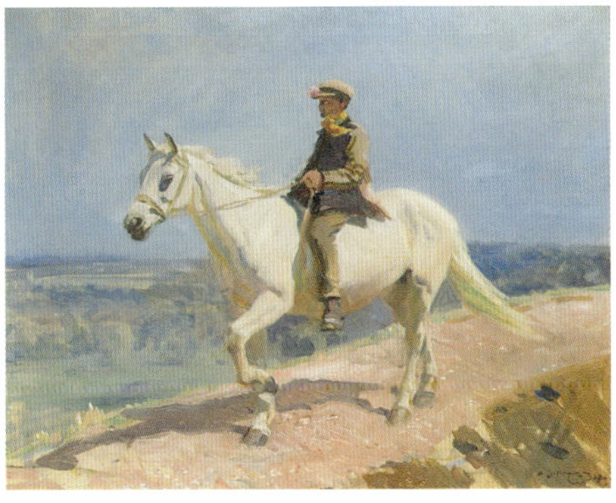

Munnings, Alfred James 1878–1959
'Shrimp' on a White Welsh Pony
oil on canvas 61 x 76.2
686

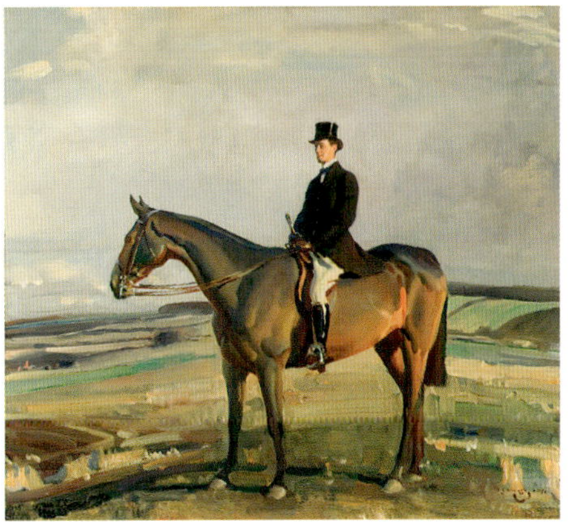

Munnings, Alfred James 1878–1959
Sir Raymond Greene, DSO, MP, on Horseback, 1919
oil on canvas 71.1 x 76.2
652

Munnings, Alfred James 1878–1959
Sky Study
oil on board 20.3 x 29.8
312

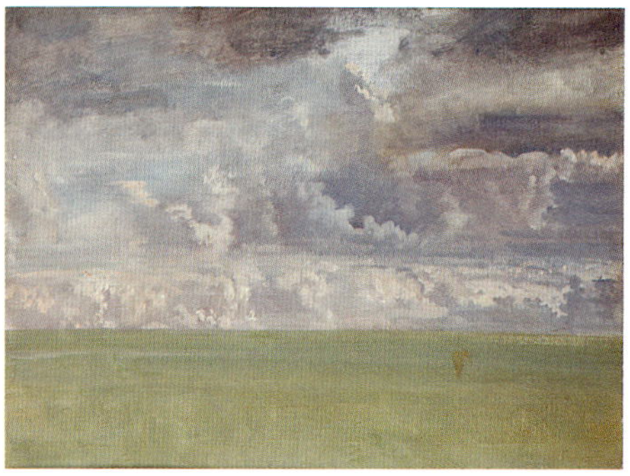

Munnings, Alfred James 1878–1959
Sky Study
oil on canvas 56.5 x 71.8
325

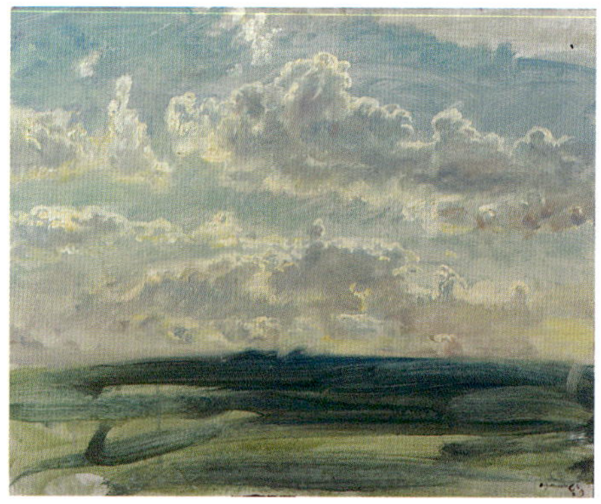

Munnings, Alfred James 1878–1959
Sky Study
oil on canvas 50.8 x 61
365

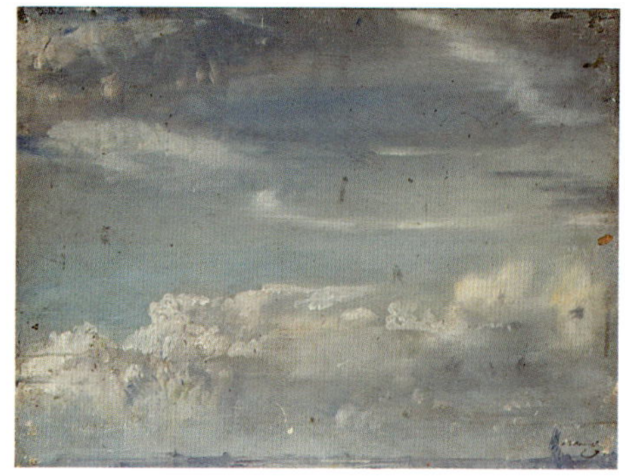

Munnings, Alfred James 1878–1959
Sky Study
oil on canvas 35.6 x 45.7
472

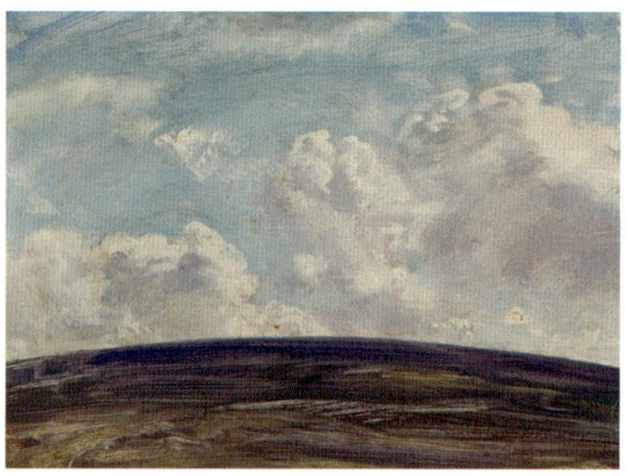

Munnings, Alfred James 1878–1959
Sky Study
oil on panel 30.5 x 40.3
680

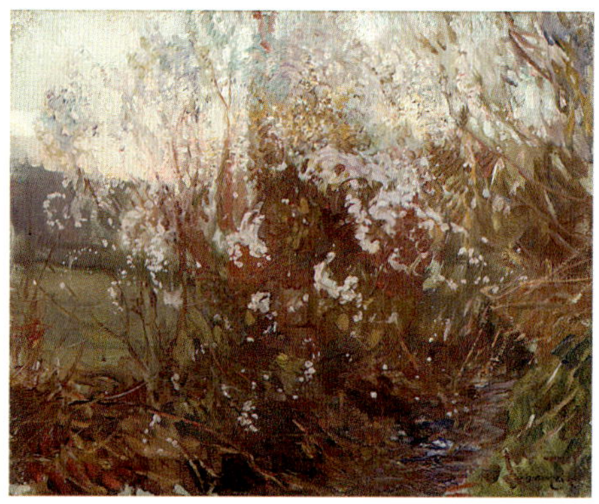

Munnings, Alfred James 1878–1959
Spring Evening, Cornwall
oil on canvas 50.8 x 61 (E)
374

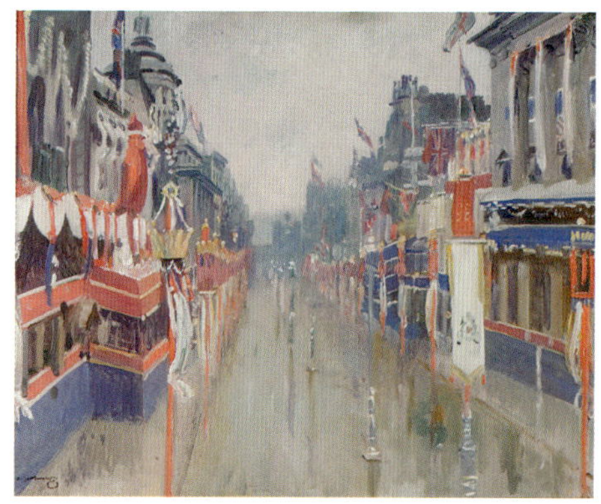

Munnings, Alfred James 1878–1959
St James's Street, Decorations for the Coronation of George VI, 1937
oil on canvas 50.8 x 61 (E)
528

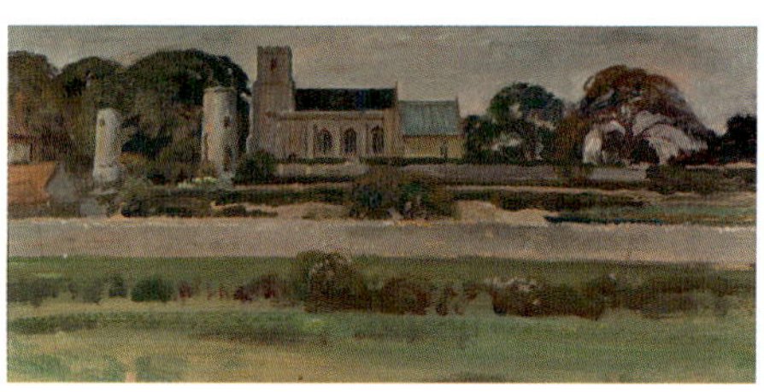

Munnings, Alfred James 1878–1959
Stiffkey Church, Norfolk
oil on board 31.8 x 68
49

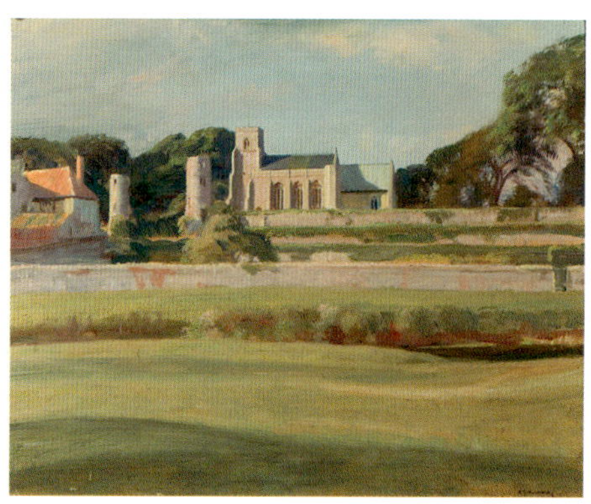

Munnings, Alfred James 1878–1959
Stiffkey Church, Norfolk
oil on canvas 48.3 x 55.9
L1:1987 (P)

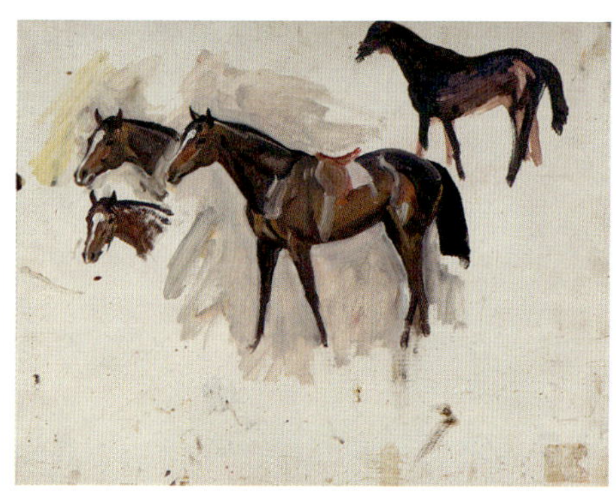

Munnings, Alfred James 1878–1959
Studies of a Bay Racehorse
oil on board 40.6 x 50.2
360

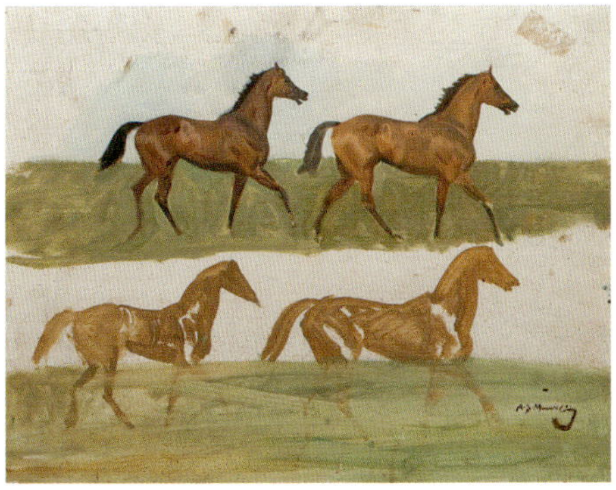

Munnings, Alfred James 1878–1959
Studies of a Bay Racehorse
oil on board 40.6 x 50.8
382

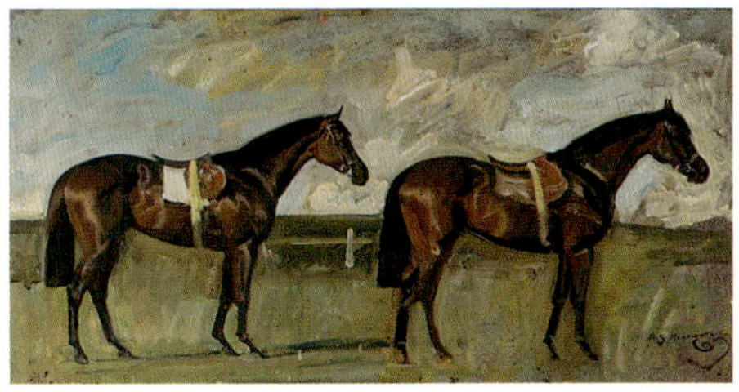

Munnings, Alfred James 1878–1959
Studies of a Bay Racehorse in a Landscape
oil on board 30.5 x 56.5
115

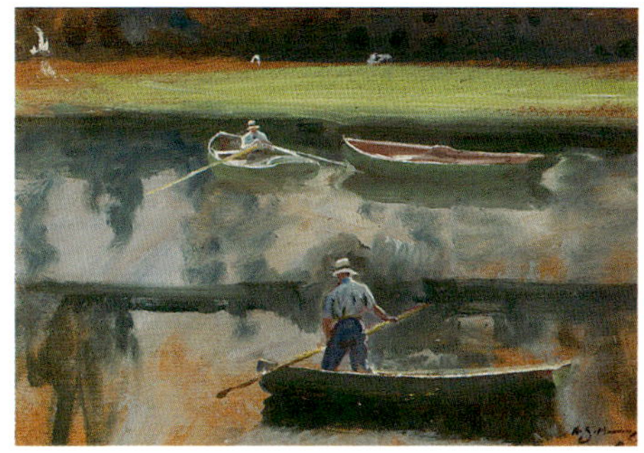

Munnings, Alfred James 1878–1959
Studies of a Boatman
oil on board 25.4 x 34.9
568

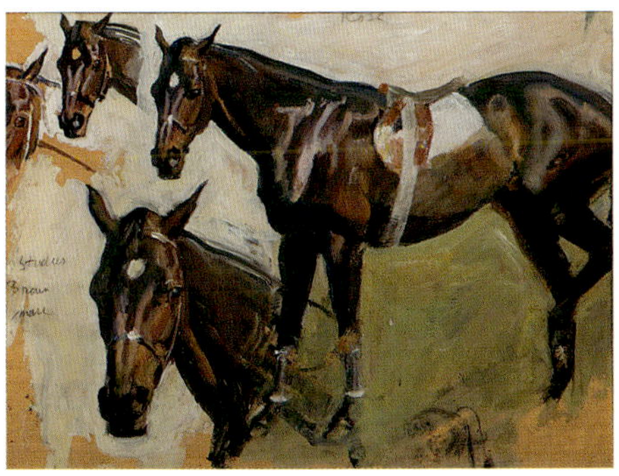

Munnings, Alfred James 1878–1959
Studies of a Brown Mare for 'Unsaddling Enclosure, Epsom'
oil on panel 33 x 41.3
186

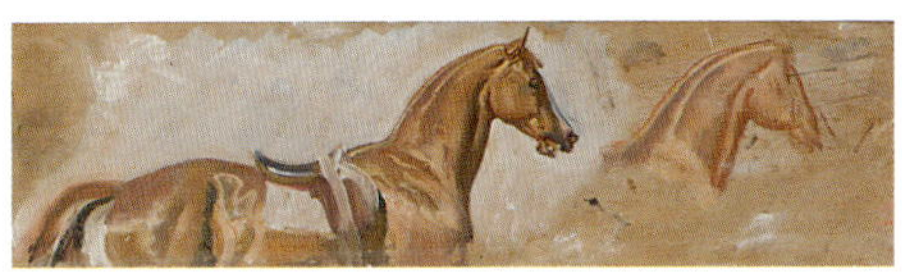

Munnings, Alfred James 1878–1959
Studies of a Chestnut Racehorse
oil on board 19.7 x 67.3
404

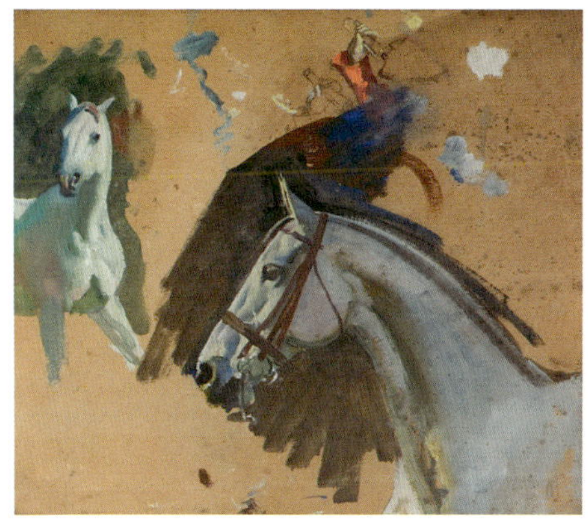

Munnings, Alfred James 1878–1959
Studies of a Grey Mare's Head
oil on board 38.7 x 44.5
278

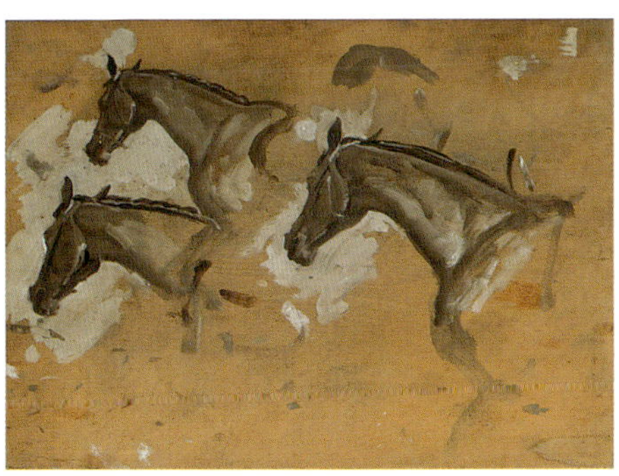

Munnings, Alfred James 1878–1959
Studies of a Horse's Head (recto)
oil on board 30.5 x 40.6
581

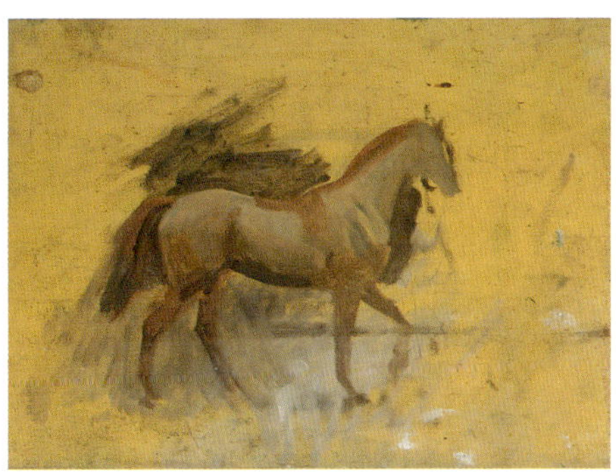

Munnings, Alfred James 1878–1959
Study of a Horse (verso)
oil on board 30.5 x 40.6
581A

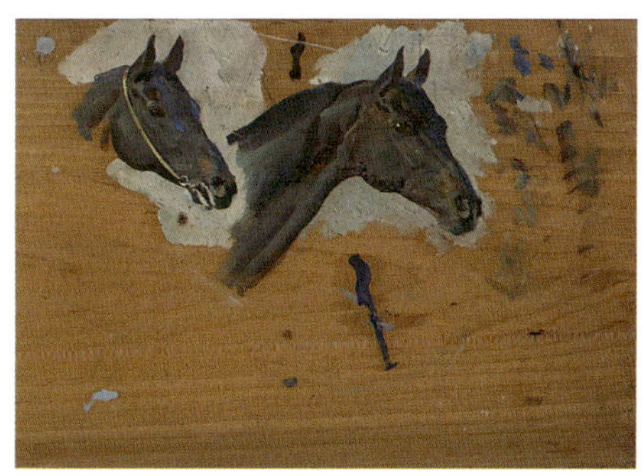

Munnings, Alfred James 1878–1959
Studies of a Horse's Head (recto)
oil on panel 30.5 x 40.6
307

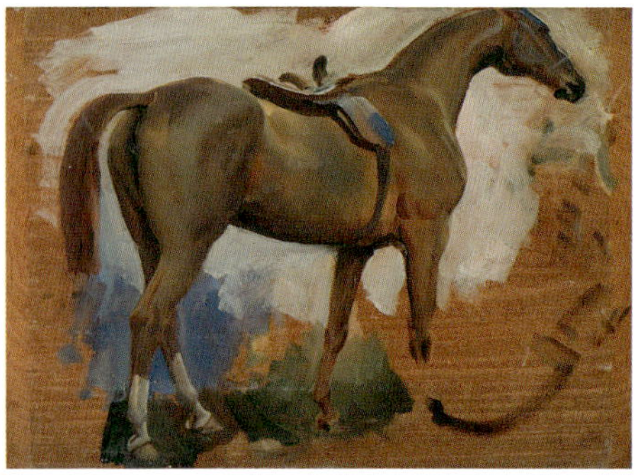

Munnings, Alfred James 1878–1959
Study of a Bay Horse (verso)
oil on panel 30.5 x 40.6
307A

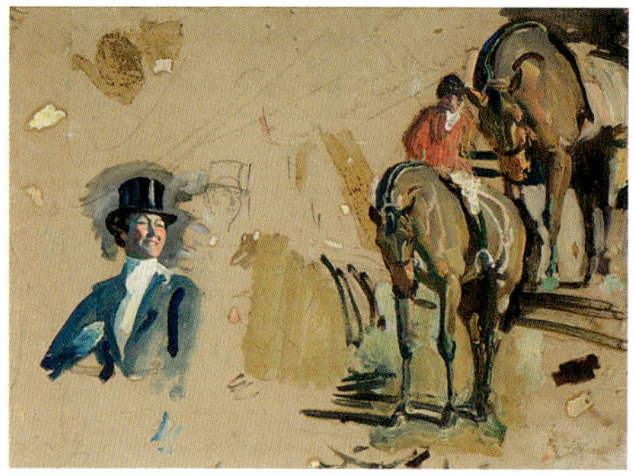

Munnings, Alfred James 1878–1959
Studies of a Huntsman and His Horse and of Lady Munnings
oil on board 35.6 x 45.1
301

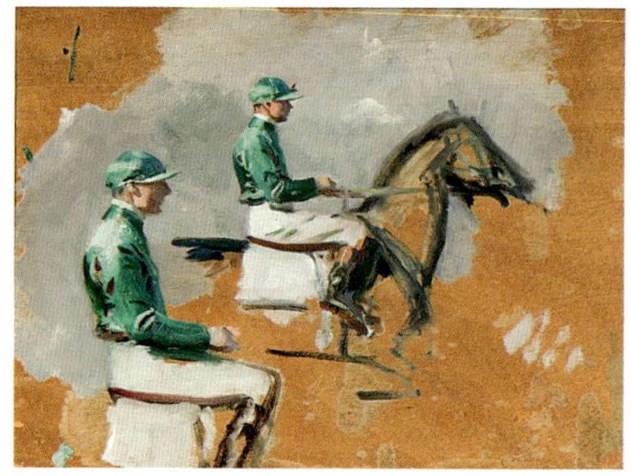

Munnings, Alfred James 1878–1959
Studies of a Jockey Wearing Green
oil on board 35.6 x 45.7
172

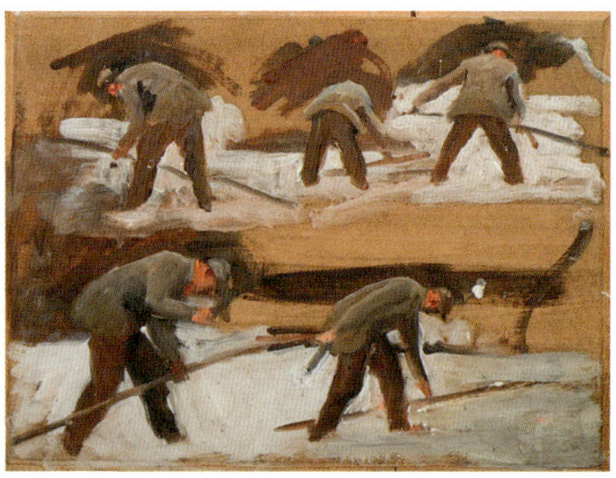

Munnings, Alfred James 1878–1959
Studies of a Man Clearing Snow
oil on panel 25.4 x 33
551

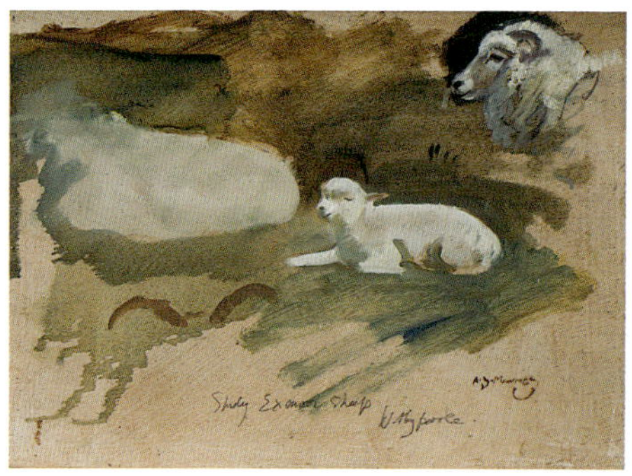

Munnings, Alfred James 1878–1959
Studies of Exmoor Sheep, Withypool
oil on board 24.8 x 33
191

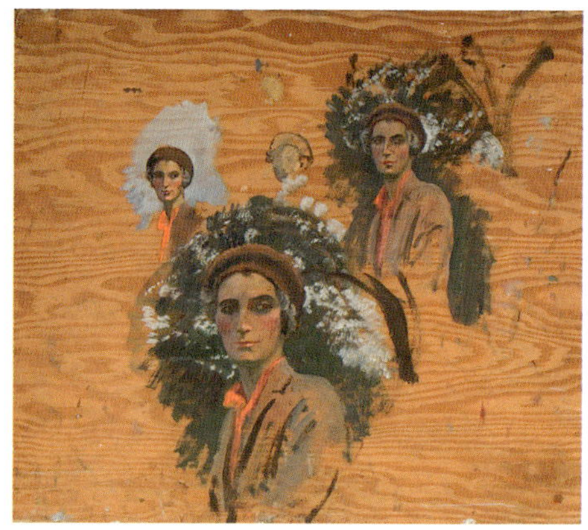

Munnings, Alfred James 1878–1959
Studies of Gladys Bawden
oil on board 40.7 x 44.5
391

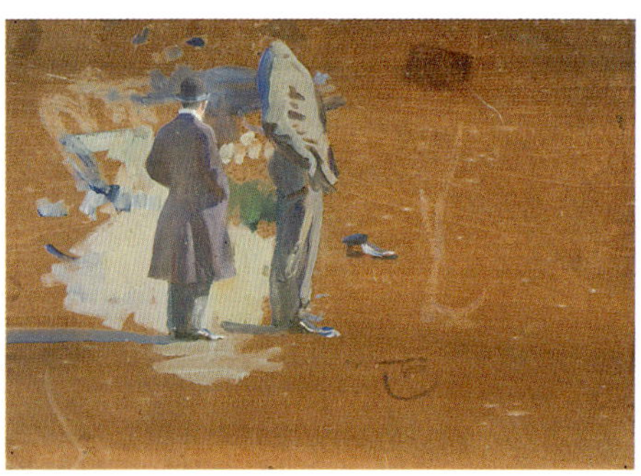

Munnings, Alfred James 1878–1959
Studies of Men Standing
oil on panel 25.4 x 35.6
556

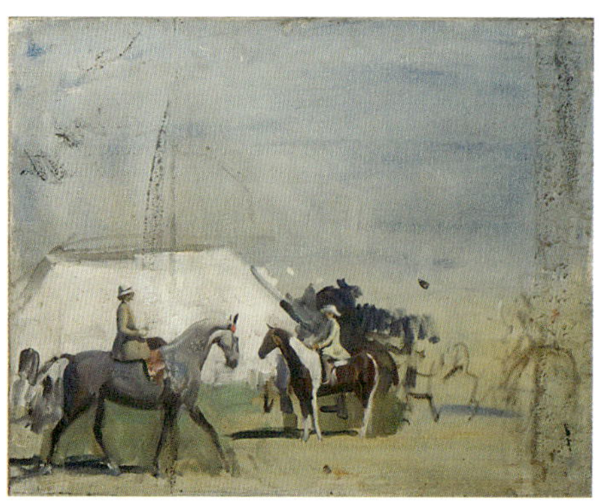

Munnings, Alfred James 1878–1959
Studies of Riders by a Marquee
oil on canvas 50.2 x 61
464

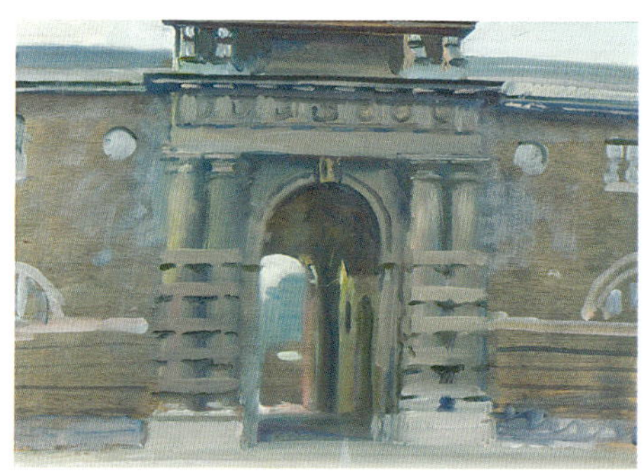

Munnings, Alfred James 1878–1959
Study at Horse Guards' Barracks
oil on board 30.5 x 41.9
582

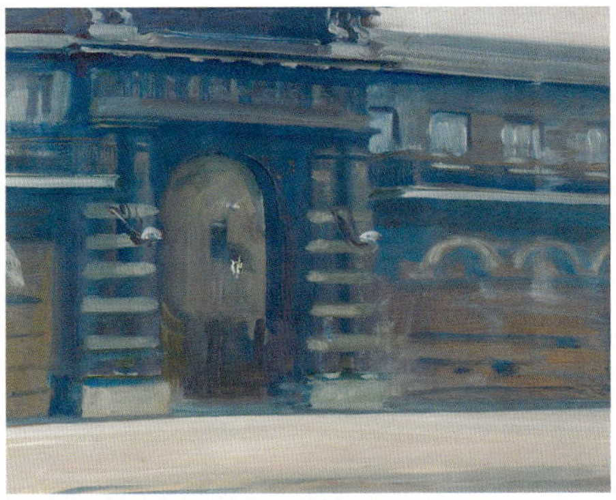

Munnings, Alfred James 1878–1959
Study at Horse Guards' Barracks
oil on board 33 x 41.3
589

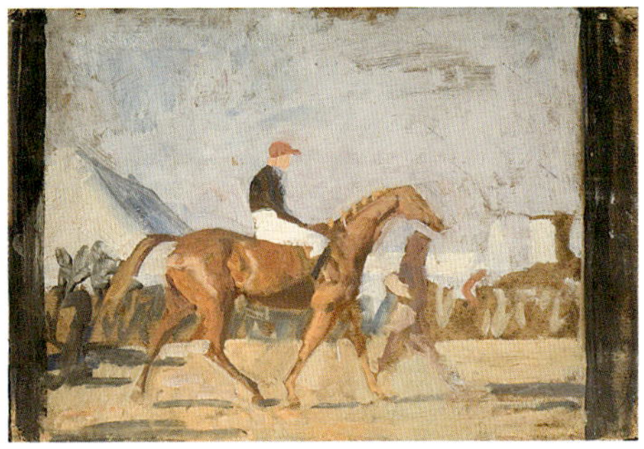

Munnings, Alfred James 1878–1959
Study at Newmarket
oil on board 34.9 x 48.9
196

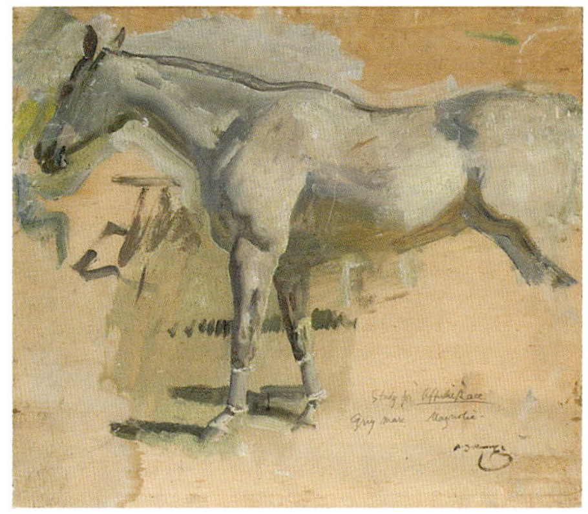

Munnings, Alfred James 1878–1959
Study for 'After the Race', the Grey Mare 'Magnolia'
oil on panel 40.6 x 45.7
481

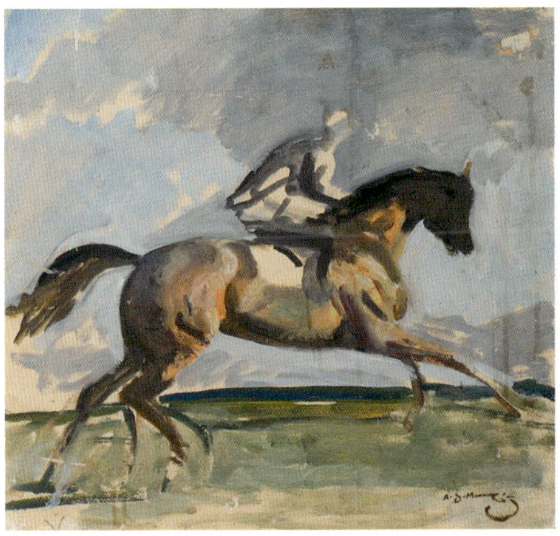

Munnings, Alfred James 1878–1959
Study for 'Coming up the Canter'
oil on board 34.9 x 36.8
178

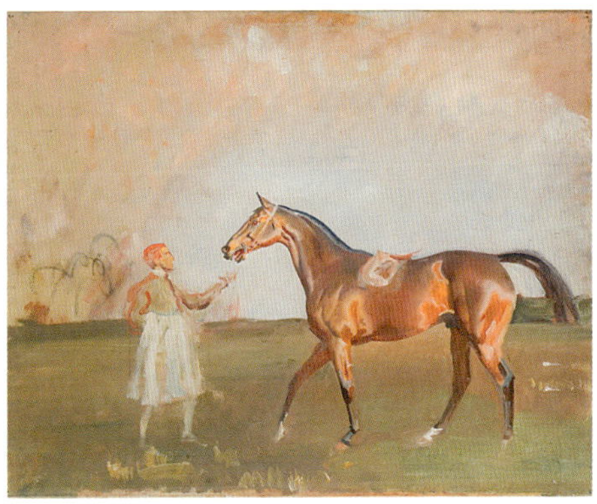

Munnings, Alfred James 1878–1959
Study for 'Coronach'
oil on canvas 67.3 x 80.6
331

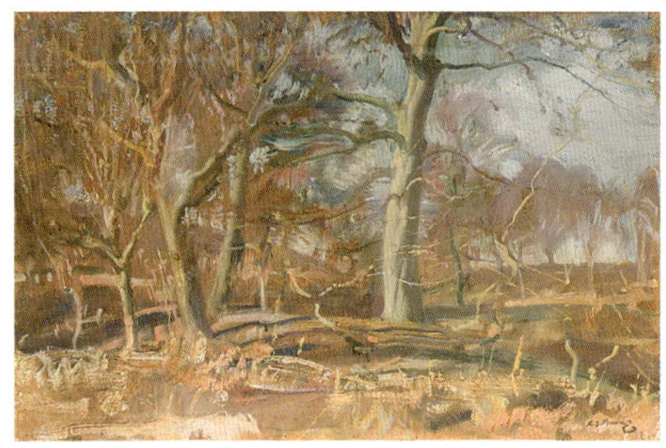

Munnings, Alfred James 1878–1959
Study for 'Edge of the Wood'
oil on board 40.6 x 61
381

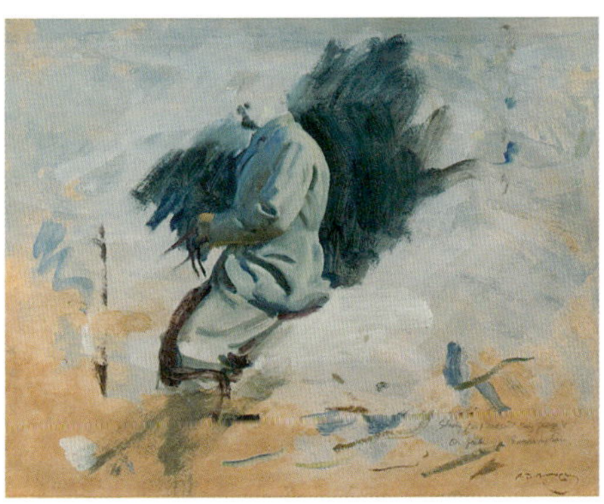

Munnings, Alfred James 1878–1959
Study for 'George V on Jock at Sandringham'
oil on board 40.6 x 50.8
377

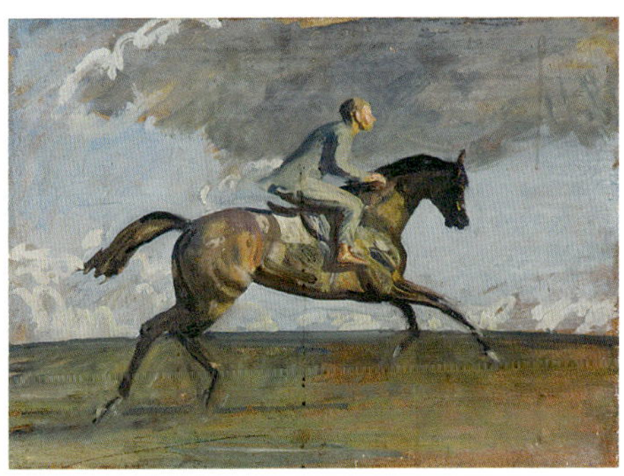

Munnings, Alfred James 1878–1959
Study for 'Going up the Canter'
oil on board 38.1 x 50.8
181

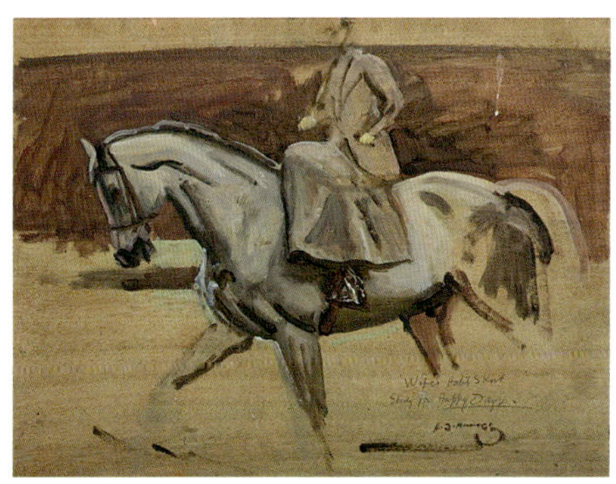

Munnings, Alfred James 1878–1959
Study for 'Happy Days'
oil on board 35.5 x 45.5
471

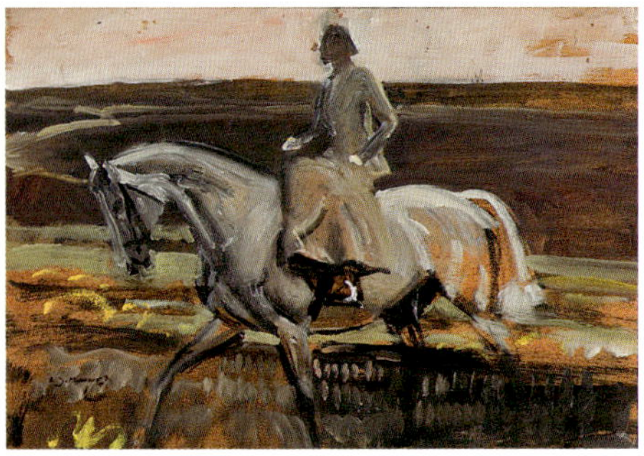

Munnings, Alfred James 1878–1959
Study for 'Lady Munnings Riding on Exmoor'
oil on panel 30.5 x 41
585

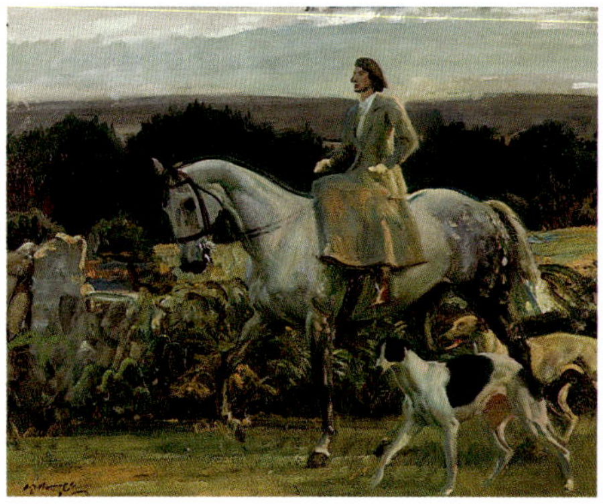

Munnings, Alfred James 1878–1959
Study for 'Lady Munnings Riding on Exmoor'
oil on canvas 48.3 x 58.4
663

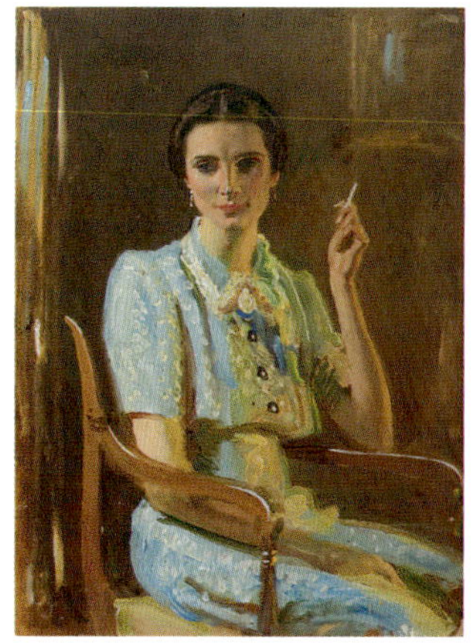

Munnings, Alfred James 1878–1959
Study for 'Miss Hancock' (recto)
oil on panel 35.6 x 25.4
552

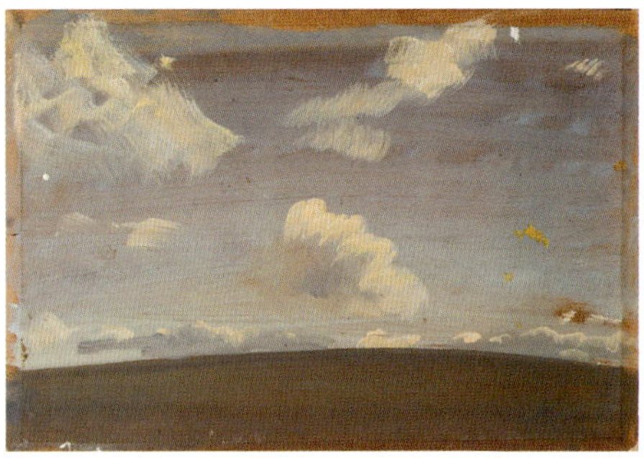

Munnings, Alfred James 1878–1959
Study of a Landscape (verso)
oil on panel 25.4 x 35.6
552A

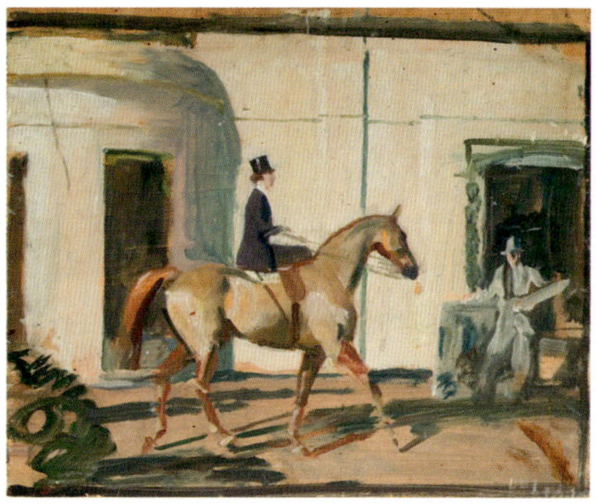

Munnings, Alfred James 1878–1959
Study for 'Our Mutual Friend the Horse' (recto)
oil on board 38 x 46
368

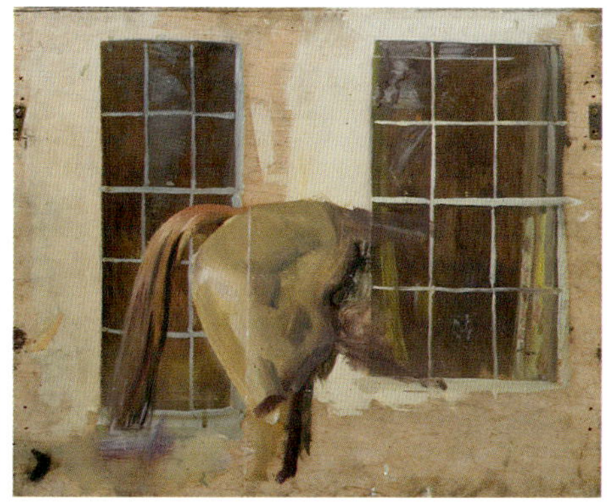

Munnings, Alfred James 1878–1959
Study (verso)
oil on board 38 x 46
368A

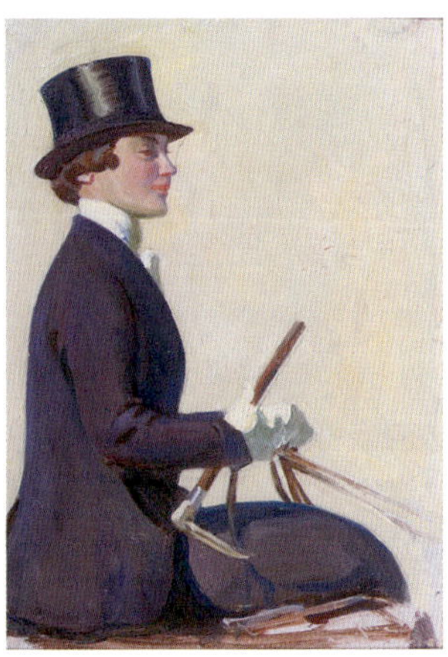

Munnings, Alfred James 1878–1959
Study for 'Our Mutual Friend the Horse'
oil on board 25 x 17
535

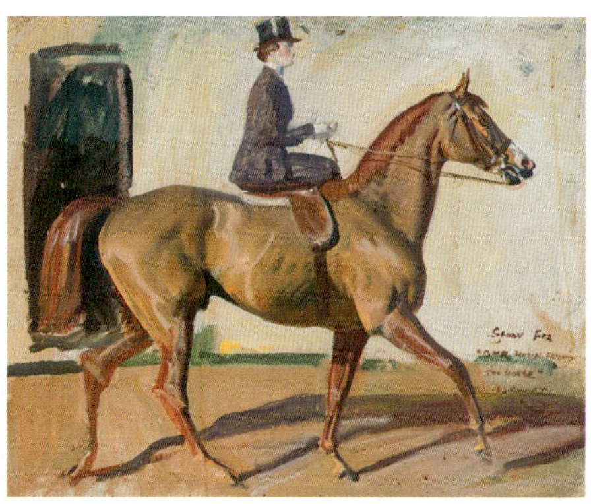

Munnings, Alfred James 1878–1959
Study for 'Our Mutual Friend the Horse', Lady Munnings on 'Rufus'
oil on board 51 x 61
467

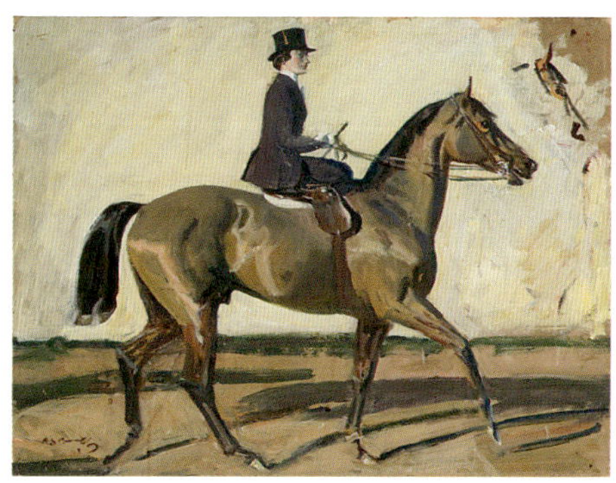

Munnings, Alfred James 1878–1959
Study for 'Our Mutual Friend the Horse', Lady Munnings Riding Side-Saddle
oil on board 46 x 58.5
440

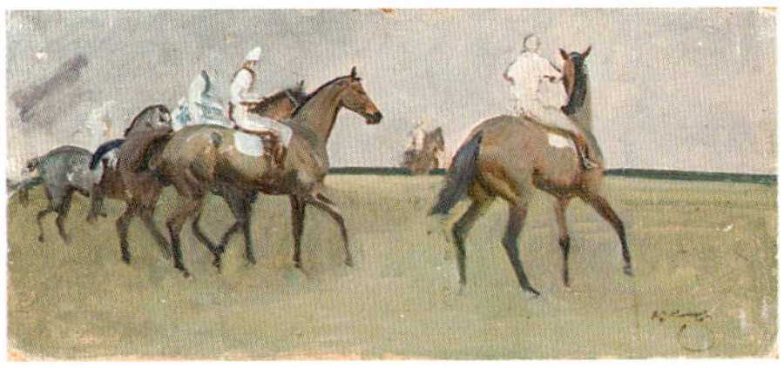

Munnings, Alfred James 1878–1959
Study for 'Start of a Steeplechase'
oil on board 21 x 45.1
399

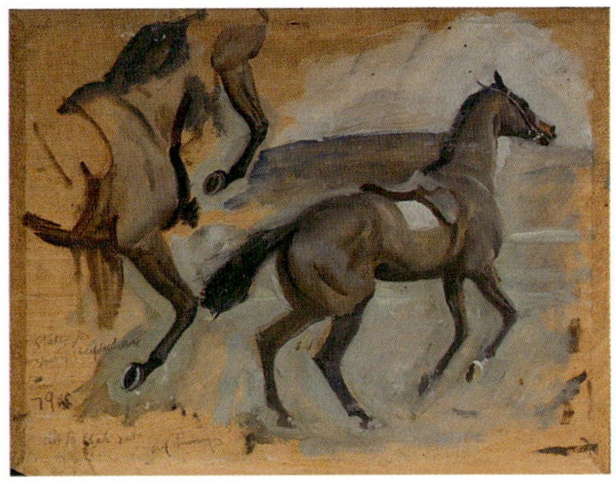

Munnings, Alfred James 1878–1959
Study for 'Start of a Steeplechase' (recto)
oil on panel 33 x 41.3
174

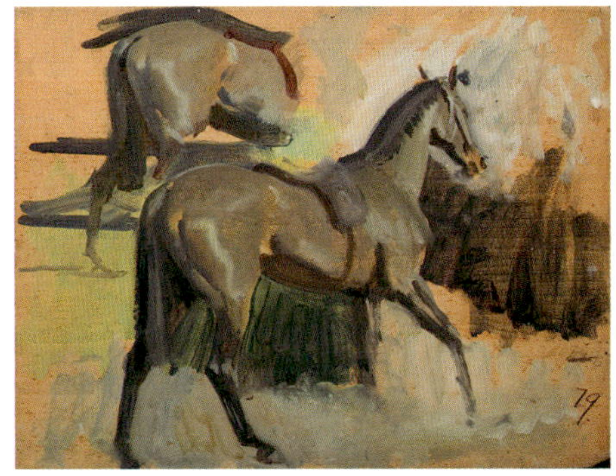

Munnings, Alfred James 1878–1959
Further Studies of Horses (verso)
oil on panel 33 x 41.3
174A

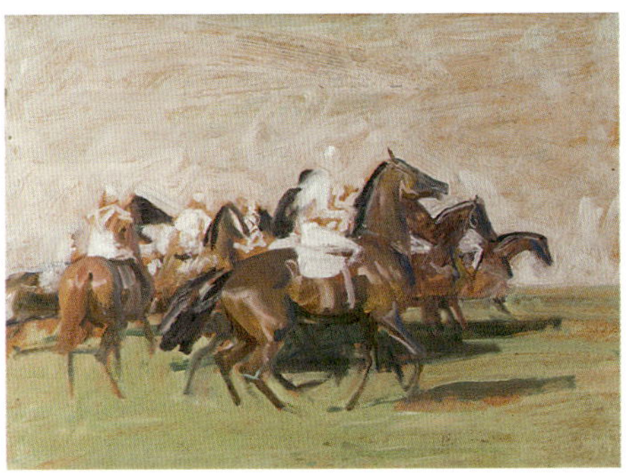

Munnings, Alfred James 1878–1959
Study for 'Starter's Orders'
oil on board 45.7 x 61
453

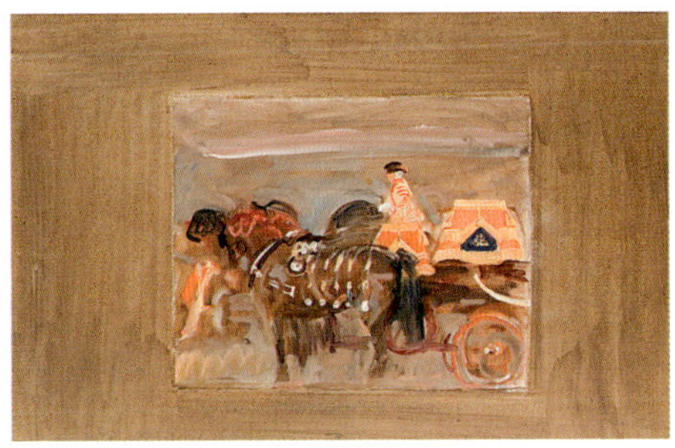

Munnings, Alfred James 1878–1959
Study for 'The Coronation'
oil on canvas 76.2 x 111.8
422

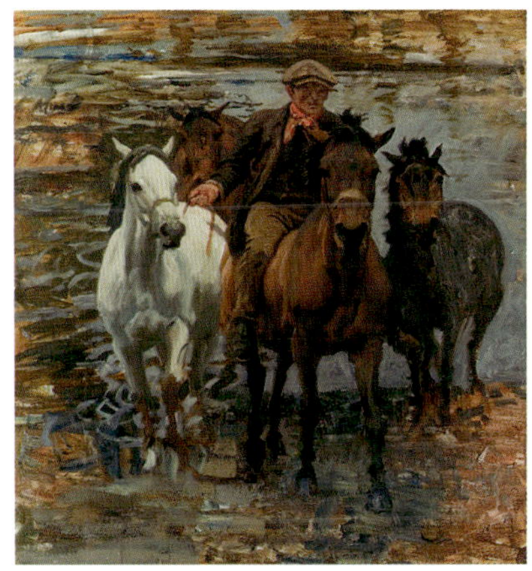

Munnings, Alfred James 1878–1959
Study for 'The Ford'
oil on canvas 114.3 x 104.1
429

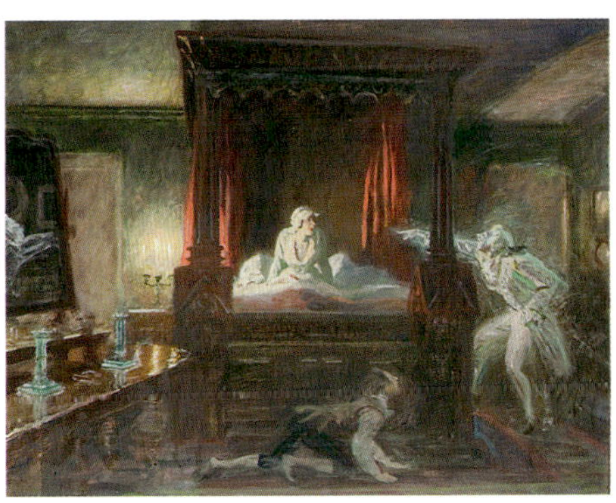

Munnings, Alfred James 1878–1959
Study for 'The Haunted House'
oil on canvas 66 x 81.3
284

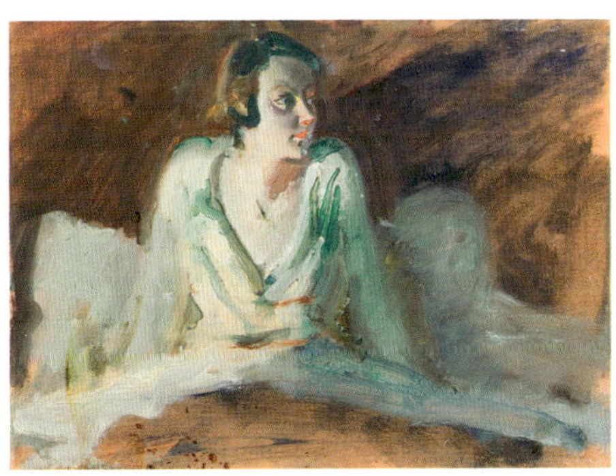

Munnings, Alfred James 1878–1959
Study for 'The Haunted House'
oil on panel 29.8 x 40.6
296

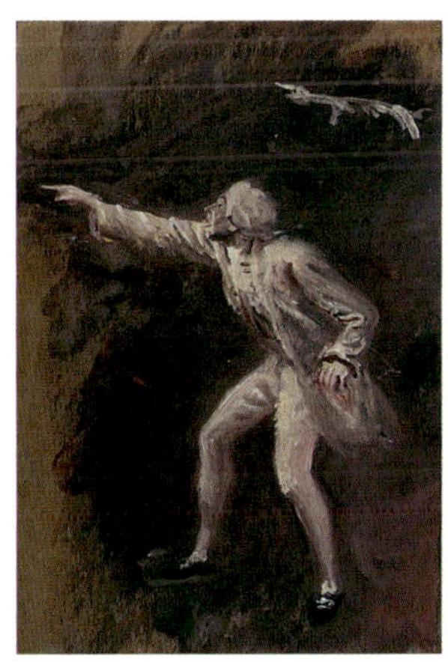

Munnings, Alfred James 1878–1959
Study for 'The Haunted House'
oil on board 40.6 x 27.9
320

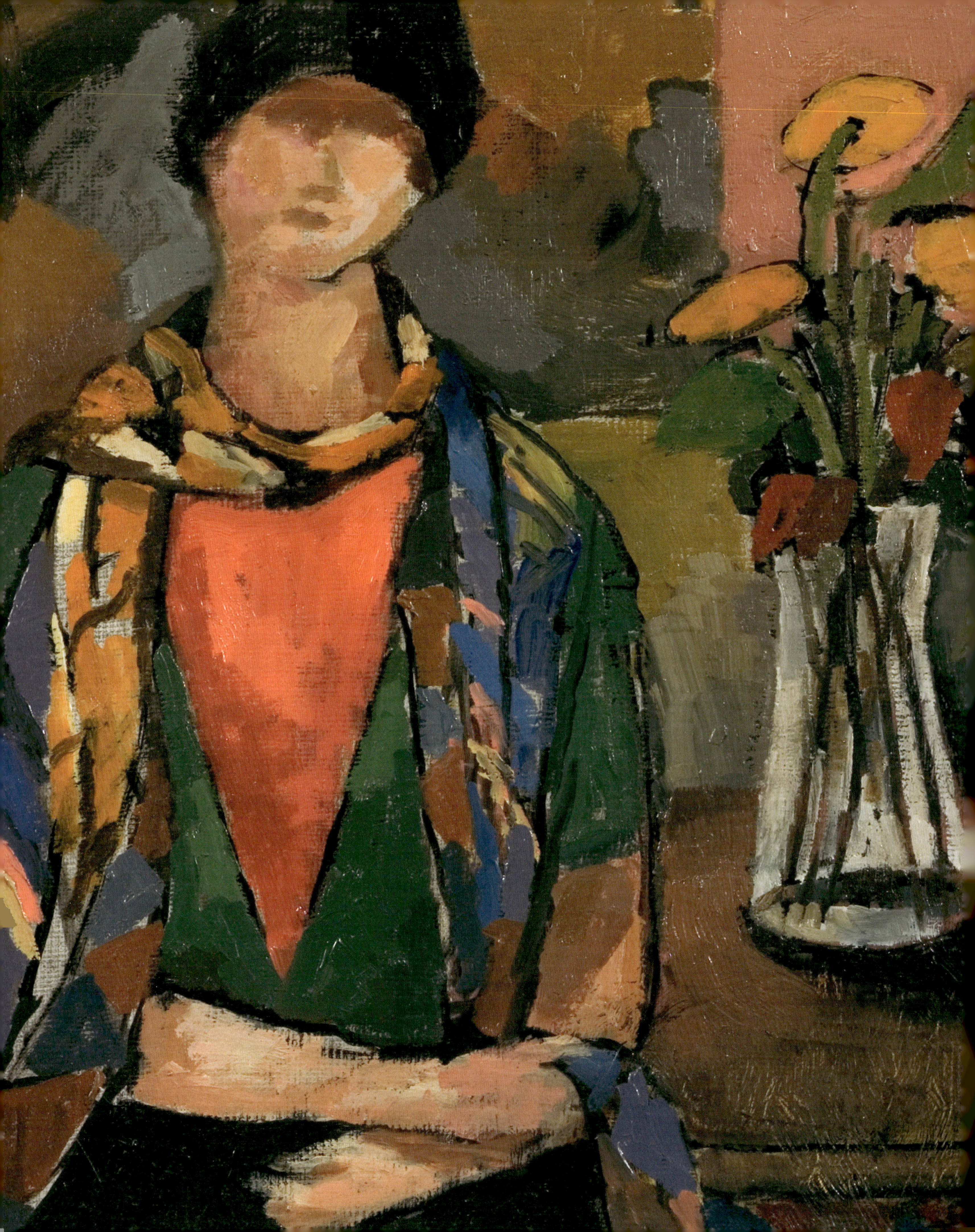

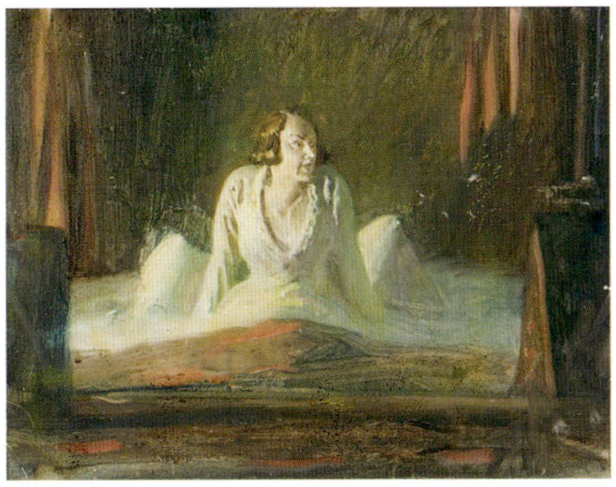

Munnings, Alfred James 1878–1959
Study for 'The Haunted House'
oil on board 35.6 x 45.1
352

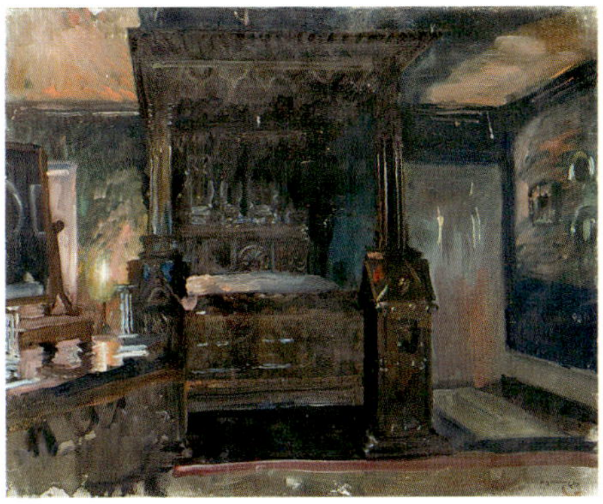

Munnings, Alfred James 1878–1959
Study for 'The Haunted House'
oil on canvas 50.8 x 61
486

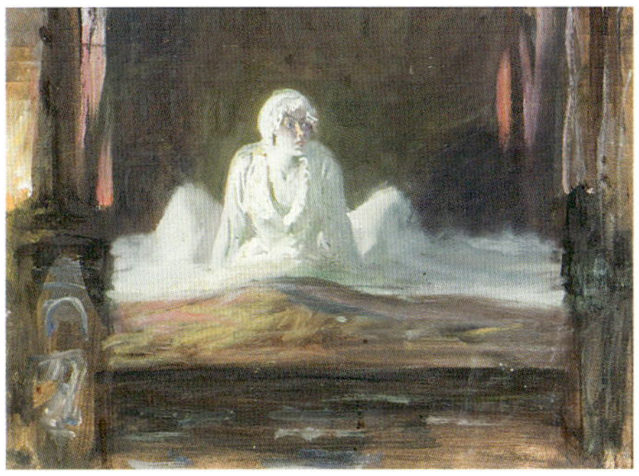

Munnings, Alfred James 1878–1959
Study for 'The Haunted House'
oil on panel 30.5 x 40.6
579

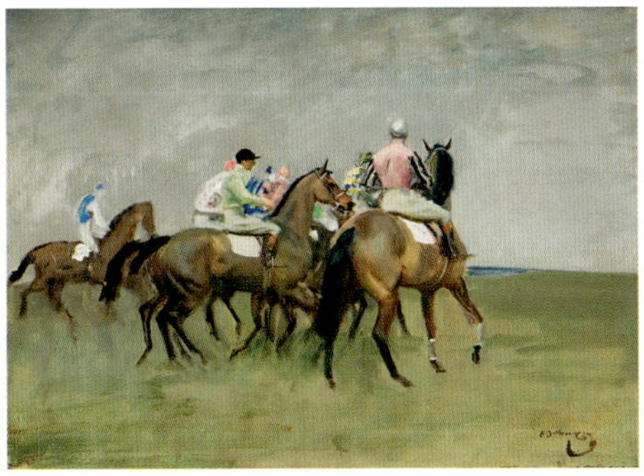

Munnings, Alfred James 1878–1959
Study for 'The Start'
oil on board 45.1 x 60.3
133

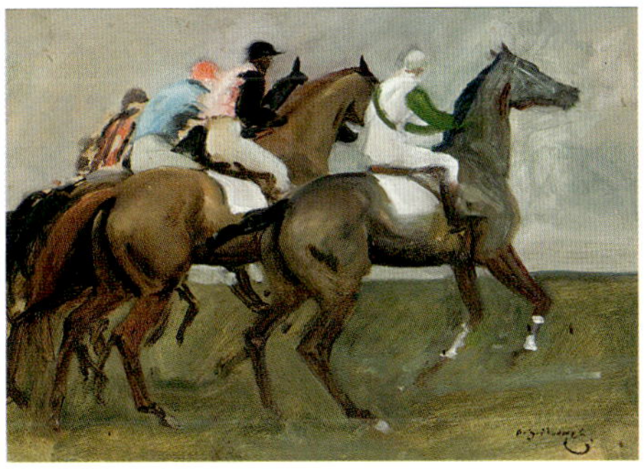

Munnings, Alfred James 1878–1959
Study for 'The Start'
oil on board 24.8 x 33
175

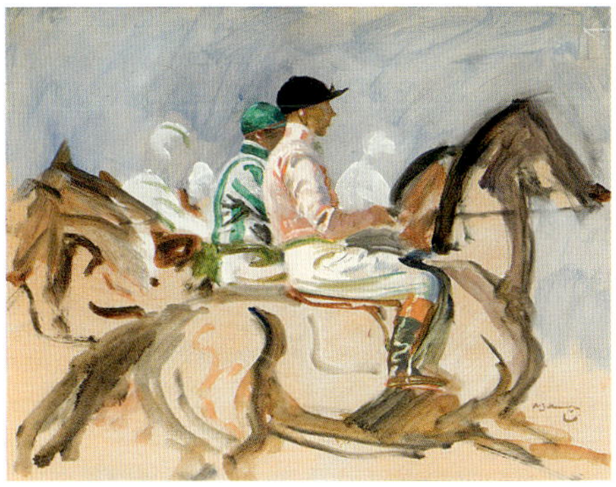

Munnings, Alfred James 1878–1959
Study for 'The Start'
oil on board 40.6 x 50.8
248

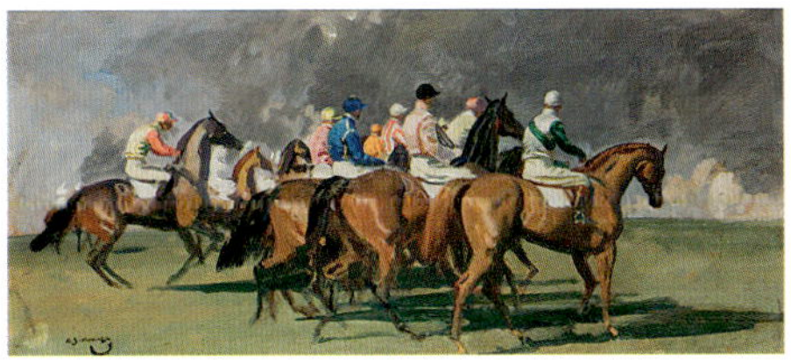

Munnings, Alfred James 1878–1959
Study for 'The Start at Newmarket'
oil on board 29.2 x 60.3
21

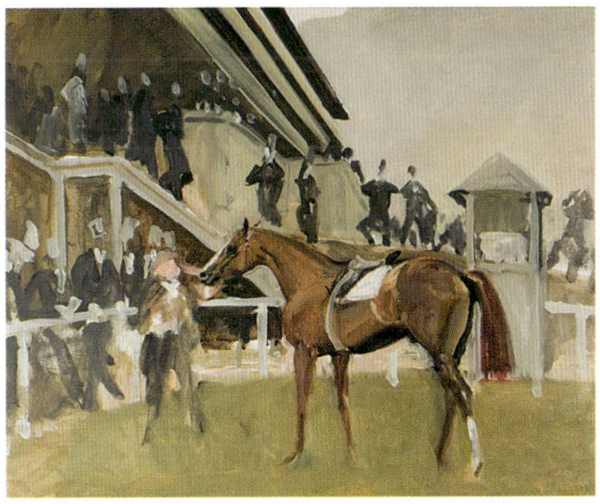

Munnings, Alfred James 1878–1959
Study for 'The Unsaddling Enclosure, Epsom'
oil on board 50.8 x 61
11

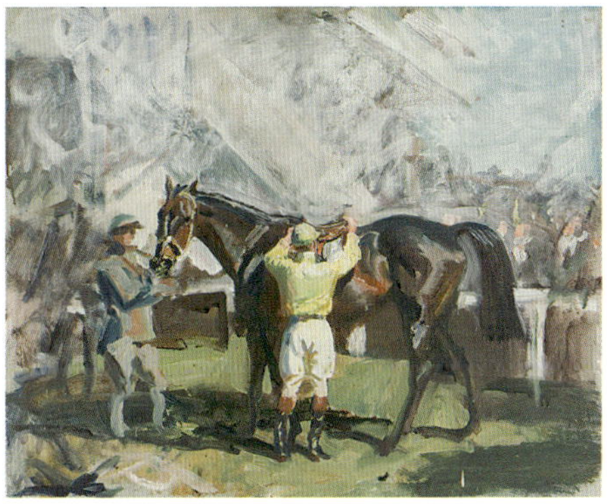

Munnings, Alfred James 1878–1959
Study for 'The Unsaddling Enclosure, Epsom'
oil on canvas 63.5 x 76.2
338

Facing page: Ayers, Duffy, b.1919, *Scarves* (detail), Fry Art Gallery, (p. 228)

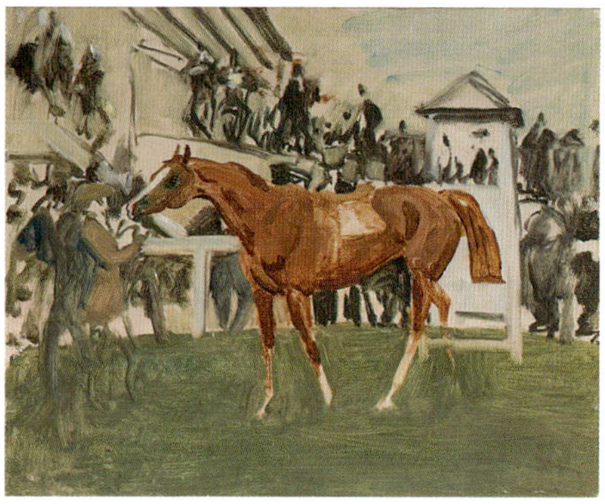

Munnings, Alfred James 1878–1959
Study for 'The Unsaddling Enclosure, Epsom'
oil on board 48.3 x 61
459

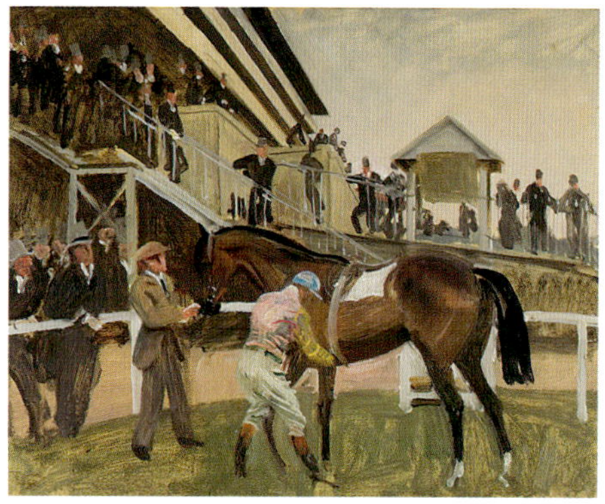

Munnings, Alfred James 1878–1959
Study for 'The Unsaddling Enclosure, Epsom'
oil on board 50.8 x 61
462

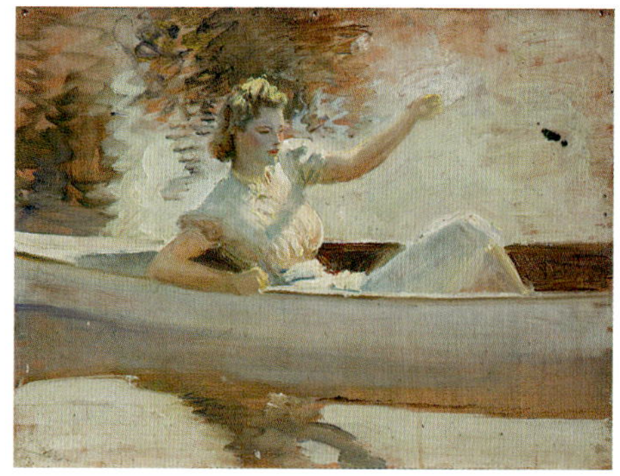

Munnings, Alfred James 1878–1959
Study for 'The White Canoe'
oil on panel 36 x 46
293

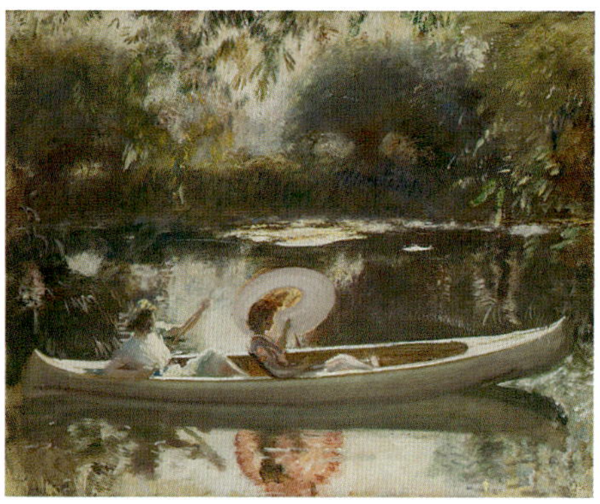

Munnings, Alfred James 1878–1959
Study for 'The White Canoe'
oil on canvas 63.5 x 76
330

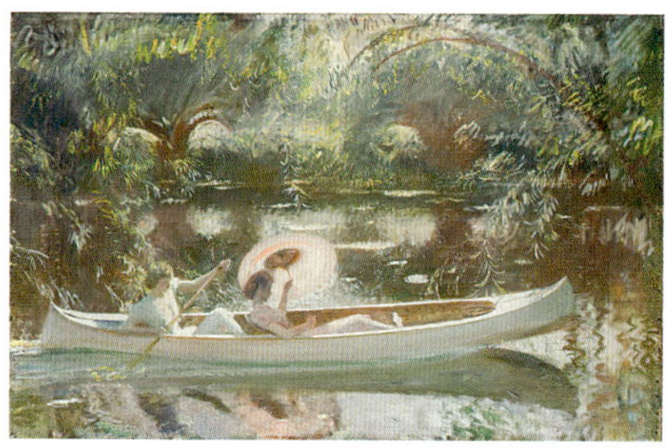

Munnings, Alfred James 1878–1959
Study for 'The White Canoe'
oil on canvas 81.5 x 123
428

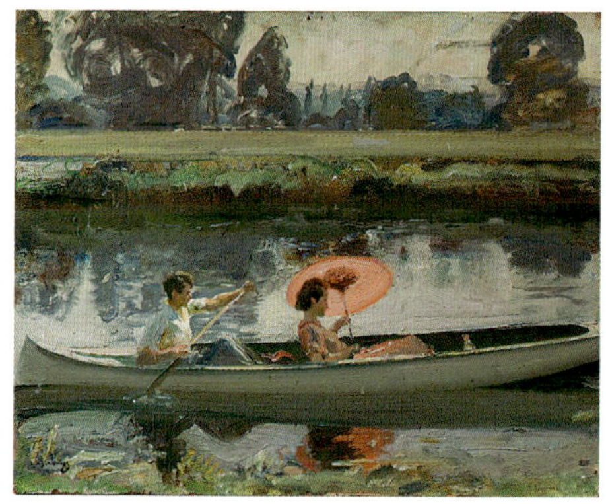

Munnings, Alfred James 1878–1959
Study for 'The White Canoe'
oil on board 51 x 61
482

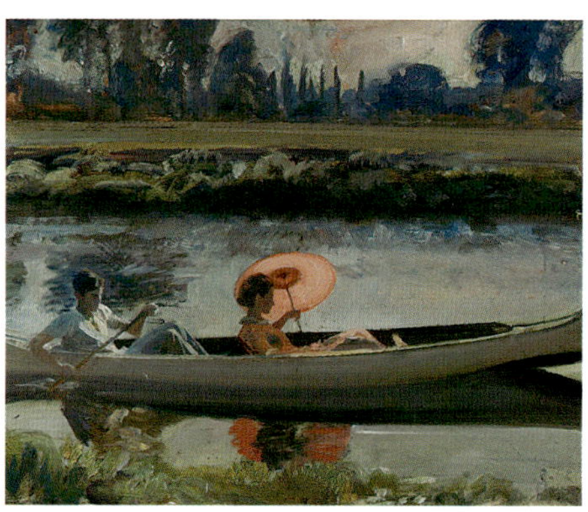

Munnings, Alfred James 1878–1959
Study for 'The White Canoe'
oil on board 51 x 61
483

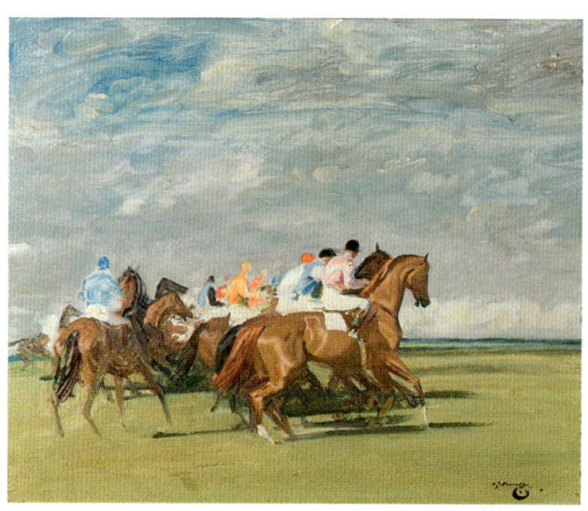

Munnings, Alfred James 1878–1959
Study for 'Under Starter's Orders'
oil on canvas 50.8 x 61
367

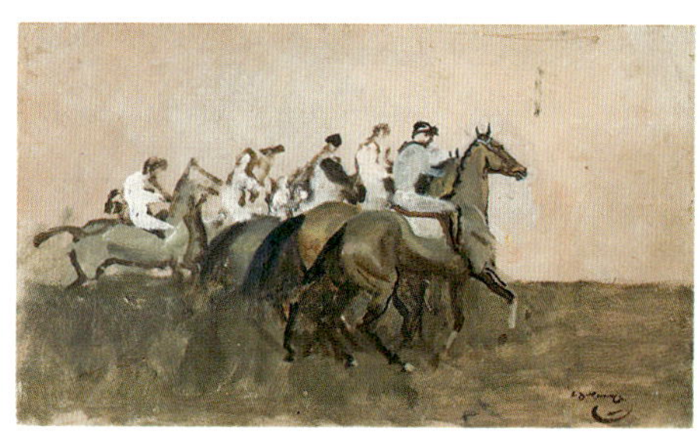

Munnings, Alfred James 1878–1959
Study for 'Under Starter's Orders'
oil on board 28.6 x 47.6
480

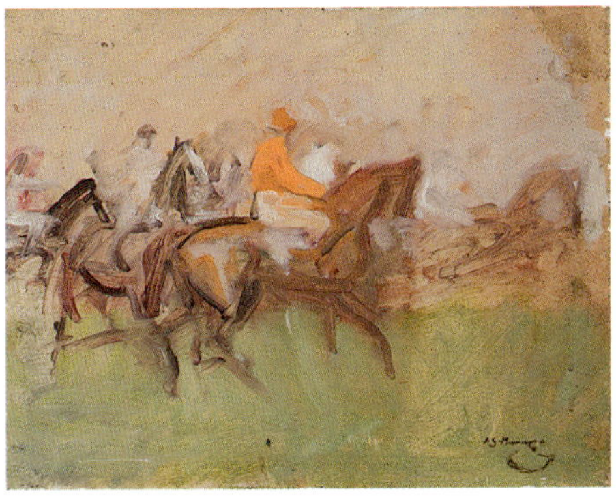

Munnings, Alfred James 1878–1959
Study for 'Under Starter's Orders'
oil on board 30.5 x 38.1
605

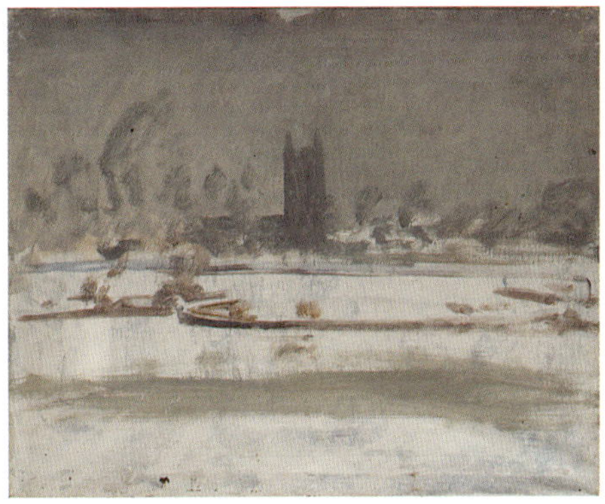

Munnings, Alfred James 1878–1959
Study of a Barge on the Stour at Dedham in Snow
oil on canvas 50.8 x 61
512

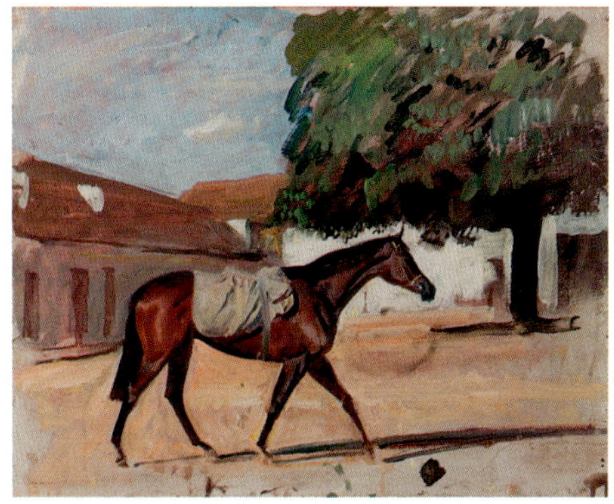

Munnings, Alfred James 1878–1959
Study of a Bay Filly in a Newmarket Yard
oil on board 50.8 x 61
123

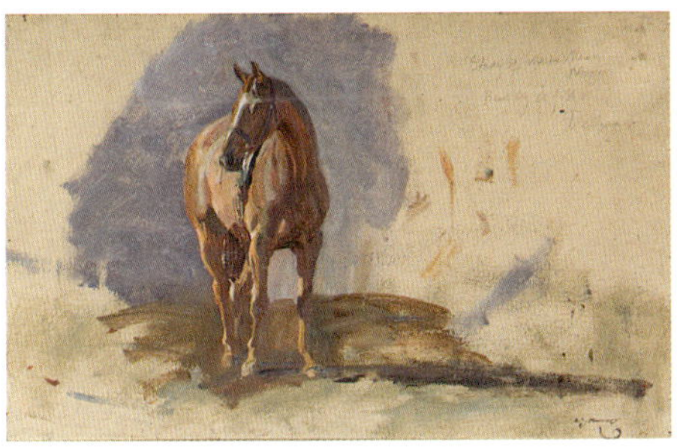

Munnings, Alfred James 1878–1959
Study of a Bay Horse, 'Master', Bred by the Artist at Dedham
oil on canvas 35.6 x 53.3
292

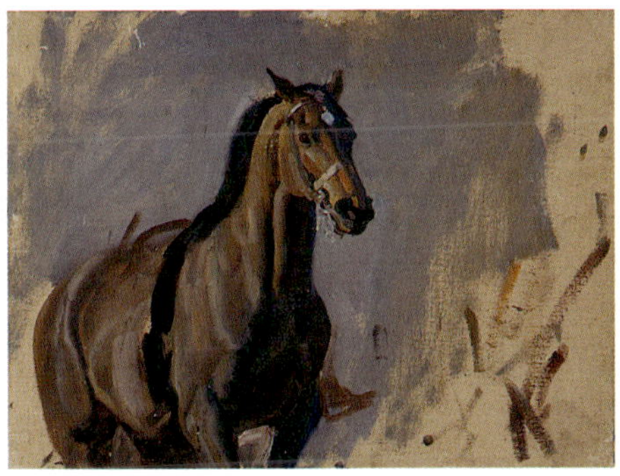

Munnings, Alfred James 1878–1959
Study of a Bay Hunter
oil on board 34.9 x 45.7
177

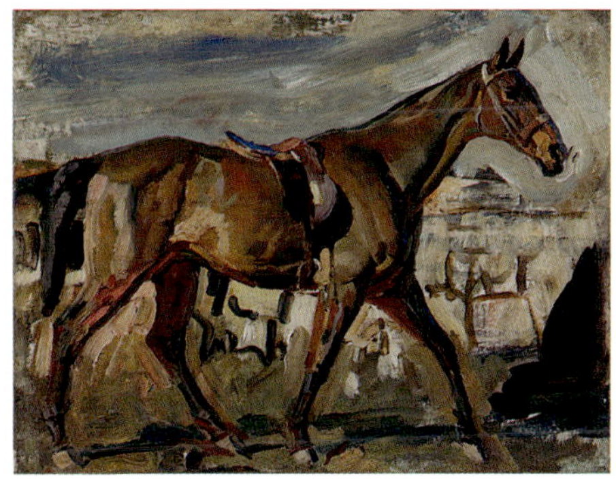

Munnings, Alfred James 1878–1959
Study of a Bay Hunter
oil on canvas 35.6 x 45.7
402

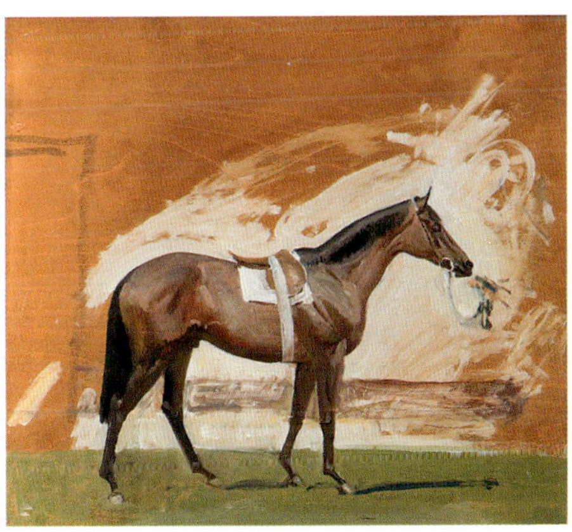

Munnings, Alfred James 1878–1959
Study of a Bay Racehorse
oil on board 45.7 x 50.8
106

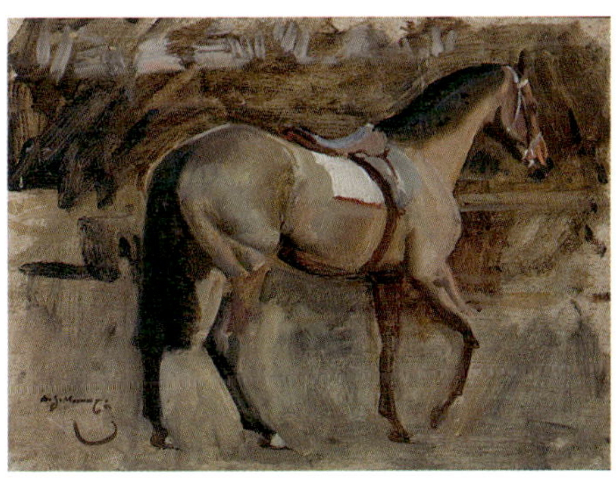

Munnings, Alfred James 1878–1959
Study of a Bay Racehorse
oil on panel 24.8 x 33
183

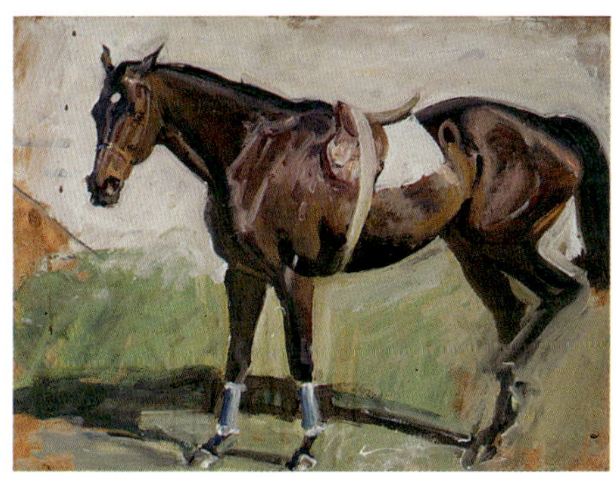

Munnings, Alfred James 1878–1959
Study of a Bay Racehorse
oil on board 38.1 x 50.2
294

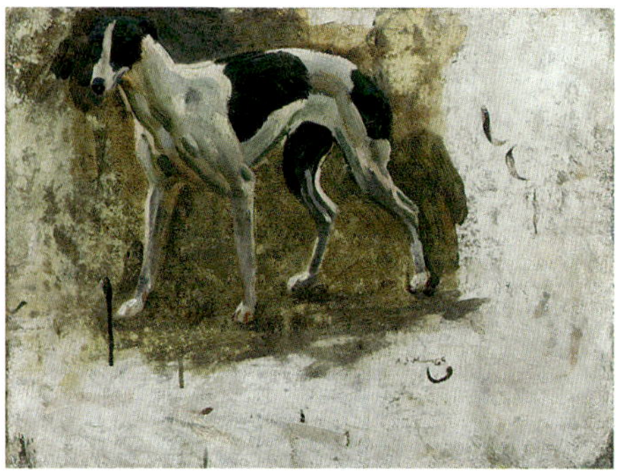

Munnings, Alfred James 1878–1959
Study of a Black and White Greyhound
oil on canvas 35.6 x 45.7
468

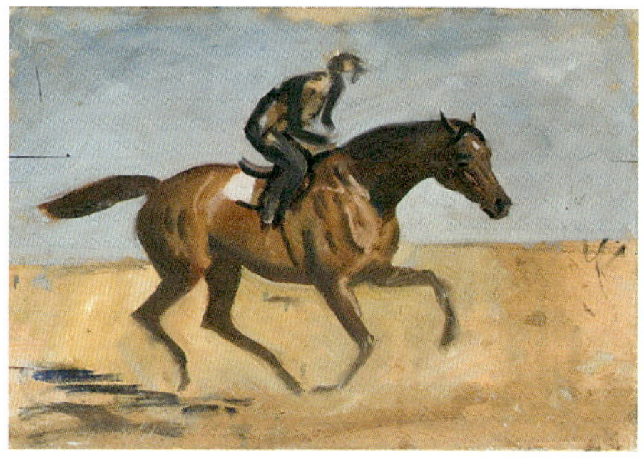

Munnings, Alfred James 1878–1959
Study of a Boy Exercising a Racehorse
oil on board 29.2 x 40.6
128

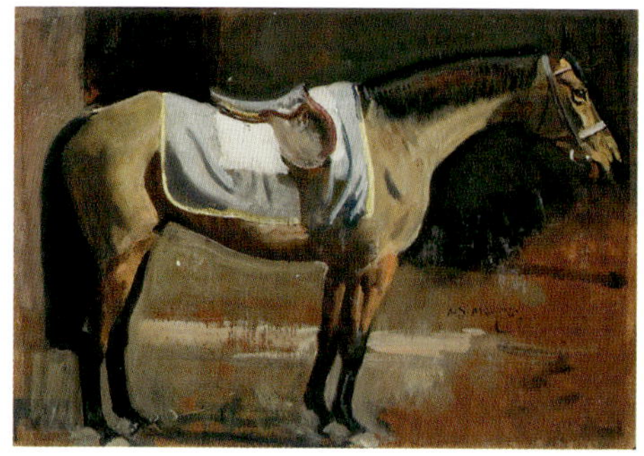

Munnings, Alfred James 1878–1959
Study of a Chaser
oil on board 25.4 x 35.6
67

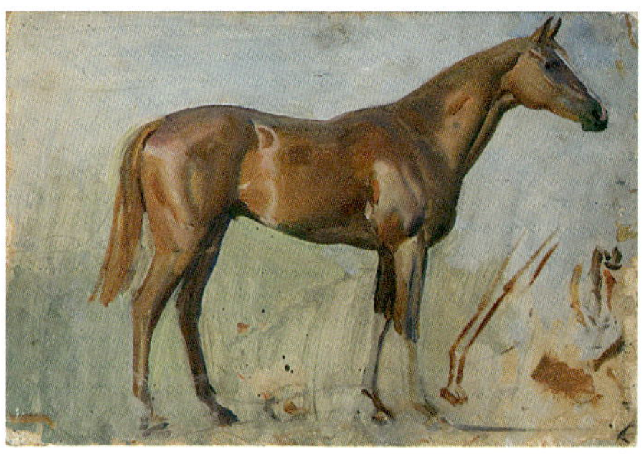

Munnings, Alfred James 1878–1959
Study of a Chestnut Horse
oil on board 39.4 x 56.5
185

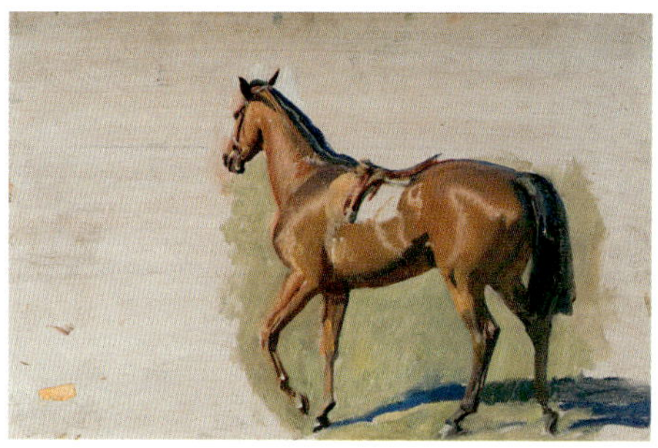

Munnings, Alfred James 1878–1959
Study of a Chestnut Racehorse from the Back
oil on board 41.3 x 61
370

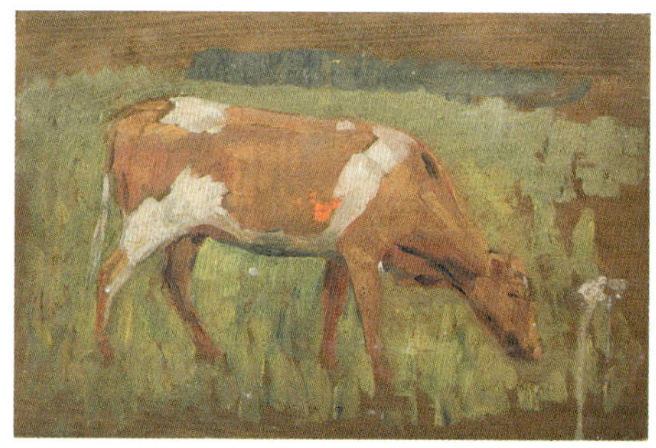

Munnings, Alfred James 1878–1959
Study of a Cow Grazing
oil on board 20.3 x 29.2
539

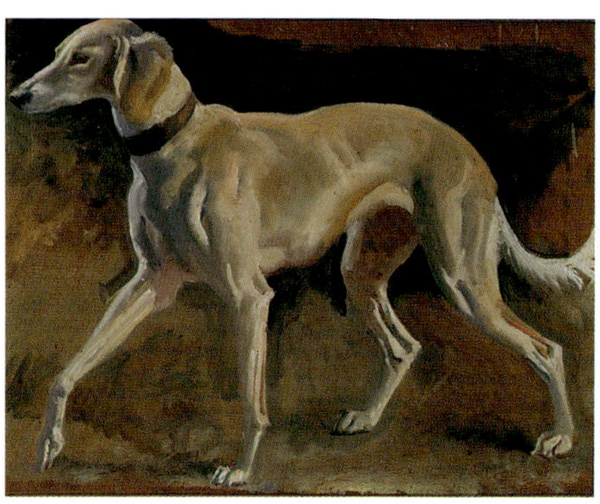

Munnings, Alfred James 1878–1959
Study of a Dog for Lady Munnings on Grey Hunter
oil on board 40.6 x 50.8
197

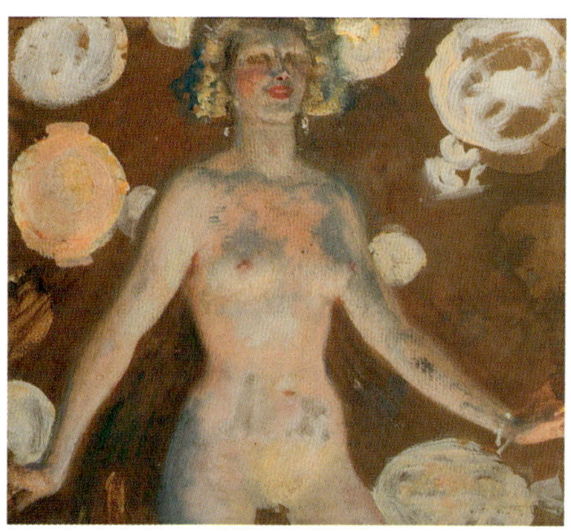

Munnings, Alfred James 1878–1959
Study of a Female Nude
oil on board 27.9 x 30.5
302

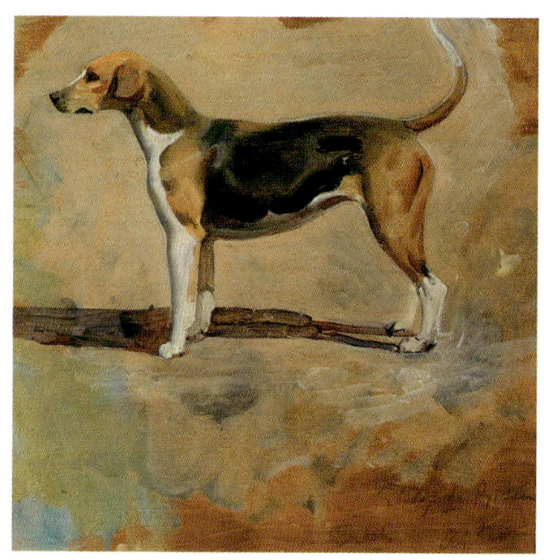

Munnings, Alfred James 1878–1959
Study of a Foxhound, 'Pytchley'
oil on board 37 x 37 (E)
47

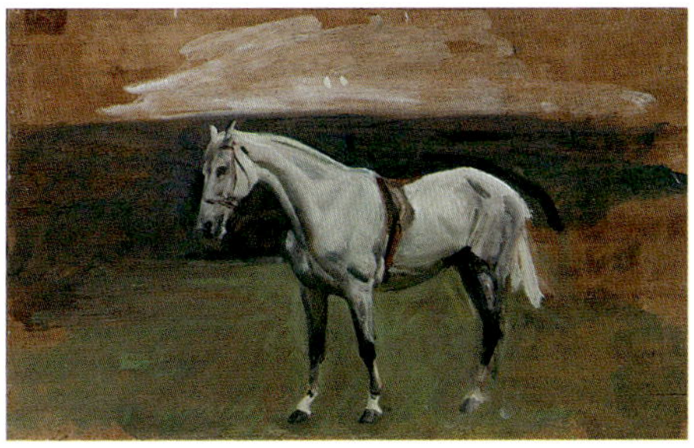

Munnings, Alfred James 1878–1959
Study of a Grey Hunter
oil on board 36.2 x 55.9
171

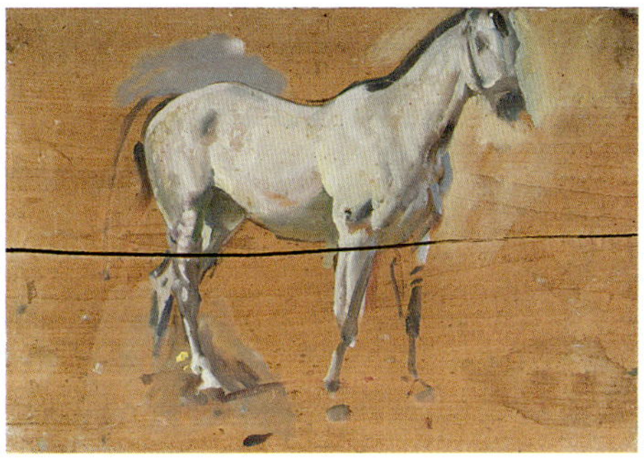

Munnings, Alfred James 1878–1959
Study of a Grey Hunter
oil on panel 25.4 x 35.6
553

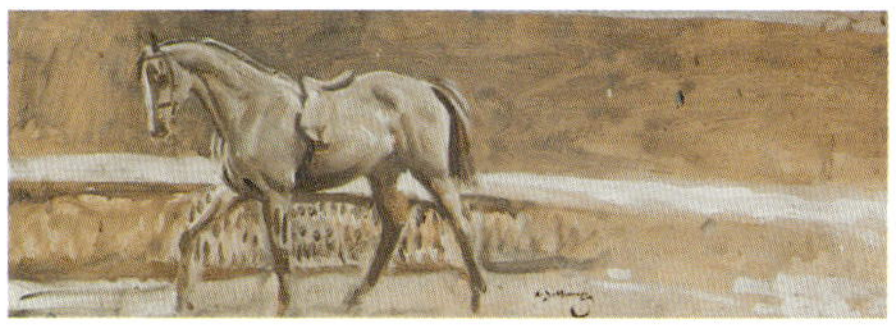

Munnings, Alfred James 1878–1959
Study of a Grey Hunter in a Landscape
oil on board 24.5 x 66.5
277

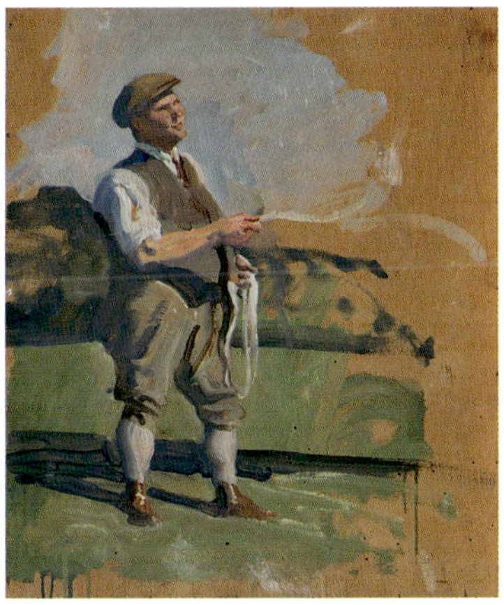

Munnings, Alfred James 1878–1959
Study of a Groom
oil on board 43.2 x 35.6
591

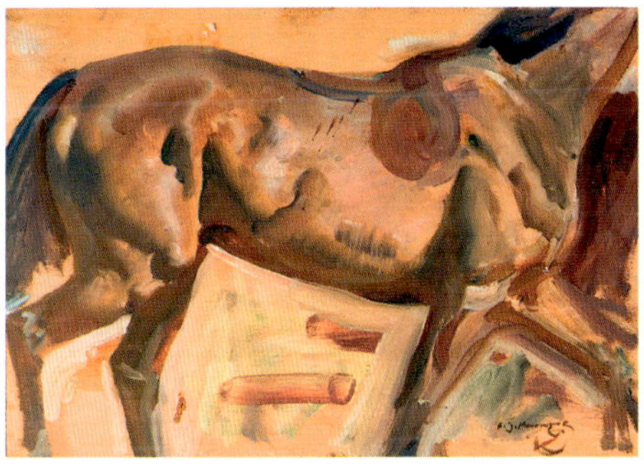

Munnings, Alfred James 1878–1959
Study of a Horse
oil on board 29.2 x 40.6
282

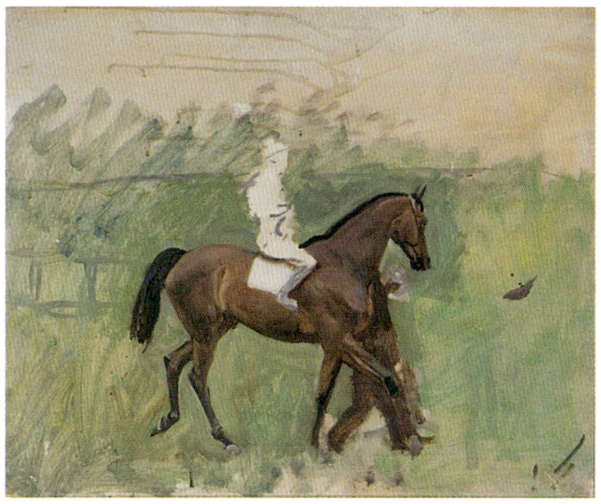

Munnings, Alfred James 1878–1959
Study of a Horse and Jockey
oil on board 50.8 x 61
461

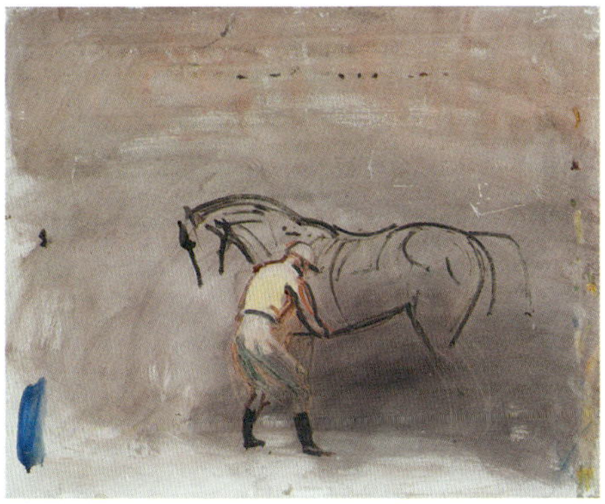

Munnings, Alfred James 1878–1959
Study of a Horse and Jockey
oil on board 50.8 x 61
511

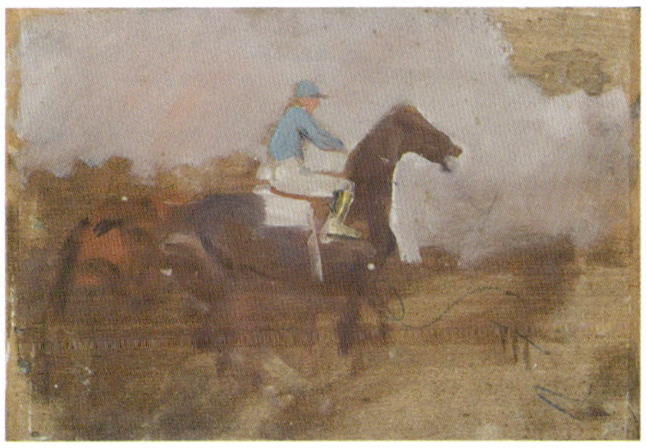

Munnings, Alfred James 1878–1959
Study of a Horse and Jockey (recto)
oil on panel 19.7 x 27.9 (E)
540

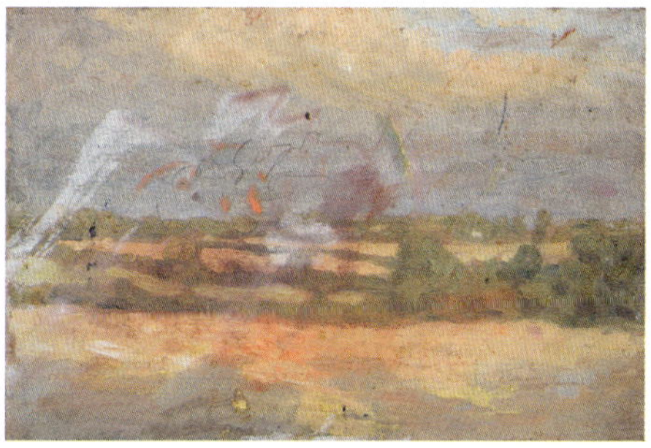

Munnings, Alfred James 1878–1959
A Landscape Study (verso)
oil on panel 19.7 x 27.9 (E)
540A

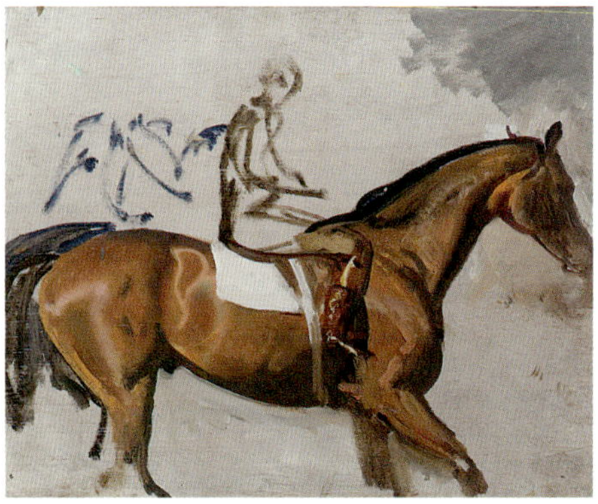

Munnings, Alfred James 1878–1959
Study of a Horse and Rider
oil on board 48.3 x 61
460

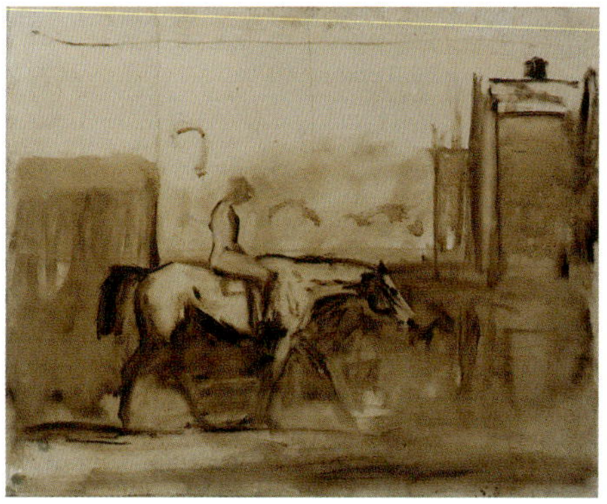

Munnings, Alfred James 1878–1959
Study of a Horse and Rider
oil on canvas 50.8 x 61
510

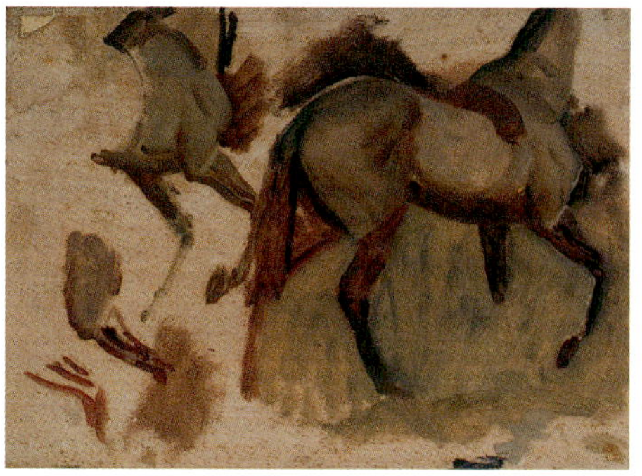

Munnings, Alfred James 1878–1959
Study of a Horse with Anatomical Parts (recto)
oil on panel 33 x 42.5
173

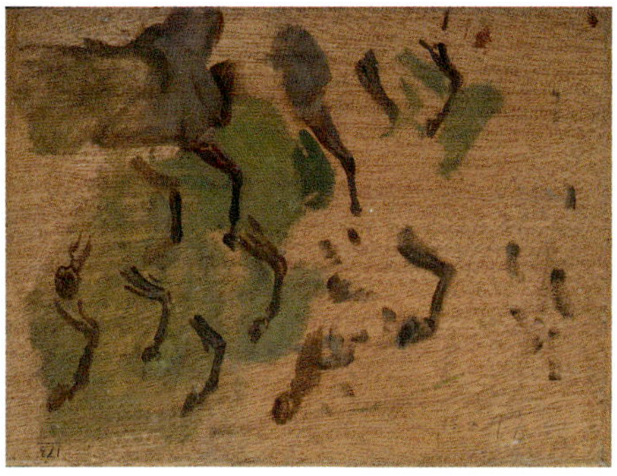

Munnings, Alfred James 1878–1959
Studies of Horses' Limbs (verso)
oil on panel 33 x 42.5
173A

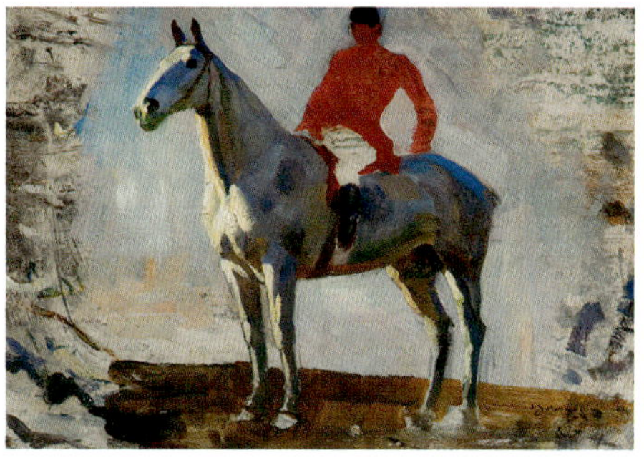

Munnings, Alfred James 1878–1959
Study of a Horse with Huntsman up
oil on canvas 30.5 x 40.6
261

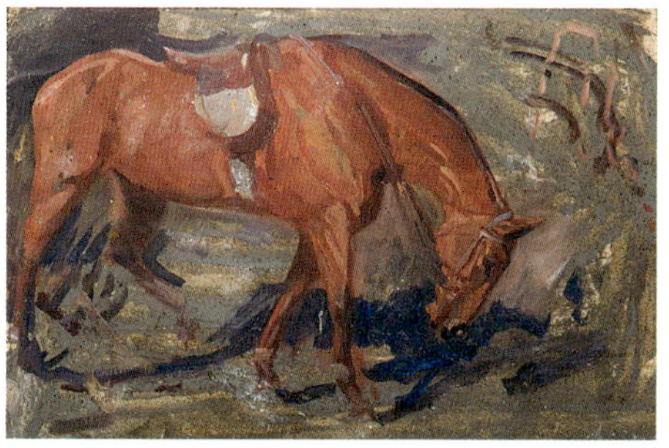

Munnings, Alfred James 1878–1959
Study of a Hunter
oil on board 34.9 x 50.8
351

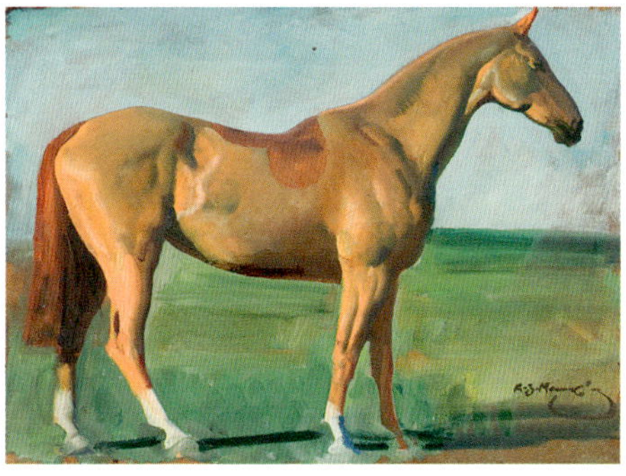

Munnings, Alfred James 1878–1959
Study of a Hunter
oil on panel 30.5 x 40.6
578

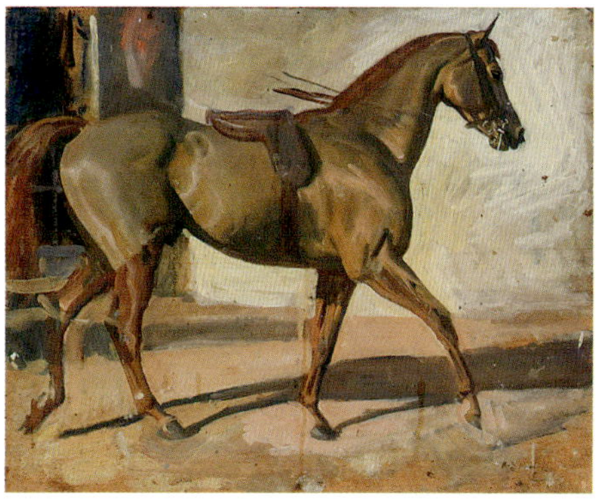

Munnings, Alfred James 1878–1959
Study of a Hunter 'Rufus'
oil on board 51 x 61
446

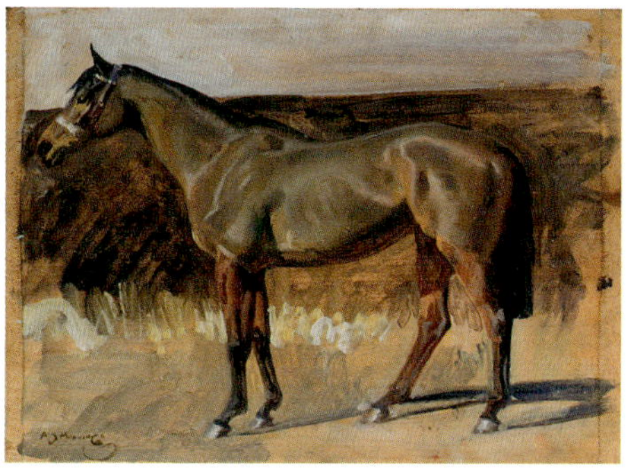

Munnings, Alfred James 1878–1959
Study of a Hunter Mare (recto)
oil on panel 30.5 x 40.6 (E)
72

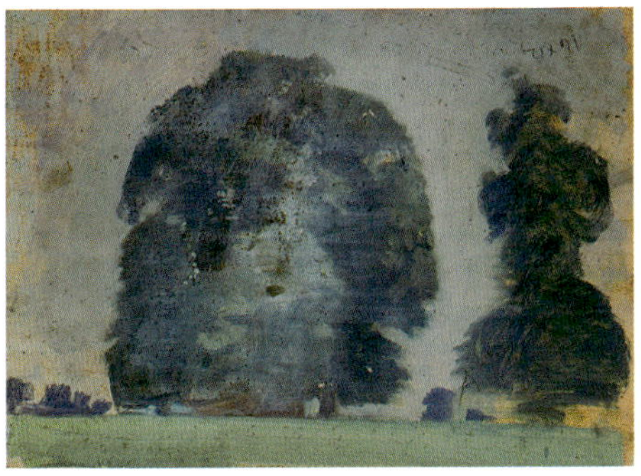

Munnings, Alfred James 1878–1959
Study of Trees (verso)
oil on panel 30.5 x 40.6 (E)
72A

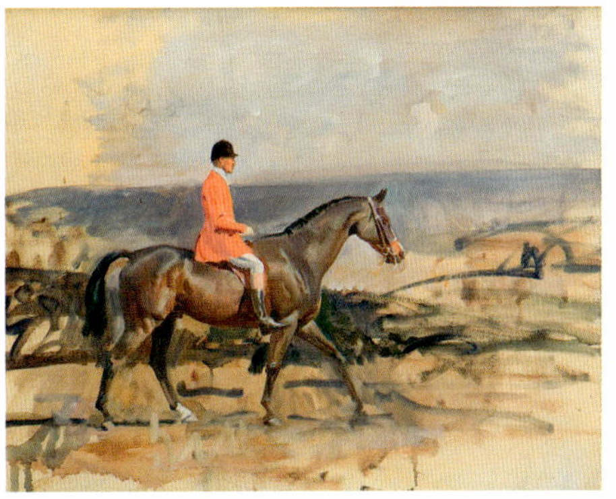

Munnings, Alfred James 1878–1959
Study of a Huntsman and a Bay Mare
oil on canvas 58.4 x 71.1
327

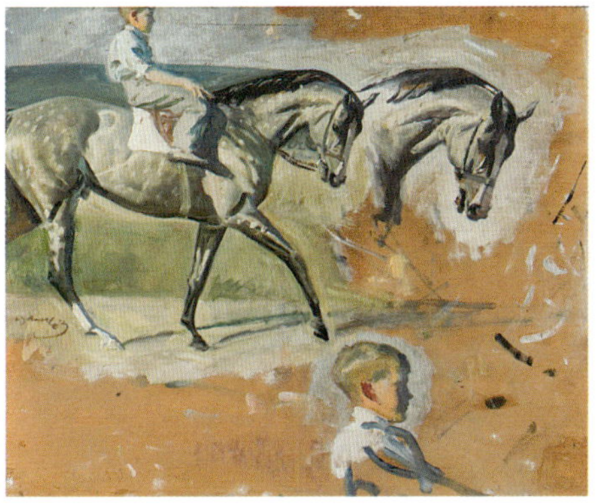

Munnings, Alfred James 1878–1959
Study of a Lad and a Two-Year-Old Racehorse
oil on board 50.8 x 61
126

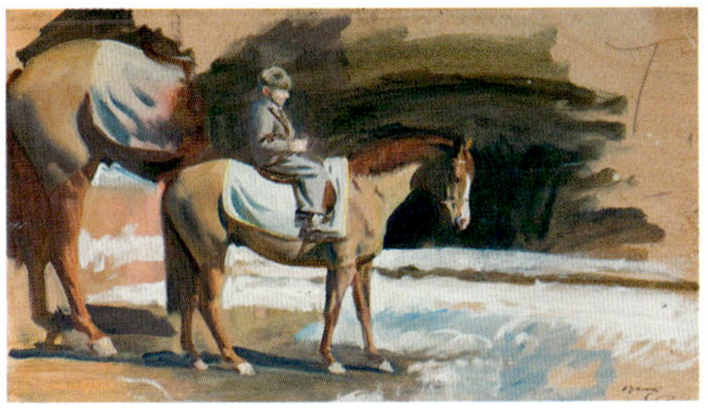

Munnings, Alfred James 1878–1959
Study of a Lad on a Pony
oil on board 35.6 x 61
130

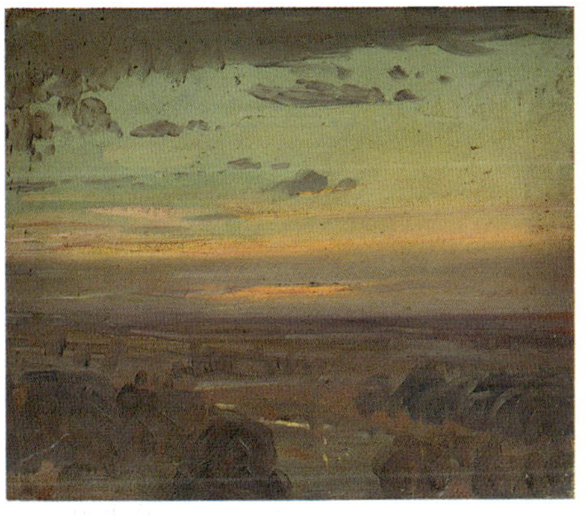

Munnings, Alfred James 1878–1959
Study of a Landscape at Sunset
oil on canvas 31 x 36
576

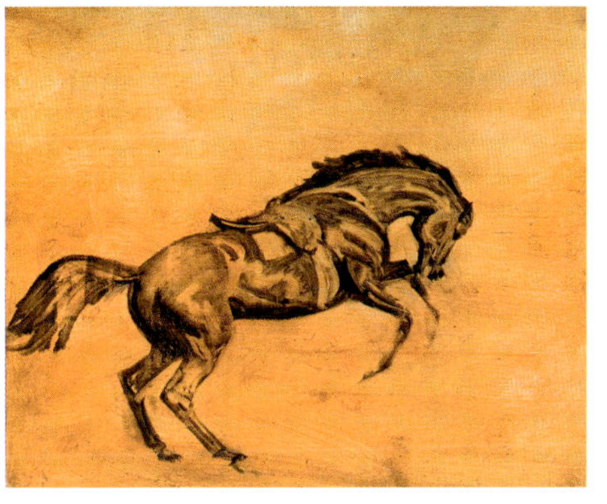

Munnings, Alfred James 1878–1959
Study of a Leaping Horse
oil on panel 50.8 x 60.3
463

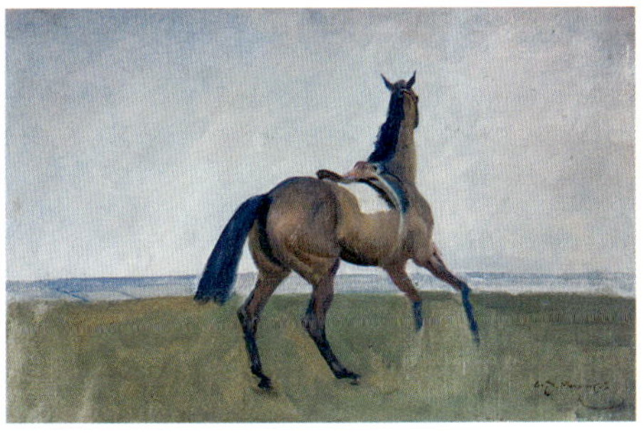

Munnings, Alfred James 1878–1959
Study of a Loose Horse
oil on canvas 26.7 x 40.6
182

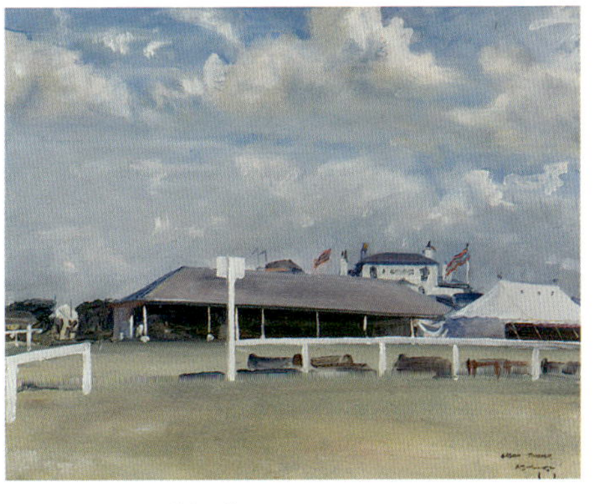

Munnings, Alfred James 1878–1959
Study of a Paddock at Epsom
oil on board 50.8 x 61
516

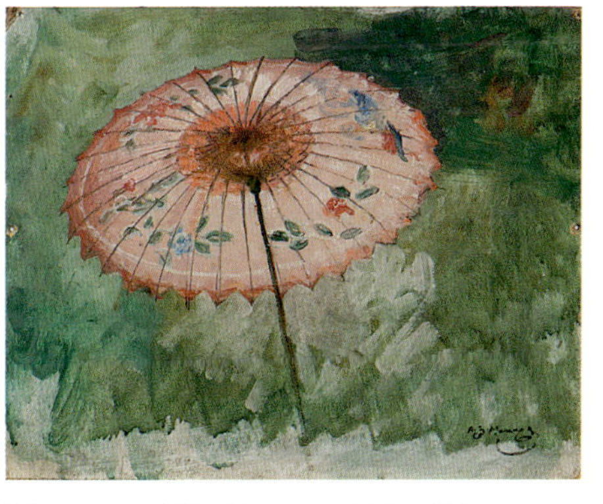

Munnings, Alfred James 1878–1959
Study of a Parasol, possibly for 'The White Canoe'
oil on board 33 x 38
300

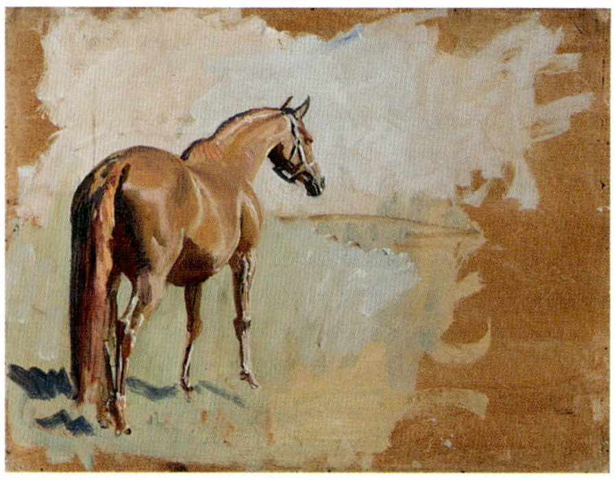

Munnings, Alfred James 1878–1959
Study of a Racehorse
oil on panel 35.6 x 45.7
180

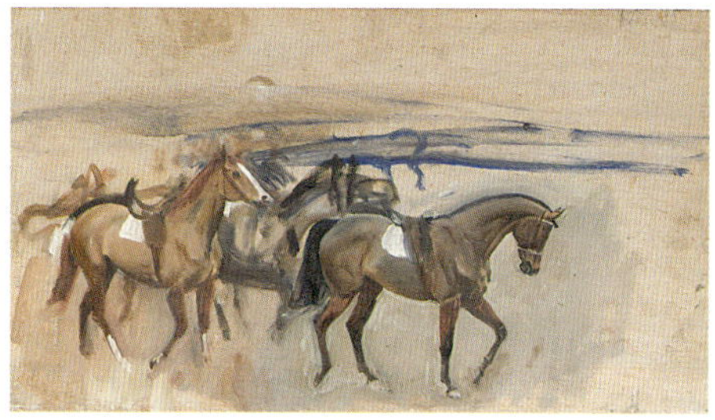

Munnings, Alfred James 1878–1959
Study of a Racehorse
oil on board 35.6 x 61
290

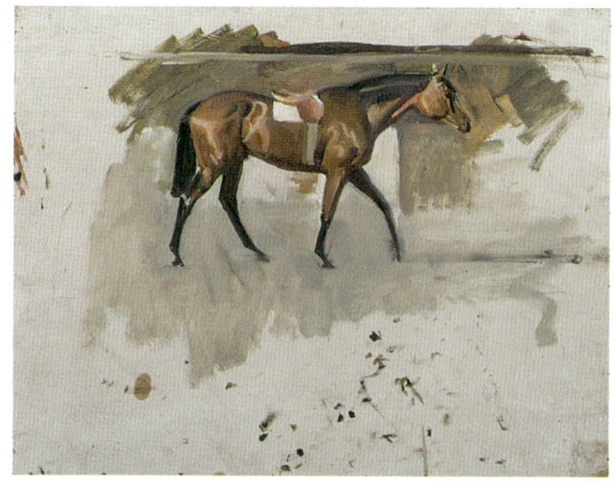

Munnings, Alfred James 1878–1959
Study of a Racehorse
oil on board 40.6 x 50.8
379

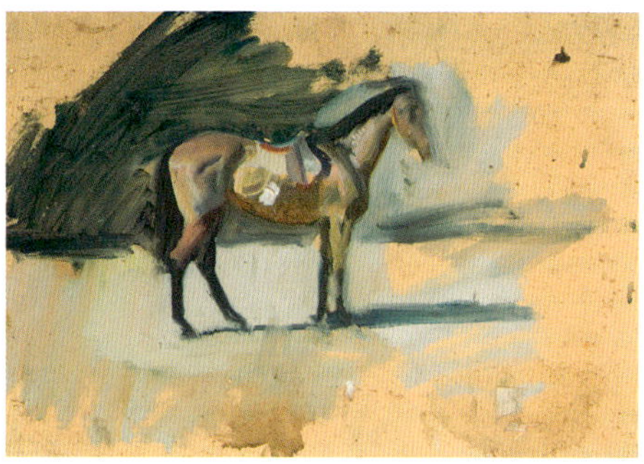

Munnings, Alfred James 1878–1959
Study of a Racehorse
oil on board 25.4 x 35.6
615

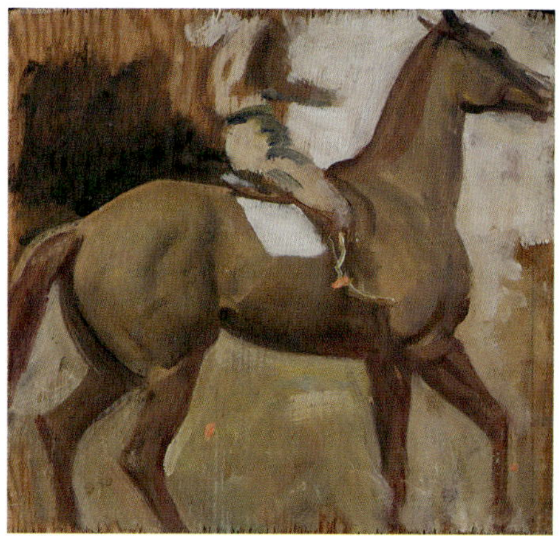

Munnings, Alfred James 1878–1959
Study of a Racehorse and Rider
oil on board 27.3 x 28.6
533

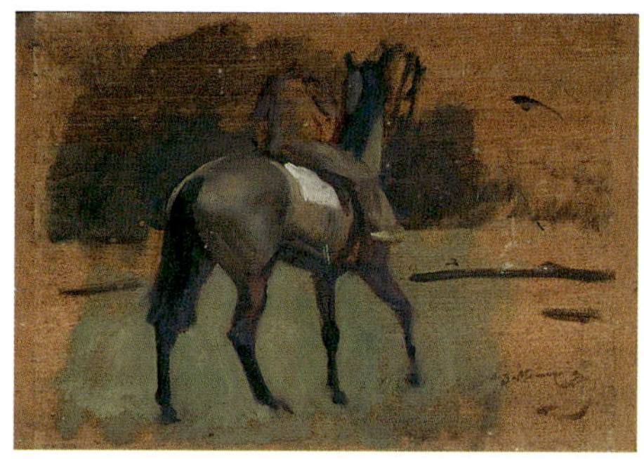

Munnings, Alfred James 1878–1959
Study of a Racehorse from the Back (recto)
oil on panel 24.8 x 33
564

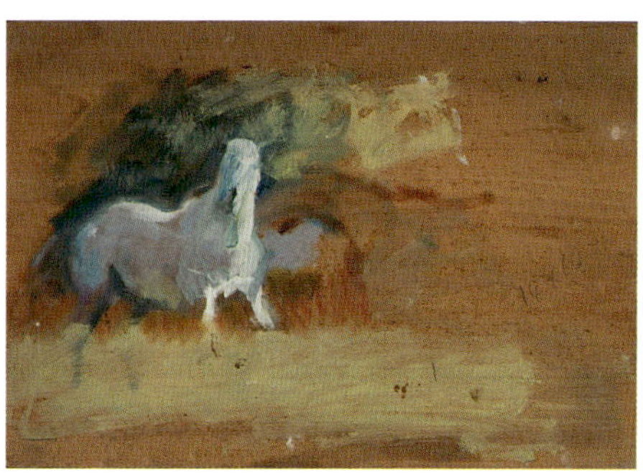

Munnings, Alfred James 1878–1959
Study (verso)
oil on panel 24.8 x 33
564A

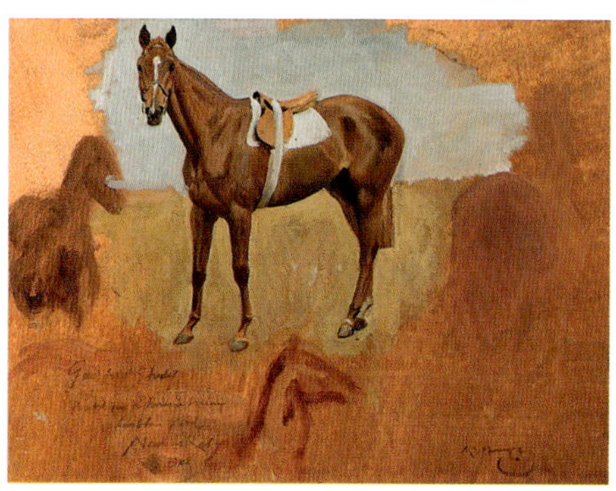

Munnings, Alfred James 1878–1959
Study of a Racehorse in Training at George Lambton's Yard
oil on board 35.6 x 45.7
179

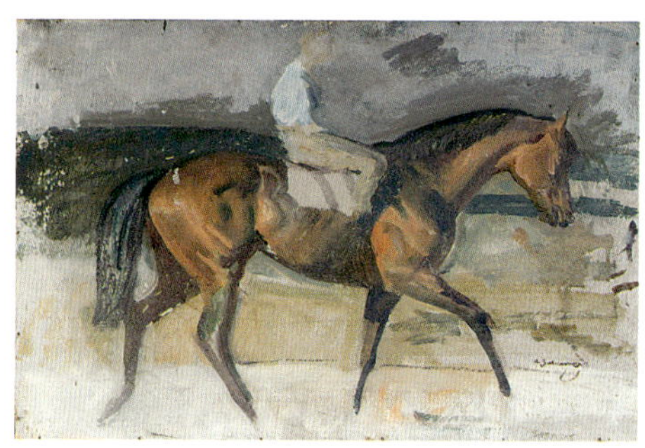

Munnings, Alfred James 1878–1959
Study of a Racehorse with a Lad up
oil on board 34.9 x 50.8
469

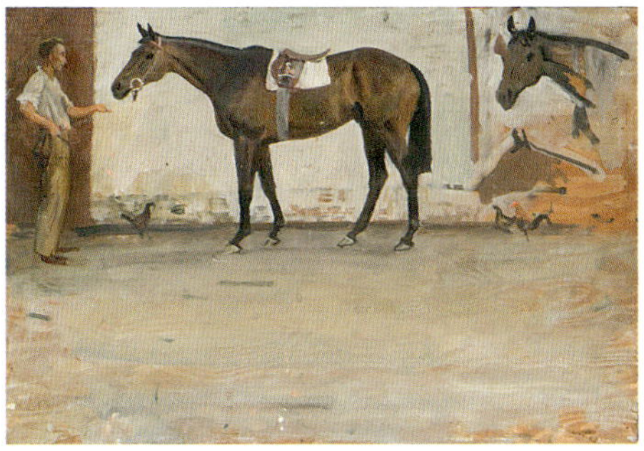

Munnings, Alfred James 1878–1959
Study of a Racehorse with a Stable Lad
oil on board 34.9 x 53.3
276

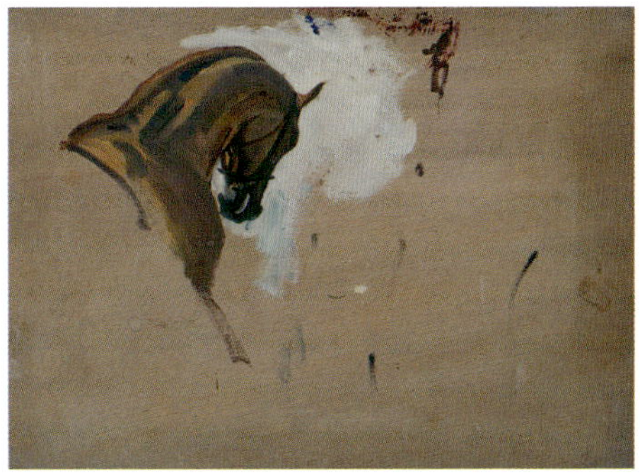

Munnings, Alfred James 1878–1959
Study of a Racehorse's Head
oil on panel 24.8 x 33
544

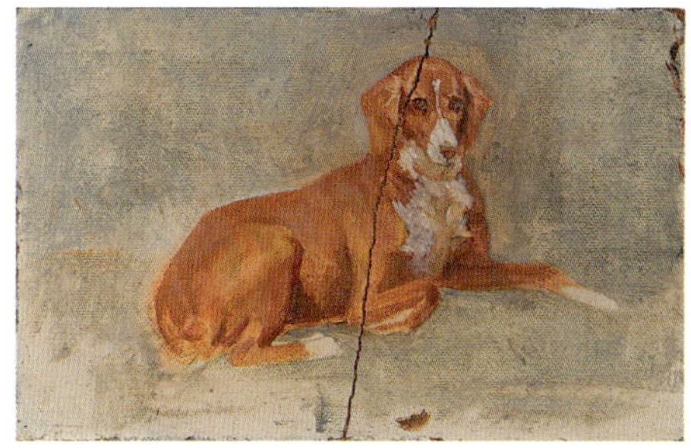

Munnings, Alfred James 1878–1959
Study of a Red Setter
oil on board 29.8 x 45.1
665

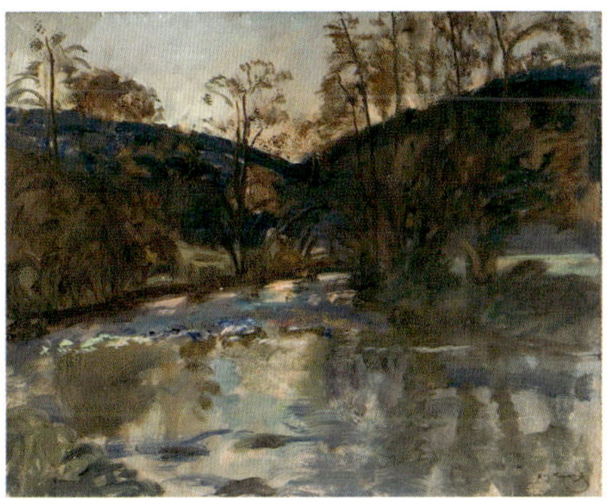

Munnings, Alfred James 1878–1959
Study of a River Landscape
oil on board 50.8 x 61
517

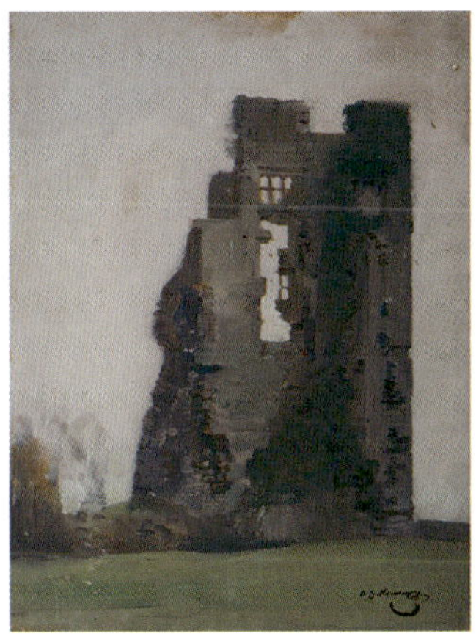

Munnings, Alfred James 1878–1959
Study of a Ruined Building
oil on panel 40.6 x 30.5
588

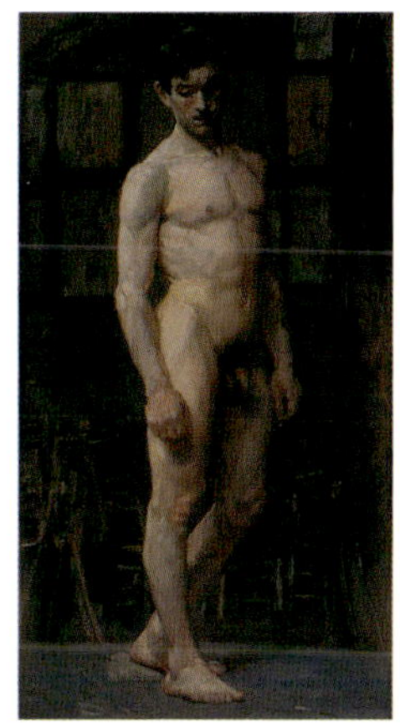

Munnings, Alfred James 1878–1959
Study of a Standing Male Nude, Julian's Atelier
oil on canvas 81.3 x 45.1
431

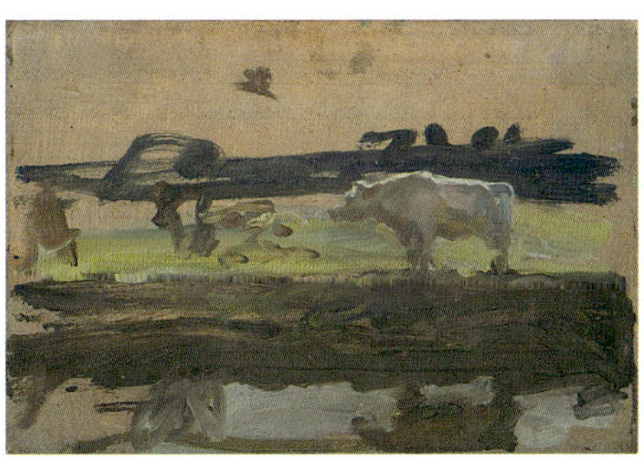

Munnings, Alfred James 1878–1959
Study of a White Bull
oil on panel 17.8 x 25.4
592

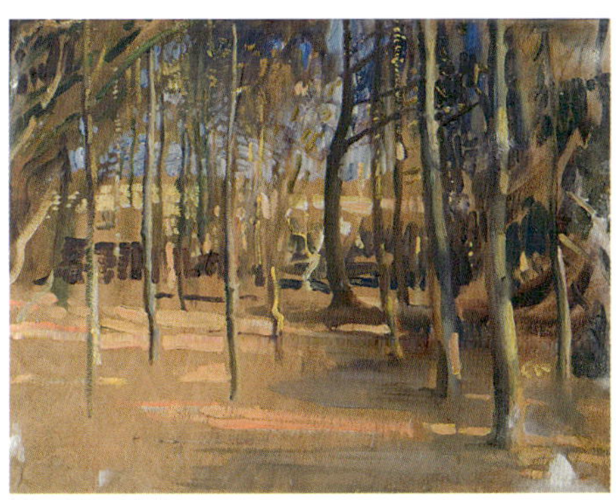

Munnings, Alfred James 1878–1959
Study of a Wood (recto)
oil on board 41.9 x 53.3 (E)
344

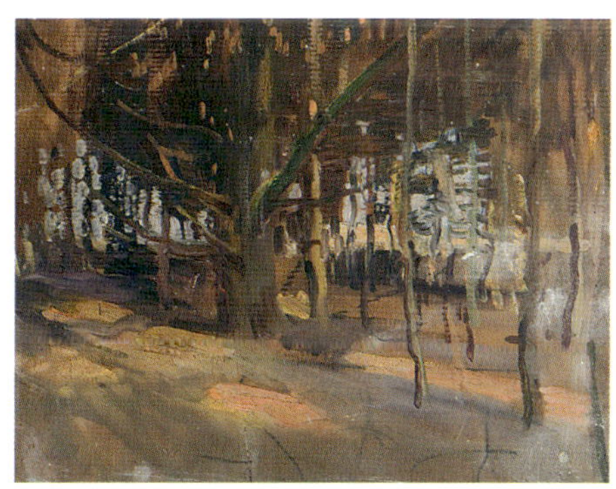

Munnings, Alfred James 1878–1959
Study of a Wood (verso)
oil on board 41.9 x 53.3 (E)
344A

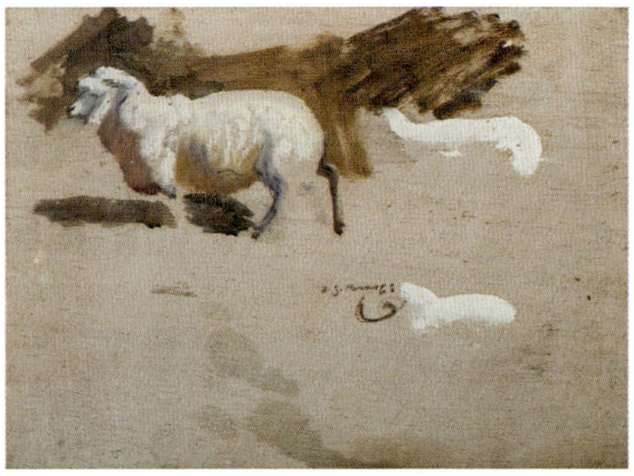

Munnings, Alfred James 1878–1959
Study of an Exmoor Sheep
oil on panel 24.8 x 33
546

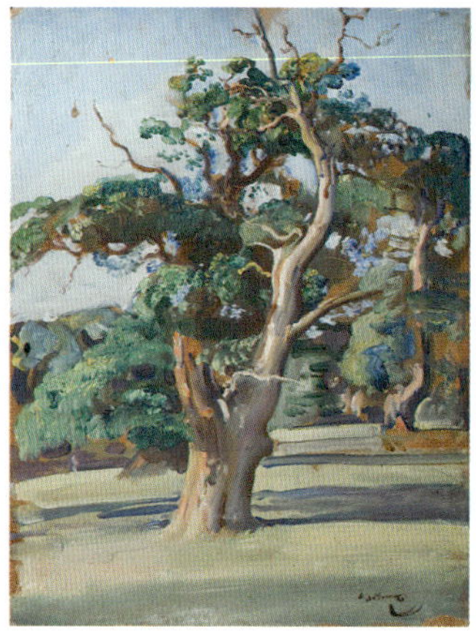

Munnings, Alfred James 1878–1959
Study of an Oak Tree
oil on panel 38.1 x 27.9
263

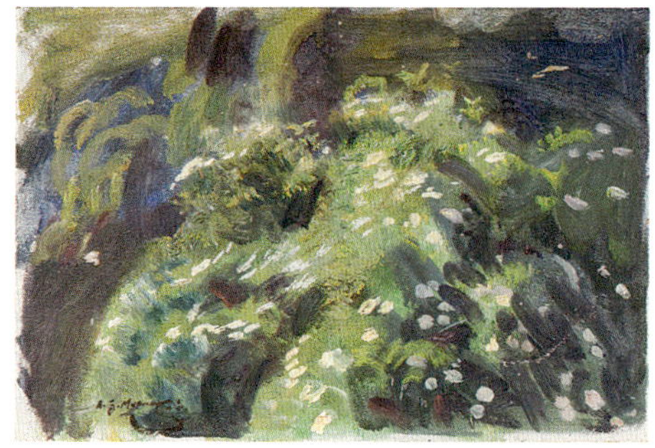

Munnings, Alfred James 1878–1959
Study of Blossom
oil on panel 17.8 x 25.4
557

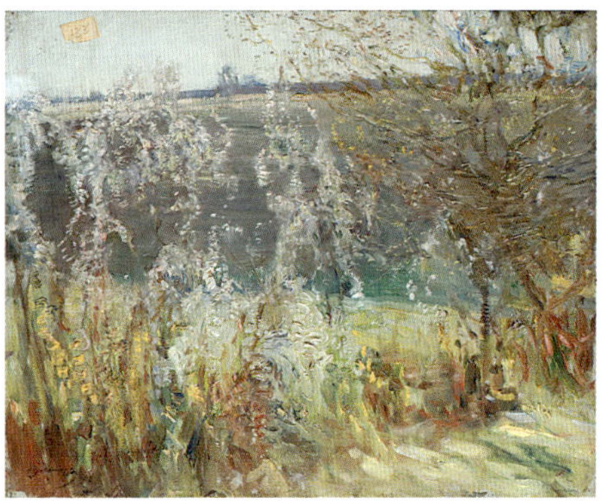

Munnings, Alfred James 1878–1959
Study of Blossoms, Cornwall
oil on canvas 50.8 x 61
489

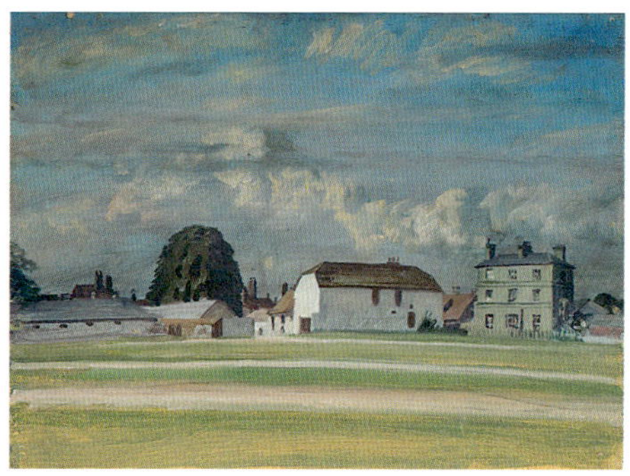

Munnings, Alfred James 1878–1959
Study of Buildings and Newmarket Stables
oil on panel 45.7 x 61
484

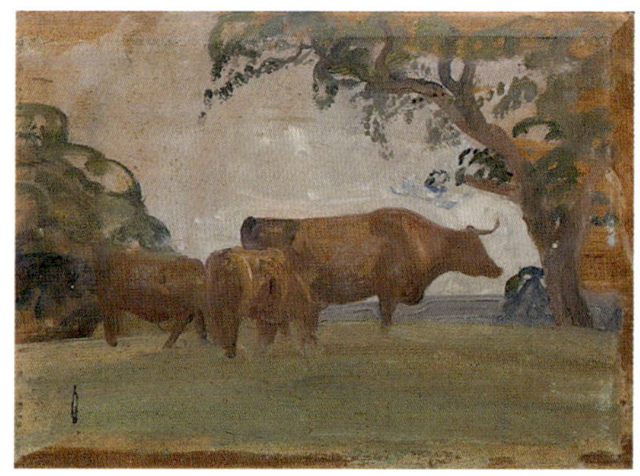

Munnings, Alfred James 1878–1959
Study of Cattle (recto)
oil on panel 25.4 x 33
562

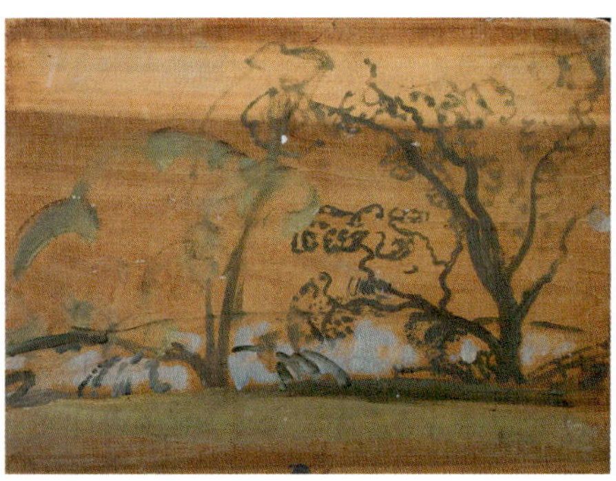

Munnings, Alfred James 1878–1959
Tree Study (verso)
oil on panel 25.4 x 33
562A

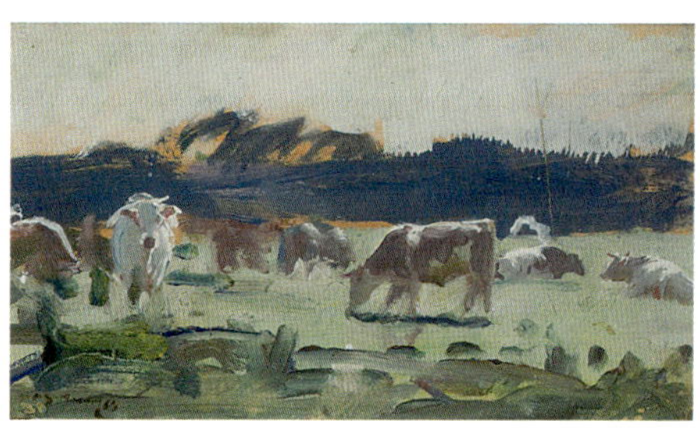

Munnings, Alfred James 1878–1959
Study of Cattle, Thorington Street, Stour Valley
oil on panel 14.6 x 24.8
611

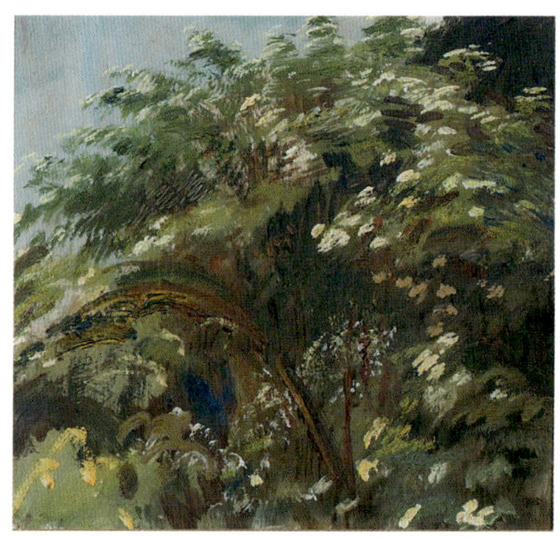

Munnings, Alfred James 1878–1959
Study of Elder Blossom
oil on board 30.5 x 31.8
319

Facing page: Bridge, Jack, *Essex Police, 1916 (L.33 over Little Wigborough)* (detail), 1990, Essex Police Museum, (p. 60)

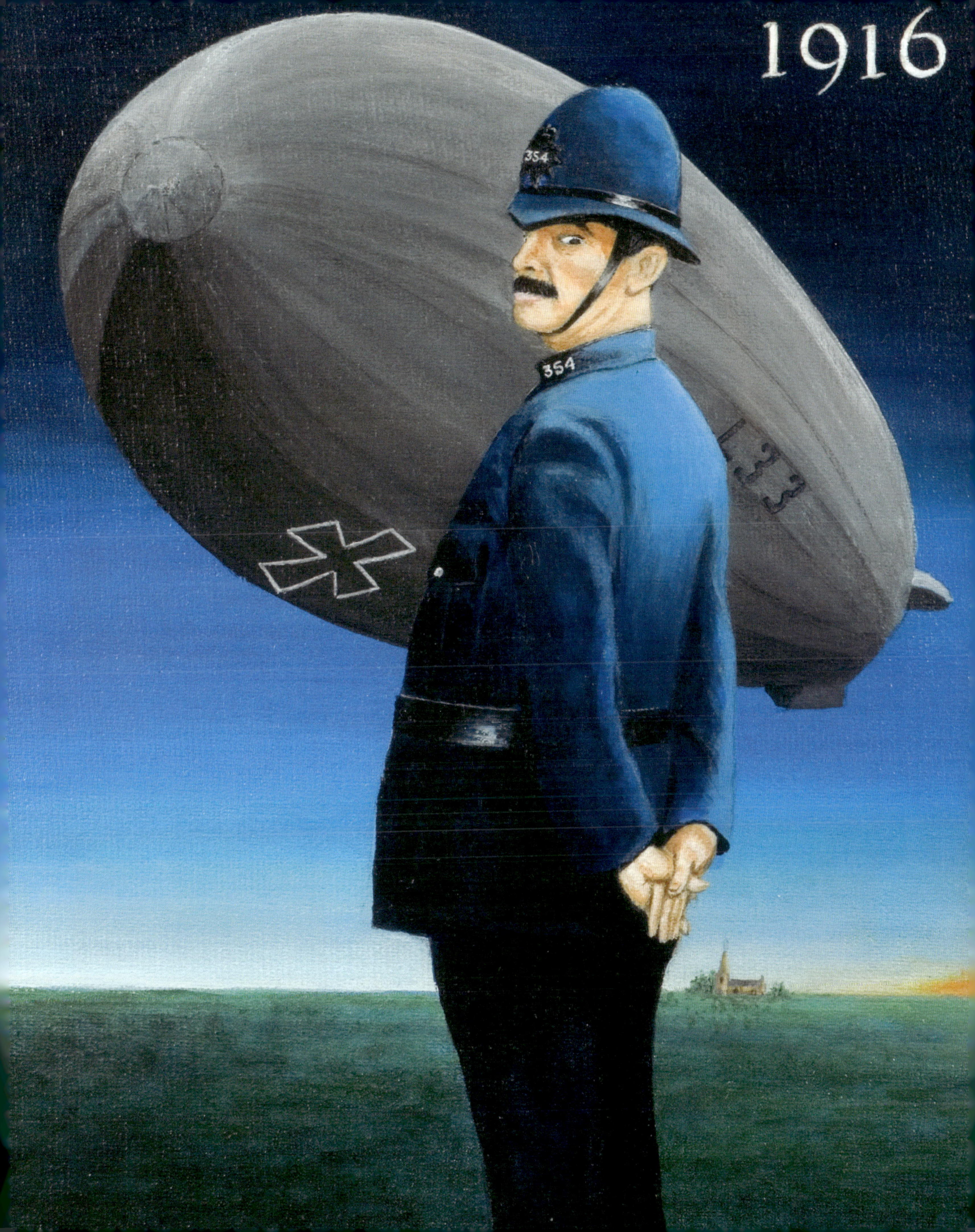
1916
354
354
L33

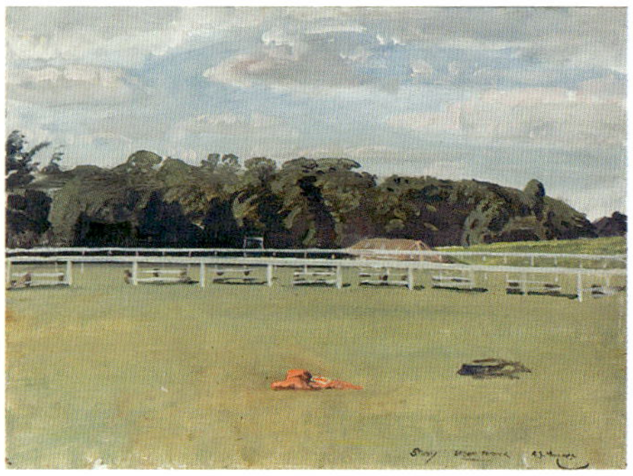

Munnings, Alfred James 1878–1959
Study of Epsom Paddock
oil on board 45.7 x 61
154

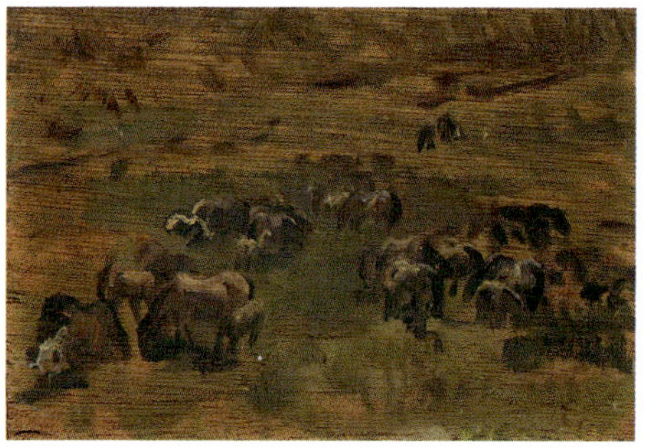

Munnings, Alfred James 1878–1959
Study of Exmoor Ponies (recto)
oil on board 16.5 x 25.1
664

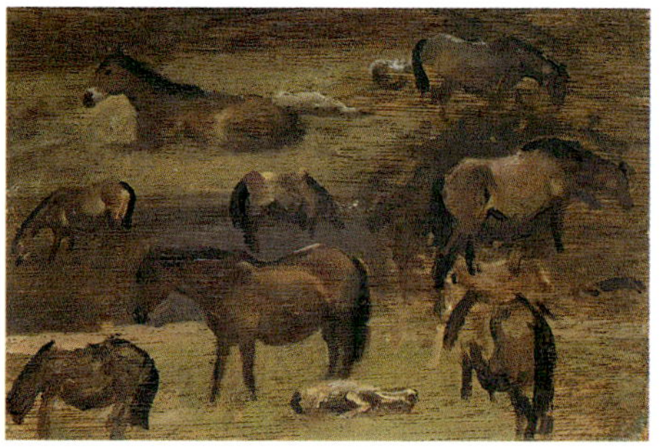

Munnings, Alfred James 1878–1959
Studies of Exmoor Ponies (verso)
oil on board 16.5 x 25.1
664A

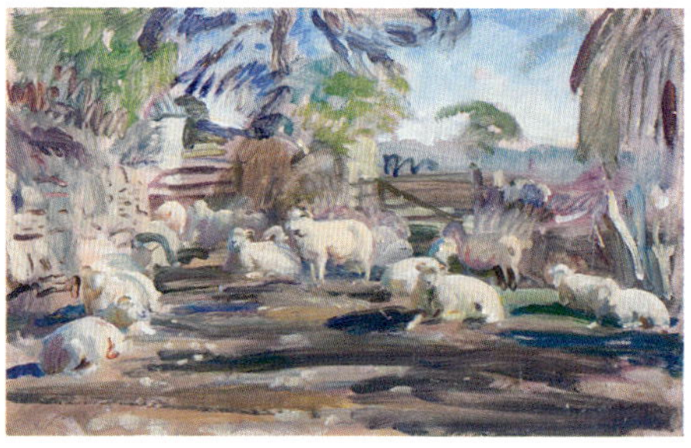

Munnings, Alfred James 1878–1959
Study of Exmoor Sheep
oil on board 27.9 x 43.8
297

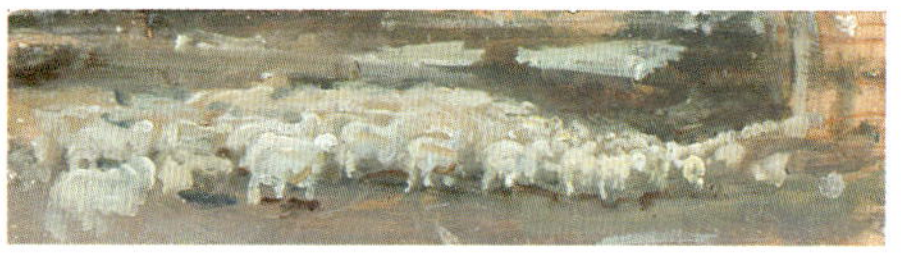

Munnings, Alfred James 1878–1959
Study of Exmoor Sheep
oil on board 15.2 x 55.9
403

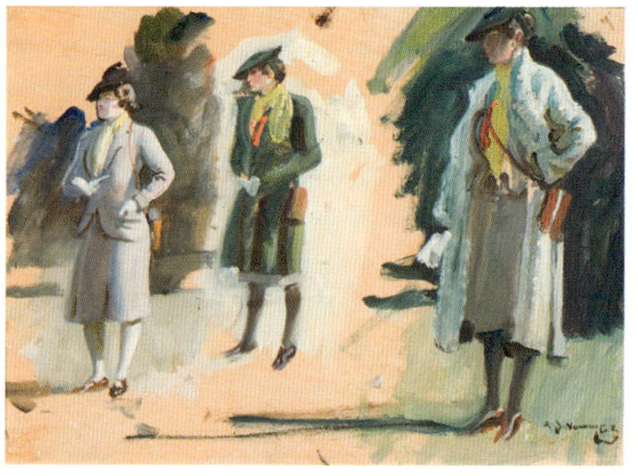

Munnings, Alfred James 1878–1959
Study of Figures at the Races
oil on board 26.7 x 35.6
73

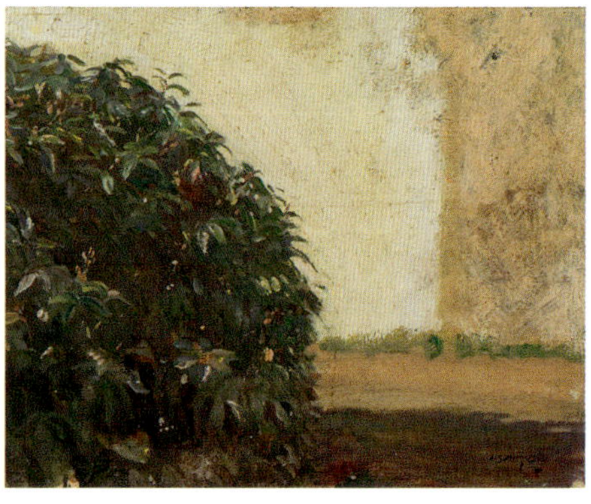

Munnings, Alfred James 1878–1959
Study of Foliage
oil on canvas 33 x 41.3
298

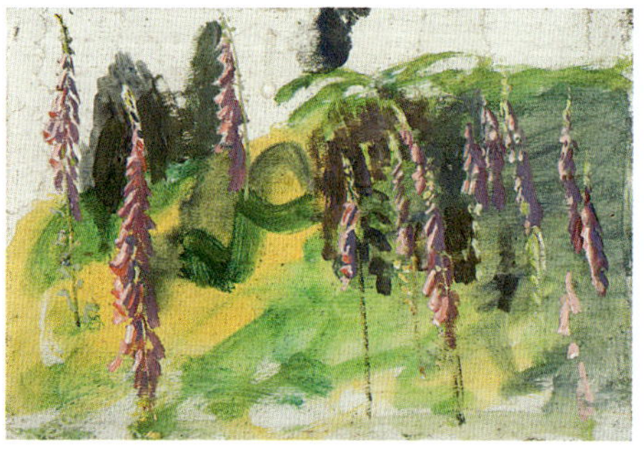

Munnings, Alfred James 1878–1959
Study of Foxgloves
oil on board 17.8 x 24.8
601

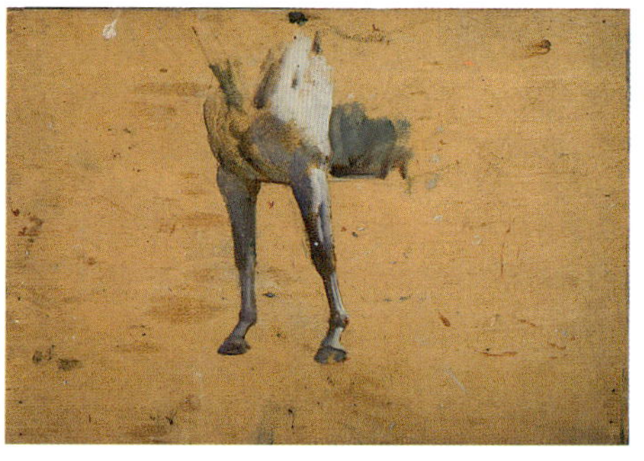

Munnings, Alfred James 1878–1959
Study of Front Legs of a Horse
oil on board 25.4 x 35.6
569

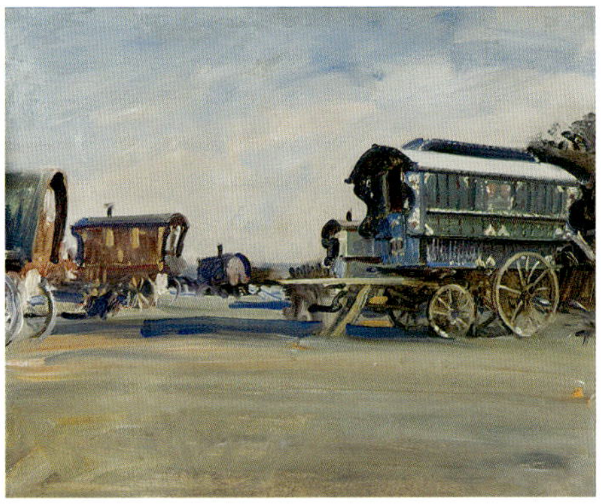

Munnings, Alfred James 1878–1959
Study of Gipsy Caravans
oil on board 50.8 x 61
515

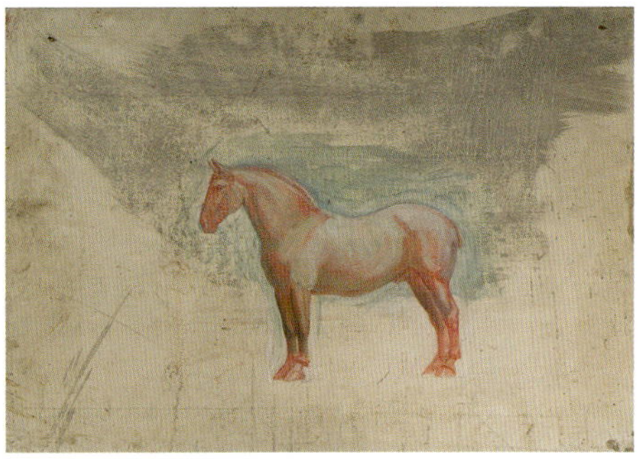

Munnings, Alfred James 1878–1959
Study of Heavy Horse
oil on board 58.4 x 81.3
677

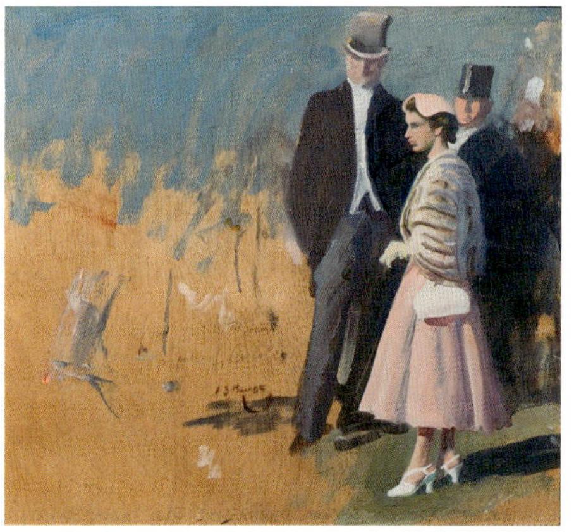

Munnings, Alfred James 1878–1959
Study of HM the Queen for 'Aureole'
oil on panel 43.2 x 45.7
157

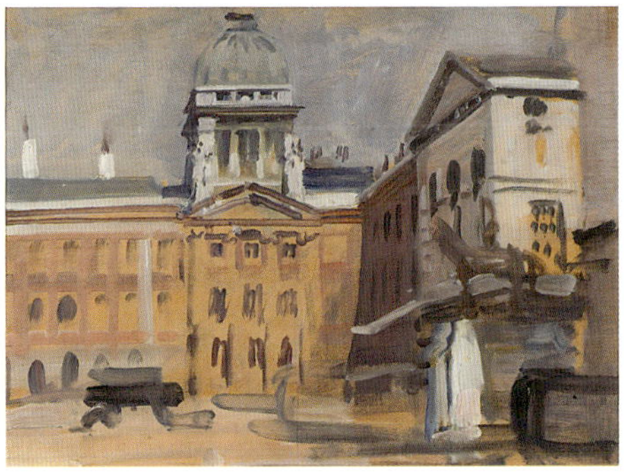

Munnings, Alfred James 1878–1959
Study of Horse Guards' Barracks, Parade Ground
oil on board 30.5 x 40.6
587

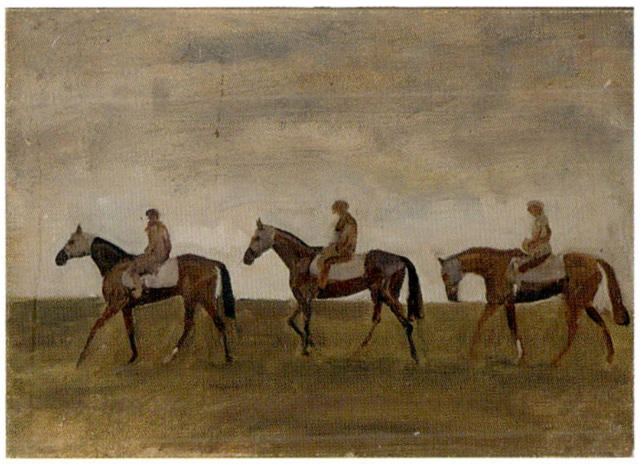

Munnings, Alfred James 1878–1959
Study of Horses and Riders
oil on canvas 40.6 x 55.9
420

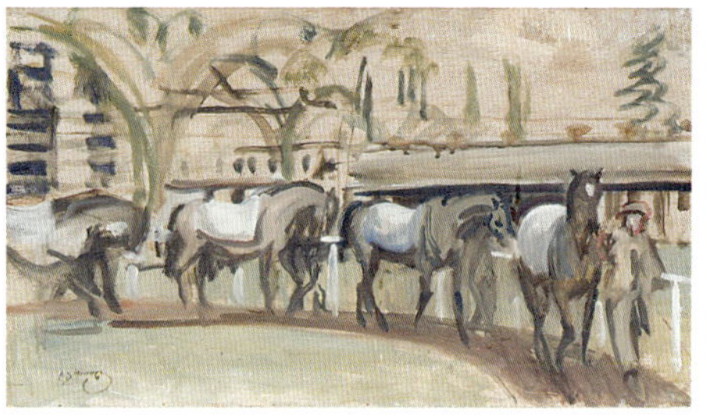

Munnings, Alfred James 1878–1959
Study of Horses in Kempton Paddock
oil on board 35.6 x 61
306

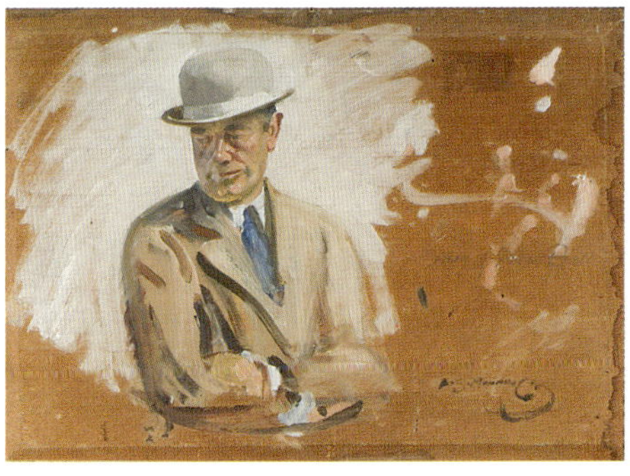

Munnings, Alfred James 1878–1959
Study of Isaac Bell
oil on board 24.1 x 33
202

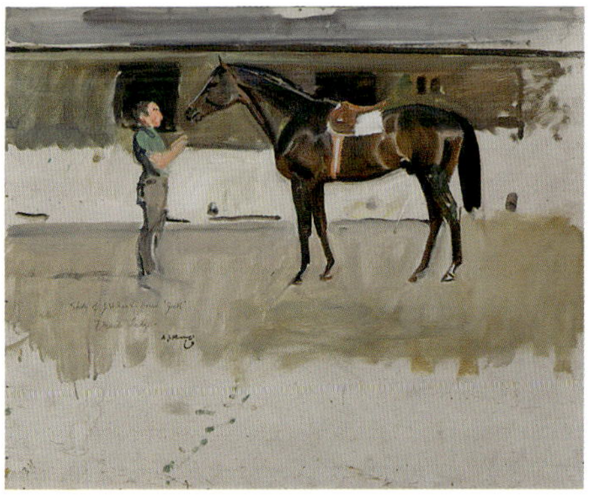

Munnings, Alfred James 1878–1959
Study of J. B. Rank's Horse, 'Jock', Druids' Lodge
oil on board 61 x 61 (E)
454

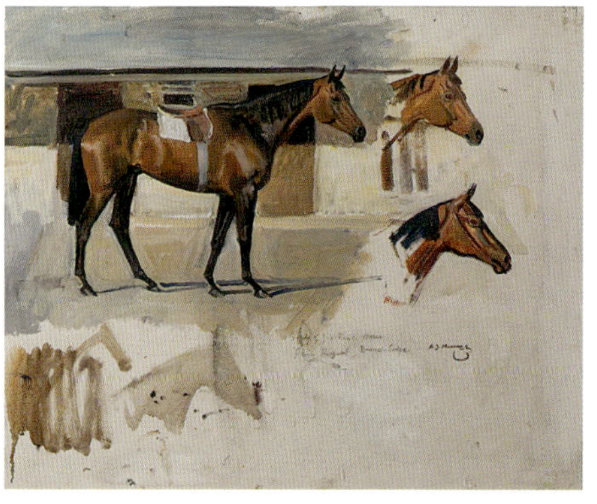

Munnings, Alfred James 1878–1959
Study of J. B. Rank's Horse, 'Prince Regent', Druids' Lodge
oil on board 50.8 x 61 (E)
112

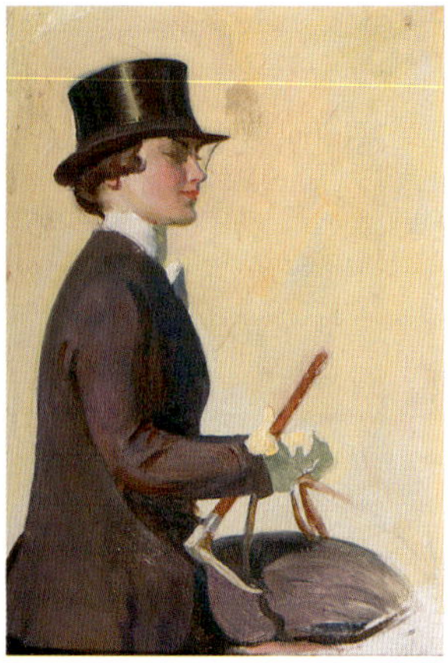

Munnings, Alfred James 1878–1959
Study of Lady Munnings for 'Our Mutual Friend the Horse'
oil on board 24 x 16
612A

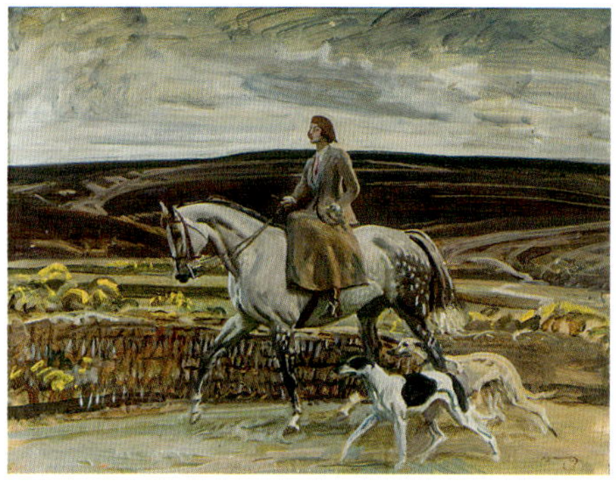

Munnings, Alfred James 1878–1959
Study of Lady Munnings Riding with Her Dogs on Exmoor
oil on panel 54 x 70
250

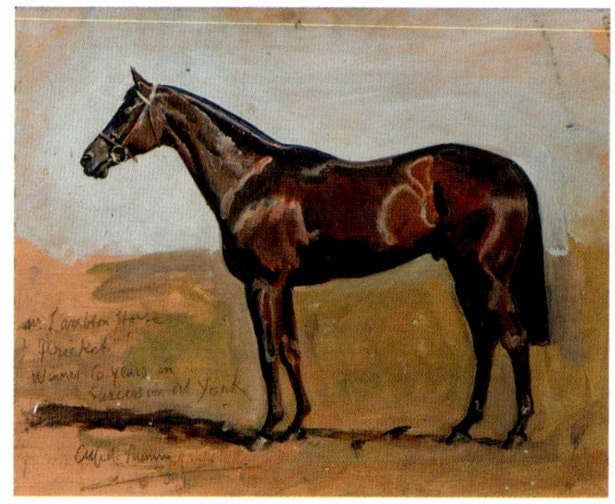

Munnings, Alfred James 1878–1959
Study of Mr Lambton's Horse, 'Pricket'
oil on board 35.6 x 43.2
156

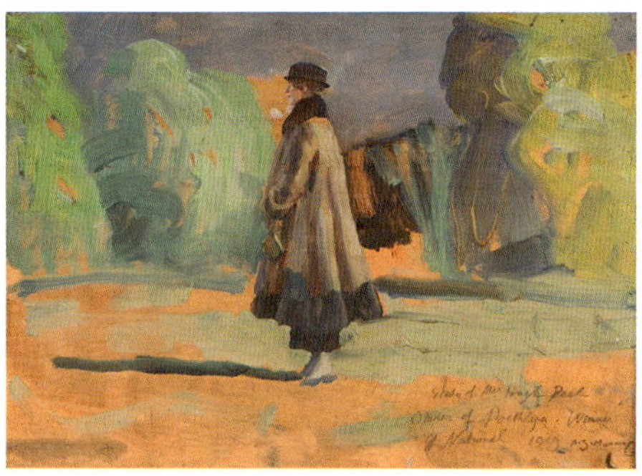

Munnings, Alfred James 1878–1959
Study of Mrs Hugh Peel, Owner of 'Poethlyn', Winner of the Grand National, 1919
oil on panel 24.8 x 35.6
65

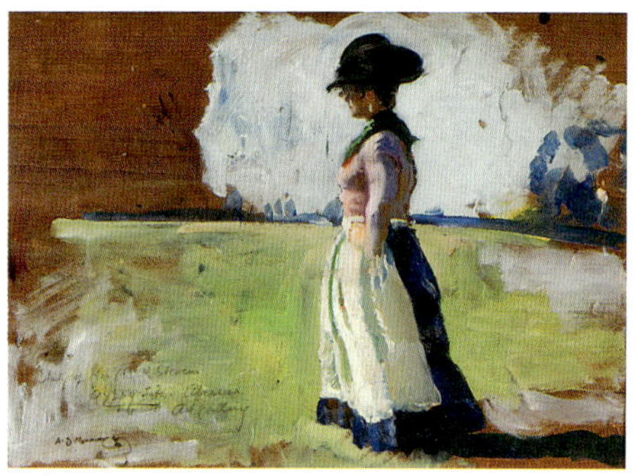

Munnings, Alfred James 1878–1959
Study of Mrs Mark Stevens, 'Gipsy Life'
oil on panel 30.5 x 40.6
575

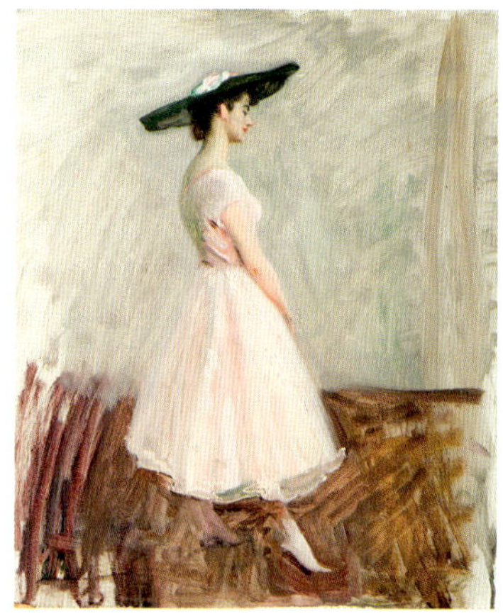

Munnings, Alfred James 1878–1959
Study of One of Selfridge's Young Ladies, in a Pink Selfridge's Dress, for 'Does the Subject Matter?'
oil on board 50.8 x 40.6
158

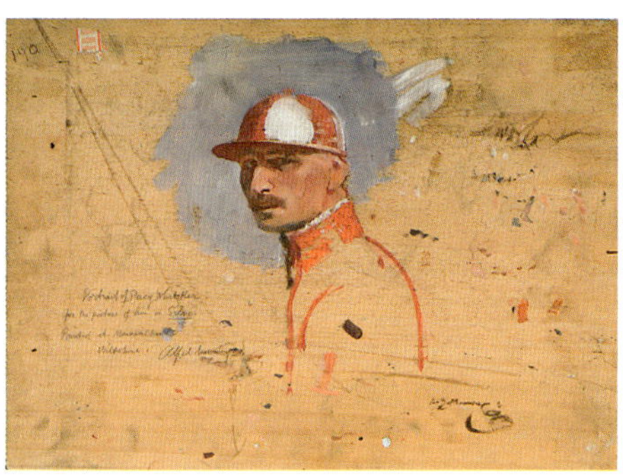

Munnings, Alfred James 1878–1959
Study of Percy Whitaker on 'Silvo' (recto)
oil on board 30.5 x 40.6
190

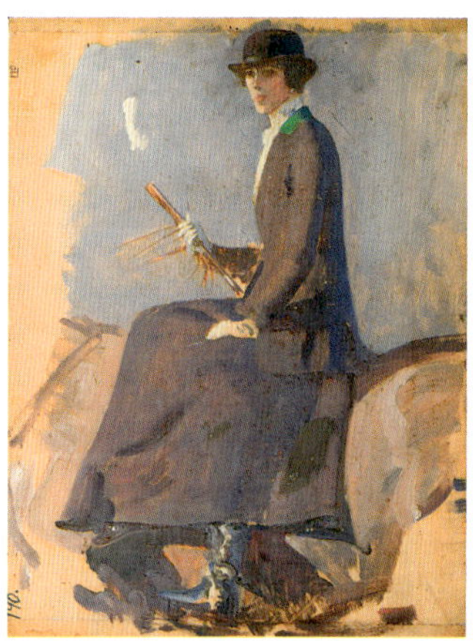

Munnings, Alfred James 1878–1959
A Portrait Study of the Duchess of Westminster (verso)
oil on board 40.6 x 30.5
190A

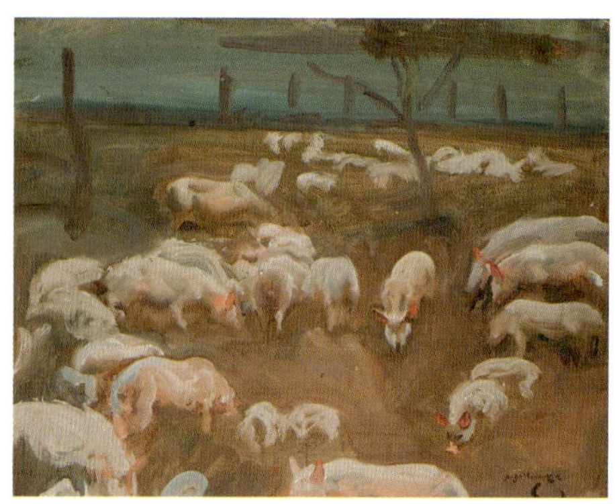

Munnings, Alfred James 1878–1959
Study of Pigs
oil on board 42.5 x 49.5
318

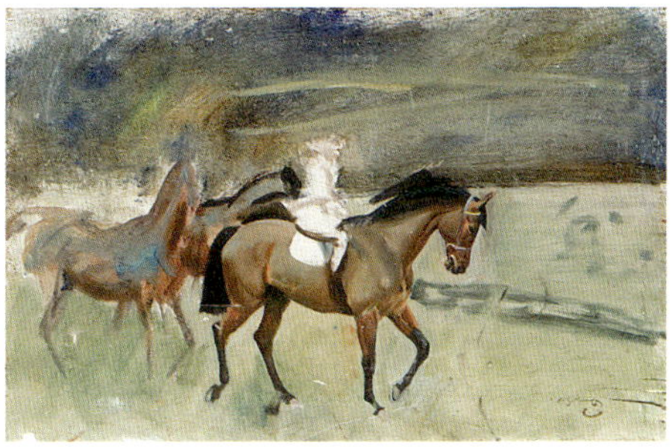

Munnings, Alfred James 1878–1959
Study of Racehorses
oil on board 40.6 x 61
444

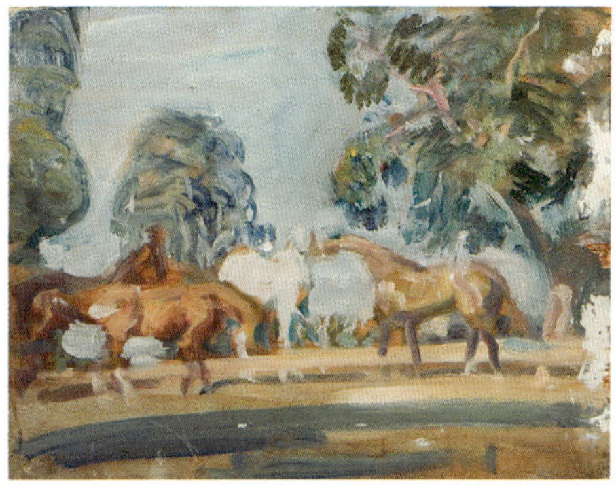

Munnings, Alfred James 1878–1959
Study of 'Rose', 'Wild Bird', 'Peggy' and 'Stockings'
oil on board 36.8 x 47
390

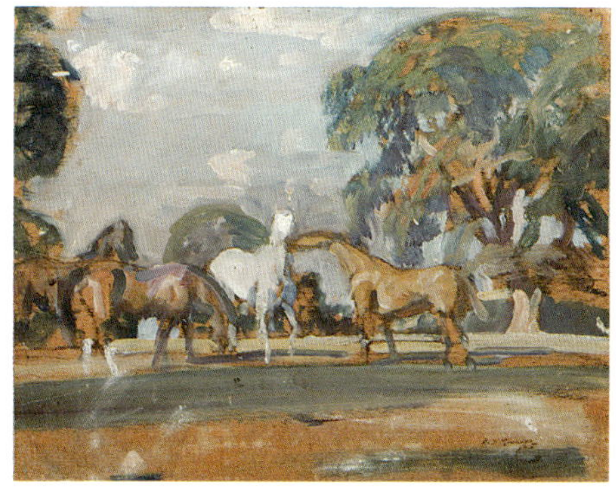

Munnings, Alfred James 1878–1959
Study of 'Rose', 'Wild Bird', 'Peggy' and 'Stockings'
oil on board 38.1 x 48.3
392

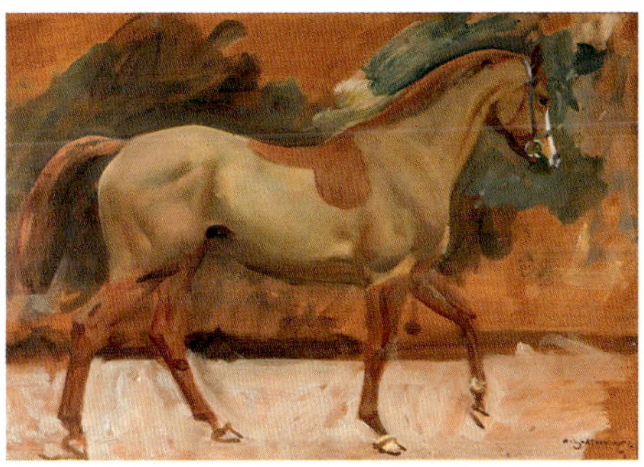

Munnings, Alfred James 1878–1959
Study of 'Rufus', a Chestnut Horse, Bought at Exmoor 1951, Bred in Ireland, 16 Years Old
oil on panel 25.4 x 34.9
71

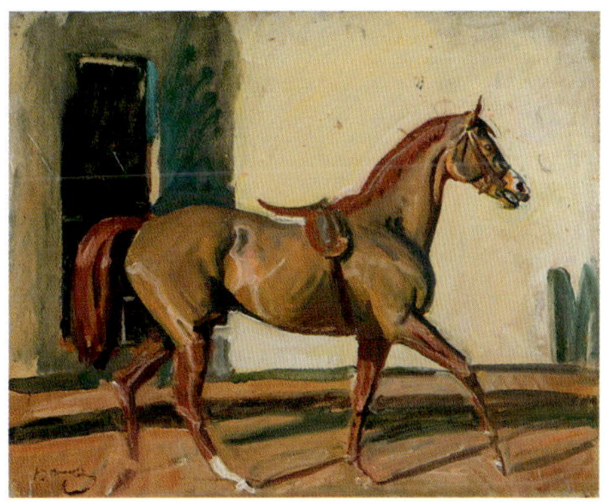

Munnings, Alfred James 1878–1959
Study of 'Rufus' for 'Our Mutual Friend the Horse'
oil on board 51 x 61
441

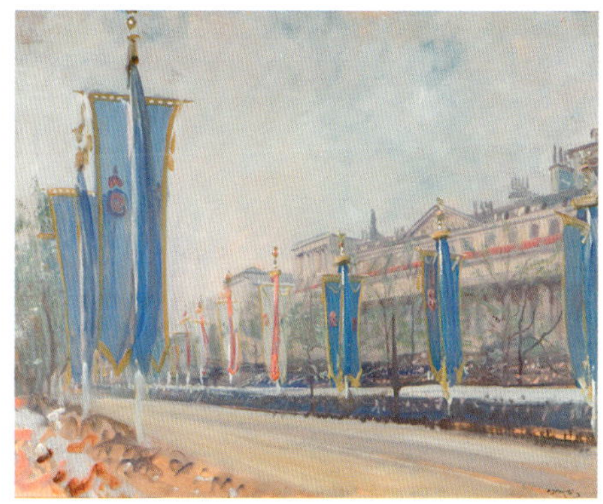

Munnings, Alfred James 1878–1959
Study of the Decorations in the Mall for the Coronation of George VI, 1937
oil on canvas 63.5 x 76.2
336

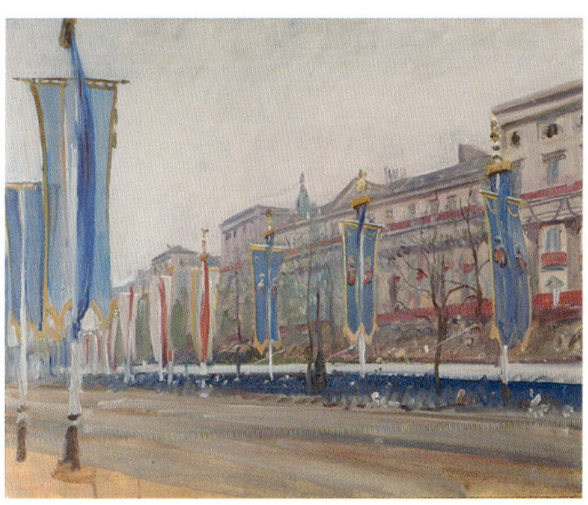

Munnings, Alfred James 1878–1959
Study of the Decorations in the Mall for the Coronation of George VI, 1937
oil on canvas 63.5 x 76.2
337

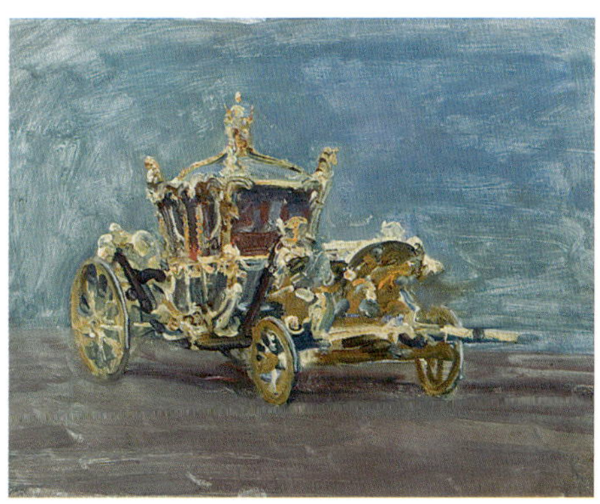

Munnings, Alfred James 1878–1959
Study of the Gold Coach in the Palace Yard
oil on board 33 x 40.6
237

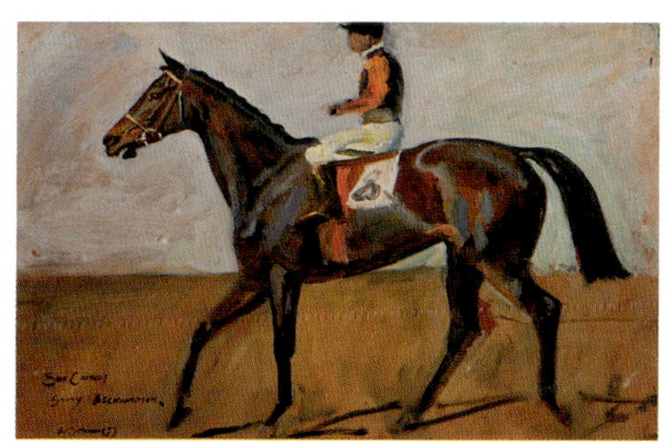

Munnings, Alfred James 1878–1959
Study of the King's Filly, 'Sun Chariot', Beckhampton
oil on panel 23.5 x 35.6
314

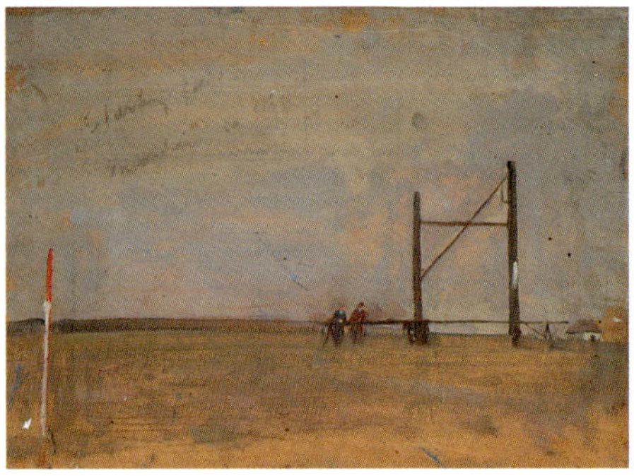

Munnings, Alfred James 1878–1959
Study of the Starting Post (recto)
oil on board 30.5 x 40.6
584

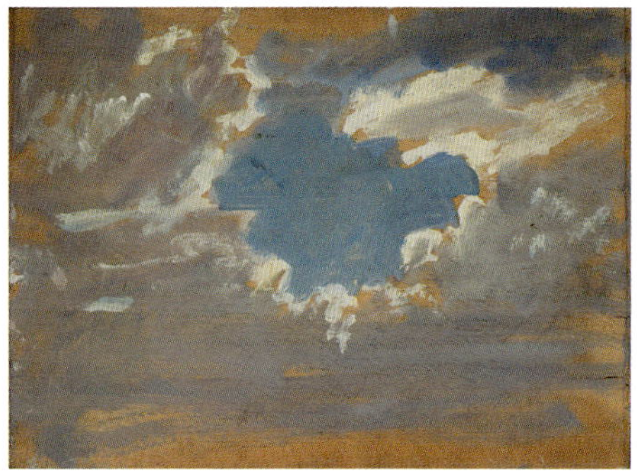

Munnings, Alfred James 1878–1959
A Sky Study (verso)
oil on board 30.5 x 40.6
584A

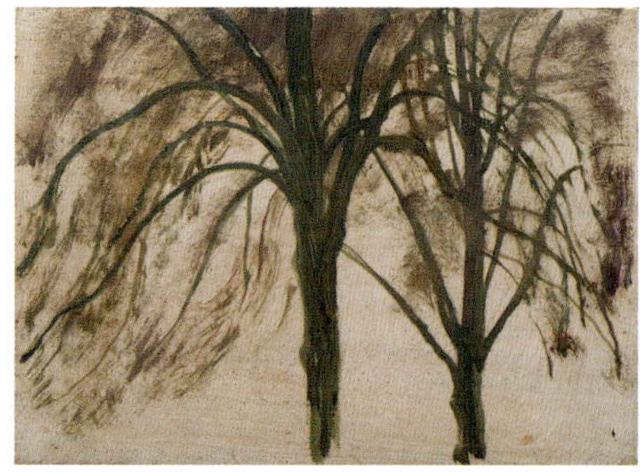

Munnings, Alfred James 1878–1959
Study of Trees (recto)
oil on panel 24.8 x 33
541

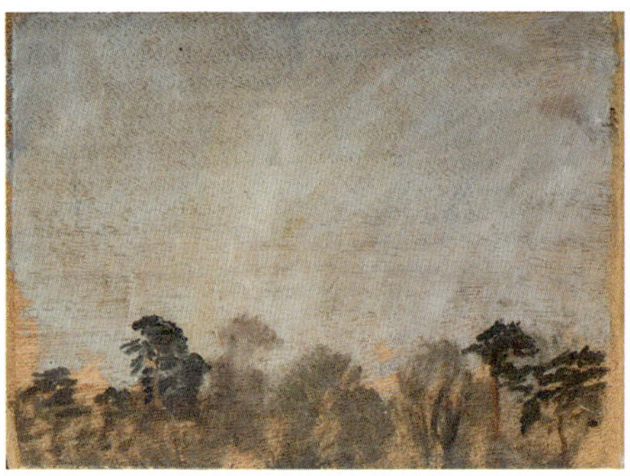

Munnings, Alfred James 1878–1959
Study of Trees (verso)
oil on panel 24.8 x 33
541A

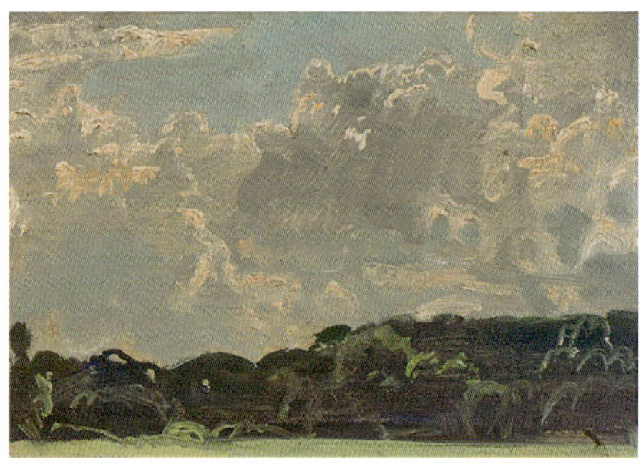

Munnings, Alfred James 1878–1959
Study of Trees (recto)
oil on board 17.8 x 25.4
599

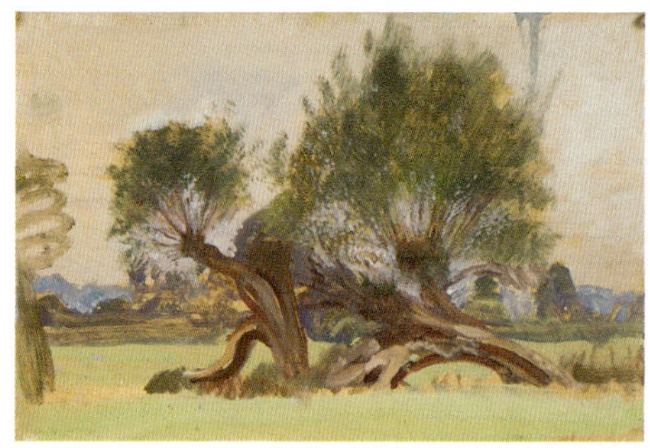

Munnings, Alfred James 1878–1959
Study of Willows (verso)
oil on board 17.8 x 25.4
599A

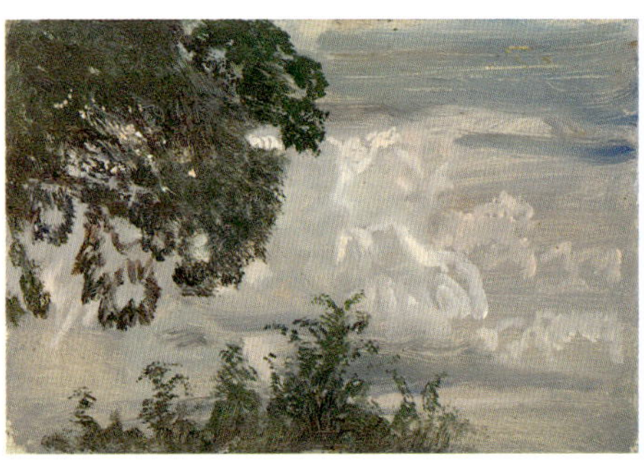

Munnings, Alfred James 1878–1959
Study of Trees and Sky
oil on board 17.8 x 25.4 (E)
538

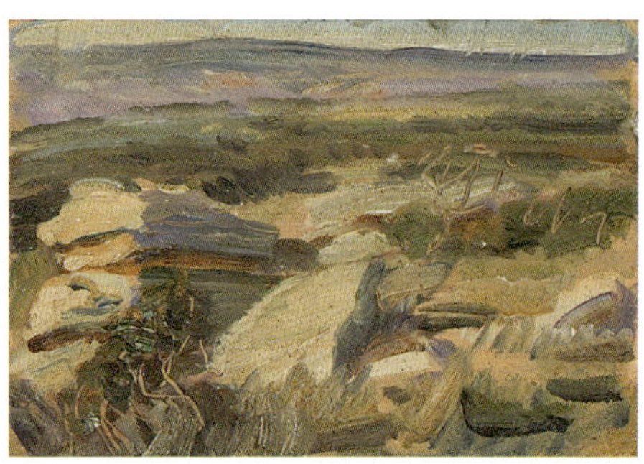

Munnings, Alfred James 1878–1959
Study on Exmoor
oil on panel 17.8 x 25.4 (E)
667

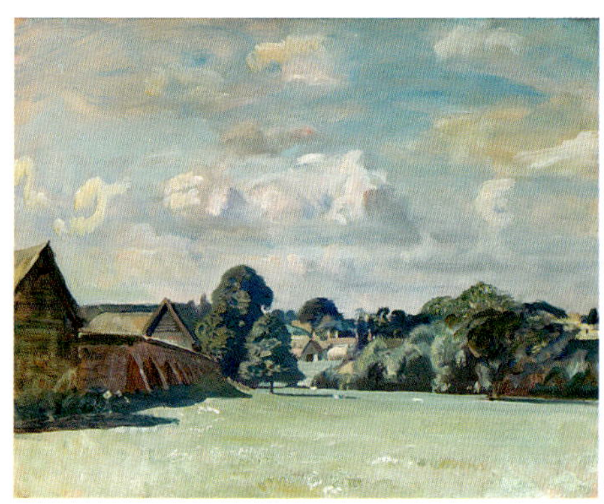

Munnings, Alfred James 1878–1959
Suffolk Landscape with Farm Buildings
oil on canvas 63.5 x 76.2
249

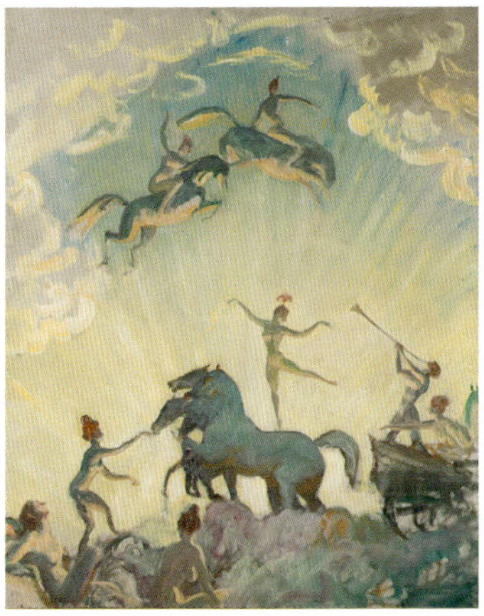

Munnings, Alfred James 1878–1959
'Sun Worship', a Design for a Drop Cloth for the Chelsea Arts Ball
oil on canvas 127.5 x 101
240

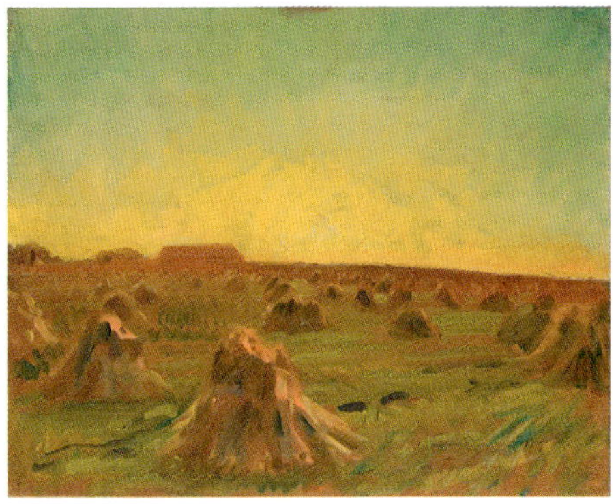

Munnings, Alfred James 1878–1959
Sunset over a Harvest Field
oil on canvas 50.8 x 61
26

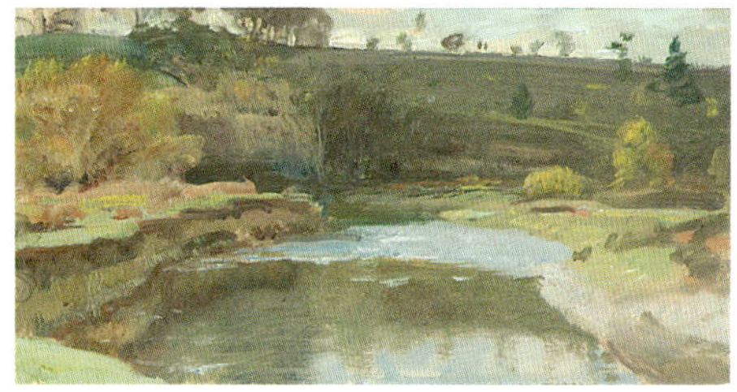

Munnings, Alfred James 1878–1959
The Barle at Withypool, Exmoor
oil on board 33 x 60.3
103

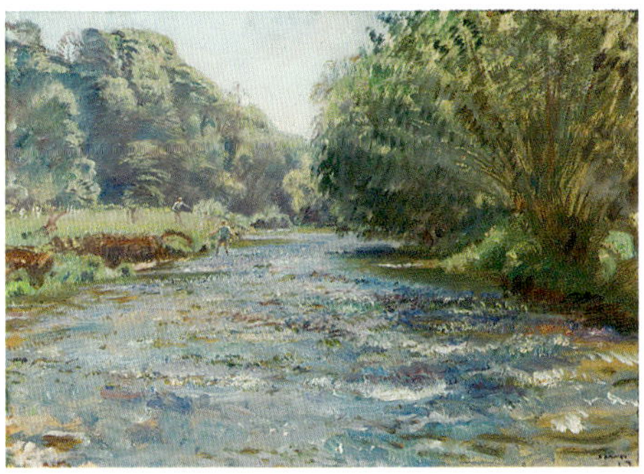

Munnings, Alfred James 1878–1959
The Barle near Brightworthy, Withypool, Exmoor
oil on board 44.5 x 61
46

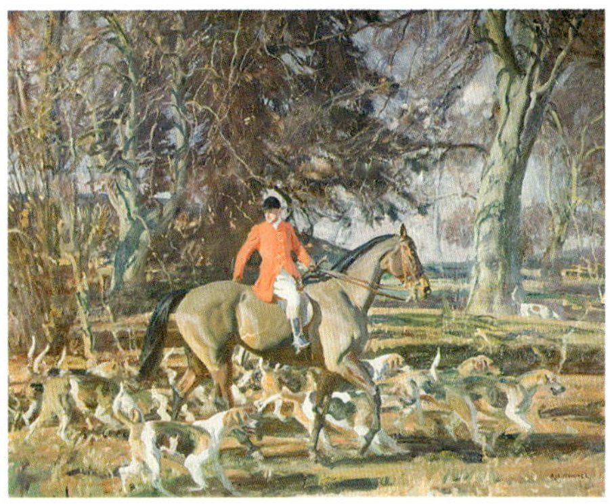

Munnings, Alfred James 1878–1959
The Edge of the Wood
oil on canvas 100.3 x 125.7
1938.253

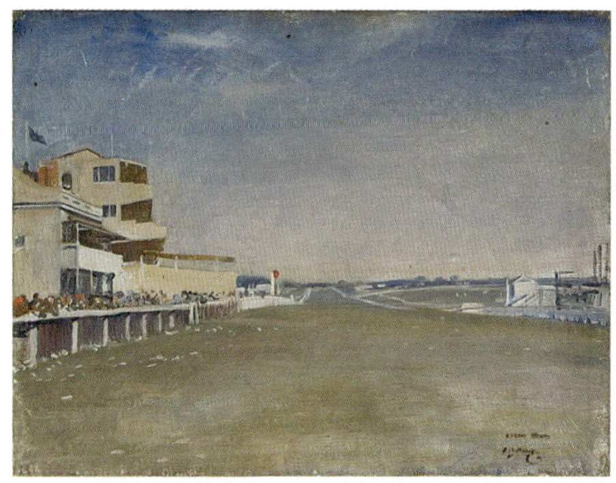

Munnings, Alfred James 1878–1959
The Epsom Stand
oil on canvas 55.9 x 71.1
326

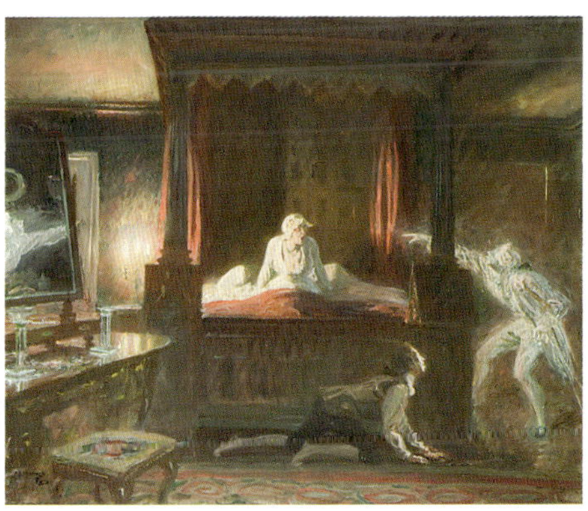

Munnings, Alfred James 1878–1959
The Haunted Room, Painted at a Farmhouse on Exmoor
oil on canvas 102.2 x 115.6
101

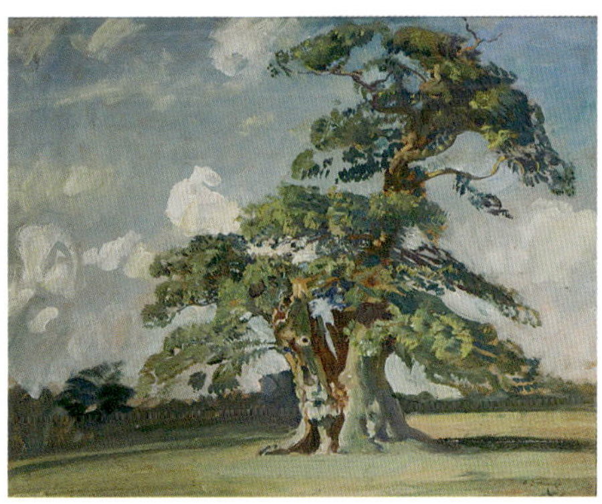

Munnings, Alfred James 1878–1959
The Old Oak, Mistley Park
oil on board 50.8 x 61
151

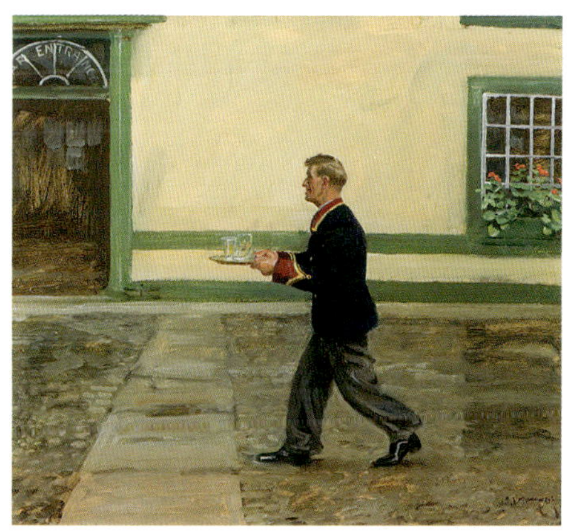

Munnings, Alfred James 1878–1959
The Porter at 'The Rutland Arms', Newmarket
oil on board 55.9 x 61
100

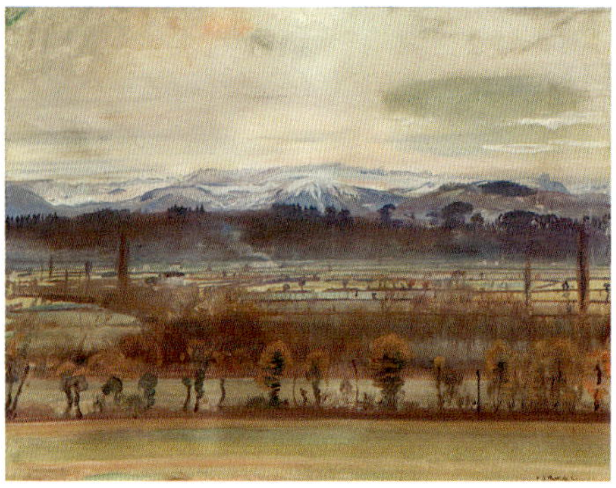

Munnings, Alfred James 1878–1959
The Pyrenees and the Plain of Tarbes
oil on canvas 122.6 x 154.8
L6:2000 (P)

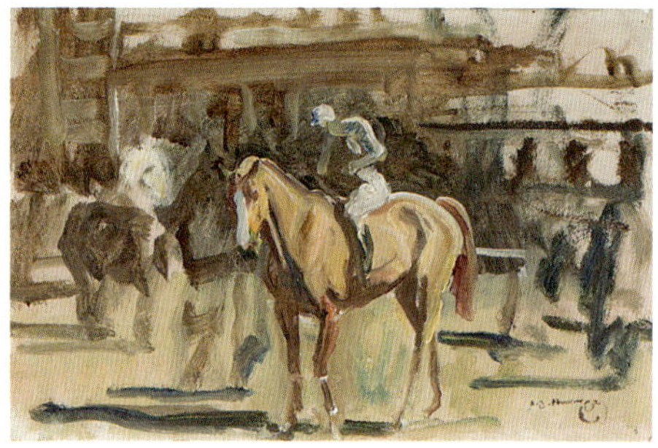

Munnings, Alfred James 1878–1959
The Saddling Paddock
oil on board 26 x 38.7
308

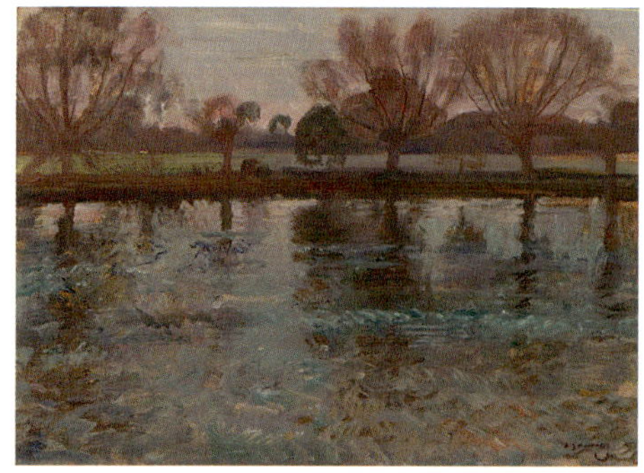

Munnings, Alfred James 1878–1959
The Stour at Dedham
oil on board 45.1 x 64.8
281

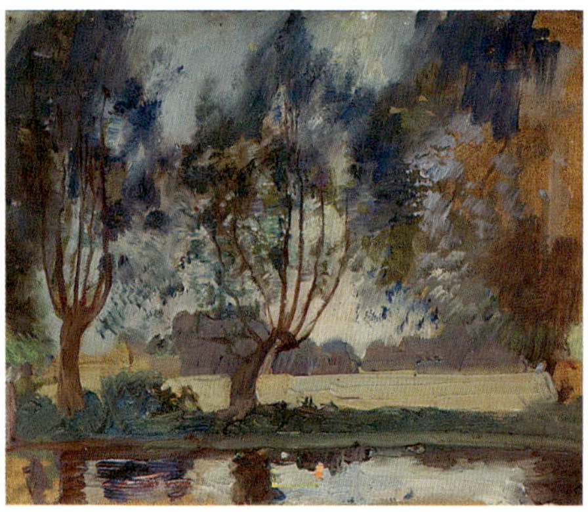

Munnings, Alfred James 1878–1959
The Stour at Dedham
oil on panel 30.5 x 35.6
283

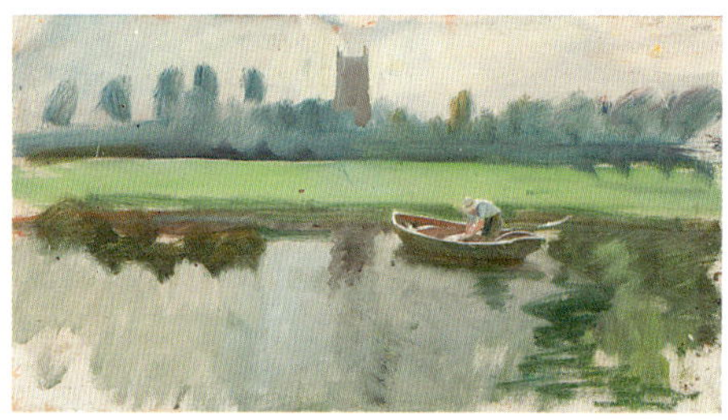

Munnings, Alfred James 1878–1959
The Stour at Dedham, with a Man in a Boat
oil on board 30.5 x 54
474

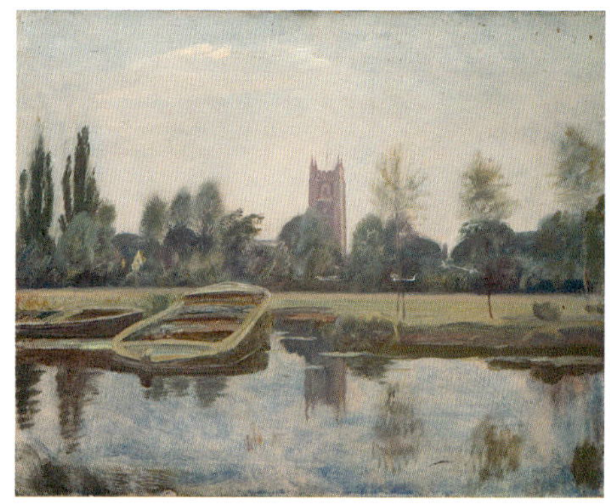

Munnings, Alfred James 1878–1959
The Stour at Dedham with Barges
oil on canvas 50.8 x 61
524

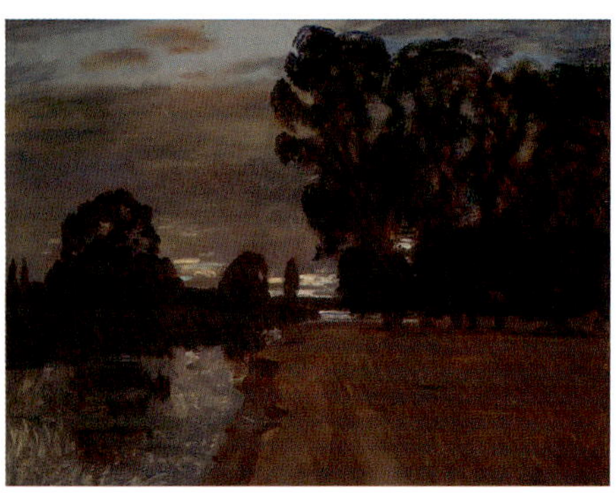

Munnings, Alfred James 1878–1959
The Stour at Night, Dedham
oil on canvas 63.5 x 76.2
285

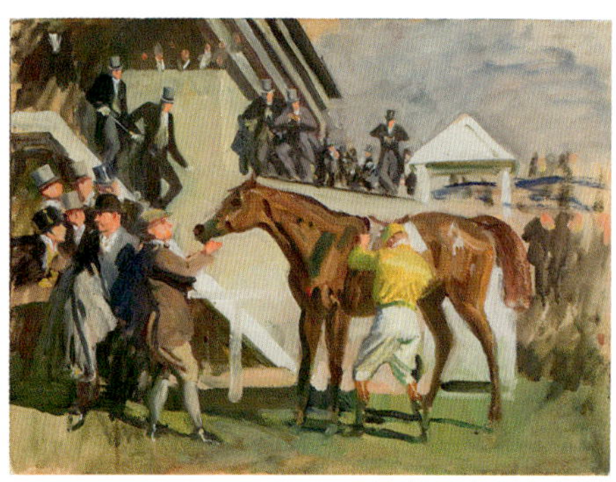

Munnings, Alfred James 1878–1959
The Unsaddling Enclosure, Epsom
oil on board 43.2 x 55.9
369

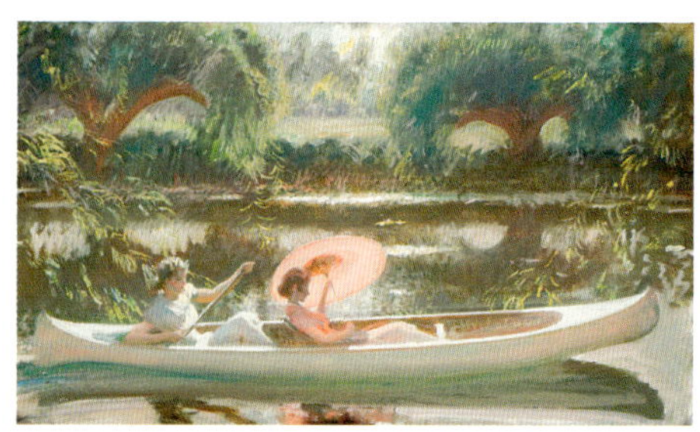

Munnings, Alfred James 1878–1959
The White Canoe on the Stour at Dedham
oil on canvas 75 x 121.5
201

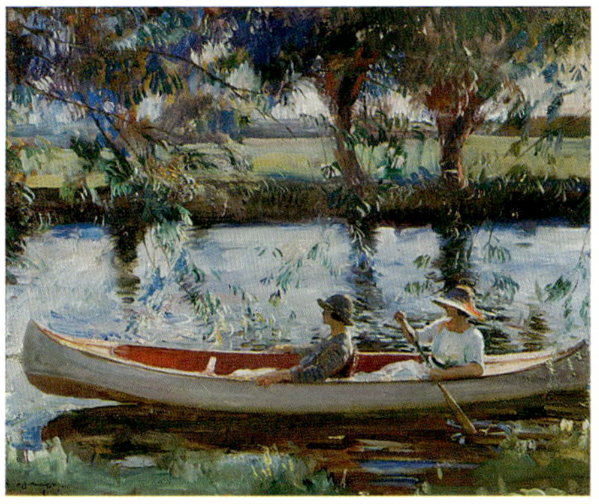

Munnings, Alfred James 1878–1959
The White Canoe on the Stour at Flatford
oil on canvas 50.8 x 60.3
138

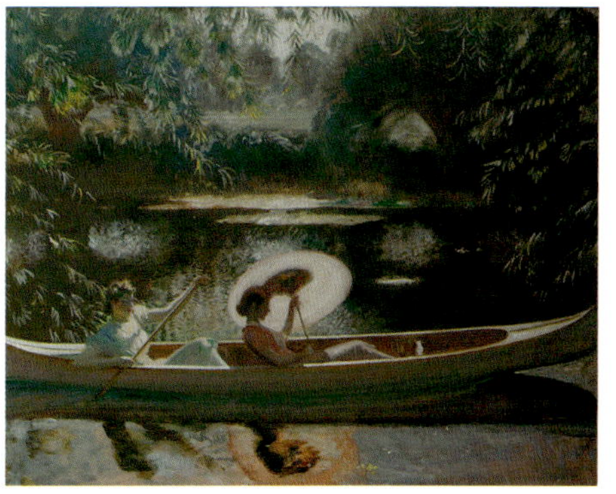

Munnings, Alfred James 1878–1959
The White Canoe, Two Young Ladies Reclining in a Canoe on the Stour at Flatford
oil on canvas 117 x 137
83

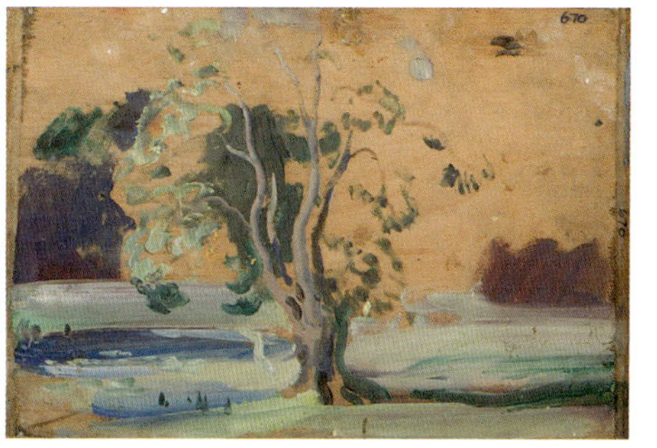

Munnings, Alfred James 1878–1959
Tree Study (recto)
oil on panel 24.8 x 35.6
670

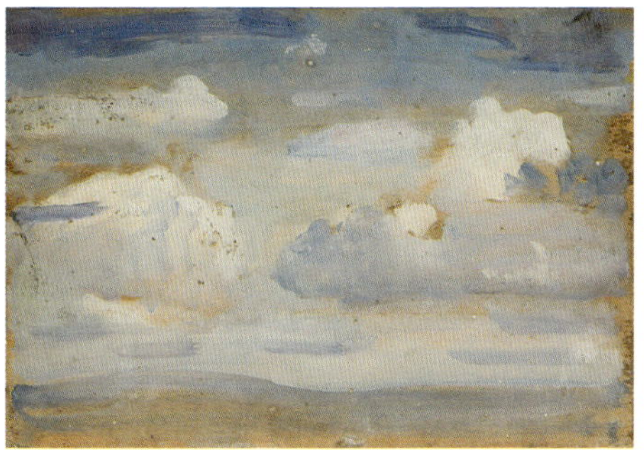

Munnings, Alfred James 1878–1959
Sky Study (verso)
oil on panel 24.8 x 35.6
670A

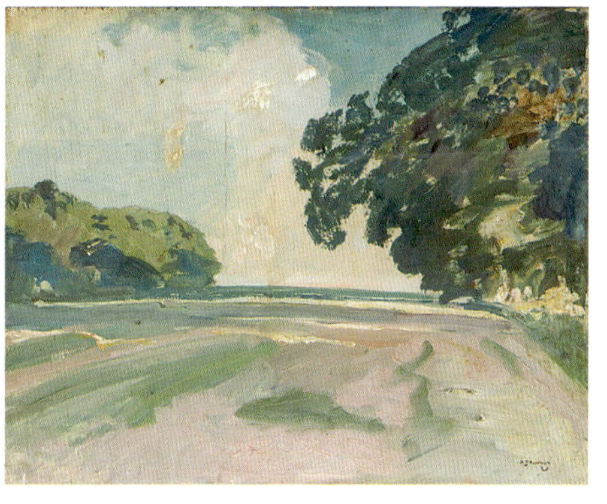

Munnings, Alfred James 1878–1959
Trees by a Field
oil on panel 50.8 x 61 (E)
487

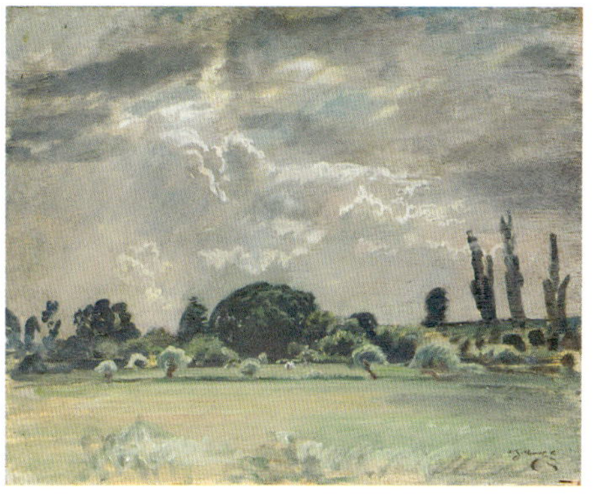

Munnings, Alfred James 1878–1959
Trees by a Field
oil on board 50.8 x 61 (E)
529

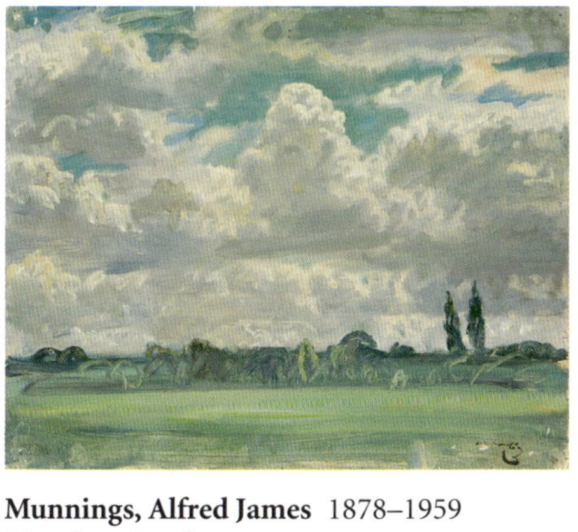

Munnings, Alfred James 1878–1959
Trees by a Landscape
oil on board 50.8 x 61
520

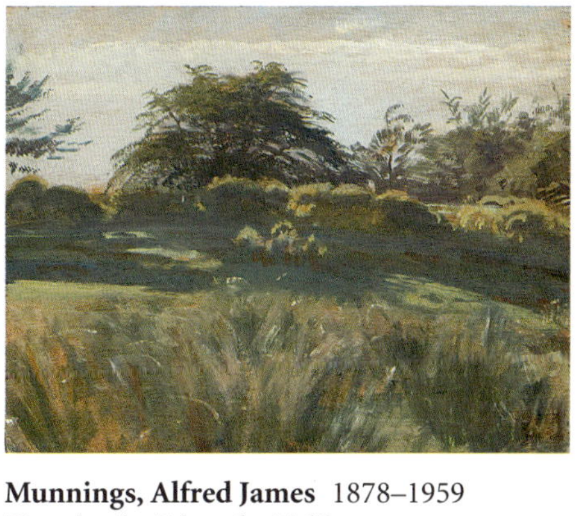

Munnings, Alfred James 1878–1959
Trees by the Edge of a Field
oil on board 40.6 x 50.8
385

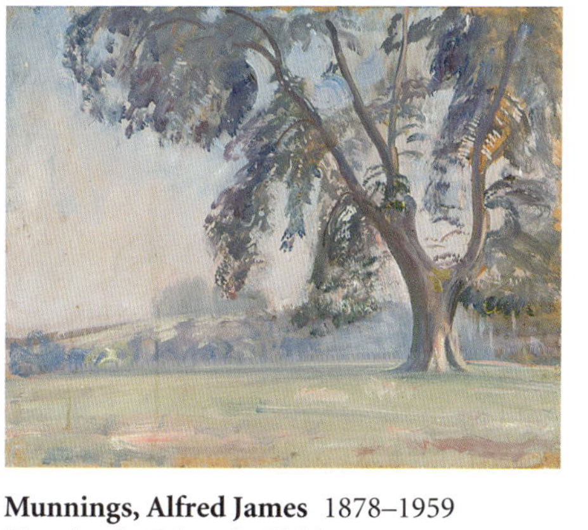

Munnings, Alfred James 1878–1959
Trees by the Edge of a Field
oil on board 50.8 x 61
407

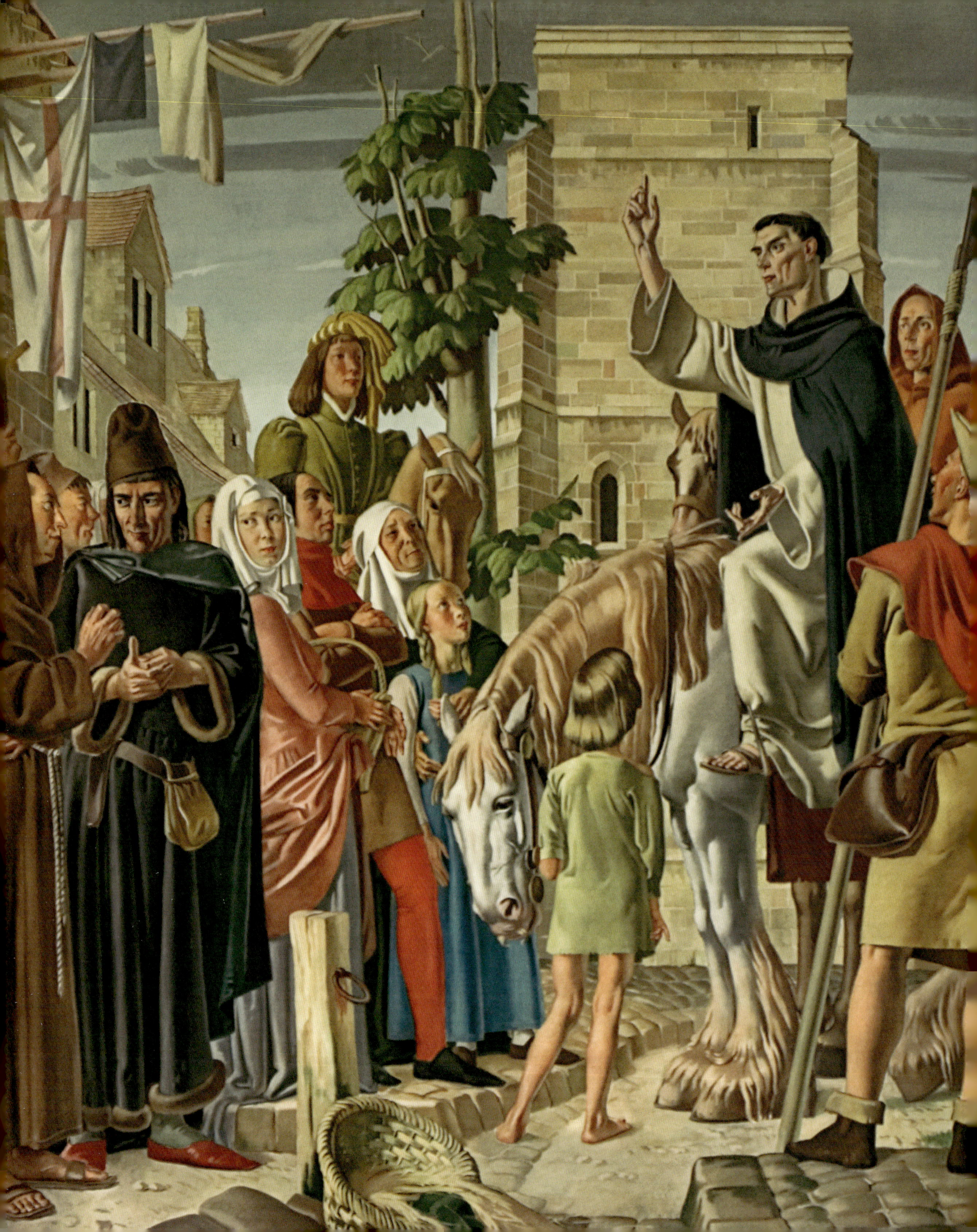

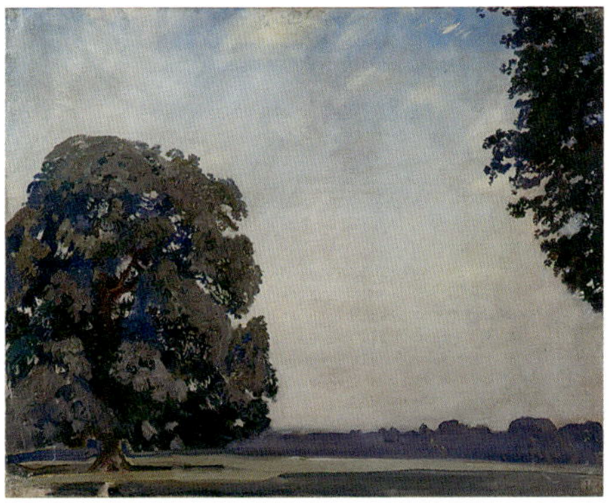

Munnings, Alfred James 1878–1959
Trees by the Edge of a Field
oil on canvas 50.8 x 61 (E)
410

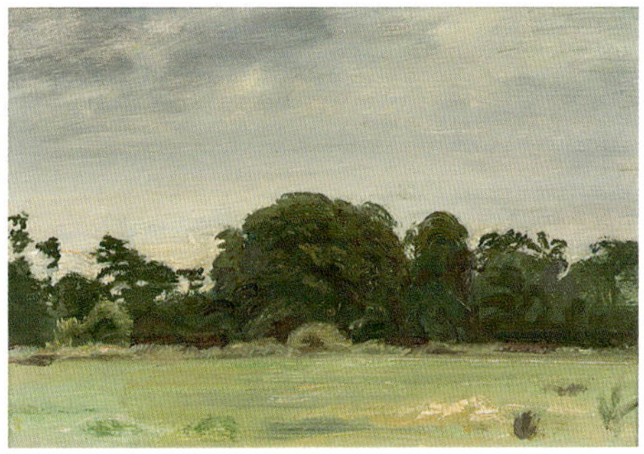

Munnings, Alfred James 1878–1959
Trees by the Edge of a Field
oil on panel 17.8 x 25.4
594

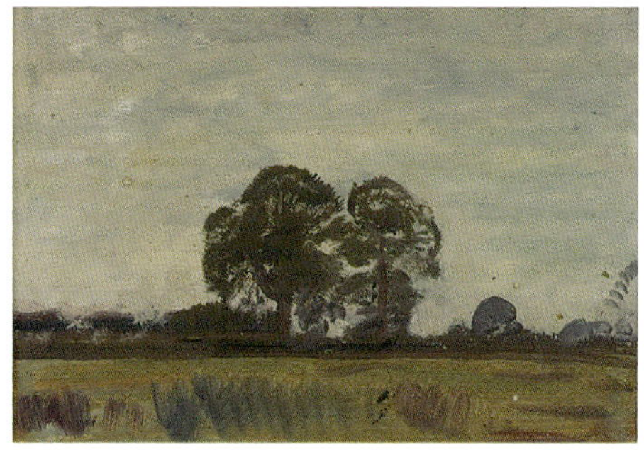

Munnings, Alfred James 1878–1959
Trees by the Edge of a Field (recto)
oil on board 17.8 x 25.4 (E)
598

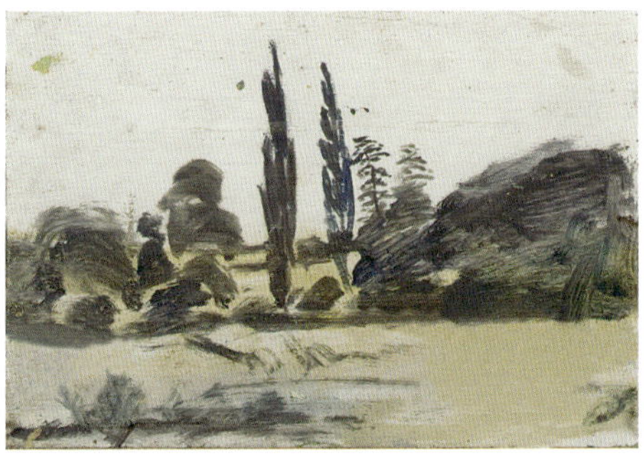

Munnings, Alfred James 1878–1959
Landscape Study (verso)
oil on board 17.8 x 25.4 (E)
598A

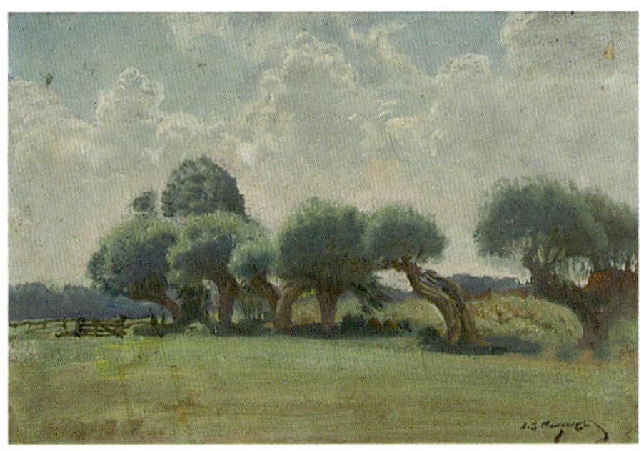

Munnings, Alfred James 1878–1959
Trees by the Edge of a Field (recto)
oil on board 25.4 x 35.6
607

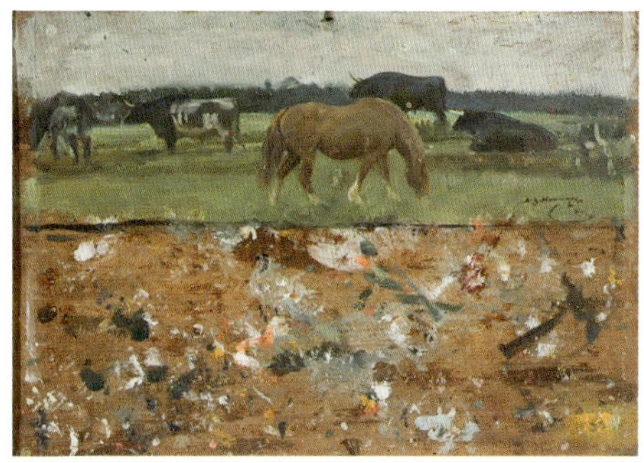

Munnings, Alfred James 1878–1959
Study of a Horse and Bullocks Grazing (verso)
oil on board 25.4 x 35.6
607A

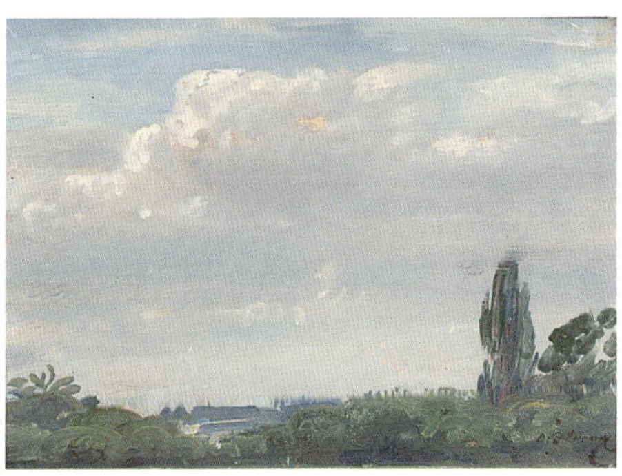

Munnings, Alfred James 1878–1959
Trees by the Edge of a Field
oil on board 17.8 x 22.9
610

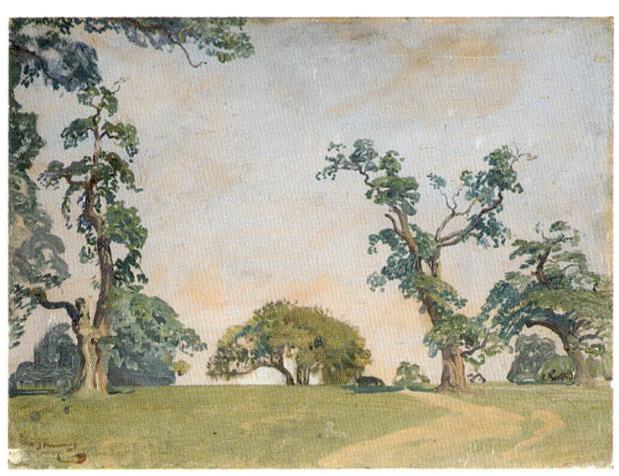

Munnings, Alfred James 1878–1959
Trees by the Edge of a Field
oil on board 30.5 x 40.6
614

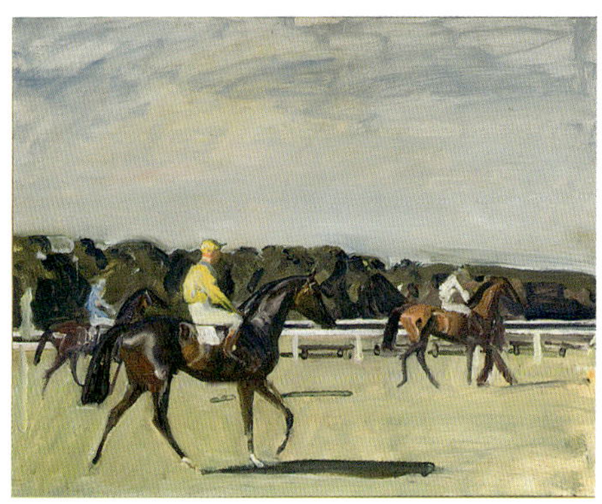

Munnings, Alfred James 1878–1959
Trotting to the Start
oil on board 50.8 x 61 (E)
12

Facing page: Fleetwood-Walker, Bernard, 1893–1965, *John Ball Preaching at Brentwood, 1381* (detail), 1938, Essex County Council, (p. 51)

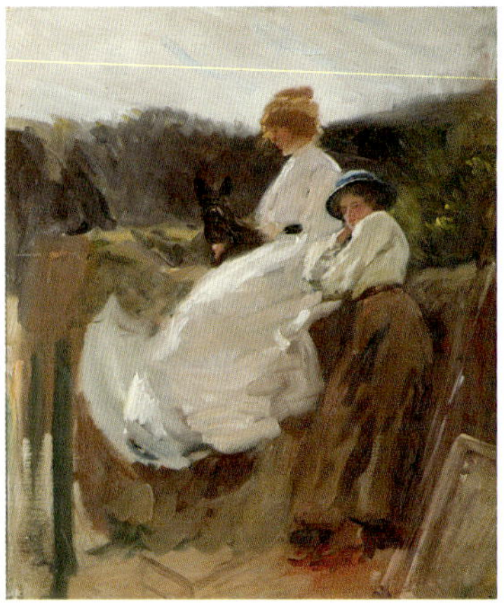

Munnings, Alfred James 1878–1959
Two Girls and a Dog
oil on canvas 76.2 x 63.5
211

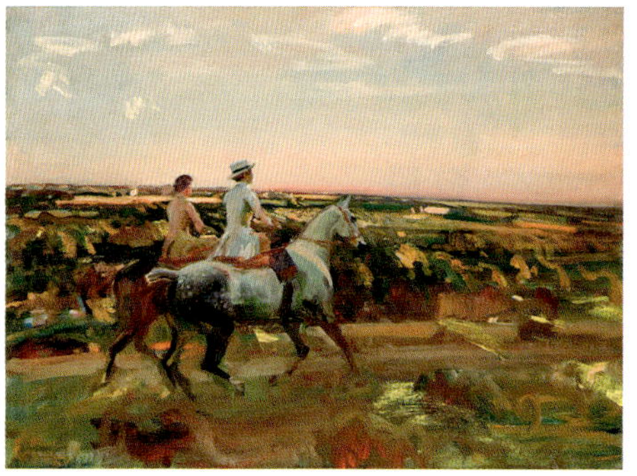

Munnings, Alfred James 1878–1959
Two Lady Riders under an Evening Sky
oil on canvas 71.1 x 91.4
247

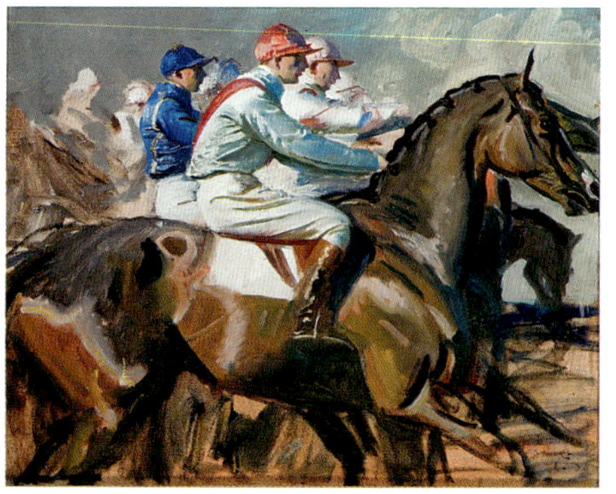

Munnings, Alfred James 1878–1959
Under Starter's Orders
oil on canvas 50.8 x 63.5
135

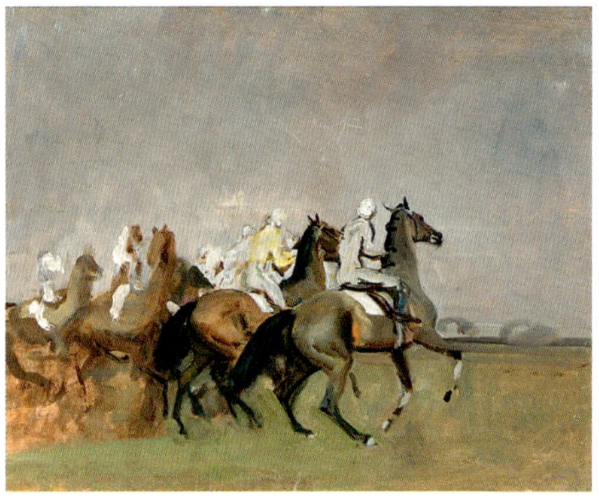

Munnings, Alfred James 1878–1959
Under Starter's Orders
oil on panel 50.8 x 61
456

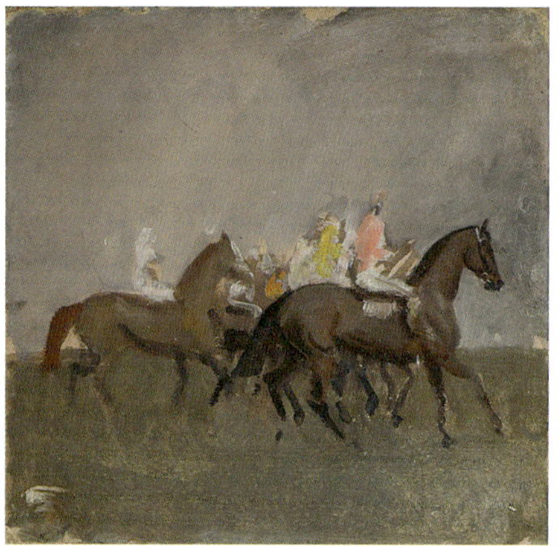

Munnings, Alfred James 1878–1959
Under Starter's Orders
oil on board 31.8 x 31.8
572

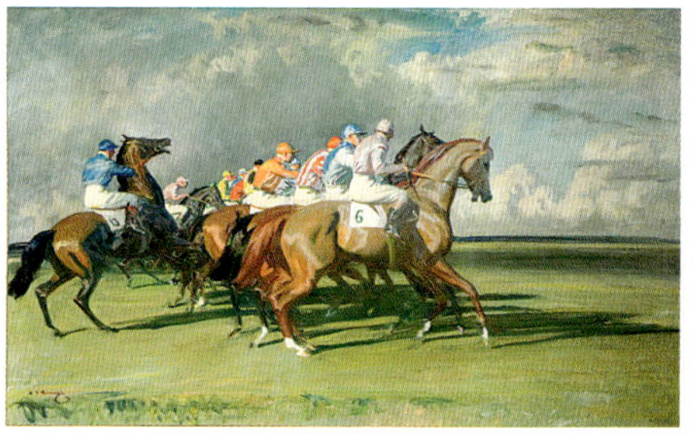

Munnings, Alfred James 1878–1959
Under Starter's Orders, Newmarket Start, Cries of 'No, No, Sir'
oil on canvas 112.4 x 177.8
131

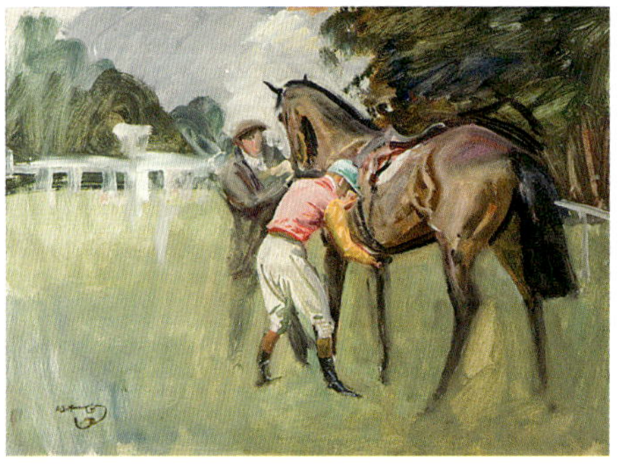

Munnings, Alfred James 1878–1959
Unsaddling of a Bay Racehorse, Stanley Wooton Colours
oil on board 45.7 x 63.5
447

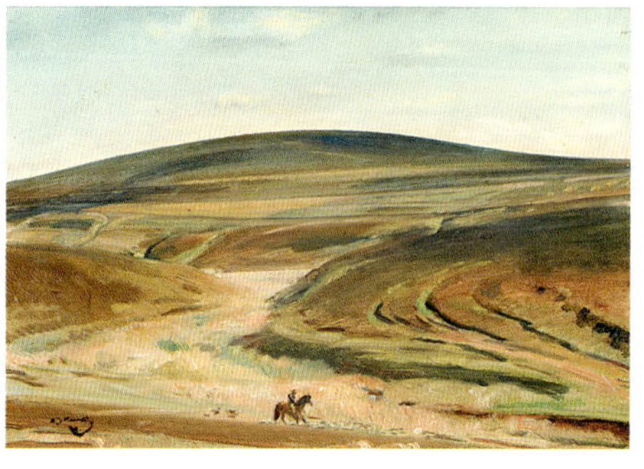

Munnings, Alfred James 1878–1959
View of Exmoor, a Rider in the Foreground
oil on board 43 x 59.5
514

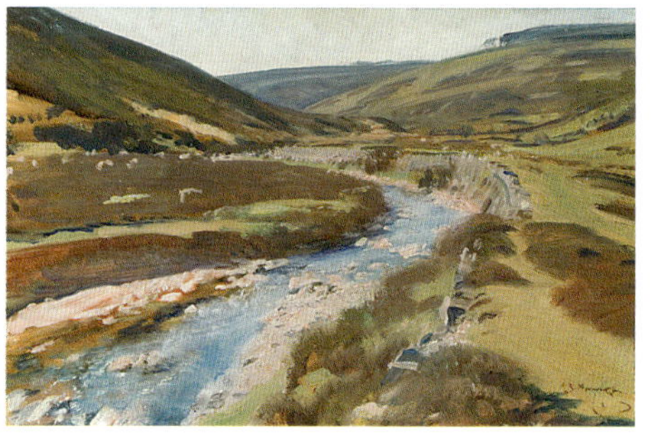

Munnings, Alfred James 1878–1959
View of Exmoor with Stream
oil on board 41 x 61
137

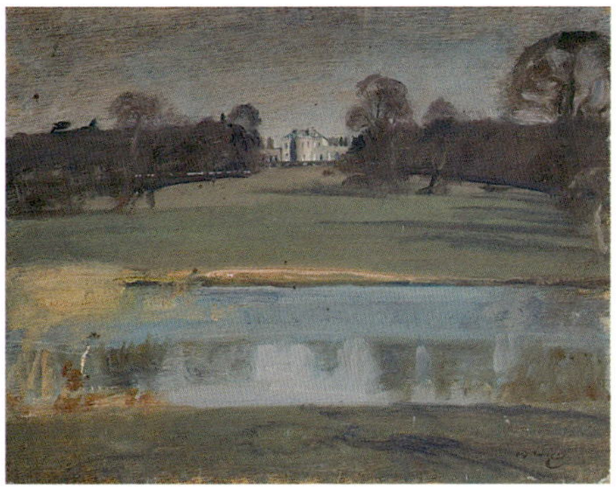

Munnings, Alfred James 1878–1959
View with Tendring Hall, Suffolk (demolished in 1955)
oil on board 40.6 x 50.8
383

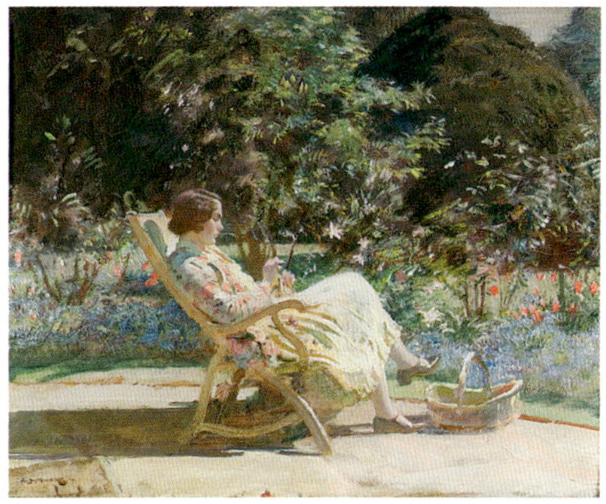

Munnings, Alfred James 1878–1959
Violet, My Wife, in the Garden
oil on canvas 50.8 x 61
58

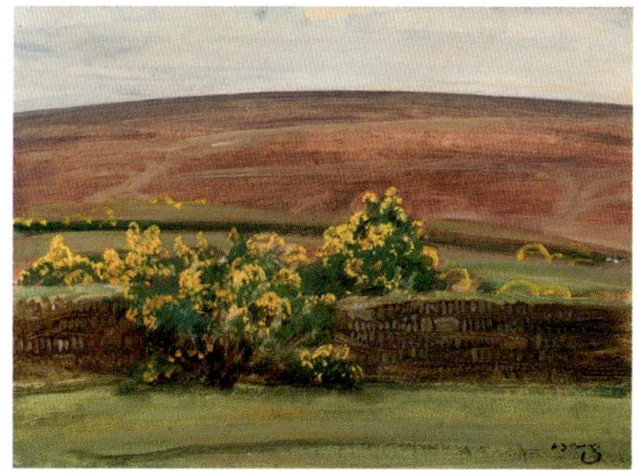

Munnings, Alfred James 1878–1959
Wall and Gorse on Exmoor
oil on board 37.5 x 50.8
246

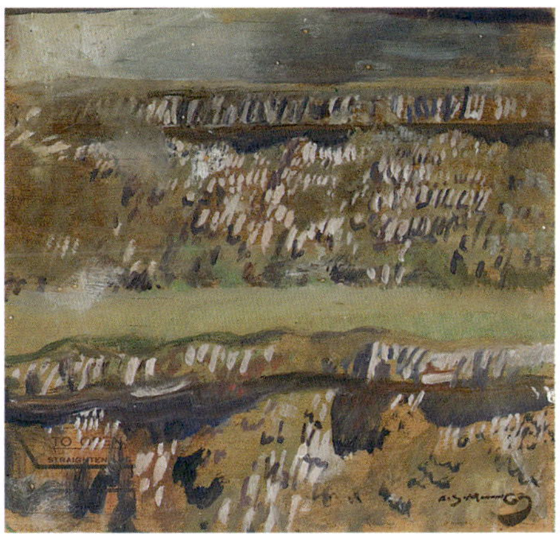

Munnings, Alfred James 1878–1959
Wall on Bradmoor, Withypool, Exmoor
oil on board 33 x 33 (E)
192

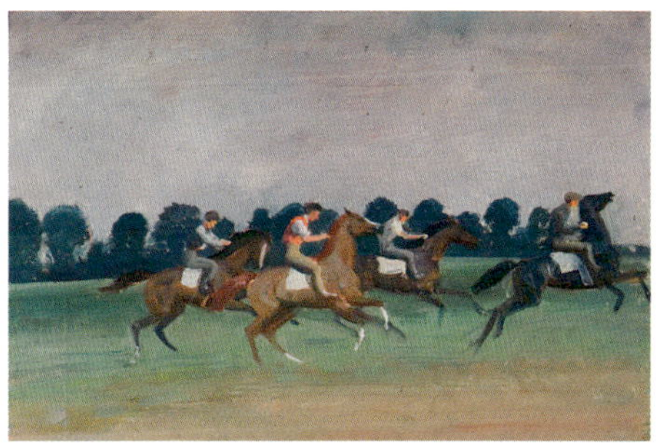

Munnings, Alfred James 1878–1959
Warren Hill, Newmarket
oil on board 27.3 x 40.6
616

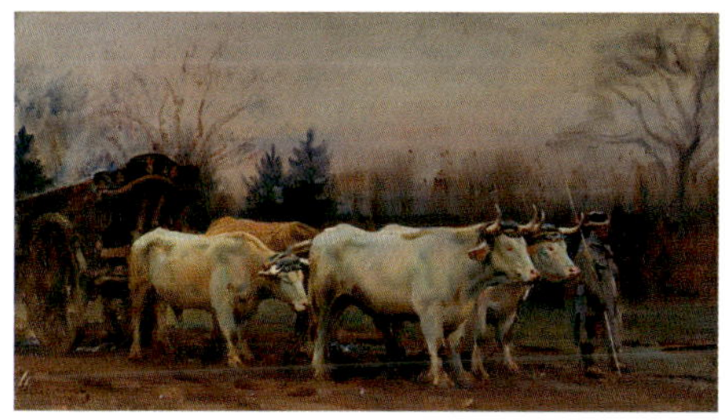

Munnings, Alfred James 1878–1959
White Oxen, Baron Robert's Estate, Chantilly
oil on canvas 35.6 x 61
102

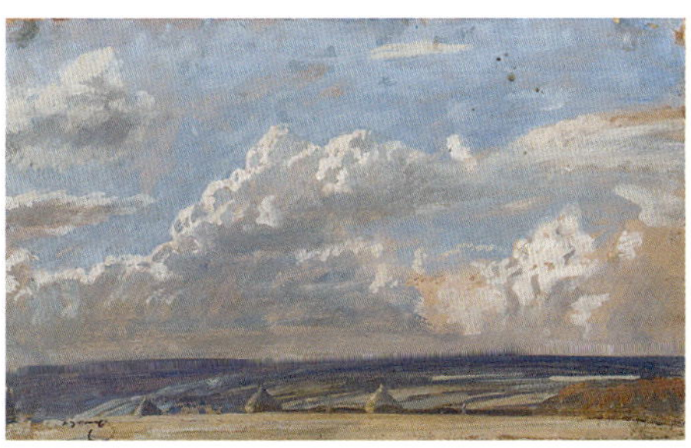

Munnings, Alfred James 1878–1959
Wide Landscape with Stacks
oil on canvas 31.8 x 50.8
473

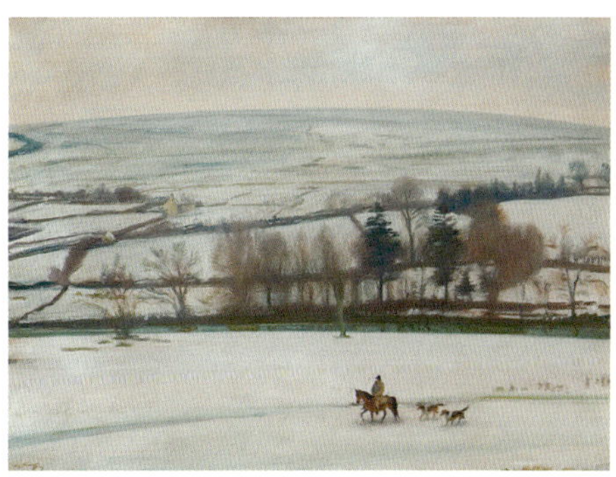

Munnings, Alfred James 1878–1959
Winter at Withypool, Exmoor: A Winter Landscape, a Rider and Two Hounds in the Foreground
oil on canvas 75 x 95.5
44

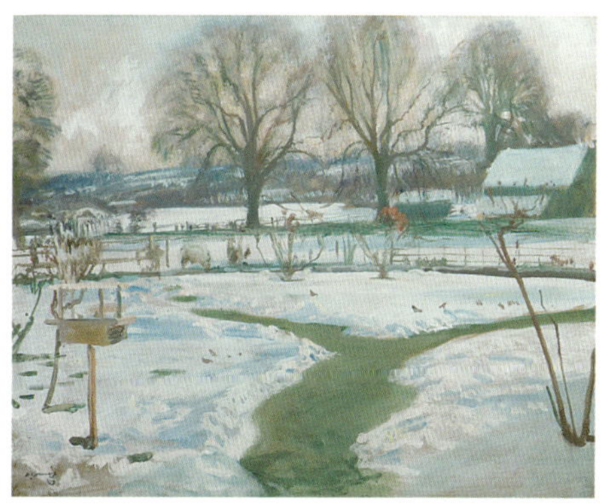

Munnings, Alfred James 1878–1959
Winter, Castle House
oil on canvas 64.1 x 76.2
235

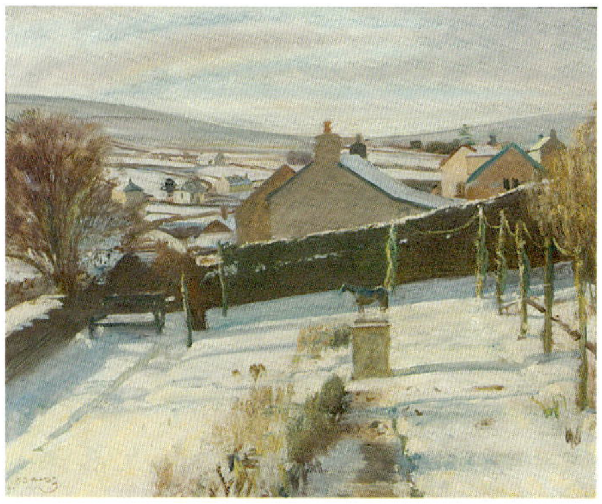

Munnings, Alfred James 1878–1959
Winter in Our Garden at Withypool, Exmoor
oil on board 50.8 x 61
48

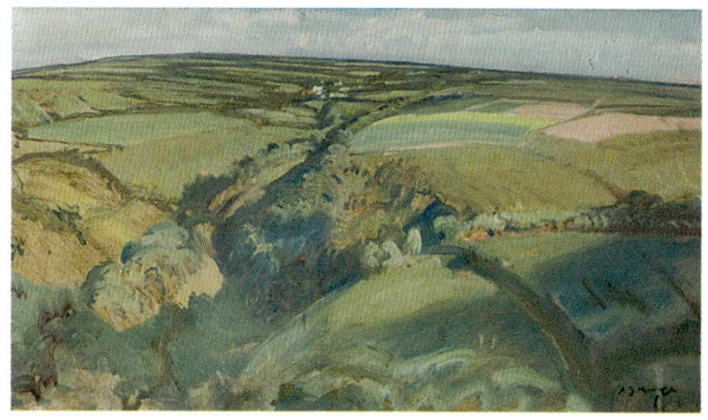

Munnings, Alfred James 1878–1959
Withypool Hill, Exmoor
oil on board 35.5 x 61
25

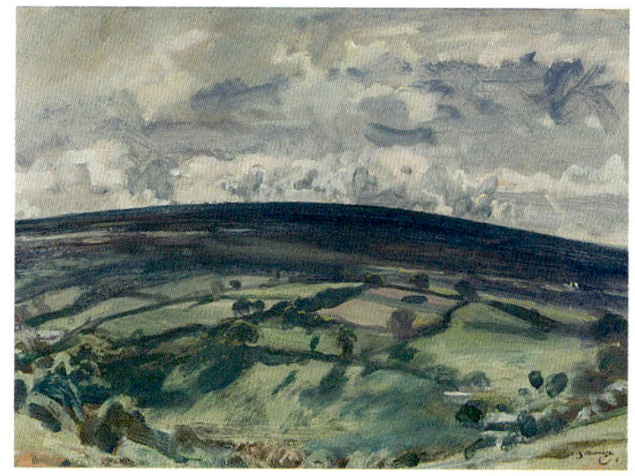

Munnings, Alfred James 1878–1959
Withypool Hill, Exmoor
oil on board 38.1 x 50.8
288

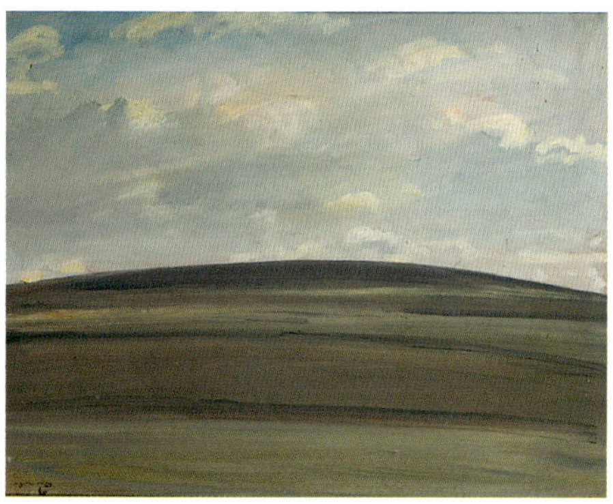

Munnings, Alfred James 1878–1959
Withypool Hill, Exmoor
oil on board 40.6 x 55.9
420B

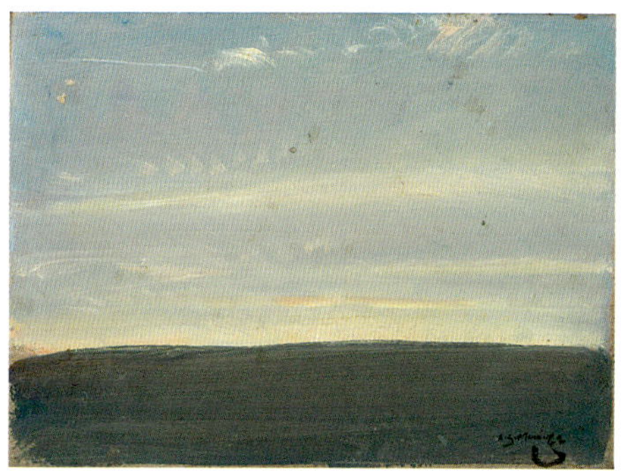

Munnings, Alfred James 1878–1959
Withypool Hill, Exmoor (recto)
oil on panel 22.9 x 35.6 (E)
561

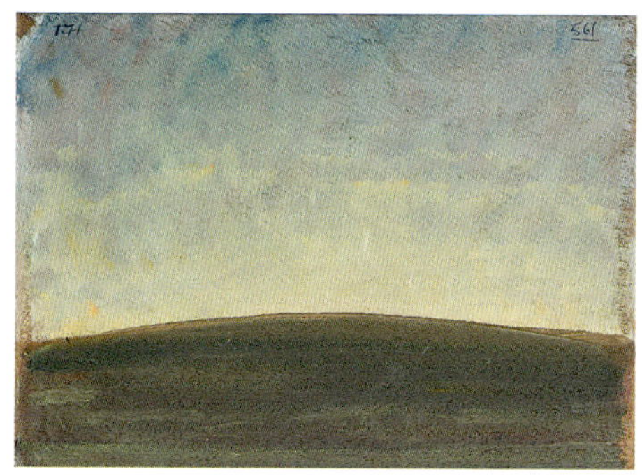

Munnings, Alfred James 1878–1959
Withypool Hill, Exmoor (verso)
oil on panel 22.9 x 35.6 (E)
561A

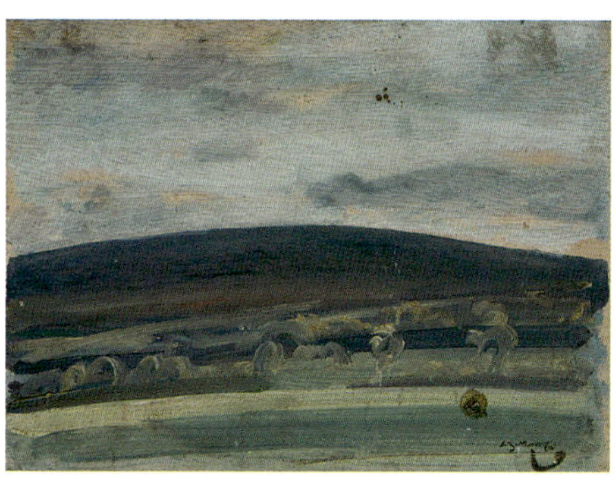

Munnings, Alfred James 1878–1959
Withypool Hill, Exmoor (recto)
oil on board 24.8 x 33
563

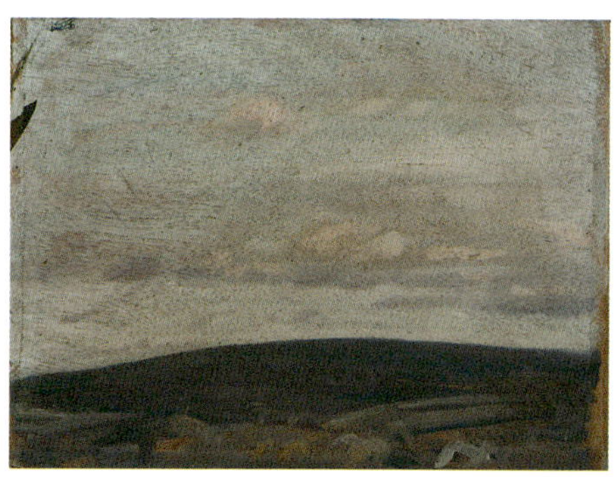

Munnings, Alfred James 1878–1959
Landscape (verso)
oil on board 24.8 x 33
563A

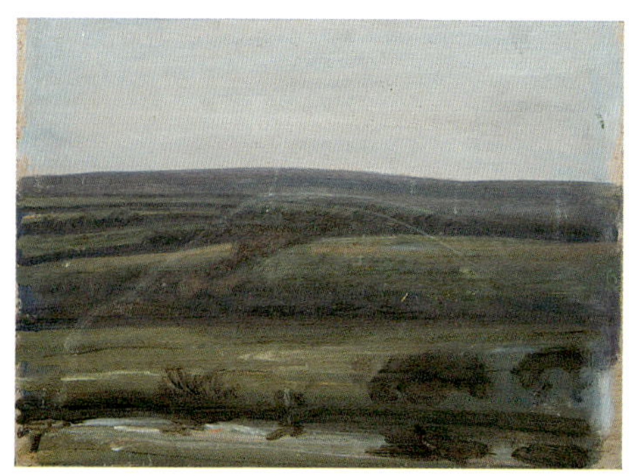

Munnings, Alfred James 1878–1959
Withypool Hill, Exmoor (recto)
oil on panel 24.8 x 33
566

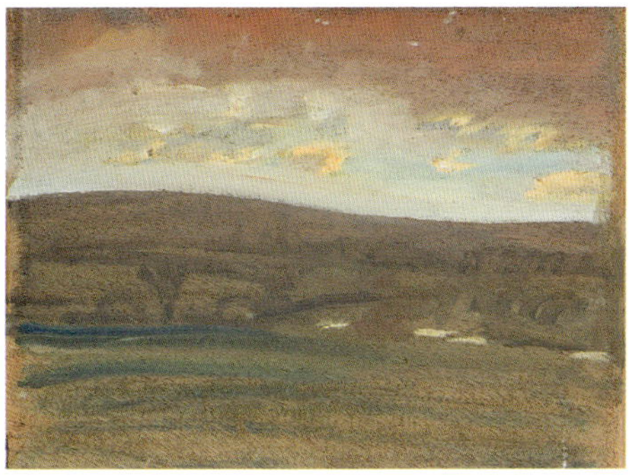

Munnings, Alfred James 1878–1959
Landscape Study (verso)
oil on panel 24.8 x 33
566A

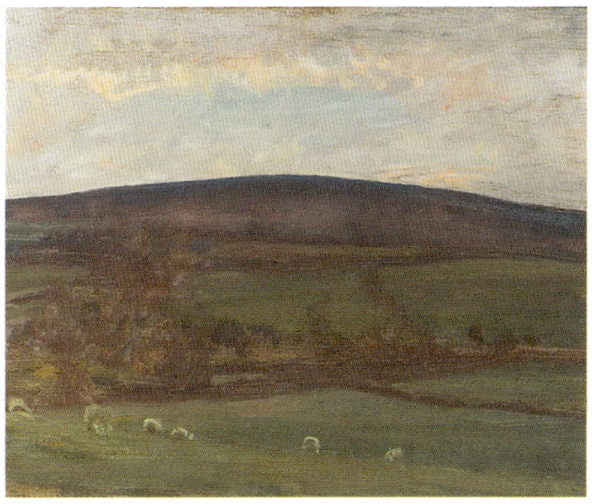

Munnings, Alfred James 1878–1959
Withypool Hill, Exmoor, Sheep in the Foreground
oil on board 50.8 x 59.1
287

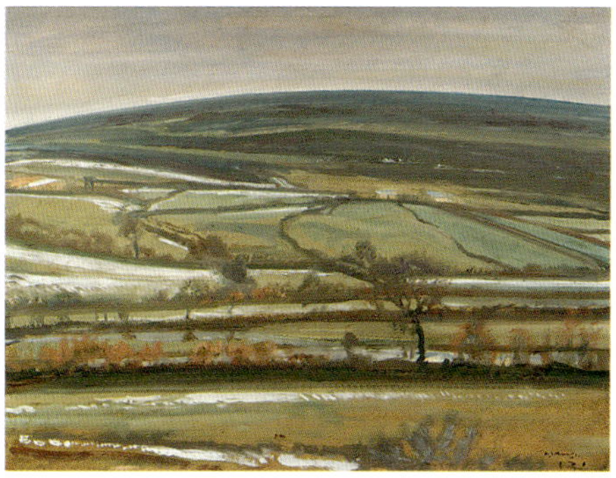

Munnings, Alfred James 1878–1959
Withypool Thaw, Exmoor
oil on board 50.8 x 66
254

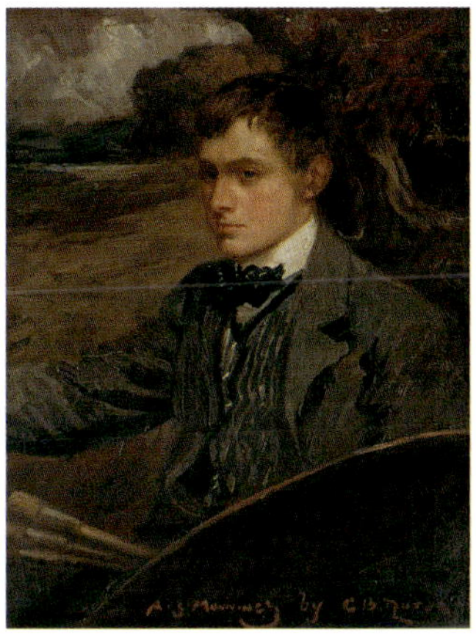

Nurse, Charles Baxter active 1895–1915
Alfred Munnings c.1898
oil on canvas 61.5 x 41
639

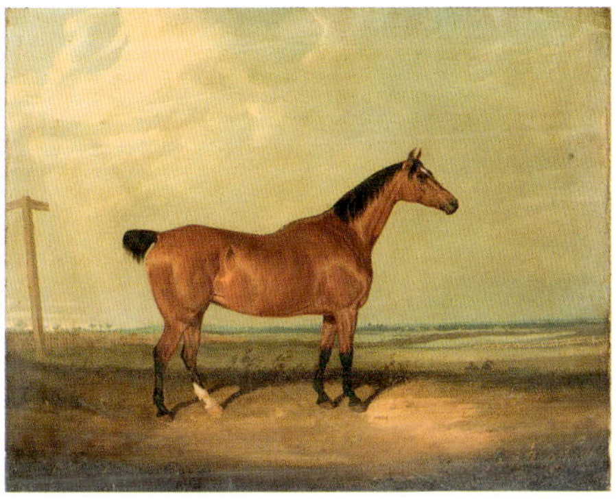

unknown artist 19th C
A Bay Hunter
oil on canvas 58 x 71
NM10

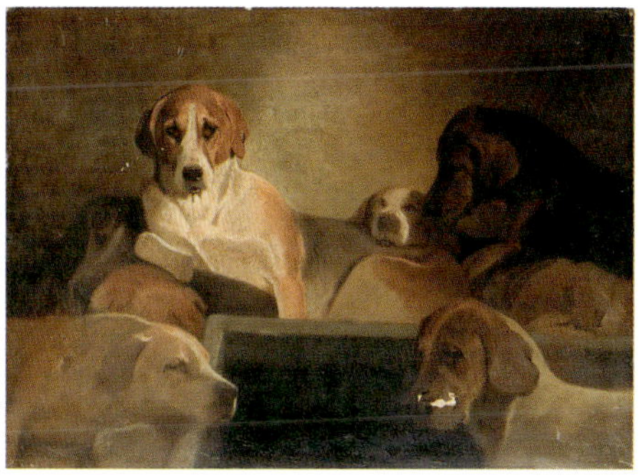

unknown artist 19th C
Hounds
oil on canvas 45 x 61
NM9

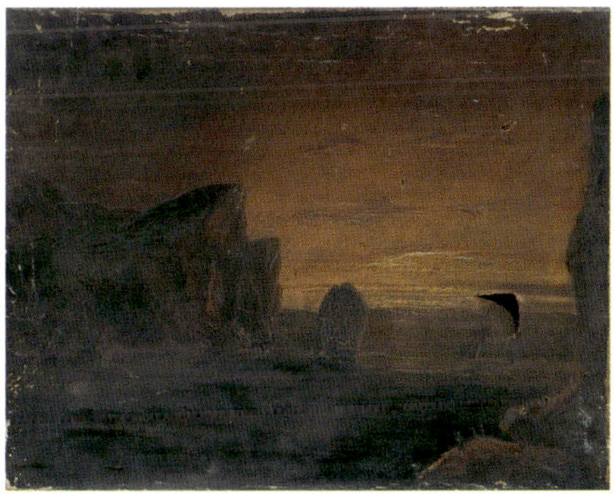

unknown artist 19th C
Shipwreck at Sunset
oil on canvas 43 x 53.5
Misc6

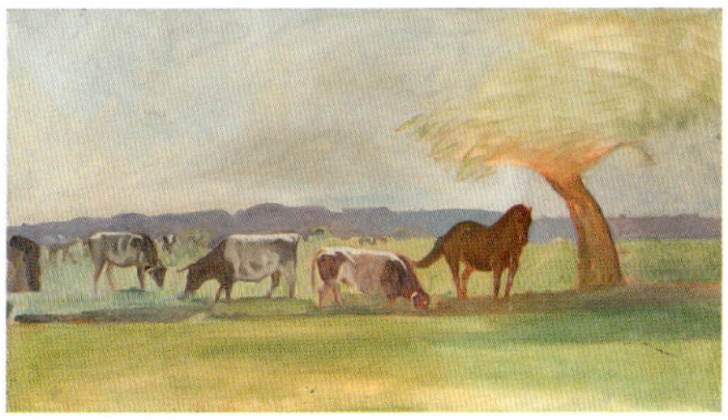

unknown artist
Cows and a Horse Beneath a Tree
oil on canvas 53 x 94.5
NM7

The Nottage Maritime Institute

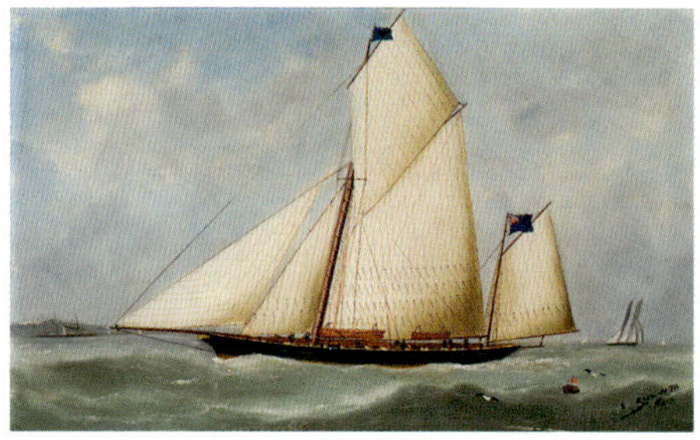

Adam, Edmond 1868–1938
Yawl 'Jullanar' 1883
oil on canvas 35 x 55
575

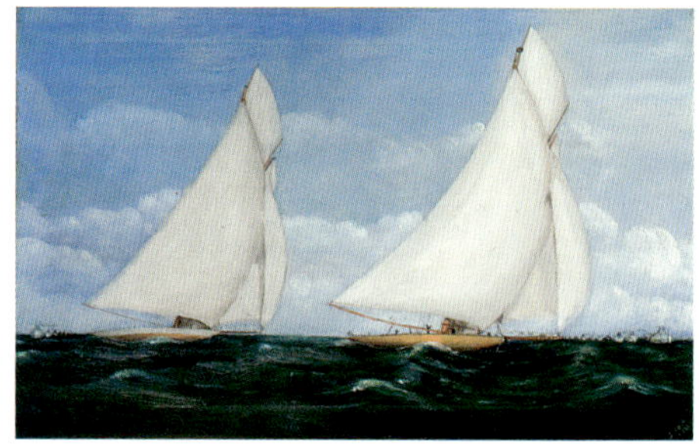

Fale, John
'Shamrock' and 'Columbia' 1901
oil on canvas 41 x 61
447

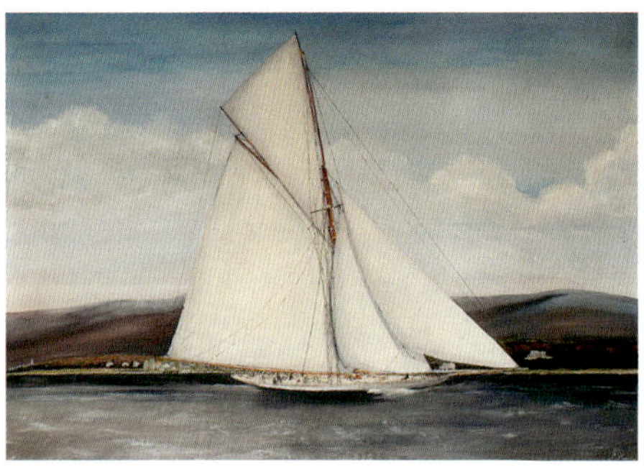

Fale, John
'Valkyrie III', America's Cup Challenger, 1895
oil on canvas 56.2 x 77
445

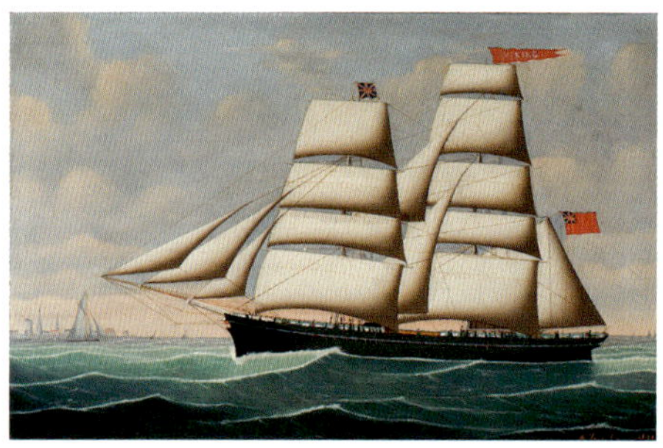

Loos, Henry active 1871–1904
Brig 'Viking' 1871
oil on canvas 52 x 76.9
438

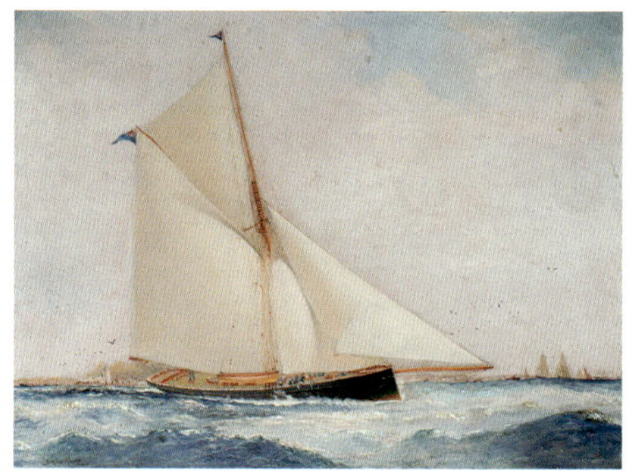

Moore, Barlow 1834–1897
Cutter Yacht 'Moina' 1896
oil on canvas 35.5 x 45.7
421

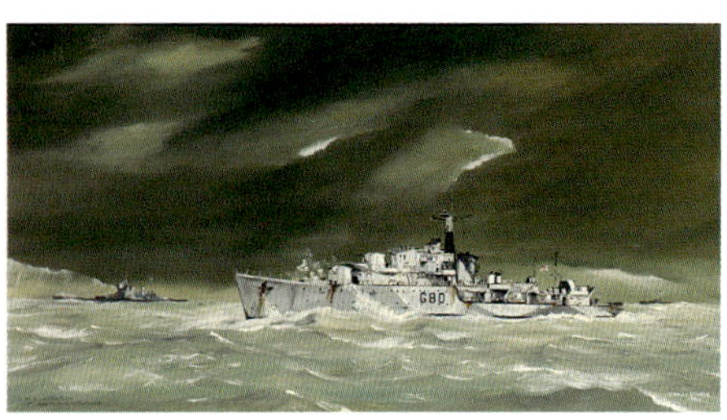

Rogers, Stanley d.c.1961
HMS Opportune', G80, 17th Destroyer Flotilla
oil on board 43 x 79
2552

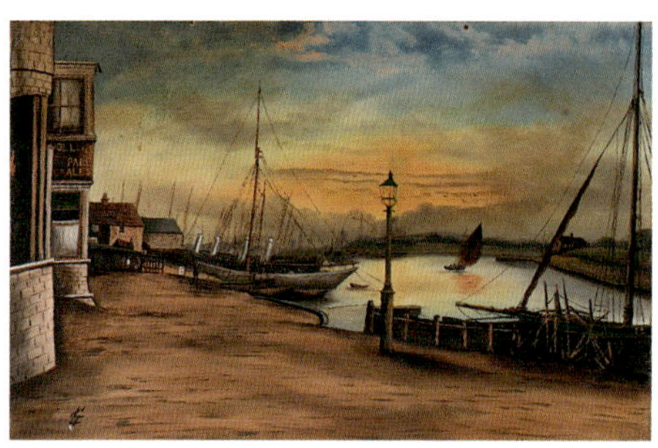

unknown artist
Waterside Scene c.1900
oil on board 50.9 x 76.2
621

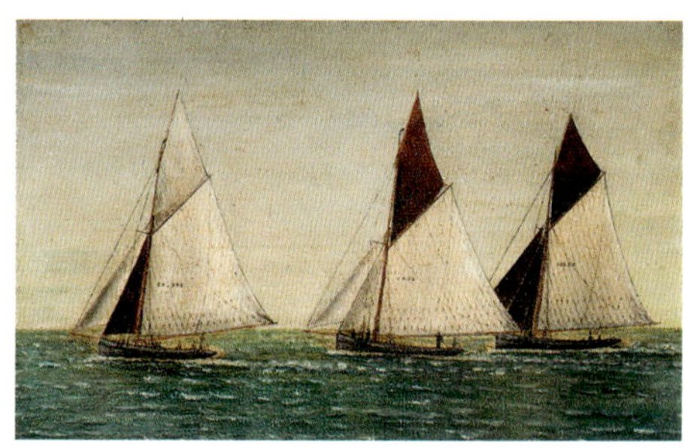

unknown artist
Smacks CK328, CK86 and CK103
oil on canvas 36.1 x 54.5
439

University of Essex

Jim Ede, a former Curator of the Tate Gallery, made the founding donation to the University of Essex. For many years he collected art from the first part of the twentieth century, developing a close relationship with the St Ives artists, including Alfred Wallis, Christopher Wood, Ben Nicholson and Barbara Hepworth. His own home, Kettle's Yard in Cambridge was dedicated to their art but he said that it was not 'an art gallery or museum, nor … simply a collection of works of art reflecting my taste or the taste of a given period. It is, rather, a continuing way of life from these last 50 years …' In 1966, while Cambridge University deliberated about taking over Kettle's Yard, Jim Ede looked towards the new university in the region, Essex, as a safe repository for a number of works from his collection. These works were to 'make a fledgling collection of your own that might grow into something unique and special …' creating an environment on campus where students could have access to the inspiration that art can bring.

Over the years the University of Essex has seen the collection expand and now includes works in different media by internationally renowned artists such as Francisco Goya, as well as nationally respected artists like Roderic Barrett, and has offered a helping hand to young emerging artists such as James Dodds. In recent years, our attention has turned towards the University's Collection of Latin American Art, which has continued the ethos of collecting by donation and has now over 700 works of its own.

Jessica Kenny, Gallery Director

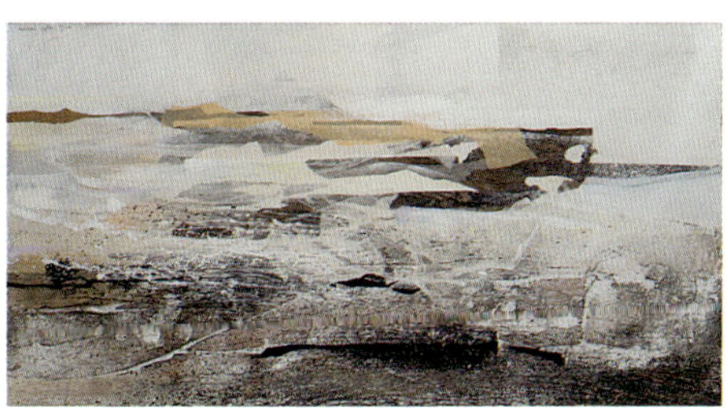

Ayrton, Michael 1921–1975
Seascape 1960
oil on board 61 x 111
14

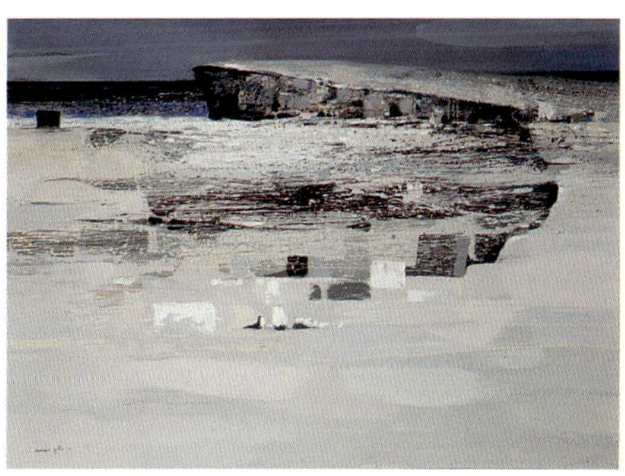

Ayrton, Michael 1921–1975
Tidal Landscape 1960
oil on canvas 74.6 x 100
8

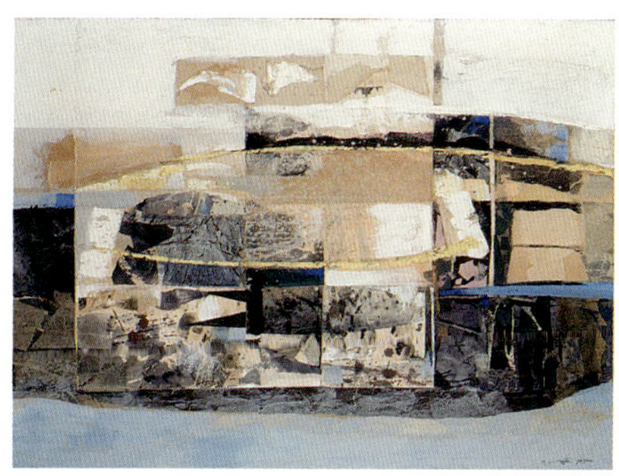

Ayrton, Michael 1921–1975
Naxos Marble 1965
oil on canvas 76 x 116
10

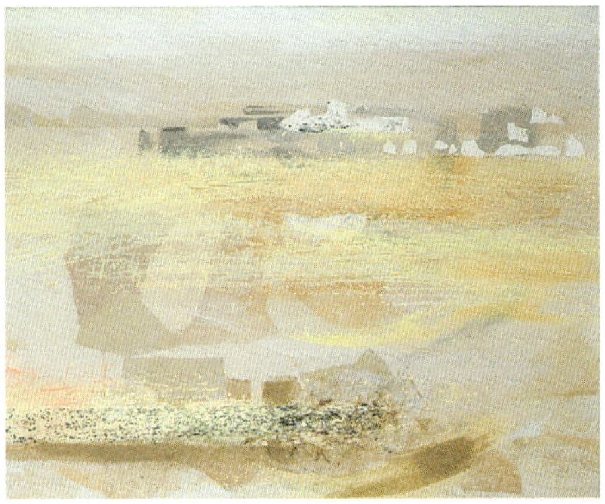

Ayrton, Michael 1921–1975
Pale Sun Landscape
acrylic on canvas 73.5 x 91.2
9

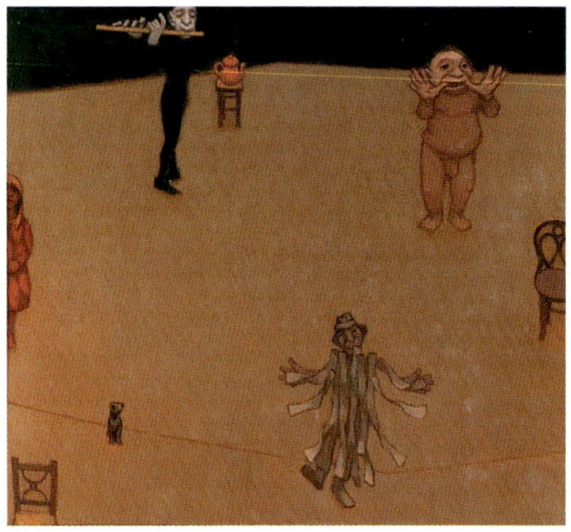

Barrett, Roderic 1920–2000
Song and Dance
oil on canvas 137.1 x 152.2
17

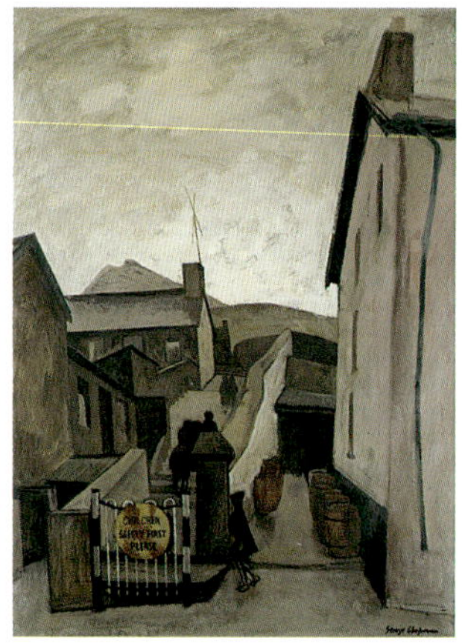

Chapman, George 1908–1993
Children Going to School
oil on canvas 112 x 79
23

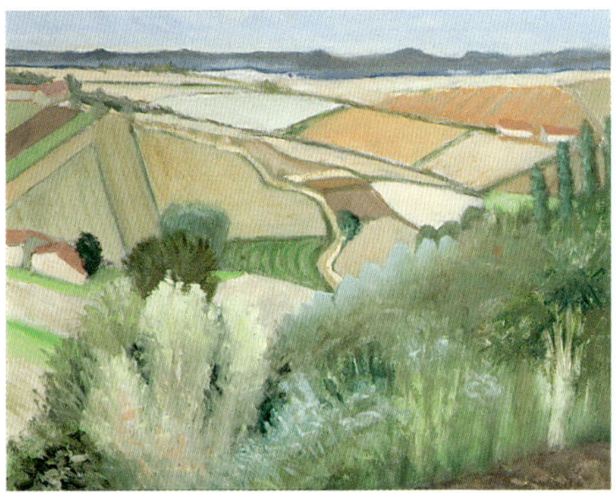

Crittall, Ariel b.1914
Landscape near Riberac
oil on canvas 44 x 54
20

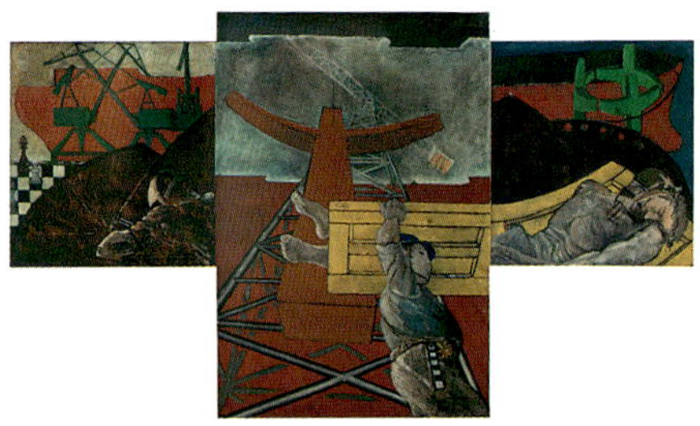

Dodds, James Foster b.1957
Solidarnosc 1982
oil on canvas 220 x 260
18

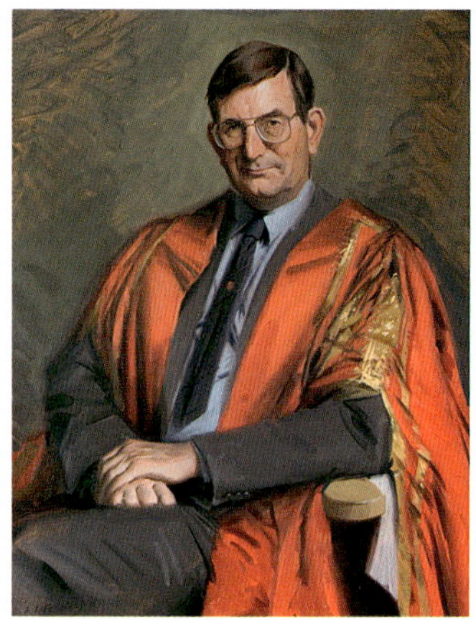

Festing, Andrew b.1941
Martin Best Harris
oil on canvas 110 x 90
1

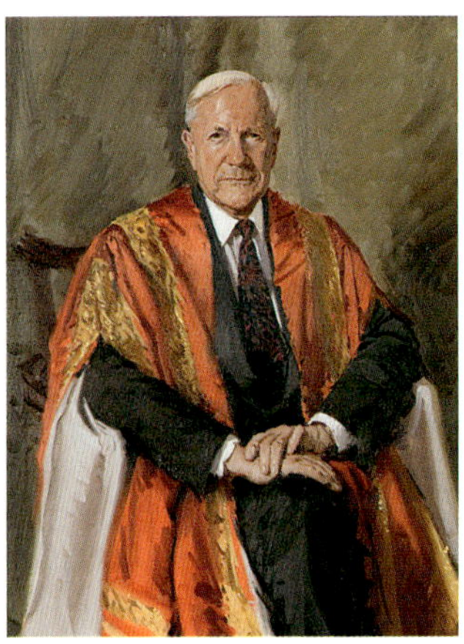

Festing, Andrew b.1941
Sir Patrick Nairne
oil on canvas 110 x 90
2

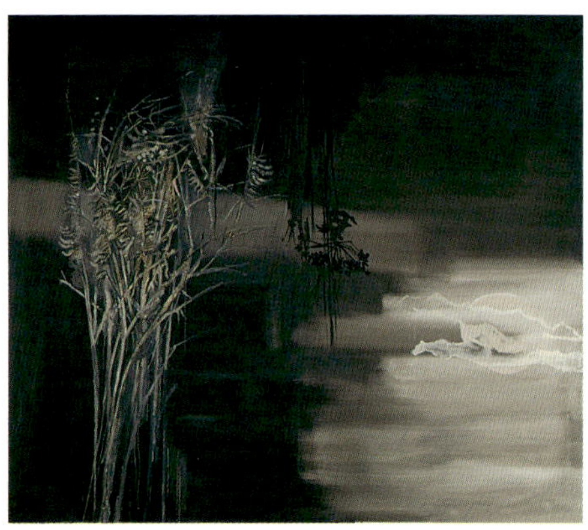

Middleditch, Edward 1923–1987
Night Reflections
oil on canvas 161 x 182.6
19

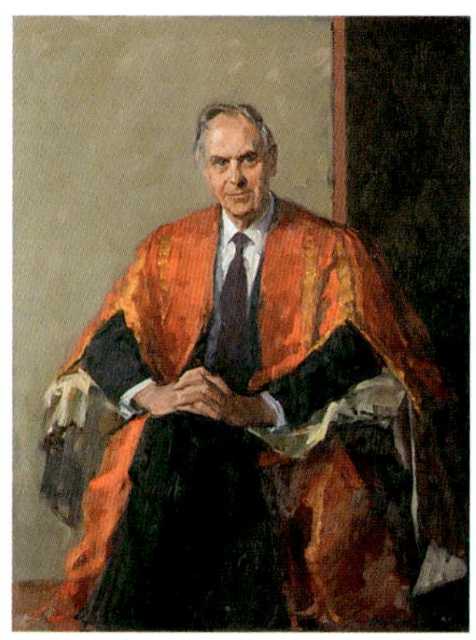

Poole, David b.1931
Sir Albert Sloman
oil on canvas 124 x 102
4

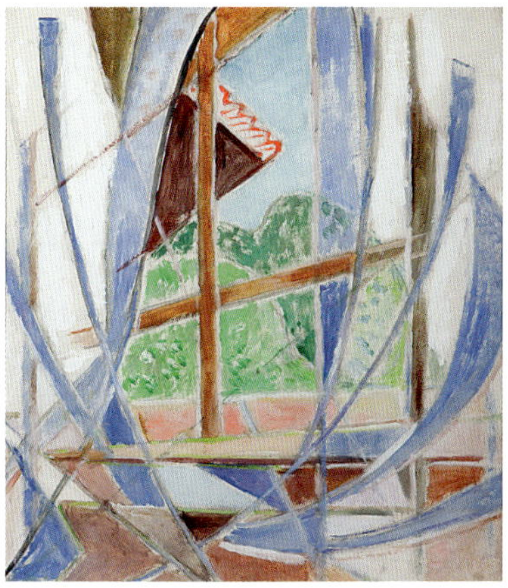

Ramsay, Patricia 1886–1974
Windowscape
oil on canvas 40.1 x 34.6
5

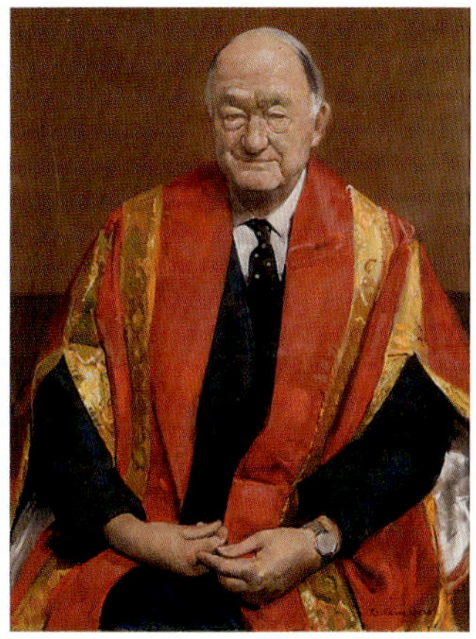

Spear, Ruskin (attributed to) 1911–1990
Lord Butler
oil on canvas 118 x 96
3

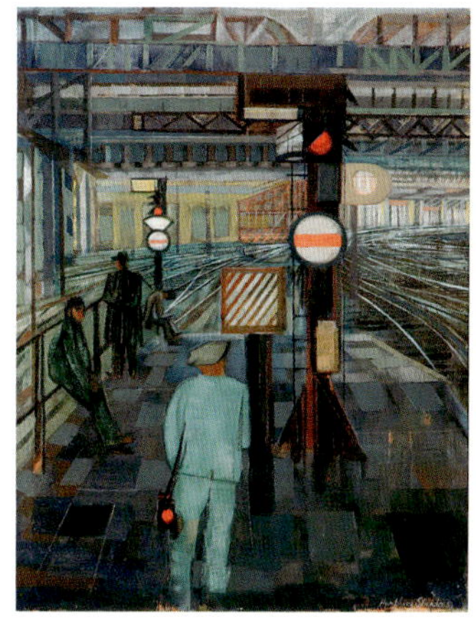

Spender, John Humphrey 1910–2005
Station Scene 1953
oil on canvas 91.7 x 69.8
22

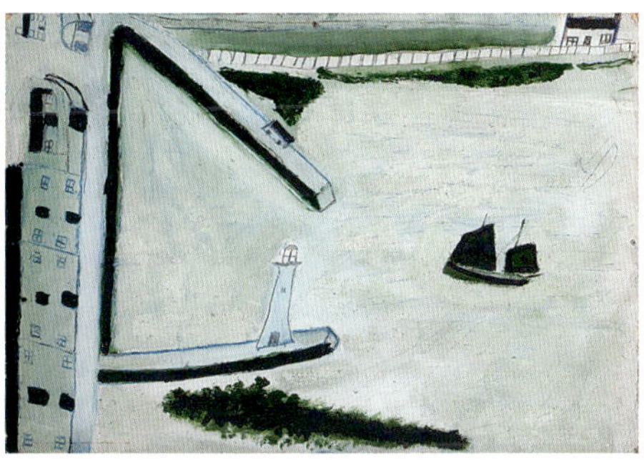

Wallis, Alfred 1855–1942
Harbour and Sailing Ship
oil on board 35 x 51.1
11

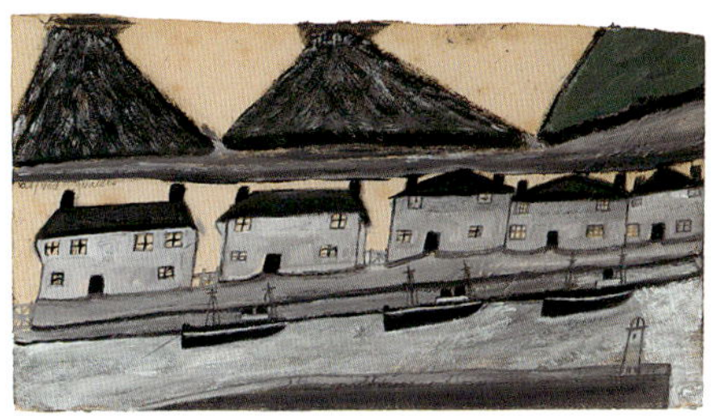

Wallis, Alfred 1855–1942
Houses and Kilns
oil on board 27.3 x 41.1
15

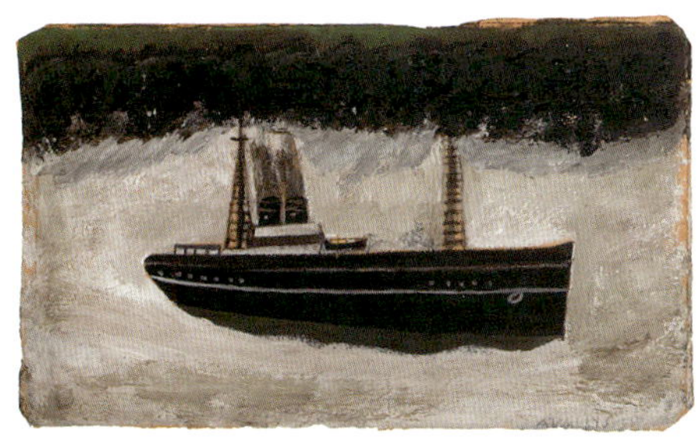

Wallis, Alfred 1855–1942
Ship
oil on board 31.1 x 51
12

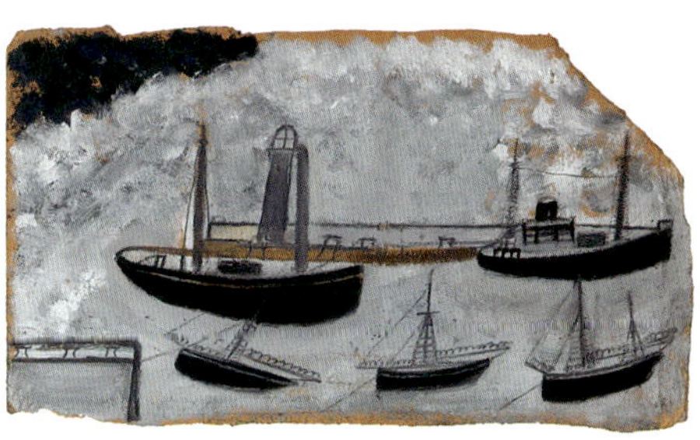

Wallis, Alfred 1855–1942
Ships in Harbour
oil on board 21 x 37.4
6

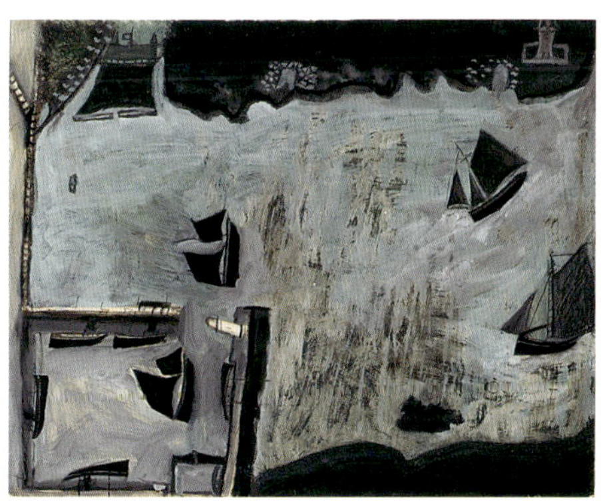

Wallis, Alfred 1855–1942
St Michael's Mount Harbour
oil on board 37 x 45.5
16

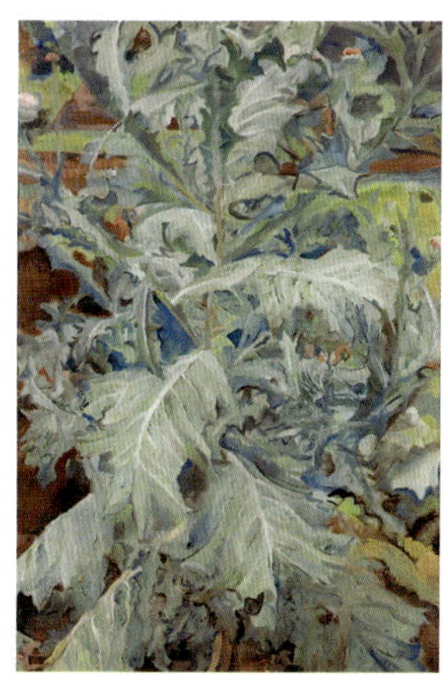

Waterfield, Margaret Helen 1863–1953
Giant Thistle
oil on canvas 91.4 x 61
21

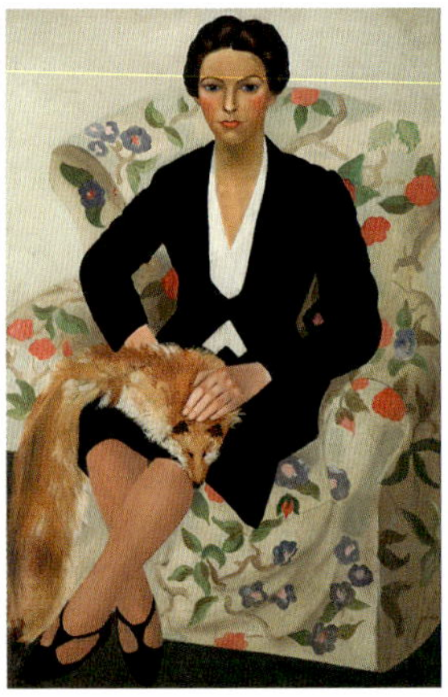

Wood, Christopher 1901–1930
Mlle Bourgoint 1929
oil on canvas 88 x 64
13

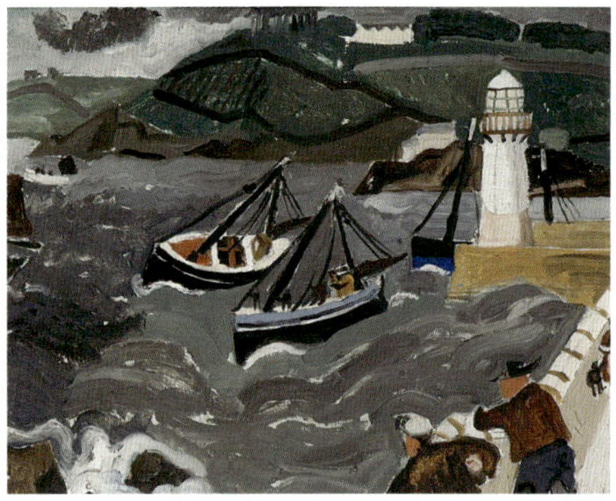

Wood, Christopher 1901–1930
Harbour in Hills
oil on canvas 36 x 43.6
7

University of Essex, Collection of Latin American Art

The University of Essex Collection of Latin American Art (UECLAA) was founded in 1993 following an initial donation by Charles Cosac, then a student in the Department of Art History and Theory, of a work by the eminent contemporary Brazilian artist Siron Franco: *Memória* of 1992. This is an intriguing and multivalent painting. The spectator is first attracted by the shimmering silver surface but on closer inspection this is not a celebratory memorial. Details hint at two different but equally destructive aspects of Brazil's involvement in the global economy: shadowy animals and animal pelts refer to the illegal trade in fur from the Amazonian rainforests, while a suggestion of a child's coffin and the silver paint surface itself commemorate a disaster that occurred in 1987 in the district of Goiânia in which Franco himself lives. An international company illegally dumped canisters of the dangerous chemical Cesium in the area and children played with this attractive shiny substance. As a result many died and many more continue to suffer health problems. Franco's *Memória* was certainly a challenging and powerful work on which to build a new collection of Latin American art, and it can usefully serve as a metaphor for the responsibilities of those in charge of building such a collection in the UK. Researching a work of art in depth involves investigating both its formal qualities and the ideas that lie behind it and then working to understand and interpret the broader aesthetic and ideological context. This is what UECLAA aims to do.

Since this initial donation UECLAA has grown to over 700 works of art in all media from most countries in the region with the emphasis on works produced in the last 50 years. Although paintings in oil or acrylic constitute only a relatively small percentage of the collection key early donations ensured that these media are represented by works of the highest calibre by some of the most important modern and contemporary artists of Latin America including Matta, Senise, Kuitca and Szyszlo. Matta's *Composition in Magenta: The End of Everything* was painted in 1942 while he was living in New York, and at a time when Jackson Pollock and Robert Motherwell would come to his studio to discuss possible new directions for painting. In this work Matta, deeply interested in both physics and psychoanalysis, explores a multidimensional space, perhaps of the mind, perhaps of the cosmos, spinning around a brilliant white central vortex. Painted in the middle of the Second World War, the title hints at the anguish and uncertainty of the times. A very different but equally painterly work, Kuitca's *Idea of a Passion* of 1984, deals with similar themes, but this time relating to a period of bloody political repression in Argentina and in a figurative mode. However, there is no one visual characteristic that can identify our paintings as Latin American. Some artists (such as Alisio, Piña and Szyszlo) make reference to aspects of the Pre-Columbian past; others to present-day indigenous and popular culture (Crousillat, Pereda, Zambrano); many are unashamedly abstract (Costigliolo, Sanín); while others draw inspiration from the art of the European past (Arango, D'Arienzo). Until comparatively recently, art school training in Latin America continued to emphasise the central importance of drawing from life, and of working in oil on canvas, and UECLAA includes numerous examples that demonstrate the continuing strength of these traditions in the region.

UECLAA is a valuable resource for undergraduate and post-graduate students at the University of Essex, not only for those taking courses in art history but also in a range of different disciplines including literature, history, sociology and human rights. Research into material in UECLAA is supported by specialist holdings in Latin American art in the University's Albert Sloman Library and by the UECLAA Archive, a unique and ever-growing collection of pamphlets, private view cards, exhibition leaflets, newspaper cuttings, artists' curricula vitae, letters, photographs, videos and other memorabilia relating to UECLAA artists and Latin American art more generally.

UECLAA has no permanent museum or gallery space. A changing selection of work is displayed in the university's Albert Sloman Library, and exhibitions of material from UECLAA are regularly included in the University Gallery exhibitions programme. A long-term collaboration with the contemporary arts organisation firstsite in Colchester will expand further in 2007, when firstsite's new building is scheduled to open. This purpose-built visual arts venue will provide UECLAA with a designated display area and many more opportunities for temporary exhibitions. Most of UECLAA will however continue to be held in store although this disadvantage has recently been offset by a generous grant from the Arts and Humanities Research Council which has enabled us to make the whole collection accessible in the form of an illustrated online catalogue. Further information about the paintings included here, about the rest of the collection and about Latin American art more generally can be found at www.ueclaa.org.uk

Valerie Fraser, Professor of Art History and Co-director of UECLAA

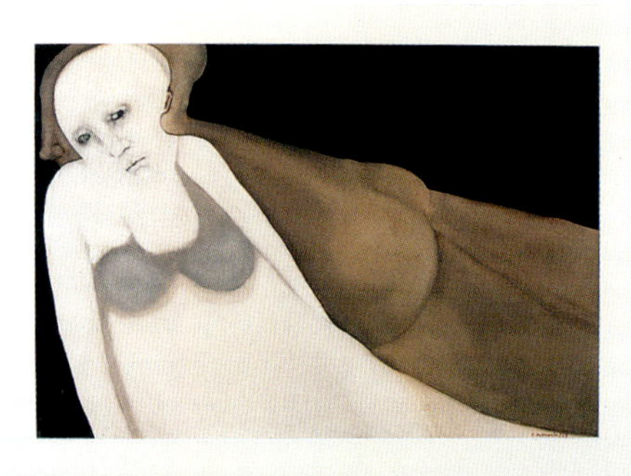

Aldunate, Carmen b.1940
Dream 1969
acrylic on paper 54 x 75
584 (P)

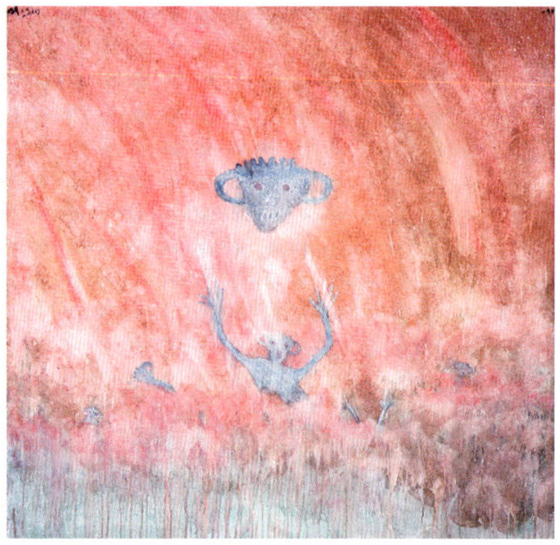

Alisio, Artemio 1942–2006
The Messenger (Popol Vuh) 1994
acrylic on canvas 130 x 130 (E)
181

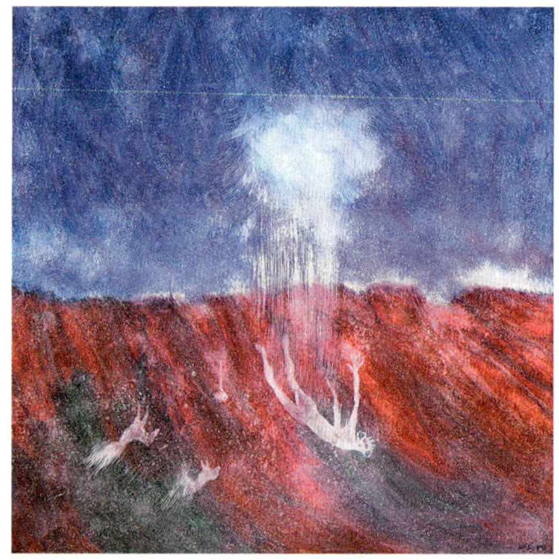

Alisio, Artemio 1942–2006
Yesterdays 1994
acrylic on card 129 x 124 (E)
180

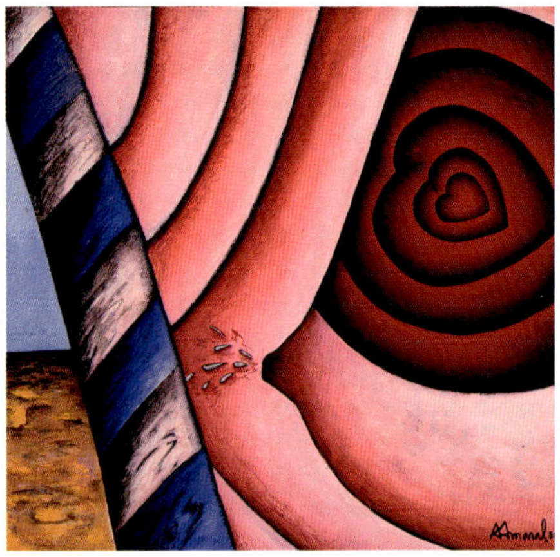

Amaral, Antonio Henrique b.1935
Chromo and Time II 1986
oil on canvas 180 x 180
245

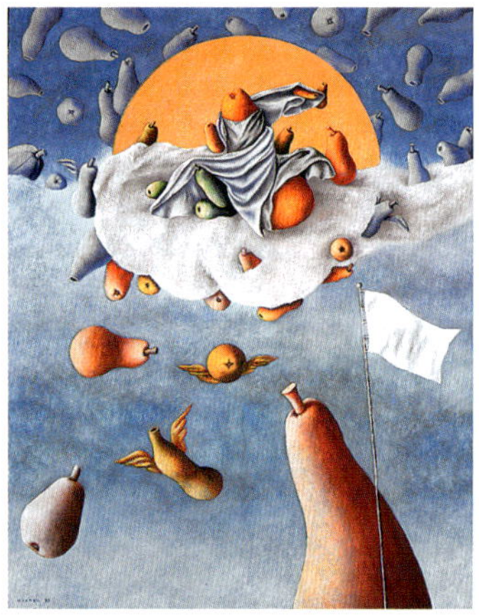

Arango, Ramiro b.1946
Assumption with the Artist 1995
oil on canvas 116 x 89
437

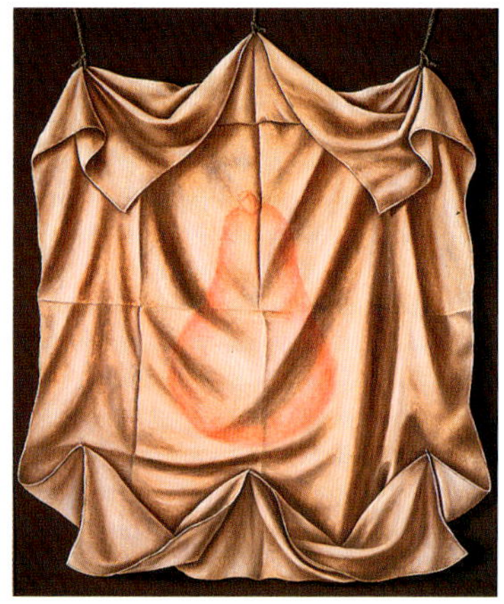

Arango, Ramiro b.1946
The Shroud (Veronica's Veil?) 1996
oil on canvas 100 x 81
436

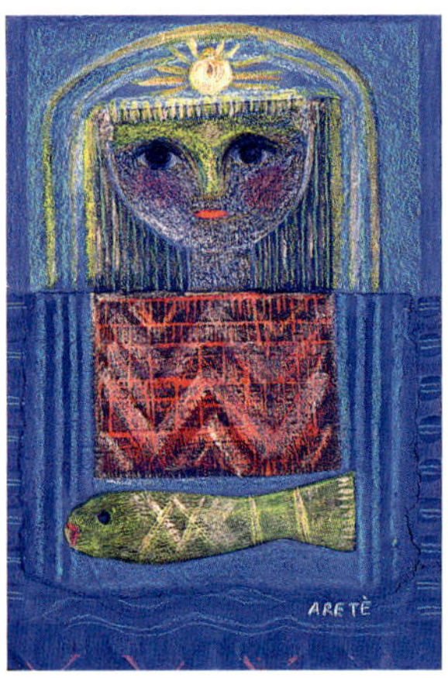

Arete b.1940
The Goddess of Fish
pastel & oil on card 36 x 23.5
226

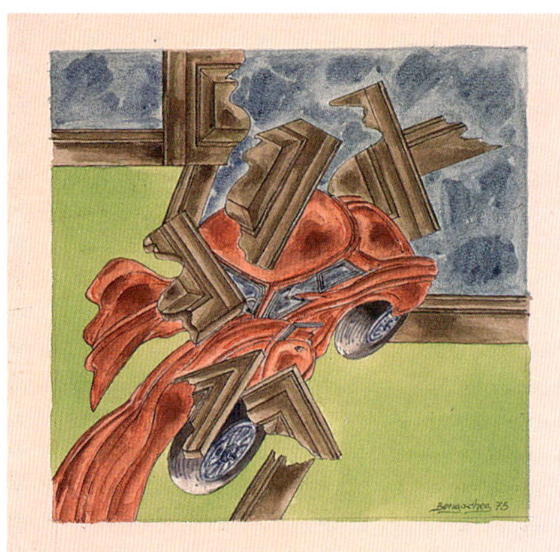

Bengochea, Miguel Angel b.1945
Untitled 1975
acrylic on card 35 x 35
2

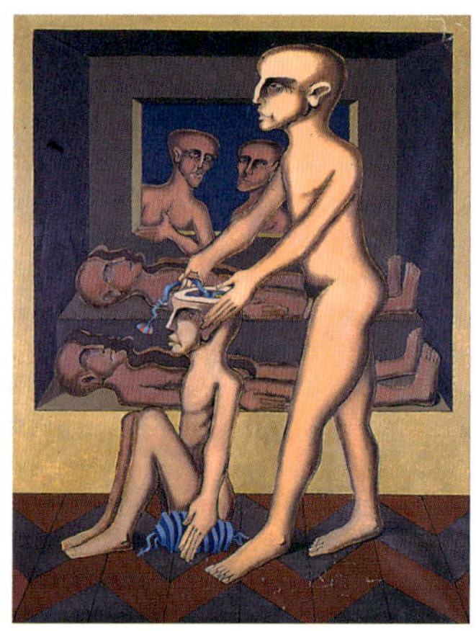

Borda, Osvaldo
Special Treatment 1971
oil on canvas 150 x 110
332

Facing page: Peake, Robert, c.1551–1619, *Portrait of a Lady (said to be Elizabeth Throckmorton (d.c.1647), Queen Elizabeth's Maid of Honour and Wife of Sir Walter Raleigh)* (detail), c.1595–1600, Maldon Town Council, (p. 213)

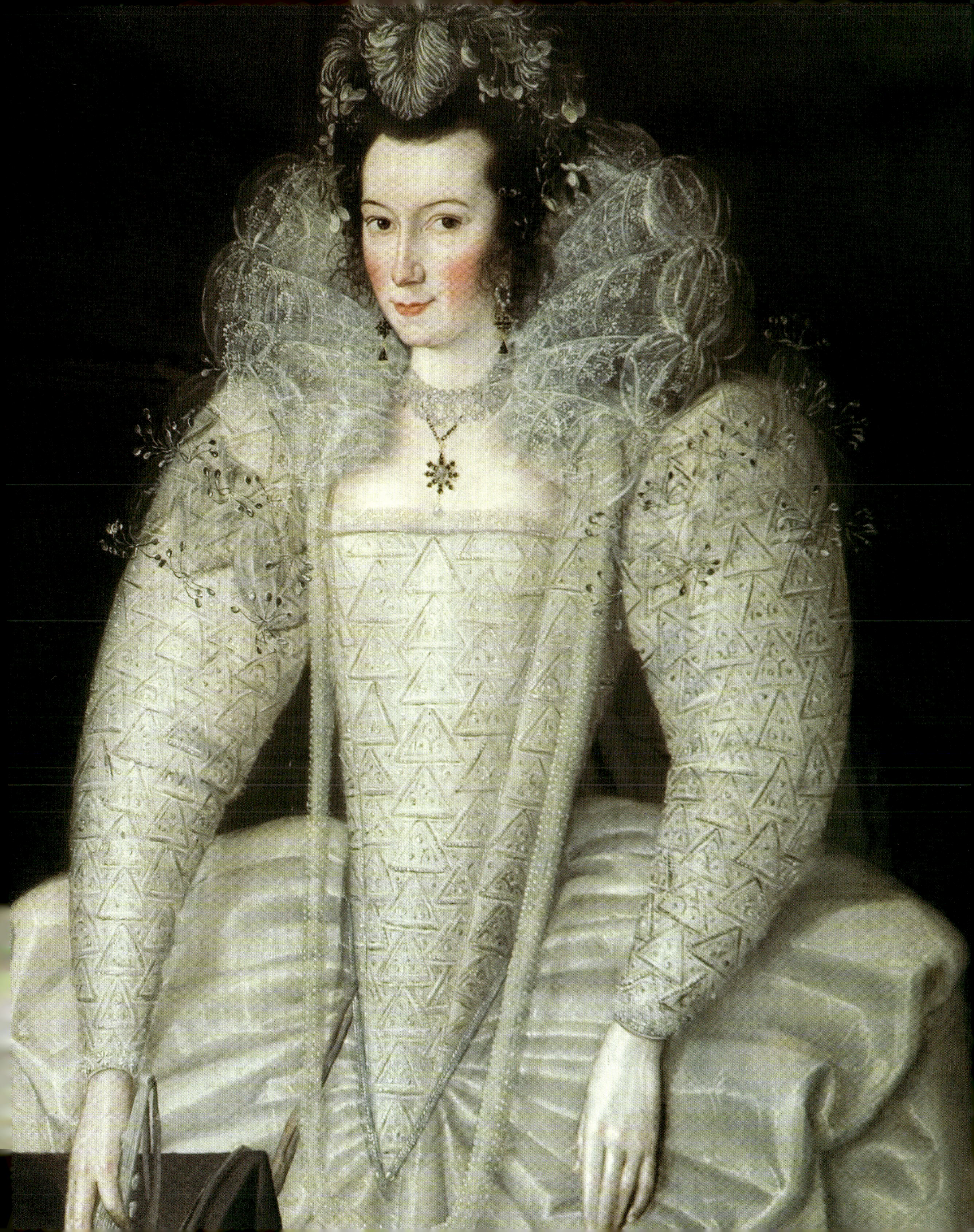

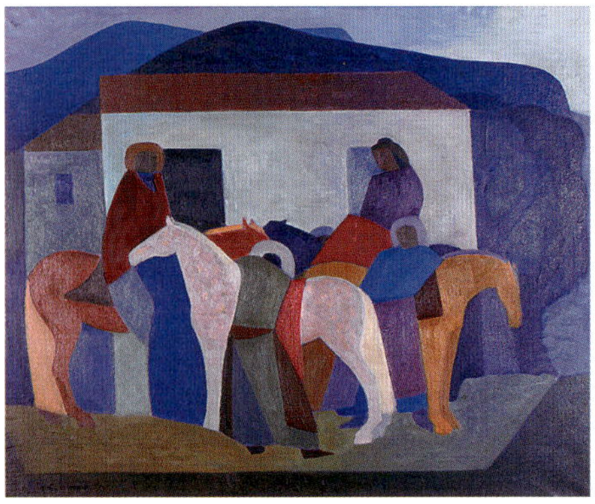

Buitrago, Guillermo b.1905
Untitled
oil on canvas 93 x 118
240

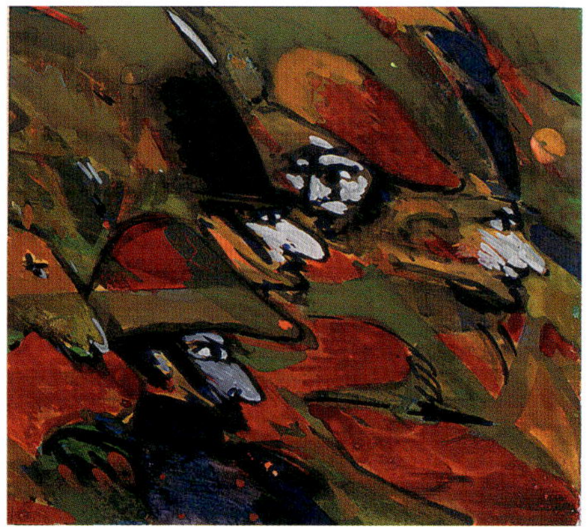

Cáceres, Juan Carlos b.1936
From the Series 'The French Revolution'
tempera on card 16 x 17.5
139

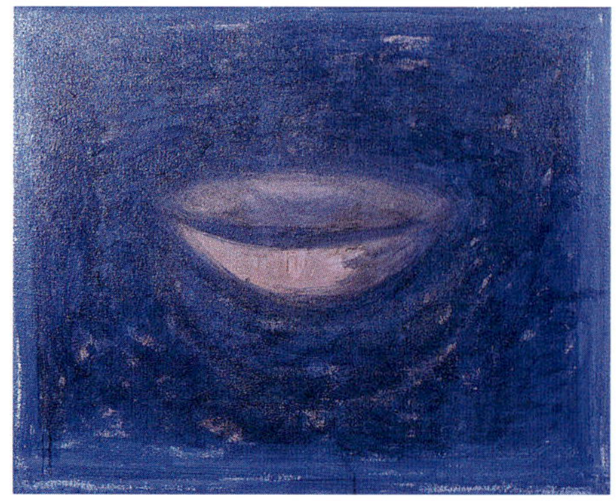

Cambre, Juan José b.1948
Untitled 1991
acrylic on canvas 39 x 59
182

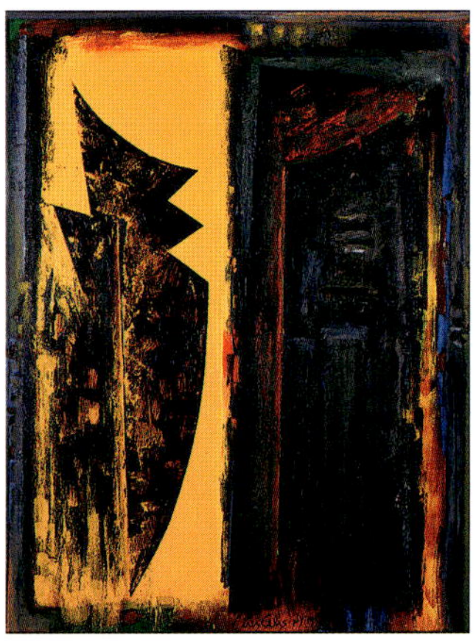

Celis, Pérez b.1939
Yellow Dancing 1990
oil on canvas 142 x 107
183

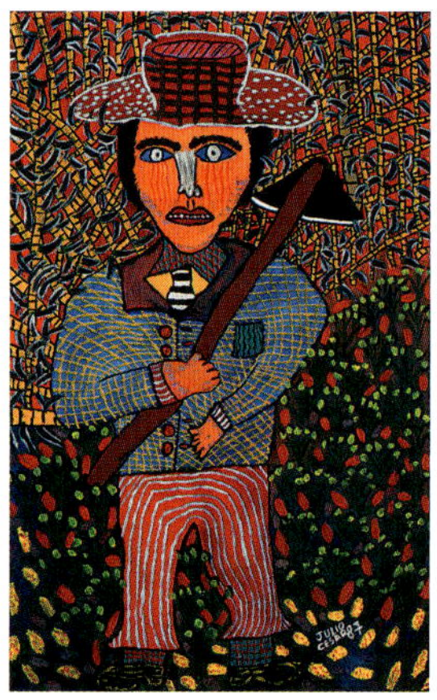

César, Julio
Untitled 1987
oil on canvas 112 x 71
135

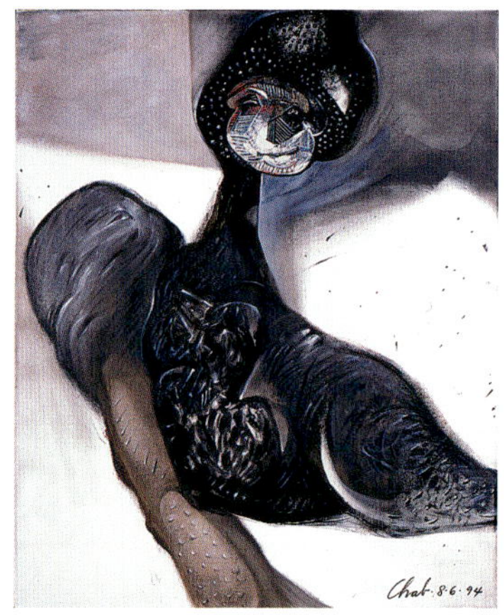

Chab, Víctor b.1930
A Thousand Tears (Fourth Song Suite) 1994
oil on canvas 99.5 x 80
109

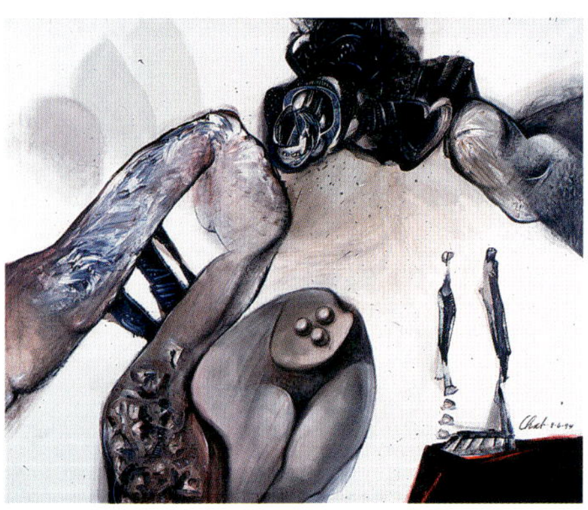

Chab, Víctor b.1930
Almond Nest (Fourth Song Suite) 1994
acrylic on canvas 150 x 180
333

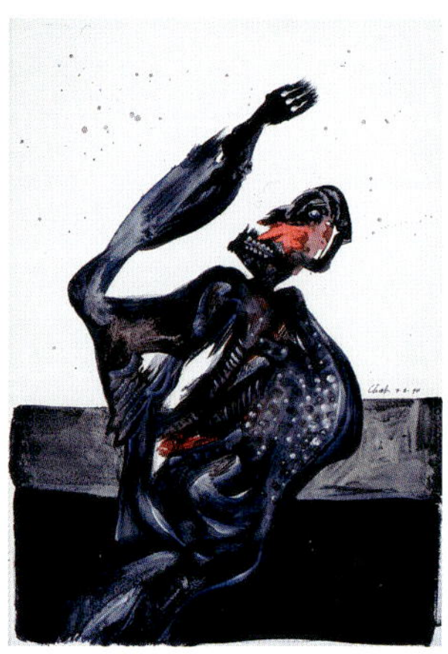

Chab, Víctor b.1930
Untitled 1994
oil on canvas 100 x 70
110

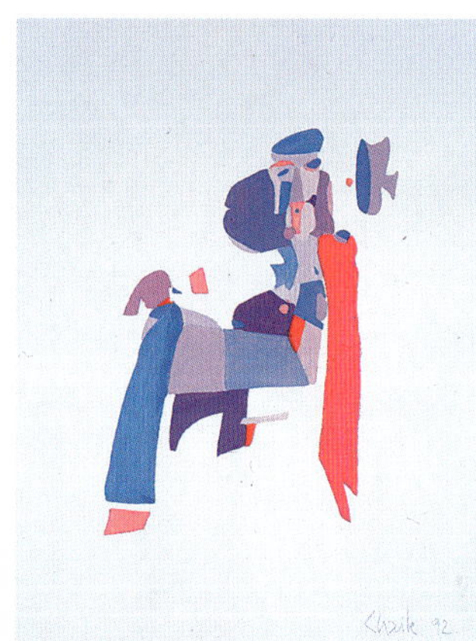

Chaile, Julio b.1964
Figure 1 1992
acrylic on paper 52.5 x 39 (E)
17

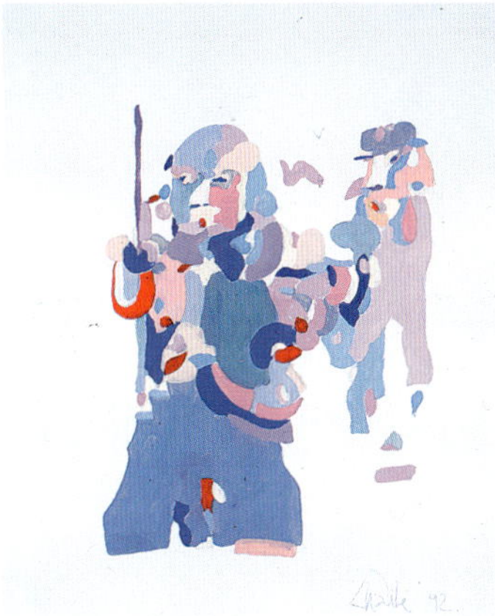

Chaile, Julio b.1964
Figure 2 1992
acrylic on paper 52.5 x 39 (E)
18

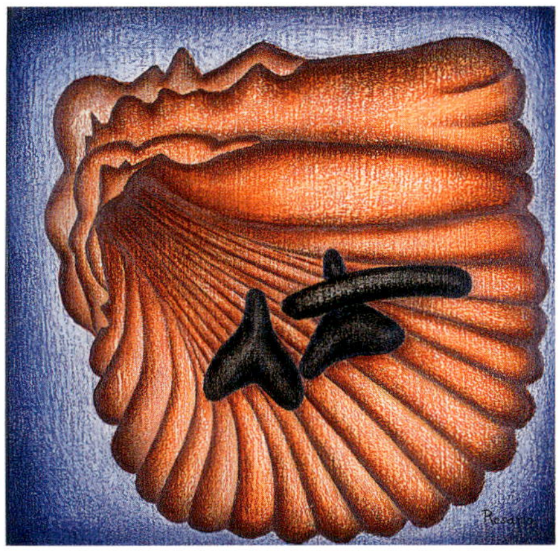

Chamorro, Rosario
Shell 1993
oil on canvas 50 x 50
54

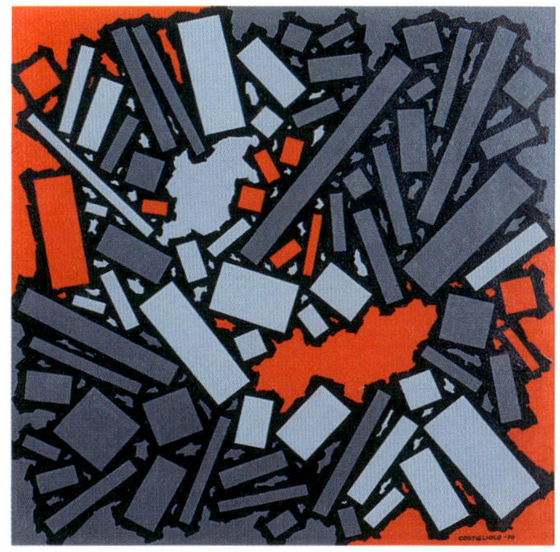

Costigliolo, José Pedro 1902–1985
From the Series 'Squares and Rectangles' 1970
acrylic on paper 46 x 46
58

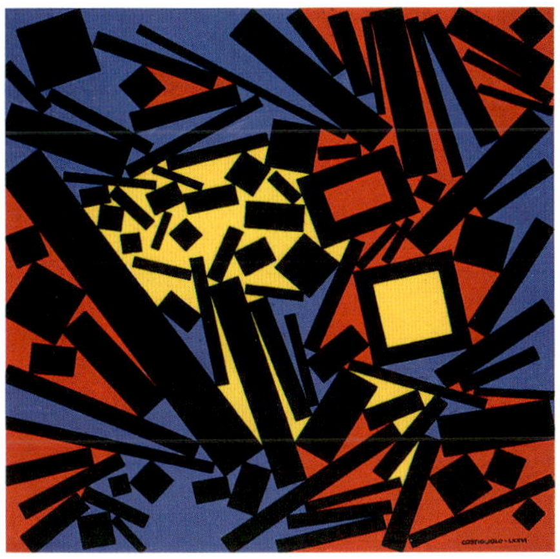

Costigliolo, José Pedro 1902–1985
From the Series 'Squares and Rectangles' 1976
acrylic on paper 50 x 50
59

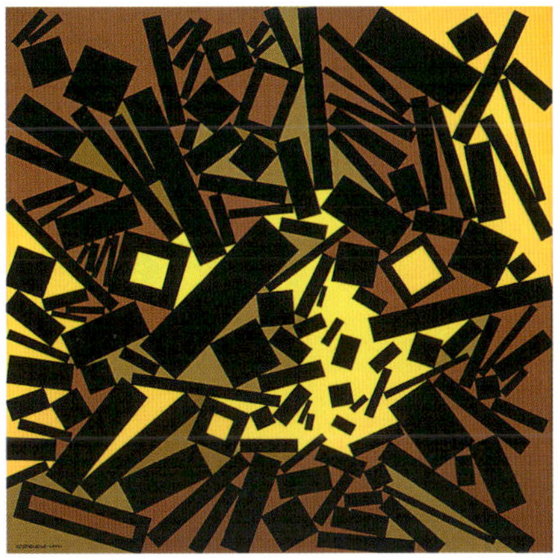

Costigliolo, José Pedro 1902–1985
Rectangles and Squares CLXIV 1976
oil on canvas 120 x 120
123

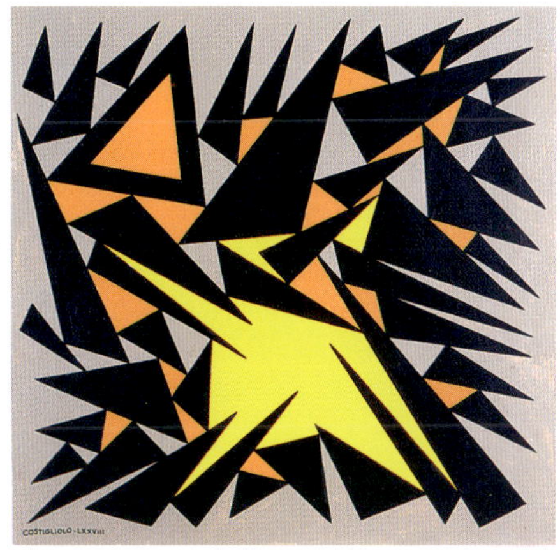

Costigliolo, José Pedro 1902–1985
From the Series 'Triangles', Triangles 102 1978
acrylic on paper 40 x 40
166

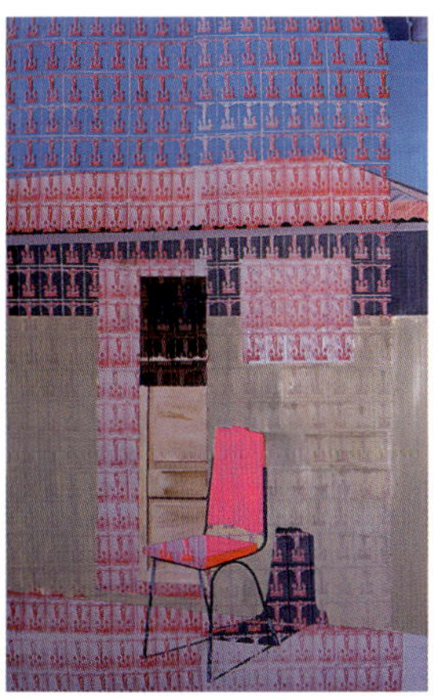

Crousillat, Paloma b.1980
Chair in Taquile, Peru 2002
mixed media on canvas 270 x 176
489

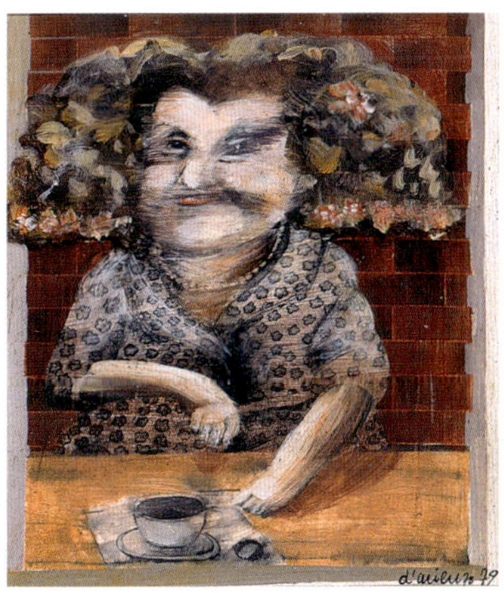

D'Arienzo, Miguel Angel b.1950
Old Menina 1979
oil on canvas 36.5 x 28
20

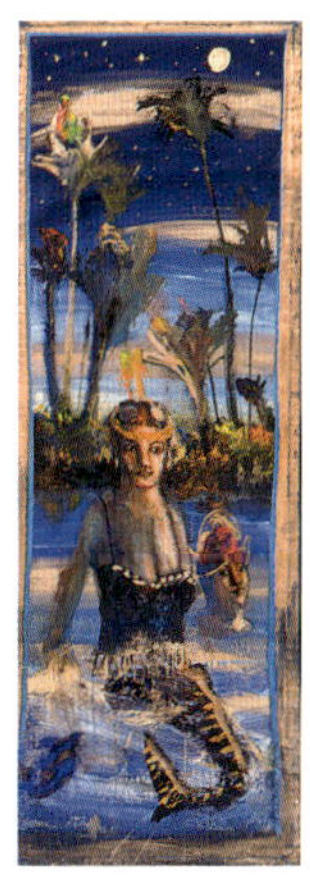

D'Arienzo, Miguel Angel b.1950
The Mermaid 1993
oil on canvas 182 x 63
19

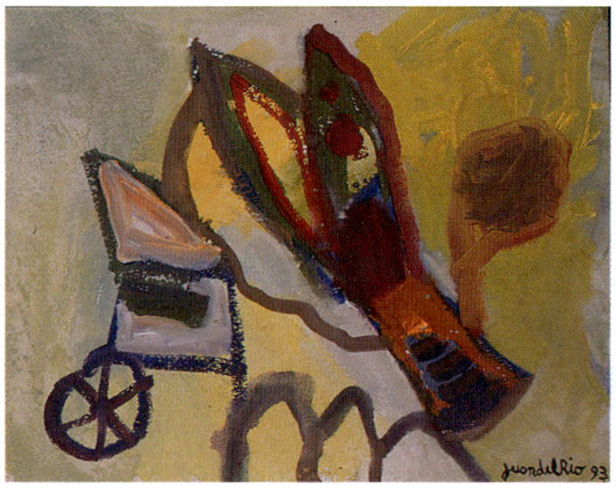

Del Rio, Juan
Untitled 1993
tempera on board 20 x 25.5
258

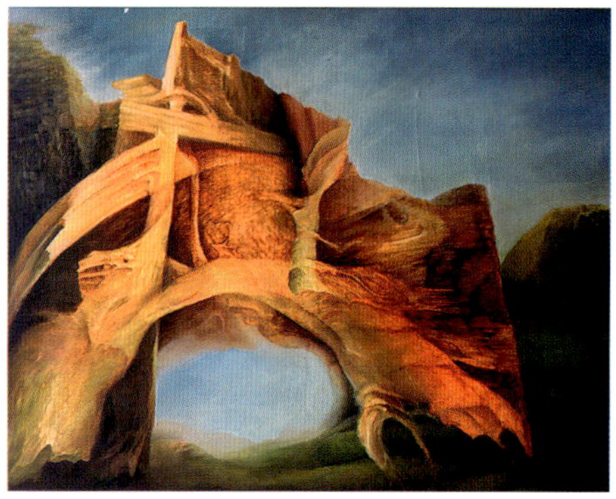

Delpino, Sara
Entrance
oil on canvas 80 x 100
177

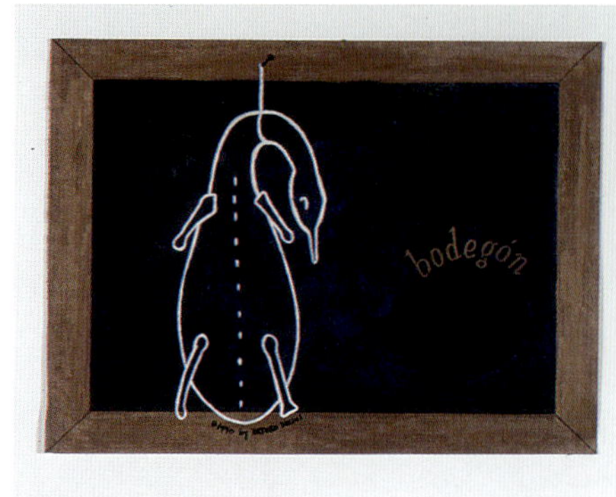

Duclos, Arturo b.1959
Still Life 1990
acrylic on paper 25.5 x 33
160

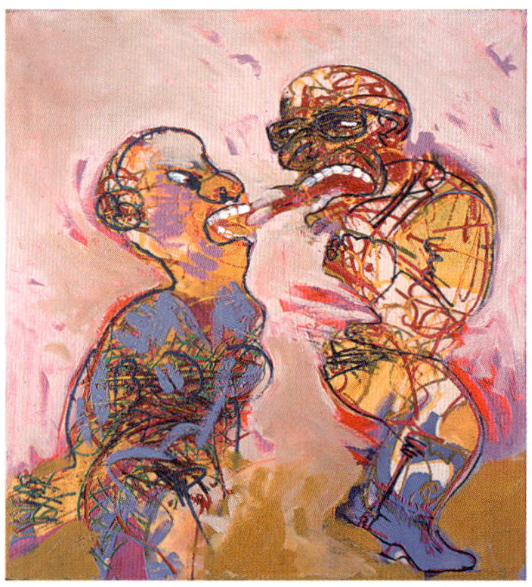

Eckell, Ana b.1947
Untitled 1985
oil on canvas 100 x 93
296

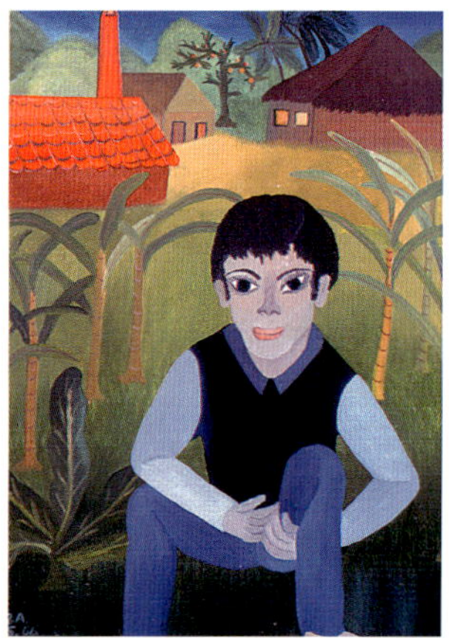

Elza O. S. b.1928
Untitled 1966
oil on canvas 60 x 45
593 (P)

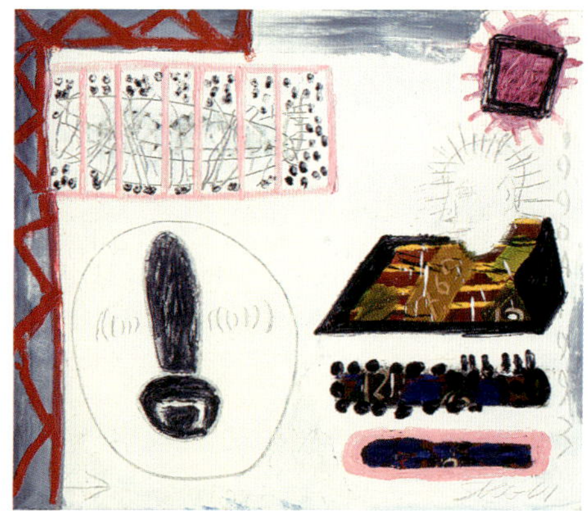

Franco, Siron b.1947
Yesterday 1990–1993
oil on canvas 80 x 90
111

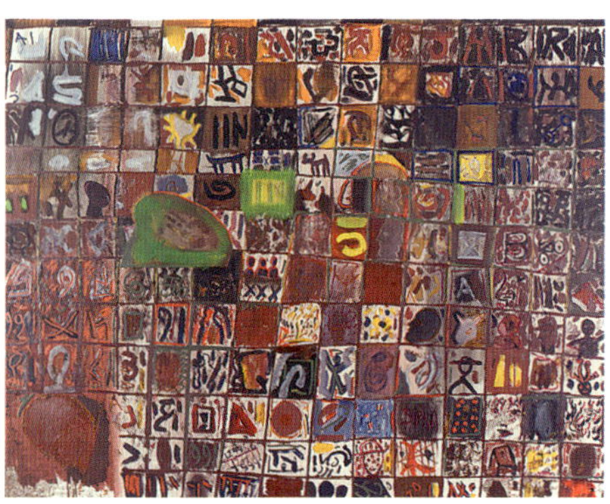

Franco, Siron b.1947
A Suspicious Story 1991
oil on canvas 160 x 199
510 (P)

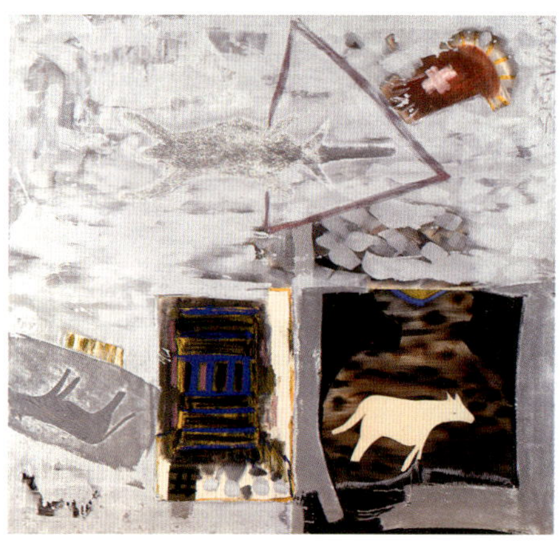

Franco, Siron b.1947
Memória 1992
acrylic & mixed media on canvas 180 x 191
1

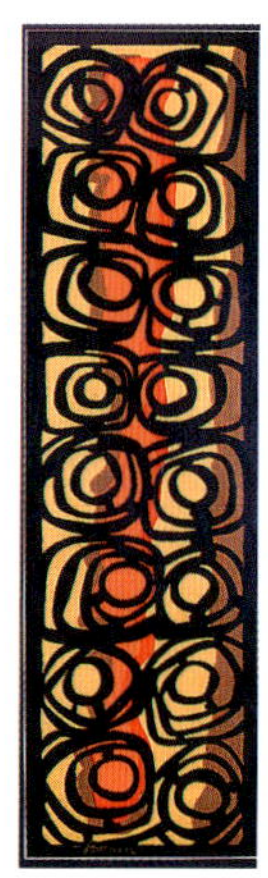

Freire, Maria b.1917
Capricorn II 1965–1993
acrylic on paper 104 x 31
55

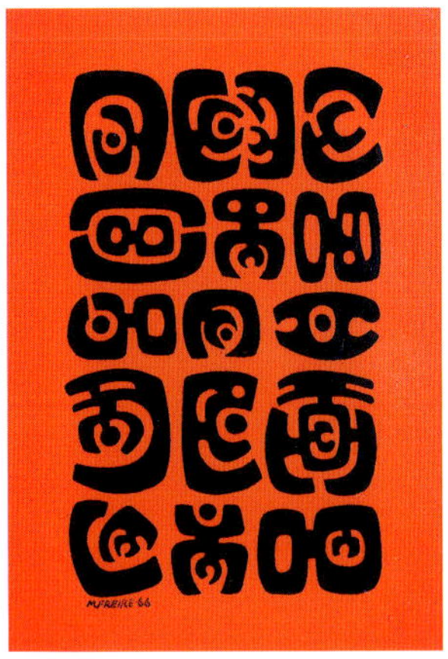

Freire, Maria b.1917
Córdoba 1966
acrylic on card 62 x 51
57

Freire, Maria b.1917
Variant 1975
acrylic on paper 59 x 39
56

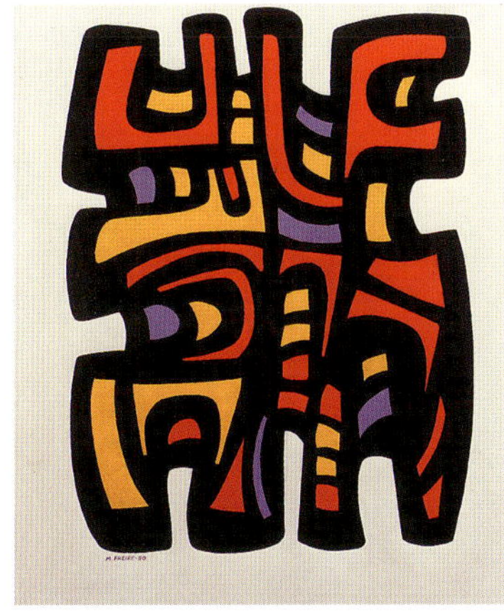

Freire, Maria b.1917
South America 1990
acrylic on canvas 130 x 100
122

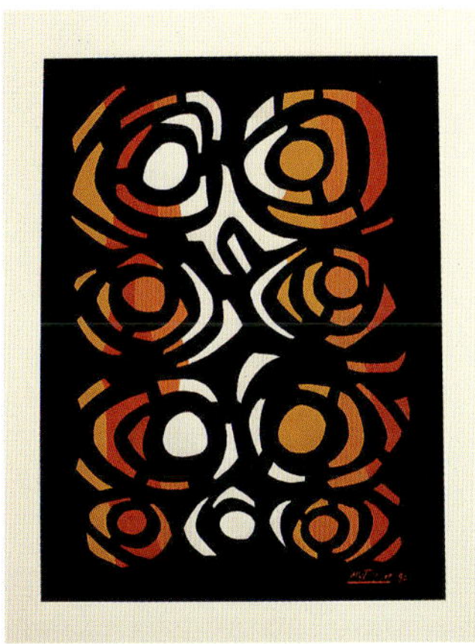

Freire, Maria b.1917
The Gold of the Tigers No.6 1994
acrylic on card 60 x 45
167

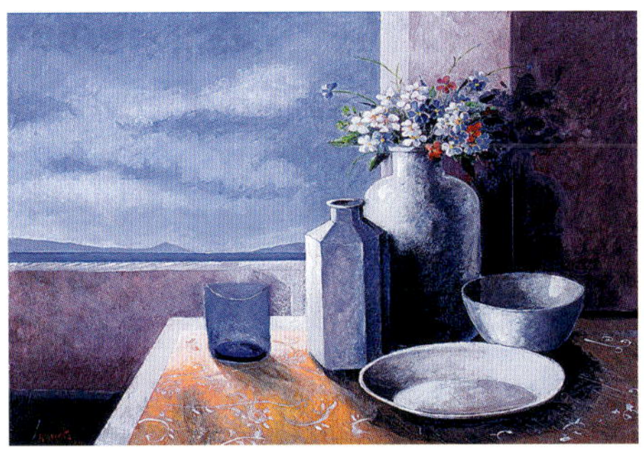

Gandía, Vicente b.1935
White Porcelain and Blue Vase 2000
oil on board 51 x 63
439

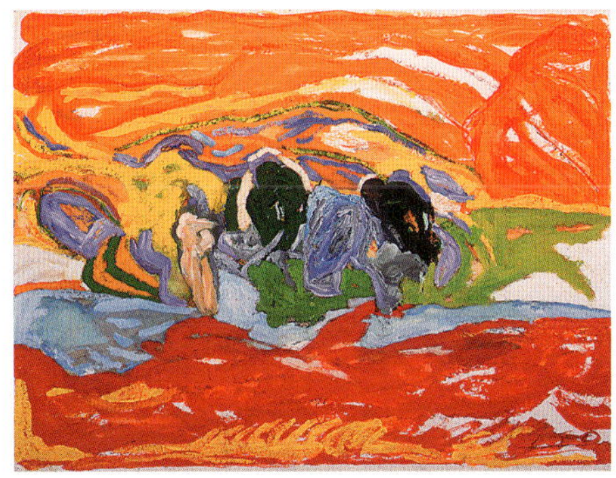

Gárgano, Germán
Turmoil 1995
acrylic & gouache on paper 38.5 x 50
315

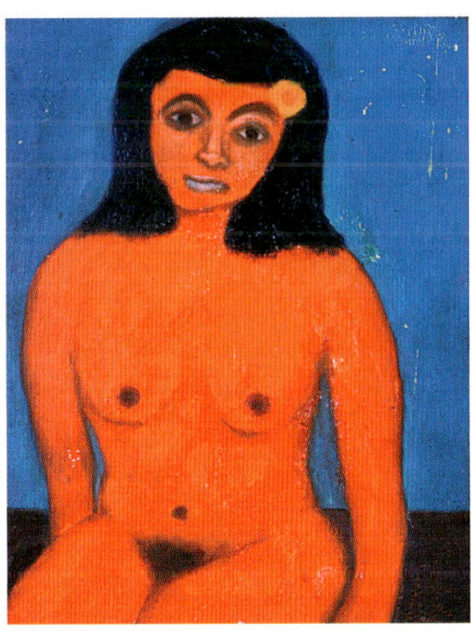

Gerson
Untitled 1960
oil on canvas 24 x 18.5
594 (P)

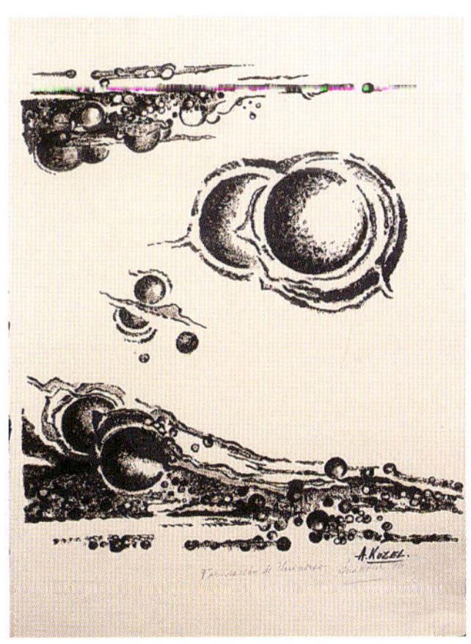

Kozel, Ana b.1937
Formation of the Universe 1996
acrylic on paper 62.5 x 46
317

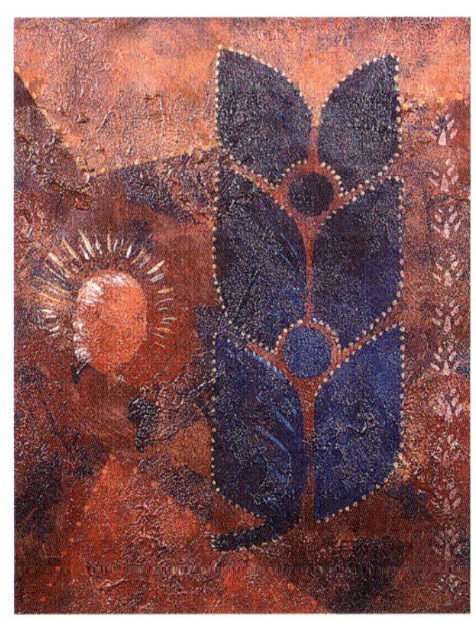

Kravetz, Carlos b.1951
The Power of the Myth, Eva 1996
oil on board 42 x 32
323

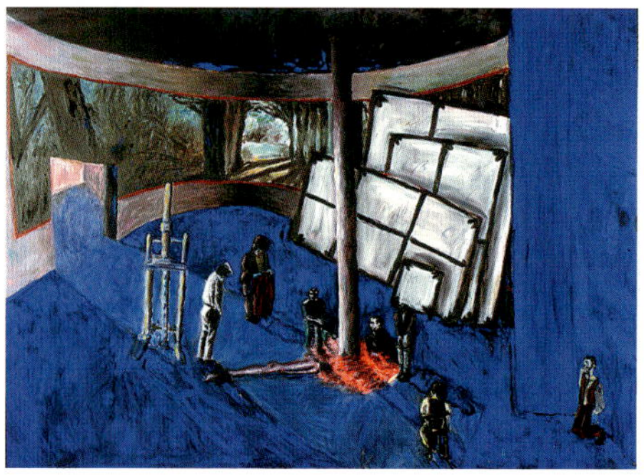

Kuitca, Guillermo b.1961
Idea of a Passion 1984
acrylic on canvas 145 x 195
509 (P)

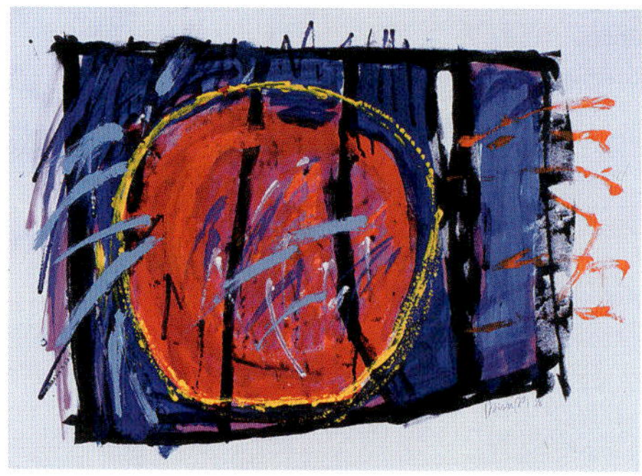

Laurencich, Diana b.1963
Enclosure 1988
acrylic on paper 55 x 74
12

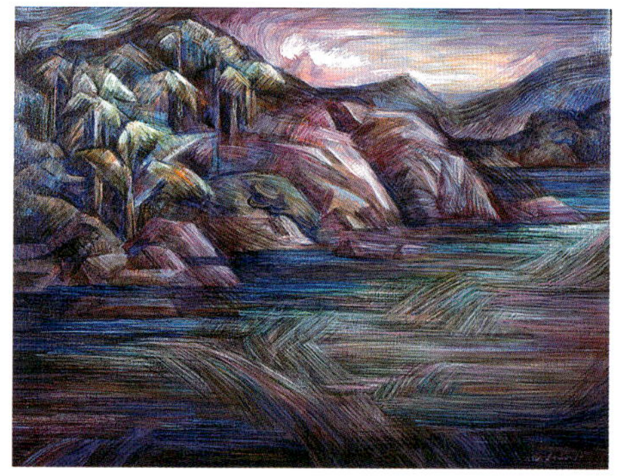

Leão, Maria Luiza b.1932
Sad Island (Angra) 1989
oil on canvas 57 x 73
336

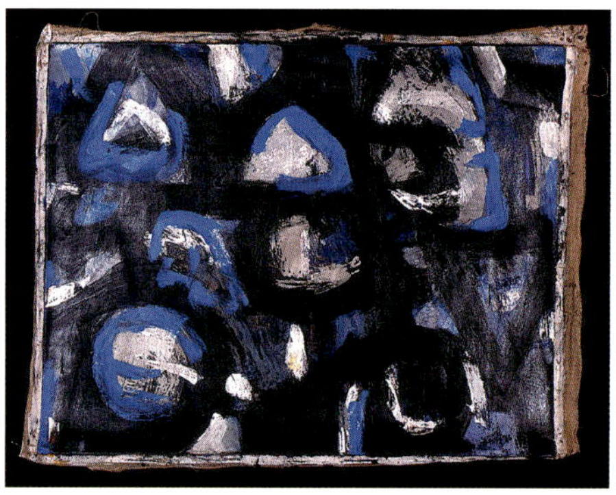

Llinás, Guido 1923–2005
Untitled 1978–1986
oil on canvas 80 x 100
223

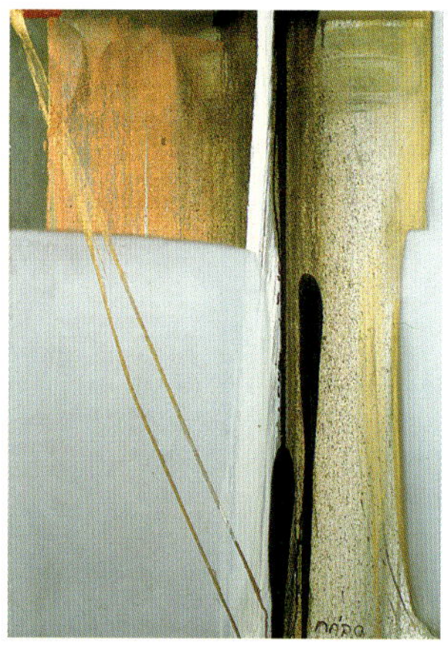

Máro, Antonio b.1928
Profile 1991
oil & gold paint on canvas 120 x 100
36

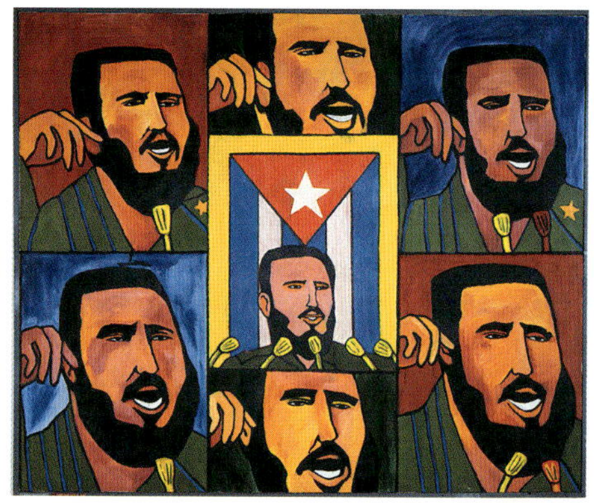

Martínez, Raúl 1927–1995
Repetitions with a Flag c.1966
oil on canvas 127 x 147
516 (P)

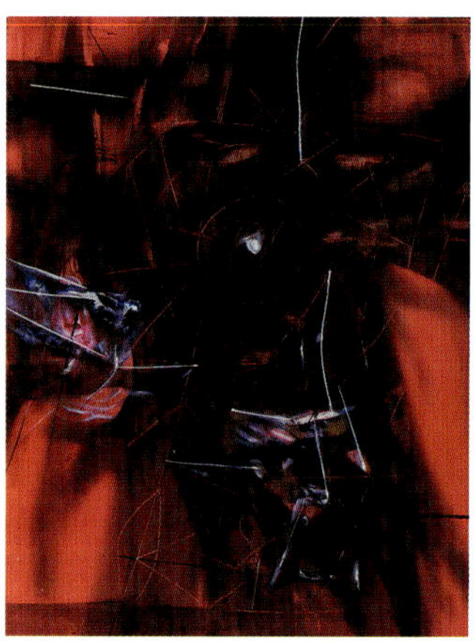

Matta, Roberto 1911–2002
Composition in Magenta: The End of Everything 1942
oil on canvas 92 x 74
508 (P)

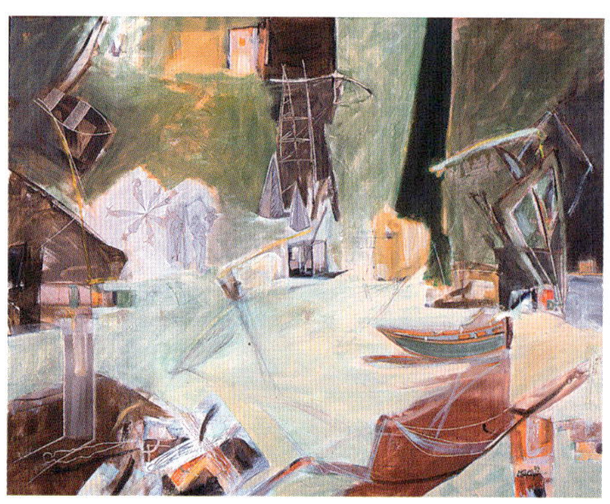

Mazuera, Diego b.1950
Stop There! 2000
acrylic on canvas 105 x 129
480

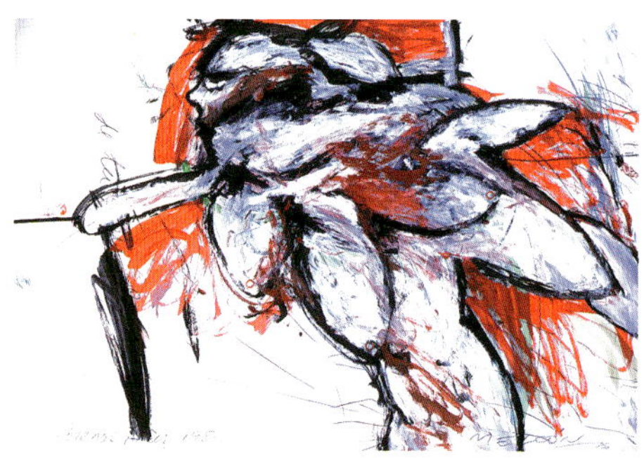

Melcon, Miguel b.1940
Untitled 1985
acrylic on paper 70 x 90
325

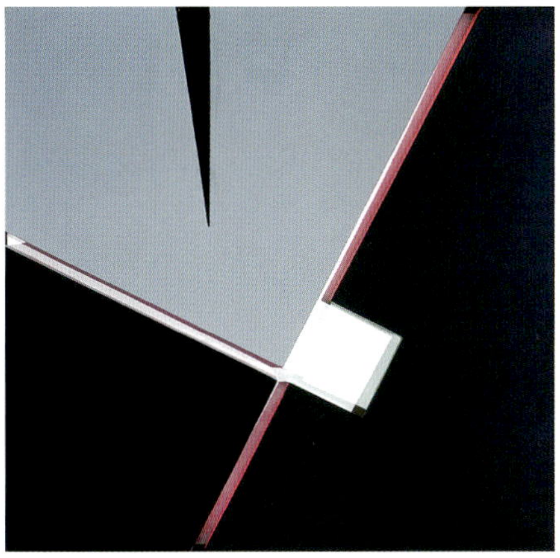

Melé, Juan b.1923
R.643 1998
acrylic on wood 60 x 60
429

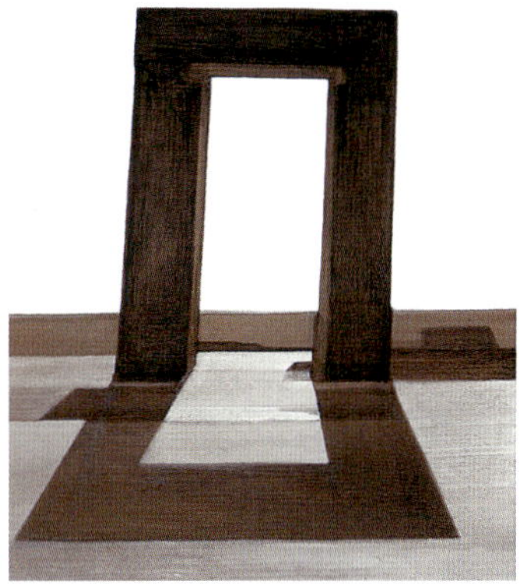

Montes, Fernando b.1930
Shadow of the Moon 1998
tempera on canvas 152 x 122
430

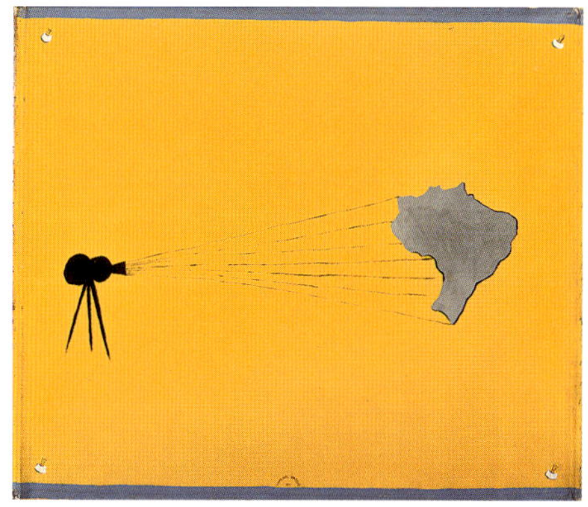

Nassar, Emmanuel b.1949
Untitled 1987
oil on canvas 125 x 144
120

Paternosto, César b.1931
Marginality and Displacement No.7 2002
emulsion, oil & acrylic on canvas 120 x 120
605

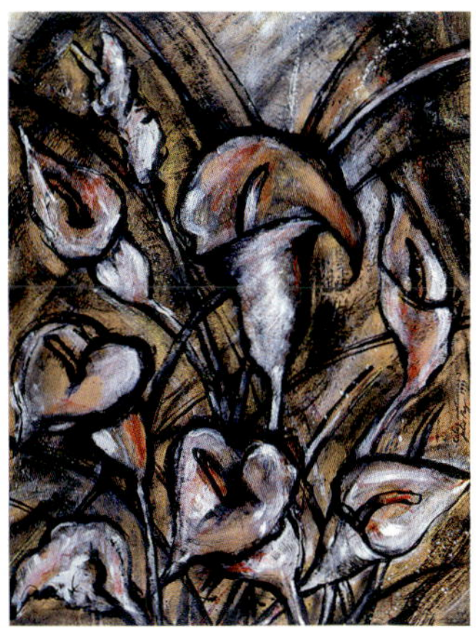

Paz, Julio b.1939
Night Lilies 1993
acrylic on paper 102 x 76
44

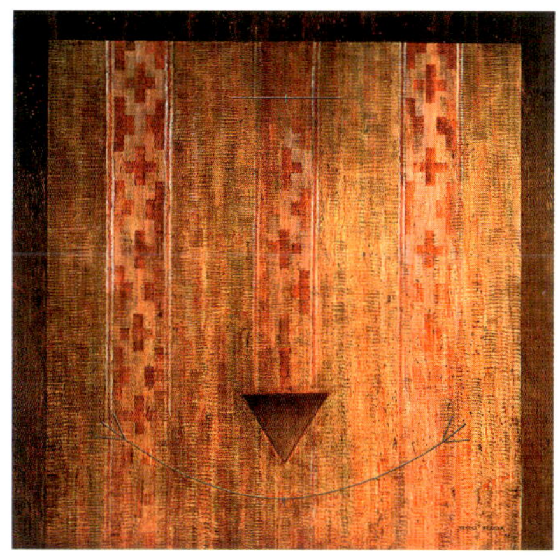

Pereda, Teresa b.1956
Chods, Colour of Gold 1997
oil on hessian 150 x 150
366

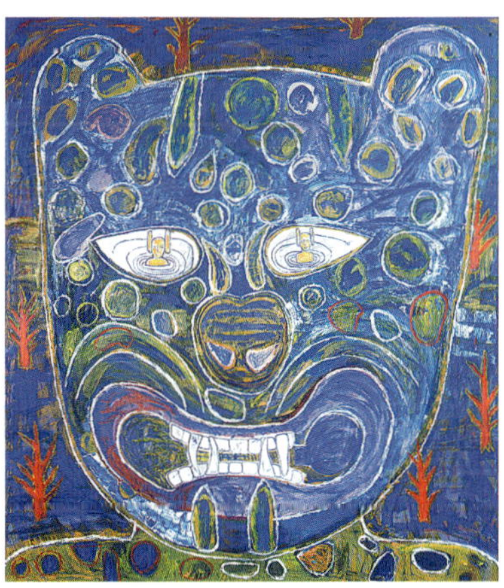

Piña, Raúl b.1961
Double Eclipse of the Moon 1998
oil on canvas 240 x 220
378

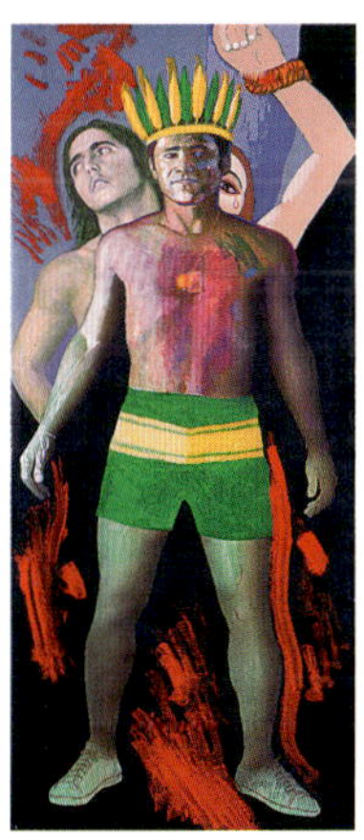

Rodrigues, Glauco Otavio Castilho
1929–2004
Saint Sebastian in June 1985
oil on canvas 97 x 38.5
125

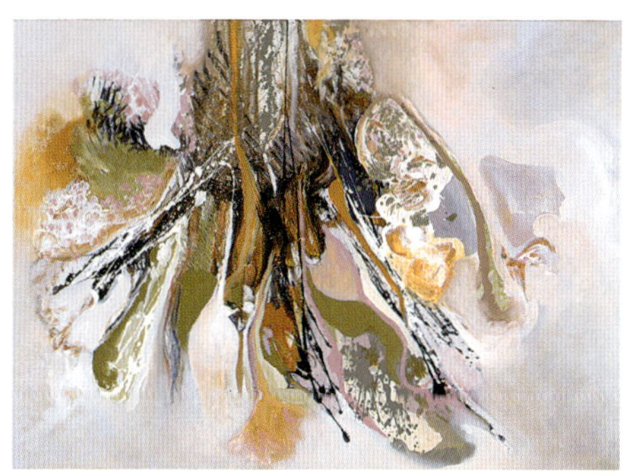

Sánchez, Beatriz
From the Wild and Magnificent Light
acrylic on canvas 70 x 95
24

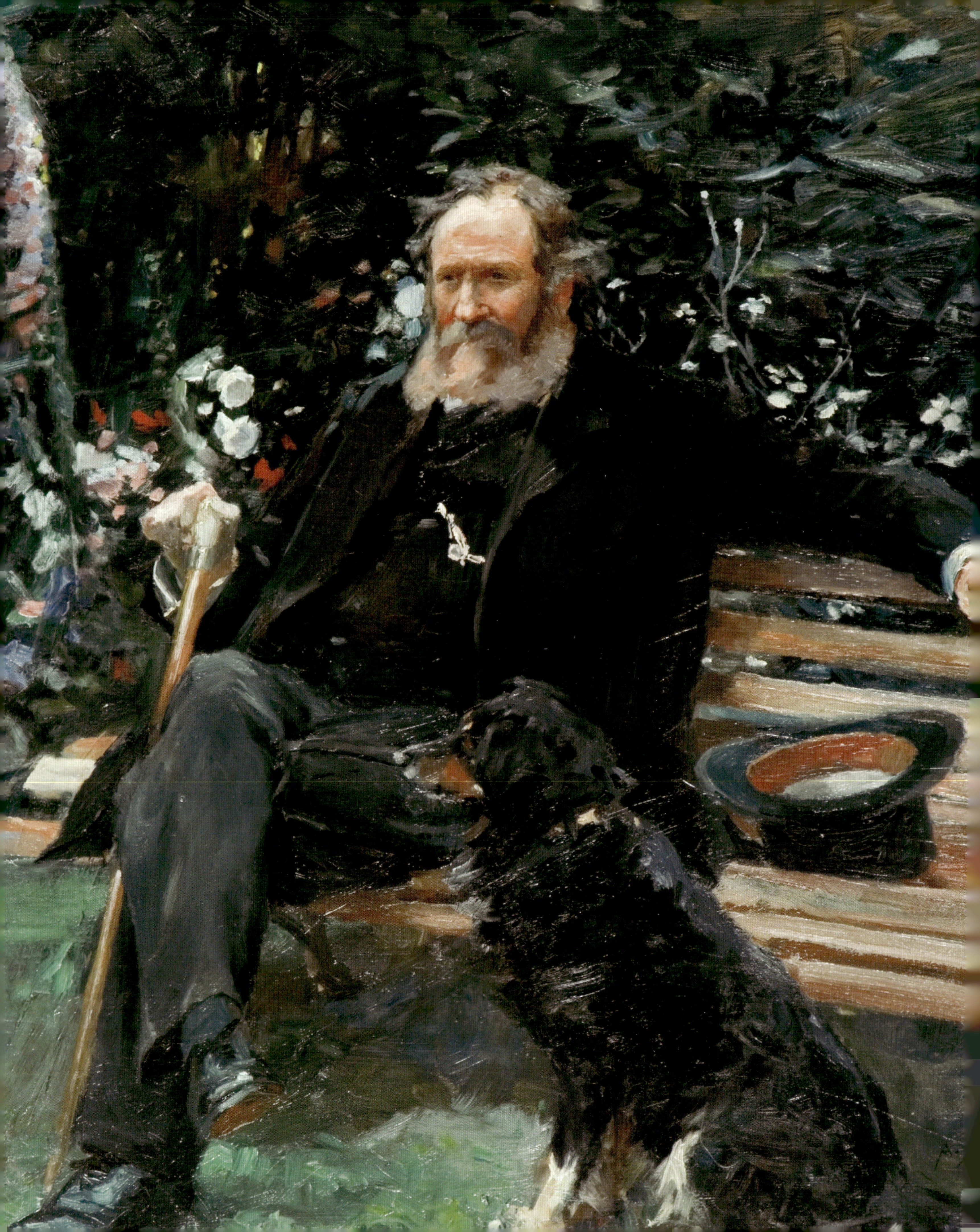

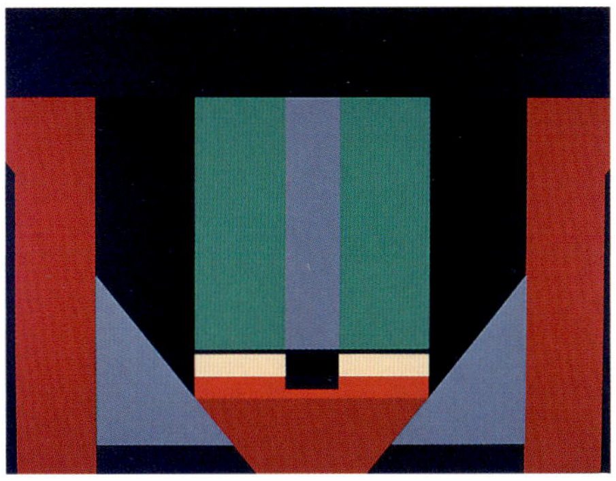

Sanín, Fanny b.1938
Acrylic No.1 1989
acrylic on canvas 100 x 130
604

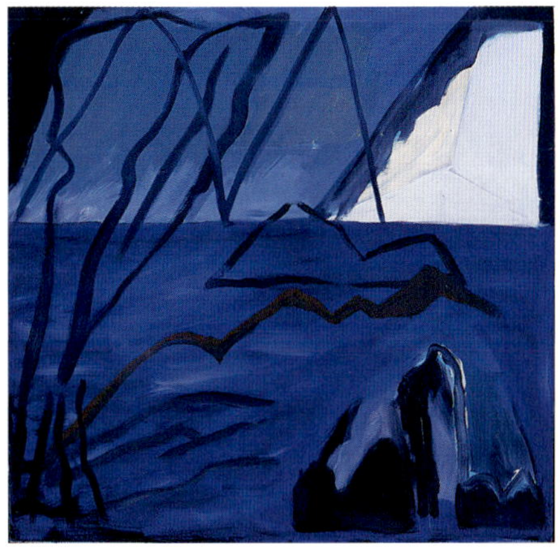

Scheihing, Vivian b.1947
Tidal Wave 1992
oil on canvas 120 x 120
224

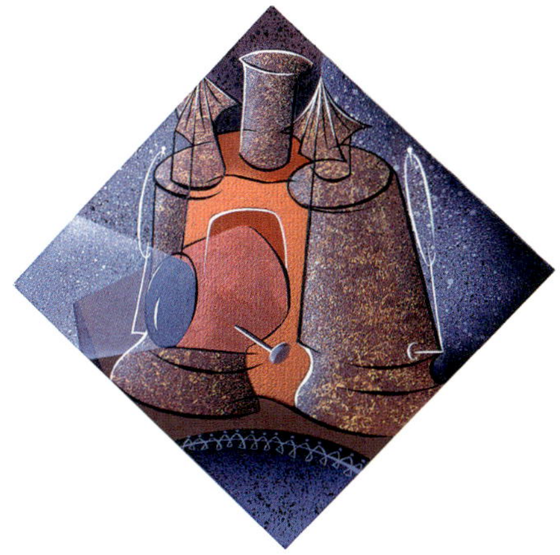

Schnell, Marcellus
Magic Lantern 1997
oil-based household paint & acrylic on canvas 30 x 30
337

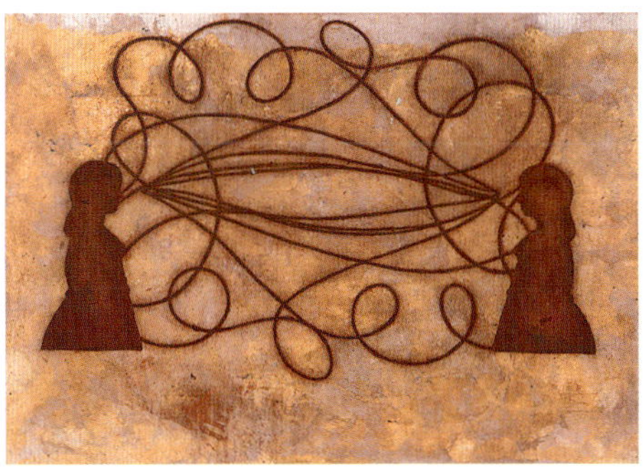

Senise, Daniel b.1955
Three Paths 1995
oil & mixed media on canvas 193 x 267
246

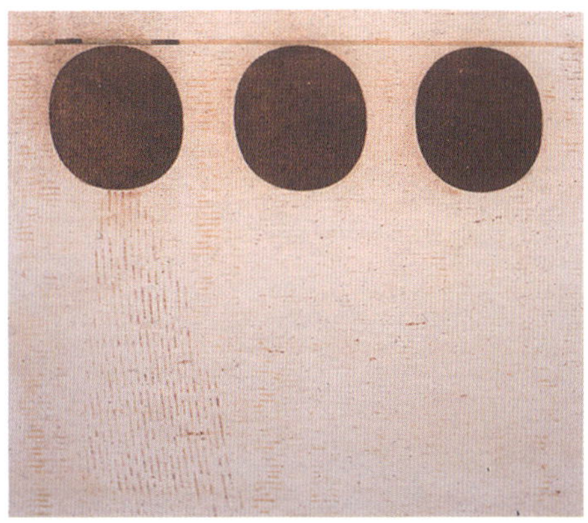

Soto-Diaz, Mariángeles b.1970
On Sugar, Spice and Other Delectable Abstractions No.018 2002
spices & acrylic on canvas 25.5 x 25.5
610

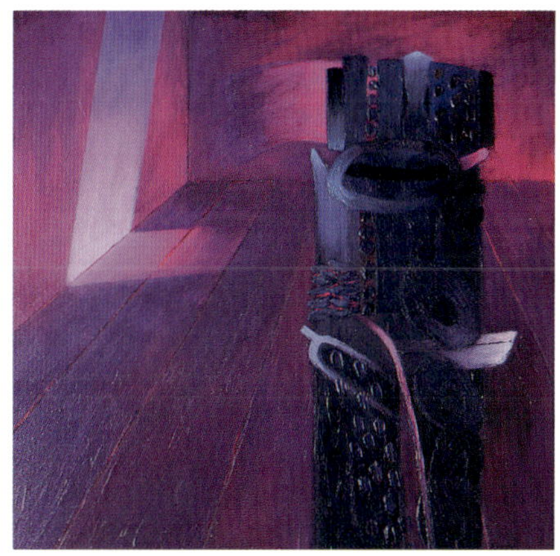

Szyszlo, Fernando de b.1925
Room No.23 1994
oil on canvas 120 x 120
134

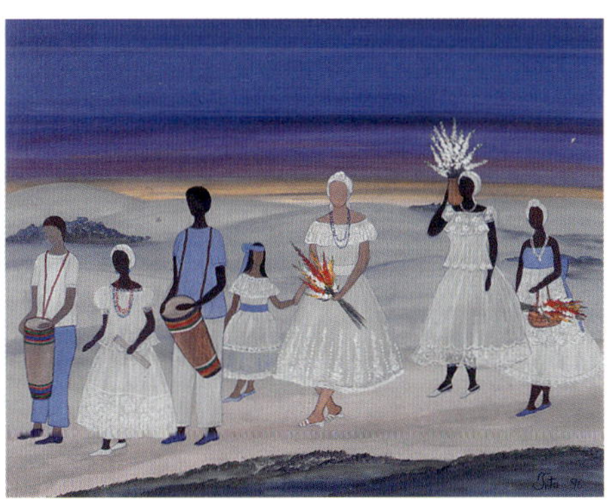

Tiíta b.1929
The Procession of Iemanja's Feast Day 1996
acrylic on canvas 50 x 64
377

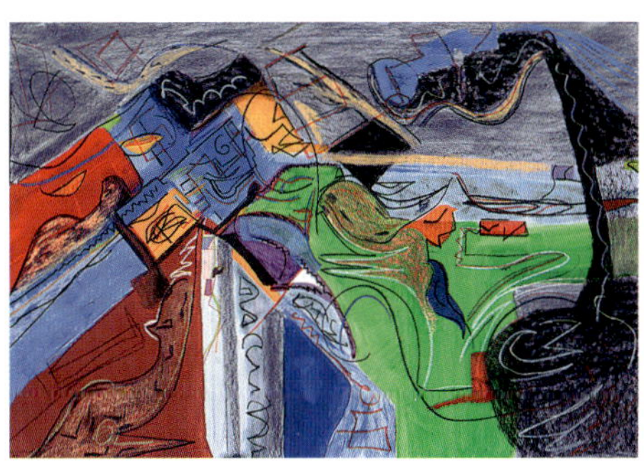

Trevisanello, Mauro
The Indian Town 1994
acrylic on paper 70 x 100
237

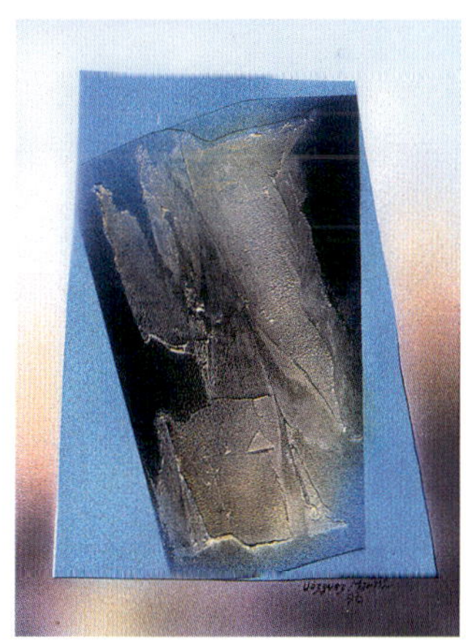

Vázquez Martín, Juan Teódulo b.1941
'Windows' Series No.2 1996
acrylic on card 24.5 x 18
285

Facing page: Munnings, Alfred James, 1878–1959, *Daniel Tomkins and His Dog* (detail), 1898, Sir Alfred Munnings Art Museum, (p. 97)

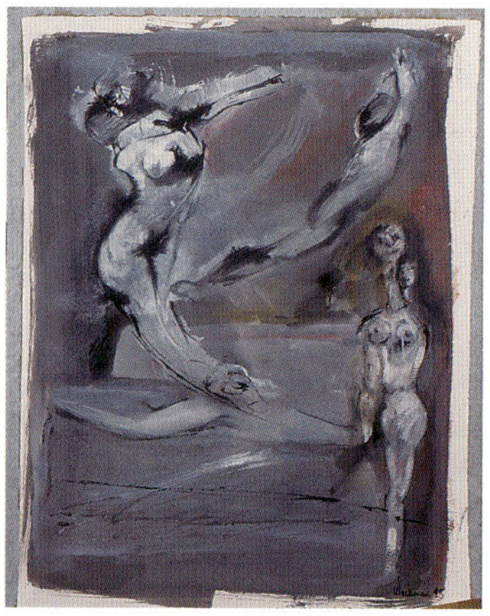

Waissman, Andres b.1955
Still Feel Like Dancing 1995
ink & acrylic on paper 53 x 41
320

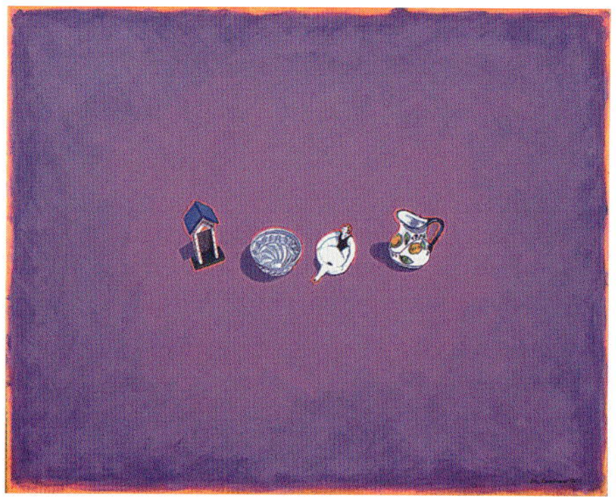

Zambrano, Elsa b.1951
Still Life 2001
acrylic on canvas 90 x 109.5
481

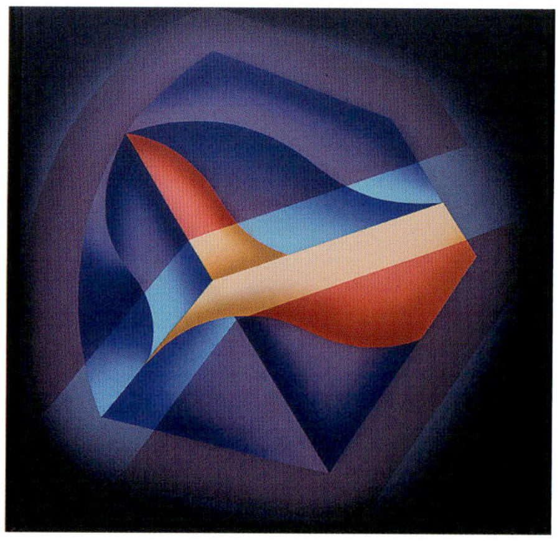

Zapisek, Adriana b.1949
Gema X Piscis 1991
acrylic on canvas 80 x 80 (E)
26

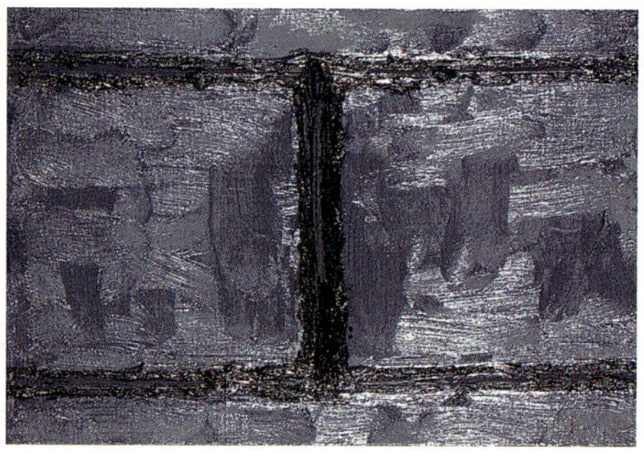

Zílio, Carlos b.1944
794AO/94–10 (from the series '794AO') 1994
oil on canvas 40 x 57
164

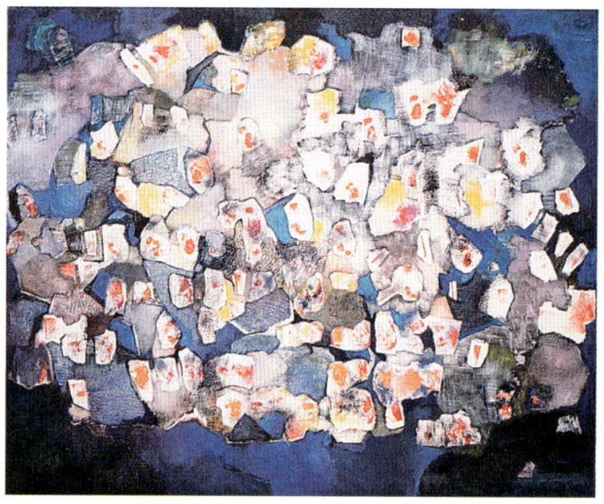

Zuik, Martha
Tree 1991
oil on canvas 100 x 120
231

Victor Batte-Lay Trust

Clarence Victor Lay, whose collection is recorded here, was born in Holy Trinity Parish, in Colchester in 1865. He was educated at Colchester Royal Grammar School and later made his reputation in the brewing industry in the King's Lynn area. He changed his name to Batte-Lay by deed poll in 1922 and, on his retirement, went back to Colchester, where he died in 1935, following a fall from his pony during his daily ride. He was a hereditary freeman, whose ancestors can be traced back to the days of the bay trade. Victor Batte-Lay was an avid collector of furniture and paintings. After his death, his widow, Margaret Eleanore Batte-Lay looked after his collection for 20 years. In January 1955, before she died, she directed her Trustees to purchase and endow a building in Colchester as a memorial to her husband 'for the benefit and advantage of the inhabitants of Colchester and in particular those who shall take an interest in the artistic and antiquarian features of that town'. A venue was therefore required and the Minories, then owned by Dr Butt, a second generation woman doctor and sister-in-law of Lucien Pissaro, was purchased in 1956. The Minories was opened to the public as an Art Gallery on 30 May 1958 by the then Director of the Victoria & Albert Museum, later knighted as Sir Trenchard Cox and Mr R. A. Butler, Home Secretary.

The original bequest focused on British art and artists from the seventeenth century onwards. It included still lifes, regency portraits, eighteenth century prints and drawings, nineteenth century samplers and oil paintings.

The Victor Batte-Lay Collection includes works by internationally celebrated artists with local relevance, such as Roderic Barrett whose work is at the Victoria & Albert Museum, Peter Coker, Maggi Hambling, B. Hughes-Stanton and Humphrey Spender with a watercolour entitled *Gross National Product*. There are a few John and Paul Nash lithographs, which are remaining after 70 wood engravings by John Nash, executed between 1919 and 1927, were offered to the Tate Gallery in 1992. The collection also includes 14 drawings of figures by Camille Pissarro, three prints by Michael Rothenstein and a book of prints and watercolours by Gino Severini entitled *Fleurs et masques*.

There is also a significant representation of important painters such as John Sell Cotman with an 1838 series of sketches and studies entitled *Liber Studorium*. There are two mezzotints by Richard Houston after John Cotes's portraits of *the Countess of Coventry* and *the Duchess of Hamilton*. It also owns an important Venetian painting attributed to Otto Hoynk of Constantinople entitled *The Spotted Dog*, on loan to Colchester Museums, and there are three drawings attributed to John Constable.

The collection includes 23 photographs of the Mersea Oysterage, now on loan to Mersea Museum, and a number of bronze sculptures such as the sculpture of a head by Eduardo Paolozzi and two cast iron fire back panels after Leonardo Da Vinci.

Altogether the Victor Batte-Lay Collection, with its 135 acquisitions, gives an insight into East Anglian culture. It explores works by local British artists of national and international standing and provides inspiration for future generations of painters and sculptors at local as well as national and international levels. Some of these works of art are on occasional display at firstsite at the Minories, as part of their Function Room programme.

Evelyne Bell, Curator

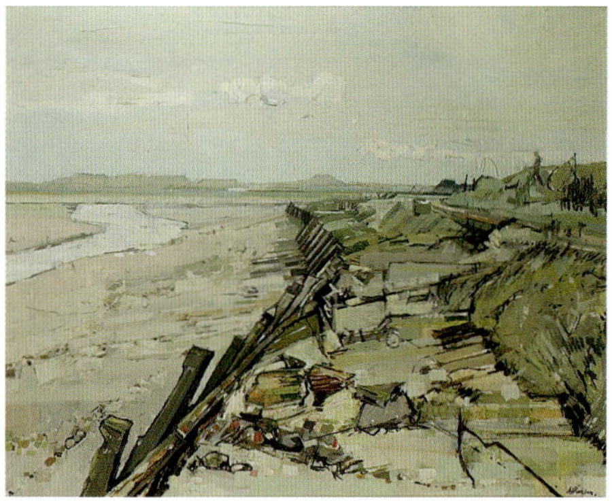

Atkinson, Anthony b.1929
Norfolk Coast
oil on canvas 62 x 74.5
303.P.84

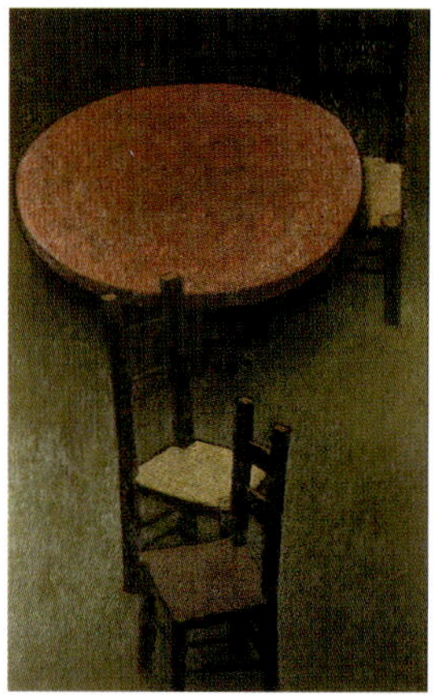

Barrett, Roderic 1920–2000
Round Table and Three Chairs 1963
oil on canvas 137 x 92
322.P.88

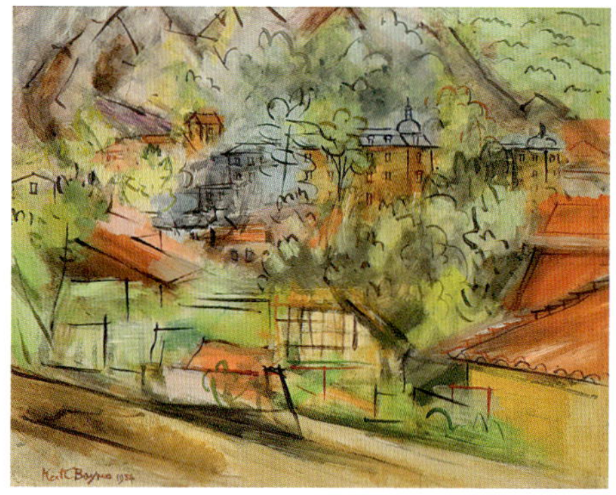

Baynes, Keith 1887–1977
Hôtel du Portugal 1954
oil on canvas 70 x 81
219.P.83

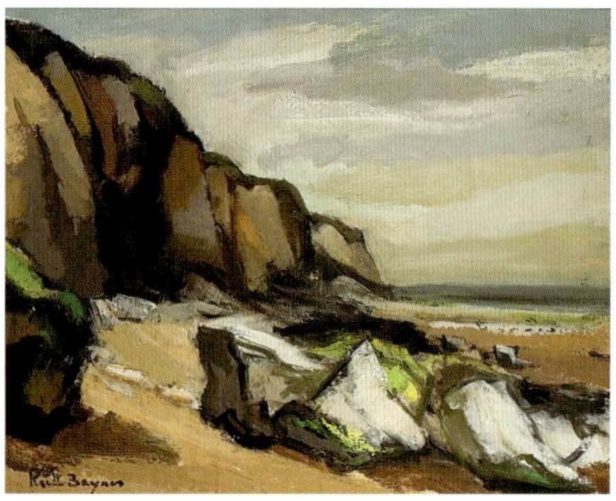

Baynes, Keith 1887–1977
Varengeville-sur-Mer, 1938
oil on canvas 65 x 76
220.P.83

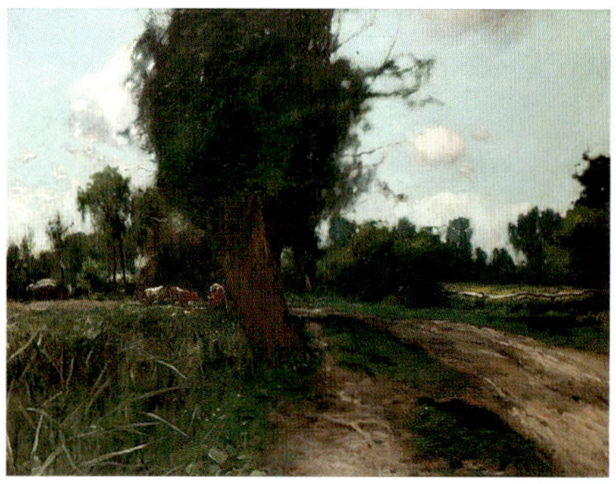

Becker, Harry 1865–1928
Landscape, Suffolk Meadows
oil on canvas 71 x 91
158.P.83

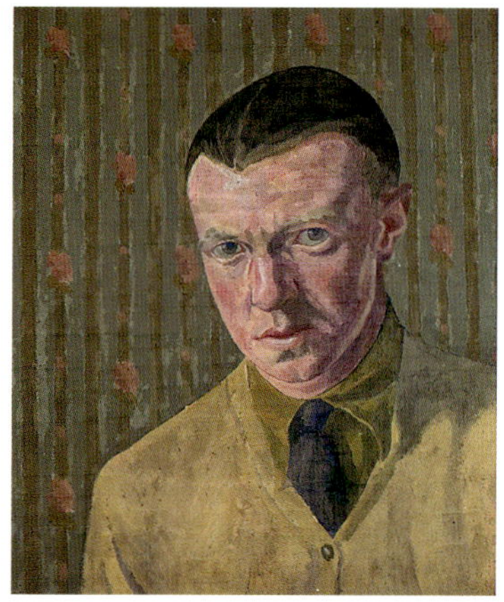

Bevan, Robert Polhill 1865–1925
Portrait of a Man Wearing Green Shirt and Tie against Striped Wall (Dickie)
oil on canvas 50 x 38
241.P.83

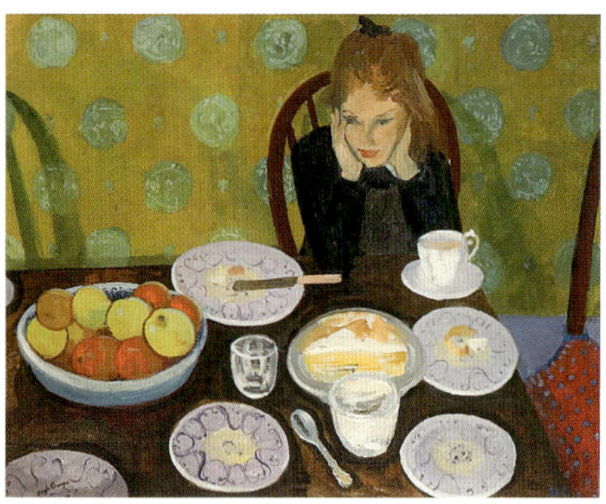

Cronyn, Hugh Verschoyle 1905–1996
Anna at Table
oil on canvas 77 x 90
304.P.84

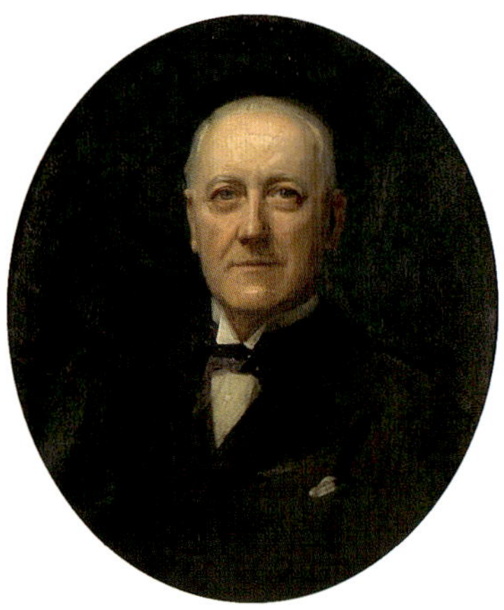

Daniell, Frank 1866–1932
Victor Batte-Lay 1926
oil on canvas 66.5 x 56.5
127.P.83

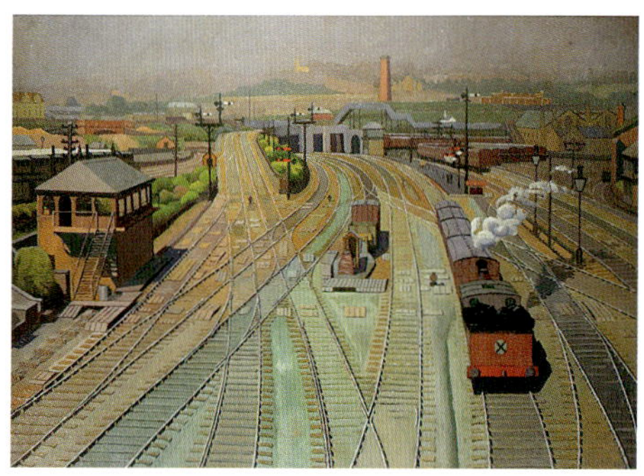

Dickey, Edward Montague O'Rourke
1894–1977
Kentish Town Railway Station 1919
oil on canvas 92 x 118
245.P.83

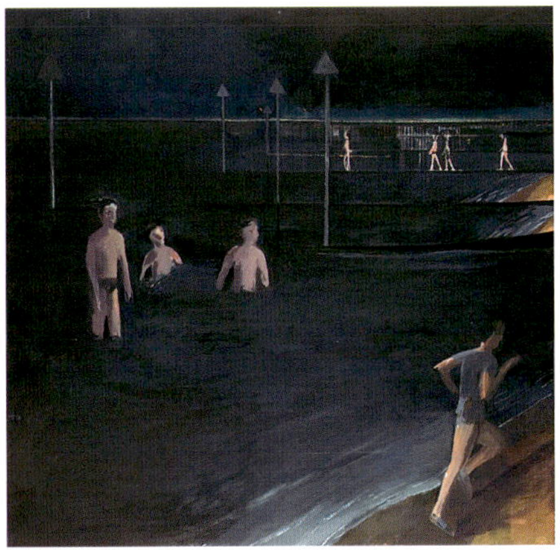

Farrell, Anthony b.1945
Summer at Night 1982/1983
oil on canvas 137 x 127 (E)
282.P.83

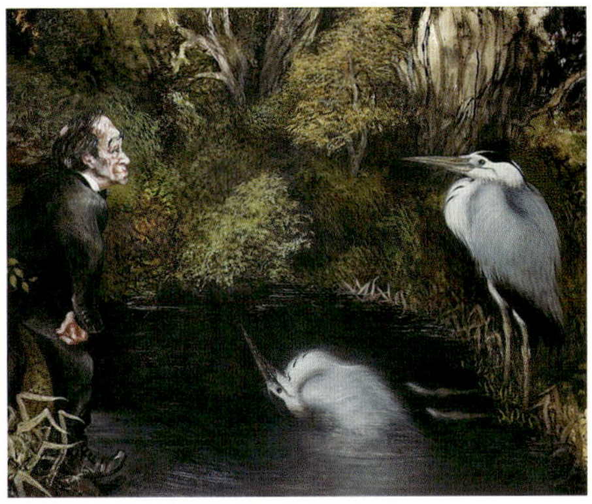

Hambling, Maggi b.1945
Encounter (from the 'Paintings of Max Wall' series) 1982
oil on canvas 137 x 158
280.P.83

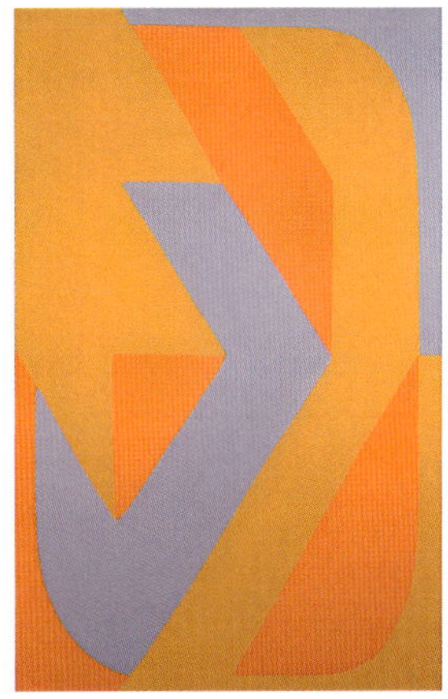

Mellis, Margaret b.1914
Lilac Yellow 1970
oil on canvas 40 x 25
264.P.83

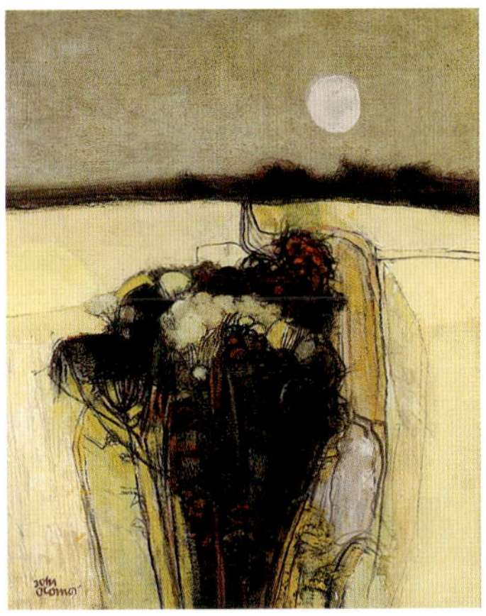

O'Connor, John Scorror 1913–2004
Lingley's Field
oil on canvas 76 x 61
236.P.83

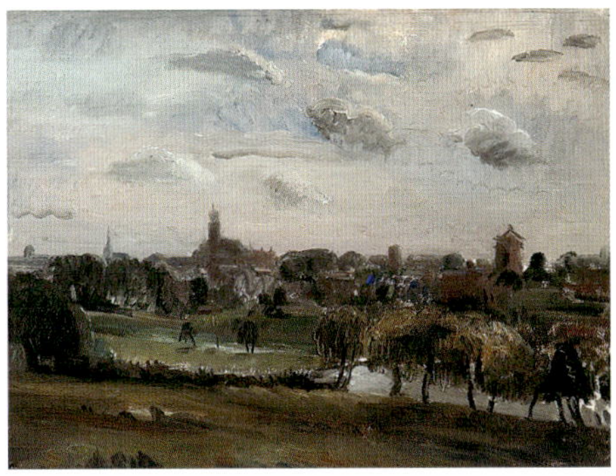

St George, Sylvia 1881–1950
Colchester from the North 1936
oil on canvas covered board 38.5 x 46.5
292.P.83

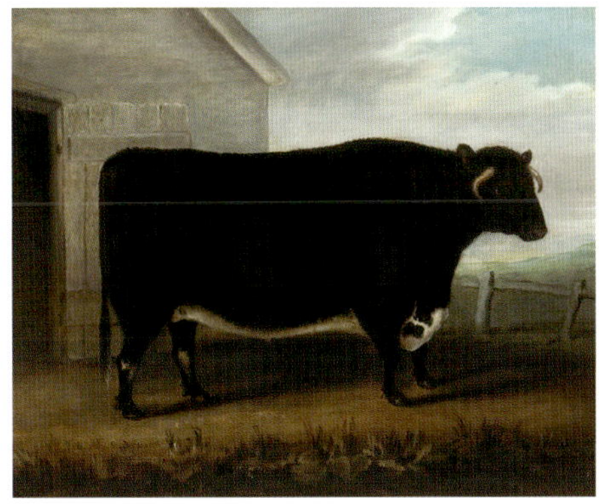

Vine, John c.1809–1867
Black Bull 1850
oil on board 46.5 x 58
197.P.83

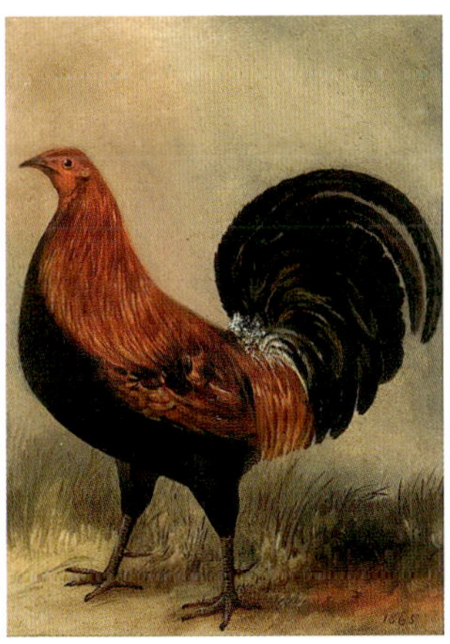

Vine, John c.1809–1867
Cockerel 1865
oil on board 43 x 31
194.P.83

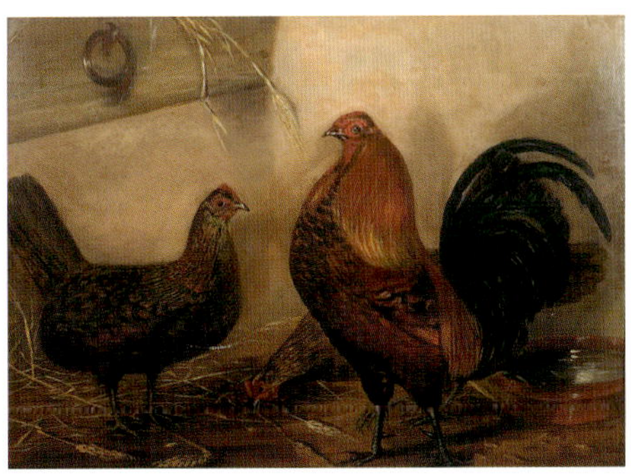

Vine, John c.1809–1867
Cock and Two Hens
oil on board 47 x 62
195.P.83

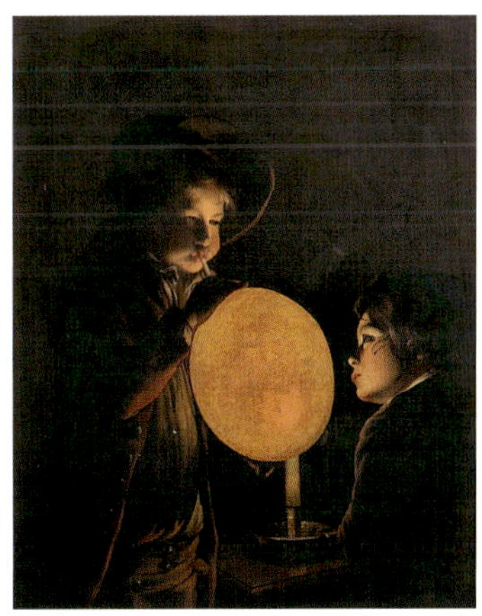

Wright, Joseph of Derby (after) 1734–1797
Boys Blowing up a Bladder
oil on canvas 90.5 x 71
137.P.83

Great Dunmow Town Council

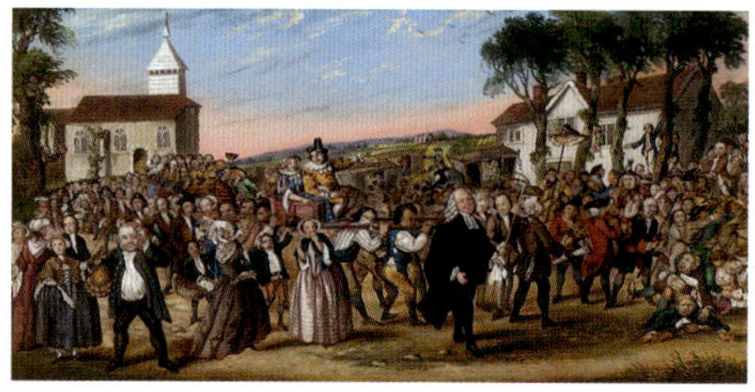

Ogborne, David c.1700–1768
The Flitch Procession Moving away from Little Dunmow Priory Church c.1751
oil on canvas 60 x 109
H/F.3.2

Earls Colne Parish Council

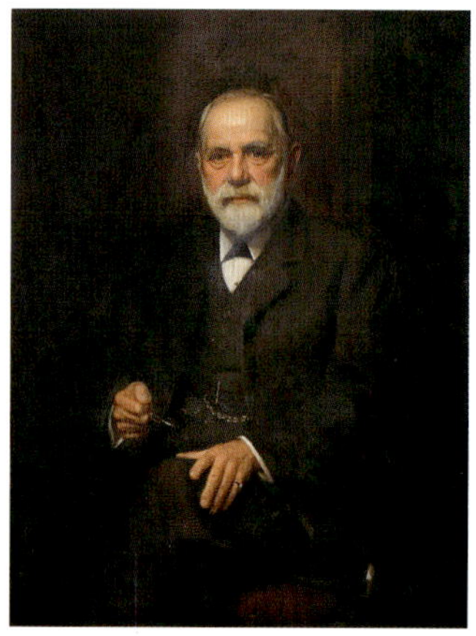

Daniell, Frank 1866–1932
Reuben Hunt of Earls Colne, Justice of the Peace for Essex, Chairman of the Governors of the Earls Colne Grammar School 1911
oil on canvas 112 x 86.5
ECPC.2

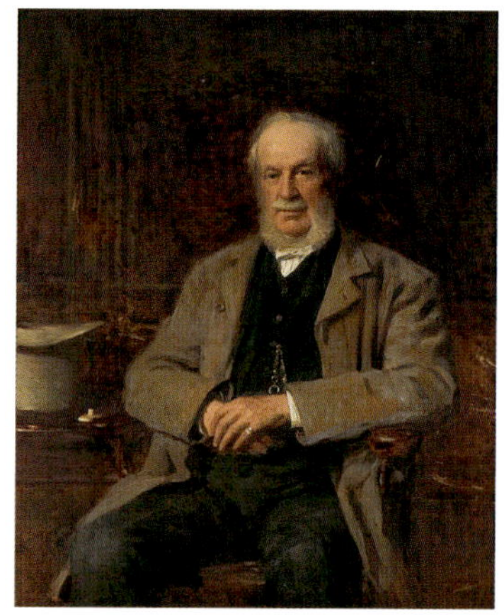

Miller, William Edwards active 1872–1929
John Taylor, MRCS 1899
oil on canvas 127 x 101.5
ECPC.1

North Weald Airfield Museum

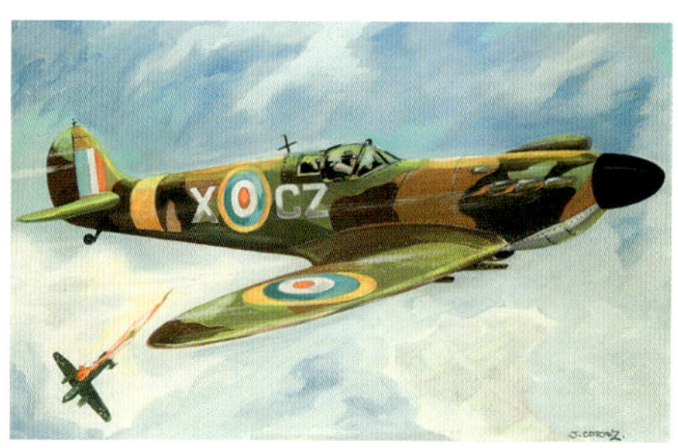

Cortez, J.
The Immortal 'Spitfire', 1940
oil on board 57.5 x 87.5
16

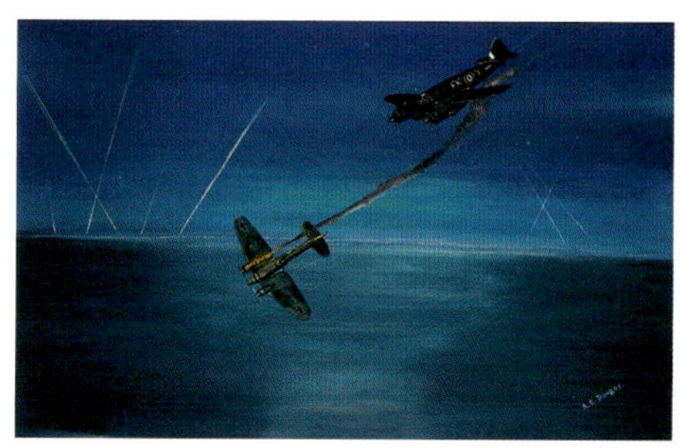

Dungey, A. E.
Beaufighter v He111 at Night c.1960
oil on canvas 59.5 x 90
8

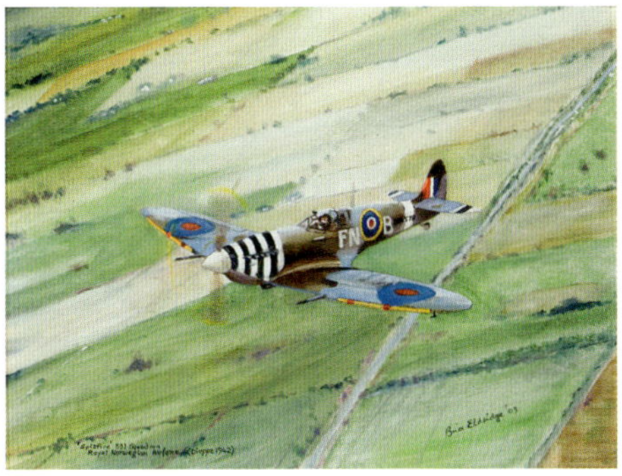

Eldridge, Brian
'Spitfire' 331 Squadron, Royal Norwegian Air Force (Dieppe, 1942) 2003
oil on board 36 x 44.5
3

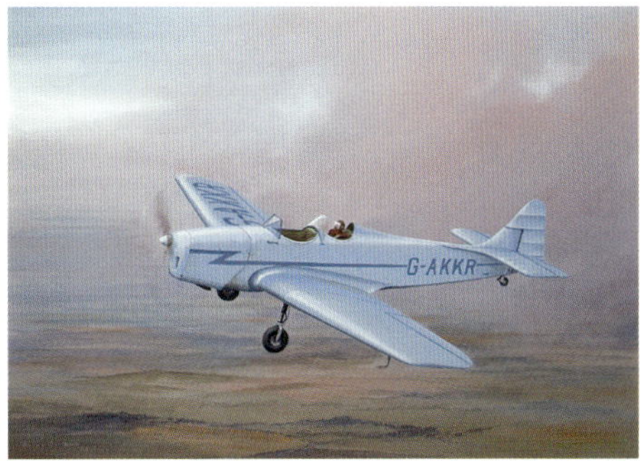

Garland, Harold active 1986–1988
Miles Magister G-AKKR 1988
acrylic on canvas 45 x 60
14

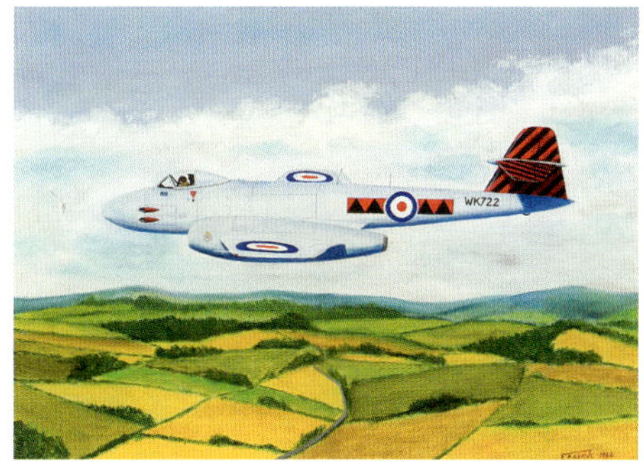

Reeve, Edward. P. active 1995–1998
Meteor WK722 1995
oil on board 29 x 34.5
6 (P)

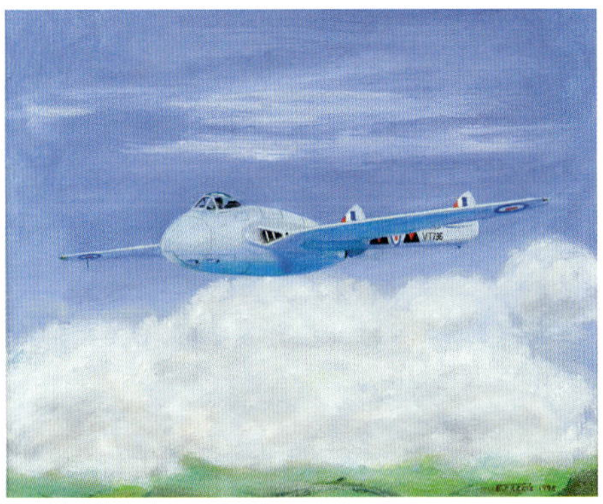

Reeve, Edward. P. active 1995–1998
Vampire VT796 1995
oil on board 24.5 x 29.5
7 (P)

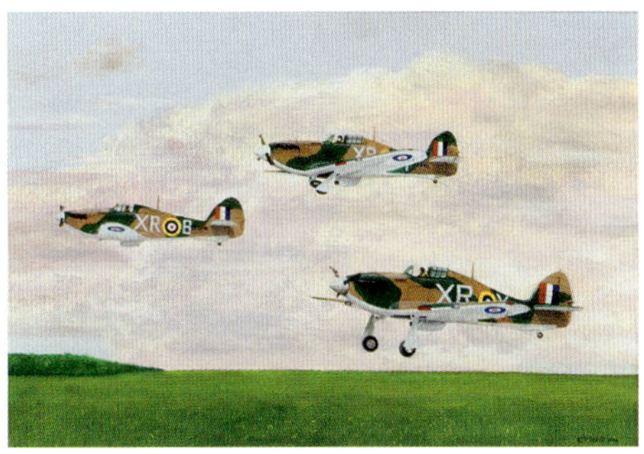

Reeve, Edward. P. active 1995–1998
Hawker Hurricane, 71 Squadron RAF, 'First from the Eyries', No.1 American Eagle Squadron 1998
oil on board 30.5 x 44
4

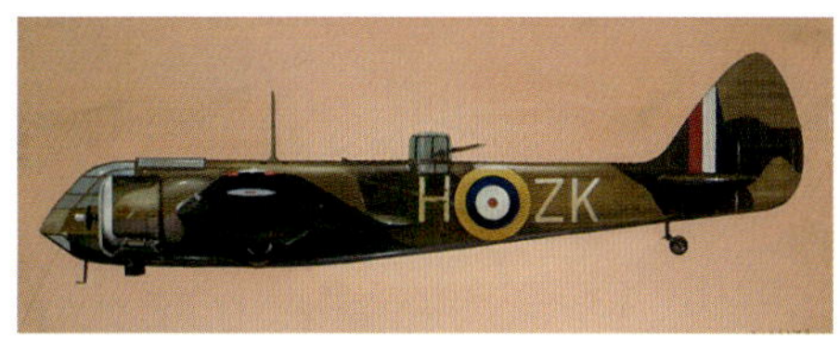

Siggins, James
*Blenheim H*ZK* c.1982
oil on board 29 x 73.5
13

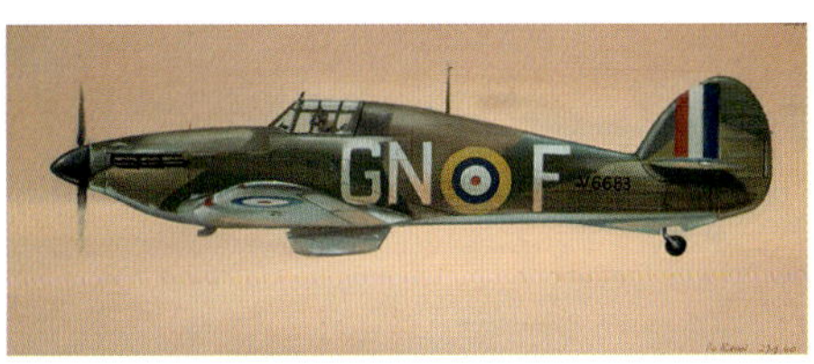

Siggins, James
*Hurricane GN*F* c.1982
oil on board 29 x 69.5
12

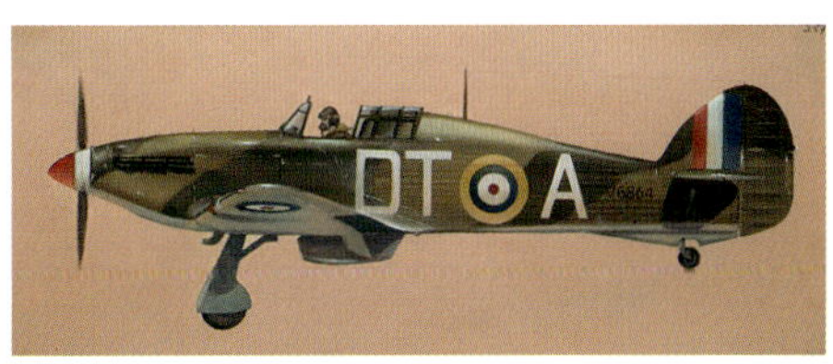

Siggins, James (attributed to)
*Hurricane DT*A* c.1982
oil on board 28 x 68.5
11

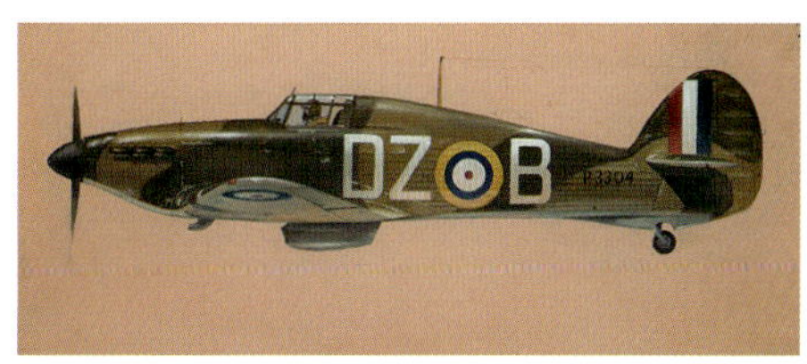

Siggins, James (attributed to)
*Hurricane DZ*B* c.1982
oil on board 29.5 x 68.5
10

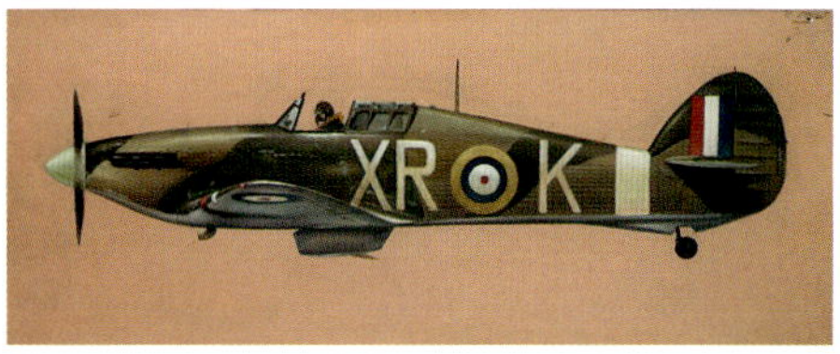

Siggins, James (attributed to)
*Hurricane XR*K* c.1982
oil on board 29 x 70
9

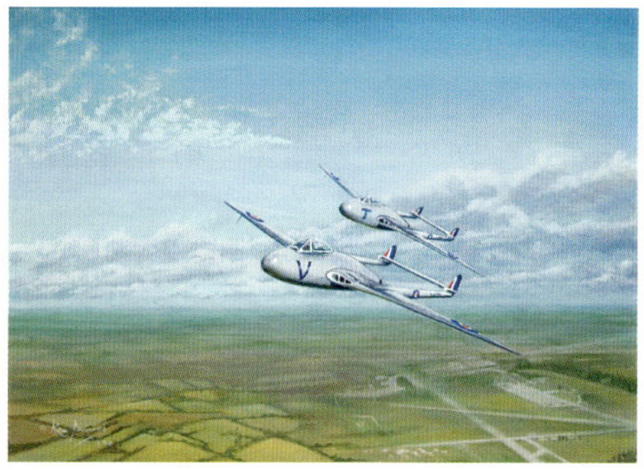

Summers, Ken
North Weald Below, Two Vampires 1998
oil on board 45 x 60.5
1

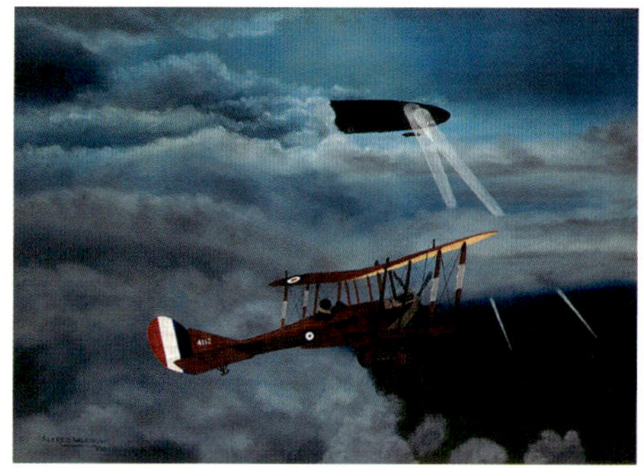

Worrow, Alfred active 1993–1998
BE2 4112 Attack on Airship L31 at Night 1993
oil on canvas 46 x 60.5
17

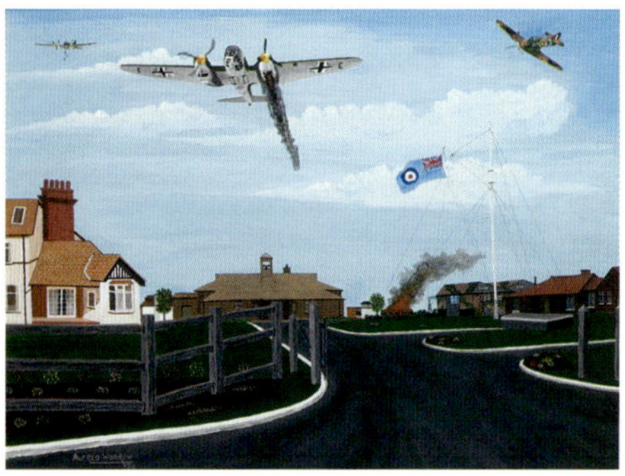

Worrow, Alfred active 1993–1998
Heinkel Attack on North Weald Airfield 1998
acrylic on board 35 x 45
15

Frinton & Walton Town Council

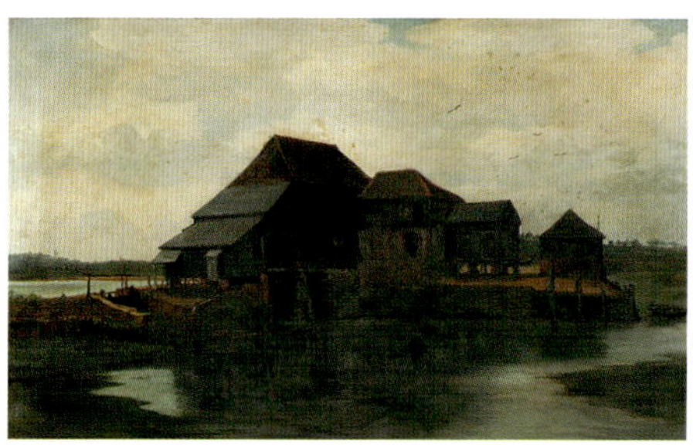

Moore, A. Harvey d.1905
The Old Water Mill, Walton-on-the-Naze 1900
oil on canvas 62 x 100
1

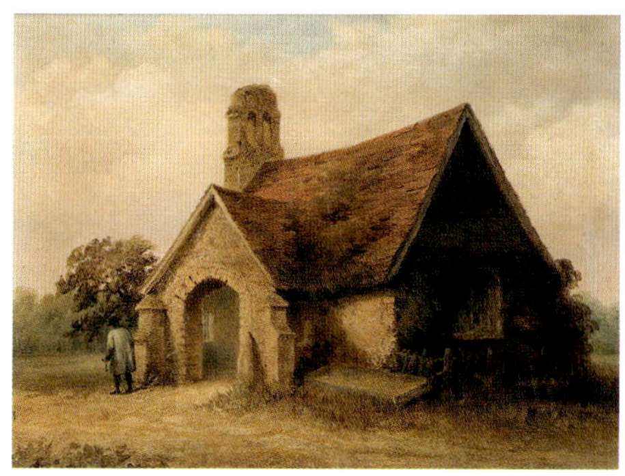

unknown artist 19th C
The Old Parish Church of St Mary the Virgin, Frinton-on-Sea
oil on canvas 34 x 44
2

Thurrock Museum

Thurrock, sited on the north banks of the River Thames, opposite Kent and the East of London, forms part of the southern boundary of Essex. It was established as a Unitary Authority on 1 April, 1998, having been granted Borough status in 1974. It was formed in 1936 by amalgamating Purfleet and Orsett Rural District Councils with Grays and Tilbury Town Councils into Thurrock Urban District Council.

Thurrock's landscape of agriculture, industry, regional shopping centres, quarries, housing estates and diverse communities within that palimpsest are often ignored, misunderstood and by-passed fast on the M25 as having nothing much to offer. In fact, with over 240 listed buildings, 13 National Monuments, 23 historic woods and 6 conservation areas, linked to the extensive collections in Thurrock Museum, our Borough offers a unique opportunity to discover a continuous chain of human development.

The collection of oil paintings is not extensive or of great quality, but it is a collection of local scenes and people, reflecting the history and industry of the area, which includes a number of pictures of Thames sailing barges, the training ships, which were once anchored off Grays, as well as a paddle steamer, '*La Marguerite*'. There are two fine *Sea Battles* by Richard Barnett Spencer.

Built in the time of Charles II when the Dutch were menacing our shores, the impressive gatehouse at Tilbury Fort, is featured in *Wind and Tide, the Thames at Tilbury Fort*, after Clarkson Stanfield. In *Queen Elizabeth, Tilbury, 1588*, the monarch is shown encouraging her troops before the Armada in front of a particularly handsome tent. This picture was once a shop advertisement for Edgingtons Tent Manufacturers on the Old Kent Road.

In the Shire Hall in Chelmsford there is a portrait of Colonel Sir Francis Whitmore, Lord Lieutenant of Essex from 1936 to 1958, he lived at Orsett Hall. We hold two portraits painted by him: *Captain Sir Ion Hamilton-Benn*, and the *Admiral of the Fleet 12th Earl of Cork and Orrery*.

Essex has lost a number of important country houses and one of these, whose estate is now bisected by the M25, is Belhus, two miles from the Thames. In the museum gallery there is a large oil painting depicting the house, gardens and estate c.1710, by an unknown artist. This picture once hung in the house and was unsold in the sale of 1923; it was acquired by Essex County Council and has been transferred to us. A Tudor house, described as 'newly builded' in 1526, it was gothicised by Lord Dacre, a friend of Sanderson Miller, in the eighteenth century.

In the main, our picture collection has not been on public display so we welcome the opportunity to have it included in the current catalogue.

Jonathan Catton, Heritage and Museum Officer

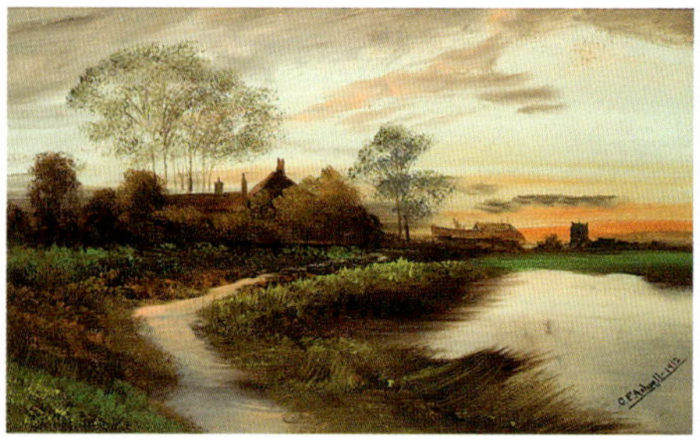

Ashwell, C. F.
Landscape (possibly West Thurrock) 1912
oil on board 43 x 68
3828

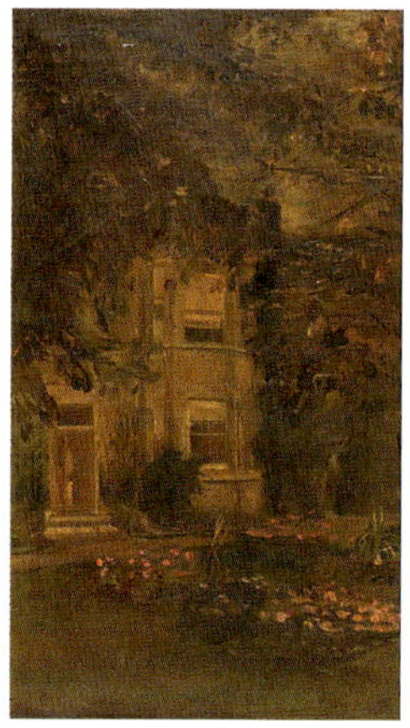

Ashwell, C. F.
Little Thurrock Rectory
oil on canvas 45.5 x 25.5
3886

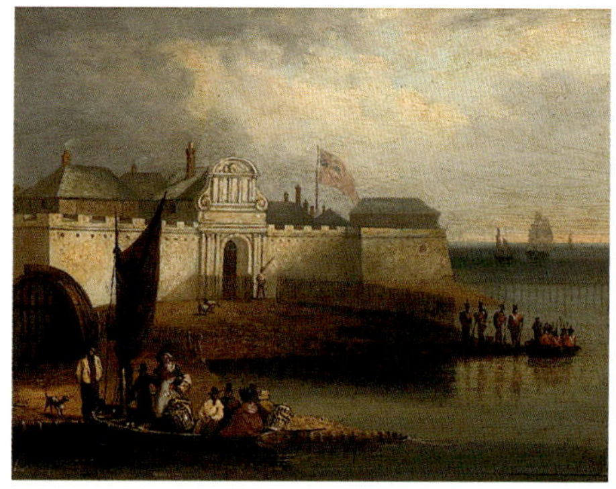

British (English) School
Tilbury Fort and Ferry c.1810
oil on panel 19 x 24.2
548

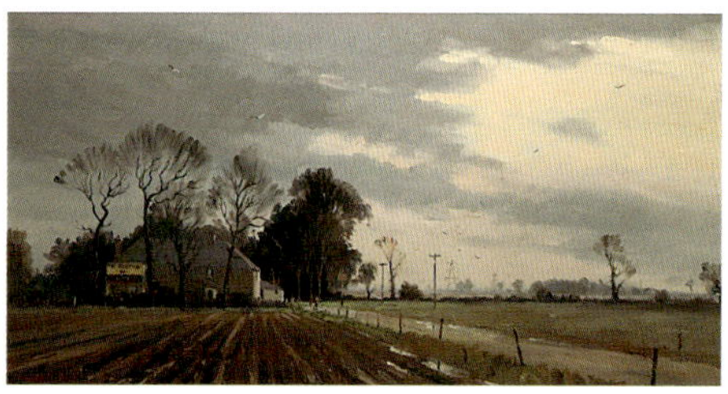

Ford, Marcus b.1914
The Harrow Inn, Bulphan c.1966
oil on canvas 46 x 84
722

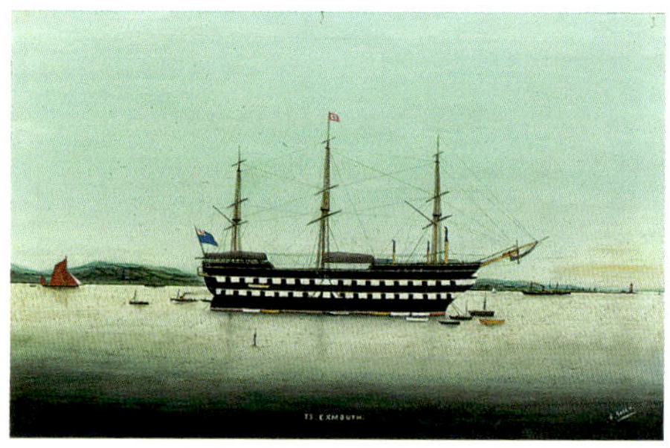

Green, F.
Training Ship 'TS Exmouth' (moored off Grays Beach, 1876–1939) c.1910
oil on canvas 61 x 91.5
918

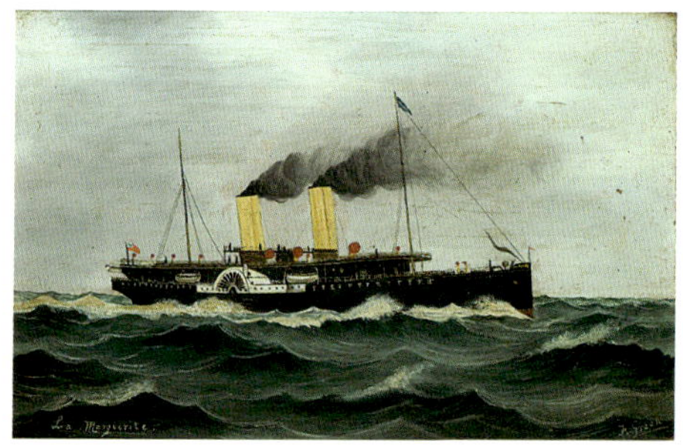

Green, F.
Paddle Steamer 'La Marguerite'
oil on board 30 x 46.5
2942.1

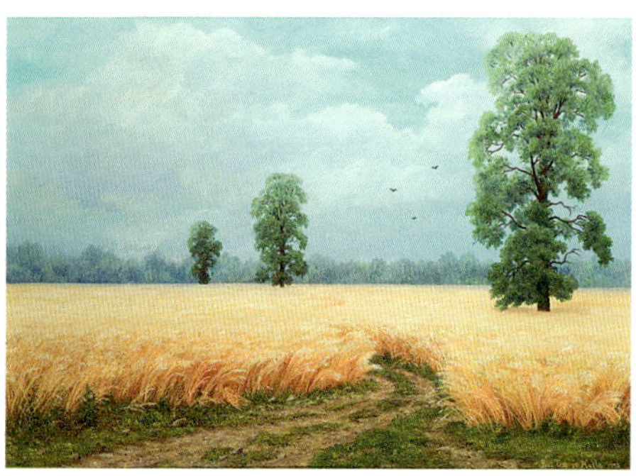

Halle, Paul George
A Passing Shower, Elms 1990
oil on canvas 46 x 61
3887

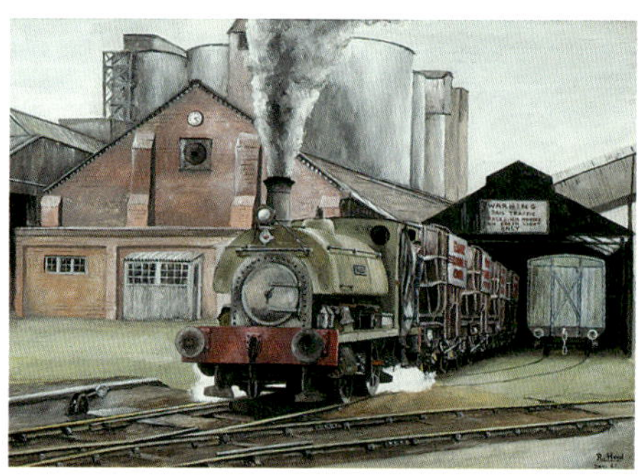

Head, R.
Tunnel Locomotive 1967
oil on paper 24.5 x 35.5
1233

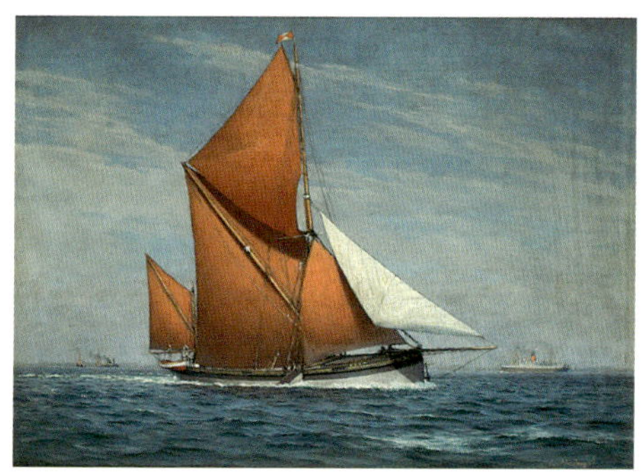

MacDougall, Ian
Sailing Barge 'Sara'
oil on canvas 44 x 59.5
1456.1 (P)

Facing page: Dodds, James, b.1957, *Maldon Shipwrights* (detail), 1988, South Essex Partnership NHS Trust, (p. 209)

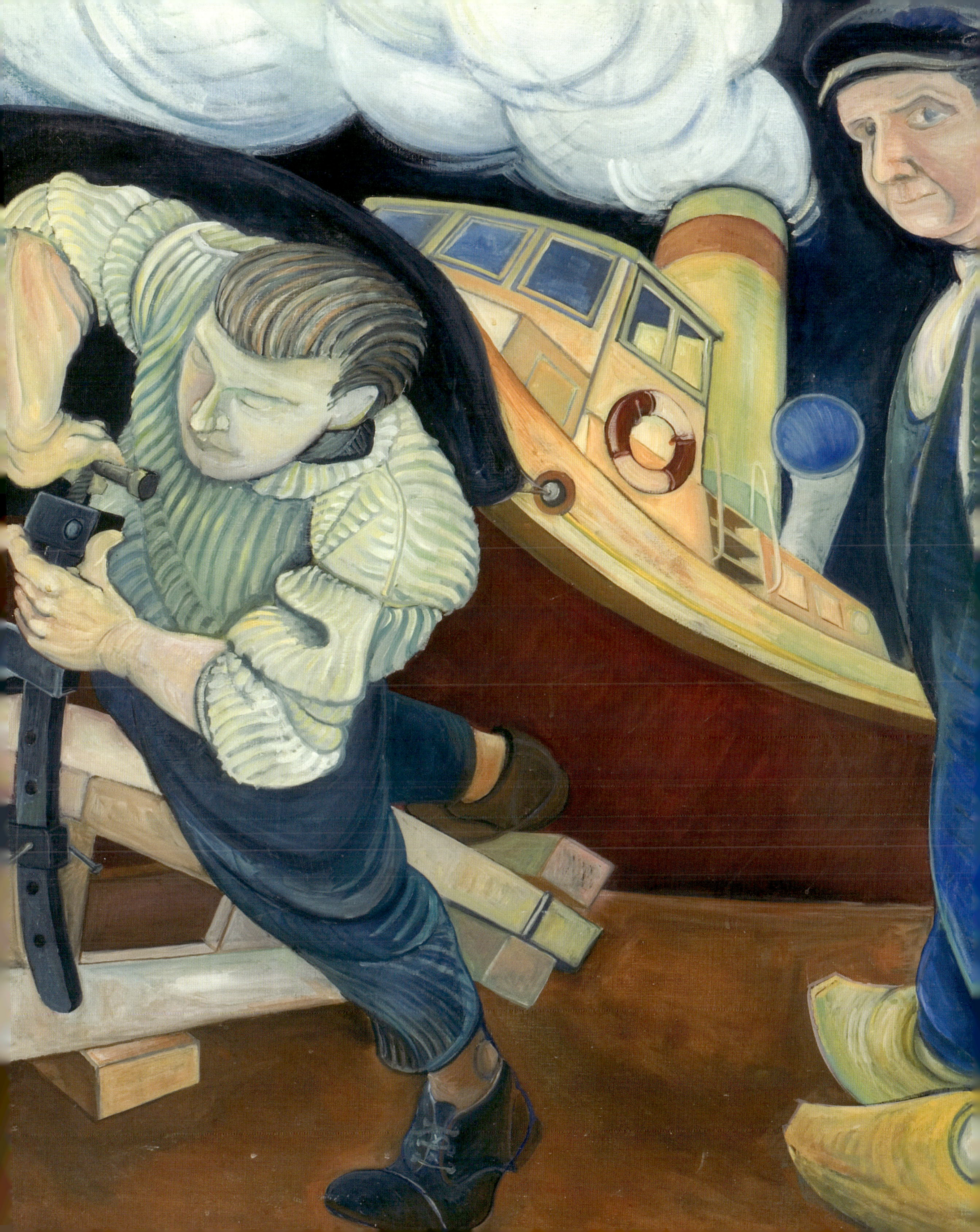

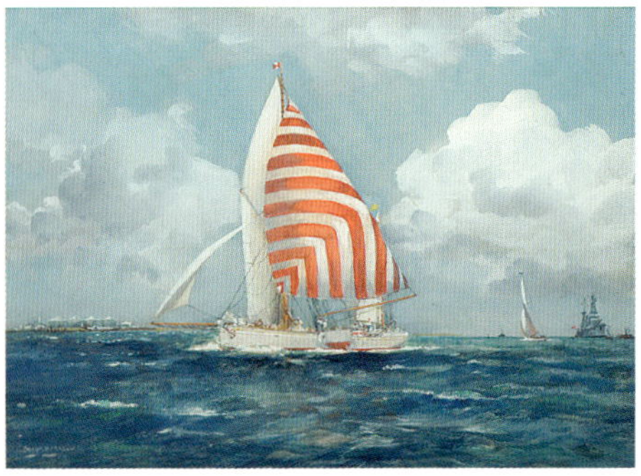

Mason, Frank Henry 1876–1965
Sailing Barge 'Veronica' Winning the Medway Race, 1957 c.1957
oil on paper 29 x 39
1456.3 (P)

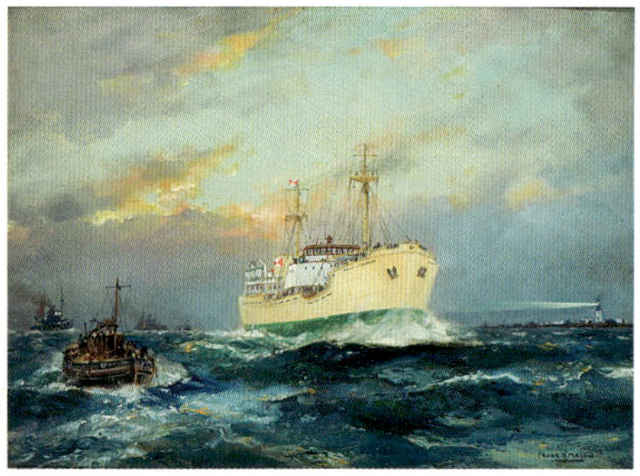

Mason, Frank Henry 1876–1965
'Frederick T. Everard' Passing Spurn Head, River Humber
oil on paper 30 x 39.5
1456.2 (P)

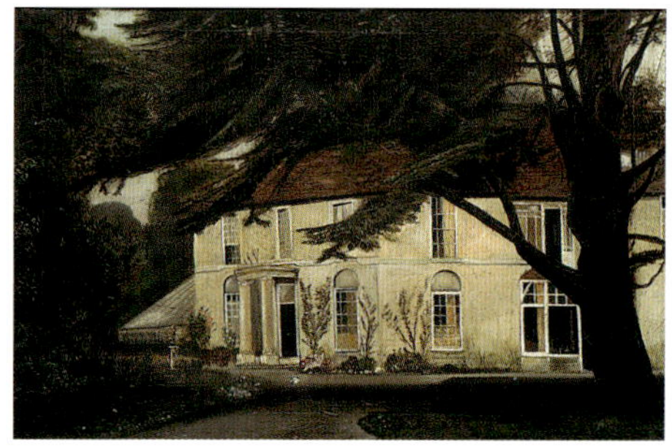

Roddam, A. E.
Moore Place, Stanford-le-Hope
oil on canvas 56 x 81.5
3884

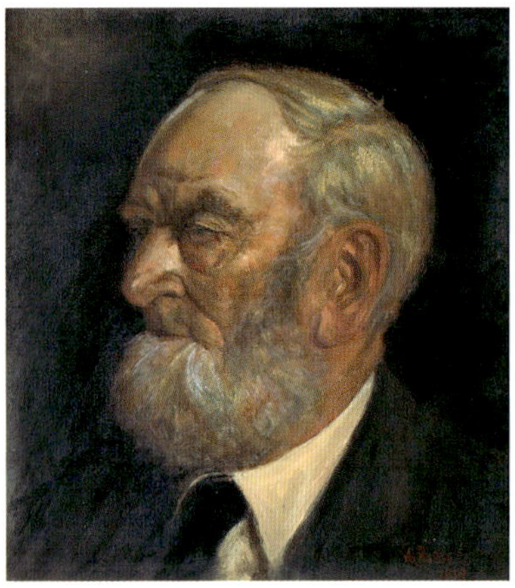

Russell, Alfred
Portrait of an Old Gentleman 1934
oil on canvas 38.5 x 35
3888

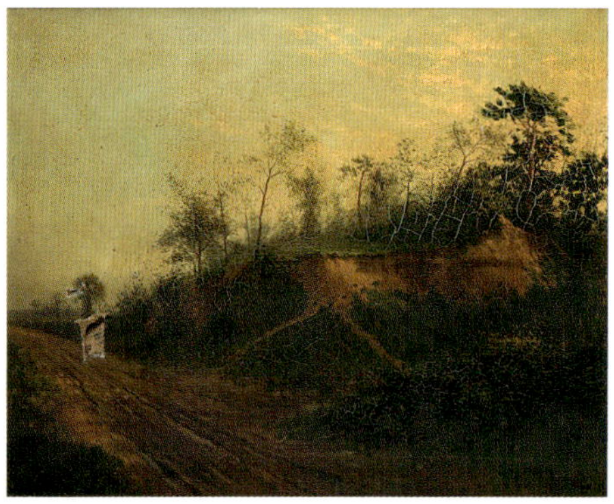

Russell, Alfred
Titan Pit, Grays
oil on canvas 49 x 59.5
1545

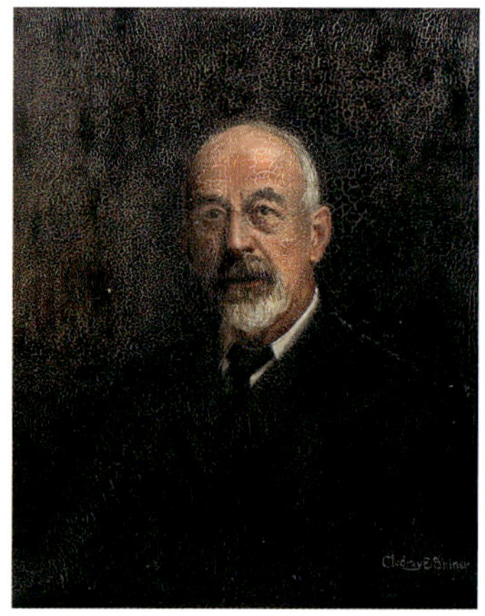

Shiner, Audrey E. 1900–c.1980
George Henry Silverwood, BA, LLB, Headmaster of Palmer's School (1893–1918)
oil on canvas 75 x 62
3881

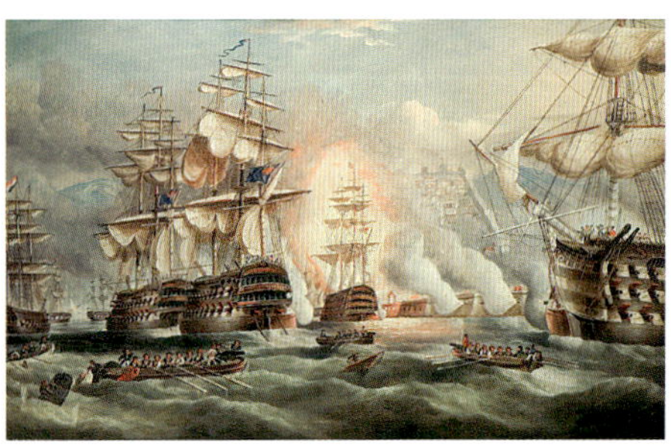

Spencer, Richard Barnett d.1874
Sea Battle
oil on canvas 57.5 x 88
3883

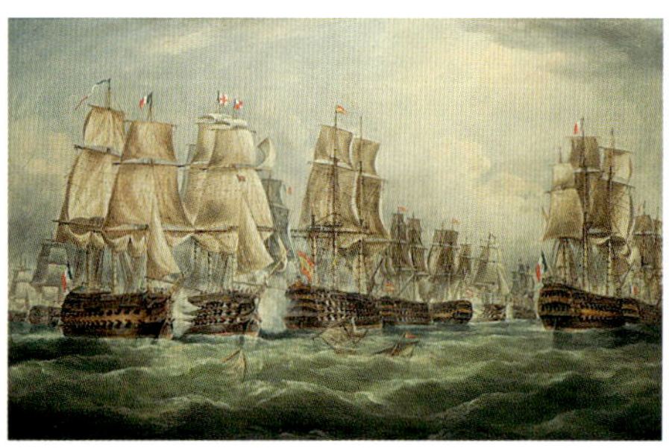

Spencer, Richard Barnett d.1874
Sea Battle
oil on canvas 57.5 x 88
3885

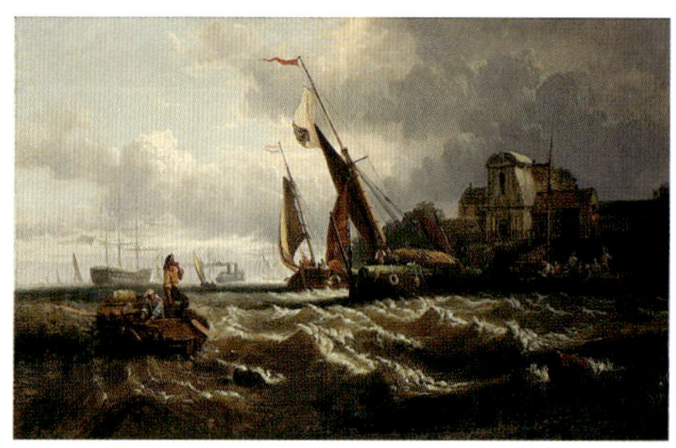

Stanfield, Clarkson (after) 1793–1867
Wind against Tide, the Thames at Tilbury Fort
c.1850
oil on canvas 76 x 127
711

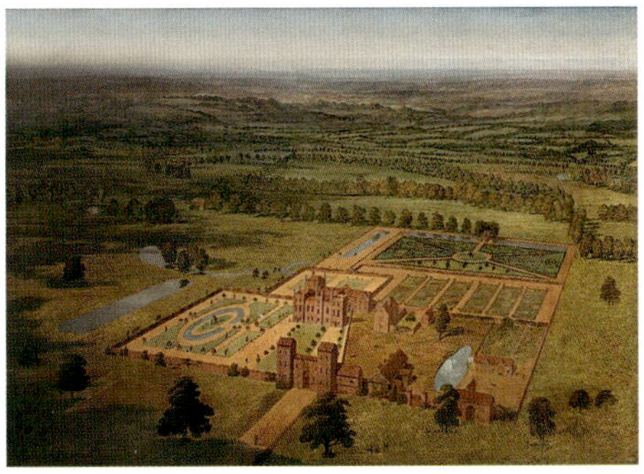

unknown artist 18th C
Belhus House and Park, c.1710 (demolished in 1957)
oil on canvas 110 x 178
3581

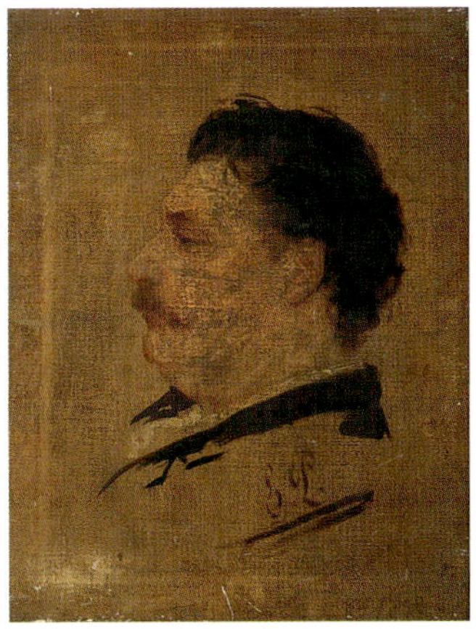

unknown artist 19th C
Portrait of a Gentleman
oil on canvas 51 x 38
1515

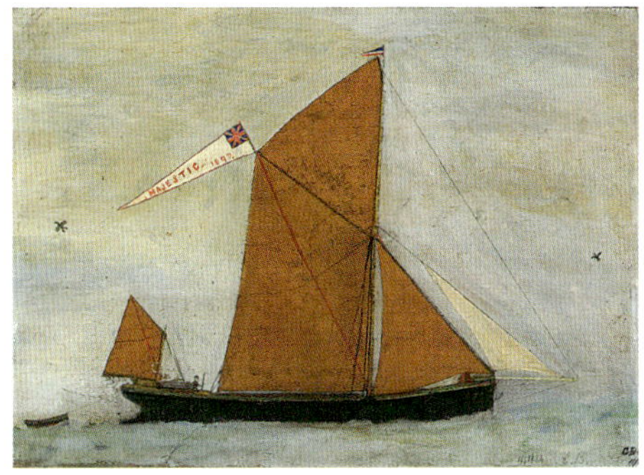

unknown artist
Thames Sailing Barge 'Majestic, 1897' (Goldsmith and Cory of Gravesend) 1914
oil on canvas 33 x 44
1442

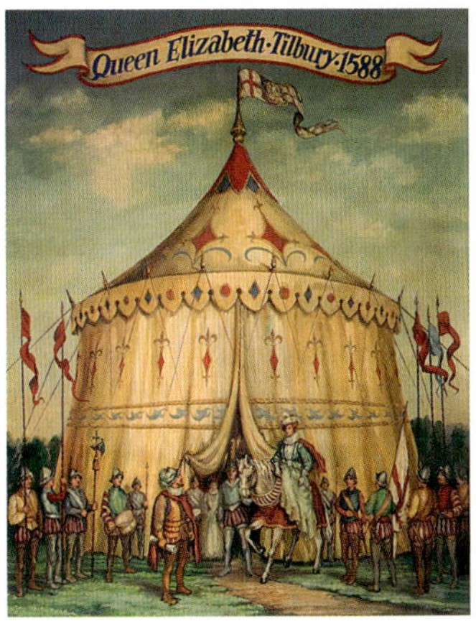

unknown artist
Queen Elizabeth, Tilbury, 1588 1920s
oil on canvas on board 177 x 156
1511 (P)

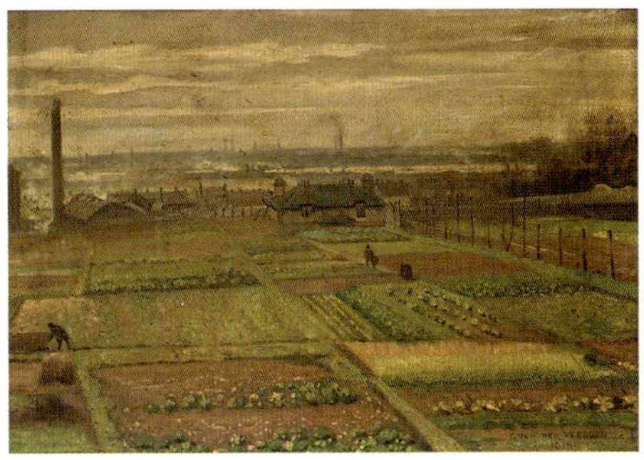

Van der Weegen, F. active 1918–1928
Allotments 1918
oil on canvas 44.6 x 61
3882

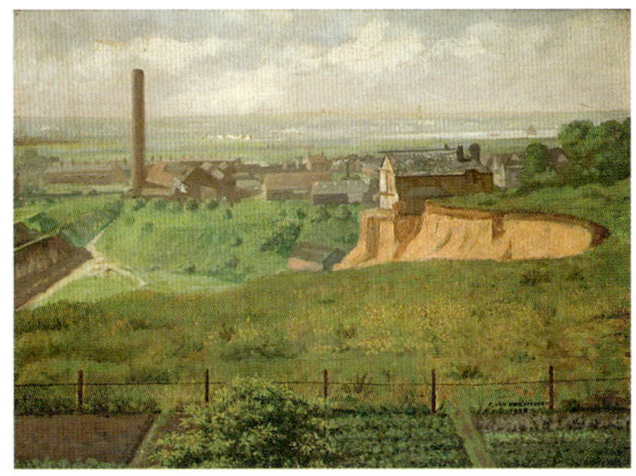

Van der Weegen, F. active 1918–1928
Globe Pit, Grays 1928
oil on canvas 56 x 63
609

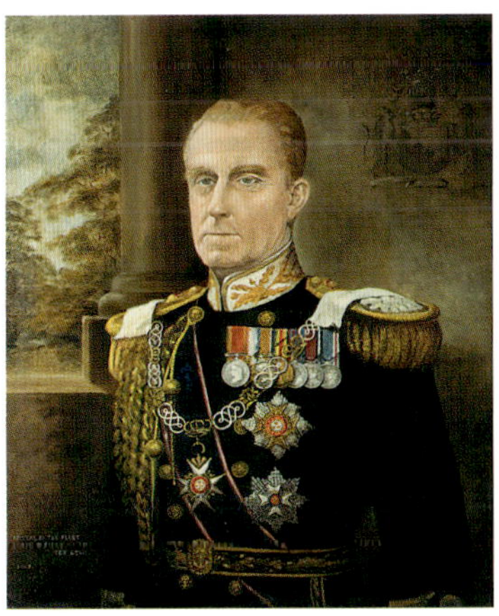

Whitmore, Francis 1872–1962
Admiral of the Fleet, 12th Earl of Cork and Orrery, GCB, GCVO 1943
oil on canvas 75 x 62
1392.2

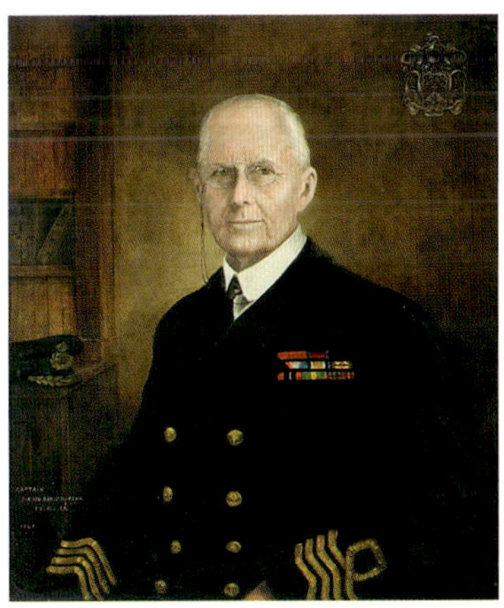

Whitmore, Francis 1872–1962
Captain Sir Ion Hamilton-Benn, 1st Bt, CB, DSO, TD 1943
oil on canvas 75.5 x 63
1392.1

Birdbrook Community House

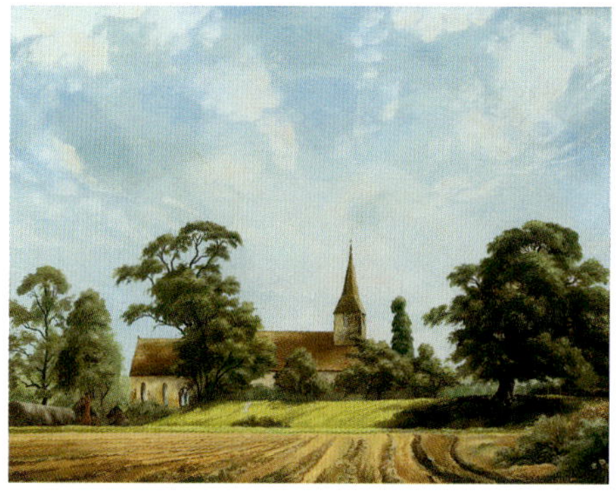

Gilbert, Stanley Victor b.1915
Birdbrook Church from the North 1968
oil on canvas 61 x 76
4

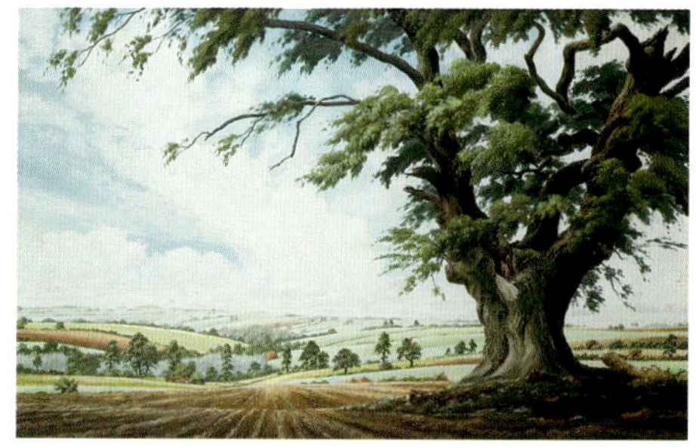

Gilbert, Stanley Victor b.1915
View from the Back of Birdbrook Hall 1968
oil on canvas 81 x 122
1

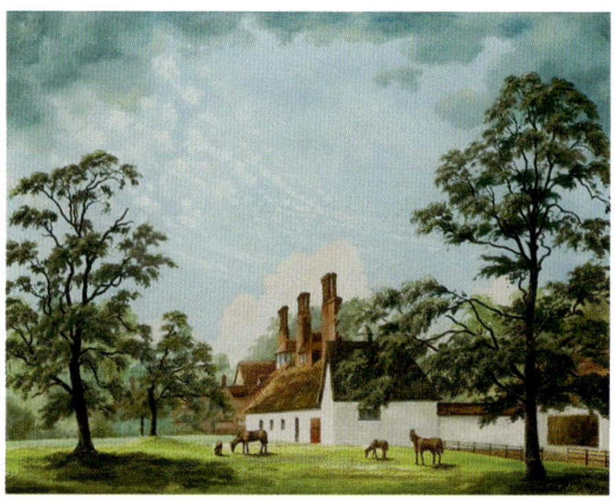

Gilbert, Stanley Victor b.1915
The Stables at Moyns Park 1969
oil on canvas 60 x 75
3

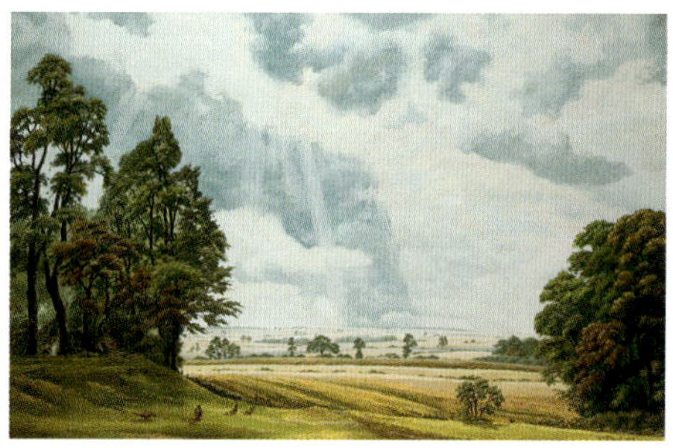

Gilbert, Stanley Victor b.1915
View from Birdbrook Hall Looking North 1969
oil on canvas 79 x 120
2

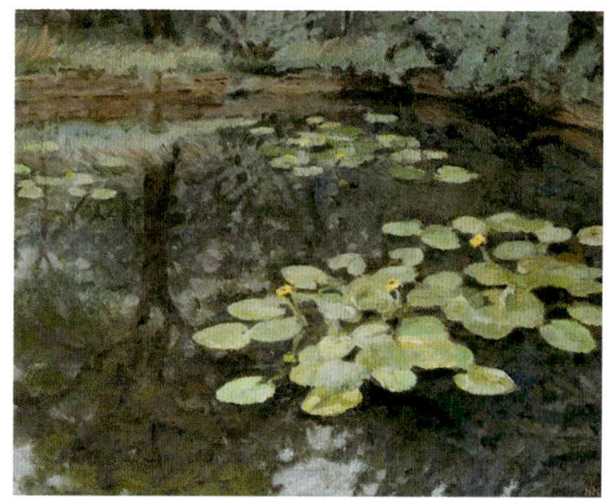

Norman, Hope
Water Lilies 1962
oil on canvas 49 x 59.5
5

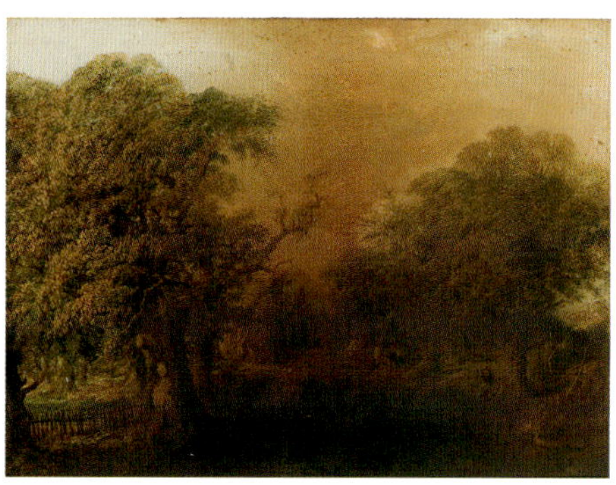

unknown artist
Woodland
oil on canvas 70 x 90
6

Halstead Town Council

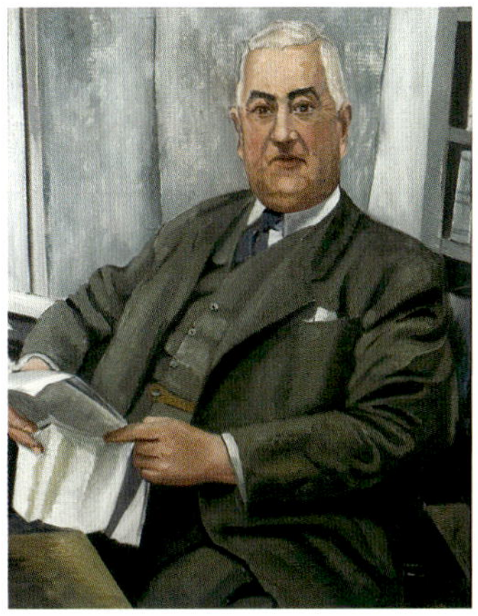

de Maistre, Leroy Leveson Laurent Joseph
1894–1968
Portrait of a Man Reading a Paper c.1950
oil & acrylic on canvas 91 x 71
1

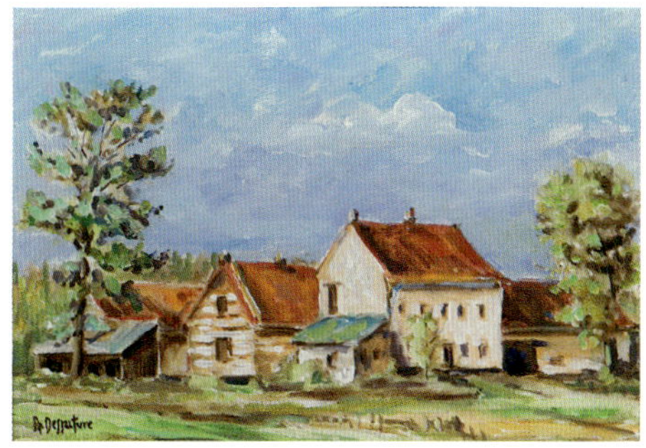

Despature, A.
Ferme du Bocquiau, Haubourdin c.1990
oil on canvas 40 x 50 (E)
5 (P)

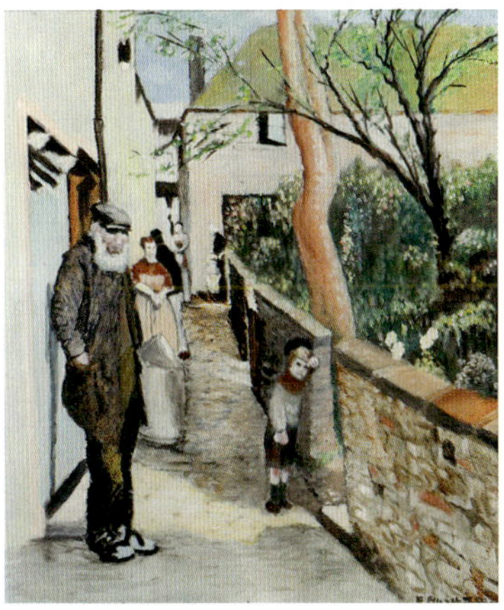

Elliott, Eric
Bygone Halstead 1979
oil on hardboard 61 x 51.5
2

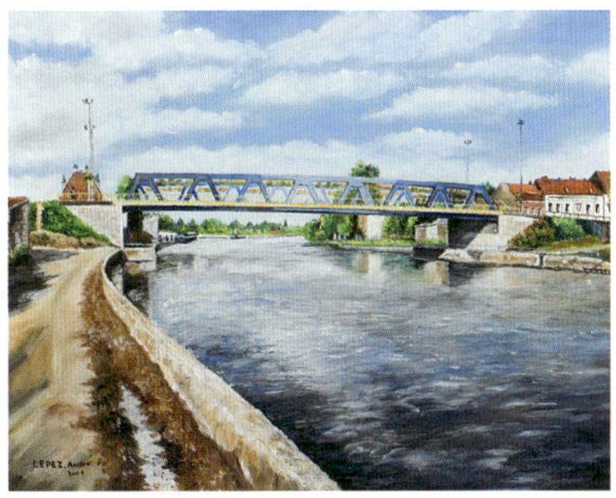

Lepez, André
Le pont d'Haubourdin 2001
oil on canvas 38.5 x 48.5
3 (P)

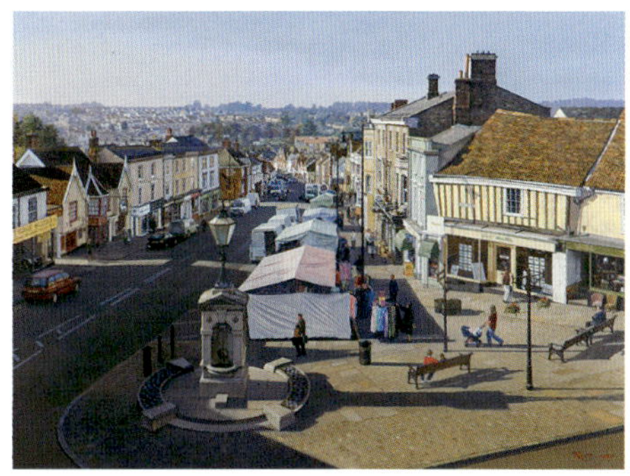

Root, Malcolm b.1950
Market Day in Halstead 1999
oil on canvas 74.5 x 99.8
4

Harlow Art Trust

Five of the seven pictures owned by Harlow Art Trust are decorative panels from the Gallery Deck Bar of the Festival of Britain Ship, *'Campania'*. They depict working boats from around the British coast. The 1951 Festival of Britain was held on London's South Bank but part of the celebration was a Sea Travelling Exhibition housed on *HMS 'Campania'*. The ship began her Festival tour at Southampton and docked at Britain's major ports of Dundee, Newcastle, Hull, Plymouth, Cardiff, Belfast, Birkenhead and Glasgow. *'Campania'*, a refrigerated cargo ship weighing 16,000 tons, was converted into an aircraft carrier in the Second World War. In 1946 she was laid up in Gareloch where James Holland, the resident designer at the Festival Office, hurried to see her when the Admiralty gave its permission for the ship to be loaned and converted into a mobile exhibition. Holland described her as 'an uncompromising lump of grey and rusty steel, but with a large hangar deck well suited for our purposes … but white paint, skeleton masts and plentiful bunting transformed a rather graceless hulk into the semblance of a floating fairground that certainly must have astonished those foreign skippers who encountered the *Campania* on her way up channel in the course of her Festival tour.' The travelling exhibition celebrated Britain's technological ingenuity and status as a world economic power; her arrival in port was greeted with great excitement and thousands of visitors.

Like many other towns, Harlow organised an exhibition as part of the Festival of Britain. However, unlike others, Harlow New Town was then in its infancy, being laid out by Sir Frederick Gibberd, and its Festival exhibition displayed works completed and in progress. At the closure of the Festival, Harlow Art Trust acquired these five panels, the work of the Southend artist, Alan Sorrell (1904–1974). A mural painter, one of his first commissions was to decorate the Central Library at Southend with four large panels, which are now part of the Beecroft Gallery collection.

Kelly Lean, Arts Development Officer & Julia Abel Smith, Essex County Co-ordinator

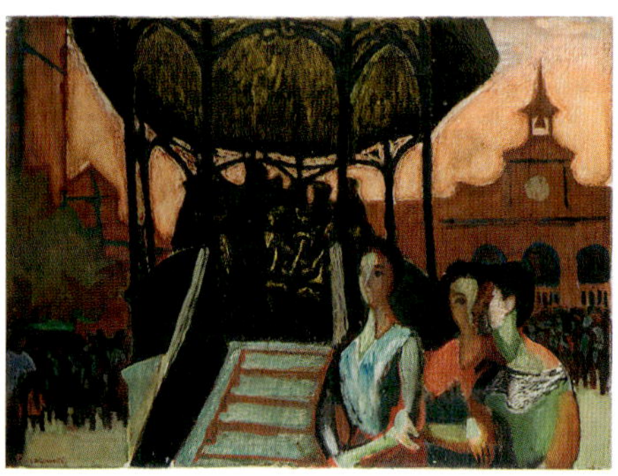

Ruszkowski, Zdzislaw 1907–1991
Sunday Evening in Ecija (Andalucia) 1956
oil on canvas 85 x 114
1

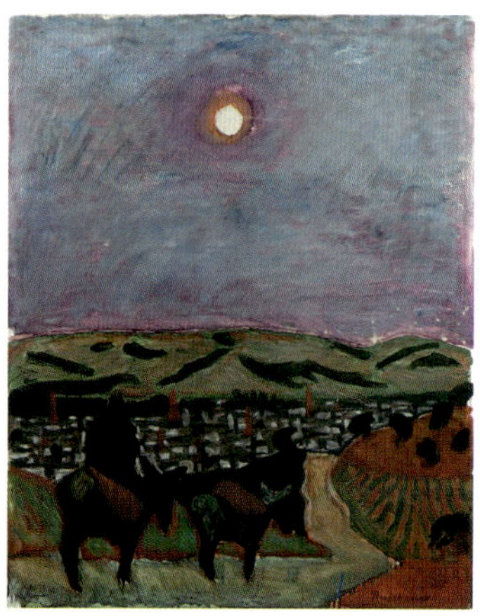

Ruszkowski, Zdzislaw 1907–1991
A Spanish Landscape by Moonlight
oil on canvas 90 x 71
2

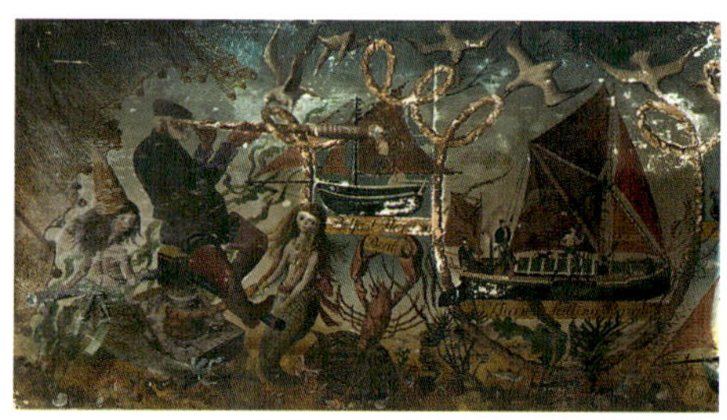

Sorrell, Alan 1904–1974
Panel from the Gallery Deck Bar of the Festival of Britain Ship 'Campania' Featuring a Belfast Herring Boat and a Thames (…) 1951
oil on plywood 122 x 213
4

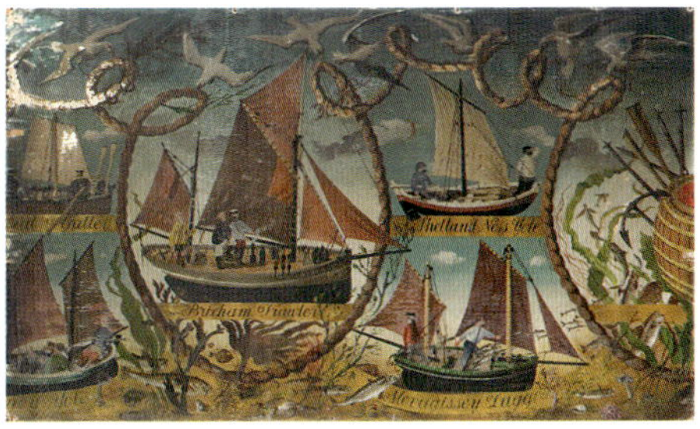

Sorrell, Alan 1904–1974
Panel from the Gallery Deck Bar of the Festival of Britain Ship 'Campania' Featuring a Deal Galley, an Orkeney Yole, a (…) 1951
oil on plywood 122 x 198
7

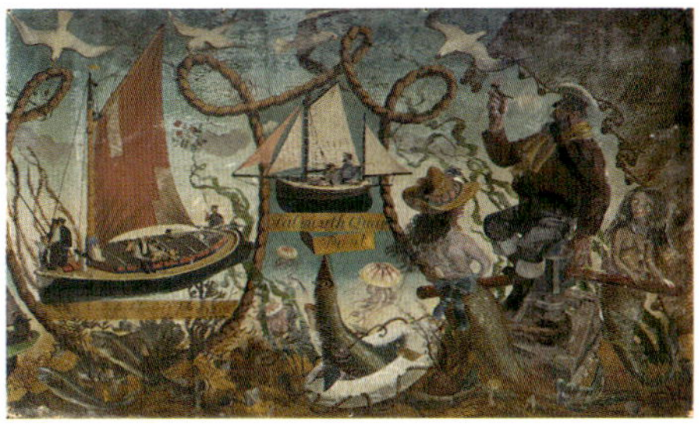

Sorrell, Alan 1904–1974
Panel from the Gallery Deck Bar of the Festival of Britain Ship 'Campania' Featuring a Norfolk Wherry and a Falmouth Quay Punt 1951
oil on plywood 122 x 198
6

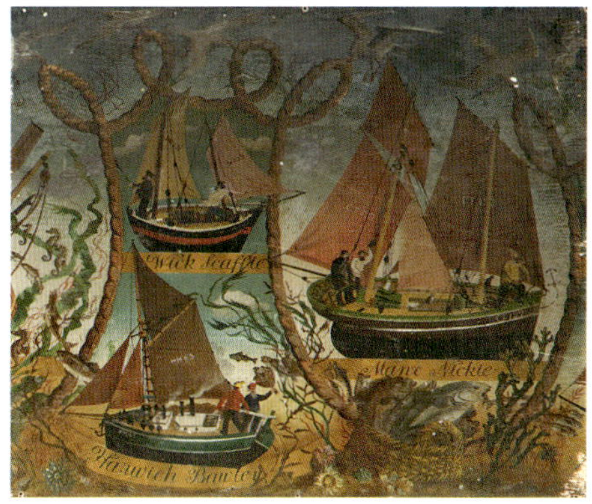

Sorrell, Alan 1904–1974
Panel from the Gallery Deck Bar of the Festival of Britain Ship 'Campania' Featuring a Wick Scaffie, a Harwich Bawley and a Manx 1951
oil on plywood 122 x 141
3

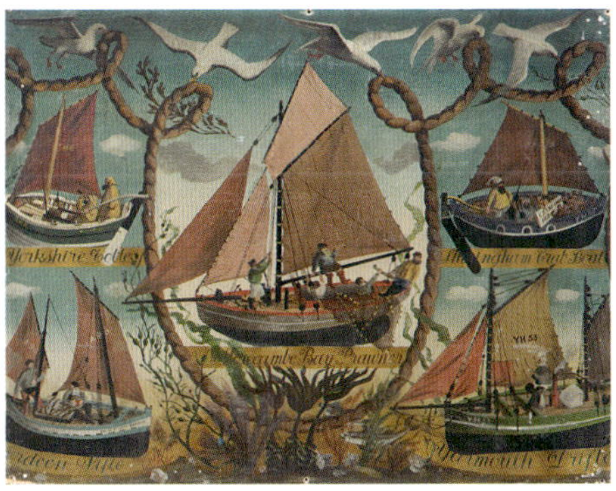

Sorrell, Alan 1904–1974
Panel from the Gallery Deck Bar of the Festival of Britain Ship 'Campania' Featuring a Yorkshire Coble, an Aberdeen Fifie, (…) 1951
oil on plywood 122 x 152
5

Harlow Council

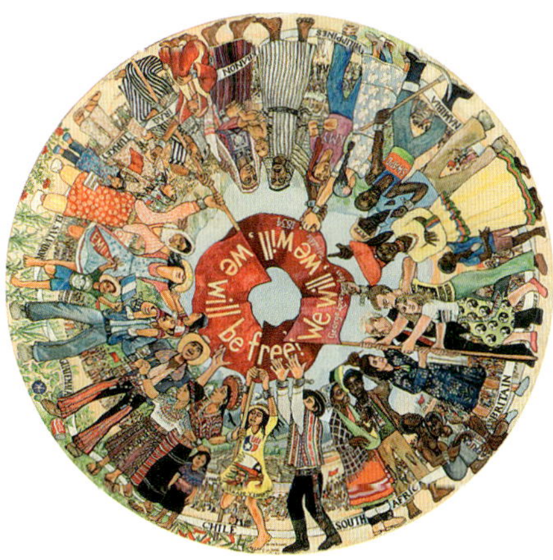

Jones, Dan
'We will, we will, we will be free!' 1984
oil on board 131
2

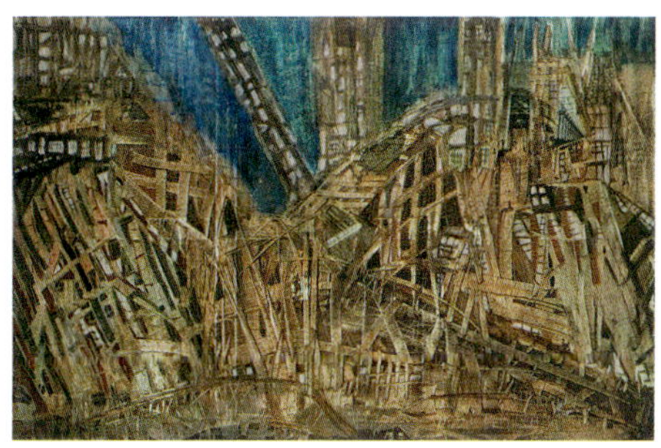

Verlon, André 1917–1993
Barrage 1964
oil on canvas 129.5 x 194.5
1

Harwich Town Council

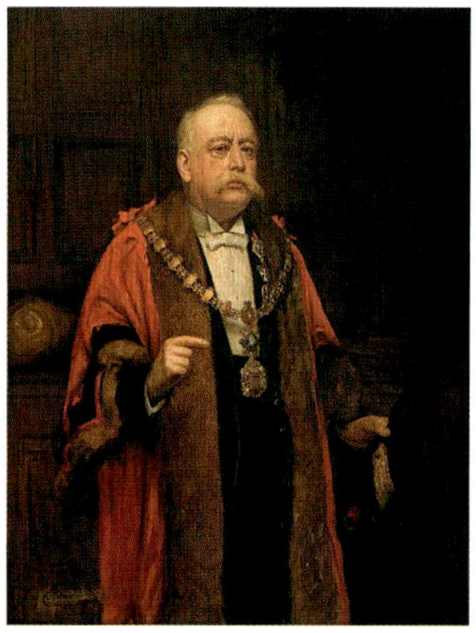

Cotman, Frederick George 1850–1920
Alderman William Groom, KD, CC, JP, VR 1903
oil on canvas 140 x 110
3

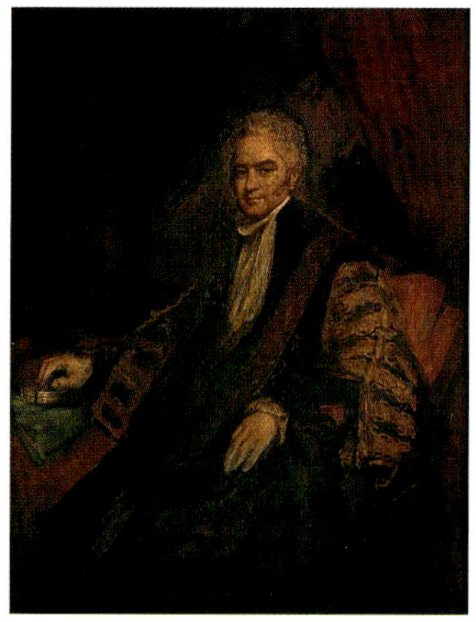

Owen, William 1769–1825
Nicholas Vansittart, 1st Baron Bexley, High Steward and MP for Harwich, Chancellor of the Exchequer (1766–1851) 1823
oil on canvas 140 x 110
2

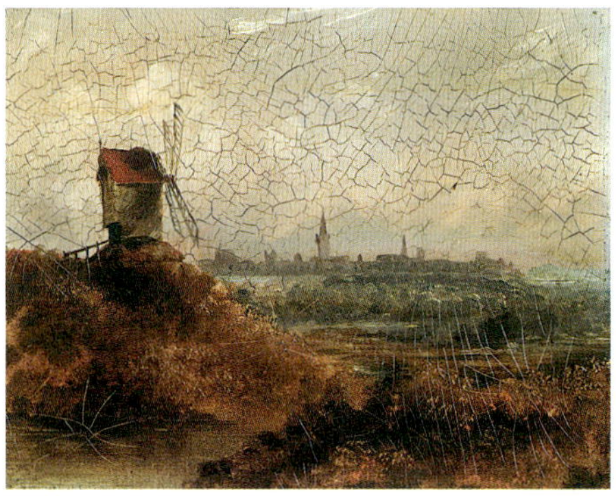

unknown artist
The Mill, Beacon Hill, Harwich 1807
oil on board 16.5 x 21
1

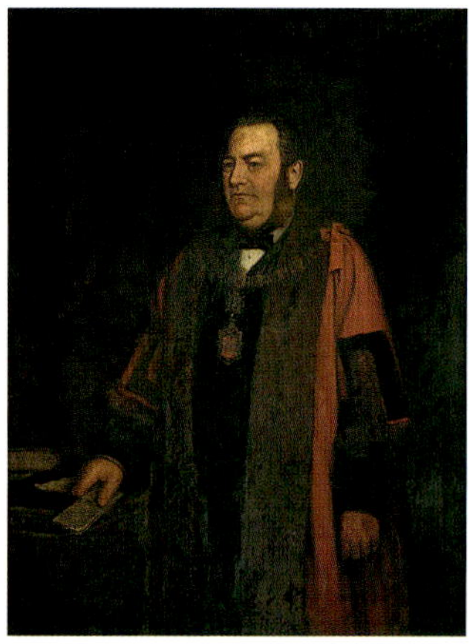

unknown artist
Alderman John Henry Vaux, JP 1887
oil on canvas 142 x 110
6

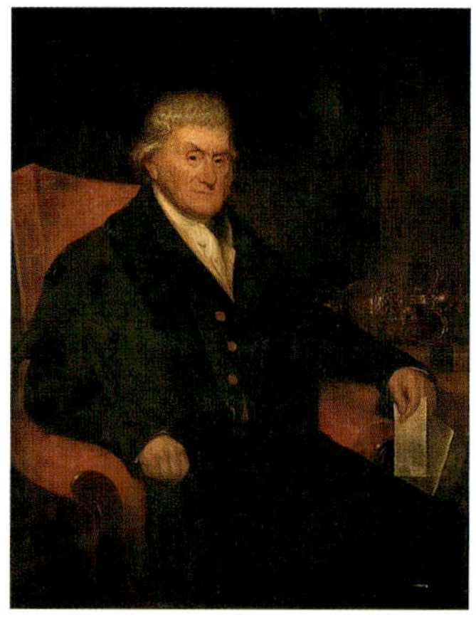

unknown artist
Alderman John Hopkins (1750–1828)
oil on canvas 139 x 108
4

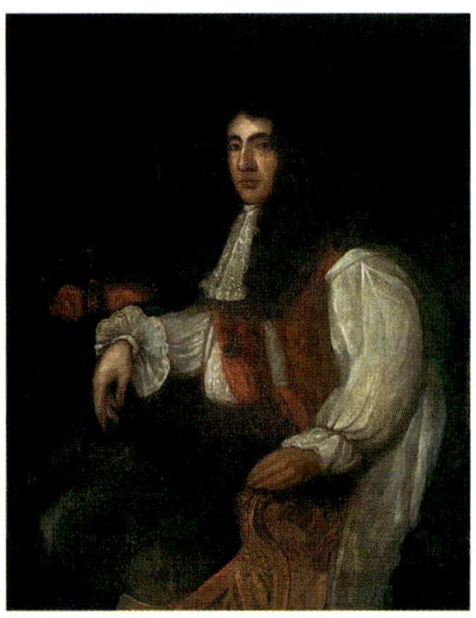

unknown artist
Charles II (1630–1685)
oil on canvas 126 x 100
5

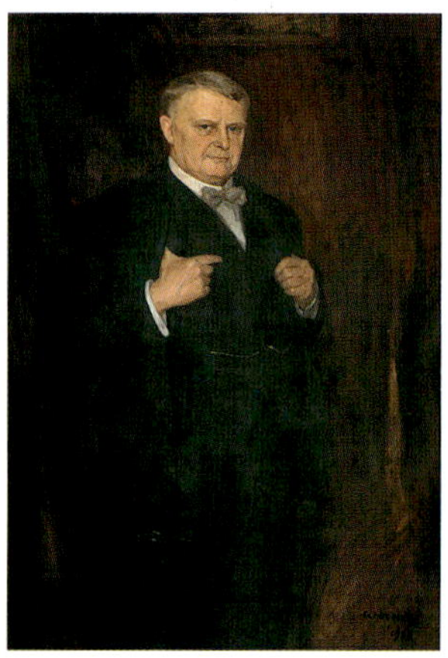

Werner
Richard Coombe Abdy, High Steward of Harwich 1926
oil on canvas 160 x 97 (E)
7

South Essex Partnership NHS Foundation Trust

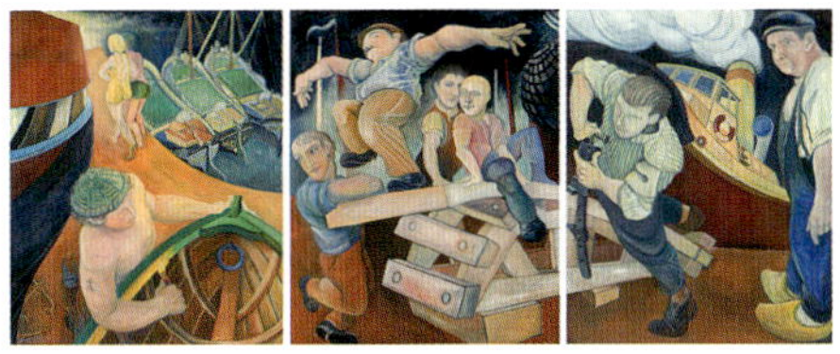

Dodds, James Foster b.1957
Maldon Shipwrights 1988
oil on canvas 132 x 303
1

Leigh Heritage Centre

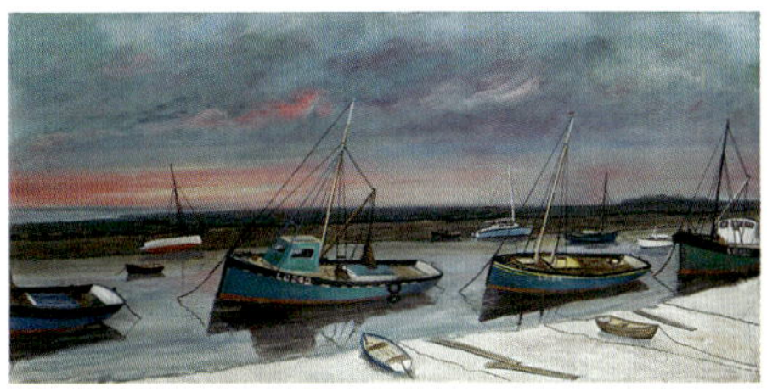

Baxter, James
Early Morning, Leigh Creek 1985
oil on canvas 46 x 91.5
4

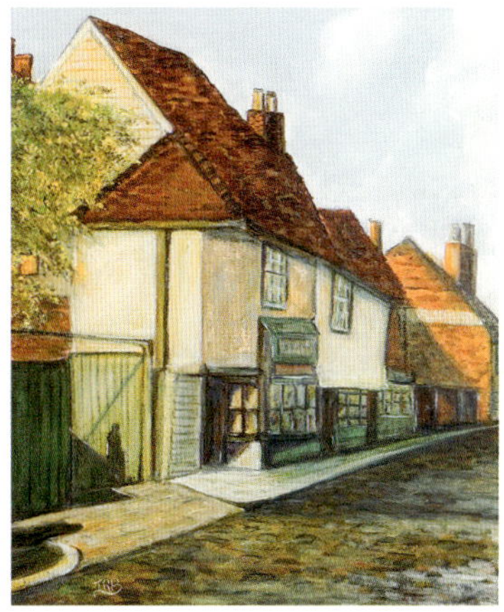

Beard, Thelma
Juniper's Cottage c.1970
oil on board 29.5 x 24
3

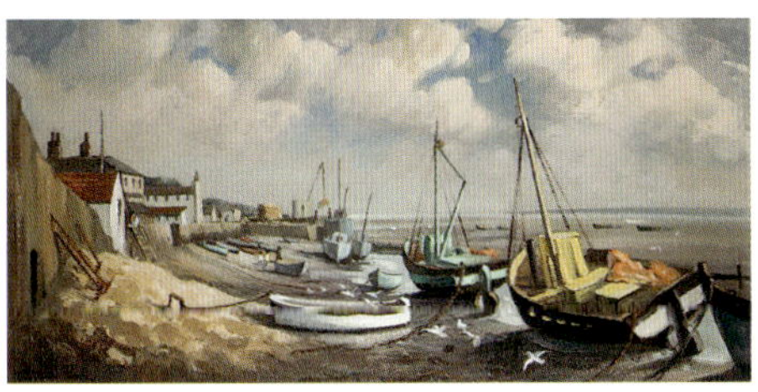

Fears, Constance 1895–late 1980s
Low Tide at Leigh-on-Sea 1979
oil on canvas 39 x 75
2

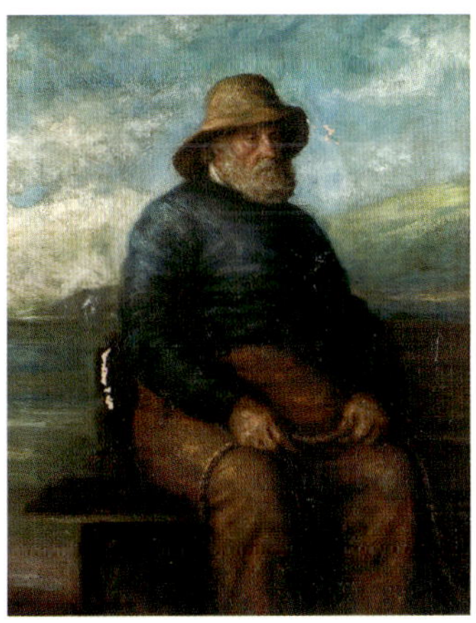

Saunders, Marion (attributed to)
Joe Juniper c.1945
oil on canvas 49.5 x 39
1

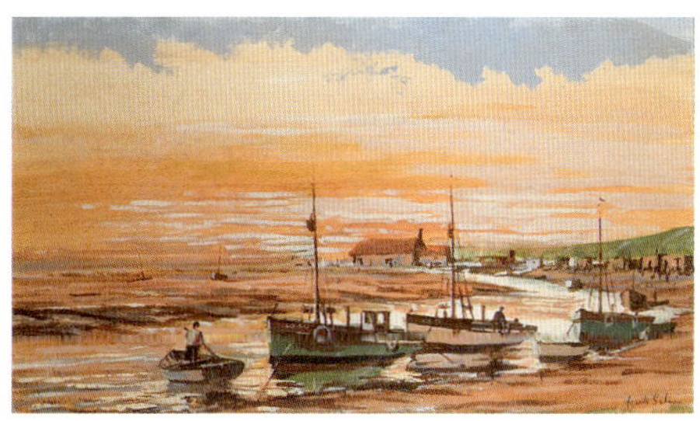

Selman, Frank
Leigh Creek c.1960
oil on canvas 44.5 x 74
5

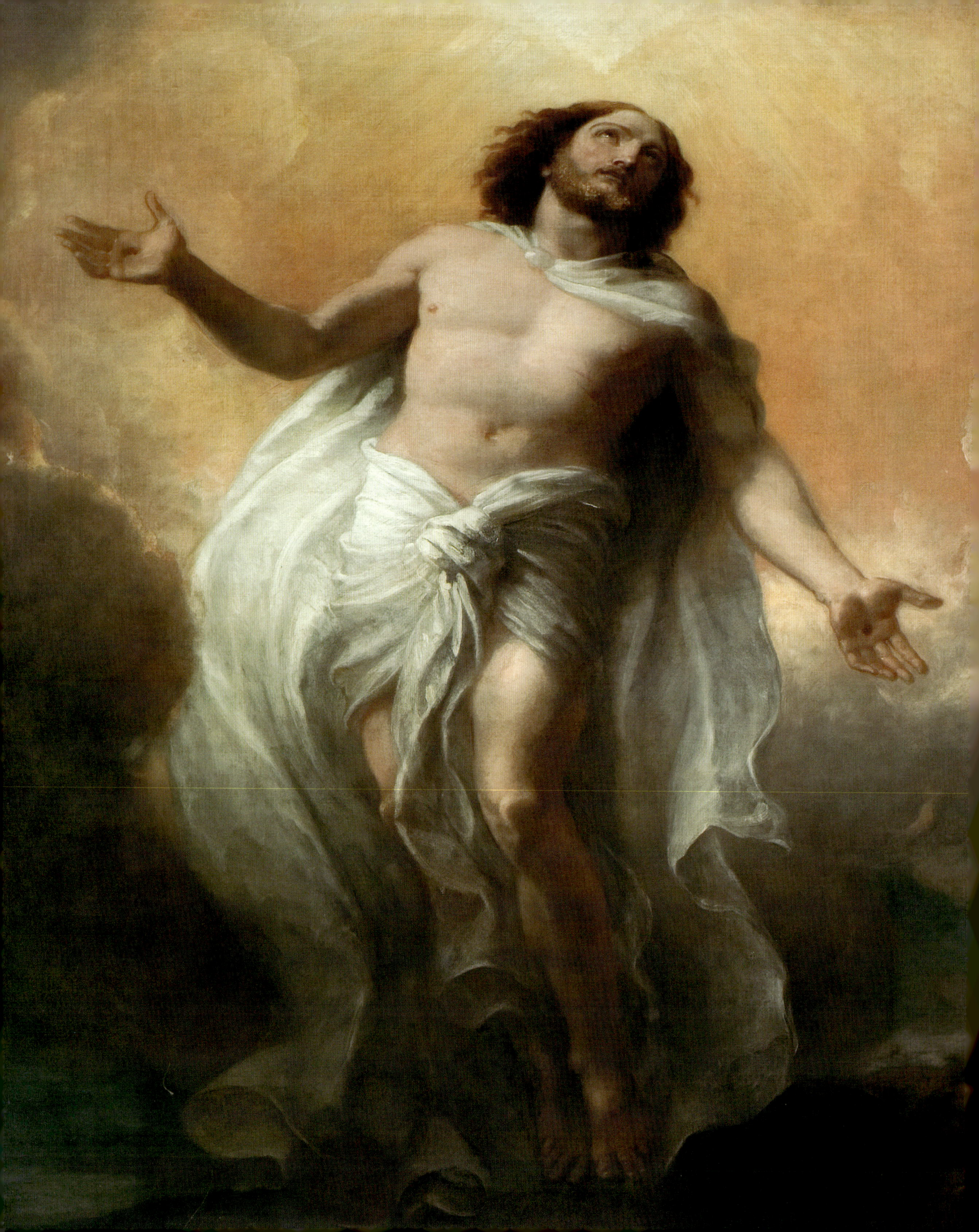

Combined Military Services Museum

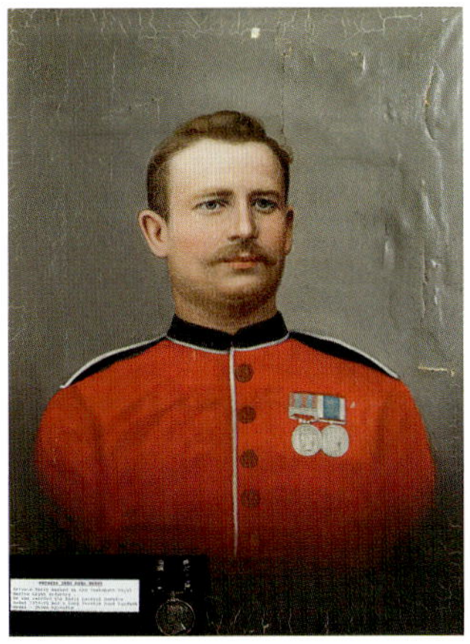

unknown artist
Charles Terry (Private 2882, Portsmouth Royal Marine Light Infantry) 1900
oil on canvas 83 x 66.6
2003.1.5

Maldon District Museum

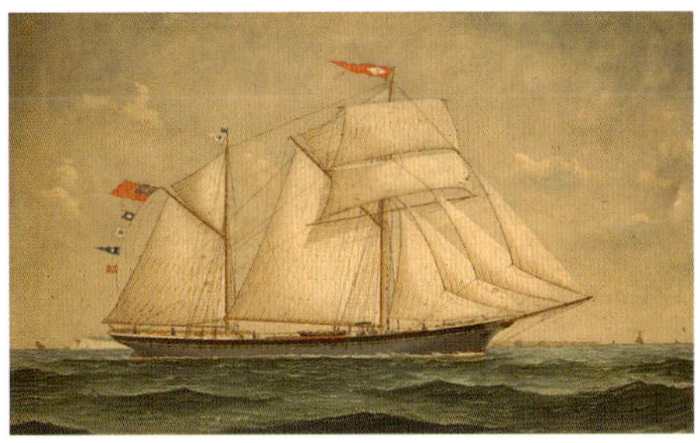

Fanner, J.
Coasting Barge, 'Record Reign' 1902
oil on canvas 39.5 x 75
1997.063.01 (P)

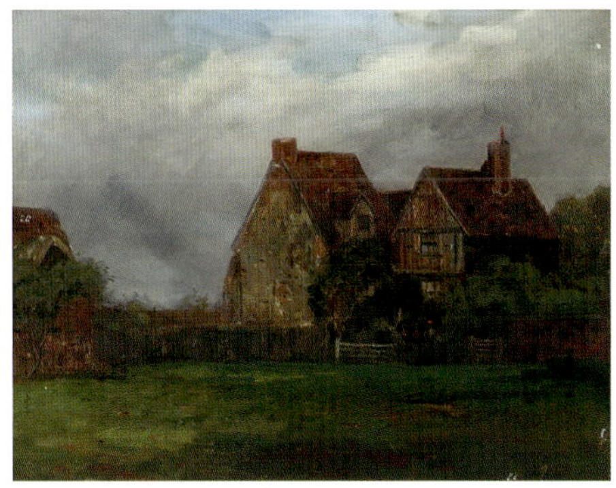

Hollingdale, Horatio R. active 1880–1899
Beeleigh Abbey before Restoration
oil on canvas 36 x 45
MM1066

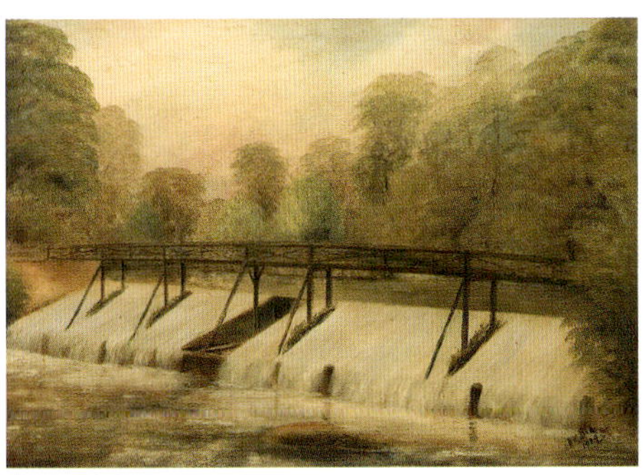

Miller, H.
Beeleigh Weir 1929
oil on canvas 40.5 x 56
MM1067

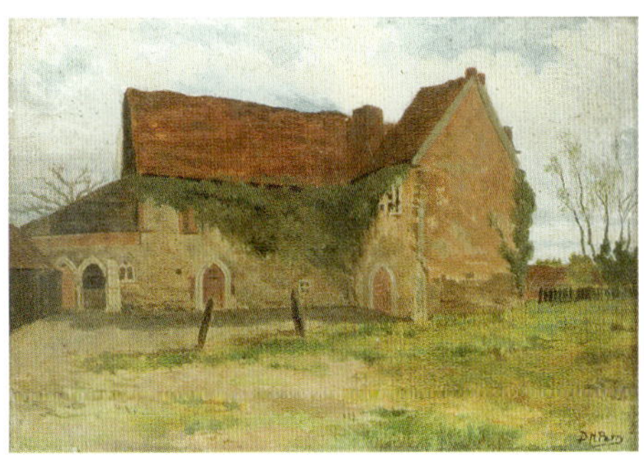

Parry, D. H.
Back of Beeleigh Abbey from the Stable Door before Restoration 1912
oil on panel 17.5 x 25.5 (E)
MM82

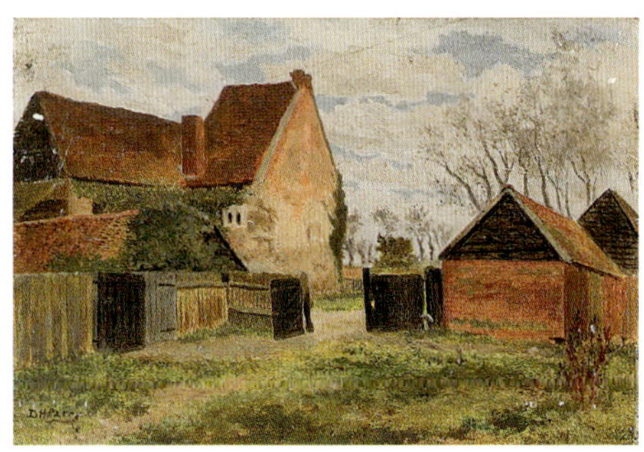

Parry, D. H.
Beeleigh Abbey before Restoration 1912
oil on panel 17.5 x 25.5 (E)
MM79

Facing page: Constable, John, 1776–1837, *The Ascension* (detail), 1821/1822, The Constable Trust, (p. 218)

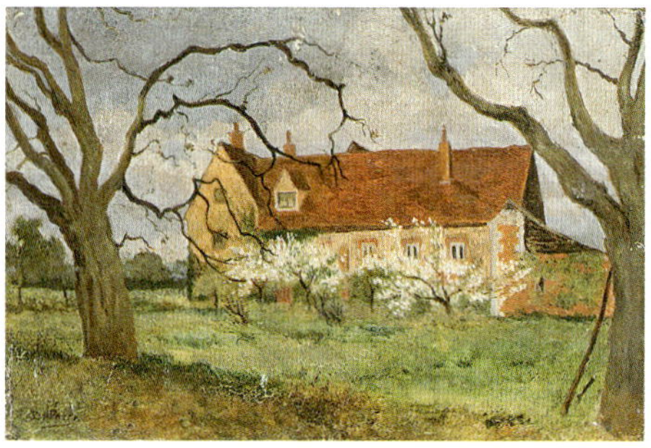

Parry, D. H.
Front of Beeleigh Abbey before Restoration
1912
oil on panel 17.5 x 25.5 (E)
MM80

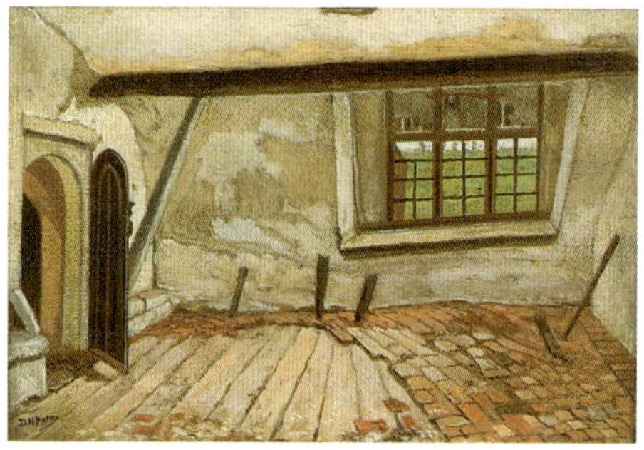

Parry, D. H.
Pentice Chamber, Beeleigh Abbey before Restoration 1912
oil on panel 17.5 x 25.5 (E)
MM81

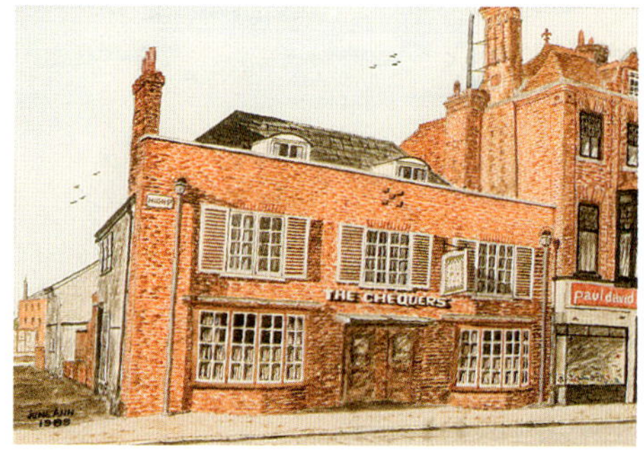

Prime, June 1936–2001
The Chequers, High Street (now Barclays Bank) 1989
tempera on paper 13 x 17.5
MM746

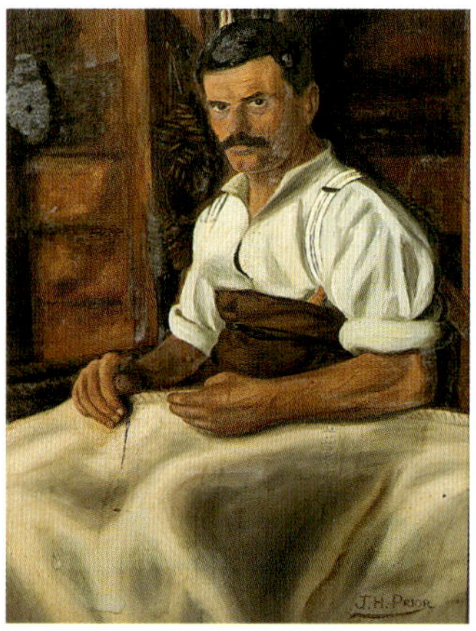

Prior, Joe H.
William Raven, Sail-Maker (1878–1959)
oil on canvas 66 x 51
E.375.2004.15.1 (P)

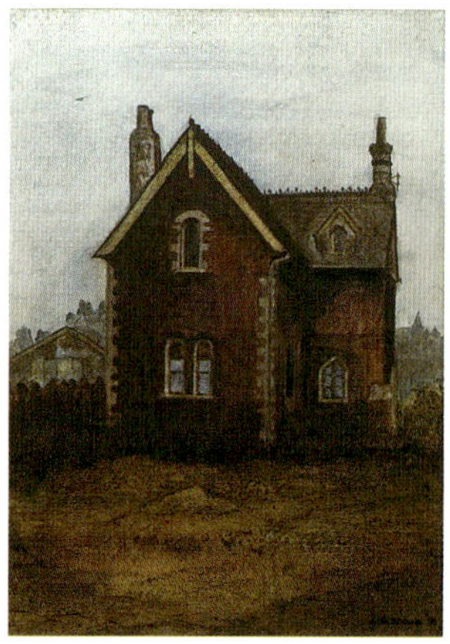

Spong, Caroline b.1939
Crossing Keeper's House before Demolition in 1978 1975
oil on canvas 41 x 30
E.470.2006.8.1

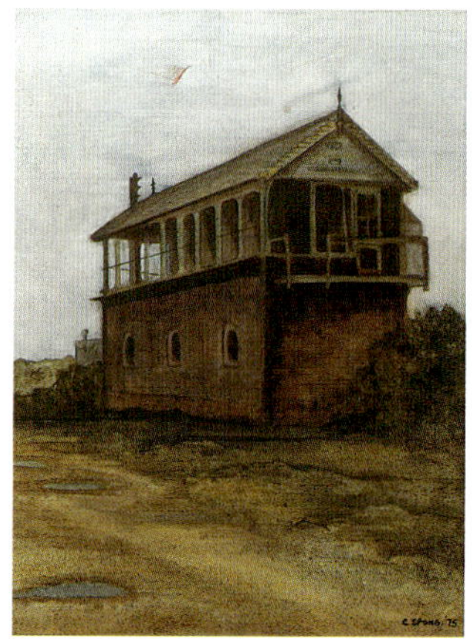

Spong, Caroline b.1939
Maldon East Signal Box before Demolition in 1982 1975
oil on canvas 41 x 30
E.470.2006.8.2

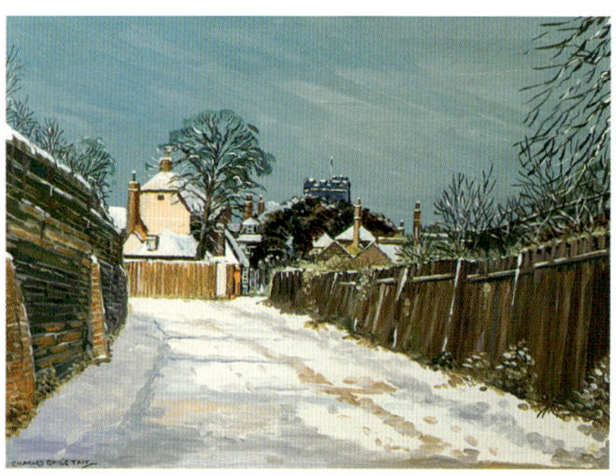

Tait, Charles Grigg 1915–1995
St Peter's Tower and Rear High Street from 'Chase' to Longfields c.1975
oil on board 44 x 58.5
MM1063

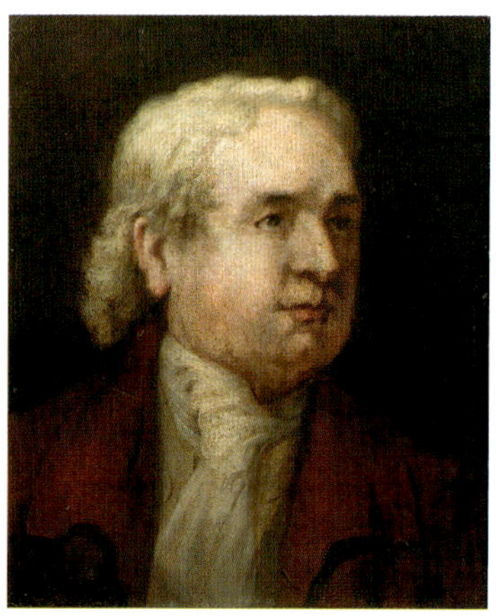

unknown artist
Horatio Gates (1728–1806), American General
oil on canvas on board 39 x 32
1112

Maldon Library

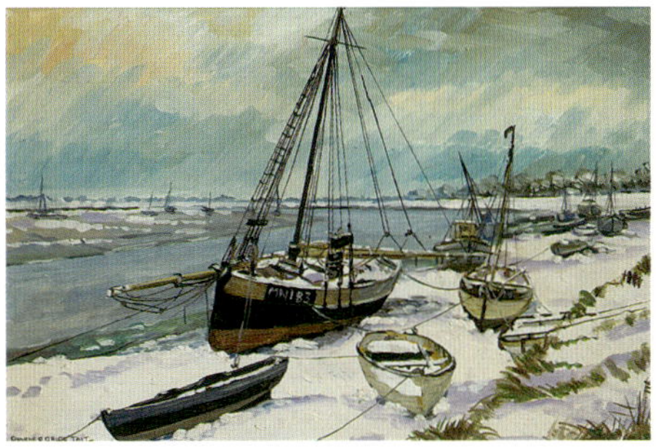

Tait, Charles Grigg 1915–1995
Boats on the River Blackwater
oil on canvas 38 x 57
1

Maldon Town Council

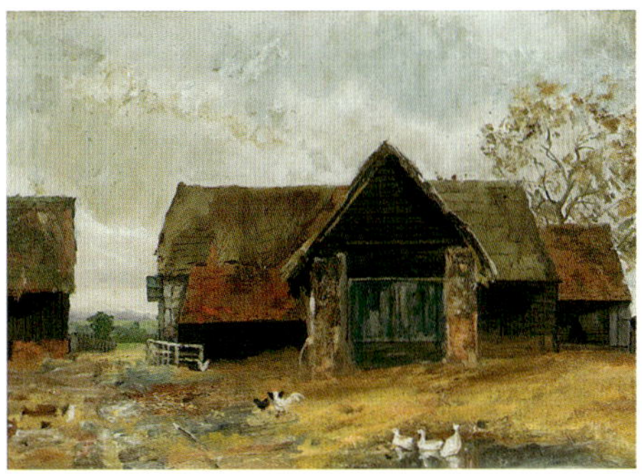

Abberley, Tessie b.1883
St Giles Leper Hospital, Spital Road, Maldon (founded by Henry II) 1902
oil on canvas 39 x 54
4

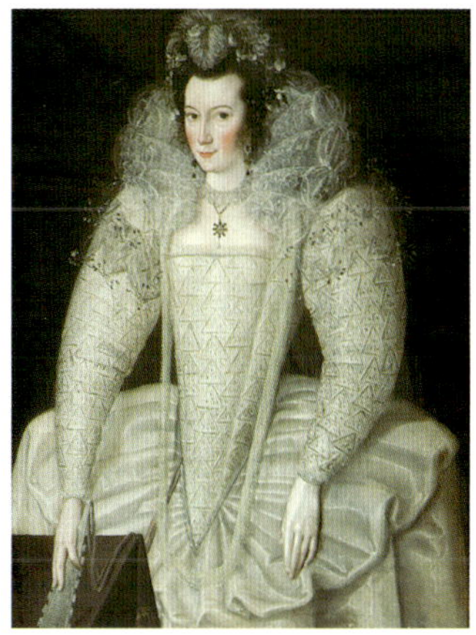

Peake, Robert c.1551–1619
Portrait of a Lady (said to be Elizabeth Throckmorton (d.c.1647), Queen Elizabeth's Maid of Honour and (...) c.1595–1600
oil on panel 111 x 89
3

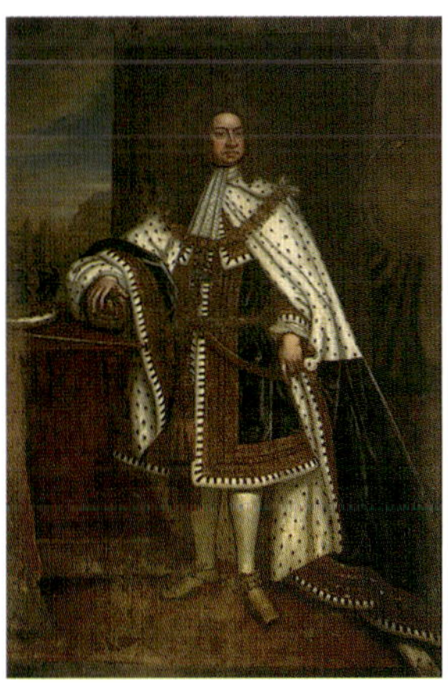

unknown artist 18th C
George I (1714–1727)
oil on canvas 220 x 121 (E)
2

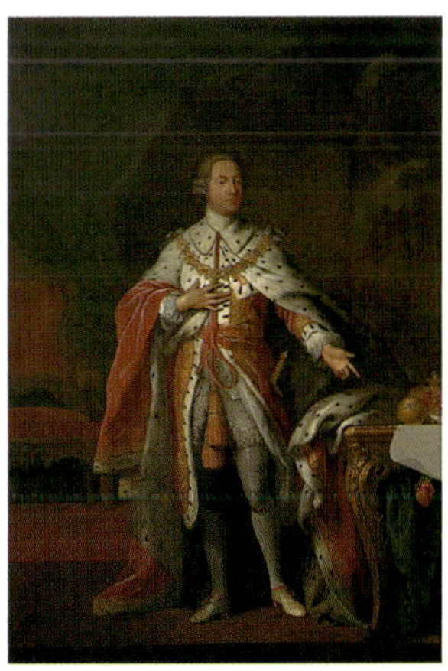

unknown artist 18th C
George III (1760–1820)
oil on canvas 230 x 173 (E)
1

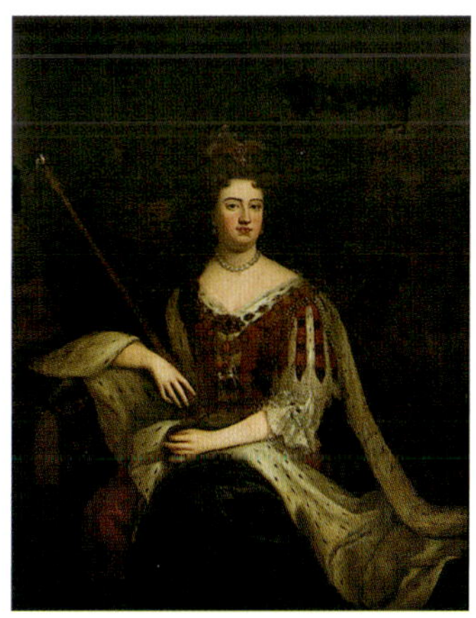

unknown artist
Queen Anne (1665–1714)
oil on canvas 140 x 124 (E)
6

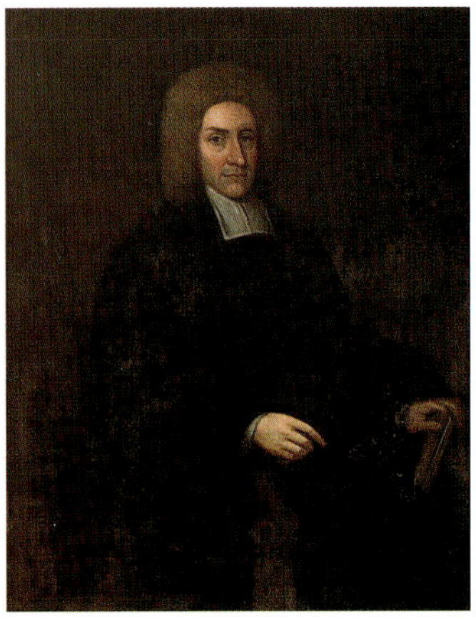

unknown artist
Thomas Plume, DD (1630–1704)
oil on canvas 120 x 99
5

Thomas Plume's Library

Thomas Plume was born in Maldon in 1630. Facts about his life are few, but we know that he was educated at King Edward VI Grammar School in Chelmsford and at Christ's College, Cambridge. At the age of 28 he became Vicar of Greenwich and later, in 1679, he was also installed as Archdeacon of Rochester. He held both of these posts for the rest of his life. Whilst Plume was Vicar of Greenwich, the first Royal Observatory was built in his parish and later he founded the Chair of Astronomy and Natural Philosophy at Cambridge University. He is mentioned in the diaries of Samuel Pepys, and John Evelyn, who heard him preach in his church at Greenwich. When he died in 1704 he was buried at Longfield in Kent, and as was his wish, his tombstone omits his name.

At his death, his books and pictures were bequeathed to the town of Maldon with the intention that they were to be used by the local clergy and any gentleman or scholar who so desired. During his lifetime, Plume had provided a permanent home for his library by converting the derelict church of St Peter's, the nave of which had collapsed shortly after 1664. Thomas Plume paid for this to be replaced by a handsome red brick building in the domestic fashion of the time and he had the tower rebuilt in a traditional Gothic style. The upper storey housed his library and Maldon Grammar School, and later the National School occupied the lower room.

As can be seen from the catalogue below, all but three of the paintings form part of the original bequest. Plume lived through a turbulent time in English history: he held strong Royalist sympathies and was deeply committed to the Church of England, as established by law. This is reflected in his collection of paintings, which include portraits of Charles I, James II and Archbishop Laud (the largest in the collection), while the *Salvator Mundi* illustrates Plume's devotion to Jesus Christ.

Thomas Plume's portrait now hangs in the Moot Hall at Maldon. By the terms of his will, he forbade 'my picture now in Mr Pond's house to be ever brought into my Library'. However, the nineteenth century Library Rules, illustrated by the artist, Robert Nightingale, does contain a miniature of the portrait in the top left hand corner.

Due to the foresight of the bequest, the library of around 7,000 volumes is still managed as a trust. Since 1988, the Trustees have had the support and assistance of the Friends of Thomas Plume's Library.

Erica Wylie, Librarian

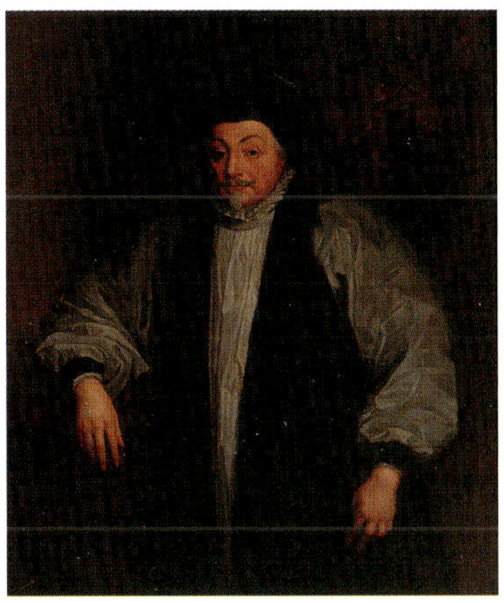

Dyck, Anthony van (copy after) 1599–1641
William Laud (1573–1645), Archbishop of Canterbury
oil on canvas 127 x 104 (E)
X.2.7

Largillière, Nicolas de (copy after)
1656–1746
James II (1633–1701)
oil on canvas 68 x 53
X.2.8

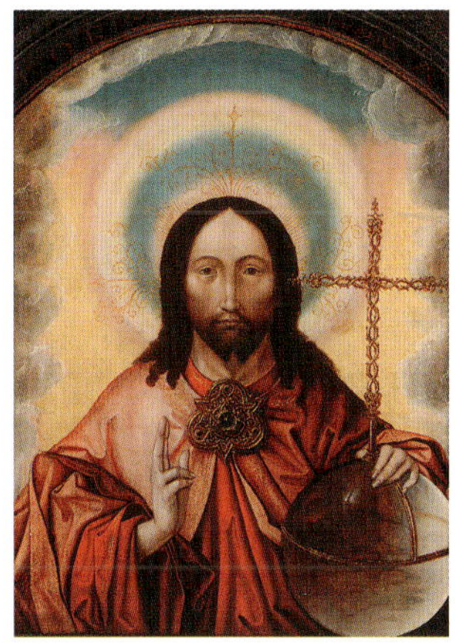

Memling, Hans (follower of)
1430–1440–1494
Salvator Mundi 16th C
oil on panel 71 x 52 (E)
X.1.2

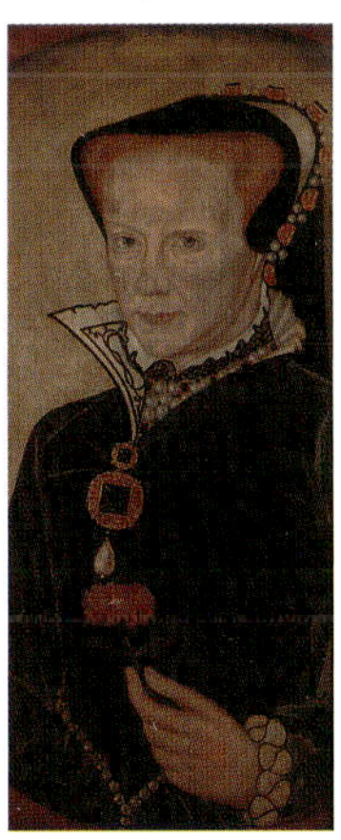

Mor, Antonis (copy after)
1512–1516–c.1576
Mary I (1516–1558) early 17th C
oil on panel 68 x 28
X.1.6

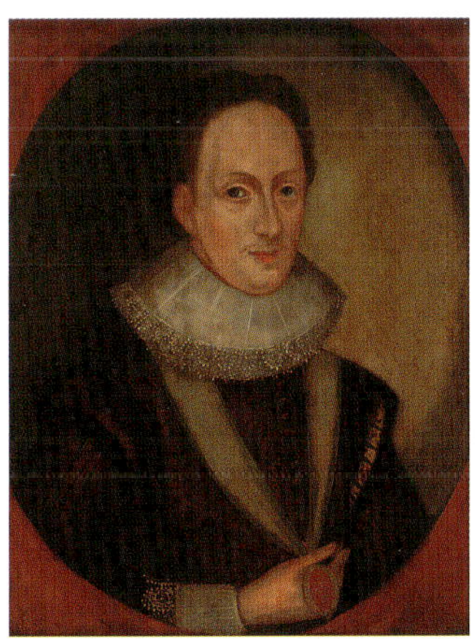

Mytens, Daniel I (circle of)
c.1590–before 1648
Charles I (1600–1649)
oil on panel 68 x 52
X.2.6

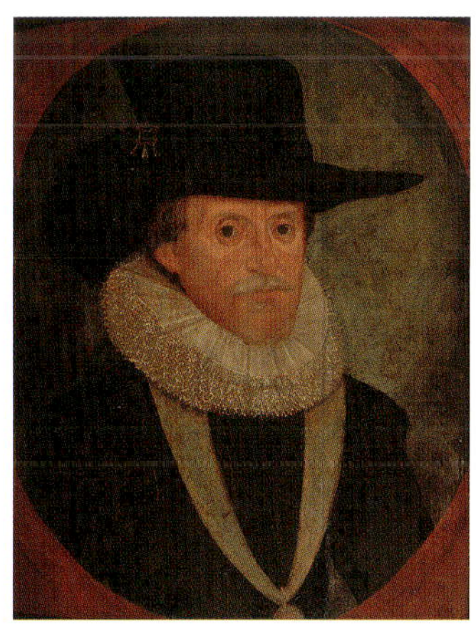

Somer, Bernaert van (follower of)
before 1575–1612
James I (1566–1625) c.1603
oil on panel 68 x 51.5
X.1.5

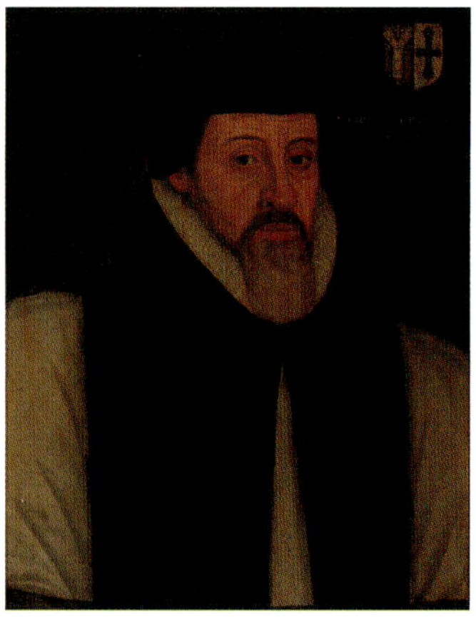

unknown artist
John Whitgift (1530?–1604), Archbishop of Canterbury c.1598
oil on panel 58 x 43.5
X.1.4

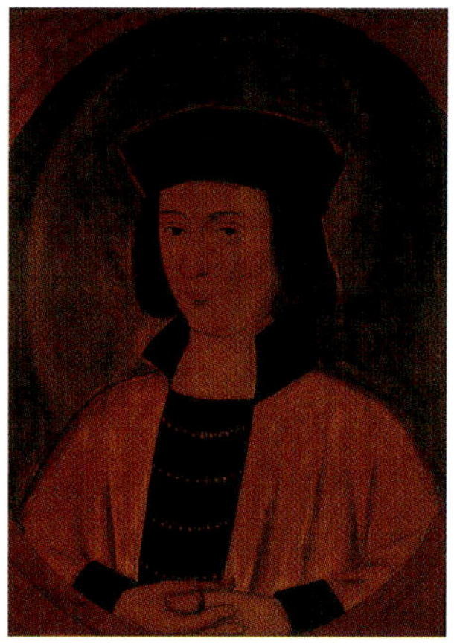

unknown artist early 17th C
Edward IV (1442–1483)
oil on panel 69 x 53
X.2.9

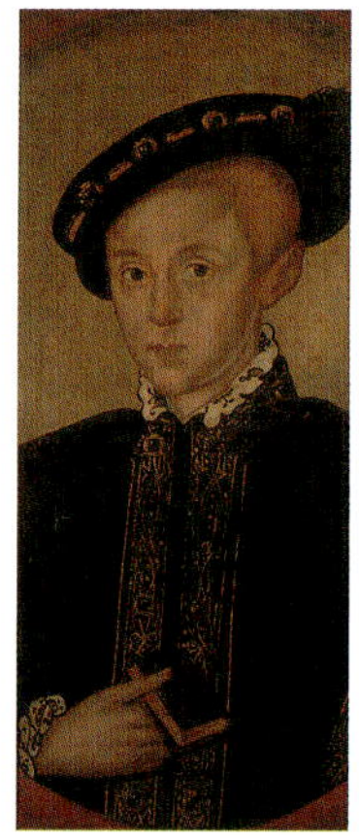

unknown artist early 17th C
Edward VI (1537–1553)
oil on panel 68 x 28
X.1.7

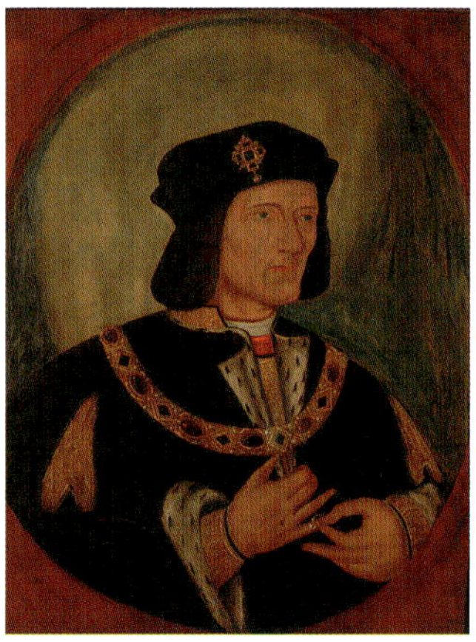

unknown artist early 17th C
Richard III (1452–1485)
oil on panel 68 x 51
X.1.3

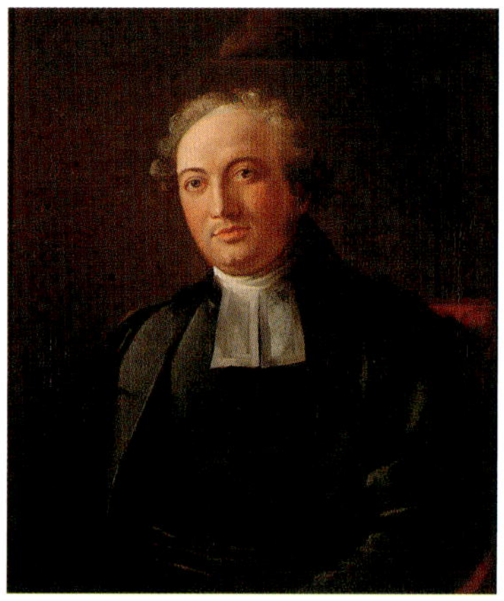

unknown artist late 19th C
Reverend Robert P. Crane, Librarian to Dr Plume's Library
oil on canvas 80 x 67 (E)
X.2.10

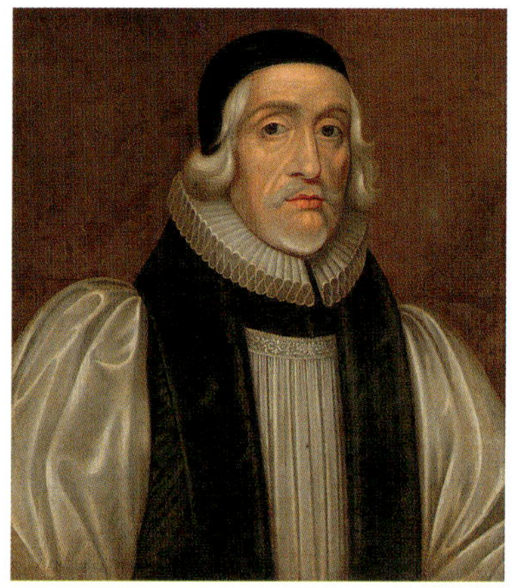

unknown artist
Dr James Ussher (1581–1656), Archbishop of Armagh
oil on canvas 59.5 x 51
X.2.5

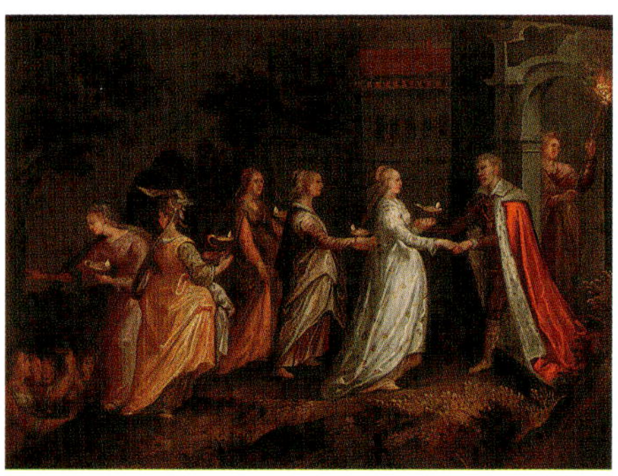

unknown artist
Five Wise Virgins
oil on canvas 42 x 54
X.2.1

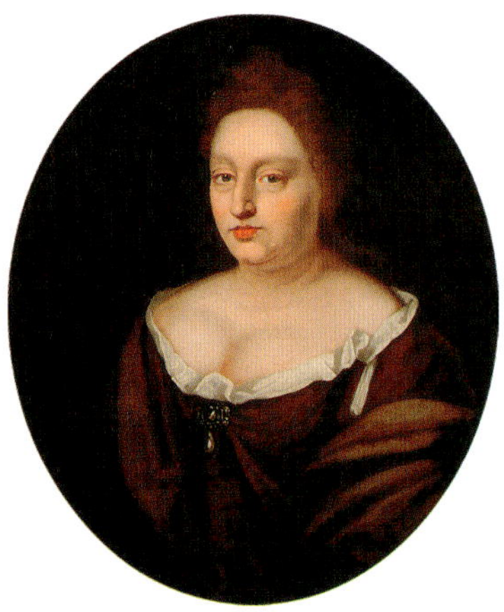

unknown artist
Mrs Margaret Oakley, Mother-in-Law of John Ray, the Botanist
oil on canvas 77 x 65
X.2.2

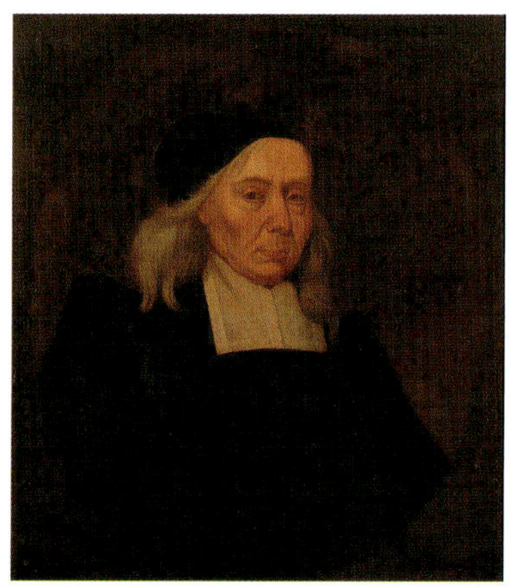

unknown artist
Unknown Divine (once believed to be John Ray, the botanist)
oil on canvas 77 x 65 (E)
X.2.3

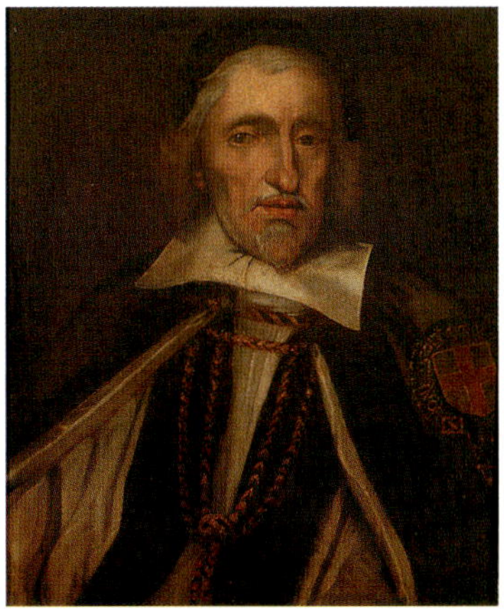

Wright, John Michael (copy after)
1617–1694
Brian Duppa (1588–1662), Dean of Christ Church, Oxford
oil on canvas 66 x 54
X.2.4

The Constable Trust

The Constable Trust was founded in 1999 to 'acquire, preserve, protect and display, for the benefit of the public, works of art having a relationship with East Anglia'. Its first act was to buy this painting, which was offered for sale in 1998 by the Parochial Church Council of All Saints, Feering.

The Ascension was commissioned for £200 by Edward Alston, a brewer from Manningtree, and Constable's cousin by marriage, because he wanted to gain favour with the Archdeacon of Colchester, the Reverend John Jefferson, who was responsible for licensing public houses. When Jefferson refused to license Alston's hostelries and subsequently died in December, 1821, Alston reneged on the contract. In spite of the financial loss this entailed, Constable completed the painting and it was installed in 1822 in the reredos of the newly built chancel of St Michael's Church, Manningtree, where it remained until the building was demolished in 1965. The painting was subsequently acquired by the Reverend Aubrey Moody for All Saints Church at Feering, a village which Constable knew through his friendship with an earlier incumbent, the Reverend Walter Wren Driffield.

Michael Archer, Chairman of the Trustees

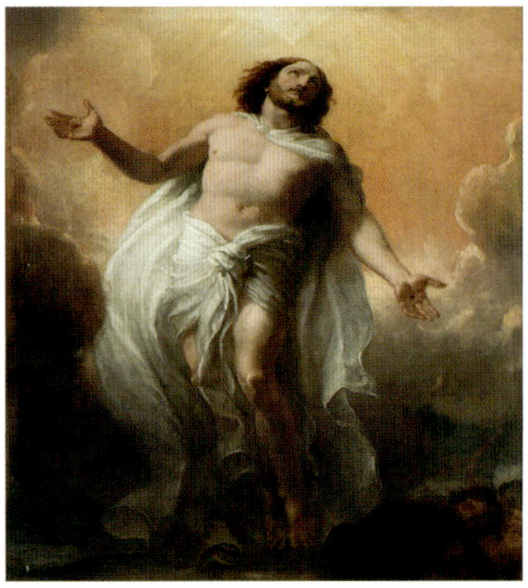

Constable, John 1776–1837
The Ascension 1821/1822
oil on canvas 160 x 127
1

Ongar War Memorial Hospital

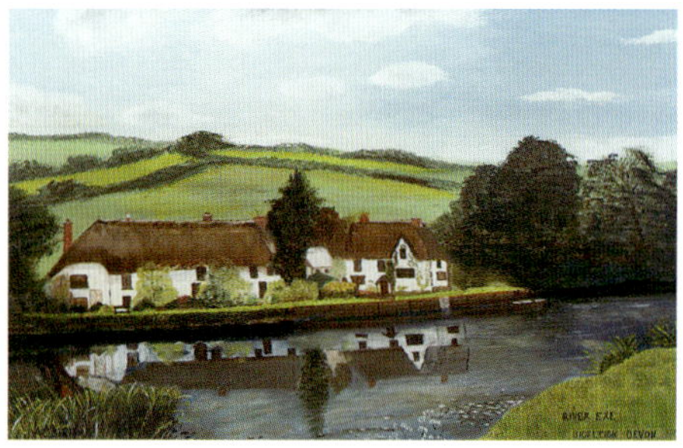

Bunton, A. C.
River Exe, Bickleigh, Devon
oil on hardboard 34 x 51.5
5

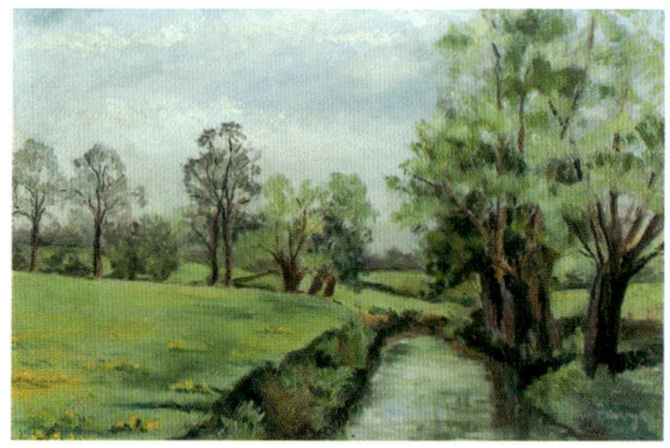

Furze, Mary
River Scene
oil on hardboard 38 x 56.5
3

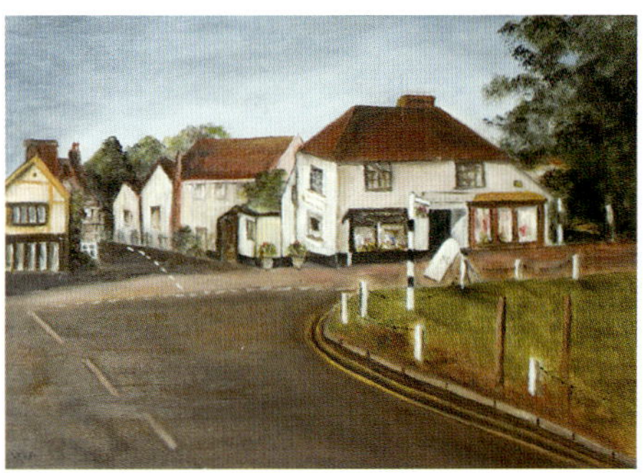

Reeder, Vera
Blackmore Village 1994
oil on hardboard 29 x 39
2

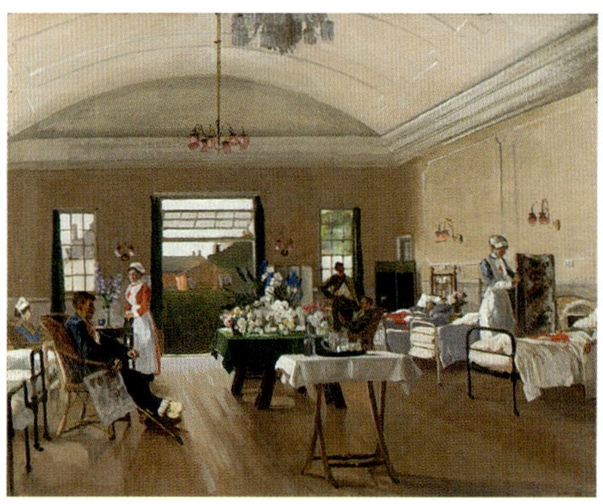

Rose, George 1882–1955
The Ballroom at Budworth Hall, Ongar 1915
oil on canvas 50 x 60
1

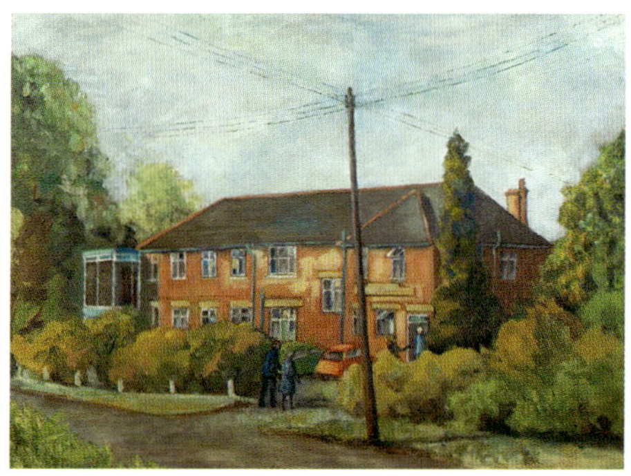

unknown artist
Ongar War Memorial Hospital c.1965
oil on hardboard 37.5 x 50
4

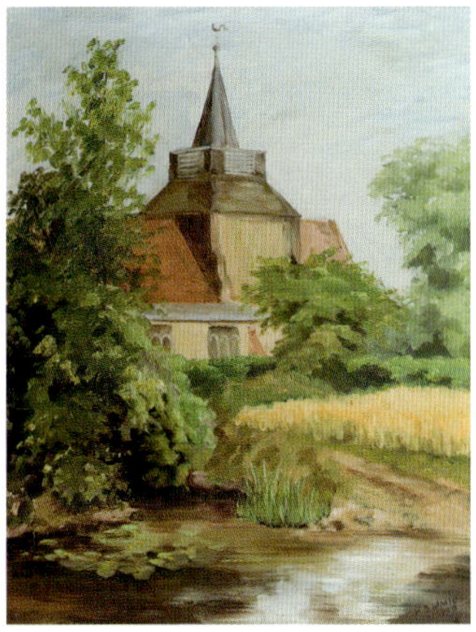

White, F. D.
Greensted Church 1969
oil on hardboard 60 x 45
6

English Heritage, Audley End House

The publicly-owned paintings at Audley End House constitute only a small proportion of the historic collection, which remains on display at the House by kind permission of Lord Braybrooke.

The first group of publicly-owned paintings was bought by the Department of the Environment in 1971 with advice from the Victoria & Albert Museum, at the same time as furniture, textiles and ceramics. The aim was to secure the key eighteenth century paintings, particularly those recording the landscape, as well as portraits of the patron and his wives. These topographical paintings record the landscape at the end of the eighteenth century and form one of the largest groups of their type in the country comparable with those at Saltram House, Devon. These paintings were not at Audley End in the eighteenth century, and are thought to have hung in the family's London house. They were subsequently transferred to Billingbear, Berkshire, the ancestral home of the Neville family. In 1797, the Nevilles inherited the Audley End estate, being moved there in 1917.

Subsequently, in 1986, English Heritage bought the group of fixed portraits set into the Saloon panelling. Generation-by-generation, it records the ownership of the house from Lord Audley of Walden's acquisition on the dissolution of the Abbey in 1538, to Sir John Griffin Griffin, 4th Lord Howard de Walden (1719–1797). Though relatively commonplace in Europe, such fixed ancestral galleries are rarer in Britain (Sudbury Hall and Arbury Hall being two examples). The scheme was created by Sir John to record his descent, and comprises seventeenth century paintings from the Griffin family collection, as well as specially commissioned works executed by Biagio Rebecca.

The rare group of painted chimneyboards (four of the original five survive) is also by Rebecca. They were installed into a fireplace during the summer when the grate was not in use. At the time of their commission in 1769, such pieces were not seen as works of art, but as decorative pieces; today their quality seems equal to the grisaille paintings supplied by Cipriani, four of which, commissioned for the Library, may be seen at Saffron Walden Museum.

The final group comprises individual Old Master paintings which had left the collection at various times in the late twentieth century and which have been returned to the house with the support of the Heritage Lottery Fund, the National Art Collections Fund and the Friends of Audley End House. Most of them can be traced back to the 1797 inventory and are representative of Sir John's cabinet paintings. The Holbein *Unknown Gentleman* (one of several optimistically ascribed to the artist in the 1797 Inventory, in this case correctly) is a fine late work. The most recent acquisition, *A Mediterranean Coastal Scene with Shipping and Mariners by a Fort* by Jan Asselyn is a good example of an artist otherwise poorly represented in British collections.

A single work has no provenance with Audley End House: the portrait of *Sir Charles Lucas* (also identified as *Colonel Richard Neville of Billingbear*). This copy was bought to replace the original, which is now in the National Portrait Gallery.

As far as possible the paintings are hung in their historic locations, largely unchanged since the 1830s and recorded in Richard, 3rd Lord Braybrooke's *History of Audley End and Saffron Walden*, 1836, and in a privately-printed picture catalogue of 1871.

Gareth Hughes, Curator

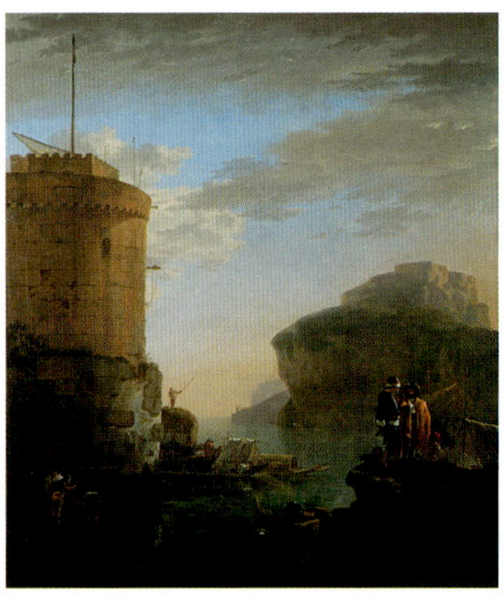

Asselyn, Jan after 1610–1652
A Mediterranean Coastal View with Shipping and Mariners by a Fort c.1650
oil on canvas 99.1 x 85.7
88096674

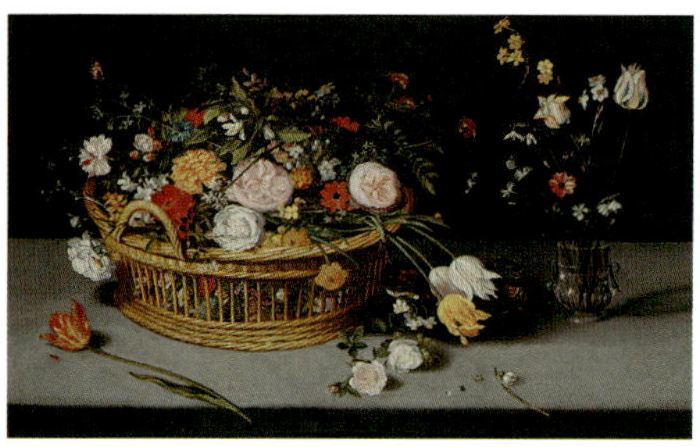

Brueghel, Jan the younger 1601–1678
Flower Piece c.1620
oil on canvas 56 x 89.5
81033498

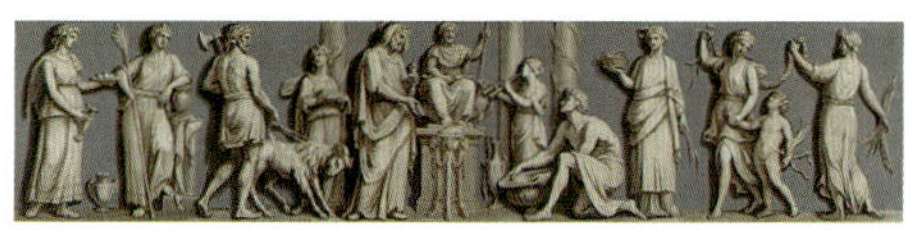

Cipriani, Giovanni Battista 1727–1785
Panel from the Robert Adam Library Representing Religion and the Arts 1770
oil on canvas 68 x 296
81030298

Facing page: Carter, Mary, b.1947, *Two for Joy* (detail), c.1972, Southend Museums Service, (p. 256)

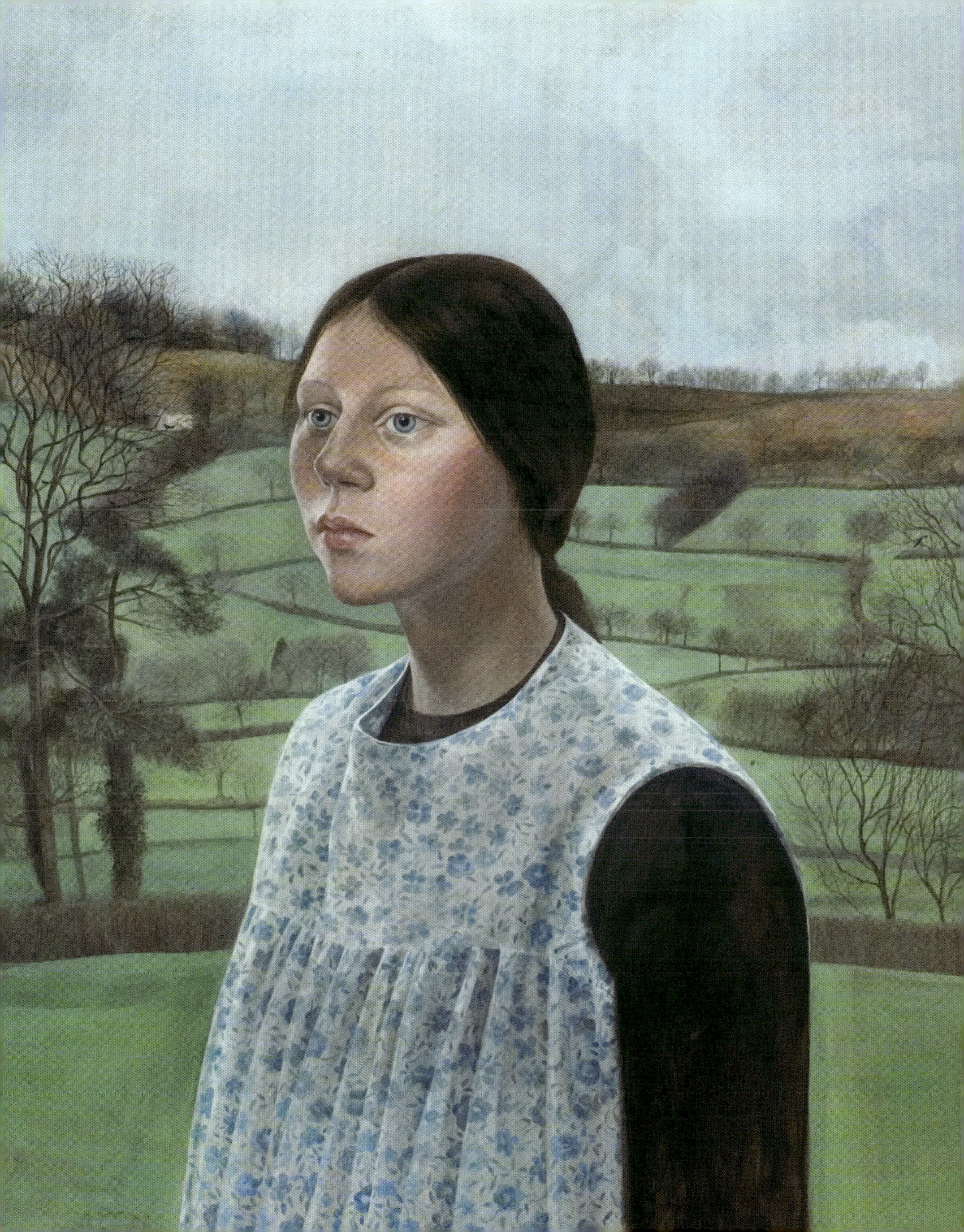

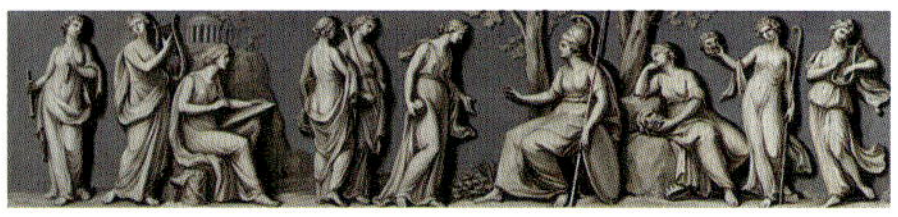

Cipriani, Giovanni Battista 1727–1785
Panel from the Robert Adam Library Representing Science and Learning 1770
oil on canvas 67.5 x 296
81030297

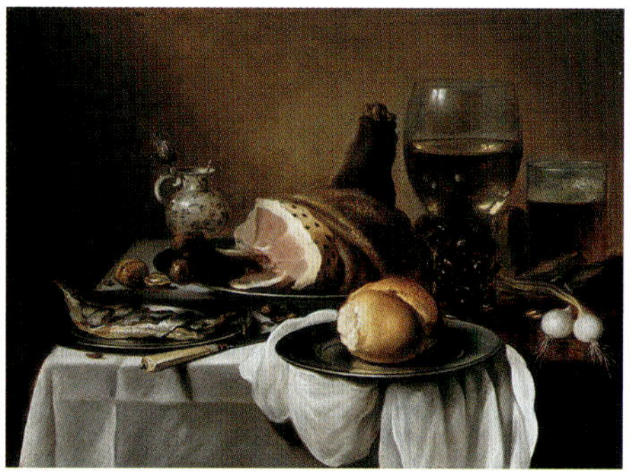

Claesz., Pieter 1597/1598–1660
Breakfast Piece c.1640
oil on oak panel 46 x 63
81031000

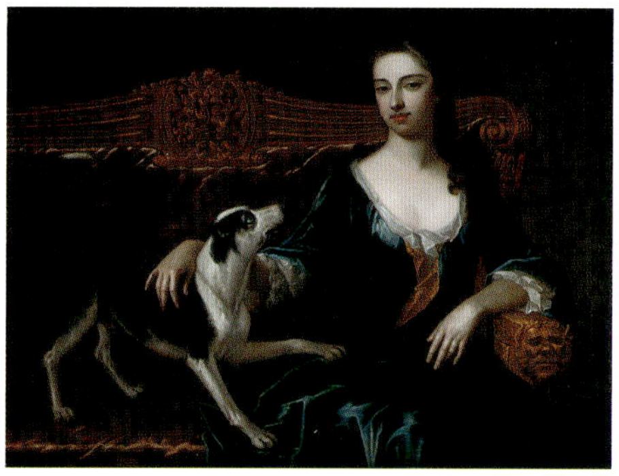

Dahl, Michael I (attributed to) 1656/1659–1743
Elizabeth Grey (later Countess of Portsmouth)
oil on canvas 102 x 132
81031326

Dobson, William (after) 1611–1646
Sir Charles Lucas (also identified as Colonel Richard Neville of Billingbear) 18th C
oil on canvas 127 x 102
81030317

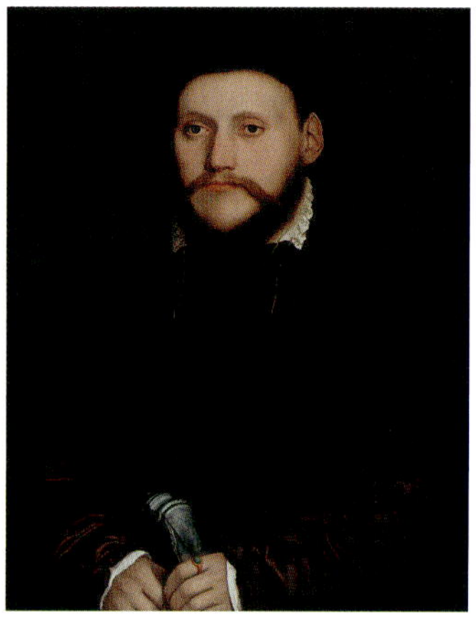

Holbein, Hans the younger 1497/1498–1543
Unknown Gentleman c.1540
oil on oak panel 44.4 x 34.2
81033497

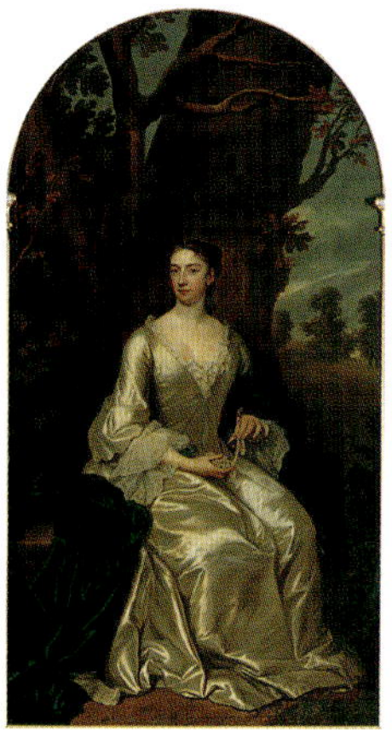

Jervas, Charles (attributed to) c.1675–1739
Elizabeth, Countess of Portsmouth
oil on canvas 239 x 122
81030149

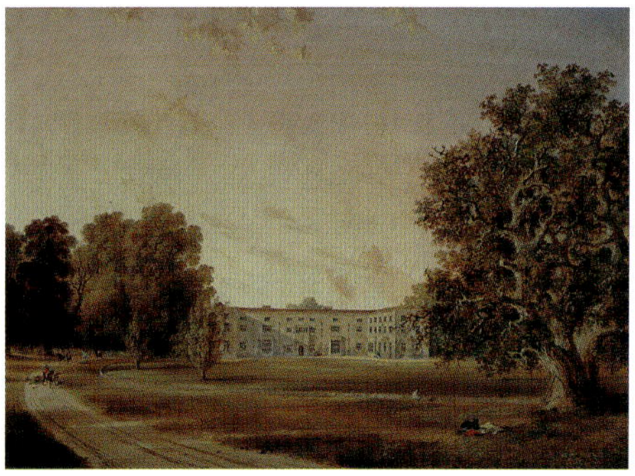

Niemann, Edmund John 1813–1876
View of Billingbear, Berkshire
oil on canvas 44 x 60
81031162

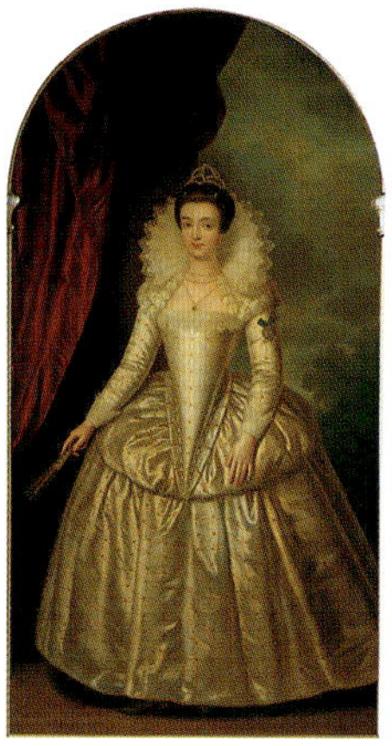

Rebecca, Biagio 1735–1808
Margaret Audley, Duchess of Norfolk 1774
oil on canvas 239 x 122
81030145

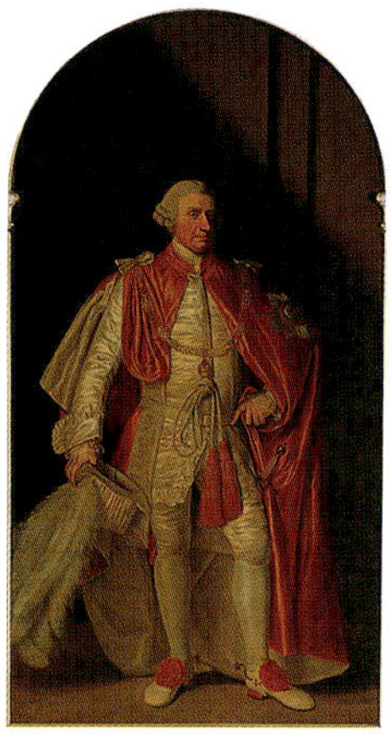

Rebecca, Biagio 1735–1808
Sir John Griffin Griffin, 4th Lord Howard de Walden 1774
oil on canvas 239 x 122
81030148

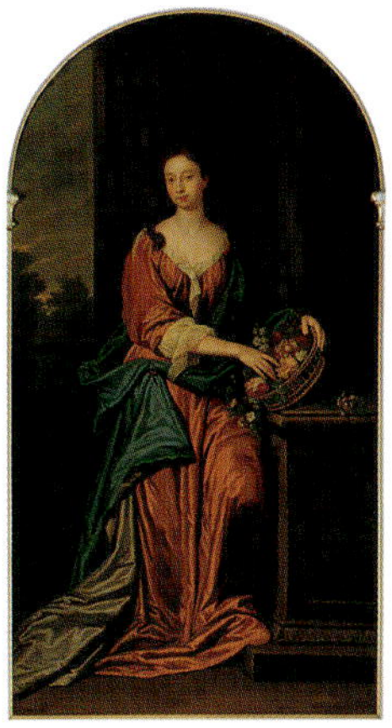

Rebecca, Biagio 1735–1808
The Honourable Anne Griffin, Mrs Whitwell 1774
oil on canvas 239 x 122
81030147

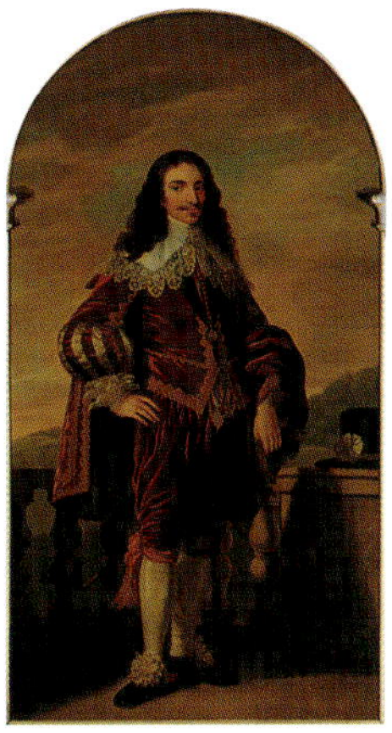

Rebecca, Biagio 1735–1808
Theophilus Howard, 2nd Earl of Suffolk 1774
oil on canvas 239 x 122
81030142

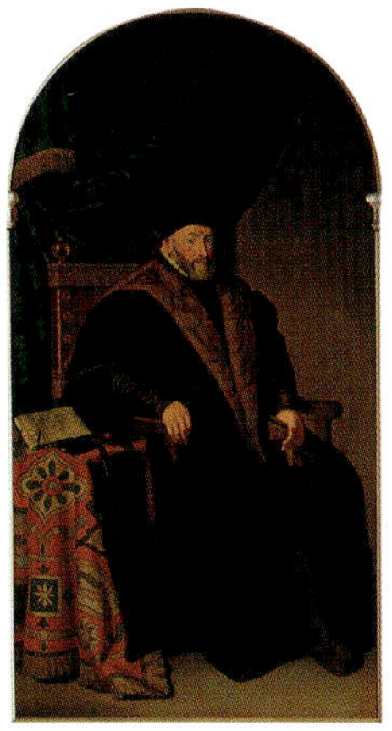

Rebecca, Biagio 1735–1808
Thomas Audley, Lord Audley 1774
oil on canvas 239 x 122
81030146

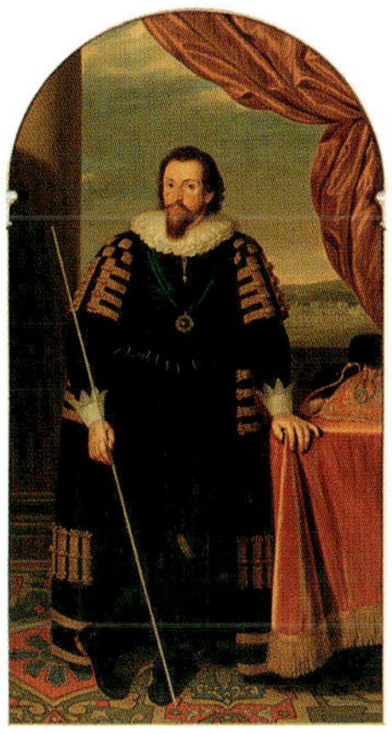

Rebecca, Biagio 1735–1808
Thomas Howard, 1st Earl of Suffolk 1774
oil on canvas 239 x 122
81030143

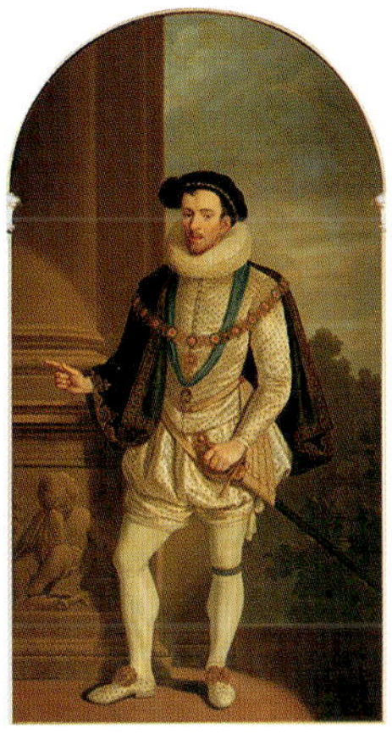

Rebecca, Biagio 1735–1808
Thomas Howard, 4th Duke of Norfolk 1774
oil on canvas 239 x 122
81030144

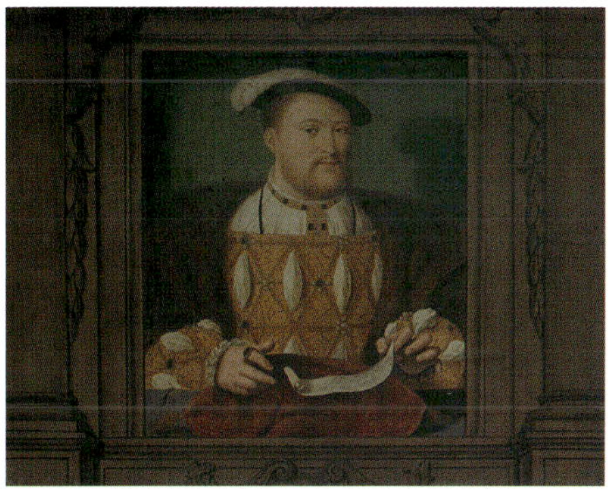

Rebecca, Biagio 1735–1808
King Henry VIII (1491–1547) 1786
oil on canvas 86 x 109
81030139

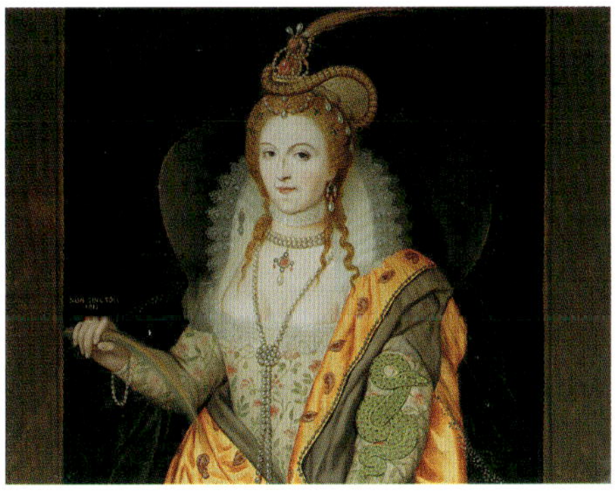

Rebecca, Biagio 1735–1808
Queen Elizabeth I (1533–1603) 1786
oil on canvas 89 x 109
81030140

Rebecca, Biagio 1735–1808
Chimney Board
oil on canvas 125 x 149
81030229

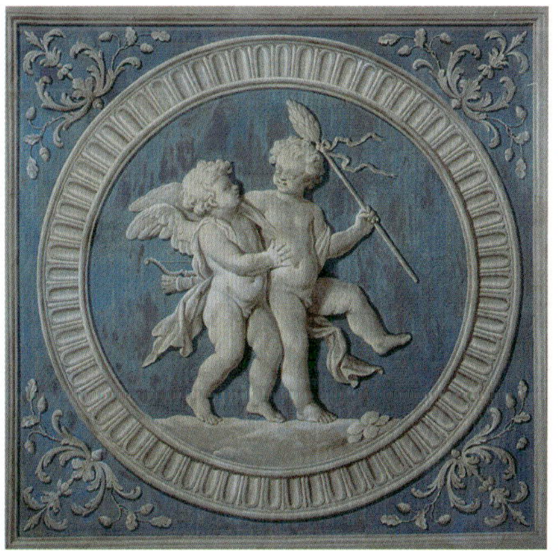

Rebecca, Biagio 1735–1808
Chimney Board
oil on canvas 110 x 110
81030247

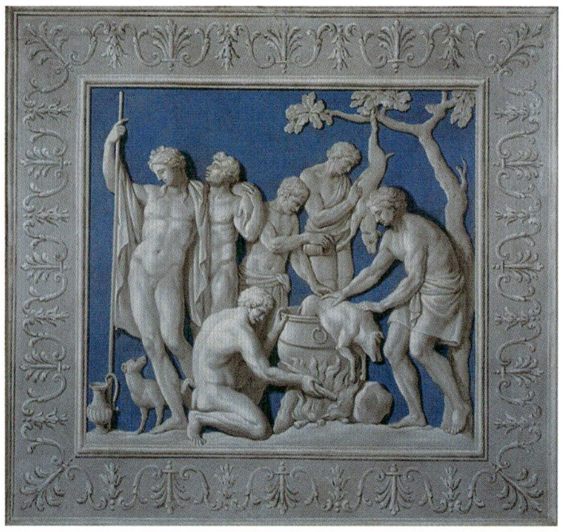

Rebecca, Biagio 1735–1808
Chimney Board
oil on canvas 118 x 123
81030248

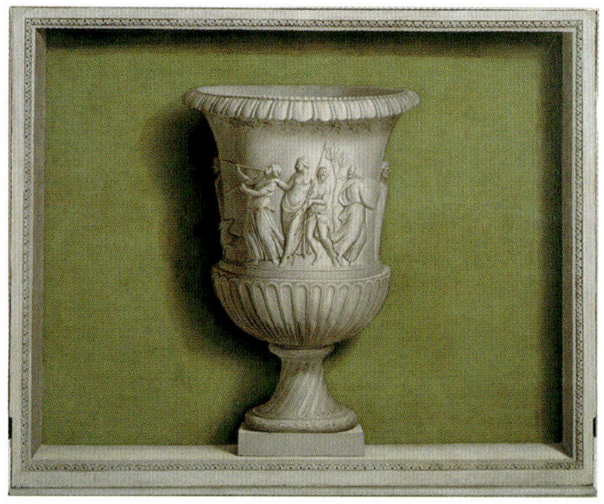

Rebecca, Biagio 1735–1808
Chimney Board
oil on canvas 125 x 151
81035843

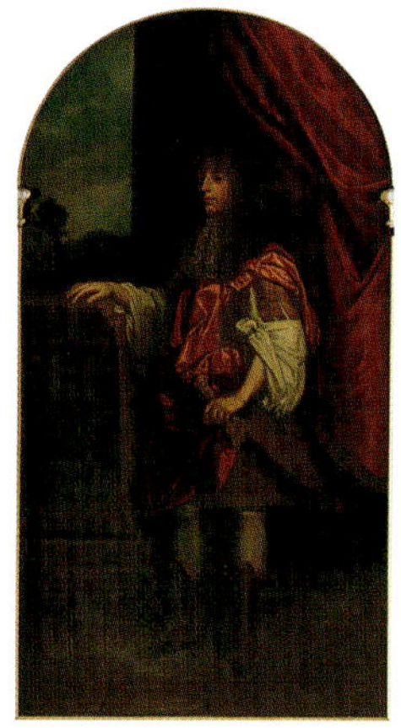

Seemann, Enoch the younger 1694–1744
Edward Griffin, 1st Lord Griffin
oil on canvas 239 x 122
81030151

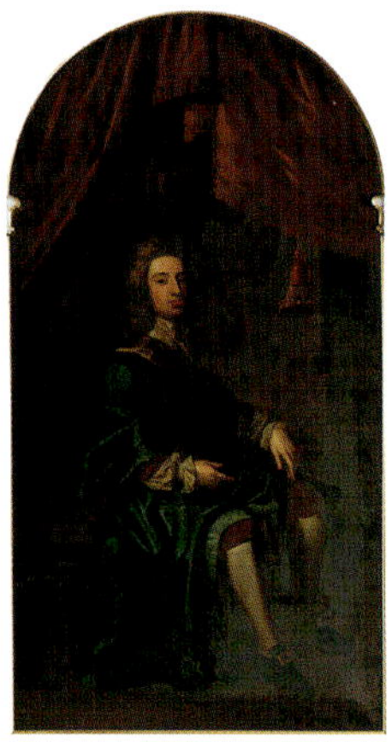

Seemann, Enoch the younger 1694–1744
James Griffin, 2nd Lord Griffin
oil on canvas 239 x 122
81030150

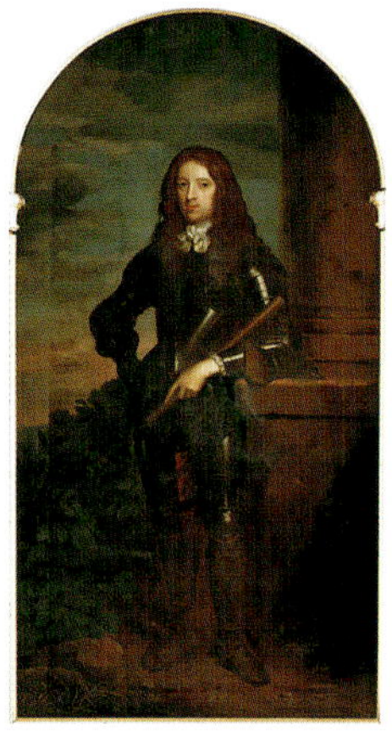

Seemann, Enoch the younger 1694–1744
James Howard, 3rd Earl of Suffolk
oil on canvas 239 x 122
81030141

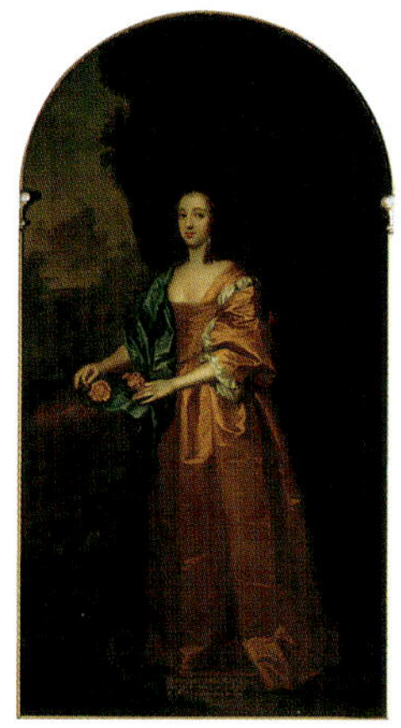

Seemann, Enoch the younger 1694–1744
Lady Susannah Rich, Countess of Suffolk
oil on canvas 239 x 122
81030153

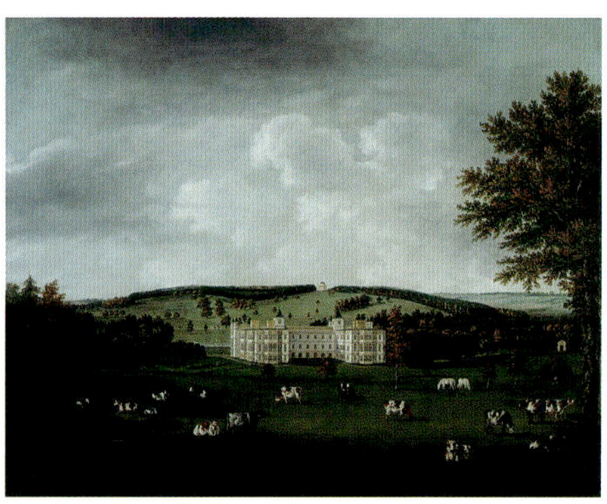

Tomkins, William c.1732–1792
Audley End and Ring Hill Temple 1788
oil on canvas 102 x 127
81030133

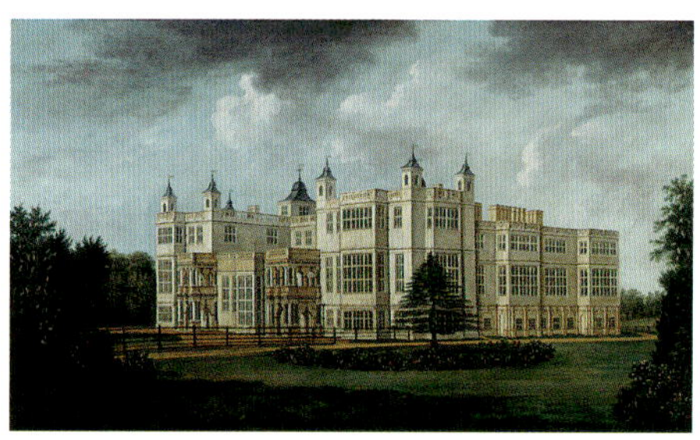

Tomkins, William c.1732–1792
Audley End from the South West 1788
oil on canvas 79 x 127
81030132

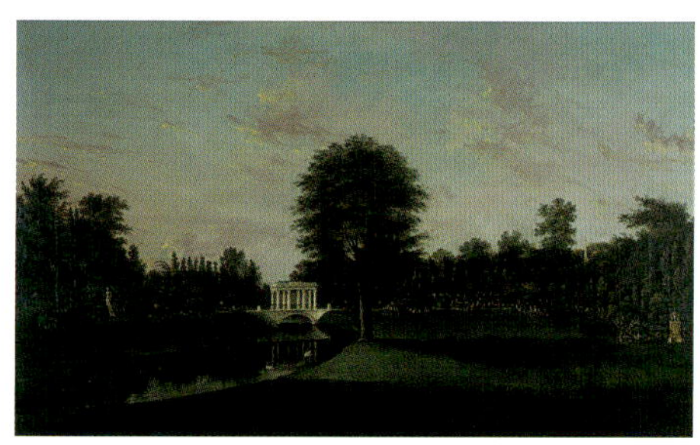

Tomkins, William c.1732–1792
Audley End, the Tea House Bridge 1788
oil on canvas 63.5 x 103
81030131

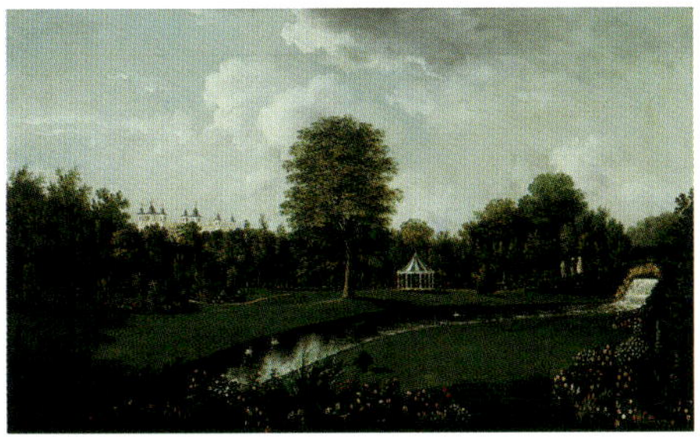

Tomkins, William c.1732–1792
Audley End, View from the Tea House Bridge 1788
oil on canvas 63.5 x 102
81030130

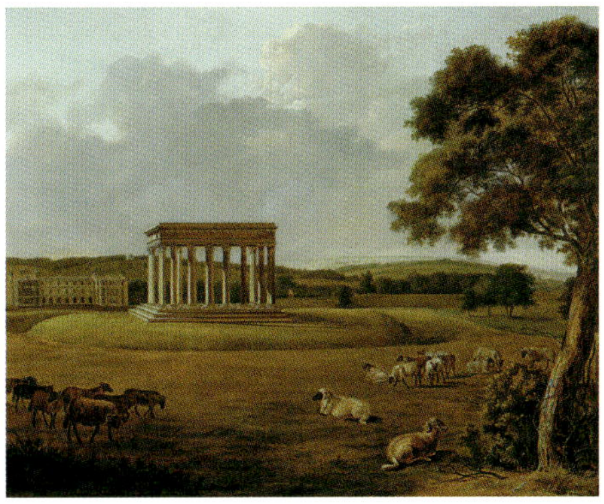

Tomkins, William c.1732–1792
Audley End and the Temple of Concord c.1792
oil on panel 58 x 74
81030134

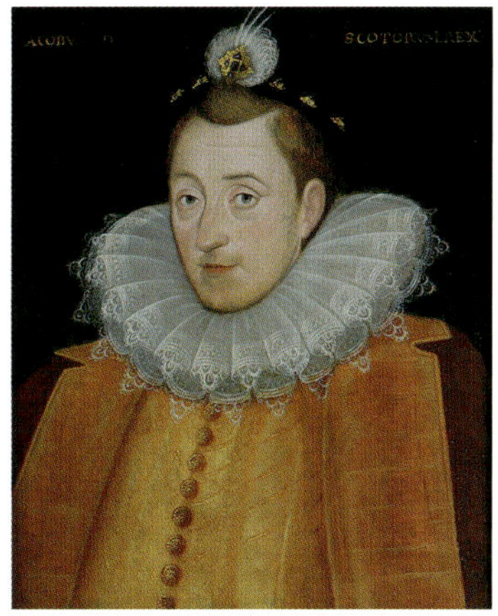

unknown artist late 16th C
King James VI of Scotland and I of England (1566–1625)
oil on panel 46 x 37
81031044

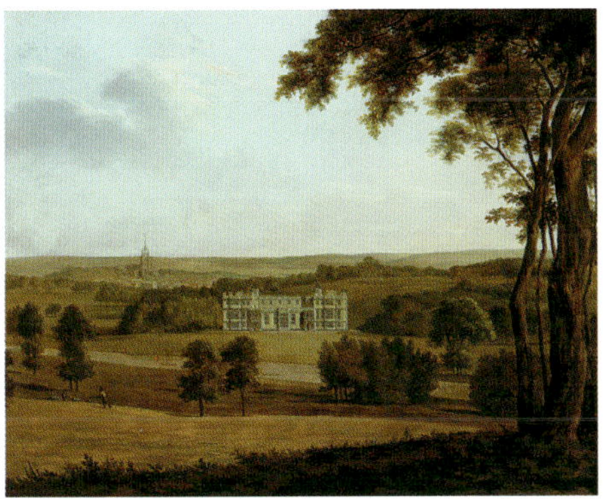

unknown artist
Audley End from the West c.1792
oil on panel 58 x 74
81030135

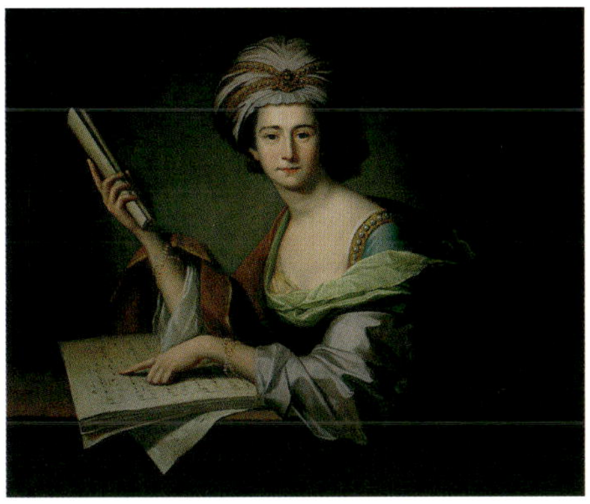

West, Benjamin 1738–1820
Anna Maria Shutz, Lady Griffin 1772
oil on canvas 89 x 107
81030136

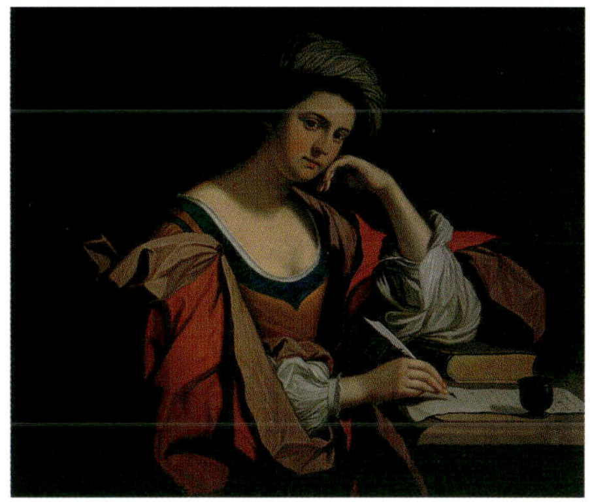

West, Benjamin 1738–1820
Katherine Clayton, Lady Howard de Walden 1772
oil on canvas 89 x 107
81030138

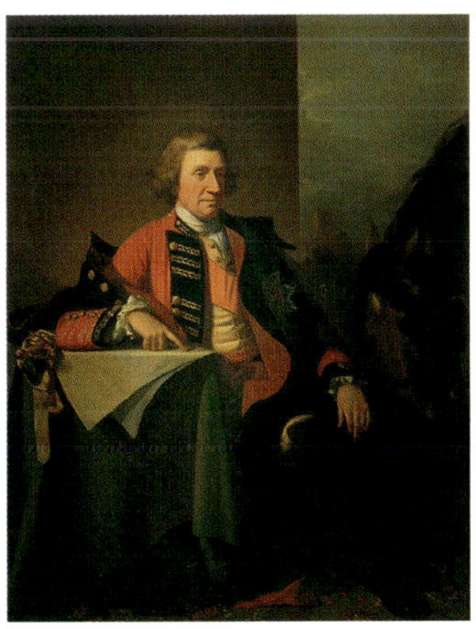

West, Benjamin 1738–1820
Sir John Griffin Griffin, 4th Lord Howard de Walden 1772
oil on canvas 170 x 130
81030137

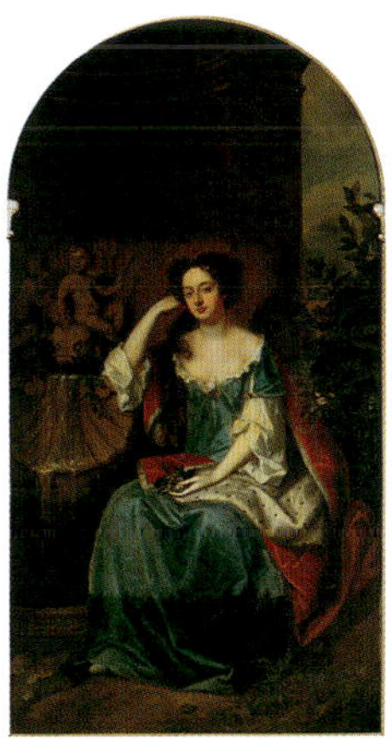

Wissing, Willem (after) c.1656–1687
Lady Essex Howard, Lady Griffin 1774
oil on canvas 239 x 122
81030152

Fry Art Gallery

The Fry Art Gallery, a perfect two-roomed miniature example of Victorian museum architecture, was built in 1856 by Francis Gibson, a Quaker banker and amateur painter, to house the pictures he had been collecting since 1830. His gallery as well as the picturesque Bridge End Gardens in which it stands, and which he had designed, were open to the public. Only three years after the completion of the gallery, Francis Gibson died and the building passed by descent to the Fry family. After Dr Fry's death in 1970, the Trustees of his estate closed the gallery but in 1985 they leased the building to the Fry Art Gallery Society. This charity was started to create the North West Essex Collection, with the Fry family collection of work by L. G. Fry (1860–1933) also being exhibited for a period each year in continuation of the tradition started by Francis Gibson.

The Gallery is primarily dedicated to the work of twentieth and twenty-first century artists who have lived and worked in North-West Essex. The particular focus of this collection is to bring together, for the first time, paintings, prints and designs by a community of artists who made their homes in and near the village of Great Bardfield from the 1930s to the 1970s. The arrival of Eric Ravilious and Edward Bawden in their bachelor days predated John Aldridge, who was followed by Michael Rothenstein and his wife Duffy Ayers, Kenneth Rowntree, Stanley Clifford Smith and George Chapman, amongst many others. At great pains to insist that they were not a school or colony, the artists began to disperse in the 1970s. Bawden moved to Saffron Walden where he joined John Bolam, Edwin Smith the photographer and artist, and his wife, Olive Cook, also an artist, and author. Of the following collection of 65 oils, the work of Smith and Cook makes up a third.

St Ives is now a by-word in twentieth century English art. Bardfield has yet to be fully assessed, although *Artists at the Fry*, edited by Martin Salisbury, 2003, and *An Inward Laugh: Edward Bawden & His Circle*, by Malcolm Yorke, 2005, go some way in this direction. This spontaneous gathering of talent was united 'by a stylistic similarity … assiduous observers of what is going on in the local scene … not imitative in the sense that they are attempting to reproduce nature on the page, but they introduce a certain stylistic formality, an organisation that is probably unique in British art', as Sir Roger de Grey PRA said when he opened the Fry Art Gallery in 1987.

The Fry Art Gallery is now recognised as a major resource and enjoys the support of the Art Fund, the MLA/Victoria & Albert Museum Purchase Grant Fund and the Essex Heritage Trust. As will be seen by those who visit us, painting in oil was not the medium of choice for most of our artists; the English watercolour tradition being preferred, with printmaking a strong suite. Two special exhibitions complement the permanent display each year. Admission is free.

Nigel Weaver, Chairman, Fry Art Gallery Society

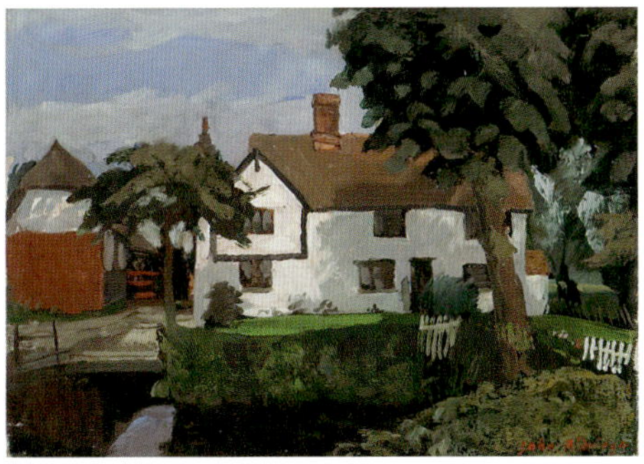

Aldridge, John Arthur Malcolm 1905–1983
Farm near Mole Hill Green 1959
oil on board 25.9 x 35.4
85

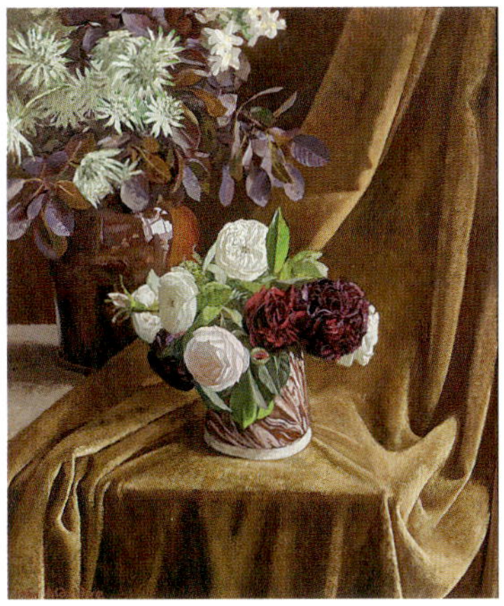

Aldridge, John Arthur Malcolm 1905–1983
Roses and Astrantia Major 1965
oil on canvas 61 x 50.5
690

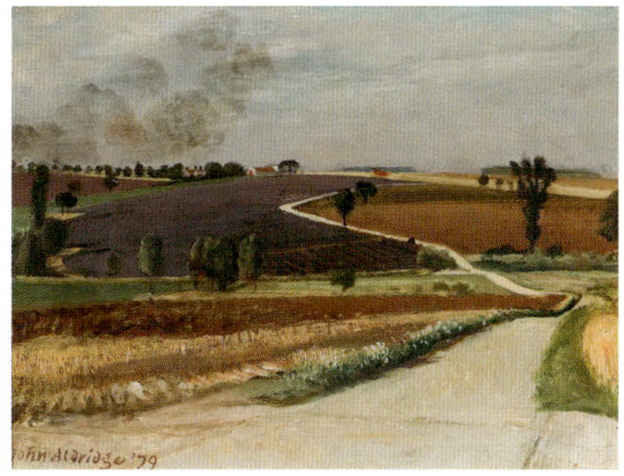

Aldridge, John Arthur Malcolm 1905–1983
The Hyde from Further Moor Hall 1979
oil on board 25.4 x 34.5
84

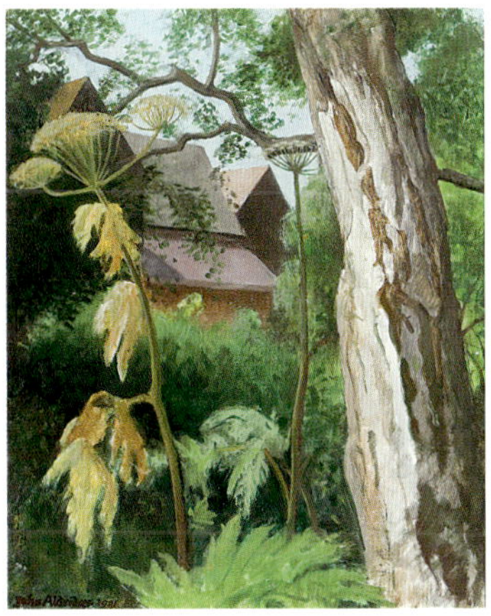

Aldridge, John Arthur Malcolm 1905–1983
Silver Birch 1981
oil on canvas 62.2 x 49.6
60

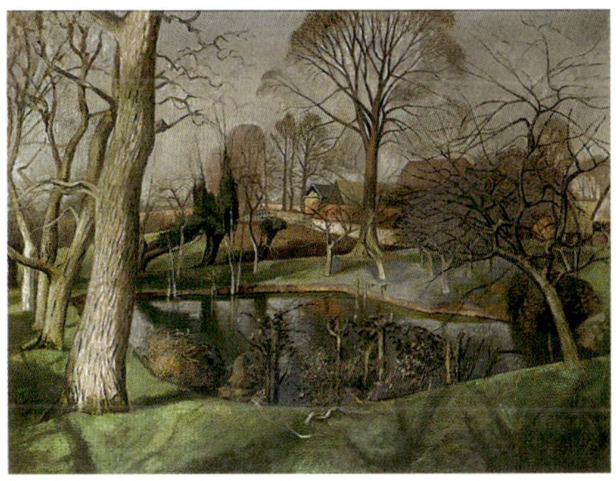

Aldridge, John Arthur Malcolm 1905–1983
Beslyn's Pond, Great Bardfield
oil on canvas 62.2 x 80.4
309

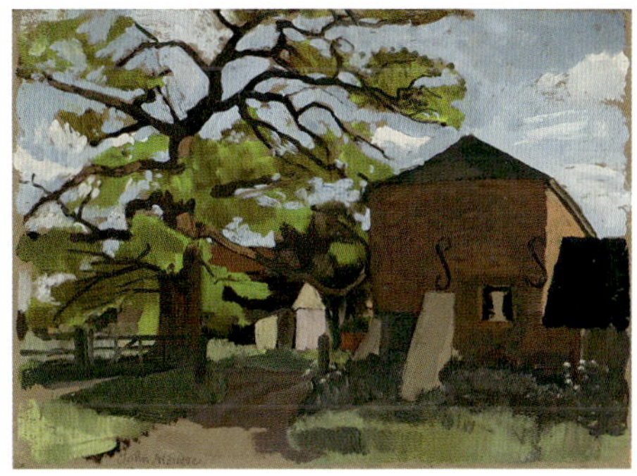

Aldridge, John Arthur Malcolm 1905–1983
Blue Gate Hall
oil on board 26.8 x 35.7
86

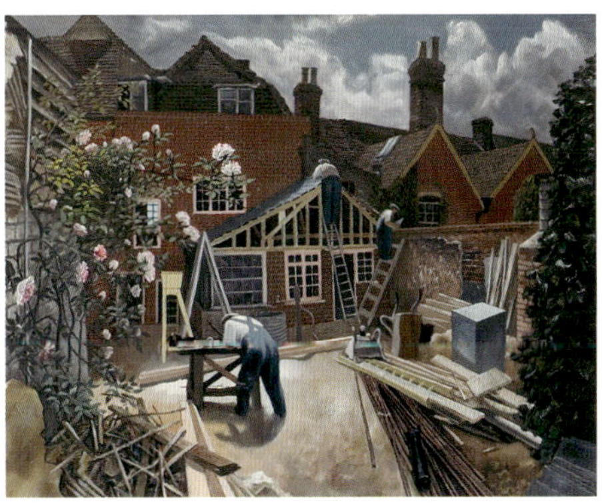

Aldridge, John Arthur Malcolm 1905–1983
Builders at Work, Brick House, Great Bardfield
oil on canvas 62.1 x 74.3
692

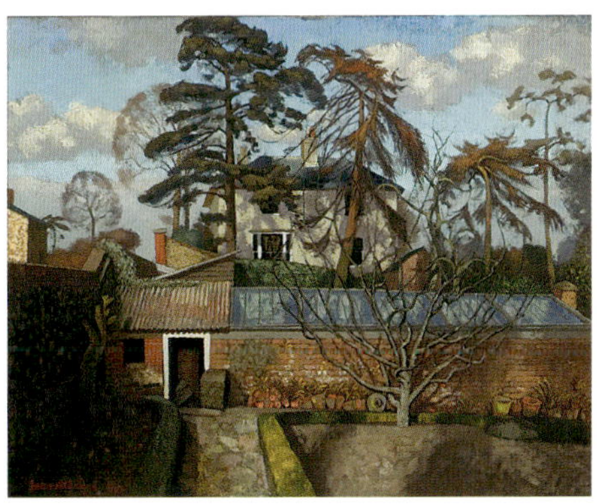

Aldridge, John Arthur Malcolm 1905–1983
February Afternoon
oil on canvas 76.5 x 92
689

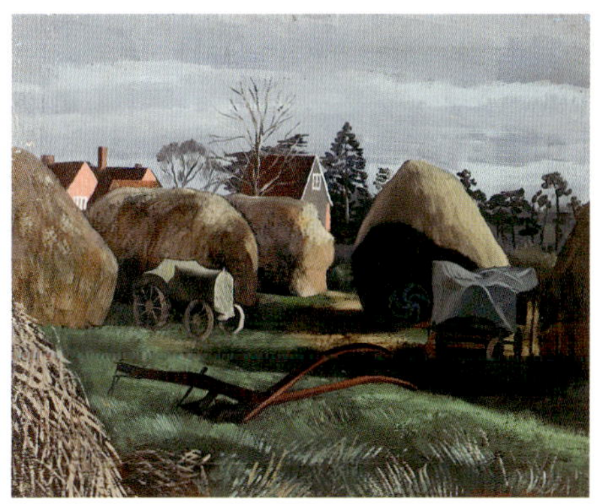

Aldridge, John Arthur Malcolm 1905–1983
Haystacks, the Place Farm
oil on canvas 49.5 x 59.7
693

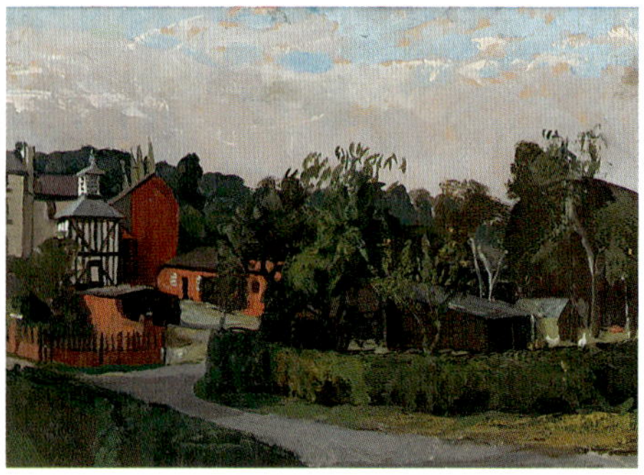

Aldridge, John Arthur Malcolm 1905–1983
King's Pyon, Shropshire
oil on board 24.5 x 34
58

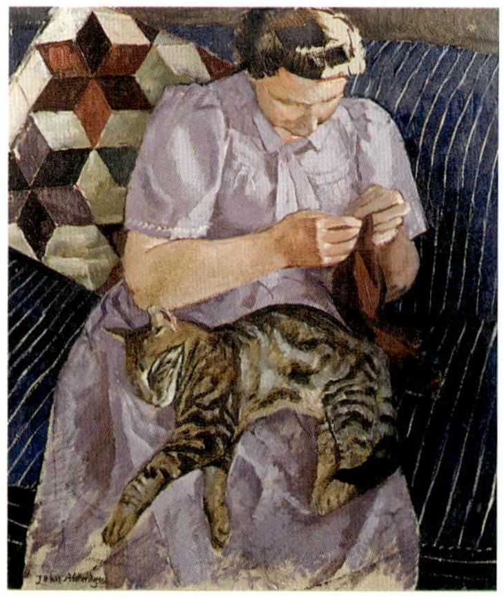

Aldridge, John Arthur Malcolm 1905–1983
Lady with Cat
oil on canvas 66.4 x 56
691

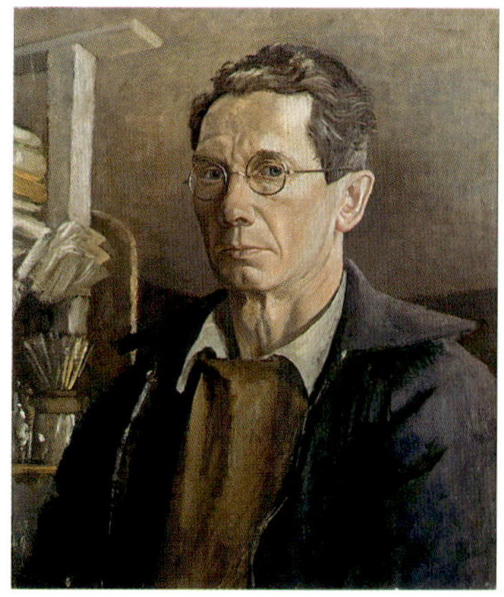

Aldridge, John Arthur Malcolm 1905–1983
Self Portrait in Oils
oil on canvas 61 x 51
653

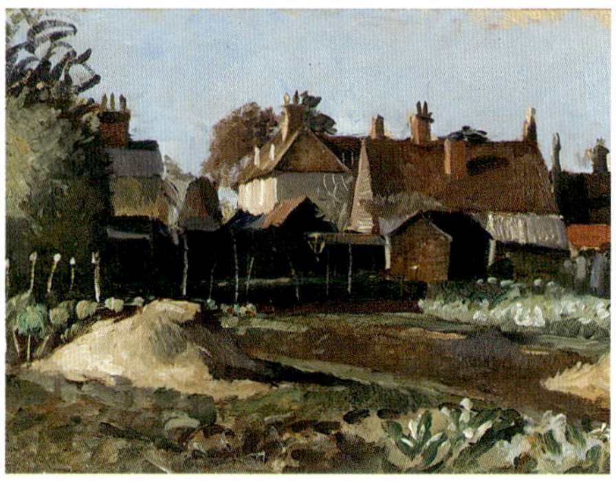

Aldridge, John Arthur Malcolm 1905–1983
The Allotments
oil on board 24.5 x 33.5
59

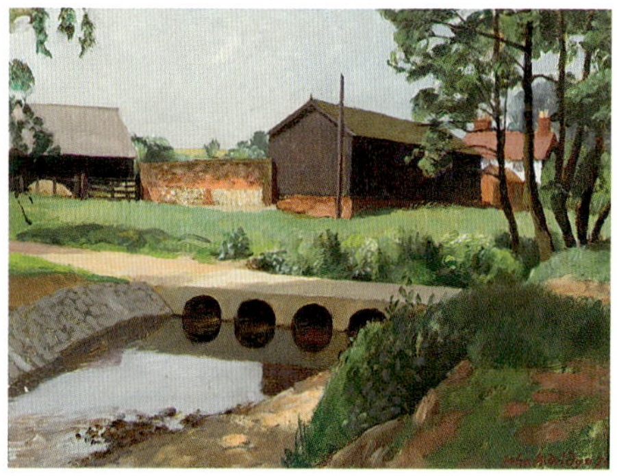

Aldridge, John Arthur Malcolm 1905–1983
The New Culvert, Copford Hall
oil on canvas 25.7 x 34.5
13

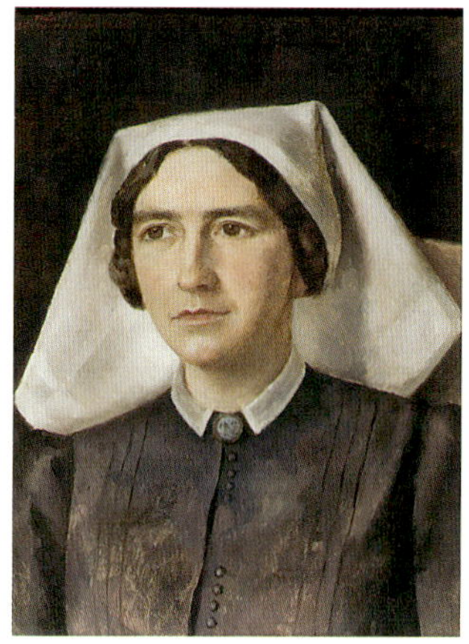

Ayers, Duffy b.1919
Kitty Wilson
oil on canvas 49.2 x 33.5
38

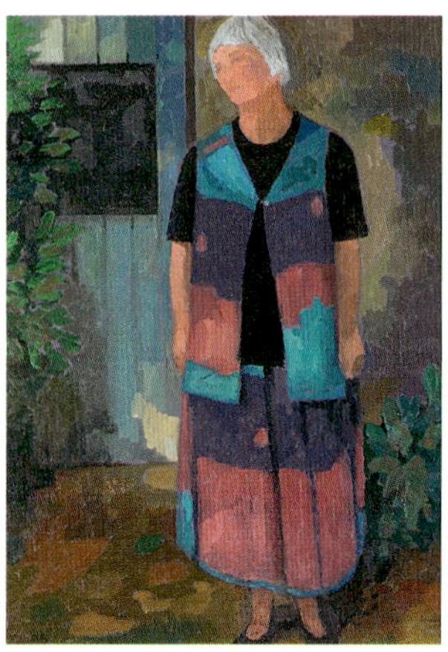

Ayers, Duffy b.1919
Olive in Her Garden
oil on hardboard 35 x 24.5
1488

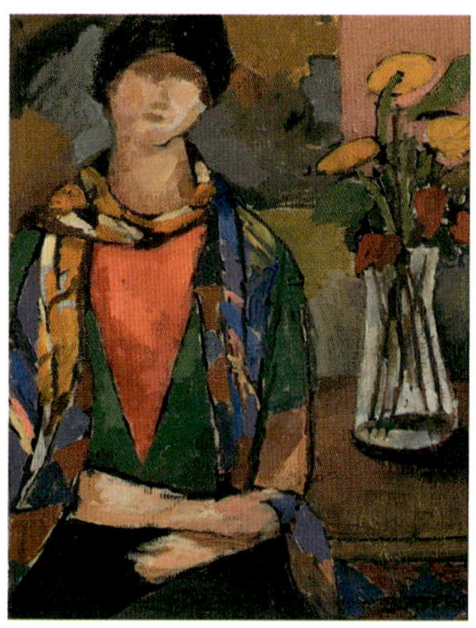

Ayers, Duffy b.1919
Scarves
oil on board 26.5 x 21.1
1023

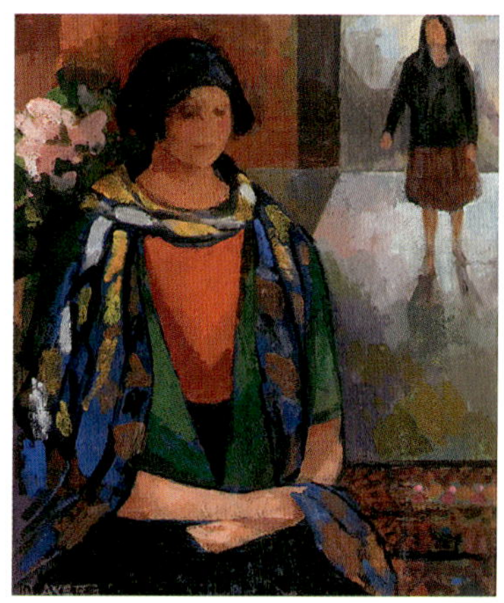

Ayers, Duffy b.1919
The Arrival
oil on board 24 x 18.8
325

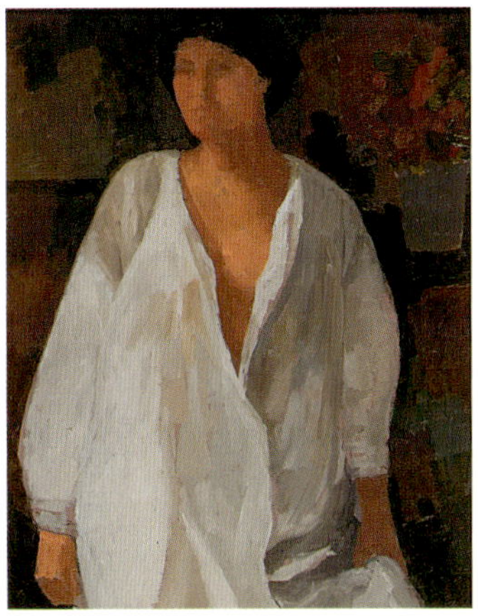

Ayers, Duffy b.1919
The White Nightdress
oil on board 29.3 x 21.8
338

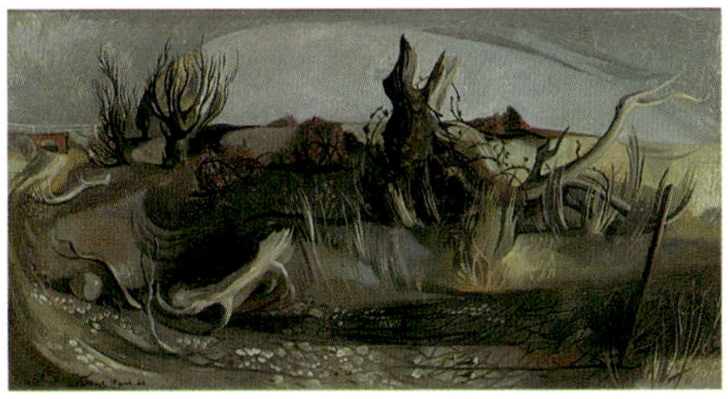

Ayrton, Michael 1921–1975
Winter Drought
oil on board 29 x 54.8
133

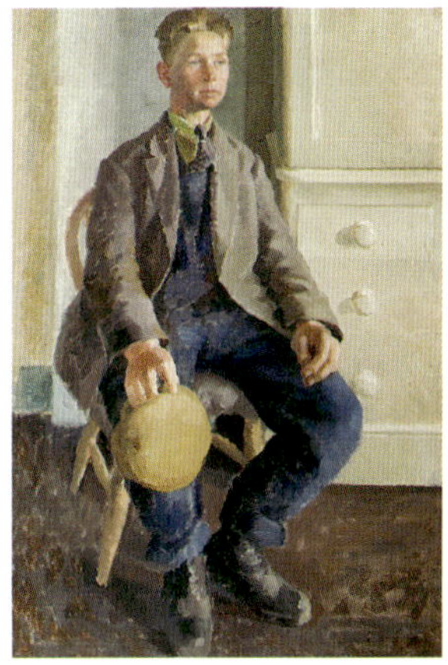

Bawden, Charlotte 1902–1969
Eric Townsend
oil on canvas 76 x 49
55

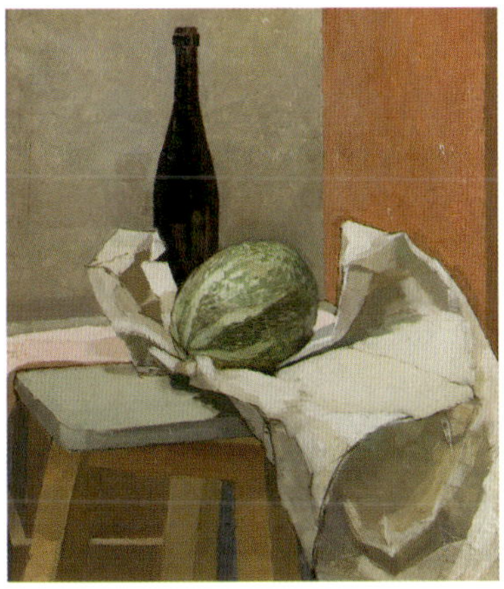

Bawden, Joanna b.1935
Still Life with Melon and Bottle
oil on board 43.8 x 40.5
312

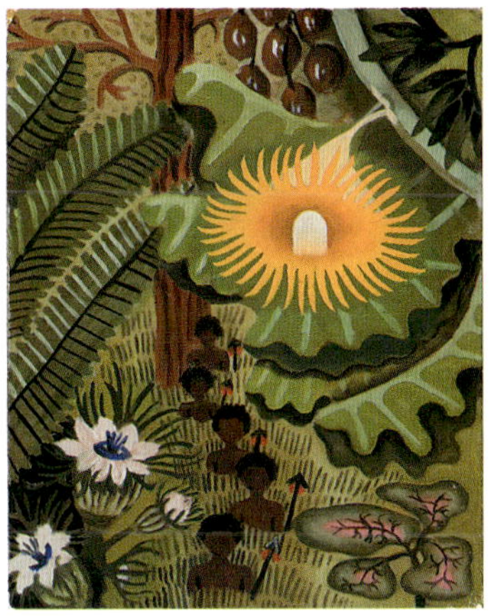

Bawden, Joanna b.1935
Sunflower
oil on board 45.7 x 35.6
313

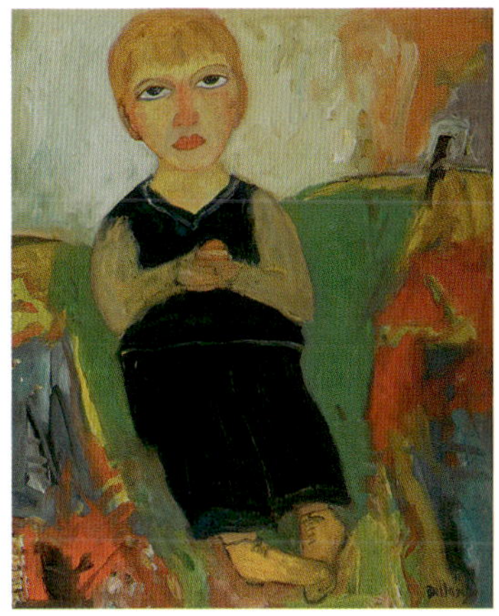

Bellany, John b.1942
My Grandson Luke
oil on canvas 76 x 61
990

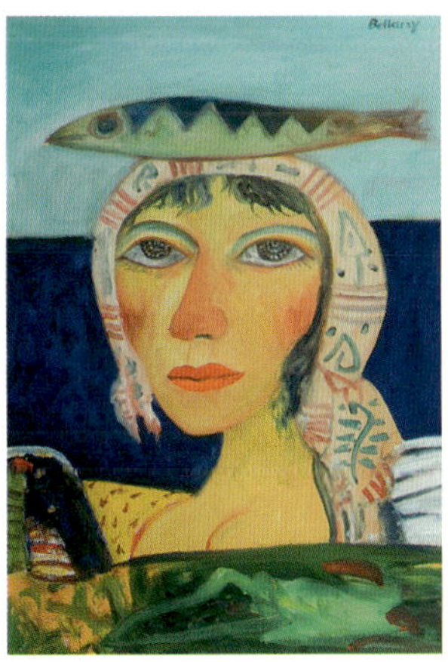

Bellany, John b.1942
Woman of the North Sea
oil on canvas 76.2 x 51
989

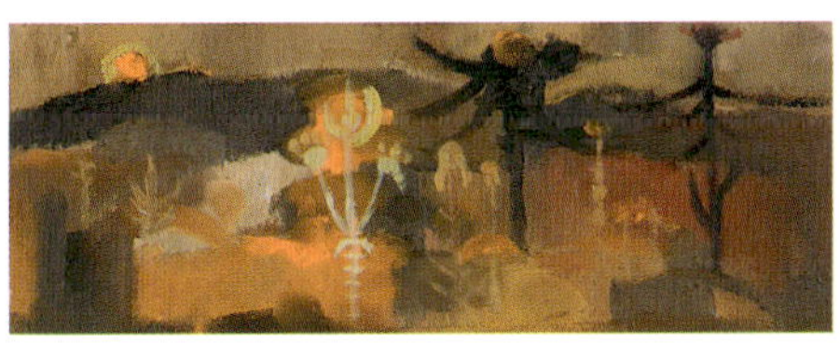

Bolam, John b.1922
Early Morning c.1955
oil on board 12.5 x 32.5
1022

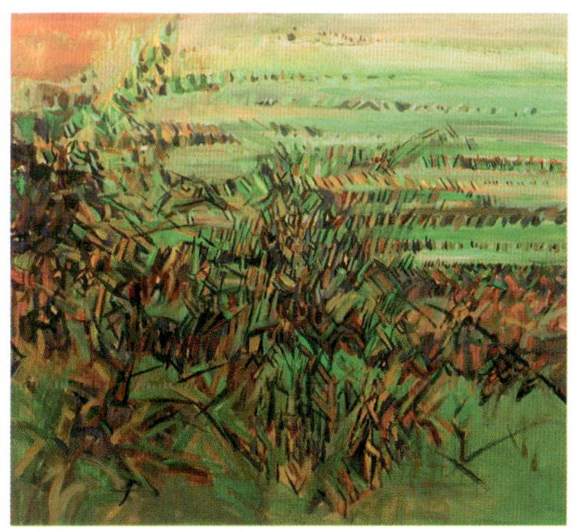

Bolam, John b.1922
Green Landscape
oil on hardboard 87 x 95
114

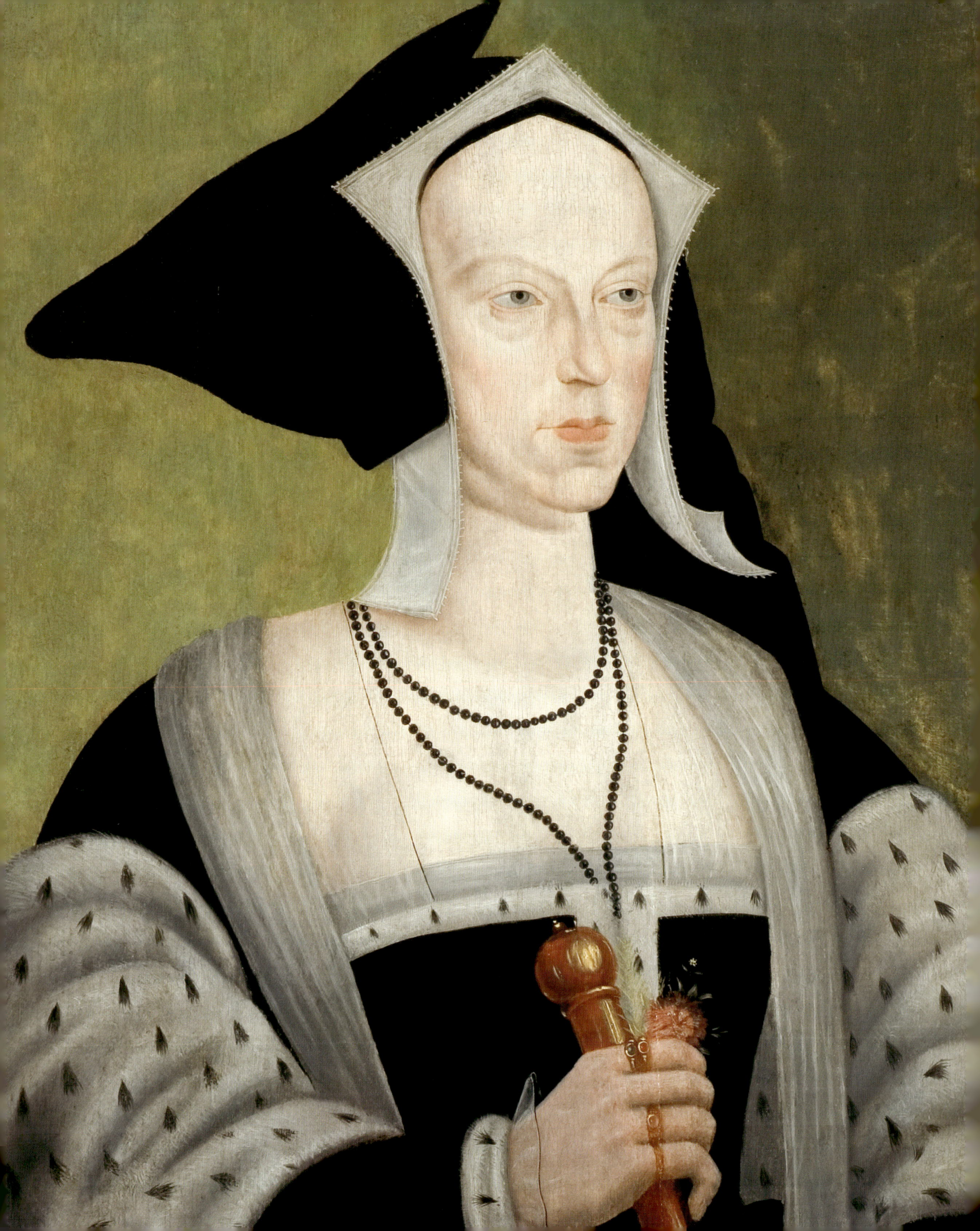

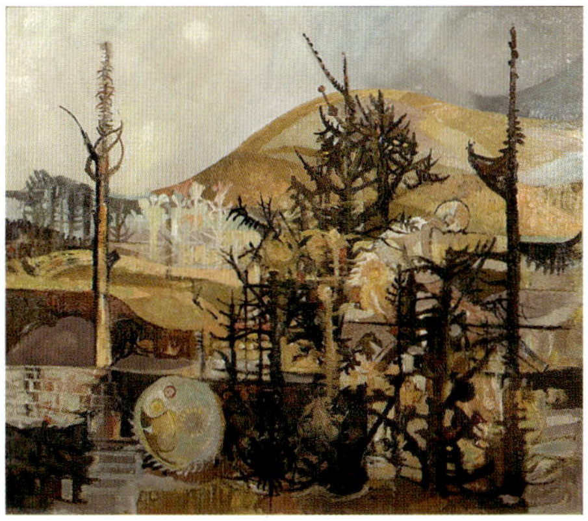

Bolam, John b.1922
Hill Worker
oil on hardboard 77.5 x 91.8
238

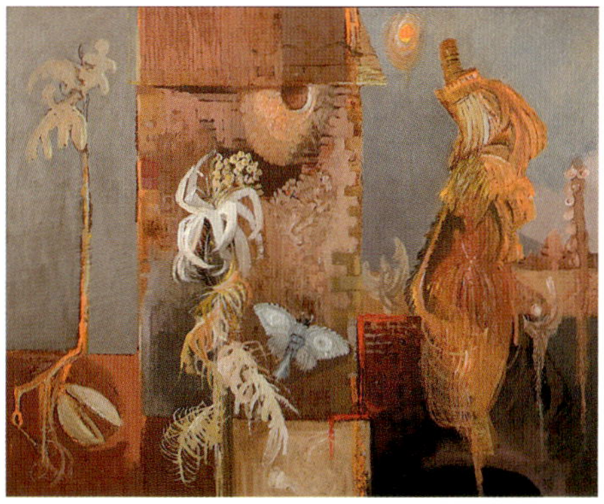

Bolam, John b.1922
October
oil on board 60 x 77
194

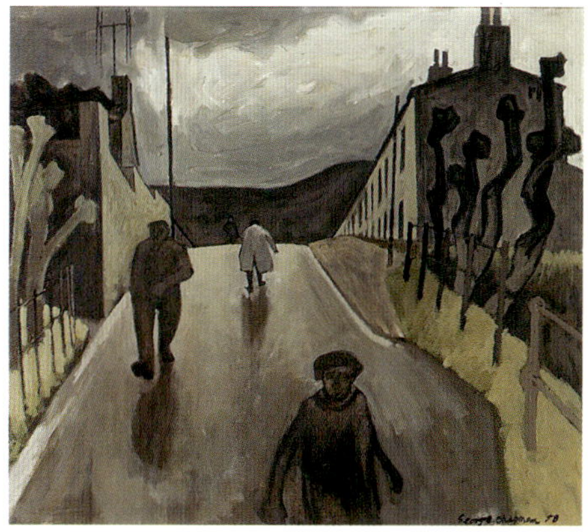

Chapman, George 1908–1993
A Steep Road 1958
oil on canvas 55.5 x 61.5
140

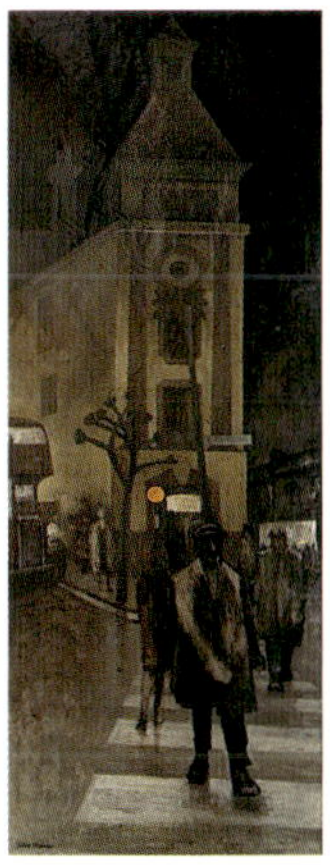

Chapman, George 1908–1993
Pontypridd
oil on canvas 217.3 x 77.3
37

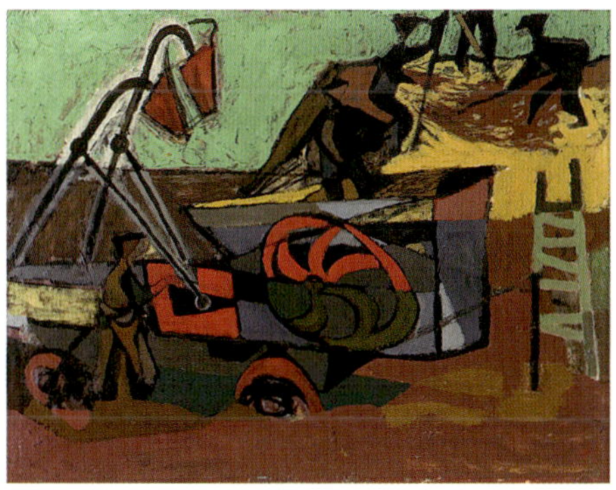

Chapman, George 1908–1993
The Threshing Machine
oil on board 45.7 x 59
695

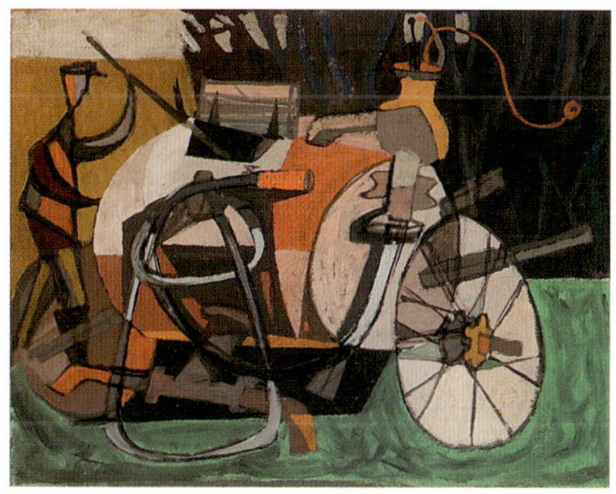

Chapman, George 1908–1993
The Water Bowser
oil on board 45.7 x 58.5
694

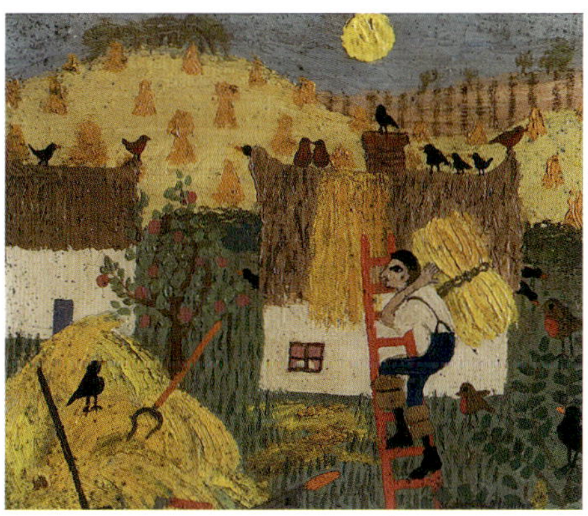

Chapman, Kate b.1926
The Thatcher 1953
oil on card 18.7 x 22.8
336

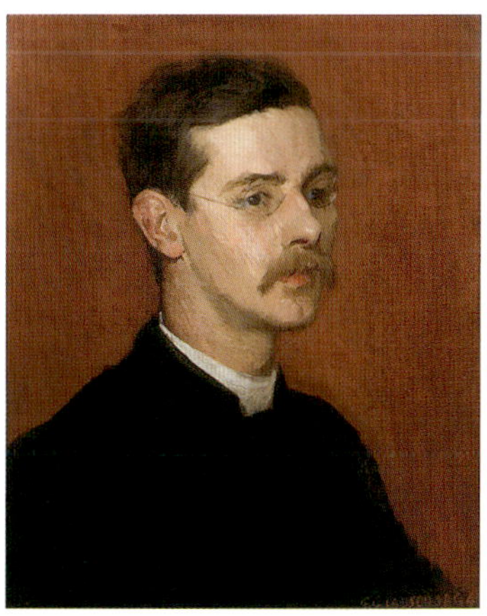

Clausen, George 1852–1944
The Reverend J. W. Court, MA 1894
oil on canvas 49.8 x 39.5
943

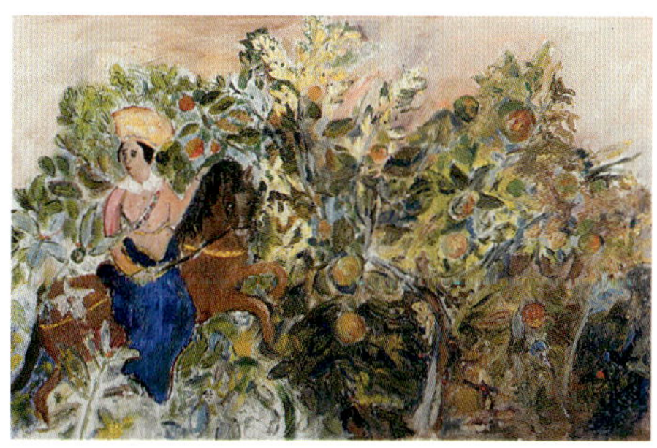

Cook, Olive 1912–2002
I Am the Ancient Apple Queen
oil on board 49 x 74.2
40

Facing page: British (English) School, *The Marchioness of Dorset* (detail), c.1555, Southend Museums Service, (p. 254)

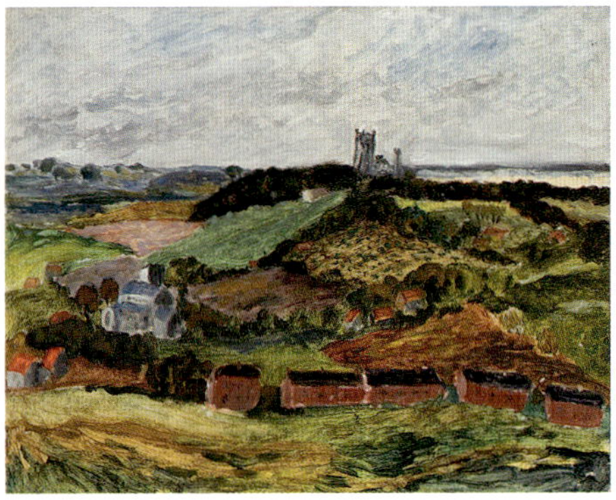

Cook, Olive 1912–2002
Cley, Norfolk
oil on board 49.5 x 60
1017

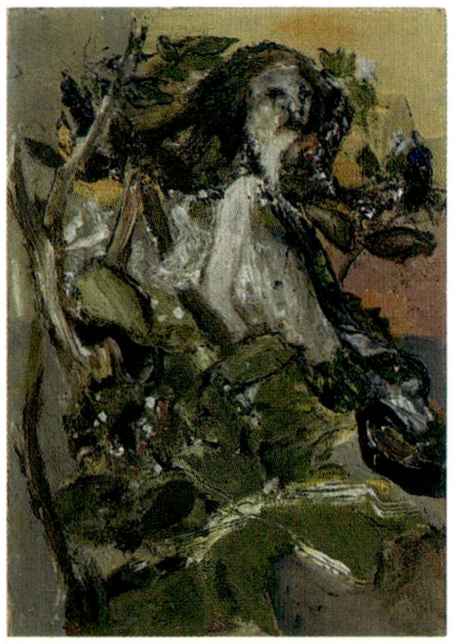

Cook, Olive 1912–2002
Lady into Tree
oil on board 29.3 x 20.4
1009

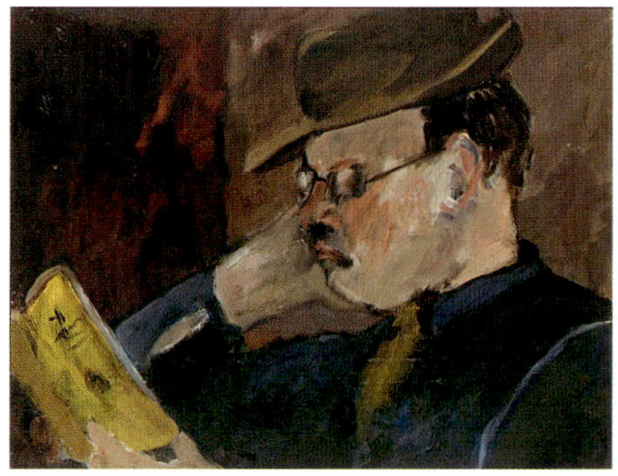

Cook, Olive 1912–2002
Michael Rothenstein Reading
oil on canvas 41 x 51
318

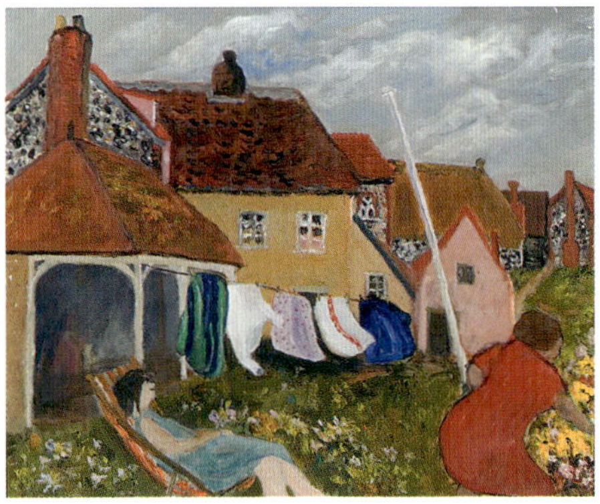

Cook, Olive 1912–2002
Norfolk Afternoon
oil on board 51 x 61.2
1012

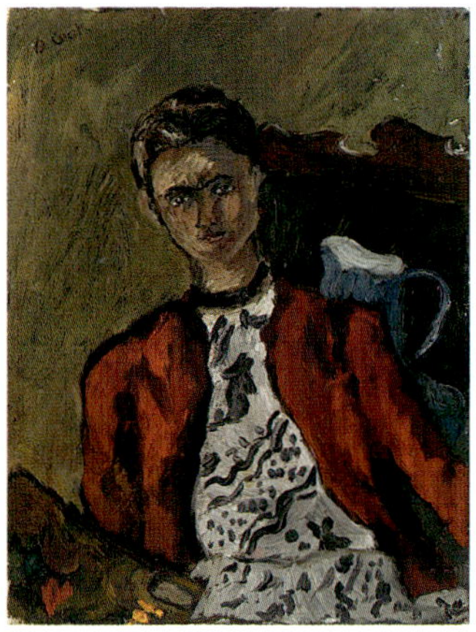

Cook, Olive 1912–2002
Portrait of a Lady
oil on card 29.5 x 22.5
1010

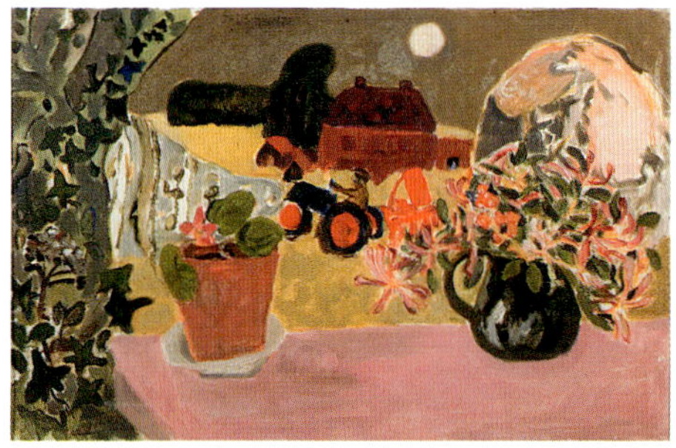

Cook, Olive 1912–2002
Remembered Suffolk Summer
oil on board 51 x 76.5
1015

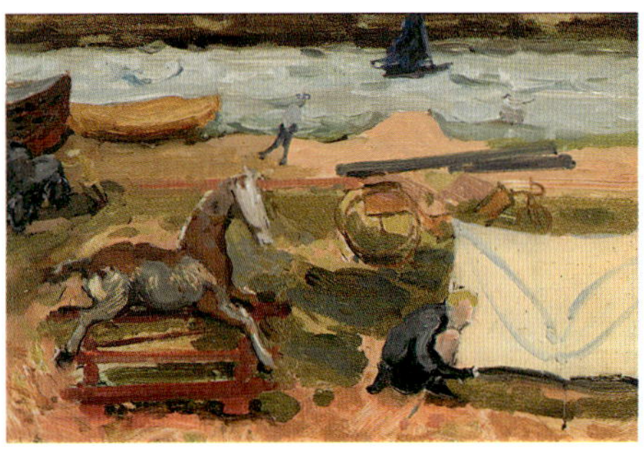

Cook, Olive 1912–2002
Rocking Horse, Seashore
oil on board 40.7 x 61
1011

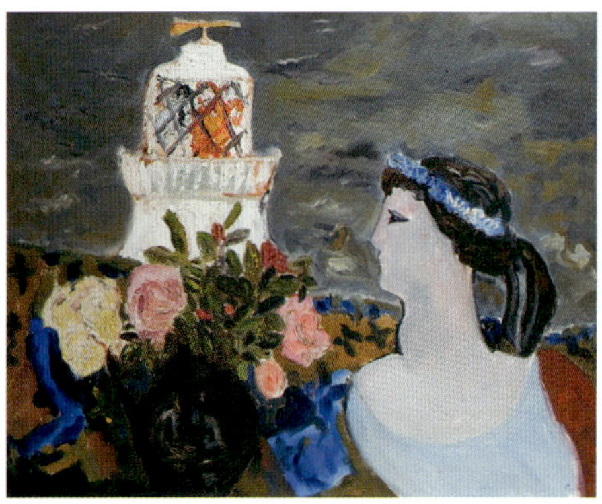

Cook, Olive 1912–2002
Ship's Figurehead and Lighthouse, Southwold
oil on board 63.5 x 76
1013

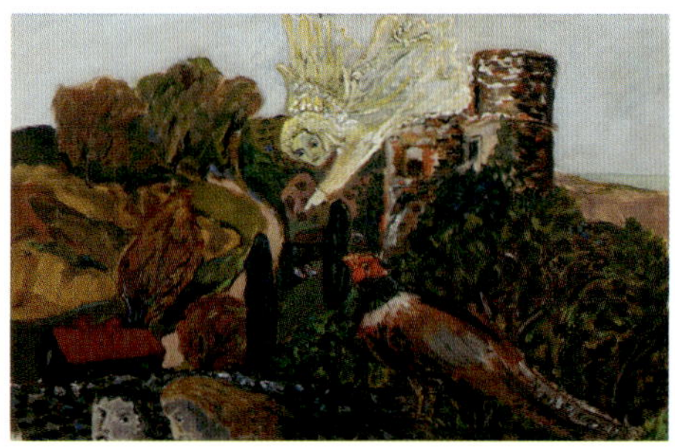

Cook, Olive 1912–2002
The Expulsion
oil on canvas 51 x 76
1016

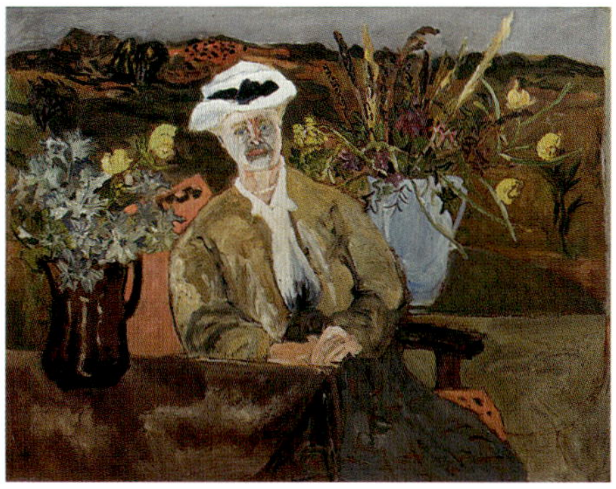

Cook, Olive 1912–2002
The White Hat
oil on hardboard 92.6 x 112.8
371

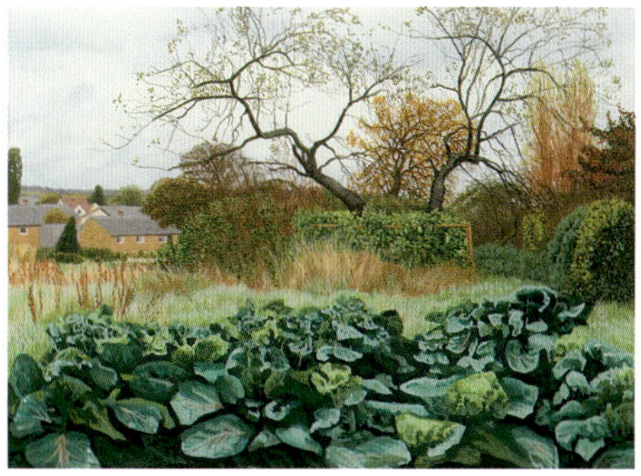

Deakins, Thomas William b.1957
Apple Tree, Dunmow Allotments
oil on board 19 x 24
330

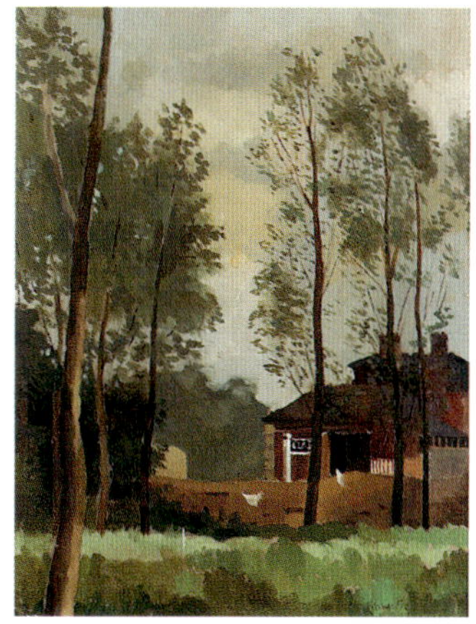

Rowntree, Kenneth 1915–1997
The Station Willows, Clare, Suffolk c.1941
oil on canvas 45.6 x 35.5
360

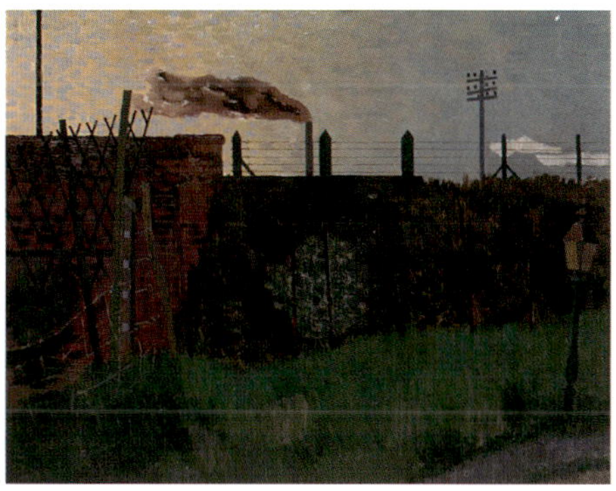

Rowntree, Kenneth 1915–1997
Dunmow Station, Dusk
oil on board 37 x 45
57

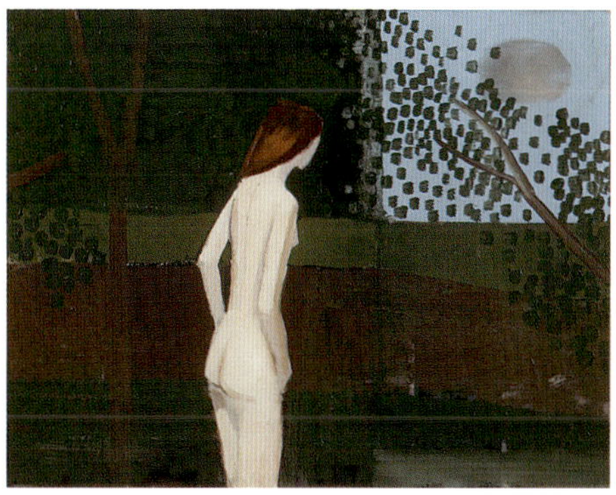

Rowntree, Kenneth 1915–1997
Evening Bather, Essex
oil on canvas 40.5 x 51
769

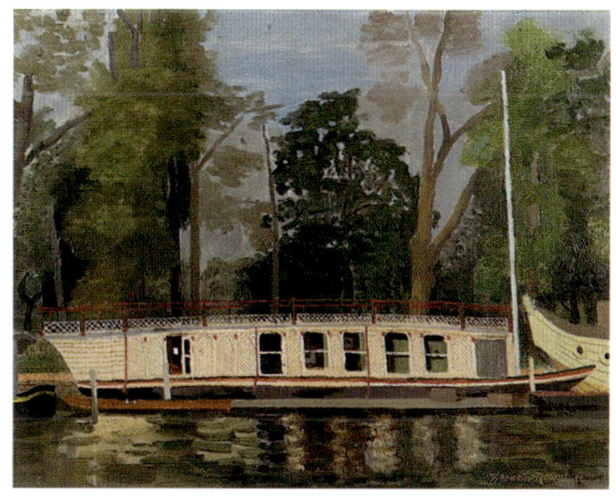

Rowntree, Kenneth 1915–1997
Exeter College Barge, Oxford
oil on canvas 40.8 x 50.8
716

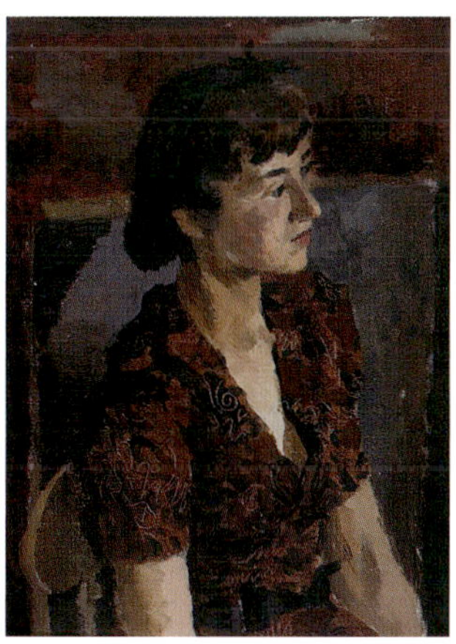

Rowntree, Kenneth 1915–1997
The Artist's Wife
oil on canvas 25.5 x 17.8
754

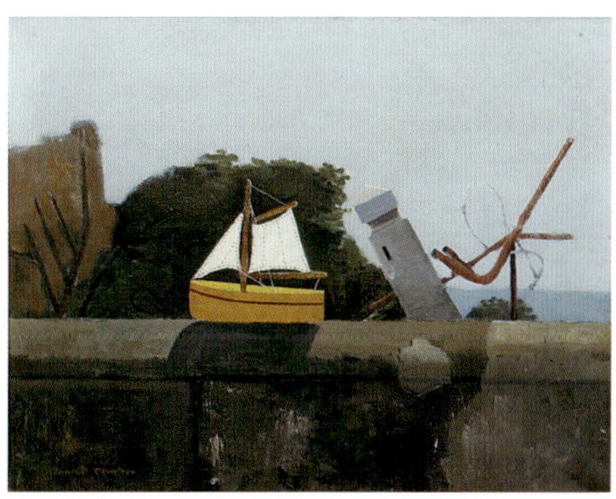

Rowntree, Kenneth 1915–1997
Toy Boat at Selsey
oil on canvas 61.4 x 76.5
715

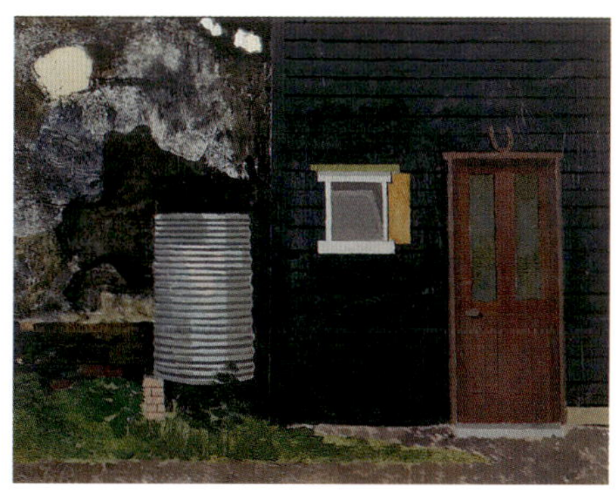

Rowntree, Kenneth 1915–1997
Water Butt, Simpkins' Cottage, Lindsell
oil on hardboard 35.8 x 45.6
352

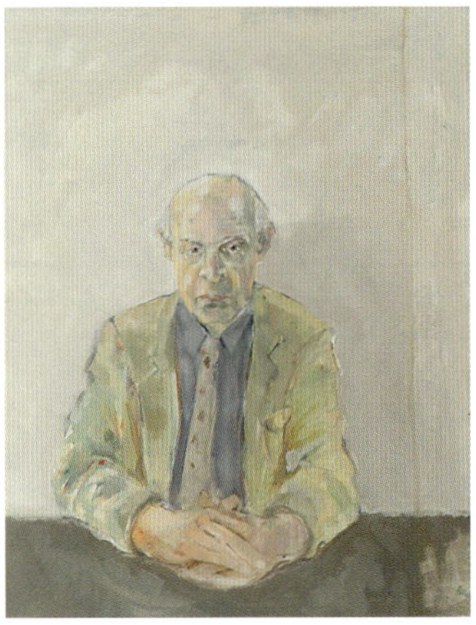

Russell, Tom b.1963
Edward Bawden
oil on canvas 60.2 x 45
242

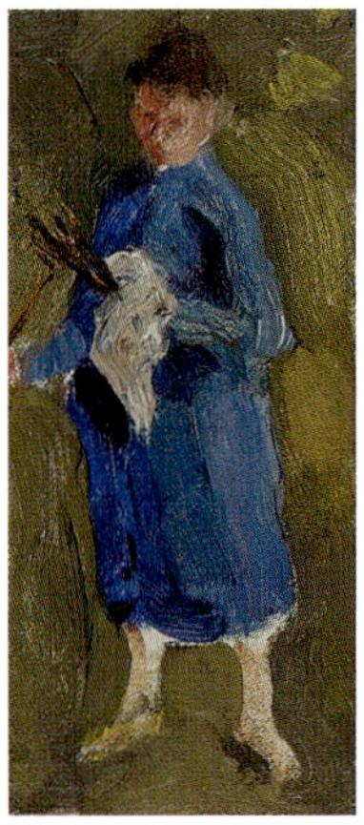

Smith, Edwin 1912–1971
Olive Cook Painting 1953
oil on board 9 x 4.5 (E)
996

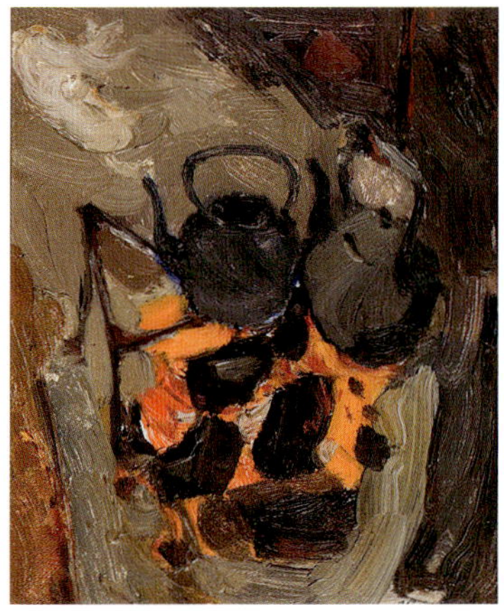

Smith, Edwin 1912–1971
Turf Fire 1953
oil on board 24 x 19.5
995

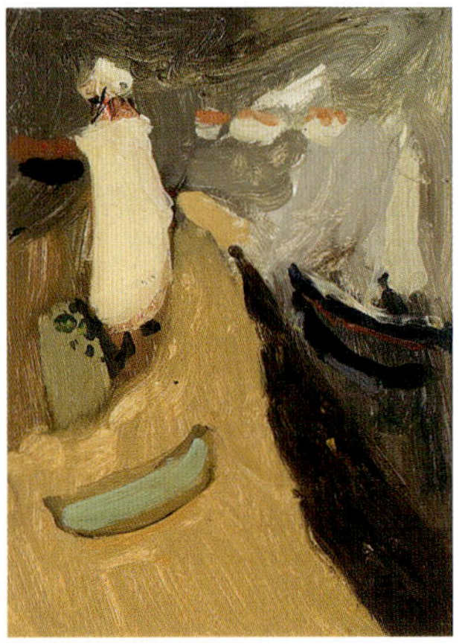

Smith, Edwin 1912–1971
Lighthouse Going for a Walk 1959
oil on paper 33 x 24
1002

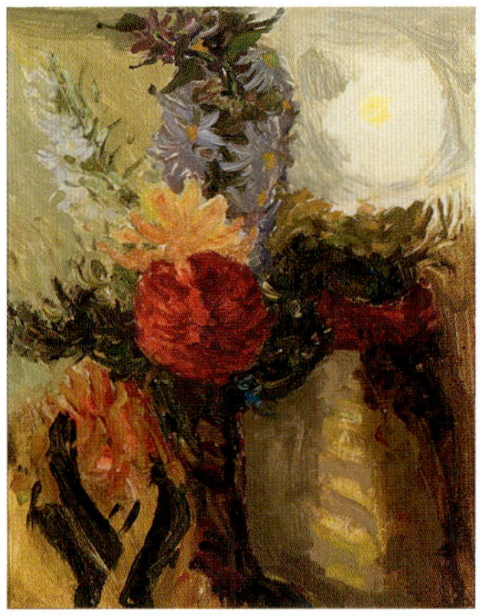

Smith, Edwin 1912–1971
Flower Piece 1961
oil on hardboard 47 x 37
1003

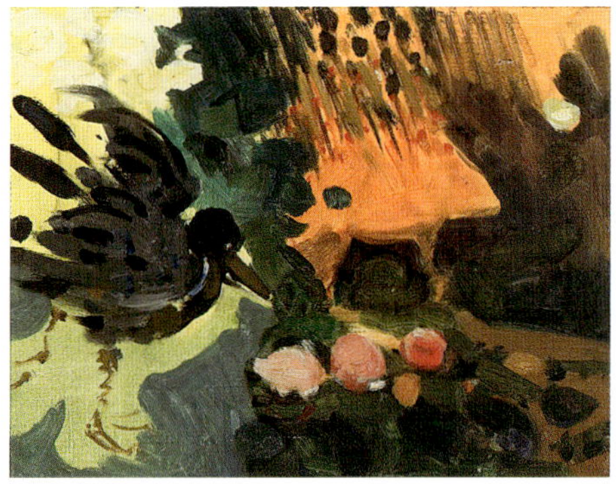

Smith, Edwin 1912–1971
A Blackbird and Roses 1963
oil on canvas 39 x 49.5
1006

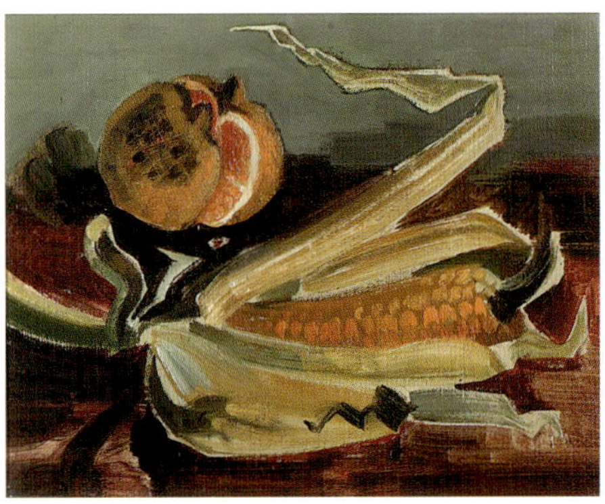

Smith, Edwin 1912–1971
Corn and Pomegranate
oil on canvas 33.5 x 41
1005

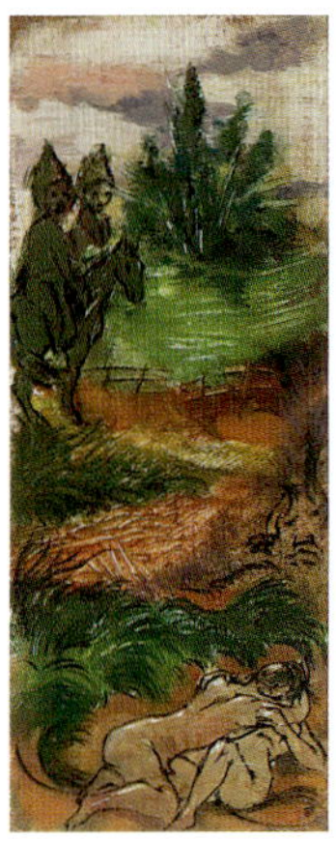

Smith, Edwin 1912–1971
Riding By
oil on board 90 x 23
994

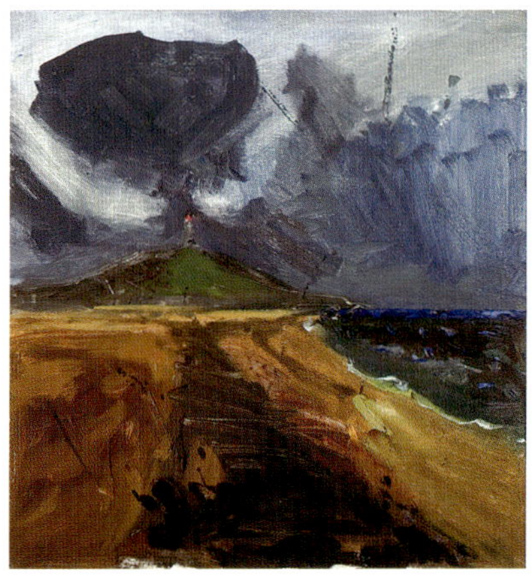

Smith, Edwin 1912–1971
Storm over Southwold
oil on canvas 64.7 x 60
331

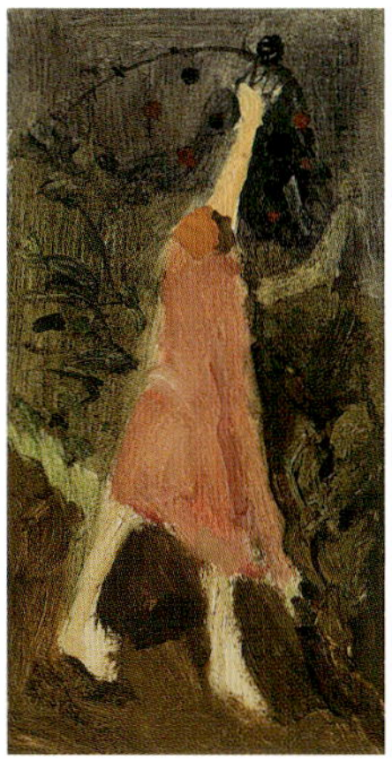

Smith, Edwin 1912–1971
The Pink Dress
oil on paper 40 x 23
1001

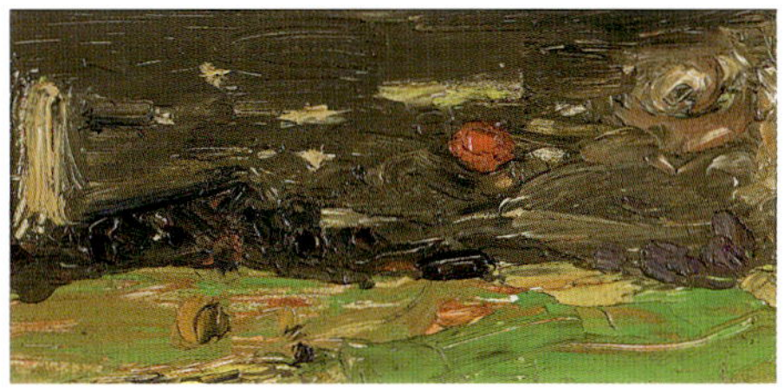

Smith, Edwin 1912–1971
View from Blackshore, Southwold
oil on board 11.5 x 23.5
997

Saffron Walden Community Hospital

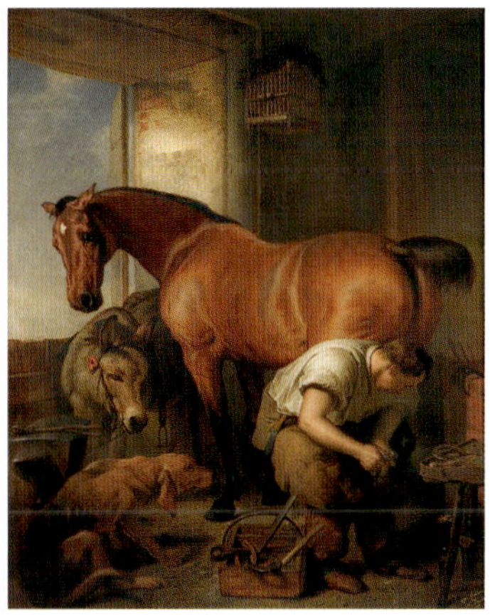

Gambardella, Julia active 1899–1906
The Blacksmith (copy after Edwin Henry Landseer) 1906
oil on canvas 140 x 102 (E)
1

Saffron Walden Library

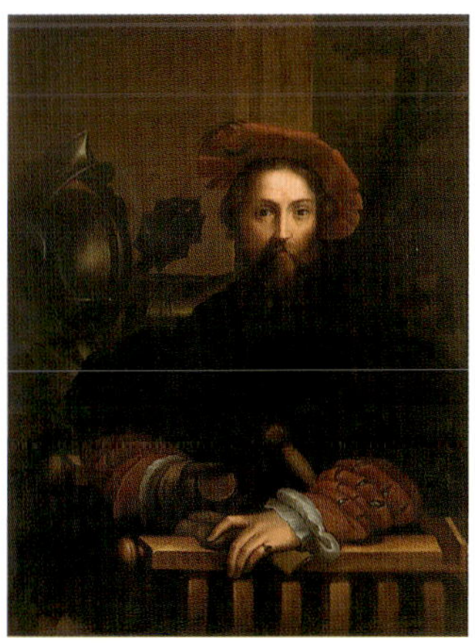

Furse, W. H. active 1831–1850
Christopher Columbus (c.1451–1506) (copy after Parmigianino)
oil on canvas 109 x 79
L040

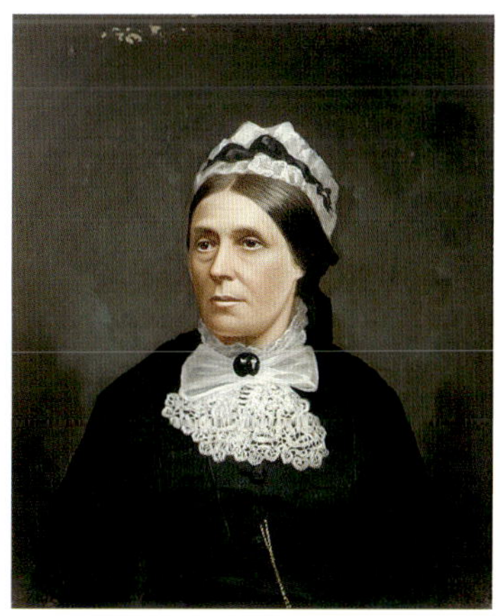

Tuke, Henry Scott (attributed to) 1858–1929
Elizabeth Gibson, née Tuke
oil on canvas 30 x 24.2
V39

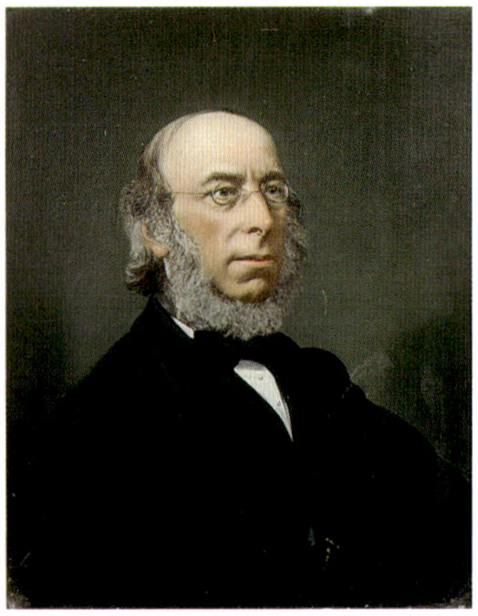

Tuke, Henry Scott (attributed to) 1858–1929
George Stacey Gibson (1818–1883)
oil on canvas 30 x 24
V38

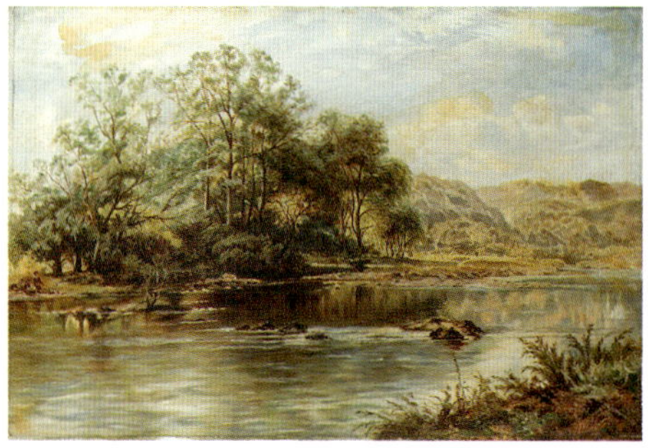

unknown artist 19th C
A Stream in Summer
oil on canvas 46 x 66.2
23

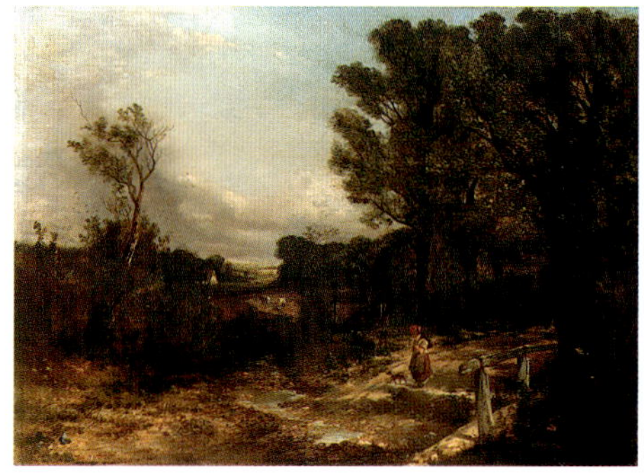

unknown artist 19th C
Pastoral Scene with a Girl and Her Dog
oil on canvas 45.6 x 61
43

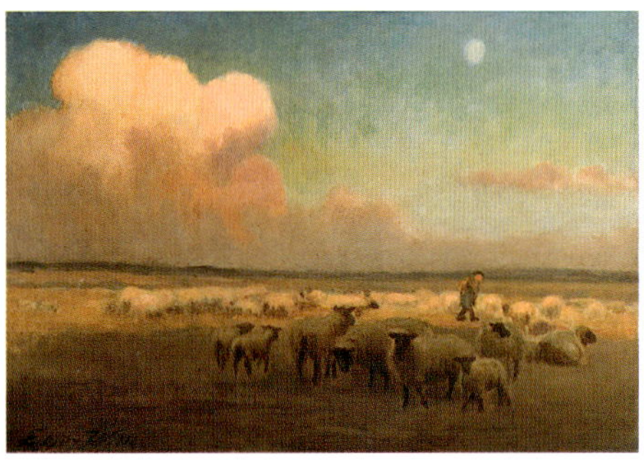

Wills, Edgar W. active 1874–1907
Sheep and Shepherd, Evening
oil on canvas 35.5 x 50.5
42

Saffron Walden Museum

Saffron Walden Museum, situated next to the Castle, first opened to the public on 12 May 1835. It is an early example of a purpose-built museum, and was founded by several local benefactors: Lord Braybrooke, John Player (whose portrait hangs in the Local History Gallery), Jabez Gibson, a banker, his brother Francis, and Thomas Spurgin. During its early history, the museum collection contained natural history specimens and other 'curious' objects. Rooms were also provided for the Horticultural Society, Walden Agricultural Society and the Literary Society, whose members occasionally assembled to hear papers.

Today the Museum has a large collection, which ranges from ceramics and glass to geology and toys. Oil paintings are only a small proportion of the decorative and fine art collections. The size and content of the oil painting collection generally reflects a period in the nineteenth century when the founders of the museum and successful local residents were acquiring works of art or commissioning portraits for posterity. The lack of a clear collecting policy has resulted in a diverse group of oil paintings ranging from four of the panels painted by Giovanni Battista Cipriani for the library at Audley End designed by Robert Adam, to a copy of Turner's *Ulysses and Polyphemus.*

The history of some of the oil paintings is interesting. One of the largest paintings in the collection, *Cock Fight* by Melchior de Hondecoeter was purchased and presented to the museum by Jabez Gibson. The museum register of that period notes the 'great value' of this piece yet ironically it once hung over the mantelpiece in a Saffron Walden public house. Jabez Gibson also presented the fine *View of the Thames* with the Monument and Southwark Cathedral in the background, described in the museum register as by the son of 'moonlight Pether'. The Italianate building in the foreground has been identified as Billingsgate Market, erected in 1850 to the designs of J. B. Bunning. However, it proved inadequate and was replaced by the present building in 1874. The identification of the former building has enabled us to pinpoint the artist – there are four artists by the name of Pether and two of them painted moonlit views – as Henry Pether, active from 1828–1865.

Hanging in the Local Studies Gallery is the self portrait by Henry Winstanley, presented by George Stacey Gibson. Winstanley was a native of Saffron Walden and designed the first Eddystone Lighthouse, eight miles off Rame Head, Cornwall. Winstanley perished at the lighthouse when it was demolished by a ferocious storm on a winter night in November, 1703.

Thanks to the Public Catalogue Foundation's project, further research has been carried out on the oil painting collection. The photographic lights highlighted the date, 1633, on the *Portrait of a Lady with a Lace Collar Holding a Tulip* in the Ceramics Gallery, which Sir Roy Strong believes is probably by Gilbert Jackson. Featuring the museum's paintings in this catalogue will improve access to this small but intriguing collection.

Sarah Wilson, Documentation and Exhibition Officer

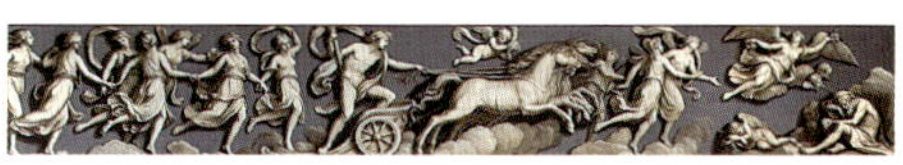

Cipriani, Giovanni Battista 1727–1785
Panel from the Robert Adam Library at Audley End Representing Air 1770
oil on canvas 68 x 440 (E)
1839.29a

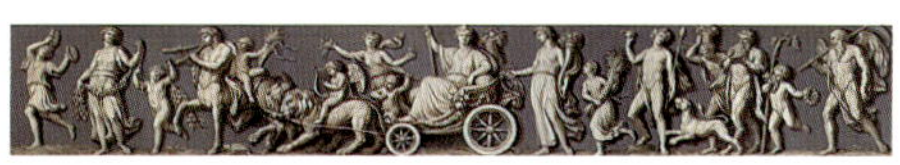

Cipriani, Giovanni Battista 1727–1785
Panel from the Robert Adam Library at Audley End Representing Earth 1770
oil on canvas 68 x 440 (E)
1839.29d

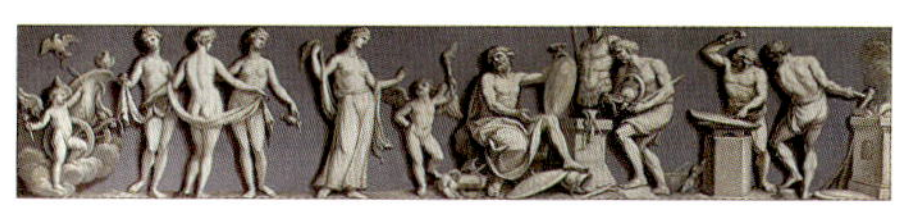

Cipriani, Giovanni Battista 1727–1785
Panel from the Robert Adam Library at Audley End Representing Fire 1770
oil on canvas 68 x 296 (E)
1839.29b

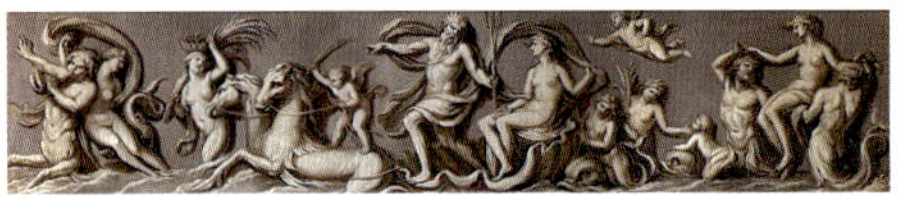

Cipriani, Giovanni Battista 1727–1785
Panel from the Robert Adam Library at Audley End Representing Water 1770
oil on canvas 68 x 296 (E)
1839.29c

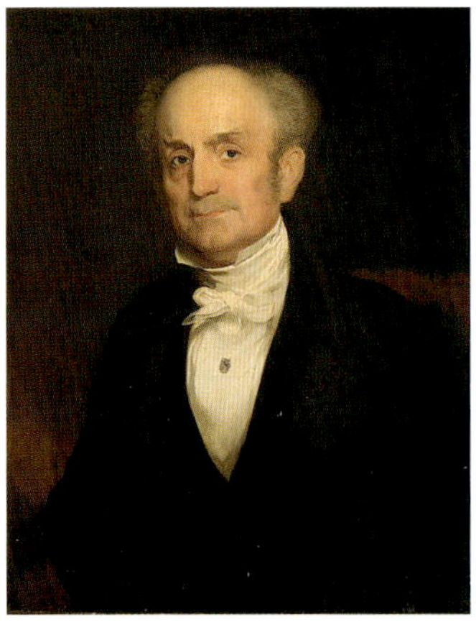

Davison, William active 1813–1843
John Player (1786–1846) 1842
oil on canvas 75 x 61.5
XXII

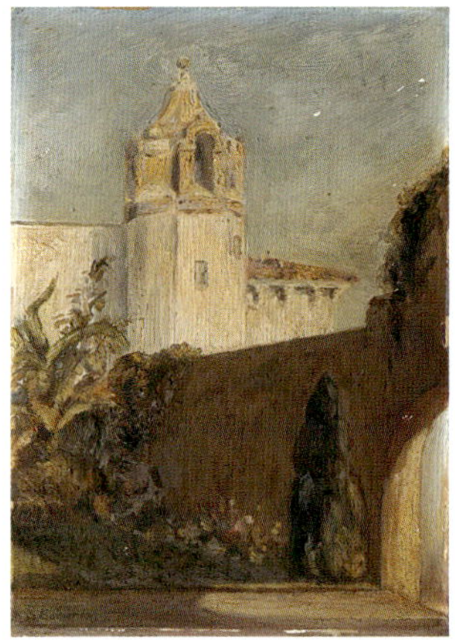

Edmonds, Stuart (attributed to)
active 1925 1927
Scene with Tower
oil on board 23 x 16.5
31302

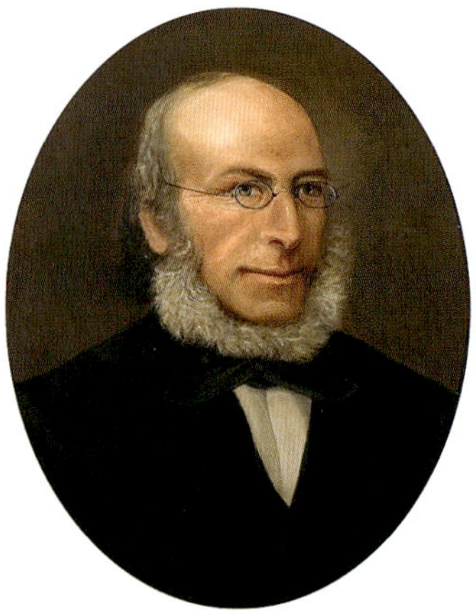

Foster, G. active 19th C
George Stacey Gibson (1818–1883)
oil on canvas 60 x 39
1885.3

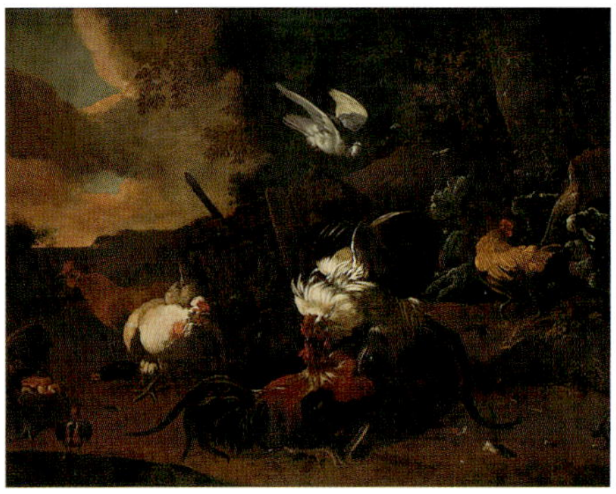

Hondecoeter, Melchior de (attributed to)
1636–1695
Cock Fight
oil on canvas 152 x 188
31291

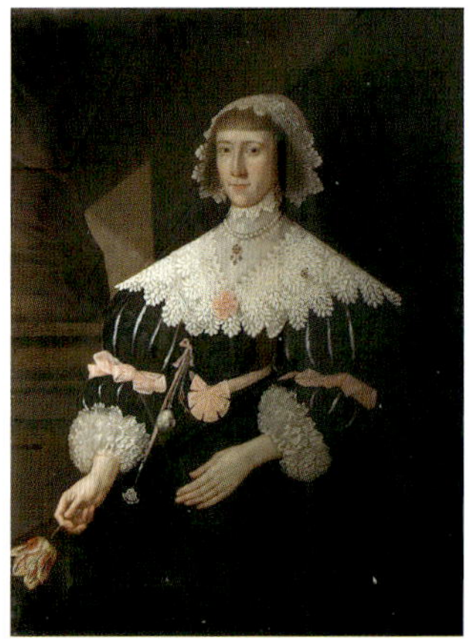

Jackson, Gilbert (attributed to)
active 1621–1640
Portrait of a Lady with a Lace Collar Holding a Tulip 1633
oil on canvas 124 x 93
X

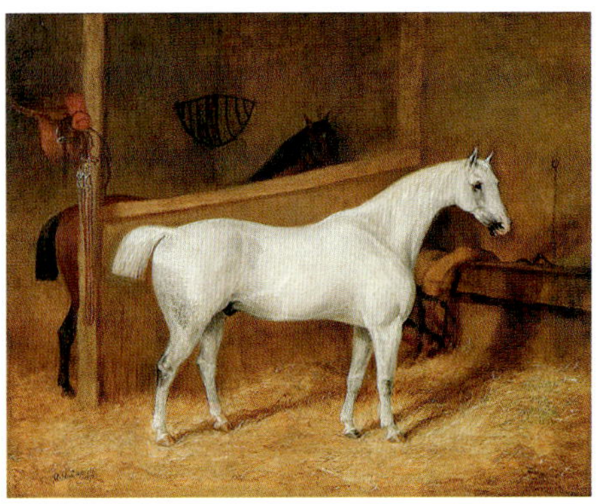

Laporte, George Henry 1799–1873
White Stallion 1871
oil on canvas 49.5 x 60
LN366 (P)

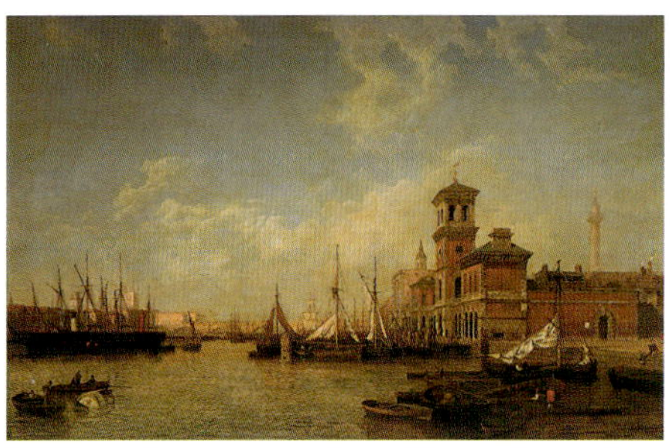

Pether, Henry active 1828–1865
View of the Thames, Pool of London, from Billingsgate to London Bridge c.1862
oil on canvas 91 x 137
31273

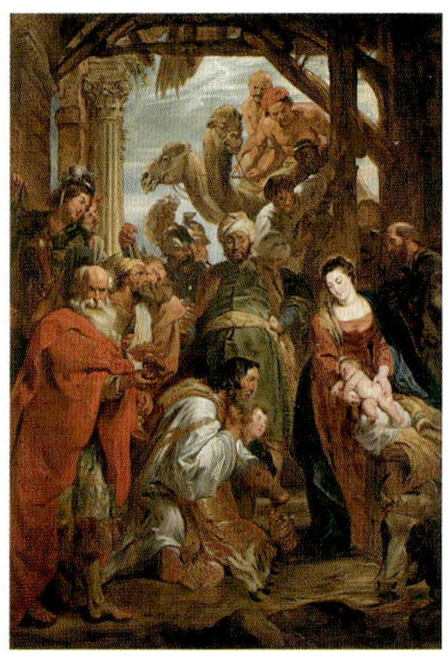

Reinagle, Philip 1749–1833
Adoration of the Magi (copy after Peter Paul Rubens)
oil on canvas 416.5 x 304.8
XL

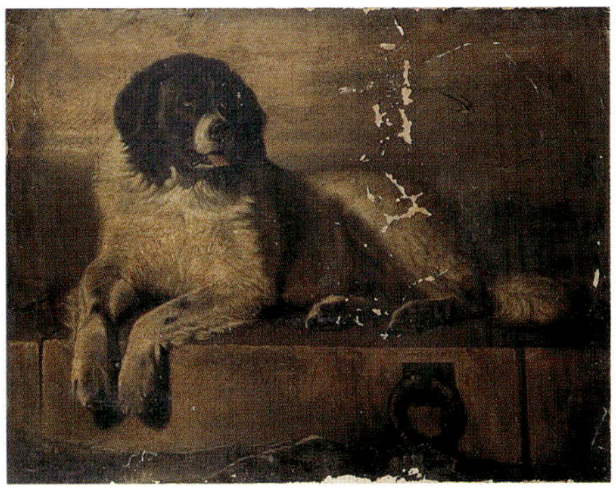

Ruggles, William Henry (copy of) active 1833–1846
A Distinguished Member of the Humane Society
oil on canvas 77 x 90.5
31293

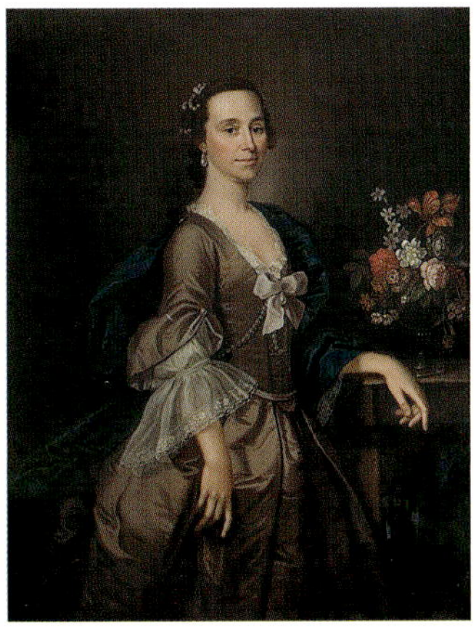

unknown artist
Mrs Thomas Wolfe 1740–1750
oil on canvas 125 x 100
1877.10.2

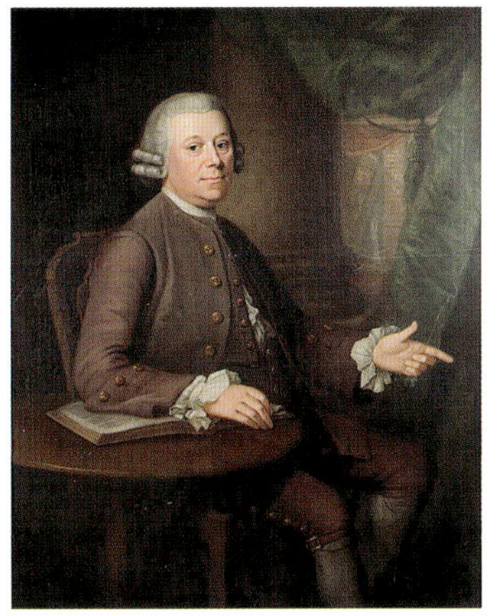

unknown artist
Thomas Wolfe 1740–1750
oil on canvas 125 x 99
1877.10.1

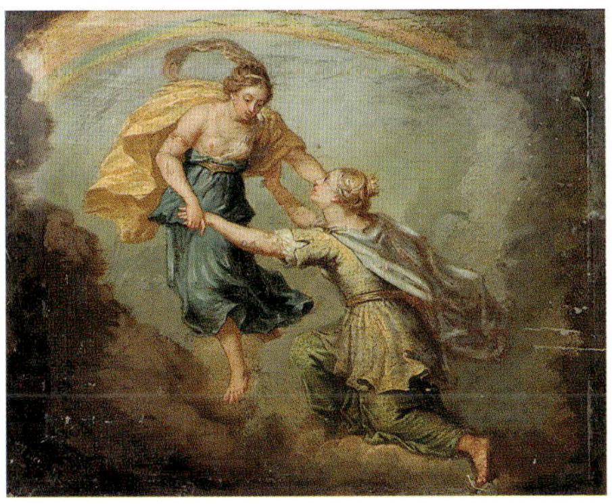

unknown artist
Adoration of Goddess Juno c.1760
oil on panel 39 x 47
F16

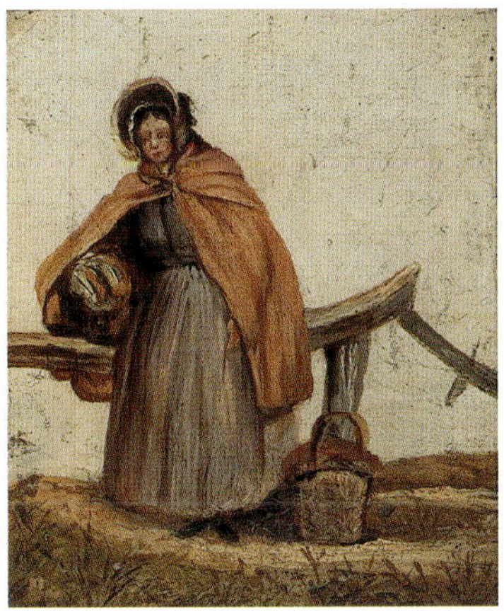

unknown artist
Woman Resting Her Basket on a Stile c.1845
oil on canvas 13 x 10.5
LN17 (P)

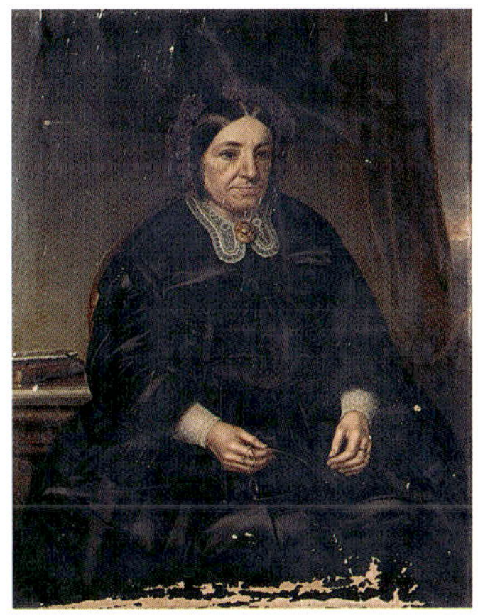

unknown artist 19th C
Portrait of a Lady Holding Her Spectacles
oil on canvas 112 x 86
31271

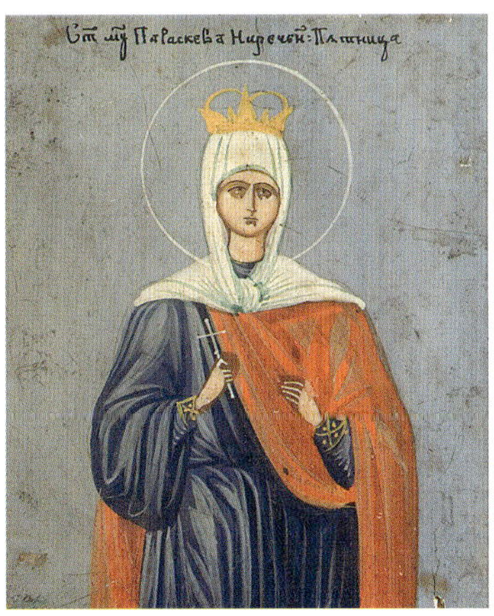

unknown artist
A Saint
oil on board 10.5 x 9
F1

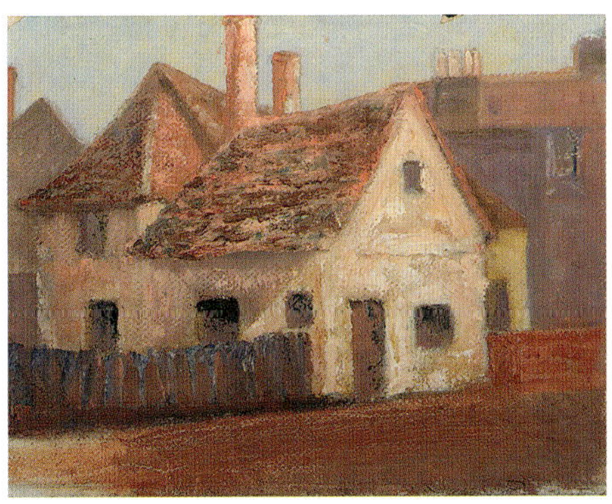

unknown artist
Cottage
oil on paper 30 x 37.5
31298

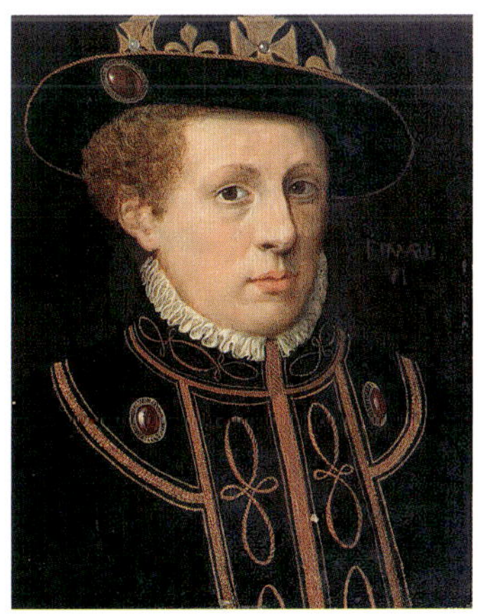

unknown artist
Edward VI (1537–1553)
oil on board 42 x 33
30302.2

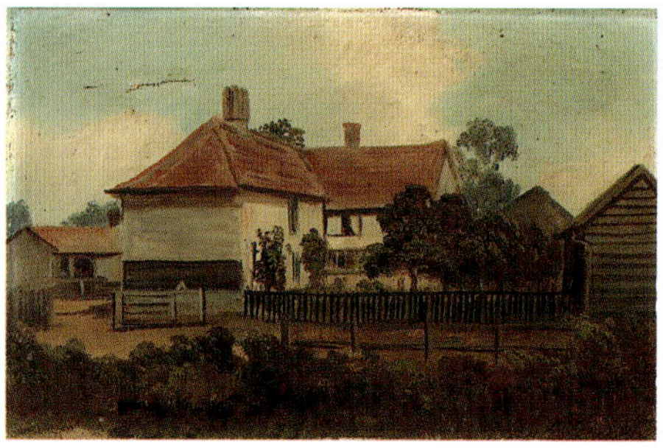

unknown artist
Freeman's Farm
oil on canvas 20 x 30.5
1978.11

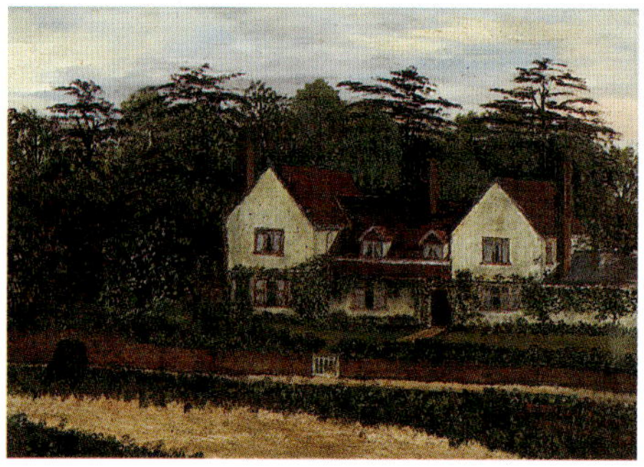

unknown artist
Hospital Farm, Newport
oil on hardboard 24 x 34
31288

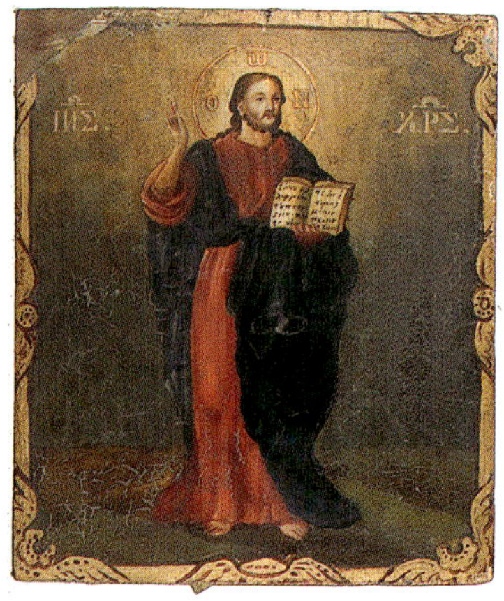

unknown artist
Icon
oil on panel 33 x 26
1894.63

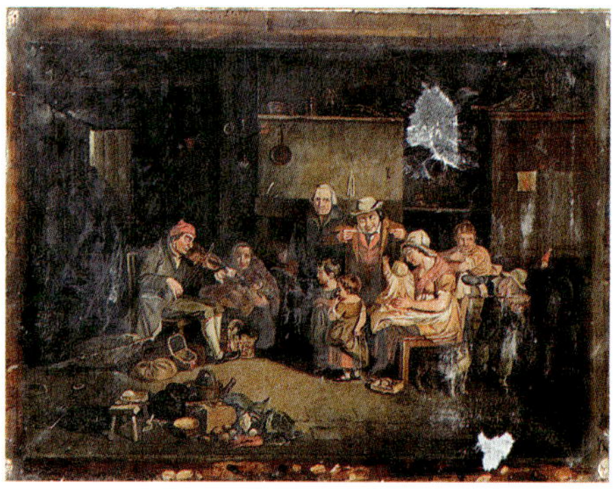

unknown artist
Interior with Figures, a Man Playing the Fiddle
oil on canvas 47.5 x 60.7
31287

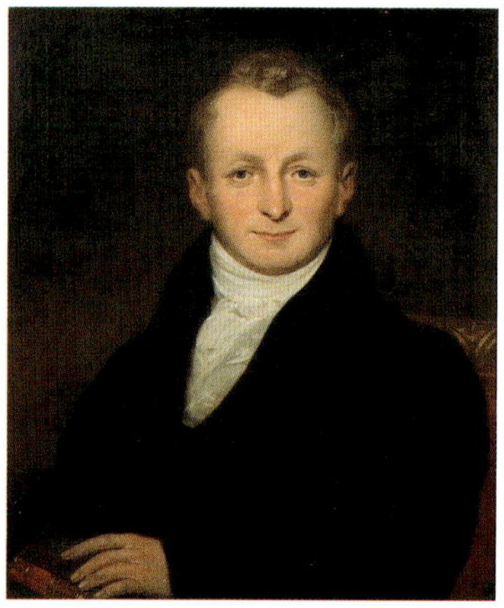

unknown artist
James Humphry of Saffron Walden (1759–1858)
oil on canvas 74.2 x 61.5
1886.22

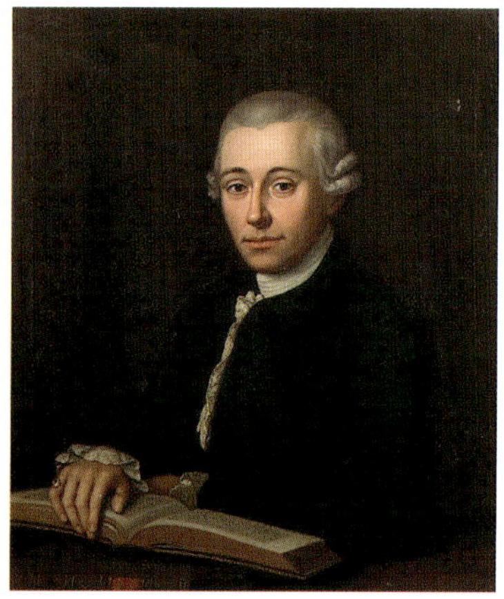

unknown artist
John Wolfe
oil on canvas 74 x 61
1877.10.3

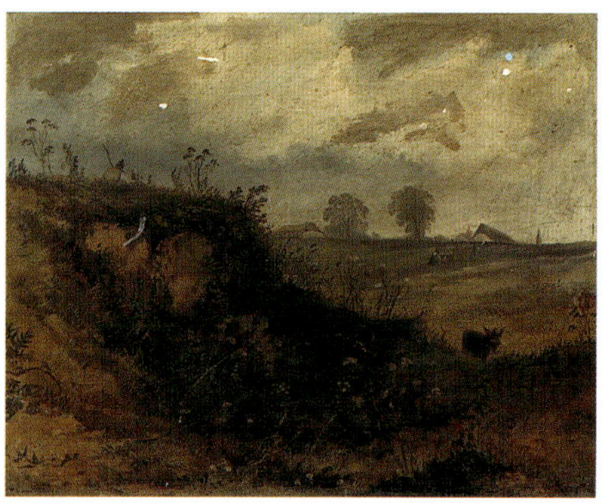

unknown artist
Landscape with a Donkey
oil on canvas 33 x 40
F15

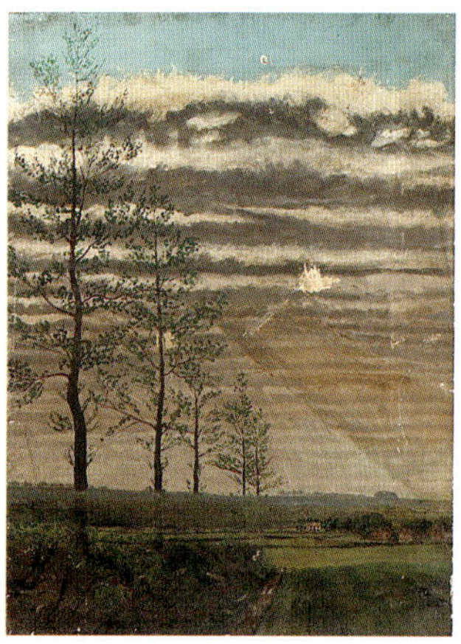

unknown artist
Landscape with Five Trees
oil on canvas 60.8 x 45.5
31285

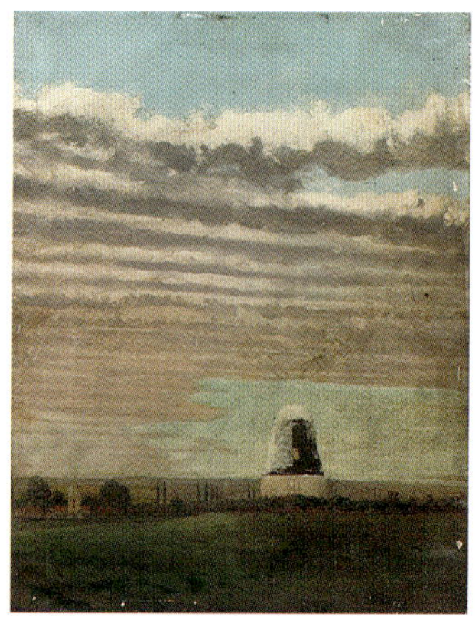

unknown artist
Landscape with Windmill and Village
oil on canvas 60.8 x 45.5
31284

Facing page: Munnings, Alfred James, 1878–1959, *Nobby Gray with the Hunt* (detail), Sir Alfred Munnings Art Museum, (p. 139)

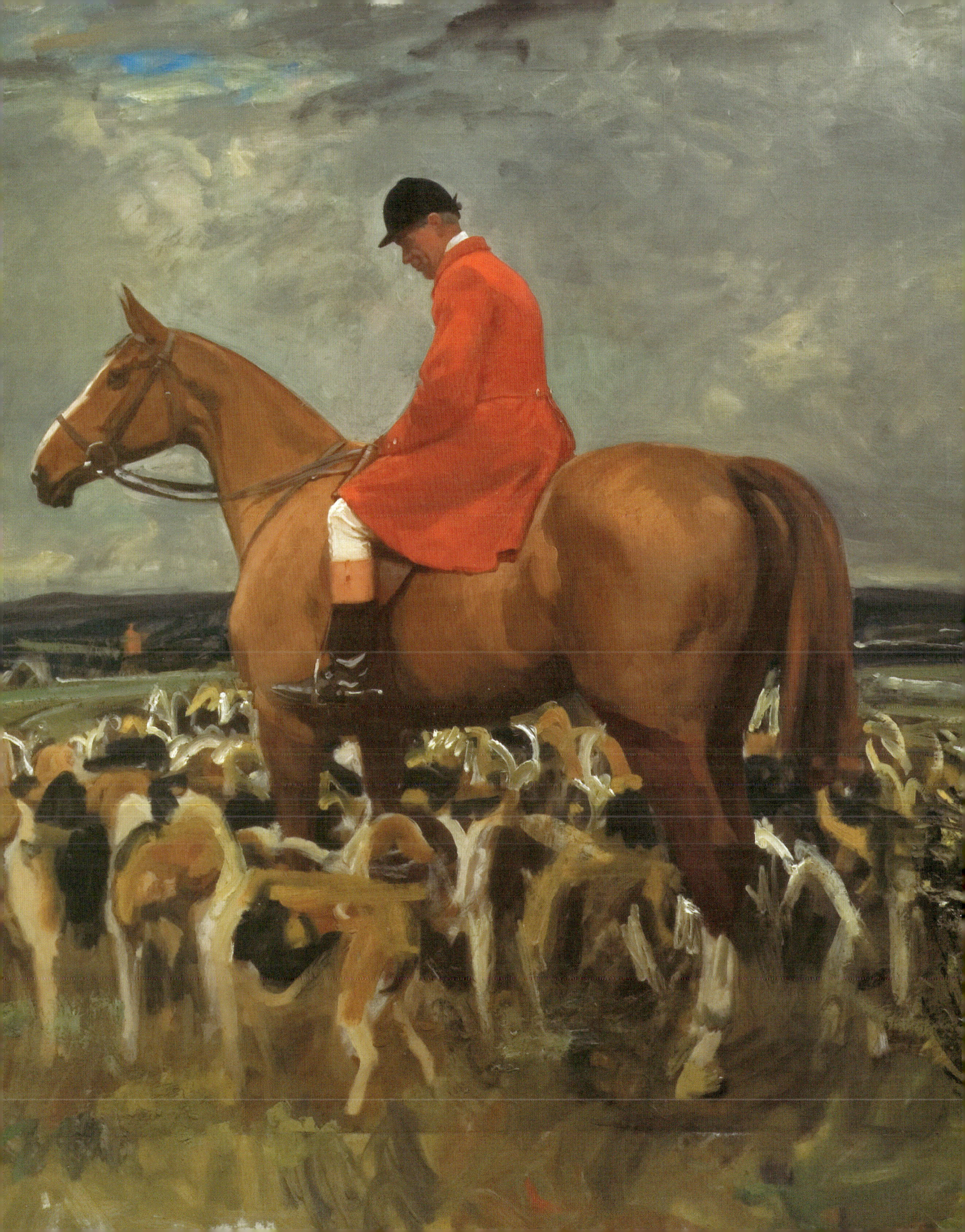

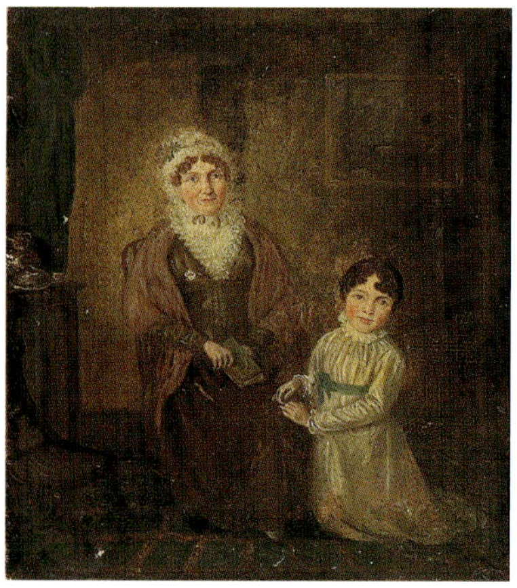

unknown artist
Old Woman and Child
oil on canvas 37 x 32
31276

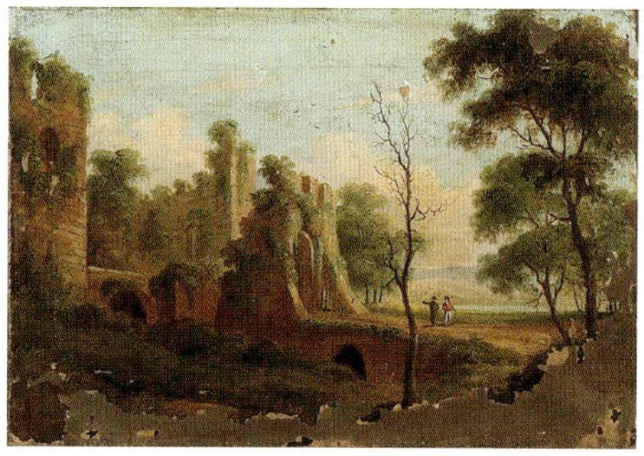

unknown artist
Restormel Castle, Cornwall
oil on canvas 22 x 30
31301

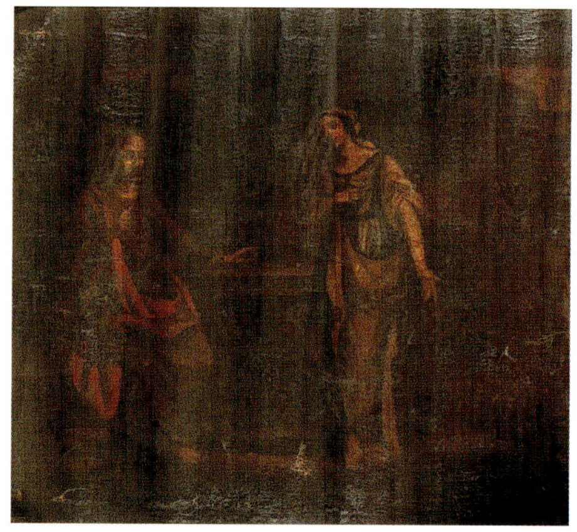

unknown artist
Seated Figure (possibly Christ) with a Woman
oil on canvas 94 x 100 (E)
31433

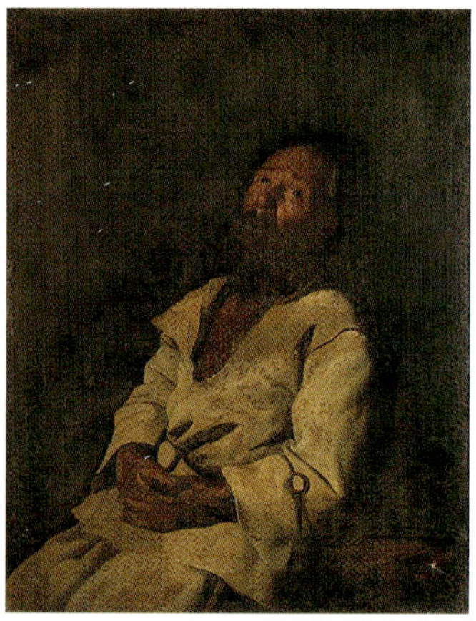

unknown artist
St Peter Repenting
oil on canvas 109 x 86.5
1921.2

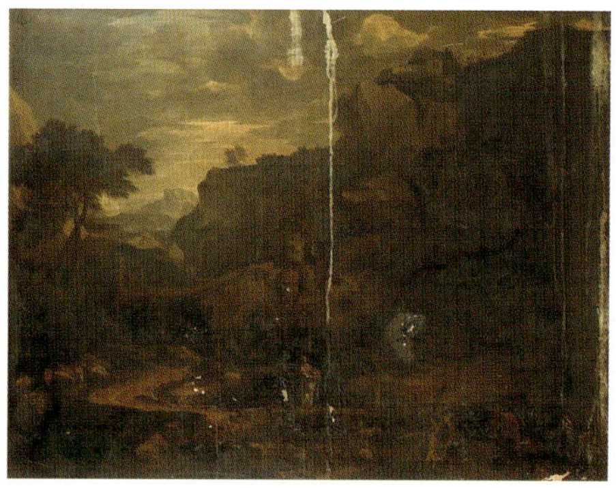

unknown artist
The Flight into Egypt
oil on canvas 87 x 107
1921.17

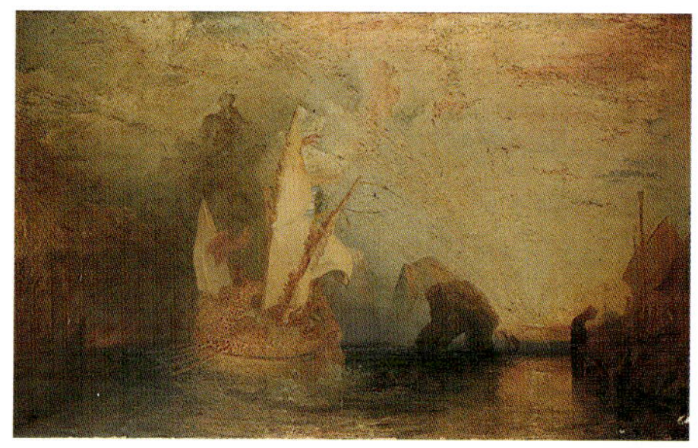

unknown artist
Ulysses and Polyphemus (copy after Joseph Mallord William Turner)
oil on board 69 x 122
1921.15

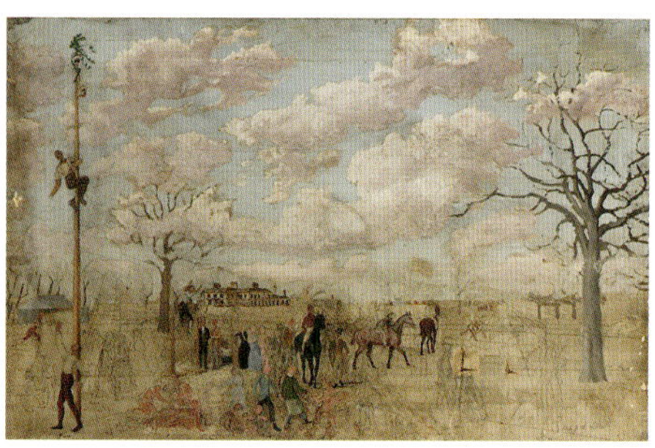

unknown artist
Unfinished Racing Scene
oil on canvas 61 x 91.5
31286

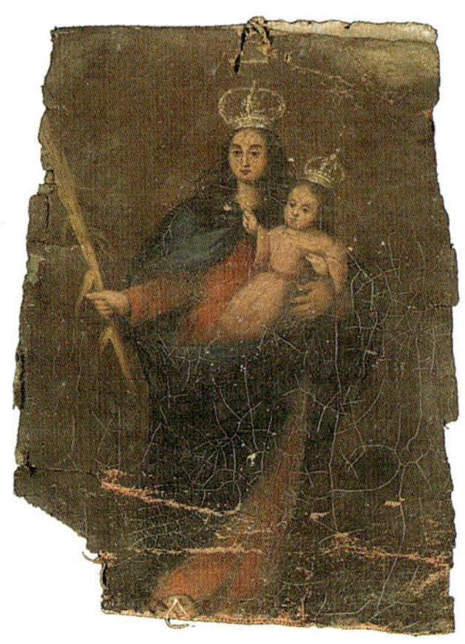

unknown artist
Virgin and Child
oil on canvas 38.5 x 24
31299

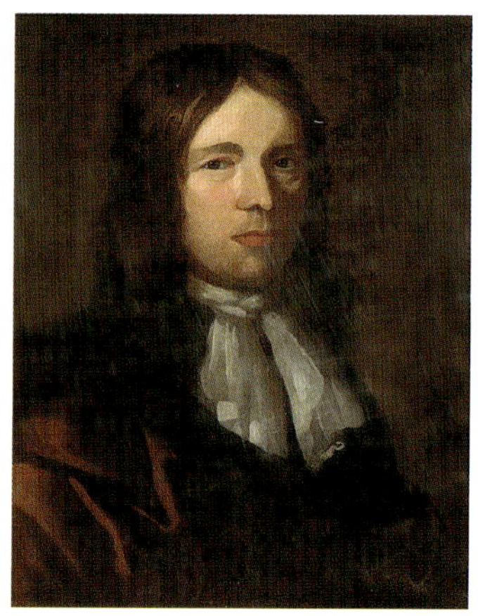

Winstanley, Henry 1644–1703
Self Portrait
oil on panel 52 x 40.5
1880.2

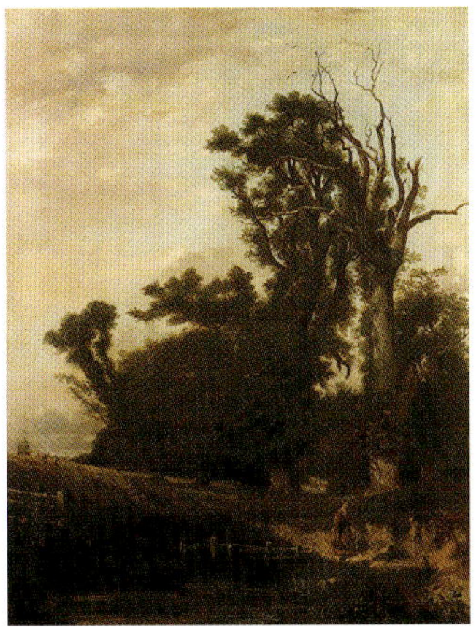

Youngman, John Mallows 1817–1899
The Withered Elm, Audley End Park
oil on canvas 101 x 74
31266

Saffron Walden Town Council

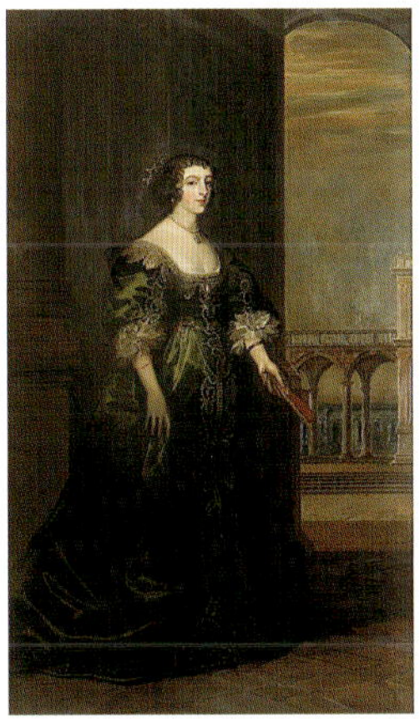

Mytens, Daniel I (after) c.1590–before 1648
Queen Henrietta Maria (1609–1669)
oil on canvas 220 x 134 (E)
001

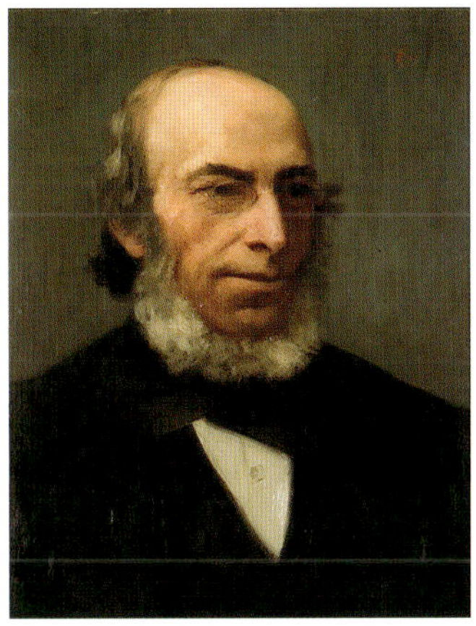

Tuke, Henry Scott 1858–1929
George Stacey Gibson (1818–1883), Mayor (1875–1877) 1880
oil on board 34.2 x 26
007

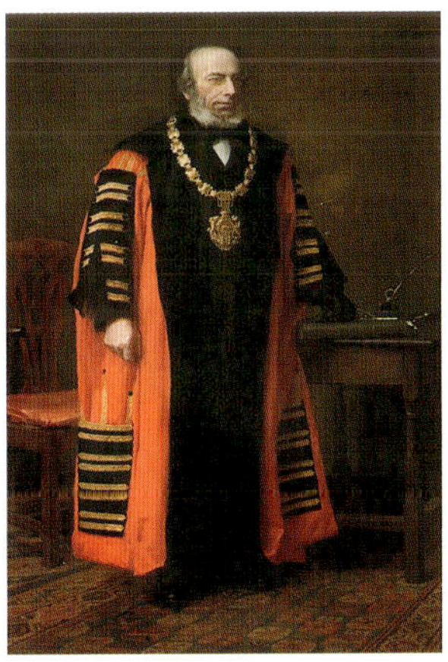

Tuke, Henry Scott 1858–1929
George Stacey Gibson (1818–1883), Mayor (1875–1877) c.1880
oil on canvas 210 x 126 (E)
003

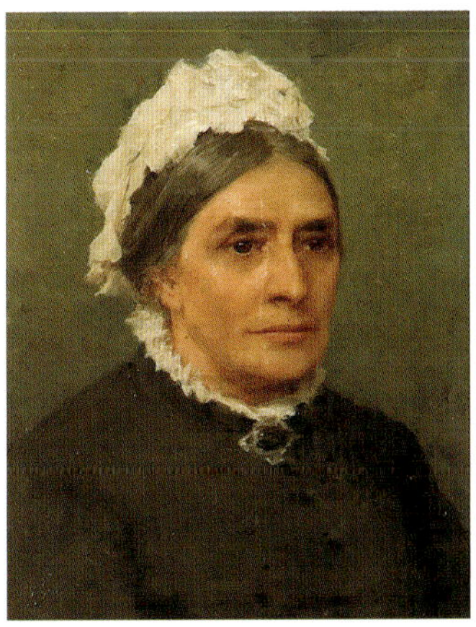

Tuke, Henry Scott (attributed to) 1858–1929
Elizabeth Gibson c.1880
oil on board 35.5 x 26.2
009

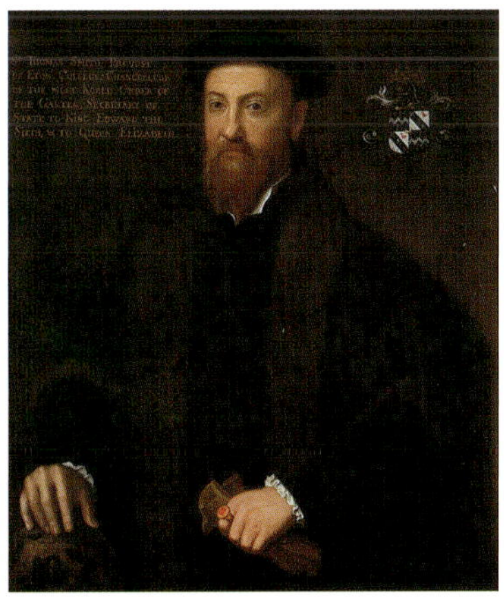

unknown artist
Sir Thomas Smith of Hill Hall, Theydon Mount c.1546
oil on canvas 74.5 x 61.5
008

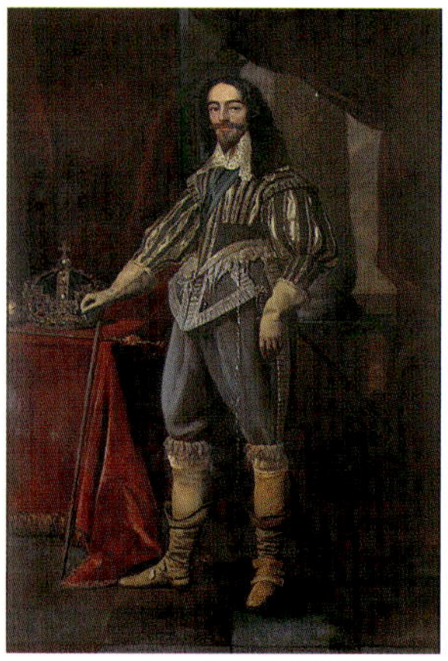

unknown artist 17th C
King Charles I (1600–1649)
oil on canvas 220 x 134 (E)
002

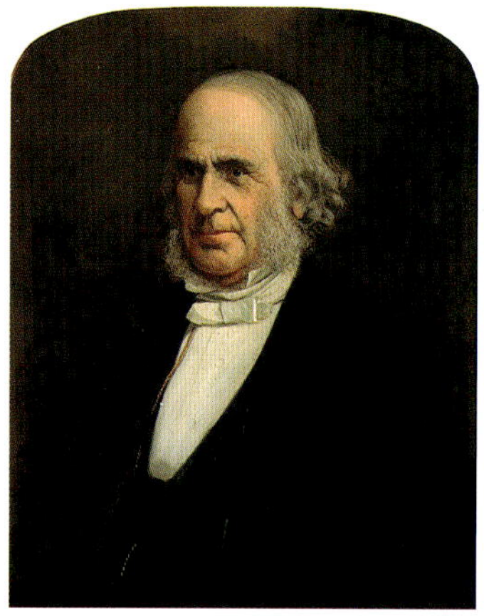

unknown artist 19th C
Joshua Clarke, JP
oil on canvas 60 x 49.5
004

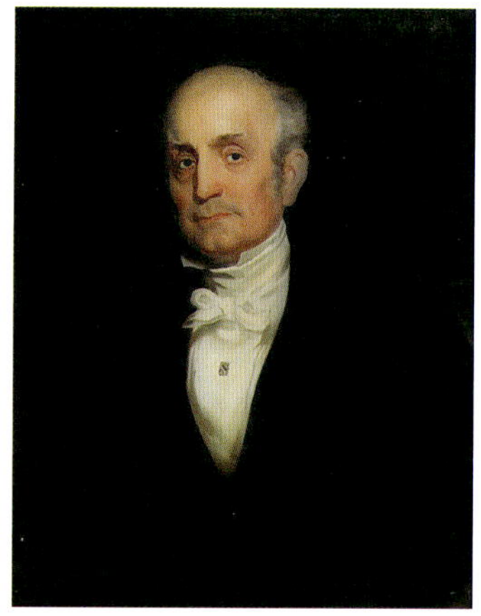

unknown artist 19th C
John Player, JP (1785–1846)
oil on canvas 75.5 x 62
006

Uttlesford District Council

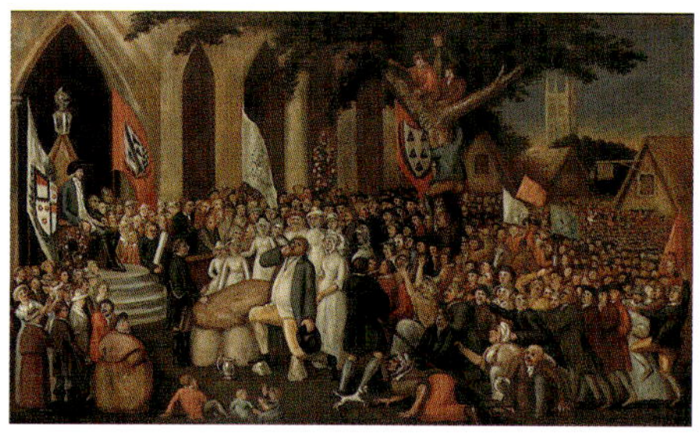

unknown artist
A Flitch Trial c.1800
oil on canvas 75.3 x 123.1
C216

Southend-on-Sea Borough Council

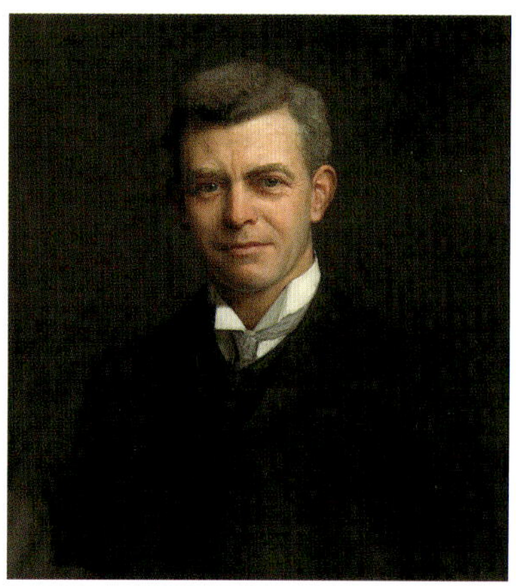

Olivier, Herbert Arnould (attributed to) 1861–1952
Sir Charles Archibald Nicholson, 2nd Bt (1867–1949), Architect and (...) 1909?
oil on canvas 80 x 65 (E)
2

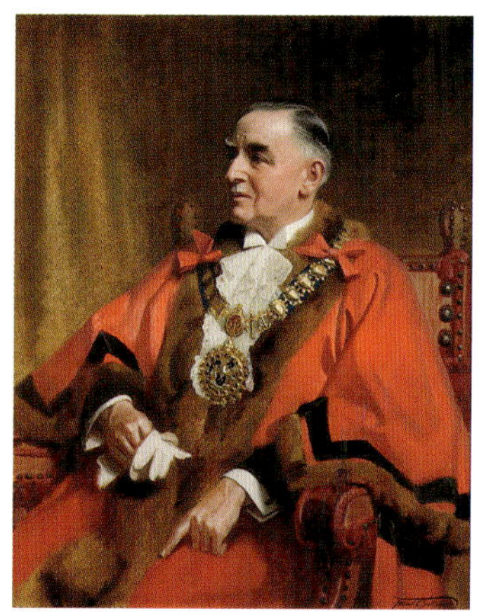

Salisbury, Frank O. 1874–1962
Alderman William Miles, CBE, JP, Mayor of Southend-on-Sea (1922–1924, 1936–1937 & 1939–1945) c.1945
oil on canvas 109 x 84
4

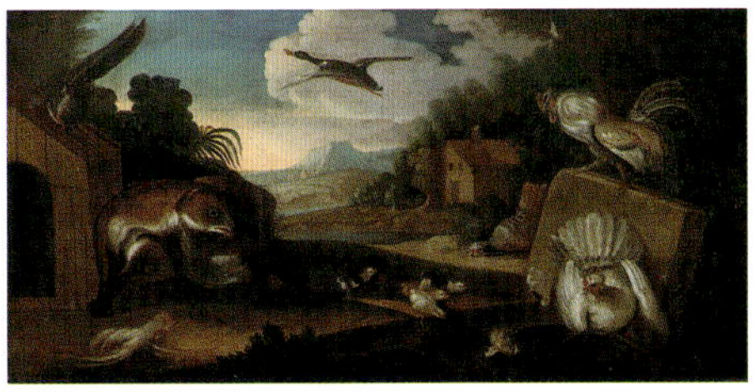

unknown artist 17th C
Fox amongst the Chickens
oil on canvas 66 x 130
1

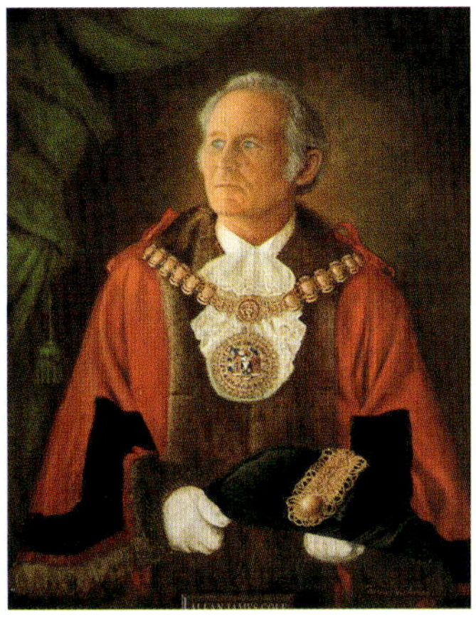

Vickress, Terence
Allan James Cole, Centenary Mayor (1992–1993) 1993
oil on canvas 100 x 75 (E)
3

Southend Pier Museum Foundation

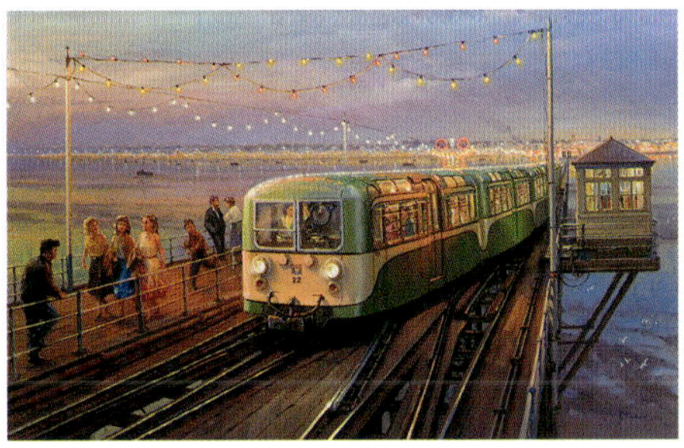

Pinnock, Robin J. b.1954
Twilight Promenade 1995
oil on canvas 49.5 x 79
1

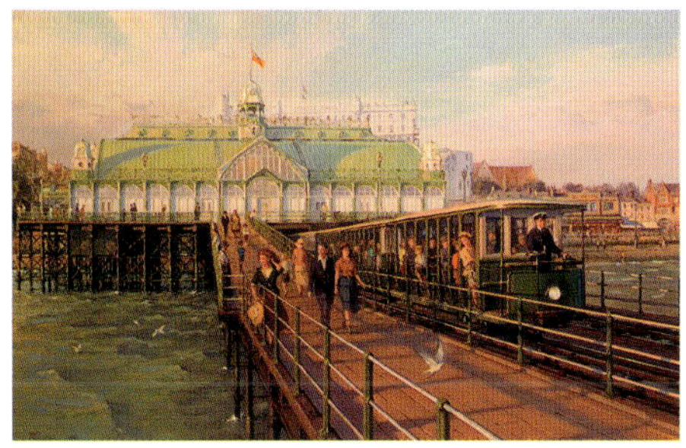

Pinnock, Robin J. b.1954
Pavilion Sunset, Southend Pier, c.1930 1998
oil on canvas 49.5 x 74.5
3

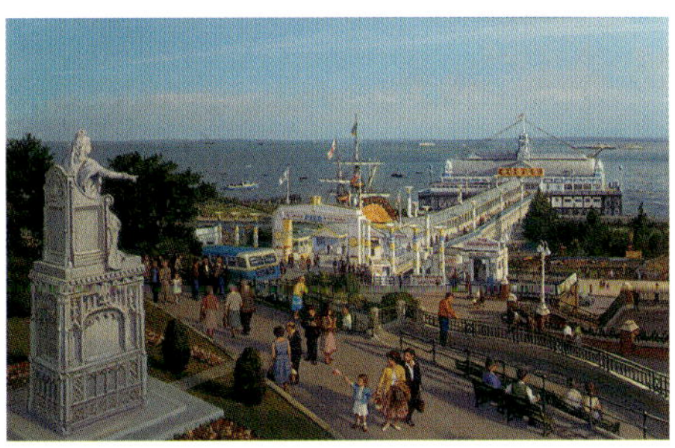

Pinnock, Robin J. b.1954
'Royal View', Southend Pier from Royal Hill, c.1950 2000
oil on canvas 50 x 74
4

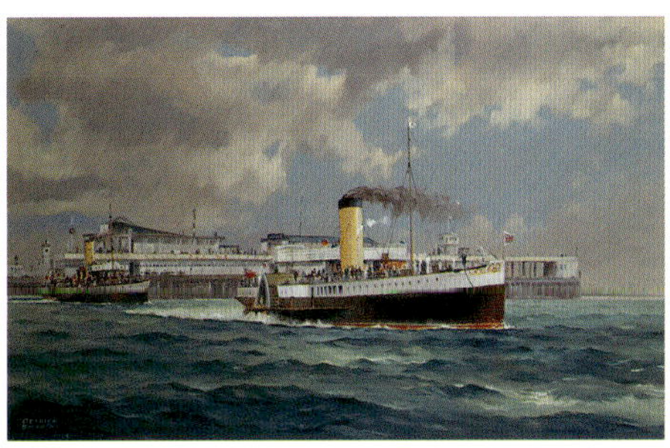

Smoothy, Derrick b.1923
'Golden Eagle' Leaving Southend Pier 1996
oil on canvas 49.5 x 75
2

Southend Museums Service

Southend Museums Service includes the Beecroft Art Gallery, Southend Central Museum, Prittlewell Priory and Southchurch Hall. Prittlewell Priory, a former Cluniac priory now houses a number of works which are too large to be displayed at the Beecroft including Stephen Pearce's *Daniel Robert Scratton of Prittlewell Priory, Essex* and a number of Alan Sorrell's paintings. It is hoped that in the future, after improvements to the building, the other Scratton portraits currently stored at the Beecroft Art Gallery will be displayed again at Prittlewell Priory, the Scratton family's former home.

The story of the Beecroft Art Gallery is that of one man's relentless pursuit of his goal, the establishment of a first class art gallery for the citizens of Southend. The man was Walter G. Beecroft, a bachelor solicitor who had practised in Leigh since 1908. In 1927, the Libraries and Museums Committee of Southend Council discussed a proposal by Beecroft that a municipal art gallery be established in the town. The committee decided not to implement the idea at the time but instead to inaugurate a Municipal Art Collection, the works were to be hung at the Central Library (now Southend Central Museum). Beecroft donated the first two paintings.

The idea of an art gallery for the town was not again given serious consideration by the council until 1947 when Beecroft offered to provide and endow a building to be used as an art gallery and cultural centre. Unfortunately, despite the general euphoria, there was no chance in those post war years, of obtaining a building licence and the scheme had to be shelved. Beecroft's response was to form the Friends of the Beecroft Art Gallery in May 1948, with an annual subscription of 10s 6d and the motto 'Forever Art Endureth'. The Friends, under the stewardship of Walter Beecroft, were to become a major driving force for the establishment of an art gallery in the town.

In July 1951, Beecroft announced that the Corporation Trustees had acquired the Warwick Hotel, which would be converted into a temporary art gallery 'until such time as a permanent gallery would be erected in Chalkwell Park'. The Warwick Hotel, with 20 bedrooms, four reception rooms and a basement kitchen, was refurbished by the Trustees (with lighting by E. K. Cole), opening as the Beecroft Art Gallery on 9th October 1953. The works of art on show when the Gallery opened were primarily those given by Beecroft, augmented by works purchased from the Art Purchase Fund. This fund started with a £1,000 donation by Beecroft, matched by a pledge by the Corporation to give £500 a year until the gallery was built. Records seem to show that the collection was somewhat fluid, paintings being traded for better examples when opportunities arose.

As it stands today, the Beecroft's collection is divided into three distinct sections: The Beecroft Collection, the Municipal Collection and the Thorpe-Smith Collection. The Beecroft Collection was collected partly by Walter Beecroft himself, and later with the assistance of the Friends of the Beecroft Art Gallery. It consists of 157 works, mainly oils, among the most important of which is the fine collection of Dutch and Flemish seascapes, landscapes, still lifes and portraits. These include a village snow scene by Molenaer and a small, minutely executed, oil on copper picture of *Tobias and the Angel* by Cornelius van Poelenburgh, a Dutch Italianate artist of the seventeenth century. Significant French works include a large river landscape by Barbizon school artist Henri Harpignies and a tranquil river scene by Trouillebert, an important contemporary of Corot. Amongst the early Italian pictures are a large and elaborately framed *Virgin and Child* attributed to sixteenth century Venetian School artist Francesco Bissolo, and a gilt cross depicting Christ and the Four Evangelists.

The Municipal Collection consists of several hundred pictures acquired with the Art Purchase Fund, which was provided by Southend Council until 1980 and mainly consists of twentieth century works, many of them purchased from Royal Academy summer exhibitions. The very first purchase, made in 1953, was the John Constable oil sketch *On the Stour*, an early work dated 1804 and with an impeccable provenance which can be traced back to the daughter of the artist, Isabel Constable. This small picture remains a firm favourite with gallery visitors and was, in retrospect, an extremely wise investment for the gallery's collections. Another wonderful work is the Frank Brangwyn picture *The Lower Reaches of the Thames* of 1887, an atmospheric depiction of Thames boatmen at work on the river, whilst a major donation to the collection in 1965 came from the Reverend Jarvis of Norwich who gave three stunning Edward Seago paintings, the likes of which the gallery could never have afforded to buy with its own funds.

The Municipal collection also includes in its ranks several works by important mid-twentieth century, Essex artists including John Aldridge and Edward Bawden, both of the Great Bardfield Group, and John Nash who had settled near Colchester after the War.

The Thorpe-Smith Collection consists of paintings, prints and drawings of the Southend area, the core of which was bequeathed by Sydney Thorpe-Smith, a resident of Cliff Town Parade, Southend. Thorpe-Smith himself collected around 100 of these works, some of the finest of which are the oils depicting the Thames estuary and its shipping by Victorian artists. These include Norwich School artist Henry Bright who painted the large oil of Hadleigh Castle, no doubt inspired by Constable's famous picture of the same subject. Also, George Shalders whose exquisite summer sunset scene of Hadleigh is a great favourite, and William Anderson whose depiction of working life on the Thames is one of the earliest in the collection dating to 1808. Some of the more obscure artists' works hold a special interest too: C. C. Coventry's view of Royal Terrace dated 1807 is the earliest oil of Southend itself and was painted before the town's famous pier was built. It depicts pleasure boats being rowed and sailed in the area where the pier would be built some decades later.

As well as being the largest in Essex, the Beecroft Art Gallery's collections are unique and unusual in their breadth. At the same time as being a historical record of the Thames estuary and Southend area, the works in the collection demonstrate the taste and collecting capabilities of the individuals who first amassed them, Walter Beecroft and Sydney Thorpe-Smith, both of whom, especially Walter Beecroft, collected fairly indiscriminately and made the occasional poor as well as excellent purchase. It is hoped that in the future, the collections may be housed in a new building with improved facilities and which can display more of the works at any one time, better exploiting the incredible fruits of 50 years of collecting.

Clare Hunt, Keeper of Art

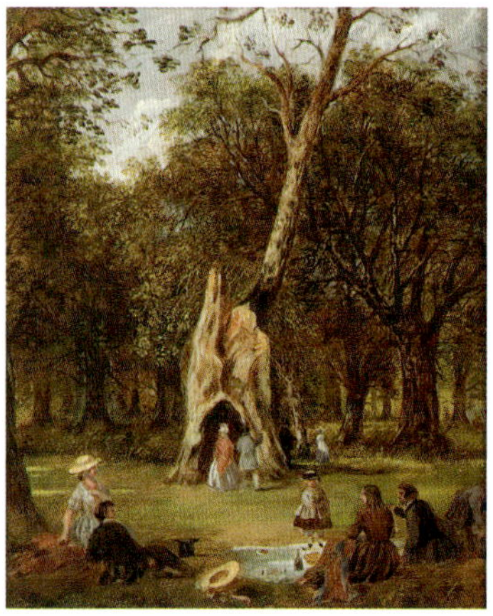

Adams, Caroline 1792–1886
Woodland Picnic Scene
oil on canvas 40.5 x 33 (E)
SOUAG.S442

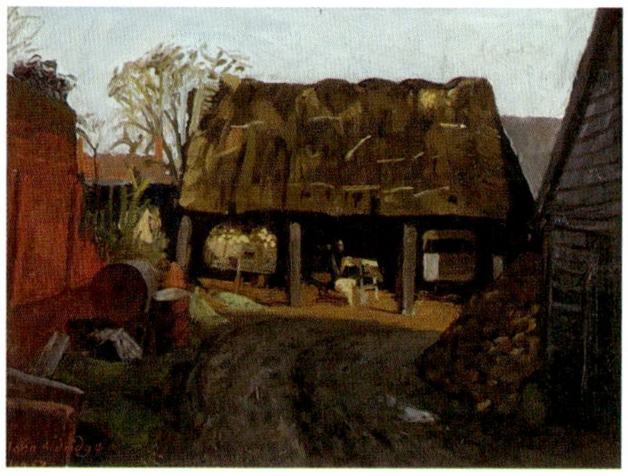

Aldridge, John Arthur Malcolm 1905–1983
The Cart Shed 1957
oil on board 27 x 35.5 (E)
SOUAG.B134

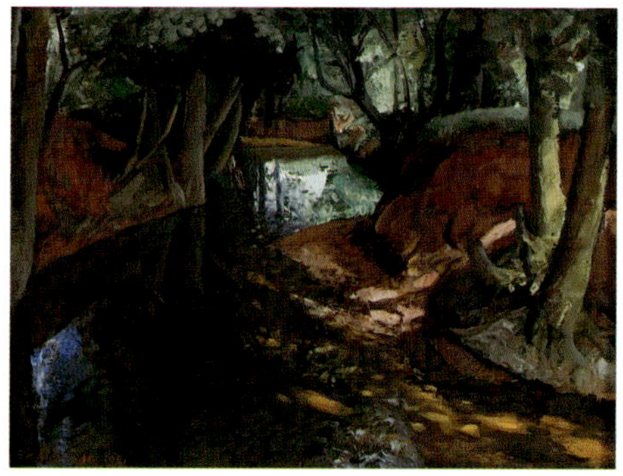

Aldridge, John Arthur Malcolm 1905–1983
River Pant, Great Bardfield 1961
oil on panel 27 x 36 (E)
SOUAG.B135

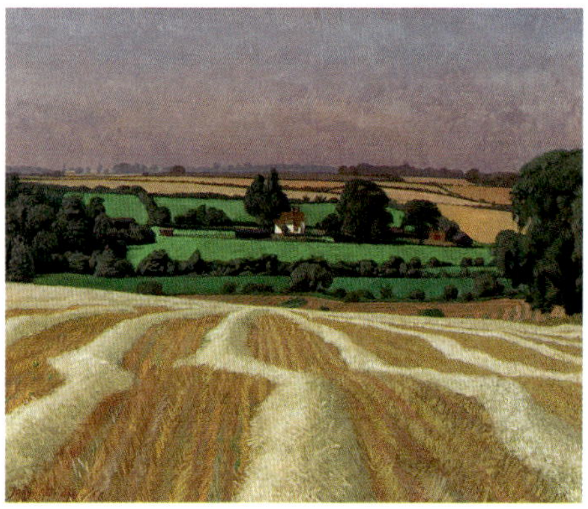

Aldridge, John Arthur Malcolm 1905–1983
Stubble Field, Thaxted 1968
oil on canvas 51 x 61 (E)
SOUAG.S112

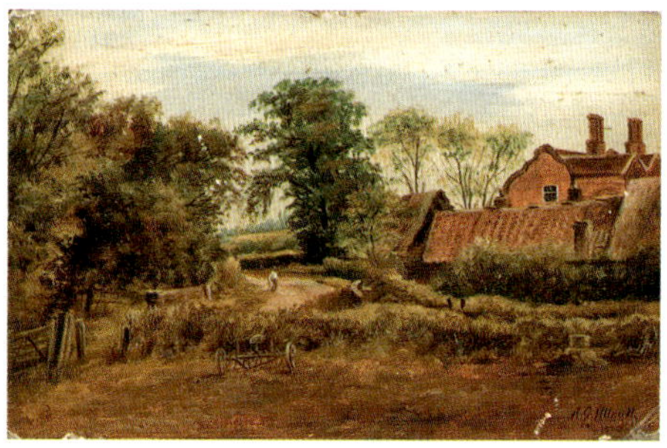

Allnutt, H. G. active 1920–1932
Cockethurst Farm, Eastwoodbury Lane 1920
oil on board 15 x 23 (E)
SOUAG.TS242

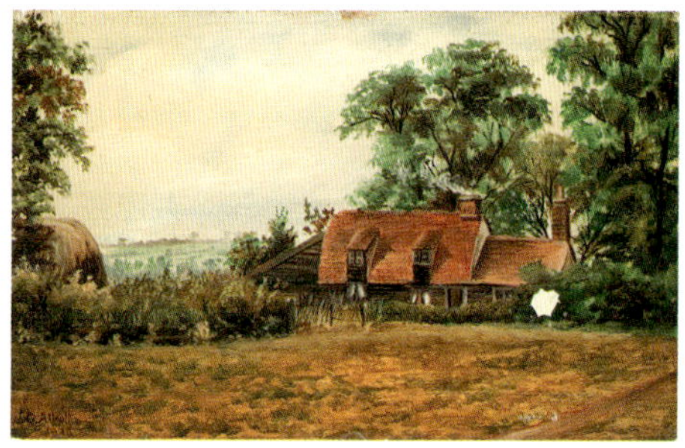

Allnutt, H. G. active 1920–1932
Eastwood Lane, Eastwood 1920
oil on board 15 x 23 (E)
SOUAG.TS716

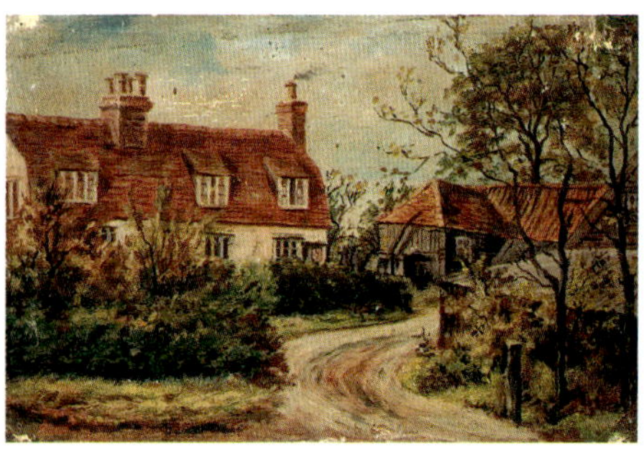

Allnutt, H. G. active 1920–1932
Eastwoodbury Lane, Eastwood 1920
oil on board 15 x 23 (E)
SOUAG.TS243

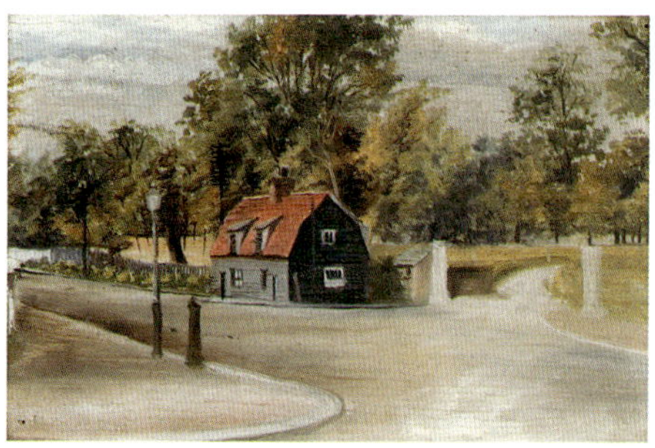

Allnutt, H. G. active 1920–1932
Eastwood 1920s
oil on board 12.5 x 20.5 (E)
SOUAG.TS718

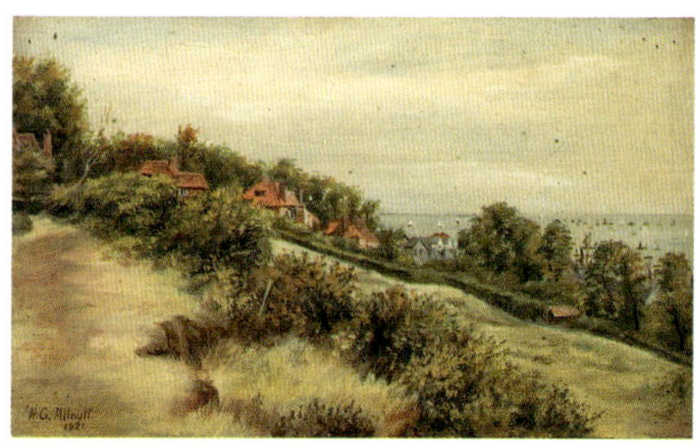

Allnutt, H. G. active 1920–1932
Billet Lane, Leigh, from Belton Hills 1921
oil on board 15 x 20.5 (E)
SOUAG.TS237

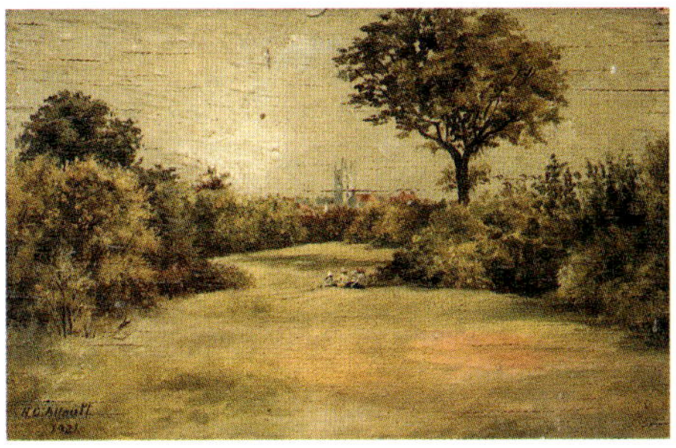

Allnutt, H. G. active 1920–1932
Prittlewell from the North-West 1921
oil on board 14.5 x 21.5 (E)
SOUAG.TS239

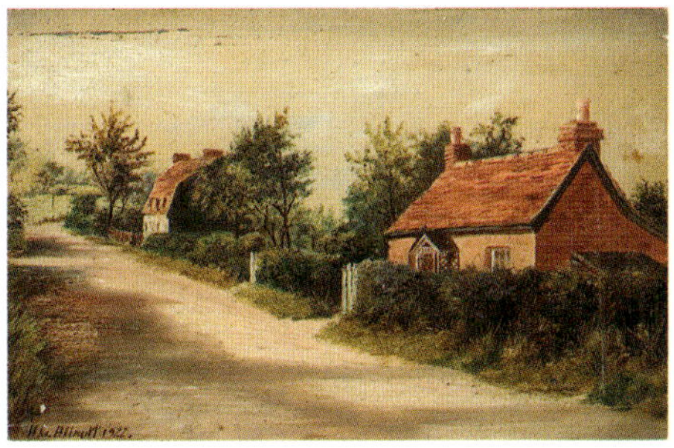

Allnutt, H. G. active 1920–1932
Hart Road, Thundersley 1922
oil on board 15 x 23 (E)
SOUAG.TS245

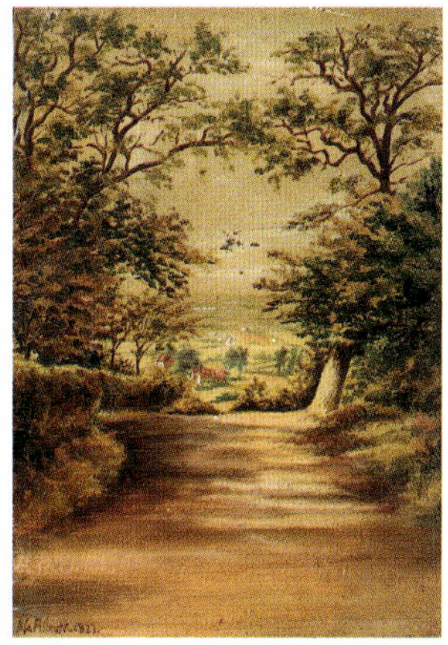

Allnutt, H. G. active 1920–1932
Landscape 1923
oil on board 23 x 15 (E)
SOUAG.TS248

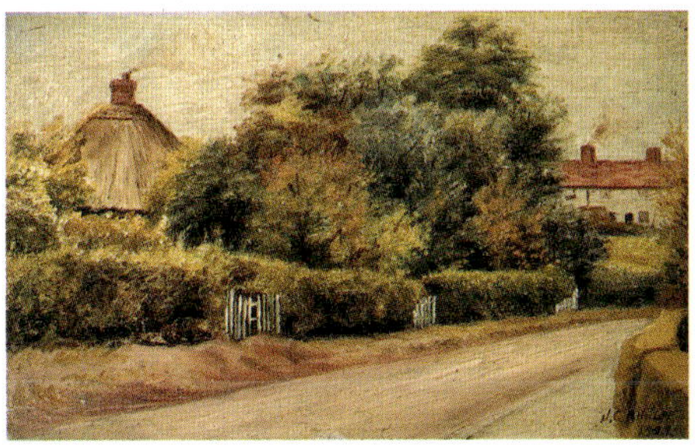

Allnutt, H. G. active 1920–1932
Old Dutch Cottage, Rayleigh 1923
oil on board 12.5 x 20.5 (E)
SOUAG.TS241

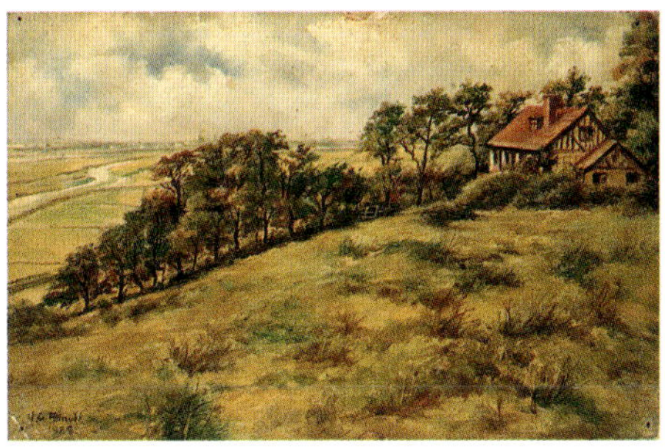

Allnutt, H. G. active 1920–1932
From Belton Hills Looking West 1928
oil on board 15 x 23 (E)
SOUAG.TS238

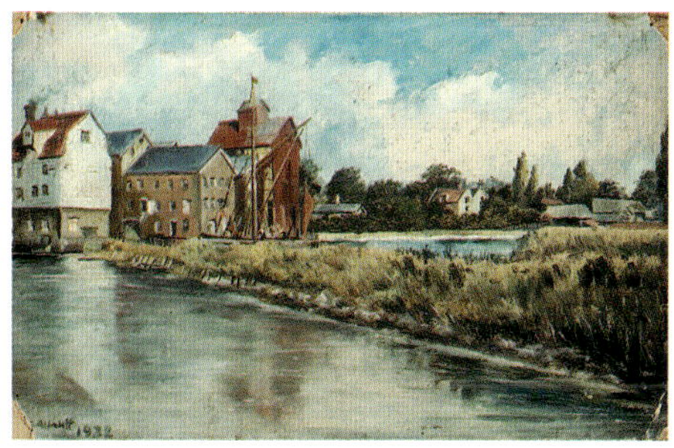

Allnutt, H. G. active 1920–1932
Stambridge Mills 1932
oil on board 15 x 23 (E)
SOUAG.TS240

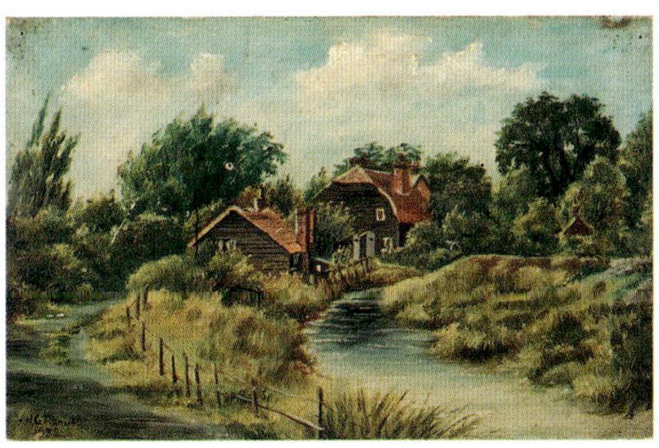

Allnutt, H. G. active 1920–1932
Watts Lane, Rochford 1932
oil on board 15 x 23 (E)
SOUAG.TS717

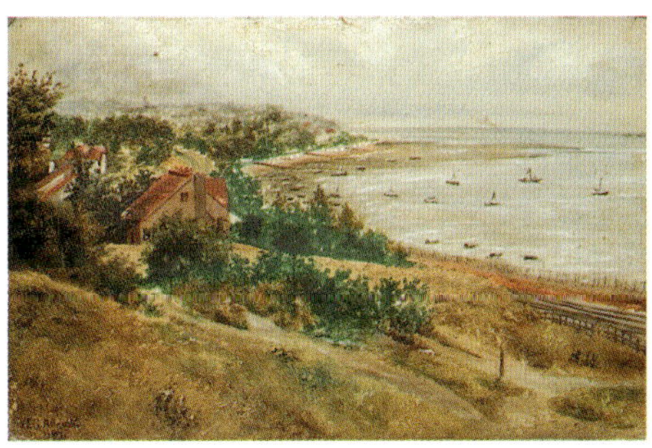

Allnutt, H. G. active 1920–1932
Chalkwell Bay from Belton Hills, Leigh
oil on board 15 x 23 (E)
SOUAG.TS236

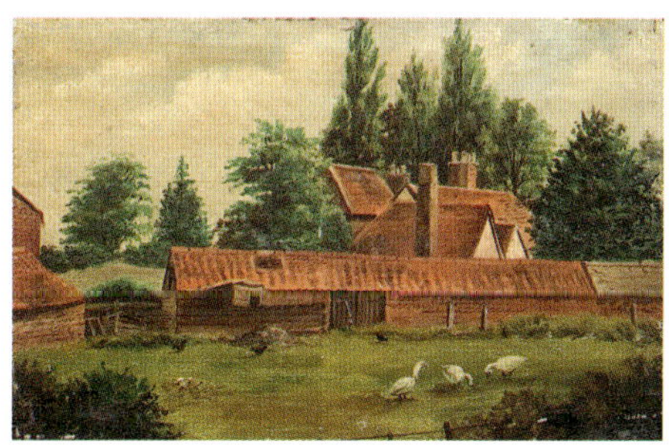

Allnutt, H. G. active 1920–1932
Farm Buildings
oil on board 14 x 20 (E)
SOUAG.TS247

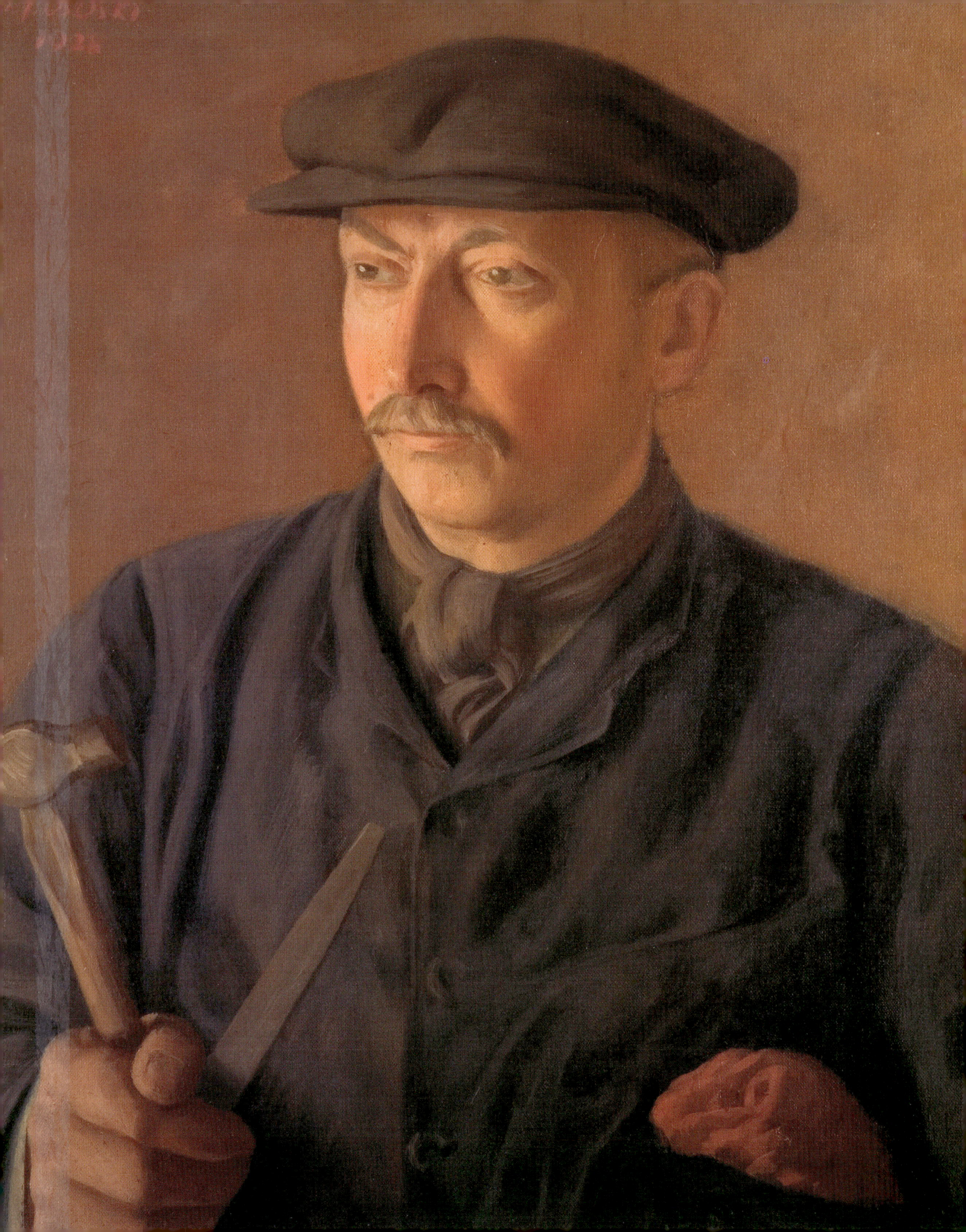

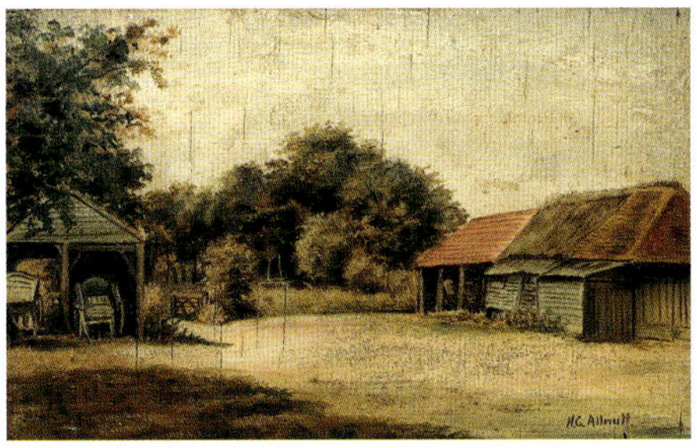

Allnutt, H. G. active 1920–1932
Farm Buildings
oil on board 13 x 20.5 (E)
SOUAG.TS249

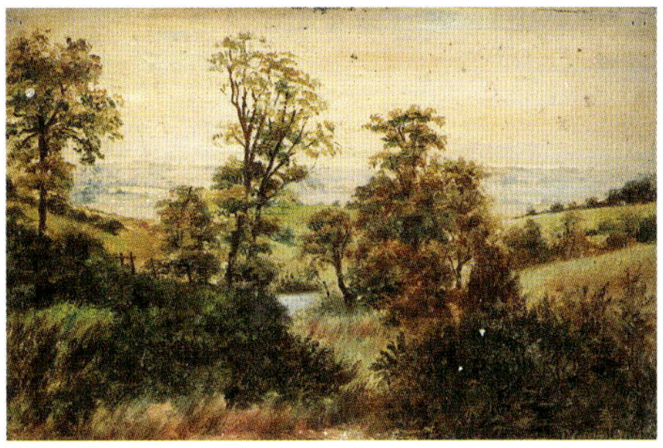

Allnutt, H. G. active 1920–1932
Landscape
oil on board 15 x 23 (E)
SOUAG.TS246

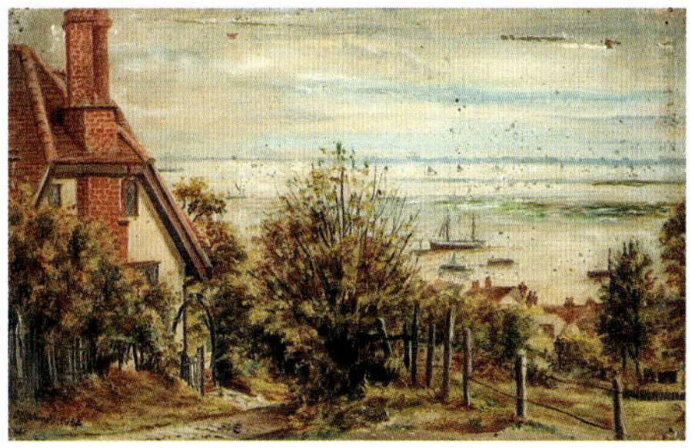

Allnutt, H. G. active 1920–1932
Looking down Billet Lane, Leigh
oil on board 15 x 23 (E)
SOUAG.TS244

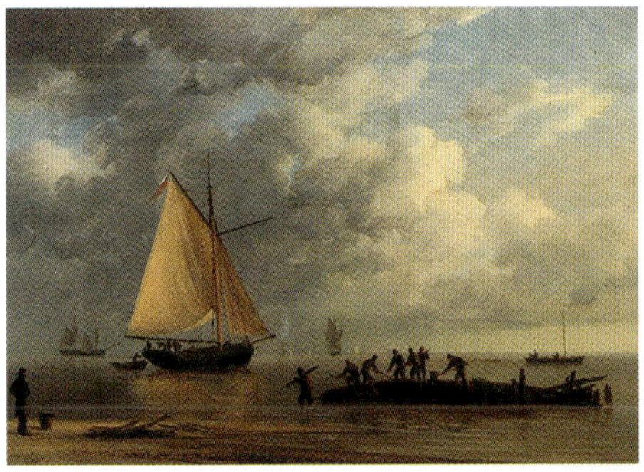

Anderson, William 1757–1837
View at the Mouth of the Thames 1808
oil on canvas 41.5 x 52 (E)
SOUAG.TS1

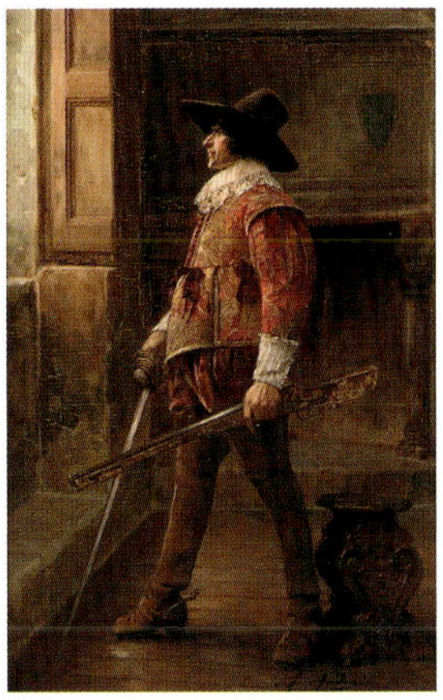

Andreis, Alex de 1871–1939
The Cavalier
oil on panel 69 x 42.5 (E)
SOUAG.S63

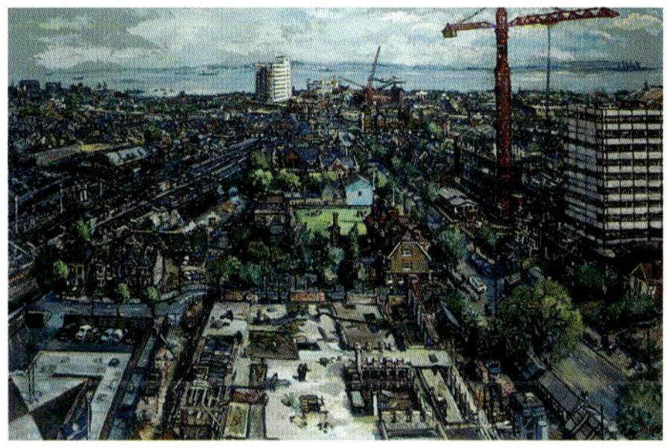

Appleton, Sheila b.1931
Jubilee Rebuilding, Southend Looking South as Seen from Floor 13 of the Civic Centre 1964
oil on board 101 x 151.5 (E)
SOUAG.TS220

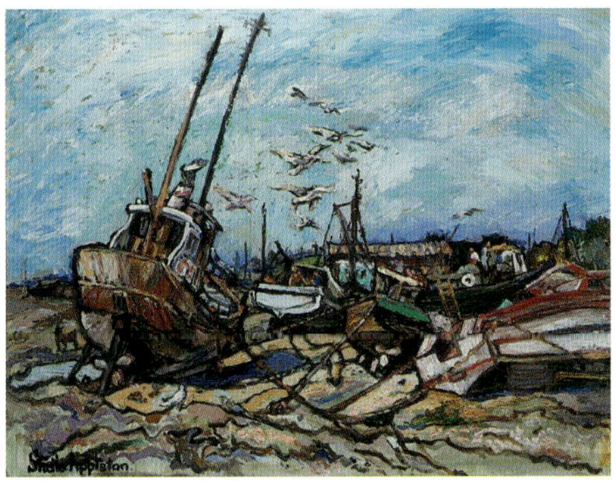

Appleton, Sheila b.1931
Boats at Leigh 1982
oil on canvas 60.5 x 75
SOUAG.TS844

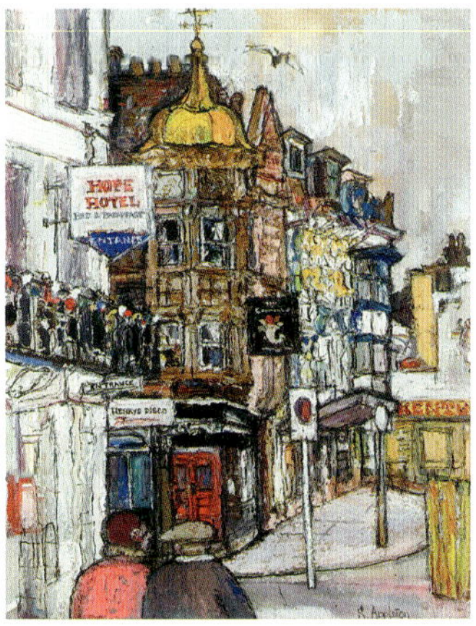

Appleton, Sheila b.1931
Seafront, Southend
oil & ink on canvas 45 x 34 (E)
SOUAG.S542

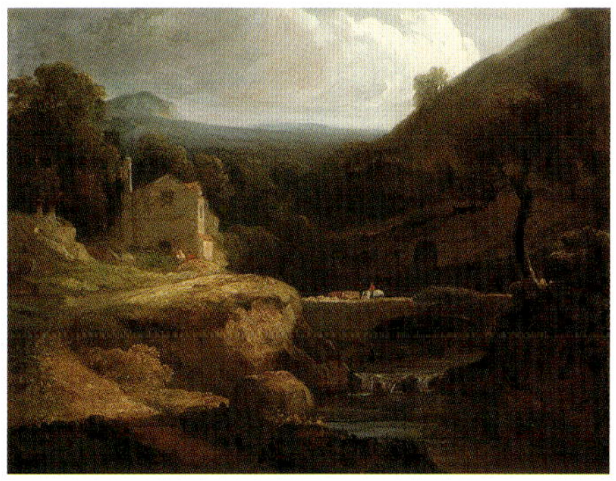

Arnald, George 1763–1841
Greta Bridge, Rokeby, Durham 1818
oil on canvas 43 x 55 (E)
SOUAG.B8

Facing page: Ososki, Gerald Judah, 1903–1981, *A. Franklin (Old Iron Portrait Collection)* (detail), 1928, Braintree District Museum, (p. 15)

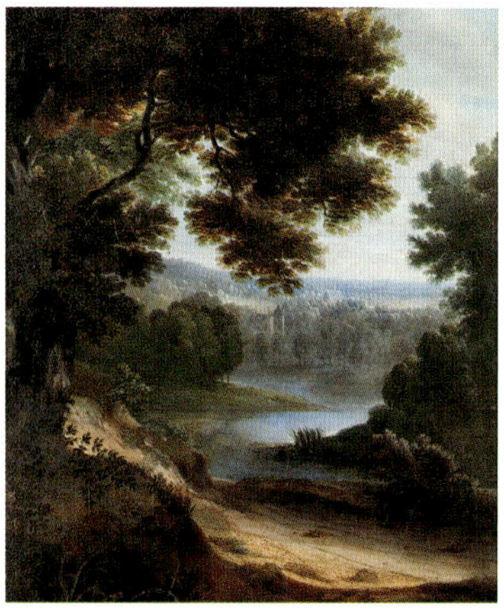

Arthois, Jacques d' 1613–1686
Flemish Landscape
oil on canvas 62.5 x 53.5 (E)
SOUAG.B32

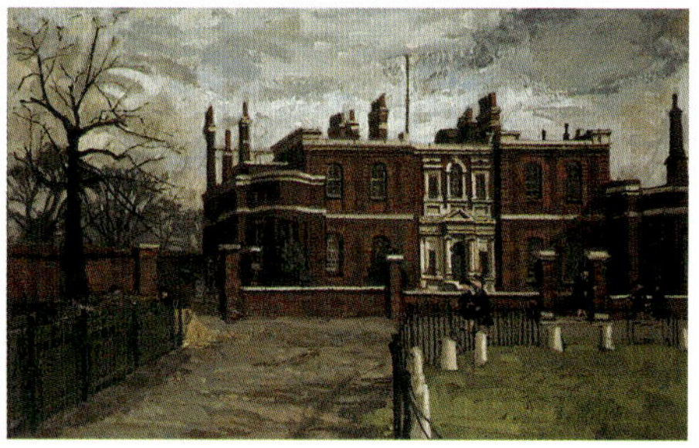

Ashby, Derek b.1926
Greenwich Park c.1956
oil on hardboard 50 x 76
SOUAG.B74

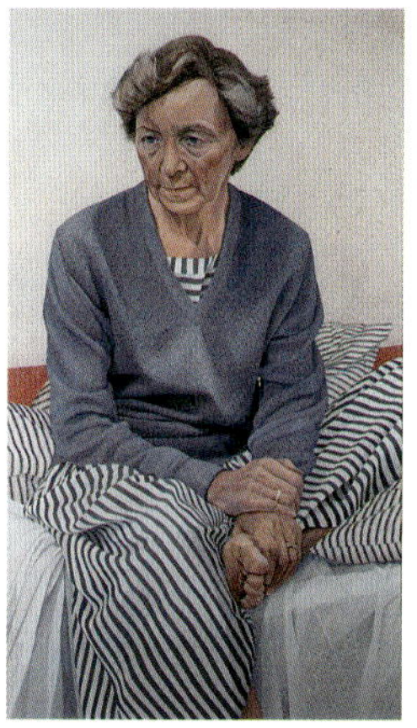

Baldwin, Warren b.1956
Large Portrait c.1985
acrylic on paper 105.5 x 58.5 (E)
SOUAG.S355

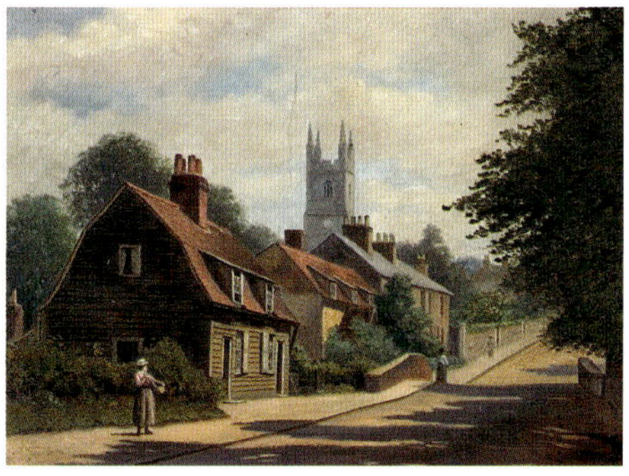

Bamford, Alfred Bennett 1857–1939
Prittlewell 1919
oil on canvas 23 x 30.5 (E)
SOUAG.TS224

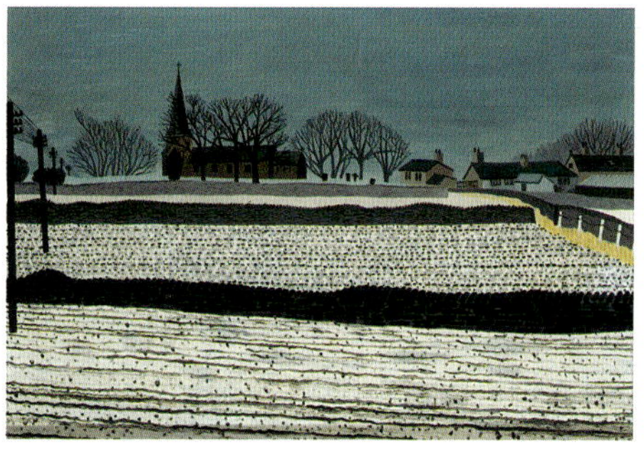

Barden, Kenneth 1924–1988
Farnley Tyas, West Yorkshire c.1972
oil on board 33 x 45.5 (E)
SOUAG.S110

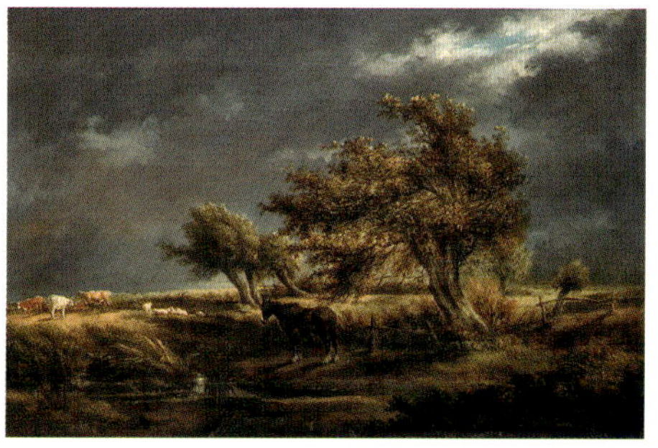

Barker, Thomas 1769–1847
Stormy Landscape
oil on canvas 36 x 50 (E)
SOUAG.B9

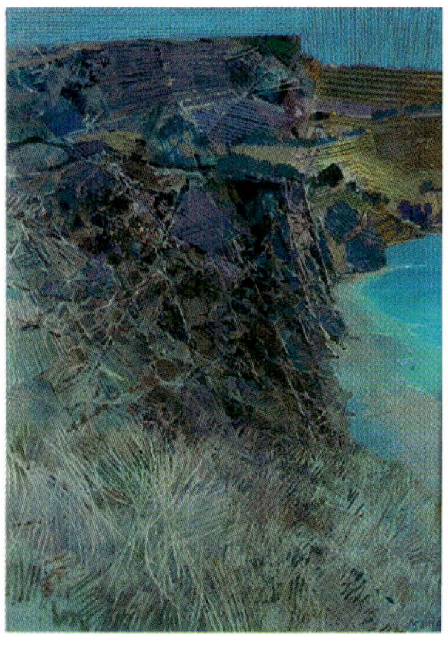

Barratt, Krome 1924–1990
West Country
oil on board 122 x 86
SOUAG.S380

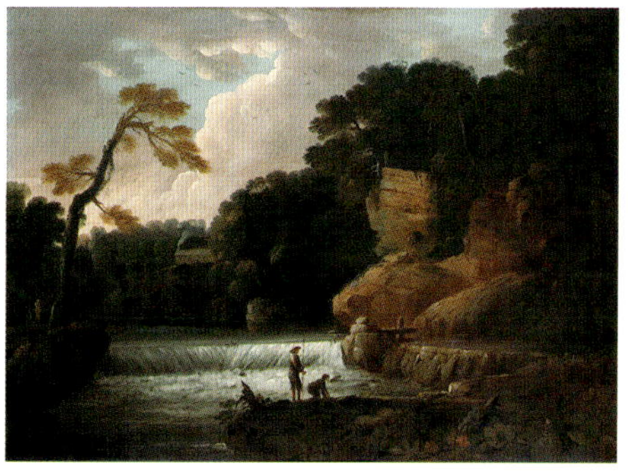

Barret, George 1728/1732–1784
Powerscourt Falls
oil on canvas 71 x 95 (E)
SOUAG.B5

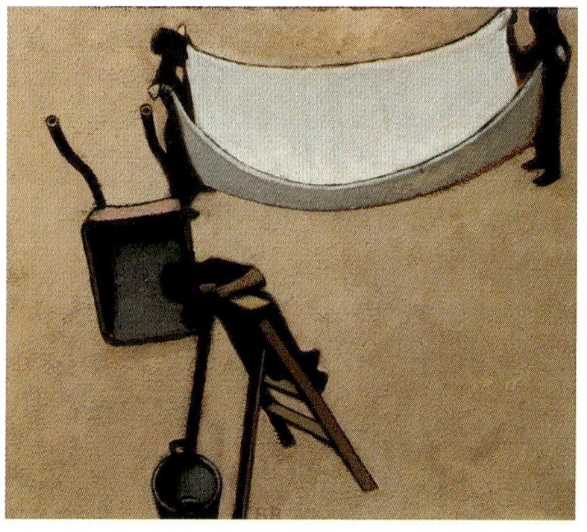

Barrett, Roderic 1920–2000
Silences II 1967
oil on board 30.5 x 35.5 (E)
SOUAG.S161

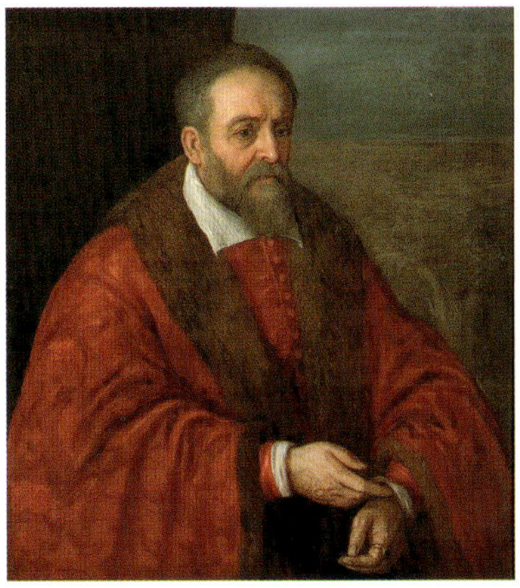

Bassano family active 16th–17th C
Portrait of a Nobleman (said to be Silva Capello) 1572?
oil on canvas 91 x 79 (E)
SOUAG.B64

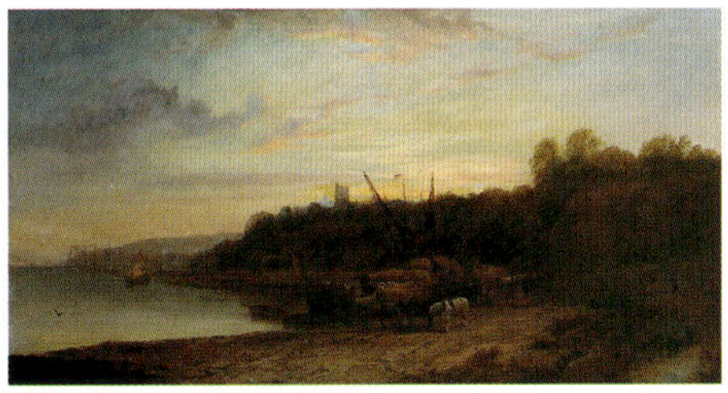

Bates, W. E. 1812–1872
View of Leigh 1861
oil on canvas 53.5 x 100 (E)
SOUAG.TS313

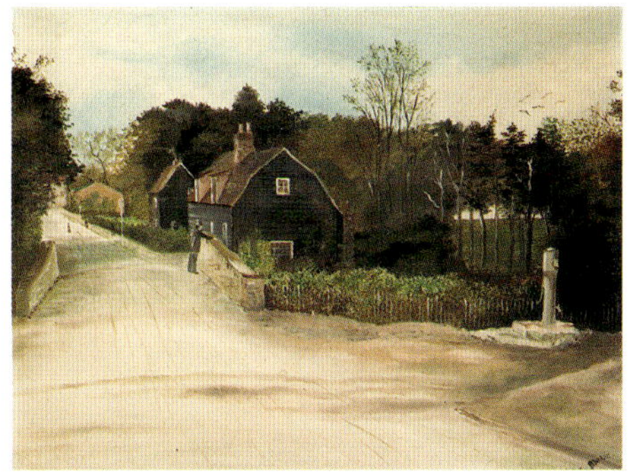

Bayliss, F.
Prittlewell Bridge c.1900
oil on board 55 x 70 (E)
SOUAG.TS494

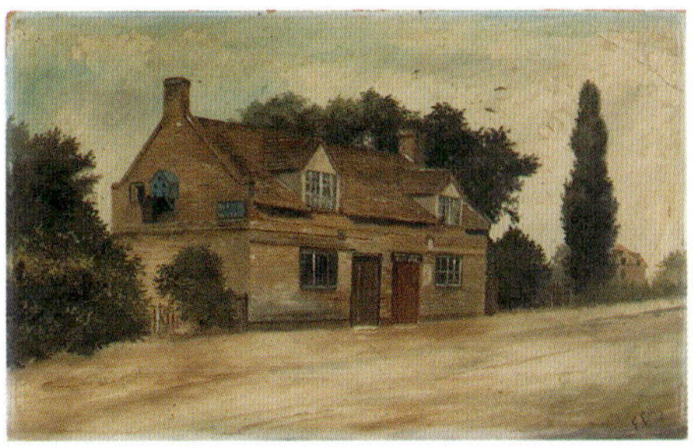

Bayliss, F.
Southchurch Post Office c.1900
oil on board 30.5 x 48 (E)
SOUAG.TS498

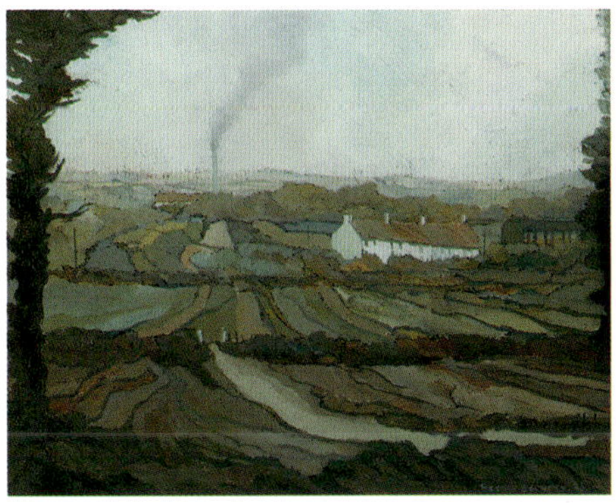

Bennett, Terence b.1935
Landscape with Cottages, Clayworth, Nottinghamshire c.1985
oil on canvas 29 x 37 (E)
SOUAG.S356

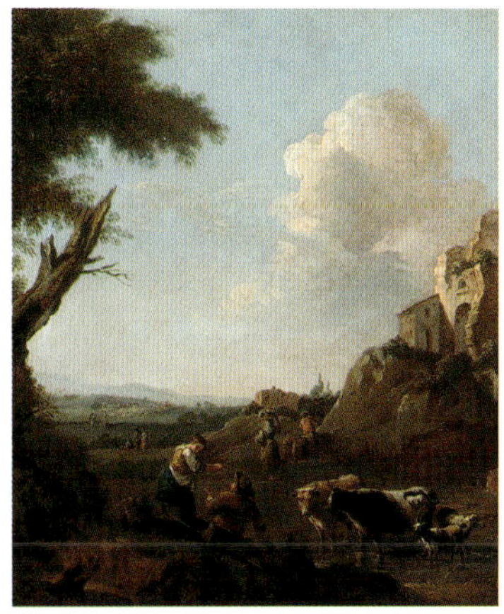

Berchem, Nicolaes 1620–1683
Landscape
oil on canvas 61.5 x 51 (E)
SOUAG.B43

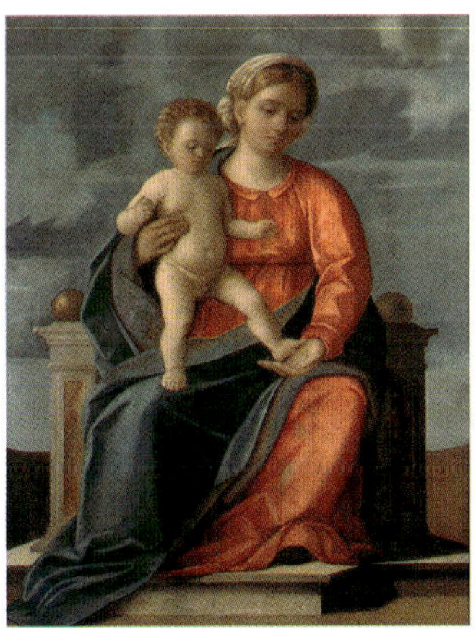

Bissolo, Francesco c.1470–1554
Virgin and Child
oil on canvas 119.5 x 89.5 (E)
SOUAG.B41

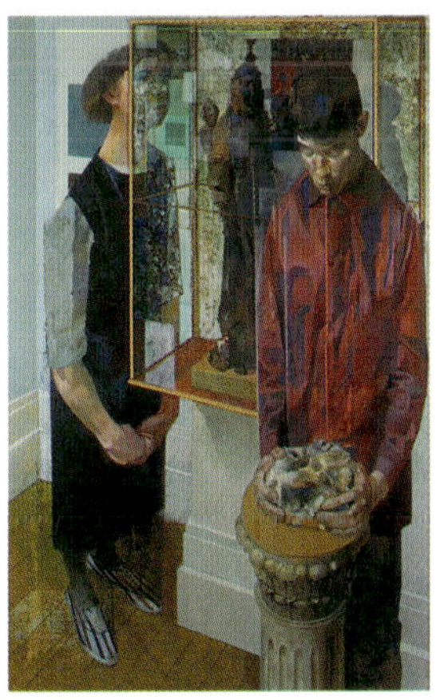

Blamey, Norman Charles 1914–1999
Proximity 1960s
oil on board 167.5 x 104 (E)
SOUAG.S64

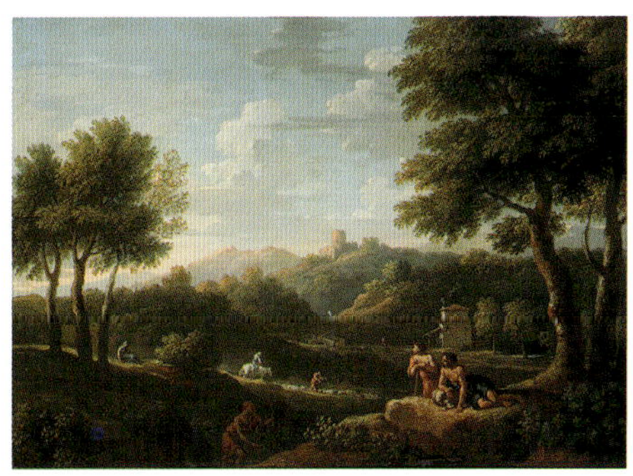

Bloemen, Jan Frans van 1662–1749
Romantic Landscape
oil on canvas 49 x 64 (E)
SOUAG.B105

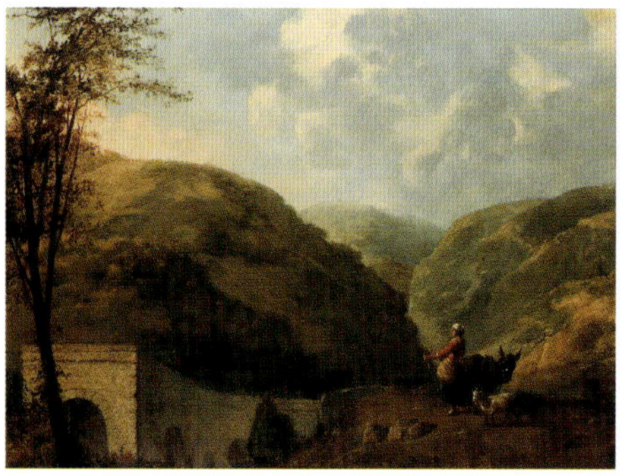

Both, Jan c.1618–1652
Landscape near Rome 1630s?
oil on canvas 68 x 86 (E)
SOUAG.B77

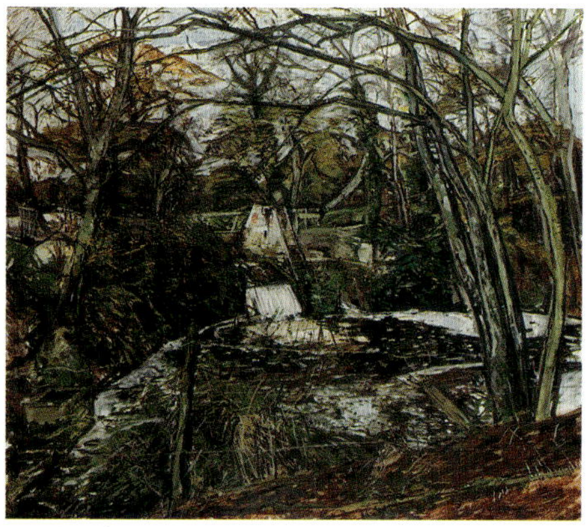

Bowey, Olwyn b.1936
Rowner Millpond in Autumn c.1973
oil on canvas 91 x 101.5 (E)
SOUAG.S122

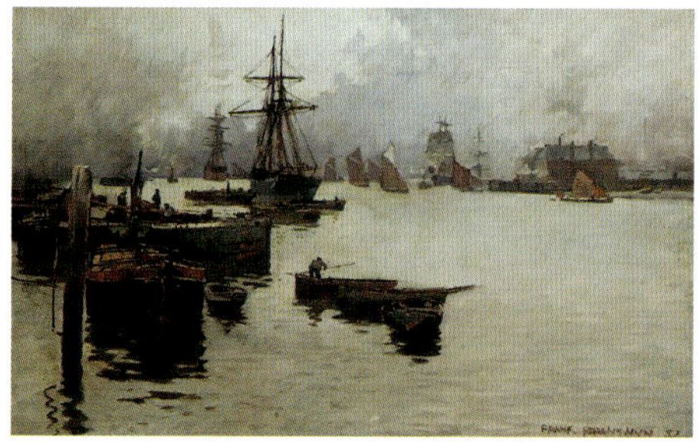

Brangwyn, Frank 1867–1956
The Lower Reaches of the Thames 1887
oil on canvas 49.5 x 75
SOUAG.S53

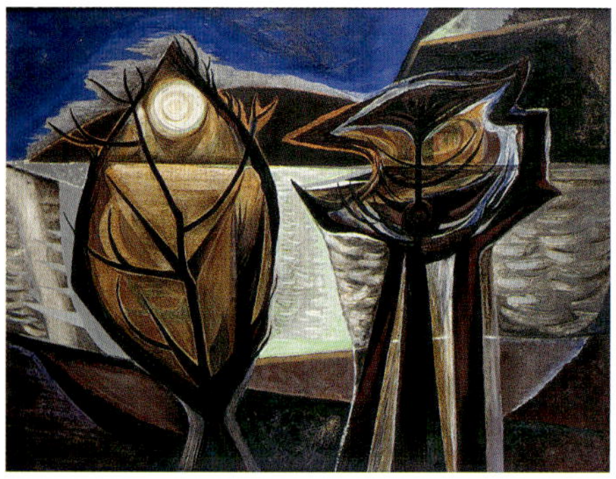

Braund, Allin 1915–2004
The Estuary
oil on hardboard 71 x 91.5 (E)
SOUAG.S54

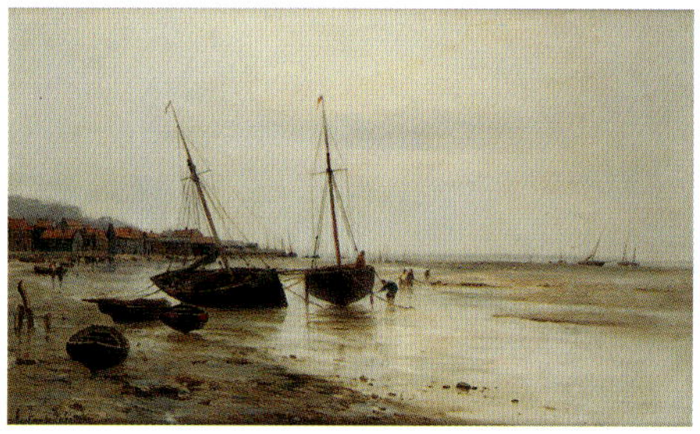

Breanski, Gustave de c.1856–1898
At Leigh, Essex c.1880–1890
oil on canvas 57 x 90
SOUAG.TS2

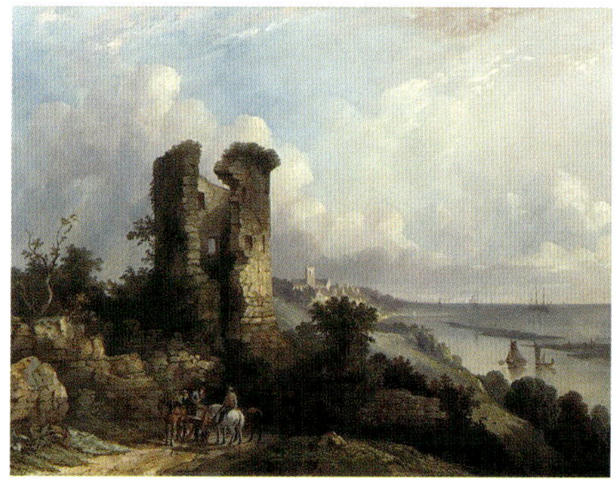

Bright, Henry 1814–1873
Hadleigh Castle c.1840
oil on canvas 70 x 90
SOUAG.TS258

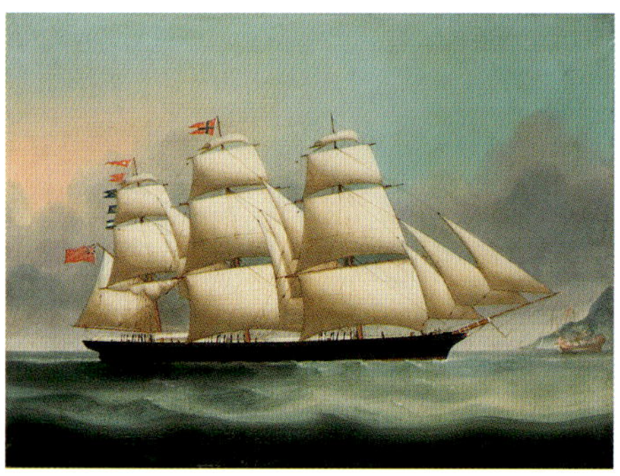

British (Chinese) School mid-19th C
'Red Riding Hood' of London
oil on canvas 30.5 x 61 (E)
SOUAG.TS492

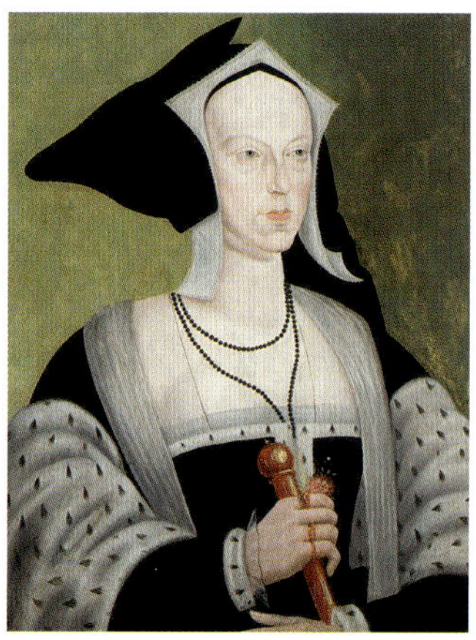

British (English) School
The Marchioness of Dorset c.1555
oil on panel 75 x 60 (E)
SOUAG.B1

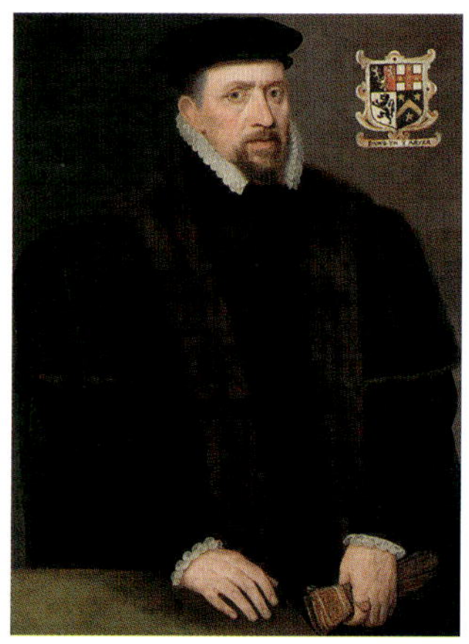

British (English) School 16th C
Portrait of a Gentleman
oil on panel 79 x 57 (E)
SOUAG.B23

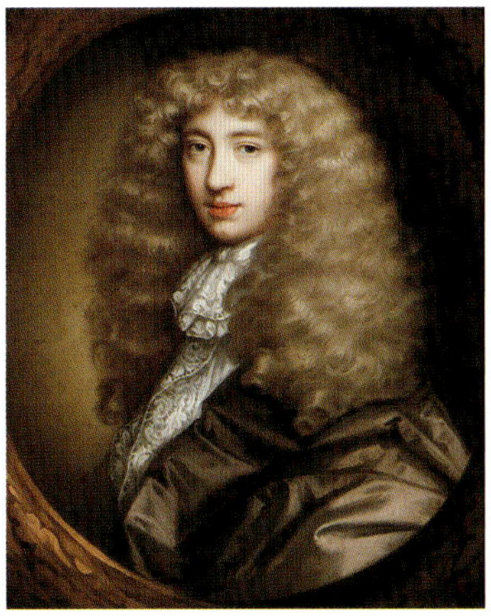

British (English) School mid-17th C
Portrait of a Young Man
oil on canvas 74 x 62.5 (E)
SOUAG.B3

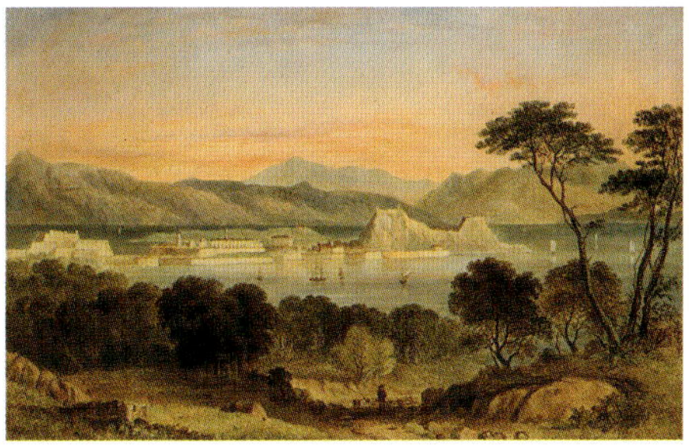

British (English) School
Italian Landscape c.1830
oil on panel 25.5 x 38 (E)
SOUAG.S3

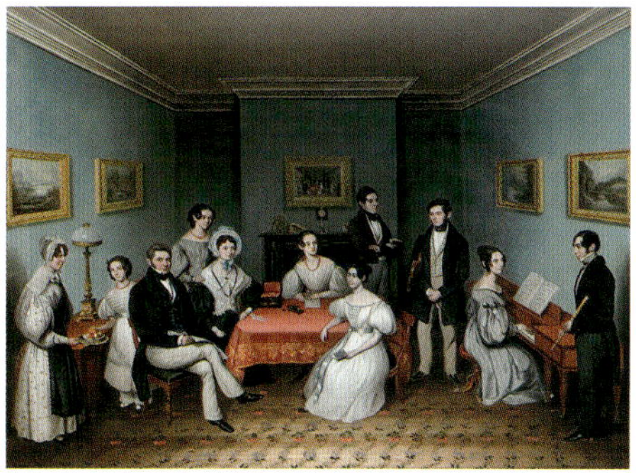

British (English) School
The Harris Family 1830s
oil on canvas 70 x 89 (E)
SOUAG.S91

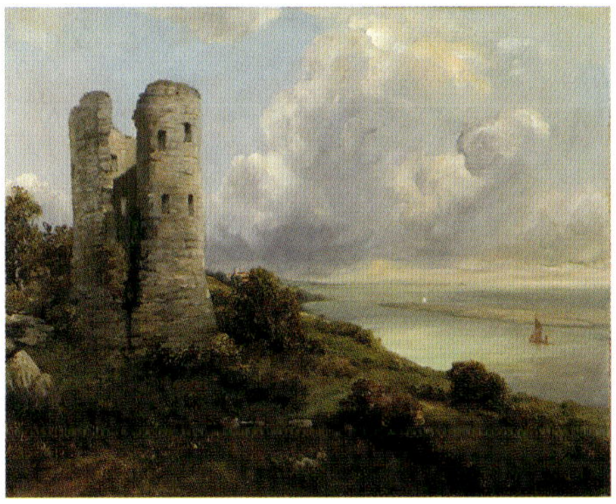

British (English) School 19th C
Hadleigh Castle
oil on canvas 63.5 x 76 (E)
SOUAG.TS314

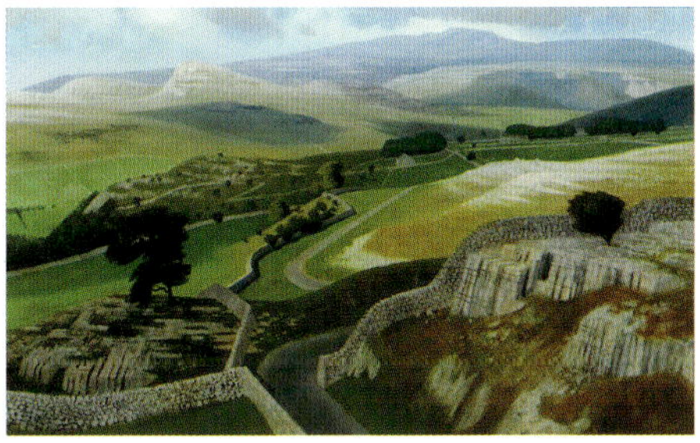

Brooke, Anne Isabella b.1916
Towards Ingleborough, across Ribblesdale
c.1973
oil on canvas 35.5 x 56 (E)
SOUAG.S124

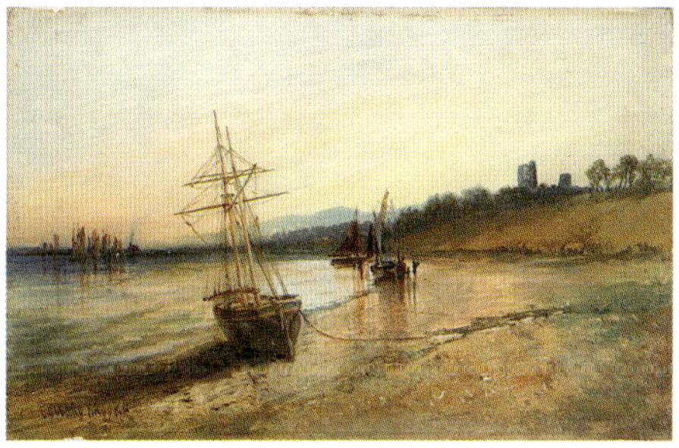

Brooke, Edward Adveno 1821–1910
Near Southend
oil on panel 15 x 24.5 (E)
SOUAG.TS437

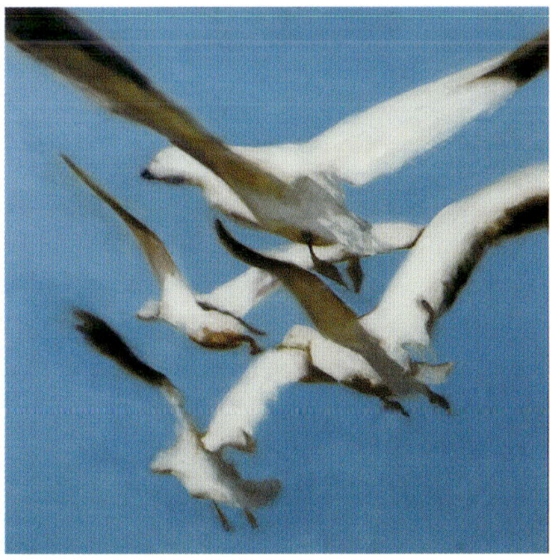

Bullen, Patricia
Seagulls c.1978
oil on board 61 x 60
SOUAG.S170

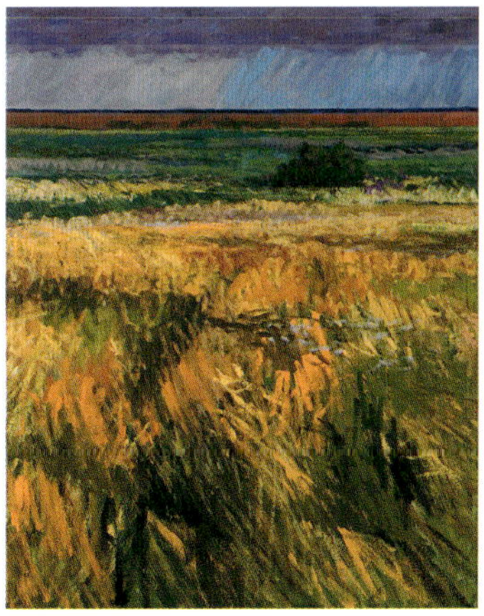

Burgess, Alan b.1936
Suffolk Triptych (centre panel)
oil on canvas 91.5 x 71
SOUAG.S388

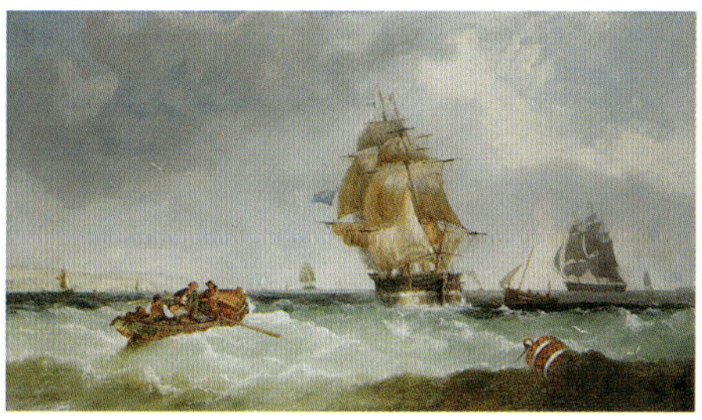

Callow, John 1822–1878
Homeward Bound, J. D. Clink's Famous Three-Masted Barque 'Oimara' Entering the Thames 1876
oil on canvas 76 x 127 (E)
SOUAG.TS3

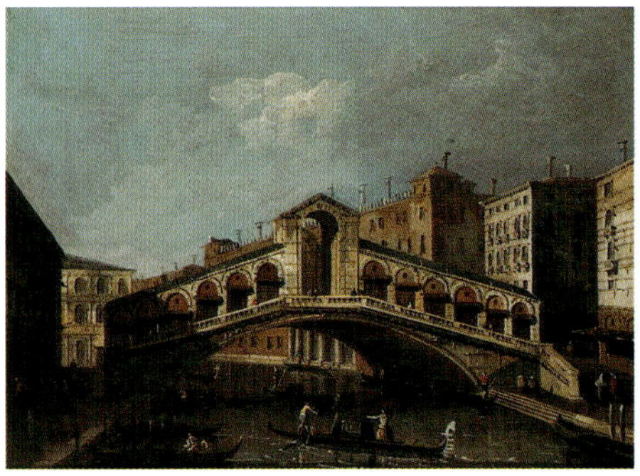

Canaletto (follower of) 1697–1768
View of the Rialto Bridge, Venice
oil on canvas 53 x 71 (E)
SOUAG.B42

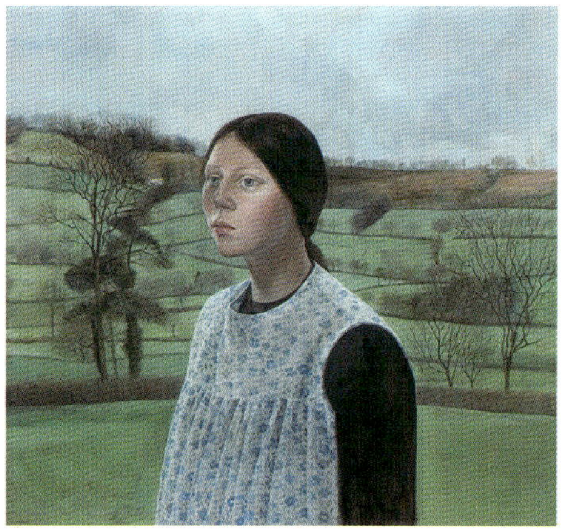

Carter, Mary b.1947
Two for Joy c.1972
oil on board 45.5 x 52 (E)
SOUAG.S108

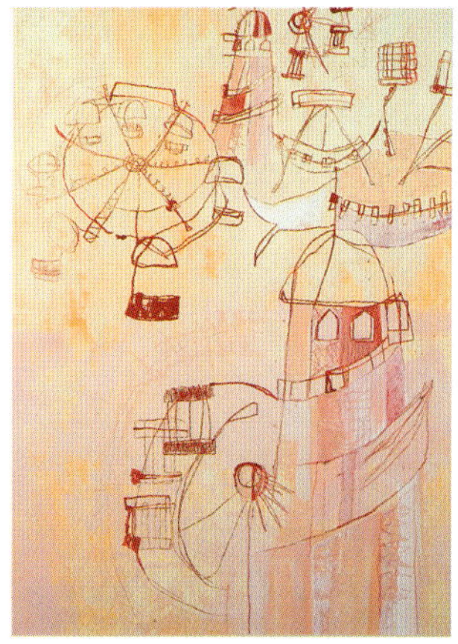

Castle, Lucy b.1977
Helter Skelter 2000
acrylic on paper 54 x 37
SOUAG.TS856

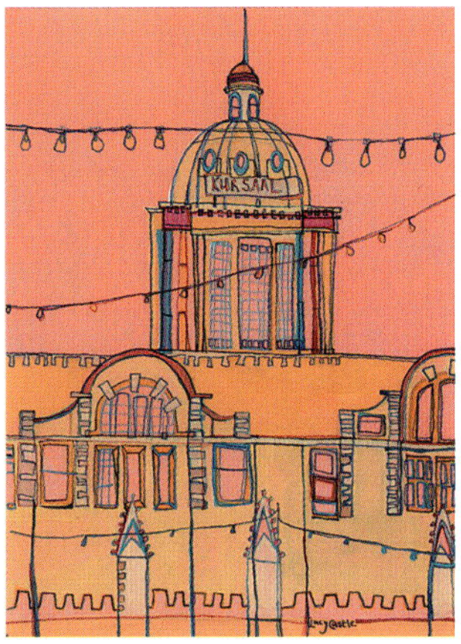

Castle, Lucy b.1977
The Kursaal II 2001
acrylic & ink on paper 28.5 x 23.5 (E)
SOUAG.TS858

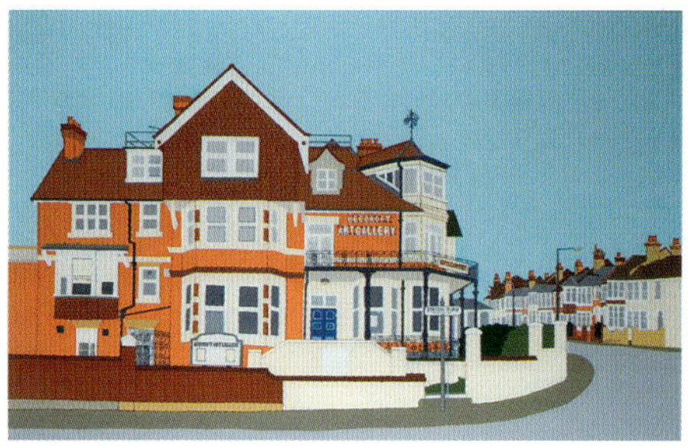

Castle, Lucy b.1977
The Beecroft Art Gallery 2003
acrylic on paper 70 x 108 (E)
SOUAG.S535

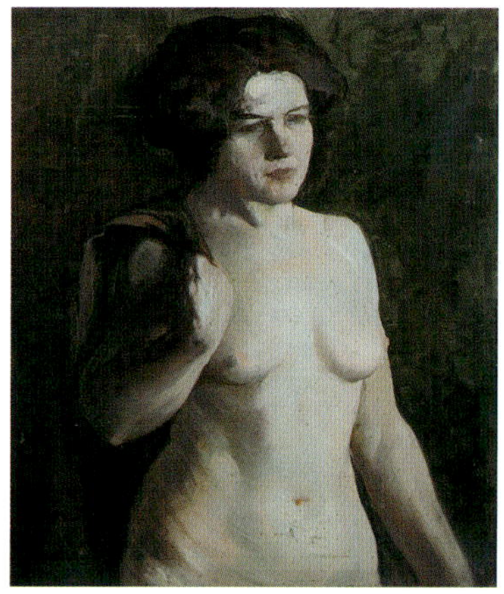

Cattle, J. T. active 1920–1977
Female Nude
oil on canvas 61 x 50.5 (E)
SOUAG.S202

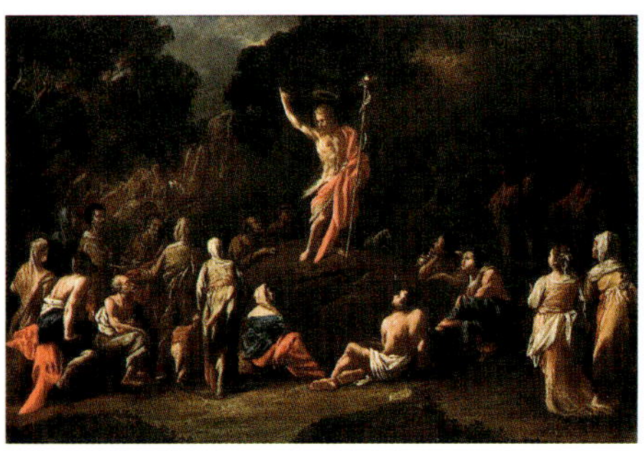

Cerquozzi, Michelangelo 1602–1660
St John the Baptist Preaching in the Wilderness
oil on canvas 35 x 49 (E)
SOUAG.S45

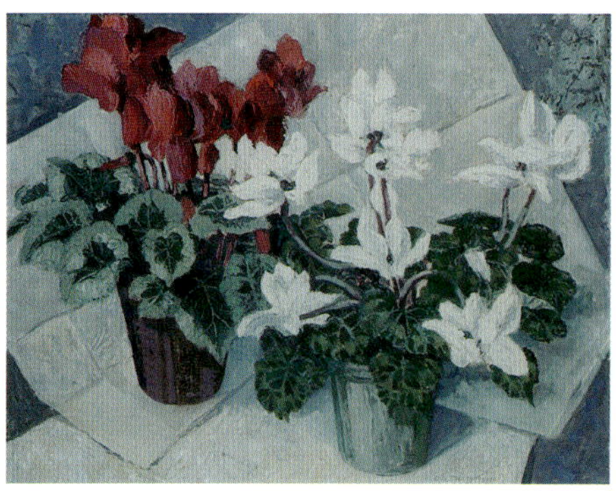

Christison, C. G.
Cyclamen
oil on board 39 x 49 (E)
SOUAG.S541

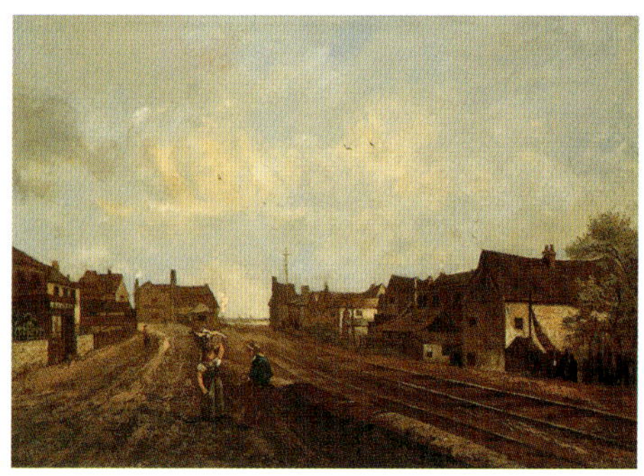

Cleminson, Robert active c.1864–c.1903 &
Fisher, G.
Old Leigh High Street
oil on canvas 44.5 x 61 (E)
SOUAG.TS462

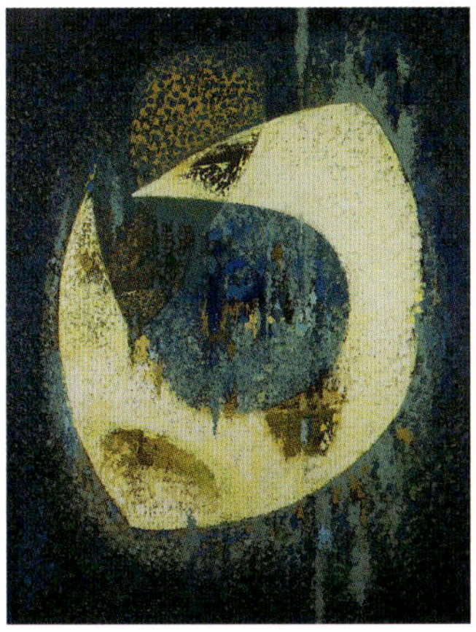

Clifford Smith, Stanley 1906–1968
Claire de la lune 1965–1967
oil on board 122 x 90 (E)
SOUAG.S87

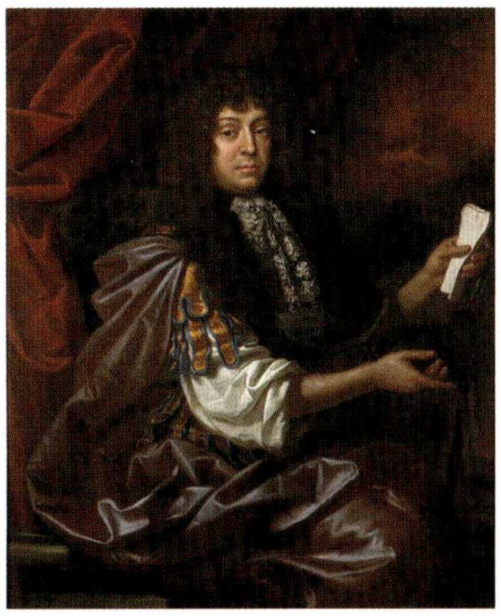

Closterman, John 1660–1711
Sir William Temple
oil on canvas 122.5 x 97.5 (E)
SOUAG.B38

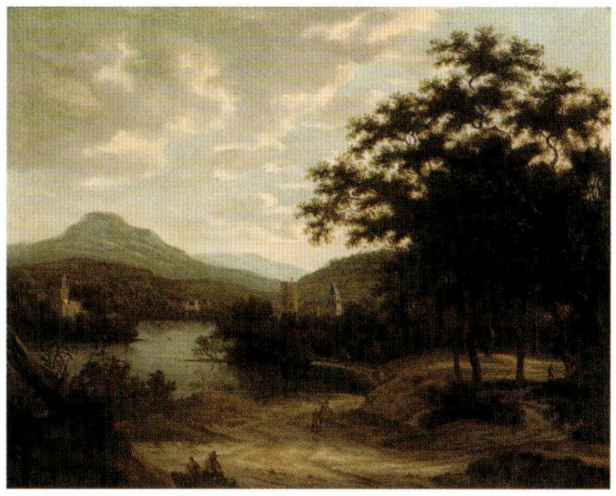

Codde, Pieter Jacobsz. 1599–1678
Landscape with a Lake and Castle 1666
oil on canvas 65 x 80 (E)
SOUAG.B58

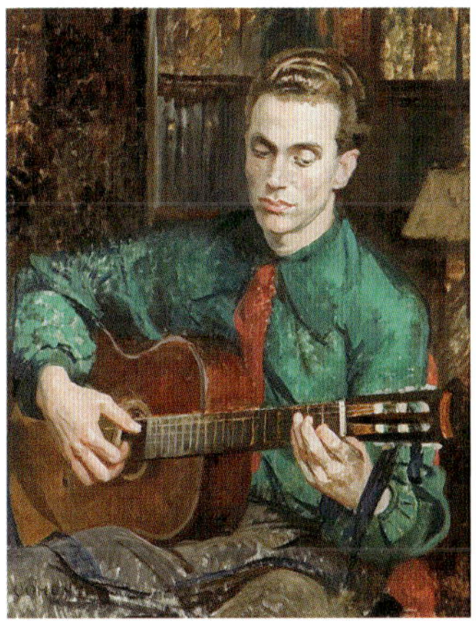

Cohen, Dorothy A. d.1960
The Guitar Player 1930s
oil on canvas 91.5 x 71 (E)
SOUAG.S49

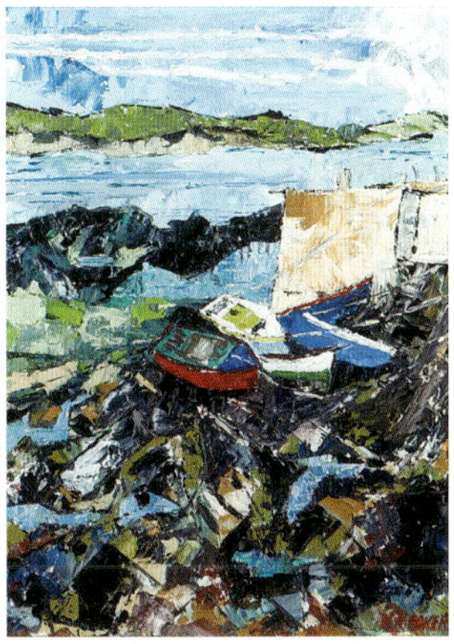

Coker, K. A.
Rocks and Boats
oil on board 39 x 28 (E)
SOUAG.S540

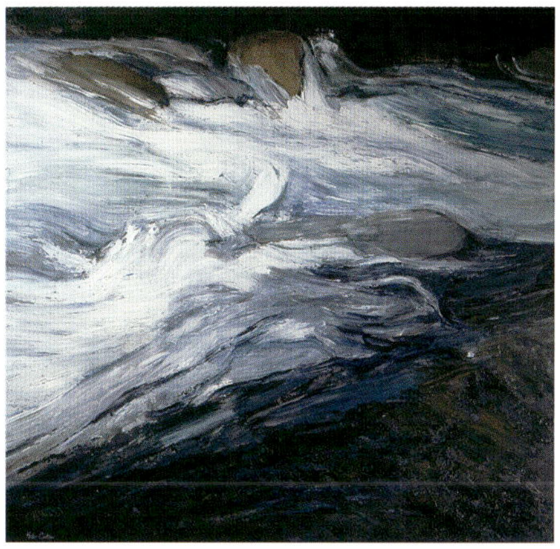

Coker, Peter 1926–2004
Mountain Stream, Pyrenees 1960s
oil on board 121 x 121
SOUAG.S83

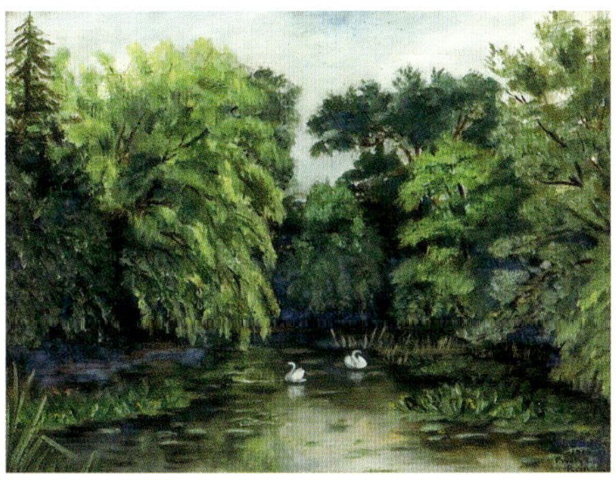

Comber, N. F.
Priory Lake, Prittlewell 1903
oil on canvas board 26.5 x 34 (E)
SOUAG.TS449

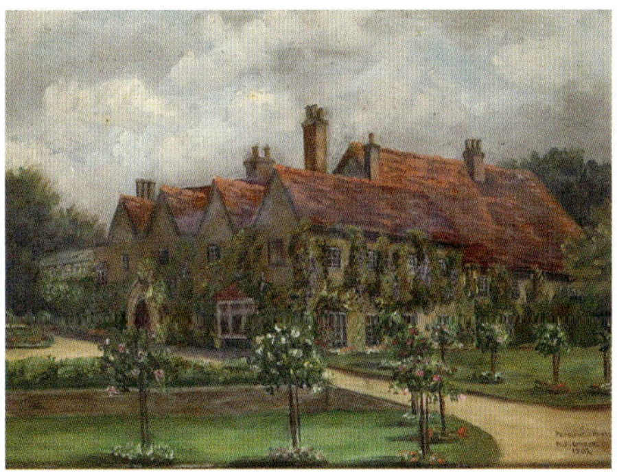

Comber, N. F.
Prittlewell Priory 1903
oil on canvas 25.5 x 33 (E)
SOUAG.TS445

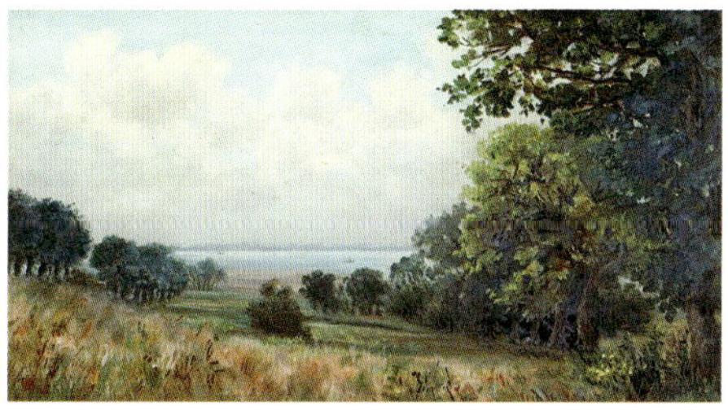

Conabeer, A. J. active 1894–1902
Westcliff 1899
oil on canvas board 19 x 33 (E)
SOUAG.TS460

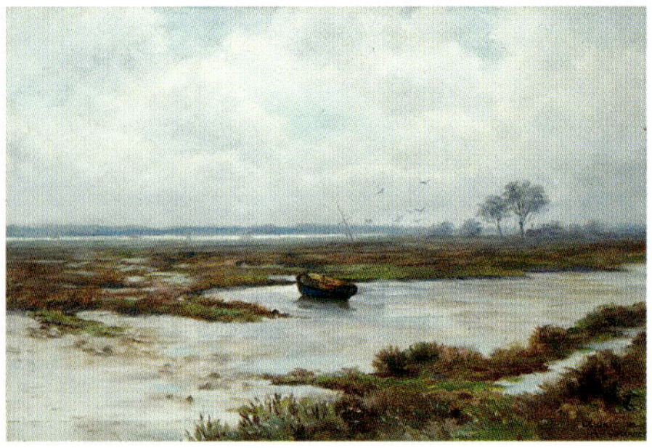

Conabeer, A. J. active 1894–1902
Leigh Creek 1902
oil on card 23 x 33 (E)
SOUAG.TS471

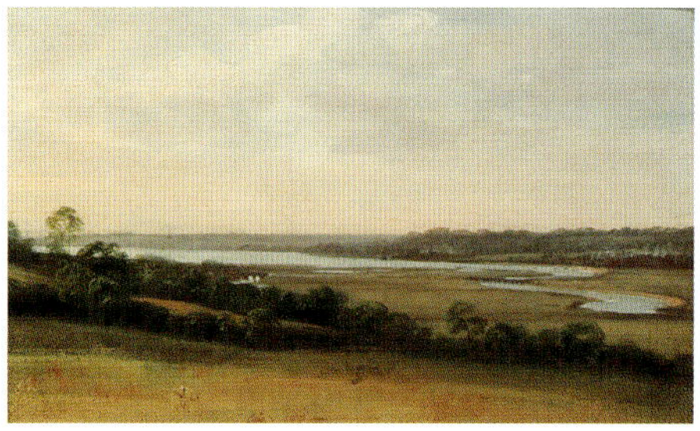

Constable, John 1776–1837
River Stour Looking towards Manningtree
1804
oil on canvas 20.5 x 33 (E)
SOUAG.S1

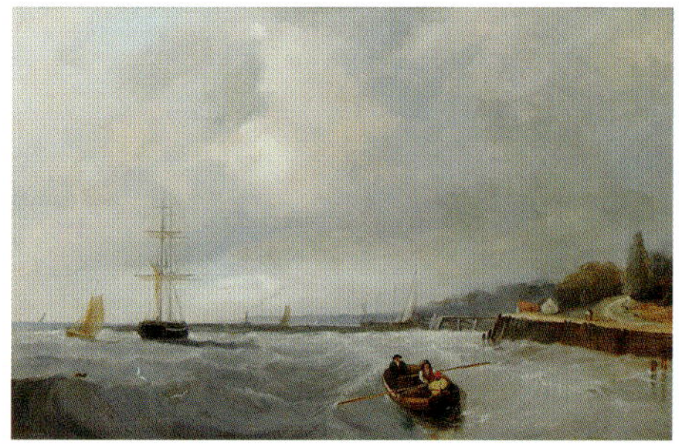

Cotman, John Sell 1782–1842
Southend, Pier Hill c.1828
oil on canvas 44 x 59 (E)
SOUAG.TS4

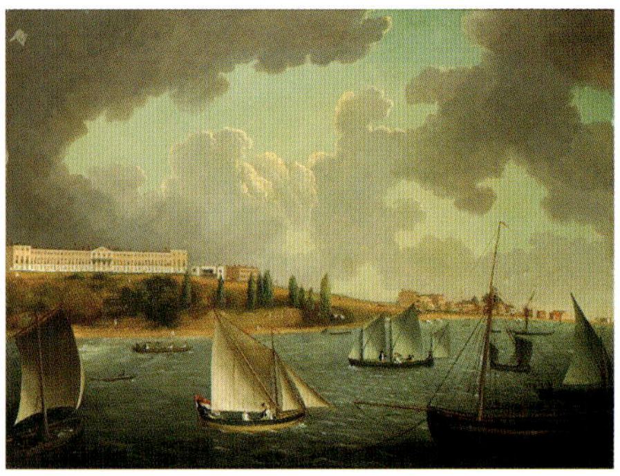

Coventry, C.C. active c.1802-1819
Royal Terrace from the Sea 1807
oil on canvas 71 x 92
SOUAG.TS5

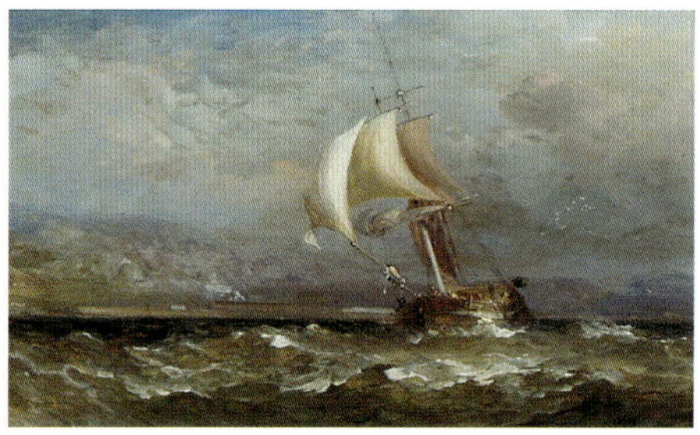

Cox, David the elder 1783–1859
Seascape
oil on panel 15 x 24 (E)
SOUAG.B12

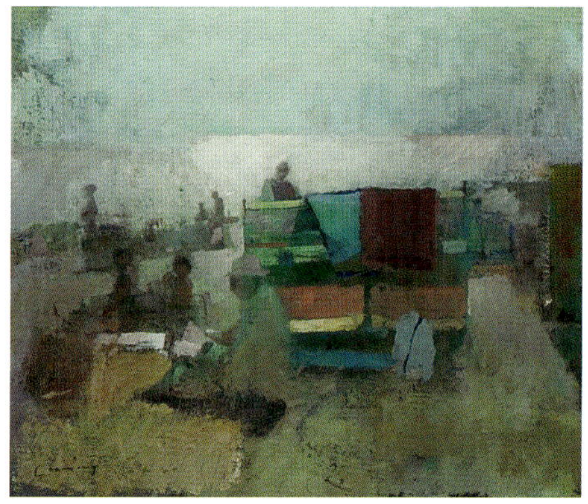

Cuming, Frederick b.1930
Landscape, August
oil on hardboard 23 x 38 (E)
SOUAG.S364

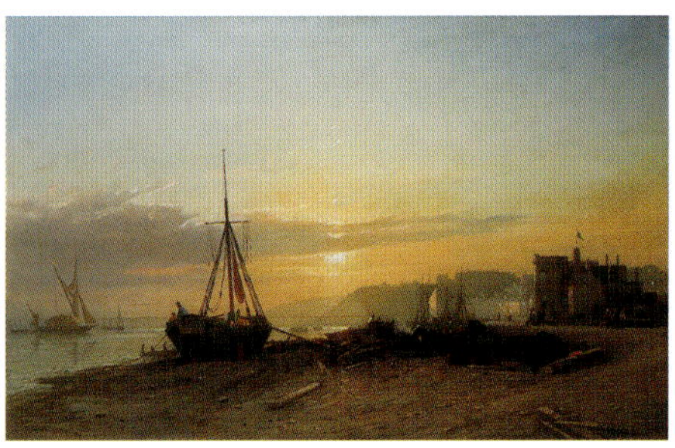

Danby, James Francis 1816–1875
Southend Beach 1865
oil on canvas 45.5 x 76 (E)
SOUAG.S46

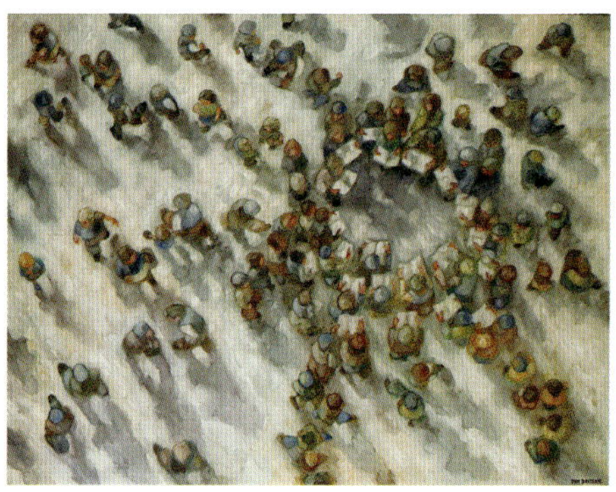

Davison, Thomas
Gathering 1970s
oil on canvas 81 x 101.5 (E)
SOUAG.B157

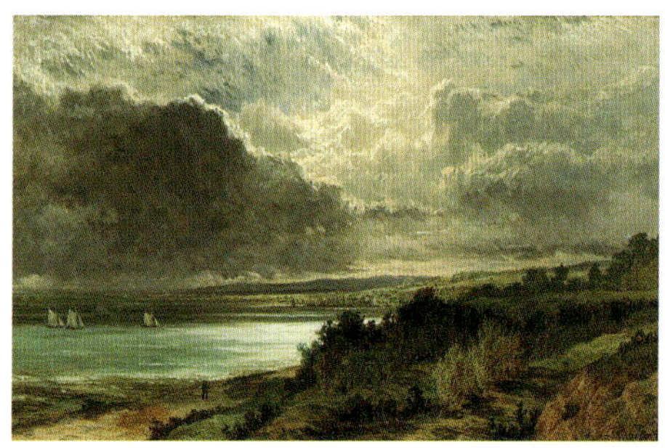

Dawson, Henry 1811–1878
Leigh Ray 1875
oil on canvas 40.5 x 61 (E)
SOUAG.TS6

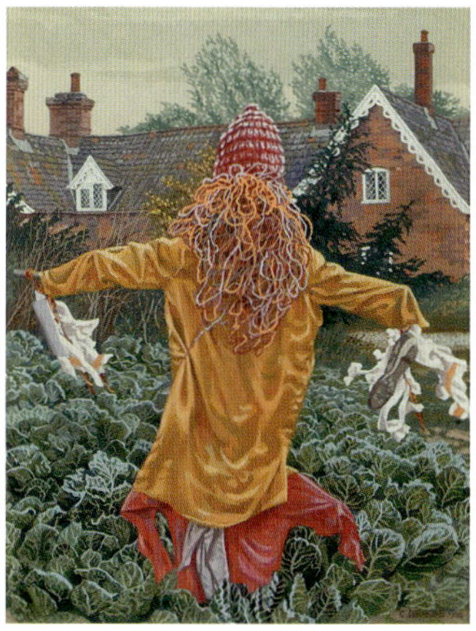

Deakins, Cyril Edward 1916–2002
Suffolk Scarecrow 1984
tempera on board 24 x 19 (E)
SOUAG.S391

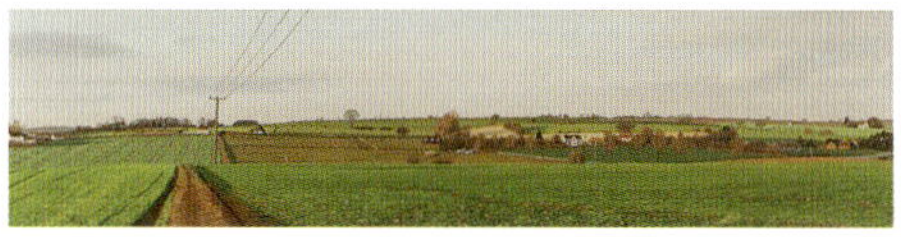

Deakins, Thomas William b.1957
A Winter's Afternoon, Duton Hill, near Dunmow c.1985
oil on board 12.5 x 48 (E)
SOUAG.S354

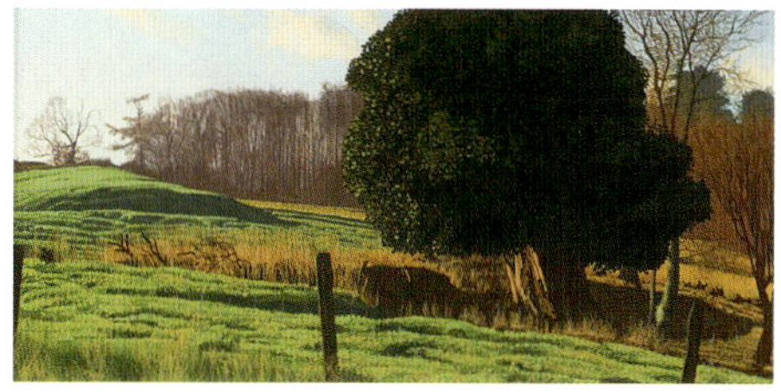

Deakins, Thomas William b.1957
January Sunshine 1995
oil on canvas panel 14 x 29.5
SOUAG.S561

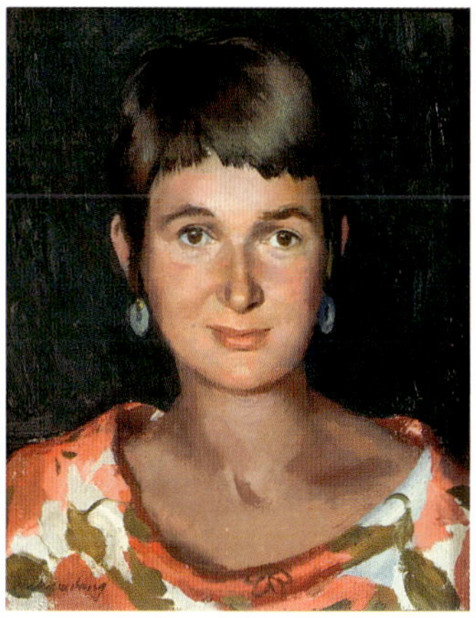

Dring, William D. 1904–1990
Portrait of a Girl, possibly Melissa c.1989
oil on canvas 26 x 20.5
SOUAG.S444

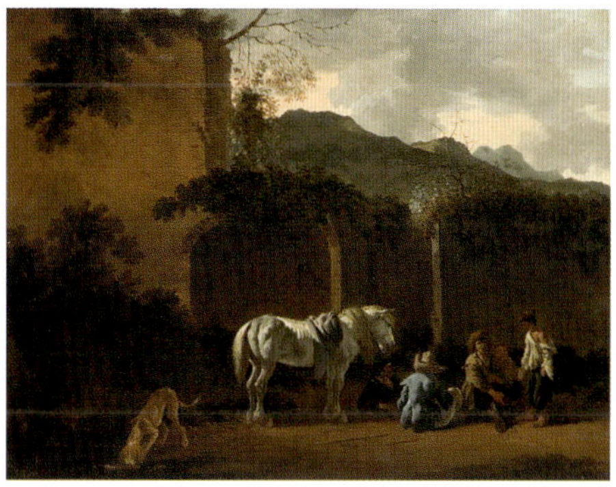

Dujardin, Karel 1626–1678
Halt of the Gypsies
oil on canvas 42.5 x 52.5 (E)
SOUAG.B34

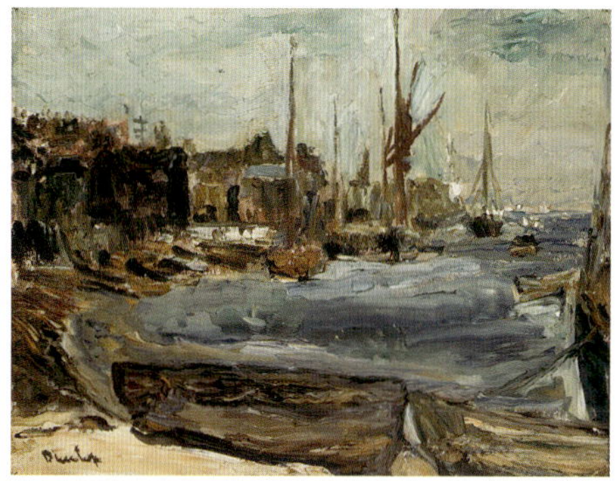

Dunlop, Ronald Ossory 1894–1973
The Harbour, Leigh-on-Sea
oil on canvas 40.5 x 51 (E)
SOUAG.TS251

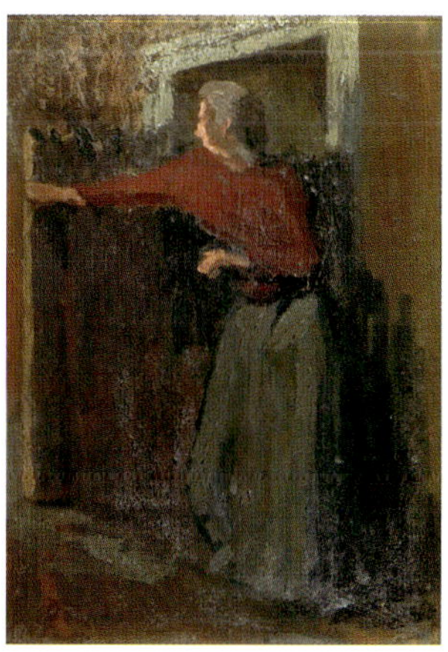

Dunstan, Bernard b.1920
Old Woman at a Gate
oil on board 32 x 23 (E)
SOUAG.S383

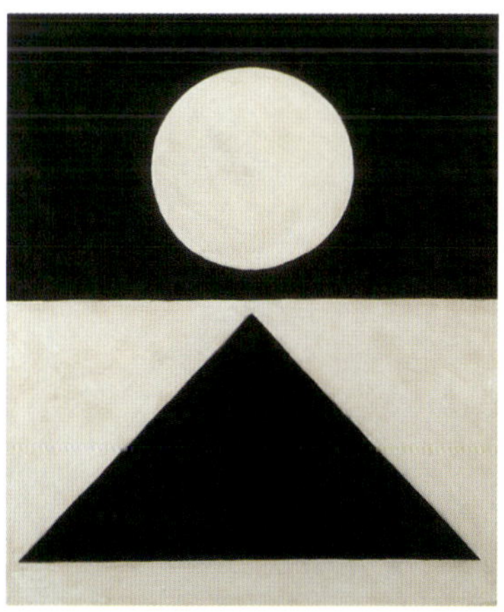

Durrant, Roy Turner 1925–1998
Inscape: The Monument 1981
tempera & acrylic on board 80 x 67
SOUAG.S251

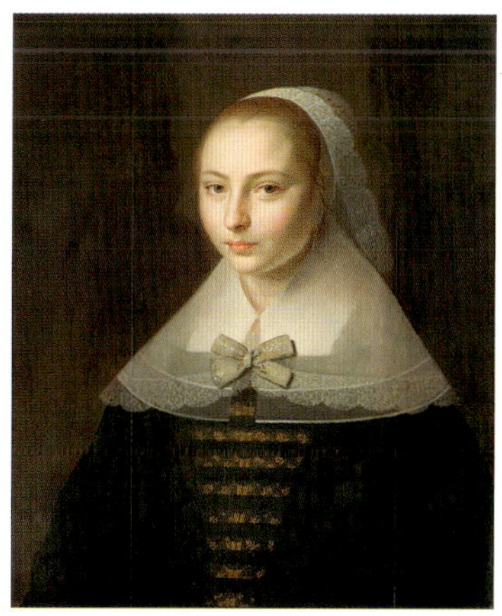

Dutch School
Portrait of a Young Woman c.1640s
oil on panel 70 x 57.5 (E)
SOUAG.S97

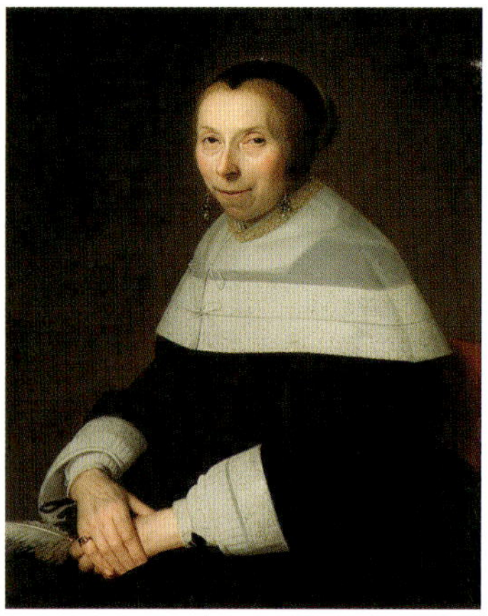

Dutch School
Portrait of a Lady c.1665
oil on panel 80 x 62.5 (E)
SOUAG.B2

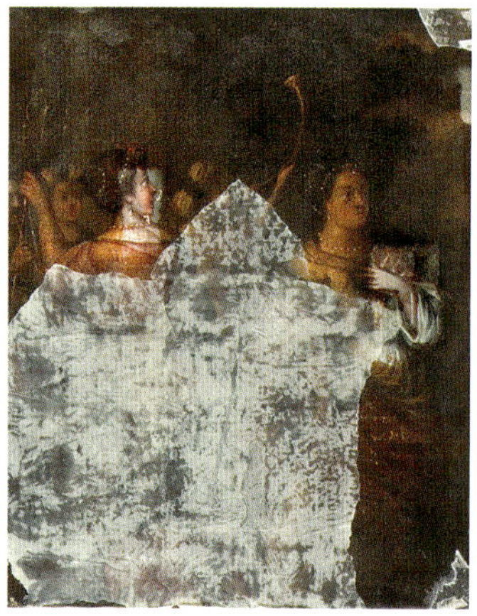

Dutch School 18th C
Women Making Music
oil on canvas 48.5 x 38
SOUAG.S106

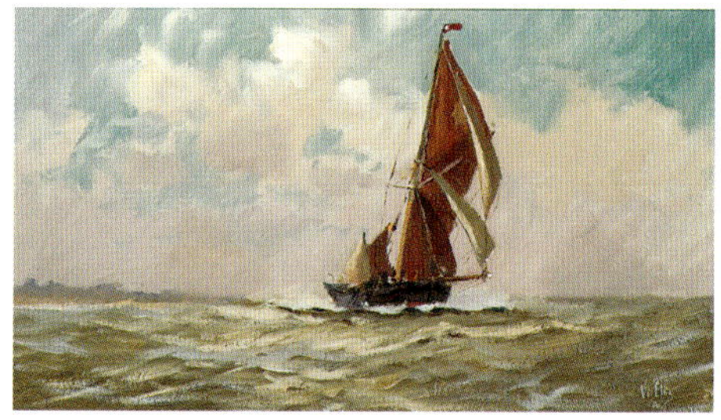

Ellis, Victor William b.1921
The Thames Barge, 'Kitty' c.1980
oil on canvas 36 x 61
SOUAG.TS855

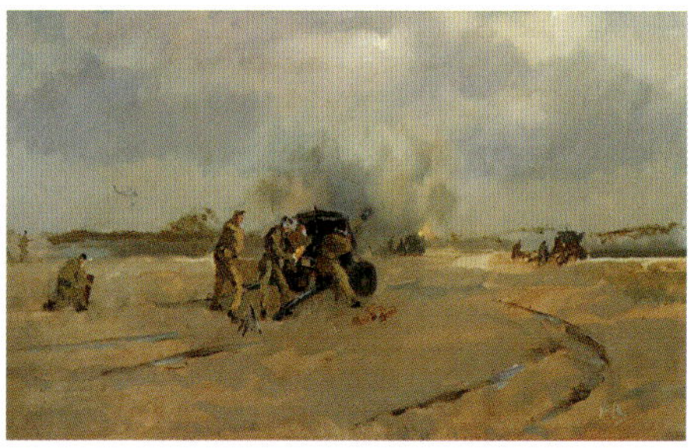

Ellis, Victor William b.1921
Trial Canvas for '25 Pounders on Salisbury Plain' c.1980
oil on canvas 46 x 71.5 (E)
SOUAG.S341

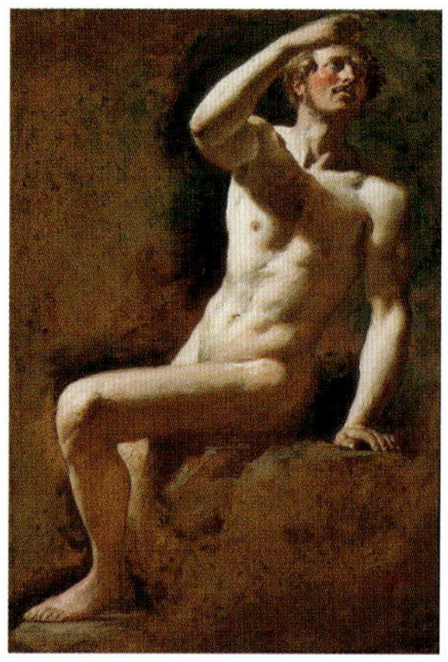

Etty, William 1787–1849
Study of a Male Nude
oil on canvas 56 x 40 (E)
SOUAG.B73

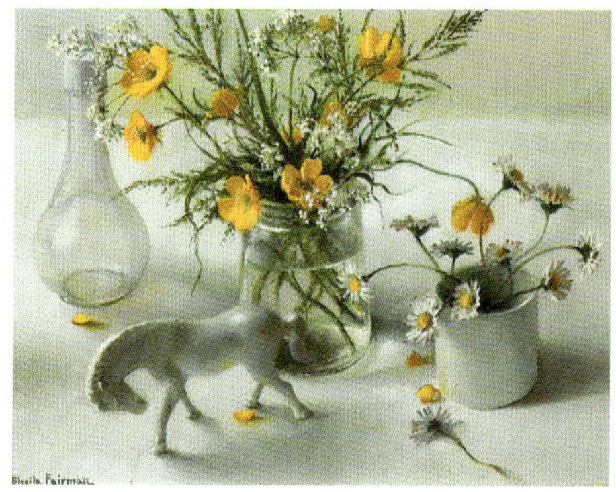

Fairman, Sheila b.1924
Still Life in White c.1986
oil on canvas 20 x 25.5 (E)
SOUAG.S389

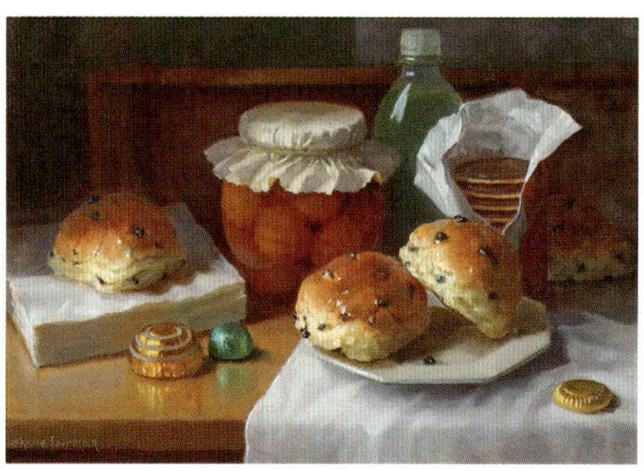

Fairman, Sheila b.1924
Biscuits and Buns 1990s
oil on board 20.4 x 30.4
SOUAG.TS908

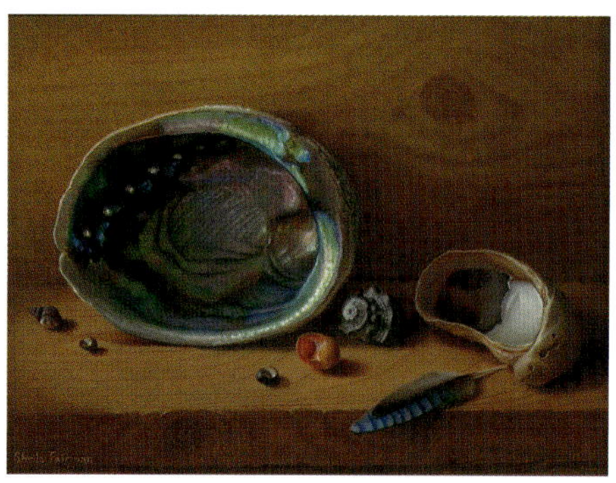

Fairman, Sheila b.1924
Abalone Shell
oil on canvas board 14.5 x 19.5 (E)
SOUAG.S373

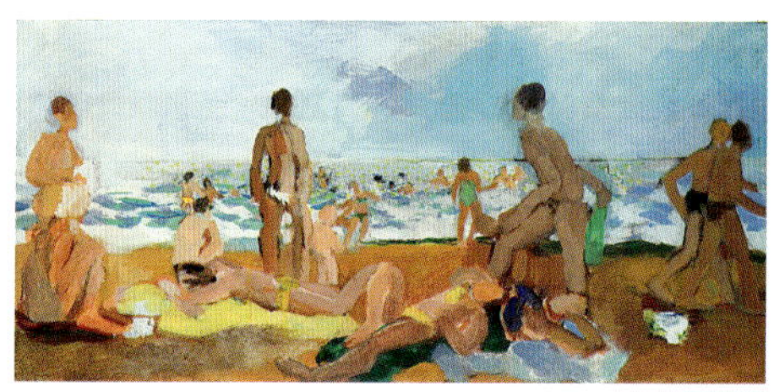

Farrell, Anthony b.1945
Study of Bathers on the Beach c.1975
oil on board 30 x 61 (E)
SOUAG.S150

Facing page: to Rowe, Ian Alan, b.1963, *Two Men on a Tram* (detail), 1989, Epping Forest District Museum, (p. 296)

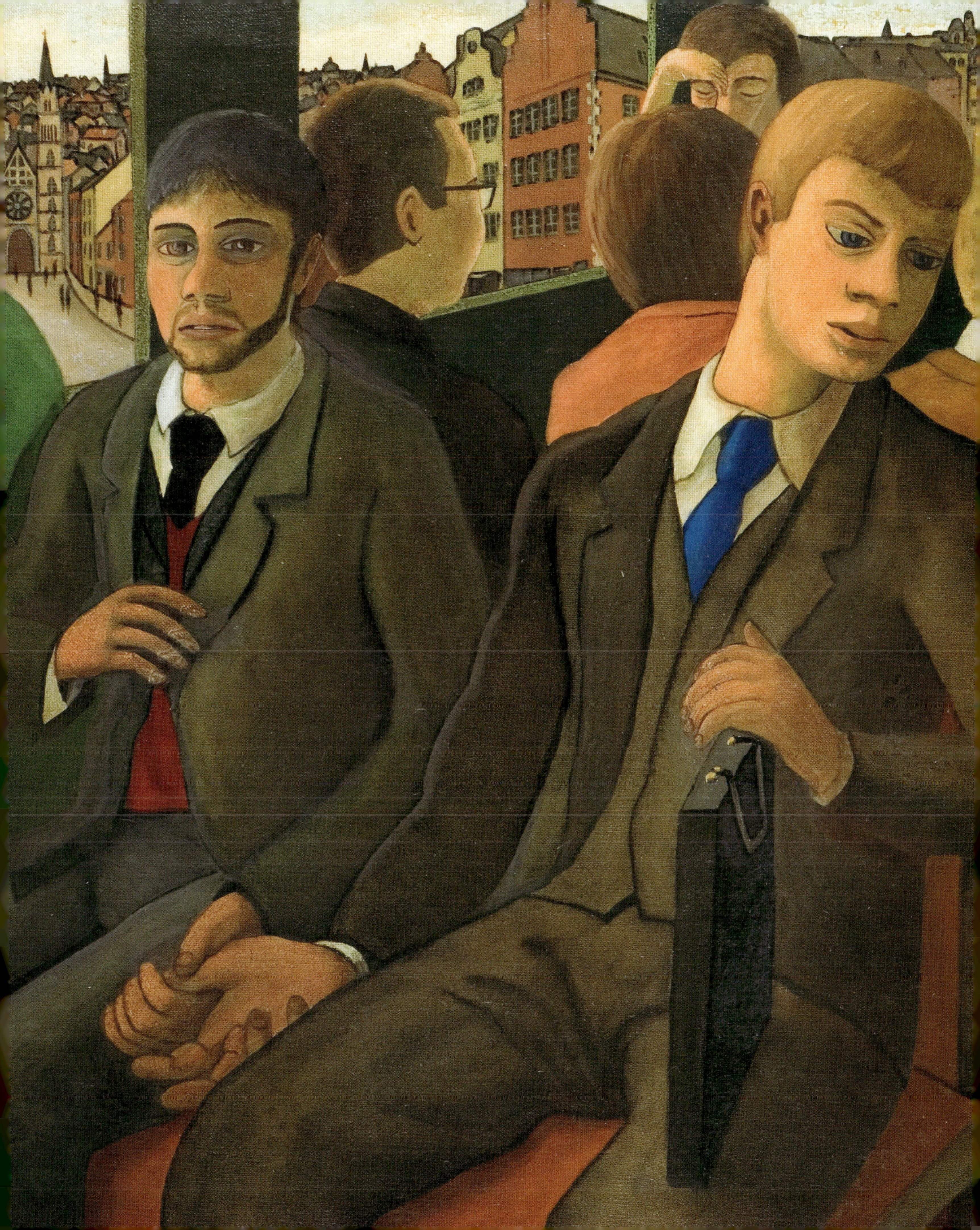

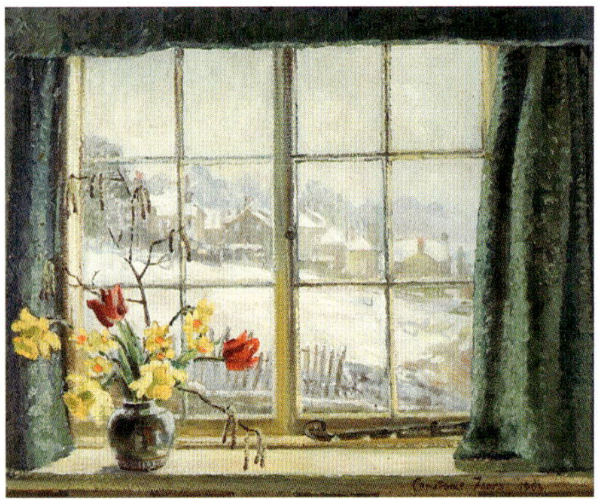

Fears, Constance 1895–late 1980s
Winter Scene from Billet Cottage 1963
oil on board 49.5 x 59.5 (E)
SOUAG.TS826

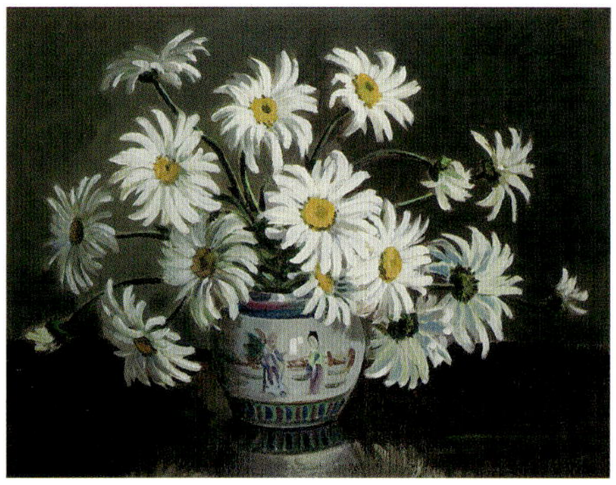

Fears, Constance 1895–late 1980s
Daisies in a Chinese Vase 1969
oil on board 51 x 61.5 (E)
SOUAG.S539

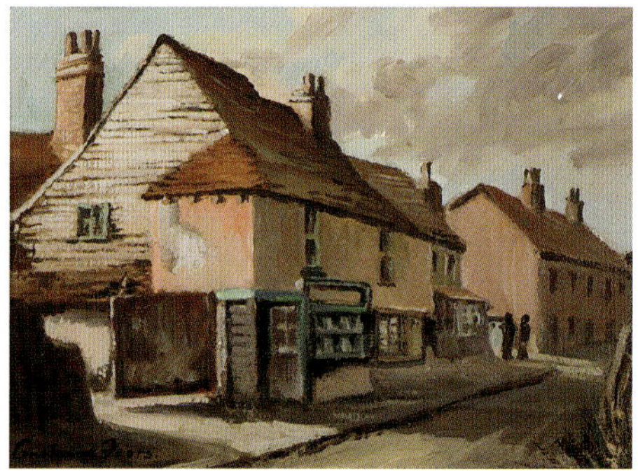

Fears, Constance 1895–late 1980s
Juniper's Cottage
oil on board 21.5 x 29 (E)
SOUAG.TS827

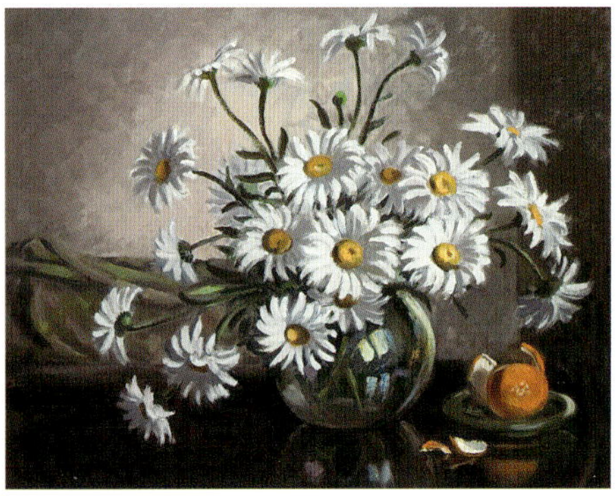

Fears, Constance 1895–late 1980s
Marguerites and Oranges
oil on board 51 x 61 (E)
SOUAG.S237

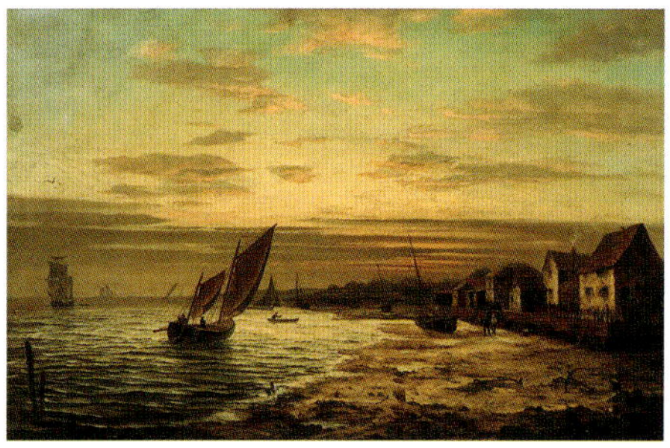

Fisher, Charles d.1890
Leigh, Essex 1878
oil on canvas 50 x 76 (E)
SOUAG.TS214

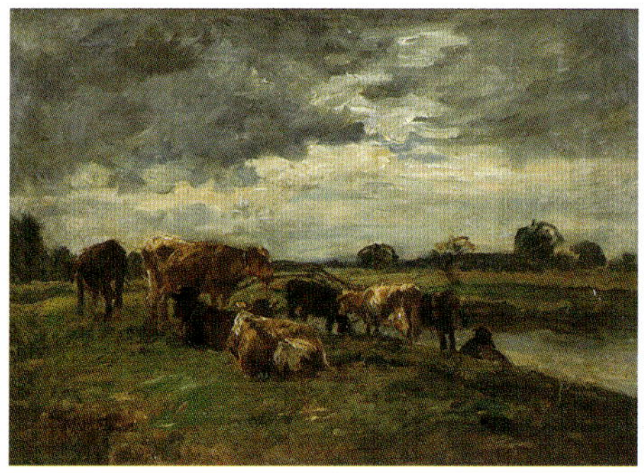

Fisher, Mark 1841–1923
Cattle at Bourne End
oil on canvas 30 x 41 (E)
SOUAG.B15

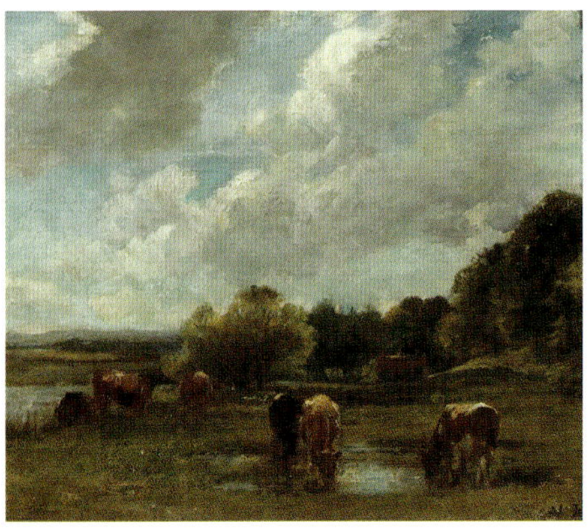

Fisher, Mark 1841–1923
Cattle by the River
oil on canvas 30.5 x 35.5 (E)
SOUAG.B116

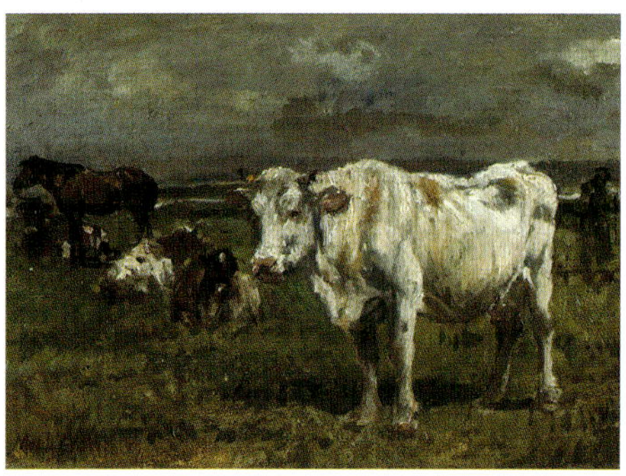

Fisher, Mark 1841–1923
Cattle in a Landscape
oil on canvas 24 x 32 (E)
SOUAG.B117

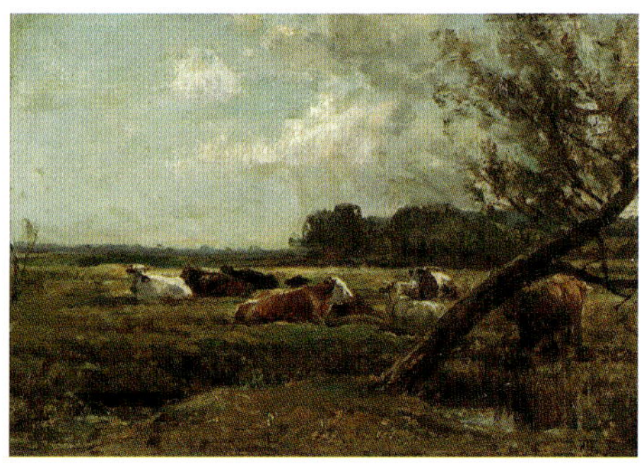

Fisher, Mark 1841–1923
Cattle Resting in Marshland
oil on canvas 25 x 34 (E)
SOUAG.B16

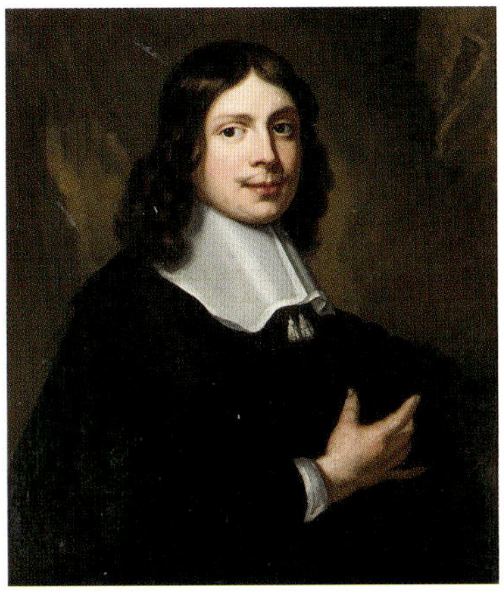

Flemish School
Portrait of a Gentleman 1650s
oil on canvas 71 x 60 (E)
SOUAG.B31

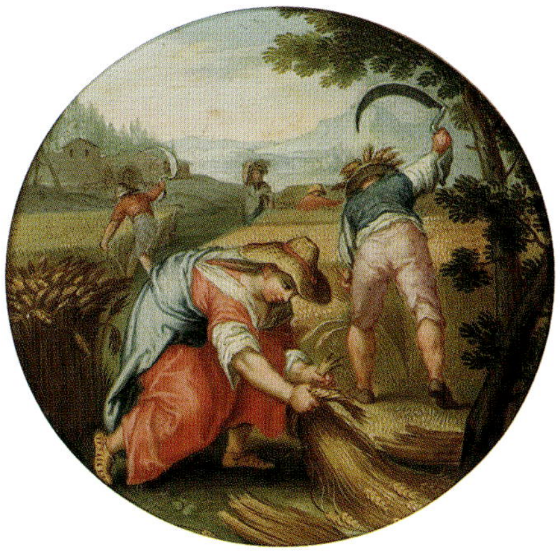

Flemish School
Harvesting Scene c.1700
oil on panel 23 (E)
SOUAG.B49

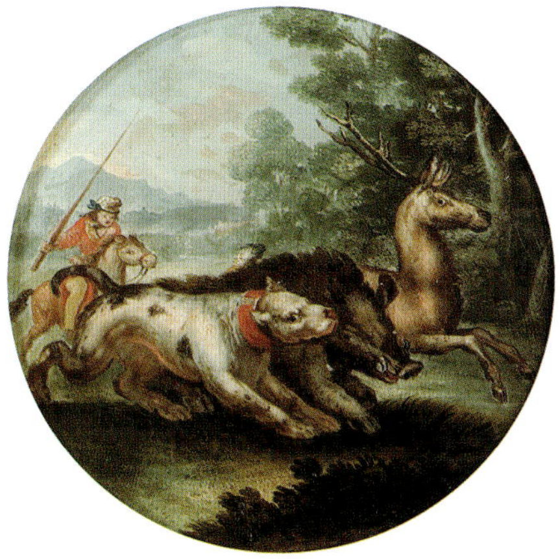

Flemish School
Hunting Scene c.1700
oil on panel 23 (E)
SOUAG.B48

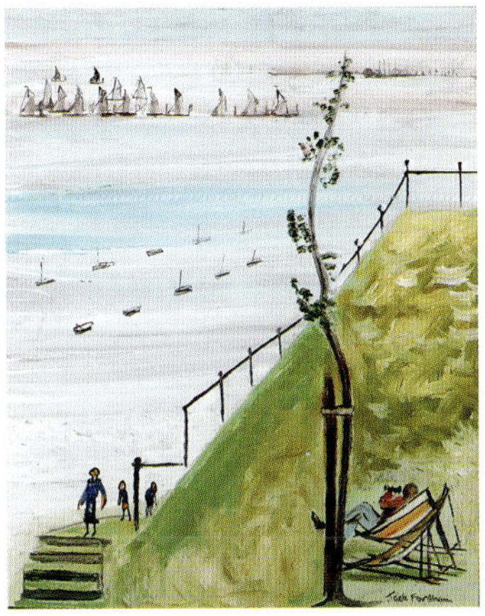

Fordham, Jack d.1982
Southend Barge Race 1979
oil on board 70.5 x 58.5 (E)
SOUAG.TS788

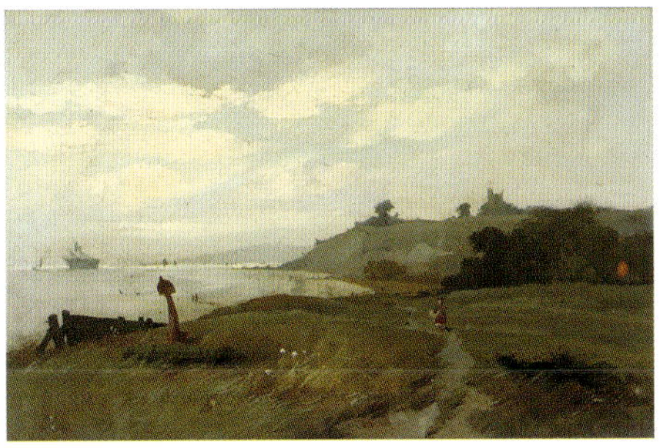

Fraser, John 1858–1927
From the Leas
oil on canvas 29 x 45.5 (E)
SOUAG.TS436

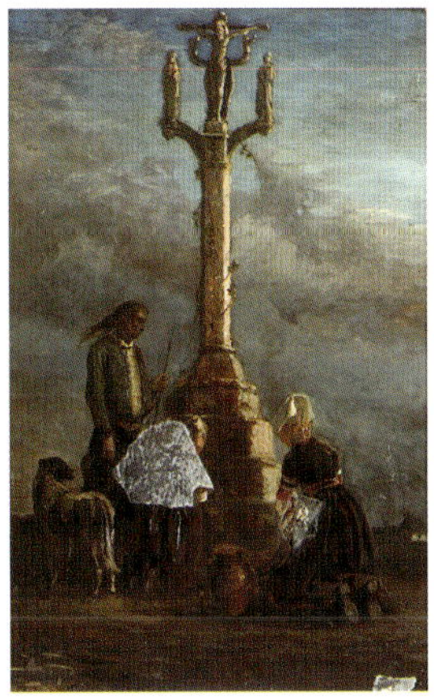

French School 19th C
A Wayside Shrine
oil on canvas 46 x 30.5 (E)
SOUAG.B47

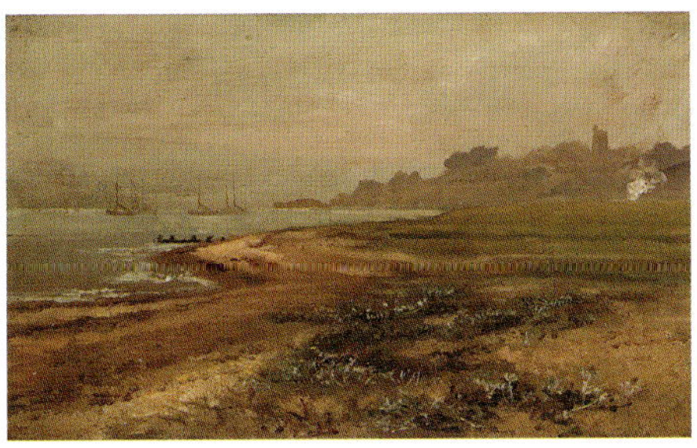

Gallon, Robert 1845–1925
Leigh from Southend 1888
oil on panel 19 x 31.5 (E)
SOUAG.TS666

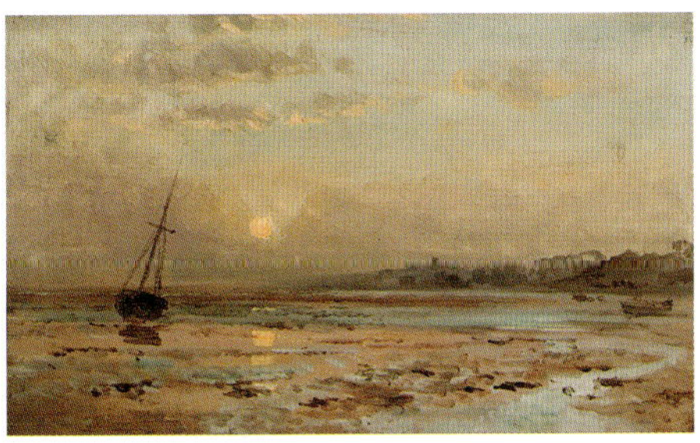

Gallon, Robert 1845–1925
Leigh from Southend Pier 1888
oil on panel 19 x 31.5 (E)
SOUAG.TS665

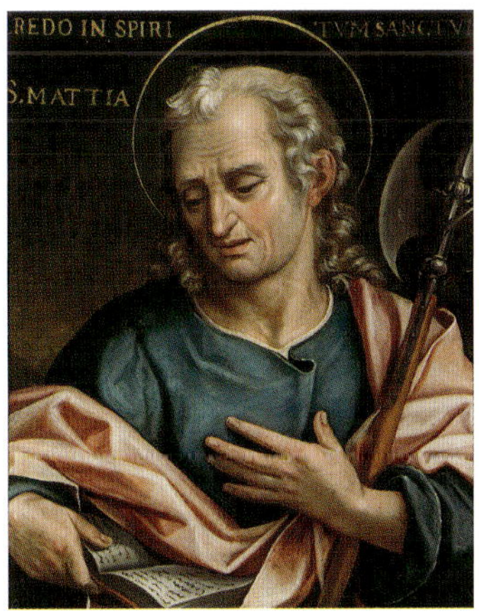

German School 17th C
St Matthias
oil on canvas 70 x 56 (E)
SOUAG.B75

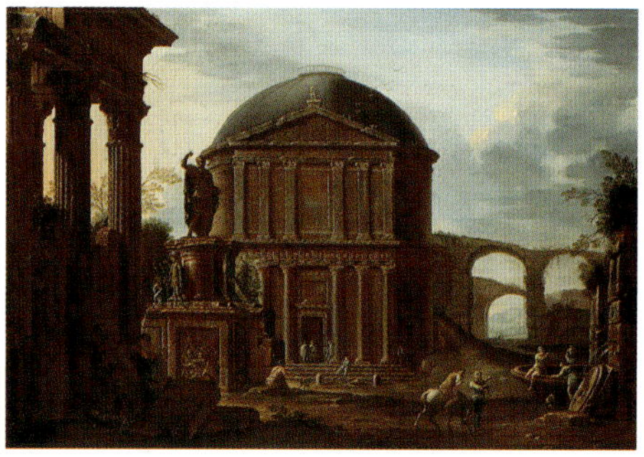

Ghisolfi, Giovanni c.1623–1683
Capriccio
oil on canvas 72 x 97.5 (E)
SOUAG.B121

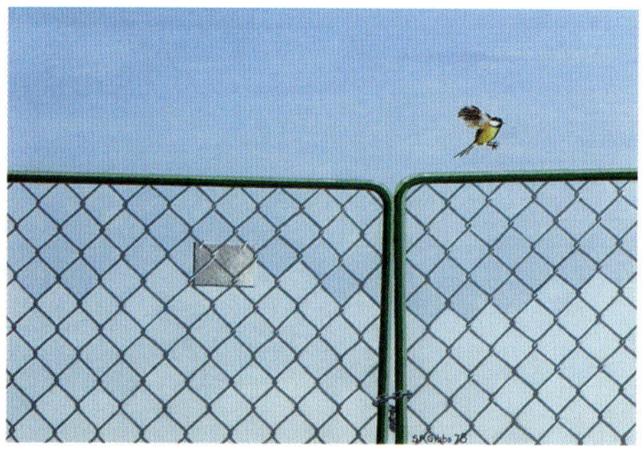

Gibbs, Stephen b.1957
Free Flight c.1978
acrylic on paper 23 x 33
SOUAG.S175

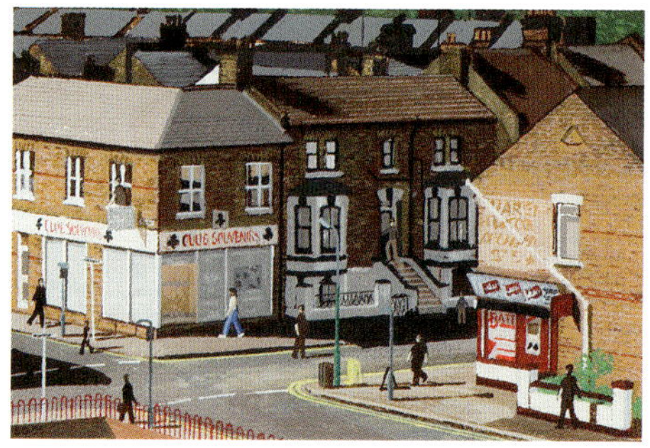

Gibbs, Stephen b.1957
Summer on the Corner of Gordon 1995
acrylic on board 13.3 x 19
SOUAG.TS871

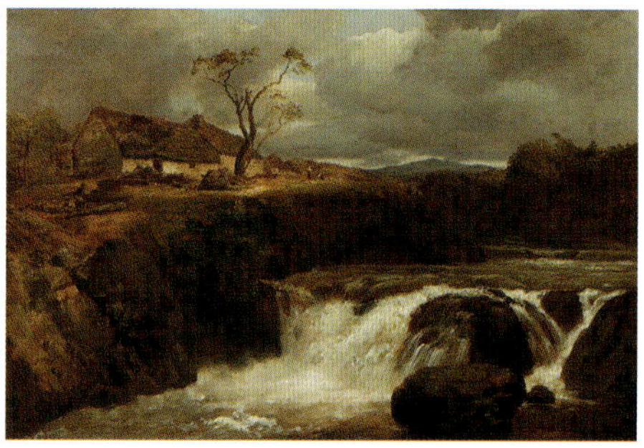

Gill, Edmund Ward 1820–1894
The Waterfall 1867
oil on canvas 35.5 x 51 (E)
SOUAG.B65

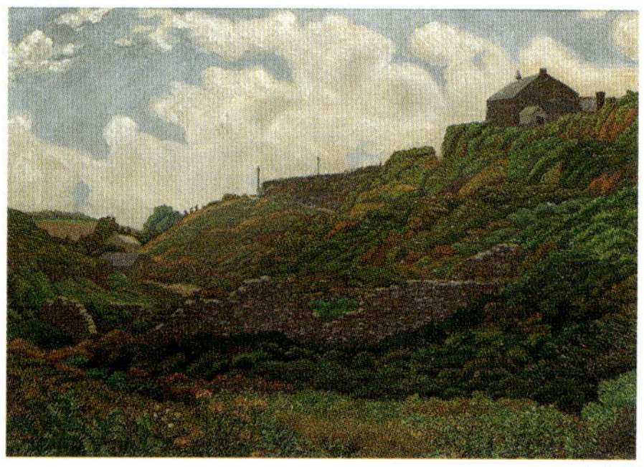

Ginner, Charles 1878–1952
Cottages at Shipley, Sussex
oil on canvas 51 x 69 (E)
SOUAG.S101

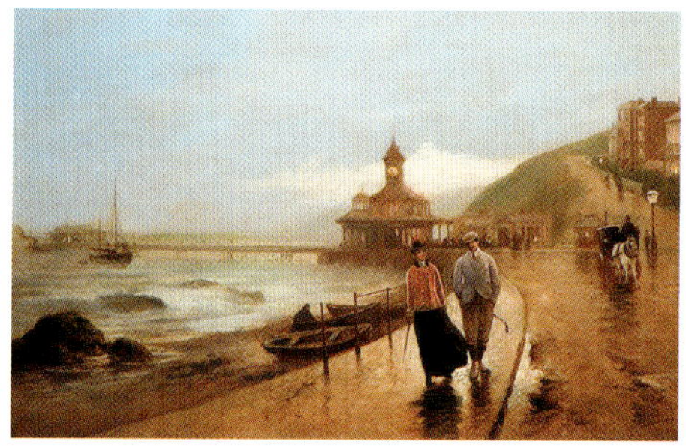

Gozzard, K.
The Wane of the Season c.1890
oil on canvas 51 x 76 (E)
SOUAG.TS7

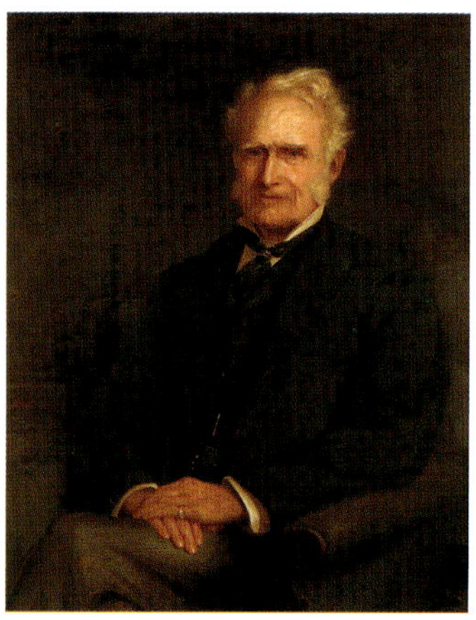

Grant, Henry active 1868–1895
Charles Woosnam, JP, Chairman of the Southend Gas Company 1895
oil on canvas 91.5 x 76 (E)
SOUAG.S439

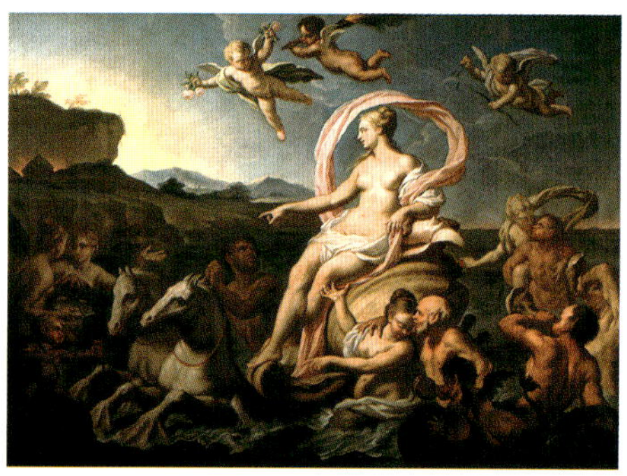

Grassi, Nicola 1682–1748
The Triumph of Amphitrite
oil on canvas 152.5 x 198 (E)
SOUAG.S213

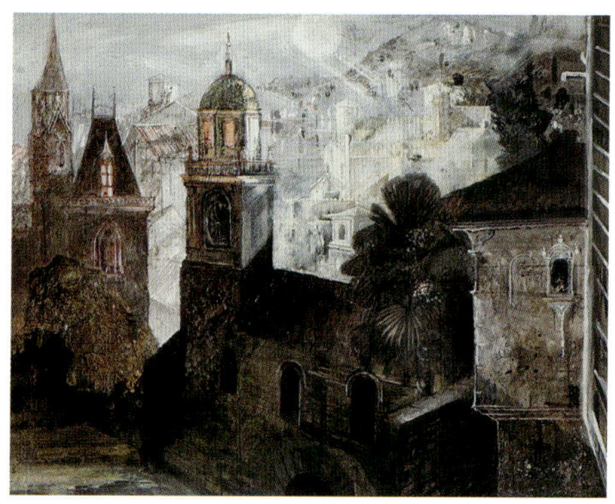

Greenwood, Ernest b.1913
Rooftops and Towers, Lecco, North Italy 1960s
oil on paper 68.5 x 84 (E)
SOUAG.S67

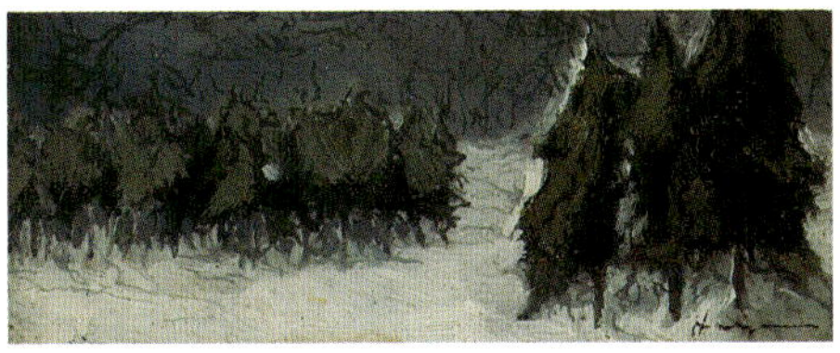

Haagensen, F. H. active 1930
Winter in Norway
oil on board 6.5 x 15 (E)
SOUAG.S434

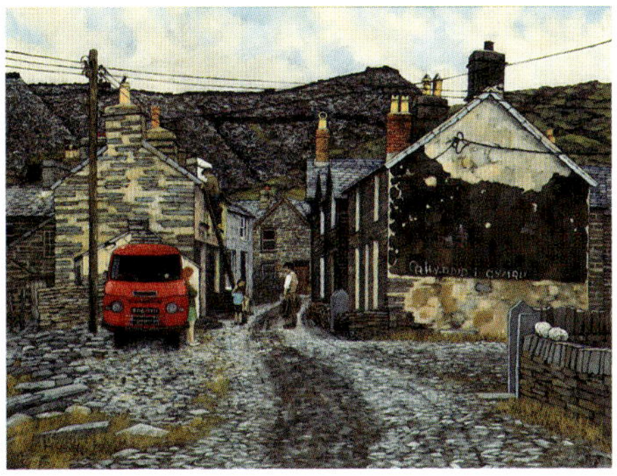

Hall, Christopher b.1930
Blaenau Ffestiniog c.1970
oil on canvas 39 x 49.5 (E)
SOUAG.S103

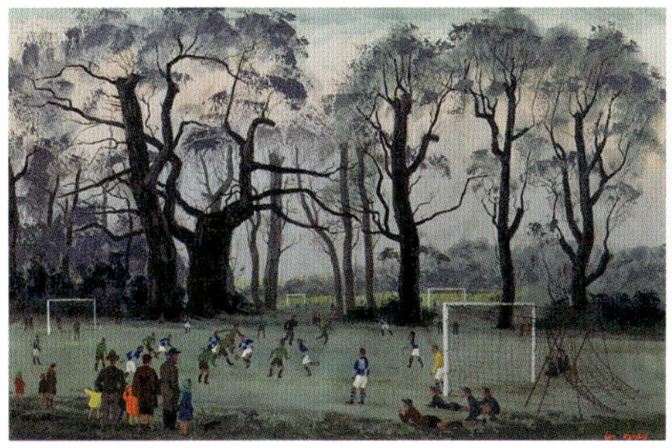

Hardy, Leo active 1936–1952
Saturday Morning at Priory Park c.1952
oil on board 49 x 74.5
SOUAG.B155

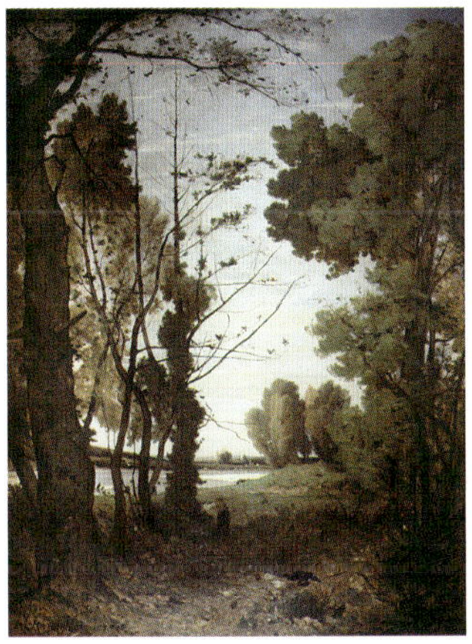

Harpignies, Henri-Joseph 1819–1916
Duck Shooting on the Banks of the River Allier
1861
oil on canvas 181 x 146 (E)
SOUAG.B97

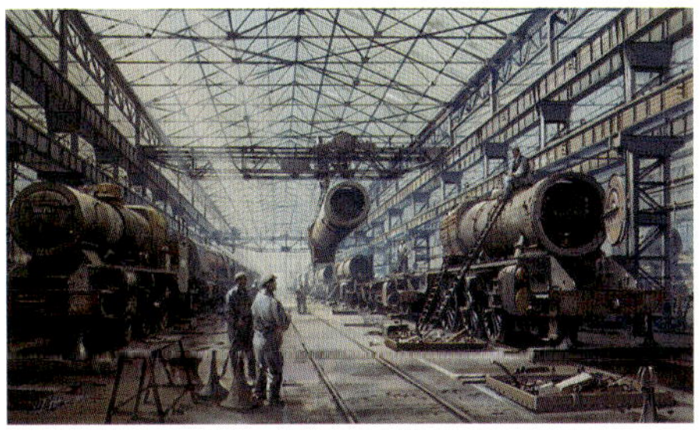

Harris, Alfred Peter b.1932
Perspective in Steel 1987
oil on board 43.5 x 70
SOUAG.S399

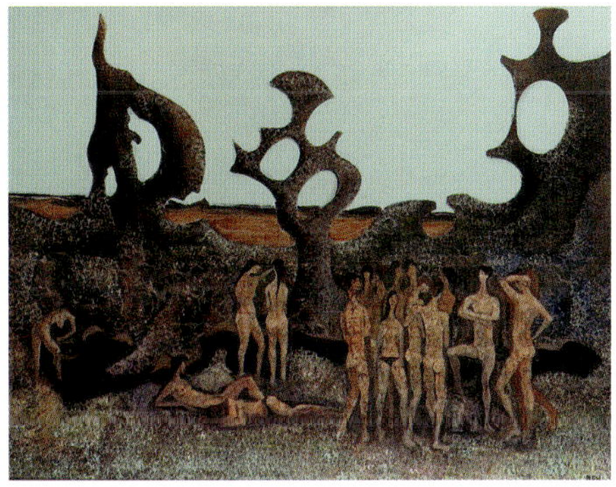

Harris, Robert E. b.1927
The Bathers 1968
oil on canvas 72.5 x 80.5 (E)
SOUAG.S78

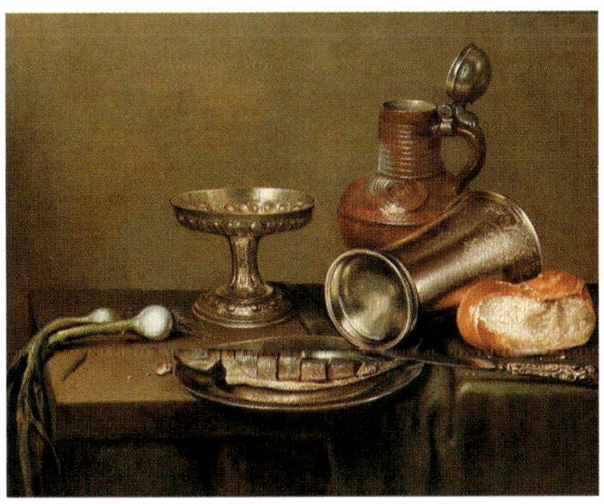

Heda, Gerrit Willemsz. c.1620–before 1702
Breakfast Still Life
oil on canvas 45 x 52.5 (E)
SOUAG.B107

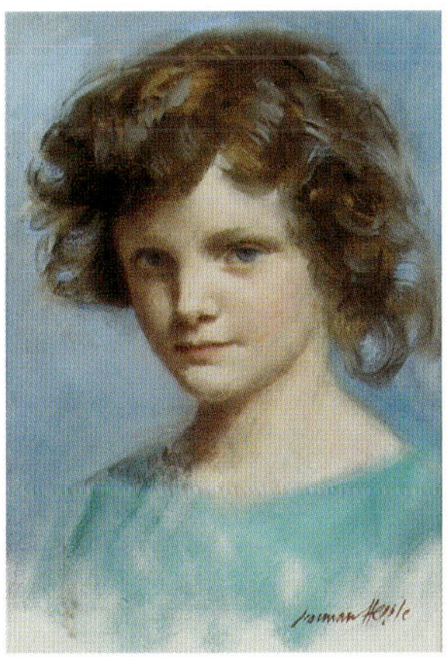

Hepple, Norman 1908–1994
Portrait of a Little Girl in Blue
oil on canvas 42 x 30.5 (E)
SOUAG.S377

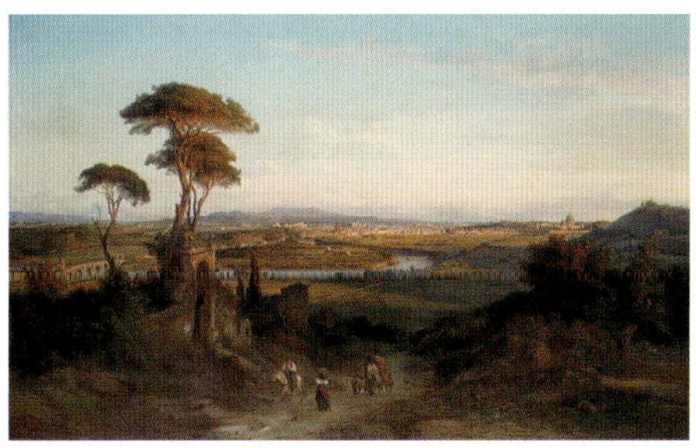

Hering, George Edwards 1805–1879
A Distant View of Rome
oil on canvas 43 x 70 (E)
SOUAG.B14

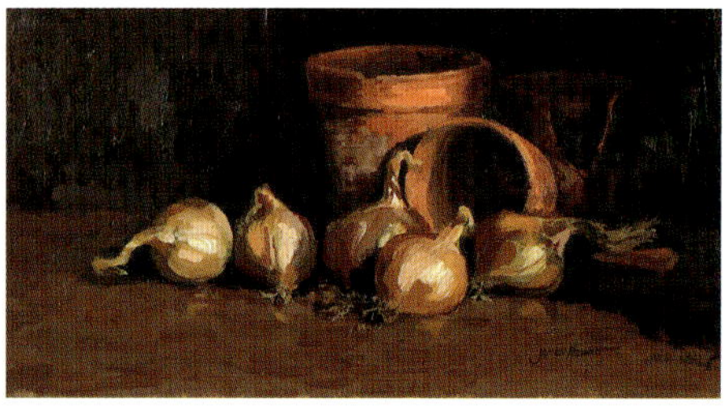

Hewitt, James
Garden Shed, Still Life c.1978
oil on canvas 20 x 35.5 (E)
SOUAG.S167

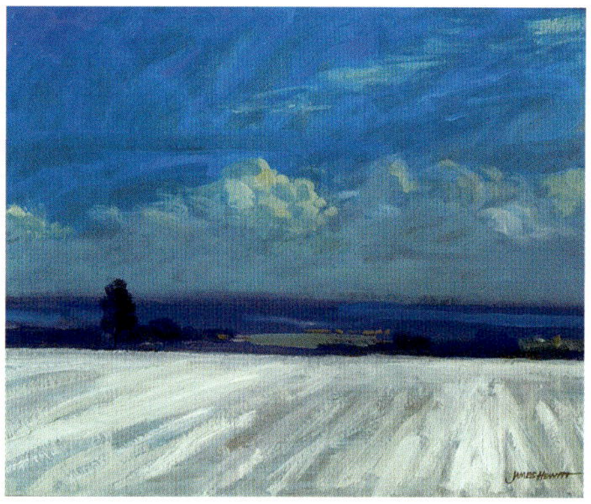

Hewitt, James
Snow at Great Totham c.1978
oil on canvas 28 x 34 (E)
SOUAG.S168

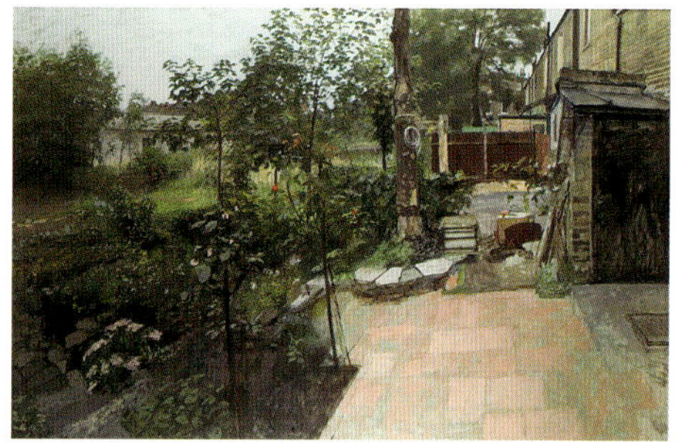

Heyworth, Alfred 1926–1976
Gardens in Chiswick c.1969
oil on board 122 x 183 (E)
SOUAG.S80

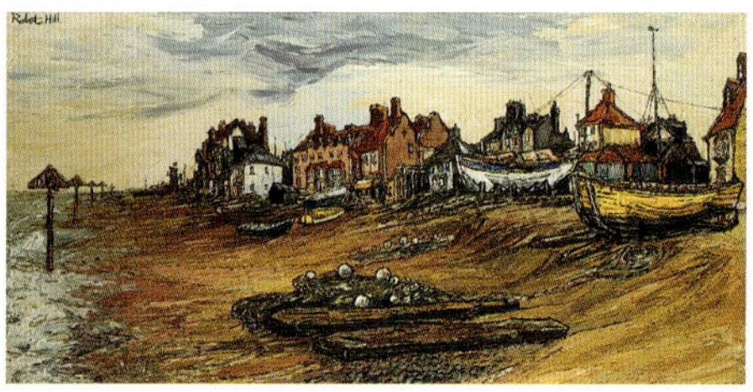

Hill, Robert W. b.1932
Aldeburgh Beach
oil on board 61 x 122 (E)
SOUAG.S94

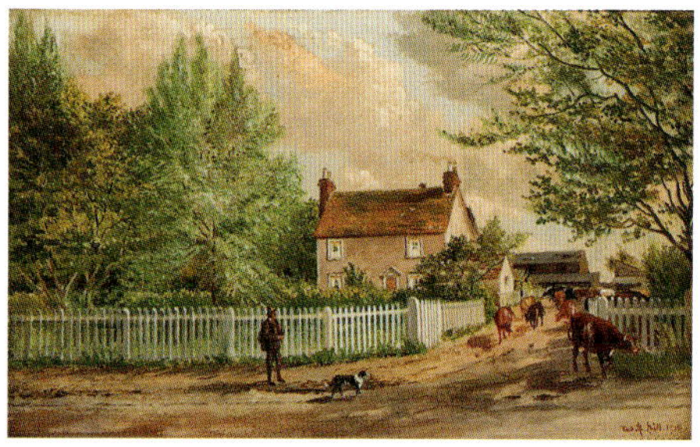

Hill, W. H.
Folly Farm, Westcliff 1910
oil on canvas 22 x 35 (E)
SOUAG.TS502

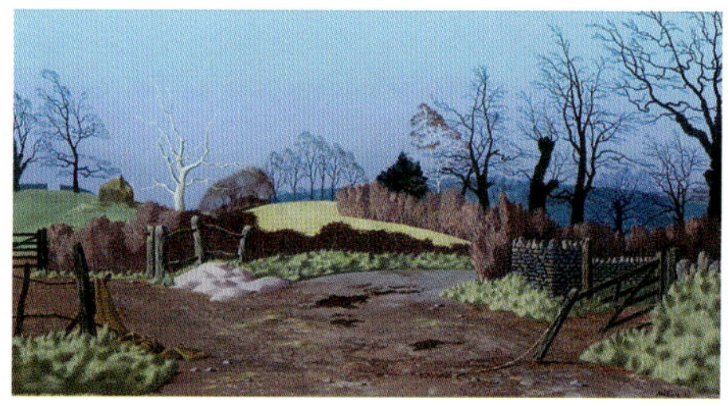

Hillier, Tristram Paul 1905–1983
Cutlers Green 1944
tempera on board 25.5 x 45.5 (E)
SOUAG.S42

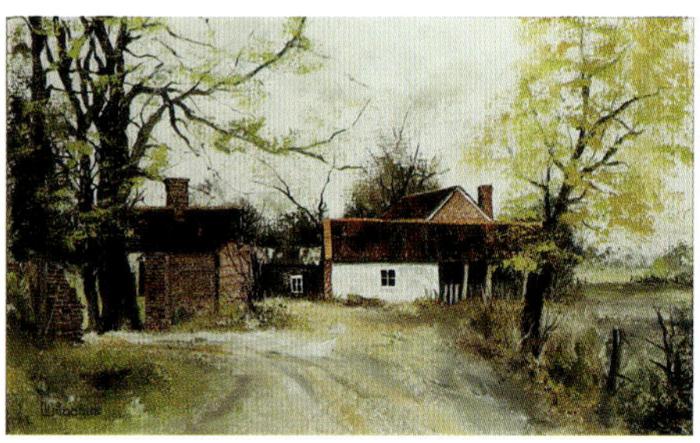

Hinde, Phil b.1938
Barns at Shelley, near Ongar c.1982
oil on canvas 37.5 x 58.5 (E)
SOUAG.S241

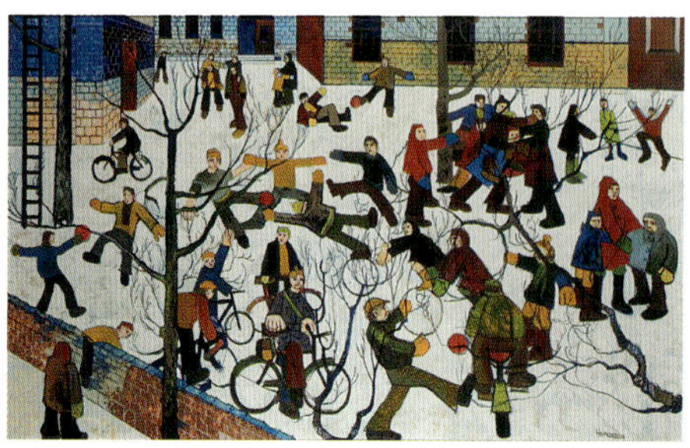

Hopkinson, John b.1941
Children's Games No.2 1970s
oil on board 82.5 x 129 (E)
SOUAG.S126

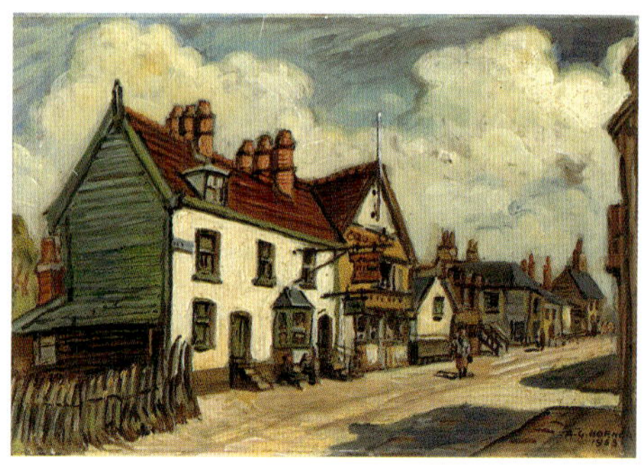

Horner, A. G. active 1953–1957
The Crooked Billet, Leigh-on-Sea 1953
oil on paper 32.5 x 40 (E)
SOUAG.TS853

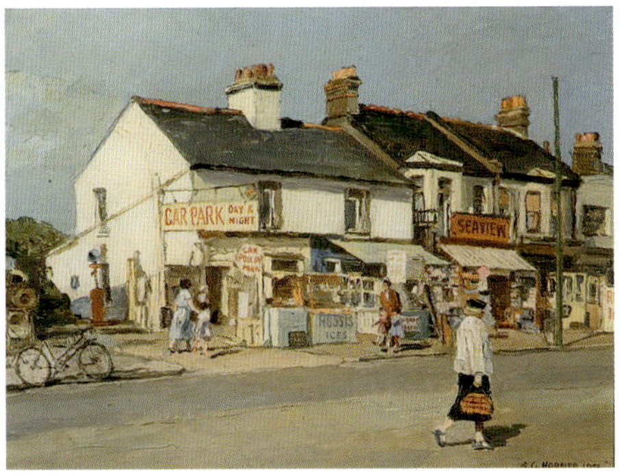

Horner, A. G. active 1953–1957
Seafront, Thorpe Bay 1956
oil on canvas 38 x 49 (E)
SOUAG.S32

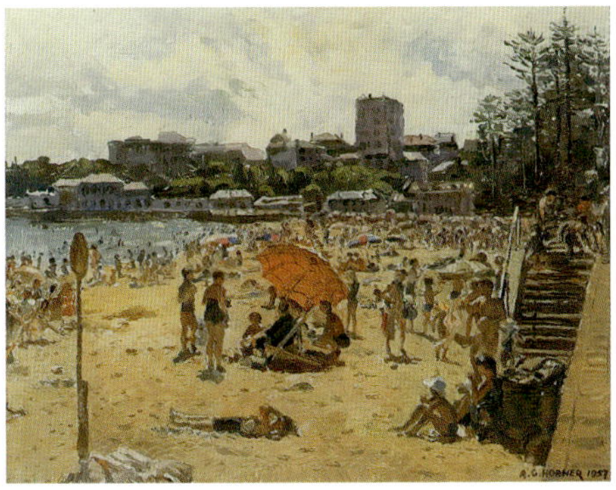

Horner, A. G. active 1953–1957
Manly Beach, Australia 1957
oil on canvas 42 x 51 (E)
SOUAG.S31

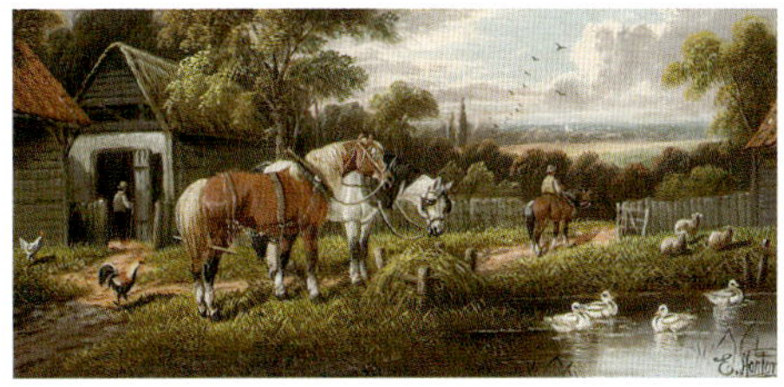

Horton, Etty d.1905
Pastoral Scene
oil on canvas 20 x 40.5 (E)
SOUAG.S252

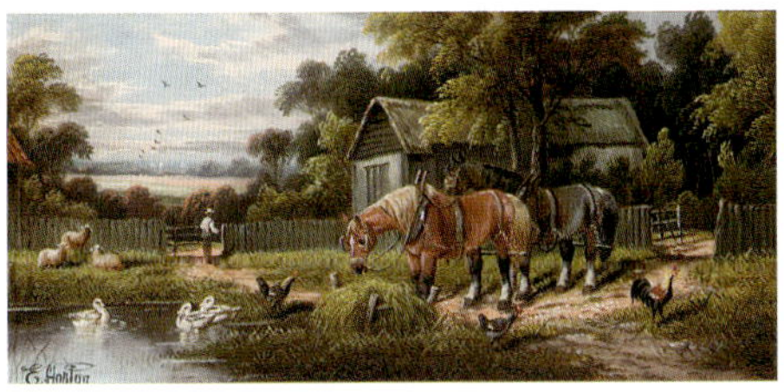

Horton, Etty d.1905
Pastoral Scene
oil on canvas 20 x 40.5 (E)
SOUAG.S253

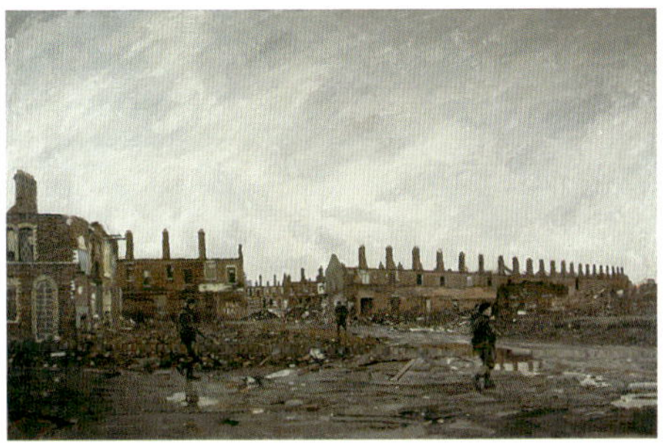

Howard, Ken b.1932
Street Patrol, Belfast 1974
oil on canvas 124 x 183 (E)
SOUAG.S363

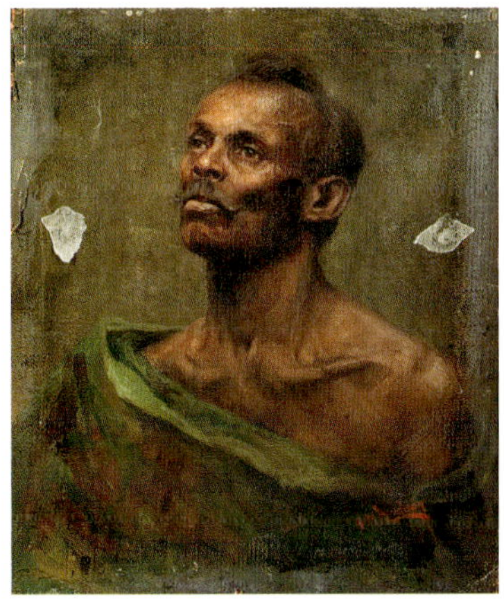

Hudson, G. M. active 1909–1935
Negro Slave
oil on canvas 62 x 51
SOUAG.S264

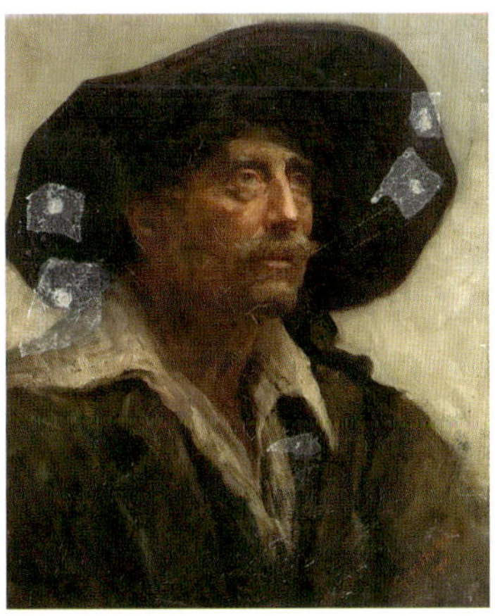

Hudson, Gwynedd M. active 1881–1935
Portrait of an Artist 1911
oil on canvas 53.5 x 43
SOUAG.S436

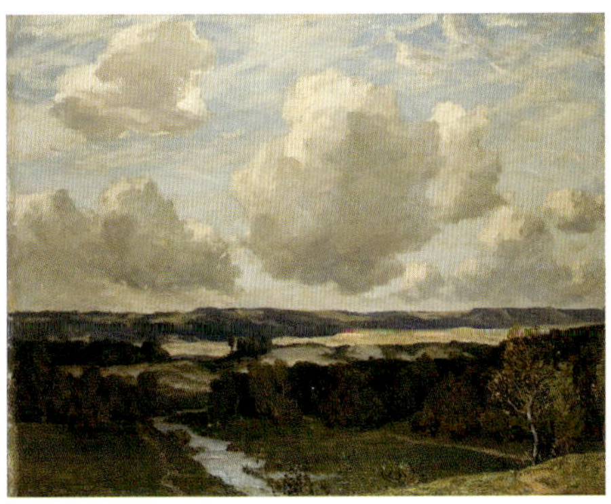

Hughes-Stanton, Herbert Edwin Pelham
1870–1937
Pas de Calais
oil on canvas 94 x 112 (E)
SOUAG.B76

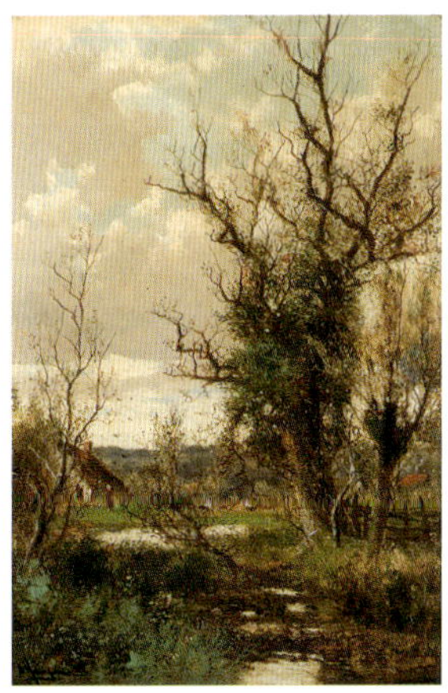

Hulk, Abraham 1813–1897
Landscape
oil on canvas 76 x 51 (E)
SOUAG.S55

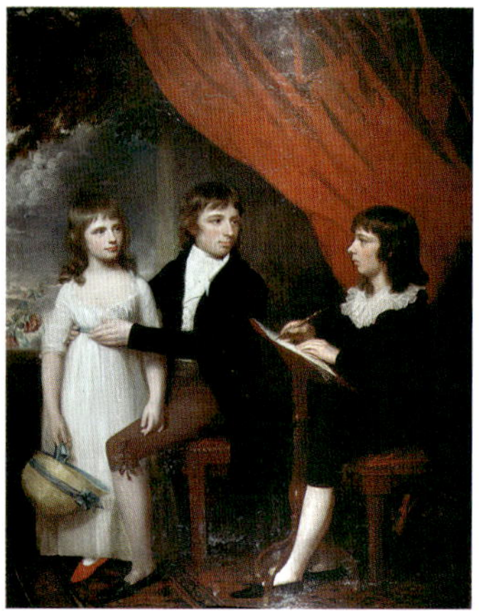

Humphry, Ozias 1742–1810
The Heygate Family c.1800
oil on canvas 177.5 x 135 (E)
SOUAG.TS8

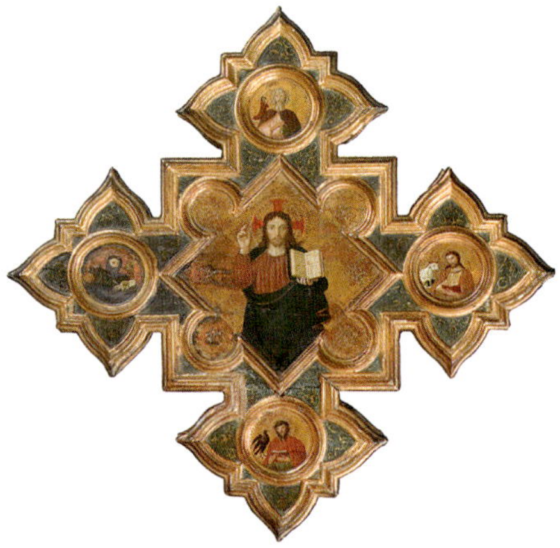

Italian School 16th C
Christ and the Four Evangelists
oil & gilt on wood 61 x 61 (E)
SOUAG.B39

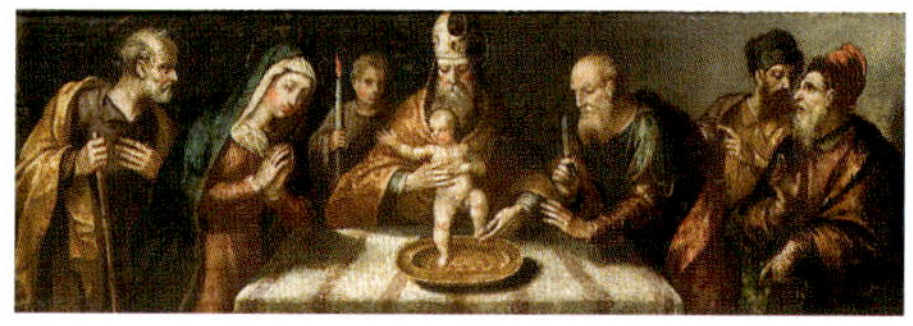

Italian School 16th C
The Circumcision of Christ
oil on panel 13 x 37.5 (E)
SOUAG.B90

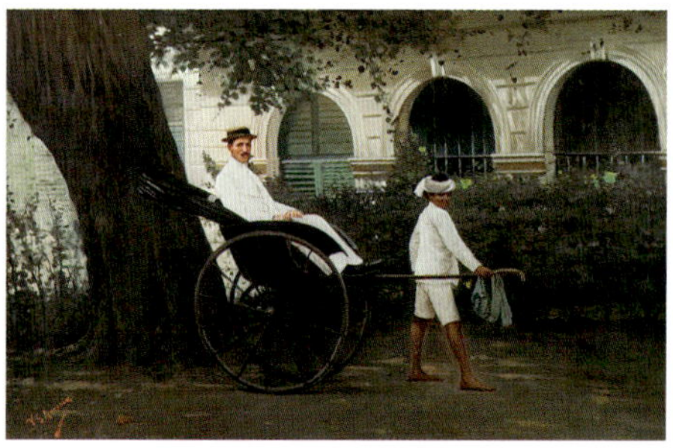

Italian School
Gentleman in a Rickshaw 1880
oil on canvas 49.5 x 75 (E)
SOUAG.S261

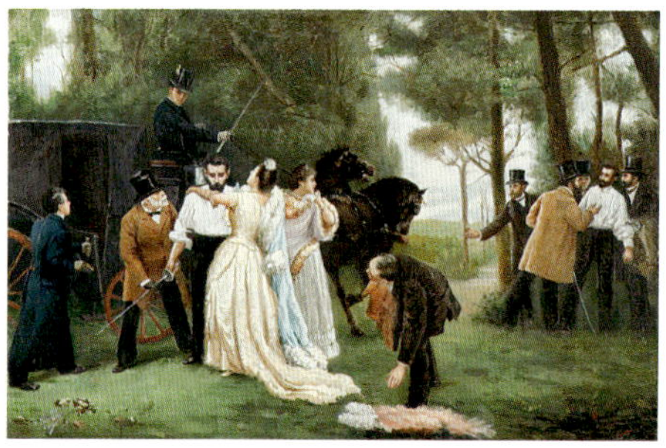

Italian School
The Duel 1880
oil on canvas 49.5 x 79 (E)
SOUAG.S260

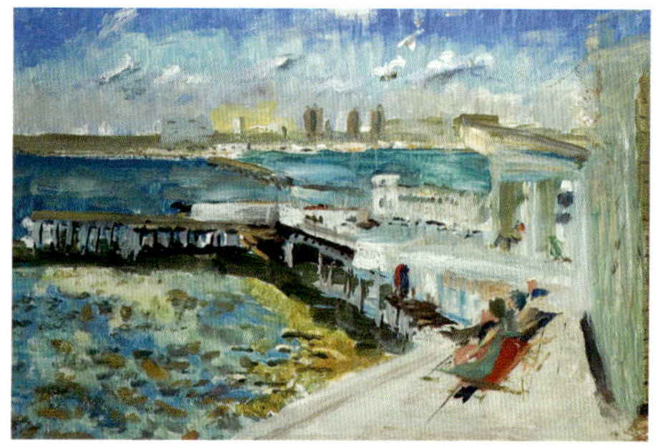

Jackson, Gloria active 1976–1985
The End of the Pier, Prior to the Fire
late 1970s
oil on board 61 x 86 (E)
SOUAG.TS823

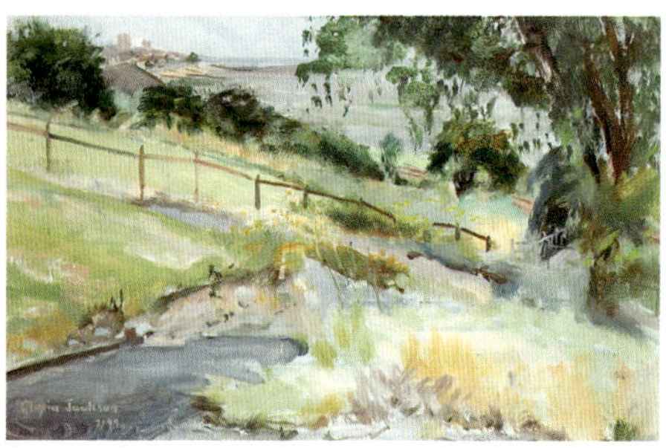

Jackson, Gloria active 1976–1985
Leighcliff Gardens 1979
oil on board 43 x 63.5 (E)
SOUAG.TS820

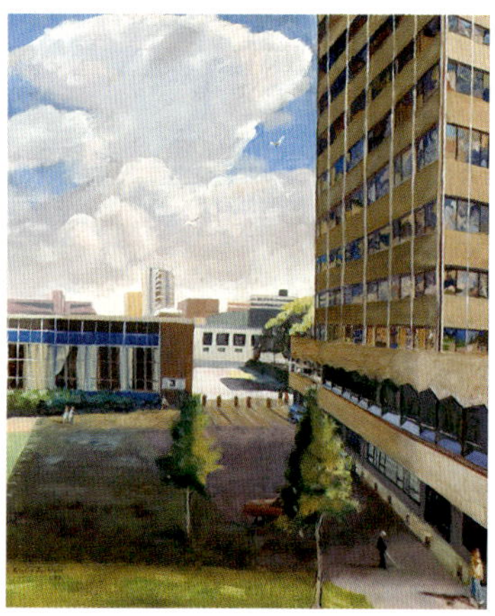

Jackson, Gloria active 1976–1985
Rear View of Civic Centre 1983
oil on board 75.5 x 61 (E)
SOUAG.TS821

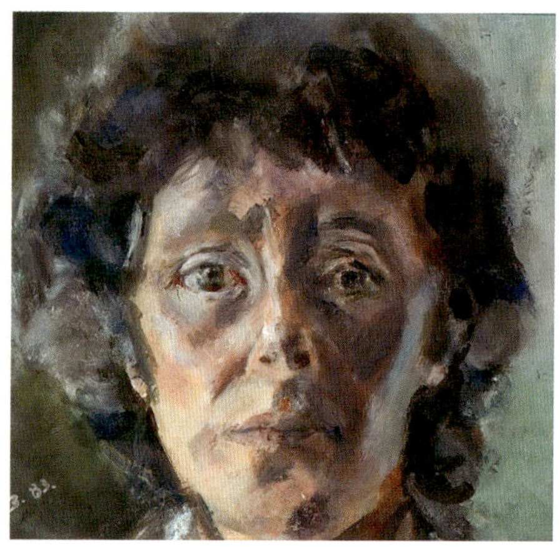

Jackson, Gloria active 1976–1985
Self Portrait 1983
oil on board 23 x 23 (E)
SOUAG.S351

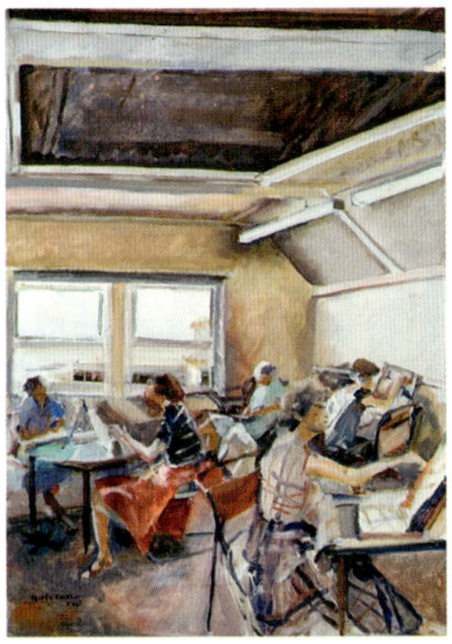

Jackson, Gloria active 1976–1985
Scene in Gallery 9 at the Beecroft 1984
oil on board 84 x 58.5 (E)
SOUAG.TS822

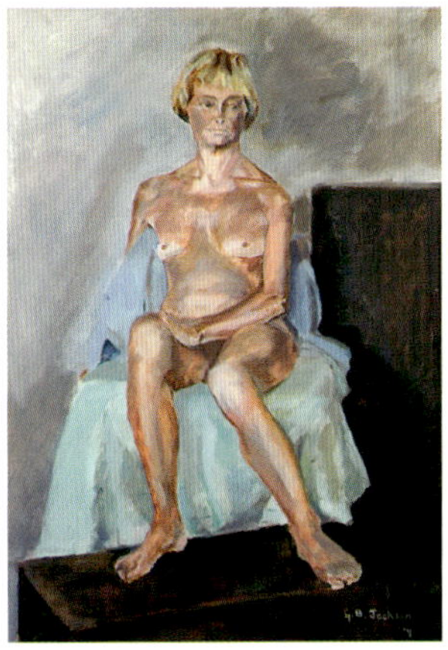

Jackson, Gloria active 1976–1985
Fair-Haired Seated Nude on Green and Blue Drapery, 1979
oil on board 80 x 54.5 (E)
SOUAG.S348

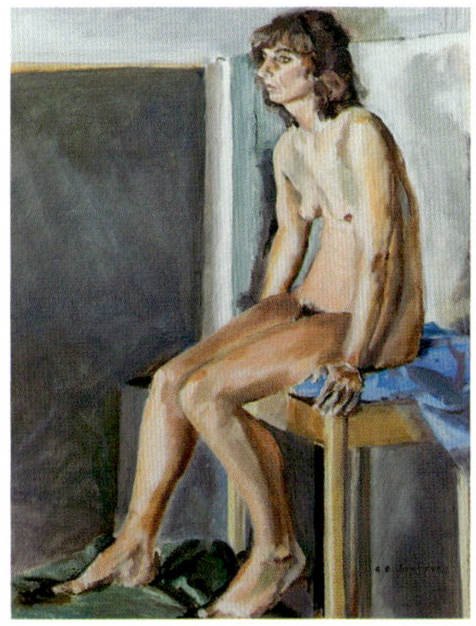

Jackson, Gloria active 1976–1985
Nude Seated on Blue-Cushioned Stool
oil on board 81 x 61 (E)
SOUAG.S349

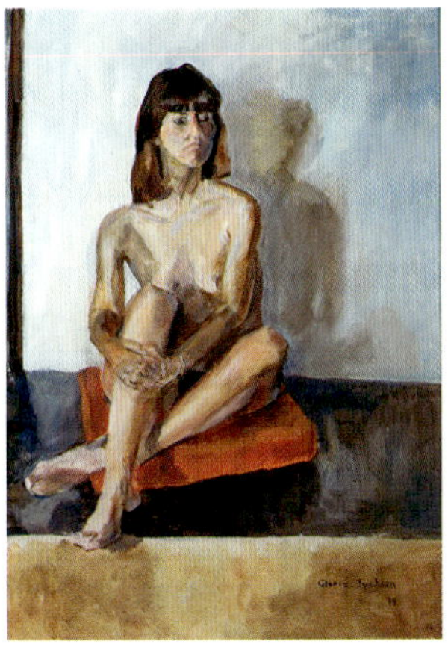

Jackson, Gloria active 1976–1985
Nude Seated on Red Cushion, 1979
oil on board 75.5 x 54.5 (E)
SOUAG.S350

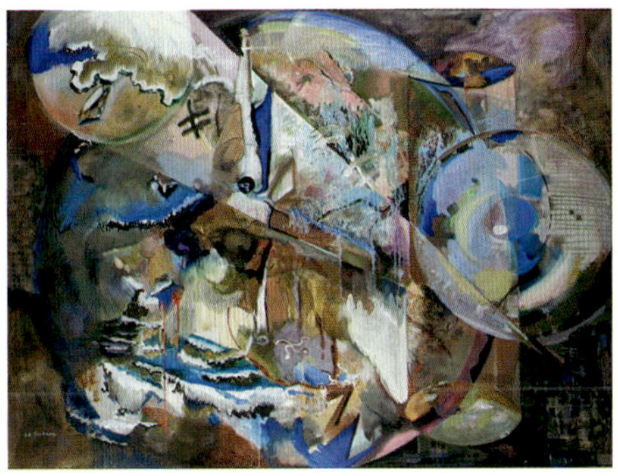

Jackson, Gloria active 1976–1985
Untitled Abstract
oil on board 122 x 162.5 (E)
SOUAG.S346

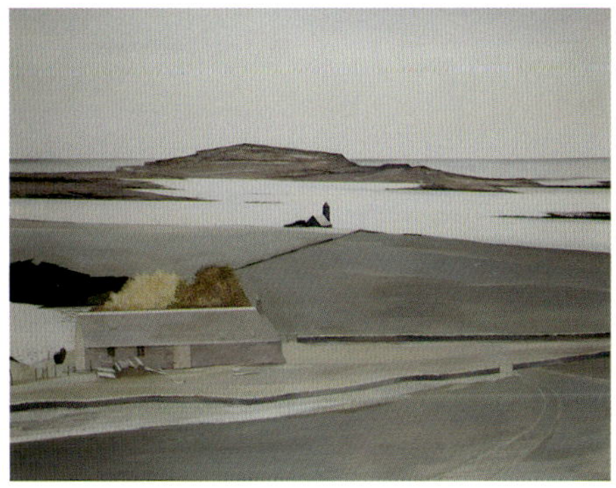

James, Owen b.1934
Canna 1975
oil & acrylic on board 101.5 x 127 (E)
SOUAG.S154

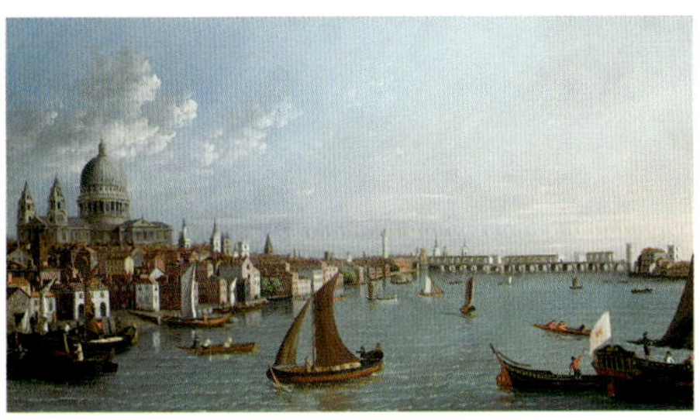

James, William active 1745–1771
London Bridge c.1756–1759
oil on canvas 75 x 125 (E)
SOUAG.TS9

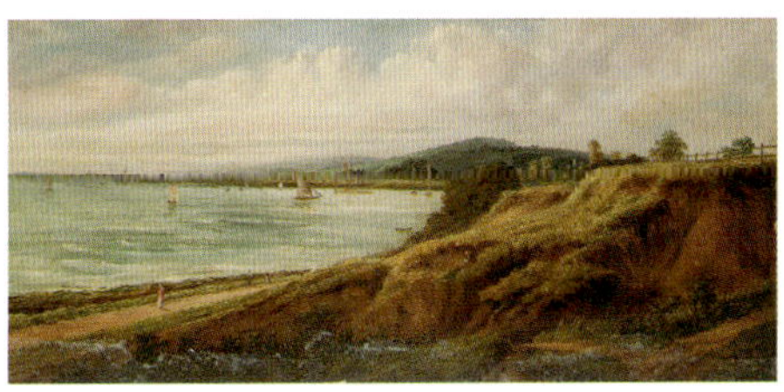

Jayne, Charles active 1838–1879
Landslip, Cliff Town, Southend c.1870
oil on canvas 45.5 x 64.5 (E)
SOUAG.TS429

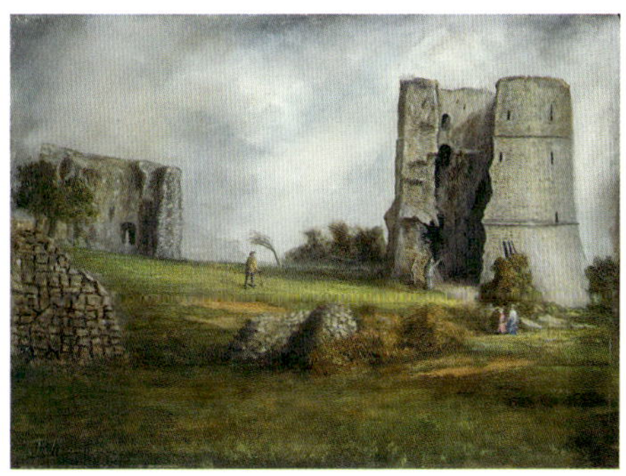

Jenkins, J.
Hadleigh Castle
oil on canvas 35 x 45.5 (E)
SOUAG.TS491

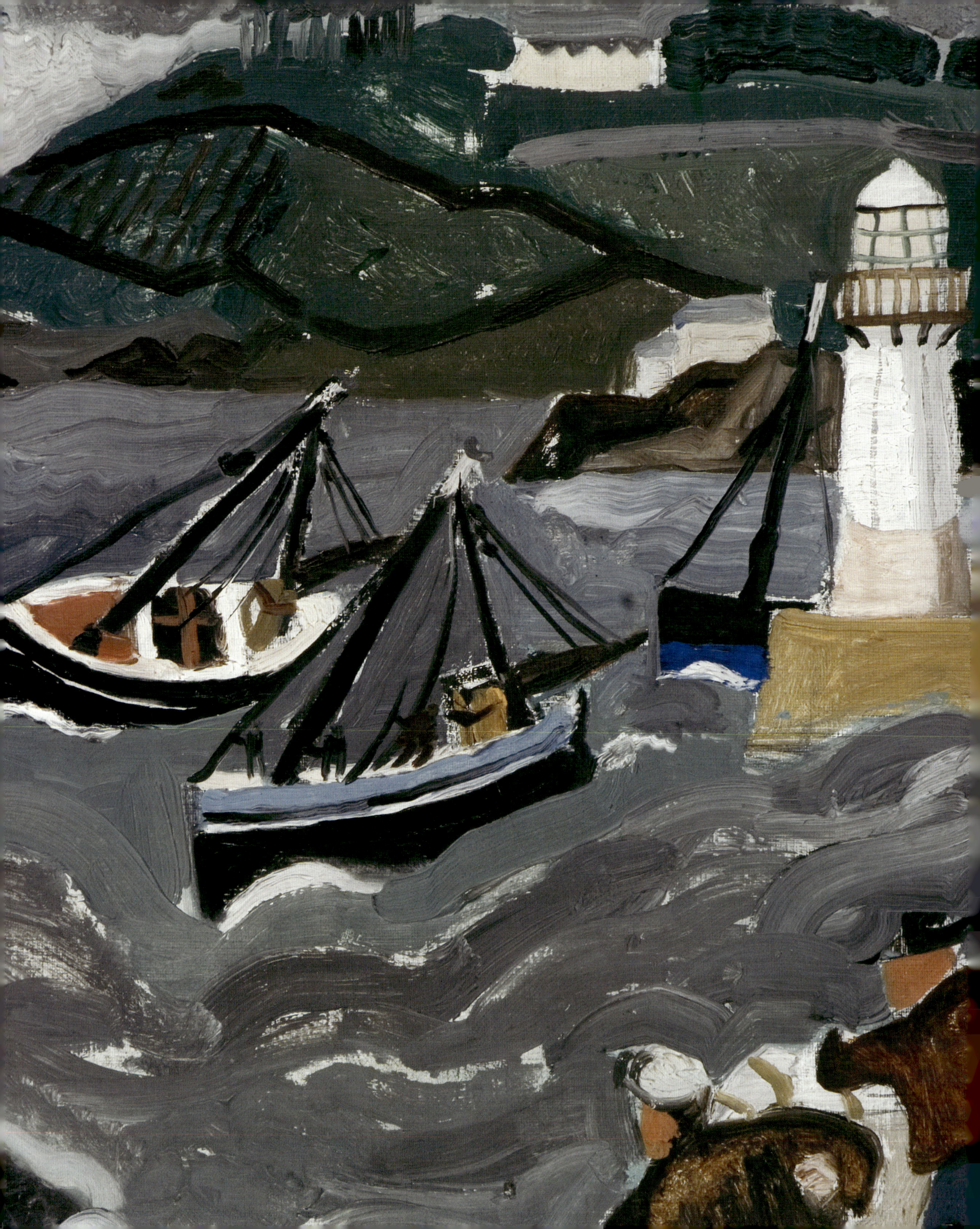

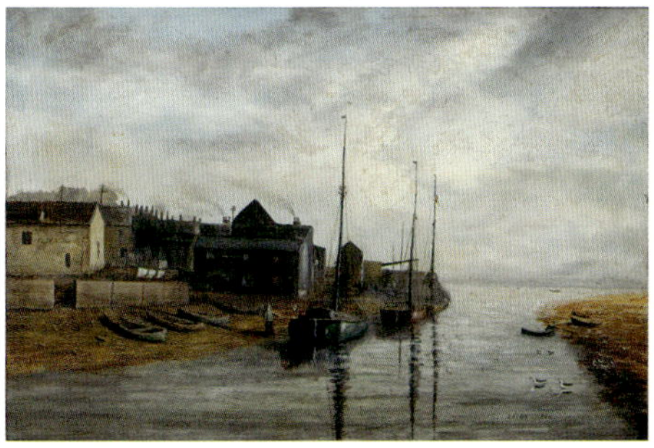

Jenkins, J.
Leigh Creek
oil on board 45.5 x 64.5 (E)
SOUAG.TS493

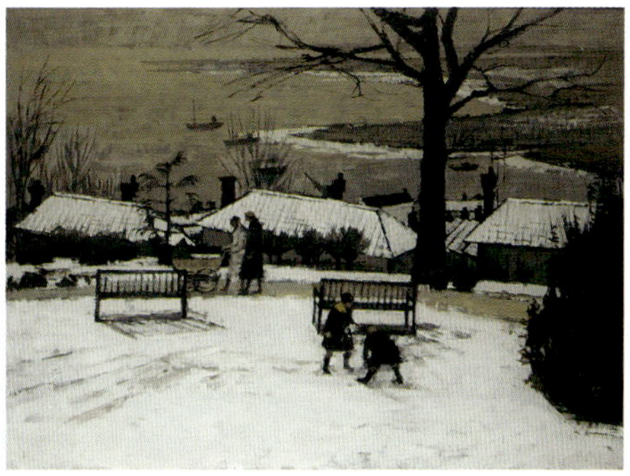

Johnson, Valerie
Winter Morning, Leigh 1950s
oil on hardboard 90 x 117 (E)
SOUAG.B88

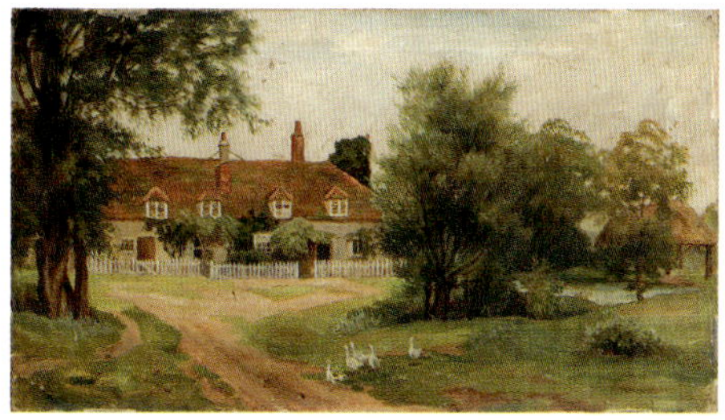

Keyes, S. K.
Southchurch Hall c.1900
oil on canvas 35.5 x 61 (E)
SOUAG.TS480

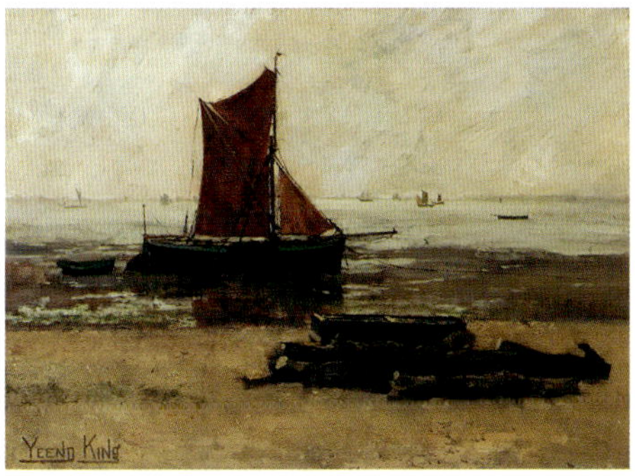

King, Yeend 1855–1924
Southend c.1887
oil on canvas 46 x 57 (E)
SOUAG.TS10

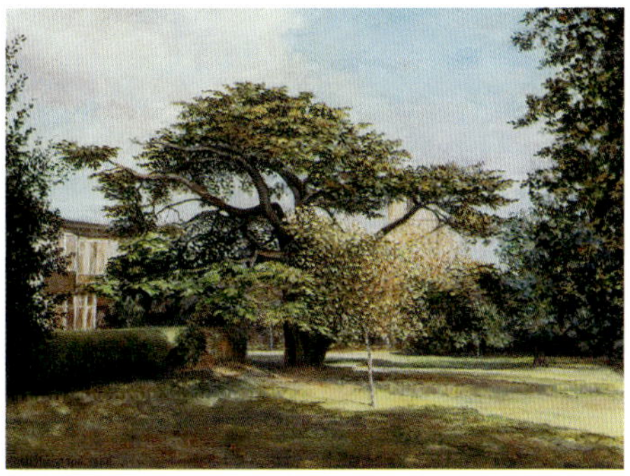

Kingston, Joyce
Cedar Tree in Prittlewell Park 1980
oil on canvas 30 x 40
SOUAG.TS915

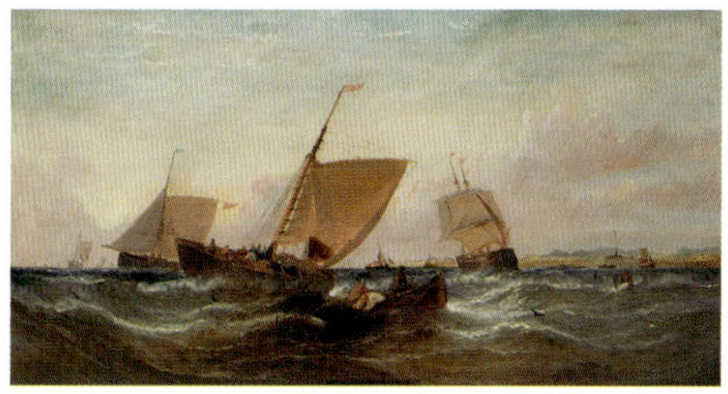

Knell, William Calcott active 1848–1885
Evening Oyster Boat off Southend Pier 1867
oil on canvas 64 x 105 (E)
SOUAG.TS11

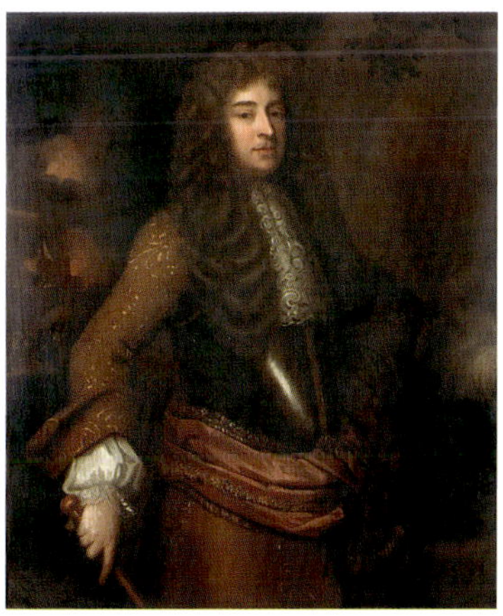

Kneller, Godfrey 1646–1723
The Earl of Rochester
oil on canvas 124 x 100 (E)
SOUAG.B125

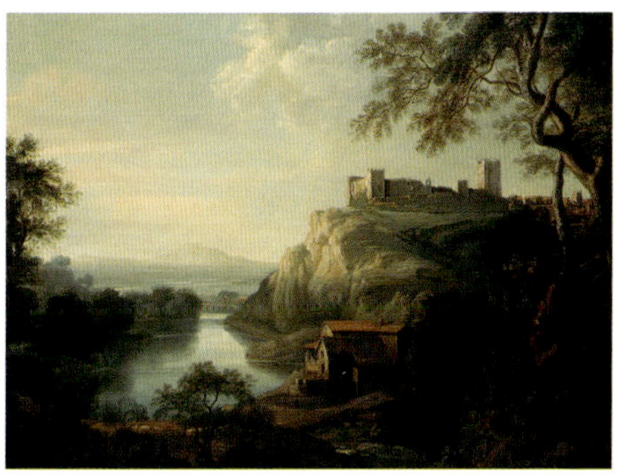

Lambert, George c.1700–1765
Richmond Castle, Yorkshire
oil on canvas 63 x 67 (E)
SOUAG.B4

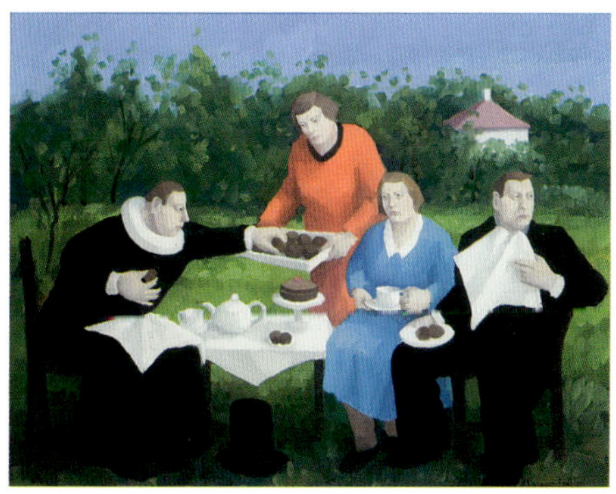

Larusdottir, Karolina b.1944
Sunday Visit to the Summerhouse 1994
oil on canvas 39.5 x 49.5
SOUAG.S556

Facing page: Wood, Christopher, 1901–1930, *Harbour in Hills* (detail), University of Essex, (p. 180)

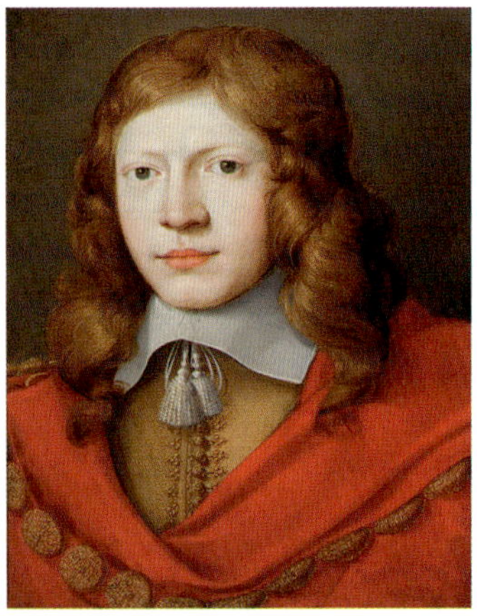

Le Nain family active 17th C
Portrait of a Youth
oil on canvas 39 x 30 (E)
SOUAG.B50

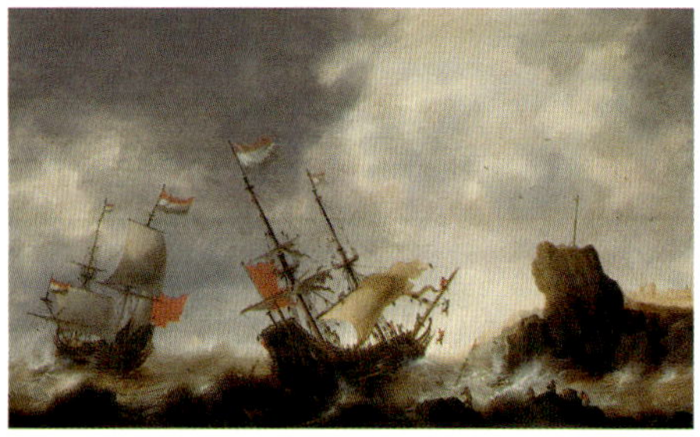

Leyden, Jan van active 1652–1669
The Shipwreck
oil on panel 58.5 x 91.5 (E)
SOUAG.B67

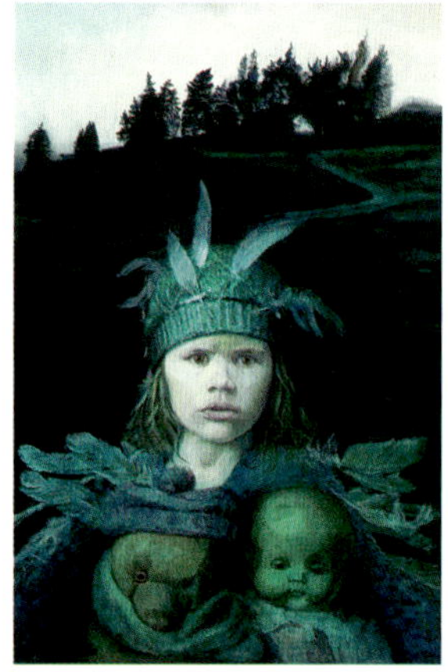

Licence, Geoffrey b.1944
Bird Girl, Belton Hills c.1982
oil on board 61.5 x 40.5 (E)
SOUAG.S242

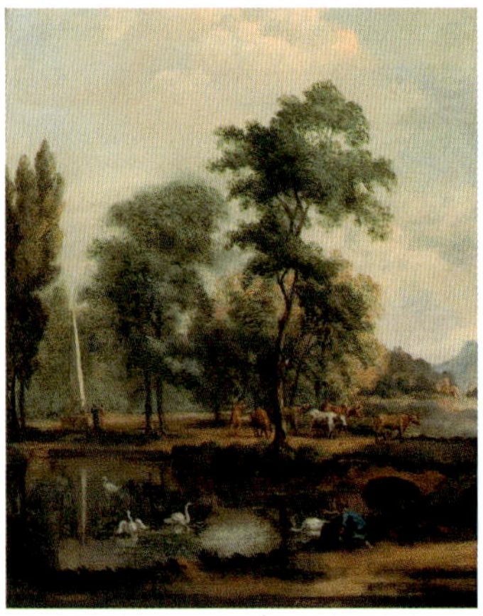

Lint, Hendrik Frans van 1684–1763
Landscape by a River
oil on canvas 32.5 x 27.5 (E)
SOUAG.B127

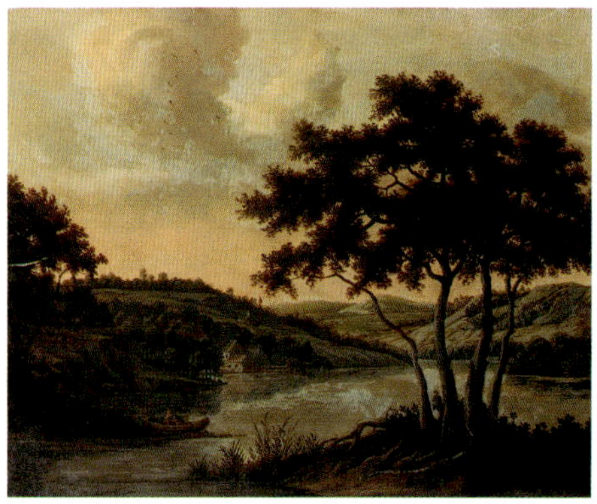

Looten, Jan c.1618–c.1681
River Landscape
oil on canvas 62.5 x 75 (E)
SOUAG.B33

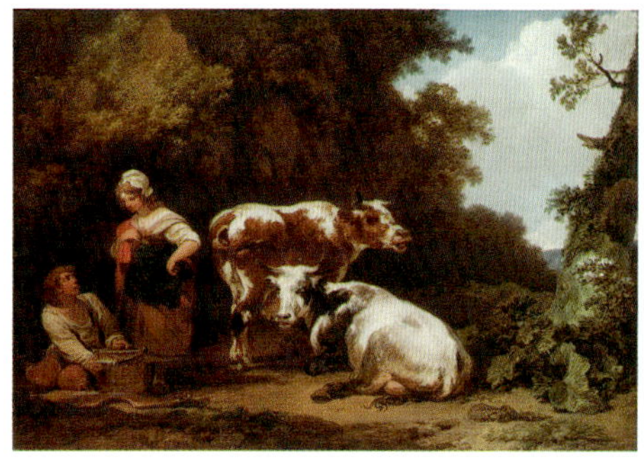

Loutherbourg, Philip James de 1740–1812
Pastoral Scene 1797
oil on canvas 27 x 36 (E)
SOUAG.B108

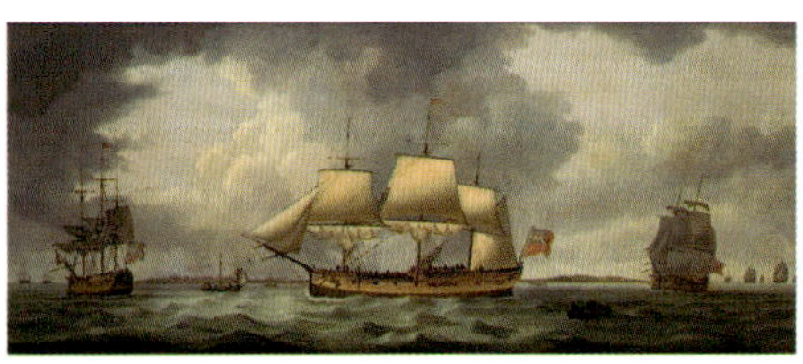

Luny, Thomas 1759–1837
The 'Duke William', Homeward Bound off the Entrance to the River Thames 1783
oil on canvas 61 x 141 (E)
SOUAG.TS12

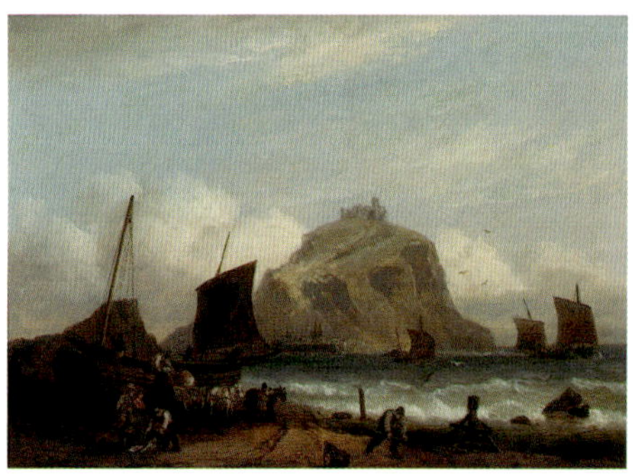

Luny, Thomas 1759–1837
St Michael's Mount 1835
oil on canvas 37 x 50 (E)
SOUAG.B66

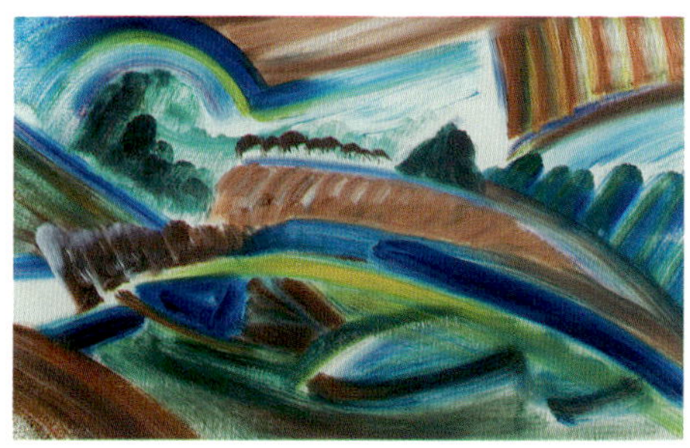

Lygo-Baker, Owen Neil b.1940
Valley, Autumn 1966
oil on board 35.5 x 56 (E)
SOUAG.S104

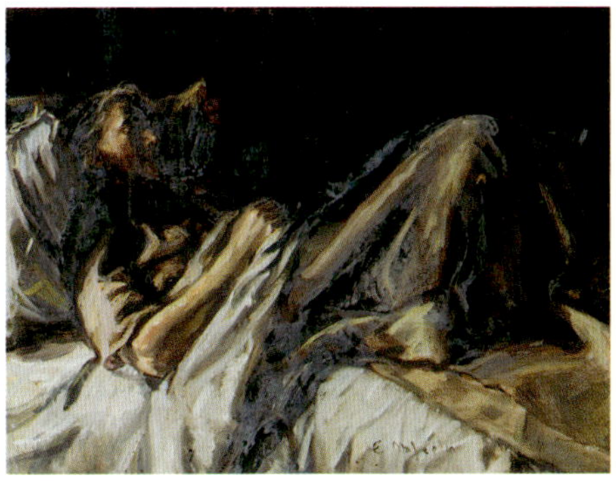

Malcolm, Ellen 1923–2002
Night Shadows
oil on canvas 56 x 68.5 (E)
SOUAG.B69

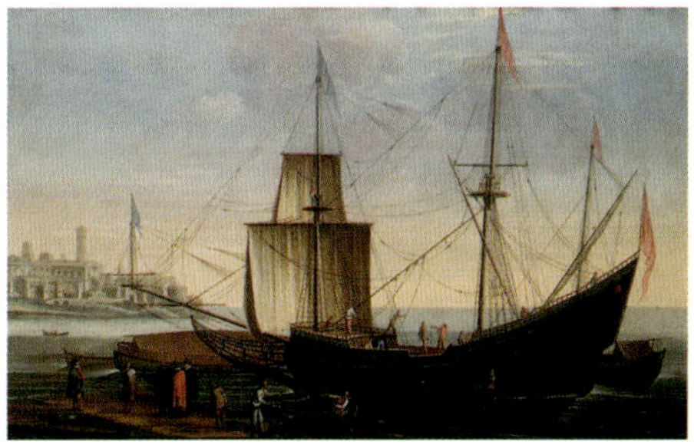

Manglard, Adrien 1695–1760
Shipping off the Italian Coast
oil on canvas 48 x 74
SOUAG.B129

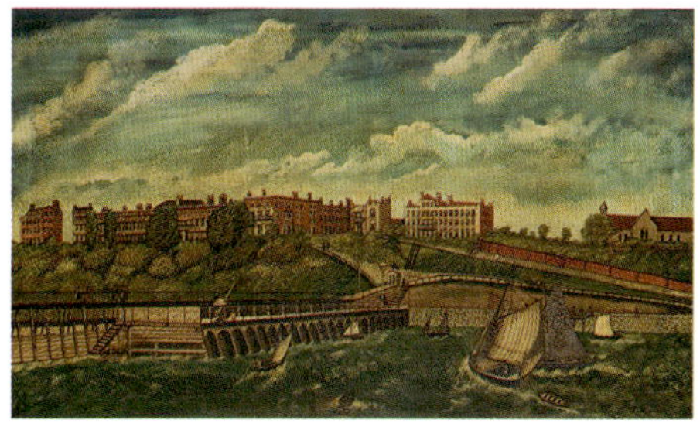

Marder, J.
View of Southend Seafront
oil on canvas 52.5 x 85 (E)
SOUAG.TS782

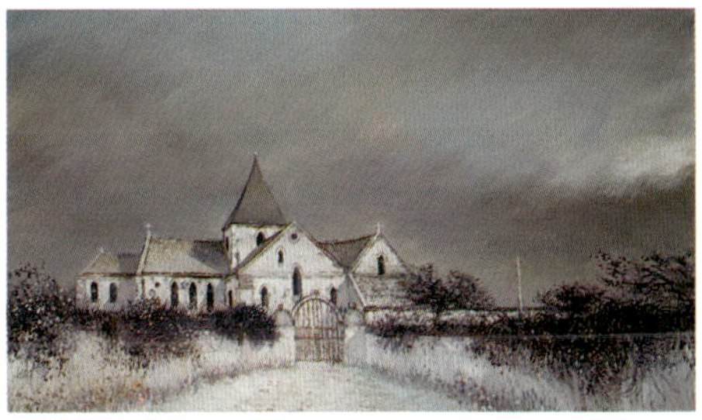

Mason, Bateson 1910–1977
Near Vouvray c.1973
oil on hardboard 76 x 122.5 (E)
SOUAG.S121

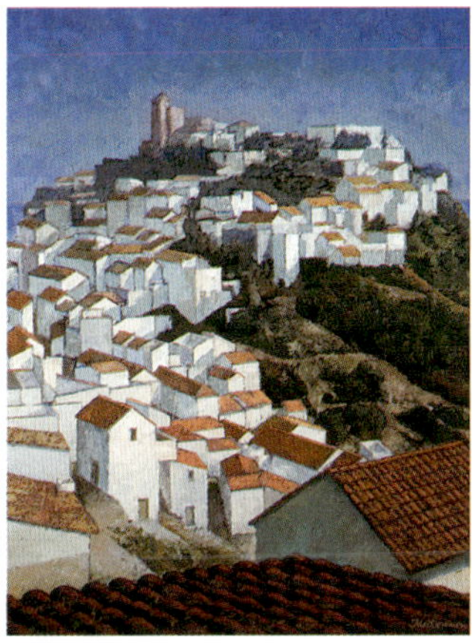

Meddemmen, George 1920–2004
Casares, Costa del Sol
oil on board 56 x 40.5 (E)
SOUAG.S384

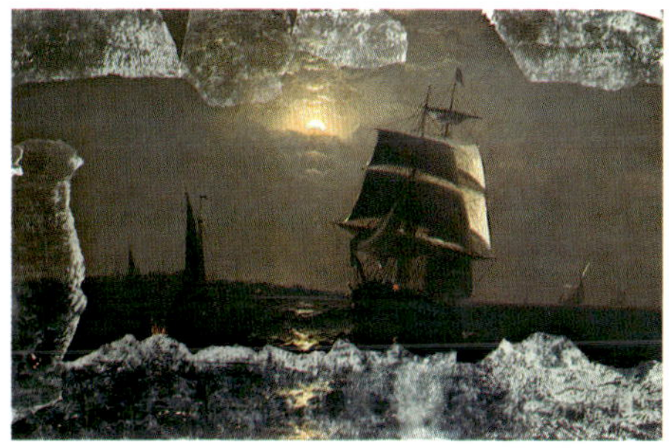

Melbye, Anton 1818 1875
Midnight off Sheerness
oil on canvas 61 x 91.5 (E)
SOUAG.TS13

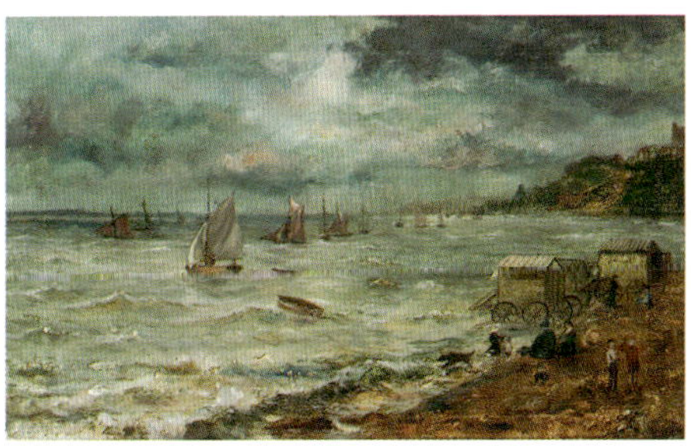

Melville, Eliza Anne Leslie active from 1894
Leigh Cliffs
oil on canvas 40.5 x 61 (E)
SOUAG.TS482

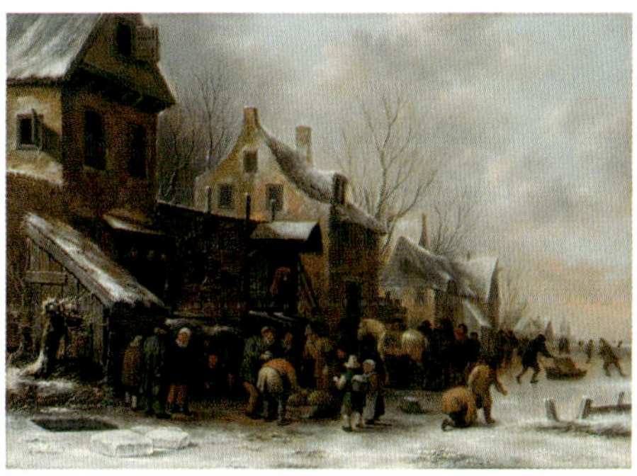

Molenaer, Klaes c.1630–1676
Winter Scene in Holland
oil on panel 49 x 65 (E)
SOUAG.B35

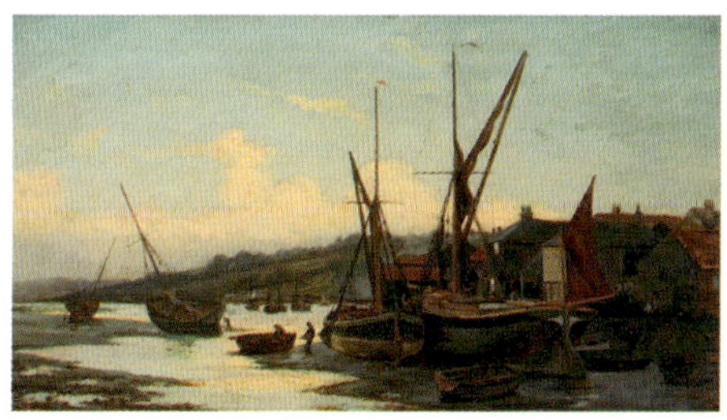

Moore, A. Harvey d.1905
Leigh c.1900
oil on canvas 29 x 52
SOUAG.TS916

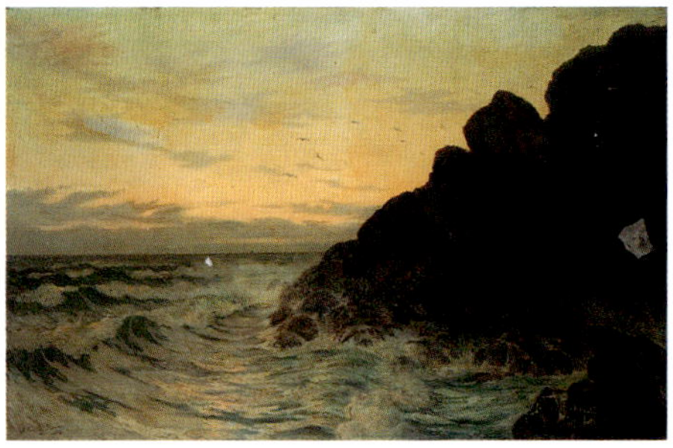

Moore, A. Harvey d.1905
Seascape 1904
oil on canvas 99 x 137 (E)
SOUAG.S262

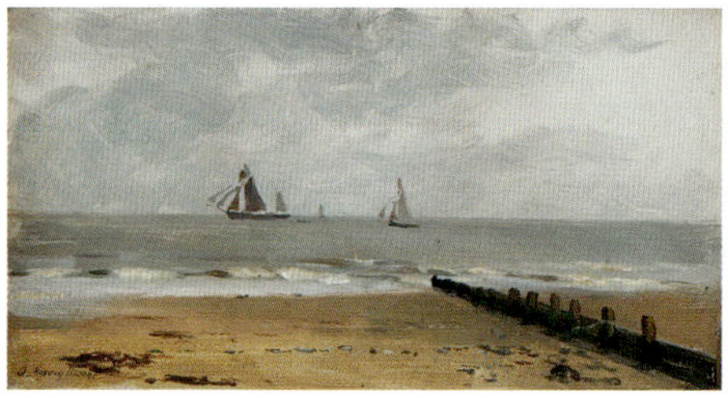

Moore, A. Harvey d.1905
Crowstone Beach
oil on canvas 15 x 28 (E)
SOUAG.S48

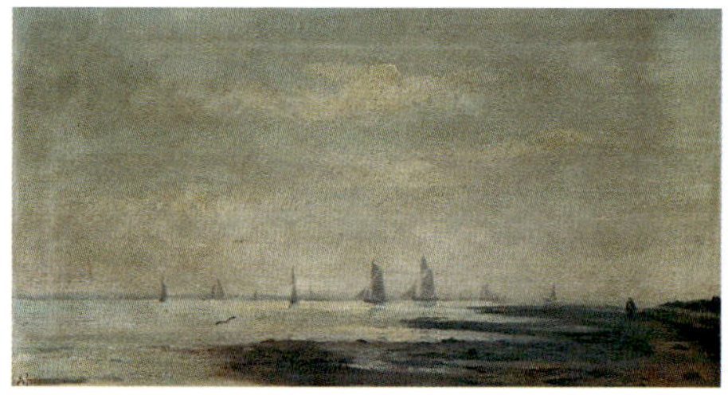

Moore, A. Harvey d.1905
The Estuary Looking West
oil on canvas 30.5 x 53.5 (E)
SOUAG.TS669

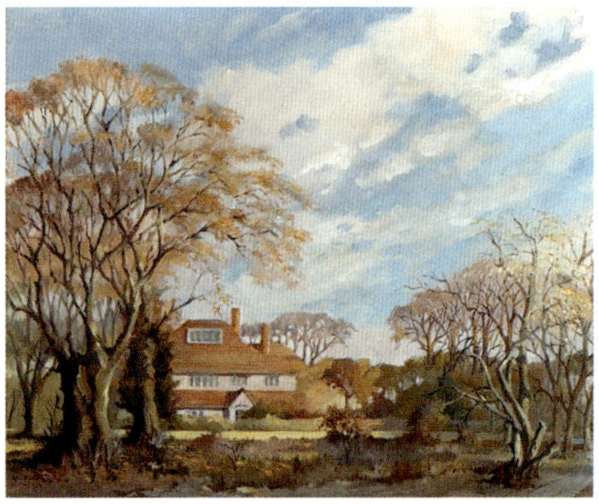

Moore, F. J.
The Clubhouse, Belfairs 1965
oil on board 39 x 50
SOUAG.TS259

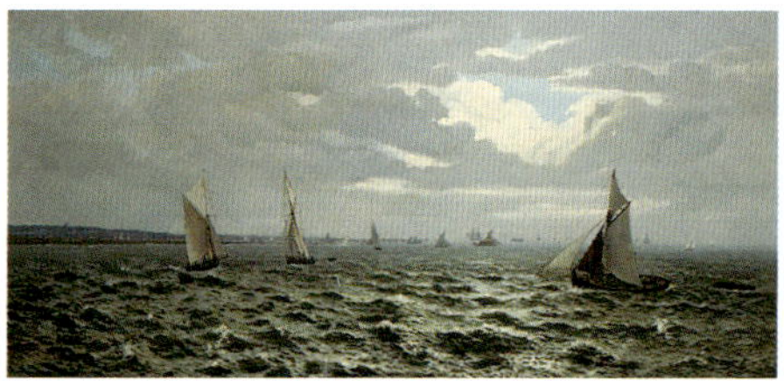

Moore, Henry 1831–1895
Off Leigh-on-Sea, Essex
oil on canvas 51 x 101.5 (E)
SOUAG.S99

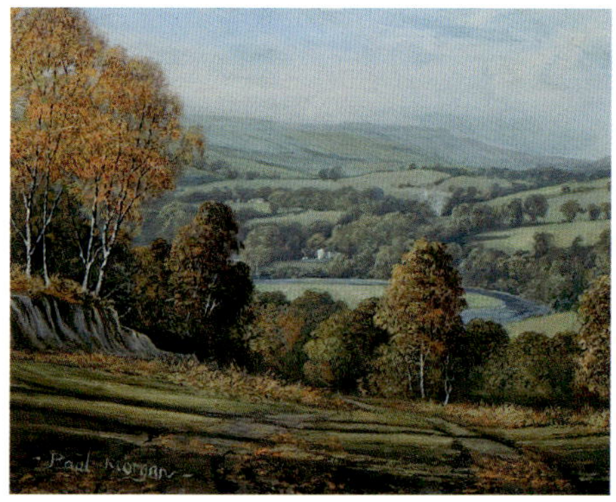

Morgan, Paul Robert b.1940
The Bend in the River
oil on board 19 x 24 (E)
SOUAG.S345

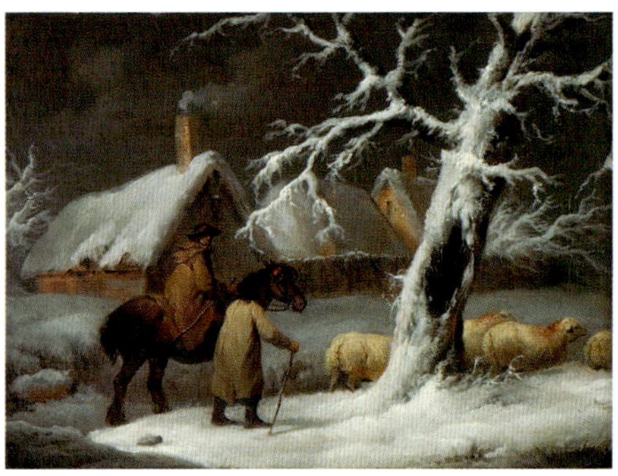

Morland, George 1763–1804
Winter Landscape
oil on panel 24 x 30.5 (E)
SOUAG.B109

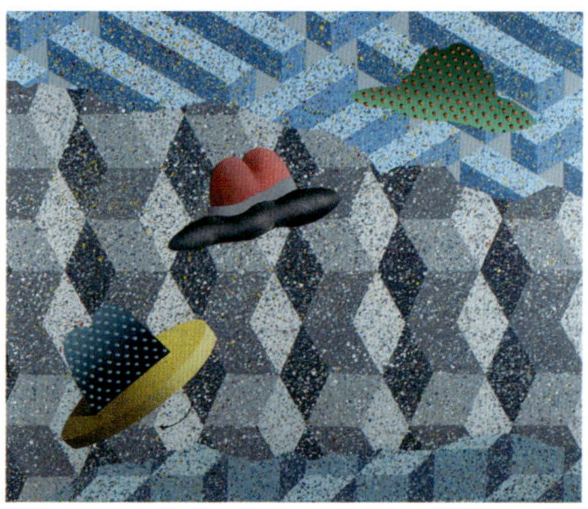

Moune, John
Monomorphosis (detail) 1980
acrylic on canvas 185 x 231
SOUAG.S250

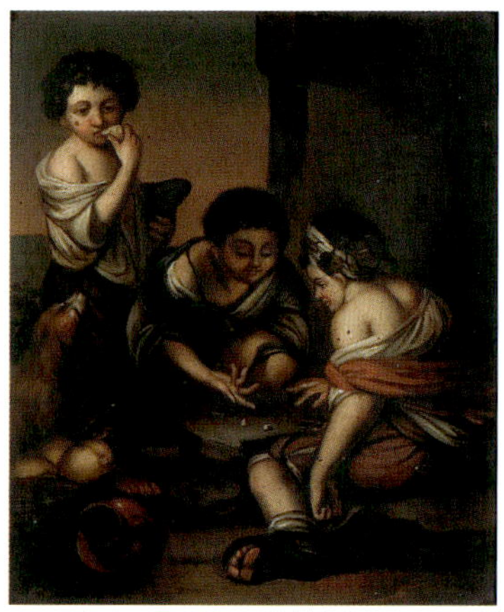

Murillo, Bartolomé Esteban (after)
1618–1682
Beggar Boys Playing Dice 18th C?
oil on copper 25.5 x 15 (E)
SOUAG.S438

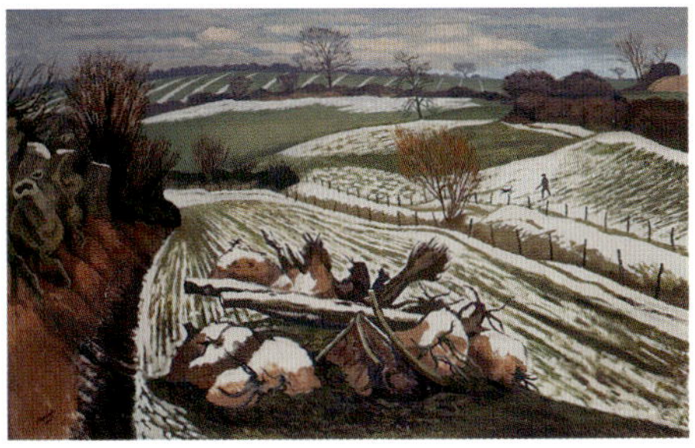

Nash, John Northcote 1893–1977
Melting Snow at Wormingford 1962
oil on canvas 46 x 75 (E)
SOUAG.B132

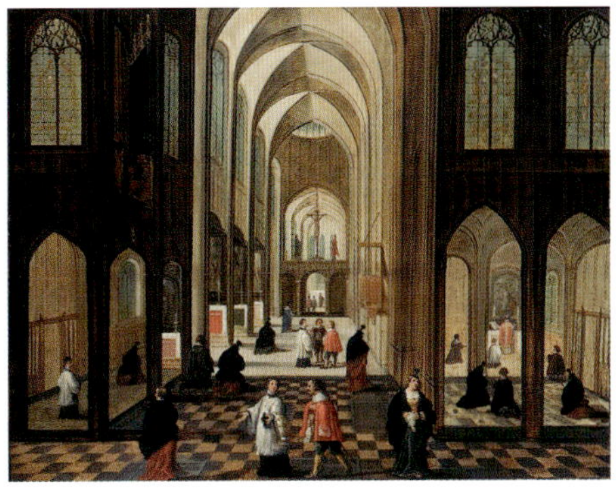

Neeffs, Peeter the younger 1620–1675
Cathedral Interior
oil on panel 37 x 44.5 (E)
SOUAG.B28

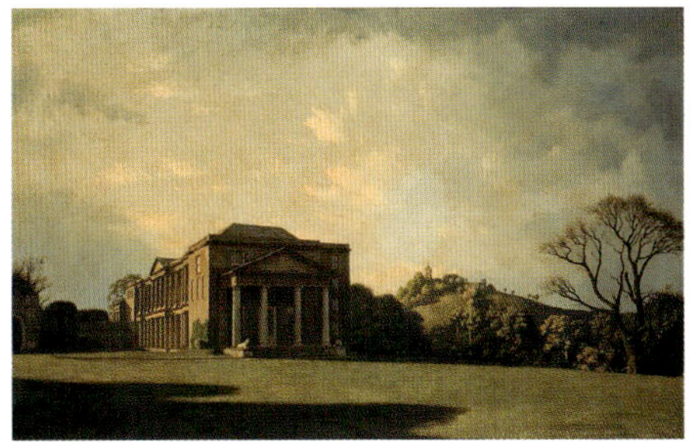

Newton, Algernon Cecil 1880–1968
West Wycombe Park 1933
oil on canvas 61 x 91.5 (E)
SOUAG.B70

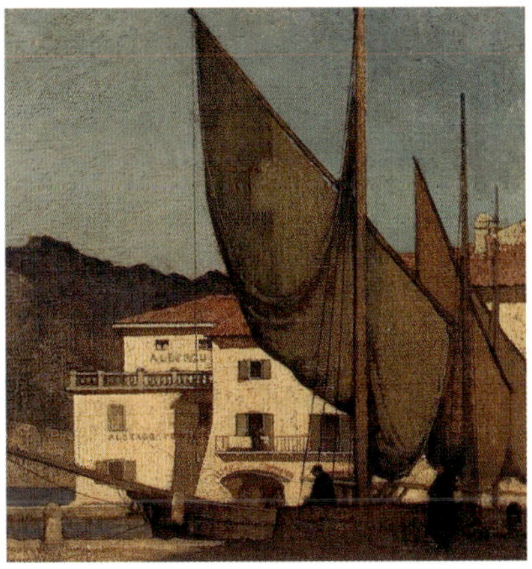

Nicholls, Bertram 1883–1974
Quay in Italy 1928
oil on canvas 40 x 38 (E)
SOUAG.B21

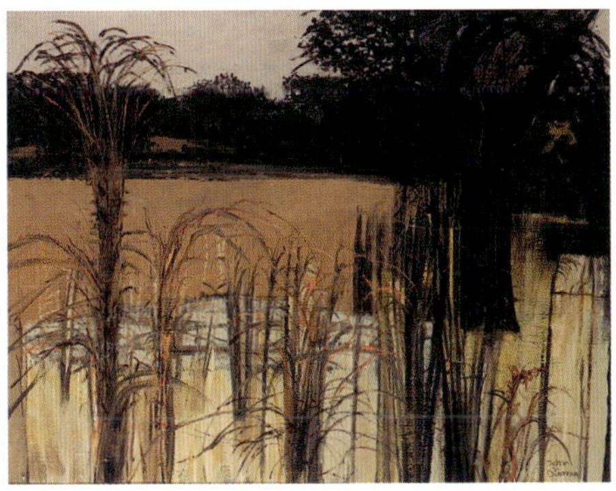

O'Connor, John Scorror 1913–2004
Botany Pool c.1955
oil on canvas 61 x 76 (E)
SOUAG.S52

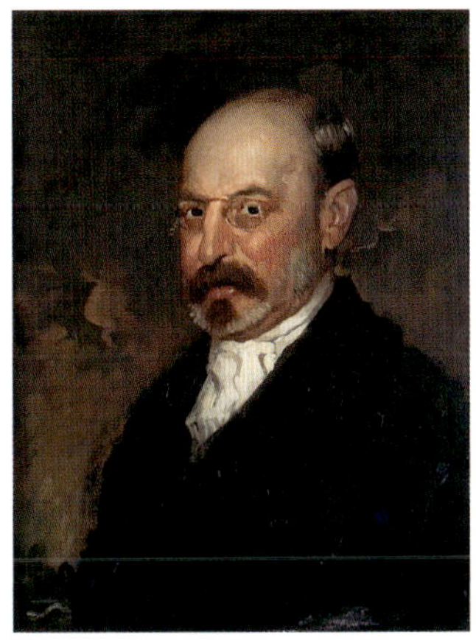

Orpen, William 1878–1931
Charles Wertheim
oil on canvas 61 x 46 (E)
SOUAG.B20

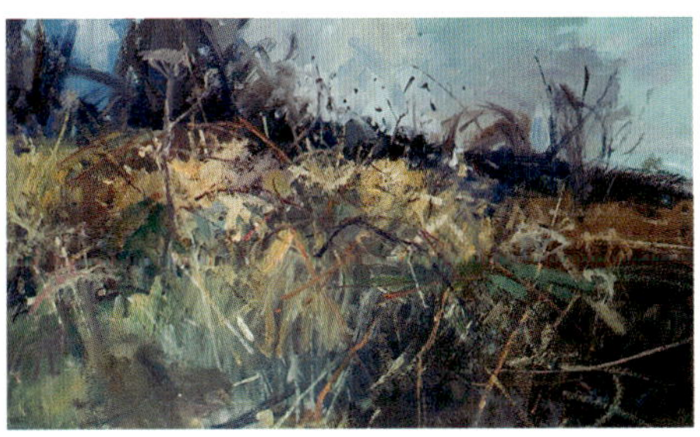

Osborne, John b.1939
Bushes, Winter 1960s
oil on canvas 58.5 x 91.5 (E)
SOUAG.S77

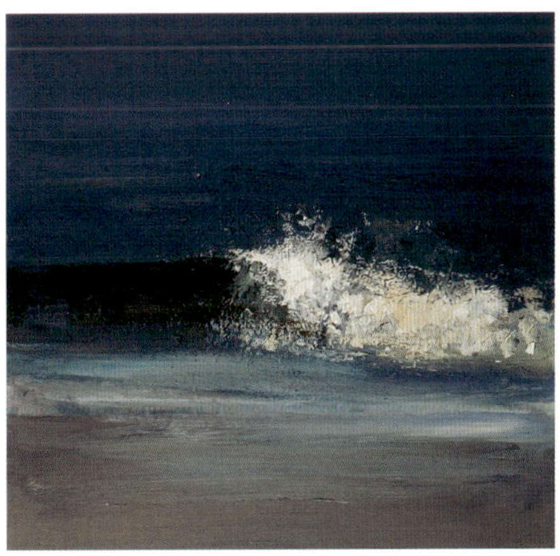

Osborne, John b.1939
Breaking Wave
oil on canvas 60 x 60
SOUAG.TS901

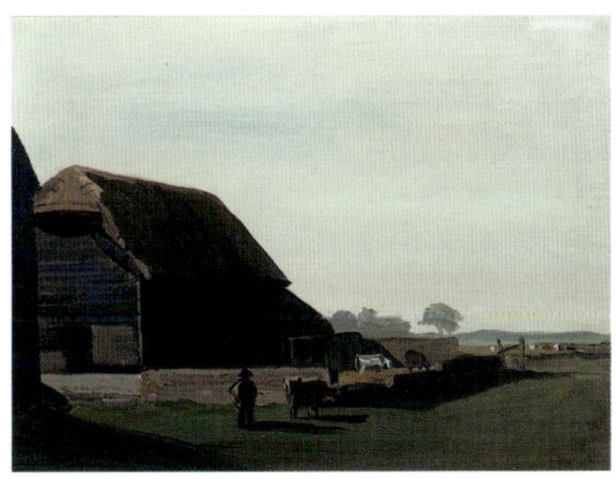

Padwick, Philip Hugh 1876–1958
Barns at Clymping, West Sussex
oil on board 30.5 x 40.5 (E)
SOUAG.S5

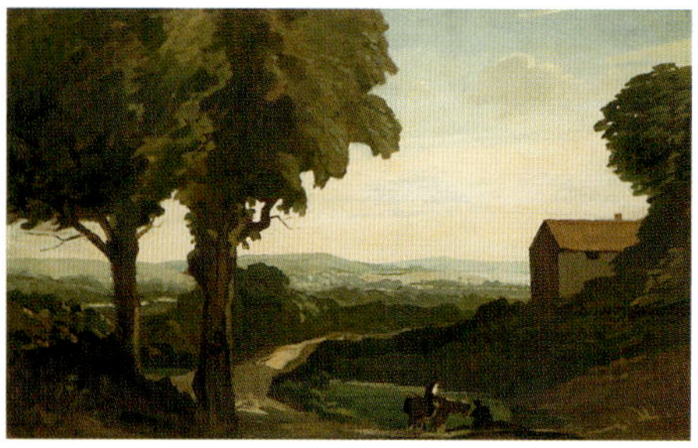

Padwick, Philip Hugh 1876–1958
Sussex Landscape
oil on canvas 58 x 89
SOUAG.B19

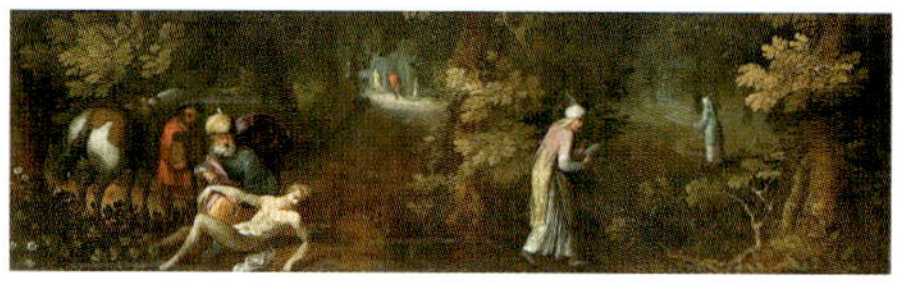

Paolo Fiammingo 1540–1596
The Good Samaritan
oil on panel 32.5 x 100 (E)
SOUAG.B120

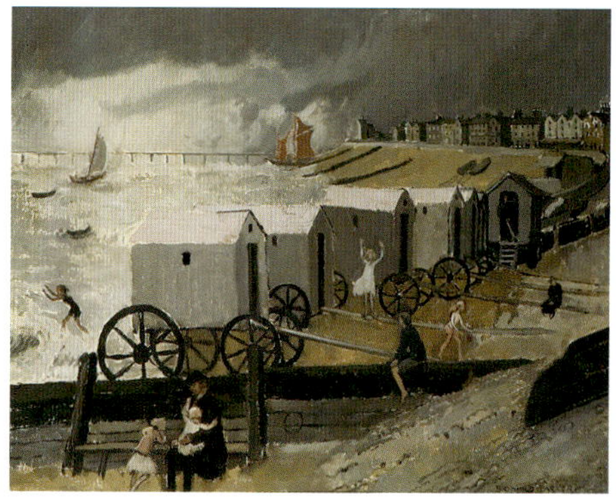

Parker, Brynhild 1907–1987
Windy Day on Marine Parade, Southend
c.1925
oil on canvas 49 x 59.5
SOUAG.TS14

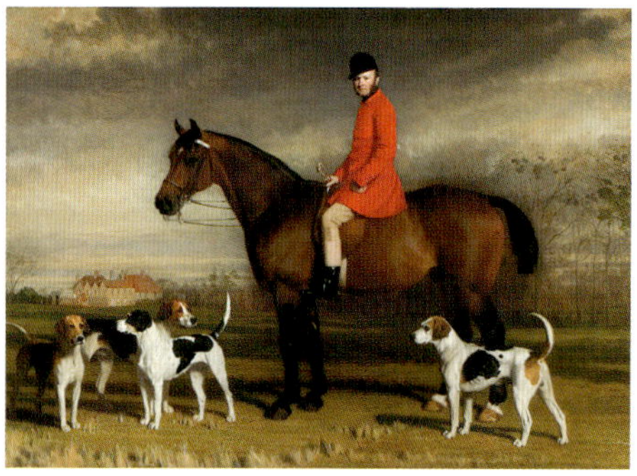

Pearce, Stephen 1819–1904
Daniel Robert Scratton of Prittlewell Priory, Essex 1867
oil on canvas 162.5 x 216 (E)
SOUAG.TS715

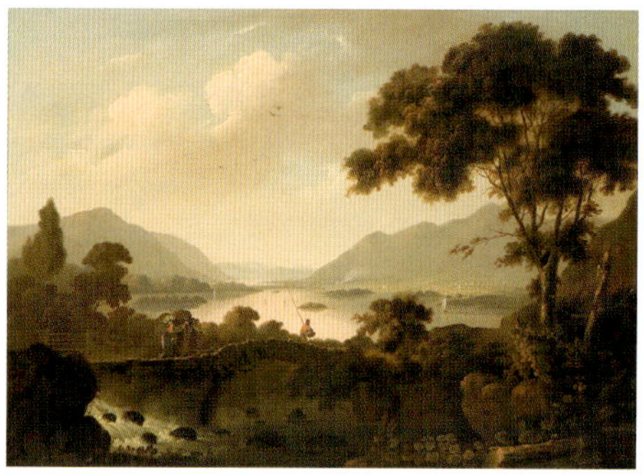

Pennington, John 1773–1841
Lake District Landscape 1808
oil on canvas 48 x 63.5 (E)
SOUAG.B103

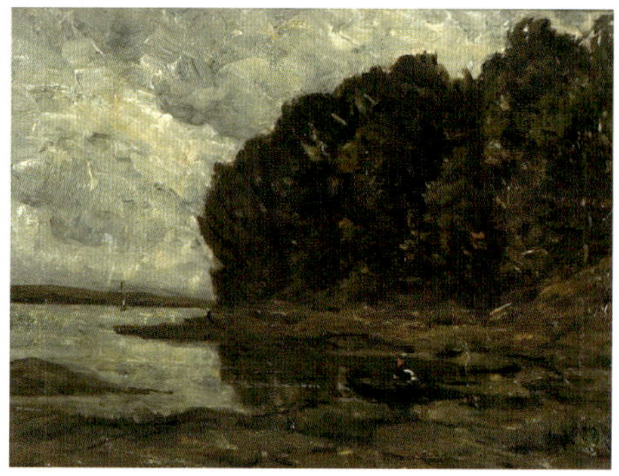

Peppercorn, Arthur Douglas 1847–1926
Devon River
oil on canvas 45.5 x 61 (E)
SOUAG.B56

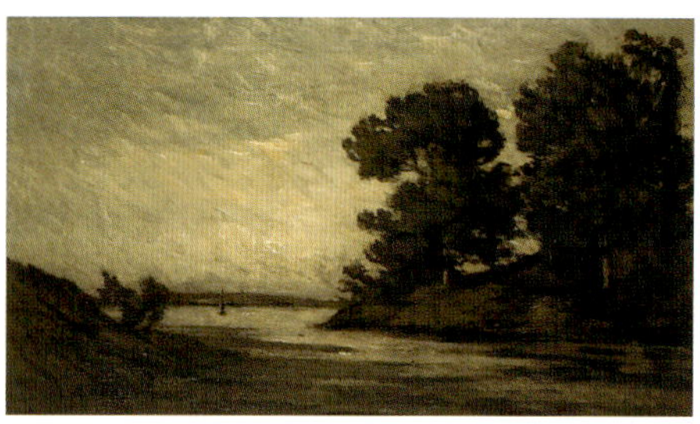

Peppercorn, Arthur Douglas 1847–1926
Near Falmouth
oil on canvas 76 x 127 (E)
SOUAG.B68

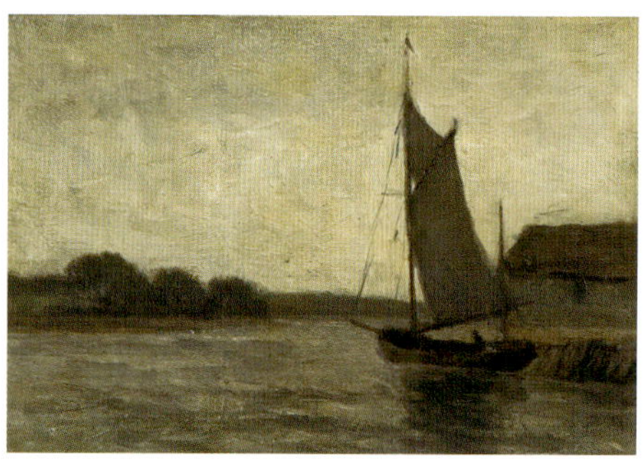

Peppercorn, Arthur Douglas 1847–1926
Quay at Bosham Harbour
oil on canvas 30.5 x 43 (E)
SOUAG.S4

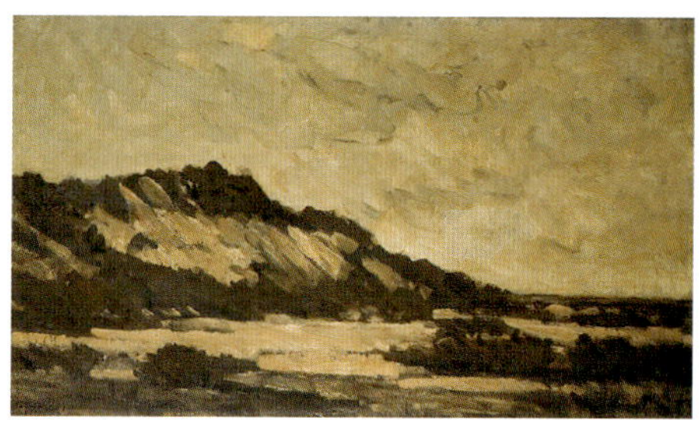

Peppercorn, Arthur Douglas 1847–1926
The Cliff
oil on canvas 76 x 127 (E)
SOUAG.B55

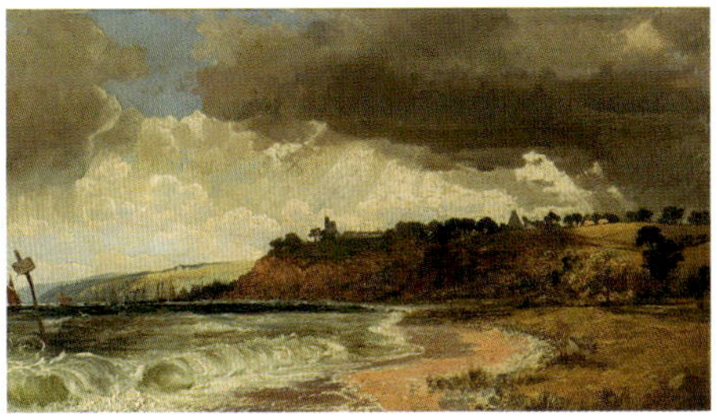

Pettitt, Edwin Alfred 1840–1912
Leigh from the East c.1864
oil on canvas 35 x 61 (E)
SOUAG.TS272

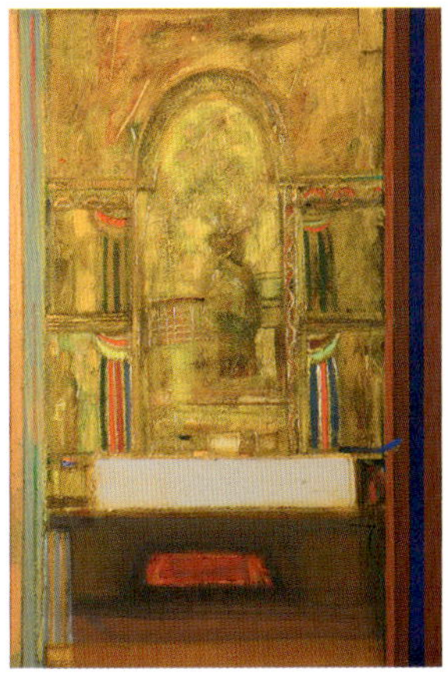

Philipson, Robin 1916–1992
Retablo c.1976
oil on board 91 x 60
SOUAG.S156

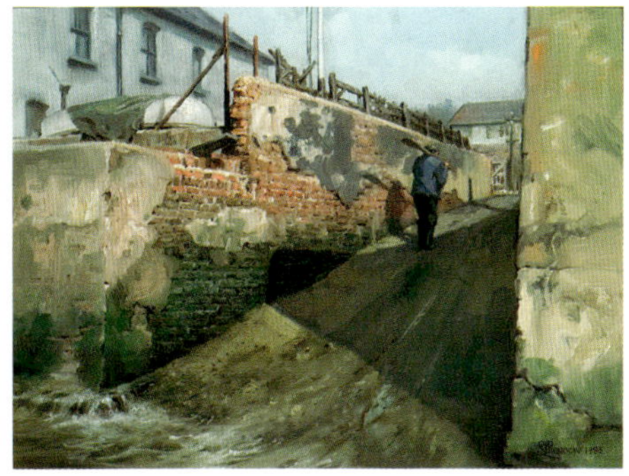

Pinnock, Robin J. b.1954
Fisherman's Walk 1983
oil on board 42.5 x 52 (E)
SOUAG.TS798

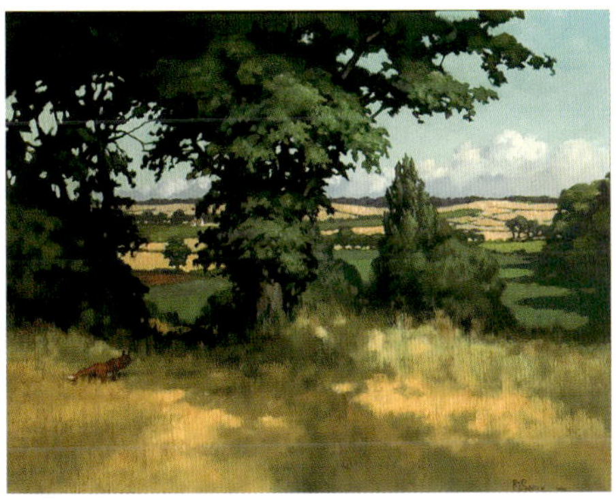

Pinnock, Robin J. b.1954
Near Shelley, Suffolk c.1984
oil on canvas 50 x 61 (E)
SOUAG.S324

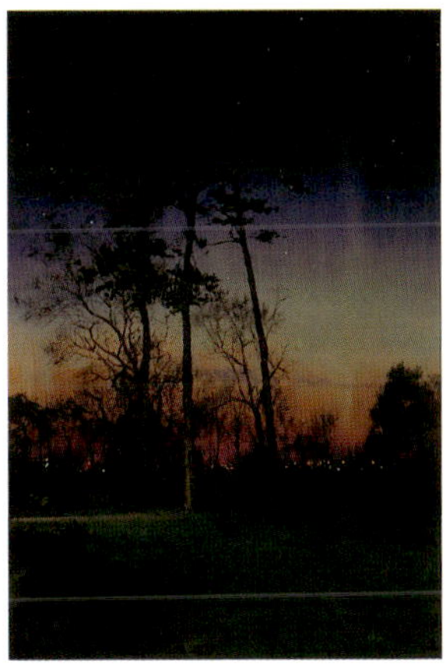

Pinnock, Robin J. b.1954
Chalkwell Park with Aurora Borealis
oil on canvas 76 x 50 (E)
SOUAG.S382

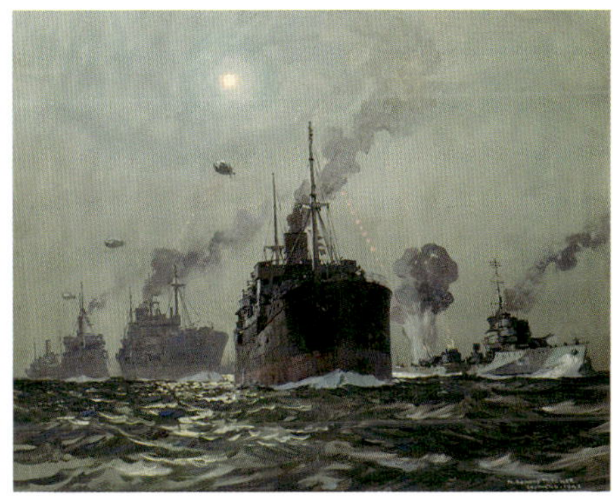

Pitcher, Neville Sotheby 1889–1959
Convoy off Southend Pier: Attack by Moonlight
1943
oil on canvas 62 x 75.5 (E)
SOUAG.TS15

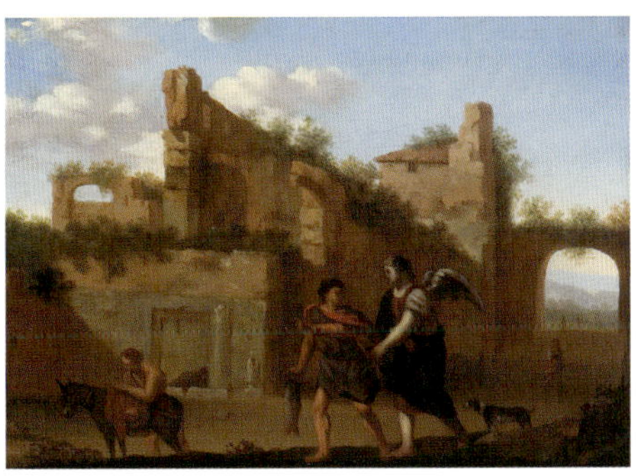

Poelenburgh, Cornelis van 1594/1595–1667
Tobias and the Angel
oil on copper 13 x 17.5 (E)
SOUAG.B112

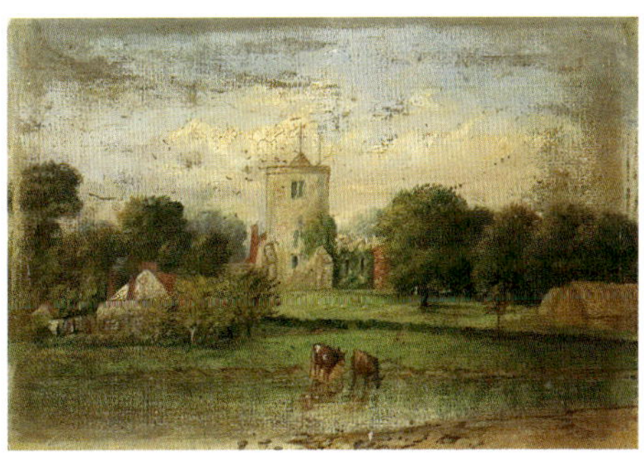

Poole, H. J. active c.1900
St Mary's Church Overlooking Benfleet Creek
oil on board 17.5 x 25.5 (E)
SOUAG.TS706

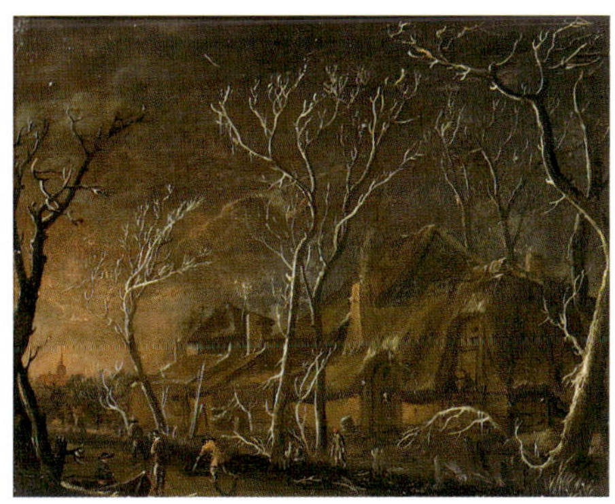

Rombouts, Salomon c.1652–c.1702
A Winter Scene at Night
oil on panel 25 x 30.5 (E)
SOUAG.B128

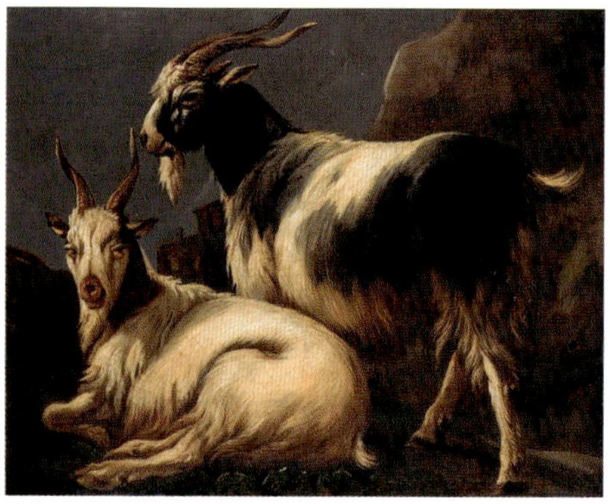

Roos, Philipp Peter 1657–1706
Study of Goats
oil on canvas 48.5 x 57.5 (E)
SOUAG.B62

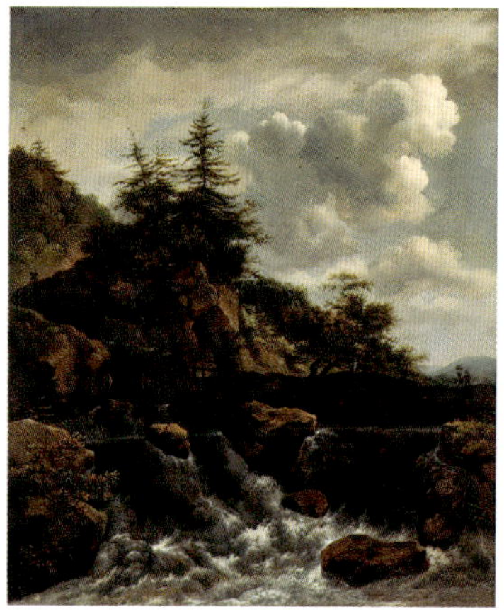

Ruisdael, Jacob van 1628/1629–1682
The Waterfall
oil on canvas 69 x 57.5 (E)
SOUAG.B113

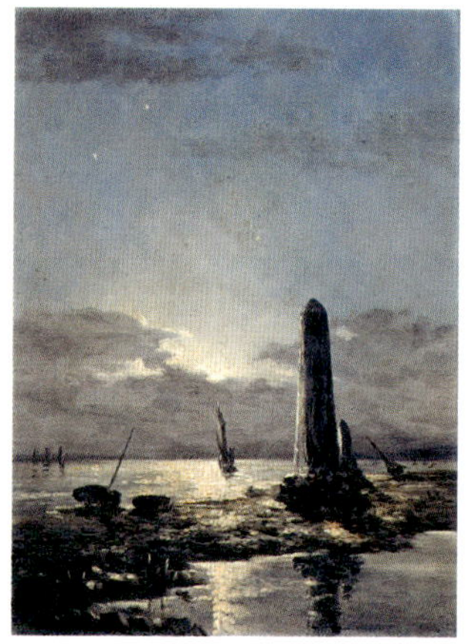

Rule, A. E.
The Crowstone at Night
oil on canvas 43 x 32 (E)
SOUAG.TS852

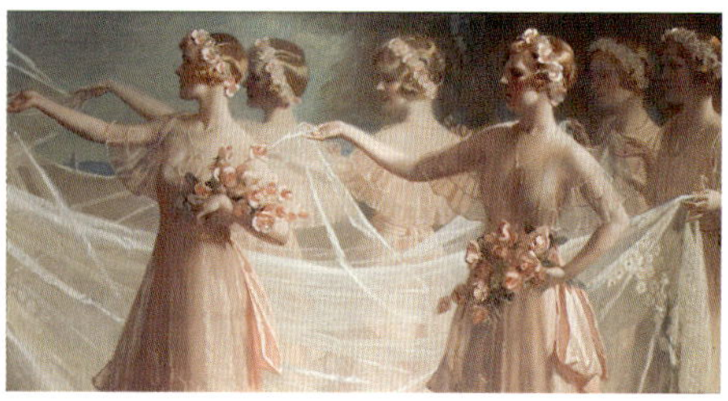

Salisbury, Frank O. 1874–1962
The Bridal Train 1933
oil on canvas 104 x 184
SOUAG.B18

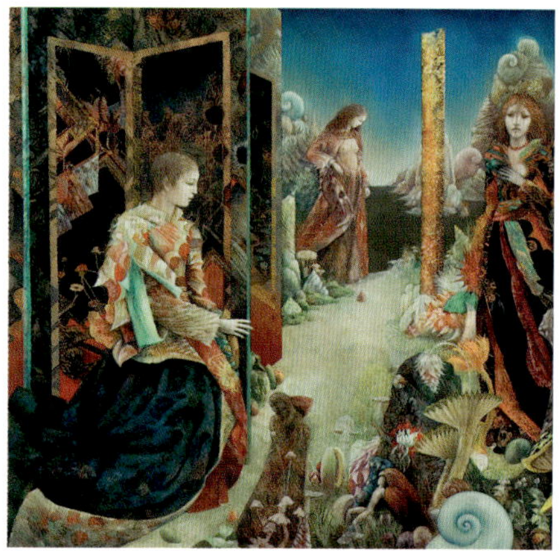

Salmon, Robert
Islands I 1977
oil on canvas 91.5 x 91.5 (E)
SOUAG.S164

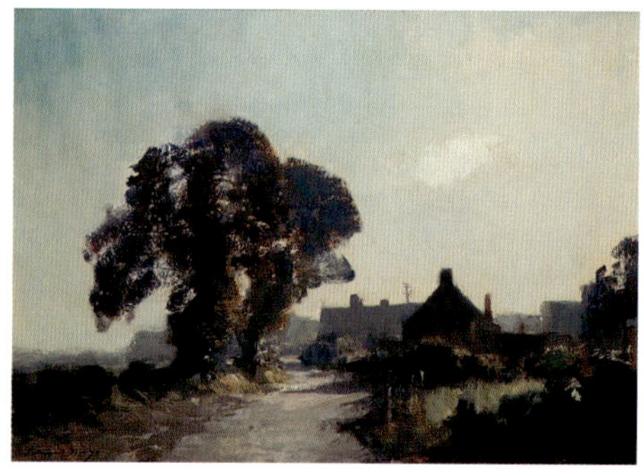

Seago, Edward Brian 1910–1974
Early Morning, September
oil on board 51 x 67.5 (E)
SOUAG.S61

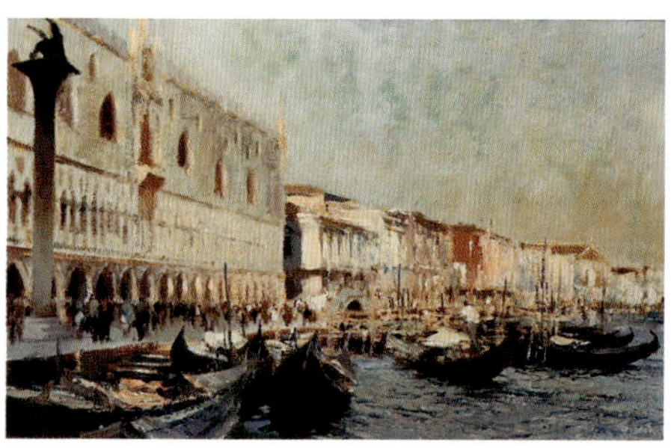

Seago, Edward Brian 1910–1974
The Doge's Palace, Venice
oil on board 57.5 x 77 (E)
SOUAG.S59

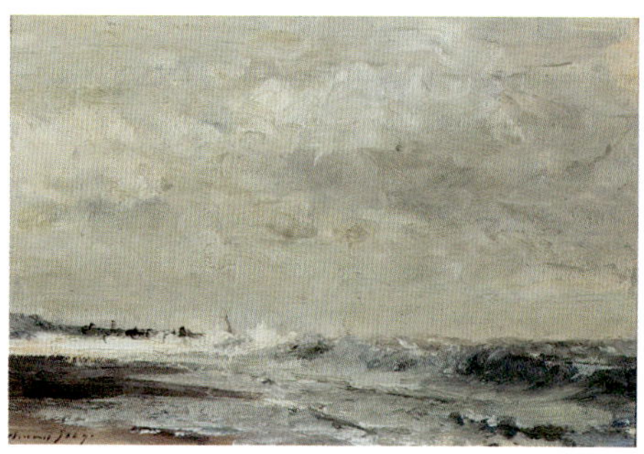

Seago, Edward Brian 1910–1974
The Foreshore
oil on board 28.5 x 41.5 (E)
SOUAG.S60

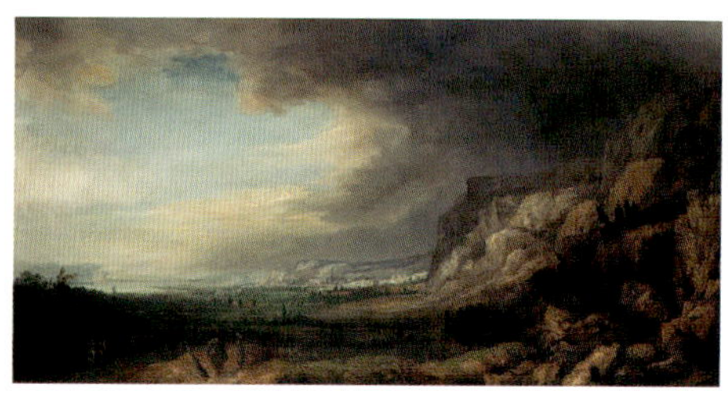

Segers, Hercules Pietersz. (after)
c.1589–c.1638
Landscape
oil on canvas 57.5 x 103 (E)
SOUAG.B36

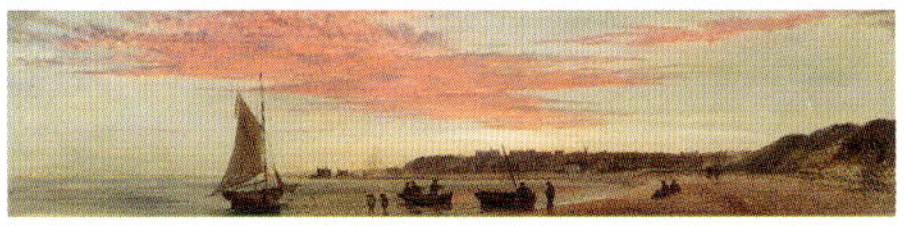

Shalders, George c.1826–1873
Southend at Sunset c.1860
oil on canvas 15 x 61 (E)
SOUAG.TS271

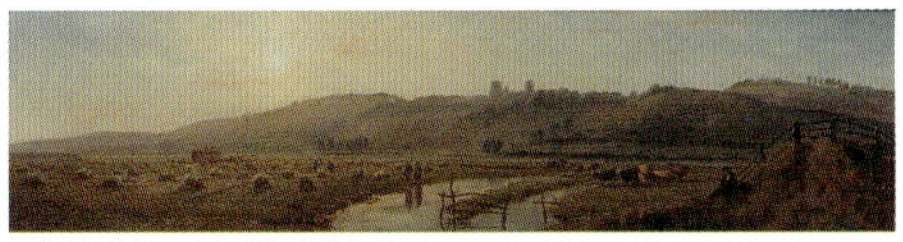

Shalders, George c.1826–1873
Afternoon, Hadleigh
oil on canvas 15 x 59.5
SOUAG.TS847

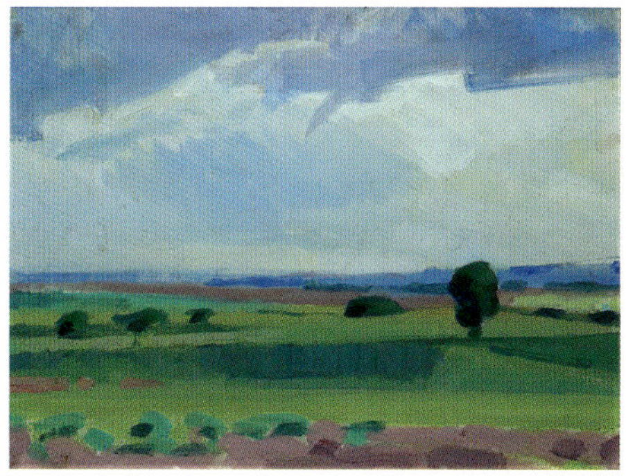

Shaw, Leslie active late 20th C
Landscape
oil on paper & board 30 x 40 (E)
SOUAG.S247

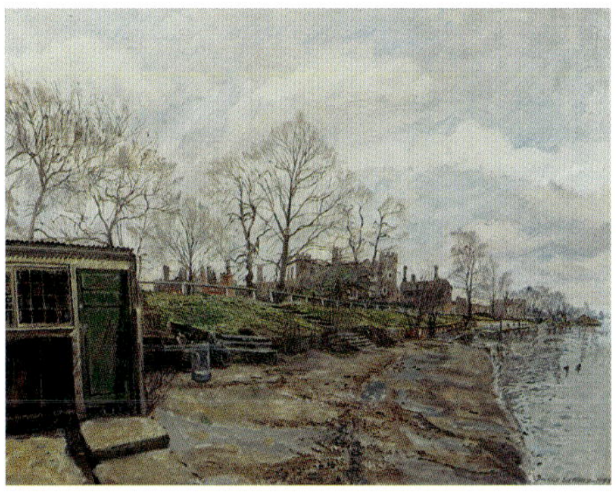

Sheppard, Maurice Raymond b.1947
Boat House, Hampton Court Palace 1977
oil on board 40.5 x 51 (E)
SOUAG.S162

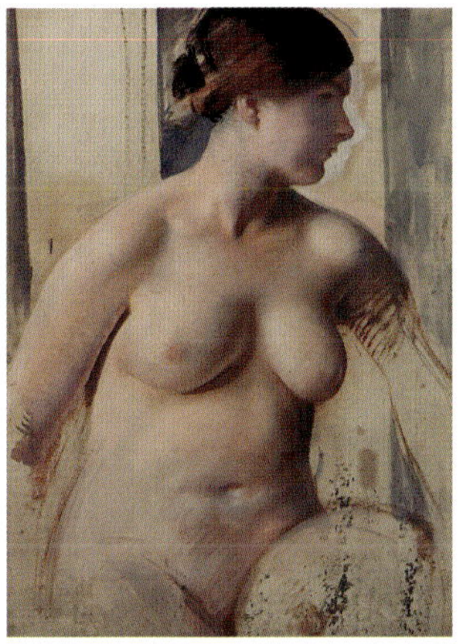

Sims, Charles 1873–1928
Study of a Nude
oil on canvas 75.5 x 55 (E)
SOUAG.S50

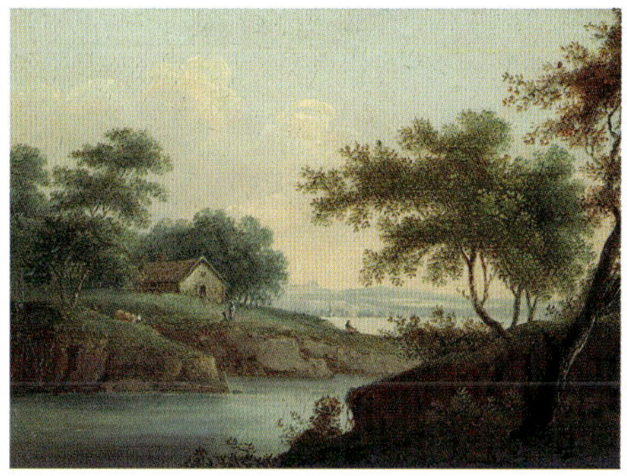

Smith, George 1714–1776
By the River
oil on canvas 11.5 x 15 (E)
SOUAG.B111

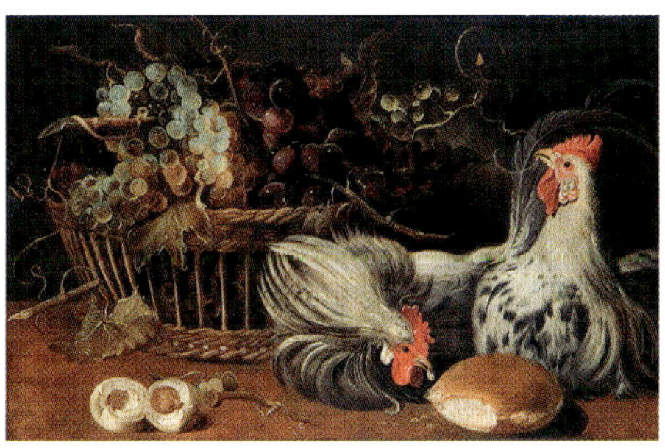

Snyders, Frans 1579–1657
Still Life with Cocks c.1610–1612
oil on panel 44.5 x 64 (E)
SOUAG.B26

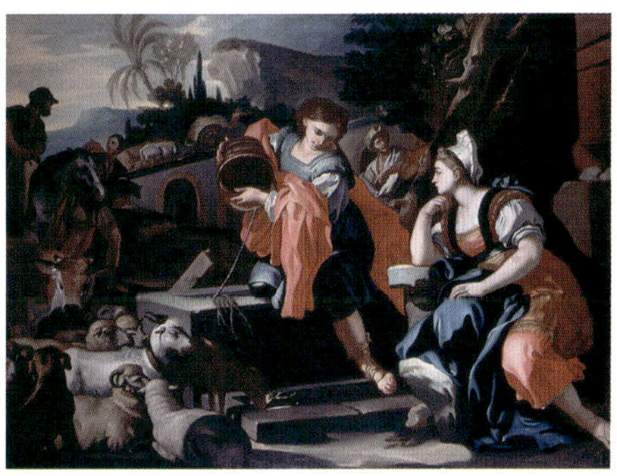

Solimena, Francesco 1657–1747
Rebecca at the Well
oil on canvas 121 x 159.5 (E)
SOUAG.S10

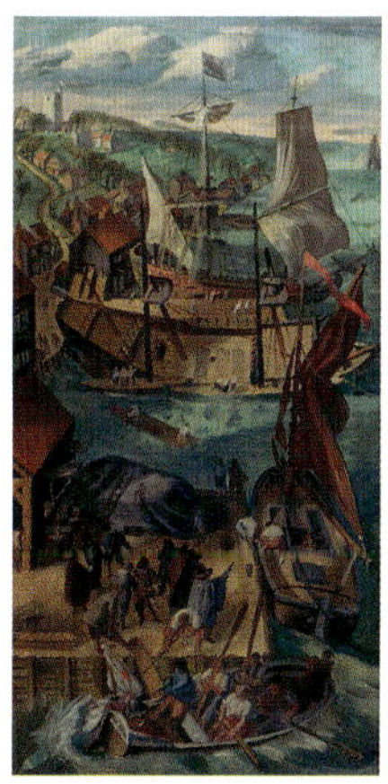

Sorrell, Alan 1904–1974
Study for 'The Refitting of Admiral Blake's Fleet at Leigh, during the First Dutch War' 1933
oil on board 68.5 x 33 (E)
SOUAG.TS490.1

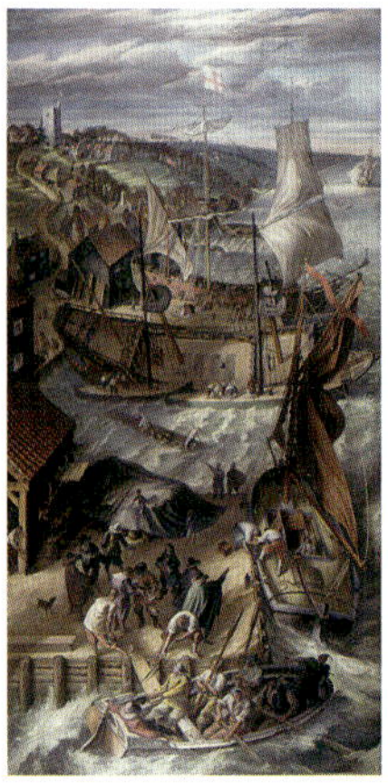

Sorrell, Alan 1904–1974
The Refitting of Admiral Blake's Fleet at Leigh, during the First Dutch War 1933
oil on board 280 x 137 (E)
SOUAG.TS490

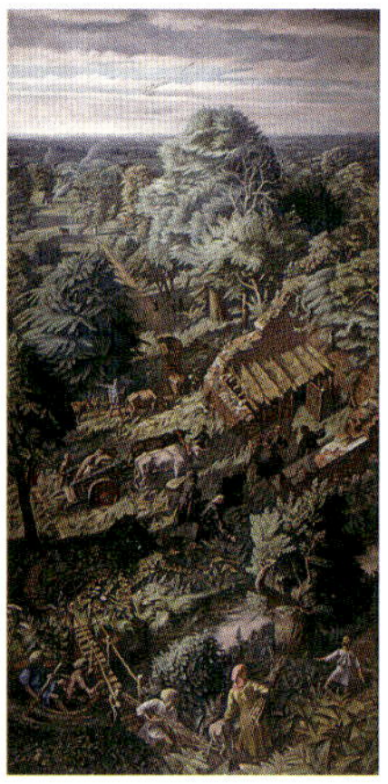

Sorrell, Alan 1904–1974
The Building of Prittlewell Priory c.1935
oil on board 280 x 137 (E)
SOUAG.TS714

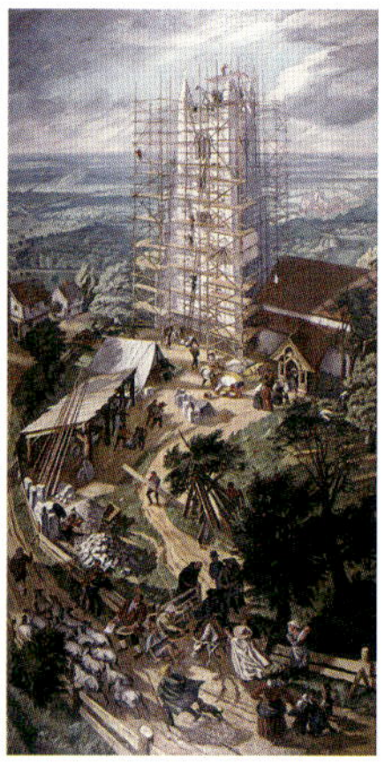

Sorrell, Alan 1904–1974
The Building of Prittlewell Church Tower c.1936
oil on board 280 x 137 (E)
SOUAG.TS842

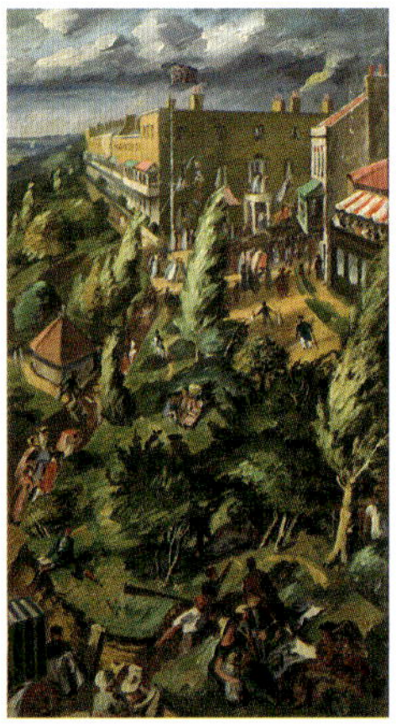

Sorrell, Alan 1904–1974
Study for 'The Arrival of the First Mail Coach at Southend' 1937
oil on canvas 70 x 36
SOUAG.TS917

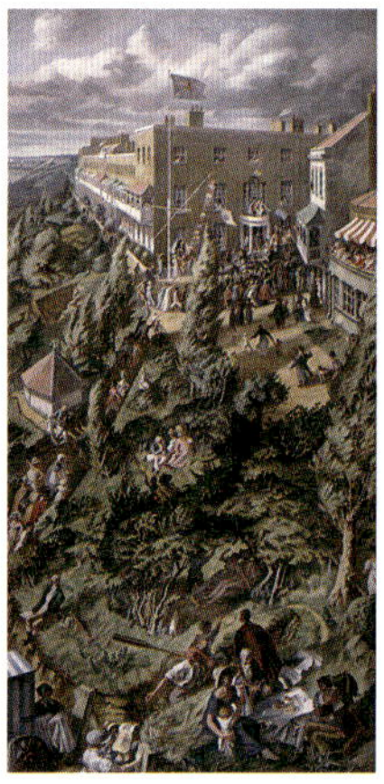

Sorrell, Alan 1904–1974
The Arrival of the First Mail Coach at Southend c.1937
oil on board 280 x 137 (E)
SOUAG.TS878

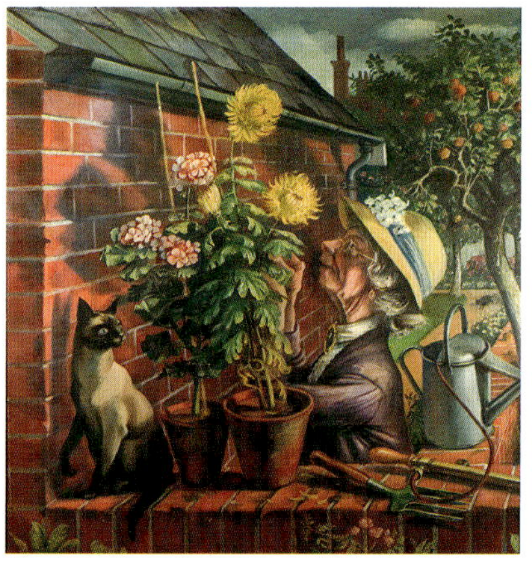

Sorrell, Alan 1904–1974
Summer Scene Triptych (left wing) 1956
oil on board 123 x 114
SOUAG.S437A

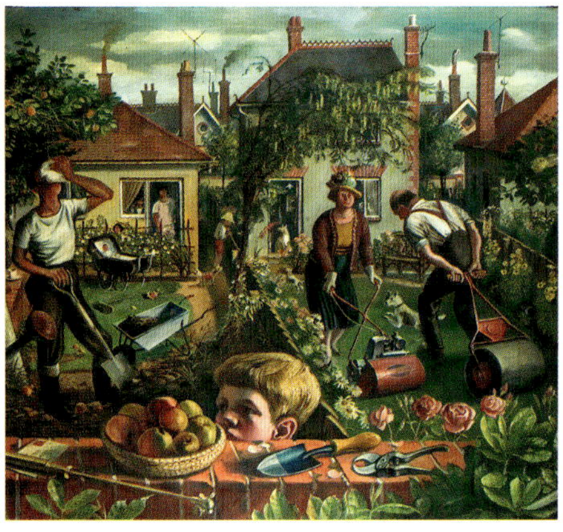

Sorrell, Alan 1904–1974
Summer Scene Triptych (right wing) 1956
oil on board 123 x 132
SOUAG.S437

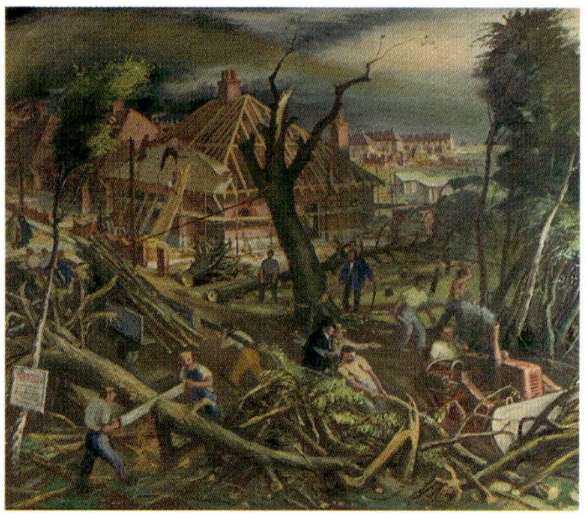

Sorrell, Alan 1904–1974
The Spoilers (detail) 1958
oil on board 123 x 243
SOUAG.S39

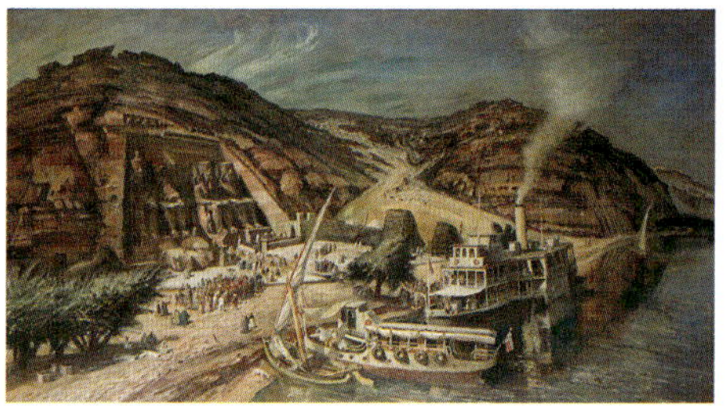

Sorrell, Alan 1904–1974
Abu Simbel, Nubia 1964
oil on board 104 x 181 (E)
SOUAG.S538

Facing page: Campion, Oliver, 1928–2000, *J. W. Caton* (detail), 1958, Braintree District Museum, (p. 11)

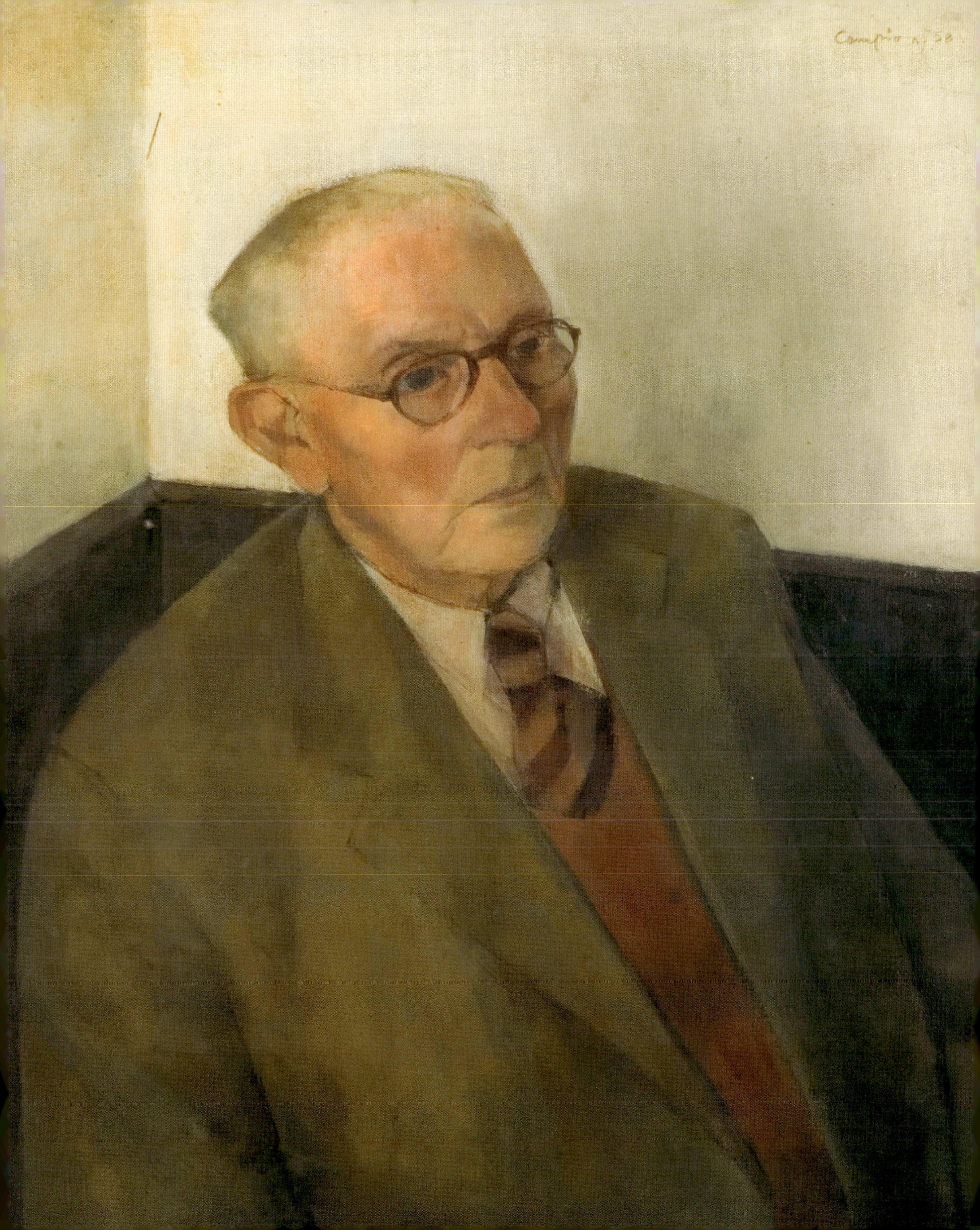

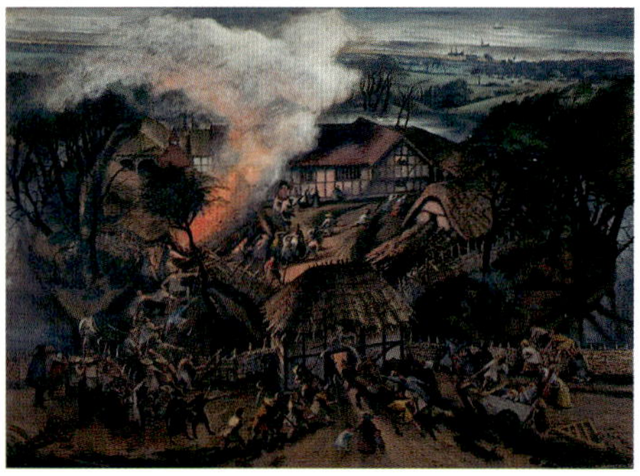

Sorrell, Alan 1904–1974
Attack on Southchurch Hall during the Peasants' Revolt, 1381 1969
oil on board 170 x 206 (E)
SOUAG.S396

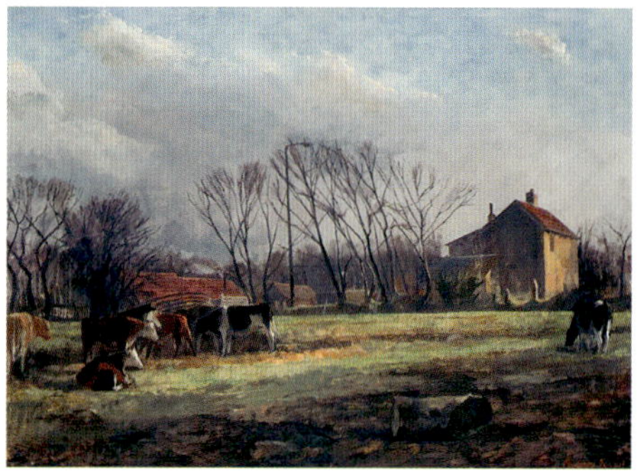

Sorrell, Richard b.1948
Mr King's Cattle c.1980
oil on board 73.5 x 91.5 (E)
SOUAG.TS789

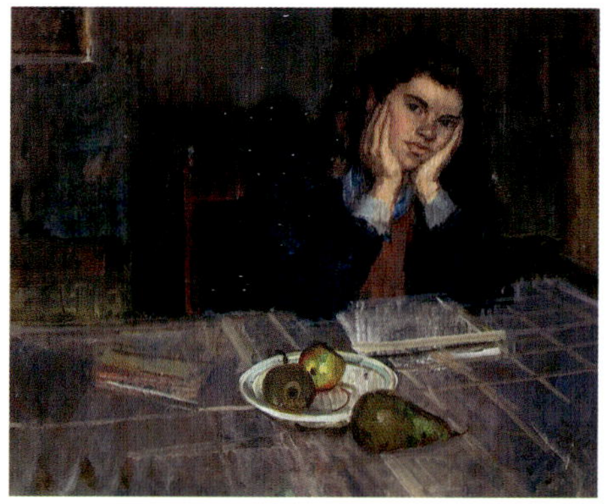

Spear, Ruskin 1911–1990
Daydreaming, Portrait of the Artist's Wife
1930s
oil on canvas 49 x 56 (E)
SOUAG.B143

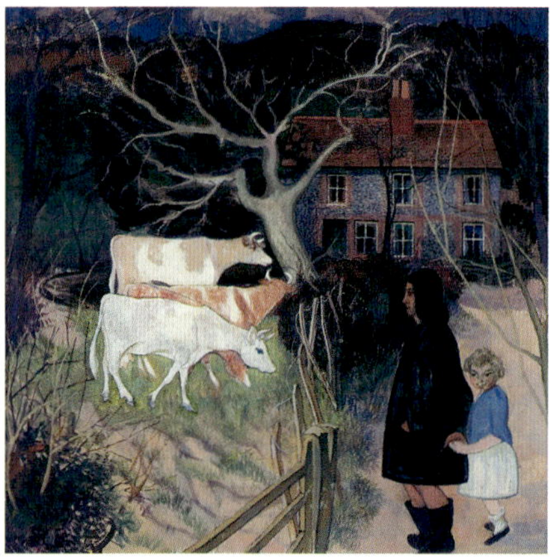

Spencer, Gilbert 1893–1979
Clarissa c.1963
oil on canvas 64 x 63.5 (E)
SOUAG.B137

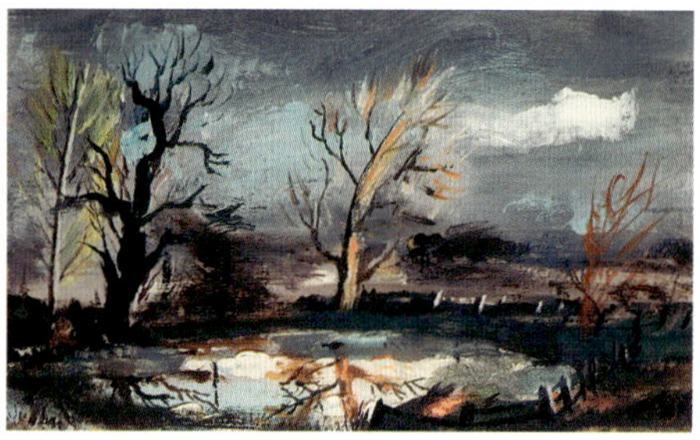

Suddaby, Rowland 1912–1972
Landscape
oil on paper 13.5 x 21 (E)
SOUAG.S343

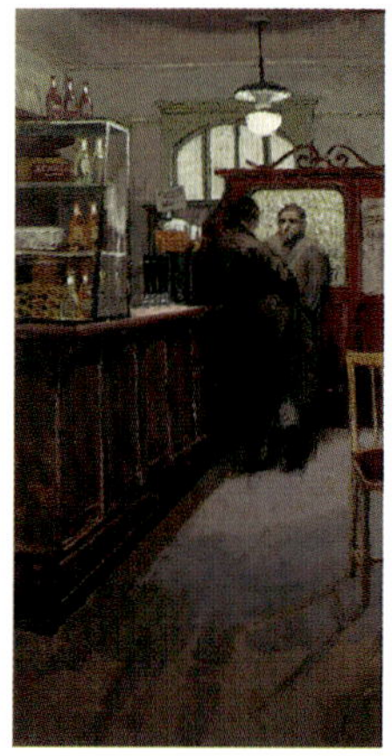

Taylor, Arthur H. active from 1953
Waiting Room 1950s
oil on canvas 115.5 x 58.5 (E)
SOUAG.B89

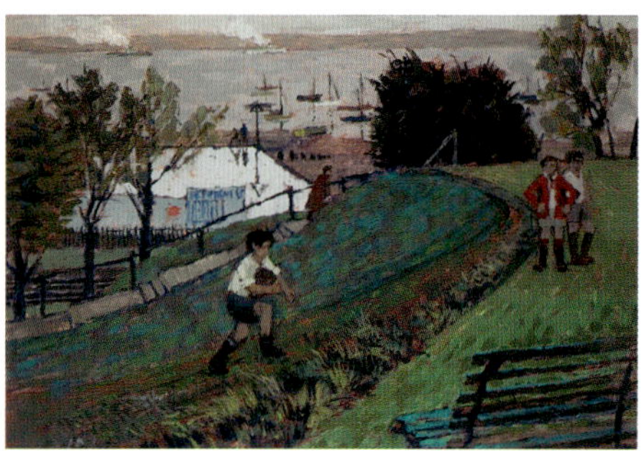

Taylor, Arthur H. active from 1953
Cliff Parade, Leigh-on-Sea
oil on board 54.5 x 76 (E)
SOUAG.B139

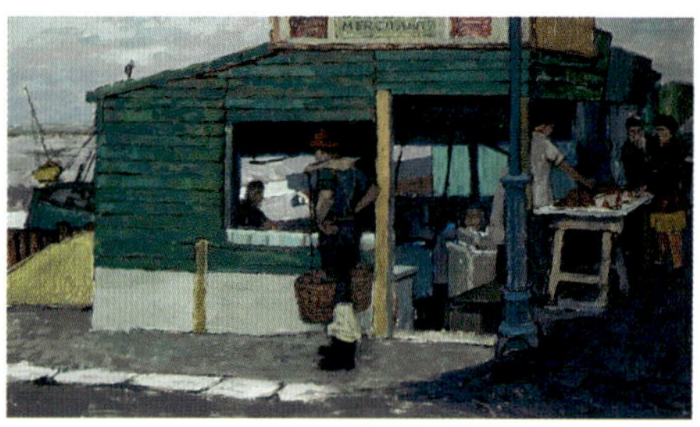

Taylor, Arthur H. active from 1953
The Cockle Shed, Leigh
oil on board 49.5 x 82.5
SOUAG.B138

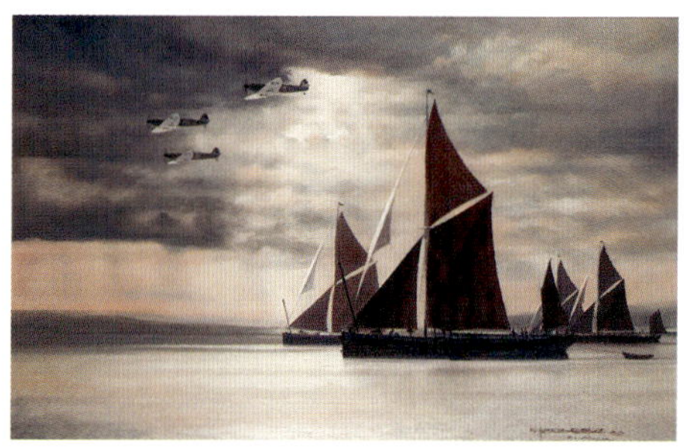

Thompson, Charles John b.1931
Southend's Own Spitfires from 54th Squadron from Rochford, 1940
oil on board 64.5 x 91.5 (E)
SOUAG.S447

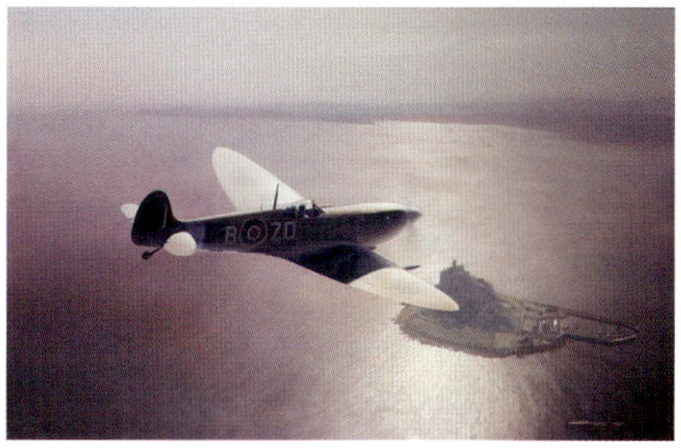

Thompson, Charles John b.1931
Supermarine Spitfire MkIX MH434, over St Michael's Mount, Cornwall
oil on canvas 60 x 90.5
SOUAG.S421

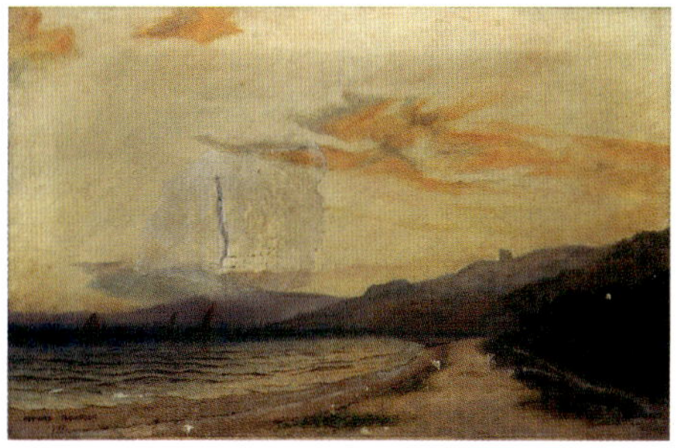

Thompson, Howard
View of Sea and Coast 1902
oil on canvas 41 x 61
SOUAG.S336

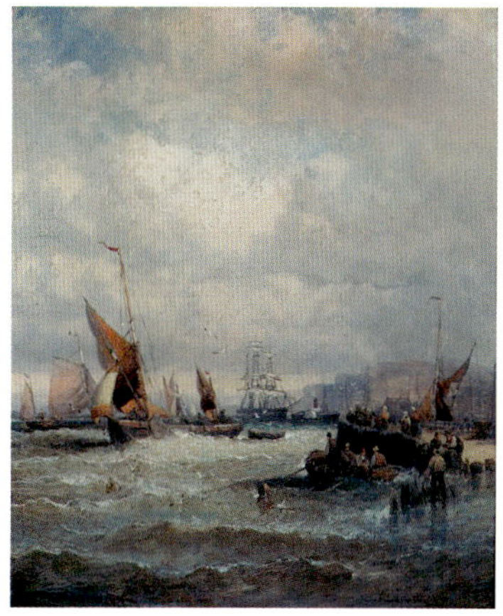

Thornbury, Willam Anslow
active 1858–1906
A Breezy Day, Mouth of the Thames
oil on canvas 44 x 39 (E)
SOUAG.TS16

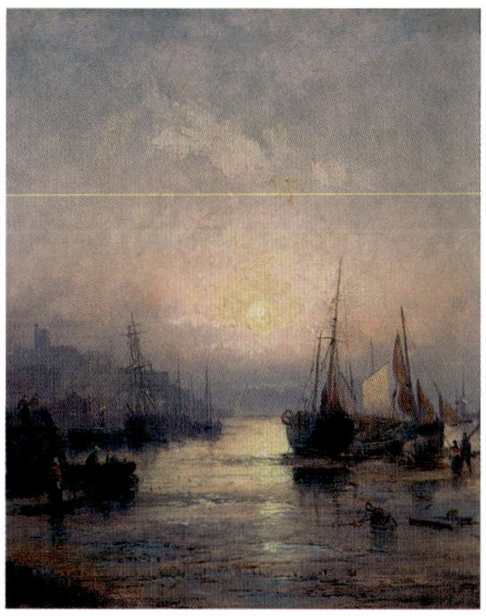

Thornbury, William Anslow
active 1858–1906
Sunrise, Low Tide, Leigh
oil on canvas 44 x 39 (E)
SOUAG.TS17

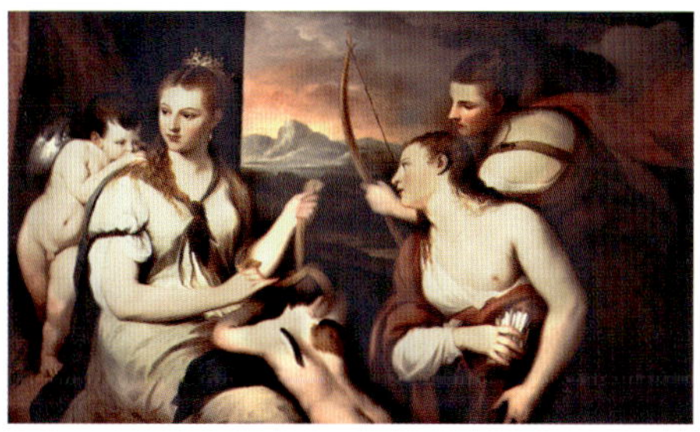

Titian (after) c.1488–1576
The Education of Love
oil on canvas 118 x 189 (E)
SOUAG.B124

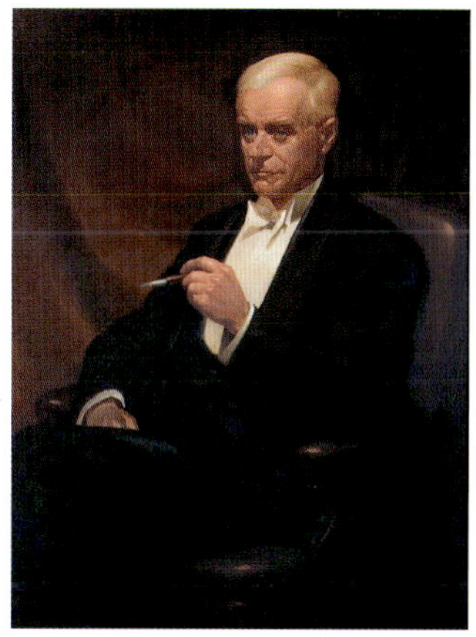

Tombleson, J. B.
Philip C. Humphreys 1934
oil on canvas 100 x 75
SOUAG.TS900

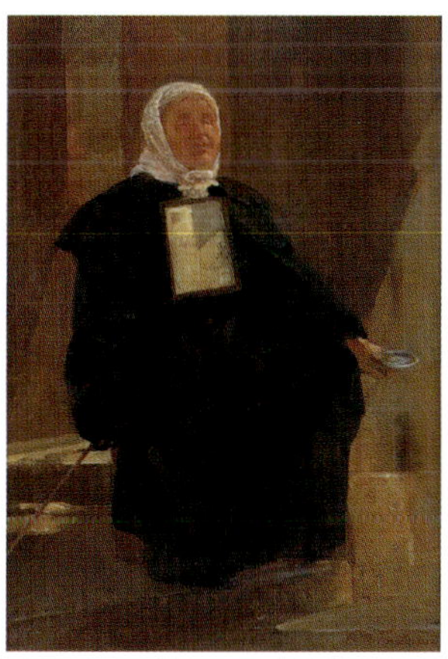

Tomlinson, Reginald R. 1885–1978
Licensed Breton Beggar c.1977
oil on canvas 35.5 x 25.5 (E)
SOUAG.S166

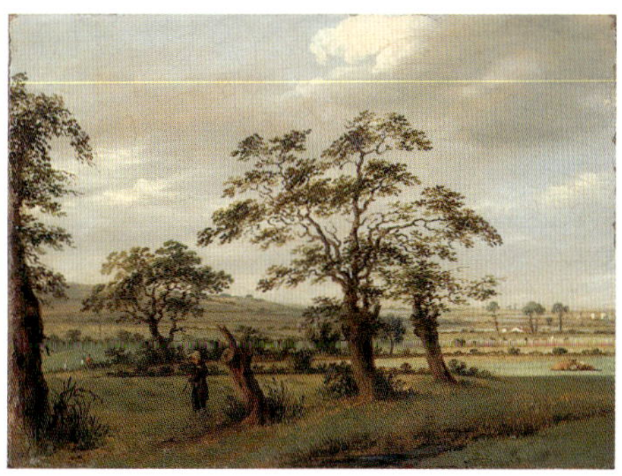

Towne, Charles 1763–1840
Landscape with Two Cows
oil on canvas 17.5 x 22.5 (E)
SOUAG.B114

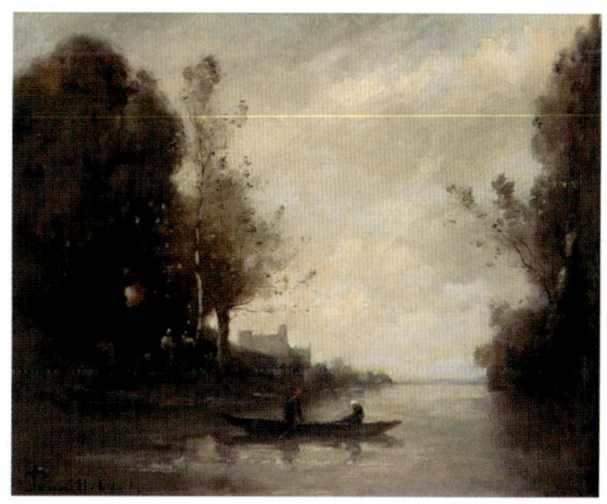

Trouillebert, Paul Désiré 1829–1900
A Quiet Backwater 1870s–1880s
oil on canvas 38 x 45 (E)
SOUAG.B115

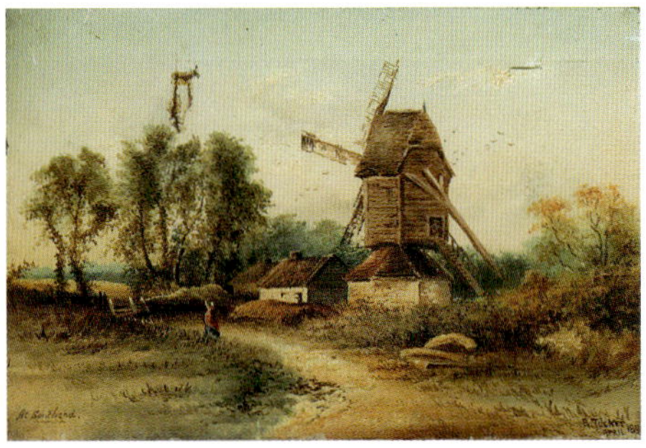

Tucker, Raymond active 1852–1903
At Southend 1894
oil on canvas 23 x 33 (E)
SOUAG.TS662

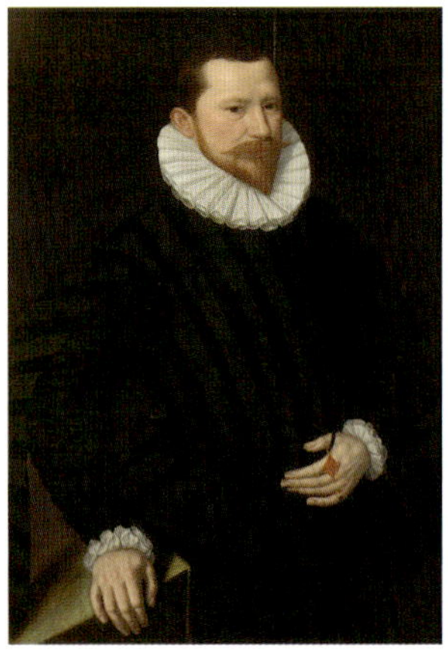

unknown artist
Portrait of a Nobleman 1586
oil on panel 101 x 74 (E)
SOUAG.B44

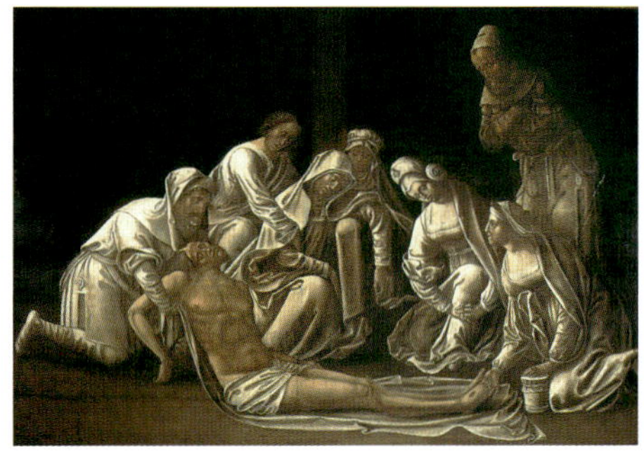

unknown artist 16th C
Deposition from the Cross
oil on canvas 112.5 x 161 (E)
SOUAG.B40

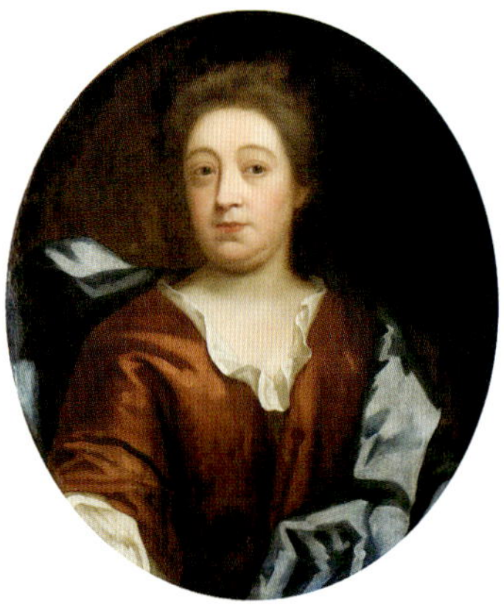

unknown artist 18th C
Portrait of a Lady, possibly Elizabeth Appleton of Coggeshall
oil on canvas 73.5 x 63.5 (E)
SOUAG.TS517

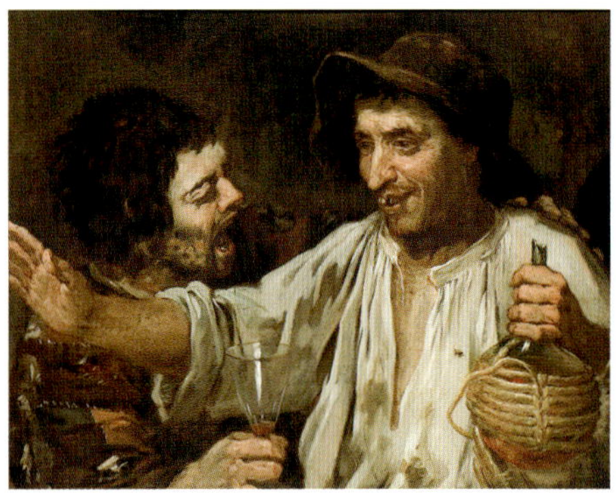

unknown artist 18th C
The Wine Seller
oil on canvas 60 x 72.5 (E)
SOUAG.B46

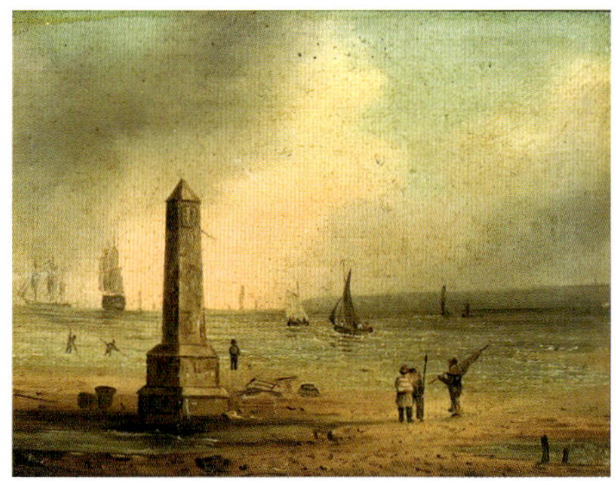

unknown artist
The Crowstone 1809
oil on canvas 18 x 23
SOUAG.TS920

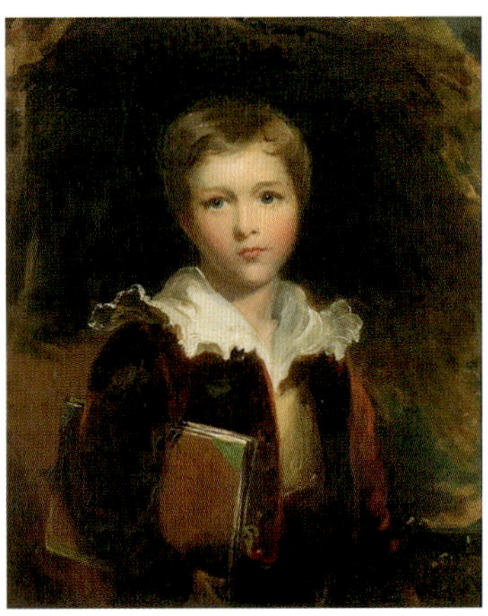

unknown artist
Daniel Robert Scratton in a Red Jacket c.1830
oil on board 30.5 x 25.5 (E)
SOUAG.S454

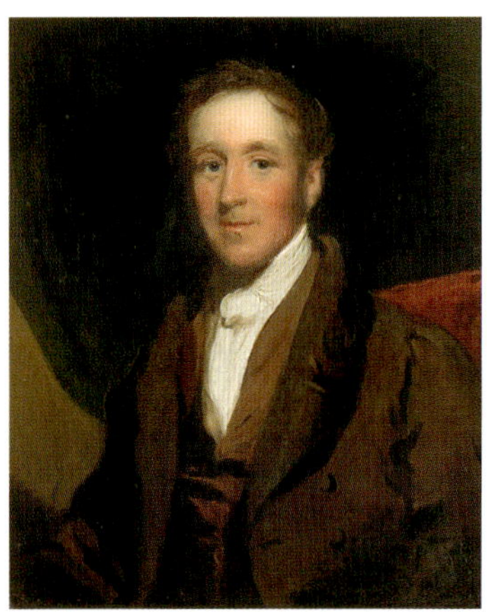

unknown artist
John Baynton Scratton c.1830
oil on board 30.5 x 25.5 (E)
SOUAG.S450

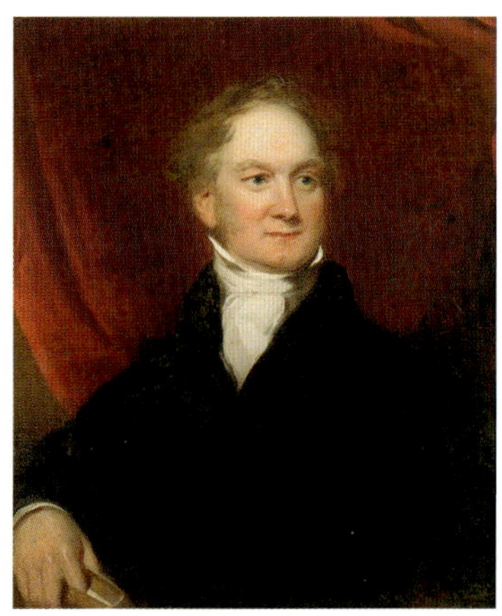

unknown artist
Portrait of a Gentleman in a Black Coat (possibly Reverend Frederick Nolan) c.1830
oil on board 30.5 x 25.5 (E)
SOUAG.S456

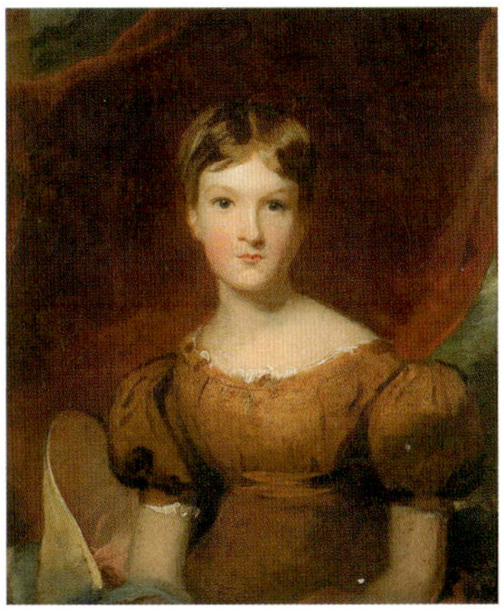

unknown artist
Portrait of a Girl in a Bronze Dress, possibly Jane Scratton c.1830
oil on board 30.5 x 25.5 (E)
SOUAG.S453

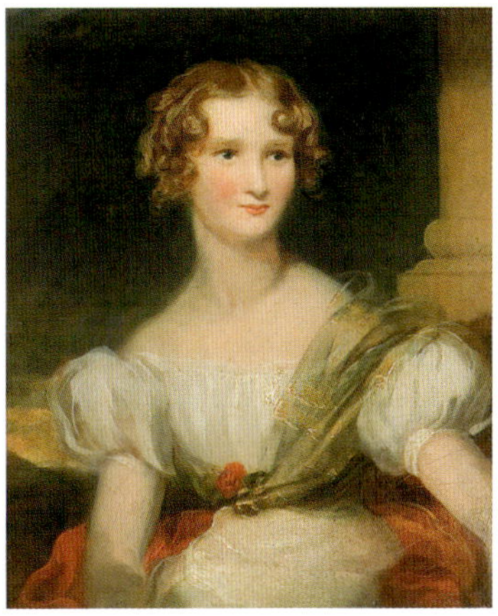

unknown artist
Portrait of a Girl in a White Dress (possibly Harriet Scratton) c.1830
oil on board 30.5 x 25.5 (E)
SOUAG.S452

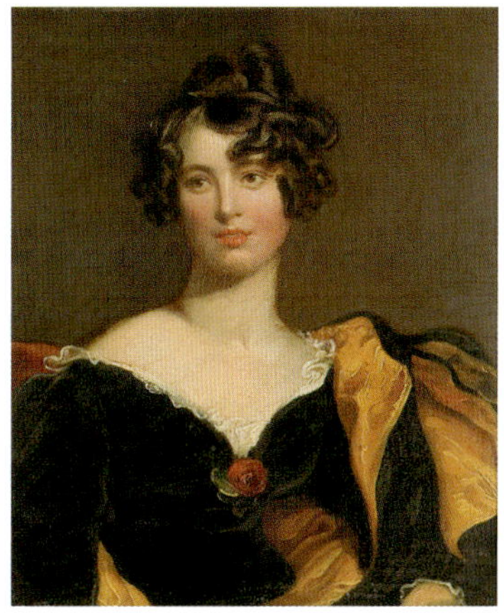

unknown artist
Portrait of a Lady in a Black Dress (possibly Elizabeth Boone) c.1830
oil on board 30.5 x 25.5 (E)
SOUAG.S455

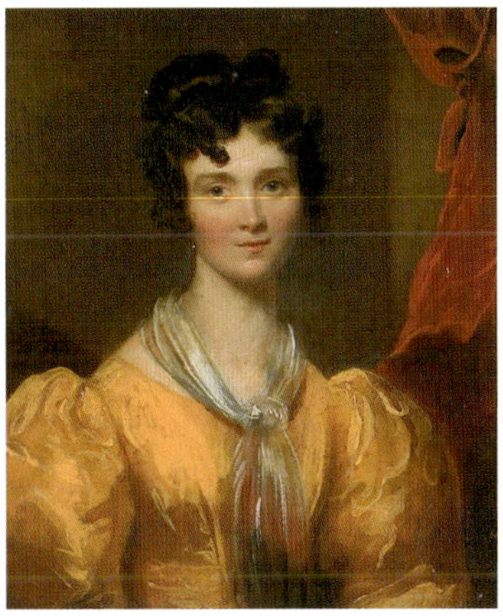

unknown artist
Portrait of a Young Lady in a Yellow Dress (possibly Harriet Scratton) c.1830
oil on board 30.5 x 25.5 (E)
SOUAG.S451

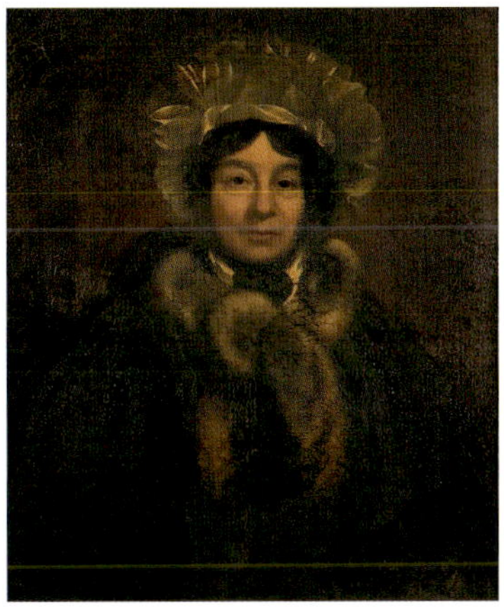

unknown artist
Jane Langworthy, Wife of John Offin of Hutton Park c.1850
oil on canvas 73.5 x 61
SOUAG.TS903

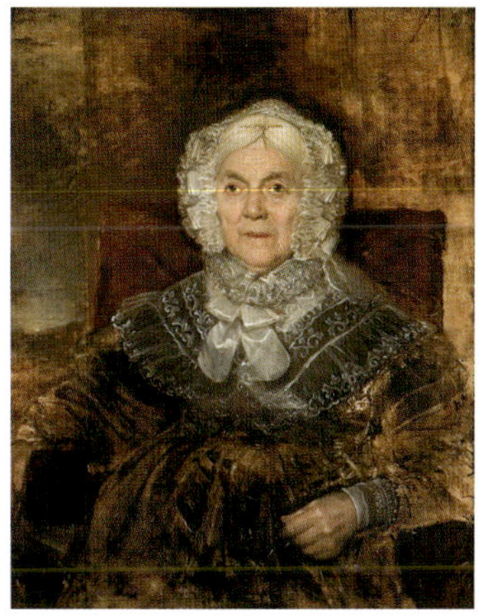

unknown artist
Catherine Elizabeth Offin c.1870
oil on canvas 90 x 70
SOUAG.TS904

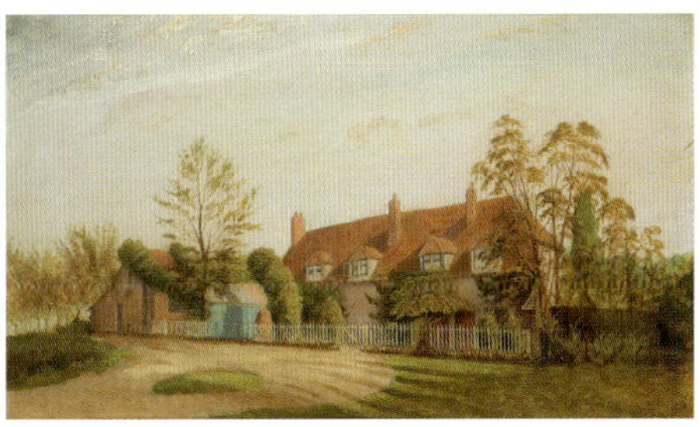

unknown artist
Southchurch Hall 1898
oil on canvas 25.5 x 40.5 (E)
SOUAG.TS448

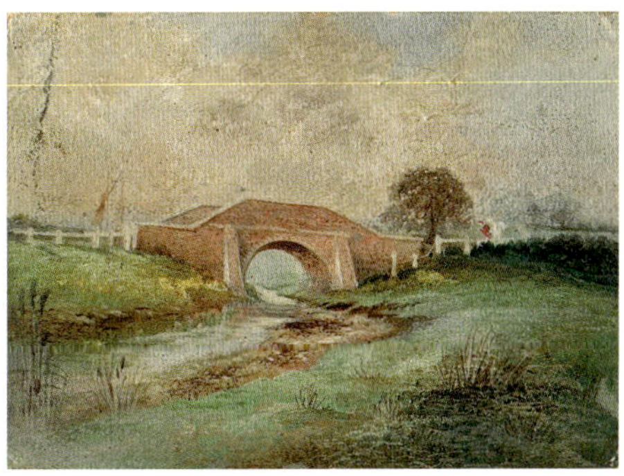

unknown artist 19th C
Bridge at Little Stambridge
oil on board 15 x 20.5 (E)
SOUAG.TS306

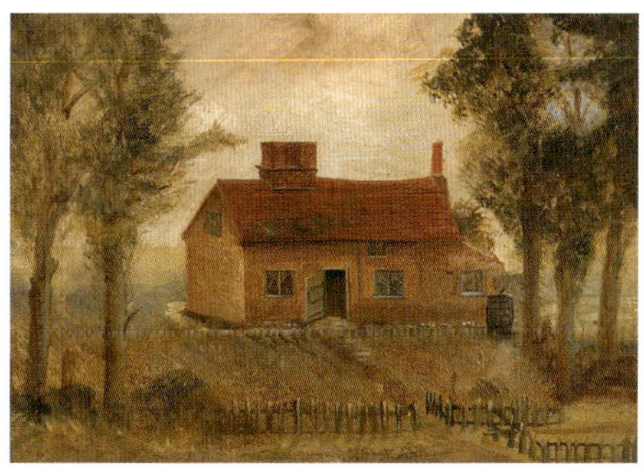

unknown artist 19th C
Cottage near Southend
oil on canvas 25.5 x 37 (E)
SOUAG.TS516

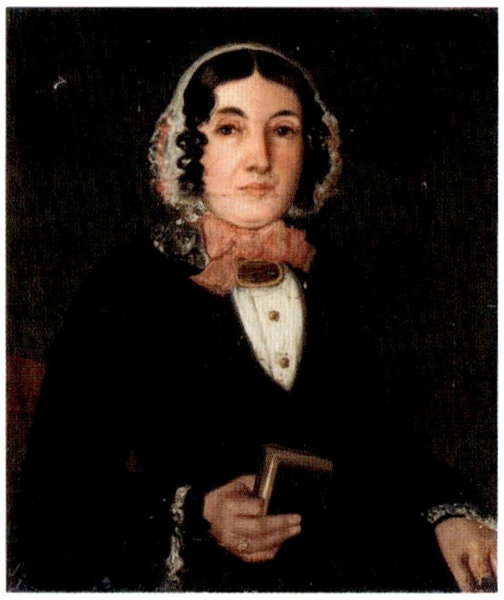

unknown artist 19th C
Portrait of a Lady Holding a Book
oil on canvas 76 x 63
SOUAG.TS910

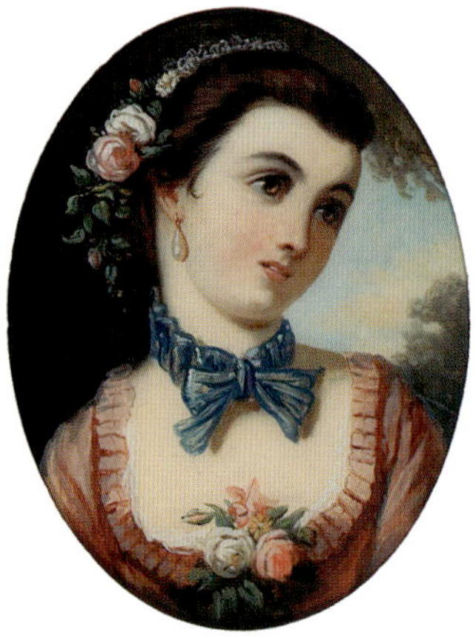

unknown artist 19th C
Portrait of a Young Lady
oil on glass 31 x 23
SOUAG.TS912

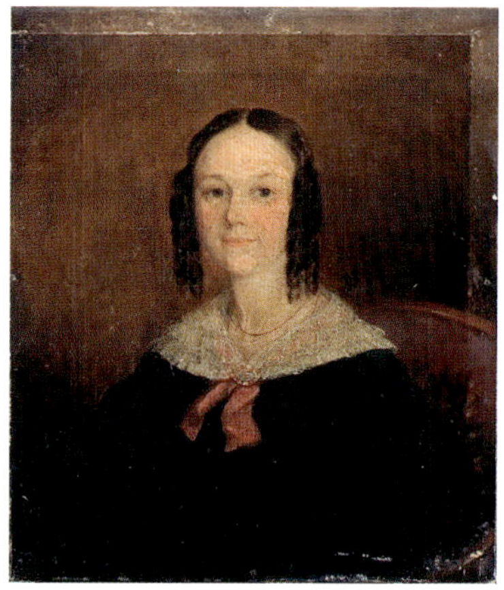

unknown artist 19th C
Portrait of a Young Lady with Red Ribbon
oil on canvas 30 x 25.5
SOUAG.TS911

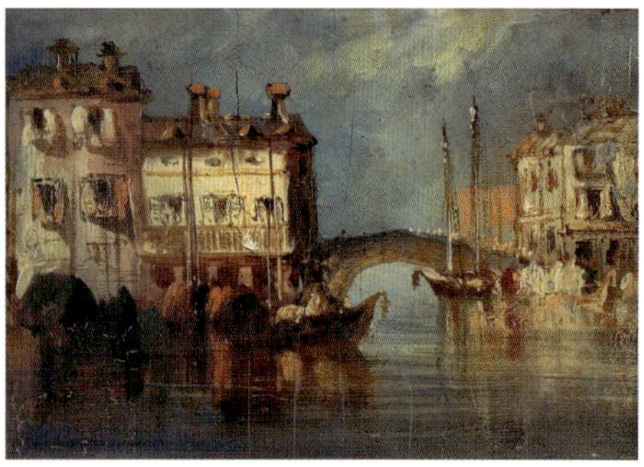

unknown artist 19th C
River Scene
oil on board 17 x 25
SOUAG.TS907

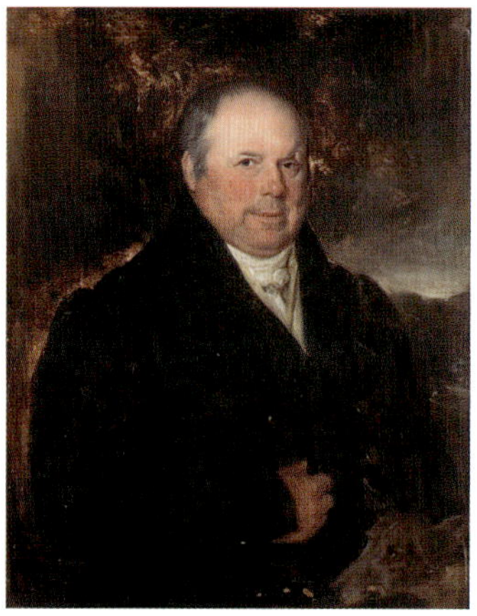

unknown artist late 19th C
Abraham Offin (b.1830)?
oil on canvas 90 x 69.5
SOUAG.TS906

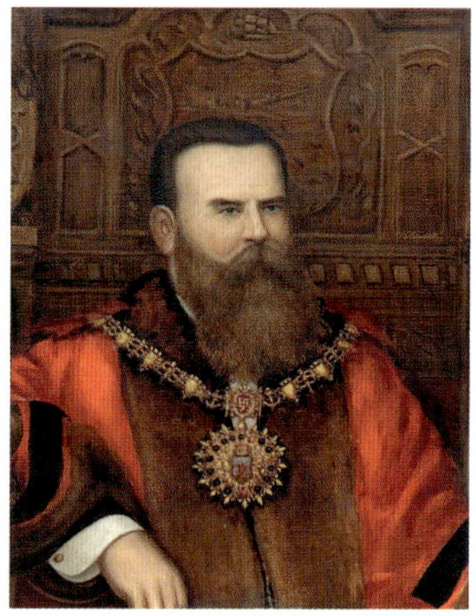

unknown artist late 19th C
Alderman Dowsett, First Mayor of Southend (1892–1893)
oil on canvas 71.5 x 53 (E)
SOUAG.S267

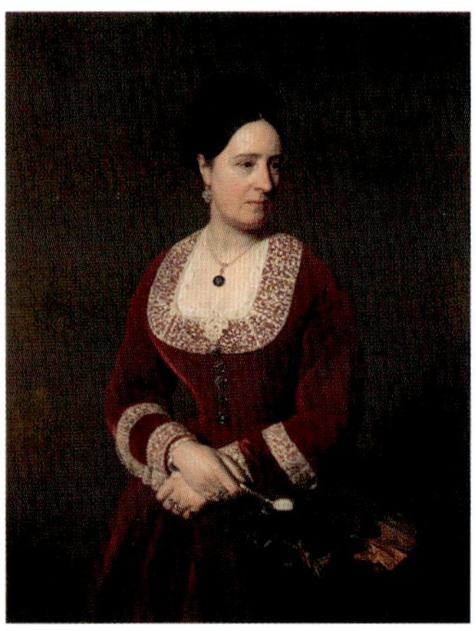

unknown artist late 19th C
Mrs Scratton of Prittlewell Priory
oil on canvas 110 x 84.5 (E)
SOUAG.L.75.1

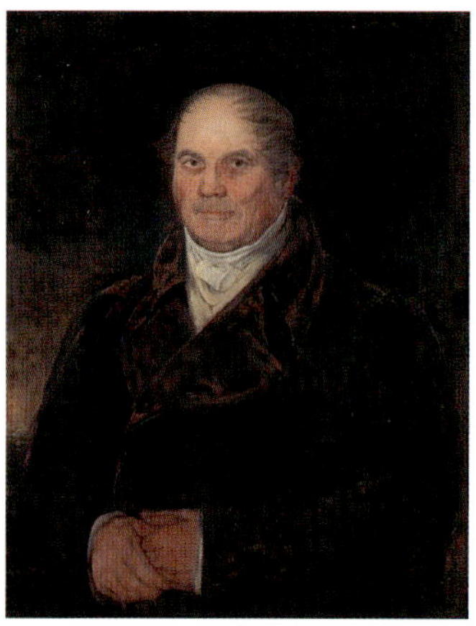

unknown artist late 19th C
Thomas William Offin (1834–1934)?
oil on canvas 90 x 68
SOUAG.TS905

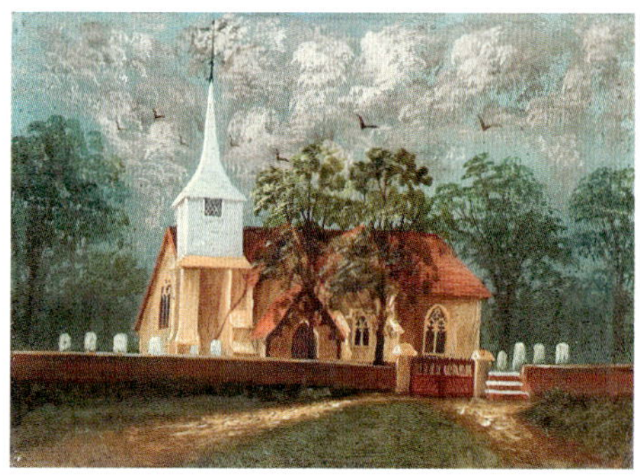

unknown artist
Eastwood Church c.1900
oil on canvas board 15 x 20 (E)
SOUAG.TS779

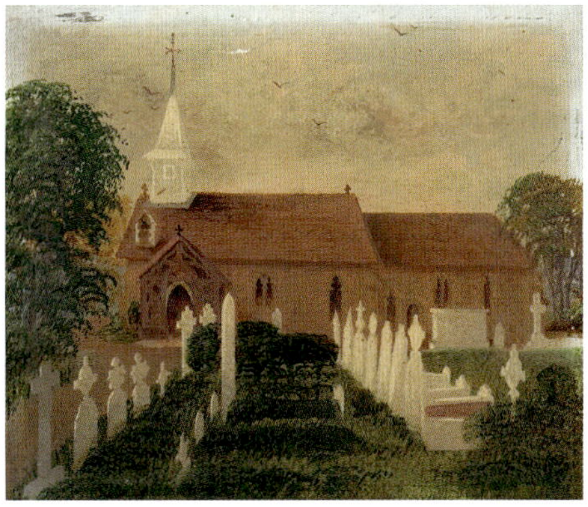

unknown artist
Holy Trinity, Southchurch c.1900
oil on canvas board 17.5 x 20 (E)
SOUAG.TS499

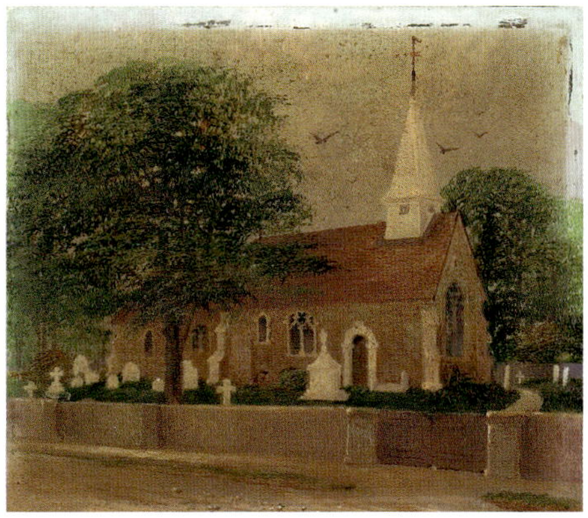

unknown artist
Holy Trinity, Southchurch c.1900
oil on canvas board 17.5 x 20 (E)
SOUAG.TS500

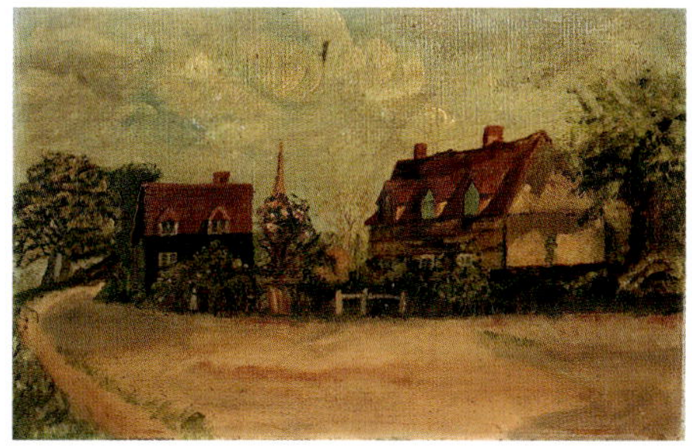

unknown artist
Road Junction, Southchurch c.1900
oil on canvas board 20 x 30.5 (E)
SOUAG.TS501

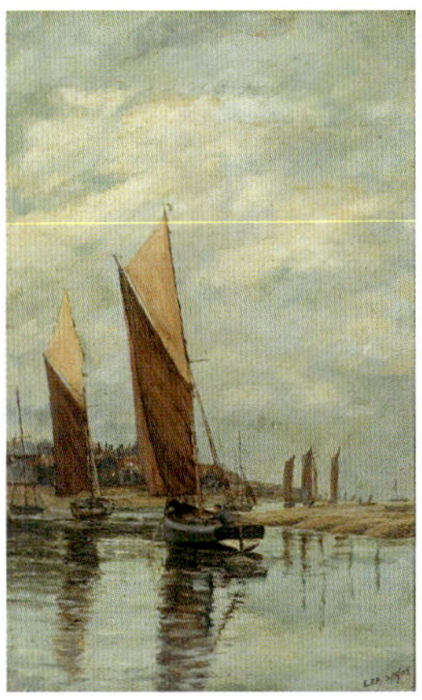

unknown artist
Fishing Boats in Leigh Creek, Looking West 1905
oil on canvas 40.5 x 25.5 (E)
SOUAG.TS430

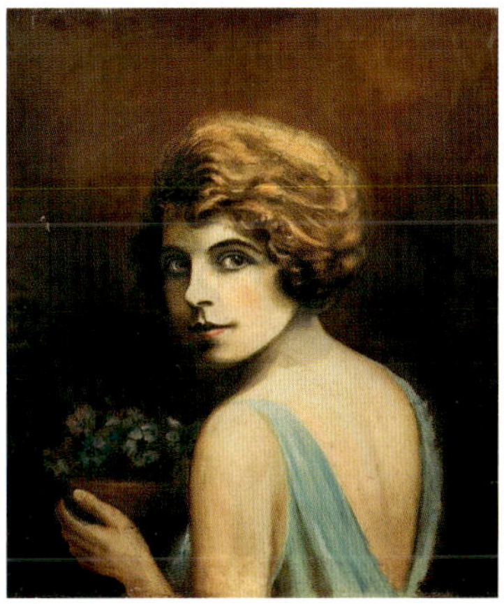

unknown artist
Girl in a Blue Dress c.1930
oil on canvas 60 x 50 (E)
SOUAG.S265

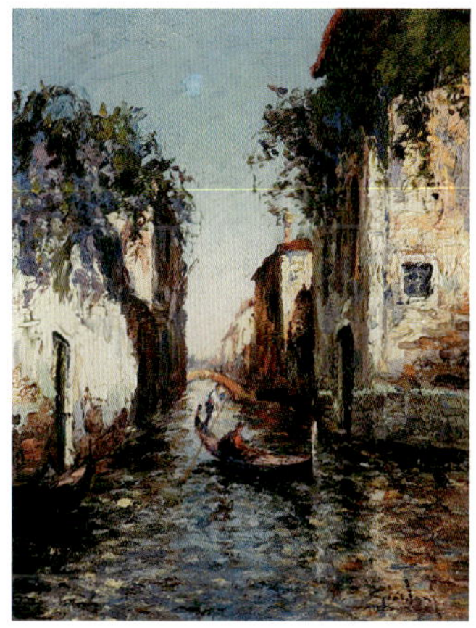

unknown artist
Venetian Canal Scene c.1930
oil on canvas 68.5 x 52 (E)
SOUAG.S56

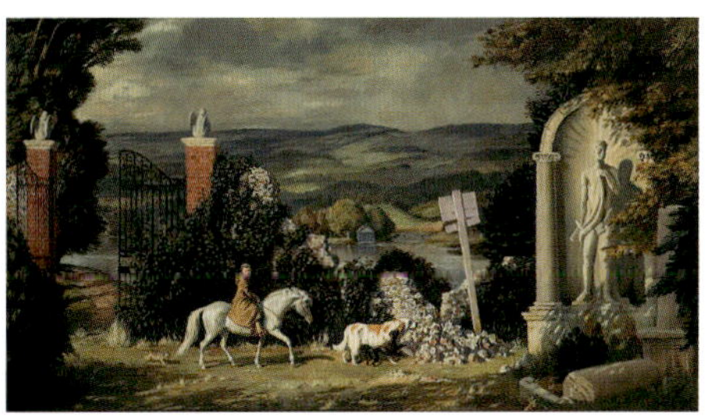

unknown artist
Landscape with Rider on a White Horse and Dogs 1946
oil on canvas 60 x 101
SOUAG.TS902

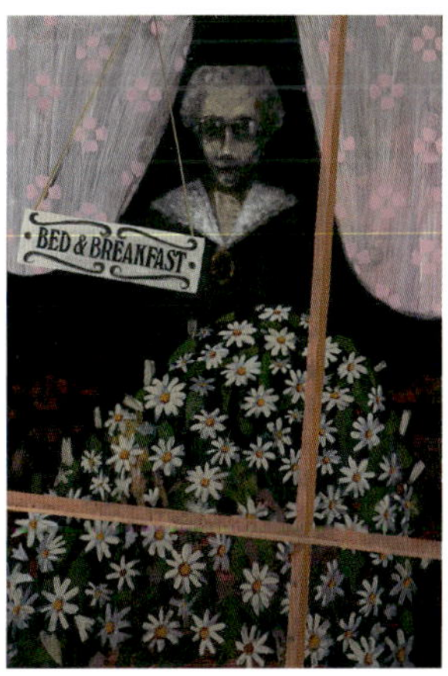

unknown artist
Bed and Breakfast 1980s
oil on board 91 x 60.5
SOUAG.S328

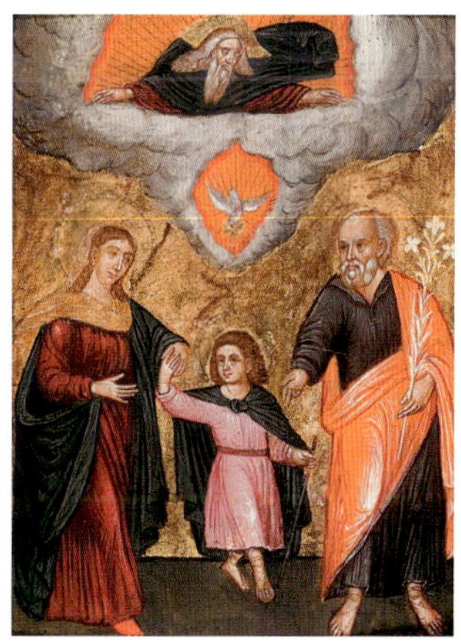

unknown artist
Holy Family
oil on panel 43 x 30 (E)
SOUAG.B126

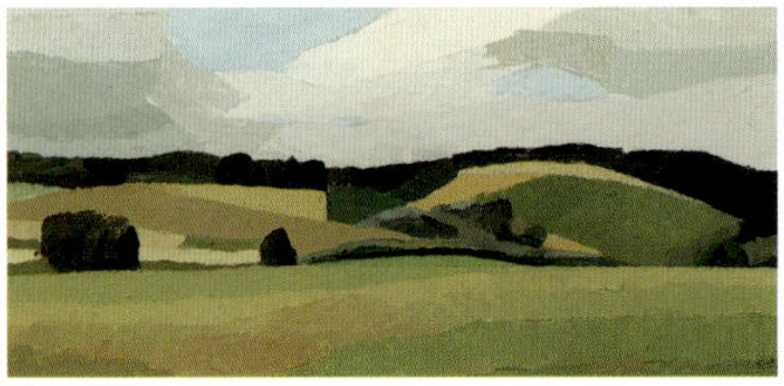

Vaesen, Guy 1912–2002
Suffolk Landscape c.1972
oil on board 30.5 x 61 (E)
SOUAG.S109

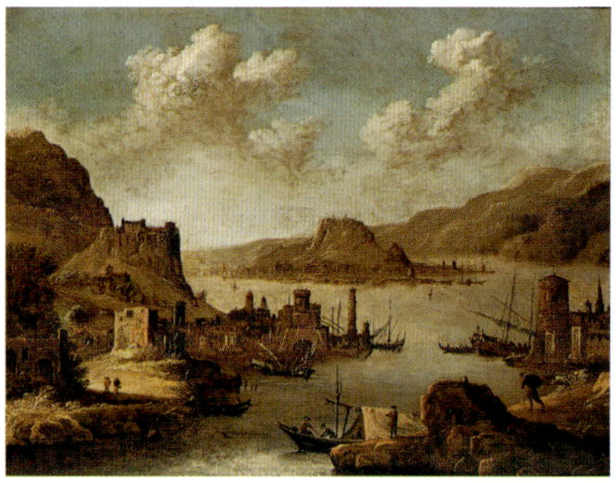

Verburgh, Dionys 1655–1722
Coast and Harbour Scene
oil on panel 39 x 48 (E)
SOUAG.B24

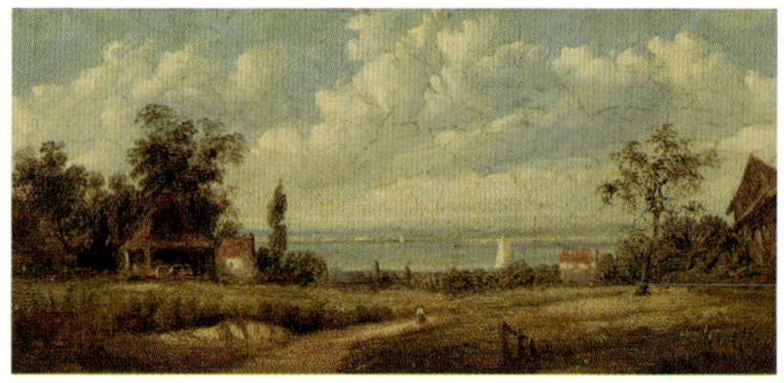

Vickers, Alfred 1786–1868
Southchurch c.1860
oil on canvas 33.5 x 53.5 (E)
SOUAG.TS18

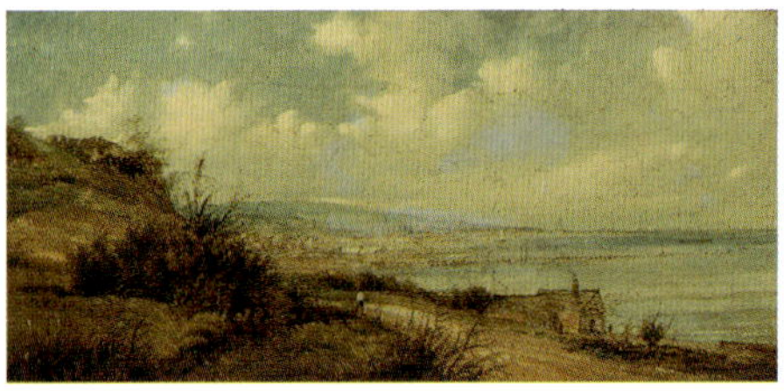

Vickers, Alfred 1786–1868
Southend from the Cliffs, Looking East c.1860
oil on canvas 33.5 x 53.5 (E)
SOUAG.TS19

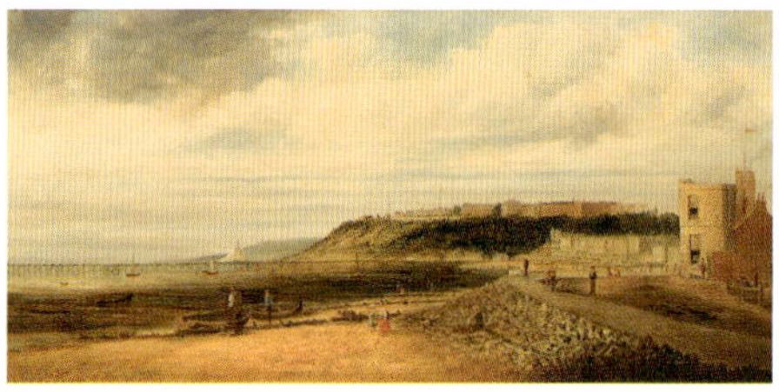

Vickers, Alfred 1786–1868
Southend from the Old Town, Looking West
c.1860
oil on canvas 38 x 76 (E)
SOUAG.TS20

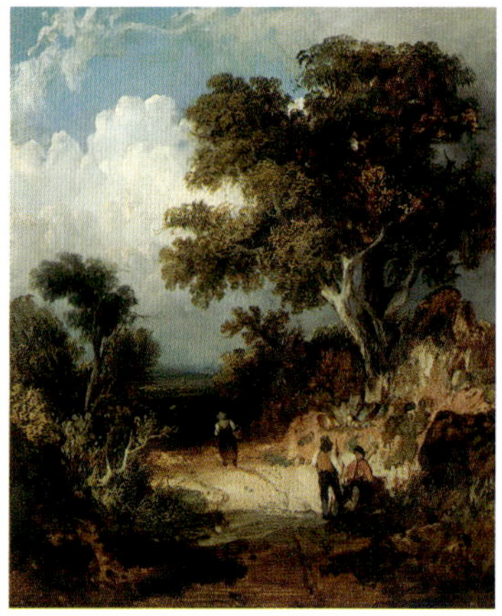

Vickers, Alfred 1786–1868
Landscape
oil on canvas 34 x 28 (E)
SOUAG.S2

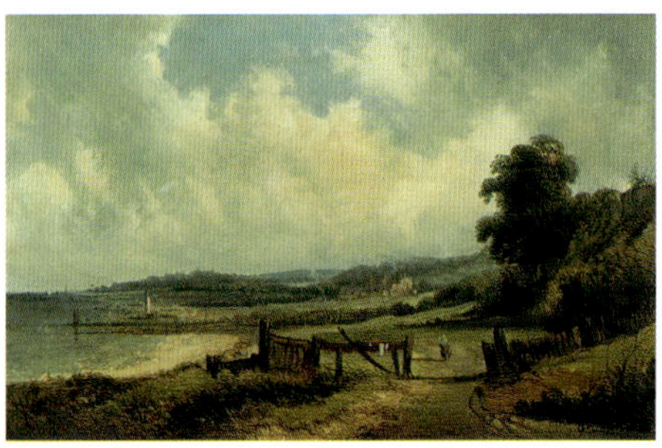

Vickers, Alfred 1786–1868
View near Southend
oil on canvas 39 x 50 (E)
SOUAG.TS326

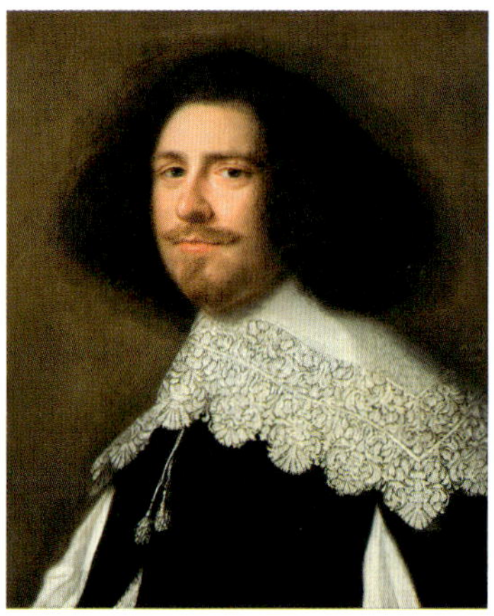

Vries, Abraham de c.1590–c.1650
Portrait of a Gentleman c.1639
oil on canvas 57.5 x 47.5 (E)
SOUAG.B29

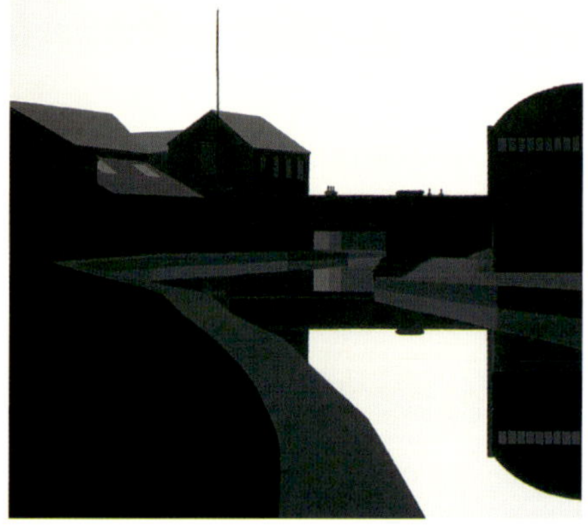

Wade, Maurice 1917–1991
Canal at Longport
oil on board 68.5 x 68.5 (E)
SOUAG.S93

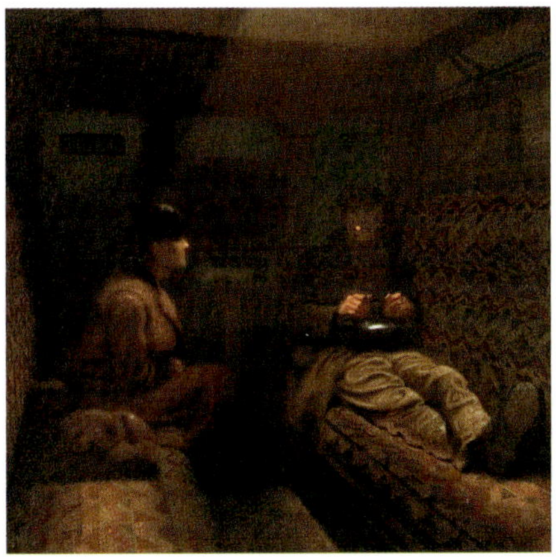

Wallcousins, Ernest 1883–1976
Conversation Piece 1943
oil on board 60 x 58.5
SOUAG.S157

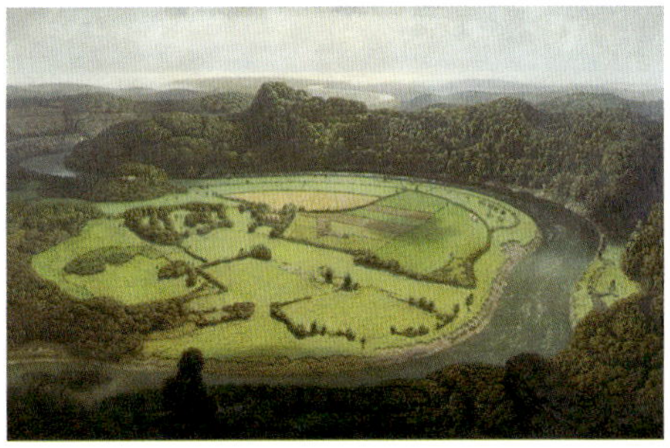

Wallcousins, Ernest 1883–1976
River Wye Approaching the Severn Estuary c.1947
oil on canvas 88 x 134 (E)
SOUAG.B122

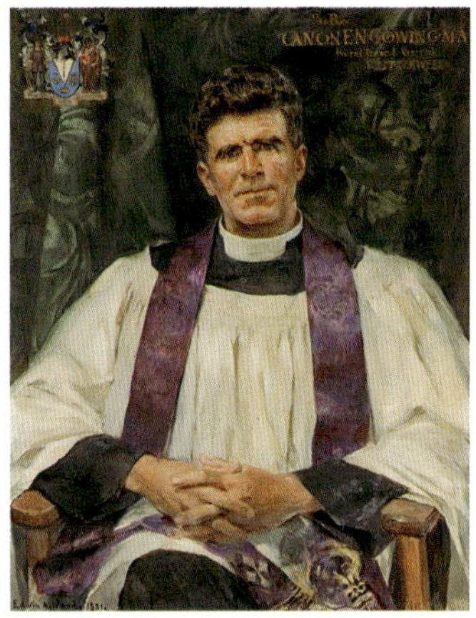

Ward, Edwin Arthur 1859–1933
The Reverend Canon E. N. Gowing, MA, Rural Dean and Vicar of Prittlewell 1931
oil on canvas 90 x 70 (E)
SOUAG.S259

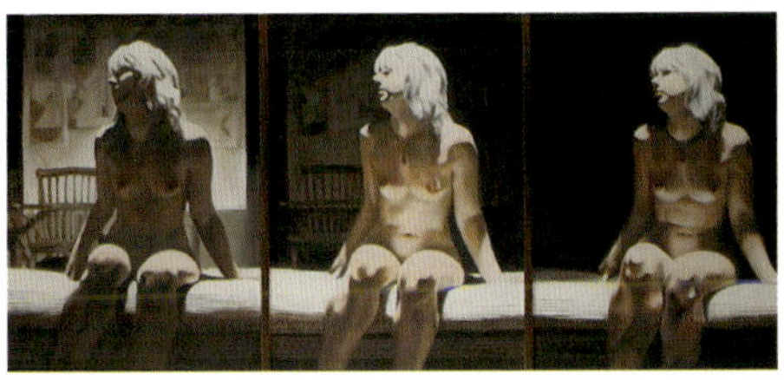

Ward-Robinson, Neil b.1943
Nude under a Swinging Light Source
oil on canvas 45 x 65 (E)
SOUAG.S379

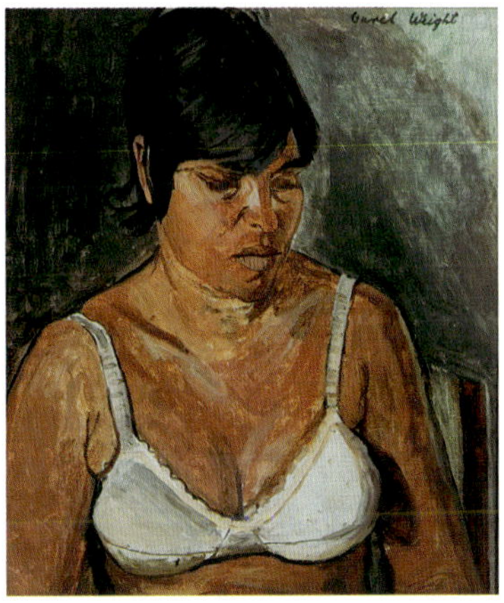

Weight, Carel Victor Morlais 1908–1997
Girl in a White Bra c.1969
oil on board 35.5 x 30.5 (E)
SOUAG.S342

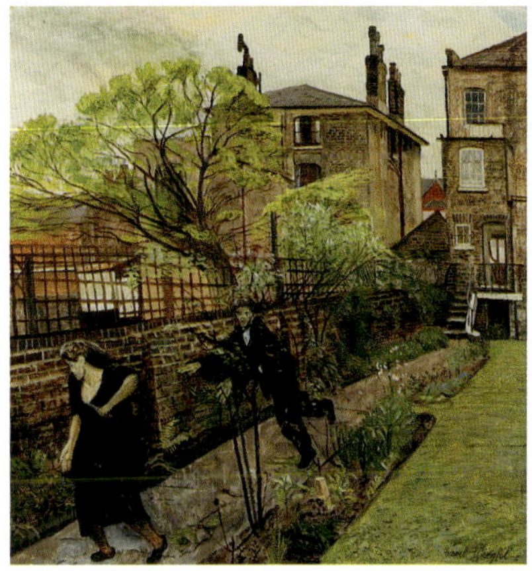

Weight, Carel Victor Morlais 1908–1997
Death of Lucretia No.1
oil on board 83 x 80 (E)
SOUAG.B142

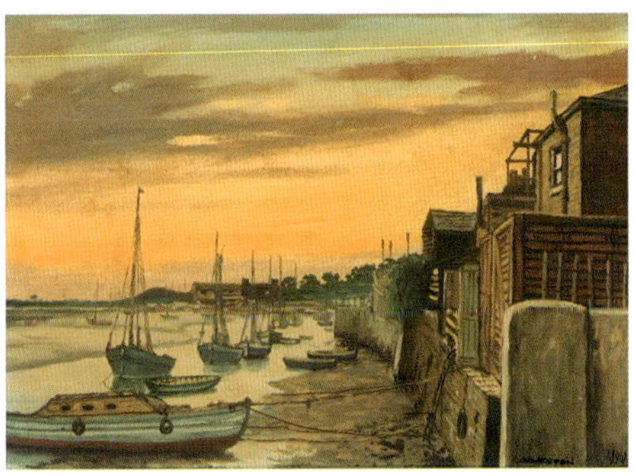

Weston, A.
The Creek, Leigh-on-Sea 1961
oil on board 21.5 x 30 (E)
SOUAG.TS839

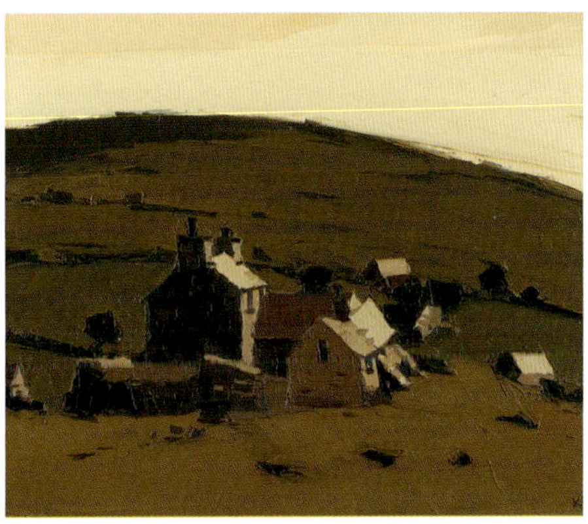

Williams, Kyffin b.1918
Deserted Farm, Llanrhuddlad c.1970
oil on canvas 51 x 61 (E)
SOUAG.S100

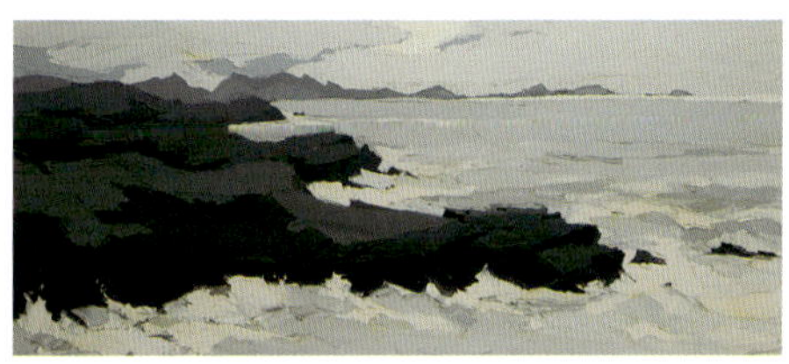

Williams, Kyffin b.1918
Sea at Trearddur c.1976
oil on board 50 x 114 (E)
SOUAG.S159

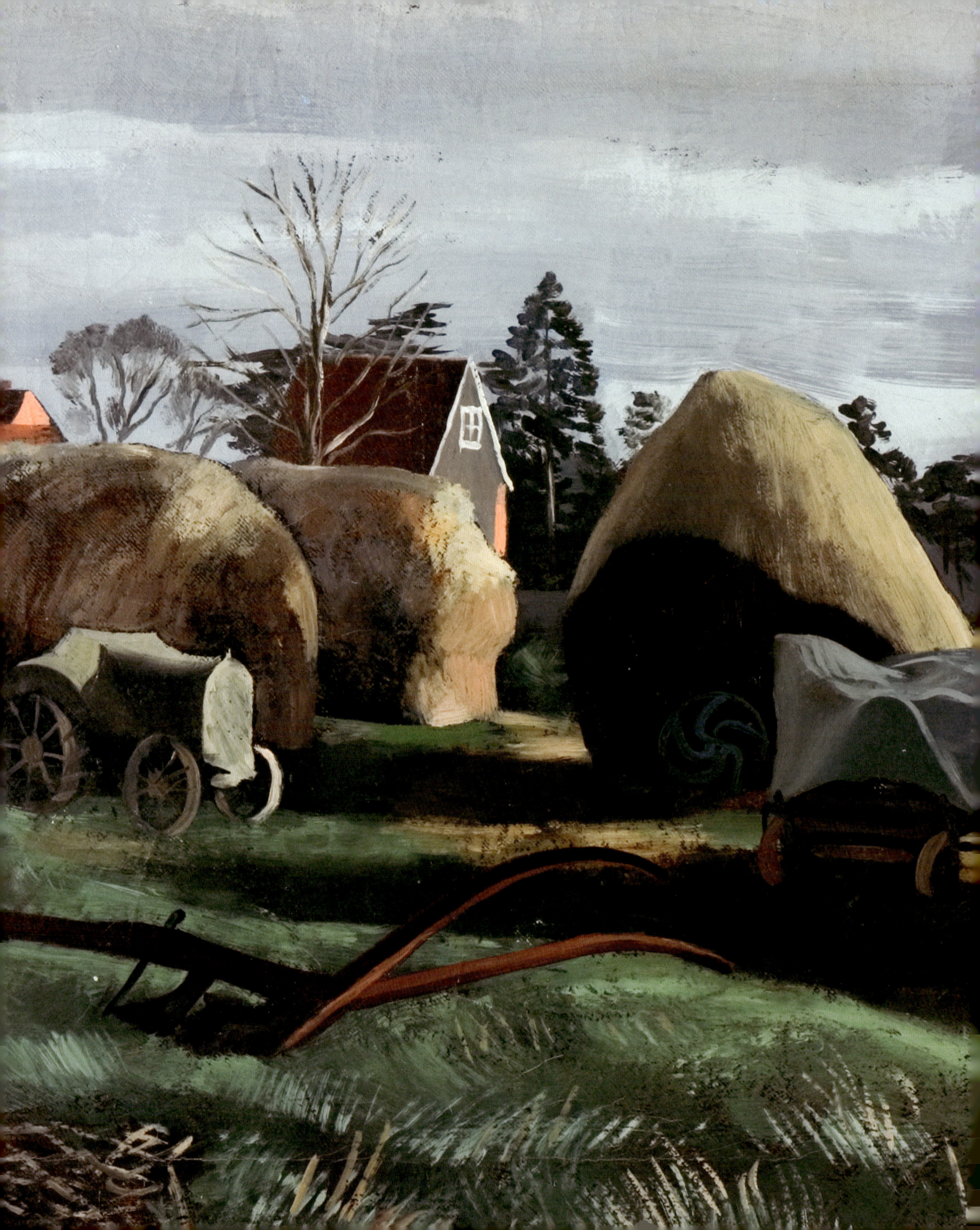

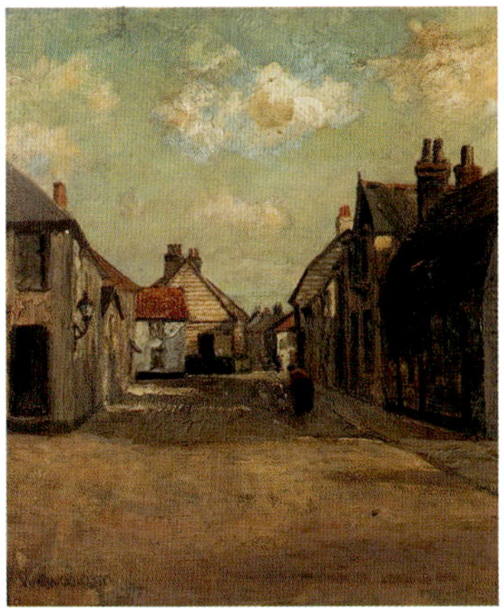

Woolcott, Wilfred Robert b.1892
High Street, Leigh-on-Sea 1919
oil on canvas 24 x 20.5
SOUAG.TS207

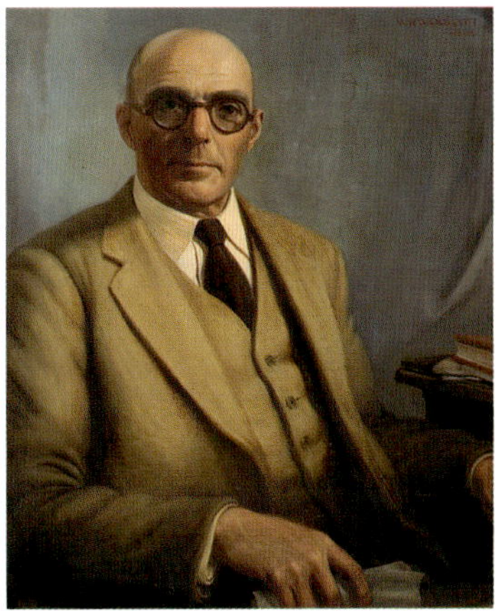

Woolcott, Wilfred Robert b.1892
Walter G. Beecroft 1950
oil on canvas 66 x 56 (E)
SOUAG.B22

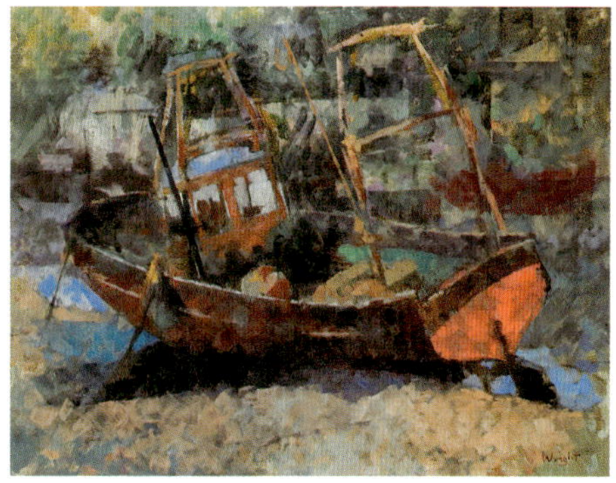

Wright, Frank Alan
Cockle Boat at Leigh c.1980s
oil on canvas board 47.5 x 59.6
SOUAG.TS919

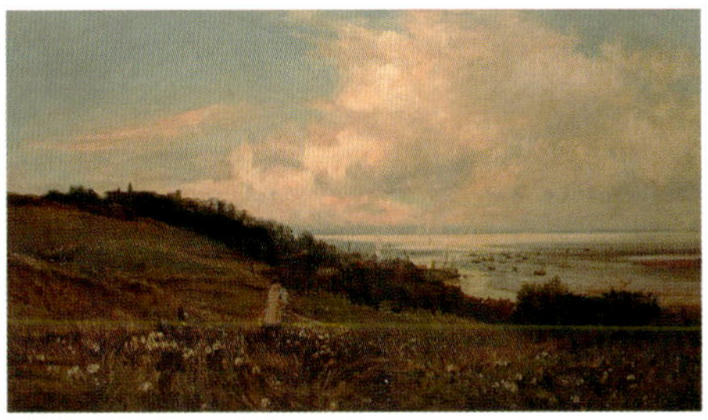

Wyllie, Charles William 1853–1923
Leigh, at the Estuary of the River Thames
c.1885
oil on canvas 76 x 127 (E)
SOUAG.TS22

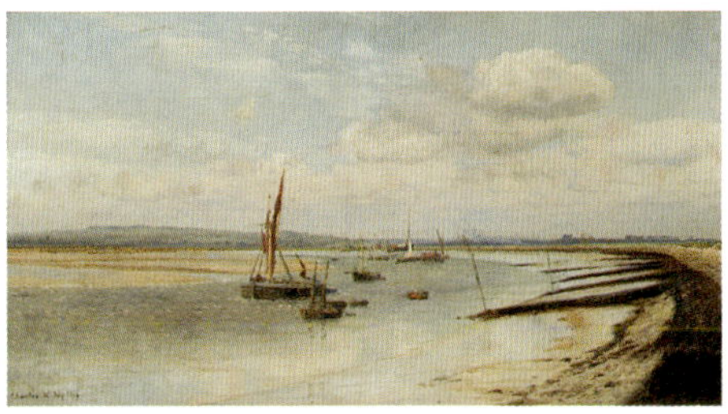

Wyllie, Charles William 1853–1923
Hole Haven
oil on canvas 25.5 x 45.5 (E)
SOUAG.TS21

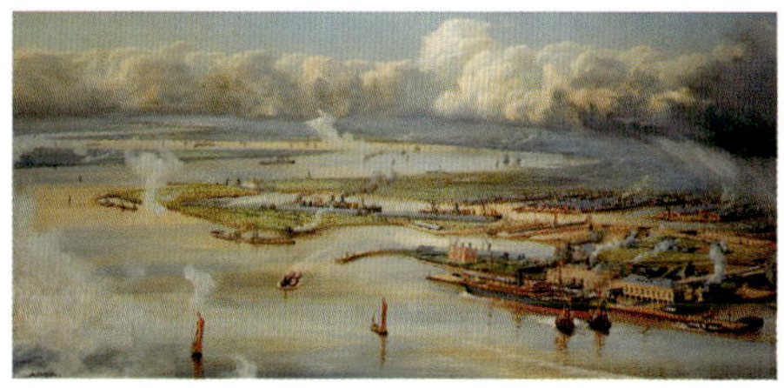

Wyllie, Harold 1880–1973
Tilbury, Essex
oil on canvas 60 x 120.5 (E)
SOUAG.TS23

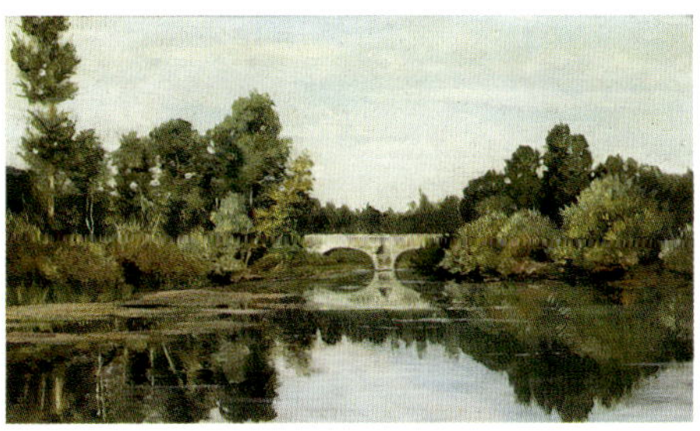

Yon, Edmond Charles 1836–1897
Bridge over a River
oil on board 14 x 23.5 (E)
SOUAG.B119

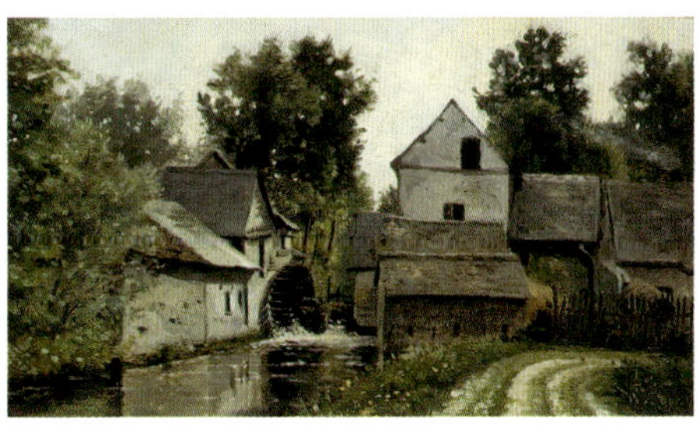

Yon, Edmond Charles 1836–1897
The Watermill
oil on card 14.5 x 23.5 (E)
SOUAG.B118

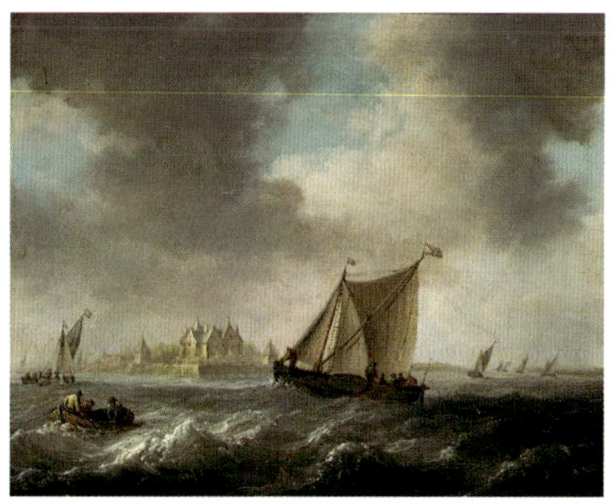

Zeeman, Reinier c.1623–c.1668
Off Scheveningen
oil on canvas 30 x 36 (E)
SOUAG.B27

Facing page: Aldridge, John Arthur Malcolm, 1905–1983, *Haystacks, the Place Farm* (detail), Fry Art Gallery, (p. 227)

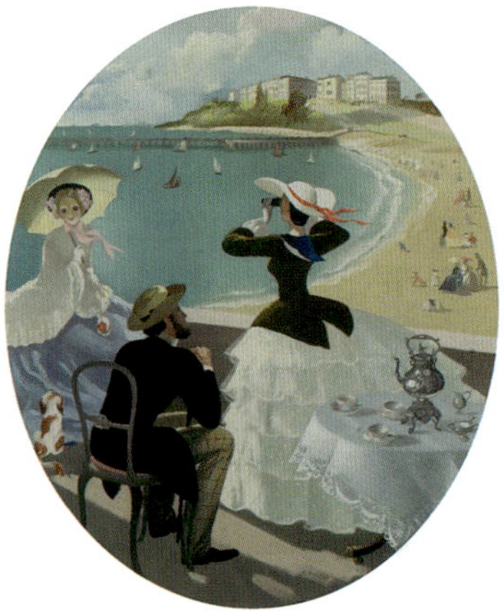

Zinkeisen, Anna Katrina 1901–1976
Promenade Scene, 'Old Southend' c.1930s
oil on canvas 58 x 23 (E)
SOUAG.S372

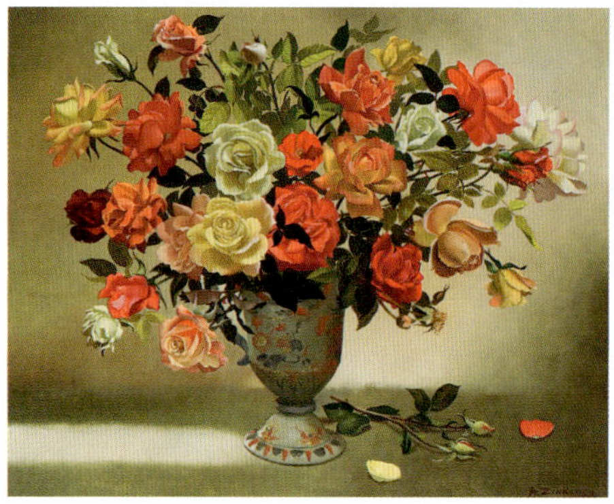

Zinkeisen, Anna Katrina 1901–1976
Still Life of Flowers c.1930s
oil on canvas 63.5 x 75 (E)
SOUAG.S371

Thaxted Guildhall

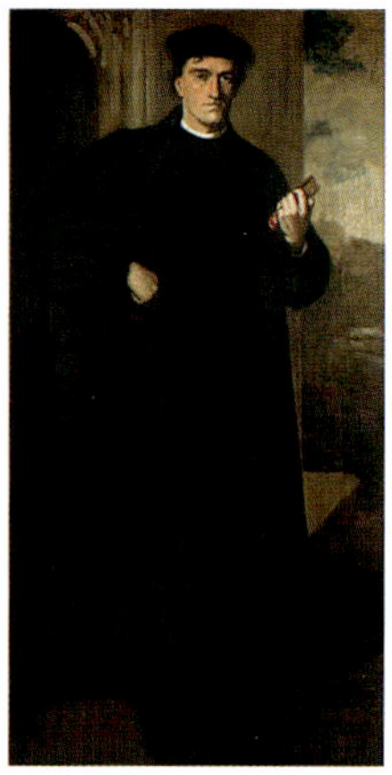

Carter, Frank W. 1870–1933
The Reverend Conrad Noel (1869–1942)
oil on board 173 x 90
TGH.1 (P)

Epping Forest District Museum

Epping Forest District Museum is a relatively young institution. The collections began to be formed in 1969 by Chigwell Urban District Council, but with local government reorganization in 1975, this collection was acquired by the newly formed Epping Forest District Council. A part-time museum service operated from the Recreation Department in Hemnall Street, Epping. By 1978 it became necessary to develop this service, and in November 1981, 39–41 Sun Street, Waltham Abbey opened as the Epping Forest District Museum.

The Museum's remit is to collect and present the social history of the district and the fine art collection reflects this aim. Making up approximately 5% of our total collection, most of the works are on paper, but our small collection of oils and acrylics is broad in style and subject, including abstract and imaginative work in addition to portraiture and landscapes. The Forest itself is a recurring subject, as in *Autumn, High Beach*, 1988 by Alec Dixon and *After Sunset, Epping Forest*, 1984–2002 by Charles Potter. It is also a theme for more abstract works such as *Save the Forest*, 1975 by Sylvia Tyers, which was an expression of opposition to the expansion of the local road network and fears as to its effect on the environment. However, other local landmarks, like the Abbey Church (as seen in *Waltham Abbey Gateway* by an unknown artist), and Copped Hall, also feature and these, together with representations of historic events, as in Henry Pierce Bone's romanticised 1815 rendering of *Burial of King Harold at Waltham Abbey, October, 1066*, demonstrate the strength of local pride in the district and its history.

Many artists have been drawn to the locality, and we are lucky to have significant collections of work by Walter Spradbery and Haydn Reynolds Mackey and, with the support of the Heritage Lottery Fund and the Victoria & Albert Museum, we have recently been able to acquire Lucien Pissarro's *The Garden, Epping*, painted during his residence at 44 Hemnall Street between 1893–1897. In July 1893, he wrote to his father, Camille: 'Epping resembles Eragny considerably, but the views are more extensive. There are pretty cottages and a great forest in which some parts are very wild. Most of the trees however are like willows: that is, a large trunk with branches growing at the top. This also applies to the oaks and ash trees, and gives a curious effect'. In 1897 Lucien Pissarro suffered a stroke and he moved back to London, with his wife, Esther, and daughter, Orovida.

Our prime criteria for acquisition are that the subject matter relates to the Epping Forest District or that the artist is connected to the district by birth or residence. We have also collected work by living artists through the biennial *Artists in Essex* exhibition, at which time our scope is extended to the whole of the historic county of Essex.

We are pleased to have this opportunity to publish our collection and, as a recently appointed member of staff, I would personally like to thank the Public Catalogue Foundation for providing me with a chance to familiarise myself with our varied and interesting collection of paintings.

Jill Holmen, Collections Manager

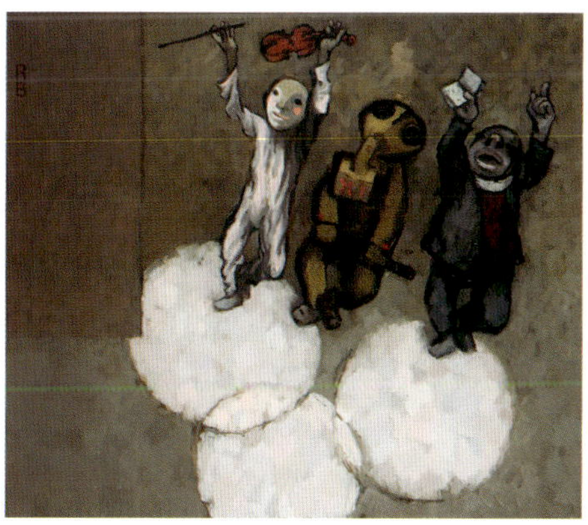

Barrett, Roderic 1920–2000
The Arts, Army and Church Dance 1989
oil on canvas 80 x 92
1989.46

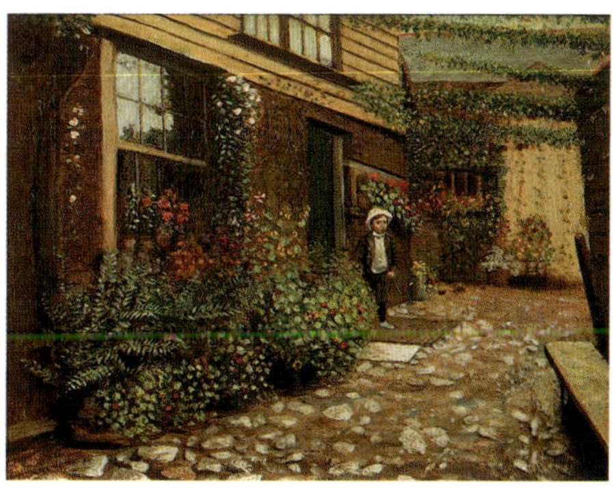

Bascombe, K. N.
'The Old Spotted Cow' Public House, Waltham Abbey
oil on canvas 35.5 x 46
1983.40.1

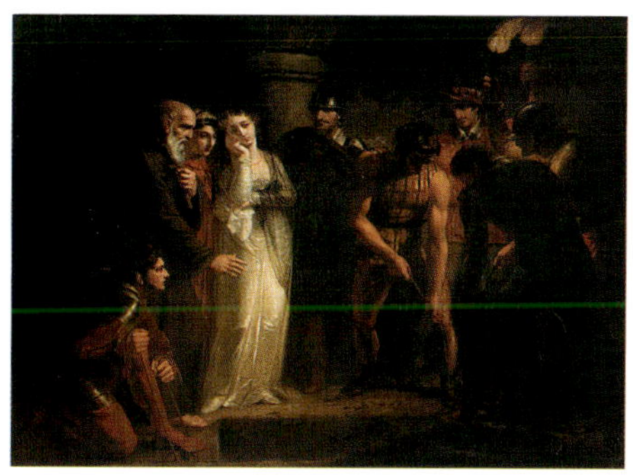

Bone, Henry Pierce 1779–1855
Burial of King Harold at Waltham Abbey, October, 1066 1815
oil on canvas 98 x 122
1993.1129

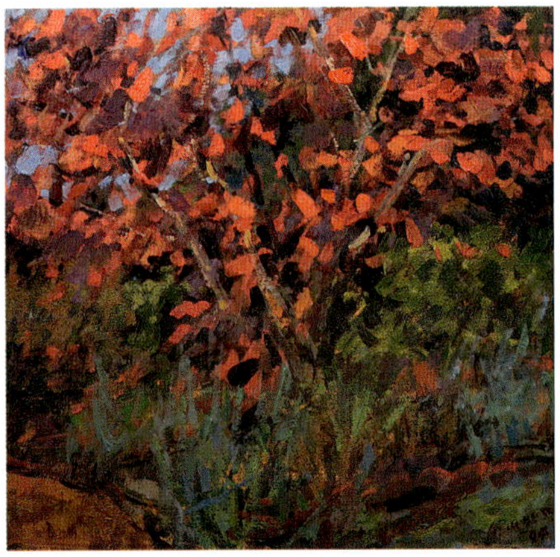

Burgess, Alan b.1936
Autumn Acer, Benington Lordship (Hertfordshire) 1996
oil on canvas 50.5 x 51
1996.86.4

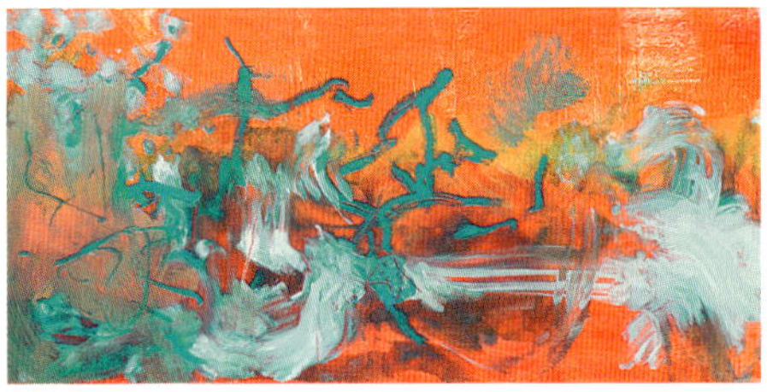

Byrne, Sharon
Greetings 2
acrylic on paper 48 x 93.5
2000.337

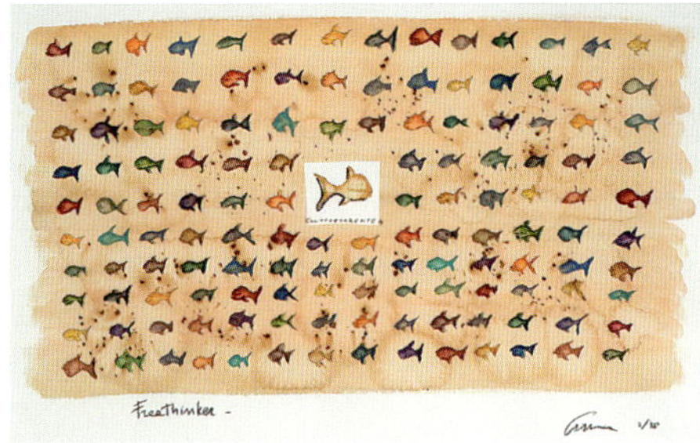

Castellano, Cinzia b.1961
Freethinker
acrylic & watercolour on panel 62.8 x 83.1
1998.773

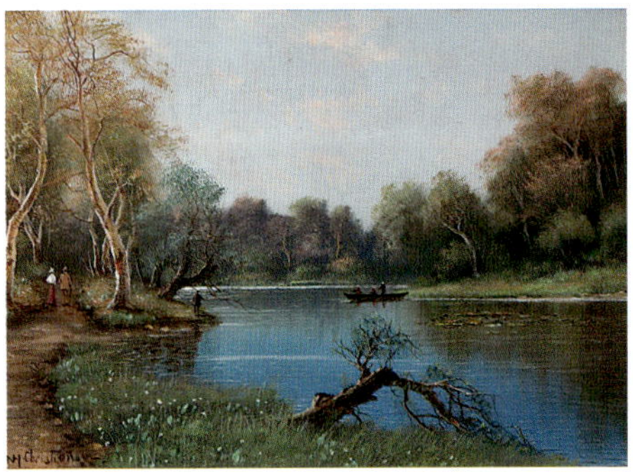

Christiansen, Niels H. active 1874–c.1903
Connaught Water
oil on board 29.5 x 39.5
1994.481

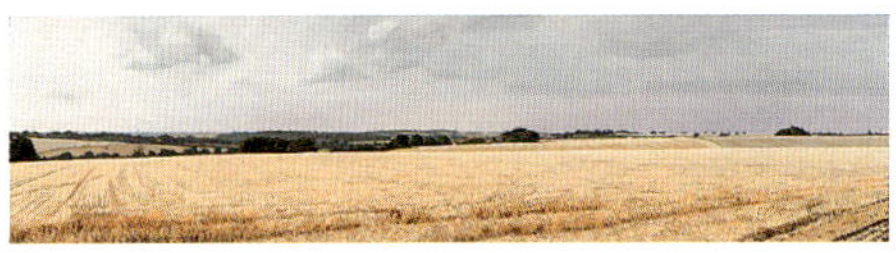

Deakins, Thomas William b.1957
Last Summer, Duton Hill and Tilty, the Chelmer Valley, from Great Easton 1985
oil on board 13.5 x 50.5
1985.76

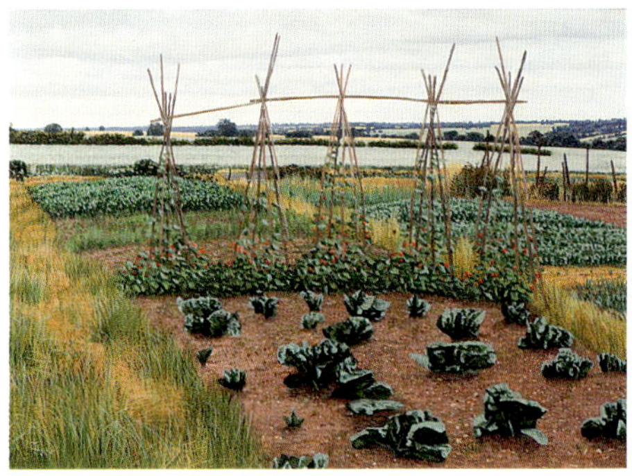

Deakins, Thomas William b.1957
Bean Row, Felsted Allotments
oil on board 15 x 20
1990.4

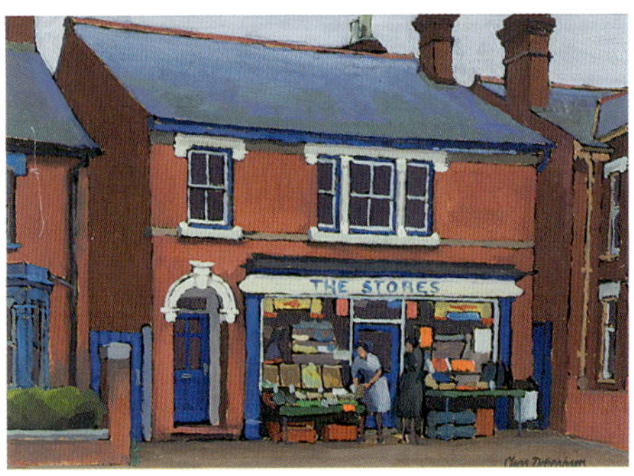

Debenham, Charles b.1933
The Stores
oil on board 15 x 20
1982.125

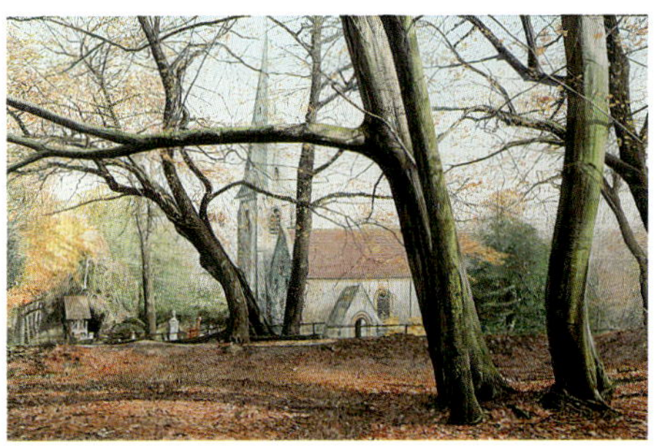

Dixon, Alec active 1933–1988
Autumn, High Beach 1988
oil on canvas 41 x 61
1988.16

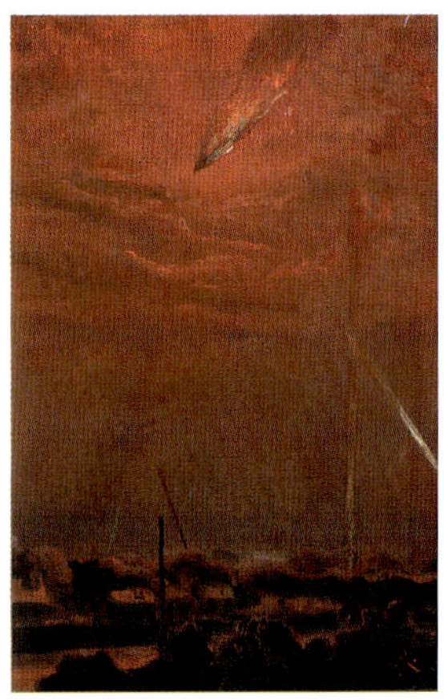

Enfield, J. K.
The Doom of 'Zeppelin L.21' at Cuffley, 2.30 am, 3 September 1916 1916
oil on board 37.5 x 23.5
1993.832

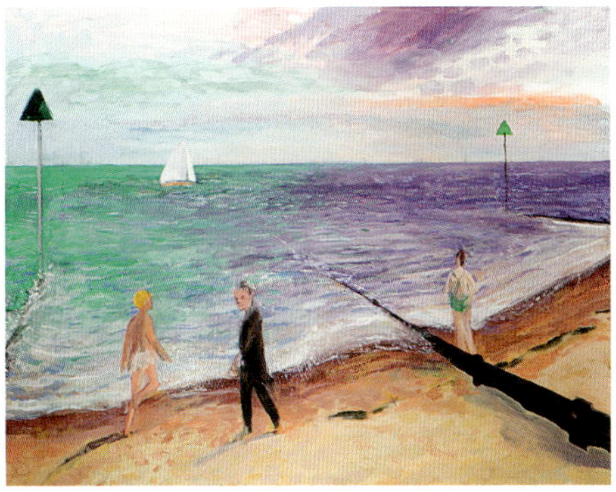

Farrell, Anthony b.1945
Purple Sea, Leigh-on-Sea 1983
oil on canvas 115 x 145
1983.77

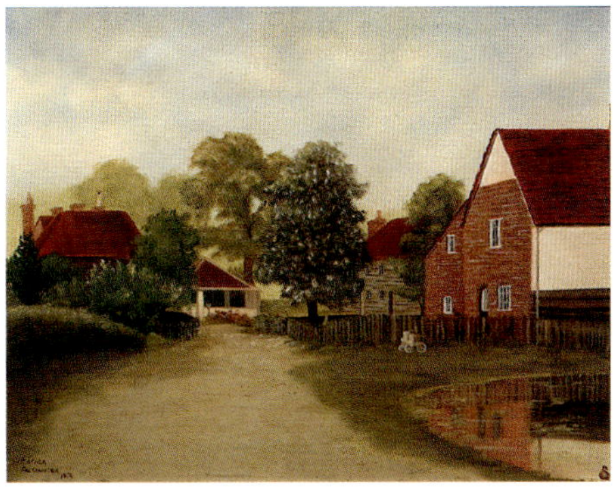

Freshwater, Heather
Theydon Mount, 1890 1976
oil on canvas 40.5 x 51
1993.830

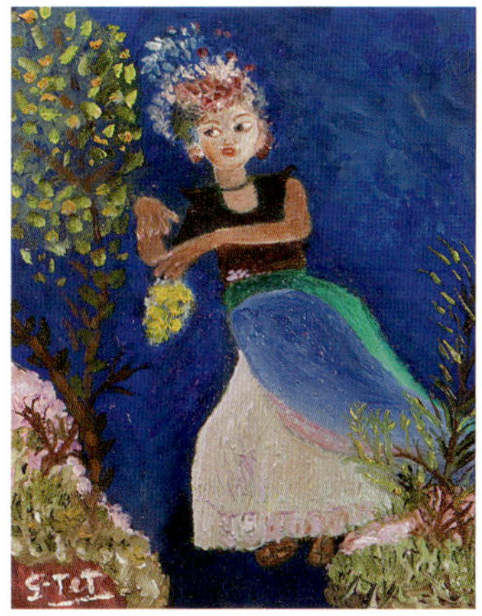

G-Tet
Joy of Dancing 1992
oil on canvas 24 x 19
1992.429

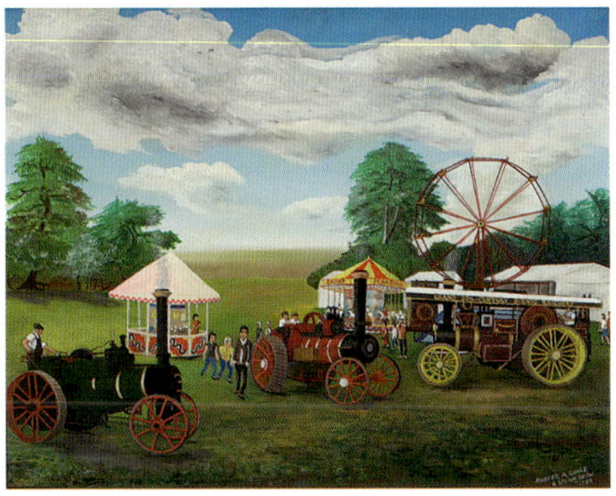

Gould, Robert A.
A Day at the Steam Engine Show 1985
oil on board 60 x 74.5
1985.77

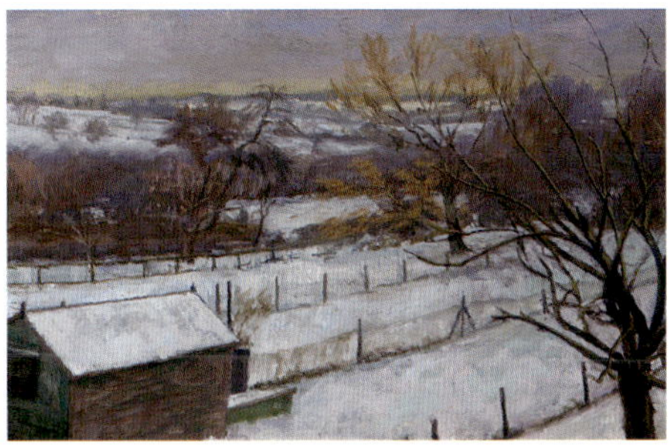

Gower, Valerie
Snow in Essex 1984
oil on canvas 37 x 55
1984.75

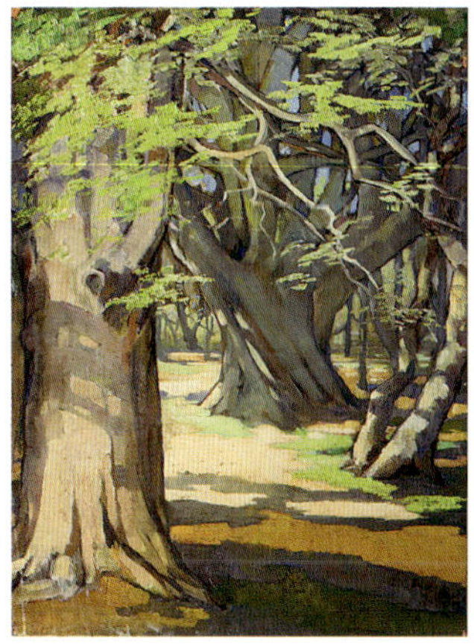

Harris, D. R.
Epping Forest
oil on board 79.5 x 57
1993.109

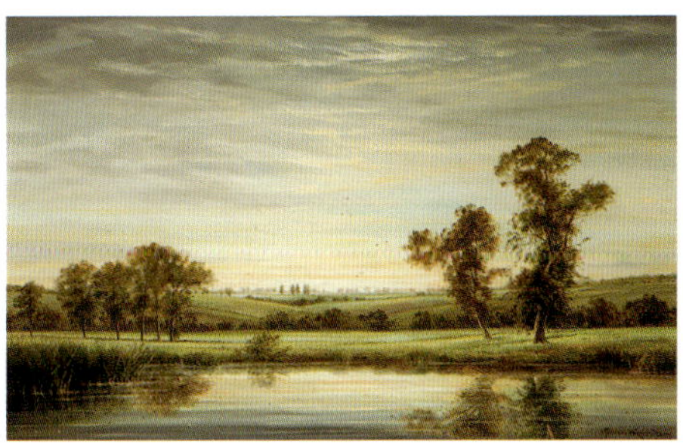

Kennedy, Thomas 1900–1982
On the River Roding
oil on canvas 59.5 x 105
1984.32.1

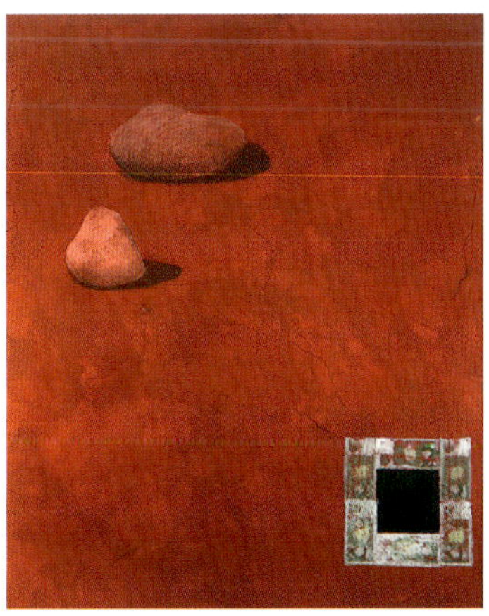

Kite, Roger b.1947
Untitled Red 1984
oil on canvas 126 x 100
1984.76

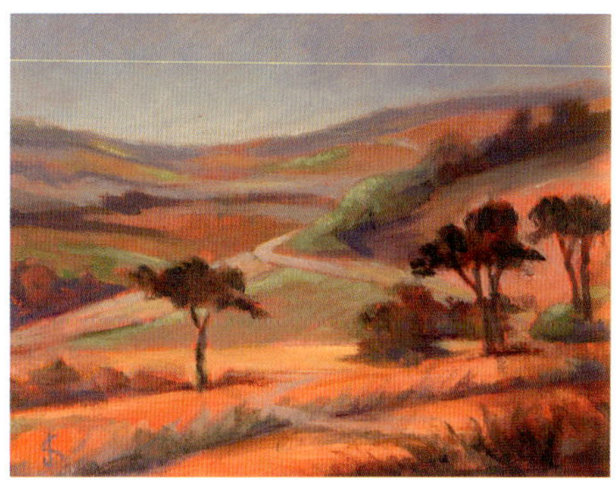

Langley, J.
Anderida Legacy
oil on board 14 x 19
1998.770

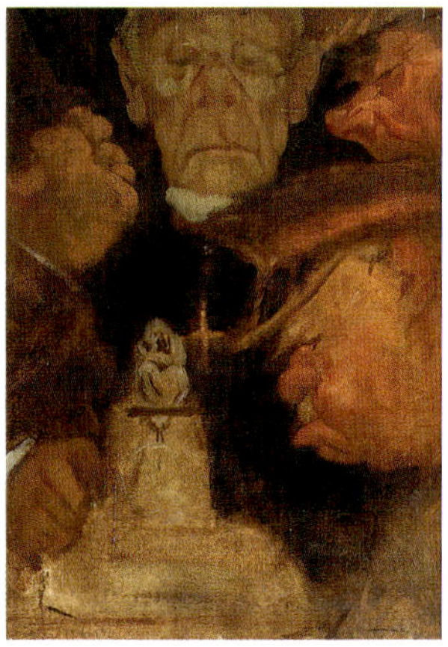

Mackey, Haydn Reynolds 1883–1979
Allegory of Finance, Religion, the Military and the Working Classes 1920–1930
oil on canvas 48.5 x 33
2002.30

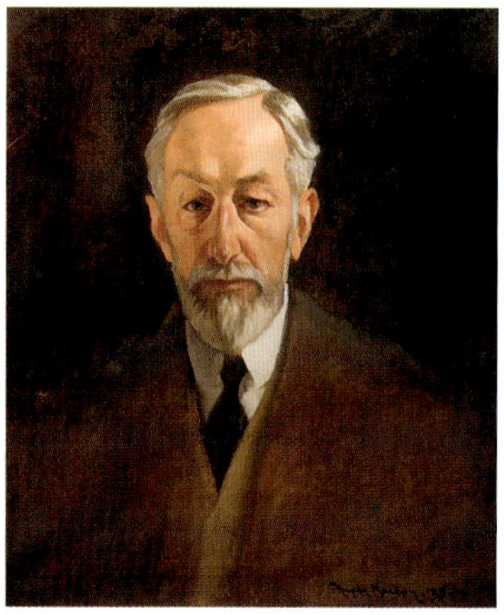

Mackey, Haydn Reynolds 1883–1979
The Right Honourable Lord Noel Buxton 1935
oil on canvas 58 x 48
1998.324

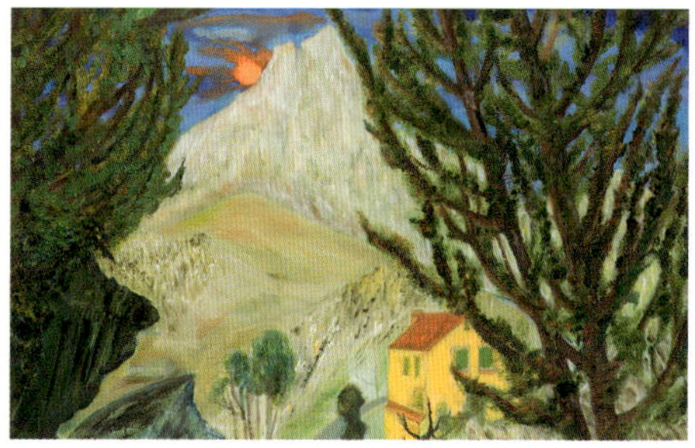

Metson, Graham Peter b.1950
The Yellow House on the Road to Puerto de Soller, Majorca, Evening Light
oil on canvas 60 x 86
1990.1

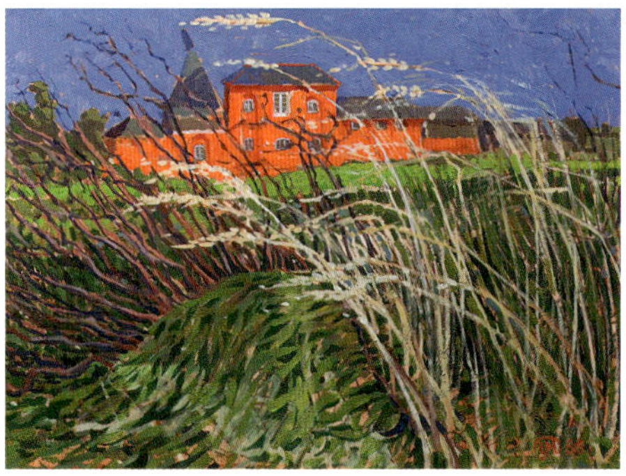

Murray, Brian b.1918
Battlesbridge 1985
oil on paper 44.5 x 60
1985.79

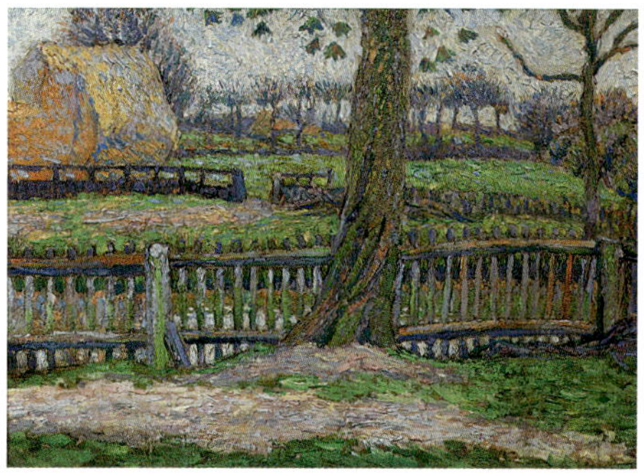

Pissarro, Lucien 1863–1944
The Garden, Epping 1893–1895
oil on canvas 26.5 x 38
2003.447

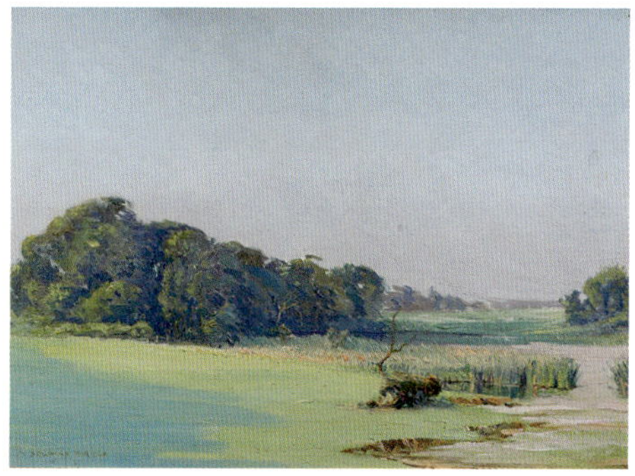

Porter, Arthur Bowmar 1876–1960
An Essex Landscape
oil on board 25.5 x 33
1982.93.1

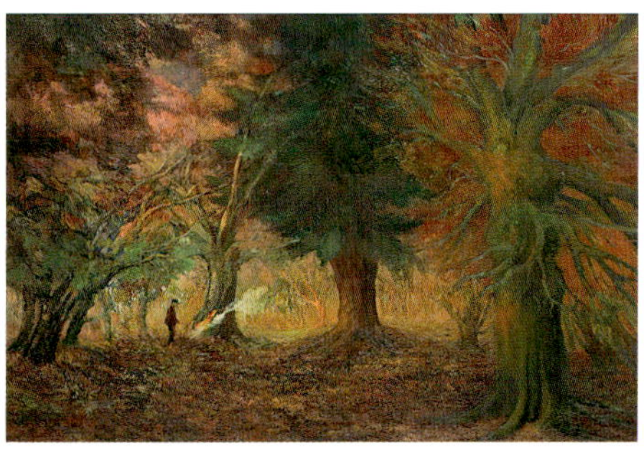

Potter, Charles 1904–2002
After Sunset, Epping Forest 1984–2002
oil on canvas 62 x 90
2004.63

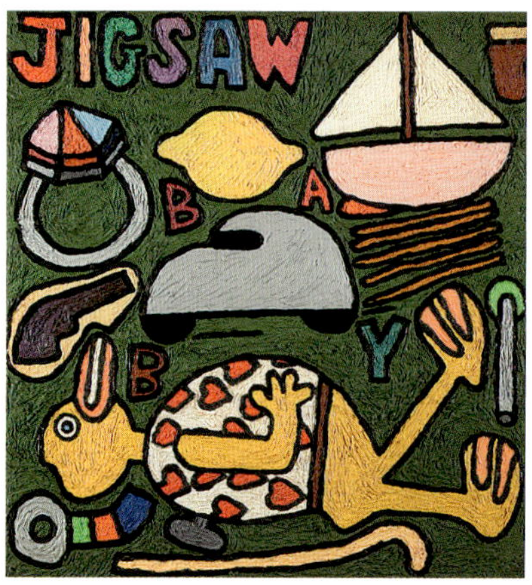

Robinson, Peter b.1957
Jigsaw Baby 1986
oil on canvas 115 x 91
1986.108

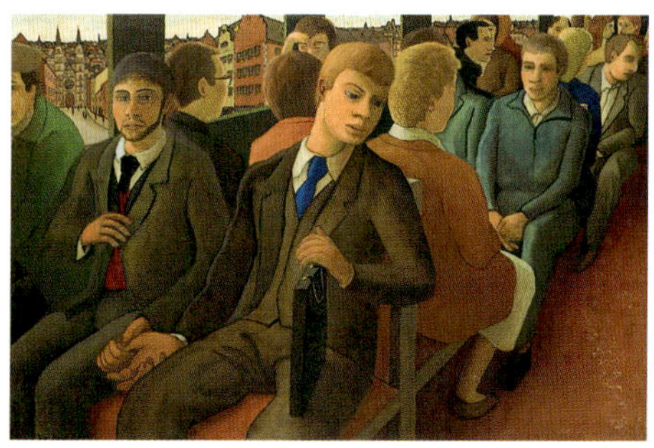

Rowe, Ian Alan b.1963
Two Men on a Tram 1989
oil on canvas 66 x 94
1989.49

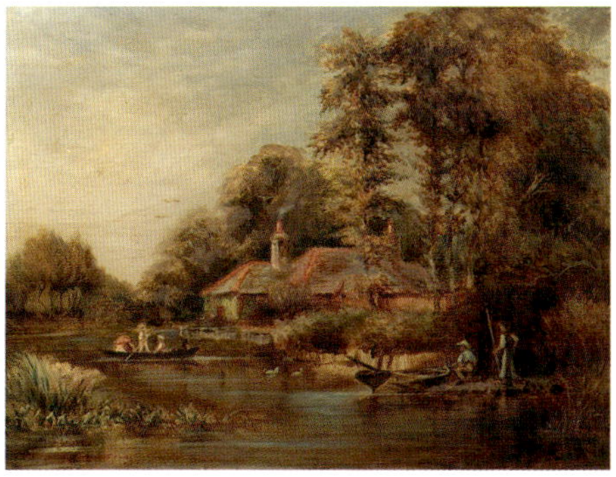

Simcox, A.
Lower Island, Waltham Abbey 1808
oil on canvas 41 x 51
1986.93

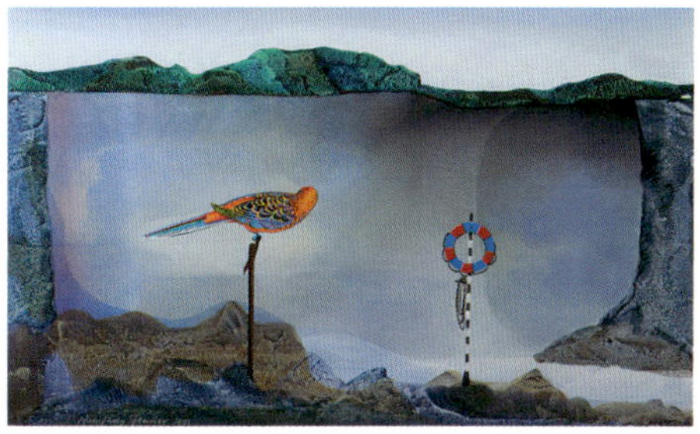

Spender, John Humphrey 1910–2005
Competition 1981
acrylic on paper 33 x 54
1983.76

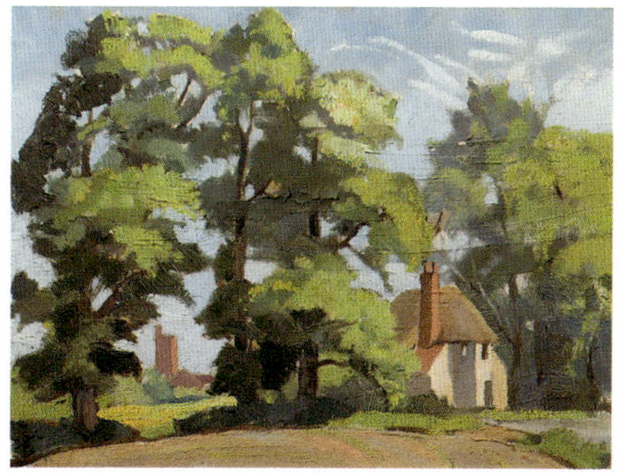

Thoday, Betty
Bury Lane Cottage, Epping 1950–1960
oil on canvas 36 x 45.5
1995.14.2

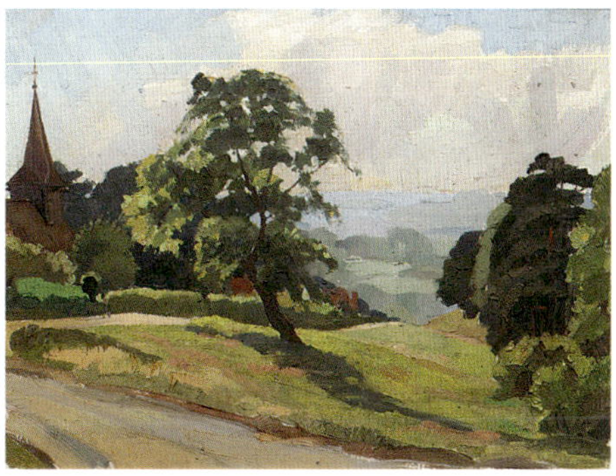

Thoday, Betty
St Thomas Church, Horseshoe Hill, Upshire
1950–1960
oil on canvas 35.5 x 45
1995.14.1

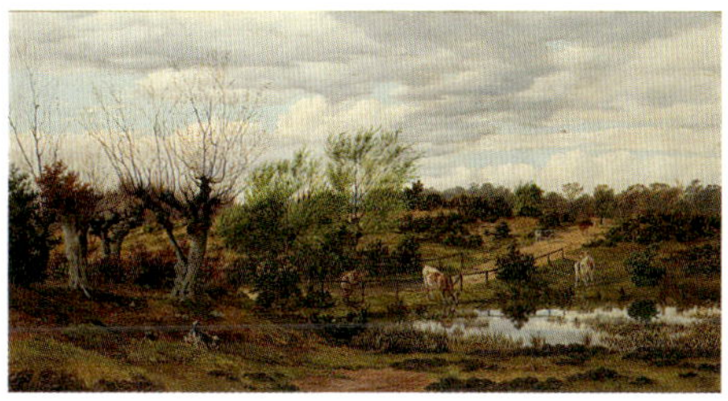

Trappes, Francis M. active 1868–1885
Road to Copped Hall 1875
oil on canvas 50 x 90
1984.64

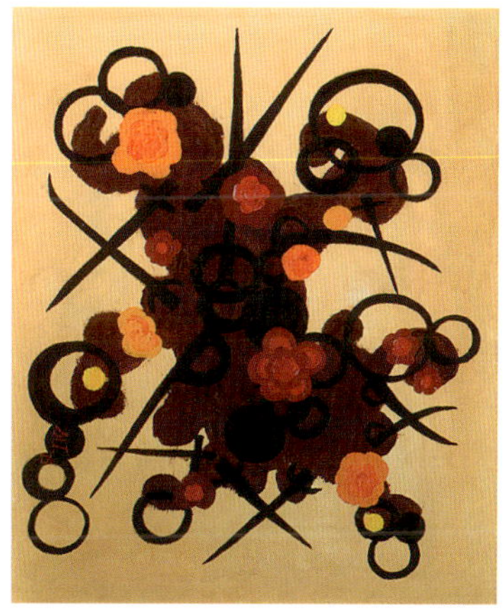

Tyers, Sylvia b.1933
Save the Forest 1975
oil on canvas 59.5 x 49.5
2003.378

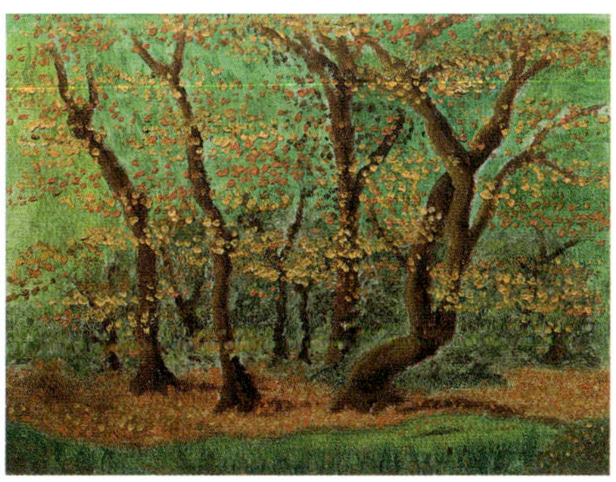

Tyers, Sylvia b.1933
Epping Forest before the M25 c.1975
oil on canvas 35 x 45.5
2003.379

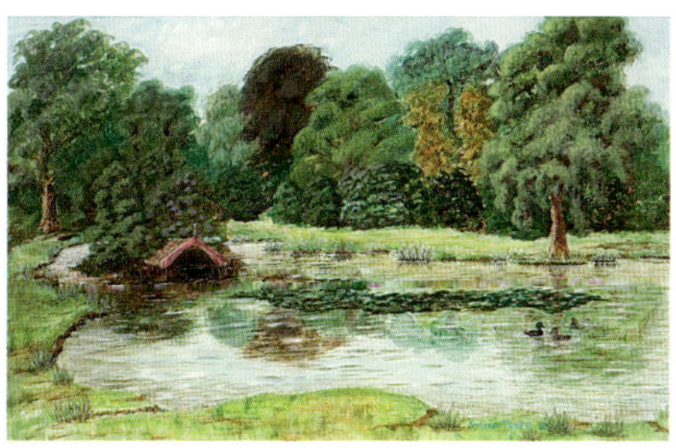

Tyers, Sylvia b.1933
The Lake, Copped Hall 1985
acrylic on canvas 50 x 77
2003.377

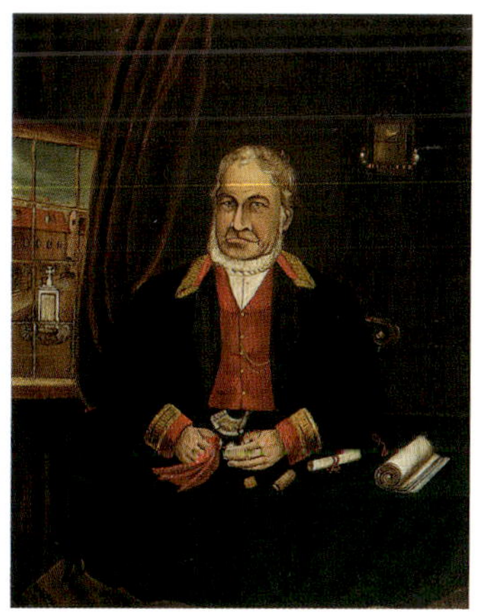

unknown artist
William Bradley, Town Beadle 1887
oil on canvas 50 x 40
1993.956

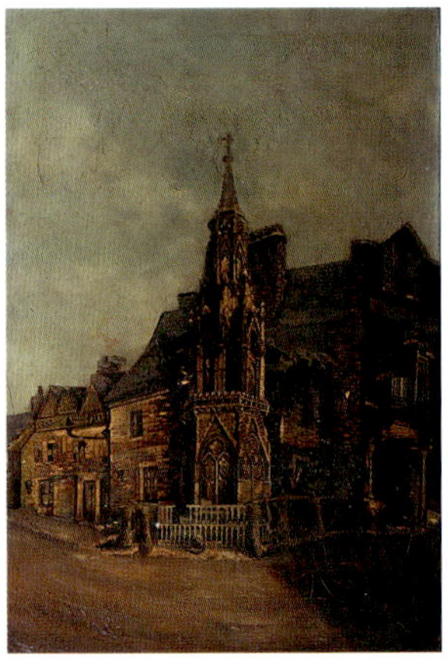

unknown artist
Waltham Cross 1891
oil on canvas 63 x 40
1988.39

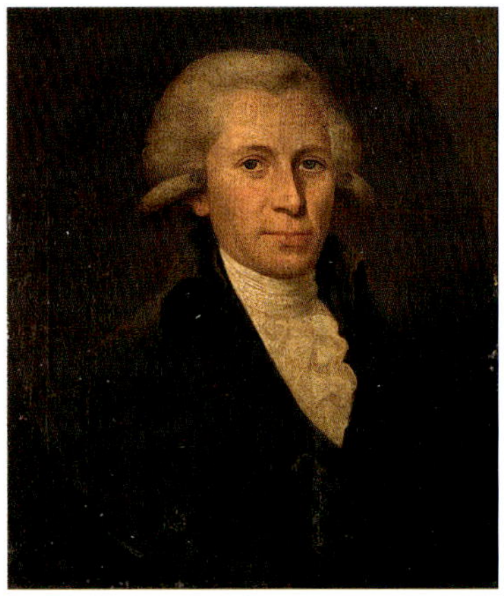

unknown artist
Portrait of a Gentleman
oil on canvas 61 x 51
1982.903.2

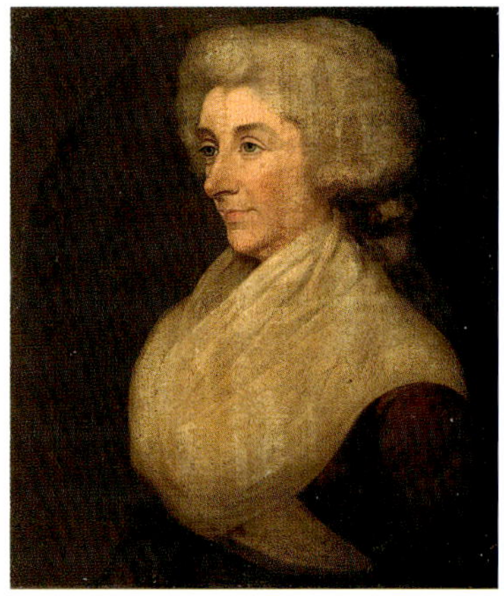

unknown artist
Portrait of a Lady
oil on canvas 61 x 51
1982.903.1

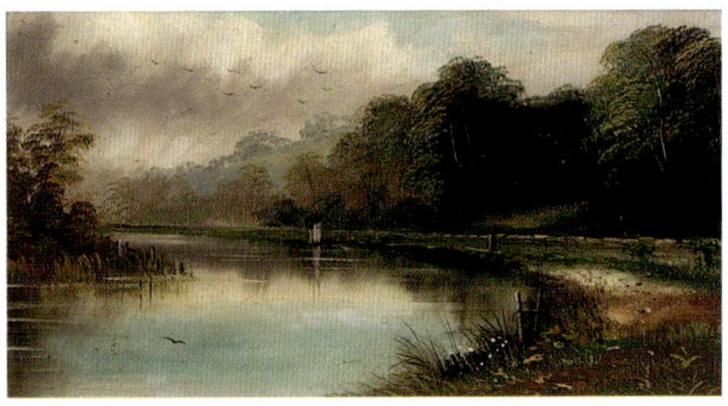

unknown artist
River Landscape
oil on canvas 20 x 36
2000.340

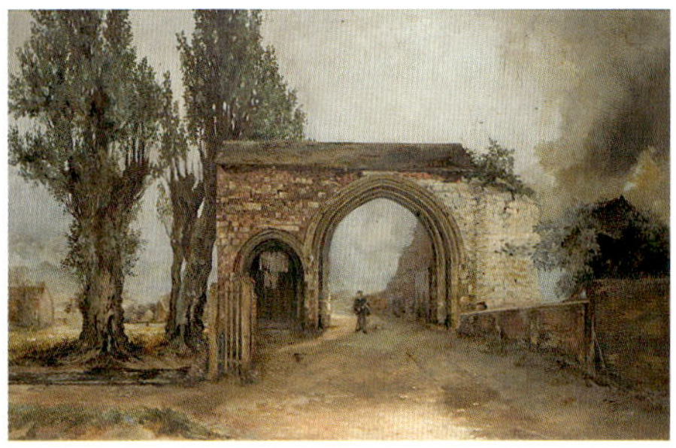

unknown artist
Waltham Abbey Gateway
oil on canvas 69.5 x 105
1993.1128

Royal Gunpowder Mills, Waltham Abbey

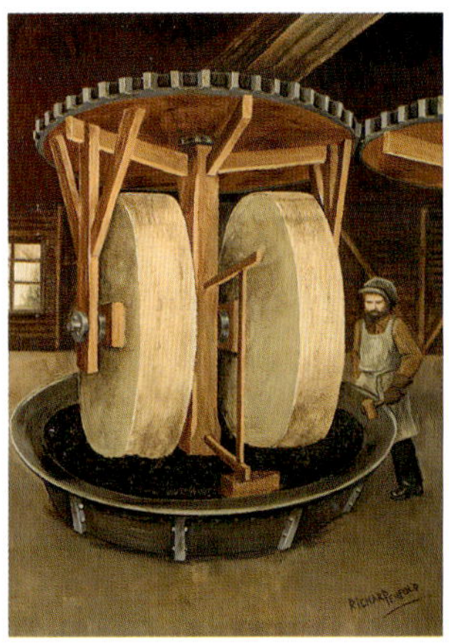

Penfold, Richard W. b.1946
Gunpowder Incorporating Mill, c.1780 1978
acrylic on canvas 70 x 50
1

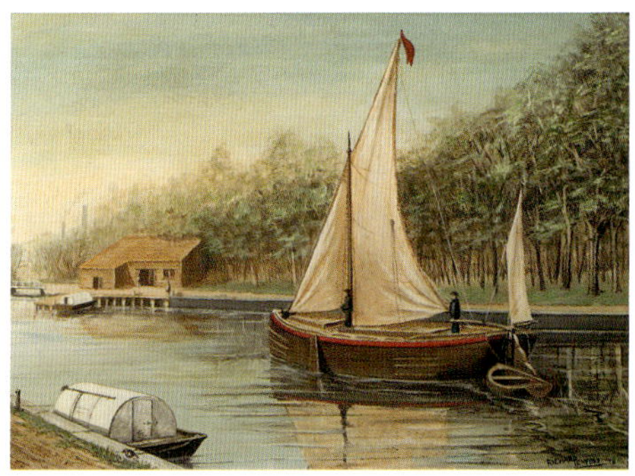

Penfold, Richard W. b.1946
'Lady of the Lea' Explosives Barge 1978
acrylic on canvas 45 x 60
2

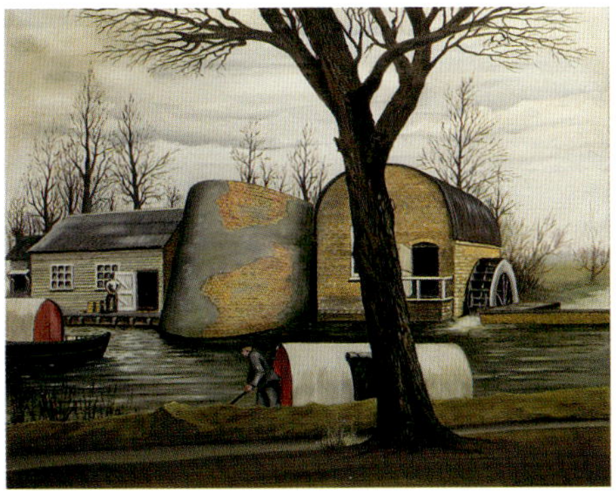

Tinniswood, Robert 1936–1991
Gunpowder Press House, c.1880 1981
oil on canvas 50 x 60
3

Southend University Hospital

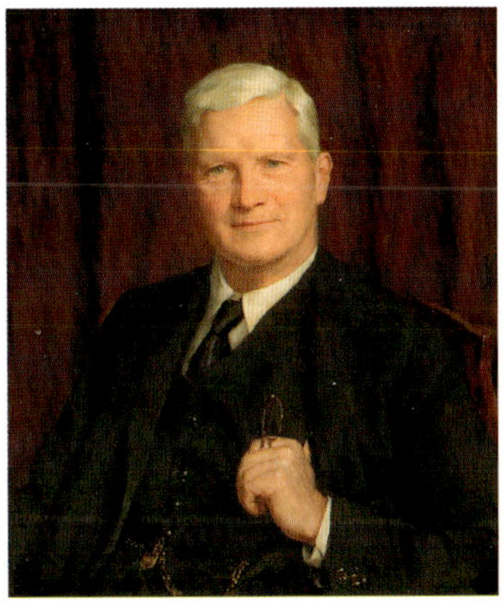

Olivier, Herbert Arnould 1861–1952
The Right Honourable the Earl Iveagh, KG, FRS (1874–1967) 1936
oil on canvas 74 x 61
2

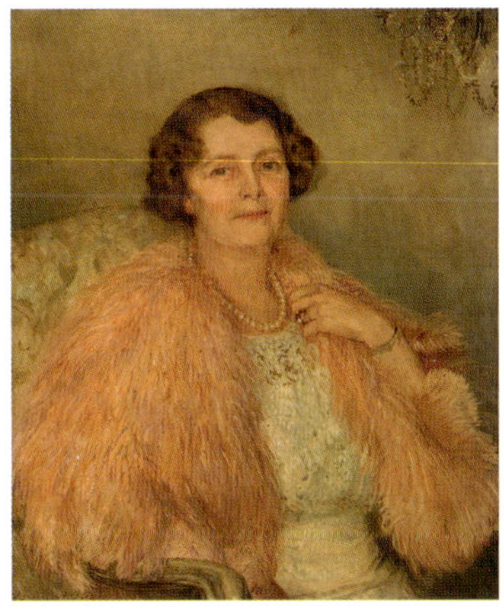

Olivier, Herbert Arnould 1861–1952
The Lady Gwendolen Iveagh, CBE (d.1966)
1937
oil on canvas 74 x 61
1

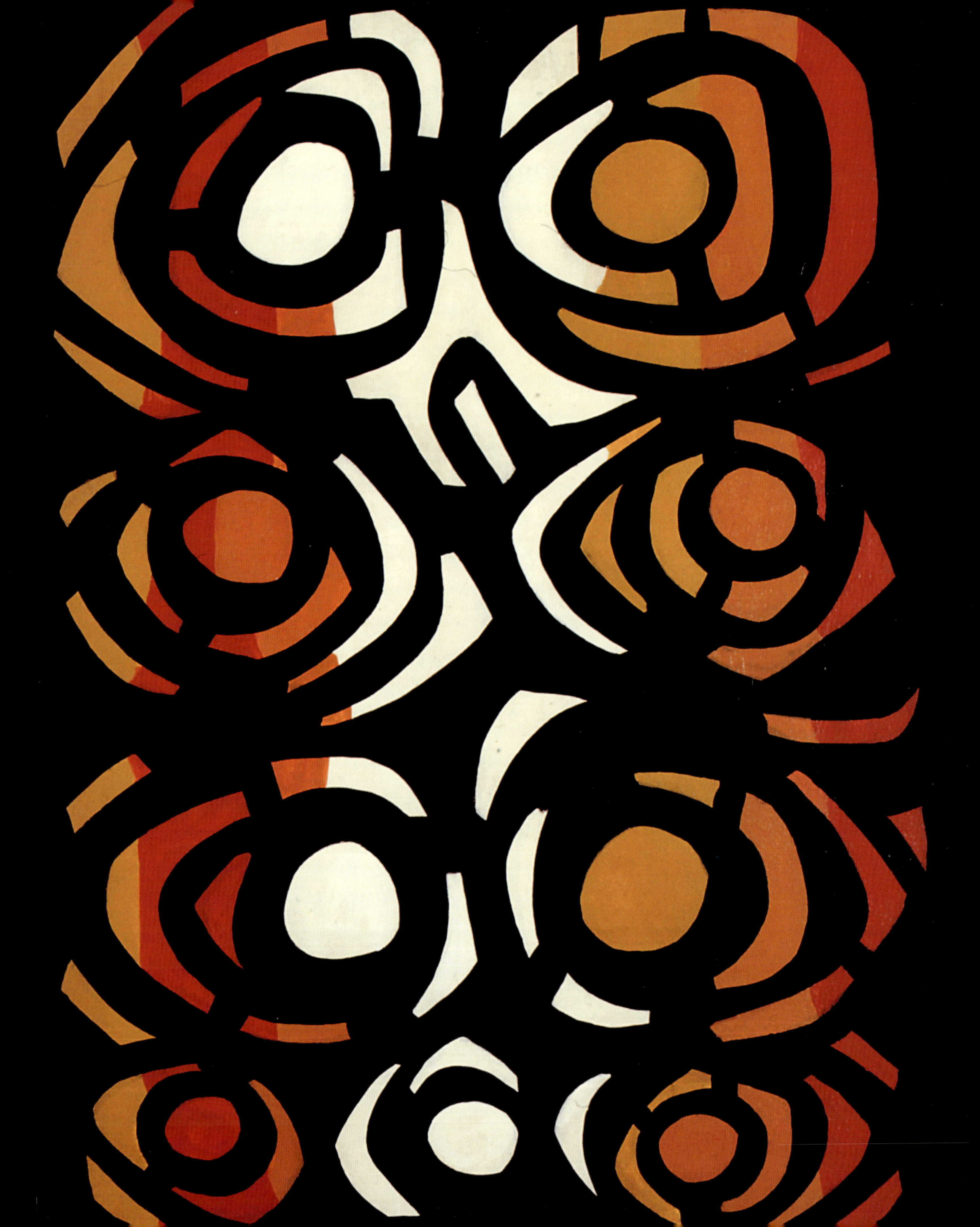

Paintings Without Reproductions

This section lists all the paintings that have not been included in the main pages of the catalogue. They were excluded as it was not possible to photograph them for this project. Additional information relating to acquisition credit lines or loan details is also included. For this reason the information below is not repeated in the Further Information section.

Broomfield Hospital

Harley-Peters, Jonet, *Heligan Blue*, painting, 95, commissioned by the Broomfield Arts Project, 2005, not available at the time of photography

Harley-Peters, Jonet, *Turquoise*, painting, 96, commissioned by the Broomfield Arts Project, 2005, not available at the time of photography

Lindop, Matthew b.1978, *The Conversation*, 100 x 200, household gloss paint on canvas, 91, commissioned by the Broomfield Arts Project, 2005, not available at the time of photography

Ridley, Annabel, *Aldeburgh Beach*, 112 x 163, screen-printed, painted & collaged on linen, 4, commissioned, 2000, not available at the time of photography

Chelmsford Museums

Adkins, Arthur Montressor active 1901–1914, *The Bridge, Wanstead*, oil on canvas, M28294, donated, 1930, not available at the time of photography

Boulton-Maude, Doris 1893–1961, *Gun Hut in Winter, Study of a Pillbox*, 1945, 51.3 x 71, oil on canvas, 1971.006, bequeathed, 1971, not available at the time of photography

Robson, Elsie May active c.1910–1938, *Old Railway Bridge, Maldon*, c.1910, 24 x 34.5, oil on canvas, 1974.006, donated, 1974, not available at the time of photography

unknown artist, *Lieutenant Colonel A. C. Newman Winning the Victoria Cross in the St Nazaire Raid*, c.1955, 119.3 x 154.5, oil on board, ER00289, donated, 1973, not available at the time of photography

Veyre, Agnès, *Untitled*, oil, MP1998.072, gift from twin town of Annonay, France, 1998?, not available at the time of photography

Essex County Council

Chamberlain, Mason (attributed to) active c.1786–1826, *Mr and Mrs John Bridges*, 13.8 x 19.3, oil on panel, 5, presented by D. P. Sellar, 1898, not available at the time of photography

Teniers, David II (follower of) 1610–1690, *Interior with Figures at a Table*, 15 x 21.5, oil on canvas, 7, presented by D. P. Sellar, 1898, not available at the time of photography

unknown artist, *Three Fishing Smacks and a Blazing Sky*, 30 x 21, oil on canvas, 73, not available at the time of photography

University of Essex, Collection of Latin American Art

Bernal Ponce, Juan b.1938, *Jack-in-the-Box*, 1970, 128 x 130, oil on canvas, 598, not available at the time of photography

Gama, Alex b.1950, *Untitled*, 2002, 100 x 14.5, acrylic on wood, 627, donated by the artist, 2004, not available at the time of photography

Guzmán, Antonia b.1954, *The Idea*, 2004, 50 x 70, acrylic on canvas, 540, donated by the artist, not available at the time of photography

Tendring District Council

Kleijn, Lodewijk Johannes 1817–1897, *Dutch Skating Scene*, 41 x 71, oil on canvas, 1, not available at the time of photography

South Essex Partnership NHS Trust

Dodds, James Foster b.1957, *Springtide*, 1988, 132 x 303, oil on canvas?, 2

Southend Museums Service

Burgess, Alan b.1936, *Suffolk Triptych (left wing)*, oil on canvas, SOUAG.5388, not available at the time of photography

Burgess, Alan b.1936, *Suffolk Triptych (right wing)*, oil on canvas, SOUAG.5388, not available at the time of photography

Sorrell, Alan 1904–1974, *Summer Scene Triptych (centre panel)*, 1956, oil on board, SOUAG.S437b, not available at the time of photography

Epping Forest District Museum

Adams, J., *Epping High Street*, 1990, 62 x 77, oil on paper, 1994.48, acquired, 1984, not available at the time of photography

Blank, Jeremy Nicholas b.1957, *Forlorn Angels*, 1982, 112 x 61, oil & encaustic on wood, 1982.121, purchased by the artist, 1982, not available at the time of photography

Burgess, Howard J., *Narrow Street*, 21 x 15.4, oil on wood, 1998.769, purchased from the artist, 1998, not available at the time of photography

Spradbery, Walter 1889–1969, *View of a Park*, 39 x 24.6, watercolour, oil & pencil on paper, 1996.8, donated by John Spradbery, 1996, not available at the time of photography

Facing page: Freire, Maria, b.1917, *The Gold of the Tigers No.6* (detail), 1994, University of Essex, Collection of Latin American Art, (p. 187)

Further Information

The paintings listed in this section have additional information relating to one or more of the five categories outlined below. This extra information is only provided where it is applicable and where it exists. Paintings listed in this section follow the same order as in the illustrated pages of the catalogue.

I	The full name of the artist if this was too long to display in the illustrated pages of the catalogue. Such cases are marked in the catalogue with a (…).

II	The full title of the painting if this was too long to display in the illustrated pages of the catalogue. Such cases are marked in the catalogue with a (…).

III	Acquisition information or acquisition credit lines as well as information about loans, copied from the records of the owner collection.

IV	Artist copyright credit lines where the copyright owner has been traced. Exhaustive efforts have been made to locate the copyright owners of all the images included within this catalogue and to meet their requirements. Any omissions or mistakes brought to our attention will be duly attended to and corrected in future publications.

V	The credit line of the lender of the transparency if the transparency has been borrowed. Bridgeman images are available subject to any relevant copyright approvals from the Bridgeman Art Library at www.bridgeman.co.uk

Basildon Arts Trust

Crowley, Graham b.1950, *3B*, © the artist
Davie, Alan b.1920, *White Magician*, © the artist
Donaldson, Antony b.1939, *Zigzag Past an Aurelia*, © the artist
Frost, Terry 1915–2003, *Red and Black*, © the artist's estate
Heron, Patrick 1920–1999, *Study in Blue**, © estate of Patrick Heron 2006. All rights reserved, DACS
Hitchens, Ivon 1893–1979, *Blue November*, © Ivon Hitchens' estate/Jonathan Clark & Co
Mullaniff, Kathleen b.1957, *Birds and Animals by a Tree*, © the artist
Outram, Steven b.1953, *Landscape: A Late February Afternoon*, © Steven Outram RBA
Redfern, David b.1947, *The Shah's Riot*, © the artist
Scott, William George 1913–1989, *Blue Form on White*, © William Scott estate
Sedgley, Peter b.1930, *Oranges and Lemons*, © the artist
Unsworth, Peter b.1937, *Owl and Clergyman*
Waldron, Dylan b.1953, *Farmhouse Corner*, © the artist
Wells, John 1907–2000, *Study in Grey and Brown**

Basildon District Council

Benjamins, Arthur b.1953, *Estelle IV' at Detroit, 1930 (Miss Carstairs leading the race for the Harmsworth Trophy)*, commissioned with financial assistance from the Basildon Arts Trust and the Friends of Wat Tyler Country Park, 1989, © the artist
Franks, Dave *Eric Blunden in 'Flamin' 'Ell!'*, donated, 2004
Hawkins, G. *Burt Noone in His Racing Boat 'Fugitive'*, donated by Burt Noone, 2005

Belchamp St Paul Community House

May, Margaret d. after 1993, *The House by the Lake (Kyrenia)*, presented by the artist, 1993
Wilson, Cecil active c.1900–1934, *The Stagecoach, 'Venture'*, gift as part of the Community House furnishings when it was built

Castle Point Borough Council

Etherington, E. *Children Lying in the Surf*
Etherington, E. *Countryside River Scene*
Etherington, E. *Farmyard Scene*
Loxton, J. E. *Hadleigh Castle*
Parker, Mary *Old Canvey Council Offices; Benfleet Council Offices, South Benfleet; St Mary the Virgin; Dutch Cottage Museum, Canvey Island*, presented by the artist to the Chairman of the Council on the occasion of the Castle Point Festival, 1976
Pound, F. C. *Folding Bridge and Creek between the Mainland and Canvey Island*

Dutch Cottage Museum

Amos, Gay *The Dutch Cottage Museum*, donated
Kerwood, G. *Dutch Cottage, Haven Road*, donated
unknown artist *The Lobster Smack, Canvey Island*, donated
unknown artist *The Dutch Cottage Museum*, donated, 1962/1963

Braintree District Museum

Aldridge, John Arthur Malcolm 1905–1983, *The Orchard, the Place House, Great Bardfield*, purchased, 1999
Aldridge, John Arthur Malcolm 1905–1983, *The Vegetable Garden, the Place House, Great Bardfield*, purchased, 2001
Brooks, Marjorie 1904–1980, *W. Griggs (Old Iron Portrait Collection)*, gift, 1989
Burn, Rodney Joseph 1899–1984, *A. North (Old Iron Portrait Collection)*, gift, 1989, © the artist's estate
Burn, Rodney Joseph 1899–1984, *A. T. Strutt (Old Iron Portrait Collection)*, on loan from Crittall Windows Ltd, © the artist's estate
Campion, Oliver 1928–2000, *J. W. Caton*, gift, 1996, © the artist's estate
Carr, Henry Marvell 1894–1970, *Miss H. Dearlove (Old Iron Portrait Collection)*, on loan from Crittall Windows Ltd
Choate, Francis Desmond 1916–2001, *Iorwerth Williams, CBE (b.1926)*, gift, 2000
Christie, Alexander b.1901, *G. Monk (Old Iron Portrait Collection)*, on loan from Crittall Windows Ltd
Clausen, Katharine Frances 1886–1936, *I. M. Coope (Old Iron Portrait Collection)*, on loan from Crittall Windows Ltd
Cole, Elsie Vera 1885–1968, *Rear of 23 Bradford Street, Bocking*, gift, 2000
Couilliot, Marguerite *Purple Landscape*, gift, 1998
Coxon, Raymond James 1896–1997, *H. S. Usher (Old Iron Portrait Collection)*, gift, 1989, © the artist's estate
de Horne Vaizey, Olive active c.1932–1959, *Old Six Bells Inn, Church Lane, Bocking*, gift, 2000
de Horne Vaizey, Olive active c.1932–1959, *Cane's Mill, Bocking*, gift, 1975
de Horne Vaizey, Olive active c.1932–1959, *My Peaceful Home*, gift, 1975
de Horne Vaizey, Olive active c.1932–1959, *Back of Maysent House, Bradford Street, Bocking*, gift, 1975
Dodd, Phyllis 1899–1995, *F. Rogers (Old Iron Portrait Collection)*, gift, 1989, © P. and R. Bliss
Downey, Steve b.1945, *Yantra 2: Circle of Indifference*, purchased, 1994
Druard, R. *L'étang, St Pierre*, gift, 1998
Gines, A. *H. S. Usher*, gift, 1989
Greenham, Robert Duckworth 1906–1976, *E. Byford (Old Iron Portrait Collection)*, on loan from Crittall Windows Ltd
Greiffenhagen, Maurice 1862–1931, *Sir William Julien Courtauld, BT, JP, CC (1870–1940), the Donor of the Town Hall to Braintree*, presented by Lady Cicely Courtauld, 1928
Greiffenhagen, Maurice 1862–1931, *George Thomas Thorpe Bartram, JP, CA*, presented by 1,400 friends in Braintree and the county in recognition of 50 years of public service (1879–1929)
Greiffenhagen, Maurice 1862–1931, *Battle of Maldon, 991*, presented by William Julien Courtauld, JP, CC, 1930
Greiffenhagen, Maurice 1862–1931, *Huguenots Spinning, Weaving and Dyeing, 1690*, presented by William Julien Courtauld, JP, CC, 1930
Greiffenhagen, Maurice 1862–1931, *John Ray (1628–1705)*, presented by William Julien Courtauld, JP, CC, 1930
Greiffenhagen, Maurice 1862–1931, *King John Presents the Bishop of London with the Charter for Braintree, 1199*, presented by William Julien Courtauld, JP, CC, 1930
Greiffenhagen, Maurice 1862–1931, *Ploughing, Sowing and Harrowing, c.1060*, presented by William Julien Courtauld, JP, CC, 1930
Greiffenhagen, Maurice 1862–1931, *Sailing of the Braintree Company in the 'Lyon', 1632*, presented by William Julien Courtauld, JP, CC, 1930
Greiffenhagen, Maurice 1862–1931, *Soldier on a Horse, Depicting*

the History of the Township of Braintree, presented by William Julien Courtauld, JP, CC, 1930
Greiffenhagen, Maurice 1862–1931, *William Pygot, Protestant Martyred at Braintree, 28 March 1555*, presented by William Julien Courtauld, JP, CC, 1930
Guthrie, Robin 1902–1971, *H. Walford (Old Iron Portrait Collection)*, gift, 1989, © the artist's estate
Hawkes, S. *Mary's Cottage, Rayne*, gift, c.1989
Hood, William T. *Essex Landscape: The Heybridge Canal near Maldon*
H. M. *High Street, Braintree*, gift, 1995
Ososki, Gerald Judah 1903–1981, *A. Franklin (Old Iron Portrait Collection)*, on loan from Crittall Windows Ltd, © the artist's estate
Ososki, Gerald Judah 1903–1981, *George 'Doc' Harvey (Old Iron Portrait Collection)*, gift, 1998, © the artist's estate
Ososki, Gerald Judah 1903–1981, *H. White (Old Iron Portrait Collection)*, gift, 1989, © the artist's estate
Ososki, Gerald Judah 1903–1981, *S. H. Wordley (Old Iron Portrait Collection)*, on loan from Crittall Windows Ltd, © the artist's estate
Ososki, Gerald Judah 1903–1981, *Sir Valentine Crittall, JP (1884–1961), Lord Braintree (Old Iron Portrait Collection)*, on loan from Crittall Windows Ltd, © the artist's estate
Phillips, A. active 1927–1939, *Sir Valentine Crittall, JP (1884–1961), Lord Braintree*, gift, 1989
Sands, Henry Southgate b.1900, *H. S. Munns (Old Iron Portrait Collection)*, on loan from Crittall Windows Ltd
Sands, Henry Southgate b.1900, *W. C. C. Bywater (Old Iron Portrait Collection)*, on loan from Crittall Windows Ltd
Schwabe, Randolph 1885–1948, *Frederick Gold Rogers (Old Iron Portrait Collection)*, gift, 2000, © the artist's estate
Towner, Donald Chisholm 1903–1985, *C. Conroy (Old Iron Portrait Collection)*, gift, 1989, © the artist's estate
unknown artist early 19th C, *George Courtauld, Donor of Braintree Literary and Mechanics Institution (1802–1861)*, gift
unknown artist *Victor Attwood*, gift, 1989
Vaizey, A. early 19th C, *Bocking Post Mill*, on loan from the Friends of Bocking Windmill
Wells, Leonard Harry b.1903, *J. 'Ramsey' Willison (Old Iron Portrait Collection)*, gift, 1989
Wells, Leonard Harry b.1903, *G. Usher (Old Iron Portrait Collection)*, on loan from Crittall Windows Ltd
Wilkie, James 1890–1957, *H. H. Wrate (Old Iron Portrait Collection)*, on loan from Crittall Windows Ltd
Winn, Hugh b.1940, *Resurrection*, purchased, 1999, © the artist
Zinkeisen, Anna Katrina 1901–1976, *The Evolution of the Textile Industry*, gift from Sara Lee Courtauld, 2002, © the artist's estate

Braintree Library

Crittall, Ariel b.1914, *Venetian Bottles*, purchased, 1997, © the artist

Great Bardfield Historical Society

Thomas, Philippa Mary b.1919, *Mrs Arlington*, gift, © the artist

Brentwood Museum

Gutheridge, W. G. active 1902–1910, *St Peter, South Weald*, gift from Brentwood Borough Council, 1991
unknown artist *Roger Chester Nightingale (1909–1944)*, gift from Moyna Thompson, secretary at Brentwood School, 1999

Burnham-on-Crouch and District Local Society

Christison, C. G. *Betty Perren, Founder of the Museum*, donated by Geoffrey Wickham, 1989
Cossey, George *The Thames Barge 'Truelove'*, bequeathed
Hackman, Frederick James active 1908–1922, *Schooner and Barge Loading at Bradwell Quay*, donated by Kevin Bruce, 1983

Anglia Ruskin University

Gibbs, Andrew Robert *Harmonics of Duality*, purchased, 1994

Broomfield Hospital

Bicknell, John b.1958, *Untitled*, donated by L. J. T. Risk Solutions, 2001
Cain, Jean *Still Life*, purchased from Colchester and District Visual Arts Trust, 2003
Hocombe, Sarah b.1963, *Dolphin Mural*, commissioned by the Broomfield Arts Project, 2000, © the artist
Hocombe, Sarah b.1963, *Hadleigh Castle*, commissioned by the Broomfield Arts Project, 2002, © the artist
Hocombe, Sarah b.1963, *Hadleigh Castle*, commissioned by the Broomfield Arts Project, 2002, © the artist
Hocombe, Sarah b.1963, *Hadleigh Castle*, commissioned by the Broomfield Arts Project, 2002, © the artist
Hocombe, Sarah b.1963, *Landscape 1*, commissioned by the Broomfield Arts Project, 2003, © the artist
Hocombe, Sarah b.1963, *Landscape 2*, commissioned by the Broomfield Arts Project, 2003, © the artist
Hocombe, Sarah b.1963, *Orca*, commissioned by the Broomfield Arts Project, 2005, © the artist
Hocombe, Sarah b.1963, *Penguins in an Icy Landscape*, commissioned by the Broomfield Arts Project, 2005, © the artist
Hocombe, Sarah b.1963, *Porthole*, commissioned by the Broomfield Arts Project, 2000, © the artist
Hocombe, Sarah b.1963, *Skyscape 1, View of Wivenhoe*, commissioned by the Broomfield Arts Project, 2003, © the artist
Hocombe, Sarah b.1963, *Skyscape 2, View of Maldon*, commissioned by the Broomfield Arts Project, 2003, © the artist
Hocombe, Sarah b.1963, *Tropical Forest, Day*, commissioned by the Broomfield Arts Project, 2005, © the artist
Hocombe, Sarah b.1963, *Tropical Forest, Night*, commissioned by the Broomfield Arts Project, 2005, © the artist
Hocombe, Sarah b.1963, *Turtle Mural*, commissioned by the Broomfield Arts Project, 2000, © the artist
Marine, Tom b.1956 & **Relton, Christine** b.1959 *White Text*, commissioned by the Broomfield Arts Project, 2001, © the artists
Priseman, Robert b.1965, *Hatfield Forest, Night and Day*, commissioned by the Broomfield Arts Project, 2001, © the artist
Smith, Dilwyn b.1958, *Untitled*, donated by L. J. T. Risk Solutions, 2001, © the artist
Thompson, Estelle b.1960, *Garden Picture*, donated by L. J. T. Risk Solutions, 2001, © the artist
unknown artist *Brown Abstract*, acquired from the Arts Council of England Collection, 2003

Chelmsford Museums

Abraham, Esmond b.1935, *Hylands in 1803 (after George Whitmore)*, donated by the artist (formerly the borough architect), 1999, © the artist
Aldridge, John Arthur Malcolm 1905–1983, *The River Pant near Sculpin's Bridge*, purchased, 1962
Aldridge, John Arthur Malcolm 1905–1983, *Garden in January*, purchased, 1988
Aldridge, John Arthur Malcolm 1905–1983, *Harvest Fields, Duton Hill, near Dunmow*, purchased, 1988
Archer, Charles 1904–1993, *The Old Corn Exchange and Market*, acquired, 1966, © the artist's estate
Archer, Charles 1904–1993, *Moulsham Mill, Chelmsford*, purchased, 1980, © the artist's estate
Atkinson, Anthony b.1929, *Water Meadows, Boxted*, purchased, 1967, © the artist
Atkinson, Anthony b.1929, *Farm at West Bergholt*, acquired, 1974, © the artist
Austen, David b.1960, *Giotto's Basket*, donated by the Contemporary Art Society, 1988, © the artist
Bamford, Alfred Bennett 1857–1939, *Old Houses, the Friars, Moulsham Street, Chelmsford*
Bamford, Alfred Bennett 1857–1939, *North Ambulatory, Westminster Abbey*, purchased, 1997
Barrett, Roderic 1920–2000, *Separate Relations*, purchased, 1979, © the artist's estate
Bartlett, Charles b.1921, *Essex Estuary*, purchased, 1976, © the artist
Barton, Charles H. 1908–1979, *Imaginary Townscape*, bequeathed, 1979
Barton, Charles H. 1908–1979, *Zambezi Ritual Dance*, bequeathed, 1979
Barton, Charles H. 1908–1979, *S. H. Tunstall*, bequeathed, 1979
Beckingham, Arthur 1855–1920, *Village Street, Danbury*, purchased, 1997
Bellingham-Smith, Elinor 1906–1988, *Orchard Snowscape, Felsted*, purchased with assistance from Resource/Victoria & Albert Museum Purchase Grant Fund, 2003, © the artist's estate
Bliss, Douglas Percy 1900–1984, *High Noon, Windley*, grant-aided purchase, 1985, © P and R. Bliss
Bottefer, M. (attributed to) *Vase of Flowers with Mountain View*
Boulton-Maude, Doris 1893–1961, *View of a Village and River (possibly the Nile)*, bequeathed, 1971, © the artist's estate
Boulton-Maude, Doris 1893–1961, *The Return*, bequeathed, 1971, © the artist's estate
Boulton-Maude, Doris 1893–1961, *Orchard in Blossom*, bequeathed, 1971, © the artist's estate
Boulton-Maude, Doris 1893–1961, *Mayes Farm, Sandon*, donated, 2002, © the artist's estate
Boulton-Maude, Doris 1893–1961, *Point of View*, bequeathed, 1971, © the artist's estate
Boulton-Maude, Doris 1893–1961, *Farmyard, Fordingbridge*, bequeathed, 1971, © the artist's estate
Boulton-Maude, Doris 1893–1961, *The Garden Window*, bequeathed, 1971, © the artist's estate
Boulton-Maude, Doris 1893–1961, *Isobel Barnes*, bequeathed, 1971, © the artist's estate
Boulton-Maude, Doris 1893–1961, *Lionel Maude*, on loan from the Maude Family Trust, © the artist's estate
Boulton-Maude, Doris 1893–1961, *Louise Maude, née Shanks (1855–1939)*, on loan from the Maude Family Trust, © the artist's estate
Brill, Reginald 1902–1974, *Smoke*, purchased, 1974, © the artist's estate
Brill, Reginald 1902–1974, *Three Men ('Have You Heard This One?')*, purchased, 1974, © the artist's estate
British (English) School *The Hunt at Galleywood?*, donated or transferred from the Passmore Edwards Museum, 1996
British (English) School *Captain William Thorne, 56th Regiment (d.1844)*, donated, 1973
Brown, William 1822/1823–1899, *Widford Old Church*, purchased, 1973
Brown, William 1822/1823–1899, *Chelmsford High Street, from above the Stone Bridge*, purchased, 1973
Brown, William 1822/1823–1899, *River Chelmer at Broomfield*, purchased, 1973
Brown, William (attributed to) 1822/1823–1899, *Friars' Place and Moulsham Street*, donated, 1964
Brown, William (attributed to) 1822/1823–1899, *Springfield Wharf*, acquired, before 1970
Buchel, Charles A. 1872–1950, *Christine, Mrs John Hanbury*, donated, 1997
Buchel, Charles A. 1872–1950, *John Hanbury*, donated, 1997
Buckler, E. *The Iron Bridge, Chelmsford*, purchased, 1966
Buckner, Richard 1812–1883, *Margaret Laetitia, Lady Western, née Bushby (1798–1872)*, bequeathed by Elizabeth Ellen, Lady Western, 1939
Burnand, Geoffrey Norman 1912–1996, *Mrs Kathleen May Andrews*, donated by the sitter's son, 1980
Burnand, Geoffrey Norman 1912–1996, *The Carpenter*, grant-aided purchase, 1986
Chapman, George 1908–1993, *Mr Bone, the Butcher of Great Bardfield*, purchased, 1990, © Nicholas Chapman
Cleverly, Peter b.1943, *Oaklands House, Moulsham Street, Chelmsford*, donated by the artist, 1994
Coker, Peter 1926–2004, *Still Life with Hare and Grapes*, grant-aided purchase, 1987, © Peter Coker, RA
Coker, Peter 1926–2004, *Leadgate, Cumbria*, purchased, 1973, © Peter Coker, RA
Colkett, Samuel David (attributed to) 1806–1863, *Chelmsford from Springfield Hill*, purchased with the assistance of the MGC/Victoria & Albert Museum Purchase Grant Fund, 1960
Cooper, Thomas Sidney (circle of)

1803–1902, *Pastoral Scene with Cows*, acquired, 1933
Crome, Douglas H. *Councillor Fred Richardson*, donated, 1986
Crossley, Gordon b.1929, *Gladwyns Farmhouse, Sheering*, purchased, 1975
Crossley, Gordon b.1929, *Edge of a Wood*, acquired, 1975
Cuthbert, Rosalind b.1951, *Cecil Collins at the Central School of Art, London (detail of full-length)*, donated by the Contemporary Art Society, 1986, © the artist
Danvers, Joan b.1919, *Pots from the Little Waltham Dig*, purchased, 1973
Deakins, Thomas William b.1957, *December Dusk*, purchased, 1997, © the artist
Derry, Pamela 1932–2002, *Now Summer Has Come*, acquired, 1978, © the artist's estate
Dudley, Robert d.c.1893, *River Scene with View of a Mill*, acquired, before 1970
Feldh, F. C. active 19th C, *Mountain Lake*, acquired, before 1988
Francis, Mark b.1962, *Trassey*, purchased, 1990
Fraser, Alexander b.1940, *Guild Street No.3*, donated by the Contemporary Art Society, 1985–1986, © the artist
Gilbey, Kathrine b.1932, *Bundles*, acquired, 1977, © the artist
Gopal-Chowdhury, Paul b.1949, *Still Life with Bread*, donated by the Contemporary Art Society, 1981, © the artist
Grant, Francis 1803–1878, *Sir Thomas Burch Western, Lord Lieutenant and Custos Rotulorum of the County of Essex*, bequeathed by Elizabeth Ellen, Lady Western, 1939
Hailstone, Bernard 1910–1987, *District Officer F. G. Keen of Chelmsford, OBE, Auxiliary Fire Service*, donated, 1949, transferred from the War Artists Advisory Committee/Imperial War Museum, © the artist's estate
Hambling, Maggi b.1945, *Mourning Sunset*, donated by the Contemporary Art Society, 1992, © the artist
Hambling, Maggi b.1945, *Lett Dreaming*, purchased with the assistance of the MGC/Victoria & Albert Museum Purchase Grant Fund, 1986, © the artist
Harraden, Richard Banks 1778–1862, *John Ray (1628–1705) (copy after Thomas Hudson)*, acquired, by or before 1966
Haughton, Benjamin 1865–1924, *A Woodland Vista*, donated by the artist's widow, 1937
Haughton, Benjamin 1865–1924, *On the Yeo*, donated by the artist's widow, 1937
Haughton, Benjamin 1865–1924, *Spring Evening*, donated by the artist's widow, 1937
Hughes, Diane b.1943, *Across the Fields after Harvest*, purchased, 2005, © the artist
Jackson, John 1778–1831, *Robert Tindal of Coval Hall (1749–1833), Father of Sir Nicholas Tindal*, purchased, 1986
Janssens van Ceulen, Cornelis (circle of) 1593–1661, *Jemima Waldegrave, Lady Crewe*, donated, 1962
Johnson, Sidney Yates active 1892–1929, *Landscape*, donated, 1935
Jordan, R. E. *Bradford Street, Bocking*, acquired, 1979
Jordan, R. E. *Baddow Road, Chelmsford*, acquired, 1973
Jordan, R. E. *Duke Street, Chelmsford*, acquired, 1976
Jordan, R. E. *Snow at Writtle*, acquired, 1975
Juel, Jens 1745–1802, *Juliana Margaretta Waltersdorff (later Mrs Cornelius Kortright)*, purchased with the assistance of Resource/ Victoria & Albert Museum Purchase Grant Fund, the National Art Collections Fund, the Essex Heritage Fund, the Friends of Chelmsford Museums and an anonymous donor, 2001
Juel, Jens 1745–1802, *Juliana, Wife of Cornelius Kortright*, purchased with the assistance of Resource/ Victoria & Albert Museum Purchase Grant Fund, the National Art Collections Fund, the Friends of Chelmsford Museums and an anonymous donor, 2002
Kinnaird, Henry John active 1880–1920, *Old Mill near Little Baddow*, purchased with the assistance of the MGC/Victoria & Albert Museum Purchase Grant Fund, 1999
Kneller, Godfrey (circle of) 1646–1723, *Dorothy, Lady Monoux*, donated, 1962
Lamb, Lynton Harold 1907–1977, *Lila*, grant-aided purchase, 1991, © the artist's estate
Lamb, Lynton Harold 1907–1977, *Rooftops*, purchased, 1997, © the artist's estate
Lamb, Lynton Harold 1907–1977, *Elms, Sydenham*, purchased with the assistance of the MGC/Victoria & Albert Museum Purchase Grant Fund, 1999, © the artist's estate
Lamb, Lynton Harold 1907–1977, *Geoffrey Luling*, grant-aided purchase, 1991, © the artist's estate
Lamb, Lynton Harold 1907–1977, *Mr Mayhew of Sandon*, acquired, 1963, © the artist's estate
Lamb, Lynton Harold 1907–1977, *A Lane near Ludlow by Moonlight*, grant-aided purchase, 1990, © the artist's estate
Lamb, Lynton Harold 1907–1977, *Self Portrait*, purchased with the assistance of the MGC/Victoria & Albert Museum Purchase Grant Fund and the Pilgrim Trust, 1991, © the artist's estate
Lamb, Lynton Harold 1907–1977, *Biddy, Mrs Lynton Lamb*, gift from a private collection, 2003, © the artist's estate
Lamb, Lynton Harold 1907–1977, *Jocelyn Newbery*, grant-aided purchase, 1991, © the artist's estate
Lamb, Lynton Harold 1907–1977, *Still Life with Flowers*, grant-aided purchase, 1991, © the artist's estate
Lamb, Lynton Harold 1907–1977, *The Garden at Rose Cottage, Sandon*, donated by a private collector, 1999, © the artist's estate
Lamb, Lynton Harold 1907–1977, *Old Rectory, Sandon (Football Match)*, purchased with the assistance of the MGC/Victoria & Albert Museum Purchase Grant Fund, 1999, © the artist's estate
Lamb, Lynton Harold 1907–1977, *Winter Landscape: Essex*, purchased with the assistance of the MGC/ Victoria & Albert Museum Purchase Grant Fund, 1994, © the artist's estate
Lamb, Lynton Harold 1907–1977, *Calabria*, purchased, 1965, © the artist's estate
Lamb, Lynton Harold 1907–1977, *No.1 Ballast Workings, Sandon*, purchased, 1967, © the artist's estate
Longley, F. C. active 1970s, *The Dawn of Christianity*, donated, 1975
Lucas, John 1807–1874, *Sir Nicholas Tindal (1776–1846), Chief Justice of the Common Pleas*, acquired, 1977
Lysaght, Edward 1902–1997, *Late Autumn, Whitebrook Valley*, acquired, before 1980
Massey-Ryan, Roger b.1959, *Chelmsford Town and Market in 1591*, commissioned on Chelmsford's 800th anniversary, 1999, © Chelmsford Museums Service
McKenna, Stephen b.1939, *Heroic Still Life*, purchased with the assistance of the MGC/Victoria & Albert Museum Purchase Grant Fund, 1983, © the artist
Mellon, Campbell A. 1876–1955, *Baddow Meads, Chelmsford*, purchased, 1995
Middleton, Charles *Chelmsford Shoppers*, purchased, 1981
Mileham, Anthony active 1950–1975, *Landscape: Galleywood Common*, acquired, 1977
Morris, Cedric Lockwood 1889–1982, *The Swiss Visitor*, purchased with the assistance of the MGC/ Victoria & Albert Museum Purchase Grant Fund, 1982, © trustees of the Cedric Lockwood Morris Estate/ Foundation
Norman, R. F. d.1978?, *Progress*, purchased, 1964
O'Connor, John Scorror 1913–2004, *Track to Corbel's Farm*, purchased with the assistance of the MGC/Victoria & Albert Museum Purchase Grant Fund, 1966, © the artist's estate
O'Connor, John Scorror 1913–2004, *Pond on Tollesbury Marshes*, purchased, 1961, © the artist's estate
Popham, James Kidwell 1884–c.1960, *The Road to Little Waltham*, purchased?, 1967
Popham, James Kidwell 1884–c.1960, *The Wood in Autumn*, acquired, by or before 1967
Rankin, Stella b.1915, *London Fog*, donated by the artist, 1996, © Stella Rankin
Rankin, Stella b.1915, *Jug and Apples*, donated by the artist, 1992, © Stella Rankin
Rankin, Stella b.1915, *Estuary Threatened by a Marina*, purchased, 1992, © Stella Rankin
Rankin, Stella b.1915, *Still Life and Landscape*, donated by artist, 1992, © Stella Rankin
Redworth, William Josiah 1873–1947, *Captain Arthur Hill's 'Mike'*, acquired, before 1970
Redworth, William Josiah 1873–1947, *'Rocketer'*, acquired, before 1971
Reinagle, Philip 1749–1833, *The Shire Hall, Chelmsford*, purchased with the assistance of the MGC/ Victoria & Albert Museum Purchase Grant Fund, 1964
Ridgewell, John b.1937, *Gate*, purchased, 1981
Robson, Elsie May active c.1910–1938, *Landscape with Ruined Castle*, donated, 1974
Robson, Elsie May active c.1910–1938, *Landscape (Rocky Bay)*, donated, 1974
Robson, Elsie May active c.1910–1938, *Seascape (from cliffs)*, donated, 1974
Robson, Elsie May active c.1910–1938, *Landscape with Highland Cattle*, donated, 1974
Rowntree, Kenneth 1915–1997, *Summer Gardens, Bardfield*, purchased with the assistance of the MGC/Victoria & Albert Museum Purchase Grant Fund, 1986, © the artist's estate
Rowntree, Kenneth 1915–1997, *Ethel House, Great Bardfield*, purchased with the assistance of the MGC/Victoria & Albert Museum Purchase Grant Fund, 1986, © the artist's estate
Schwegmann-Fielding, Anne b.1967, *Piranha*, purchased, 1977, © the artist
Self, Lawrence 1924–2002, *Saltings, Shingle Street*, purchased, 1968, © the artist's estate
Self, Lawrence 1924–2002, *Sunlight and Sea Wall, Walberswick*, purchased, 1968, © the artist's estate
Shanks, Emily 1857–1936, *Ear Inspection in a Russian Hospital*, presented by Lionel Maude, nephew of artist, 1966
Shirlaw, George 1934–2005, *Sunflower*, purchased, 1979, © the artist's estate
Smith, Edwin 1912–1971, *War Unmasked*, bequeathed by Olive Cook, the artist's widow, 2002, © Chelmsford Museums Service
Smith, Edwin 1912–1971, *The Eloquent Backs*, bequeathed by Olive Cook, the artist's widow, 2002, © Chelmsford Museums Service
Smith, Edwin 1912–1971, *Boy Shapes*, bequeathed by Olive Cook, the artist's widow, 2002, © Chelmsford Museums Service
Smith, Edwin 1912–1971, *Still Life with Pens, Ink and Jug*, bequeathed by Olive Cook, the artist's widow, 2002, © Chelmsford Museums Service
Smith, Edwin 1912–1971, *The Red Gate*, bequeathed by Olive Cook, the artist's widow, 2002, © Chelmsford Museums Service
Smith, Edwin 1912–1971, *Stacking Peas (with a view of Waveney Church, Norfolk)*, bequeathed by Olive Cook, the artist's widow, 2002, © Chelmsford Museums Service
Smith, Edwin 1912–1971, *Norfolk Sandpit*, bequeathed by Olive Cook, the artist's widow, 2002, © Chelmsford Museums Service
Smith, Edwin 1912–1971, *Southwold (Landscape with Jet)*, bequeathed by Olive Cook, the artist's widow, 2002, © Chelmsford Museums Service
Smith, Edwin 1912–1971, *Playing for the Painter*, bequeathed by Olive Cook, the artist's widow, 2002, © Chelmsford Museums Service
Smith, Edwin 1912–1971, *Cherry Picker*, bequeathed by Olive Cook, the artist's widow, 2002, © Chelmsford Museums Service
Smith, Edwin 1912–1971, *Gypsy Encampment*, bequeathed by Olive Cook, the artist's widow, 2002, © Chelmsford Museums Service
Smith, Edwin 1912–1971, *Steam Roller*, bequeathed by Olive Cook, the artist's widow, 2002, © Chelmsford Museums Service
Spencer-Phillips, Valerie b.1923, *Chelmsford in Winter (The Old Cattle Market)*, © the artist
Spencer-Pryse, Tessa b.1940, *Poverty*, acquired, 1986, © the artist
Spender, John Humphrey 1910–2005, *Paper Mills*, acquired, 1986, © the Humphrey Spender Archive
Tebby, Arthur Kemp c.1865–c.1935, *Ashingdon, St Andrew (before the north vestry was added by Sir Charles Nicholson, 1921)*, donated, 1975
unknown artist early 15th C, *King with Gold Crown, possibly Edward the Confessor*, donated by Colonel W. J. Lucas, c.1850
unknown artist early 15th C, *Pope with Tiara with Gold Ball and Cross*, donated by Colonel W. J. Lucas, c.1850
unknown artist early 15th C, *Saint with Book*, on loan from South Hanningfield Church
unknown artist early 15th C, *St Bartholomew*, donated by Colonel W. J. Lucas, c.1850

unknown artist early 15th C, *St Catherine of Alexandria*, donated by Colonel W. J. Lucas, c.1850
unknown artist early 15th C, *St James the Great*, donated by Colonel W. J. Lucas, c.1850
unknown artist early 15th C, *St James the Less*, donated by Colonel W. J. Lucas, c.1850
unknown artist early 15th C, *St John Baptist*, donated by Colonel W. J. Lucas, c.1850
unknown artist early 15th C, *St Peter*, on loan from South Hanningfield Church
unknown artist early 15th C, *St Simon*, donated by Colonel W. J. Lucas, c.1850
unknown artist *Sally, née Pocock (1755–1818), Wife of Robert Tindal, Mother of Sir Nicholas Tindal*, purchased, 1986
unknown artist *Mr Brady Wood of Sparrows Farm, Terling*, purchased, 1979
unknown artist *Captain George Cheveley of the Roxwell Volunteers*, acquired with the collections of Chelmsford Philosophical Society
unknown artist *Richard Coates of Maldon (1763–1822)*, bequeathed by Coates' daughter
unknown artist *Old Cottages, Duke Street, Chelmsford*, donated, 1974
unknown artist *Old Cottages, Duke Street, Chelmsford*, presented by Gerald Ridley, 1925
unknown artist *Sergeant-Major James Mitchell*, acquired from the sitter's family, 1971
unknown artist early 19th C, *Major-General George O'Malley GCB, 88th Regiment (1780–1843)*, purchased with the assistance of the MGC/Victoria & Albert Museum Purchase Grant Fund, 1981
unknown artist late 19th C, *Saint with Book*, on loan from South Hanningfield Church
unknown artist late 19th C, *Saint with Book*, donated by Colonel W. J. Lucas, c.1850
unknown artist late 19th C, *Saint with Canister*, on loan from South Hanningfield Church
unknown artist late 19th C, *Saint with Cross (possibly St Paul)*, on loan from South Hanningfield Church
unknown artist late 19th C, *Saint with Staff*, on loan from South Hanningfield Church
unknown artist late 19th C, *Saint with Stick and Book*, on loan from South Hanningfield Church
unknown artist late 19th C, *St Bartholomew with Knife*, on loan from South Hanningfield Church
unknown artist late 19th C, *St Peter*, donated by Colonel W. J. Lucas, c.1850
Wardle, Arthur 1864–1949, *Study of a Pointer*, acquired, before 1971
White, Ethelbert 1891–1972, *New Hall Farm, Boreham*, purchased, 1988, © the Ethelbert White estate
Winter, Frederick Charles active 1891–1930s, *An Officer of the 56th Foot, 1843*, donated, 1973
Winter, Frederick Charles active 1891–1930s, *An Officer of the Pompadours (56th Light Foot, 1799)*, donated, 1973
Wollen, William Barnes 1857–1936, *The Last Stand of the 44th Foot at Gundermuck, 1842*, purchased by the officers of the 1st Battalion Essex Regiment 1911, 1939

Essex County Council

Appelbee, Leonard 1914–2000, *Tree and Stream with Stile*
Bega, Cornelis Pietersz. (follower of) 1631/1632–1664, *Interior with Mother Suckling Her Child*, presented by D. P. Sellar, 1898
Boden, Leonard 1911–1999, *Colonel Sir John Ruggles-Brise, Bt, CB, OBE, TD, JP of Spains Hall, Finchingfield, Lord Lieutenant of Essex (1958–1978)*, © the artist's estate
British (English) School *Portrait of a Bearded Gentleman (possibly Francis Bacon, 1st Baron Verulam and Viscount St Albans)*
British (English) School 17th C, *Reverend Thomas Brand*
British (English) School *Wooded Landscape with Thatched Cottage*, presented by D. P. Sellar, 1898
British (English) School 19th C, *Portrait of a Lady*
British (English) School 20th C, *Joseph Hewett, JP*
Carlson, Ronald b.1936, *Welsh Street*
Carr, Henry Marvell 1894–1970, *George Frederick Chaplin, CBE, JP, DL*
Codner, John b.1913, *Charles Edward Leatherland, OBE, JP, DL*
Codner, Maurice Frederick 1888–1958, *Colonel Sir Gilbertson Smith, TD, DL*
Codner, Maurice Frederick 1888–1958, *Percy Astins, CBE, JP*
Codner, Maurice Frederick 1888–1958, *Frank Savin Foster, CBE, JP*
Codner, Maurice Frederick 1888–1958, *William James Bennett, CBE, JP, DL*
Constable, John (follower of) 1776–1837, *View of Hampstead Heath*, presented by D. P. Sellar, 1898, on loan to Essex Record Office
Cooper, John Riley *Councillor Thomas Edward Dale, DL, Chairman (1994–1995)*
Daniell, Frank 1866–1932, *Andrew Johnston, First Chairman of the Essex County Council (1835–1922)*
Daniell, Frank 1866–1932, *J. H. Burrows, JP (1854-1935), Chairman (1931)*
Dicksee, Frank 1853–1928, *Colonel Sir Francis H. D. C. Whitmore, Bt, KCB, CMG, DSO, TD, JP of Orsett Hall, Lord Lieutenant of Essex (1936–1958)*, presented by Essex Yeomanry Association, on loan to Chelmsford Territorial Army HQ
Dou, Gerrit (after) 1613–1675, *Girl Playing a Virginal*, presented by D. P. Sellar, 1898
Dugdale, Thomas Cantrell 1880–1952, *Sir Christopher Musgrave, JP, CA (1856–1929)*, presented by his colleagues of the Essex County Council in recognition of his public services to the county, © Joanna Dunham
Dyckmans, Josephus Laurentius 1811–1888, *Lady Standing at a Wash Tub*, presented by D. P. Sellar, 1898
Eastman, Frank S. 1878–1964, *W. Swaine Chisenhale-Marsh (1857–1929), Chairman (1916–1929), High Sheriff of Essex (1892)*
Eastman, Frank S. 1878–1964, *Herbert Edmund Brooks, DL, JP (1860–1931), Chairman (1929)*
Eastman, Mary active c.1932–1970, *H. de Havilland, MA*
Fleetwood-Walker, Bernard 1893–1965, *John Ball Preaching at Brentwood, 1381*, commissioned by Councillor William Julien Courtauld, 1938
Froste, Peter b.1935, *Medieval Farmstead at Stebbingford*, produced by Essex County Council, © DACS 2006
Froste, Peter b.1935, *Roman Villa at Great Holts, Boreham*, produced by Essex County Council, © DACS 2006
Froste, Peter b.1935, *Plotlands at Basildon in the 1940s*, produced by Essex County Council, © DACS 2006
Froste, Peter b.1935, *Roman Settlement at Great Chesterford*, produced by Essex County Council, © DACS 2006
Garvey, Edmund (after) c.1740–1813, *View of Bath*, presented by D. P. Sellar, 1898
Gill, Colin Unwin 1892–1940, *Boadicea at Colchester, 61 AD*, commissioned by Councillor William Julien Courtauld, 1938, © the artist's estate
Green, Kenneth 1905–1986, *Elizabeth Coker*, © the artist's estate
Gunn, Herbert James 1893–1964, *Colonel Sir Francis H. D. C. Whitmore, Bt, KCB, CMG, DSO, TD, JP of Orsett Hall, Lord Lieutenant of Essex (1936–1958)*, presented by Essex Yeomanry Association, © estate of the artist
Haecken, Alexander van 1701–1758, *A Fashionable Music Party*, presented by D. P. Sellar, 1898
Herp, Willem van I c.1614–1677, *Interior with Figures Eating and Drinking*, presented by D. P. Sellar, 1898
Highmore, Joseph (follower of) 1692–1780, *Reverend Joseph Avery of Kirby-le-Soken*, presented by Lord Methuen, 1960
Hobbema, Meindert (after) 1638–1709, *The Avenue at Middleharnis*, presented by D. P. Sellar, 1898
Hobbema, Meindert (style of) 1638–1709, *Wooded Landscape with Horsemen Resting by a House*, presented by D. P. Sellar, 1898
Hoppner, John (follower of) 1758–1810, *Portrait of a Lady*, presented by D. P. Sellar, 1898
Hysing, Hans (attributed to) 1678–1753, *Timothy Brand, Sheriff of Essex (1721)*
Janssens van Ceulen, Cornelis (style of) 1593–1661, *Sir John Bramston, Lord Chief Justice (1635)*, secured for the County by Andrew Johnston, on loan to Chelmsford Borough Council
Kneller, Godfrey (attributed to) 1646–1723, *Edmund Humfrey of Rettendon*
Kwarte, Felix *Sidney Woodfull Millard*
Lamb, Lynton Harold 1907–1977, *The Crown*, © the artist's estate
Lamb, Lynton Harold 1907–1977, *Work Table*, © the artist's estate
Lawrence, Alfred Kingsley 1893–1975, *Queen Elizabeth I at Tilbury, 1588*
Lawrence, Thomas (follower of) 1769–1830, *Queen Caroline (1768–1821)*, presented by D. P. Sellar, 1898
Lewis, Neville 1895–1972, *Queen Victoria at Epping Forest, 1882*, © the artist's estate
Lonsdale, James (attributed to) 1777–1839, *Sir John Tyssen Tyrell, Bt, MP of Boreham (1795–1877)*, presented by Lord Kenyon of Gredington, on loan to Chelmsford Borough Council
Lorrain, Claude (follower of) 1604–1682, *Capriccio with Harbour*, presented by D. P. Sellar, 1898
Lundens, Gerrit 1622–after 1683, *Dutch Company Merrymaking*, presented by D. P. Sellar, 1898
Lundens, Gerrit 1622–after 1683, *'La main chaude', Dutch Party Playing Games in an Interior*, presented by D. P. Sellar, 1898
Lyon, Robert 1894–1978, *Harwich in the Late XVII Century (Samuel Pepys, MP for Harwich inspecting the King's Navy)*, commissioned by Councillor William Julien Courtauld, 1938, © the artist's estate
Massey-Ryan, Roger b.1959, *Iron Age Settlement at Lofts Farm, near Maldon, c.850 BC*, produced by Essex County Council, © Essex County Council
Massey-Ryan, Roger b.1959, *Late Bronze Age Landscape at South Hornchurch*, produced by Essex County Council, © Essex County Council
Massey-Ryan, Roger b.1959, *Medieval Manorial Complex at Southchurch Hall, c.1400*, produced by Essex County Council, © Essex County Council
Massey-Ryan, Roger b.1959, *Saxon Cemetery within Prehistoric Remains at Orsett*, produced by Essex County Council, © Essex County Council
Massey-Ryan, Roger b.1959, *Roman Villa at Mucking*, produced by Essex County Council, © Essex County Council
Massey-Ryan, Roger b.1959, *Bronze Age Landscape at Ardleigh, c.1200 BC*, produced by Essex County Council, © Essex County Council
Massey-Ryan, Roger b.1959, *Triple-Ditch, Pre-Conquest, Iron Age Enclosure at Orsett Cock*, produced by Essex County Council, © Essex County Council
Meijer, Hendrick de c.1600–c.1690, *Horsemen Resting by a House*, presented by D. P. Sellar, 1898
Mendoza, June active 1960–2006, *Councillor Mrs Kathleen Nolan, DL, Chairman (1992–1993)*
Mendoza, June active 1960–2006, *Councillor Paul Edward Winston White, DL (Lord Hanningfield), Chairman (1989–1992)*
Moore, Ernest 1865–1940, *Arthur Porter, JP*
Oakshea, Anthony *Anthony Peel in front of the Police Headquarters at Springfield*
Osborne, John b.1939, *A White Blossom Tree*, © the artist
Osborne, John b.1939, *Field at Sunset*, © the artist
Ostade, Adriaen van (follower of) 1610–1685, *Interior with Dutch Peasants Drinking*, presented by D. P. Sellar, 1898
Phillips, Thomas (circle of) 1770–1845, *Thomas Gardiner Bramston*, secured for the County by Andrew Johnston
Pickersgill, Henry William (circle of) 1782–1875, *William Bramston*, presented by his constituents and friends on his retirement from Parliament after having represented South Essex for 30 years
Poussin, Nicolas (school of) 1594–1665, *Bacchanalia*, presented by D. P. Sellar, 1898, on loan to Essex Record Office
Rushbury, Henry 1889–1968, *Elizabeth Fry of Plashet (East Ham), the Friend of Prisoners (1780–1845)*, © the artist's estate
Rushbury, Henry 1889–1968, *John Ray of Black Notley, Father of Natural History (1627–1703)*, © the artist's estate
Rushbury, Henry 1889–1968, *Lord Rayleigh of Terling, President of the Royal Society (1842–1919)*, © the artist's estate
Rushbury, Henry 1889–1968, *Sir Evelyn Wood of Harlow, Soldier (1858–1919)*, © the artist's estate
Rushbury, Henry 1889–1968, *William Byrd of Stondon Place, Composer and Musician (1558–1625)*, © the artist's estate
Rushbury, Henry 1889–1968, *William Gilberd of Colchester, Pioneer of Electrical Science (1540–1603)*, © the artist's estate
Rushbury, Henry 1889–1968, *William Morris of Walthamstow, Poet and Craftsman (1834–1896)*, ©

the artist's estate
Sancha, Carlos Luis 1920–2001, *Thomas Frederick James Collins, CBE, DL*
Sancha, Carlos Luis 1920–2001, *Geoffrey Claud Waterer, DL*
Sancha, Carlos Luis 1920–2001, *Robert George Reginald Daniels, JP, DL*
Sancha, Carlos Luis 1920–2001, *Ronald Millward Williams, DL*
Sancha, Carlos Luis 1920–2001, *Stanley George Barnett*
Sancha, Carlos Luis 1920–2001, *Robert William Dixon Smith*
Sancha, Carlos Luis 1920–2001, *Admiral Sir Andrew Lewis, KCB, JP, Lord Lieutenant of Essex (1978–1992)*
Serres, John Thomas (follower of) 1759–1825, *Capriccio with a British Man o' War*, presented by D. P. Sellar, 1898
Smith, John (attributed to) c.1717–1764, *Wooded Lake with Thatched Cottage*, presented by D. P. Sellar, 1898
Stone, Richard b.1951, *The Right Honourable the Lord Braybrooke, Knight of St John, MA, JP, Lord Lieutenant of Essex (1992–2002)*, © the artist
Stranovius, Tobias (studio of) 1684–1731, *Still Life with a Monkey, Jay and Parrot*, presented by D. P. Sellar, 1898
Teniers, David II (after) 1610–1690, *Rural Scene with Figures Playing Skittles*, presented by D. P. Sellar, 1898
Teniers, David II (follower of) 1610–1690, *Surgery with Chiropodist*, presented by D. P. Sellar, 1898
Terborch, Gerard II (after) 1617–1681, *Interior with Lady Washing Her Hands*, presented by D. P. Sellar, 1898
Terborch, Gerard II (follower of) 1617–1681, *Interior with Peasants*, presented by D. P. Sellar, 1898
Thompson, Anthony *The 'Mayflower' Leaving Plymouth, 1620*, commissioned by Councillor William Julien Courtauld, 1938
Wigley, Eileen b.1946, *My Personal View of Essex*, © the artist
Williams, Edward (circle of) 1782–1855, *Wooded Landscape with Thatched Cottage*, presented by D. P. Sellar, 1898

Essex Police Museum

Bridge, Jack *Essex Police, 1840 (Tilbury)*, commissioned for the 150th anniversary, 1990
Bridge, Jack *Essex Police, 1870 (Chappel)*, commissioned for the 150th anniversary, 1990
Bridge, Jack *Essex Police, 1890*, commissioned for the 150th anniversary, 1990
Bridge, Jack *Essex Police, 1916 (L.33 over Little Wigborough)*, commissioned for the 150th anniversary, 1990
Bridge, Jack *Essex Police, 1930 (Colchester)*, commissioned for the 150th anniversary, 1990
Bridge, Jack *Essex Police, 1940 (Thaxted)*, commissioned for the 150th anniversary, 1990
Bridge, Jack *Essex Police, 1965 (Southend-on-Sea)*, commissioned for the 150th anniversary, 1990
Bridge, Jack *Essex Police, 1990 (Bradwell-on-Sea)*, commissioned for the 150th anniversary, 1990
Bridge, Jack *Admiral John McHardy, Chief Constable of Essex (1840–1881)*, commissioned
Bridge, Jack *Constable Charles 'Zepp' Smith (arrested the crew of a zeppelin which crashed at Little Wigborough, 1916), 1916*, commissioned
Bridge, Jack *James Lee (hanged for the murder of Inspector Simmons)*, commissioned
Bridge, Jack *John Bausor, an Early Inspector of the Essex Constabulary*, commissioned
Bridge, Jack *Samuel Dougal in Staff Sergeant's Military Dress (Murderer of Camille Holland, Moat Farm, Clavering)*, commissioned
Bridge, Jack *Sergeant Bill Gosling (Southend-on-Sea Constabulary)*, commissioned
Hodges, George d.1980s, *Dorothy Jordan, First Woman Police Inspector of Essex Constabulary (1944)*, donated, 1991
Woon, Des *Police Launch*, donated

Essex Record Office

Burgoyne, P. *Mary Brewster, Wife of William Mildmay*
Carse, James (attributed to) active c.1836–1848, *Ellys Anderson Stephens of Bower Hall (demolished in 1926), Steeple Bumpstead*, on loan from a private individual
Hogarth, William (school of) 1697–1764, *Lucy Baynes Plucking an Orange*, acquired from Ilford Ltd, 1960
Priseman, Robert b.1965, *The Search Room at Essex Record Office*, presented by the Friends of Historic Essex, 2003, © the artist
J. S. *A View of the North Front of Bower House, Havering atte Bower*, acquired from Ilford Ltd, 1960
unknown artist early 17th C, *Portrait of a Gentleman in a Black Doublet and Lace Collar*, acquired from Ilford Ltd, 1960
unknown artist early 17th C, *Portrait of a Lady in an Embroidered Dress*, acquired from Ilford Ltd, 1960
unknown artist late 17th C, *Portrait of a Gentleman in a Long Wig and a Brown Cloak, with a Dog*, acquired from Ilford Ltd, 1960
unknown artist late 17th C, *Portrait of a Young Lady in a Brown Dress and Pink Cloak*, acquired from Ilford Ltd, 1960
unknown artist *Frances Carswell, Mother of Edmund Humfrey of Rettendon*
unknown artist *George Bramston, LLD, of Woodham Walter*
unknown artist *Sir Charles Barrington of Hatfield Broad Oak, Aged 31*
unknown artist *Mary Beke (d.1771), Wife of John Baynes*, acquired from Ilford Ltd, 1960
unknown artist early 18th C, *Portrait of a Gentleman in a Brown Coat (believed to be Francis Lee, possibly the husband of Lucy Baynes)*, acquired from Ilford Ltd, 1960
unknown artist *A View of the South Front of Bower House, Havering atte Bower*, acquired from Ilford Ltd, 1960
Vanderbank, John c.1694–1739, *John Baynes, Sergeant-at-Law, d.1737 (builder of Bower House, Havering atte Bower)*, acquired from Ilford Ltd, 1960
Vanderbank, John c.1694–1739, *Mary (d.1771), Wife of John Baynes*, acquired from Ilford Ltd, 1960

Colchester Archaeological Trust

Froste, Peter b.1935, *Balkerne Gate, Colchester*, commissioned by the Colchester Archaeological Trust, © DACS 2006
Froste, Peter b.1935, *Roman Theatre and Temple of Claudius, Colchester*, commissioned by the Colchester Archaeological Trust, © DACS 2006
Froste, Peter b.1935, *West Front, St Botolph's Priory, Colchester*, commissioned by the Colchester Archaeological Trust, © DACS 2006
Froste, Peter b.1935, *The Stanway Burials c.65 AD*, commissioned by the Colchester Archaeological Trust, © DACS 2006

Colchester County High School

Pallot, Joyce 1912–2004, *Cranes*, donated by the artist's family, © the artist's estate
Pallot, Joyce 1912–2004, *Flamingoes and Fish*, donated by the artist's family, © the artist's estate
Pallot, Joyce 1912–2004, *Glazed Vestibule*, donated by the artist's family, © the artist's estate
Pallot, Joyce 1912–2004, *Quayside Reflections*, donated by the artist's family, © the artist's estate

Colchester Museums

Aiken, John MacDonald 1880–1961, *Annie, Viscountess Cowdray, High Steward of Colchester (copy after William Orpen)*, presented by the sitter, 1931
Aiken, John MacDonald 1880–1961, *The Right Honourable Weetman Dickinson Pearson, 1st Viscount Cowdray PC, GCVO (1856–1927) (copy after William Orpen)*, presented by the High Steward of Colchester, Annie, Viscountess Cowdray, 1931
Archer, Archibald active 1810–1845, *Sir George Henry Smythe*, gift from P. G. Laver
Bamfield, W. B. *Susannah Wiseman (after William Allsworth)*, gift from Mrs Lyon-Campbell
Barber, Alfred R. 1841–1925, *Langham Mill*, gift from A. S. Mason
Barber, Alfred R. 1841–1925, *Five Rabbits*, untraced find
Barber, Alfred R. 1841–1925, *Four White Rabbits*, purchased from the Johae Art Centre
Bashall, Nick b.1956, *Bed Street, Kabul*, presented by 16 Air Assault Brigade and Colchester Garrison, © the artist
Baskett, Charles E. 1845–1929, *Still Life with Wine Glass*, gift from L. J. Watts
Becker, Harry 1865–1928, *Lucas and Lisle Descending the Great Stair, Colchester Castle*, untraced find
Becker, Harry 1865–1928, *Dutch Refugees Fleeing from the Persecution of the Duke of Alva, Praying Permission of the Bailiffs of Colchester to Settle in the Town, 1570 AD*, presented to the town of Colchester by Charles O. G. Becker
Becker, Harry 1865–1928, *An Incident at the Siege of Colchester, 1648*, presented by Alderman Wilson Marriage
Becker, Harry 1865–1928, *Harvesters, Suffolk*, purchased from Christie's
Bell, Thomas Currie 1873–1946, *A Country Inn*
Benham, Barbara J. 1912–1999, *The Maltings at the Hythe, Colchester*, purchased from Wivenhoe Arts Club
Beyerhaus, E. active 1857–1862, *Charlotte Eleanor Cooper*
Breanski, Alfred de 1852–1928, *Evening, Wonders of the Loch*, transferred from the public library
Bryans, H. W. active 1891–c.1922, *The Three Marys at the Sepulchre*, gift from the Borough architect
Buck, William active 1864–1900, *Choppings Mill, Colchester*, gift from Mrs W. W. Smith
Bull, J. *Colchester, Dawn*, gift from C. E. Owen
Burton, Hal *Tram Crossing the North Bridge, Colchester*, gift from P. M. Skoulding
Burton, William Francis 1907–1995, *Colchester Castle*, gift from the Friends of Colchester Museum
Campion, C. S. *Sir William Campion (killed at the Siege of Colchester, 1648)*, gift from the Campion family, descendants of the sitter
Carter, H. Malcolm *Abberton Reservoir at Sunset*, gift from Miss Irene Carter
Codner, Maurice Frederick 1888–1958, *Sir Gurney Benham (1859–1944), Mayor of Colchester*
Codner, Maurice Frederick 1888–1958, *Alderman Percy A. Sanders, CBE, DG, JP (Mayor of Colchester 1922 & 1939–1942)*
Codner, Maurice Frederick 1888–1958, *Bernard Mason*, gift from the sitter
Collins, Henry 1910–1994, *Sheepen, Colchester*, gift from Cheltenham and Gloucester Building Society
Constable, John 1776–1837, *Reverend Thomas Lechmere Grimwood, DD (1740–1809), Headmaster of Dedham Grammar School*, gift from P. G. Laver
Cope, Arthur Stockdale 1857–1940, *The Right Honourable James Round of Birch Hall, PC (1842–1916)*, presented to Colchester Town Council by Major J. G. Round, JP, 1955
Cope, Arthur Stockdale (copy of) 1857–1940, *The Right Honourable James Round of Birch Hall, PC (1842–1916)*, gift from Captain Charles Round and Mr J. Horace Round, 1922
Corsi, Santi b.1871 & **Lavery, John** 1856–1941 *Pitti Palace, Florence*, donated by the Honourable Diana, Lady Darling
Cotman, Frederick George 1850–1920, *At Fordwich, Kent*
Cross, Gail *Culver Street, Colchester*, commissioned from the artist
Cunningham, C. H. *Field Marshal Sir Evelyn Wood, VC, GCB, GCMG (commanded Colchester Garrison, 1886–1889)*, gift from Alfred Hills
Dance, George the younger (copy of) 1741–1825, *Reverend Samuel Parr, LLD (1742–1825), Headmaster of Colchester Grammar School*, presented by the pupils of Colchester Royal Grammar School, 1902
Daniell, Frank 1866–1932, *Canon Irvine, MA*
Daniell, Frank 1866–1932, *John Kavanagh*, gift from John Kavanagh Ltd
Daniell, Frank 1866–1932, *Colchester Blue Coat School Boy*, presented by public subscription
Daniell, Frank 1866–1932, *Colchester Blue Coat School Girl*, presented by public subscription
Daniell, Frank 1866–1932, *Alderman Henry Goody, JP, Mayor of Colchester (1893, 1894 & 1905–1906)*
Daniell, Frank 1866–1932, *Henry Charles Wanklyn, Town Clerk*, presented by public subscription
Daniell, Frank 1866–1932, *Councillor Catherine Buchanan Alderton, JP (The first woman Mayor of Colchester, 1923–1924)*, presented by subscription by the inhabitants of Colchester
Daniell, Frank 1866–1932, *Alderman Alfred Francis, Mayor of*

Colchester (1883), presented by Francis Kershaw, the sitter's brother
Daniell, Frank 1866–1932, *Alderman Claude Egerton-Green, JP, Mayor of Colchester (1894–1895 & 1900–1901)*, presented by public subscription
Daniell, Frank 1866–1932, *Alderman Edwin Beard, JP*, gift from E. S. Beard
Daniell, Frank 1866–1932, *Alderman Henry Laver, JP, FSA*, gift from the Colchester Arts Club
Daniell, Frank 1866–1932, *Alderman Horace-Egerton Green, JP, DL, Mayor of Colchester (1886–1887 & 1898–1899)*, presented by public subscription
Daniell, Frank 1866–1932, *Alderman James N. Paxman, CE (1832–1922), Mayor of Colchester (1887–1888 & 1897–1898)*
Daniell, Frank 1866–1932, *Alderman James Wicks, JP, Mayor of Colchester (1895–1896)*, presented by public subscription
Daniell, Frank 1866–1932, *Alderman John Kent (1805–1896), Mayor (1879)*, presented by sitter's daughter, Mrs E. F. Blaxill
Daniell, Frank 1866–1932, *Alderman Wilson Marriage, JP, Portreeve of Colchester*, presented by public subscription by the inhabitants of Colchester
Daniell, Frank 1866–1932, *Entrance at Middleburg, Holland*, purchased from Albert Hall Art Gallery
Daniell, Frank 1866–1932, *George Bawtree*, gift from George, Emily and Katherine Bawtree, children of the sitter
Daniell, Frank 1866–1932, *Toledo Cathedral*, transferred from the Borough Art Collection
Daniell, Frank 1866–1932, *William Gilberd of Colchester (1540–1603), Physician to Queen Elizabeth and King James, Founder of the Science of Magnetism*, presented by Charles F. Benham
Daniell, Frank 1866–1932, *William Sparling*, gift from Arthur Sparling, grandson of the sitter
Debenham, Charles b.1933, *High Street, Colchester, 1950*, presented by Friends of Colchester Museum, © the artist
Debenham, Charles b.1933, *Bourne Road Bookies, Colchester*, purchased from the artist, © the artist
Debenham, Charles b.1933, *Cavalry Barracks, Colchester*, purchased from the artist, © the artist
Debenham, Charles b.1933, *Married Quarters, Abbey Fields*, purchased from the artist, © the artist
Debenham, Charles b.1933, *North Station Road, Colchester*, purchased from the artist, © the artist
Dunthorne, James I (attributed to) 1730–1815, *Colchester from Middle Mill*, gift from Bernard Mason
Dunthorne, James I (attributed to) 1730–1815, *Colchester from the North-West*, gift from Bernard Mason
Dunthorne, James I (attributed to) 1730–1815, *St Botolph's Priory, Colchester*
Dunthorne, John III 1770–1844, *Flatford Lock, Suffolk*
Dunthorne, John IV 1798–1832, *A Country Lane*
Dunthorne, John IV 1798–1832, *Cows on a Country Lane*
Dunthorne, John IV 1798–1832, *Lane with Stile and Field, Dedham Vale*, gift
Dyck, Anthony van (after) 1599–1641, *Arthur Capel*
Felmingham, E. *Kelvedon High Street*, bequeathed by Miss Peggy Marian Jones
Flemish School *The Transfiguration*, presented by Reverend W. E. Spencer, MA
Flemish School *The Visitation*, presented by Reverend W. E. Spencer, MA
Friswell, Harry P. Hain 1857–after 1906, *Flatford Bridge, Suffolk*
Froste, Peter b.1935, *Sack of the Temple of Claudius, Colchester*, purchased from the artist, © DACS 2006
Froste, Peter b.1935, *Colchester Castle under Construction*, purchased from the artist, © DACS 2006
Froste, Peter b.1935, *Roman Theatre, Colchester*, purchased from the artist, © DACS 2006
Froste, Peter b.1935, *View of Roman Colchester from the South-West*, purchased from the artist, © DACS 2006
Fry, Roger Eliot 1866–1934, *Willy Lott's Cottage, Flatford*, purchased from Christie's, 1993
Fussell, Michael 1927–1974, *A Scene from the Siege of Colchester*, gift from Dr Douglas Rossdale
Gale, Charles T. *The Peep Show Man*, gift from R. M. Gale
Gilbert, Josiah 1814–1892, *Isaac Taylor II*, bequeathed by Miss M. Herbert
Grone, Ferdinand E. c.1845–1920, *Edward Marriage, President of the Colchester Friends' Adult Schools*
Grone, Ferdinand E. c.1845–1920, *Flatford Mill, Suffolk*, gift from the artist to the town of Colchester
Haddock, Jesse E. *Charles H. Hawkins, JP (Mayor of Colchester 1848–1849, 1865, 1870 & 1871)*
Halls, John James 1776–1834, *Julia Halls Holding an Umbrella*, gift from Madame S. Mennessuer
Halls, John James 1776–1834, *Reverend John Savill (1780–1826)*
Hansard, W. D. *Middle Mill, Colchester*, gift from Miss E. Stebbing
Hatcher, E. W. *'Cloriana'*, gift from F. W. Anderson
Head, Charles 1850–1926, *Reverend Sabine Baring-Gould (1834–1924), Rector of East Mersea (1871–1881)*
Head, Charles 1850–1926, *Benjamin Revett Cant, the Eminent Rosarian*, presented by the sitter's family
Head, Charles 1850–1926, *Charles Henry Hawkins, JP*, gift from the Hawkins family
Head, Charles 1850–1926, *Reverend Philip Morant (1700–1770), Historian of Essex and Colchester*, presented by Mr and Mrs P. R. Green
Head, Charles 1850–1926, *William Mason (d.1802) Alderman of the Borough of Colchester, Mayor (1796–1797)*, presented by the sitter's great-great granddaughters, H. and L. J. Bawtree
Henry, George F. 1858–1943, *The Honourable Mr Justice Darling (1849–1936), Judge of the King's Bench (1897–1936)*, presented by the sitter's daughters
Hoynk, Otto (attributed to) c.1630–c.1686, *The Spotted Dog (The Golden Horn at Constantinople)*, on loan from the Victor Batte-Lay Trust
Hunt, Arthur Ackland active 1865–1902, *Dr William Gilberd Showing His Experiments on Electricity to Queen Elizabeth and Her Court*, presented by the Institute of Electrical Engineers
Italian (Venetian) School *The Last Supper*, untraced find
Jensen, Alfred 1859–1935, *'SS Colchester'*, purchased from Paskell and Cann
Jensen, Alfred 1859–1935, *'SS Dresden'*, purchased from Reeman, Dansie, Howe and Son
Jensen, Alfred 1859–1935, *'SS St Petersburg'*, purchased from Reeman, Dansie, Howe and Son
Jensen, Alfred 1859–1935, *'SS Cromer'*, purchased from Reeman, Dansie, Howe and Son
Jensen, Alfred 1859–1935, *'SS Brussels'*, purchased from Reeman, Dansie, Howe and Son
Jensen, Alfred 1859–1935, *'SS St Denis'*, purchased from Reeman, Dansie, Howe and Son
Johnson, Cyrus 1848–1925, *George Henry Errington, High Steward of Colchester*
Johnson, F. R. active 1978–1979, *Bourne Mill, Colchester*, untraced find
Johnson, F. R. active 1978–1979, *Mevagissey, Cornwall*
Ladell, Edward 1821–1886, *Still Life with Fruit and a Bird's Nest*, gift from Lieutenant Colonel J. Walter
Ladell, Edward 1821–1886, *Still Life with Pheasant, Partridge and Duck*, gift from Mrs H. Joslin
Lance, George 1802–1864, *Still Life with Monkey, Sparrow and Fruit*, gift from Miss Ada Lance
Landon, Charles Paul 1760–1826, *Landscape: Water, Clouds and Moon*, gift from A. H. Mackmurdo
Lang, Peter *Wivenhoe Quay*, purchased from the artist
Largillière, Nicolas de (after) 1656–1746, *The Crucifixion*, bequeathed by Mrs George Round
Lely, Peter (after) 1618–1680, *Arthur Barnadiston, Recorder of Colchester (1649)*, presented by Councillor W. Gurney Benham
Lonsdale, James 1777–1839, *Charles Abbot, 1st Baron Colchester (1757–1829)*, bequeathed by the sitter's grandson, Reginald Charles Edward, 3rd Baron Colchester
Lucas, John 1807–1874, *George Round (1803–1857), High Sheriff of Essex (1845)*
Lucas, John 1807–1874, *Charles Gray Round, MA*, presented by the town council and inhabitants of Colchester
Miles, G. *Colchester Castle*, untraced find
Muirhead, David 1867–1930, *The Fen Bridge, near Dedham (Constable's Country)*, presented by the Right Honourable Justice Darling
Nagle, I. *Middle Mill, Colchester*, gift from Mrs Percy King
Nash, John Northcote 1893–1977, *The Garden in Winter*, purchased from Christie's, 1993
Nicholson, E. W. active 1901–1902, *John Bawtree Harvey, JP (1809–1890), Mayor of Colchester (1881–1883)*, presented by the family of the sitter
Nicholson, E. W. active 1901–1902, *Henry Sidney Goody*, gift from the Goody family
Nightingale, Robert 1815–1895, *William Philip Honywood of Markshall, near Coggeshall (1823–1859), High Sheriff (1851)*
Parish, Josiah 1834–1882, *Nether Hall, Roydon*, gift from Mrs P. F. Turner
Peake, Robert (attributed to) c.1551–1619, *Sir Thomas Lucas, Knight of St John, Colchester*, purchased with the assistance of the National Art Collections Fund, 1993
Percival, W. H. active 1862–1906, *North Bridge, Colchester*, gift from Mrs Mason, 1937
Peterson, Otto Fredrik 1672–1729, *King Charles I*
Pissarro, Lucien 1863–1944, *St Lawrence's Church, near Southminster*, presented by Samuel Bensusan, the brother of the artist's wife
Pissarro, Lucien 1863–1944, *Colchester from Sheepen Hill*, presented by Alderman John Bensusan-Butt, nephew of the artist's wife
Pissarro, Lucien 1863–1944, *The Acacia Tree at the Minories, Colchester*, bequeathed by David Bensusan-Butt, 1998
Prentice, James active 1846, *A Yokel*, purchased from Reeman, Dansie, Howe and Son
Reilly, John Lewis active 1857–1899, *Charles Gray (1696–1782), MP for Colchester in Five Parliaments (copy after Thomas Gainsborough)*, presented by James Round, MP
Reilly, John Lewis active 1857–1899, *Colonel Neville (copy after William Charles Thomas Dobson)*, gift from Frederick John Keeling, 1899
Reilly, John Lewis active 1857–1899, *Sir Charles Lucas, Leader of the Royalist Forces at the Siege of Colchester (after William Charles Thomas Dobson)*, gift from Mrs Keeling
Reilly, John Lewis active 1857–1899, *Sir Francis Walsingham, Secretary of State, Recorder of Colchester (d.1590)*
Reilly, John Lewis active 1857–1899, *Charles Gray Round (copy after John Lucas)*, purchased from Reeman, Dansie, Howe and Son
Reinagle, Ramsay Richard (copy of) 1775–1862, *Ann Constable (1748–1815)*, gift from Alderman Wilson Marriage, 1926
Roberts, Henry Benjamin 1832–1915, *London Stage Coach*
Root, Malcolm b.1950, *Train at Colchester Station*, purchased from the artist, © the artist
Rushbury, Henry 1889–1968, *John Ray of Black Notley, Father of Natural History (1627–1703)*, untraced find, © the artist's estate
Savage, James Henry active c.1820–1853, *Greenstead Church, Colchester (copy after John Greig)*, purchased
Savage, James Henry active c.1820–1853, *The Old Moot Hall, Colchester*, gift from Councillor Cave
Saville, Josephine active 1863–1906, *John Stock Barnes, Clerk of the Peace (1836–1887)*, presented by the artist
Smythe, Thomas 1825–1907, *Country Scene with Two Windmills*
St George, Sylvia 1881–1950, *Air Raid over Colchester at Night*, gift from Miss I. M. St George Brett
St George, Sylvia 1881–1950, *St Botolph's, Colchester, a Bombed House*, gift from Miss I. M. St George Brett
St George, Sylvia 1881–1950, *Cherry Blossom, Boxted*, bequeathed by Miss I. M. St George Brett
St George, Sylvia 1881–1950, *Colchester in Winter*, purchased from Reeman, Dansie, Howe and Son
St George, Sylvia 1881–1950, *Flowers in the Sink*, bequeathed by Miss I. M. St George Brett
St George, Sylvia 1881–1950, *Malaga, Spain*, bequeathed by Miss I. M. St George Brett
St George, Sylvia 1881–1950, *Regatta at Burnham-on-Crouch*, bequeathed by Miss I. M. St George Brett
St George, Sylvia 1881–1950, *River Stour in Flood, Essex*, bequeathed by Miss I. M. St George Brett
St George, Sylvia 1881–1950, *The Parks, Colchester*, purchased from

Reeman, Dansie, Howe and Son
Stannard, F. *Nayland Mill, Suffolk*, gift from the artist
Stannard, F. *Wissington Locks, Barges and Floodgate*, gift from the artist
Stannard, F. *Wissington Mill, Suffolk*, gift from the artist
Stone, Richard b.1951, *Queen Elizabeth II (b.1926)*, commissioned by Colchester Borough Council, © the artist
Strutt, Benjamin 1754–1857, *Execution of Sir Charles Lucas and Sir George Lisle at Colchester, 28 August 1648*, gift
Summers, S. N. active 1764–1806, *Dr Robert Potter*, gift from Councillor Laver
Taylor, R. *Lady in an Ermine Robe*, gift from Mr E. M. Gonet
Todd, F. G. *Still Life with Fruit*, gift from F. Robinson
Turner, Ernie d.1977, *Fingringhoe*, purchased from Reeman, Dansie, Howe and Son
Turner, Ernie d.1977, *Wivenhoe*, purchased from Reeman, Dansie, Howe and Son
Turner, F. Claridge active 1872–1893, *The Haywain (after John Constable)*, presented by Sydney Claridge Turner, 1927
unknown artist *The Virgin*, gift from the artist
unknown artist *Dr William Gilberd, MD*
unknown artist 17th C, *Bower Hall, Steeple Bumpstead (demolished in 1926)*, on long-term loan from Walthamstow Public Library
unknown artist 17th C, *Mary Honywood (née Waters) of Markshall, Essex (d.1625)*
unknown artist 17th C, *Mary Honywood (née Waters) of Markshall, Essex (d.1625)*
unknown artist 18th C, *Bishop Warburton (1698–1769)*
unknown artist 18th C, *Miss Anne Lisle*
unknown artist 18th C, *Mr Boys*, gift from Mrs Lyon-Campbell
unknown artist 18th C, *Samuel Claye (b.1752)*, purchased
unknown artist *Colchester Castle*
unknown artist *North-West View of Colchester Castle*, gift from the Borough Art Collection
unknown artist *Cliffs and Seashore, Harwich and Dovercourt*, gift from Dr John Penfold
unknown artist *Harwich and Dovercourt*, gift from Dr John Penfold
unknown artist *Mr Thomas Moore*, bequeathed by Michael Piquet-Wicks
unknown artist *Mrs Thomas Moore*, bequeathed by Michael Piquet-Wicks
unknown artist *Portrait of a Gentleman in a Gothic Hall*, bequeathed by Michael Piquet-Wicks
unknown artist *North Hill, Colchester*, gift from Mr H. A. Cook
unknown artist *Middle Mill, Colchester from East Stream*, gift from F. Bardsley
unknown artist early 19th C, *John Bawtree (1760–1824), Deputy Lieutenant for the County of Essex, JP*, presented to the town of Colchester by the sitter's great granddaughter, Louisa Mary Bawtree
unknown artist early 19th C, *Portrait of a Boy*
unknown artist early 19th C, *Reverend Samuel Carr, MA (1791–1854), Vicar of St Peter's, Colchester (1829–1854)*, gift from Miss Mary Anna Carr
unknown artist 19th C, *Alderman William Cheshire*
unknown artist 19th C, *Benjamin Monson, the First Colchester Photographer*, gift from F. Rehburger
unknown artist 19th C, *Bourne Mill, Colchester*, untraced find
unknown artist 19th C, *Colchester Castle*
unknown artist 19th C, *General Francis Slater Rebow (1770–1845), Owner of Wivenhoe Park and Patron of John Constable*
unknown artist 19th C, *John Eley of Kelvedon*, gift from Vestry House Museum
unknown artist 19th C, *John Grimwade*, gift from H. J. Grimwade
unknown artist 19th C, *Lieutenant John Andrews (d.1817)*, presented by the National Art Collections Fund
unknown artist 19th C, *Middle Mill, Colchester*, purchased
unknown artist 19th C, *Sergeant Lay*, gift from Mrs Lyon-Campbell
unknown artist 19th C, *The Old Moot Hall, Colchester*, gift from Mrs Humm
unknown artist 19th C, *Three Bunches of First Prize Black Grapes*, purchased from Paskell and Cann
unknown artist 19th C, *Three Bunches of First Prize Green Grapes*, purchased from Paskell and Cann
unknown artist 19th C, *Walter Swinborne*, gift from executors of Joshua Baker
unknown artist *Alderman Walter Littlebury, JP*, gift from Mrs Littlebury, widow of the sitter
unknown artist *Eld Lane, Colchester*, bequeathed by Miss Phyllis Edith Pigg
unknown artist 20th C, *Councillor Chopping*, gift from R. Chopping
unknown artist *Charles Tayspill (1600–1662)*, purchased
unknown artist *Giles Tayspill*, purchased
unknown artist *Hester, Lady Honywood, née Lamont (1607–1681)*, gift from Sir W. Gurney Benham
unknown artist *John Chaplin (1795–1858), Mayor of Colchester (1836)*, gift from the sitter's son, Samuel Chaplin, JP
unknown artist *John King, Mayor of Colchester (1775–1778 & 1781)*, gift
unknown artist *Roger Nunn, MD, Mayor of Colchester (1834 & 1842)*, gift from George Bawtree
unknown artist *Sir Harbottle Grimston, PC (1603–1685), Speaker of the House of Commons, Master of the Rolls*, presented by James Round, MP
unknown artist *Sir Harbottle Grimston, PC (1603–1685) Speaker of the House of Commons, Master of the Rolls*, gift from David Mintors
unknown artist *Sir Thomas Honywood (1586–1666)*, gift from Sir W. Gurney Benham
unknown artist *The Casting Out of Hagar*, gift from A. H. Mackmurdo
unknown artist *Thomas, 3rd Lord Fairfax (1612–1671), and His Wife, Anne (1614–1665) (after William Charles Thomas Dobson)*, presented by Mrs Edward Benham
Vinckboons, David 1576–c.1632, *Flemish Village Merrymaking*, presented by Mr Charles Godfrey, 1918
Vine, John c.1809–1867, *James Cobb of 16 High Street, Colchester*, presented by Miss Mann, 1922
Vine, John c.1809–1867, *Mrs James Cobb of Colchester*, presented by Miss Mann, 1922
Vine, John c.1809–1867, *Chestnut Horse*, gift from K. W. Everitt
Vine, John c.1809–1867, *Black Horse*, gift from K. W. Everitt
Walker, Robert (after) c.1600–c.1659, *General Henry Ireton*
Williams, R. active 1842, *Peel Castle, Isle of Man*, gift from A. H. Mackmurdo, 1932
Winch, Miller J. active 1891–c.1920, *High Street, Colchester at Night*, gift from Miss V. Paice

Feering & Kelvedon Local History Museum

Durell, Amy Clara b.1865, *Miss Ada Cecilia Lance (b.1866) of the Red House, Kelvedon*, gift, c.1978
Foster, C. *Chrysanthemums in a Jug*, gift from Mr C. J. Deal, 1977

Sir Alfred Munnings Art Museum

Codner, Maurice Frederick 1888–1958, *Sir Alfred Munnings*, acquired by Sir Alfred Munnings
Codner, Maurice Frederick 1888–1958, *Sir Alfred Munnings Seated*, acquired by Sir Alfred Munnings
Eves, Reginald Grenville 1876–1941, *Lily, Carnation, Lily, Rose' (copy of John Singer Sargent)*, acquired by Sir Alfred Munnings
Haigh, Alfred G. 1870–1963, *The Inch*, acquired through Lady Munnings
Haigh, Alfred G. 1870–1963, *Bonny Rose*, acquired through Lady Munnings
E. F. M. *Fountain of Lights*
Munnings, Alfred James 1878–1959, *After the Party*, donated by the artist, © the artist's estate
Munnings, Alfred James 1878–1959, *Daniel Tomkins and His Dog*, purchased from Copeman, 1975, © the artist's estate
Munnings, Alfred James 1878–1959, *A Shoot in a Swede Field*, purchased from Frost and Reed, 1973, © the artist's estate
Munnings, Alfred James 1878–1959, *A Suffolk Horse Fair, Lavenham*, purchased from Christie's, 1973, © the artist's estate
Munnings, Alfred James 1878–1959, *Study of a Male Nude in Julian's Atelier*, donated by the artist, © the artist's estate
Munnings, Alfred James 1878–1959, *The Fancy Dress Ball*, on loan from Mr Peter Mogg, © the artist's estate
Munnings, Alfred James 1878–1959, *A Female Nude Seated at Julian's Atelier, Rue du Dragon*, donated by the artist, © the artist's estate
Munnings, Alfred James 1878–1959, *Colt Breaker's Gig*, donated by the artist, © the artist's estate
Munnings, Alfred James 1878–1959, *The Timber Gill*, donated by the artist, © the artist's estate
Munnings, Alfred James 1878–1959, *A Lady Seated in a Park*, purchased from Mr R. C. Porter, 1983, © the artist's estate
Munnings, Alfred James 1878–1959, *Hornberg, Black Forest*, purchased from Sotheby's, 1979, © the artist's estate
Munnings, Alfred James 1878–1959, *Old Gray*, purchased from Richard Green, 1985, © the artist's estate
Munnings, Alfred James 1878–1959, *Flower Girl, Violets*, purchased from Mr Roy Miles, 1973, © the artist's estate
Munnings, Alfred James 1878–1959, *The Grey Pony, Augereau, in a Sandpit with Groom, George Curzon*, donated by the artist, © the artist's estate
Munnings, Alfred James 1878–1959, *Nelly Gray*, purchased from Sotheby's, 1981, © the artist's estate
Munnings, Alfred James 1878–1959, *Path to the Orchard*, purchased from Mr Roy Miles, 1974, © the artist's estate
Munnings, Alfred James 1878–1959, *Study of George Curzon, Groom*, donated by the artist, © the artist's estate
Munnings, Alfred James 1878–1959, *Cassie Jeweller*, purchased from Mr T. Watts, 1979, © the artist's estate
Munnings, Alfred James 1878–1959, *A Gipsy Campfire*, purchased from Frost and Reed, 1973, © the artist's estate
Munnings, Alfred James 1878–1959, *The Ford*, donated by the artist, © the artist's estate
Munnings, Alfred James 1878–1959, *Poplars, River Waveney*, donated by the artist, © the artist's estate
Munnings, Alfred James 1878–1959, *'Shrimp' Leading Ponies across a Norfolk Common*, purchased from Sotheby's, 1981, © the artist's estate
Munnings, Alfred James 1878–1959, *Cattle Watering in a Stream, Zennor, Cornwall*, donated by the artist, © the artist's estate
Munnings, Alfred James 1878–1959, *Cornwall, Blossom*, donated by the artist, © the artist's estate
Munnings, Alfred James 1878–1959, *Cows at Water, Lamorna*, donated by the artist, © the artist's estate
Munnings, Alfred James 1878–1959, *Spring in a Cornish Valley*, donated by the artist, © the artist's estate
Munnings, Alfred James 1878–1959, *The Harness Room*, donated by the artist, © the artist's estate
Munnings, Alfred James 1878–1959, *Hunting Morning*, purchased from Sotheby's, 1974, © the artist's estate
Munnings, Alfred James 1878–1959, *Phyllis Crocker*, donated by the artist, © the artist's estate
Munnings, Alfred James 1878–1959, *The Bay Horse, 'Patrick', Bought in Dublin with Grey Mare*, donated by the artist, © the artist's estate
Munnings, Alfred James 1878–1959, *Lamorna Inn*, purchased from Newhouse Galleries, USA, 1975, © the artist's estate
Munnings, Alfred James 1878–1959, *R. W. Sutherland, Cavalry Officer*, donated by the artist, © the artist's estate
Munnings, Alfred James 1878–1959, *A Girl on a Bed*, donated by the artist, © the artist's estate
Munnings, Alfred James 1878–1959, *Study in the Eure Valley, France, with the Canadian Army*, donated by the artist, © the artist's estate
Munnings, Alfred James 1878–1959, *Study of Dawn Effect, France, 2 April 1918*, donated by the artist, © the artist's estate
Munnings, Alfred James 1878–1959, *Tagg's Island*, purchased from Mr Roy Miles, 1973, © the artist's estate
Munnings, Alfred James 1878–1959, *A Dark Bay Hunter*, donated by the artist, © the artist's estate
Munnings, Alfred James 1878–1959, *Lady Munnings Riding a Grey Hunter ('Magnolia') Side-Saddle, with Her Dogs on Exmoor*, donated by the artist, © the artist's estate
Munnings, Alfred James 1878–1959, *Sow and Pigs, Great Thurlow, Suffolk*, donated by the artist, © the artist's estate
Munnings, Alfred James 1878–1959, *Elder Blossom*, donated by

the artist, © the artist's estate
Munnings, Alfred James 1878–1959, *Horse Studies (recto)*, donated by the artist, © the artist's estate
Munnings, Alfred James 1878–1959, *Horse Study (verso)*, donated by the artist, © the artist's estate
Munnings, Alfred James 1878–1959, *Study of a Clipped Hunter Mare*, donated by the artist, © the artist's estate
Munnings, Alfred James 1878–1959, *The Gilded Coach, Painted in the Palace Yard in Grey Weather*, donated by the artist, © the artist's estate
Munnings, Alfred James 1878–1959, *Dunster Castle, Somerset*, donated by the artist, © the artist's estate
Munnings, Alfred James 1878–1959, *Thatching an Oat Stack with Rushes, Exmoor*, donated by the artist, © the artist's estate
Munnings, Alfred James 1878–1959, *Study for 'The White Canoe'*, donated by the artist, © the artist's estate
Munnings, Alfred James 1878–1959, *Study for 'The White Canoe'*, donated by the artist, © the artist's estate
Munnings, Alfred James 1878–1959, *Study for 'The White Canoe' (recto)*, donated by the artist, © the artist's estate
Munnings, Alfred James 1878–1959, *Study of a Huntsman for 'Who's the Lady?' (verso)*, donated by the artist, © the artist's estate
Munnings, Alfred James 1878–1959, *Two Studies of Mr George Lambton's Horse, 'Pricket'*, donated by the artist, © the artist's estate
Munnings, Alfred James 1878–1959, *'Cheena', a Study of Lady Munnings' Mare*, donated by the artist, © the artist's estate
Munnings, Alfred James 1878–1959, *Exmoor Sheep (recto)*, © the artist's estate
Munnings, Alfred James 1878–1959, *Sheep Studies (verso)*, © the artist's estate
Munnings, Alfred James 1878–1959, *Study for 'Southern Hero'*, donated by the artist, © the artist's estate
Munnings, Alfred James 1878–1959, *A Sheepdog at Withypool, Exmoor*, donated by the artist, © the artist's estate
Munnings, Alfred James 1878–1959, *Brightworthy Ford, Withypool, Exmoor, Evening*, donated by the artist, © the artist's estate
Munnings, Alfred James 1878–1959, *'Dear Cheena', a Bay Hunter*, donated by the artist, © the artist's estate
Munnings, Alfred James 1878–1959, *Garden at Withypool, Exmoor*, donated by the artist, © the artist's estate
Munnings, Alfred James 1878–1959, *Study of Paul Delaney, Withypool, Exmoor*, donated by the artist, © the artist's estate
Munnings, Alfred James 1878–1959, *Stables at Withypool, Exmoor, Studies of 'Cherrybounce' and 'Anarchist'*, donated by the artist, © the artist's estate
Munnings, Alfred James 1878–1959, *Exmoor Ponies*, donated by the artist, © the artist's estate
Munnings, Alfred James 1878–1959, *An Old Gravel Pit*, donated by the artist, © the artist's estate
Munnings, Alfred James 1878–1959, *The Unsaddling Enclosure, Epsom*, donated by the artist, © the artist's estate
Munnings, Alfred James 1878–1959, *Before the Start, Newmarket*, donated by the artist, © the artist's estate
Munnings, Alfred James 1878–1959, *Studies of Mr Rank's Horse, 'Strathspey', Winner of 1949 Cesarewitch (painted at Druids' Lodge)*, donated by the artist, © the artist's estate
Munnings, Alfred James 1878–1959, *Studies of 'Rufus'*, donated by the artist, © the artist's estate
Munnings, Alfred James 1878–1959, *Study for 'Early Morning, Newmarket'*, donated by the artist, © the artist's estate
Munnings, Alfred James 1878–1959, *A Black Horse at Newmarket*, donated by the artist, © the artist's estate
Munnings, Alfred James 1878–1959, *Moving up for the Start (painted after the last race in the artist's studio, Newmarket)*, donated by the artist, © the artist's estate
Munnings, Alfred James 1878–1959, *Studies of 'Rufus's' Head*, donated by the artist, © the artist's estate
Munnings, Alfred James 1878–1959, *Trees by the Edge of a Field*, donated by the artist, © the artist's estate
Munnings, Alfred James 1878–1959, *Study for 'The Unsaddling Enclosure, Epsom'*, donated by the artist, © the artist's estate
Munnings, Alfred James 1878–1959, *Study of Foliage and Sky*, donated by the artist, © the artist's estate
Munnings, Alfred James 1878–1959, *Study of 'The Start' (done in studio on heath after racing)*, donated by the artist, © the artist's estate
Munnings, Alfred James 1878–1959, *'Black Knight' Finishes His Diary*, donated by the artist, © the artist's estate
Munnings, Alfred James 1878–1959, *Study of a Yellow Jockey on My Mare, 'Irish Smock'*, donated by the artist, © the artist's estate
Munnings, Alfred James 1878–1959, *Study of the Yellow Jockey*, donated by the artist, © the artist's estate
Munnings, Alfred James 1878–1959, *A Barge on the Stour at Dedham*, donated by the artist, © the artist's estate
Munnings, Alfred James 1878–1959, *A Barge on the Stour at Dedham*, donated by the artist, © the artist's estate
Munnings, Alfred James 1878–1959, *A Bay Horse*, donated by the artist, © the artist's estate
Munnings, Alfred James 1878–1959, *A Bay Horse in a Landscape*, donated by the artist, © the artist's estate
Munnings, Alfred James 1878–1959, *A Bay Horse in a Landscape*, donated by the artist, © the artist's estate
Munnings, Alfred James 1878–1959, *A Bay Horse in a Stable (recto)*, donated by the artist, © the artist's estate
Munnings, Alfred James 1878–1959, *Studies of a Horse's Head (verso)*, donated by the artist, © the artist's estate
Munnings, Alfred James 1878–1959, *A Bay Horse near a Building*, donated by the artist, © the artist's estate
Munnings, Alfred James 1878–1959, *A Bay Hunter*, donated by the artist, © the artist's estate
Munnings, Alfred James 1878–1959, *A Bay Racehorse by a Stable*, donated by the artist, © the artist's estate
Munnings, Alfred James 1878–1959, *A Bay Racehorse with a Groom*, donated by the artist, © the artist's estate
Munnings, Alfred James 1878–1959, *A Bay Racehorse with Jockey up, in Pink and White Striped Colours, in a Landscape*, donated by the artist, © the artist's estate
Munnings, Alfred James 1878–1959, *A Chestnut Horse in a Landscape*, donated by the artist, © the artist's estate
Munnings, Alfred James 1878–1959, *A Chestnut Horse in a Landscape ('Happy Laughter')*, donated by the artist, © the artist's estate
Munnings, Alfred James 1878–1959, *A Chestnut Horse in a Stable*, donated by the artist, © the artist's estate
Munnings, Alfred James 1878–1959, *A Chestnut Racehorse Held by a Boy in a Landscape*, donated by the artist, © the artist's estate
Munnings, Alfred James 1878–1959, *A Chestnut Racehorse Painted at George Lambton's Yard, Newmarket*, donated by the artist, © the artist's estate
Munnings, Alfred James 1878–1959, *A Chestnut Racehorse with Jockey up in a Landscape*, donated by the artist, © the artist's estate
Munnings, Alfred James 1878–1959, *A Chestnut with Jockey up*, donated by the artist, © the artist's estate
Munnings, Alfred James 1878–1959, *A Cloud Study*, donated by the artist, © the artist's estate
Munnings, Alfred James 1878–1959, *A Cloud Study*, donated by the artist, © the artist's estate
Munnings, Alfred James 1878–1959, *A Cloud Study*, donated by the artist, © the artist's estate
Munnings, Alfred James 1878–1959, *A Cloud Study, Exmoor*, donated by the artist, © the artist's estate
Munnings, Alfred James 1878–1959, *A Cow and a Figure in a Stable*, donated by the artist, © the artist's estate
Munnings, Alfred James 1878–1959, *A Dark Bay Horse in a Landscape*, donated by the artist, © the artist's estate
Munnings, Alfred James 1878–1959, *A Dark Bay Racehorse in a Stable*, donated by the artist, © the artist's estate
Munnings, Alfred James 1878–1959, *A Distant View of Dedham from the Stour at Sunset*, donated by the artist, © the artist's estate
Munnings, Alfred James 1878–1959, *A Farmyard Scene*, donated by the artist, © the artist's estate
Munnings, Alfred James 1878–1959, *A Garden Scene*, donated by the artist, © the artist's estate
Munnings, Alfred James 1878–1959, *A Garden Scene*, donated by the artist, © the artist's estate
Munnings, Alfred James 1878–1959, *A Garden Scene*, donated by the artist, © the artist's estate
Munnings, Alfred James 1878–1959, *A Grey Horse in the Unsaddling Paddock, Epsom*, donated by the artist, © the artist's estate
Munnings, Alfred James 1878–1959, *A Grey Racehorse with a Lad up*, donated by the artist, © the artist's estate
Munnings, Alfred James 1878–1959, *A Groom Holding a Bay Horse, near Stables*, donated by the artist, © the artist's estate
Munnings, Alfred James 1878–1959, *A Horse and Rider in a Landscape*, donated by the artist, © the artist's estate
Munnings, Alfred James 1878–1959, *A Horse in a Landscape*, donated by the artist, © the artist's estate
Munnings, Alfred James 1878–1959, *A Horse with a Groom*, donated by the artist, © the artist's estate
Munnings, Alfred James 1878–1959, *A Hunter in a Stable*, donated by the artist, © the artist's estate
Munnings, Alfred James 1878–1959, *A Hunter in a Stable*, donated by the artist, © the artist's estate
Munnings, Alfred James 1878–1959, *A Huntsman on a Grey in a Landscape*, donated by the artist, © the artist's estate
Munnings, Alfred James 1878–1959, *A Lad Exercising a Racehorse*, donated by the artist, © the artist's estate
Munnings, Alfred James 1878–1959, *A Lad on a Racehorse*, donated by the artist, © the artist's estate
Munnings, Alfred James 1878–1959, *A Lady Riding a Bay Hunter*, donated by the artist, © the artist's estate
Munnings, Alfred James 1878–1959, *A Landscape*, donated by the artist, © the artist's estate
Munnings, Alfred James 1878–1959, *A Landscape (recto)*, donated by the artist, © the artist's estate
Munnings, Alfred James 1878–1959, *Study of Trees (verso)*, donated by the artist, © the artist's estate
Munnings, Alfred James 1878–1959, *A Landscape of Fields and Hedgerows in Deep Shadow*, donated by the artist, © the artist's estate
Munnings, Alfred James 1878–1959, *A Landscape of Trees and Grazing Sheep*, donated by the artist, © the artist's estate
Munnings, Alfred James 1878–1959, *A Landscape, Study with Trees*, donated by the artist, © the artist's estate
Munnings, Alfred James 1878–1959, *A Landscape with a Distant Village (possibly French)*, donated by the artist, © the artist's estate
Munnings, Alfred James 1878–1959, *A Landscape with Cottage*, donated by the artist, © the artist's estate
Munnings, Alfred James 1878–1959, *A Landscape with Farm Buildings*, donated by the artist, © the artist's estate
Munnings, Alfred James 1878–1959, *A Landscape with Farm Buildings*, donated by the artist, © the artist's estate
Munnings, Alfred James 1878–1959, *A Landscape with Foliage*, donated by the artist, © the artist's estate
Munnings, Alfred James 1878–1959, *A Landscape with Foxgloves*, donated by the artist, © the artist's estate
Munnings, Alfred James 1878–1959, *A Landscape with Foxgloves in the Foreground*, donated by the artist, © the artist's estate
Munnings, Alfred James 1878–1959, *A Landscape with Trees*, donated by the artist, © the artist's estate
Munnings, Alfred James 1878–1959, *A Landscape with Trees by a Field*, donated by the artist, © the artist's estate
Munnings, Alfred James 1878–1959, *A Landscape with Trees on the Edge of a Field (recto)*, donated by the artist, © the artist's estate
Munnings, Alfred James 1878–1959, *Study of Trees (verso)*, donated by the artist, © the artist's estate
Munnings, Alfred James 1878–1959, *A Landscape with Trees on the Edge of a Field*, donated by the

artist, © the artist's estate
Munnings, Alfred James 1878–1959, *A Lane at Exford, Exmoor (study of a tree)*, donated by the artist, © the artist's estate
Munnings, Alfred James 1878–1959, *A Light Bay Horse with a Stable Boy*, donated by the artist, © the artist's estate
Munnings, Alfred James 1878–1959, *A Mare and Foal*, donated by the artist, © the artist's estate
Munnings, Alfred James 1878–1959, *A Parkland Scene with Trees*, donated by the artist, © the artist's estate
Munnings, Alfred James 1878–1959, *A Parkland Scene with Trees*, donated by the artist, © the artist's estate
Munnings, Alfred James 1878–1959, *A Pastoral Scene with Trees and a Stream in the Foreground*, donated by the artist, © the artist's estate
Munnings, Alfred James 1878–1959, *A Pollarded Willow (recto)*, donated by the artist, © the artist's estate
Munnings, Alfred James 1878–1959, *Studies of Ponies and Cattle (verso)*, donated by the artist, © the artist's estate
Munnings, Alfred James 1878–1959, *A Racecourse*, donated by the artist, © the artist's estate
Munnings, Alfred James 1878–1959, *A Racehorse Held by a Groom*, donated by the artist, © the artist's estate
Munnings, Alfred James 1878–1959, *A Racehorse in a Landscape*, donated by the artist, © the artist's estate
Munnings, Alfred James 1878–1959, *A Racehorse in a Landscape*, donated by the artist, © the artist's estate
Munnings, Alfred James 1878–1959, *A Racehorse with Jockey up, Wearing Blue with Yellow Ribbon*, donated by the artist, © the artist's estate
Munnings, Alfred James 1878–1959, *A River Landscape on Exmoor*, donated by the artist, © the artist's estate
Munnings, Alfred James 1878–1959, *A River Scene with a Tug*, donated by the artist, © the artist's estate
Munnings, Alfred James 1878–1959, *A River Scene with Trees*, donated by the artist, © the artist's estate
Munnings, Alfred James 1878–1959, *A Scene at Newmarket*, donated by the artist, © the artist's estate
Munnings, Alfred James 1878–1959, *A Sky Study*, donated by the artist, © the artist's estate
Munnings, Alfred James 1878–1959, *A Spring Landscape, Raydon, Suffolk*, donated by the artist, © the artist's estate
Munnings, Alfred James 1878–1959, *A Stream Overhung by Trees*, donated by the artist, © the artist's estate
Munnings, Alfred James 1878–1959, *A Study from Memory of an Eager Horse*, donated by the artist, © the artist's estate
Munnings, Alfred James 1878–1959, *A Study of a Hound (recto)*, donated by the artist, © the artist's estate
Munnings, Alfred James 1878–1959, *Study of a Rider with Man and Calf (verso)*, donated by the artist, © the artist's estate
Munnings, Alfred James 1878–1959, *A Study of Blossom*, donated by the artist, © the artist's estate
Munnings, Alfred James 1878–1959, *A Study of Rocks, Lamorna Cove*, donated by the artist, © the artist's estate
Munnings, Alfred James 1878–1959, *A Study of the Windsor Greys*, donated by the artist, © the artist's estate
Munnings, Alfred James 1878–1959, *A Suffolk Landscape*, donated by the artist, © the artist's estate
Munnings, Alfred James 1878–1959, *A Tree Study (recto)*, donated by the artist, © the artist's estate
Munnings, Alfred James 1878–1959, *A Tree Study (verso)*, donated by the artist, © the artist's estate
Munnings, Alfred James 1878–1959, *A View at Castle House*, donated by the artist, © the artist's estate
Munnings, Alfred James 1878–1959, *A View in Exmoor, Distant Hill in Shadow*, donated by the artist, © the artist's estate
Munnings, Alfred James 1878–1959, *A View in Suffolk*, donated by the artist, © the artist's estate
Munnings, Alfred James 1878–1959, *A View near Withypool, Exmoor, with Flood Water*, donated by the artist, © the artist's estate
Munnings, Alfred James 1878–1959, *A View of Boxted Mill*, donated by the artist, © the artist's estate
Munnings, Alfred James 1878–1959, *A View of Dedham Vale with Stacks in a Field*, donated by the artist, © the artist's estate
Munnings, Alfred James 1878–1959, *A View of Exmoor, Gorse Bushes in Foreground*, donated by the artist, © the artist's estate
Munnings, Alfred James 1878–1959, *A View of Exmoor, Sheep by the Wall in the Foreground*, donated by the artist, © the artist's estate
Munnings, Alfred James 1878–1959, *A View of Great Thurlow, Suffolk*, donated by the artist, © the artist's estate
Munnings, Alfred James 1878–1959, *A View of the Pyrenees from Pau*, donated by the artist, © the artist's estate
Munnings, Alfred James 1878–1959, *A View of Whitehall*, donated by the artist, © the artist's estate
Munnings, Alfred James 1878–1959, *A View on Exmoor*, donated by the artist, © the artist's estate
Munnings, Alfred James 1878–1959, *A View on Exmoor*, donated by the artist, © the artist's estate
Munnings, Alfred James 1878–1959, *A View on Exmoor*, donated by the artist, © the artist's estate
Munnings, Alfred James 1878–1959, *A View on Exmoor*, donated by the artist, © the artist's estate
Munnings, Alfred James 1878–1959, *A View on Exmoor, Ponies in the Foreground (recto)*, donated by the artist, © the artist's estate
Munnings, Alfred James 1878–1959, *Study of a Landscape (verso)*, donated by the artist, © the artist's estate
Munnings, Alfred James 1878–1959, *A View on Exmoor with Bushes in Blossom*, donated by the artist, © the artist's estate
Munnings, Alfred James 1878–1959, *A Winter Landscape*, donated by the artist, © the artist's estate
Munnings, Alfred James 1878–1959, *A Winter Landscape, Exmoor, Figures on Horseback in the Foreground*, donated by the artist, © the artist's estate
Munnings, Alfred James 1878–1959, *A Winter Landscape with Trees*, donated by the artist, © the artist's estate
Munnings, Alfred James 1878–1959, *A Winter Scene at Castle House with Birds Feeding*, donated by the artist, © the artist's estate
Munnings, Alfred James 1878–1959, *A Winter Scene at Castle House with Birds in the Foreground*, donated by the artist, © the artist's estate
Munnings, Alfred James 1878–1959, *A Wooded Landscape*, donated by the artist, © the artist's estate
Munnings, Alfred James 1878–1959, *A Wooded Landscape*, donated by the artist, © the artist's estate
Munnings, Alfred James 1878–1959, *A Wooded Landscape*, donated by the artist, © the artist's estate
Munnings, Alfred James 1878–1959, *A Woodland Scene*, donated by the artist, © the artist's estate
Munnings, Alfred James 1878–1959, *An Autumn Exmoor Landscape*, donated by the artist, © the artist's estate
Munnings, Alfred James 1878–1959, *An Avenue of Trees*, donated by the artist, © the artist's estate
Munnings, Alfred James 1878–1959, *An Exmoor Landscape (recto)*, donated by the artist, © the artist's estate
Munnings, Alfred James 1878–1959, *Study of a Horse (verso)*, donated by the artist, © the artist's estate
Munnings, Alfred James 1878–1959, *An Exmoor Landscape*, donated by the artist, © the artist's estate
Munnings, Alfred James 1878–1959, *An Exmoor Landscape*, donated by the artist, © the artist's estate
Munnings, Alfred James 1878–1959, *An Exmoor Landscape*, donated by the artist, © the artist's estate
Munnings, Alfred James 1878–1959, *An Exmoor Landscape (recto)*, donated by the artist, © the artist's estate
Munnings, Alfred James 1878–1959, *An Exmoor Landscape (verso)*, donated by the artist, © the artist's estate
Munnings, Alfred James 1878–1959, *An Exmoor Landscape (recto)*, donated by the artist, © the artist's estate
Munnings, Alfred James 1878–1959, *Study of Clouds (verso)*, donated by the artist, © the artist's estate
Munnings, Alfred James 1878–1959, *An Exmoor Landscape with a Wall (recto)*, donated by the artist, © the artist's estate
Munnings, Alfred James 1878–1959, *Horse Studies (verso)*, donated by the artist, © the artist's estate
Munnings, Alfred James 1878–1959, *An Exmoor Landscape with Gorse (recto)*, donated by the artist, © the artist's estate
Munnings, Alfred James 1878–1959, *Trees in a Landscape (verso)*, donated by the artist, © the artist's estate
Munnings, Alfred James 1878–1959, *An Exmoor Scene*, donated by the artist, © the artist's estate
Munnings, Alfred James 1878–1959, *An Exmoor View (recto)*, donated by the artist, © the artist's estate
Munnings, Alfred James 1878–1959, *An Exmoor View (verso)*, donated by the artist, © the artist's estate
Munnings, Alfred James 1878–1959, *An Exmoor View (recto)*, donated by the artist, © the artist's estate
Munnings, Alfred James 1878–1959, *An Exmoor View (verso)*, donated by the artist, © the artist's estate
Munnings, Alfred James 1878–1959, *An Extensive Landscape*, donated by the artist, © the artist's estate
Munnings, Alfred James 1878–1959, *An Extensive Landscape*, donated by the artist, © the artist's estate
Munnings, Alfred James 1878–1959, *An Extensive Landscape with a Road*, donated by the artist, © the artist's estate
Munnings, Alfred James 1878–1959, *An Extensive Landscape with Sheep Grazing in the Fields*, donated by the artist, © the artist's estate
Munnings, Alfred James 1878–1959, *An Extensive View of Exmoor*, donated by the artist, © the artist's estate
Munnings, Alfred James 1878–1959, *An Extensive View of Exmoor*, donated by the artist, © the artist's estate
Munnings, Alfred James 1878–1959, *An Extensive View of Exmoor*, donated by the artist, © the artist's estate
Munnings, Alfred James 1878–1959, *An Extensive Winter Landscape, Exmoor (recto)*, donated by the artist, © the artist's estate
Munnings, Alfred James 1878–1959, *Study of a Winter Landscape (verso)*, donated by the artist, © the artist's estate
Munnings, Alfred James 1878–1959, *An Extensive Winter Landscape, Withypool, Exmoor*, donated by the artist, © the artist's estate
Munnings, Alfred James 1878–1959, *An Oak Grove, Nayland, Suffolk*, donated by the artist, © the artist's estate
Munnings, Alfred James 1878–1959, *An Open Landscape*, donated by the artist, © the artist's estate
Munnings, Alfred James 1878–1959, *'Anarchist'*, donated by the artist, on loan to the National Horseracing Museum, Newmarket, © the artist's estate
Munnings, Alfred James 1878–1959, *At the Half Mile, Newmarket, Three Runners*, donated by the artist, © the artist's estate
Munnings, Alfred James 1878–1959, *Autumn, near Stoke by Nayland*, donated by the artist, © the artist's estate
Munnings, Alfred James 1878–1959, *Autumn, Richmond Park*, donated by the artist, © the artist's estate
Munnings, Alfred James 1878–1959, *Bagsworthy Water, Exmoor*, donated by the artist, © the artist's estate
Munnings, Alfred James 1878–1959, *Bagsworthy Water, Exmoor, at Cloud*, donated by the artist, © the artist's estate
Munnings, Alfred James 1878–1959, *Barge on the Stour at Dedham*, on loan from Miss I. Maynard, © the artist's estate
Munnings, Alfred James 1878–1959, *Barges on a River*, donated by the artist, © the artist's estate
Munnings, Alfred James 1878–1959, *Before the Race*, donated by the artist, © the artist's estate
Munnings, Alfred James 1878–1959, *Before the Race*, donated by the artist, © the artist's estate
Munnings, Alfred James 1878–1959, *Before the Race*, donated by the artist, © the artist's estate
Munnings, Alfred James 1878–1959, *Before the Race*, donated by the artist, © the artist's estate
Munnings, Alfred James 1878–1959, *Before the Start*, donated by the artist, © the artist's estate
Munnings, Alfred James 1878–1959, *Before the Start*, donated by

the artist, © the artist's estate
Munnings, Alfred James 1878–1959, *Before the Start, Newmarket*, donated by the artist, © the artist's estate
Munnings, Alfred James 1878–1959, *Blossom*, donated by the artist, © the artist's estate
Munnings, Alfred James 1878–1959, *Boy and Racehorse Study*, donated by the artist, © the artist's estate
Munnings, Alfred James 1878–1959, *Boys on a Barge*, donated by the artist, © the artist's estate
Munnings, Alfred James 1878–1959, *Brightworthy Ford, Withypool, Exmoor (recto)*, donated by the artist, © the artist's estate
Munnings, Alfred James 1878–1959, *Brightworthy Ford, Withypool, Exmoor (verso)*, donated by the artist, © the artist's estate
Munnings, Alfred James 1878–1959, *Brightworthy Ford, Withypool, Exmoor (recto)*, donated by the artist, © the artist's estate
Munnings, Alfred James 1878–1959, *Elm Trees (verso)*, donated by the artist, © the artist's estate
Munnings, Alfred James 1878–1959, *Brightworthy Ford, Withypool, Exmoor (recto)*, donated by the artist, © the artist's estate
Munnings, Alfred James 1878–1959, *Brightworthy Ford, Withypool, Exmoor (verso)*, donated by the artist, © the artist's estate
Munnings, Alfred James 1878–1959, *Brightworthy Ford, Withypool, Exmoor*, donated by the artist, © the artist's estate
Munnings, Alfred James 1878–1959, *Brightworthy Ford, Withypool, Exmoor*, donated by the artist, © the artist's estate
Munnings, Alfred James 1878–1959, *Brightworthy Ford, Withypool, Exmoor*, donated by the artist, © the artist's estate
Munnings, Alfred James 1878–1959, *Brightworthy Ford, Withypool, Exmoor (recto)*, donated by the artist, © the artist's estate
Munnings, Alfred James 1878–1959, *Study (verso)*, donated by the artist, © the artist's estate
Munnings, Alfred James 1878–1959, *Brightworthy Ford, Withypool, Exmoor*, donated by the artist, © the artist's estate
Munnings, Alfred James 1878–1959, *Brightworthy Ford, Withypool, Exmoor*, donated by the artist, © the artist's estate
Munnings, Alfred James 1878–1959, *Brightworthy Ford, Withypool, Exmoor*, donated by the artist, © the artist's estate
Munnings, Alfred James 1878–1959, *Brightworthy Ford, Withypool, Exmoor*, donated by the artist, © the artist's estate
Munnings, Alfred James 1878–1959, *Brightworthy Ford, Withypool, Exmoor*, donated by the artist, © the artist's estate
Munnings, Alfred James 1878–1959, *Brightworthy Ford, Withypool, Exmoor*, donated by the artist, © the artist's estate
Munnings, Alfred James 1878–1959, *Brightworthy Ford, Withypool, Exmoor*, donated by the artist, © the artist's estate
Munnings, Alfred James 1878–1959, *Brightworthy Ford, Withypool, Exmoor*, donated by the artist, © the artist's estate
Munnings, Alfred James 1878–1959, *Brightworthy Ford, Withypool, Exmoor*, donated by the artist, © the artist's estate
Munnings, Alfred James 1878–1959, *Brightworthy Ford, Withypool, Exmoor*, donated by the artist, © the artist's estate
Munnings, Alfred James 1878–1959, *Brightworthy Ford, Withypool, Exmoor*, donated by the artist, © the artist's estate
Munnings, Alfred James 1878–1959, *Brightworthy Ford, Withypool, Exmoor*, donated by the artist, © the artist's estate
Munnings, Alfred James 1878–1959, *Bringing Home the Sheep, Withypool, Exmoor*, © the artist's estate
Munnings, Alfred James 1878–1959, *Bringing Home the Sheep, Withypool, Exmoor*, donated by the artist, © the artist's estate
Munnings, Alfred James 1878–1959, *Bringing Home the Sheep, Withypool, Exmoor*, donated by the artist, © the artist's estate
Munnings, Alfred James 1878–1959, *'Bunker II', a Bay Racehorse*, donated by the artist, © the artist's estate
Munnings, Alfred James 1878–1959, *Cavalry Charge Led by Lieutenant G. M. Flowerdew, VC*, donated by the artist, © the artist's estate
Munnings, Alfred James 1878–1959, *'Cherrybounce'*, donated by the artist, © the artist's estate
Munnings, Alfred James 1878–1959, *Cloud Studies (recto)*, donated by the artist, © the artist's estate
Munnings, Alfred James 1878–1959, *Cloud Studies (verso)*, donated by the artist, © the artist's estate
Munnings, Alfred James 1878–1959, *Cloud Study (recto)*, donated by the artist, © the artist's estate
Munnings, Alfred James 1878–1959, *Cloud Study (verso)*, donated by the artist, © the artist's estate
Munnings, Alfred James 1878–1959, *Cloud Study, Exmoor*, donated by the artist, © the artist's estate
Munnings, Alfred James 1878–1959, *Cloud Study on Exmoor*, donated by the artist, © the artist's estate
Munnings, Alfred James 1878–1959, *Clouds on Exmoor*, donated by the artist, © the artist's estate
Munnings, Alfred James 1878–1959, *Coming off the Heath, Exercising the Horses, Newmarket*, donated by the artist, © the artist's estate
Munnings, Alfred James 1878–1959, *Cottages by a River*, © the artist's estate
Munnings, Alfred James 1878–1959, *Crossing the Ford*, donated by the artist, © the artist's estate
Munnings, Alfred James 1878–1959, *Dedham Painted from Lock Cottage*, donated by the artist, © the artist's estate
Munnings, Alfred James 1878–1959, *Design for Happy New Year Greeting*, donated by the artist, © the artist's estate
Munnings, Alfred James 1878–1959, *Does the Subject Matter?*, donated by the artist, © the artist's estate
Munnings, Alfred James 1878–1959, *Early Morning, Newmarket*, donated by the artist, © the artist's estate
Munnings, Alfred James 1878–1959, *Early Spring Landscape, Dedham*, donated by the artist, © the artist's estate
Munnings, Alfred James 1878–1959, *Epsom Paddock*, donated by the artist, © the artist's estate
Munnings, Alfred James 1878–1959, *Epsom Paddock and Stands*, donated by the artist, © the artist's estate
Munnings, Alfred James 1878–1959, *Exercising Horses on Warren Hill, Newmarket*, donated by the artist, © the artist's estate
Munnings, Alfred James 1878–1959, *Exercising the Horses*, donated by the artist, © the artist's estate
Munnings, Alfred James 1878–1959, *Exercising the Horses*, donated by the artist, © the artist's estate
Munnings, Alfred James 1878–1959, *Exercising the Horses*, donated by the artist, © the artist's estate
Munnings, Alfred James 1878–1959, *Exercising the Horses*, donated by the artist, © the artist's estate
Munnings, Alfred James 1878–1959, *Exmoor*, donated by the artist, © the artist's estate
Munnings, Alfred James 1878–1959, *Exmoor*, donated by the artist, © the artist's estate
Munnings, Alfred James 1878–1959, *Exmoor, Blackthorne*, donated by the artist, © the artist's estate
Munnings, Alfred James 1878–1959, *Exmoor Landscape*, donated by the artist, © the artist's estate
Munnings, Alfred James 1878–1959, *Exmoor Ponies*, donated by the artist, © the artist's estate
Munnings, Alfred James 1878–1959, *Exmoor Ponies*, donated by the artist, © the artist's estate
Munnings, Alfred James 1878–1959, *Exmoor Sheep*, © the artist's estate
Munnings, Alfred James 1878–1959, *Exmoor with Gorse*, donated by the artist, © the artist's estate
Munnings, Alfred James 1878–1959, *Figures on a Beach below Cliffs (possibly Cornwall)*, donated by the artist, © the artist's estate
Munnings, Alfred James 1878–1959, *First Study for 'Frozen River'*, donated by the artist, © the artist's estate
Munnings, Alfred James 1878–1959, *Floods near Nayland*, donated by the artist, © the artist's estate
Munnings, Alfred James 1878–1959, *Gardens, Dedham*, donated by the artist, © the artist's estate
Munnings, Alfred James 1878–1959, *Going to the Start*, donated by the artist, © the artist's estate
Munnings, Alfred James 1878–1959, *Going up the Canter, a Boy Exercising a Racehorse*, donated by the artist, © the artist's estate
Munnings, Alfred James 1878–1959, *Good Pasture beyond the Gate*, donated by the artist, © the artist's estate
Munnings, Alfred James 1878–1959, *Grisaille Study of a Hunter*, donated by the artist, © the artist's estate
Munnings, Alfred James 1878–1959, *'Happy Laughter', a Chestnut Racehorse, with Jockey up in a Landscape*, donated by the artist, © the artist's estate
Munnings, Alfred James 1878–1959, *'High Stakes', Lord Astor's Horse*, donated by the artist, © the artist's estate
Munnings, Alfred James 1878–1959, *HM Queen Mary, a Study for 'Driving to Ascot'*, donated by the artist, © the artist's estate
Munnings, Alfred James 1878–1959, *Horse Studies*, donated by the artist, © the artist's estate
Munnings, Alfred James 1878–1959, *Horses with Stable Lads up at Newmarket*, donated by the artist, © the artist's estate
Munnings, Alfred James 1878–1959, *Huntsman Crossing the Dunkery Beacon, Exmoor*, donated by the artist, © the artist's estate
Munnings, Alfred James 1878–1959, *Idle Moments*, on long-term loan, © the artist's estate
Munnings, Alfred James 1878–1959, *Knight Riding by a Lake (recto)*, donated by the artist, © the artist's estate
Munnings, Alfred James 1878–1959, *A Scene from the New Testament (verso)*, donated by the artist, © the artist's estate
Munnings, Alfred James 1878–1959, *Lady Munnings on a Grey Hunter*, donated by the artist, © the artist's estate
Munnings, Alfred James 1878–1959, *Lady Munnings on a Grey Hunter*, donated by the artist, © the artist's estate
Munnings, Alfred James 1878–1959, *Lady Munnings Riding a Bay Hunter*, donated by the artist, © the artist's estate
Munnings, Alfred James 1878–1959, *Lamorna Cove, Cornwall*, donated by the artist, © the artist's estate
Munnings, Alfred James 1878–1959, *Lamorna Cove, Cornwall*, donated by the artist, © the artist's estate
Munnings, Alfred James 1878–1959, *Landscape with a Barn*, donated by the artist, © the artist's estate
Munnings, Alfred James 1878–1959, *Landscape with a Windmill*, donated by the artist, © the artist's estate
Munnings, Alfred James 1878–1959, *Landscape with Trees*, donated by the artist, © the artist's estate
Munnings, Alfred James 1878–1959, *Landscape with Trees*, on loan from Mr Christopher Greenwood, © the artist's estate
Munnings, Alfred James 1878–1959, *Landscape, Withypool, Exmoor, Winter*, donated by the artist, © the artist's estate
Munnings, Alfred James 1878–1959, *Langham Mill Pool on the Stour*, donated by the artist, © the artist's estate
Munnings, Alfred James 1878–1959, *Major E. Shackle, Buckinghamshire Farmers' Hunt*, purchased from Sotheby's, 1979, © the artist's estate
Munnings, Alfred James 1878–1959, *May Blossom*, donated by the artist, © the artist's estate
Munnings, Alfred James 1878–1959, *May on Exmoor*, donated by the artist, © the artist's estate
Munnings, Alfred James 1878–1959, *Mill Hill, Oar, Exmoor*, donated by the artist, © the artist's estate
Munnings, Alfred James 1878–1959, *Miss Hancock, Seated Smoking with a Dog in an Interior*, donated by the artist, © the artist's estate
Munnings, Alfred James 1878–1959, *Moving up to the Start*, donated by the artist, © the artist's estate
Munnings, Alfred James 1878–1959, *Mr Sponge on the Go*, donated by the artist, © the artist's estate
Munnings, Alfred James 1878–1959, *Mrs J. V. Rank at Druids' Lodge by the Swimming Pool*, purchased from a private collector, Sotheby's, 1981, © the artist's estate
Munnings, Alfred James 1878–1959, *My Grey Mare*, donated by the artist, © the artist's estate
Munnings, Alfred James 1878–1959, *My Wife, My Horse and*

Myself, donated by the artist, © the artist's estate
Munnings, Alfred James 1878–1959, *Nobby Gray with the Hunt*, donated by the artist, © the artist's estate
Munnings, Alfred James 1878–1959, *Old Gentleman in Period Costume with Walking Stick*, purchased from Mrs M. E. Austin, 1984, © the artist's estate
Munnings, Alfred James 1878–1959, *Old Man in Period Costume Holding a Bottle and Glass*, purchased from Mrs M. E. Austin, 1984, © the artist's estate
Munnings, Alfred James 1878–1959, *On the Stour, Dedham*, donated by the artist, © the artist's estate
Munnings, Alfred James 1878–1959, *Oxen at an Archway Being Yoked, at Baron Robert's Estate, Chantilly*, donated by the artist, © the artist's estate
Munnings, Alfred James 1878–1959, *Pigs at Great Thurlow, Suffolk*, donated by the artist, © the artist's estate
Munnings, Alfred James 1878–1959, *Point-to-Point*, on loan from the City Museum and Art Gallery, Stoke-on-Trent, © the artist's estate
Munnings, Alfred James 1878–1959, *Ponies in a Sandpit, Ringland Hills, Norfolk*, donated by the artist, © the artist's estate
Munnings, Alfred James 1878–1959, *Porlock Studies, Trees by the Edge of a Field (recto)*, donated by the artist, © the artist's estate
Munnings, Alfred James 1878–1959, *Study of Cattle Grazing (verso)*, donated by the artist, © the artist's estate
Munnings, Alfred James 1878–1959, *Racehorses in a Landscape*, donated by the artist, © the artist's estate
Munnings, Alfred James 1878–1959, *Racehorses in a Landscape*, donated by the artist, © the artist's estate
Munnings, Alfred James 1878–1959, *Racehorses Training in a Landscape*, donated by the artist, © the artist's estate
Munnings, Alfred James 1878–1959, *'Rich Gift'*, donated by the artist, © the artist's estate
Munnings, Alfred James 1878–1959, *Riderless Horse*, donated by the artist, © the artist's estate
Munnings, Alfred James 1878–1959, *Riding to the Start*, donated by the artist, © the artist's estate
Munnings, Alfred James 1878–1959, *River Landscape with Trees*, donated by the artist, © the artist's estate
Munnings, Alfred James 1878–1959, *River Scene at Brightworthy, Withypool, Exmoor, Evening Light*, donated by the artist, © the artist's estate
Munnings, Alfred James 1878–1959, *River Scene, Boxted Mill*, donated by the artist, © the artist's estate
Munnings, Alfred James 1878–1959, *'Rufus', a Study for 'Our Mutual Friend the Horse'*, donated by the artist, © the artist's estate
Munnings, Alfred James 1878–1959, *Self Portrait*, donated by the artist, © the artist's estate
Munnings, Alfred James 1878–1959, *Study*, donated by the artist, © the artist's estate
Munnings, Alfred James 1878–1959, *Selworthy, West Somerset*, donated by the artist, © the artist's estate
Munnings, Alfred James 1878–1959, *September Afternoon on the Stour, Dedham*, donated by the artist, © the artist's estate
Munnings, Alfred James 1878–1959, *Sheep on Exmoor*, donated by the artist, © the artist's estate
Munnings, Alfred James 1878–1959, *'Shrimp' and 'Augereau' in Ringland Hills*, purchased from Miss M. Chadburn, 1977, © the artist's estate
Munnings, Alfred James 1878–1959, *'Shrimp' on a White Welsh Pony*, bequeathed by Mrs V. Legge, 2002, © the artist's estate
Munnings, Alfred James 1878–1959, *Sir Raymond Greene, DSO, MP, on Horseback, 1919*, purchased through Oscar and Peter Johnson Ltd, 1980, © the artist's estate
Munnings, Alfred James 1878–1959, *Sky Study*, donated by the artist, © the artist's estate
Munnings, Alfred James 1878–1959, *Sky Study*, donated by the artist, © the artist's estate
Munnings, Alfred James 1878–1959, *Sky Study*, donated by the artist, © the artist's estate
Munnings, Alfred James 1878–1959, *Sky Study*, donated by the artist, © the artist's estate
Munnings, Alfred James 1878–1959, *Sky Study*, donated by the artist, © the artist's estate
Munnings, Alfred James 1878–1959, *Spring Evening, Cornwall*, donated by the artist, © the artist's estate
Munnings, Alfred James 1878–1959, *St James's Street, Decorations for the Coronation of George VI, 1937*, donated by the artist, © the artist's estate
Munnings, Alfred James 1878–1959, *Stiffkey Church, Norfolk*, donated by the artist, © the artist's estate
Munnings, Alfred James 1878–1959, *Stiffkey Church, Norfolk*, on loan from Miss I. Maynard, © the artist's estate
Munnings, Alfred James 1878–1959, *Studies of a Bay Racehorse*, donated by the artist, © the artist's estate
Munnings, Alfred James 1878–1959, *Studies of a Bay Racehorse*, donated by the artist, © the artist's estate
Munnings, Alfred James 1878–1959, *Studies of a Bay Racehorse in a Landscape*, donated by the artist, © the artist's estate
Munnings, Alfred James 1878–1959, *Studies of a Boatman*, donated by the artist, © the artist's estate
Munnings, Alfred James 1878–1959, *Studies of a Brown Mare for 'Unsaddling Enclosure, Epsom'*, donated by the artist, © the artist's estate
Munnings, Alfred James 1878–1959, *Studies of a Chestnut Racehorse*, donated by the artist, © the artist's estate
Munnings, Alfred James 1878–1959, *Studies of a Grey Mare's Head*, donated by the artist, © the artist's estate
Munnings, Alfred James 1878–1959, *Studies of a Horse's Head (recto)*, donated by the artist, © the artist's estate
Munnings, Alfred James 1878–1959, *Study of a Horse (verso)*, donated by the artist, © the artist's estate
Munnings, Alfred James 1878–1959, *Studies of a Horse's Head (recto)*, donated by the artist, © the artist's estate
Munnings, Alfred James 1878–1959, *Study of a Bay Horse (verso)*, donated by the artist, © the artist's estate
Munnings, Alfred James 1878–1959, *Studies of a Huntsman and His Horse and of Lady Munnings*, donated by the artist, © the artist's estate
Munnings, Alfred James 1878–1959, *Studies of a Jockey Wearing Green*, donated by the artist, © the artist's estate
Munnings, Alfred James 1878–1959, *Studies of a Man Clearing Snow*, donated by the artist, © the artist's estate
Munnings, Alfred James 1878–1959, *Studies of Exmoor Sheep, Withypool*, donated by the artist, © the artist's estate
Munnings, Alfred James 1878–1959, *Studies of Gladys Bawden*, donated by the artist, © the artist's estate
Munnings, Alfred James 1878–1959, *Studies of Men Standing*, donated by the artist, © the artist's estate
Munnings, Alfred James 1878–1959, *Studies of Riders by a Marquee*, donated by the artist, © the artist's estate
Munnings, Alfred James 1878–1959, *Study at Horse Guards' Barracks*, donated by the artist, © the artist's estate
Munnings, Alfred James 1878–1959, *Study at Horse Guards' Barracks*, donated by the artist, © the artist's estate
Munnings, Alfred James 1878–1959, *Study at Newmarket*, donated by the artist, © the artist's estate
Munnings, Alfred James 1878–1959, *Study for 'After the Race', the Grey Mare 'Magnolia'*, donated by the artist, © the artist's estate
Munnings, Alfred James 1878–1959, *Study for 'Coming up the Canter'*, donated by the artist, © the artist's estate
Munnings, Alfred James 1878–1959, *Study for 'Coronach'*, donated by the artist, © the artist's estate
Munnings, Alfred James 1878–1959, *Study for 'Edge of the Wood'*, donated by the artist, © the artist's estate
Munnings, Alfred James 1878–1959, *Study for 'George V on Jock at Sandringham'*, donated by the artist, © the artist's estate
Munnings, Alfred James 1878–1959, *Study for 'Going up the Canter'*, donated by the artist, © the artist's estate
Munnings, Alfred James 1878–1959, *Study for 'Happy Days'*, donated by the artist, © the artist's estate
Munnings, Alfred James 1878–1959, *Study for 'Lady Munnings Riding on Exmoor'*, donated by the artist, © the artist's estate
Munnings, Alfred James 1878–1959, *Study for 'Lady Munnings Riding on Exmoor'*, donated by the artist, © the artist's estate
Munnings, Alfred James 1878–1959, *Study for 'Miss Hancock' (recto)*, donated by the artist, © the artist's estate
Munnings, Alfred James 1878–1959, *Study of a Landscape (verso)*, donated by the artist, © the artist's estate
Munnings, Alfred James 1878–1959, *Study for 'Our Mutual Friend the Horse'*, donated by the artist, © the artist's estate
Munnings, Alfred James 1878–1959, *Study*, donated by the artist, © the artist's estate
Munnings, Alfred James 1878–1959, *Study for 'Our Mutual Friend the Horse'*, donated by the artist, © the artist's estate
Munnings, Alfred James 1878–1959, *Study for 'Our Mutual Friend the Horse', Lady Munnings on 'Rufus'*, donated by the artist, © the artist's estate
Munnings, Alfred James 1878–1959, *Study for 'Our Mutual Friend the Horse', Lady Munnings Riding Side-Saddle*, donated by the artist, © the artist's estate
Munnings, Alfred James 1878–1959, *Study for 'Start of a Steeplechase' (recto)*, donated by the artist, © the artist's estate
Munnings, Alfred James 1878–1959, *Further Studies of Horses (verso)*, donated by the artist, © the artist's estate
Munnings, Alfred James 1878–1959, *Study for 'Start of a Steeplechase'*, donated by the artist, © the artist's estate
Munnings, Alfred James 1878–1959, *Study for 'Starter's Orders'*, donated by the artist, © the artist's estate
Munnings, Alfred James 1878–1959, *Study for 'The Coronation'*, donated by the artist, © the artist's estate
Munnings, Alfred James 1878–1959, *Study for 'The Ford'*, donated by the artist, © the artist's estate
Munnings, Alfred James 1878–1959, *Study for 'The Haunted House'*, donated by the artist, © the artist's estate
Munnings, Alfred James 1878–1959, *Study for 'The Haunted House'*, donated by the artist, © the artist's estate
Munnings, Alfred James 1878–1959, *Study for 'The Haunted House'*, donated by the artist, © the artist's estate
Munnings, Alfred James 1878–1959, *Study for 'The Haunted House'*, donated by the artist, © the artist's estate
Munnings, Alfred James 1878–1959, *Study for 'The Haunted House'*, donated by the artist, © the artist's estate
Munnings, Alfred James 1878–1959, *Study for 'The Haunted House'*, donated by the artist, © the artist's estate
Munnings, Alfred James 1878–1959, *Study for 'The Start'*, donated by the artist, © the artist's estate
Munnings, Alfred James 1878–1959, *Study for 'The Start'*, donated by the artist, © the artist's estate
Munnings, Alfred James 1878–1959, *Study for 'The Start'*, donated by the artist, © the artist's estate
Munnings, Alfred James 1878–1959, *Study for 'The Start at Newmarket'*, donated by the artist, © the artist's estate
Munnings, Alfred James 1878–1959, *Study for 'The Unsaddling Enclosure, Epsom'*, donated by the artist, © the artist's estate
Munnings, Alfred James 1878–1959, *Study for 'The Unsaddling Enclosure, Epsom'*, donated by the artist, © the artist's estate
Munnings, Alfred James 1878–1959, *Study for 'The Unsaddling Enclosure, Epsom'*, donated by the artist, © the artist's estate
Munnings, Alfred James 1878–1959, *Study for 'The Unsaddling Enclosure, Epsom'*, donated by the artist, © the artist's estate
Munnings, Alfred James 1878–1959, *Study for 'The White Canoe'*, donated by the artist, © the artist's estate
Munnings, Alfred James 1878–1959, *Study for 'The White Canoe'*, donated by the artist, © the artist's estate
Munnings, Alfred James 1878–1959, *Study for 'The White Canoe'*, donated by the artist, © the artist's estate
Munnings, Alfred James 1878–1959, *Study for 'The White Canoe'*, donated by the artist, © the artist's estate
Munnings, Alfred James 1878–1959, *Study for 'The White Canoe'*, donated by the artist, © the artist's

estate
Munnings, Alfred James 1878–1959, *Study for 'Under Starter's Orders'*, donated by the artist, © the artist's estate
Munnings, Alfred James 1878–1959, *Study for 'Under Starter's Orders'*, donated by the artist, © the artist's estate
Munnings, Alfred James 1878–1959, *Study for 'Under Starter's Orders'*, donated by the artist, © the artist's estate
Munnings, Alfred James 1878–1959, *Study of a Barge on the Stour at Dedham in Snow*, donated by the artist, © the artist's estate
Munnings, Alfred James 1878–1959, *Study of a Bay Filly in a Newmarket Yard*, donated by the artist, © the artist's estate
Munnings, Alfred James 1878–1959, *Study of a Bay Horse, 'Master', Bred by the Artist at Dedham*, donated by the artist, © the artist's estate
Munnings, Alfred James 1878–1959, *Study of a Bay Hunter*, donated by the artist, © the artist's estate
Munnings, Alfred James 1878–1959, *Study of a Bay Hunter*, donated by the artist, © the artist's estate
Munnings, Alfred James 1878–1959, *Study of a Bay Racehorse*, donated by the artist, © the artist's estate
Munnings, Alfred James 1878–1959, *Study of a Bay Racehorse*, donated by the artist, © the artist's estate
Munnings, Alfred James 1878–1959, *Study of a Bay Racehorse*, donated by the artist, © the artist's estate
Munnings, Alfred James 1878–1959, *Study of a Black and White Greyhound*, donated by the artist, © the artist's estate
Munnings, Alfred James 1878–1959, *Study of a Boy Exercising a Racehorse*, donated by the artist, © the artist's estate
Munnings, Alfred James 1878–1959, *Study of a Chaser*, donated by the artist, © the artist's estate
Munnings, Alfred James 1878–1959, *Study of a Chestnut Horse*, donated by the artist, © the artist's estate
Munnings, Alfred James 1878–1959, *Study of a Chestnut Racehorse from the Back*, donated by the artist, © the artist's estate
Munnings, Alfred James 1878–1959, *Study of a Cow Grazing*, donated by the artist, © the artist's estate
Munnings, Alfred James 1878–1959, *Study of a Dog for Lady Munnings on Grey Hunter*, donated by the artist, © the artist's estate
Munnings, Alfred James 1878–1959, *Study of a Female Nude*, donated by the artist, © the artist's estate
Munnings, Alfred James 1878–1959, *Study of a Foxhound, 'Pytchley'*, donated by the artist, © the artist's estate
Munnings, Alfred James 1878–1959, *Study of a Grey Hunter*, donated by the artist, © the artist's estate
Munnings, Alfred James 1878–1959, *Study of a Grey Hunter*, donated by the artist, © the artist's estate
Munnings, Alfred James 1878–1959, *Study of a Grey Hunter in a Landscape*, donated by the artist, © the artist's estate
Munnings, Alfred James 1878–1959, *Study of a Groom*, donated by the artist, © the artist's estate
Munnings, Alfred James 1878–1959, *Study of a Horse*, donated by the artist, © the artist's estate
Munnings, Alfred James 1878–1959, *Study of a Horse and Jockey*, donated by the artist, © the artist's estate
Munnings, Alfred James 1878–1959, *Study of a Horse and Jockey*, donated by the artist, © the artist's estate
Munnings, Alfred James 1878–1959, *Study of a Horse and Jockey (recto)*, donated by the artist, © the artist's estate
Munnings, Alfred James 1878–1959, *A Landscape Study (verso)*, donated by the artist, © the artist's estate
Munnings, Alfred James 1878–1959, *Study of a Horse and Rider*, donated by the artist, © the artist's estate
Munnings, Alfred James 1878–1959, *Study of a Horse and Rider*, donated by the artist, © the artist's estate
Munnings, Alfred James 1878–1959, *Study of a Horse with Anatomical Parts (recto)*, donated by the artist, © the artist's estate
Munnings, Alfred James 1878–1959, *Studies of Horses' Limbs (verso)*, donated by the artist, © the artist's estate
Munnings, Alfred James 1878–1959, *Study of a Horse with Huntsman up*, donated by the artist, © the artist's estate
Munnings, Alfred James 1878–1959, *Study of a Hunter*, donated by the artist, © the artist's estate
Munnings, Alfred James 1878–1959, *Study of a Hunter*, donated by the artist, © the artist's estate
Munnings, Alfred James 1878–1959, *Study of a Hunter 'Rufus'*, donated by the artist, © the artist's estate
Munnings, Alfred James 1878–1959, *Study of a Hunter Mare (recto)*, donated by the artist, © the artist's estate
Munnings, Alfred James 1878–1959, *Study of Trees (verso)*, donated by the artist, © the artist's estate
Munnings, Alfred James 1878–1959, *Study of a Huntsman and a Bay Mare*, donated by the artist, © the artist's estate
Munnings, Alfred James 1878–1959, *Study of a Lad and a Two-Year-Old Racehorse*, donated by the artist, © the artist's estate
Munnings, Alfred James 1878–1959, *Study of a Lad on a Pony*, donated by the artist, © the artist's estate
Munnings, Alfred James 1878–1959, *Study of a Landscape at Sunset*, donated by the artist, © the artist's estate
Munnings, Alfred James 1878–1959, *Study of a Leaping Horse*, donated by the artist, © the artist's estate
Munnings, Alfred James 1878–1959, *Study of a Loose Horse*, donated by the artist, © the artist's estate
Munnings, Alfred James 1878–1959, *Study of a Paddock at Epsom*, donated by the artist, © the artist's estate
Munnings, Alfred James 1878–1959, *Study of a Parasol, possibly for 'The White Canoe'*, donated by the artist, © the artist's estate
Munnings, Alfred James 1878–1959, *Study of a Racehorse*, donated by the artist, © the artist's estate
Munnings, Alfred James 1878–1959, *Study of a Racehorse*, donated by the artist, © the artist's estate
Munnings, Alfred James 1878–1959, *Study of a Racehorse*, donated by the artist, © the artist's estate
Munnings, Alfred James 1878–1959, *Study of a Racehorse*, donated by the artist, © the artist's estate
Munnings, Alfred James 1878–1959, *Study of a Racehorse and Rider*, donated by the artist, © the artist's estate
Munnings, Alfred James 1878–1959, *Study of a Racehorse from the Back (recto)*, donated by the artist, © the artist's estate
Munnings, Alfred James 1878–1959, *Study (verso)*, donated by the artist, © the artist's estate
Munnings, Alfred James 1878–1959, *Study of a Racehorse in Training at George Lambton's Yard*, donated by the artist, © the artist's estate
Munnings, Alfred James 1878–1959, *Study of a Racehorse with a Lad up*, donated by the artist, © the artist's estate
Munnings, Alfred James 1878–1959, *Study of a Racehorse with a Stable Lad*, donated by the artist, © the artist's estate
Munnings, Alfred James 1878–1959, *Study of a Racehorse's Head*, donated by the artist, © the artist's estate
Munnings, Alfred James 1878–1959, *Study of a Red Setter*, donated by the artist, © the artist's estate
Munnings, Alfred James 1878–1959, *Study of a River Landscape*, donated by the artist, © the artist's estate
Munnings, Alfred James 1878–1959, *Study of a Ruined Building*, donated by the artist, © the artist's estate
Munnings, Alfred James 1878–1959, *Study of a Standing Male Nude, Julian's Atelier*, donated by the artist, © the artist's estate
Munnings, Alfred James 1878–1959, *Study of a White Bull*, donated by the artist, © the artist's estate
Munnings, Alfred James 1878–1959, *Study of a Wood (recto)*, donated by the artist, © the artist's estate
Munnings, Alfred James 1878–1959, *Study of a Wood (verso)*, donated by the artist, © the artist's estate
Munnings, Alfred James 1878–1959, *Study of an Exmoor Sheep*, donated by the artist, © the artist's estate
Munnings, Alfred James 1878–1959, *Study of an Oak Tree*, donated by the artist, © the artist's estate
Munnings, Alfred James 1878–1959, *Study of Blossom*, donated by the artist, © the artist's estate
Munnings, Alfred James 1878–1959, *Study of Blossoms, Cornwall*, donated by the artist, © the artist's estate
Munnings, Alfred James 1878–1959, *Study of Buildings and Newmarket Stables*, donated by the artist, © the artist's estate
Munnings, Alfred James 1878–1959, *Study of Cattle (recto)*, donated by the artist, © the artist's estate
Munnings, Alfred James 1878–1959, *Tree Study (verso)*, donated by the artist, © the artist's estate
Munnings, Alfred James 1878–1959, *Study of Cattle, Thorington Street, Stour Valley*, donated by the artist, © the artist's estate
Munnings, Alfred James 1878–1959, *Study of Elder Blossom*, donated by the artist, © the artist's estate
Munnings, Alfred James 1878–1959, *Study of Epsom Paddock*, donated by the artist, © the artist's estate
Munnings, Alfred James 1878–1959, *Study of Exmoor Ponies (recto)*, donated by the artist, © the artist's estate
Munnings, Alfred James 1878–1959, *Studies of Exmoor Ponies (verso)*, donated by the artist, © the artist's estate
Munnings, Alfred James 1878–1959, *Study of Exmoor Sheep*, donated by the artist, © the artist's estate
Munnings, Alfred James 1878–1959, *Study of Exmoor Sheep*, donated by the artist, © the artist's estate
Munnings, Alfred James 1878–1959, *Study of Figures at the Races*, donated by the artist, © the artist's estate
Munnings, Alfred James 1878–1959, *Study of Foliage*, donated by the artist, © the artist's estate
Munnings, Alfred James 1878–1959, *Study of Foxgloves*, donated by the artist, © the artist's estate
Munnings, Alfred James 1878–1959, *Study of Front Legs of a Horse*, donated by the artist, © the artist's estate
Munnings, Alfred James 1878–1959, *Study of Gipsy Caravans*, donated by the artist, © the artist's estate
Munnings, Alfred James 1878–1959, *Study of Heavy Horse*, donated by the artist, © the artist's estate
Munnings, Alfred James 1878–1959, *Study of HM the Queen for 'Aureole'*, donated by the artist, © the artist's estate
Munnings, Alfred James 1878–1959, *Study of Horse Guards' Barracks, Parade Ground*, donated by the artist, © the artist's estate
Munnings, Alfred James 1878–1959, *Study of Horses and Riders*, donated by the artist, © the artist's estate
Munnings, Alfred James 1878–1959, *Study of Horses in Kempton Paddock*, donated by the artist, © the artist's estate
Munnings, Alfred James 1878–1959, *Study of Isaac Bell*, donated by the artist, © the artist's estate
Munnings, Alfred James 1878–1959, *Study of J. B. Rank's Horse, 'Jock', Druids' Lodge*, donated by the artist, © the artist's estate
Munnings, Alfred James 1878–1959, *Study of J. B. Rank's Horse, 'Prince Regent', Druids' Lodge*, donated by the artist, © the artist's estate
Munnings, Alfred James 1878–1959, *Study of Lady Munnings for 'Our Mutual Friend the Horse'*, donated by the artist, © the artist's estate
Munnings, Alfred James 1878–1959, *Study of Lady Munnings Riding with Her Dogs on Exmoor*, donated by the artist, © the artist's estate
Munnings, Alfred James 1878–1959, *Study of Mr Lambton's Horse, 'Pricket'*, donated by the artist, on loan to the National Horseracing Museum, Newmarket, © the artist's estate
Munnings, Alfred James 1878–1959, *Study of Mrs Hugh Peel, Owner of 'Poethlyn', Winner of the Grand National, 1919*, donated by the artist, © the artist's estate
Munnings, Alfred James 1878–1959, *Study of Mrs Mark Stevens, 'Gipsy Life'*, donated by the artist, © the artist's estate
Munnings, Alfred James 1878–1959, *Study of One of Selfridge's Young Ladies, in a Pink Selfridge's Dress, for 'Does the Subject Matter?'*, donated by the artist, © the artist's estate
Munnings, Alfred James 1878–1959, *Study of Percy Whitaker on 'Silvo' (recto)*, donated by the artist,

© the artist's estate
Munnings, Alfred James 1878–1959, *A Portrait Study of the Duchess of Westminster (verso)*, donated by the artist, © the artist's estate
Munnings, Alfred James 1878–1959, *Study of Pigs*, donated by the artist, © the artist's estate
Munnings, Alfred James 1878–1959, *Study of Racehorses*, donated by the artist, © the artist's estate
Munnings, Alfred James 1878–1959, *Study of 'Rose', 'Wild Bird', 'Peggy' and 'Stockings'*, donated by the artist, © the artist's estate
Munnings, Alfred James 1878–1959, *Study of 'Rose', 'Wild Bird', 'Peggy' and 'Stockings'*, donated by the artist, © the artist's estate
Munnings, Alfred James 1878–1959, *Study of 'Rufus', a Chestnut Horse, Bought at Exmoor 1951, Bred in Ireland, 16 Years Old*, donated by the artist, © the artist's estate
Munnings, Alfred James 1878–1959, *Study of 'Rufus' for 'Our Mutual Friend the Horse'*, donated by the artist, © the artist's estate
Munnings, Alfred James 1878–1959, *Study of the Decorations in the Mall for the Coronation of George VI, 1937*, donated by the artist, © the artist's estate
Munnings, Alfred James 1878–1959, *Study of the Decorations in the Mall for the Coronation of George VI, 1937*, donated by the artist, © the artist's estate
Munnings, Alfred James 1878–1959, *Study of the Gold Coach in the Palace Yard*, donated by the artist, © the artist's estate
Munnings, Alfred James 1878–1959, *Study of the King's Filly, 'Sun Chariot', Beckhampton*, donated by the artist, © the artist's estate
Munnings, Alfred James 1878–1959, *Study of the Starting Post (recto)*, donated by the artist, © the artist's estate
Munnings, Alfred James 1878–1959, *A Sky Study (verso)*, donated by the artist, © the artist's estate
Munnings, Alfred James 1878–1959, *Study of Trees (recto)*, donated by the artist, © the artist's estate
Munnings, Alfred James 1878–1959, *Study of Trees (verso)*, donated by the artist, © the artist's estate
Munnings, Alfred James 1878–1959, *Study of Trees (recto)*, donated by the artist, © the artist's estate
Munnings, Alfred James 1878–1959, *Study of Willows (verso)*, donated by the artist, © the artist's estate
Munnings, Alfred James 1878–1959, *Study of Trees and Sky*, donated by the artist, © the artist's estate
Munnings, Alfred James 1878–1959, *Study on Exmoor*, donated by the artist, © the artist's estate
Munnings, Alfred James 1878–1959, *Suffolk Landscape with Farm Buildings*, donated by the artist, © the artist's estate
Munnings, Alfred James 1878–1959, *'Sun Worship', a Design for a Drop Cloth for the Chelsea Arts Ball*, donated by the artist, © the artist's estate
Munnings, Alfred James 1878–1959, *Sunset over a Harvest Field*, donated by the artist, © the artist's estate
Munnings, Alfred James 1878–1959, *The Barle at Withypool, Exmoor*, donated by the artist, © the artist's estate
Munnings, Alfred James 1878–1959, *The Barle near Brightworthy, Withypool, Exmoor*, donated by the artist, © the artist's estate
Munnings, Alfred James 1878–1959, *The Edge of the Wood*, on loan from Manchester City Art Galleries, © the artist's estate
Munnings, Alfred James 1878–1959, *The Epsom Stand*, donated by the artist, © the artist's estate
Munnings, Alfred James 1878–1959, *The Haunted Room, Painted at a Farmhouse on Exmoor*, donated by the artist, © the artist's estate
Munnings, Alfred James 1878–1959, *The Old Oak, Mistley Park*, donated by the artist, © the artist's estate
Munnings, Alfred James 1878–1959, *The Porter at 'The Rutland Arms', Newmarket*, donated by the artist, © the artist's estate
Munnings, Alfred James 1878–1959, *The Pyrenees and the Plain of Tarbes*, on loan from Ms Margaret Haunton, © the artist's estate
Munnings, Alfred James 1878–1959, *The Saddling Paddock*, donated by the artist, © the artist's estate
Munnings, Alfred James 1878–1959, *The Stour at Dedham*, donated by the artist, © the artist's estate
Munnings, Alfred James 1878–1959, *The Stour at Dedham*, donated by the artist, © the artist's estate
Munnings, Alfred James 1878–1959, *The Stour at Dedham, with a Man in a Boat*, donated by the artist, © the artist's estate
Munnings, Alfred James 1878–1959, *The Stour at Dedham with Barges*, donated by the artist, © the artist's estate
Munnings, Alfred James 1878–1959, *The Stour at Night, Dedham*, donated by the artist, © the artist's estate
Munnings, Alfred James 1878–1959, *The Unsaddling Enclosure, Epsom*, donated by the artist, © the artist's estate
Munnings, Alfred James 1878–1959, *The White Canoe on the Stour at Dedham*, donated by the artist, © the artist's estate
Munnings, Alfred James 1878–1959, *The White Canoe on the Stour at Flatford*, donated by the artist, © the artist's estate
Munnings, Alfred James 1878–1959, *The White Canoe, Two Young Ladies Reclining in a Canoe on the Stour at Flatford*, donated by the artist, © the artist's estate
Munnings, Alfred James 1878–1959, *Tree Study (recto)*, donated by the artist, © the artist's estate
Munnings, Alfred James 1878–1959, *Sky Study (verso)*, donated by the artist, © the artist's estate
Munnings, Alfred James 1878–1959, *Trees by a Field*, donated by the artist, © the artist's estate
Munnings, Alfred James 1878–1959, *Trees by a Field*, donated by the artist, © the artist's estate
Munnings, Alfred James 1878–1959, *Trees by a Landscape*, donated by the artist, © the artist's estate
Munnings, Alfred James 1878–1959, *Trees by the Edge of a Field*, donated by the artist, © the artist's estate
Munnings, Alfred James 1878–1959, *Trees by the Edge of a Field*, donated by the artist, © the artist's estate
Munnings, Alfred James 1878–1959, *Trees by the Edge of a Field*, donated by the artist, © the artist's estate
Munnings, Alfred James 1878–1959, *Trees by the Edge of a Field*, donated by the artist, © the artist's estate
Munnings, Alfred James 1878–1959, *Trees by the Edge of a Field (recto)*, donated by the artist, © the artist's estate
Munnings, Alfred James 1878–1959, *Study of a Horse and Bullocks Grazing (verso)*, donated by the artist, © the artist's estate
Munnings, Alfred James 1878–1959, *Trees by the Edge of a Field*, donated by the artist, © the artist's estate
Munnings, Alfred James 1878–1959, *Trees by the Edge of a Field*, donated by the artist, © the artist's estate
Munnings, Alfred James 1878–1959, *Trees by the Edge of a Field (recto)*, donated by the artist, © the artist's estate
Munnings, Alfred James 1878–1959, *Landscape Study (verso)*, donated by the artist, © the artist's estate
Munnings, Alfred James 1878–1959, *Trotting to the Start*, donated by the artist, © the artist's estate
Munnings, Alfred James 1878–1959, *Two Girls and a Dog*, donated by the artist, © the artist's estate
Munnings, Alfred James 1878–1959, *Two Lady Riders under an Evening Sky*, donated by the artist, © the artist's estate
Munnings, Alfred James 1878–1959, *Under Starter's Orders*, donated by the artist, © the artist's estate
Munnings, Alfred James 1878–1959, *Under Starter's Orders*, donated by the artist, © the artist's estate
Munnings, Alfred James 1878–1959, *Under Starter's Orders*, donated by the artist, © the artist's estate
Munnings, Alfred James 1878–1959, *Under Starter's Orders, Newmarket Start, Cries of 'No, No, Sir'*, donated by the artist, © the artist's estate
Munnings, Alfred James 1878–1959, *Unsaddling of a Bay Racehorse, Stanley Wooton Colours*, donated by the artist, © the artist's estate
Munnings, Alfred James 1878–1959, *View of Exmoor, a Rider in the Foreground*, donated by the artist, © the artist's estate
Munnings, Alfred James 1878–1959, *View of Exmoor with Stream*, donated by the artist, © the artist's estate
Munnings, Alfred James 1878–1959, *View with Tendring Hall, Suffolk (demolished in 1955)*, donated by the artist, © the artist's estate
Munnings, Alfred James 1878–1959, *Violet, My Wife, in the Garden*, donated by the artist, © the artist's estate
Munnings, Alfred James 1878–1959, *Wall and Gorse on Exmoor*, donated by the artist, © the artist's estate
Munnings, Alfred James 1878–1959, *Wall on Bradmoor, Withypool, Exmoor*, donated by the artist, © the artist's estate
Munnings, Alfred James 1878–1959, *Warren Hill, Newmarket*, donated by the artist, © the artist's estate
Munnings, Alfred James 1878–1959, *White Oxen, Baron Robert's Estate, Chantilly*, donated by the artist, © the artist's estate
Munnings, Alfred James 1878–1959, *Wide Landscape with Stacks*, donated by the artist, © the artist's estate
Munnings, Alfred James 1878–1959, *Winter at Withypool, Exmoor: A Winter Landscape, a Rider and Two Hounds in the Foreground*, donated by the artist, © the artist's estate
Munnings, Alfred James 1878–1959, *Winter, Castle House*, donated by the artist, © the artist's estate
Munnings, Alfred James 1878–1959, *Winter in Our Garden at Withypool, Exmoor*, donated by the artist, © the artist's estate
Munnings, Alfred James 1878–1959, *Withypool Hill, Exmoor*, donated by the artist, © the artist's estate
Munnings, Alfred James 1878–1959, *Withypool Hill, Exmoor*, donated by the artist, © the artist's estate
Munnings, Alfred James 1878–1959, *Withypool Hill, Exmoor*, donated by the artist, © the artist's estate
Munnings, Alfred James 1878–1959, *Withypool Hill, Exmoor(recto)*, donated by the artist, © the artist's estate
Munnings, Alfred James 1878–1959, *Withypool Hill, Exmoor (verso)*, donated by the artist, © the artist's estate
Munnings, Alfred James 1878–1959, *Withypool Hill, Exmoor (recto)*, donated by the artist, © the artist's estate
Munnings, Alfred James 1878–1959, *Landscape (verso)*, donated by the artist, © the artist's estate
Munnings, Alfred James 1878–1959, *Withypool Hill, Exmoor (recto)*, donated by the artist, © the artist's estate
Munnings, Alfred James 1878–1959, *Landscape Study (verso)*, donated by the artist, © the artist's estate
Munnings, Alfred James 1878–1959, *Withypool Hill, Exmoor, Sheep in the Foreground*, donated by the artist, © the artist's estate
Munnings, Alfred James 1878–1959, *Withypool Thaw, Exmoor*, donated by the artist, © the artist's estate
Nurse, Charles Baxter active 1895–1915, *Alfred Munnings*
unknown artist 19th C, *A Bay Hunter*
unknown artist 19th C, *Hounds*
unknown artist 19th C, *Shipwreck at Sunset*
unknown artist *Cows and a Horse Beneath a Tree*

The Nottage Maritime Institute

Adam, Edmond 1868–1938, *Yawl 'Jullanar'*
Fale, John *'Shamrock' and 'Columbia'*
Fale, John *'Valkyrie III', America's Cup Challenger, 1895*
Loos, Henry active 1871–1904, *Brig 'Viking'*
Moore, Barlow 1834–1897, *Cutter Yacht 'Moina'*, donated by Sir H. Wrey
Rogers, Stanley d.c.1961, *HMS Opportune', G80, 17th Destroyer Flotilla*, donated by Miss S. Lee-Barber
unknown artist *Waterside Scene*
unknown artist *Smacks CK328, CK86 and CK103*

University of Essex

Ayrton, Michael 1921–1975, *Seascape*, donated by Andrew Carnwath, © the artist's estate
Ayrton, Michael 1921–1975, *Tidal Landscape*, donated by Andrew Carnwath, © the artist's estate
Ayrton, Michael 1921–1975, *Naxos Marble*, donated by Andrew Carnwath, © the artist's estate

Ayrton, Michael 1921–1975, *Pale Sun Landscape*, donated by Andrew Carnwath, © the artist's estate
Barrett, Roderic 1920–2000, *Song and Dance*, donated by the artist, © the artist's estate
Chapman, George 1908–1993, *Children Going to School*, donated by Andrew Carnwath, © Nicholas Chapman
Crittall, Ariel b.1914, *Landscape near Riberac*, © the artist
Dodds, James Foster b.1957, *Solidarnosc*, donated by the artist, © the artist
Festing, Andrew b.1941, *Martin Best Harris*, © the artist
Festing, Andrew b.1941, *Sir Patrick Nairne*, © the artist
Middleditch, Edward 1923–1987, *Night Reflections*
Poole, David b.1931, *Sir Albert Sloman*, © the artist
Ramsay, Patricia 1886–1974, *Windowscape*, donated by Jim Ede, 1966, © the artist's estate
Spear, Ruskin (attributed to) 1911–1990, *Lord Butler*, © courtesy of the artist's estate/www.bridgeman.co.uk
Spender, John Humphrey 1910–2005, *Station Scene*, donated by Andrew Carnwath, © the Humphrey Spender Archive
Wallis, Alfred 1855–1942, *Harbour and Sailing Ship*, donated by Jim Ede, 1966, © DACS 2006
Wallis, Alfred 1855–1942, *Houses and Kilns*, donated by Jim Ede, 1966, © DACS 2006
Wallis, Alfred 1855–1942, *Ship*, donated by Jim Ede, 1966, © DACS 2006
Wallis, Alfred 1855–1942, *Ships in Harbour*, donated by Jim Ede, 1966, © DACS 2006
Wallis, Alfred 1855–1942, *St Michael's Mount Harbour*, donated by Jim Ede, 1966, © DACS 2006
Waterfield, Margaret Helen 1863–1953, *Giant Thistle*, donated by Andrew Carnwath
Wood, Christopher 1901–1930, *Mlle Bourgoint*, donated by Jim Ede, 1966
Wood, Christopher 1901–1930, *Harbour in Hills*, donated by Jim Ede, 1966

University of Essex, Collection of Latin American Art

Aldunate, Carmen b.1940, *Dream*, on loan from Ruby Reid Thompson, © University of Essex Collection of Latin American Art
Alisio, Artemio 1942–2006, *The Messenger (Popol Vuh)*, donated by the artist, 1995, © University of Essex Collection of Latin American Art
Alisio, Artemio 1942–2006, *Yesterdays*, donated by the artist, 1995, © University of Essex Collection of Latin American Art
Amaral, Antonio Henrique b.1935, *Chromo and Time II*, donated by the artist, 1996, © University of Essex Collection of Latin American Art
Arango, Ramiro b.1946, *Assumption with the Artist*, donated by the artist, 2000, © University of Essex Collection of Latin American Art
Arango, Ramiro b.1946, *The Shroud (Veronica's Veil?)*, donated by the artist, 2000, © University of Essex Collection of Latin American Art
Arete b.1940, *The Goddess of Fish*, donated by the artist, 1996, © University of Essex Collection of Latin American Art
Bengochea, Miguel Angel b.1945, *Untitled*, donated by Marcos Curi, 1993, © University of Essex Collection of Latin American Art
Borda, Osvaldo *Special Treatment*, donated by Museo de Arte Contemporáneo, Buenos Aires, 1997, © University of Essex Collection of Latin American Art
Buitrago, Guillermo b.1905, *Untitled*, donated by Jacqueline Rothschild, 1996, © University of Essex Collection of Latin American Art
Cáceres, Juan Carlos b.1936, *From the Series 'The French Revolution'*, donated by Albino Dieguez Videla, 1995, © University of Essex Collection of Latin American Art
Cambre, Juan José b.1948, *Untitled*, donated by the artist, 1995, © University of Essex Collection of Latin American Art
Celis, Pérez b.1939, *Yellow Dancing*, donated by the artist, 1990, © University of Essex Collection of Latin American Art
César, Julio *Untitled*, donated by Martin Gree, 1995, © University of Essex Collection of Latin American Art
Chab, Víctor b.1930, *A Thousand Tears (Fourth Song Suite)*, donated by the artist, 1994, © University of Essex Collection of Latin American Art
Chab, Víctor b.1930, *Almond Nest (Fourth Song Suite)*, donated by the artist, 1997, © University of Essex Collection of Latin American Art
Chab, Víctor b.1930, *Untitled*, donated by the artist, 1994, © University of Essex Collection of Latin American Art
Chaile, Julio b.1964, *Figure 1*, donated by Josefina Durini, 1993, © University of Essex Collection of Latin American Art
Chaile, Julio b.1964, *Figure 2*, donated by Josefina Durini, 1993, © University of Essex Collection of Latin American Art
Chamorro, Rosario *Shell*, donated by the artist, 1995, © University of Essex Collection of Latin American Art
Costigliolo, José Pedro 1902–1985, *From the Series 'Squares and Rectangles'*, donated by Maria Freire, 1994, © University of Essex Collection of Latin American Art
Costigliolo, José Pedro 1902–1985, *From the Series 'Squares and Rectangles'*, donated by Maria Freire, 1994, © University of Essex Collection of Latin American Art
Costigliolo, José Pedro 1902–1985, *Rectangles and Squares CLXIV*, donated by Maria Freire, 1994, © University of Essex Collection of Latin American Art
Costigliolo, José Pedro 1902–1985, *From the Series 'Triangles', Triangles 102*, donated by Maria Freire, 1995, © University of Essex Collection of Latin American Art
Crousillat, Paloma b.1980, *Chair in Taquile, Peru*, donated by the artist, 2002, © University of Essex Collection of Latin American Art
D'Arienzo, Miguel Angel b.1950, *Old Menina*, donated by Josefina Durini, 1993, © University of Essex Collection of Latin American Art
D'Arienzo, Miguel Angel b.1950, *The Mermaid*, donated by Josefina Durini, 1993, © University of Essex Collection of Latin American Art
Del Rio, Juan *Untitled*, donated by Guillermo Whitelow, 1996, © University of Essex Collection of Latin American Art
Delpino, Sara *Entrance*, donated by the artist, 1995, © University of Essex Collection of Latin American Art
Duclos, Arturo b.1959, *Still Life*, donated by the artist, 1995, © University of Essex Collection of Latin American Art
Eckell, Ana b.1947, *Untitled*, donated by the artist, 1997, © University of Essex Collection of Latin American Art
Elza O. S. b.1928, *Untitled*, on loan from Ruby Reid Thompson, © University of Essex Collection of Latin American Art
Franco, Siron b.1947, *Yesterday*, donated by Martin Gree, 1994, © University of Essex Collection of Latin American Art
Franco, Siron b.1947, *A Suspicious Story*, on loan from Michael and Simone Naify, © University of Essex Collection of Latin American Art
Franco, Siron b.1947, *Memória*, donated by Charles Cosac, 1993, © University of Essex Collection of Latin American Art
Freire, Maria b.1917, *Capricorn II*, donated by the artist, 1994, © University of Essex Collection of Latin American Art
Freire, Maria b.1917, *Córdoba*, donated by the artist, 1994, © University of Essex Collection of Latin American Art
Freire, Maria b.1917, *Variant*, donated by the artist, 1994, © University of Essex Collection of Latin American Art
Freire, Maria b.1917, *South America*, donated by the artist, 1994, © University of Essex Collection of Latin American Art
Freire, Maria b.1917, *The Gold of the Tigers No.6*, donated by the artist, 1995, © University of Essex Collection of Latin American Art
Gandía, Vicente b.1935, *White Porcelain and Blue Vase*, donated by the artist, 2000, © University of Essex Collection of Latin American Art
Gárgano, Germán *Turmoil*, donated by the artist, 1997, © University of Essex Collection of Latin American Art
Gerson *Untitled*, on loan from Ruby Reid Thompson, © University of Essex Collection of Latin American Art
Kozel, Ana b.1937, *Formation of the Universe*, donated by the artist, 1997, © University of Essex Collection of Latin American Art
Kravetz, Carlos b.1951, *The Power of the Myth, Eva*, donated by the artist, 1997, © University of Essex Collection of Latin American Art
Kuitca, Guillermo b.1961, *Idea of a Passion*, on loan from Michael and Simone Naify, © University of Essex Collection of Latin American Art
Laurencich, Diana b.1963, *Enclosure*, donated by Roque de Bonis, © University of Essex Collection of Latin American Art
Leão, Maria Luiza b.1932, *Sad Island (Angra)*, donated by the artist, 1997, © University of Essex Collection of Latin American Art
Linás, Guido 1923–2005, *Untitled*, donated by Ruta Correa, 1996, © University of Essex Collection of Latin American Art
Máro, Antonio b.1928, *Profile*, donated by Latin American Arts Association, 1993, © University of Essex Collection of Latin American Art
Martínez, Raúl 1927–1995, *Repetitions with a Flag*, on loan from Miriam Glucksmann, © University of Essex Collection of Latin American Art
Matta, Roberto 1911–2002, *Composition in Magenta: The End of Everything*, on loan from Michael and Simone Naify, © University of Essex Collection of Latin American Art
Mazuera, Diego b.1950, *Stop There!*, donated by the artist, 2002, © University of Essex Collection of Latin American Art
Melcon, Miguel b.1940, *Untitled*, donated by Museo de Arte Contemporáneo, Buenos Aires, 1997, © University of Essex Collection of Latin American Art
Melé, Juan b.1923, *R.643*, donated by the artist, 1999, © University of Essex Collection of Latin American Art
Montes, Fernando b.1930, *Shadow of the Moon*, donated by the artist, 1999, © University of Essex Collection of Latin American Art
Nassar, Emmanuel b.1949, *Untitled*, donated by Siron Franco, 1995, © University of Essex Collection of Latin American Art
Paternosto, César b.1931, *Marginality and Displacement No.7*, donated by the artist, 2003, © University of Essex Collection of Latin American Art
Paz, Julio b.1939, *Night Lilies*, donated by the Museo de Arte Contemporáneo, Buenos Aires, 1993, © University of Essex Collection of Latin American Art
Pereda, Teresa b.1956, *Chods, Colour of Gold*, donated by Josefina Durini, 1998, © University of Essex Collection of Latin American Art
Piña, Raúl b.1961, *Double Eclipse of the Moon*, donated by the artist, 1998, © University of Essex Collection of Latin American Art
Rodrigues, Glauco Otavio Castilho 1929–2004, *Saint Sebastian in June*, donated by Gottfried Stuetzer Jr, 1995, © University of Essex Collection of Latin American Art
Sánchez, Beatriz *From the Wild and Magnificent Light*, donated by Josefina Durini, 1993, © University of Essex Collection of Latin American Art
Sanín, Fanny b.1938, *Acrylic No.1*, donated by the artist, 2003, © University of Essex Collection of Latin American Art
Scheihing, Vivian b.1947, *Tidal Wave*, donated by Ruta Correa, © University of Essex Collection of Latin American Art
Schnell, Marcellus *Magic Lantern*, donated by the artist, 1997, © University of Essex Collection of Latin American Art
Senise, Daniel b.1955, *Three Paths*, donated by the artist, 1996, © University of Essex Collection of Latin American Art
Soto-Diaz, Mariángeles b.1970, *On Sugar, Spice and Other Delectable Abstractions No.018*, donated by the artist, 2004, © University of Essex Collection of Latin American Art
Szyszlo, Fernando de b.1925, *Room No.23*, donated by the artist, 1995, © University of Essex Collection of Latin American Art
Tiíta b.1929, *The Procession of Iemanja's Feast Day*, donated by the artist, 1998, © University of Essex Collection of Latin American Art
Trevisanello, Mauro *The Indian Town*, donated by Museo de Arte Contemporáneo, Buenos Aires, 1996, © University of Essex Collection of Latin American Art
Vázquez Martín, Juan Teódulo b.1941, *'Windows' Series No.2*, donated by Raymond Bowen, 1996, © University of Essex Collection of Latin American Art
Waissman, Andres b.1955, *Still Feel Like Dancing*, donated by Museo de Arte Contemporáneo, Buenos Aires, 1997, © University of Essex Collection of Latin American Art
Zambrano, Elsa b.1951, *Still Life*, donated by the artist, 2002, © University of Essex Collection of Latin American Art

Zapisek, Adriana b.1949, *Gema X Piscis*, donated by Josefina Durini, 1993, © University of Essex Collection of Latin American Art
Zílio, Carlos b.1944, *794AO/94–10 (from the series '794AO')*, donated by Paula Terra Neale, 1995, © University of Essex Collection of Latin American Art
Zuik, Martha *Tree*, donated by Museo de Arte Contemporáneo, Buenos Aires, 1996, © University of Essex Collection of Latin American Art

Victor Batte-Lay Trust

Atkinson, Anthony b.1929, *Norfolk Coast*, gift from Marion Bentham, 1984, © the artist
Barrett, Roderic 1920–2000, *Round Table and Three Chairs*, gift from Colin Benham, 1987, © the artist's estate
Baynes, Keith 1887–1977, *Hôtel du Portugal*
Baynes, Keith 1887–1977, *Varengeville-sur-Mer, 1938*
Becker, Harry 1865–1928, *Landscape, Suffolk Meadows*, gift from Miss Lazell, 1959
Bevan, Robert Polhill 1865–1925, *Portrait of a Man Wearing Green Shirt and Tie against Striped Wall (Dickie)*
Cronyn, Hugh Verschoyle 1905–1996, *Anna at Table*, gift from Marion Bentham, 1984
Daniell, Frank 1866–1932, *Victor Batte-Lay*, bequeathed by Victor Batte-Lay, 1955
Dickey, Edward Montague O'Rourke 1894–1977, *Kentish Town Railway Station*, gift from the National Art Collections Fund, 1968
Farrell, Anthony b.1945, *Summer at Night*, purchased, 1983, © the artist
Hambling, Maggi b.1945, *Encounter (from the 'Paintings of Max Wall' series)*, purchased from a National Portrait Gallery exhibition with the assistance of the National Art Collections Fund and the Contemporary Art Society, © the artist
Mellis, Margaret b.1914, *Lilac Yellow*, gift from the Contemporary Art Society, 1979, © Margaret Mellis estate
O'Connor, John Scorror 1913–2004, *Lingley's Field*, © the artist's estate
St George, Sylvia 1881–1950, *Colchester from the North*, gift from Miss I. M. St George Brett, 1983
Vine, John c.1809–1867, *Black Bull*, purchased from Mrs N. Francis, 1961
Vine, John c.1809–1867, *Cockerel*, purchased from Mrs N. Francis, 1961
Vine, John c.1809–1867, *Cock and Two Hens*, purchased from Mrs N. Francis, 1961
Wright, Joseph of Derby (after) 1734–1797, *Boys Blowing up a Bladder*, gift from John Bensusan-Butt, 1958

Great Dunmow Town Council

Ogborne, David c.1700–1768, *The Flitch Procession Moving away from Little Dunmow Priory Church*, purchased by Great Dunmow Parish Council, 1950

Earls Colne Parish Council

Daniell, Frank 1866–1932, *Reuben Hunt of Earls Colne, Justice of the Peace for Essex, Chairman of the Governors of the Earls Colne Grammar School*, presented to Earls Colne Grammar School, 1975?
Miller, William Edwards active 1872–1929, *John Taylor, MRCS*

North Weald Airfield Museum

Cortez, J. *The Immortal 'Spitfire', 1940*, gift, 2004
Dungey, A. E. *Beaufighter v He111 at Night*, gift, 2004
Eldridge, Brian *'Spitfire' 331 Squadron, Royal Norwegian Air Force (Dieppe, 1942)*, gift, 2004
Garland, Harold active 1986–1988, *Miles Magister G-AKKR*, gift, 2005
Reeve, Edward. P. active 1995–1998, *Meteor WK722*, acquired, 2002, on loan from the artist
Reeve, Edward. P. active 1995–1998, *Vampire VT796*, acquired, 2002, on loan from the artist
Reeve, Edward. P. active 1995–1998, *Hawker Hurricane, 71 Squadron RAF, 'First from the Eyries', No.1 American Eagle Squadron*
Siggins, James *Blenheim H*ZK*, gift, 1991
Siggins, James *Hurricane GN*F*, gift, 1991
Siggins, James (attributed to) *Hurricane DT*A*, gift, 1991
Siggins, James (attributed to) *Hurricane DZ*B*, gift, 1991
Siggins, James (attributed to) *Hurricane XR*K*, gift, 1991
Summers, Ken *North Weald Below, Two Vampires*, gift, 2002
Worrow, Alfred active 1993–1998, *BE2 4112 Attack on Airship L31 at Night*, gift, 2002
Worrow, Alfred active 1993–1998, *Heinkel Attack on North Weald Airfield*, acquired, 2004

Frinton & Walton Town Council

Moore, A. Harvey d.1905, *The Old Water Mill, Walton-on-the-Naze*
unknown artist 19th C, *The Old Parish Church of St Mary the Virgin, Frinton-on-Sea*, bequeathed to the Urban District Council of Frinton and Walton by Mr John Ashworth Jones, JP, of Walton-on-the-Naze, 1938

Thurrock Museum

Ashwell, C. F. *Landscape (possibly West Thurrock)*
Ashwell, C. F. *Little Thurrock Rectory*
British (English) School *Tilbury Fort and Ferry*, purchased from the Parker Gallery
Ford, Marcus b.1914, *The Harrow Inn, Bulphan*
Green, F. *Training Ship 'TS Exmouth' (moored off Grays Beach, 1876–1939)*, donated
Green, F. *Paddle Steamer 'La Marguerite'*, donated by Sherwin Clare, 1992
Halle, Paul George *A Passing Shower, Elms*, purchased
Head, R. *Tunnel Locomotive*, acquired, 1971
MacDougall, Ian *Sailing Barge 'Sara'*, on loan from F. T. Everard & Sons
Mason, Frank Henry 1876–1965, *Sailing Barge 'Veronica' Winning the Medway Race, 1957*, on loan from F. T. Everard & Sons
Mason, Frank Henry 1876–1965, *'Frederick T. Everard' Passing Spurn Head, River Humber*, on loan from F. T. Everard & Sons
Roddam, A. E. *Moore Place, Stanford-le-Hope*
Russell, Alfred *Portrait of an Old Gentleman*
Russell, Alfred *Titan Pit, Grays*
Shiner, Audrey E. 1900–c.1980, *George Henry Silverwood, BA, LLB, Headmaster of Palmer's School (1893–1918)*
Spencer, Richard Barnett d.1874, *Sea Battle*
Spencer, Richard Barnett d.1874, *Sea Battle*
Stanfield, Clarkson (after) 1793–1867, *Wind against Tide, the Thames at Tilbury Fort*
unknown artist 18th C, *Belhus House and Park, c.1710 (demolished in 1957)*, on loan from Essex County Council
unknown artist 19th C, *Portrait of a Gentleman*
unknown artist *Thames Sailing Barge 'Majestic, 1897' (Goldsmith and Cory of Gravesend)*
unknown artist *Queen Elizabeth, Tilbury, 1588*, on loan from Edgington Tent Manufacturers
Van der Weegen, F. active 1918–1928, *Allotments*
Van der Weegen, F. active 1918–1928, *Globe Pit, Grays*
Whitmore, Francis 1872–1962, *Admiral of the Fleet, 12th Earl of Cork and Orrery, GCB, GCVO*
Whitmore, Francis 1872–1962, *Captain Sir Ion Hamilton-Benn, 1st Bt, CB, DSO, TD*

Birdbrook Community House

Gilbert, Stanley Victor b.1915, *Birdbrook Church from the North*, © the artist
Gilbert, Stanley Victor b.1915, *View from the Back of Birdbrook Hall*, © the artist
Gilbert, Stanley Victor b.1915, *The Stables at Moyns Park*, © the artist
Gilbert, Stanley Victor b.1915, *View from Birdbrook Hall Looking North*, © the artist
Norman, Hope *Water Lilies*
unknown artist *Woodland*

Halstead Town Council

de Maistre, Leroy Leveson Laurent Joseph 1894–1968, *Portrait of a Man Reading a Paper*, © the artist's estate
Despature, A. *Ferme du Bocquiau, Haubourdin*, on loan from Halstead Twinning Association, on display at Halstead Library
Elliott, Eric *Bygone Halstead*
Lepez, André *Le pont d'Haubourdin*, on loan from Halstead Twinning Association, on display at Halstead Library
Root, Malcolm b.1950, *Market Day in Halstead*, commissioned by Halstead Town Council for the Millennium, on display at Halstead Library, © the artist

Harlow Art Trust

Ruszkowski, Zdzislaw 1907–1991, *Sunday Evening in Ecija (Andalucia)*
Ruszkowski, Zdzislaw 1907–1991, *A Spanish Landscape by Moonlight*
Sorrell, Alan 1904–1974, *Panel from the Gallery Deck Bar of the Festival of Britain Ship 'Campania' Featuring a Belfast Herring Boat and a Thames Sailing Barge*, acquired from the Festival of Britain, 1951, © the artist's estate
Sorrell, Alan 1904–1974, *Panel from the Gallery Deck Bar of the Festival of Britain Ship 'Campania' Featuring a Deal Galley, an Orkeney Yole, a Brixham Trawler, a Shetland Ness Yole and a Mevagissey Lugger*, acquired from the Festival of Britain, 1951, © the artist's estate
Sorrell, Alan 1904–1974, *Panel from the Gallery Deck Bar of the Festival of Britain Ship 'Campania' Featuring a Norfolk Wherry and a Falmouth Quay Punt*, acquired from the Festival of Britain, 1951, © the artist's estate
Sorrell, Alan 1904–1974, *Panel from the Gallery Deck Bar of the Festival of Britain Ship 'Campania' Featuring a Wick Scaffie, a Harwich Bawley and a Manx*, acquired from the Festival of Britain, 1951, © the artist's estate
Sorrell, Alan 1904–1974, *Panel from the Gallery Deck Bar of the Festival of Britain Ship 'Campania' Featuring a Yorkshire Coble, an Aberdeen Fifie, a Morecombe Bay Prawner, a Sheringham Crab Boat and a Yarmouth Drifter*, acquired from the Festival of Britain, 1951, © the artist's estate

Harlow Council

Jones, Dan *We will, we will, we will be free!*
Verlon, André 1917–1993, *Barrage*, © DACS 2006

Harwich Town Council

Cotman, Frederick George 1850–1920, *Alderman William Groom, KD, CC, JP, VR*, presented by his fellow townsmen in recognition of his valued public services to his native borough, 1903
Owen, William 1769–1825, *Nicholas Vansittart, 1st Baron Bexley, High Steward and MP for Harwich, Chancellor of the Exchequer (1766–1851)*
unknown artist *The Mill, Beacon Hill, Harwich*
unknown artist *Alderman John Henry Vaux, JP*
unknown artist *Alderman John Hopkins (1750–1828)*
unknown artist *Charles II (1630–1685)*, acquired, 1682
Werner *Richard Coombe Abdy, High Steward of Harwich*

South Essex Partnership NHS Foundation Trust

Dodds, James Foster b.1957, *Maldon Shipwrights*, © the artist

Leigh Heritage Centre

Baxter, James *Early Morning, Leigh Creek*, gift
Beard, Thelma *Juniper's Cottage*, gift
Fears, Constance 1895–late 1980s, *Low Tide at Leigh-on-Sea*, gift
Saunders, Marion (attributed to) *Joe Juniper*, gift
Selman, Frank *Leigh Creek*, gift

Combined Military Services Museum

unknown artist *Charles Terry (Private 2882, Portsmouth Royal Marine Light Infantry)*, purchased from Keith Turner (dealer), Hornchurch, 1995

Maldon District Museum

Fanner, J. *Coasting Barge, 'Record Reign'*, accessioned, 1997, on loan
Hollingdale, Horatio R. active 1880–1899, *Beeleigh Abbey before Restoration*

Miller, H. *Beeleigh Weir*
Parry, D. H. *Back of Beeleigh Abbey from the Stable Door before Restoration*
Parry, D. H. *Beeleigh Abbey before Restoration*
Parry, D. H. *Front of Beeleigh Abbey before Restoration*
Parry, D. H. *Pentice Chamber, Beeleigh Abbey before Restoration*
Prime, June 1936–2001, *The Chequers, High Street (now Barclays Bank)*, presented by P. J. Lacey, 1989, © the artist's estate
Prior, Joe H. *William Raven, Sail-Maker (1878–1959)*, on loan from a private individual
Spong, Caroline b.1939, *Crossing Keeper's House before Demolition in 1978*, presented by P. J. Lacey, 1998, © the artist
Spong, Caroline b.1939, *Maldon East Signal Box before Demolition in 1982*, presented by P. J. Lacey, 1998, © the artist
Tait, Charles Grigg 1915–1995, *St Peter's Tower and Rear High Street from 'Chase' to Longfields*, purchased, 1976, © the artist's estate
unknown artist *Horatio Gates (1728–1806), American General*

Maldon Library

Tait, Charles Grigg 1915–1995, *Boats on the River Blackwater*, donated by the Maldon Art Society, © the artist's estate

Maldon Town Council

Abberley, Tessie b.1883, *St Giles Leper Hospital, Spital Road, Maldon (founded by Henry II)*, donated by Miss Abberley, daughter of the artist, 1995
Peake, Robert c.1551–1619, *Portrait of a Lady (said to be Elizabeth Throckmorton (d.c.1647), Queen Elizabeth's Maid of Honour and Wife of Sir Walter Raleigh)*
unknown artist 18th C, *George I (1714–1727)*
unknown artist 18th C, *George III (1760–1820)*
unknown artist *Queen Anne (1665–1714)*
unknown artist *Thomas Plume, DD (1630–1704)*

Thomas Plume's Library

Dyck, Anthony van (copy after) 1599–1641, *William Laud (1573–1645), Archbishop of Canterbury*, bequeathed by Thomas Plume, 1704
Largillière, Nicolas de (copy after) 1656–1746, *James II (1633–1701)*, bequeathed by Thomas Plume, 1704
Memling, Hans (follower of) 1430–1440–1494, *Salvator Mundi*, bequeathed by Thomas Plume, 1704
Mor, Antonis (copy after) 1512–1516–c.1576, *Mary I (1516–1558)*, bequeathed by Thomas Plume, 1704
Mytens, Daniel I (circle of) c.1590–before 1648, *Charles I (1600–1649)*, bequeathed by Thomas Plume, 1704
Somer, Bernaert van (follower of) before 1575–1612, *James I (1566–1625)*, bequeathed by Thomas Plume, 1704
unknown artist *John Whitgift (1530?–1604), Archbishop of Canterbury*, bequeathed by Thomas Plume, 1704
unknown artist early 17th C, *Edward IV (1442–1483)*, bequeathed by Thomas Plume, 1704
unknown artist early 17th C, *Edward VI (1537–1553)*, bequeathed by Thomas Plume, 1704
unknown artist early 17th C, *Richard III (1452–1485)*, bequeathed by Thomas Plume, 1704
unknown artist late 19th C, *Reverend Robert P. Crane, Librarian to Dr Plume's Library*, presented by Mr Crane's third daughter, Miss Caroline Sarah Crane, 1891
unknown artist *Dr James Ussher (1581–1656), Archbishop of Armagh*, bequeathed by Thomas Plume, 1704
unknown artist *Five Wise Virgins*
unknown artist *Mrs Margaret Oakley, Mother-in-Law of John Ray, the Botanist*, purchased by the Trustees, 1860
unknown artist *Unknown Divine (once believed to be John Ray, the botanist)*, bequeathed by Thomas Plume, 1704
Wright, John Michael (copy after) 1617–1694, *Brian Duppa (1588–1662), Dean of Christ Church, Oxford*, bequeathed by Thomas Plume, 1704

The Constable Trust

Constable, John 1776–1837, *The Ascension*, purchased, 1999, on loan to Church of St Mary the Virgin, Dedham

Ongar War Memorial Hospital

Bunton, A. C. *River Exe, Bickleigh, Devon*
Furze, Mary *River Scene*, donated by the artist
Reeder, Vera *Blackmore Village*
Rose, George 1882–1955, *The Ballroom at Budworth Hall, Ongar*
unknown artist *Ongar War Memorial Hospital*
White, F. D. *Greensted Church*

English Heritage, Audley End House

Asselyn, Jan after 1610–1652, *A Mediterranean Coastal View with Shipping and Mariners by a Fort*, purchased from Johnny Van Haeften, 2002
Brueghel, Jan the younger 1601–1678, *Flower Piece*, purchased by private treaty sale, 1998
Cipriani, Giovanni Battista 1727–1785, *Panel from the Robert Adam Library Representing Religion and the Arts*, presented by Jane, Lady Braybrooke, 1839, on loan from Saffron Walden Museum
Cipriani, Giovanni Battista 1727–1785, *Panel from the Robert Adam Library Representing Science and Learning*, presented by Jane, Lady Braybrooke, 1839, on loan from Saffron Walden Museum
Claesz., Pieter 1597/1598–1660, *Breakfast Piece*, purchased at Christie's, 1993
Dahl, Michael I (attributed to) 1656/1659–1743, *Elizabeth Grey (later Countess of Portsmouth)*, purchased by private treaty sale, 1986
Dobson, William (after) 1611–1646, *Sir Charles Lucas (also identified as Colonel Richard Neville of Billingbear)*, purchased at Sotheby's Sale of Contents of Tyningham, lot 540, 1987
Holbein, Hans the younger 1497/1498–1543, *Unknown Gentleman*, purchased by private treaty sale, 1998
Jervas, Charles (attributed to) c.1675–1739, *Elizabeth, Countess of Portsmouth*, purchased, 1971
Niemann, Edmund John 1813–1876, *View of Billingbear, Berkshire*, purchased by private treaty sale, 1986
Rebecca, Biagio 1735–1808, *Margaret Audley, Duchess of Norfolk*, purchased, 1971
Rebecca, Biagio 1735–1808, *Sir John Griffin Griffin, 4th Lord Howard de Walden*, purchased, 1971
Rebecca, Biagio 1735–1808, *The Honourable Anne Griffin, Mrs Whitwell*, purchased, 1971
Rebecca, Biagio 1735–1808, *Theophilus Howard, 2nd Earl of Suffolk*, purchased, 1971
Rebecca, Biagio 1735–1808, *Thomas Audley, Lord Audley*, purchased, 1971
Rebecca, Biagio 1735–1808, *Thomas Howard, 1st Earl of Suffolk*, purchased, 1971
Rebecca, Biagio 1735–1808, *Thomas Howard, 4th Duke of Norfolk*, purchased, 1971
Rebecca, Biagio 1735–1808, *King Henry VIII (1491–1547)*, purchased, 1971
Rebecca, Biagio 1735–1808, *Queen Elizabeth I (1533–1603)*, purchased, 1971
Rebecca, Biagio 1735–1808, *Chimney Board*, purchased by private treaty sale, 1986
Rebecca, Biagio 1735–1808, *Chimney Board*, purchased by private treaty sale, 1986
Rebecca, Biagio 1735–1808, *Chimney Board*, purchased by private treaty sale, 1986
Rebecca, Biagio 1735–1808, *Chimney Board*, purchased by private treaty sale, 1986
Seemann, Enoch the younger 1694–1744, *Edward Griffin, 1st Lord Griffin*, purchased, 1971
Seemann, Enoch the younger 1694–1744, *James Griffin, 2nd Lord Griffin*, purchased, 1971
Seemann, Enoch the younger 1694–1744, *James Howard, 3rd Earl of Suffolk*, purchased, 1971
Seemann, Enoch the younger 1694–1744, *Lady Susannah Rich, Countess of Suffolk*, purchased, 1971
Tomkins, William c.1732–1792, *Audley End and Ring Hill Temple*, purchased, 1971
Tomkins, William c.1732–1792, *Audley End from the South West*, purchased, 1971
Tomkins, William c.1732–1792, *Audley End, the Tea House Bridge*, purchased, 1971
Tomkins, William c.1732–1792, *Audley End, View from the Tea House Bridge*, purchased, 1971
Tomkins, William c.1732–1792, *Audley End and the Temple of Concord*, purchased, 1971
unknown artist late 16th C, *King James VI of Scotland and I of England (1566–1625)*, purchased by private treaty sale, 1986
unknown artist *Audley End from the West*, purchased, 1971
West, Benjamin 1738–1820, *Anna Maria Shutz, Lady Griffin*, purchased, 1971
West, Benjamin 1738–1820, *Katherine Clayton, Lady Howard de Walden*, purchased, 1971
West, Benjamin 1738–1820, *Sir John Griffin Griffin, 4th Lord Howard de Walden*, purchased, 1971
Wissing, Willem (after) c.1656–1687, *Lady Essex Howard, Lady Griffin*, purchased, 1971

Fry Art Gallery

Aldridge, John Arthur Malcolm 1905–1983, *Farm near Mole Hill Green*, donated by the executors of the Aldridge estate
Aldridge, John Arthur Malcolm 1905–1983, *Roses and Astrantia Major*, purchased
Aldridge, John Arthur Malcolm 1905–1983, *The Hyde from Further Moor Hall*, donated by the executors of the Aldridge estate
Aldridge, John Arthur Malcolm 1905–1983, *Silver Birch*, donated by the executors of the Aldridge estate
Aldridge, John Arthur Malcolm 1905–1983, *Beslyn's Pond, Great Bardfield*, purchased with the assistance of the Essex Heritage Trust
Aldridge, John Arthur Malcolm 1905–1983, *Blue Gate Hall*, donated by the executors of the Aldridge estate
Aldridge, John Arthur Malcolm 1905–1983, *Builders at Work, Brick House, Great Bardfield*, purchased
Aldridge, John Arthur Malcolm 1905–1983, *February Afternoon*, purchased
Aldridge, John Arthur Malcolm 1905–1983, *Haystacks, the Place Farm*, purchased
Aldridge, John Arthur Malcolm 1905–1983, *King's Pyon, Shropshire*, donated by the executors of the Aldridge estate
Aldridge, John Arthur Malcolm 1905–1983, *Lady with Cat*, purchased
Aldridge, John Arthur Malcolm 1905–1983, *Self Portrait in Oils*, donated by the executors of the Aldridge estate
Aldridge, John Arthur Malcolm 1905–1983, *The Allotments*, donated by the executors of the Aldridge estate
Aldridge, John Arthur Malcolm 1905–1983, *The New Culvert, Copford Hall*, donated by the executors of the Aldridge estate
Ayers, Duffy b.1919, *Kitty Wilson*, donated by the sitter, © the artist
Ayers, Duffy b.1919, *Olive in Her Garden*, purchased, 2005, © the artist
Ayers, Duffy b.1919, *Scarves*, donated, © the artist
Ayers, Duffy b.1919, *The Arrival*, purchased, © the artist
Ayers, Duffy b.1919, *The White Nightdress*, purchased, © the artist
Ayrton, Michael 1921–1975, *Winter Drought*, donated by Isabel Lambert, © the artist's estate
Bawden, Charlotte 1902–1969, *Eric Townsend*, donated by Edward Bawden
Bawden, Joanna b.1935, *Still Life with Melon and Bottle*, donated by the artist
Bawden, Joanna b.1935, *Sunflower*, donated by the artist
Bellany, John b.1942, *My Grandson Luke*, donated by the artist, © the artist/www.bridgeman.co.uk
Bellany, John b.1942, *Woman of the North Sea*, donated by the artist, © the artist/www.bridgeman.co.uk
Bolam, John b.1922, *Early Morning*, donated by Olive Cook, © the artist
Bolam, John b.1922, *Green Landscape*, donated by the artist, © the artist
Bolam, John b.1922, *Hill Worker*, donated by the artist, © the artist
Bolam, John b.1922, *October*, donated by Mrs P. Hill, © the artist
Chapman, George 1908–1993, *A Steep Road*, purchased, © Nicholas Chapman
Chapman, George 1908–1993,

Pontypridd, donated by Mr & Mrs Yarborough, © Nicholas Chapman
Chapman, George 1908–1993, *The Threshing Machine*, purchased, © Nicholas Chapman
Chapman, George 1908–1993, *The Water Bowser*, purchased, © Nicholas Chapman
Chapman, Kate b.1926, *The Thatcher*, donated by Mr & Mrs M. Mann
Clausen, George 1852–1944, *The Reverend J. W. Court, MA*, donated by Mr D. G. Pelly, © Clausen estate
Cook, Olive 1912–2002, *I Am the Ancient Apple Queen*, donated by the artist, © Fry Art Gallery
Cook, Olive 1912–2002, *Cley, Norfolk*, bequeathed by the artist, 2002, © Fry Art Gallery
Cook, Olive 1912–2002, *Lady into Tree*, bequeathed by the artist, © Fry Art Gallery
Cook, Olive 1912–2002, *Michael Rothenstein Reading*, purchased, © Fry Art Gallery
Cook, Olive 1912–2002, *Norfolk Afternoon*, bequeathed by the artist, © Fry Art Gallery
Cook, Olive 1912–2002, *Portrait of a Lady*, bequeathed by the artist, © Fry Art Gallery
Cook, Olive 1912–2002, *Remembered Suffolk Summer*, bequeathed by the artist, © Fry Art Gallery
Cook, Olive 1912–2002, *Rocking Horse, Seashore*, bequeathed by the artist, © Fry Art Gallery
Cook, Olive 1912–2002, *Ship's Figurehead and Lighthouse, Southwold*, bequeathed by the artist, © Fry Art Gallery
Cook, Olive 1912–2002, *The Expulsion*, bequeathed by the artist, © Fry Art Gallery
Cook, Olive 1912–2002, *The White Hat*, purchased, © Fry Art Gallery
Deakins, Thomas William b.1957, *Apple Tree, Dunmow Allotments*, purchased, © the artist
Rowntree, Kenneth 1915–1997, *The Station Willows, Clare, Suffolk*, purchased, 1996, © the artist's estate
Rowntree, Kenneth 1915–1997, *Dunmow Station, Dusk*, on long-term loan, © the artist's estate
Rowntree, Kenneth 1915–1997, *Evening Bather, Essex*, purchased from the artist's widow with the assistance of a grant from the Britton-Pears Foundation, © the artist's estate
Rowntree, Kenneth 1915–1997, *Exeter College Barge, Oxford*, presented by the National Art Collections Fund, © the artist's estate
Rowntree, Kenneth 1915–1997, *The Artist's Wife*, purchased, © the artist's estate
Rowntree, Kenneth 1915–1997, *Toy Boat at Selsey*, presented by the National Art Collections Fund, © the artist's estate
Rowntree, Kenneth 1915–1997, *Water Butt, Simpkins' Cottage, Lindsell*, purchased, © the artist's estate
Russell, Tom b.1963, *Edward Bawden*, donated by the artist, the sitter's grandson
Smith, Edwin 1912–1971, *Olive Cook Painting*, bequeathed by Olive Cook, © Fry Art Gallery
Smith, Edwin 1912–1971, *Turf Fire*, bequeathed by Olive Cook, © Fry Art Gallery
Smith, Edwin 1912–1971, *Lighthouse Going for a Walk*, bequeathed by Olive Cook, © Fry Art Gallery
Smith, Edwin 1912–1971, *Flower Piece*, donated, © Fry Art Gallery
Smith, Edwin 1912–1971, *A Blackbird and Roses*, bequeathed by Olive Cook, © Fry Art Gallery
Smith, Edwin 1912–1971, *Corn and Pomegranate*, bequeathed by Olive Cook, © Fry Art Gallery
Smith, Edwin 1912–1971, *Riding By*, donated, © Fry Art Gallery
Smith, Edwin 1912–1971, *Storm over Southwold*, purchased, © Fry Art Gallery
Smith, Edwin 1912–1971, *The Pink Dress*, donated, © Fry Art Gallery
Smith, Edwin 1912–1971, *View from Blackshore, Southwold*, bequeathed by Olive Cook, © Fry Art Gallery

Saffron Walden Community Hospital

Gambardella, Julia active 1899–1906, *The Blacksmith (copy after Edwin Henry Landseer)*

Saffron Walden Library

Furse, W. H. active 1831–1850, *Christopher Columbus (c.1451–1506) (copy after Parmigianino)*
Tuke, Henry Scott (attributed to) 1858–1929, *Elizabeth Gibson, née Tuke*
Tuke, Henry Scott (attributed to) 1858–1929, *George Stacey Gibson (1818–1883)*
unknown artist 19th C, *A Stream in Summer*
unknown artist 19th C, *Pastoral Scene with a Girl and Her Dog*
Wills, Edgar W. active 1874–1907, *Sheep and Shepherd, Evening*

Saffron Walden Museum

Cipriani, Giovanni Battista 1727–1785, *Panel from the Robert Adam Library at Audley End Representing Air*, presented by Jane, Lady Braybrooke, 1839
Cipriani, Giovanni Battista 1727–1785, *Panel from the Robert Adam Library at Audley End Representing Earth*, presented by Jane, Lady Braybrooke, 1839
Cipriani, Giovanni Battista 1727–1785, *Panel from the Robert Adam Library at Audley End Representing Fire*, presented by Jane, Lady Braybrooke, 1839
Cipriani, Giovanni Battista 1727–1785, *Panel from the Robert Adam Library at Audley End Representing Water*, presented by Jane, Lady Braybrooke, 1839
Davison, William active 1813–1843, *John Player (1786–1846)*
Edmonds, Stuart (attributed to) active 1925–1927, *Scene with Tower*
Foster, G. active 19th C, *George Stacey Gibson (1818–1883)*, presented by Mrs George Stacey Gibson, 1885
Hondecoeter, Melchior de (attributed to) 1636–1695, *Cock Fight*, presented by Jabez Gibson
Jackson, Gilbert (attributed to) active 1621–1640, *Portrait of a Lady with a Lace Collar Holding a Tulip*, purchased at Mr Fry's sale
Laporte, George Henry 1799–1873, *White Stallion*, on permanent loan
Pether, Henry active 1828–1865, *View of the Thames, Pool of London, from Billingsgate to London Bridge*, presented by Jabez Gibson
Reinagle, Philip 1749–1833, *Adoration of the Magi (copy after Peter Paul Rubens)*, donated by Francis Gibson, 1835–1882, on loan to Chrishall Church
Ruggles, William Henry (copy of) active 1833–1846), *A Distinguished Member of the Human Society*
unknown artist *Mrs Thomas Wolfe*, presented by Mr J. Wolfe, 1877
unknown artist *Thomas Wolfe*, gift, 1877
unknown artist *Adoration of Goddess Juno*, presented by Joseph Clark
unknown artist *Woman Resting Her Basket on a Stile*, on permanent loan
unknown artist 19th C, *Portrait of a Lady Holding Her Spectacles*
unknown artist *A Saint*
unknown artist *Cottage*
unknown artist *Edward VI (1537–1553)*
unknown artist *Freeman's Farm*, gift, 1978
unknown artist *Hospital Farm, Newport*
unknown artist *Icon*, gift, 1894
unknown artist *Interior with Figures, a Man Playing the Fiddle*
unknown artist *James Humphry of Saffron Walden (1759–1858)*, gift, 1886
unknown artist *John Wolfe*, gift, 1877
unknown artist *Landscape with a Donkey*
unknown artist *Landscape with Five Trees*
unknown artist *Landscape with Windmill and Village*
unknown artist *Old Woman and Child*
unknown artist *Restormel Castle, Cornwall*
unknown artist *Seated Figure (possibly Christ) with a Woman*
unknown artist *St Peter Repenting*, gift, 1921
unknown artist *The Flight into Egypt*, gift, 1921
unknown artist *Ulysses and Polyphemus (copy after Joseph Mallord William Turner)*, gift, 1921
unknown artist *Unfinished Racing Scene*
unknown artist *Virgin and Child*
Winstanley, Henry 1644–1703, *Self Portrait*, presented by George Stacey Gibson, 1880
Youngman, John Mallows 1817–1899, *The Withered Elm, Audley End Park*, gift

Saffron Walden Town Council

Mytens, Daniel I (after) c.1590–before 1648, *Queen Henrietta Maria (1609–1669)*, presented by Captain F. J. O. Montagu, OBE, MC, DL, 1935
Tuke, Henry Scott 1858–1929, *George Stacey Gibson (1818–1883), Mayor (1875–1877)*, presented by George P. Horton, JP
Tuke, Henry Scott 1858–1929, *George Stacey Gibson (1818–1883), Mayor (1875–1877)*, commissioned by the borough of Saffron Walden
Tuke, Henry Scott (attributed to) 1858–1929, *Elizabeth Gibson*
unknown artist *Sir Thomas Smith of Hill Hall, Theydon Mount*
unknown artist 17th C, *King Charles I (1600–1649)*, presented by Captain F. J .O. Montagu, OBE, MC, DL, 1935
unknown artist 19th C, *Joshua Clarke, JP*
unknown artist 19th C, *John Player, JP (1785–1846)*, presented by J. D. Player and W. C. Player of Nottingham

Uttlesford District Council

unknown artist *A Flitch Trial*, transferred from Great Dunmow Rural District Council, 1974

Southend-on-Sea Borough Council

Olivier, Herbert Arnould (attributed to) 1861–1952, *Sir Charles Archibald Nicholson, 2nd Bt (1867–1949), Architect and Inhabitant of Porters*, purchased as part of a property from Sir Charles Archibald Nicholson, 1932
Salisbury, Frank O. 1874–1962, *Alderman William Miles, CBE, JP, Mayor of Southend-on-Sea (1922–1924, 1936–1937 & 1939–1945)*, © estate of Frank O. Salisbury/DACS 2006
unknown artist 17th C, *Fox amongst the Chickens*
Vickress, Terence *Allan James Cole, Centenary Mayor (1992–1993)*, commissioned to commemorate the Council's centenary, 1992

Southend Pier Museum Foundation

Pinnock, Robin J. b.1954, *Twilight Promenade*, commissioned by Southend Pier Museum Foundation, © Southend Pier Museum Foundation
Pinnock, Robin J. b.1954, *Pavilion Sunset, Southend Pier, c.1930*, commissioned by Southend Pier Museum Foundation, © Southend Pier Museum Foundation
Pinnock, Robin J. b.1954, *'Royal View', Southend Pier from Royal Hill, c.1950*, commissioned by Southend Pier Museum Foundation, © Southend Pier Museum Foundation
Smoothy, Derrick b.1923, *'Golden Eagle' Leaving Southend Pier*, commissioned by Southend Pier Museum Foundation, © Southend Pier Museum Foundation

Southend Museums Service

Adams, Caroline 1792–1886, *Woodland Picnic Scene*, purchased from the Simon Carter Gallery, Woodbridge, 1989
Aldridge, John Arthur Malcolm 1905–1983, *The Cart Shed*, purchased from the home of the artist with the Emily Briggs Bequest, c.1964
Aldridge, John Arthur Malcolm 1905–1983, *River Pant, Great Bardfield*, purchased from the home of the artist with the Emily Briggs Bequest, c.1964
Aldridge, John Arthur Malcolm 1905–1983, *Stubble Field, Thaxted*, purchased from the Essex Royal Academy's Exhibition, 1972
Allnutt, H. G. active 1920–1932, *Cockethurst Farm, Eastwoodbury Lane*, gift from Mrs H. G. Allnutt, c.1965
Allnutt, H. G. active 1920–1932, *Eastwood Lane, Eastwood*, gift from Mrs H. G. Allnutt
Allnutt, H. G. active 1920–1932, *Eastwoodbury Lane, Eastwood*, gift from Mrs H. G. Allnutt, c.1965
Allnutt, H. G. active 1920–1932, *Eastwood*, gift from Mrs H. G. Allnutt
Allnutt, H. G. active 1920–1932, *Billet Lane, Leigh, from Belton Hills*, gift from Mrs H. G. Allnutt, c.1965
Allnutt, H. G. active 1920–1932, *Prittlewell from the North-West*, gift from Mrs H. G. Allnutt, c.1968
Allnutt, H. G. active 1920–1932, *Hart Road, Thundersley*, gift from Mrs H. G. Allnutt, c.1965
Allnutt, H. G. active 1920–1932, *Landscape*, gift from Mrs H. G. Allnutt, c.1965
Allnutt, H. G. active 1920–1932, *Old Dutch Cottage, Rayleigh*, gift from Mrs H. G. Allnutt, c.1965
Allnutt, H. G. active 1920–1932, *From Belton Hills Looking West*, gift from Mrs H. G. Allnutt, c.1965
Allnutt, H. G. active 1920–1932,

Stambridge Mills, gift from Mrs H. G. Allnutt, c.1965
Allnutt, H. G. active 1920–1932, *Watts Lane, Rochford*, gift from Mrs H. G. Allnutt
Allnutt, H. G. active 1920–1932, *Chalkwell Bay from Belton Hills, Leigh*, gift from Mrs H. G. Allnutt, c.1965
Allnutt, H. G. active 1920–1932, *Farm Buildings*, gift from Mrs H. G. Allnutt, c.1965
Allnutt, H. G. active 1920–1932, *Farm Buildings*, gift from Mrs H. G. Allnutt, c.1965
Allnutt, H. G. active 1920–1932, *Landscape*, gift from Mrs H. G. Allnutt, c.1965
Allnutt, H. G. active 1920–1932, *Looking down Billet Lane, Leigh*, gift from Mrs H. G. Allnutt, c.1965
Anderson, William 1757–1837, *View at the Mouth of the Thames*, bequeathed by Sidney Thorpe-Smith, 1961
Andreis, Alex de 1871–1939, *The Cavalier*, bequeathed by Mrs B. E. Pattison, c.1965
Appleton, Sheila b.1931, *Jubilee Rebuilding, Southend Looking South as Seen from Floor 13 of the Civic Centre*, purchased with the Thorpe-Smith Bequest from the eighth Southend Open Exhibition at the Beecroft Art Gallery, 1964, © the artist
Appleton, Sheila b.1931, *Boats at Leigh*, purchased from the artist, 1982, © the artist
Appleton, Sheila b.1931, *Seafront, Southend*, purchased, © the artist
Arnald, George 1763–1841, *Greta Bridge, Rokeby, Durham*, gift from Mr W. G. Beecroft
Arthois, Jacques d' 1613–1686, *Flemish Landscape*, gift from Mr Lumley and Mrs D. Francis
Ashby, Derek b.1926, *Greenwich Park*, purchased from the Selections from the Royal Academy Exhibition, 1956 at the Beecroft Art Gallery, © the artist
Baldwin, Warren b.1956, *Large Portrait*, purchased from the Royal Academy, 1985, © the artist
Bamford, Alfred Bennett 1857–1939, *Prittlewell*, gift from Mrs D. U. Gowing
Barden, Kenneth 1924–1988, *Farnley Tyas, West Yorkshire*, purchased from the Royal Academy, 1972
Barker, Thomas 1769–1847, *Stormy Landscape*, gift from Mr W. G. Beecroft
Barratt, Krome 1924–1990, *West Country*, purchased from the Krome Barratt Exhibition, 1986
Barret, George 1728/1732–1784, *Powerscourt Falls*, gift from Mr W. G. Beecroft, c.1953
Barrett, Roderic 1920–2000, *Silences II*, purchased from the Thackery Gallery, 1976, © the artist's estate
Bassano family active 16th 17th C, *Portrait of a Nobleman (said to be Silva Capello)*, gift from Mr W. G. Beecroft
Bates, W. E. 1812–1872, *View of Leigh*, gift from Mr and Mrs G. W. McClure
Bayliss, F. *Prittlewell Bridge*
Bayliss, F. *Southchurch Post Office*
Bennett, Terence b.1935, *Landscape with Cottages, Clayworth, Nottinghamshire*, purchased from the Royal Academy, 1985, © the artist
Berchem, Nicolaes 1620–1683, *Landscape*, acquired, c.1957
Bissolo, Francesco c.1470–1554, *Virgin and Child*, gift from Miss Emily Briggs
Blamey, Norman Charles 1914–1999, *Proximity*, purchased from the Royal Academy, 1966, © estate of Norman Blamey/licensed by DACS 2006
Bloemen, Jan Frans van 1662–1749, *Romantic Landscape*, gift from Mr W. G. Beecroft, c.1961
Both, Jan c.1618–1652, *Landscape near Rome*, acquired, c.1957
Bowey, Olwyn b.1936, *Rowner Millpond in Autumn*, purchased from the Royal Academy, 1973, © the artist
Brangwyn, Frank 1867–1956, *The Lower Reaches of the Thames*, purchased from the Fine Art Society, London, 1961, © courtesy of the artist's estate/www.bridgeman.co.uk
Braund, Allin 1915–2004, *The Estuary*, presented by the Contemporary Art Society, 1962, © the artist's estate
Breanski, Gustave de c.1856–1898, *At Leigh, Essex*, bequeathed by Sidney Thorpe-Smith, 1961
Bright, Henry 1814–1873, *Hadleigh Castle*, purchased from Sotheby's, London, 1967
British (Chinese) School mid 19th C, *'Red Riding Hood' of London*
British (English) School *The Marchioness of Dorset*, gift from Mr W. G. Beecroft, 1953
British (English) School 16th C, *Portrait of a Gentleman*, gift from Mr W. G. Beecroft
British (English) School mid-17th C, *Portrait of a Young Man*, gift from Mr W. G. Beecroft, 1953
British (English) School *Italian Landscape*, gift from Mr P. Poole
British (English) School *The Harris Family*, gift from Miss Z. Harris (descendant of sitters), 1970
British (English) School 19th C, *Hadleigh Castle*, gift from Mr and Mrs G. W. McClure
Brooke, Anne Isabella b.1916, *Towards Ingleborough, across Ribblesdale*, purchased from the Royal Academy, 1973
Brooke, Edward Adveno 1821–1910, *Near Southend*
Bullen, Patricia *Seagulls*, purchased from Wildlife of Essex Exhibition, 1978
Burgess, Alan b.1936, *Suffolk Triptych (centre panel)*, purchased from Alan Burgess Exhibition, 1986, © the artist
Callow, John 1822–1878, *Homeward Bound, J. D. Clink's Famous Three-Masted Barque 'Oimara' Entering the Thames*, bequeathed by Sidney Thorpe-Smith, 1961
Canaletto (follower of) 1697–1768, *View of the Rialto Bridge, Venice*
Carter, Mary b.1947, *Two for Joy*, purchased from the Royal Academy, 1972, © the artist
Castle, Lucy b.1977, *Helter Skelter*, purchased from the Lucy Castle Exhibition at the Beecroft Art Gallery, 2001, © the artist
Castle, Lucy b.1977, *The Kursaal II*, purchased from the Beecroft Art Gallery Christmas Exhibition, 2001, © the artist
Castle, Lucy b.1977, *The Beecroft Art Gallery*, commissioned on the occasion of the Gallery's 50th anniversary, 2003, © the artist
Cattle, J. T. active 1920–1977, *Female Nude*, gift from the artist, 1977
Cerquozzi, Michelangelo 1602–1660, *St John the Baptist Preaching in the Wilderness*, purchased from the S. F. Johnson Bequest, c.1960
Christison, C. G. *Cyclamen*, purchased
Cleminson, Robert active c.1864–c.1903 & **Fisher, G.**, *Old Leigh High Street*
Clifford Smith, Stanley 1906–1968, *Claire de la lune*, purchased from the Commemorative Exhibition at The Minories, Colchester, 1970, © the artist's estate
Closterman, John 1660–1711, *Sir William Temple*, gift from Mr W. G. Beecroft
Codde, Pieter Jacobsz. 1599–1678, *Landscape with a Lake and Castle*, purchased from K. Graham, London
Cohen, Dorothy A. d.1960, *The Guitar Player*, bequeathed by the artist, 1960
Coker, K. A. *Rocks and Boats*, purchased
Coker, Peter 1926–2004, *Mountain Stream, Pyrenees*, purchased from the Thackery Gallery, London, 1970, © Peter Coker, RA
Comber, N. F. *Priory Lake, Prittlewell*
Comber, N. F. *Prittlewell Priory*
Conabeer, A. J. active 1894–1902, *Westcliff*
Conabeer, A. J. active 1894–1902, *Leigh Creek*
Constable, John 1776–1837, *River Stour Looking towards Manningtree*, purchased from Agnews, London, 1953
Cotman, John Sell 1782–1842, *Southend, Pier Hill*, bequeathed by Sidney Thorpe-Smith, 1961
Coventry, C.C. active c.1802-1819, *Royal Terrace from the Sea*, bequeathed by Sidney Thorpe-Smith, 1961
Cox, David the elder 1783–1859, *Seascape*, gift from Mr W. G. Beecroft, 1947
Cuming, Frederick b.1930, *Landscape, August*, purchased from the Brandler Galleries, Brentwood, © the artist
Danby, James Francis 1816–1875, *Southend Beach*, purchased from H. Linden, London, c.1959
Davison, Thomas *Gathering*, purchased, 1976
Dawson, Henry 1811–1878, *Leigh Ray*, bequeathed by Sidney Thorpe-Smith, 1961
Deakins, Cyril Edward 1916–2002, *Suffolk Scarecrow*, purchased from the artist, 1986, © the artist's estate
Deakins, Thomas William b.1957, *A Winter's Afternoon, Duton Hill, near Dunmow*, purchased from the Southend Open Exhibition, 1985, © the artist
Deakins, Thomas William b.1957, *January Sunshine*, purchased from the 38th Essex Open Exhibition, 1996, © the artist
Dring, William D. 1904–1990, *Portrait of a Girl, possibly Melissa*, purchased from the Brandler Galleries, 1989, © courtesy of the artist's estate/www.bridgeman.co.uk
Dujardin, Karel 1626–1678, *Halt of the Gypsies*, gift from Mr W. G. Beecroft
Dunlop, Ronald Ossory 1894–1973, *The Harbour, Leigh-on-Sea*, purchased from Sotheby's, London, 1966
Dunstan, Bernard b.1920, *Old Woman at a Gate*, purchased from the Brandler Galleries, Brentwood, 1986, © courtesy of the artist/www.bridgeman.co.uk
Durrant, Roy Turner 1925–1998, *Inscape: The Monument*, gift from the artist, 1981, © the artist's estate
Dutch School *Portrait of a Young Woman*, purchased from Ronald Cooke, London, c.1970
Dutch School *Portrait of a Lady*, gift from Mr W. G. Beecroft, 1953
Dutch School 18th C, *Women Making Music*, bequeathed by Mrs H. M. Luyken
Ellis, Victor William b.1921, *The Thames Barge, 'Kitty'*, bequeathed by Mr F. I. Royston, 2001
Ellis, Victor William b.1921, *Trial Canvas for '25 Pounders on Salisbury Plain'*, purchased from Selwood Fine Arts, 1985
Etty, William 1787–1849, *Study of a Male Nude*, purchased from K. Graham, London, c.1956
Fairman, Sheila b.1924, *Still Life in White*, gift from Miss Gracey Summer, 1986, © the artist
Fairman, Sheila b.1924, *Biscuits and Buns*, © the artist
Fairman, Sheila b.1924, *Abalone Shell*, purchased, 1978?, © the artist
Farrell, Anthony b.1945, *Study of Bathers on the Beach*, purchased from the Royal Academy, 1975, © the artist
Fears, Constance 1895–late 1980s, *Winter Scene from Billet Cottage*, gift from the artist, 1985
Fears, Constance 1895–late 1980s, *Daisies in a Chinese Vase*, gift from Mrs Joan Goldspink, 2004
Fears, Constance 1895–late 1980s, *Juniper's Cottage*, gift from the artist, 1985
Fears, Constance 1895–late 1980s, *Marguerites and Oranges*, purchased from the Constance Fears, Looking at Life Retrospective Exhibition, 1981
Fisher, Charles d.1890, *Leigh, Essex*, purchased from Mr E. C. Socarro, © Southend Borough Council
Fisher, Mark 1841–1923, *Cattle at Bourne End*, gift from Mr W. G. Beecroft
Fisher, Mark 1841–1923, *Cattle by the River*, gift from Mr W. G. Beecroft, c.1965
Fisher, Mark 1841–1923, *Cattle in a Landscape*, gift from Mr W. G. Beecroft, c.1965
Fisher, Mark 1841–1923, *Cattle Resting in Marshland*, gift from Mr W. G. Beecroft
Flemish School *Portrait of a Gentleman*, gift from Mr W. G. Beecroft
Flemish School *Harvesting Scene*, purchased through the Friends of Beecroft Art Gallery, 1950s
Flemish School *Hunting Scene*, purchased through the Friends of Beecroft Art Gallery, 1950s
Fordham, Jack d.1982, *Southend Barge Race*, gift from the artist
Fraser, John 1858–1927, *From the Leas*
French School 19th C, *A Wayside Shrine*, gift from Mrs A. M. Cater
Gallon, Robert 1845–1925, *Leigh from Southend*, purchased from Sotheby's, London, 1970s
Gallon, Robert 1845–1925, *Leigh from Southend Pier*, purchased from Sotheby's, London, 1970s
German School 17th C, *St Matthias*, gift from Mr W. G. Beecroft, c.1957
Ghisolfi, Giovanni c.1623–1683, *Capriccio*, bequeathed by Mr W. G. Beecroft, c.1961
Gibbs, Stephen b.1957, *Free Flight*, purchased from the Wildlife of Essex Exhibition, 1978, © the artist
Gibbs, Stephen b.1957, *Summer on the Corner of Gordon*, acquired, c.1995, © the artist
Gill, Edmund Ward 1820–1894, *The Waterfall*, gift from Mr W. G. Beecroft, c.1955
Ginner, Charles 1878–1952, *Cottages at Shipley, Sussex*, purchased from the Fine Art Society, 1970s
Gozzard, K. *The Wane of the Season*, bequeathed by Sidney Thorpe-Smith, 1961
Grant, Henry active 1868–1895, *Charles Woosnam, JP, Chairman of the Southend Gas Company*, acquired, 1980s
Grassi, Nicola 1682–1748, *The Triumph of Amphitrite*, gift from Miss Z. Harris, before 1975
Greenwood, Ernest b.1913,

Rooftops and Towers, Lecco, North Italy, purchased from the Fine Art Society, London, 1967
Haagensen, F. H. active 1930, *Winter in Norway*, purchased from the Simon Carter Gallery, Woodbridge, 1980s
Hall, Christopher b.1930, *Blaenau Ffestiniog*, purchased from the Royal Academy, 1972, © the artist
Hardy, Leo active 1936–1952, *Saturday Morning at Priory Park*, purchased from the artist, c.1972
Harpignies, Henri-Joseph 1819–1916, *Duck Shooting on the Banks of the River Allier*, gift from Mr W. G. Beecroft in memory of his sister, Jenny, c.1959
Harris, Alfred Peter b.1932, *Perspective in Steel*, purchased from rail art exhibition at Beecroft Art Gallery, 1987
Harris, Robert E. b.1927, *The Bathers*, purchased from John Whibley Gallery, London, 1968
Heda, Gerrit Willemsz. c.1620–before 1702, *Breakfast Still Life*, bequeathed by Mr W. G. Beecroft, c.1961
Hepple, Norman 1908–1994, *Portrait of a Little Girl in Blue*, purchased from the Brandler Galleries, Brentwood, 1986, © courtesy of the artist's estate/www.bridgeman.co.uk
Hering, George Edwards 1805–1879, *A Distant View of Rome*, gift from Edmund Stone, c.1953
Hewitt, James *Garden Shed, Still Life*, purchased from the Chelmsford Festival at Chelmsford Museum, 1978
Hewitt, James *Snow at Great Totham*, purchased from the Chelmsford Festival at Chelmsford Museum, 1978
Heyworth, Alfred 1926–1976, *Gardens in Chiswick*, purchased from the Royal Academy, 1969
Hill, Robert W. b.1932, *Aldeburgh Beach*, purchased from the John Whibley Gallery, London, 1971
Hill, W. H. *Folly Farm, Westcliff*, gift from Mrs H. G. Howard
Hillier, Tristram Paul 1905–1983, *Cutlers Green*, gift from the Contemporary Art Society, 1959, © the artist's estate
Hinde, Phil b.1938, *Barns at Shelley, near Ongar*, purchased from the Southend Open Exhibition, 1982, © the artist
Hopkinson, John b.1941, *Children's Games No.2*, purchased from the John Whibley Gallery, London, 1980s, © the artist
Horner, A. G. active 1953–1957, *The Crooked Billet, Leigh-on-Sea*, purchased from Mr J. Bates, 2000
Horner, A. G. active 1953–1957, *Seafront, Thorpe Bay*, gift from Alderman B. S. Clarke
Horner, A. G. active 1953–1957, *Manly Beach, Australia*, gift from Alderman P. B. Renshaw, 1957
Horton, Etty d.1905, *Pastoral Scene*, gift from Mr W. G. Wakerly, 1983
Horton, Etty d.1905, *Pastoral Scene*, gift from Mr W. G. Wakerly, 1983
Howard, Ken b.1932, *Street Patrol, Belfast*, purchased from the Brandler Galleries, Brentwood, c.1980, © courtesy of the artist/www.bridgeman.co.uk
Hudson, G. M. active 1909–1935, *Negro Slave*, acquired, 1980s
Hudson, Gwynedd M. active 1881–1935, *Portrait of an Artist*
Hughes-Stanton, Herbert Edwin Pelham 1870–1937, *Pas de Calais*, gift from Mr and Mrs K. Graham, 1950s
Hulk, Abraham 1813–1897, *Landscape*, gift from Mrs H. C. Reeves, 1963
Humphry, Ozias 1742–1810, *The Heygate Family*, bequeathed by Sidney Thorpe-Smith, 1961
Italian School 16th C, *Christ and the Four Evangelists*, gift from Mr W. G. Beecroft
Italian School 16th C, *The Circumcision of Christ*, gift from Mr W. G. Beecroft, c.1958
Italian School *Gentleman in a Rickshaw*
Italian School *The Duel*
Jackson, Gloria active 1976–1985, *The End of the Pier, Prior to the Fire*, gift from the artist, 1985
Jackson, Gloria active 1976–1985, *Leighcliff Gardens*, gift from the artist, 1985
Jackson, Gloria active 1976–1985, *Rear View of Civic Centre*, gift from the artist, 1985
Jackson, Gloria active 1976–1985, *Self Portrait*, gift from the artist, 1985
Jackson, Gloria active 1976–1985, *Scene in Gallery 9 at the Beecroft*, gift from the artist, 1985
Jackson, Gloria active 1976–1985, *Fair-Haired Seated Nude on Green and Blue Drapery, 1979*, gift from the artist, 1985
Jackson, Gloria active 1976–1985, *Nude Seated on Blue-Cushioned Stool*, gift from the artist, 1985
Jackson, Gloria active 1976–1985, *Nude Seated on Red Cushion, 1979*, gift from the artist, 1985
Jackson, Gloria active 1976–1985, *Untitled Abstract*, gift from the artist, 1985
James, Owen b.1934, *Canna*, purchased from the Royal Academy, 1975
James, William active 1745–1771, *London Bridge*, bequeathed by Sidney Thorpe-Smith, 1961
Jayne, Charles active 1838–1879, *Landslip, Cliff Town, Southend*
Jenkins, J. *Hadleigh Castle*
Jenkins, J. *Leigh Creek*
Johnson, Valerie *Winter Morning, Leigh*, purchased, c.1958
Keyes, S. K. *Southchurch Hall*
King, Yeend 1855–1924, *Southend*, bequeathed by Sidney Thorpe-Smith, 1961
Kingston, Joyce *Cedar Tree in Prittlewell Park*
Knell, William Calcott active 1848–1885, *Evening Oyster Boat off Southend Pier*, bequeathed by Sidney Thorpe-Smith, 1961
Kneller, Godfrey 1646–1723, *The Earl of Rochester*, purchased from J. Wentworth Day
Lambert, George c.1700–1765, *Richmond Castle, Yorkshire*, gift from Mrs Susannah Halley, 1953
Larusdottir, Karolina b.1944, *Sunday Visit to the Summerhouse*, purchased from the Royal Academy summer exhibition, 1994, © the artist
Le Nain family active 17th C, *Portrait of a Youth*, purchased through the Friends of Beecroft Art Gallery
Leyden, Jan van active 1652–1669, *The Shipwreck*, purchased from K. Graham, London, c.1955
Licence, Geoffrey b.1944, *Bird Girl, Belton Hills*, purchased from the Southend Open Exhibition, 1982, © the artist
Lint, Hendrik Frans van 1684–1763, *Landscape by a River*, bequeathed by Mr W. G. Beecroft, 1961
Looten, Jan c.1618–c.1681, *River Landscape*, gift from Mr W. G. Beecroft
Loutherbourg, Philip James de 1740–1812, *Pastoral Scene*, bequeathed by Mr W. G. Beecroft, 1961
Luny, Thomas 1759–1837, *The 'Duke William', Homeward Bound off the Entrance to the River Thames*, bequeathed by Sidney Thorpe-Smith, 1961
Luny, Thomas 1759–1837, *St Michael's Mount*, purchased from K. Graham, London, c.1955
Lygo-Baker, Owen Neil b.1940, *Valley, Autumn*, gift from the Contemporary Art Society, c.1970, © the artist
Malcolm, Ellen 1923–2002, *Night Shadows*, gift from Mr E. Cecil Jones, c.1955
Manglard, Adrien 1695–1760, *Shipping off the Italian Coast*, acquired, c.1960
Marder, J. *View of Southend Seafront*, gift from Mr Fenner
Mason, Bateson 1910–1977, *Near Vouvray*, purchased from the Royal Academy, 1973
Meddemmen, George 1920–2004, *Casares, Costa del Sol*, purchased from the 28th Open Exhibition at the Beecroft Art Gallery, 1986
Melbye, Anton 1818–1875, *Midnight off Sheerness*, bequeathed by Sidney Thorpe-Smith, 1961
Melville, Eliza Anne Leslie active from 1894, *Leigh Cliffs*, acquired, c.1970
Molenaer, Klaes c.1630–1676, *Winter Scene in Holland*, acquired from K. Graham, London, 1950s
Moore, A. Harvey d.1905, *Leigh*
Moore, A. Harvey d.1905, *Seascape*
Moore, A. Harvey d.1905, *Crowstone Beach*, gift from Mr W. G. Beecroft, c.1960
Moore, A. Harvey d.1905, *The Estuary Looking West*, gift from the family of Dr and Mrs Watson, 1976
Moore, F. J. *The Clubhouse, Belfairs*
Moore, Henry 1831–1895, *Off Leigh-on-Sea, Essex*, purchased from the Fine Art Society, 1971
Morgan, Paul Robert b.1940, *The Bend in the River*, purchased from the Brandler Galleries, Brentwood, 1985, © the artist
Morland, George 1763–1804, *Winter Landscape*, gift from Mr W. G. Beecroft, c.1960
Moune, John *Monomorphosis (detail)*, gift from the Contemporary Art Society, 1983
Murillo, Bartolomé Esteban (after) 1618–1682, *Beggar Boys Playing Dice*
Nash, John Northcote 1893–1977, *Melting Snow at Wormingford*, purchased from Agnews, London, as the Ethel M. Stuart Bequest, c.1964, © artistic trustee of the estate of John Nash
Neeffs, Peeter the younger 1620–1675, *Cathedral Interior*, gift from Mr W. G. Beecroft, c.1953
Newton, Algernon Cecil 1880–1968, *West Wycombe Park*, gift from Mr W. G. Beecroft and Mr E. K. Cole, c.1956
Nicholls, Bertram 1883–1974, *Quay in Italy*, gift from Mr W. G. Beecroft, c.1953
O'Connor, John Scorror 1913–2004, *Botany Pool*, gift from Mr E. Cecil Jones, 1961, © the artist's estate
Orpen, William 1878–1931, *Charles Wertheim*, gift from Alderman S. H. J. Bates, 1953
Osborne, John b.1939, *Bushes, Winter*, purchased from the 12th Southend Open Exhibition, 1968, © the artist
Osborne, John b.1939, *Breaking Wave*, © the artist
Padwick, Philip Hugh 1876–1958, *Barns at Clymping, West Sussex*, gift from Mr W. G. Beecroft to the Southend Corporation (now Southend Borough Council), c.1928
Padwick, Philip Hugh 1876–1958, *Sussex Landscape*, gift from Mr W. G. Beecroft, c.1953
Paolo Fiammingo 1540–1596, *The Good Samaritan*, gift from Mr W. G. Beecroft, c.1953
Parker, Brynhild 1907–1987, *Windy Day on Marine Parade, Southend*, bequeathed by Sidney Thorpe-Smith, 1961
Pearce, Stephen 1819–1904, *Daniel Robert Scratton of Prittlewell Priory, Essex*, acquired from the Scratton family
Pennington, John 1773–1841, *Lake District Landscape*, purchased from Mr W. G. Beecroft, as the Montefiore Memorial Picture in memory of Dorothy Cohen, c.1960
Peppercorn, Arthur Douglas 1847–1926, *Devon River*, gift from Mr E. C. Howell, c.1953
Peppercorn, Arthur Douglas 1847–1926, *Near Falmouth*, gift from Mr W. G. Beecroft and Mr E. C. Howell, c.1953
Peppercorn, Arthur Douglas 1847–1926, *Quay at Bosham Harbour*, gift from Mr W. G. Beecroft, c.1953
Peppercorn, Arthur Douglas 1847–1926, *The Cliff*, gift from Lady Duckham, daughter of the artist, c.1953
Pettitt, Edwin Alfred 1840–1912, *Leigh from the East*, purchased from Mr Goodwin-Bailey, c.1967
Philipson, Robin 1916–1992, *Retablo*, gift from the Contemporary Art Society, 1976
Pinnock, Robin J. b.1954, *Fisherman's Walk*, purchased from one man show at Beecroft Art Gallery, 1984, © the artist
Pinnock, Robin J. b.1954, *Near Shelley, Suffolk*, purchased from the Robin Pinnock Exhibition, 1984, © the artist
Pinnock, Robin J. b.1954, *Chalkwell Park with Aurora Borealis*, purchased from the Parks, Flowers, Gardens Exhibition, 1986, © the artist
Pitcher, Neville Sotheby 1889–1959, *Convoy off Southend Pier: Attack by Moonlight*, bequeathed by Sidney Thorpe-Smith, 1961
Poelenburgh, Cornelis van 1594/1595–1667, *Tobias and the Angel*, bequeathed by Mr W. G. Beecroft
Poole, H. J. active c.1900, *St Mary's Church Overlooking Benfleet Creek*
Rombouts, Salomon c.1652–c.1702, *A Winter Scene at Night*, bequeathed by Mr W. G. Beecroft, c.1961
Roos, Philipp Peter 1657–1706, *Study of Goats*, bequeathed by Mr W. G. Beecroft
Ruisdael, Jacob van 1628/1629–1682, *The Waterfall*, bequeathed by Mr W. G. Beecroft
Rule, A. E. *The Crowstone at Night*, gift from M. G. Gracey, 1980
Salisbury, Frank O. 1874–1962, *The Bridal Train*, gift from the artist, 1953, © estate of Frank O. Salisbury/DACS 2006
Salmon, Robert *Islands I*, purchased from the Royal Academy, 1977
Seago, Edward Brian 1910–1974, *Early Morning, September*, bequeathed by the Reverend F. S. Jarvis, c.1965, © by kind permission of the Trustees of the estate of Edward Seago, courtesy of Thomas Gibson Fine Art Limited
Seago, Edward Brian 1910–1974, *The Doge's Palace, Venice*, bequeathed by the Reverend F. S. Jarvis, c.1965, © by kind permission of the Trustees of the estate of Edward Seago, courtesy of Thomas Gibson Fine Art Limited
Seago, Edward Brian 1910–1974, *The Foreshore*, bequeathed by the Reverend F. S. Jarvis, c.1965, © by kind permission of the Trustees of the estate of Edward Seago, courtesy of Thomas Gibson Fine

Art Limited
Segers, Hercules Pietersz. (after) c.1589–c.1638, *Landscape*, gift from Mr E. C. Howell, c.1950s
Shalders, George c.1826–1873, *Southend at Sunset*, purchased from Sotheby's, London, 1967
Shalders, George c.1826–1873, *Afternoon, Hadleigh*, purchased from the Simon Carter Gallery, Woodbridge, 1988
Shaw, Leslie active late 20th C, *Landscape*, purchased from the artist, 1983
Sheppard, Maurice Raymond b.1947, *Boat House, Hampton Court Palace*, purchased from the Leonie Jonleigh Studio, 1977
Sims, Charles 1873–1928, *Study of a Nude*, bequeathed by Dorothy Cohen, 1960
Smith, George 1714–1776, *By the River*, bequeathed by Mr W. G. Beecroft, c.1961
Snyders, Frans 1579–1657, *Still Life with Cocks*, gift from Mr W. G. Beecroft, c.1953
Solimena, Francesco 1657–1747, *Rebecca at the Well*, gift to Southend Corporation (now Southend Borough Council) from Councillor Mitchell, 1922
Sorrell, Alan 1904–1974, *Study for 'The Refitting of Admiral Blake's Fleet at Leigh, during the First Dutch War'*, © the artist's estate
Sorrell, Alan 1904–1974, *The Refitting of Admiral Blake's Fleet at Leigh, during the First Dutch War*, commissioned for Southend Central Library and presented by Councillor W. B. Hawken in memory of his wife, © the artist's estate
Sorrell, Alan 1904–1974, *The Building of Prittlewell Priory*, commissioned for Southend Central Library and presented by Mr E. Cecil Jones, as a memorial to his father, R. A. Jones, © the artist's estate
Sorrell, Alan 1904–1974, *The Building of Prittlewell Church Tower*, commissioned for Southend Central Library and presented by Mrs H. E. Frith to commemorate the mayoralty of her husband, © the artist's estate
Sorrell, Alan 1904–1974, *Study for 'The Arrival of the First Mail Coach at Southend'*, © the artist's estate
Sorrell, Alan 1904–1974, *The Arrival of the First Mail Coach at Southend*, commissioned for Southend Central Library and presented by Mr J. W. Burrows, JP, FSA, © the artist's estate
Sorrell, Alan 1904–1974, *Summer Scene Triptych (left wing)*, © the artist's estate
Sorrell, Alan 1904–1974, *Summer Scene Triptych (right wing)*, © the artist's estate
Sorrell, Alan 1904–1974, *The Spoilers (detail)*, gift from Mr E. Cecil Jones, c.1958, © the artist's estate
Sorrell, Alan 1904–1974, *Abu Simbel, Nubia*, gift from the artist's daughter, Julia Sanders, 2003, © the artist's estate
Sorrell, Alan 1904–1974, *Attack on Southchurch Hall during the Peasants' Revolt, 1381*, presented in memory of John William Burrows, JP, FSA (1879–1940) by his son and daughters, © the artist's estate
Sorrell, Richard b.1948, *Mr King's Cattle*, purchased from the Sorrell family exhibition at Southend Central Library, 1982, © the artist
Spear, Ruskin 1911–1990, *Daydreaming, Portrait of the Artist's Wife*, purchased from the Fine Art Society, 1966, © courtesy of the artist's estate/www.bridgeman.co.uk
Spencer, Gilbert 1893–1979, *Clarissa*, purchased from the Emily Briggs Bequest, 1960s, © courtesy of the artist's estate/www.bridgeman.co.uk
Suddaby, Rowland 1912–1972, *Landscape*, purchased from the Brandler Galleries, Brentwood, 1985, © the artist's estate
Taylor, Arthur H. active from 1953, *Waiting Room*, purchased, c.1958
Taylor, Arthur H. active from 1953, *Cliff Parade, Leigh on Sea*, commissioned to meet the terms of the Eunice Beecroft Bequest, c.1964
Taylor, Arthur H. active from 1953, *The Cockle Shed, Leigh*, commissioned to meet the terms of the Eunice Beecroft Bequest, c.1964
Thompson, Charles John b.1931, *Southend's Own Spitfires from 54th Squadron from Rochford, 1940*, purchased from the 31st Essex Open Exhibition, Beecroft Art Gallery, 1989, © the artist
Thompson, Charles John b.1931, *Supermarine Spitfire MkIX MH434, over St Michael's Mount, Cornwall*, purchased from A Brush with 3 Artists Exhibition, Beecroft Art Gallery, 1988, © the artist
Thompson, Howard *View of Sea and Coast*, gift from Mrs M. Forbes, 1958
Thornbury, William Anslow active 1858–1906, *A Breezy Day, Mouth of the Thames*, bequeathed by Sidney Thorpe-Smith, 1961
Thornbury, William Anslow active 1858–1906, *Sunrise, Low Tide, Leigh*, bequeathed by Sidney Thorpe-Smith, 1961
Titian (after) c.1488–1576, *The Education of Love*, purchased from J. Wentworth Day, c.1962
Tombleson, J. B. *Philip C. Humphreys*
Tomlinson, Reginald R. 1885–1978, *Licensed Breton Beggar*, purchased from the Royal Academy, 1977
Towne, Charles 1763–1840, *Landscape with Two Cows*, bequeathed by Mr W. G. Beecroft, c.1961
Trouillebert, Paul Désiré 1829–1900, *A Quiet Backwater*, bequeathed by Mr W. G. Beecroft, c.1961
Tucker, Raymond active 1852–1903, *At Southend*, purchased from the Alexander Galleries, Harrogate, 1975
unknown artist *Portrait of a Nobleman*, acquired, c.1957
unknown artist 16th C, *Deposition from the Cross*, gift from Mr W. G. Beecroft, 1957
unknown artist 18th C, *Portrait of a Lady, possibly Elizabeth Appleton of Coggeshall*, gift from Mr R. F. Martin to the Southend Corporation (now Southend Borough Council), 1924
unknown artist 18th C, *The Wine Seller*, purchased from Exhibition of Old Masters at under £200, 1952
unknown artist *The Crowstone*
unknown artist *Daniel Robert Scratton in a Red Jacket*, purchased from E. M. Scratton, 1990s
unknown artist *John Baynton Scratton*, purchased from E. M. Scratton, 1990s
unknown artist *Portrait of a Gentleman in a Black Coat (possibly Reverend Frederick Nolan)*, purchased from E. M. Scratton, 1990s
unknown artist *Portrait of a Girl in a Bronze Dress (possibly Jane Scratton)*, purchased from E. M. Scratton, 1990s
unknown artist *Portrait of a Girl in a White Dress (possibly Harriet Scratton)*, purchased from E. M. Scratton, 1990s
unknown artist *Portrait of a Lady in a Black Dress (possibly Elizabeth Boone)*, purchased from E. M. Scratton, 1990s
unknown artist *Portrait of a Young Lady in a Yellow Dress (possibly Harriet Scratton)*, purchased from E. M. Scratton
unknown artist *Jane Langworthy, Wife of John Offin of Hutton Park*
unknown artist *Catherine Elizabeth Offin*
unknown artist *Southchurch Hall*, acquired, 2001
unknown artist 19th C, *Bridge at Little Stambridge*, acquired, 1968
unknown artist 19th C, *Cottage near Southend*
unknown artist 19th C, *Portrait of a Lady Holding a Book*
unknown artist 19th C, *Portrait of a Young Lady*
unknown artist 19th C, *Portrait of a Young Lady with Red Ribbon*
unknown artist 19th C, *River Scene*
unknown artist late 19th C, *Abraham Offin (b.1830)?*
unknown artist late 19th C, *Alderman Dowsett, First Mayor of Southend (1892–1893)*, presented by Councillor David Garston, 1984
unknown artist late 19th C, *Mrs Scratton of Prittlewell Priory*, purchased from Mrs R. Knight (née Scratton), c.1975
unknown artist late 19th C, *Thomas William Offin (1834–1934)?*
unknown artist *Eastwood Church*, gift from Mr and Mrs D. A. Wright
unknown artist *Holy Trinity, Southchurch*
unknown artist *Holy Trinity, Southchurch*
unknown artist *Road Junction, Southchurch*
unknown artist *Fishing Boats in Leigh Creek, Looking West*, gift from Mr N. A. Wray
unknown artist *Girl in a Blue Dress*, acquired, c.1980
unknown artist *Venetian Canal Scene*, bequeathed by Percy B. Renshaw
unknown artist *Landscape with Rider on a White Horse and Dogs*
unknown artist *Bed and Breakfast*
unknown artist *Holy Family*, bequeathed by Mr W. G. Beecroft, c.1961
Vaesen, Guy 1912–2002, *Suffolk Landscape*, purchased from the Royal Academy, 1972, © the artist's estate
Verburgh, Dionys 1655–1722, *Coast and Harbour Scene*, gift from Mr W. G. Beecroft, 1953
Vickers, Alfred 1786–1868, *Southchurch*, bequeathed by Sidney Thorpe-Smith, 1961
Vickers, Alfred 1786–1868, *Southend from the Cliffs, Looking East*, bequeathed by Sidney Thorpe-Smith, 1961
Vickers, Alfred 1786–1868, *Southend from the Old Town, Looking West*, bequeathed by Sidney Thorpe-Smith, 1961
Vickers, Alfred 1786–1868, *Landscape*, gift from Mr P. Poole
Vickers, Alfred 1786–1868, *View near Southend*, purchased from Christie's, London, 1971
Vries, Abraham de c.1590–c.1650, *Portrait of a Gentleman*, gift from Mr W. G. Beecroft, c.1950
Wade, Maurice 1917–1991, *Canal at Longport*, purchased from the Thackery Gallery, London, 1971, © the artist's estate
Wallcousins, Ernest 1883–1976, *Conversation Piece*, gift from Mrs H. Wallcousins, 1976
Wallcousins, Ernest 1883–1976, *River Wye Approaching the Severn Estuary*, presented by the Friends of the Beecroft Art Gallery, c.1962
Ward, Edwin Arthur 1859–1933, *The Reverend Canon E. N. Gowing, MA, Rural Dean and Vicar of Prittlewell*
Ward-Robinson, Neil b.1943, *Nude under a Swinging Light Source*, purchased from the Madeline Liverick and Neil Ward-Robinson Exhibition, 1986, © the artist
Weight, Carel Victor Morlais 1908–1997, *Girl in a White Bra*, purchased from the Brandler Galleries, Brentwood, 1985, © the estate of the artist
Weight, Carel Victor Morlais 1908–1997, *Death of Lucretia No.1*, purchased from the Zwemmer Gallery, 1965, © the estate of the artist
Weston, A. *The Creek, Leigh-on-Sea*, gift from Miss M. E. McDermott
Williams, Kyffin b.1918, *Deserted Farm, Llanrhuddlad*, purchased from the Royal Academy, 1971, © the artist
Williams, Kyffin b.1918, *Sea at Trearddur*, purchased from the Royal Academy exhibition, 1976, © the artist
Woolcott, Wilfred Robert b.1892, *High Street, Leigh-on-Sea*, gift from Mr G. McClure
Woolcott, Wilfred Robert b.1892, *Walter G. Beecroft*, gift from Mr W. G. Beecroft, 1953
Wright, Frank Alan *Cockle Boat at Leigh*
Wyllie, Charles William 1853–1923, *Leigh, at the Estuary of the River Thames*, bequeathed by Sidney Thorpe-Smith, 1961
Wyllie, Charles William 1853–1923, *Hole Haven*, bequeathed by Sidney Thorpe-Smith, 1961
Wyllie, Harold 1880–1973, *Tilbury, Essex*, bequeathed by Sidney Thorpe-Smith, 1961
Yon, Edmond Charles 1836–1897, *Bridge over a River*, bequeathed by Mr W. G. Beecroft, 1961
Yon, Edmond Charles 1836–1897, *The Watermill*, gift from Mr W. G. Beecroft, c.1961
Zeeman, Reiner c.1623–c.1668, *Off Scheveningen*, gift from Mr W. G. Beecroft
Zinkeisen, Anna Katrina 1901–1976, *Promenade Scene, 'Old Southend'*, bequeathed by Miss Doris Eleanor Burrows, 1986, © the artist's estate
Zinkeisen, Anna Katrina 1901–1976, *Still Life of Flowers*, bequeathed by Miss Doris Eleanor Burrows, 1986, © the artist's estate

Thaxted Guildhall

Carter, Frank W. 1870–1933, *The Reverend Conrad Noel (1869–1942)*, on indefinite loan

Epping Forest District Museum

Barrett, Roderic 1920–2000, *The Arts, Army and Church Dance*, purchased from the artist, 1989, © the artist's estate
Bascombe, K. N. *'The Old Spotted Cow' Public House, Waltham Abbey*, acquired, 1983
Bone, Henry Pierce 1779–1855, *Burial of King Harold at Waltham Abbey, October, 1066*, acquired, 1993
Burgess, Alan b.1936, *Autumn Acer, Benington Lordship (Hertfordshire)*, purchased from the artist, 1996, © the artist
Byrne, Sharon *Greetings 2*, purchased

Castellano, Cinzia b.1961, *Freethinker*, purchased, 1998, © the artist
Christiansen, Niels H. active 1874–c.1903, *Connaught Water*, acquired, 1994
Deakins, Thomas William b.1957, *Last Summer, Duton Hill and Tilty, the Chelmer Valley, from Great Easton*, purchased from the artist, 1985, © the artist
Deakins, Thomas William b.1957, *Bean Row, Felsted Allotments*, purchased from the artist, © the artist
Debenham, Charles b.1933, *The Stores*, purchased from the artist, 1982, © the artist
Dixon, Alec active 1933–1988, *Autumn, High Beach*, purchased from the artist, 1988
Enfield, J. K. *The Doom of 'Zeppelin L.21' at Cuffley, 2.30 am, 3 September 1916*, acquired, 1993
Farrell, Anthony b.1945, *Purple Sea, Leigh-on-Sea*, purchased, 1983, © the artist
Freshwater, Heather *Theydon Mount, 1890*, acquired, 1993
G-Tet *Joy of Dancing*, purchased from Mrs L. C. Fells (the artist), 1992
Gould, Robert A. *A Day at the Steam Engine Show*, acquired, 1985
Gower, Valerie *Snow in Essex*, purchased, 1984
Harris, D. R. *Epping Forest*, acquired, 1993
Kennedy, Thomas 1900–1982, *On the River Roding*, purchased from Black Horse Agencies, 1984, © the artist
Kite, Roger b.1947, *Untitled Red*, © the artist
Langley, J. *Anderida Legacy*, purchased from the artist, 1998
Mackey, Haydn Reynolds 1883–1979, *Allegory of Finance, Religion, the Military and the Working Classes*, purchased from Gregory Page Turner, Commission a Portrait, 2001, © the artist's estate
Mackey, Haydn Reynolds 1883–1979, *The Right Honourable Lord Noel Buxton*, donated by Helen Power, daughter of the artist, 1997, © the artist's estate
Metson, Graham Peter b.1950, *The Yellow House on the Road to Puerto de Soller, Majorca, Evening Light*, purchased from the artist, 1990, © the artist
Murray, Brian b.1918, *Battlesbridge*, acquired, 1985, © the artist
Pissarro, Lucien 1863–1944, *The Garden, Epping*, purchased from Stern Pissarro Gallery, 2003, © the artist's estate
Porter, Arthur Bowmar 1876–1960, *An Essex Landscape*, purchased from Ambrose Auctioneers, 1982
Potter, Charles 1904–2002, *After Sunset, Epping Forest*, donated by Joyce Potter, 2004, © the artist's estate
Robinson, Peter b.1957, *Jigsaw Baby*, purchased from the artist, 1986, © the artist
Rowe, Ian Alan b.1963, *Two Men on a Tram*, purchased from the artist, 1993, © the artist
Simcox, A. *Lower Island, Waltham Abbey*, acquired, 1986
Spender, John Humphrey 1910–2005, *Competition*, purchased, © the Humphrey Spender Archive
Thoday, Betty *Bury Lane Cottage, Epping*, purchased from Black Horse Agencies, 1995
Thoday, Betty *St Thomas Church, Horseshoe Hill, Upshire*, purchased from Black Horse Agencies, 1995
Trappes, Francis M. active 1868–1885, *Road to Copped Hall*
Tyers, Sylvia b.1933, *Save the Forest*, donated by the artist, 2003, © the artist
Tyers, Sylvia b.1933, *Epping Forest before the M25*, donated by the artist, 2003, © the artist
Tyers, Sylvia b.1933, *The Lake, Copped Hall*, donated, 2003, © the artist
unknown artist *William Bradley, Town Beadle*, gift from Waltham Abbey Historical Society, 1993
unknown artist *Waltham Cross*, acquired, 1988
unknown artist *Portrait of a Gentleman*, acquired, 1982
unknown artist *Portrait of a Lady*, acquired, 1982
unknown artist *River Landscape*, donated by Waltham Abbey Historical Society, 2000
unknown artist *Waltham Abbey Gateway*, acquired, 1993

Royal Gunpower Mills, Waltham Abbey

Penfold, Richard W. b.1946, *Gunpowder Incorporating Mill, c.1780*, gift from the artist, 2001, © the artist
Penfold, Richard W. b.1946, *'Lady of the Lea' Explosives Barge*, gift from the artist, 2001, © the artist
Tinniswood, Robert 1936–1991, *Gunpowder Press House, c.1880*, bequeathed by the artist, 2001

Southend University Hospital

Olivier, Herbert Arnould 1861–1952, *The Right Honourable the Earl Iveagh, KG, FRS (1874–1967)*
Olivier, Herbert Arnould 1861–1952, *The Lady Gwendolen Iveagh, CBE (d.1966)*

Collection Addresses

Basildon

Basildon Arts Trust
The Basildon Centre, St Martin's Square
Basildon SS14 1DL
Telephone 01268 294994

Basildon District Council:

> The Motor Boat Museum
> Wat Tyler County Park, Pitsea Hall Lane
> Basildon SS16 4UH
> Telephone 01268 550077

Belchamp St Paul

Belchamp St Paul Community House
Belchamp Place, Gages Road
Belchamp St Paul CO10 7BX
Telephone 01787 277291

Benfleet

Castle Point Borough Council
Council Offices, Kiln Road, Thundersley, Benfleet SS7 1TF
Telephone 01268 882200

Dutch Cottage Museum
Benfleet Road, Canvey Island, Benfleet SS7 5NS
Telephone 01268 794005

Braintree

Braintree District Museum:

> Braintree District Museum
> The Town Hall Centre, Market Square
> Braintree CM7 3YG
> Telephone 01376 325266

> Braintree Town Hall
> The Town Hall Centre, Market Square
> Braintree CM7 3YG
> Telephone 01376 557776

Braintree Library
Fairfield Road, Braintree CM7 3YL
Telephone 01376 320752

Great Bardfield Historical Society
Strachan House, Dunmow Road, Great Bardfield
Braintree CM7 4SD
Telephone 01371 810919

Brentwood

Brentwood Museum
Cemetery Lodge, Lorne Road, Warley
Brentwood CM14 5HH
Telephone 01277 212142

Burnham-on-Crouch

Burnham-on-Crouch and District Local Society
District Museum, Coronation Road
Burnham-on-Crouch CM0 8AS
Telephone 01621 783444

Chelmsford

Anglia Ruskin University
Bishop Hall Lane, Rivermead, Chelmsford CM1 1SQ
Telephone 01245 493131

Broomfield Hospital
Broomfield Court, Chelmsford CM1 7ET
Telephone 01245 514460

Chelmsford Museums:

> Chelmsford Museum
> Oaklands Park, Moulsham Street
> Chelmsford CM2 9AQ
> Telephone 01245 605700

> Essex Regiment Museum
> Oaklands Park, Moulsham Street
> Chelmsford CM2 9AQ
> Telephone 01245 605701

> Hylands House
> Hylands Park, London Road
> Chelmsford CM2 8WQ
> Telephone 01245 605500

Essex County Council:

Essex County Council
County Hall, Market Road, Chelmsford CM1 1LX
Telephone 01245 435517

County Hall
Market Road, Chelmsford CM1 1QH
Telephone 01245 435517

Shire Hall
Tindal Square, Chelmsford Town Hall,
Chelmsford CM1 1EH
Telephone 01245 435517

Essex Police Museum
Essex Police Headquarters, PO Box 2, Springfield
Chelmsford CM2 6DA
Telephone 01245 457150

Essex Record Office
Wharf Road, Chelmsford CM2 6YT
Telephone 01245 244644

Clacton-on-Sea

Tendring District Council
Town Hall, Station Road, Clacton-on-Sea CO15 1SE
Telephone 01255 686868

Colchester

Colchester Archaeological Trust
12 Lexden Road, Colchester CO3 3NF
Telephone 01206 541051

Colchester County High School
Norman Way, Colchester CO3 3US
Telephone 01206 576973

Colchester Museums:

Colchester Museums
Museums Resource Centre, 14 Ryegate Road
Colchester CO1 1YG
Telephone 01206 282931

Colchester Castle Museum
Castle Park, Colchester CO1 1TJ
Telephone 01206 282939

Hollytrees Museum
High Street, Colchester CO1 1UG
Telephone 01206 282940

Tymperleys Clock Museum
Trinity Street, Colchester CO1 1JN
Telephone 01206 282943

Feering & Kelvedon Local History Museum
Aylett's Building, Maldon Road, Kelvedon
Colchester CO5 9BA
Telephone 01376 571206

Sir Alfred Munnings Art Museum
Castle House, Dedham, Colchester CO7 6AZ
Telephone 01206 322127

The Nottage Maritime Institute
The Quay, Wivenhoe, Colchester CO7 9BX
Telephone 01206 824142

University of Essex
Arts Office, Wivenhoe Park, Colchester CO4 3SQ
Telephone 01206 872074

University of Essex, Collection of Latin American Art
University of Essex, Wivenhoe Park, Colchester CO4 3SQ
Telephone 01206 873971

Victor Batte-Lay Trust
1 Chapel Lane, West Bergholt, Colchester CO6 3EF
Telephone 01206 241916

Dunmow

Great Dunmow Town Council
Foakes House, 47 Stortford Road
Great Dunmow CM6 1DG
Telephone 01371 872406

Earls Colne

Earls Colne Parish Council
Village Hall, York Road, Earls Colne CO6 2RN
Telephone 01787 224370

Epping

North Weald Airfield Museum
6 Hurricane Way, North Weald, Epping CM16 6AA
Telephone 01992 523010

Frinton-on-Sea

Frinton & Walton Town Council
The Council House, Triangle Shopping Centre
Frinton-on-Sea CO13 0AU
Telephone 01255 676666

Grays

Thurrock Museum
Thameside Complex, Orsett Road, Grays RM17 5DX
Telephone 01375 382555

Halstead

Birdbrook Community House
The Street, Birdbrook, Halstead CO9 4BU

Halstead Town Council
The Mill House, The Causeway, Halstead CO9 1ET
Telephone 01787 476480

Harlow

Harlow Art Trust
The Playhouse, Playhouse Square, Harlow CM20 1LS
Telephone 01279 446760

Harlow Council
Arts Development, The Playhouse, Harlow CM20 1LS
Telephone 01279 446760

Harwich

Harwich Town Council
Guildhall, 11 Church Street, Harwich CO12 3DS
Telephone 01255 507211

Laindon

South Essex Partnership NHS Foundation Trust
Dunton Court, Aston Road, High Road
Laindon SS15 6NX
Telephone 01375 364650

Leigh-on-Sea

Leigh Heritage Centre
13A High Street, Leigh Old Town, Leigh-on-Sea SS9 2EN
Telephone 01702 470834

Maldon

Combined Military Services Museum
Station Road, Maldon CM9 4LQ
Telephone 01621 841826

Maldon District Museum
47 Mill Road, Maldon CM9 5HX
Telephone 01621 842688

Maldon Library
Carmelite House, White Horse Lane, Maldon CM9 5FW
Telephone 01621 853556

Maldon Town Council
Town Council Offices, Town Hall, Market Hill
Maldon CM9 4RL
Telephone 01621 857373

Thomas Plume's Library
Maldon Town Council, Market Hill, Maldon CM9 4PZ
Telephone 01621 854850

Manningtree

The Constable Trust
North House, The Walls, Manningtree CO11 1AS
Telephone 01206 392717

Ongar

Ongar War Memorial Hospital
55 Fyfield Road, Ongar CM5 0AL
Telephone 01277 362629

Saffron Walden

English Heritage, Audley End House
Audley End, Saffron Walden CB11 4JF
Telephone 01223 5827100

Fry Art Gallery
Bridge End Gardens, Castle Street
Saffron Walden CB10 1BD
Telephone 01799 513779

Saffron Walden Community Hospital
Radwinter Road, Saffron Walden CB11 3HY
Telephone 01799 562900

Saffron Walden Library
2 King Street, Saffron Walden CB10 1ES
Telephone 01799 523178

Saffron Walden Museum
Museum Street, Saffron Walden CB10 1JL
Telephone 01799 510333

Saffron Walden Town Council
11 Emson Close, Saffron Walden CB10 1HL
Telephone 01799 516501

Uttlesford District Council
Council Offices, London Road, Saffron Walden CB11 4ER
Telephone 01799 510510

Southend-on-Sea

Southend-on-Sea Borough Council
Civic Centre, Victoria Avenue, Southend-on-Sea SS2 6ER
Telephone 01702 215141

Southend Pier Museum Foundation
Southend Pier, Western Esplanade, Marine Parade
Southend-on-Sea SS1 1EE
Telephone 01702 611214

Southend Museums Service:

Southend Museums Service
Central Museum, Victoria Avenue
Southend-on-Sea SS2 6EW
Telephone 01702 215131

Beecroft Art Gallery
Station Road, Westcliff-on-Sea SS0 7RA
Telephone 01702 347418

Prittlewell Priory
Priory Park, Victoria Avenue
Southend-on-Sea SS2
Telephone 01702 342878

Southchurch Hall
Southchurch Hall Close, Southchurch
Southend-on-Sea SS1 2TE
Telephone 01702 467671

Thaxted

Thaxted Guildhall
28 Town Street, Thaxted CM6 2LA
Telephone 01371 831281

Waltham Abbey

Epping Forest District Museum
39–41 Sun Street, Waltham Abbey EN9 1EL
Telephone 01992 716882

Royal Gunpowder Mills
Beaulieu Drive, Waltham Abbey EN9 1JY
Telephone 01992 707370

Westcliff-on-Sea

Southend University Hospital
NHS Foundation Trust, Prittlewell Chase,
Westcliff-on-Sea SS0 0RY
Telephone 01702 221045

Index of Artists

In this catalogue, artists' names and the spelling of their names follow the preferred presentation of the name in the Getty Union List of Artist Names (ULAN) as of February 2004, if the artist is listed in ULAN.

The page numbers next to each artist's name below direct readers to paintings that are by the artist; are attributed to the artist; or, in a few cases, are more loosely related to the artist being, for example, 'after', 'the circle of' or copies of a painting by the artist. The precise relationship between the artist and the painting is listed in the catalogue.

Supporters of the Public Catalogue Foundation

Master Patrons

The Public Catalogue Foundation is greatly indebted to the following Master Patrons who have helped it in the past or are currently working with it to raise funds for the publication of their county catalogues. All of them have given freely of their time and have made an enormous contribution to the work of the Foundation.

Peter Andreae, High Sheriff for Hampshire *(Hampshire)*
Sir Nicholas Bacon, DL, High Sheriff for Norfolk *(Norfolk)*
Peter Bretherton *(West Yorkshire: Leeds)*
Richard Compton *(North Yorkshire)*
George Courtauld, DL, Vice Lord Lieutenant for Essex *(Essex)*
The Marquess of Downshire *(North Yorkshire)*
Patricia Grayburn, MBE DL *(Surrey)*
Tommy Jowitt *(West Yorkshire)*
Sir Michael Lickiss *(Cornwall)*
Lord Marlesford, DL *(Suffolk)*
Phyllida Stewart-Roberts, OBE, Lord Lieutenant for East Sussex *(East Sussex)*
Leslie Weller, DL *(West Sussex)*

Financial Support

The Public Catalogue Foundation is particularly grateful to the following organisations and individuals who have given it generous financial support since the project started in 2003.

National Sponsor

Christie's

Benefactors (£10,000–£50,000)

City of Bradford Metropolitan District Council
Deborah Loeb Brice Foundation
The Bulldog Trust
A. & S. Burton 1960 Charitable Trust
The John S. Cohen Foundation
Christie's
Mr Lloyd Dorfman
The Foyle Foundation
Hampshire County Council
Peter Harrison Foundation
Hiscox plc
ICAP plc
Kent County Council
The Linbury Trust
The Manifold Trust
Robert Warren Miller
The Monument Trust
Miles Morland
National Gallery Trust
Stavros S. Niarchos Foundation
Norfolk County Council
Provident Financial
P. F. Charitable Trust
RAB Capital
Renaissance West Midlands
Saga Group Ltd
University College, London
University of Leeds
Garfield Weston Foundation

Series Patrons (Minimum donation of £2,500)

Harry Bott
Janey Buchan
Dr Peter Cannon-Brookes
Mrs Greta Fenston
G. Laurence Harbottle
Paul & Kathrine Haworth
Neil Honebon
The Keatley Trust
Michael A. Lambert
David & Amanda Leathers
Miles Morland
Sir Harry & Lady Soloman
Stuart M. Southall
University of Surrey
Mr & Mrs Charles Wyvill

Catalogue Patrons (£1,000–£10,000)

ACE Study Tours
Adams and Remers
Marcus & Kate Agius
The AIM Foundation
John Alston, CBE
Amberley Castle
Archant Ltd
Mr Ian Askew
Basingstoke and Deane Borough Council
Barlow Robbins LLP
Mr James & Lady Emma Barnard
Sir Christopher Bland
The Charlotte Bonham-Carter Charitable Trust
H. R. Pratt Boorman Family Foundation
The Bowerman Charitable Trust
Bramdean Asset Management LLP
Peter Bretherton
Mrs T. Brotherton-Ratcliffe
Mr & Mrs Patrick Burgess
Mr & Mrs Mark Burrell
Arnold J. Burton Charitable Trust
C. J. R. & Mrs C. L. Calderwood
Chichester District Council
The Timothy Colman Charitable Trust
Cornwall County Council
Mr S. J. D. Corsan
Graeme Cottam & Gloriana Marks de Chabris
Elaine Craven, Earl Street Employment Consultants Ltd
Harriett Cullen
Deborah Gage (Works of Art) Ltd
The Duke of Devonshire's Charitable Trust
Sir Harry Djanogly, CBE
Professor Patrick & Dr Grace Dowling
Lord Douro
East Sussex County Council
Eastbourne Borough Council
EEMLAC, through the Association for Suffolk Museums
Lord & Lady Egremont
Sir John & Lady Elliott
Andrew & Lucy Ellis
Essex County Council
Mrs M. A. G. Fenston
Marc Fitch Fund
Elizabeth & Val Fleming
The Friends of Historic Essex
The Friends of the Royal Pavilion, Art Gallery & Museums, Brighton
The Friends of York Art Gallery (E. J. Swift Bequest)
Christopher & Catherine Foyle
Lewis & Jacqueline Golden
Gorringes
Mrs Patricia Grayburn, MBE DL
Charles Gregson
The Gulland Family
David Gurney
Philip Gwyn
G. Laurence Harbottle
The Hartnett Charitable Trust
Hazlitt, Gooden & Fox Ltd
Heartwood Wealth Management Ltd
Lady Hind Trust
Hobart Charitable Trust
David & Prue Hopkinson
Isle of Wight Council
The J. and S. B. Charitable Trust
The Keatley Trust
Kent Messenger Group
Garrett Kirk, Jr
The Leche Trust
Leeds Art Collections Fund
Leeds City Council
Leeds Philosophical and Literary Society
Mark & Sophie Lewisohn
Maidstone Borough Council
The Marlay Group
The Mercers' Company
Rupert Nabarro
Newcastle City Council
Oakmoor Trust
Sir Idris Pearce
The Pennycress Trust
Portsmouth City Council
Mr John Rank
The Hans and Märit Rausing Charitable Trust
Roger & Jane Reed
Michael Renshall, CBE MA FCA
Sir Miles & Lady Rivett-Carnac
Rothschild Foundation
Royal Cornwall Museum
Russell New
Scarfe Charitable Trust
Shaftesbury plc
Smith & Williamson
South West of England Regional Development Agency
Caroline M. Southall
Stuart M. Southall
Southampton City Council
Mrs Andrew Stewart-Roberts, OBE
Mr Peter Stormonth Darling
Strutt and Parker
Suffolk County Council, through the Association for Suffolk Museums
The Bernard Sunley Charitable Foundation
Surrey County Council
The John Swire 1989 Charitable Trust
The Tanner Trust
Chloe Teacher
The Thistle Trust
Trusthouse Charitable Foundation
University of Essex
The Walland Trust Fund
John Wates Charitable Trust
Leslie Weller, DL
West Sussex County Council
Wilkin & Sons Ltd
Peter Wolton Charitable Trust